Marketing Research

An Applied Orientation

THIRD EDITION

Naresh K. Malhotra
Georgia Institute of Technology

Prentice Hall, Upper Saddle River, New Jersey 07458

Featuring Burke, Inc., and other research firms.

The assistance of James Agarwal with the international marketing research example, the assistance of Mark Leach and Gina Miller in writing the ethics section, and the assistance of Mark Peterson in writing the computer applications section is gratefully acknowledged.

Acquisitons Editor: *Whitney Blake*
Editorial Assistant: *Michele Foresta*
Editor-in-Chief: *Natalie Anderson*
Marketing Manager: *Shannon Moore*
Production Editor: *Michelle Rich*
Permissions Coordinator: *Monica Stipanov*
Associate Managing Editor: *John Roberts*
Managing Editor: *Dee Josephson*
Manufacturing Buyer: *Diane Peirano*
Manufacturing Supervisor: *Arnold Vila*
Manufacturing Manager: *Vincent Scelta*
Designer: *Kevin Kall*
Design Manager: *Patricia Smythe*
Interior Design: *Karen Quigley*
Photo Research Supervisor: *Melinda Lee Reo*
Image Permission Supervisor: *Kay Dellosa*
Photo Researcher: *Melinda Alexander*
Cover Design: *Joe De Pinho*
Illustrator *(Interior): TSI Graphics, Inc.*
Cover Illustration/Photo: *Digital Vision*
Composition: *TSI Graphics, Inc.*

Credits and acknowledgments for materials borrowed from other sources and reproduced, with permission, in this textbook appear on page C1.

Library of Congress Cataloging-in-Publication Data
Malhotra, Naresh K.
Marketing research: an applied orientation / Naresh K. Malhotra. —3rd ed.
p. cm.
Includes bibliographical references and index.
ISBN 0-13-083044-5 (case)
1. Marketing research. 2. Marketing research—Methodology.
I. Title.
HF5415.2.M29 1999
658.8'3—dc21 98-38880
CIP

Prentice-Hall International (UK) Limited, London
Prentice-Hall of Australia Pty. Limited, Sydney
Prentice-Hall Canada, Inc., Toronto
Prentice-Hall Hispanoamericana, S.A., Mexico
Prentice-Hall of India Private Limited, New Delhi
Prentice-Hall of Japan, Inc., Tokyo
Pearson Education Asia Pte. Ltd., Singapore
Editora Prentice-Hall do Brasil, Ltda., Rio de Janeiro

Printed in the United States of America

10 9 8 7 6 5 4 3 2

To my parents
Mr. and Mrs. H. N. Malhotra

and

To my wife Veena

and

children Ruth and Paul

The love, encouragement, and support of my parents, wife, and children has been exemplary.

"The greatest of these is love."
I Corinthians 13:13

Brief Contents

PART I: INTRODUCTION AND EARLY PHASES OF MARKETING RESEARCH 1

PART II: RESEARCH DESIGN FORMULATION 79

PART III: DATA COLLECTION, PREPARATION, AND ANALYSIS 401

Contents

PART II: RESEARCH DESIGN FORMULATION 79

Chapter 10 Questionnaire and Form Design 292

PART IV: COMMUNICATION, INTERNATIONAL AND ETHICAL DIMENSIONS WITH APPLICATIONS 691

Foreword

The world of business is moving more rapidly than ever. Critical to keeping pace is the intelligent and thoughtful use of research in managing our businesses. The most successful will undoubtedly have a broad base of education, high levels of communication skills, and creative approaches to the opportunities that are racing toward us. It is marvelous when a textbook, such as Dr. Malhotra's, allows the classroom to become a source of these skills.

This text has already proven its worth as one of the most successful in the field, with well over 100 universities using it. As a basis for students to become researchers and intelligent users of research it is unsurpassed. The real-life examples bring the student closer to the world businesspeople face every day. At every step, the student can relate to the ongoing "Department Store Patronage Project" and to the practical vignettes that bring the educational material to a realistic and practical level. The success in keeping the material at the leading edge of research also can be seen in the integration of modern tools of research such as the Internet, computer analytic software, and the latest management practices.

We at Burke, Inc. are pleased to be asked to contribute further from our experiences for this third edition. We have shared these experiences as well as our philosophies, technical skills, and thoughts about the future of research. This third edition of *Marketing Research: An Applied Orientation* provides the foundation that we believe every student should have. We know you will find the combination of theory, practice, and sound advice to be of great value to you.

Ron Tatham
Chairman, Burke, Inc.

Preface

The motivation in writing this book was to provide a Marketing Research text that is comprehensive, practical, applied, and managerial, and presents a balanced coverage of both qualitative and quantitative material. This book is written from the perspective of users of marketing research. It reflects the current trends in international marketing, ethics, and the use of the Internet and computers, as well as a focus on the practice of marketing research by featuring Burke, Inc. and other marketing research organizations.

The response to the first and second editions was truly gratifying, and more than 100 universities adopted the book in the United States. Moreover, an International Edition and an Australia and New Zealand Edition have been published as well as a Spanish translation. A European Edition is in progress. I want to express my sincere thanks and appreciation to all the professors and students who have contributed to the success of the book as users, reviewers, and providers of valuable feedback and encouragement. This third edition attempts to build on this success to make the book even more current, contemporary, illustrative, and sensitive to user needs. Several unique features in terms of the content and presentation of the material make it distinctive.

AUDIENCE

This book is suitable for use at both the undergraduate and graduate levels. This positioning is confirmed by the response to the first two editions, which included adoptions at both levels. The coverage is comprehensive and the depth and breadth of topics encompass both levels. The material is presented in a manner that is easy to read and understand. There are numerous diagrams, tables, pictures, illustrations, and examples that help explain the basic concepts. Special features designed for undergraduate students include definitions, acronyms, and exercises (questions, problems, and Internet and computer exercises). Features that will appeal to graduate students include extensive notes and comprehensive coverage. The *Instructor's Manual* offers specific suggestions for teaching each chapter at the undergraduate and graduate levels. Not only is the book suitable for use in courses on Marketing Research, but it can also be used effectively in courses on Marketing Data Analysis. All the commonly used univariate and multivariate data analysis techniques are discussed extensively yet simply.

ORGANIZATION

The book is organized into four parts, based on a six-step framework for conducting marketing research. Part I provides an introduction and discusses problem definition, the first and most important step. The nature and scope of research undertaken to develop an approach to the problem, the second step in the marketing research process, is also described. Part II covers research design, the third step, and describes in detail exploratory, descriptive, and causal designs. We describe the types of information commonly obtained in marketing research and the appropriate scales for obtaining such information. We present several guidelines for designing questionnaires and explain the procedures, techniques, and statistical considerations involved in sampling. Part III presents a practical and managerially oriented discussion of field work, the fourth step in the marketing research process. It also covers data preparation and analysis, the fifth step of the marketing research process. We discuss in detail the basic and advanced statistical techniques, with emphasis on explaining the procedures, interpreting the results, and managerial implications rather than on statistical elegance. Communicating the research by preparing and presenting a formal report constitutes the sixth step in the marketing research process and forms the subject of Part IV. This last part is also devoted to the complex process of international marketing research and the ethical issues that arise in marketing research. Throughout the book, the orientation is applied and managerial.

NEW FOR THE THIRD EDITION

While retaining the desirable features of earlier editions, the third edition contains major revisions. Several significant changes have been made. These changes were identified by conducting surveys of professors (users and nonusers) and students, and by obtaining critical reviews and detailed evaluations. Major changes include:

1. *Integrated coverage of the Internet.* A section on "Internet and Computer Applications" has been added to each chapter. This section discusses and illustrates how the Internet and computers can be used to elucidate the concepts in that chapter. In addition, use of the Internet is integrated throughout several of the chapters. For example, chapter 6 presents e-mail surveys and Internet surveys as two new methods of survey administration. These methods, along with seven others (telephone, CATI, in-home, mall intercept, CAPI, mail, and mail panels) are evaluated on various criteria for survey selection. Each chapter also includes a section called "Internet and Computer Exercises," which provides an opportunity to apply some of these concepts in real-life settings.
2. *A new feature provided by Burke, Inc., a premier marketing research firm.* Each chapter opens with a quotation from a Burke professional providing a perspective on the subject matter of that chapter. Each chapter also contains a section, "Focus on Burke," placed just before the "Summary" section. "Focus on Burke," contributed by Burke professionals, illustrates how the concepts in that chapter are being implemented by Burke. In addition, at the end of each part is a section, "Professional Perspectives," which contains articles by members of the Burke staff.
3. *Addition of Minitab and Excel to statistical software.* Because it is a popular software used for teaching introductory statistics and marketing data analysis, Minitab has been added. Likewise, the use of Excel—and spreadsheets in general—is becoming increasingly popular. The data analysis chapters now feature five statistical packages: SPSS, SAS, BMDP, Minitab, and Excel, along with other popular programs. This book can be used as a text regardless of the statistical package being used by the instructor.
4. *Modifications of some data analysis chapters.* Chapters 15 ("Frequency Distribution, Cross-Tabulation, and Hypothesis Testing"), 16 ("Analysis of Variance and Covariance"), and 19 ("Factor Analysis") have been modified so that all the data used to illustrate these techniques are presented at the beginning of the chapter. Thus all the data analysis techniques in chapters 15 through 21 are now uniformly illustrated by providing the entire data set at the beginning of each chapter. The students should be encouraged to reanalyze these data using software specified by the instructor and compare the results to those given in the book.

5. *New figures, tables, exhibits, Research in Practice boxes and text.* Where appropriate, new material has been added to present new ideas, update the technology, or clarify the subject. Such additions have been made throughout the text.
6. *New and updated examples and cases.* Several new examples have been added, some old ones deleted, and the remaining examples have been updated as appropriate. Some new cases have been added and all the rest updated to reflect the current marketing and marketing research environment.
7. *Updated references.* The references have been updated. Each chapter contains many references from 1997 or later. Some of the classic references have been retained.

KEY FEATURES OF THE TEXT

The book has several salient and unique features, both in terms of content and pedagogy.

Content Features

1. A separate chapter has been devoted to problem definition and developing an approach. These important steps in the marketing research process are discussed thoroughly and extensively (chapter 2).
2. A separate chapter covers secondary data analysis. In addition to the traditional sources, computerized databases and syndicate sources are also covered extensively. Use of the Internet for secondary data analysis is discussed in detail (chapter 4).
3. Qualitative research is discussed in a separate chapter. Focus groups, depth interviews, and projective techniques are discussed in detail, with emphasis on the applications of these procedures. Use of the Internet for qualitative research is discussed in detail (chapter 5).
4. A separate chapter presents survey and observation methods (chapter 6), while another discusses experimentation (chapter 7). Thus, descriptive and causal designs are covered in detail.
5. Two chapters have been devoted to scaling techniques. One chapter is devoted to the fundamentals and comparative scaling techniques (chapter 8). The other covers noncomparative techniques, including multiitem scales, and procedures for assessing their reliability, validity, and generalizability (chapter 9).
6. A separate chapter discusses questionnaire design. A step-by-step procedure and several guidelines are provided for constructing questionnaires (chapter 10).
7. Two chapters cover sampling techniques. One chapter discusses the qualitative issues involved in sampling and the various nonprobability and probability sampling techniques (chapter 11). The other chapter explains statistical issues as well as final and initial sample size determination (chapter 12).
8. A separate chapter presents field work. We give several guidelines on interviewer training, interviewing, and supervision of field workers (chapter 13).
9. The book is unique in the treatment of marketing research data analysis. Separate chapters have been devoted to:
   - **a.** Data preparation (chapter 14)
   - **b.** Frequency distribution, cross-tabulation, and hypothesis testing (chapter 15)
   - **c.** Analysis of variance and covariance (chapter 16)
   - **d.** Regression analysis (chapter 17)
   - **e.** Discriminant analysis (chapter 18)
   - **f.** Factor analysis (chapter 19)
   - **g.** Cluster analysis (chapter 20)
   - **h.** Multidimensional scaling and conjoint analysis (chapter 21)

   The data set used to explain each technique is provided in the beginning of the chapter. Data analysis is illustrated for five statistical packages: SPSS, SAS, BMDP, Minitab, and Excel.

10. To supplement the discussions throughout the text, an additional chapter explains international marketing research. The environment in which international marketing research is conducted is described, followed by a discussion of some advanced concepts (chapter 23).
11. In addition to discussions throughout the text, another chapter has been devoted to ethics in marketing research. We describe some of the guidelines that aid managers and researchers in ethical decision making. A framework for ethics in marketing research is then proposed. The way in which ethics influence each step of the marketing research process is explained (chapter 24).

Pedagogical Features

1. Scholarship is appropriately blended with a highly applied and managerial orientation. We illustrate throughout the application of concepts and techniques by marketing researchers and implementation of findings by managers to improve marketing practice. The emphasis on applied marketing research is further reinforced by featuring Burke, Inc., in a significant way in each chapter.
2. Numerous real-life examples are given. These examples describe in some detail the kind of marketing research used to address a specific managerial problem and the decision that was based on the findings. Where appropriate, the sources cited have been supplemented by additional marketing research information to enhance the usefulness of these examples. Additional examples have been integrated throughout the text to further explain and illustrate the concepts in each chapter.
3. In addition, a real-life project is used as a running example to illustrate the various concepts throughout the text. These illustrations have been blocked, entitled "Department Store Patronage Project," and highlighted using a colored background. To make the running example comprehensive so that it covers all aspects of marketing research, an actual department store project that I conducted is supplemented with other similar projects with which I was involved, although several aspects of these projects have been disguised. In other instances, as in the case of causal research design, I show how the relevant concepts can be applied in a department store setting. Thus, the department store example spans the whole book and is easy to pick up in any chapter.
4. Each chapter contains Research in Practice boxes. These provide a further illustration of how marketing research concepts are being implemented in practice.
5. Another way in which a contemporary focus is achieved is by integrating the coverage of international marketing research and ethics in marketing research throughout the text. We show how the concepts discussed in each chapter can be applied in an international setting and discuss the ethical issues that may arise when implementing those concepts domestically and internationally.
6. The use of the Internet and computers has also been integrated throughout the text. Each chapter has a section entitled "Internet and Computer Applications." We show how the Internet and computers can be integrated in each step of the marketing research process and how they can be used to implement the concepts discussed in each chapter. Each chapter also contains "Internet and Computer Exercises" which present opportunities to apply these concepts in real-life settings.
7. Data analysis procedures are illustrated with respect to SPSS, SAS, BMDP, Minitab, and Excel, along with other popular programs. This book can be used as a text, regardless of the statistical package being used by the instructor.
8. Each chapter contains one or more helpful acronyms, which summarize the salient concepts. Acronyms are the most popular mnemonic technique used by college students. Theoretical and empirical evidence supporting the effectiveness of mnemonic techniques and their usefulness as a pedagogical tool has been discussed in a paper I published in the *Journal of the Academy of Marketing Science* (Spring 1991): 141–150.

9. Each part contains "Professional Perspectives," which feature articles by some of the leading marketing research practitioners from Burke and other organizations. These articles complement the material in the chapters and further strengthen the applied orientation of the book.
10. Short and long real-life cases. Each part of the book contains some short cases. These cases illustrate the concepts discussed. The conciseness of the cases will allow for their use in examinations. Some long cases are also provided—including some cases with statistical data. These cases are current and deal with topics of interest to students.
11. Extensive "Exercises" and "Activities" sections include questions, problems, Internet and computer exercises, role playing, field work, and group discussion, are found at the conclusion of each chapter or in the *Instructor's Manual*. This provides ample opportunities for learning and testing the concepts covered in the chapter.
12. A complete set of learning aids including a functional and useful Web site, an *Instructor's Manual*, PowerPoint slides, Exercises in Marketing Research, and Test Bank have been provided.

INSTRUCTIONAL SUPPORT

The Web site can be accessed at www.prenhall.com/phbusiness or www.dupree.gatech.edu. To access the book page from the Prentice Hall site, click on the Book Specific Sites. To access the book page from the DuPree site, click on the Faculty button, then click on Naresh K. Malhotra, and then on Marketing Research: An Applied Orientation, Third Edition. The complete Web site address is www.dupree.gatech/faculty/malhotra/index.html.

The Web site contains:

- The entire *Instructors' Manual*
- Test Item File
- PowerPoint Slides containing a chapter outline and all the figures, tables, and Research in Practice boxes for each chapter.
- All the blocked examples for each chapter.
- Data for Cases 3.4 (Matsushita), 3.5 (Pampers), and 3.6 (Chrysler) given in the book. These data can also be downloaded with ease.
- Four comprehensive cases with data. These cases are DuPont carpets (consumer products), Gucci catalog (direct marketing), Kosair Children's Hospital (services), and Astec (industrial marketing). Each case has associated with it: (1) questions for each of the 24 chapters, (2) questionnaire, (3) coding sheet, (4) file extract, (5) data that can be down loaded, and (6) answers to case questions that are contained in a password-protected directory. To obtain the password, please contact your local Prentice Hall representative or contact me (e-mail: naresh.malhotra @mgt.gatech.edu, tel: 404-894-4358, fax: 404-894-6030).
- Links to other useful Web sites.

The Web site is being enhanced continually.

Instructor's Manual. The *Instructor's Manual*, written by the author, is very closely tied to the text. The manual shows how to tailor the material in each chapter to the undergraduate and graduate levels. Each chapter contains transparency masters, chapter objectives, author's notes, chapter outline, teaching suggestions, and answers to all end-of-chapter exercises and activities (questions, problems, Internet and computer exercises). In addition, solutions are provided to all the cases, including those that involve data analysis. The *Instructor's Manual* also contains the four comprehensive cases with data: DuPont carpets (consumer products), Gucci catalog (direct marketing), Kosair Children's Hospital (services), and Astec (industrial marketing). The enclosed disk contains statistical data for Cases 3.4 (Matsushita), 3.5 (Pampers), and 3.6 (Chrysler) given in the book. This disk also contains the four comprehensive cases, DuPont, Gucci catalog, Kosair Children's Hospital, and Astec, including for each case: (1) questions for each of the 24 chapters, (2) questionnaire, (3) coding sheet, (4) file extract, (5) statistical data, and (6) and answers to case questions.

Test Item File. Available for both the IBM and the Macintosh, this valuable test item file contains a wide variety of tests for each chapter that allow you to "create" your own exams.

Note that *Exercises in Marketing Research* written by Naresh K. Malhotra and Chulwan Kim is no longer available in hard copy. Instead these cases (DuPont, Gucci, Kosair Children's Hospital, and Astec), along with the questions, questionnaire, coding sheet, data, and answers, can be obtained from either the Web site or the *Instructor's Manual.*

ACKNOWLEDGMENTS

Several people have been extremely helpful in writing this textbook. I would like to acknowledge Professor Arun K. Jain (University of Buffalo) who taught me Marketing Research in a way I will never forget. My students, particularly former doctoral students (James Agarwal, Imad Baalbaki, Dan McCort, Charla Mathwick, Gina Miller, and Mark Peterson) and current doctoral students (Ashutosh Dixit, Rick McFarland, Harriet Outland, Jamie Pleasant, and Cassandra Wells) as well as other doctoral students (Mark Leach and Tyra Mitchell), have been very helpful in many ways. I particularly want to acknowledge the assistance of Mark Leach and Gina Miller in writing the ethics sections and chapter, the assistance of Mark Peterson in writing the computer applications sections, and the assistance of James Agarwal with the international marketing research examples in the earlier two editions. The students in my Marketing Research courses have provided useful feedback as the material was class tested for several years. My colleagues at Georgia Tech, especially Fred Allvine, have been very supportive. I also want to thank Ronald L. Tatham (chairman, Burke, Inc.) for his encouragement, support, and the many contributions from Burke that appear throughout the book. William D. Neal (founder and senior executive officer of SDR, Inc.) has been very helpful and supportive over the years. Lawrence W. Labash (Market Facts, Inc.), Roger L. Bacik (Elrick & Lavidge, Inc.), Brian Lunde (Walker Information, Inc.), and the other practitioners who have contributed to the book.

The reviewers have provided many constructive and valuable suggestions. Among others, the help of the following reviewers is gratefully acknowledged.

Reviewers for the third edition:

Tom Anastasti, Boston University
John Weiss, Colorado State University
Subash Lonial, University of Louisville
Joel Herche, University of the Pacific
Paul L. Sauer, Canisius College

Reviewers for the second edition:

Rick Andrews, University of Delaware
Holland Blades Jr., Missouri Southern State College
Sharmila Chatterjee, Santa Clara University
Rajshekhar Javalgi, Cleveland State University
Mushtaq Luqmani, Western Michigan University
Jeanne Munger, University of Southern Maine
Audesh Paswan, University of South Dakota
Venkatram Ramaswamy, University of Michigan
Gillian Rice, Thunderbird University
Paul L. Sauer, Canisius College
Hans Srinivasan, University of Connecticut

Reviewers for the first edition:

David M. Andrus, Kansas State University
Joe Ballenger, Stephen F. Austin State University
Joseph D. Brown, Ball State University
Thomas E. Buzas, Eastern Michigan University
Rajendar K. Garg, Northeastern Illinois University
Lawrence D. Gibson, Consultant
Ronald E. Goldsmith, Florida State University
Rajshekhar G. Javalgi, Cleveland State University
Charlotte H. Mason, University of North Carolina
Kent Nakamoto, University of Colorado
Thomas J. Page Jr., Michigan State University
William S. Perkins, Pennsylvania State University
Sudhi Seshadri, University of Maryland at College Park
David Shani, Baruch College

The team at Prentice Hall provided outstanding support. Special thanks are due to Sandra Steiner, President; James C. Boyd, Editorial Director; Natalie E. Anderson, Editor in Chief; Whitney Blake, Senior Marketing Editor; John Larkin, Associate Marketing Editor; Brian Kibby, Director of Marketing; Shannon Moore, Marketing Manager; Michelle Rich, Production Editor; Michele Foresta, Editorial Assistant. Special recognition is due to the several field representatives and sales people who have done an outstanding job in marketing the book.

I want to acknowledge with great respect my parents, Mr. and Mrs. H. N. Malhotra. Their love, encouragement, support, and the sacrificial giving of themselves have been exemplary. My heartfelt love and gratitude go to my wife, Veena, and my children, Ruth and Paul, for their faith, hope, and love.

Most of all, I want to acknowledge and thank my Savior and Lord, Jesus Christ, for the many miracles He has performed in my life. This book is, truly, the result of His grace—"This is the Lord's doing; it is marvelous in our eyes" (Psalm 118:23).

Naresh K. Malhotra

About the Author

Dr. Naresh K. Malhotra is Regents' Professor, DuPree College of Management, Georgia Institute of Technology. He is listed in *Marquis Who's Who in America*, 51st Edition (1997), 52nd Edition (1998), 53rd Edition (1999), and in the *National Registry of Who's Who* (1999).

In an article by Wheatley and Wilson (1987 AMA Educators' Proceedings), Professor Malhotra was ranked number one in the country based on articles published in the *Journal of Marketing Research* from 1980 to 1985. He also holds the all-time record for the most publications in the *Journal of Health Care Marketing*. He is ranked number one based on publications in the *Journal of the Academy of Marketing Science* (JAMS) from its inception through volume 23, 1995. He is also number one based on publications in JAMS from 1986 to 1995. He is listed as one of the best researchers in marketing in John Fraedrich, "The Best Researchers in Marketing," *Marketing Educator* (Summer 1997), p. 5.

He has published more than 75 papers in major refereed journals including the *Journal of Marketing Research, Journal of Consumer Research, Marketing Science, Journal of Marketing, Journal of Academy of Marketing Science, Journal of Retailing, Journal of Health Care Marketing*, and leading journals in statistics, management science, and psychology. In addition, he has also published numerous refereed articles in the proceedings of major national and international conferences. Several articles have received research awards.

He was Chairman, Academy of Marketing Science Foundation, 1996–1998, and was President, Academy of Marketing Science, 1994–1996, and Chairman of the Board of Governors from 1990 to 1992. He is a Distinguished Fellow of the Academy and Fellow of the Decision Sciences Institute. He serves as an Associate Editor of *Decision Sciences Journal* and has served as Section Editor, Health Care Marketing Abstracts, *Journal of Health Care Marketing*. Also, he serves on the Editorial Boards of eight journals.

His book entitled *Marketing Research: An Applied Orientation*, Second Edition, was published by Prentice Hall, Inc. An International Edition and an Australian Edition of his book have also been published, along with a Spanish translation. The book has received widespread adoption at both the graduate and undergraduate levels with more than 100 schools using it in the United States.

Dr. Malhotra has consulted for business, nonprofit, and government organizations in the United States and abroad and has served as an expert witness in legal and regulatory proceedings. He is the winner of numerous awards and honors for research, teaching, and service to the profession.

Dr. Malhotra is a member and Deacon, First Baptist Church of Atlanta. He lives in the Atlanta area with his wife, Veena, and children, Ruth and Paul.

Part I

Introduction and Early Phases of Marketing Research

In this part, we discuss the nature and scope of marketing research and its role in decision support systems. We describe the marketing research industry and the many exciting career opportunities in this field. We set out a six-step marketing research process and discuss problem definition, the first and the most important step, in detail. Finally, we describe the development of an approach to the problem, the second step in the marketing research process, and discuss in detail the various components of the approach. The perspective given in these chapters should be useful to both the decision maker and the marketing researcher.

Chapter 1

"The role of a marketing researcher must include consulting skills, technical proficiency, and sound management. The focus of the role is to provide information to identify marketing problems and solutions in such a way that action can be taken."

Ron Tatham, chairman, Burke, Inc.

Introduction to Marketing Research

OBJECTIVES

After reading this chapter, the student should be able to

1. understand the nature and scope of marketing research and its role in designing and implementing successful marketing programs
2. explain the role of marketing research in decision support systems in providing data, marketing models, and specialized software
3. discuss the types and roles of research suppliers including internal and external, full-service, and limited-service suppliers
4. describe careers available in marketing research and the backgrounds and skills needed to succeed in them
5. describe a conceptual framework for conducting marketing research as well as the six steps of the marketing research process
6. acquire an appreciation of the international dimension and the complexity involved in international marketing research
7. gain an understanding of the ethical aspects of marketing research and the responsibilities each of the marketing research stakeholders have to themselves, each other, and the research project
8. explain how the Internet and computers can facilitate the marketing research process

OVERVIEW

Marketing research comprises one of the most important and fascinating facets of marketing. In this chapter, we describe the nature of marketing research, emphasizing its role of providing information for marketing decision making and provide several real-life examples to illustrate the basic concepts of marketing research. We give a formal definition of marketing research and subdivide marketing research into two areas: problem identification and problem solving research. We show that marketing research is also an integral part of marketing information systems or decision support systems. Next we provide an overview of marketing research suppliers and services, along with guidelines for selecting a supplier.

Because of demand for well-executed marketing research, there are many exciting career opportunities in this field. We discuss these opportunities, along with a description of the stages of the marketing research process. To illustrate the marketing research process, we examine the department store patronage project, which was an actual marketing research project conducted by the author, and use it as a running example throughout the book. The topic of international marketing research is introduced and discussed systematically in the subsequent chapters. The ethical aspects of marketing research and the responsibilities each of the marketing research stakeholders have to themselves, each other, and the research project are presented and developed in more detail throughout the text. This chapter concludes with an applications-oriented discussion on the use of the Internet and computers in marketing research, another emphasis which pervades the entire book.

WHAT DOES MARKETING RESEARCH ENCOMPASS?

The term *marketing research* is broad in meaning; it is related to all aspects of marketing. The following examples will provide a flavor of the varied nature of marketing research:

EXAMPLE

Lotus Development Corporation Uses Marketing Research as a Development Tool

Recently, Lotus Development Corp. redesigned its Web site after market research revealed some improvements customers desired.

The company conducts focus groups (group interviews with 8 to 12 people at a time) of customers and business partners every four months. This routine use of focus groups recognizes the fact that Web sites are products with very short life cycles and need ongoing attention to keep them up-to-date. The focus groups evaluate Lotus' Web site and the sites of other companies. Some objectives for the focus groups include: identifying factors that lead Internet users (and nonusers) to visit a Web site; identifying what factors entice visitors to return often to a Web site; and identifying users' technological capabilities. The focus group findings are verified by survey research, which also forms the basis of quantitative projections.

The use of focus groups and survey research allows Lotus to actively collect some information that is not collected passively. Passive counters can keep track of the number of visitors to a Web site, as well as the number of visitors who actually use the site. For example, Lotus can monitor the number of visitors who use its chat rooms that pertain to specific products. However, just knowing that the number of visitors is changing does not provide a company with any insights concerning why there is a decrease or increase in visitors. Focus groups and surveys are ways to gain those insights.

From focus groups, Lotus learned that customers wanted improved navigation and a higher level of consistency. In the past, the emphasis was on making sure that information was delivered quickly to customers. Focus groups also revealed that the company needed to develop the site further to make it easier for Web site visitors to navigate through all of the information. These findings were further verified through a survey posted on its Web site.

Based on these findings, Lotus redesigned the site so that every page is consistent. The company logo has a consistent place on each page, and a navigation shortcut system remains on the left side of the page as the user switches from page to page. The redesign was a huge undertaking for Lotus, but it resulted in a substantial increase in the number of visitors to the Web site, and generated additional repeat business.[1] ■

EXAMPLE

Marketing Research Puts Sandwich Chain on a Roll

In 1972, Port of Subs began as a single shop in Reno, Nevada. The company now continues to make submarine sandwiches on a regional basis. Port of Subs has 81 units concentrated as franchises in Las Vegas, Reno, and Fresno. Franchisees function through local co-op organizations or 22 single store markets.

Not long ago, the company was having problems with competition in the area. This comprised of submarine sandwich shops and other fast food vendors like hamburger, taco, and pizza restaurants. CEO and founder, John Larsen made a decision to hire a market research team to analyze the market and make recommendations on how to improve sales. The market research group conducted customer focus groups and one-on-one in-depth interviews to understand what factors influence consumers' choice of fast food and submarine sandwiches. Then, a telephone survey was done to identify the consumer image of the sub shop.

Gail Humes, Port of Subs marketing manager, stated that the research "told us that our image needed a little shock-therapy. Instead of continuing to position ourselves vis-à-vis just our sandwich competitors, which we'd been doing for some time, the agency proposed that we go after a bigger, more profitable slice of the pie—the entire quick-service restaurant category."

Consequently, co-op markets began to utilize a new advertising plan. Since radio would provide precise and cost-effective audience targeting, it was selected as the primary medium to deliver the new Port of Subs message. Billboards and direct mail were also used to focus advertising on select geographical regions. In areas where radio and billboard advertising were not feasible due to cost restrictions, direct mail was used to target the customer. A new "Fast, Fresh, and on a Roll" campaign was launched. Colorful and inviting photography, humor, and a new logo were used to lure the consumer, and to generate a new look and attitude for Port of Subs. The result? Marketing research estimated a 5.25 percent increase in average store sales over the previous year.[2] ■

EXAMPLE

The Making of a President

President Bill Clinton used market research to develop policies and to polish those policies once they were in place. Clinton and his team made extensive use of published sources of information, focus groups (group interviews), telephone and personal surveys, and interview style meetings in order to understand what the people were expecting from the policies that are developed. To Clinton, the taxpayers of the country were his administration's "customers."

His first big test came during his first State of the Union address when Clinton unveiled his "product of uncertain demand," a new economic package that included higher taxes. The White House used market research to smooth the rough edges of the new package and to sell it to the American people. The raising of taxes was the ultimate hard sell. Clinton made use of focus groups and telephone surveys to determine how to make the new package palatable. The research indicated that the public was willing to pay higher taxes in order to reduce the national debt, but the research also revealed that it expected both the President and Congress to deal with wasteful federal spending. Thus, deficit reduction was an important aspect of this package.

One advertising executive noted that "instituting a new policy is the same as offering a new product. When you market anything you need to concentrate on the end benefit." Clinton attempted to do just that, by making extensive use of marketing research.[3] ■

EXAMPLE

Reviving an Ailing Giant

In the early 1980s, Chrysler was fighting for survival. Fortunately, a few years earlier, two men had come to the company from Ford. These men were Lee Iacocca and Howard Sperlich, and they brought with them a revolutionary idea—the minivan.

Iacocca, a senior manager, and Sperlich, a designer, used marketing research to identify a need—better family transportation. Despite skyrocketing fuel prices in the early 1980s, "overpowering" research in the form of focus groups, mall intercept and mail surveys

Marketing research gave Chrysler the confidence to enter the minivan market that GM and Ford considered too risky, and to seize a lucrative opportunity.

suggested that consumers wanted a van that handled like a car. A Chrysler executive stated that "the people we're selling [the minivan] to don't tow. A very small percentage of Americans on a regular basis tow more than a Class 1 trailer; we can tow a Class 1 trailer." It was clear that the public did not need a workhorse vehicle, but a reliable, spacious, convenient mode of transportation.

Marketing research suggested that a minivan met these characteristics. As a result, Chrysler stunned the competition with an innovative new product that eventually was dubbed an automotive "home run" for the company. Chrysler designed its product around the consumer rather than the internal perceptions of the organization. Marketing research gave the company the confidence to enter a market that GM and Ford considered too risky. GM and Ford missed the opportunity to bring the minivan to market. GM feared it would detract from its highly lucrative station wagon segment. Ford passed for the opportunity of smaller more fuel-efficient models.

Chrysler, in contrast, developed a strong linkage between the consumer problem and the product solution. Almost 20 years later, the company's product line still accounts for about one-quarter of Chrysler's sales and a significant portion of its profits. The marketing research that brought the minivan to market, has revitalized the once ailing car manufacturer.[4] ■

EXAMPLE

M/A/R/C and Peapod: Two Peas in a Pod

The M/A/R/C Group is a leading market research provider. Peapod, L. P. is an on-line grocery shopping service. Consumers can access the Peapod Web site (www.peapod.com), and place their grocery orders on-line. Peapod partners with regional grocery stores, which provide the groceries. The groceries are then delivered to the customer.

The M/A/R/C Group and Peapod recently conducted a market research study in which they used the Internet to gather observational data on on-line grocery shopping behavior. They supplemented this with data gathered through surveys. The observational data allowed them to observe actual consumer purchase behavior. The survey data allowed them to gain insights into the motivations for the purchase behavior, as well as attitudes, beliefs, and lifestyles of the consumers. The study was conducted to provide consumer goods manufacturers and retailers with insights into the behavior and motivations of on-line grocery shoppers.

The observational data was collected on-line through the Internet. Consumers make their grocery purchases on-line through the Peapod network. Peapod then has a record of the name and address of each customer, the items they purchased, and the time of the purchase. Through these observational methods, Peapod and M/A/R/C were able to observe actual, real time purchasing behavior of 20,000 on-line shoppers.

For the survey portion of the study, M/A/R/C and Peapod administered surveys to 800 Peapod customers. The purpose of the surveys was to provide insight into the motivation behind the purchasing behavior of the on-line shoppers. M/A/R/C and Peapod believe this is the first study of its type which associates on-line observational transaction data with survey data.

The study produced interesting results that give insight into the behavior and motivations of on-line shoppers. For instance, the study showed that on average, the shoppers spent $113 per visit. This is much higher than that spent on an average shopping trip in a grocery store. The average Peapod shopper spent $2,072 per year in groceries. The heavy Peapod user spent $4,155. Also, on-line shoppers were more receptive to bargains than the typical in-store, grocery shopper. Furthermore, the most commonly mentioned reasons for purchasing specific items were, in order of importance, price, brand, and nutrition. It was clear that consumers were looking for value. Based on these findings, Peapod successfully positioned itself as a high value alternative to in-store grocery shopping.[5] ■

EXAMPLE

The Jury Is in for Marketing Research

Lawyers are now turning to marketing research in order to better understand their jury. Lawyers find target marketing research to be beneficial especially when the case is difficult, the jury pool is diverse, and the facts are controversial.

Jury research consultants use techniques such as focus groups, and demographic and psychographic databases. One marketing research device is PercepTrac, a juror database. The device is used by mock jurors to determine their positive or negative responses to facts presented in the trial. The jurors record their response changes as the trial is presented. The lawyer can then review the responses to determine if the presentation of the facts is being received well. The response data can be sorted by demographic and psychographic profiles so that a lawyer will have a better understanding of the reactions of the actual jury. The device was successfully used in a Florida Department of Transportation case in securing land for a road widening project. The device pointed out a legal term for condemning land, "a taking," which was causing many negative responses from the mock jury. When the case went to court, the lawyer avoided the legal term that had caused such a negative response with the mock jurors and won the case.[6] ■

EXAMPLE

The Super Turnaround of Supertram in Sheffield, England

Sheffield, England used professional marketing research and marketing plan to turn the tram ridership around. The Sheffield City Council decided to build an environmentally friendly and economically feasible means of transportation. The tram system was originally projected to be profitable from day one. However, initial ridership was well below expectations. The system was losing more than $4 million per year.

Marketing research enabled the super turnaround of Supertram in Sheffield, England.

The City Council hired Kevin Lannigan, formerly of Procter & Gamble, to help turn the lagging Supertram system around. He was to determine why ridership was low, and then determine what actions could be taken to increase ridership. Lannigan used a classical marketing research approach to accomplish these tasks. He conducted a review of the literature, analysis of available data, one-on-one in-depth interviews, and personal surveys. His research discovered several trends. First, the critical local press helped fuel negative perceptions and hostility towards the Supertram project. Product improvements were required on the system as well. Finally, there were misconceptions regarding pricing, reliability, and speed of service.

Supertram used the responses obtained through the research projects to make several improvements. For example, it introduced longer term, or commuter-like, tickets, as well as new pricing strategies. The use of questionnaires also helped build a customer database of over 50,000 customers, segmented into various markets. The company uses these customer categories to help determine which segments get different promotions or incentives. The research results helped turn the project around in the first year. Supertram had a 42 percent increase in ridership over the previous year. It was also able to bring the system to near break-even status during the first year after the study.[7] ■

THE NATURE OF MARKETING RESEARCH

These examples illustrate the crucial role played by marketing research in designing and implementing successful marketing programs.[8] Note, that marketing research is being used by all kinds of organizations and for a wide range of purposes. It is being used by small businesses (Port of Subs), large businesses (Chrysler), manufacturing companies (Chrysler), technology companies (Lotus), on-line marketers (Peapod), policy makers (President Clinton), professional services (lawyers), and nonprofit organizations (Sheffield City Council). These examples illustrate only a few of the methods used to conduct marketing research: mail, personal, telephone, Internet surveys, observation methods, published sources of information, analysis of large databases, one-on-one in-depth interviews, and focus groups. This text will introduce you to the full complement of marketing research techniques and illustrate their applications in formulating effective marketing strategies. Perhaps the role of marketing research can be better understood in light of the basic marketing paradigm depicted in Figure 1.1.

The emphasis in marketing is on the identification and satisfaction of customer needs. In order to determine customer needs and to implement marketing strategies and programs aimed at satisfying those needs, marketing managers need information. They need information about customers, competitors, and other forces in the marketplace. In recent years, many factors have increased the need for more detailed information. As firms have become national and international in scope, the need for information on larger and more distant markets has increased. As consumers have become more affluent and sophisticated, marketing managers need better information on how consumers will respond to products and other marketing offerings. As competition has become more intense, managers need information on the effectiveness of their marketing tools. Because the environment is changing rapidly, marketing managers need more timely information.[9]

The task of marketing research is to assess the information needs and provide management with relevant, accurate, reliable, valid, and current information. Today's competitive marketing environment and the ever-increasing costs attributed to poor decision making require that marketing research provide sound information. Sound decisions are not based on gut feeling, intuition, or even pure judgment. In the absence of sound information, an incorrect management decision may result, as illustrated by the Johnson & Johnson baby aspirin example.

Figure 1.1
The Role of Marketing Research

EXAMPLE

Johnson & Johnson's Gentleness Could Not Handle Pain

Johnson & Johnson's attempt to use its company name on baby aspirin proved to be unsuccessful. Johnson & Johnson products are perceived as gentle, but gentleness is not what people want in a baby aspirin. While baby aspirin should be safe, gentleness per se is not a desirable feature. Rather, some people perceived that a gentle aspirin may not be effective enough. So, here is an example of what seemed, intuitively, to be a natural move but turned out to be an incorrect decision.[10] ■

As indicated by the Johnson & Johnson example, marketing managers make numerous strategic and tactical decisions in the process of identifying and satisfying customer needs. As shown in Figure 1.1, they make decisions about potential opportunities, target market selection, market segmentation, planning and implementing marketing programs, marketing performance, and control. These decisions are complicated by interactions between the controllable marketing variables of product, pricing, promotion, and distribution. Further complications are added by uncontrollable environmental factors such as general economic conditions, technology, public policies and laws, political environment, competition, and social and cultural changes. Another factor in this mix is the complexity of the various customer groups: consumers, employees, shareholders, suppliers, etc. Marketing research helps the marketing manager link the marketing variables with the environment and the customer groups. It helps remove some of the uncertainty by providing relevant information about the marketing variables, environment, and consumers. In the absence of relevant information, consumers' response to marketing programs cannot be predicted reliably or accurately. Ongoing marketing research programs provide information on controllable and noncontrollable factors and consumers; this information enhances the effectiveness of decisions made by marketing managers.[11]

Traditionally, marketing researchers were responsible for assessing information needs and providing the relevant information while marketing decisions were made by the managers. However, these roles are changing and marketing researchers are becoming more involved in decision making, whereas marketing managers are becoming more involved with research. This trend can be attributed to better training of marketing managers, advances in technology, and a shift in the marketing research paradigm where more and more marketing research is being undertaken on an ongoing basis rather than in response to specific marketing problems or opportunities.[12]

This crucial role of marketing research is recognized in its definition, which is given in the next section.

DEFINITION OF MARKETING RESEARCH

The American Marketing Association's formal definition of marketing research is given in Research in Practice 1.1.[13] For the purpose of this text, which emphasizes the need for information for decision making, marketing research is defined as follows:

Marketing research is the systematic and objective identification, collection, analysis, dissemination, and use of information for the purpose of improving decision making related to the identification and solution of problems (and opportunities) in marketing.

Marketing Research The systematic and objective identification, collection, analysis, dissemination, and use of information for the purpose of assisting management in decision making related to the identification and solution of problems (and opportunities) in marketing.

Several aspects of this definition are noteworthy. First, marketing research is systematic. Thus systematic planning is required at all the stages of the **marketing research process**. The procedures followed at each stage are methodologically sound, well documented, and, as much as possible, planned in advance. Marketing research uses the scientific method, in that data are collected and analyzed to test prior notions or hypotheses.

Marketing Research Process A set of six steps which defines the tasks to be accomplished in conducting a marketing research study. These include problem definition, developing an approach to the problem, research design formulation, field work, data preparation and analysis, and report generation and presentation.

Marketing research is objective. It attempts to provide accurate information that reflects a true state of affairs. It should be conducted impartially. Although research is always influenced by the researcher's research philosophy, it should be free from the personal or political biases of the researcher or the management. Research motivated by personal or political gain involves a breach of professional standards. Such research is deliberately biased so as to result in predetermined findings. The motto of every researcher should be, "Find it and tell it like it is."

Marketing research involves the identification, collection, analysis, dissemination, and use of information. Each phase of this process is important. We identify or define the marketing

RESEARCH IN PRACTICE 1.1

The American Marketing Association Redefines Marketing Research

The Board of Directors of the American Marketing Association has approved the following as the new definition of marketing research:

Marketing research is the function that links the consumer, customer, and public to the marketer through information—information used to identify and define marketing opportunities and problems; generate, refine, and evaluate marketing actions; monitor marketing performance; and improve understanding of marketing as a process.

Marketing research specifies the information required to address these issues; designs the method for collecting information; manages and implements the data collection process; analyzes the results; and communicates the findings and their implications.

research problem or opportunity and then determine what information is needed to investigate it. Because every marketing opportunity translates into a research problem to be investigated, the terms *problem* and *opportunity* are used interchangeably here. Next, the relevant information sources are identified and a range of data collection methods varying in sophistication and complexity are evaluated for their usefulness. The data are collected using the most appropriate method; they are analyzed, interpreted, and inferences are drawn. Finally, the findings, implications, and recommendations are provided in a format that allows the information to be used for marketing decision making and to be acted upon directly. The next section elaborates on this definition by classifying different types of marketing research.[14]

A CLASSIFICATION OF MARKETING RESEARCH

Our definition states that organizations engage in marketing research for two reasons: (1) to identify and (2) solve marketing problems. This distinction serves as a basis for classifying marketing research into problem identification research and problem solving research, as shown in Figure 1.2.

Problem Identification Research Research which is undertaken to help identify problems that are not necessarily apparent on the surface and yet exist or are likely to arise in the future.

Problem identification research is undertaken to help identify problems that are, perhaps, not apparent on the surface and yet exist or are likely to arise in the future. Examples of problem identification research include market potential, market share, brand or company image, market characteristics, sales analysis, short-range forecasting, long-range forecasting, and business trends research. A survey of companies conducting marketing research indicated that 97 percent of those who responded were conducting market potential, market share, and market characteristics research. About 90 percent also reported that they were using other types of problem identification research. Research of this type provides information about the marketing environment and helps diagnose a problem. For example, a declining market potential indicates that the firm is likely to have a problem achieving its growth targets. Similarly, a problem exists if the market potential is increasing but the firm is losing market share. The recognition of economic, social, or cultural trends, such as changes in consumer behavior, may point to underlying problems or opportunities.[15]

Problem Solving Research Research undertaken to help solve specific marketing problems.

Once a problem or opportunity has been identified, **problem solving research** is undertaken to arrive at a solution. The findings of problem solving research are used in making decisions which will solve specific marketing problems. Most companies conduct problem solving research.[16] Table 1.1 shows the different types of issues that are addressed by problem solving research, including segmentation, product, pricing, promotion, and distribution research.

Figure 1.2
A Classification of Marketing Research

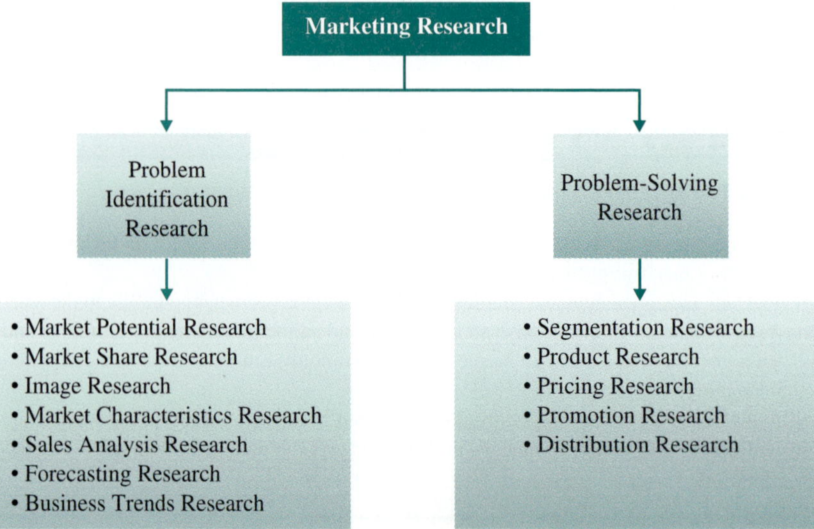

TABLE 1.1

PROBLEM SOLVING RESEARCH

Segmentation Research	Promotional Research
Determine basis of segmentation	Optimal promotional budget
Establish market potential and responsiveness for various segments	Sales promotion relationship
Select target markets and create lifestyle profiles demography, media, and product image characteristics	Optimal promotional mix
Product Research	Copy decisions
Test concept	Media decisions
Determine optimal product design	Creative advertising testing
Package tests	Claim substantiation
Product modification	Evaluation of advertising effectiveness
Brand positioning and repositioning	*Distribution Research*
Test marketing	Determine type of distribution
Control store tests	Attitudes of channel members
Pricing Research	Intensity of wholesale and retail coverage
Importance of price in brand selection	Channel margins
Pricing policies	Location of retail and wholesale outlets
Product line pricing	
Price elasticity of demand	
Initiating and responding to price changes	

Classifying marketing research into two main types is useful from a conceptual, as well as a practical, viewpoint. However, problem identification research and problem solving research go hand-in-hand, and a given marketing research project may combine both types of research. A marketing research project for Scott Paper Co. that investigated loss of market share identified the cause as increased local competition (problem identification) and the solution as the introduction of new products designed to meet this competition (problem solving). Another example is provided by Kellogg's solution to revive low cereal sales.

EXAMPLE

Cereal. Eat it for Life

Faced with a slump in the market, Kellogg's faced the challenge of reviving low cereal sales. Through marketing research, it was able to identify the problem and develop several solutions to increase cereal sales.

To identify the problem, Kellogg's used several tasks to help them in the process. The researchers spoke to decision makers within the company, interviewed industry experts, conducted analysis of available data, and performed some qualitative research. Several important issues came out of this preliminary research: current products were being targeted to the kids, bagels and muffins were winning for favored breakfast foods; high prices were turning consumers to generic brands. Some other information also came to light during the research. Adults want quick foods that require very little or no preparation. These issues helped Kellogg's identify the problem. It needed to be more creative in introducing new products to meet the needs of the adult market.

After defining the problem, Kellogg's went to work on solutions. First, it began to introduce flavors more suited to the adult palette, but were not the tasteless varieties of the past. For example, it introduced Honey-flavored Shredded Wheat and Honey Crunch Corn

Flakes. Both aimed towards the adult market. It also implemented promotions featuring Microsoft software for the entire family instead of the usual toys. Finally, it launched an ad campaign aimed at adults called *Cereal. Eat it for life.*

Through creative problem identification research followed by problem solving research, Kellogg's has not only seen an increase in sales, but also an increased consumption of cereal at times other than just breakfast.[17] ■

THE ROLE OF MARKETING RESEARCH IN MIS AND DSS

Marketing Information System (MIS) A formalized set of procedures for generating, analyzing, storing, and distributing pertinent information to marketing decision makers on an ongoing basis.

Earlier, we defined marketing research as the systematic and objective identification, collection, analysis, and dissemination of information for use in marketing decision making.[18] The information obtained through marketing research and sources such as internal records and marketing intelligence becomes an integral part of the firm's marketing information system (MIS). A **marketing information system** (MIS) is a formalized set of procedures for generating, analyzing, storing, and distributing information to marketing decision makers on an ongoing basis. Note that the definition of MIS is similar to marketing research, except that MIS provides information continuously rather than on the basis of ad hoc research studies. The design of an MIS focuses on each decision maker's responsibilities, style, and information needs. Information gathered from various sources, such as invoices and marketing intelligence, including marketing research, is combined and presented in a format which can be readily used in decision making. More information can be obtained from MIS than from ad hoc marketing research projects, but MIS is limited in the amount and nature of information it provides and the way this information can be used by the decision maker. This is because the information is rigidly structured and cannot be easily manipulated.

Decision Support System (DSS) An information system which enables decision makers to interact directly with both databases and analysis models. The important components of a DSS include hardware and a communication network, data base, model base, software base, and the DSS user (decision maker).

Developed to overcome the limitations of MIS, decision support systems (DSS) enable decision makers to interact directly with databases and analysis models. A **decision support system** (DSS) is an integrated system including hardware, communications network, database, model base, software base, and the DSS user (decision maker) that collects and interprets information for decision making. Marketing research contributes research data to the database, marketing models and analytical techniques to the model base, and specialized programs for analyzing marketing data to the software base. DSS differ from MIS in various ways (see Figure 1.3).[19] DSS combine the use of models or analytical techniques with the traditional access and retrieval functions of MIS. DSS are easier to use in an interactive mode and can adapt to changes in the environment as well as to the decision-making approach of the user. In addition to improving efficiency, DSS can

Figure 1.3
Management Information Systems versus Decision Support Systems

MIS	DSS
• Structured Problems	• Unstructured Problems
• Use of Reports	• Use of Models
• Rigid Structure	• User-Friendly Interaction
• Information Displaying Restricted	• Adaptability
• Can Improve Decision Making by Clarifying Raw Data	• Can Improve Decision Making by Using "What If" Analysis

also enhance decision making effectiveness by using "what if" analysis.[20] DSS have been further developed into expert systems, which utilize artificial intelligence procedures to incorporate expert judgment.

EXAMPLE

DSS Give FedEx a Decided Edge

Its advanced worldwide decision support systems have been major ingredients in the success of Federal Express (FedEx).

Federal Express (FedEx) has developed a reputation for being a reliable express shipping service. It has become a technology leader in the highly competitive shipping market and aims to become the best worldwide. A major ingredient in the success has been the advanced worldwide decision support systems that provide information on customers and detailed aspects of every shipment including ordering, billing, tracking, and tracing.

Its sophisticated DSS has enabled FedEx to become the first company to go from "zero to 1 billion in sales in 10 years without the aid of mergers or acquisitions, and to dominate the fast-growing overnight-cargo field." In one example of the several strategic ways in which the DSS is used, FedEx has implemented highly sophisticated "segment management marketing" (SMM). FedEx has developed a "value quotient" formula that allows marketers to analyze individual customers on a case-by-case analysis. This value quotient includes weights for strategic/competitive value of customer and profitability through a survey of 30 questions. The objectives of FedEx help define the weight given to an individual customer and provide a more strategic perspective than simply using profit to pinpoint the value of a customer. FedEx has defined 14 highly specific customer segments based on consumer attitudes relating to price, reliability, urgency, content safety of product, tracking, and proof of delivery. The current SMM includes family classifications and segments to help marketers further understand the customers they serve. Thus, FedEx has taken a very aggressive information oriented approach to competition which will be the key to continued success.[21] ■

As shown by the experience of FedEx, MIS and DSS can greatly enhance the information available to management. In making specific marketing decisions, management may also rely on marketing research suppliers and services.

MARKETING RESEARCH SUPPLIERS AND SERVICES

Internal Suppliers Marketing research departments located within a firm.

Marketing research suppliers and services provide most of the information needed for making marketing decisions. Figure 1.4 classifies marketing research suppliers and services. Broadly, research suppliers can be classified as internal or external. An **internal supplier** is a marketing research department within the firm. Many firms, particularly the big ones, ranging from automobile companies (GM, Ford, DaimlerChrysler) to consumer products firms (Procter & Gamble, Colgate Palmolive, Coca-Cola) to banks (Citigroup, BankAmerica) maintain in-house marketing research departments. The marketing research department's place in the organizational structure may vary considerably. At one extreme, the research function may be centralized and located at the corporate headquarters. At the other extreme is a decentralized structure in which the marketing research function is organized along divisional lines. In a decentralized scheme, the company may be organized into divisions by products, customers, or geographical regions, with marketing research personnel assigned to the various divisions. These personnel generally report to a division manager rather than to a corporate level executive. In addition, between these two extremes, there is a variety of organizations. The best organization for a firm depends on its marketing research needs and the structure of marketing and other functions, although in recent years there has been a trend toward centralization and a trimming of marketing research staff. Internal suppliers often rely on external suppliers to perform specific marketing research tasks. Research in Practice 1.2 illustrates the organization of the marketing research function at Oscar Mayer.[22]

External Suppliers Outside marketing research companies hired to supply marketing research services.

Full-Service Suppliers Companies that offer the full range of marketing research activities.

External suppliers are outside firms hired to supply marketing research services. These external suppliers, which collectively comprise the marketing research industry, range from small, one or a few persons, to operations to very large global corporations.[23] Research in Practice 1.3 lists the top 50 marketing research suppliers in the United States.[24] External suppliers can be classified as full-service or limited-service suppliers. **Full-service suppliers** offer the entire range of marketing research services, from problem definition, developing an approach, questionnaire design, sampling, data collection, data analysis, and interpretation,

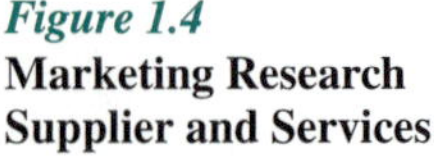

Figure 1.4
Marketing Research Supplier and Services

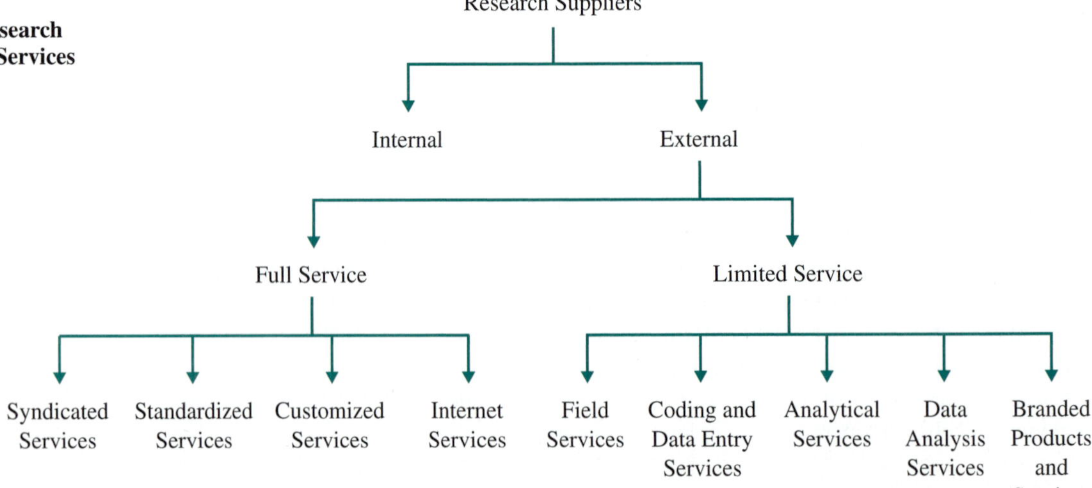

to report preparation and presentation. The services provided by these suppliers can be further broken down into syndicated services, standardized services, customized, and Internet services (Figure 1.4).

Syndicated services collect information which is then provided to subscribers. Surveys, diary panels, scanners, and audits are the main means by which these data are collected. For example, the Nielsen Television Index provides information on audience size and demographic characteristics of households watching specific television programs. Scanner volume tracking data, such as those generated by electronic scanning at check-out counters in supermarkets, are also provided by the A. C. Nielsen Company. The Stanford Research Institute, on the other hand, conducts an annual survey of consumers that is used to classify persons into homogeneous groups for segmentation purposes. The National Purchase Diary (NPD) panel maintains the largest diary panel in the United States. Syndicated services are discussed in more detail in chapter 4.[25]

Standardized services are research studies conducted for different client firms but in a standard way. For example, procedures for measuring advertising effectiveness have been standardized so that the results can be compared across studies and evaluative norms can be established. The Starch Readership Survey is the most widely used service for evaluating print advertisements; another well-known service is the Gallup and Robinson Magazine Impact Studies. These services are also sold on a syndicated basis.

Customized services offer a wide variety of marketing research services customized to suit a client's specific needs. Each marketing research project is treated uniquely. Some marketing research firms that offer these services include Burke, Inc., Market Facts, Inc., and Elrick & Lavidge.

Internet services are offered by several marketing research firms including some who have specialized in conducting marketing research on the Internet. For example, Greenfield Online Research Center Inc., of Westport, Connecticut, a subsidiary of the Greenfield Consulting firm, offers a broad range of customized qualitative and quantitative on-line marketing research for consumer, business-to-business, and professional markets. Using large, proprietary databases, this firm conducts studies within its secure Web site.

Limited-service suppliers specialize in one or a few phases of the marketing research project. Services offered by such suppliers are classified as field services, coding and data entry, data analysis, analytical services, and branded products. **Field services** collect data

Syndicated Services Companies that collect and sell common pools of data designed to serve information needs shared by a number of clients.

Standardized Services Companies that use standardized procedures to provide marketing research to various clients.

Customized Services Companies that tailor research procedures to best meet the needs of each client.

Internet Services Companies specializing in conducting marketing research on the Internet.

Limited-Service Suppliers Companies specializing in one or a few phases of the marketing research project.

Field Services Companies offering their expertise in collecting data for research projects.

RESEARCH IN PRACTICE 1.2

Organization of Marketing Research at Oscar Mayer

The Oscar Mayer marketing research department is organized into two functional areas: Brand Research and Marketing Systems and Analytics (MSA). The Brand Research group has the following responsibilities:

- Conducting primary and secondary research
- Serving as marketing consultants
- Analyzing market trends
- Advancing the state-of-the-art in marketing research

Researchers in the MSA group fulfill three main roles:

- Performing sales analysis based on shipment and store-scanner data
- Supporting computer end users within the marketing department
- Serving as a source of marketing information

RESEARCH IN PRACTICE 1.3

Top 50 U.S. Research Organizations

Rank 1997	Rank 1996	Organization	Total research revenues* (millions)	Percent and revenues from outside U.S. (in millions)	
1	1	AC Nielsen Corp.	$1,391.6	77.7%	$1,081.6
2	2	Cognizant Corp.	1,339.1	49.2	659.1
3	3	Information Resources Inc.	456.3	19.6	89.6
4	6	Westat Inc.	182.0	—	—
5	8	NFO Worldwide Inc.	190.0***	21.4	35.8
6	4	The Arbitron Co.	165.2	—	—
7	7	Maritz Marketing Research Inc.	146.0	20.0	29.2
8	9	The Kantar Group Ltd.	127.1	20.2	25.7
9	10	The NPD Group Inc.	110.3	18.3	20.2
10	11	Market Facts Inc.	100.1	7.0	7.0
11	5	Pharm. Marketing Services Inc.	91.6	46.0	42.1
12	12	Audits & Surveys Worldwide Inc.	68.9	43.5	30.0
13	14	BASES Worldwide	57.6	19.7	11.4
14	13	The M/A/R/C Group Inc.	57.3	1.5	0.1
15	15	Opinion Research Corp.	53.9	32.7	17.6
16	16	SOFRES Intersearch	53.0	15.0	8.5
17	18	NOP Information Group	52.0	—	—
18	20	J. D. Power and Associates	51.5	3.9	2.0
19	22	Burke Inc.	43.8	22.8	10.0
20	19	Macro International Inc.	42.9	38.5	16.5
21	23	Roper Starch Worldwide Inc.	40.0	17.8	7.1
22	17	Abt Associates Inc.	39.3	—	—
23	21	Elrick & Lavidge	37.1	5.7	2.1
24	38	IntelliQuest Inc.	36.5	29.0	10.6
25	26	Wirthlin Worldwide	35.5	16.0	5.7
26	28	Total Research Corp.	33.1	27.2	9.0
27	25	MORPACE International	31.2	17.9	5.6
28	27	C&R Research Services Inc.	31.1	—	—
29	24	Walker Information	30.9	21.8	6.7
30	29	Lieberman Research Worldwide	28.6	13.3	3.8
31	34	Diagnostic Research International Inc.	26.7	3.1	0.8
32	33	IPSOS-ASI Inc.	26.7	—	—
33	30	Yankelovich Partners Inc.	26.4	—	—
34	31	Custom Research Inc.	25.8	—	—
35	39	Harris Black International Ltd.	25.7	7.4	1.9
36	32	Market Strategies Inc.	25.2	1.6	0.4
37	37	ICR-Int'l Communications Research	22.3	—	—
38	36	Data Development Corp.	22.2	8.7	1.9
39	35	Chilton Research Services	21.5	—	—
40	40	Market Decisions	18.2	—	—
41	—	National Research Corp.	16.3	—	—
42	43	Response Analysis Corp.	15.9	6.0	0.9

(Continued)

RESEARCH IN PRACTICE 1.3 *(Continued)*

Rank 1997	1996	Organization	Total research revenues* (millions)	Percent and revenues from outside U.S. (in millions)	
43	—	Marketing and Planning Systems	14.2	6.0	0.9
44	46	MATRIXX Marketing Research	14.1	41.1	5.8
45	41	RDA Group Inc.	14.0	30.0	4.2
46	45	Guideline Research Corp.	13.3	2.3	0.3
47	48	Directions Research Inc.	13.2	—	—
48	44	Conway/Milliken & Associates	13.0	—	—
49	49	TVG Inc.	12.3	—	—
50	—	Savitz Research Center Inc.	12.0	—	—
Subtotal, Top 50			$5,479.7	39.3%	$2,153.2
All other (124 CASRO member companies not included in Top 50)***			535.7		
Total (174 organizations)			6,015.4		

through mail, personal, or telephone interviewing; and firms that specialize in interviewing are called field service organizations. These organizations may range from small proprietary organizations that operate locally to large multinational organizations with WATS-line interviewing facilities. Some organizations maintain extensive interviewing facilities across the country for interviewing shoppers in malls. Many offer qualitative data-collection services such as focus group interviewing (discussed in chapter 5). Some firms that offer field services are Field Facts, Inc., Field Work Chicago, Inc., Quality Controlled Services, and Survey America.

Coding and data entry services include editing completed questionnaires, developing a coding scheme, and transcribing the data on to diskettes or magnetic tapes for input into the computer. NRC Data Systems provides such services.

Coding and Data Entry Services Companies offering their expertise in converting completed surveys or interviews into a usable database for conducting statistical analysis.

Analytical services include designing and pretesting questionnaires, determining the best means of collecting data, designing sampling plans, and other aspects of the research design. Some complex marketing research projects require knowledge of sophisticated procedures, including specialized experimental designs (discussed in chapter 7), and analytical techniques such as conjoint analysis and multidimensional scaling (discussed in chapter 21). This kind of expertise can be obtained from firms and consultants specializing in analytical services.

Analytical Services Companies that provide guidance in the development of the research design.

Data analysis services are offered by firms, also known as tab houses, that specialize in computer analysis of quantitative data such as those obtained in large surveys. Initially most data analysis firms supplied only tabulations (frequency counts) and cross-tabulations (frequency counts that describe two or more variables simultaneously). Now many firms, such as SDR, Inc., offer sophisticated data analysis using advanced statistical techniques. With the proliferation of microcomputers and software, many firms now have the capability to analyze their own data, but data analysis firms are still in demand.

Data Analysis Services Firms whose primary service is to conduct statistical analysis of quantitative data.

Branded marketing research products and services are specialized data collection and analysis procedures developed to address specific types of marketing research problems. These procedures are patented, given brand names, and marketed like any other branded product. Magic Wand by DigiData Entry System is an example of a branded

Branded Marketing Research Products Specialized data collection and analysis procedures developed to address specific types of marketing research problems.

product that transcribes data from printed questionnaires into a computer readable format. It uses a handheld scanner to pick up respondent-completed checkmarks, interprets them, and writes them to a disk. Research in Practice 1.4 provides a perspective on full-service versus limited-service suppliers.[26]

SELECTING A RESEARCH SUPPLIER

A firm that cannot conduct an entire marketing research project in-house must select an external supplier for one or more phases of the project. The firm should compile a list of prospective suppliers from sources such as trade publications, professional directories, word of mouth, and the Internet. When deciding on criteria for selecting an outside supplier, a firm should ask itself why it is seeking outside marketing research support. For example, a

RESEARCH IN PRACTICE 1.4

Full-Service versus Limited-Service Marketing Research Firms

Susan Adelman and Kevin Heaken of Survey Service, Inc. and Heaken Research, respectively, both field survey firms, find that more often today, clients will perform the problem definition and designing the survey instrument in-house to subcontract the data collection. This is done in order to cut costs in market research. This has also changed the method and approach of the full-service companies to meet new customer needs. Burke Marketing Research, a large full-service company, has replaced many in-house departments for end users who have cut their in-house staff because of the trend of downsizing. An example would be Ocean Spray or Quaker Oats, which cut marketing staff and subcontract all marketing research to companies such as Burke and Maritz Marketing Research. So now, the end user simply provides the full-service company with a management decision problem, which is interpreted and articulated into the marketing research problem by a full-service company, and the other steps are also performed by the market research company. Some companies believe that they can reduce costs by going straight to the field service companies. However, according to Cathy Kneidl, VP for Quality Control Services, a branch of Maritz, this is a mistake because the steps leading up to the data collection are omitted, which renders the market research questionable. The approach and process of market research are critical to obtain data that can be useful and interpreted to improve or make sound management decisions. The issue is determining if the company requires a full-service company, which would undertake the entire research process, or is field research satisfactory, as in Samsonite. Samsonite wanted to test the market for responses to various suitcase colors. For this research, a full service firm was not necessary, only a survey had to be administered to confirm trends or preferences.

For researching well-defined problems, Samsonite often hires limited-service rather than full-service marketing research firms.

small firm that needs one project investigated may find it economically efficient to employ an outside source. Or a firm may not have the technical expertise to undertake certain phases of a project or political conflict-of-interest issues may determine that a project be conducted by an outside supplier.

When developing criteria for selecting an outside supplier, a firm should keep some basics in mind. What is the reputation of the supplier? Do they complete projects on schedule? Are they known for maintaining ethical standards? Are they flexible? Are their research projects of high quality? What kind and how much experience does the supplier have? Has the firm had experience with projects similar to this one? Do the supplier's personnel have both technical and nontechnical expertise? In other words, in addition to technical skills, are the personnel assigned to the task sensitive to the client's needs and do they share the client's research ideology? Can they communicate well with the client?

Remember that the cheapest bid is not always the best one. Competitive bids should be obtained and compared on the basis of quality, as well as price. A good practice is to get a written bid or contract before beginning the project. Decisions about marketing research suppliers, just like other management decisions, should be based on sound information.

CAREERS IN MARKETING RESEARCH

Promising career opportunities are available with marketing research firms (e.g., A. C. Nielsen, Burke, Inc., M/A/R/C). Equally appealing are careers in business and nonbusiness firms and agencies with in-house marketing research departments (e.g., Procter & Gamble, Coca-Cola, AT&T, the Federal Trade Commission, U.S. Census Bureau). Advertising agencies (e.g., BBDO International, Ogilvy & Mather, J. Walter Thompson, Young & Rubicam) also conduct substantial marketing research and employ professionals in this field. Some of the positions available in marketing research include vice president of marketing research, research director, assistant director of research, project manager, field work director, statistician/data processing specialist, senior analyst, analyst, junior analyst, and operational supervisor. Figure 1.5 lists job titles in marketing research and describes their accompanying responsibilities.[27] Research in Practice 1.5 gives several examples of job ads one might see in newspapers, journals, and trade magazines.[28]

The most common entry-level position in marketing research for people with bachelor's degrees (e.g., B.B.A.) is as operational supervisor. These people are responsible for supervising a well-defined set of operations, including field work, data editing, and coding, and may be involved in programming and data analysis. Another entry-level position for B.B.A.s is assistant project manager. An assistant project manager will learn and assist in questionnaire design, review field instructions, and monitor timing and costs of studies. In the marketing research industry, however, there is a growing preference for people with master's degrees. Those with M.B.A. or equivalent degrees are likely to be employed as project managers. In marketing research firms such as Elrick & Lavidge, the project manager works with the account director in managing the day-to-day operations of a marketing research project. The typical entry-level position in a business firm would be junior research analyst (for B.B.A.s) or research analyst (for M.B.A.s). The junior analyst and the research analyst learn about the particular industry and receive training from a senior staff member, usually the marketing research manager. The junior analyst position includes a training program to prepare individuals for the responsibilities of a research analyst, including coordinating with the marketing department and sales force to develop goals for product exposure. The research analyst responsibilities include checking all data for accuracy, comparing and contrasting new research with established norms, and analyzing primary and secondary data for the purpose of market forecasting.

As these job titles indicate, people with a variety of backgrounds and skills are needed in marketing research. Technical specialists such as statisticians obviously need strong backgrounds in statistics and data analysis. Other positions, such as research director, call

1. **Vice President of Marketing Research**: This is the senior position in marketing research. The vice president is responsible for the entire marketing research operation of the company and serves on the top management team. Sets the objectives and goals of the marketing research department.
2. **Research Director**: Also a senior position, the director has the overall responsibility for the development and execution of all the marketing research projects.
3. **Assistant Director of Research**: Serves as an administrative assistant to the director and supervises some of the other marketing research staff members.
4. **(Senior) Project Manager**: Has overall responsibility for design, implementation, and management of research projects.
5. **Statistician/Data Processing Specialist**: Serves as an expert on theory and application of statistical techniques. Responsibilities include experimental design, data processing, and analysis.
6. **Senior Analyst**: Participates in the development of projects and directs the operational execution of the assigned projects. Works closely with the analyst, junior analyst, and other personnel in developing the research design and data collection. Prepares the final report. The primary responsibility for meeting time and cost constraints rests with the senior analyst.
7. **Analyst**: Handles the details involved in executing the project. Designs and pretests the questionnaires and conducts a preliminary analysis of the data.
8. **Junior Analyst**: Handles routine assignments such as secondary data analysis, editing and coding of questionnaires, and simple statistical analysis.
9. **Field Work Director**: Responsible for the selection, training, supervision, and evaluation of interviewers and other field workers.

Figure 1.5
Selected Marketing Research Job Descriptions

for managing the work of others and require more general skills. To prepare for a career in marketing research you should:

- take all the marketing courses you can
- take courses in statistics and quantitative methods
- acquire Internet and computer skills. Knowledge of programming languages is an added asset
- take courses in psychology and consumer behavior
- acquire effective written and verbal communication skills
- think creatively. Creativity and common sense command a premium in marketing research

Marketing researchers should be liberally educated so that they can understand the problems confronting managers and address them from a broad perspective.[29] The following example shows what managers look for in entry-level employees.

EXAMPLE

Amoco Digs for the Right Stuff

Abdul Azhari, marketing research director for Amoco, Chicago, looks for the following credentials when hiring new members for his department:

"It's essential that they know how to dig into the analytical matters, that they know how to analyze things. Also, it's essential that they know how to analyze data with an eye to practicality and application to marketing needs. It is also essential that they can communicate verbally and in writing to the various client departments that we have and also adjust communication to these various departments so that when they are with R&D people, they talk the language of scientists. When the client is the director of sales, they have to be

RESEARCH IN PRACTICE 1.5

A Sample of Marketing Research Jobs

The Gallup Organization

SURVEY RESEARCH

- **RESEARCH ANALYSTS**
- **RESEARCH ASSOCIATES**
- **BUSINESS DEVELOPMENT/SALES**

- ***Do you want to lead your industry in research innovation?***
- ***Did your graduate program emphasize marketing research?***
- ***Are you an outstanding writer and analyst who conceptualizes the big picture?***
- ***Do you have a career commitment to high quality survey research and Fortune 500 consulting?***
- ***Are you an overachiever, always striving and pushing yourself to do more?***
- ***Do you build warm, supportive friendships with associates and clients, establishing long-term partnerships?***
- ***Do you have the courage to make difficult recommendations and support them when challenged?***
- ***Are you a perfectionist? Do you assume responsibility for careful completion of all phases of the research process?***
- ***Do you put your clients' needs above your own?***

The Gallup Organization will hire in a variety of US and international locations. Advanced degree required for all analysis positions. Responsibility for designing and directing studies, contributing to proposals, sample design, questionnaire design, analyzing crosstabs, analyzing complex survey data, writing reports, and presenting results to clients.

Business development professionals will generate leads, make presentations, and close sales. Any background considered, big-ticket, intangible sales strongly preferred.

The most respected name in survey research, Gallup is growing at a rate of 30% annually. We offer excellent salary plus performance incentives. If you are an innovator and leader with a desire to create a vision for the future of research, we invite you to interview.

Call: 1-800-561-5257 or 1-800-561-5258
and ask for an interview appointment with Laura Mussman

Equal Opportunity Employer

The Gallup Organization

We are focused on the future.

Yours and Ours.

SABRE is a multimillion dollar firm owned by AMR, Corp., parent company of American Airlines. SABRE is the leading provider of business decision support tools to the travel and transportation industry. SABRE currently has an opportunity for:

SENIOR MARKETING RESEARCH ANALYST

We are currently seeking a Senior Marketing Research Analyst to work closely with internal clients and travel providers to gain an understanding of customer needs, expectations and perceptions to resolve business problems and make recommendations for resolutions. Qualitative and quantitative methodologies are utilized and approximately 40% of the projects are international in scope.

The qualified candidate must possess 5+ years of primary marketing research experience and a college degree, advanced degree preferred. Strong analytical skills as well as excellent oral and written communication skills required. Must have experience working with outside research suppliers in consumer and business-to-business industries and the ability to manage 5-7 primary research studies simultaneously. Moderating experience, SPSS skills and International research a plus.

We offer an exciting, fast-paced environment with opportunities for advancement, competitive salaries, travel privileges and a Flexible Benefits Plan. If interested, please forward your resume to: **SABRE Group, P.O. Box 619615, MD4126, Dept. MN0302/SMR, D/FW Airport, TX 75261-9615; Fax: (817) 931-5697; E-mail: sabre_group_recruitment@sabre.com** No phone calls, please. If possible, send a clean, scannable resume on white paper in 12-point text. Please visit our website at **www.sabre.com** EOE

MARKET RESEARCH

- Oak Brook, IL based restaurant has three **Business Research Manager** positions available. Ideal candidate should have a strong quantitative focus with experience in trend analysis, statistical techniques, and general data analysis. $75K.
- **Account Group Manager** – Growing suppliers seek professionals with 4-10 years of account management experience. Must have strong analytical and presentation skills. Advertising or telecom experience a plus! IL, MN, OH. $55-80K + Bonus.
- **Research Managers/Directors** needed with 3+ years in business-to-business research. Consumer, financial, health, and hi-tech experience with a supplier a plus. NJ, CT, NY, CA, IL. $50-100K.
- **Market research professionals** needed for positions with consumer packaged goods and syndicated data clients. Experience in consumer packaged goods research. MBA preferred but not necessary. NY, CT, NJ, CA, IL, OH, MI, GA, NC, PA, CO. $50-70K.

SMITH HANLEY
Associates, Inc.

Please call or write:

Shirley Baron	Rhonda Leucuta
Maryann Meyer	Nancy Glaser
256 Post Road East	200 W. Madison
Westport, CT 06880	Chicago, IL 60606
Tel.: 203-221-8939	Tel.: 312-629-2400
Fax: 203-221-8938	Fax: 312-629-0615

Please visit our website @ http://www.smithhanley.com

EXECUTIVE RECRUITERS

MARKET RESEARCH

Established, dynamic, quality and value driven Westchester-based company w/a wide range of corporate clients seeking ambitious, energetic Assistant VPs. If you desire autonomy, professional challenges, growth opportunities, pleasant working environment, highly competitive compensation and benefits, then this is the job for you. Must be able to direct projects independently, including study design, proposal preparation, questionnaire development and data analysis and report writing. Successful candidates will cultivate and support clients, and train and direct project staff. Project management background in a supplier required. Position is heavily to weighted to client service. Minimum 5 years custom research supplier experience. Client side exp/MBA a plus. All replies strictly confidential.

Fax/mail resume to:
BAIGlobal Inc.
Attn: RKA
580 White Plains Road
Tarrytown, NY 10591
Fax: 914-631-8300

able to speak 'marketingese.' Their written word as well as their presentation must be appropriate to the audience.

They must look at the broad picture. They must see the forest—not only the trees. They must also understand that marketing research is one element of the process and is not the end itself."[30] ■

MARKETING RESEARCH PROCESS

We conceptualize the marketing research process as consisting of six steps. Each of these steps is discussed in great detail in the subsequent chapters; thus, the discussion here is brief.

Step 1: Problem Definition

The first step in any marketing research project is to define the problem. In defining the problem, the researcher should take into account the purpose of the study, the relevant background information, what information is needed, and how it will be used in decision making. Problem definition involves discussion with the decision makers, interviews with industry experts, analysis of secondary data, and, perhaps, some qualitative research, such as focus groups. Once the problem has been precisely defined, the research can be designed and conducted properly (see chapter 2).

Step 2: Development of an Approach to the Problem

Development of an approach to the problem includes formulating an objective or theoretical framework, analytical models, research questions, hypotheses, and identifying characteristics or factors that can influence the research design. This process is guided by discussions with management and industry experts, case studies and simulations, analysis of secondary data, qualitative research, and pragmatic considerations (see chapter 2).

Step 3: Research Design Formulation

A research design is a framework or blueprint for conducting the marketing research project. It details the procedures necessary for obtaining the required information, and its purpose is to design a study that will test the hypotheses of interest, determine possible answers to the research questions, and provide the information needed for decision making. Conducting exploratory research, precisely defining the variables, and designing appropriate scales to measure them are also a part of the research design. The issue of how the data should be obtained from the respondents (for example, by conducting a survey or an experiment) must be addressed. It is also necessary to design a questionnaire and a sampling plan to select respondents for the study. More formally, formulating the research design involves the following steps:

1. Secondary data analysis
2. Qualitative research
3. Methods of collecting quantitative data (survey, observation, and experimentation)
4. Measurement and scaling procedures
5. Questionnaire design
6. Sampling process and sample size
7. Plan of data analysis

These steps are discussed in detail in chapters 3–12.

Step 4: Field Work or Data Collection

Data collection involves a field force or staff that operates either in the field, as in the case of personal interviewing (in-home, mall intercept, or computer-assisted personal interviewing), from an office by telephone (telephone or computer-assisted telephone interviewing), through mail (traditional mail and mail panel surveys with prerecruited households), or electronically (e-mail or Internet). Proper selection, training, supervision, and evaluation of the field force helps minimize data-collection errors (see chapter 13).

Step 5: Data Preparation and Analysis

Data preparation includes the editing, coding, transcription, and verification of data. Each questionnaire or observation form is inspected, or edited, and, if necessary, corrected. Number or letter codes are assigned to represent each response to each question in the questionnaire. The data from the questionnaires are transcribed or key-punched on to magnetic tape, or disks, or inputted directly into the computer. Verification ensures that the data from the original questionnaires have been accurately transcribed, while data analysis, guided by the plan of data analysis, gives meaning to the data that have been collected. Univariate techniques are used for analyzing data when there is a single measurement of each element or unit in the sample, or, if there are several measurements of each element, each variable is analyzed in isolation. On the other hand, multivariate techniques are used for analyzing data when there are two or more measurements on each element and the variables are analyzed simultaneously (see chapters 14–21).

Step 6: Report Preparation and Presentation

The entire project should be documented in a written report which addresses the specific research questions identified, describes the approach, the research design, data collection, and data analysis procedures adopted, and presents the results and the major findings. The findings should be presented in a comprehensible format so that they can be readily used in the decision making process. In addition, an oral presentation should be made to management using tables, figures, and graphs to enhance clarity and impact (see chapter 22).

As indicated by Research in Practice 1.6, our description of the marketing research process is fairly typical of the research being done by major corporations.[31]

RESEARCH IN PRACTICE 1.6

Marketing Research at Marriott Corporation

Marriott functions in three main areas: lodging (Marriott Hotels and Resorts, Marriott Suites, Residence, Courtyard, and Fairfield Inns), contract services (Marriott Business Food and Services, Education, Health Care and In-Flight Services, and Host International, Inc.) and restaurants (family restaurants, Travel Plazas, and Hot Shoppes). However, its is probably best known for its lodging operations.

Marketing research at Marriott is done at the corporate level through the Corporate Marketing Services (CMS). CMS's goals include providing managers of the different areas of Marriott with the information that they need to better understand the market and the customer.

CMS does many different types of research. It uses quantitative and qualitative research approaches such as telephone and mail surveys, focus groups, and customer intercept to gain more information on market segmentation and sizing, product testing, price sensitivity of consumers, consumer satisfaction, and the like.

The process of research at Marriott is a simple stepwise progression. The first steps are to better define the problem to be addressed, the objectives of the client unit, and to develop an approach to the problem. The next step is to formulate a research design and design the study. CMS must decide whether to do its own research or to buy it from an outside organization. Also it must decide whether or not to use multiple firms in the latter case. Once a decision is made, the research is carried out by collecting and analyzing the data. Then CMS presents the study findings. The final step in the research process is to keep a constant dialogue between the client and CMS. During this stage, CMS may help explain the implications of the research findings or make suggestions for future actions.

THE DEPARTMENT STORE PATRONAGE PROJECT

A department store patronage project conducted by the author is used as a running example throughout this text to illustrate concepts and data analysis procedures. The purpose of this project was to assess the relative strengths and weaknesses of a major department store, relative to a group of direct and indirect competitors. This store will be referred to as Sears; the true identity of the actual store has been disguised. The goal was to formulate marketing programs designed to boost the declining sales and profits of Sears. Ten major stores, including prestigious department stores (e.g., Saks Fifth Avenue, Neiman Marcus), national chains (e.g., J.C. Penney), discount stores (e.g., K-Mart, Target), and some regional chains (e.g., Belk) were considered in this study. A nondisguised questionnaire was designed and administered, using in-home personal interviews, to a convenience sample of 271 households drawn from a major metropolitan area. A six-point scale was used (subjects were asked to check a number from 1 to 6) whenever ratings were obtained. The following information was solicited:

1. Familiarity with the 10 department stores
2. Frequency with which household members shopped at each of the 10 stores
3. Relative importance attached to each of the eight factors selected as the choice criteria utilized in selecting a department store. These factors were quality of merchandise, variety and assortment of merchandise, returns and adjustment policy, service of store personnel, prices, convenience of location, layout of store, and credit and billing policies
4. Evaluation of the 10 stores on each of the 8 factors of the choice criteria
5. Preference ratings for each store
6. Rankings of the 10 stores (from most preferred to least preferred)
7. Degree of agreement with 21 lifestyle statements
8. Standard demographic characteristics (age, education, etc.)
9. Name, address, and telephone number

The study helped the sponsor to determine consumer perceptions of and preferences for the department store. Areas of weakness were identified in terms of specific factors influencing the consumers' choice criteria and in terms of specific product categories. Appropriate marketing programs were designed to overcome these weaknesses. Finally, a positioning strategy was developed to attain a desirable store image.

Some Americans were born to shop in department stores.

INTERNATIONAL MARKETING RESEARCH

The United States accounts for only 39 percent of the marketing research expenditures worldwide. About 40 percent of all marketing research is conducted in Western Europe and 9 percent in Japan. Most of the research in Europe is done in Germany, the United Kingdom, France, Italy, and Spain.[32] With the globalization of markets, marketing research has assumed a truly international character and this trend is likely to continue. Several U.S. firms conduct international marketing research, including AC Nielsen, Information Resources, and NFO Worldwide (see Research In Practice 1.3). Foreign-based firms include IMS International, AGB (United Kingdom), Infratest and GfK (Germany).

Conducting international marketing research (research for true international products), foreign research (research carried out in a country other than the country of the research commissioning organization), or multinational research (research conducted in all or all important countries where the company is represented), is much more complex than domestic marketing research. All research of this kind, including cross-cultural research, will be discussed under the broad rubric of international marketing research. The environment prevailing in the countries, cultural units, or international markets being researched influences the way the six steps of the marketing research process should be performed. These environmental factors and their impact on the marketing research process are discussed in detail in subsequent chapters.

Despite the complexity involved, international marketing research is expected to grow at a faster rate than domestic research. A major contributing factor is that markets for many products in the United States are approaching saturation. In contrast, the markets for these products in other countries are in the early stages of development, as illustrated by the following example.

EXAMPLE

Unilever Taps Thai Lifestyles

Thanks to the rapid economic growth Thailand has known in the past few years, there are now millions of people in the middle class looking for an international lifestyle and international products. For instance, the haircare market is dominated by Procter & Gamble and Unilever with its different brands such as Sunsilk, Dimension, Organic, among others. Some Thai women seem to prefer brands directly imported from western countries and this has become an interesting market segment for Unilever.

With marketing research, it has been indeed proved that "metropolitan Thais are more eager to try new products than many other nationalities." Moreover, young women believe that changing their shampoo brands regularly makes their hair look better. The conservative appearance of many Thais has also recently changed with a turn into "radical new looks" and there is an increasing number of people becoming "fashion-conscious," especially for their hair. Last but not least, what happens in Thailand influences the consumer trends in neighboring countries such as Cambodia, Laos, or Vietnam that are looking at Thai people as a source of new and other lifestyle ideas.

International marketing research greatly helped Unilever to rethink both Thailand and international strategy on hair products. It enabled the decision makers to take into account the cultural background and the cultural evolution of the Thai population. Having acquired so much information on the growing and quickly evolving Thai market, Unilever has reoriented its strategy. Thus, Thailand has become one of Unilever's key centers for the development of new hair products and Unilever's Organic shampoo was first launched in Thailand before being available worldwide.[33] ■

ETHICS IN MARKETING RESEARCH

Several aspects of marketing research have strong ethical implications. As explained earlier, marketing research is generally conducted by commercial (i.e., for-profit) firms which are either independent research organizations (external suppliers) or departments within corporations (internal suppliers). Most marketing research is conducted for clients representing commercial firms. The profit motive may occasionally cause researchers or clients to compromise the objectivity or professionalism associated with the marketing research process, as the following example illustrates.

EXAMPLE

"Sugging" and "Frugging" Are Unethical

Sometimes directing marketing and telemarketing firms contact consumers under the pretense of conducting survey research but with the real motive of generating sales leads. Such surveys ask information about interest in the marketer's products, background and demographic variables, and respondent's desire for more information. Information on respondents who show interest or request more information is passed on to the company's salespeople with instructions to pursue these "hot leads." Clearly, the purpose of these surveys is not scientific investigation but generating sales leads. This practice is called "sugging." "Frugging" is a similar practice and involves soliciting funds under the guise of research. Both "sugging" and "frugging" are unethical and hurt the cause of marketing research. The marketing research industry has taken an aggressive stand against both these practices.[34] ■

Marketing research has often been described as having four stakeholders: (1) the marketing researcher, (2) the client, (3) the respondent, and (4) the public. These stakeholders have certain responsibilities to each other and to the research project. Ethics issues arise when the interests of these stakeholders are in conflict and when one or more of the stakeholders are lacking in their responsibilities. For example, if the researcher does not follow appropriate marketing research procedures, or if the client misrepresents the findings in the company's advertising, ethical norms are violated. Ethical issues are best resolved by the stakeholders behaving honorably. Codes of conduct, such as the American Marketing Association code of ethics, are available to guide behavior and help resolve ethical dilemmas. These ethical issues are discussed in more detail in subsequent chapters and in chapter 24 which is devoted to ethical theories and models and which presents a framework for incorporating ethics in marketing research.

INTERNET AND COMPUTER APPLICATIONS

The Internet, also known as the Information Super Highway, is possibly the greatest communication medium since the telephone. The World Wide Web (www or Web) is the dominant component of the Internet and many use the terms Web and Internet synonymously. Each document on the Web has a specific electronic address called a Uniform Resource Locator (URL). In this text we list the URLs of several sites useful for marketing research. These sites are not guaranteed to be available or to be at the same URL when you read this text, as the Internet changes rapidly.

There are many ways in which the Internet can be useful to marketing researchers. It can be used as a source of marketing research providers; a source of secondary data; a source for marketing research software; and as a source for data gathering via focus groups, surveys, etc. It is another source of information that feeds into the firm's marketing information system. One of the great advantages of doing research on the Internet is that the data can be processed as fast as they come in. Internet data do not require the extra step of data input because the data are electronically sent from the respondent. The Internet is also very useful for project management. Internet e-mail combined with software such as Lotus Notes is being used for communication by researchers and clients, and for coordinating and managing the six steps of the marketing research process. The Internet is also being used to disseminate marketing research results and reports, which can be posted on the Web and made available to managers on a worldwide basis.

One way to determine what information is on the Internet is to use search engines to do queries for information. Search engines are usually provided free of charge by the Internet service provider. Yahoo! at www.yahoo.com/, AltaVista at altavista.digital.com/, and Infoseek at guide.infoseek.com/ are three well-known search engines.

The Internet is very efficient for identifying marketing research firms that supply specific services. Using a search engine, such as Yahoo, several research firms can be identified. When selecting a research supplier, it is easy to find information on the suppliers at their Web sites. Many sites include information on company history, products, clients, and employees. For an example visit The Marketing Tools Directory at marketingtools.com/directory/index.htm and click on the market research option. To view specific Internet sites of a well-known marketing research firms visit Burke Marketing Research at www.burke.com. Research in Practice 1.7 gives the URLs of important marketing research associations.[35]

In our earlier discussion on careers in marketing research, job descriptions were given along with directions for preparing for such jobs. The Internet can be used to help find a job in marketing research. Research Info at www.researchinfo.com/ and Marketing Research Roundtable at www.drgutah.com/wwwboard/ both offer research employment boards where job postings and jobs wanted ads are placed.

The Internet is fast becoming a useful tool in the identification, collection, analysis, and dissemination of information related to marketing research. Throughout this book we show how the six steps of the marketing research process are facilitated by Internet research.[36] Computers, mainframes, and then microcomputers have had a profound impact on marketing and marketing research. In this text we show how microcomputers and mainframes can be integrated in each step of the marketing research process. We focus on both

RESEARCH IN PRACTICE 1.7

Marketing Research Associations On-Line

Domestic

AAPOR: American Association for Public Opinion Research (www.aapor.org)
AMA: American Marketing Association (www.ama.org)
ARF: The Advertising Research Foundation (www.amic.com/arf)
CASRO: The Council of American Survey Research Organizations (www.casro.org)
MRA: Marketing Research Association (www.mra-net.org)
QRCA: Qualitative Research Consultants Association (www.qrca.org)
RIC: Research Industry Coalition (www.researchindustry.org)

International

ESOMAR: European Society for Opinion and Marketing Research (www.esomar.nl)
MRS: The Market Research Society (UK) (www.marketresearch.org.uk)
MRSA: The Market Research Society of Australia (www.mrsa.com.au)
PMRS: The Professional Marketing Research Society (Canada) (www.pmrs-aprm.com)

types of computers because both systems are used in practice, and abundant software has been developed to facilitate interaction between microcomputers and mainframes. Part III of this book illustrates the use of the mainframe and microcomputer versions of some popular statistical packages, SPSS, SAS, BMDP, and Minitab, as well as spreadsheets (Excel).[37]

FOCUS ON Burke

Burke, Inc. is one of the premier international business research and consulting firms in the industry. Since its 1931 founding, Burke has helped manufacturing and service companies understand and accurately predict marketplace behavior. Burke's employee owners solve marketing and business problems by looking at the big picture, then focusing on finding and implementing solutions to the most critical problems facing businesses today in order to provide them with a competitive advantage.

All of Burke's services are offered worldwide through Infratest Burke AG, of Munich, Germany. In 1997, Infratest Burke acquired 50 percent interest in Burke, Inc., solidifying their international partnership and strengthening the organization's global capabilities. The Burke worldwide organization has offices and affiliates in 40 countries. According to industry publications, Burke, Inc. ranks among the top 50 U.S. research organizations. Infratest Burke is the world's seventh largest research company.

Burke provides business solutions through four areas of expertise:

- Burke Marketing Research
- Burke Customer Satisfaction Associates
- The Training & Development Center
- Burke Strategic Consulting Group

Burke Marketing Research (BMR) provides full-service custom marketing research, analysis, and consulting for consumer and business-to-business product and service companies to help them understand marketplace dynamics. Some of the services provided to clients include product testing, brand equity research, pricing research, market segmentation, and strategic research.

Within BMR, Burke ICE Research (Information Communications, Entertainment Research) leverages Burke's extensive research knowledge and experience in this evolving and highly competitive industry group. Representative clients for all of BMR include: Borden, Brown & Williamson, CBS, Coca-Cola, Frito-Lay, Kimberly Clark, McNeil, Microsoft, Novartis, Pepsico, US West, VISA, and others.

Burke Customer Satisfaction Associates (BCSA) offers specialized services in customer satisfaction measurement and business management to a wide range of business categories. Burke CSA's *Secure Customer Index*© provides industry "best-in-class" standards for assessing and improving customer-driven practices in order to improve customer retention and loyalty. Representative clients include Sun Microsystems, Bank of Montreal, GE Power Systems, Chevron Lubricants, Idaho Power, DirecTV, Microsoft, and others.

The Training & Development Center offers in-depth educational seminars on marketing research, data analysis, customer satisfaction measurement, employee surveys, and qualitative research techniques. Some of the coursework selections include: Measuring and Managing Customer Satisfaction, Introduction to Marketing Research, Introduction to Qualitative Research, Focus Group Moderator Training, as well as others.

Burke Strategic Consulting Group (BSCG) offers in-depth experience in consulting and implementing strategic change. Service lines include: employee surveys, work process reengineering, selection systems, and incentive compensation. Working together with BCSA, BSCG, conducts extensive analyses to link employee and customer satisfaction to bottom-line business performance. BSCG also provides executive assessments and coaching for top-level managers. Representative clients include: AtlantiCare, Bank of Montreal, Rutland Regional Medical Center, State of Georgia, and Nesbitt Burns.

For more information visit www.burke.com.

SUMMARY

Marketing research provides information about consumers, channel members, competitors, changes, and trends in the marketplace, and other aspects of the firm's environment. The purpose of marketing research is to assess information needs and provide the relevant information so as to improve marketing decision making. Marketing research is systematic and objective in its quest to identify and help solve marketing problems. Information obtained using marketing research becomes an integral part of the MIS and DSS. Marketing research contributes to the DSS by providing research data to the database, marketing models and analytical techniques to the model base, and specialized marketing research programs to the software base.

Marketing research may be conducted internally or may be purchased from external suppliers. Full-service suppliers provide the entire range of marketing research services from problem definition to report preparation and presentation. The services provided by these suppliers can be classified as syndicated, standardized, customized, or Internet services. Limited-service suppliers specialize in one or a few phases of the marketing research project. Services offered by these suppliers can be classified as field services, coding and data entry, data analysis, analytical services, or branded products.

Due to the need for marketing research, attractive career opportunities are available with marketing research firms, business and nonbusiness firms and agencies with marketing research departments, and advertising agencies. The marketing research process consists of six steps which must be followed systematically. International marketing research is much more complex than domestic research as the researcher must consider the environment prevailing in the international markets which are being researched.

Ethical issues arise when the interests of the stakeholders are in conflict and when one or more of the stakeholders are lacking in their responsibilities. Marketing research makes extensive use of the Internet and computers.

KEY TERMS AND CONCEPTS

marketing research
marketing research process
problem identification research
problem solving research
marketing information system
decision support systems (DSS)
internal suppliers
external suppliers
full-service suppliers
syndicated services
standardized services
customized services
Internet services
limited-service suppliers
field services
coding and data entry services
analytical services
data analysis services
branded marketing research products

ACRONYMS

The role and salient characteristics of marketing research may be described by the acronym RESEARCH:

R ecognition of information needs
E ffective decision making
S ystematic and objective
E xude/disseminate information
A nalysis of information
R ecommendations for action
C ollection of information
H elpful to managers

EXERCISES

Questions

1. Describe the task of marketing research.
2. What decisions are made by marketing managers? How does marketing research help in making these decisions?
3. Define marketing research.
4. Describe one classification of marketing research.
5. What is a marketing information system?
6. How is DSS different from MIS?
7. Explain one way to classify marketing research suppliers and services.
8. What are syndicated services?
9. What is the main difference between a full-service and limited-service supplier?
10. What are branded products?
11. List five guidelines for selecting an external marketing research supplier.
12. What career opportunities are available in marketing research?
13. Discuss three ethical issues in marketing research that relate to the client, the supplier, and the respondent.
14. Describe the steps in the marketing research process.

Problems

1. Look through recent issues of newspapers and magazines to identify five examples of problem identification research and five examples of problem solving research.
2. List one kind of marketing research that would be useful to each of the following organizations:
   a. Your campus bookstore
   b. The public transportation authority in your city
   c. A major department store in your area
   d. A restaurant located near your campus
   e. A zoo in a major city

INTERNET AND COMPUTER EXERCISES

1. Visit the Web sites of the top three marketing research firms in Research in Practice 1.3. Write a report on the services offered by these firms. Use the Framework of Figure 1.4. What statements can you make about the structure of the marketing research industry?
2. Visit the Sears Web site (www.sears.com). Write a report about the retailing and marketing activities of Sears. This will help you better understand the Department Store Patronage Project, which is used as a running example throughout this text.
3. Visit the Web sites of MRA, ESOMAR, and MRSA (see Research in Practice 1.7 for the URLs). Compare and contrast the information available at these sites. Of the three marketing research associations, which has the most useful Web site? Why?
4. Visit www.bls.gov. What is the employment potential for marketing researchers?
5. Examine recent issues of magazines such as *Marketing News, Advertising Age, Quirk's Marketing Research Review*, and *Marketing Research: A Magazine of Management and Applications* to identify one mainframe or one microcomputer application in each of the following areas:
   a. Identification of information needs
   b. Collection of information
   c. Analysis of information
   d. Provision of information (report preparation)

Chapter 2

Defining the Marketing Research Problem and Developing an Approach

"One of the most challenging tasks is defining the research problem such that the research yields information that directly addresses the management issue. The end result should be for management to understand the information fully and take action based on it."

Jim Roberts,
vice president,
marketing services,
Burke, Inc.

OBJECTIVES

After reading this chapter, the student should be able to

1. understand the importance of and the process used for defining the marketing research problem
2. describe the tasks involved in problem definition including discussion with decision makers, interviews with industry experts, secondary data analysis, and qualitative research
3. discuss the environmental factors affecting the definition of the research problem: past information and forecasts; resources and constraints; objectives of the decision maker; buyer behavior; legal environment; economic environment; and marketing and technological skills of the firm
4. clarify the distinction between the management decision problem and the marketing research problem
5. explain the structure of a well-defined marketing research problem including the broad statement and the specific components
6. discuss in detail the various components of the approach: objective/theoretical framework, analytical models, research questions, hypotheses, and identification of characteristics influencing the research design
7. acquire an appreciation of the complexity involved and gain an understanding of the procedures for defining the problem and developing an approach in international marketing research
8. understand the ethical issues and conflicts that arise in defining the problem and developing the approach
9. explain how the Internet and computers can facilitate the process of defining the problem and developing an approach

OVERVIEW

This chapter covers the first two of the six steps of the marketing research process described in chapter 1: defining the marketing research problem and developing an approach to the problem. Defining the problem is the most important step, because only when a problem has been identified clearly and accurately can a research project be conducted properly. Defining the marketing research problem sets the course of the entire project. In this chapter, we allow the reader to appreciate the complexities involved in defining a problem by identifying the factors to be considered and the tasks involved. Additionally, we provide guidelines for appropriately defining the marketing research problem and avoiding common types of errors. We also discuss in detail the components of an approach to the problem: objective/theoretical framework, analytical models, research questions, hypotheses, and characteristics or factors influencing the research design. The special considerations involved in defining the problem and developing an approach in international marketing research are also discussed. Several ethical issues that arise at this stage of the marketing research process are considered. Finally, we discuss the use of the Internet and computers in defining the problem and developing an approach.

We introduce our discussion with an example from Harley Davidson, which needed specific information about its customers.

EXAMPLE

Harley Goes Whole Hog

The motorcycle manufacturer Harley Davidson made such an important comeback in the 1990s that there was a two-year waiting list to get a bike. Although distributors urged Harley Davidson to build more motorcycles, the company was skeptical about investing in new production facilities.

The bad years of the early 1980s had taught top management to be more risk averse than risk prone. Harley Davidson was now performing well again, and investing in new facilities meant taking risk. Would the demand follow in the long term or would customers stop wanting Harleys when the next fad came along? The decrease in the motorcycles' quality, linked to the too-fast growth of Harley, had cost the company all its bad years. The management was afraid that the decision to invest was too early. On the other hand, investing would help Harley Davidson to expand and maybe become the market leader on the heavyweight segment.

At this point, the management decision problem was: Should Harley Davidson invest to produce more motorcycles? The marketing research problem was to determine if the customers would be loyal buyers of Harley Davidson in the long term. Specifically, the research had to address the following issues:

1. Who are the customers? What are their demographic and psychographic characteristics?
2. Can different types of customers be distinguished? Is it possible to segment the market in a meaningful way?

Appropriate problem definition and research approach helped Harley Davidson to discover that it had an army of loyal customers who view its motorcycles as a symbol of independence, freedom, and power.

3. How do customers feel about their Harleys? Are all customers motivated by the same appeal?
4. Are the customers loyal to Harley Davidson? What is the extent of their brand loyalty?

One of the research questions (RQs) examined and the associated hypotheses (Hs) were:

RQ: Can the motorcycle buyers be segmented based on psychographic characteristics?
H1: There are distinct segments of motorcycle buyers.
H2: Each segment is motivated to own a Harley for a different reason.
H3: Brand loyalty is high among Harley Davidson customers in all segments.

Both qualitative research and quantitative research were conducted. First, focus groups of current owners, would-be owners, and owners of other brands were conducted to understand the feelings of customers about Harley Davidson. Second, 16,000 surveys were mailed, to get the psychological, sociological, and demographic profiles of customers and also their subjective appraisal of Harley. Some of the major findings were as follows:

- Seven categories of customers could be distinguished: (1) the Adventure-Loving Traditionalist, (2) the Sensitive-Pragmatist, (3) the Stylish Status-Seeker, (4) the Laid-Back Camper, (5) the Classy Capitalist, (6) the Cool-Headed Loner, and (7) the Cocky Misfit. Thus, H1 was supported.
- Harley however, had the same appeal to all customers: It was a symbol of independence, freedom, and power. (This uniformity across segments was surprising, contradicting H2).
- All customers were long-term loyal customers of Harley Davidson, supporting H3.

Based on these findings, the decision was made to invest in new production facilities to increase the number of Harleys built.[1] ■

This example shows the importance of correctly defining the marketing research problem and developing an appropriate approach.

IMPORTANCE OF DEFINING THE PROBLEM

Although each step in a marketing research project is important, problem definition is the most important step. As mentioned in chapter 1, for the purpose of marketing research, problems and opportunities are treated interchangeably. **Problem definition** involves stating the general marketing research problem and identifying its specific components. Only when the marketing research problem has been defined clearly can research be designed and conducted properly. Of all the tasks in a marketing research project, none is more vital to the ultimate fulfillment of a client's needs than a proper definition of the research problem. All the effort, time, and money spent from this point on will be wasted if the problem is misunderstood or ill-defined.[2] This point is critical: Inadequate problem definition is a leading cause of failure of marketing research projects. Further, better communication and more involvement in problem definition are the most frequently mentioned ways of improving the usefulness of research. These results lead to the conclusion that the importance of clearly identifying and defining the marketing research problem cannot be overstated. Research in Practice 2.1 cites an episode from the author's personal experience to illustrate this point. Further insights on the difficulty involved in appropriately defining the problem are provided by the problem definition process.[3]

Problem Definition A broad statement of the general marketing research problem and identification of its specific components.

THE PROCESS OF DEFINING THE PROBLEM AND DEVELOPING AN APPROACH

The problem definition and approach development process is shown in Figure 2.1. The tasks involved in problem definition consist of discussions with the decision makers, interviews with industry experts and other knowledgeable individuals, analysis of secondary data, and sometimes qualitative research. These tasks help the researcher understand the background of the problem by analyzing the environmental context. Certain essential environmental factors bearing on the problem should be evaluated. Understanding the environmental context facilitates the identification of the management decision problem. Then, the management decision problem is translated into a marketing research problem. Based on the definition of the marketing research problem, an appropriate approach is developed. The components of the approach consist of: objective/theoretical framework, analytical

Figure 2.1
The Process of Defining the Problem and Developing an Approach

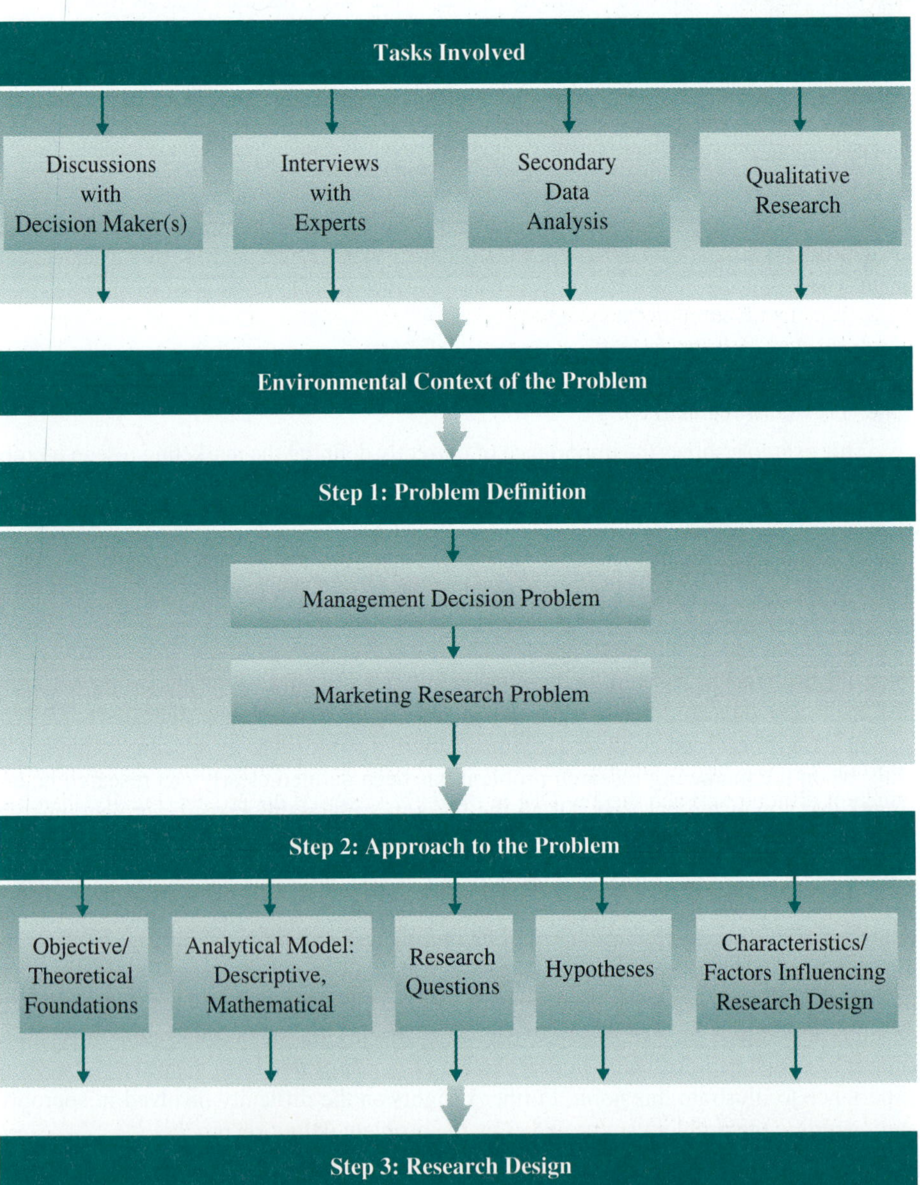

RESEARCH IN PRACTICE 2.1

Chain Restaurant Study

One day I received a telephone call from a research analyst who introduced himself as an alumnus of my university. He was working for a restaurant chain in town and wanted help in analyzing the data he had collected during a marketing research study. When we met, he presented me with a copy of the questionnaire and asked how he should analyze the data. My first question to him was, "What is the problem being addressed?" When he looked perplexed, I explained that data analysis was not an independent exercise. Rather, the goal of data analysis is to provide information related to the problem components. I was surprised to learn that he did not have a clear understanding of the marketing research problem and that a written definition of the problem did not exist. So, before proceeding any further, I had to define the marketing research problem. Once that was done, I found that much of the data collected were not relevant to the problem. In this sense, the whole study was a waste of resources. A new study had to be designed and implemented to address the problem identified.

models, research questions, hypotheses, and characteristics or factors influencing the research design. Further explanation of the problem definition process begins with a discussion of the tasks involved.

TASKS INVOLVED

The tasks involved in problem definition include discussions with the decision makers, interviews with industry experts, secondary data analysis, and qualitative research. The purpose of these tasks is to obtain information on the environmental context of the problem and help define the marketing research problem.

Discussions with the Decision Maker

Discussions with the decision maker (DM) are extremely important. The DM needs to understand the capabilities and limitations of research.[4] Research provides information relevant to management decisions, but it cannot provide solutions, because solutions require managerial judgment. Conversely, the researcher needs to understand the nature of what decision managers face—the management problem—and what they hope to learn from the research.

To identify the management problem, the researcher must possess considerable skill in interacting with the DM. Several factors may complicate this interaction. Access to the DM may be difficult, and some organizations have complicated protocols for access to top executives. The organizational status of the researcher or the research department may make it difficult to reach the key DM in the early stages of the project. Finally, there may be more than one key DM and meeting with them collectively or individually may be difficult. Despite these problems, it is necessary that the researcher interact directly with the key decision makers.[5]

Problem Audit
A comprehensive examination of a marketing problem to understand its origin and nature.

The **problem audit** provides a useful framework for interacting with the DM and identifying the underlying causes of the problem. The problem audit, like any other type of audit, is a comprehensive examination of a marketing problem with the goal of understanding its origin and nature.[6] The problem audit involves discussions with the DM on the following issues, which are illustrated with a problem facing McDonald's:

1. *The events that led to the decision that action is needed, or the history of the problem.* McDonald's, a long-time leader in the fast foods industry, was losing market share in 1997 and 1998 to competitors such as Burger King and Wendy's. This problem came

into sharper focus as these competitors launched new products and aggressive promotional campaigns, while the contemporaneous campaigns of McDonald's were less than successful.

2. *The alternative courses of action available to the DM.* The set of alternatives may be incomplete at this stage, and qualitative research may be needed to identify the more innovative courses of action. The alternatives available to the management of McDonald's included: introducing new sandwiches and menu items, reducing prices, opening more restaurants, launching special promotions, and increasing advertising.
3. *The criteria that will be used to evaluate the alternative courses of action.* For example, new product offerings might be evaluated on the basis of sales, market share, profitability, return on investment, and so forth. McDonald's must evaluate the alternatives based on contributions to market share and profits.
4. *The potential actions that are likely to be suggested based on the research findings.* The research findings will likely call for a strategic marketing response by McDonald's.
5. *The information that is needed to answer the DM's questions.* The information needed includes a comparison of McDonald's and its major competitors on all the elements of the marketing mix (product, pricing, promotion, and distribution) in order to determine relative strengths and weaknesses.
6. *The manner in which the DM will use each item of information in making the decision.* The key DMs will devise a strategy for McDonald's based on the research findings and their intuition and judgment.
7. *The corporate culture as it relates to decision making.*[7] In some firms, the decision making process is dominant; in others, the personality of the DM is more important. Awareness of corporate culture may be one of the most important factors that distinguishes researchers who affect strategic marketing decisions from those who do not. The corporate culture at McDonald's calls for a committee approach in which critical decisions are made by key decision makers.

It is important to perform a problem audit because the DM, in most cases, has only a vague idea of what the problem is. For example, the DM may know that the firm is losing market share but may not know why. DMs tend to focus on symptoms rather than on causes. Inability to meet sales forecasts, loss of market share, and decline in profits are all symptoms. The researcher should treat the underlying causes, not merely address the symptoms. For example, loss of market share may be caused by better promotion by the competition, inadequate distribution of the company's products, or any number of other factors. Only when the underlying causes are identified can the problem be successfully addressed, as exemplified by the effort of store brand jeans.

EXAMPLE

Turning "Uncool" to "Cool": It's a Matter of Image

For years, teenagers have considered store label jeans "uncool." Although the lower price tag of store brand jeans, such as J. C. Penney's Arizona brand jeans or the Gap's in-house brand, has long appealed to value-conscious parents, teenagers have preferred big brand names such as Levi's, Lee, and Wrangler. The big name brands have historically dominated the $10.6 billion industry as a result. Through marketing research problem audits, the private labels determined that the real cause for their low market share was lack of image. Therefore, the marketing research problem was defined as enhancing their image in the eyes of the target market—the lucrative teenage segment.

Arizona jeans and Gap's in-house brands have led the charge among the "generics" in changing their image. These store brand jeans, along with other store label jeans, now target the teenage market with "cutting edge" advertising. Their advertisements feature rock bands such as Aerosmith along with high tech imagery to attract teenagers. The brands also promote their trendy World Wide Web sites. Gap jeans have also scored big. The chain's strategy has been to distance their store brand jeans from the store itself. Teenagers think of the Gap as a place where older people or their parents shop, thus making it "uncool." Gap's marketing campaign now aims to separate their store name and image from their jeans that are aimed at teens. This is the opposite to a more typical or traditional brand name leveraging strategy. The results, according to Michael Wood of the research services firm Teenage Research Unlimited, are that "Teens are not putting it together that this is the house brand."

The results for the store brand jeans have been quite successful. According to the marketing research firm NPD Group, private label jeans' market share has risen from 16 percent in 1990 to 25 percent in 1997. Levi's, the market leader, has seen its market share drop from 22 percent to 20 percent over the same time period. Levi's drop is typical of the big brand names nationwide. Their share has gone from 70 percent to 65 percent overall. These impressive results are encouraging other stores to consider introducing their own label jeans to capture a portion of the teenage market.[8] ■

As in the case of the private label jeans, a problem audit, which involves extensive interaction between the DM and the researcher, can greatly facilitate problem definition by determining the underlying causes. The interaction between the researcher and the DM is facilitated when one or more people in the client organization serve as a liaison and form a team with the marketing researcher. In order to be fruitful, the interaction between the DM and the researcher should be characterized by the seven Cs:

1. *Communication*. Free exchange of ideas between the DM and researcher is essential.
2. *Cooperation*. Marketing research is a team project in which both the parties (DM and researcher) must cooperate.
3. *Confidence*. Mutual trust should underlie the interaction between the DM and the researcher.
4. *Candor*. There should not be any hidden agendas, and an attitude of openness should prevail.
5. *Closeness*. Feelings of warmth and closeness should characterize the relationship between the DM and the researcher.
6. *Continuity*. The DM and the researcher must interact continually rather than sporadically.
7. *Creativity*. The interaction between the DM and the researcher should be creative rather than formulaic.

Interviews with Industry Experts

In addition to discussions with the DM, interviews with industry experts, individuals knowledgeable about the firm and the industry, may help formulate the marketing research problem.[9] These experts may be found both inside and outside the firm. Typically, expert information is obtained by unstructured personal interviews, without administering a formal questionnaire. It is helpful, however, to prepare a list of topics to be covered during the interview. The order in which these topics are covered and the questions to ask should not be predetermined but decided as the interview progresses. This allows greater flexibility in capturing the insights of the experts. The purpose of interviewing experts is to help define the marketing research problem rather than to develop a conclusive solution. Unfortunately, two potential difficulties may arise when seeking advice from experts:

1. Some individuals who claim to be knowledgeable and are eager to participate may not really possess expertise.
2. It may be difficult to locate and obtain help from experts outside the client organization.

For these reasons, interviews with experts are more useful in conducting marketing research for industrial firms and for products of a technical nature, where it is relatively easy to identify and approach the experts. This method is also helpful in situations in which little information is available from other sources, as in the case of radically new products. Experts can provide valuable insights in modifying or repositioning existing products, as illustrated by the repositioning of Oldsmobile.

EXAMPLE

Oldsmobile Sheds Old Image

During the 1960s and early 1970s, the Oldsmobile Division of General Motors was very successful. Then the gas crunch and increasing imports of cars hurt the division badly. It lost sales as well as market share in the late 1970s and 1980s. In the early 1990s, Oldsmobile set out to regain, redefine, and rebuild its products and customer base. The first order of business was to determine what Oldsmobile was and what it could become. When outside consultants were brought in, the real problem was identified: Oldsmobile had an old image. These experts emphasized that brand image was a key factor influencing automobile sales and Oldsmobile cars were perceived as conventional and old fashioned. Subsequent research on brand image led Oldsmobile to embrace an alluring and unconventional image. The 1998 Oldsmobile Aurora was introduced with the "Defy Convention" theme and positioned to younger, better-educated, higher-income buyers. This marketing strategy has helped Oldsmobile to increase sales and improve profitability.[10] ■

The Oldsmobile example points to the key role of industry experts. However, information obtained from the DM and the industry experts should be supplemented with the available secondary data.

Secondary Data Analysis

Secondary Data Data collected for some purpose other than the problem at hand.

Primary Data Data collected or produced by the researcher specifically to address the research problem.

Secondary data are data collected for some purpose other than the problem at hand. **Primary data**, on the other hand, are collected or produced by the researcher for the specific purpose of addressing the research problem. Secondary data include information made available by business and government sources, commercial marketing research firms, and computerized databases. Secondary data are an economical and quick source of background information. Analysis of available secondary data is an essential step in the problem definition process: Primary data should not be collected until the available secondary data have been fully analyzed. Given the tremendous importance of secondary data, this topic will be discussed in detail in chapter 4, which also further discusses the differences between secondary and primary data.

Qualitative Research

Qualitative Research An unstructured, exploratory research methodology based on small samples intended to provide insight and understanding of the problem setting.

Information obtained from the DM, industry experts, and secondary data may not be sufficient to define the research problem. Sometimes qualitative research must be undertaken to gain an understanding of the problem and its underlying factors. **Qualitative research** is unstructured, exploratory in nature, based on small samples, and may utilize popular qualitative techniques such as focus groups (group interviews), word association (asking respondents to indicate their first responses to stimulus words), and depth interviews (one-on-one interviews that probe the respondents' thoughts in detail). Other exploratory research techniques, such as pilot surveys with small samples of respondents, may also be undertaken. Exploratory research is discussed in more detail in chapter 3, and qualitative research techniques are discussed in detail in chapter 5. Although research undertaken at this stage may not be conducted in a formal way, it can provide valuable insights, as illustrated by Amtrak.

EXAMPLE

Qualitative Research Helps Amtrak Stay on Track

Qualitative research helped Amtrak to create a high-speed, premium railroad service for its Boston–New York–Washington route.

Amtrak has decided to create a high-speed, premium railroad service for its Boston–New York–Washington route. The new train, scheduled to debut in October 1999, will travel at speeds of up to 150 miles an hour and will deliver passengers to their destinations on that route within three hours.

In designing this service, the problem that Amtrak was facing was how to compete with the airlines. Qualitative research in the form of focus groups helped to identify the important aspects of the problem. Initial focus groups revealed that travel time, seating, lighting, color schemes, and food/beverage services would be important to customers who were looking for a comfortable and enjoyable ride. Determining the importance consumers attached to these factors in selecting a mode of transportation became important components of the problem. Focus groups were held to further explore these factors, followed by several large sample surveys.

Participants of the focus groups sat in prototype railcars and discussed what they liked and did not like about them. For instance, researchers asked respondents whether they preferred sitting across from each other at tables or in forward or backward positions. They also questioned participants about the seat characteristics they preferred. Questions in other focus groups centered around lighting, color schemes, and food and beverage services. They also performed extensive survey research, in the form of telephone surveys before making any definite design decisions. In total, Amtrak utilized the opinions of more than 20,000 customers in the design of their new train service.

This research indicated that a travel time of under three hours would be required to compete with the airlines. Seat characteristics valued by the participants included back support, conformation to the body, provision of personal space, and comfort. The results of this research led Amtrak to consider designing seating that is comfortable and spacious. All seating, including the coach class, will provide ample legroom. For instance, even the coach class will have a 42-inch seat pitch. This is greater legroom than found in many airlines' first class seating. The results also led Amtrak to consider including both row and table layouts. Results also showed that participants preferred lighting that was adequate for reading and conducting work, but not too bright. They preferred classic colors schemes. Specifically, the majority preferred white or off-white walls and green, maroon, and blue upholstery. Questions regarding food and beverage service lead Amtrak to include a bistro-style train car as well as "service at your seat," such as that provided by airlines.

Amtrak will continue conducting research after the high speed train debuts in October 1999. This will allow it to stay in touch with customers preferences and opinions regarding the new service, and make adjustments if necessary.[11] ■

The insights gained from qualitative research—along with discussions with decision maker(s), interviews with industry experts, and secondary data analysis—help the researcher to understand the environmental context of the problem.

ENVIRONMENTAL CONTEXT OF THE PROBLEM

Environmental Context of the Problem Consists of the factors that have an impact on the definition of the marketing research problem, including past information and forecasts, resources and constraints of the firm, objectives of the decision maker, buyer behavior, legal environment, economic environment, and marketing and technological skills of the firm.

To understand the background to a marketing research problem, the researcher must understand the client's firm and industry. In particular, the researcher should analyze the factors that have an impact on the definition of the marketing research problem. These factors, encompassing the **environmental context of the problem**, include past information and forecasts pertaining to the industry and the firm; resources and constraints of the firm; objectives of the decision maker; buyer behavior; legal environment; economic environment; and marketing and technological skills of the firm, as shown in Figure 2.2. Each of these factors is discussed briefly.[12]

Past Information and Forecasts

Past information and forecasts of trends with respect to sales, market share, profitability, technology, population, demographics, and lifestyle can help the researcher understand the underlying marketing research problem. Where appropriate, this kind of analysis should be carried out at the industry *and* firm levels. For example, if a firm's sales have decreased but industry sales have increased, the problems will be very different than if the industry sales have also decreased. In the former case, the problems are likely to be specific to the firm.[13]

Past information and forecasts can be valuable in uncovering potential opportunities and problems, as the fast food industry has discovered. The following example shows how fast food chains, pizza restaurants, and other outlets for take-out food have sought to exploit potential opportunities in the recent trend toward take-out food and home delivery.

Figure 2.2
Factors to be Considered in the Environmental Context of the Problem

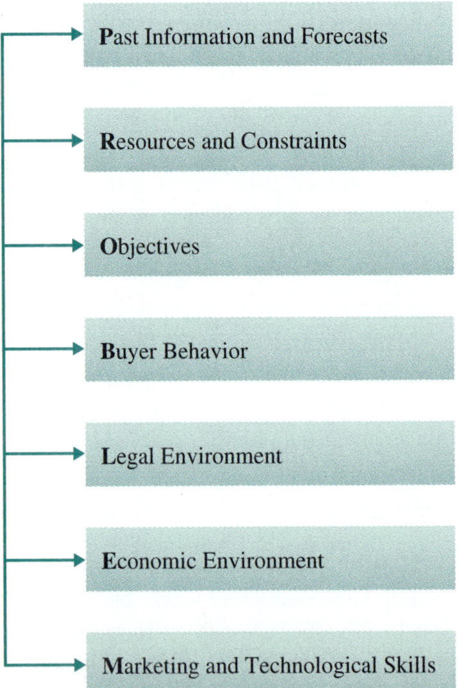

EXAMPLE

Take-Out Market Takes Off

In recent years there has been a significant trend toward take-out food. A study by Liberman Research, New York, found that an average of 81 percent of households buy take-out food at least once every four weeks and that many individuals take out food once a week, at an average weekly cost of $16.50 a person. Traditional fastfood outlets remain the most popular, with 76 percent of consumers buying takeout there, followed by 66 percent preferring take-out pizza. The study forecasts that home delivery will be the future of take-out food. Upscale entrees, soups, salads, and sandwiches will be added to the home delivery repertoire. Also, the study forecasts that one day snacks and candy will be home delivered. This presents problems for fastfood marketers that emphasize dine-in service but offers tremendous opportunities for those catering to the take-out and home delivery segments. Pizza Hut has successfully capitalized on this trend by emphasizing take-out and home delivery services. For example, it opened several take-out only (with no dine-in service) outlets to better serve this market.[14] ■

This example illustrates the usefulness of past information and forecasts, which can be especially valuable if resources are limited and there are other constraints on the organization.

Resources and Constraints

To formulate a marketing research problem of appropriate scope, it is necessary to take into account both the resources available, such as money and research skills, and the constraints on the organization, such as cost and time. Proposing a large-scale project that would cost $100,000 when only $40,000 has been budgeted obviously will not meet management approval. In many instances, the scope of the marketing research problem may have to be reduced to accommodate budget constraints. For instance, as in the department store patronage project, the investigation might be confined to major geographical markets rather than conducted on a national basis.

It is often possible to extend the scope of a project appreciably with only a marginal increase in costs. This can considerably enhance the usefulness of the project, thereby increasing the probability that management will approve it. Time constraints can be important when decisions must be made quickly.[15] A project for Fisher-Price, a major toy manufacturer, involving mall-intercept interviews in six cities (Chicago, Fresno, Kansas City, New York, Philadelphia, and San Diego) had to be completed in six weeks. Why this rush? The results had to be presented at an upcoming board meeting where a major (go/no go) decision was to be made about a new product introduction.[16]

Other constraints, such as those imposed by the client firm's personnel, organizational structure and culture, or decision-making styles, should be identified to determine the scope of the research project. However, constraints should not be allowed to diminish the value of the research to the decision maker or compromise the integrity of the research process. If a research project is worth doing, it is worth doing well. If the resources are too limited to allow a high-quality project, the firm should be advised not to undertake formal marketing research. It is essential, then, to identify resources and constraints, a task that can be better understood when examined in the light of the objectives of the organization and the decision maker.

Objectives

Objectives Goals of the organization and of the decision maker that must be considered in order to conduct successful marketing research.

Decisions are made to accomplish **objectives**. The formulation of the management decision problem must be based on a clear understanding of two types of objectives: (1) the organizational objectives (the goals of the organization), and (2) the personal objectives of the decision maker (DM). For the project to be successful, it must serve the objectives of the organization and of the DM. This, however, is not an easy task.

The DM rarely formulates personal or organizational objectives accurately. Rather, it is likely that these objectives will be stated in terms which have no operational significance, such as "to improve corporate image." Direct questioning of the DM is unlikely to reveal all of the relevant objectives. The researcher needs skill to extract these objectives. An effective technique is to confront the DM with each of the possible solutions to a problem and ask whether he or she would follow that course of action. If the answer is "no," use further probing to uncover objectives that are not served by the course of action.

Buyer Behavior

Buyer Behavior A body of knowledge useful in understanding and predicting consumers' reactions based on an individual's specific characteristics.

Buyer behavior is a central component of the environmental context. In most marketing decisions, the problem can ultimately be traced to predicting the response of buyers to specific actions by the marketer. An understanding of the underlying buyer behavior can provide valuable insights into the problem. The buyer behavior factors that should be considered include:

1. The number and geographical location of the buyers and nonbuyers
2. Demographic and psychological characteristics
3. Product consumption habits and the consumption of related product categories
4. Media consumption behavior and response to promotions
5. Price sensitivity
6. Retail outlets patronized
7. Buyer preferences

The following example shows how changes in buyer behavior may present both threats and opportunities.

EXAMPLE

Coffee Isn't Just the Same Old Grind

Innovators like Starbucks, who capitalized upon changes in consumer behavior, were able to gain a foothold in the competitive coffee market.

As recently as 1987, the three major coffee companies, Procter & Gamble, General Foods, and Nestlé, held nearly 90 percent of the multibillion dollar retail coffee market. However, consumer tastes and preferences for coffee were changing. Consumers shifted their preferences to higher quality, gourmet brands, and alternative delivery channels. These factors were ignored by the big three. As a result, innovators such as Starbucks capitalized on these changes in consumer behavior, and were able to gain a foothold in the market. By 1998, Starbucks, other regional cafes, and the gourmet, whole-bean roasters had collectively created billions in shareholder value, and together had obtained about 25 percent of the coffee market share. Had the majors stayed focused on changing customer tastes, bought better beans, changed their packaging and delivery systems, and restructured prices, they would have made it much harder for Starbucks and others to break into the market.[17] ■

The increase in the average age of the coffee drinker and the decline in coffee consumption could be attributed to changes in the sociocultural environment, which includes demographic trends and consumer tastes. In addition, the legal environment and the economic environment can have an impact on the behavior of the consumers and the definition of the marketing research problem.

Legal Environment

The **legal environment** includes public policies, laws, government agencies, and pressure groups that influence and regulate various organizations and individuals in society. Important areas of law include patents, trademarks, royalties, trade agreements, taxes, and tariffs. Federal laws have an impact on each element of the marketing mix. In addition, laws have been passed to regulate specific industries. The legal environment can have an important bearing on the definition of the marketing research problem.

Legal Environment Regulatory policies and norms within which organizations must operate.

Economic Environment

Along with the legal environment, another important component of the environmental context is the **economic environment**, which comprises purchasing power, gross income, disposable income, discretionary income, prices, savings, credit availability, and general economic conditions. The general state of the economy (rapid growth, slow growth, recession, or stagflation) influences the willingness of consumers and businesses to take on credit and spend on big ticket items. Thus, the economic environment can have important implications for marketing research problems.

Economic Environment The economic environment consists of income, prices, savings, credit, and general economic conditions.

Marketing and Technological Skills

A company's expertise with each element of the marketing mix as well as its general level of marketing and technological skills affect the nature and scope of the marketing research project. For example, the introduction of a new product that requires sophisticated technology may not be a viable course if the firm lacks the skills to manufacture or market it.

A firm's marketing and technological skills greatly influence the marketing programs and strategies that can be implemented. At a broader level, other elements of the technological environment should be considered. Technological advances, such as the continuing development of computers, have had a dramatic impact on marketing research. To illustrate, computerized check-out lanes allow supermarkets to monitor daily consumer demand for products and make the data available to the researcher. It is possible to obtain precise information on retail sales, not only of the firm's brands but also of competing brands. The speed and accuracy of data collection enable the researcher to investigate intricate problems such as the daily changes in market share during a promotion.

After gaining an adequate understanding of the environmental context of the problem, the researcher can define the management decision problem and the marketing research problem.

MANAGEMENT DECISION PROBLEM AND MARKETING RESEARCH PROBLEM

The management decision problem asks what the DM needs to do, whereas the marketing research problem asks what information is needed and how it can best be obtained. Research can provide the necessary information to make a sound decision.[18] The **management**

Management Decision Problem The problem confronting the decision maker. It asks, "What does the decision maker need to do?"

Marketing Research Problem A problem that entails determining what information is needed and how it can be obtained.

decision problem is action oriented. It is concerned with the possible actions the DM can take. How should the loss of market share be arrested? Should the market be segmented differently? Should a new product be introduced? Should the promotional budget be increased?

In contrast, the **marketing research problem** is information oriented. It involves determining what information is needed and how that information can be obtained effectively and efficiently. Consider, for example, the loss of market share for a particular product line. The management decision problem is how to recover this loss. Alternative courses of action include modifying existing products, introducing new products, changing other elements in the marketing mix, and segmenting the market. Suppose the DM and the researcher (R) believe that the problem is caused by inappropriate segmentation of the market and wanted research to provide information on this issue. The research problem would then become the identification and evaluation of an alternative basis for segmenting the market. Note that this process is interactive. The department store patronage project example illustrates further the distinction between the management decision problem and the marketing research problem as well as the interactive nature of the problem definition process.

The following examples further distinguish between the management decision problem and the marketing research problem:

Management decision problem	*Marketing research problem*
Should a new product be introduced?	To determine consumer preferences and purchase intentions for the proposed new product.
Should the advertising campaign be changed?	To determine the effectiveness of the current advertising campaign.
Should the price of the brand be increased?	To determine the price elasticity of demand and the impact on sales and profits of various levels of price changes.

DEFINING THE MARKETING RESEARCH PROBLEM

The general rule to be followed in defining the research problem is that the definition should (1) allow the researcher to obtain all the information needed to address the management decision problem, and (2) guide the researcher in proceeding with the project. Researchers make two common errors in problem definition. The first arises when the research problem is defined too broadly. A broad definition does not provide clear guidelines for the subsequent steps involved in the project. Some examples of overly broad marketing research problem definitions are: developing a marketing strategy for the brand, improving the competitive position of the firm, or improving the company's image. These are not specific enough to suggest an approach to the problem or a research design.

The second type of error is just the opposite: the marketing research problem is defined too narrowly. A narrow focus may preclude consideration of some courses of action, particularly those that are innovative and not obvious. It may also prevent the researcher from addressing important components of the management decision problem. For example, in a project conducted for a major consumer products firm the management problem was how to respond to a price cut initiated by a competitor. The alternative courses of action initially identified by the firm's research staff were (1) decrease the price of the firm's brand to match the competitor's price cut; (2) maintain price but increase advertising heavily; and (3) decrease the price somewhat, without matching the competitor's price, and moderately increase advertising. None of these alternatives seemed promising. When outside marketing research experts were brought in, the problem was redefined as improving the market share

DEPARTMENT STORE PATRONAGE PROJECT

Defining the Problem

***DM*:** We have seen a decline in the patronage of our store.
***R*:** How do you know that?
***DM*:** Well, it is reflected in our sales and market share.
***R*:** Why do you think that your patronage has declined?
***DM*:** I wish I knew!
***R*:** What about competition?
***DM*:** I suspect we are better than competition on some factors and worse on others.
***R*:** How do the customers view your store?
***DM*:** I think most of them positively, although we may have a weak area or two.

After a series of dialogues with the DM and other key managers, analysis of secondary data, and qualitative research, the problem was identified as follows:

Management decision problem
What should be done to improve the patronage of Sears?

Marketing research problem
Determine the relative strengths and weaknesses of Sears, vis-à-vis other major competitors, with respect to factors that influence store patronage.

and profitability of the product line. Qualitative research indicated that in blind tests consumers could not differentiate products offered under different brand names. Furthermore, consumers relied on price as an indicator of product quality. These findings led to a creative alternative: increase the price of the existing brand and introduce two new brands—one priced to match the competitor and the other priced to undercut it. This strategy was implemented leading to an increase in market share and profitability.

The likelihood of committing either error of problem definition can be reduced by stating the marketing research problem in broad, general terms and identifying its specific components (see Figure 2.3). The **broad statement of the problem** provides perspective and acts as a safeguard against committing the second type of error. The **specific components** focus on the key aspects of the problem and provide clear guidelines on how to proceed. Examples of appropriate marketing research problem definitions are provided in the two following examples.

Broad Statement of the Problem The initial statement of the marketing research problem, which provides an appropriate perspective on the problem.

Specific Components of the Problem The second part of the marketing research problem definition. The specific components focus on the key aspects of the problem and provide clear guidelines on how to proceed.

Figure 2.3
Proper Definition of the Marketing Research Problem

EXAMPLE

Research Serves Tennis *Magazine*

The publishers of *Tennis* magazine, a publication of the New York Times Co., wanted to obtain information about their readers. They hired Signet Research, Inc., an independent research company in Cliffside Park, New Jersey, to conduct marketing research. The management decision problem was what changes should be made in *Tennis* magazine to make it more appealing to its readers.

The broad marketing research problem was defined as gathering information about the subscribers of *Tennis* magazine. Specific components of the problem included the following:

1. *Demographics.* Who are the men and women who subscribe to the magazine?
2. *Psychological characteristics and lifestyles.* How subscribers spent their money and their free time? Lifestyle indicators to be examined were fitness, travel, car rental, apparel, consumer electronics, credit cards, and financial investments.
3. *Tennis activity.* Where and how often do subscribers play tennis? What are their skill levels?
4. *Relationship to* Tennis *magazine.* How much time do subscribers spend with the issues? How long do they keep them? Do they share the magazine with other tennis players?

Because the questions were so clearly defined, the information provided by this research helped management design specific features on tennis instruction, equipment, famous tennis players, and locations to play tennis to meet readers' specific needs. These changes made *Tennis* magazine more appealing to its readers.[19] ■

In the *Tennis* magazine example, the broad statement of the problem focused on gathering information about the subscribers, and the specific components identified the specific items of information that should be obtained. An appropriate definition of the problem helped *Tennis* to make changes to meet specific needs in the marketplace. Problem definition in the department store patronage project followed a similar pattern.

DEPARTMENT STORE PATRONAGE PROJECT

Problem Definition

In the department store patronage project, the marketing research problem was to determine the relative strengths and weaknesses of Sears, vis-à-vis other major competitors, with respect to factors that influence store patronage. Specifically, research provided information on the following questions.

1. What criteria do households use when selecting department stores?
2. How do households evaluate Sears and competing stores in terms of the choice criteria identified in question 1?
3. Which stores are patronized when shopping for specific product categories?
4. What is the market share of Sears and its competitors for specific product categories?
5. What is the demographic and psychological profile of the customers of Sears? Does it differ from the profile of customers of competing stores?
6. Can store patronage and preference be explained in terms of store evaluations and customer characteristics?

There should be a written statement of the marketing research problem that has been agreed to by the client. Burke consultant discussing the marketing research problem definition with the client.

Once the marketing research problem has been broadly stated and its specific components identified, the researcher is in a position to develop a suitable approach.

COMPONENTS OF THE APPROACH

In the process of developing an approach, we must not lose sight of the goal—the outputs. The outputs of the approach development process should include the following components: objective/theoretical framework, analytical models, research questions, hypotheses, and identification of characteristics influencing the research design (see Figure 2.1). Each of these components is discussed in the following sections.

Objective/Theoretical Framework

In general, research should be based on objective evidence and supported by theory. A **theory** is a conceptual scheme based on foundational statements called axioms, which are assumed to be true. **Objective evidence** (evidence that is unbiased and supported by empirical findings) is gathered by compiling relevant findings from secondary sources. Likewise, an appropriate theory to guide the research might be identified by reviewing academic literature contained in books, journals, and monographs. The researcher should rely on theory to determine which variables should be investigated. Furthermore, theoretical considerations provide information on how the variables should be operationalized and measured, as well as how the research design and sample should be selected. A theory also serves as a foundation on which the researcher can organize and interpret the findings: "Nothing is so practical as a good theory."[20] The role of theory in the various phases of an applied marketing research project is summarized in Table 2.1.

Theory A conceptual scheme based on foundational statements, or axioms, which are assumed to be true.

Objective Evidence Unbiased evidence that is supported by empirical findings.

Theory also plays a vital role in influencing the research procedures adopted in basic research. However, applying a theory to an applied marketing research problem requires creativity on the part of the researcher. A theory may not specify adequately how its abstract constructs (variables) can be embodied in a real-world phenomenon. Moreover, theories are incomplete. They deal with only a subset of variables that exist in the real world. Hence, the researcher must also identify and examine other, nontheoretical, variables.[21]

TABLE 2.1

THE ROLE OF THEORY IN APPLIED MARKETING RESEARCH

Research Task	*Role of Theory*
1. Conceptualizing and identifying key variables	Provides a conceptual foundation and understanding of the basic processes underlying the problem situation. These processes will suggest key dependent and independent variables.
2. Operationalizing key variables	Theoretical constructs (variables) can suggest independent and dependent variables naturally occurring in the real world.
3. Selecting a research design	Causal or associative relationships suggested by the theory may indicate whether a causal or descriptive design should be adopted (see chapter 3).
4. Selecting a sample	The theoretical framework may be useful in defining the population and suggesting variables for qualifying respondents, imposing quotas, or stratifying the population.
5. Analyzing and interpreting data	The theoretical framework (and the models, research questions and hypotheses based on it) guide the selection of a data analysis strategy and the interpretation of results (see chapter 14).
6. Integrating findings	The findings obtained in the research project can be interpreted in the light of previous research and integrated with the existing body of knowledge.

The department store patronage project illustrates how theory can be used to develop an approach. Review of the retailing literature revealed that the modeling of store patronage in terms of choice criteria had received considerable support.[22] Furthermore, as many as 42 choice criteria had been identified in the literature, and guidelines on operationalizing these variables were provided. This provided an initial pool from which the final eight characteristics included in the questionnaire were selected. Theoretical considerations also suggested that store patronage behavior could be examined via a survey of respondents familiar with department store shopping. The theoretical framework also serves as a foundation for developing an appropriate analytical model.

Analytical Model An explicit specification of a set of variables and their interrelationships designed to represent some real system or process in whole or in part.

Verbal Model Analytical models that provide a written representation of the relationships among variables.

Graphical Model Analytical models that provide a visual picture of the relationships among variables.

Mathematical Model Analytical models that explicitly describe the relationships among variables, usually in equation form.

Analytical Model

An **analytical model** is a set of variables and their interrelationships designed to represent, in whole or in part, some real system or process. Models can have many different forms. The most common are verbal, graphical, and mathematical structures. In a **verbal model**, the variables and their relationships are stated in prose form. Such models may be mere restatements of the main tenets of a theory. A **graphical model** is visual and is used to isolate variables and to suggest directions of relationships but is not designed to provide numerical results. Graphical models are logical, preliminary steps to developing mathematical models.[23] A **mathematical model** explicitly specifies the relationships among variables, usually in equation form.[24] These models can be used as guides for formulating the research design and have the advantage of being amenable to manipulation.[25] The different models are illustrated in the context of the department store patronage project.

As can be seen from this example, the verbal, graphical, and mathematical models depict the same phenomenon or theoretical framework in different ways. The phenomenon of store patronage stated verbally is represented for clarity through a figure (graphical model) and is put in equation form (mathematical model) for ease of statistical estimation and testing. Graphical models are particularly helpful in conceptualizing an approach to the problem, as the following new car purchase model illustrates.

DEPARTMENT STORE PATRONAGE PROJECT

Model Building

Verbal model

A consumer first becomes aware of a department store. That person then gains an understanding of the store by evaluating the store in terms of the factors making up the choice criteria. Based on the evaluation, the consumer forms a degree of preference for the store. If preference is strong enough, the consumer will patronize the store.

Graphical model

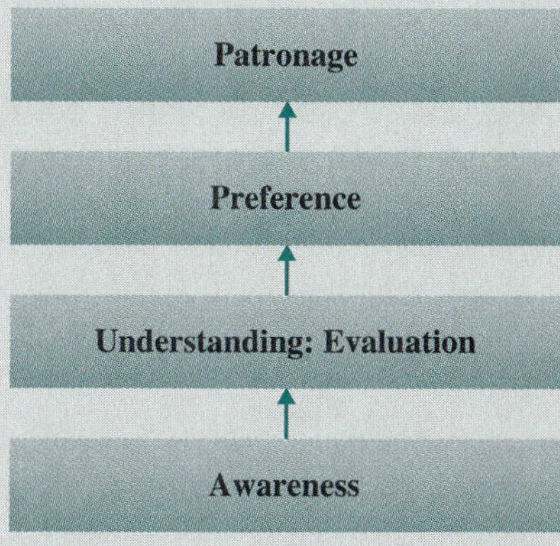

Mathematical model

$$y = a_0 + \sum_{i=1}^{n} a_i x_i$$

where

y = degree of performance

a_0, a_i = model parameters to be estimated statistically

x_i = store patronage factors that constitute the choice criteria

EXAMPLE

The True Definition of Luxury. Yours

The following graphical model illustrates the new car purchase decision process. A person starts as a passive consumer ("I am not now interested in considering the purchase of a new vehicle"). When the consumer is actively interested in purchasing a new car, the consumer creates a consideration set (limits the brands to be considered). This is followed by shopping, buying (sale), and assessing the value of products and services. Automobile firms such as Accura have used the new car purchase model to formulate marketing strategies that are consonant with consumers' underlying decision-making process. In this model, Accura is part of the consideration set for a certain group of consumers who are luxury oriented. Therefore, the marketing theme of the 1998 Accura RL, "The True Definition of Luxury. Yours," was based on this model.[26]

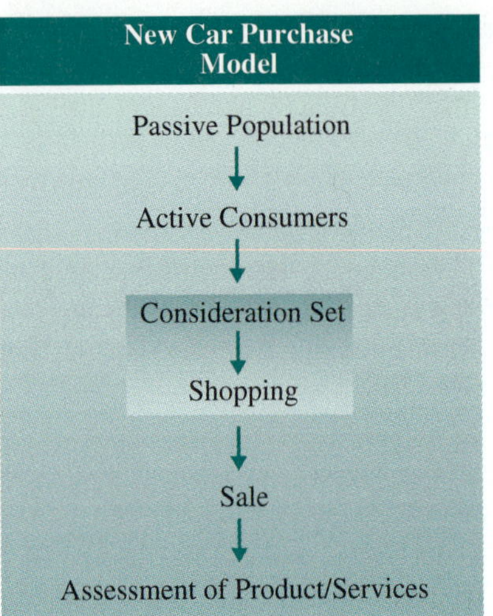

The verbal, graphical, and mathematical models complement each other and help the researcher identify relevant research questions and hypotheses.

Research Questions

Research Questions Research questions are refined statements of the specific components of the problem.

Research questions (RQs) are refined statements of the specific components of the problem. The components of the problem define the problem in specific terms, but further detail may be needed to develop an approuach. Each component of the problem may have to be broken down into subcomponents or research questions. Research questions ask what specific information is required with respect to the problem components. If the research questions are answered by the research, then the information obtained should aid the decision

DEPARTMENT STORE PATRONAGE PROJECT

Research Questions

The fifth component of the research problem was the psychological profile of Sears' customers. In the context of psychological characteristics, several research questions were asked about the customers of Sears.

- Do they exhibit store loyalty?
- Are they heavy users of credit?
- Are they more conscious of personal appearance as compared to customers of competing stores?
- Do they combine shopping with eating out?

The research questions were then further refined by precisely defining the variables and determining how they were to be operationalized. To illustrate, how should the use of store credit be measured? It could be measured any of the following ways:

1. Whether the customer holds a Sears credit card
2. Whether the customer uses the Sears credit card
3. The number of times the store credit card was used in a specified time period
4. The dollar amount charged to the store credit card during a specified time period

maker. The formulation of the research questions should be guided not only by the problem definition, but also by the theoretical framework and the analytical model adopted. For a given problem component, there are likely to be several research questions, as in the case of the department store patronage project.

The theoretical framework and the analytical model play a significant role in the operationalization and measurement of variables specified by the research questions. So, while in the department store patronage project the literature reviewed did not provide any definitive measure of store credit, the mathematical model could incorporate any of the alternative measures. Thus it was decided to include all four measures of store credit in the study. Research questions may be further refined into one or more hypotheses.

Hypotheses

Hypothesis An unproven statement or proposition about a factor or phenomenon that is of interest to the researcher.

A **hypothesis** (H) is an unproven statement or proposition about a factor or phenomenon that is of interest to the researcher. It may, for example, be a tentative statement about relationships between two or more variables as stipulated by the theoretical framework or the analytical model. Often, a hypothesis is a possible answer to the research question.[27] Hypotheses go beyond research questions because they are statements of relationships or propositions rather than merely questions to which answers are sought. While research questions are interrogative, hypotheses are declarative and can be tested empirically (see chapter 15). An important role of a hypothesis is to suggest variables to be included in the research design.[28] The relationship between the marketing research problem, research questions, and hypotheses, along with the influence of the objective/theoretical framework and analytical models, is described in Figure 2.4 and illustrated by the following example from the department store patronage project.[29]

Unfortunately, it may not be possible to formulate hypotheses in all situations. Sometimes sufficient information is not available to develop hypotheses. At other times, the most reasonable statement of a hypothesis may be a trivial restatement of the research question. For example:

RQ: Do customers of Sears exhibit store loyalty?
H: Customers of Sears are loyal.

Hypotheses are an important part of the approach to the problem. When stated in operational terms, such as H1 and H2 in the department store example, they provide guidelines on what and how data are to be collected and analyzed. When operational hypotheses are stated using symbolic notation, they are commonly referred to as statistical hypotheses. A research question may have more than one hypothesis associated with it, as in the case of Chanel. Chanel Inc. was considering advertising its Chanel brand of perfume in magazines

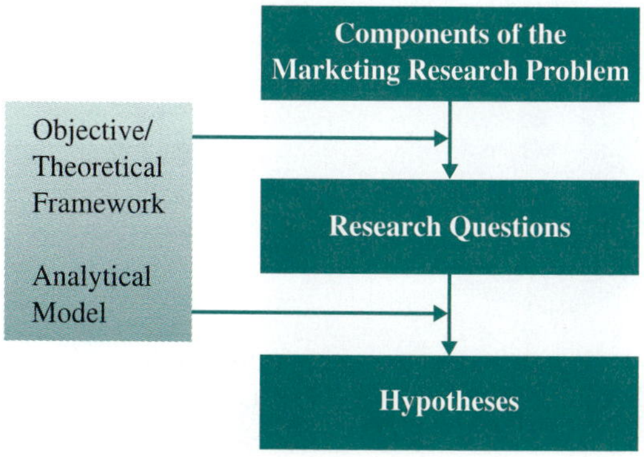

Components of the Marketing Research Problem
Objective/ Theoretical Framework
Research Questions
Analytical Model
Hypotheses

Figure 2.4
Development of Research Questions and Hypotheses

DEPARTMENT STORE PATRONAGE PROJECT

Hypotheses

The following hypotheses were formulated in relation to the research question on store loyalty:[30]

- H1: Customers who are store loyal are less knowledgeable about the shopping environment.
- H2: Store loyal customers are more risk averse than are nonloyal customers.

These hypotheses guided the research by ensuring that variables measuring knowledge of the shopping environment and propensity to take risks were included in the research design.

it formerly considered too pedestrian for its prestigious brand—*Working Woman*, *Savvy*, *Rolling Stone*, *Omni*, and *Interview*. The Chanel brand had a 2.8 percent share of department store sales (the leader is Estée Lauder with a 20.9 percent share). By expanding its advertising beyond high-fashion magazines, Chanel Inc. hoped to improve its share of department store sales. The following research question and hypotheses may be posed.[31]

RQ: Does Chanel have an upscale image?
H1: Chanel is perceived to be an expensive brand.
H2: Users of Chanel have higher-than-average incomes.
H3: Users of Chanel associate this perfume with status.

Note that to test H1, the researcher would have to operationalize and measure the perceived price associated with Chanel. Empirical testing of H2 would require that the respondents be classified as users or nonusers of Chanel and provide information on their incomes. Finally, H3 tells us that we need to operationalize another variable or a set of variables

Investigation of appropriate research questions and hypotheses lead to a broadening of the market for Chanel perfume.

which measure the status associated with Chanel. The results of this research provided support for H1 and H3 but not for H2. While Chanel did have an upscale image, its appeal was not limited to the upscale segment. Broadening of the target market by advertising in magazines formerly considered pedestrian led to improved department store sales of Chanel.

Relevant Characteristics

As mentioned earlier, a useful way of conceptualizing the development of an approach is to view it as a bridge between step 1 (problem definition) and step 3 (research design) of the marketing research process. Specifically, we focus here on one important aspect of research design: developing a questionnaire. The key question to ask, given the problem definition, research questions, and hypotheses, is what additional characteristics, factors, product attributes, or variables should be identified so that a questionnaire can be constructed? The answer to this question will result in the identification of the **relevant characteristics**. Let us consider the department store patronage project and focus on the components of the problem identified earlier in this chapter.

Relevant Characteristics
Characteristics, factors, product attributes, or variables that may affect a research design.

DEPARTMENT STORE PATRONAGE PROJECT

Relevant Characteristics

Component 1

This component involves the criteria households use to select a department store. Unless the specific factors constituting this criteria are identified, we cannot formulate a question asking the respondents which factors are important to them.

Based on the process outlined earlier, the following characteristics were identified: quality of merchandise, variety and assortment of merchandise, returns and adjustment policy, service of store personnel, prices, convenience of location, layout of store, credit and billing policies.

Component 2

This component is concerned with competition. Unless the competing stores are identified, it would be impossible to obtain information related to this component. Nine department stores were identified as competitors to Sears.

Component 3

Specific product categories are the focus of this component. Sixteen different product categories were selected, including women's dresses, women's sportswear, lingerie and body fashion, junior merchandise, men's apparel, cosmetics, jewelry, shoes, sheets and towels, furniture and bedding, and draperies.

Component 4

No additional characteristics or variables need to be identified.

Component 5

The standard demographic characteristics were included. The specific psychological characteristics selected were store loyalty, credit use, appearance consciousness, and combining shopping with eating.

Component 6

No additional characteristics or variables need to be identified.

This process is further illustrated by United Airlines in Research in Practice 2.2.[32]

RESEARCH IN PRACTICE 2.2

At United, Food Is Uniting the Airline with Travelers

United Airlines, as other major airlines, had to deal with passenger loyalty (management decision problem: how to attract more and more loyal passengers?). The broad marketing research problem was to identify the factors that influence loyalty of airline travelers. The basic answer is to improve service. Exploratory research, theoretical framework, and empirical evidence reveals that the consumers' choice of an airline is influenced by: safety, price of the ticket, frequent flyer program, convenience of scheduling, and brand name.

A graphical model stipulated that consumers evaluate competing airlines based on factors of the choice criteria to select a preferred airline. The problem was that major airlines were quite similar on these factors. Indeed, "airlines offer the same schedules, the same service, and the same fares." Consequently, United Airlines had to find a way to differentiate itself. Food turned out to be the solution.

Secondary data, such as the J. D. Power & Associates' survey on "current and future trends in airline food industry," indicated that "food service is a major contributor to customer's loyalty." Such a survey also emphasized the importance of food brands. The airline's Marketrak survey told United Airlines that "customers wanted more varied and up-to-date food." The following research questions and hypotheses may be posed.

RQ1: How important is food for airline customers?
H1: Food is an important factor for airline travelers.
H2: Travelers value branded food.
H3: Travelers prefer larger food portions, but with consistent quality.
H4: Travelers prefer exotic food.

Characteristics that influence the research design included the identification of competing airlines (Delta, American, etc.), factors of the choice criteria (already identified), measurement of airline travel and loyalty.

This kind of research helped United Airlines to define their marketing research problem, and develop the approach. Focus groups and surveys were conducted to check customers' perceptions of food in United Airlines' aircraft. The results provided support for all the hypotheses (H1 to H4). United Airlines then made a few changes: new "culinary menus," larger portions of food, new coffee and branded products (e.g., Godiva chocolates). This resulted in better service, increasing customer satisfaction and fostering loyalty.

After all the hypotheses about the importance of food were supported, United Airlines upgraded its food service, increasing customer satisfaction and fostering loyalty.

The process of identifying the relevant characteristics and the other components of the approach to the problem leads to a specification of the information needed. By focusing on each component of the problem and the related theory, models, research questions, hypotheses, and characteristics that have been identified in developing an approach, the researcher can determine what information should be obtained. This facilitates the formulation of an appropriate research design.

INTERNATIONAL MARKETING RESEARCH

The precise definition of the marketing research problem is more difficult in international marketing research than in domestic marketing research. Unfamiliarity with the environmental factors of the country in which the research is being conducted can greatly increase the difficulty of understanding the problem's environmental context and uncovering its causes.

EXAMPLE

Heinz Ketchup Couldn't Catch-Up in Brazil

Despite good track records inland and overseas, H. J. Heinz Co. failed in Brazil, a market that seemed to be South America's biggest and most promising. Heinz entered into a joint venture with Citrosuco Paulista, a giant orange juice exporter, because of the future possibility of buying the profitable company. Yet, the sales of its products, including ketchup, did not take off. Where was the problem? A problem audit revealed that the company lacked a strong local distribution system. Heinz lost control of the distribution because it worked on consignment. Distribution couldn't reach 25 percent penetration. The other related problem was that Heinz concentrated on neighborhood shops because this strategy was successful in Mexico. However, the problem audit revealed that 75 percent of the grocery shopping in São Paulo is done in supermarkets and not the smaller shops. Although, Mexico and Brazil may appear to have similar cultural and demographic characteristics, consumer behavior can vary greatly. A closer and intensive look at the Brazilian food distribution system and the behavior of consumers could have averted this failure. Heinz, however, is watching more closely in Asia, especially China, where the company markets baby food and where 22 million babies are born every year.[33] ■

As the Heinz example illustrates, many international marketing efforts fail not because research was not conducted but because the relevant environmental factors were not taken into account. Generally, this leads to a definition of the problem that is too narrow. Consider, for example the consumption of soft drinks. In many Asian countries water is consumed with meals, and soft drinks are generally served to guests and on special occasions. Therefore, the management problem of increasing the market share of a soft drink brand would translate to different marketing research problems in India than in the United States. Before defining the problem, the researcher must isolate and examine the impact of the **self-reference criterion** (SRC), or the unconscious reference to one's own cultural values. The following steps help researchers account for environmental and cultural differences when defining the problem in an international marketing context: [34]

Self-Reference Criterion The unconscious reference to one's own cultural values.

Step 1. Define the marketing research problem in terms of domestic environmental and cultural factors. This involves an identification of relevant American (or Western) traits, economics, values, needs, or habits.

Step 2. Define the marketing research problem in terms of foreign environmental and cultural factors. Make no judgments. This involves an identification of the related traits, economics, values, needs, or habits in the proposed market culture. This task requires input from researchers familiar with the foreign environment.

Step 3. Isolate the self-reference criterion (SRC) influence on the problem and examine it carefully to see how it complicates the problem. Examine the differences between steps 1 and 2. The SRC can be seen to account for these differences.

Step 4. Redefine the problem without the SRC influence and address it for the foreign market situation. If the differences in steps 3 are significant, the impact of the SRC should be carefully considered.

Consider the broad problem of the Coca-Cola Company trying to increase its penetration of the soft drink market in India. In step 1, the problem of increasing the market penetration in the United States would be considered. In the United States, virtually all households consume soft drinks, and the problem would be to increase the soft drink consumption of existing consumers. Furthermore, soft drinks are regularly consumed with meals and as thirst quenchers. So the problem of increasing market penetration would involve getting the consumers to consume more soft drinks with meals and at other times. In India, on the other hand (step 2), a much smaller percentage of households consume soft drinks, and soft drinks are not consumed with meals. Thus, in step 3, the SRC can be identified as the American notion that soft drinks are an all-purpose, all-meal, beverage. In step 4, the problem in the Indian context can be defined as how to get a greater percentage of the Indian consumers to consume soft drinks (Coca-Cola products) and how to get them to consume soft drinks (Coca-Cola products) more often for personal consumption.

While developing theoretical frameworks, models, research questions, and hypotheses, remember that differences in the environmental factors, especially the sociocultural environment, may lead to differences in the formation of perceptions, attitudes, preferences, and choice behavior. For example, orientation toward time varies considerably across cultures. In Asia, Latin America, and the Middle East, people are not as time-conscious as, say, Europeans. This influences their perceptions of and preferences for convenience foods such as frozen foods and prepared dinners. In developing an approach to the problem, the researcher should consider the equivalence of consumption and purchase behavior and the underlying factors that influence them. This is critical to the identification of the correct research questions, hypotheses, and characteristics/factors that influence the research design.

EXAMPLE

Surf Superconcentrate Faces a Super Washout in Japan

Unilever attempted to break into the Japanese detergent market with Surf Superconcentrate. It achieved 14.5 percent of the market share initially during test marketing, which fell down to a shocking 2.8 percent when the product was introduced nationally. Where did they go wrong? Surf was designed to have a distinctive premeasured packet as in tea bag–like sachets, joined in pairs, because convenience was an important attribute to Japanese consumers. It also had a "fresh smell" appeal. However, Japanese consumers noticed that the detergents did not dissolve in the wash, partly because of weather conditions and also because of the popularity of low-agitation washing machines. Surf was not designed to work in the new washing machines. Unilever also found that the "fresh smell" positioning of new Surf had little relevance because most consumers hang their wash out in the fresh air. The research approach was certainly not without flaws: Unilever failed to identify critical attributes that are relevant in the Japanese detergent market. Furthermore, it identified factors such as "smell fresh" that had no relevance in the Japanese context. Appropriate qualitative research such as focus groups across samples from the target market could have revealed the correct characteristics or factors leading to a suitable research design.[35] ■

ETHICS IN MARKETING RESEARCH

Ethical issues arise if the process of defining the problem and developing an approach is compromised by the personal agendas of the client (DM) or the researcher. This process is adversely affected when the DM has hidden objectives, such as gaining a promotion or justifying a decision that has been already made. The DM has the obligation to be candid and disclose to the researcher all the relevant information that will enable a proper definition of the marketing research problem. Likewise, the researcher is ethically bound to define the problem so as to further the best interest of the client rather than the interest of the research firm. At times this may involve making the interest of the research firm subservient to the client leading to an ethical dilemma.

EXAMPLE

Ethical or More Profitable?

A marketing research firm is hired by a major consumer electronics company (e.g., Philips) to conduct a large-scale segmentation study with the objective of improving market share. The researcher, after following the process outlined in this chapter, determines that the problem is not market segmentation but distribution. The company appears to be lacking an effective distribution system, which is limiting market share. However, the distribution problem requires a much simpler approach that will greatly reduce the cost of the project and the research firm's profits. What should the researcher do? Should the research firm conduct the research the client wants rather than the research the client needs? Ethical guidelines indicate that the research firm has an obligation to disclose the actual problem to the client. If, after the distribution problem has been discussed, the client still desires the segmentation research, the research firm should feel free to conduct the study. The reason is that the researcher can not know for certain the motivations underlying the client's behavior.[36] ■

Several ethical issues are also pertinent in developing an approach. When a client solicits proposals, not with the intent of subcontracting the research, but with the intent of gaining the expertise of research firms without pay, an ethical breach has occurred. If the client rejects the proposal of a research firm, then the approach specified in that proposal should not be implemented by the client, unless the client has paid for the development of the proposal. Likewise, the research firm has the ethical obligation to develop an appropriate approach. If the approach is going to make use of models developed in another context, then this should be disclosed to the client. For example, if the researcher is going to use a customer satisfaction model developed previously for an insurance company in a customer satisfaction study for a bank, then this information should be made known. Proprietary models and approaches developed by a research firm are the property of that firm and should not be reused by the client in subsequent studies without the permission of the research firm.

Such ethical situations would be satisfactorily resolved if both the client and the researcher adhered to the seven Cs: communication, cooperation, confidence, candor, closeness, continuity, and creativity, as discussed earlier. This would lead to a relationship of mutual trust that would check any unethical tendencies.

INTERNET AND COMPUTER APPLICATIONS

There are several ways in which the Internet can help in defining the problem and developing an approach and add value to the traditional methods. Let us first consider the tasks involved.

Discussions with the Decision Maker

The Internet can help the researcher gain access to the DM or DMs. Thanks to e-mail, it is now possible to reach decision makers anywhere, at any time. The Internet can also provide chat rooms so the DM can chat with the researcher and other DMs about the research project. A discussion could be developed around the problem audit. The audit issues could be introduced in the chat room by the researcher. The DMs could respond to the questions and to the thoughts of the other chat room respondents (other DMs, the researcher, etc.). The availability of the responses to be seen by whomever enters the chat room has the effect of getting all of the DMs together at one time without requiring that they be physically present at the same time. Because of the nature of the discussion (inside company correspondence), the participants could be given password access to the chat room, thus, keeping the information secure from those without a need to know.

Interviews with Industry Experts

The Internet can also be used to enhance the researcher's ability to obtain advice from experts. The Internet can be searched to find industry experts outside of the client's organization. To locate an expert, search the lists of Usenet FAQs to see if one covers your topic. If there is no FAQ, search the list of Usenet newsgroups or forums (www.dejanews.com) to find an appropriate forum. Then search for list servers related to the industry or type of organization to which that client belongs. Experts would probably be subscribers to such list servers. List servers are covered in more depth in chapter 3. Chat rooms can also be used to have interactive discussions with industry experts.

Secondary Data Analysis and Qualitative Research

Search engines, mentioned in chapter 1, can be used to collect secondary data quickly and economically. We will discuss the availability and acquisition of secondary information on the Internet in more detail in chapter 4. The Internet is also useful in doing qualitative research. We provide a detailed discussion of the use of chat rooms and list servers to do exploratory research in chapter 3. Conducting qualitative research, such as focus groups and in-depth interviews, via the Internet is discussed in chapter 5.

Environmental Context of the Problem

Many of the factors to be considered in the environmental context of the problem can be researched via the Internet. Past information and forecasts of trends can be found by searching for the appropriate information with the search engines mentioned earlier.

RESEARCH IN PRACTICE 2.3

The Enterprising Home Page of Coca-Cola Enterprises

The home page for Coca-Cola Enterprises (www.cokecce.com) provides:

company overview
financial information
facts and statistics
share-owner sources
investor news
daily stock prices
frequently asked questions
link to the Coca-Cola Company home page.

For client specific information the user can go to the company home page, by simply typing the company's name, after clicking on the Netsearch icon on the browser, and get the information from there. Generally, the companies provide the information about their products and services in their home page. Thus the home page of a company is the ideal starting point for information about the company.

Further, the user can search for the competitor information also on the Internet. There are various ways of doing this, the easiest being going to the competitor's home page. For example, the user can go to the Pepsi home page (www.pepsico.com) or to RC Cola's home page (www.comnet.ca).

A frequently used file for company and competitor information is Dunn's Market identifiers from Dunn & Bradstreet (www.dbisna.com). The Dow Jones News/Retrieval Service (DJNR) is the full text on-line service of Dow Jones and Company. It offers company and industry information on more than 10 million U.S. and international companies. StreetLink

FOCUS ON Burke

The most difficult task in research, in the opinion of Burke, is coming to grips with the marketing research problem or objectives. Typically, a manager thinks in terms of the symptoms of a problem or the desired outcome of implementing decisions. For example, the manager might say, "our level of repeat purchase among our customers is declining" (symptom). The manager might also say, "would this new concept perform up to our expectations if introduced into the marketplace?" (desired outcome). It is the job of the researcher to aid the manager in taking these kinds of statements and creating "researchable" definition of the marketing research problem. What Burke tries to achieve *before* designing the research is a statement of the marketing research problem that is based on:

1. specific measurements that relate to the management decision problem
2. details of the form the information is to take
3. clear understanding of how the information is to be used

Each time Burke consultants meet with the key decision makers (DMs) to discuss a research issue they fill out a brief form that includes:

1. why the research is necessary, including what is the management issue, what decisions will be made
2. what specifically will be measured (e.g. purchase interest, price elasticity over a defined range of prices, etc.)
3. how the information will be used by the DMs in decision making
4. what timing is required
5. what budget is appropriate

A manufacturer of a product for the treatment of athlete's foot was concerned that a recent erosion in sales would lead eventually to distribution problems, as retailers would refuse to stock the product. To rejuvenate sales, the company planned to update the package and restage the product. The company asked Burke to bid on a telephone survey among recent users of the product, but the objectives of the proposed research were vague. After meeting with the decision makers of the company and its ad agency, Burke determined that the broad marketing problem was "to determine the viability of the proposed restage." Burke also felt that focusing only on the users of the company's brand was a too narrow view of the problem. Recognizing that the restage would not succeed unless the product could draw users away from other brands, Burke recommended asessing the reaction of users of any athlete's foot remedy, not just users of the company's brand. The client agreed that Burke's definition of the marketing research problem would provide better information to help decision makers determine whether to proceed with the restage. This project was awarded to Burke.

provides a site at which corporate information is available on many companies. The site can be found at www.streetlink.com/.

Several commercial marketing research firms, for example, the Gallup organization (www.gallup.com), provide valuable information on buyer behavior and market trends. Many newsletters follow marketing, economic and regulatory trends and are available through on-line databases. For example, NewsNet provides access to newsletters such as *Congressional Activities* and *Congressional Research Report*. All these sources can be very useful in understanding the environmental context of the problem and in developing a suitable approach.

In addition to the Internet, computers can be used in other ways to define the problem and develop an approach. The literature review could be conveniently conducted by examining, among other sources, on-line information about catalogs, books, and articles. Spreadsheet software packages such as Lotus 1-2-3 and Excel are effective managerial tools in developing and testing simple mathematical models. Data are stored in the cells of the spreadsheet and assigned a unique location code. By entering the variables of the model and specifying their relationships with a formula, the researcher can perform sensitivity analysis of key variables and study or graph their impact on other variables. The microcomputer and mainframe versions of popular statistical packages, SPSS, SAS, BMDP, Minitab, and Excel can be used for developing and estimating mathematical models.

SUMMARY

Defining the marketing research problem is the most important step in a research project. It is a difficult step, because frequently management has not determined the actual problem or has only a vague notion about it. The researcher's role is to help management identify and isolate the problem.

The tasks involved in formulating the marketing research problem include discussions with management, including the key decision makers, interviews with industry experts, analysis of secondary data, and qualitative research. These tasks should lead to an understanding of the environmental context of the problem. The environmental context of the problem should be analyzed and certain essential factors evaluated. These factors include past information and forecasts about the industry and the firm, objectives of the DM, buyer behavior, resources and constraints of the firm, the legal and economic environment, and marketing and technological skills of the firm.

Analysis of the environmental context should assist in the identification of the management decision problem, which should then be translated into a marketing research problem. The management decision problem asks what the DM needs to do, whereas the marketing research problem asks what information is needed and how it can be obtained effectively and efficiently. The researcher should avoid defining the marketing research problem either too broadly or too narrowly. An appropriate way of defining the marketing research problem is to make a broad statement of the problem and then identify its specific components.

Developing an approach to the problem is the second step in the marketing research process. The components of an approach consist of objective/theoretical framework, analytical models, research questions, hypotheses, and characteristics influencing the research design. It is necessary that the approach developed be based on objective or empirical evidence and be grounded in theory. The relevant variables and their interrelationships may be neatly summarized via an analytical model. The most common kinds of model structures are verbal, graphical, and mathematical. The research questions are refined statements of the specific components of the problem that ask what specific information is required with respect to the problem components. Research questions may be further refined into hypotheses. Finally, given the problem definition, research questions, and hypotheses, characteristics or factors needed to construct a questionnaire should be identified.

When defining the problem in international marketing research, the researcher must isolate and examine the impact of the self-reference criterion (SRC), or the unconscious reference to one's own cultural values. Likewise, when developing an approach, the differences in the environment prevailing in the domestic market and the foreign markets should be carefully considered. Several ethical issues which have an impact on the client and the researcher can arise at this stage but can be resolved by adhering to the seven Cs: communication, cooperation, confidence, candor, closeness, continuity, and creativity. The Internet and computers can be useful in the process of defining the problem and developing an approach.

KEY TERMS AND CONCEPTS

problem definition
problem definition process
problem audit
secondary data
primary data
qualitative research
environmental context of the problem
objectives
buyer behavior
legal environment
economic environment
management decision problem
marketing research problem
broad statement of the problem
specific components of the problem
theory
objective evidence
analytical model
verbal model
graphical model
mathematical model
research questions
hypothesis
relevant characteristics
self-reference criterion

ACRONYMS

The factors to be considered while analyzing the environmental context of the problem may be summed up by the acronym PROBLEM:

P ast information and forecasts
R esources and constraints
O bjectives of the decision maker
B uyer behavior
L egal environment
E conomic environment
M arketing and technological skills

EXERCISES

Questions

1. What is the first step in conducting a marketing research project?
2. Why is it important to define the marketing research problem appropriately?
3. What are some reasons management is often not clear about the real problem?
4. What is the role of the researcher in the problem definition process?
5. What is a problem audit?
6. What is the difference between a symptom and a problem? How can a skillful researcher differentiate between the two and identify a true problem?
7. What are some differences between a management decision problem and a marketing research problem?
8. What are the common types of errors encountered in defining a marketing research problem? What can be done to reduce the incidence of such errors?
9. How are the research questions related to components of the problem?
10. What are the differences between research questions and hypotheses?
11. Is it necessary for every research project to have a set of hypotheses? Why or why not?
12. What are the most common forms of analytical models?
13. Give an example of an analytical model that includes all the three major types.
14. Describe a microcomputer software program that can be used to assist the researcher in defining the research problem.

Problems

1. State the research problems for each of the following management decision problems.
   - **a.** Should a new product be introduced?
   - **b.** Should an advertising campaign that has run for three years be changed?
   - **c.** Should the in-store promotion for an existing product line be increased?
   - **d.** What pricing strategy should be adopted for a new product?
   - **e.** Should the compensation package be changed to motivate the sales force better?
2. State management decision problems for which the following research problems might provide useful information.
   - **a.** Estimate the sales and market share of department stores in a certain metropolitan area.
   - **b.** Determine the design features for a new product which would result in maximum market share.
   - **c.** Evaluate the effectiveness of alternative TV commercials.

   d. Assess current and proposed sales territories with respect to their sales potential and workload.
   e. Determine the prices for each item in a product line so as to maximize total sales for the product line.
3. Identify five symptoms of problems facing a DM and a plausible cause for each one.
4. For the first component of the department store patronage project, identify the relevant research questions and develop suitable hypotheses. (Hint: Closely follow the example given in this chapter for the fifth component of the department store project.)
5. Suppose you are doing a project for Delta airlines. Identify, from secondary sources, the attributes or factors passengers consider when selecting an airline.

INTERNET AND COMPUTER EXERCISES

1. You are a consultant to Coca-Cola USA working on a marketing research project for Diet Coke.
   a. Use the on-line databases in your library to compile a list of articles related to the Coca-Cola Company, Diet Coke, and the soft drink industry published during the past year.
   b. Visit the Coca-Cola and PepsiCo Web sites and compare the information available at each (see Research in Practice 2.3).
   c. Based on the information collected from the Internet, write a report on the environmental context surrounding Diet Coke.
2. Select any firm. Using secondary sources, obtain information on the annual sales of the firm and the industry for the last 10 years. Use a spreadsheet package, such as Lotus 1-2-3 or Excel, or any microcomputer or mainframe statistical package, to develop a graphical model relating the firm's sales to the industry sales.
3. Visit the Web sites of competing sneaker brands (Nike, Reebok, Adidas). From an analysis of information available at these sites, determine the factors of the choice criteria used by consumers in selecting a sneaker brand.
4. BankAmerica wants to know how it can increase its market share and has hired you as a consultant. Read the 10-K reports for BankAmerica and three competing banks at www.sec.gov/edgarhp.htm and analyze the environmental context of the problem.

Professional Perspectives

1.1 The Industry Perspective

Joe Ottaviani,
Senior Vice President, General Manager, Burke Marketing Research. As senior vice president and general manager of Burke Marketing Research, a division of Burke, Inc., Joe has overall responsibility for the successful execution of research projects. In 25 years at Burke, Joe has held positions on both sales and operations. He is also a member of Burke's board of directors.

As the new millennium approaches, the marketing research industry cannot rest on its accomplishments; it must be up to the task of dealing with many important new challenges. Marketing research, as a profession, has made many important contributions to the marketing process. In fact, the industry has played a major role in researching every aspect of the marketing mix, from pricing to promotion, for the world's leading manufacturers and service organizations.

The future of marketing research holds many changes that are both exciting and challenging. The globalization of the world's economies has changed forever the way the profession operates. The top buyers of marketing research sell products globally; therefore, their marketing problems transcend national boundaries. So what was once a service that was provided on a national basis has been transformed into a service that is worldwide. Clients have learned, often the hard way, that conducting marketing research on an international basis is very tricky. Proper execution of marketing research in this setting not only requires technical competence but also knowledge of and sensitivity to cultural diversity. The overwhelming need for competent worldwide research has fueled a number of international partnerships. The industry has been characterized by many mega takeovers and mergers. Most of the top marketing research companies on both sides of the Atlantic are busy either buying up other companies or themselves being bought. The next playing field for mergers and acquisitions will be the important Pacific Rim and Asian markets.

The client base for most marketing research companies has changed as the marketing discipline has been accepted into more and more industries and service sectors. Classic marketing research developed and grew up in the packaged goods industry. Anyone who has been in the industry more than 20 years can remember when the entire client base was packaged goods companies. Today, most marketing research firms include among their client lists IT (information technology) firms, telecoms, and many companies in the ever-expanding service sectors. This trend will continue as new industries and service sectors uncover the power of information gained through marketing research. As one important ramification of this change in the client base, the professional researcher plays a greater role in every step of the research process, from problem definition to final presentation and recommendations.

There is every indication that individual client assignments will continue to grow in size and complexity. The prices for many assignments now reach into the millions of dollars and require expertise in a variety of disciplines only recently offered by marketing researchers. This has had an effect on the way marketing research companies hire and staff various functions. The definition of a full-service firm also changed. What was once a field and tab operation, full-service now includes the ability to not only conduct the research and provide recommendations but to assist the client in carrying out those recommendations. In order to be considered full-service in the future, marketing research firms will be required to hire and train professionals from academic areas, such as change management and industrial psychology, that are not currently represented in the firm.

The future of the industry's main source of information, data collection, is somewhat uncertain. Collecting information from consumers is a necessary and important step in the marketing research process. Without data there will be no analysis and no recommendations for the client. There are two very powerful forces that are affecting how data will be collected in the future: (1) respondent cooperation and (2) legislation. Consumers, the main source of the industry's data, are becoming more and more difficult to contact. Despite much effort by industry groups such as CASRO (Council of American Survey Research Organizations), the MRA (Marketing Research Association), and CMOR (Council for Marketing and Opinion Research), cooperation rates among consumers for survey participation is on a long downslide. It is the responsibility of everyone in the industry to ensure that the important relationship existing between data collectors and the general public be maintained and protected. We must take serious steps to rid our industry of practices that "turn off" the consumer to the survey experience. Attention must be given to shortening interview lengths and focusing subject matter. Consideration must also be given to the hours worked by data collectors. It is simply not acceptable to contact consumers at dinner or late at night with a long boring interview. A new and potentially powerful tool, the Internet, promises to be the data collection method of the future.

On the legislative side, it would appear that most state legislatures have a hard time differentiating between marketing research and telemarketing. In their efforts to restrict the hours during which telemarketing can be conducted, legislatures often pass laws that lump all telephone contact with the consumer under one banner. The groups mentioned above, especially CMOR, to date have managed to remove marketing research activities from legislation restricting telemarketing.

There is a widening gap between the experience levels of practitioners on the client and supplier sides of the business. Marketing research departments were often hard hit by corporate downsizing in the late 1980s and early 1990s. Many experienced employees who were let go found themselves serving as consultants to the very firms that downsized them. Perhaps one of the most unfortunate results of this downsizing, besides the vacuum of talent it created on the client side, was the effect it had on training new talent. For many years, research departments in the largest companies functioned as excellent training and proving grounds for marketing research professionals. Without these programs in place, the industry has been facing, for some time, a shortage of trained professionals. Research providers on the other hand were compelled to hire and train research professionals. The resulting experience gap has forced clients to rely more heavily on research providers for an ever-expanding variety of their needs; and research providers are now more deeply involved in the clients' business than ever before. A very recent development, which is certain to increase in favor, is for clients to make office space available to research providers so they can function as members of the client company's staff.

HOW BURKE FITS IN

As one of the oldest custom survey research companies, Burke has experienced most of the industry's growing pains. Burke, Inc. traces its roots back to a small company founded by Alberta Burke in 1931. For nearly 70 years, the Burke name has been synonymous with industry leadership and quality.

Like most of the industry, Burke, Inc. earned its spurs in the packaged goods industry. Burke, Inc. now markets its services across four diverse divisions providing services in the areas of (1) custom research, (2) customer satisfaction and loyalty retention, (3) educational seminars in marketing research, and (4) assisting clients with implementing strategic changes. Burke offers these services on a worldwide basis by a partnership with Infratest Burke AG of Munich, Germany—the seventh largest research company in the world. This alliance also provides for an intellectual exchange of ideals and methods, making both partners a stronger force in the marketplace.

One could properly infer from the above that Burke can serve a wide variety of client needs in the marketing research arena. Taking a look at just the custom research business, the chart below indicates the breadth of services offered. The Research Protocols shown in the "arrows" were developed by Burke, Inc. to solve marketing problems at the various points in the marketing process:

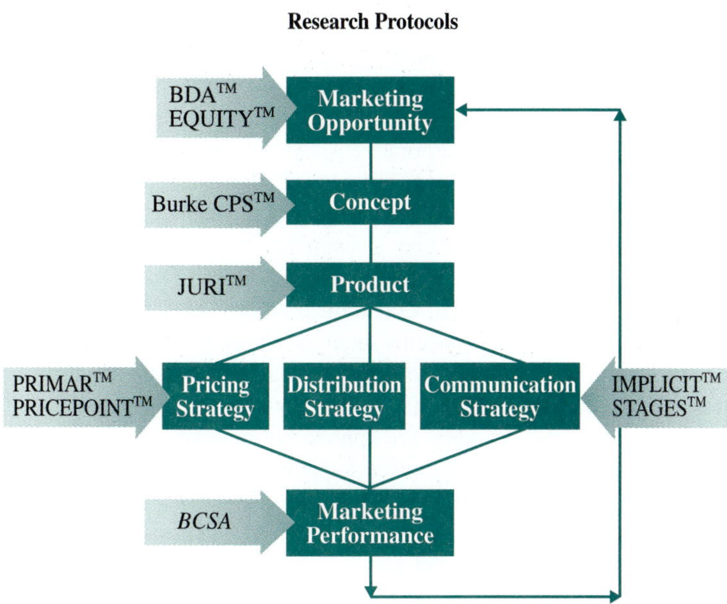

Establishing an Internet research business is very much a priority at Burke. With uncertainty surrounding the future of data collection, the Internet provides a solution with great potential. An Internet operations group has been formed to support the growing business—both qualitative as well as quantitative—in this area. Clients from all business sectors are participating in this new area of research.

In an industry where people are a firm's number one asset, Burke has invested much time and effort in recruiting, hiring, and training. Such investments are vital to the success of any organization that operates in a vibrant, people-oriented industry such as marketing research. Our growth and future success depends on our ability to attract, train, and retain the best and brightest of today's workers.

1.2 The Profession of Marketing Research: A Strategic Assessment[1]

The profession of marketing research is being redefined. To understand this redefinition, we must take a hard look at the current state of both the industry and the profession, because they are so intertwined. However, before examining the status of the profession we will consider the research purchasers, advertising agencies, and research agencies.

[1]This article is an abridged version prepared by William D. Neal. The original article entitled "The Profession of Marketing Research: A Strategic Assessment and a Prescription for Improvement" was published in *Marketing Research*, 1, (September 1989): 13–23.

William D. Neal
founder and senior executive officer of Sophisticated Data Research (SDR), Inc., Atlanta, Georgia. William D. Neal oversees all marketing and customer satisfaction programs at SDR. In addition, he conducts seminars and provides consulting services to clients in the areas of market segmentation and strategic positioning. Mr. Neal has served as vice president of the Marketing Research Division and chairman of the board of the American Marketing Association.

RESEARCH PURCHASERS

Dramatic changes that have a direct effect on the research function are taking place in the corporate environment. One is the impact of new technologies. Powerful personal computers are fostering hands-on access to marketing data throughout the corporate environment. Scanning and single-source data systems are flooding packaged goods marketers with an overflow of data. Advanced, extremely fast communications capabilities are accelerating the marketing process. This technology is having the effect of "flattening" the traditional corporate organization. Corporations no longer need a battalion of middle managers to prepare and filter information for senior corporate decision making.

For similar reasons, large corporate research departments are often seen as incompatible with today's lean and mean, fast-moving corporate environment. In many cases, corporate research departments are being reorganized, redeployed, downsized, and, in some cases, eliminated altogether. In many firms the nature of corporate investments in marketing research is also changing. We are seeing major new investments in single-source data systems, product tracking panels, audience measurement systems, and service quality measurement systems. These systems tend to be tactical. Constrained budgets have forced firms to invest in the quick-payoff research that such systems seem to represent. These tactical systems, which are often very promotion oriented, are being purchased and installed at the expense of the more strategic and long-term research that supports long-term planning.

However, emerging sectors of the economy are approaching marketing research in a different way than do the traditional packaged goods companies that have been our corporate model for so many years. The services sector is a major bright spot for our profession and the industry of marketing research. Especially noteworthy are the areas of communications, health care, travel and tourism, financial services, and professional services. All are making major investments in marketing research, but few are using the packaged goods model. High technology marketers, for the most part, continue to ignore traditional marketing research, though there are a few notable exceptions. Retailing seems to be slowly emerging as a major area for research investigations especially in service quality measurement.

ADVERTISING AGENCIES

In many advertising agencies, the trend is toward severe downsizing of research departments. Research professionals in many advertising agencies are experiencing lower status. They are being viewed as technicians rather than as consultants and managers. Agency research professionals have reduced in-house capabilities, and they are becoming less involved in high-level client consulting and advisory services. Many are simply brokering marketing research to full-service commercial firms—and, most recently, they are doing precious little of that. In general, the research professional in the advertising agency is being directed toward concept development and promotional pretesting and away from assessment, evaluation, and strategy development functions.

RESEARCH AGENCIES

Large, traditional marketing research firms are typically taking one of three paths:

1. They are building and selling huge databases, such as transaction measurement products and services, specialized panels, audience measurement systems, or service quality measurement systems.
2. They are building and selling technology-based solutions to marketing problems, such as consumer behavior models, pricing models, marketing effectiveness/efficiency models, or market forecasting models.

3. They are very efficiently providing the operational end of custom research services, namely data collection, data processing, and computer analysis services.

All three of these avenues require ever-increasing capital investments, and this requirement for capital is fueling much of the consolidation and buyout activity that is flourishing in the marketing research industry. It is becoming increasingly difficult for these larger, operationally oriented firms to compete in the custom research and expert consulting arenas because of (1) their typically high overhead and operating costs, (2) extreme pressure to "keep the plant operating at full capacity," and (3) a management philosophy directed toward operating efficiency and not scientific investigation.

Among the smaller research agencies and consultancies, we see ever-expanding numbers, increased fragmentation, and a tendency toward "custom" research services in both strategic and tactical arenas. These smaller firms are moving toward product and service category areas of specialization, and their low operational overhead makes them very price competitive. In many cases, they are putting the custom research departments of the large, full-service research companies at an extreme price and expertise disadvantage.

STATUS OF THE PROFESSION

The crossroads at which the profession finds itself is best described by the role of the professional marketing researcher in the corporate environment—which is often ill-defined. Is it the role of the marketing researcher to be the consummate critic of new things and new ideas, who subjects those new ideas to some acid test of dispassionate analysis, or is it that of the advocate of the new and faddish? Is our role that of the high-level consultant who has a finger on the pulse of the consumer or customer, or is it that of a technician who needs only to react to the demands and whims of the marketer? Is the professional marketing researcher a specialist or a generalist, an artist or a technocrat?

Another problem facing our industry and detracting severely from our professional image is the lack of specific requirements for entry into our profession. There are no explicit educational requirements, though the vast majority of us have at least one college degree. There are no requirements in terms of either field of training or experience. Literally anyone can hang out a shingle and claim to be a qualified marketing researcher.

Current professional development programs do not seem to be adequate for advancing the knowledge and expertise of the majority of marketing researchers. For the most part, colleges and universities are not providing a sufficient technical or business foundation for entry-level professionals in our field. Until very recently, there was no generally agreed upon curriculum for a career in marketing research, but the American Marketing Association now has published a draft curriculum. Few opportunities are available for independent training of marketing research professionals. Far fewer investments in professional training are being made by either client firms or research agencies, mainly because of both the expense and the lack of pertinent programs. Finally, few quality publications are targeted to the professional practitioner, though this situation is rapidly changing. Where will this lead us in the future?

FUTURE DIRECTIONS

In the future, the corporate research staff is likely to be more decentralized and dispersed into the operating units. The research staff will become smaller, because there will be fewer technical and analytical staff people. In many firms the research function will become more "managerial" in that the corporate research department will become procurers and managers of business research information and information systems, not collectors and detailed analyzers of data. They will have a major role in integrating business information from divergent sources—market scanning and transaction measurement systems, secondary sources, internal sources, and custom studies. More research emphasis will be on service quality research and measurement, customer satisfaction research and measurement, pricing research and pricing experiments, and explaining measured market behavior with sophisticated models that simulate the purchase environment. We can expect to see more true experimentation, with less emphasis on ad hoc, disjointed market analysis. Given these observations, we can expect that the corporate research staff will rely more heavily on outside, independent service companies for both market measurement and consulting services for particular product or service areas.

For the research providers, the future for business research seems bright—but it will be different! First, the split will continue to accelerate between the larger, more traditional marketing research companies and the smaller, consultancy-based research organizations. On one side, the major research firms will invest heavily in the operational aspect of the business—either providing very efficient custom data collection and data processing services or providing highly specialized database and technology-based services. The survivors will be those that continue to provide extremely efficient or unique services and have the capital resources to exploit their position.

On the other side will be an ever-expanding set of small, specialized firms that will combine custom research services with product- and service-category-specific consulting services. The secret to survival for these firms will be a top-notch reputation in a particular product/service category, a considerable capability to execute custom research studies rapidly, and a broad utilization of the newer analytical procedures.

It may be nearly impossible for any research firm to fill both roles. Each side requires a unique management philosophy and set of skills. The two sides require different financial structures and radically different marketing philosophies. Therefore, the larger, traditional "general services" research firms that have been a basic strength in our industry may be forced to jump to one side or the other of this split or, alternatively, to put an entirely separate corporate entity in each camp. Either way, marketing research professionals and firms must look toward the future, if they expect to be in it and be viable.

1.3 The Marketing Research Problem: From the DM's Desk to Study Execution

As a practicing researcher, I find that much of the satisfaction of this profession comes from the sense of discovery and achievement in the unique and interesting problems waiting to be solved. It is this uniqueness that prevents the development of a simple cookbook approach to problem solving and allows creativity in our professional lives. Still, we must have foundations for how we define or examine marketing research problems.

The decision maker (DM) tends to focus on the symptoms and usually defines problems in terms of a desired outcome, such as why are my sales down (desired outcome = high levels of sales), or how do I choose the best of the two test products (desired outcome = product that produces the largest share and/or revenue). To a researcher, on the other hand, a problem is appropriately defined when it states the needed information such that a level of measurement is specified. For example:

DM: Our sales are going down—what can we do?

Researcher: Declining sales are symptoms of problems in the marketplace in general (all products in our category are declining in popularity) or problems with our product. The resolution is sequential:

1. What are the causes of the decline? (A research issue)
2. What actions are we capable of taking against these causes once identified? (A management issue)
3. Which of these actions produces the optimal result for us? (A research issue)
4. How do we monitor the impact of these actions once they are taken? (A research issue)
5. How do we implement ongoing modifications to continue to improve sales? (Another sequence of management and research issues)

Ronald L. Tatham, Ph.D., *chairman, Burke, Inc. Ronald L. Tatham is actively involved in both the general management of the corporation and the design and analysis of research. Burke operates with the concept of the "producing manager." Every senior manager is involved in client-related activities and the delivery of Burke's research efforts.*

Thus from the researcher's point of view, the problem definition has to result in a specific set of components.

In the simplest case, a DM asks, "Which of these two proposed new products is better?" The researcher must now define "better" in such a way that specific components of the marketing research problem can be identified and appropriate measurements made. The definition stage could result in defining "better" as some combination of:

1. Has an image most consistent with that sought by our company in terms of specific measurable image characteristics.
2. Has the greatest appeal when measured in a concept test prior to product creation (appeal defined in terms of a purchase interest scale).
3. Has the highest sales forecast in a simulated test market that includes a home use period.
4. Results in the highest net sales in a minitest market.

Each of these four definitions of "better" implies a specific measurement to be taken by the researcher. However, the researcher must address the more specific issues of:

1. There are many components of image. Which are appropriate to this occasion and how do we assess them?
2. Which purchase interest scale do we use, and how do we evaluate the results?
3. There are several approaches to simulated test markets. Which do we select?

These do not exhaust the components of the problem that must be addressed, but they show that the researcher must eventually define the problem in terms of specific components and measurements. At the exploratory stage of problem development the measures may be "expert opinion." However, at later stages the measures will likely be obtained from the eventual purchasers or purchase deciders for the product or service.

A general statement of proper problem definition is as follows: "When the problem is properly defined the researcher knows all of the possible answers, but the researcher has not counted the answers yet." In other words, the best problem definition, from the researcher's point of view, leads to such a precise definition of measurement that the nature of the answers are known, only their frequencies are unknown. For example, problem definition meetings may have led the researcher to measure the following characteristics of a sample of current users of a product:

1. Age
2. Number of times the product was purchased in the past seven days
3. Number of items purchased at each purchase occasion (past seven days)
4. Number of times competitive products were purchased in past seven days
5. Number of competitive items purchased at each purchase occasion (past seven days)
6. Ratings of client's product and competitive products on five 10-point image questions

For each of the six information areas listed above, the researcher knows the form of the answer and the limits within which acceptable answers can be given. That is, we know the population distribution of ages and we know the specific units (years of age) we will get for answers; we know that only answers of the numbers 1 through 10 are permitted on information item #6, and so forth. We do not know the actual values of the answers among our target population. This may sound naively simple, but it illustrates the point that you must know what you are measuring before you attempt to gather information.

If the problem is defined rigorously, the usefulness of the information can be tested with the DM. The basic question to be asked of the DM is, "If the data the respondents give us take the following forms, what would you or could you do?" The researcher can show the DM hypothetical results based on the researcher's conjecture. If the DM says, "I'm not sure what I would do with that information," the researcher must stop and ask, "What additional information would you need to make this information more useful or what about this information limits its usefulness to you?" Because you know the form of all of the possible answers, you must test the likely results for usefulness with the DM even if you do not know the outcome of the study. A proper definition of the problem will provide the DM with the relevant information needed for decision making and guide the researcher in proceeding with the research project.

Cases

1.1 Life in the Fast Lane: Fast Food Chains Race to Be Number One

Fast food restaurants have been characterized by their limited menus, self-service, high turnover, and high percentage of take-out orders. The four market leaders—McDonald's, Burger King, Taco Bell, and Wendy's—comprise about half of the 59,960 fast food restaurants in the United States and collectively assumed 70 percent of the $467 million market in 1996. McDonald's, the market leader, had sales of over $16 million in its U.S. system alone from its 12,094 U.S. locations. Chief competitor Burger King sold over $7 million worth of fast food with about half the number of stores as McDonald's. Although the domination of these market leaders was once thought to spell doom for local regional operators, smaller chains are instead rebounding and experiencing new levels of growth. Chains such as Sonic and Carl's Jr. are invading markets that were formerly havens to their larger counterparts. With more and more chains competing for the consumers fast food buck, marketing is becoming increasingly important. McDonald's, which is expected to spend over $600 million in advertising in 1998, reorganized its management structure to better tackle the challenges posed in regional markets. Meanwhile, Burger King has made plans to challenge the leader on its chief products, the Big Mac and French fries, increasing its ad budget 4 percent to an estimated $385 million in 1998. McDonald's is still the market share leader with 42.1 percent of the U.S. market, but Burger King's share jumped 9.2 percent in 1996 alone to reach a 19.2 percent share and Wendy's gained 6.4 percent to reach 11 percent. Now more than ever, marketing to consumers' tastes is likely to be key in competing in the increasingly concentrated fast food restaurant war.

Capturing or retaining market position is intuitively tied to keeping up with the changing preferences of the American consumer. In a recent study conducted by Maritz Marketing Research, convenience of location, quality of food, menu selection, and then service were shown to be the most important influences on adults' fast food choices. Surprisingly, low price was not among the top four reasons Americans made their fast food selections. Only 8 percent of those surveyed made a fast food choice based on price.

Adults under the age of 65 cited proximity of location as the most important factor in their fast food purchase, with 26 percent of those polled stating it to be the chief criterion influencing their dining choice. After convenience of location, quality of the fast food itself was most important to consumers. This is interpreted to mean that not only do consumers want a superior product, but they want consistency in quality in each order at any location. Taco Bell recently shed its emphasis on low price for a focus on quality. The chain transformed its "Extra Value Meals" multimenu item combination package into "Border Select" meal platters by upgrading and modifying the food offered and the image presented. Arby's, a chain specializing in roast beef sandwiches, holds the phrase "a cut above" not only as an advertising slogan but as an intended view of its restaurants in general. "In everything we talk about—our uniforms, our buildings, our sandwiches—we want to be a little bit better than our competitors," proclaims the chain spokesman.

Moreover, customers are craving a variety of selections. Menu selection was also important to consumers, with 16 percent of adults polled citing it as the chief reason for choosing a fast food outlets. Chains offered diversified menus and often try to offer unique items. The Oklahoma City–based Sonic chain offers, in addition to the traditional sandwich, "things that you can't get at competitors like . . . onion rings and cherry limeades." Market leaders are also looking to capitalize on that one item that the competitor is not offering. Wendy's restaurants offered a unique four-item line of pita sandwiches in

1996, and racked up new highs in sales according to the firm. Menu selection was primarily important to senior citizens. One in four senior citizens felt that menu selection was the most important factor in their choice of dining establishments. Experts have predicted that the number of menu items will continue to grow as all fast food restaurateurs offer new items to avoid consumer boredom and maintain growth and market share. As a spokesman for Burger King said, "We'll stay with what we know best, but we have to add items to meet consumer preferences."

About 12 percent of adults surveyed felt that fast service was the basis of their fast food restaurant choice. McDonald's strategy is to "attract customers with price and keep them with service" and become "recognized as the service leader in the nation" according to the corporation's U.S. president. To emphasize this quality, McDonald's plans to extol its drive-through operations in a series of TV ads, showcasing the speed with which the hard-working staff diligently prepares the customers' orders. Taco Bell too exalts service qualities in its stores, with a mission summarized in the acronym FACT, which stands for "Fast food, Accurate orders, Cleanliness, and food served at the right Temperature." Wendy's has adopted a special "M.B.A.," which stands for "A Mop Bucket Attitude." This represents Wendy's "commitment to the traditional definition of customer satisfaction, which means putting customer service (cleanliness, quality food, and atmosphere) before numbers and computer printouts." Wendy's maintains that this is one of the major reasons for their success. Burger King has long recognized the importance of creating a favorable and memorable dining experience. Burger King was the first fast food restaurant to introduce dining rooms that allowed its customers to dine inside of its facilities. In 1992 Burger King became the first fast food restaurant to introduce table service and an expanded dinner menu in order to enhance the customer's dining experience.

The most recent trend in fast food restaurants has been toward value pricing. This trend was ushered in by Taco Bell, which dropped prices and boosted system-wide sales by 18.5 percent in only two years. While it was a novelty for a short time, value pricing has become a part of almost every major competitor. McDonald's offers its Extra Value Menu; Wendy's has a 99¢ Super Value Menu that emphasizes variety by offering items ranging from ready-to-go Side Salads to a Country Fried Steak Sandwich; and Burger King and Hardee's offer plans similar to that of McDonald's.

In a further effort to expand the fast food market, the industry has looked overseas. Because Asian and European markets are at the stage of fast food that America reached in 1960, American chains have a substantial competitive advantage there. Marketing experts have predicted that it will be easier for established American chains to expand overseas than at home. McDonald's is expected to realize about 40 percent of its operating profits outside the United States in 2000, as compared with 21 percent in 1990. Burger King has also focused on Japan as a wide-open market for its burgers and has also given much attention to the Eastern European market. It has recently opened up restaurants in Poland, the former East Germany, and Hungary, while at the same time establishing a training academy in London to service its European franchises. Wendy's has recently been recognized as a serious competitor in the international fast food market. Wendy's is currently contracted with more than 50 countries outside of the United States. Given the stiff competition, it remains to be seen if McDonald's can continue to be the leader in the domestic fast food race, as well as become the front runner in the international fast food race.

Questions

1. Describe the marketing information needs of the fast food industry.
2. What role can marketing research play in providing the information needed?
3. Give some examples of problem identification research that McDonald's can undertake to ensure their continued leadership in the fast food industry.
4. Describe the kinds of problem/solution research that Wendy's might undertake to improve its sales and market share.
5. Given the market potential overseas, should fast food chains conduct marketing research in foreign countries? What kind of opportunities and challenges will the fast foods chains encounter in conducting international marketing research?

References

Mark Hamstra, "McDonald's to Intensify Tech, Regionalization Efforts in 1998," *Nation's Restaurant News* 31(47) (November 24, 1997): 1, 97.

Cyndee Miller, "McDonald's Shifts Strategy as Competitors Get Stronger," *Marketing News* 31(9) (April 28, 1997): 1, 10.

Karen Benezra and Shannon Stevens, "BK to Boost '98 Media by $15M," *Brandweek* 38(43) (November 17, 1997): 37.

1.2 Nike Sprints Ahead of the Competition, Yet Has a Long Way to Run

Nike Inc., located in Beaverton, Oregon, is the number one U.S. athletic footwear company and the number two American brand in terms of name recognition among foreign consumers—a status shared with IBM and second only to Coca-Cola. This high degree of recognition is probably one of the main reasons Nike has been so immensely successful. For the 1997 fiscal year, the company continued to soar, earning over $795 million with sales of over $9.18 billion. Despite a $41.5 percent sales gain, analysts forecast a change in Nike's future. Although the company remains well managed with 15.8 percent growth expected for 1998, experts feel the company will have to work harder to grow in the future. Consumers are becoming less than enthralled with Nike's $100-plus prices and are rounding out their Nike-filled closets with other brand name clothing. Reebok and Adidas, the number two and three businesses in the industry, respectively, had increasing sales as of late 1997. Adidas especially is giving Nike a run for its money in women's sports—running and soccer—and is reporting triple-digit increases in worldwide orders. In response, the company is tweaking its hit marketing formula, which was started in 1985. The company hopes to shift attention to its product innovation and how the company has evolved.

Perhaps such success should be attributed in part to its wildly successful concept-based advertising campaigns. The company uses a process that is often called "image transfer." Nike ads almost never specifically place a product—or mention the brand name. A mood or atmosphere is created and then the brand is associated with that mood. "We don't set out to make ads. The ultimate goal is to make a connection," states Dan Weiden of one of Nike's ad agencies. One ad featured the Beatles and clips of Nike athletes Michael Jordan and John McEnroe juxtaposed with pictures of regular folks also engaged in sports. It was used to infer that real athletes prefer Nike and that perhaps if the general audience buys the brand they will play better too. Nike's unpredictable image-based ads have ranged from the shocking, such as its portrayal of real blood and guts in a "Search and Destroy" campaign used during the 1996 Olympic games; to humorous, such as the first ad used to launch Michael Jordan's Jordan brand wear. The latter advertising made the tongue-in-cheek suggestion that Jordan himself had a hand in production by slipping away from a Bulls' game at half time to run over to his company and then making his way back in time for the game's second half.

In 1998, Nike shifted to the new phase in its marketing campaign, emphasizing more of its product innovation skills than the jockey, edgy attitude that it displayed in previous years. "We recognize that our ads need to tell consumers that we're about product innovation and not just athletes and exposure. We need to prove to consumers that we're not just slapping a swoosh [the company trademark] on stuff to make a buck," says Chris Zimmerman, director of Nike's U.S. advertising. With the launch of the "I can" campaign, Nike is showing less of the celebrity athletes that previously adorned its marketing output and showing more product usage than in the previous "Just Do It" campaign. Competitors Reebok and Adidas have recently featured more product-focused ads and have met with a great deal of success. Despite this rearranged focus, Nike is not backing away from innovative marketing; for instance, Nike billboard ads that appeared around mid-1997 featured a static shot of a pair of shoes and directed consumers to an Internet site.

Also at the heart of Nike's new strategy is the international arena. That may prove to be the most difficult element for Nike to undertake. According to one source there seems to be a pretty strong recognition that in a few years Nike will be larger outside of the United States than inside. The problem that the company faces is that even though international sales currently make up one-third of Nike's business, international business still pales in comparison with the domestic sales. Nike would like to expand into the soccer and international sports arena, but to do so it will have to refocus marketing and distribution in order to reestablish itself as an authentic, technically superior sports shoe. Most recently Nike has bought out many of its worldwide distribution centers in order to achieve greater control of its operations. In the future, Nike would like to build up its presence in the key markets of China, Germany, Mexico, and Japan. Nike will focus its advertising on sports, and will feature sports that are of a particular interest in a specific region. Nike realizes that while it is ahead of the competition, it still has a long, long way to run.

Questions

1. How would you describe the buying behavior of consumers with respect to athletic footwear?
2. What is the management decision problem facing Nike as it attempts to retain its leadership position?

3. Define the marketing research problem facing Nike, given the management decision problem you have identified.
4. Develop two suitable research questions and formulate two hypotheses for each.
5. How can the Internet be used to help Nike in conducting marketing research, and in marketing its products.

References

Jeff Jensen, "Product Innovation Steps into Spotlight at Nike," *Advertising Age* 68(36) (September 8, 1997): 3, 48.

Isabelle Sender, "Just Do It, Abroad," *Chain Store Age* 73(10) (October 1997): 121–4.

Jeff Jensen, "Reebok and Nike Go Head to Head in Soccer Battle," *Advertising Age* 68(18) (May 5, 1997): 4.

1.3 Lexus: Imparting Value to Luxury and Luxury to Value?

In the 1980s Toyota developed a concept for a new car that was destined to be a success. The concept of the car, which was to be called Lexus, was based on the observation that there was a large, affluent market for cars that could boast exceptional performance. However, a significant portion of that market ranked value highly. Thus, they were loathe to pay the extraordinary prices that Mercedes charged for its high-performance vehicles. Toyota planned to target this market by creating a car that matched Mercedes on the performance criteria but was priced much more reasonably, providing consumers the value they desired, and making them feel that they were smart buyers.

Toyota introduced the Lexus in 1989 with much fanfare. A clever advertising campaign announced the arrival of this new car. One ad showed the Lexus next to a Mercedes with the headline, "The First Time in History That Trading a $73,000 Car for a $36,000 Car Could Be Considered Trading Up." Of course, Lexus had all the detail that the Mercedes did: a sculptured form, a quality finish, and a plush interior. The detail was not, however, limited to the car. Separate dealerships were created that had the type of atmosphere that affluent consumers expected from a luxury car maker including a grand showroom, free refreshments, and professional salespeople.

Toyota placed a strong emphasis on the performance of the new car. A package was sent to potential customers that included a 12-minute video displaying Lexus' superior engineering. The video showed that when a glass of water was placed on the engine block of a Mercedes and a Lexus, the water shook on the Mercedes while the Lexus had a virtually still glass of water. This visually told the viewer that the stability of Lexus was far better than even one of the most expensive cars around. Another video showed a Lexus making a sharp turn with a glass of water on its dashboard. The glass remained upright; again, the Lexus proved itself. These videos were successful in bringing in customers, whose expectations were surpassed.

The other luxury car makers noticed—and realized that they had to respond somehow. They could either lower their prices, admitting they were overpriced to begin with, or they could increase prices, adding more extras and reinforcing the image of the rich man's vehicle. They chose the former strategy and decided to beat Toyota at its own game. In the past three years, Mercedes, BMW, and Jaguar, which is now owned by Ford Motor Company, have kept prices low and increased quality. This has led to significant sales growth for all three auto manufacturers. Mercedes and Jaguar both saw 20 percent increases in 1994 from the previous year.

As a result of its success, Lexus decided to raise prices from $36,000 to $50,000 in 1994. This strategy did not work out as well as Lexus had hoped. Sales dropped 10 percent to 72,000 cars in the first 10 months of 1994 compared to 1993 sales. Lexus has since realized that it lacks the heritage for prestige that European luxury cars command and that people are once again willing to pay extra for that prestige. Lexus has, as a result, turned to a new advertising campaign to inspire an emotional response to its cars. The campaign must be exceptionally powerful because it also has to combat the decrease in growth of the luxury car market compared to the auto industry's overall growth. Partly responsible for this decline, the "near luxury" autos have skimmed away potential luxury auto consumers. Included in this group are the Toyota Avalon, the Nissan Maxima, the Mazda Millenia. BMW and Mercedes have also introduced products for this segment: the BMW 3 Series and the Mercedes C Class.

To combat this competition, Lexus is emphasizing nontraditional advertising and promotion, in addition to more mainstream luxury car advertisements. For example, part of the $60 million 1996 campaign for its S300 model included sending e-mail advertisements to 15,000 potential customers. These potential customers were visitors to the company's Web site who stated in an on-line questionnaire that they owned a non-Lexus automobile. The company's attempt to tap nonowners' latent interest in their products with special e-mail messages was a marketing first. Lexus plans to expand marketing efforts in the future with the aim of not only gaining new customers but retaining present clients. Although the company's plans are highly classified, their latest efforts hint that newer marketing tactics will follow in the unconventional style of ads past. For instance, Lexus' recent sponsorship of a skiing event in Colorado included an invitation to all Lexus owners to spend a luxurious, all-expenses-paid weekend in the mountains. These efforts are consistent with Lexus' philosophy of imparting value to luxury, and luxury to value.

Questions

1. Describe the management decision problem facing Lexus as it seeks to fight competition from other luxury car manufacturers such as Mercedes, BMW, and Jaguar, as well as competition from the "near luxury" autos such as the Nissan Maxima and the Mazda Millenia.
2. Formulate the marketing research problem corresponding to the management decision problem you have identified in question 1.
3. Develop a graphical model explaining the consumer choice process for luxury cars.
4. Identify two research questions based on the definition of the marketing research problem and the graphical model.
5. Develop at least one hypothesis for each research question you have identified in question 4.
6. How would you conduct an Internet search for information on the luxury car market? Summarize the results of your search in a report.

References

Bradley Johnson, "Lexus Tries E-Mail for Auto Intro," *Advertising Age* 67(41) (October 1996): 4.

Michael McCarthy, "Luxury Drive on the Web," *Adweek* (Western Edition) 46(29) (July 15, 1996): 2.

1.4 Marketing Research Lights the Way for Electric Utilities

With the impending deregulation of the electricity utility industry, the $200 billion retail market energy companies are facing a challenge that they never faced for nearly all of the industry's 100-year history—how to market their product more effectively. Under the regulated system, regional monopolies were the only game in town. Customers either paid the one power company's sometimes exorbitant bill or did without power. A huge disruption to this way of life came with the passage of the National Energy Policy Act in 1992. The act allowed companies to sell power to one another, effectively enabling competition in the wholesale electricity market. The act, which took effect in 1998, affects about two thirds of the nation's utilities. The result is likely to be an all-out free-for-all competition for customers. This competition will serve to weed out the winners from the losers in a market that had previously had little direct competition for customers.

With the influx of national and regional competition for consumers' dollars, the old traditional mainstay power company is going to have to put a lot more effort into maintaining its customer base. According to a recent study by Market Facts, in which customer commitment to their power company was studied, 31 percent stated that they were ready to switch companies with little encouragement, while 24 percent were willing to consider alternatives. As the power companies grapple with the threat of losing customers that they never expected would have an alternative source of energy, they are turning to marketing research to help solidify their grip on the market.

Several utilities have demonstrated the power of marketing research for generating new or additional business. In the late 1980s, Florida Power & Light Company of Miami started focusing its efforts on issues beyond conservation marketing. The marketing department fine-tuned its market segmentation strategies. The commercial customer segment was broken down further into hotel, hospital, and office subsegments. One of the most successful programs involved a residential outdoor security light program targeted toward the senior citizen community. The program helped increase the use of outdoor lights and helped the older community feel safer and more secure. Florida Power & Light found that its customers were more concerned with value than price.

Marketing research has shown that establishing a unique brand identity is important in any marketing approach, even when the product is electricity. Kansas City, Missouri's UtiliCorp United introduced what is believed to be the first national energy brand with EnergyOne in 1995, complete with a distinctive red-and-blue logo. "The market is changing so radically that to compete you must have a brand like AT&T or Sprint," says spokesman Al Butkus. Cincinnati's Cinergy Corp. sought visibility by securing the rights to rename Cincinnati's Riverfront Stadium to Cinergy Field for a period of five years. With nationally televised Bengals and Reds games to be played at Cinergy Field, the company realistically expects national brand name recognition.

Some competitors are expected to wage war on the price front, as occurred in the United Kingdom when deregulation set in there. A price-based competition tested in New Hampshire showed an increase in frustration for both power companies and consumers. While companies had to contend with using bare-base pricing methods, consumers faced a flood of nuisance marketing, including and not limited to telemarketer calls urging the customer to switch companies. Price marketing results in creation of very fickle customers, states Robert Cuervost, decision systems vice president of the marketing research firm Market Facts.

Marketing an invisible, intangible product such as electricity requires more than merely brand recognition and low prices; it requires satisfying consumer needs and concerns better than any other competitor. This process begins by becoming familiar with the customers. While power companies have a wealth of consumer identification information, such as names, power usage, and addresses, collected during years of service, companies have only recently undertaken marketing research to understand preferences of those customers and segment the market. The issue of technical performance, such as how outages are handled, and personal relationship issues, as in how power company employees deal with consumers, are expected to rise to the forefront of interest in the new power company wars.

Surveys of consumers indicate that energy companies will need to identify with customers more fully. Power companies, who are already leaders in customer service and response and community involvement, have a head start in humanizing the company to the consumers. This type of quality can go a long way with consumers when they are faced with new competition asking them to ditch their familiar power company in favor of some Johnny-come-lately. For example, GPU Energy of Reading, Pennsylvania, has set up an Internet site in conjunction with the local schools called "GPU Kids." The site, which features games, contests, and a library for students, has hundreds of hits daily, forming an invaluable connection with the market. Centerior Energy of Cleveland has a different approach to gaining customer loyalty through services. The company offers customers points allocated per each kilowatt used that can be traded in for merchandise. The company's marketing director states, "This is one more aspect that differentiates us from the competition." The utilities are also catering to consumer interests. Companies such as Enron Corp and Edison International are selling "green power," power obtained from renewable resources such as wind tunnels. With the current interest in protecting scarce resources, 30 percent of people in a pilot study chose the "green" supplier, even though the price was quite higher than the electricity obtained from other sources.

These examples show that marketing research can serve as a powerful tool in the electrical utility industry. Marketing research can generate new customers for the industry and light the way for more sophisticated marketing techniques.

Questions

1. Discuss the role of marketing research in the electric utilities industry.
2. Discuss the role of the Internet and computers (microcomputers and mainframes) in conducting marketing research and providing decision support in the electric utilities industry.
3. Given the success of the outdoor security light program, Florida Power & Light would like to identify the other needs of the senior citizen community. Define the management decision problem.
4. Define the marketing research problem, given the management decision problem identified above.
5. Develop two research questions and two hypotheses.
6. Develop a simple graphic model explaining how outdoor light meets the security needs of senior citizens.

References

Rebecca Piirto Heath, "The Marketing of Power," *American Demographics* 19(9) (September 1997): 59–63.

Beth Snyder, "Online Newsletter Helps Electric Utilities Market," *Advertising Age* 68(46) (November 17, 1997): 58.

Beth Snyder, "Utility Deregulation Stokes Surge of 'Green Power' Ads," *Advertising Age* 68(50) (December 15, 1997): 65.

Part II

Research Design Formulation

After the problem has been defined (step 1) and the approach developed (step 2), a research design (step 3) is formulated. This part of the text describes in detail exploratory, descriptive, and causal research designs. We describe the primary scales of measurement and the comparative and noncomparative scaling techniques commonly used. We present several guidelines for designing questionnaires and explain the procedures, techniques, and statistical considerations involved in sampling. Managers and researchers should find this material helpful.

Chapter 3

Research Design

"When designing research, one is faced with a continual series of trade-offs. Since there are typically numerous design alternatives that will work, the goal is to find the design that enhances the value of the information obtained, while reducing the cost of obtaining it."

Mike Pietrangelo,
vice president,
client services,
Burke, Inc.

OBJECTIVES

After reading this chapter, the student should be able to

1. define research design, classify various research designs, and explain the differences between exploratory and conclusive
2. compare and contrast the basic research designs: exploratory, descriptive, and causal
3. describe the major sources of errors in a research design, including random sampling error, and the various sources of nonsampling error
4. discuss managerial aspects of coordinating research projects, particularly budgeting and scheduling
5. describe the elements of a marketing research proposal and show how it addresses the steps of the marketing research process
6. explain research design formulation in international marketing research
7. understand the ethical issues and conflicts that arise in formulating a research design
8. discuss the use of the Internet and computers in research design formulation

OVERVIEW

Chapter 2 discussed how to define a marketing research problem and develop a suitable approach. These first two steps are critical to the success of the entire marketing research project. Once they have been completed, the researcher should devote attention to designing the formal research project by formulating a detailed research design (see Figure 2.1 in chapter 2).

This chapter defines and classifies research designs. We describe the two major types of research designs: exploratory and conclusive. We further classify conclusive research designs as descriptive or causal and discuss both types in detail. We then consider the differences between the two types of descriptive designs, cross-sectional and longitudinal, and identify sources of errors. We cover budgeting and scheduling of a research project and present guidelines for writing a marketing research proposal. The special considerations involved in formulating research designs in international marketing research are discussed. Several ethical issues that arise at this stage of the marketing research process are considered. Finally, we discuss the use of the Internet and computers in formulating research designs. The reader can develop a better appreciation of the concepts presented in this chapter by first considering the following examples, which illustrate cross-sectional and longitudinal research designs.

EXAMPLE

TimeOut. Women's Golf Apparel Market Is "in Full Swing"

Exploratory (focus groups) as well as descriptive longitudinal (survey) research helped TimeOut to create a full line of LPGA licensed clothing that is both functional and attractive.

Although women comprise only 20 percent of the golfers today, they purchase more than 50 percent of all golf products, excluding golf clubs, according to the Women's Sports Foundation. This trend has led to the opening of women's-only golf stores around the country to cater to the needs of female golfers. The women's golf apparel market is now over $150 million per year. This has led traditional golf brands to introduce women's lines.

To meet this growing demand, TimeOut, a division of King Louie International, now offers a full line of LPGA-licensed clothing. In order to ascertain what this large group of women golfers expects and wants in their golf clothing, TimeOut created Fairway Forum, a panel of female golf enthusiasts that provides insight into women's apparel tastes. Women who have been recruited to this panel participate in focus groups and surveys. Because the women belong to the panel, multiple surveys measuring essentially the same variables can be conducted on the same set of respondents, thus implementing a longitudinal design.

What TimeOut has learned is that women are extremely serious about their golf game and wish more LPGA events were televised. Additionally, TimeOut discovered that women are extremely eager for new brands to hit the market as traditional brands do not offer enough selection to meet their tastes. These women do not want to wear reformulated versions of men's golf apparel, nor do they want to scamper about the course in "cutesy" clothing; and finally, these women do not want to encounter other women wearing the same outfit. These consumers are hungry for more variety and demanding it in the marketplace.

This research thoroughly indicates that female golfers want apparel that is both functional and attractive. For example, they want deep pockets to hold golf balls while they go around the course. The Forum also helped determine some of the underlying psychological factors that women link with their apparel. While these women want to be treated as athletes, they also want to be treated with respect. TimeOut's Fairway Forum panel has been an excellent tool in assisting sporting goods and apparel manufacturers in designing clothing to meet the needs of this growing golf segment.[1] ■

EXAMPLE

Customer Value Means Time and Money Savings

Kurt Salmon Associates, a New York–based consulting firm, monitors trends in the apparel industry using the "Consumer Pulse Survey," a multiple cross-sectional study of 1,000 people performed every year. The most recent study, from 1996, shows that consumers guard their free time more closely and therefore spend less time shopping, they are buying more casual clothing and less career clothing such as suits and dresses, and they want value and convenience.

Of those surveyed, 39 percent said they would rather have more time than more money, and this is reflected in the average amount of time spent shopping, dropping from 4.3 hours per month in 1993 to 3 hours per month in 1996. Seven of ten respondents reported consistently shopping at stores where the check-out lines move quickly; 64 percent said they would leave a store without making a purchase if they thought checking out would take too long. The desire to save time for leisure activities has resulted in growth in home shopping. Catalog shopping was the most popular form of shopping at home, with

72 percent saying they had bought direct from a catalog outlet in the last year. Another 19 percent reported buying from one of the television shopping channels.

Value shopping is still on the increase—25 percent expected to do more shopping at discount stores, and 84 percent thought that department stores were too expensive. More than 50 percent of respondents buy their clothing at the end of the season to save money, and 70 percent said that they buy almost all of their clothes on sale.

It is projected that home shopping via catalogs, television shopping channels, and the Internet will continue to grow. In-store retailers, such as Wal-Mart, which offer quick shopping and high value, will also gain in consumer patronage and market share. By knowing how consumers define value, stores such as Wal-Mart can design marketing programs to enhance customer value and thus increase market share.[2] ■

As these examples indicate, two main types of research designs are employed in marketing research: exploratory and conclusive. An understanding of the fundamentals of research design and its components enables the researcher to formulate a design that is appropriate for the problem at hand.

RESEARCH DESIGN: DEFINITION

A **research design** is a framework or blueprint for conducting the marketing research project. It details the procedures necessary for obtaining the information needed to structure or solve marketing research problems. Although a broad approach to the problem has already been developed, the research design specifies the details—the nuts and bolts—of implementing that approach. A research design lays the foundation for conducting the project. A good research design will ensure that the marketing research project is conducted effectively and efficiently. Typically, a research design involves the following components, or tasks. Each of these components will be discussed in detail in the subsequent chapters.

Research Design A framework or blueprint for conducting the marketing research project. It specifies the details of the procedures necessary for obtaining the information needed to structure and/or solve marketing research problems.

1. Define the information needed (chapter 2).
2. Design the exploratory, descriptive, and/or causal phases of the research (chapters 3–7).
3. Specify the measurement and scaling procedures (chapters 8 and 9).
4. Construct and pretest a questionnaire (interviewing form) or an appropriate form for data collection (chapter 10).
5. Specify the sampling process and sample size (chapters 11 and 12).
6. Develop a plan of data analysis (chapter 14).

First let's classify the different types of research design.

RESEARCH DESIGN: CLASSIFICATION

Research designs may be broadly classified as exploratory or conclusive (see Figure 3.1). The differences between exploratory and conclusive research are summarized in Table 3.1. The primary objective of **exploratory research** is to provide insights into, and an understanding of, the problem confronting the researcher.[3] Exploratory research is used in cases when you must define the problem more precisely, identify relevant courses of action, or gain additional insights before an approach can be developed. The information needed is only loosely defined at this stage, and the research process that is adopted is flexible and unstructured. For example, it may consist of personal interviews with industry experts. The sample, selected to generate maximum insights, is small and nonrepresentative. The primary data are qualitative in nature and are analyzed accordingly. Given these characteristics of the research process, the findings of exploratory research should be regarded as tentative or as input to further research. Typically, such research is followed by further exploratory or

Exploratory Research One type of research design that has as its primary objective the provision of insights into and comprehension of the problem situation confronting the researcher.

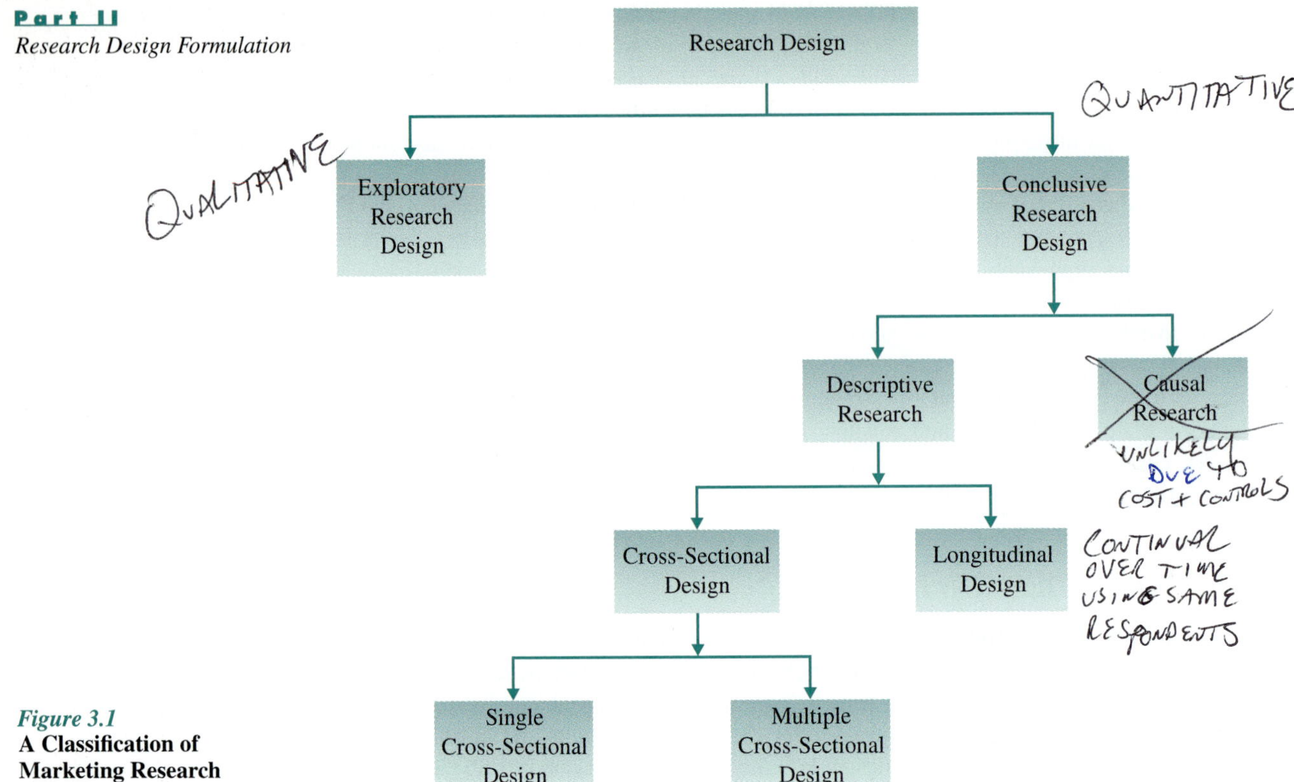

Figure 3.1
A Classification of Marketing Research Designs

conclusive research. Sometimes, exploratory research, particularly qualitative research, is all the research that is conducted. In these cases, caution should be exercised in utilizing the findings obtained. Exploratory research will be discussed in more detail in the next section.

The insights gained from exploratory research might be verified by conclusive research, as the objective of conclusive research is to test specific hypotheses and examine

TABLE 3.1

DIFFERENCES BETWEEN EXPLORATORY AND CONCLUSIVE RESEARCH

	Exploratory	*Conclusive*
Objective:	To provide insights and understanding.	To test specific hypotheses and examine relationships.
Characteristics:	Information needed is defined only loosely.	Information needed is clearly defined.
	Research process is flexible and unstructured.	Research process is formal and structured.
	Sample is small and nonrepresentative.	Sample is large and representative.
	Analysis of primary data is qualitative.	Data analysis is quantitative.
Findings/Results:	Tentative	Conclusive
Outcome:	Generally followed by further exploratory or conclusive research.	Findings used as input into decision making.

specific relationships. This requires that the information needed is clearly specified.[4] **Conclusive research** is typically more formal and structured than is exploratory research. It is based on large, representative samples, and the data obtained are subjected to quantitative analysis. The findings from this research are considered to be conclusive in nature in that they are used as input into managerial decision making. As shown in Figure 3.1, conclusive research designs may be either descriptive or causal, and descriptive research designs may be either cross-sectional or longitudinal. Each of these classifications is discussed further, beginning with exploratory research.

Conclusive Research
Research designed to assist the decision maker in determining, evaluating, and selecting the best course of action to take in a given situation.

EXPLORATORY RESEARCH

As its name implies, the objective of exploratory research is to explore or search through a problem or situation to provide insights and understanding (Table 3.2). Exploratory research could be used for any of the following purposes:

- Formulate a problem or define a problem more precisely.
- Identify alternative courses of action.
- Develop hypotheses.
- Isolate key variables and relationships for further examination.[5]
- Gain insights for developing an approach to the problem.
- Establish priorities for further research.

In general, exploratory research is meaningful in any situation in which the researcher does not have enough understanding to proceed with the research project. Exploratory research is characterized by flexibility and versatility, with respect to the methods, because formal research protocols and procedures are not employed. It rarely involves structured questionnaires, large samples, and probability sampling plans. Rather, researchers are alert to new ideas and insights as they proceed. Once a new idea or insight is discovered, they may shift their exploration in that direction. That new direction is pursued until its possibilities are exhausted or another direction is found. For this reason, the focus of the investigation may shift constantly as new insights are discovered. Thus, the creativity and

TABLE 3.2

A COMPARISON OF BASIC RESEARCH DESIGNS

	Exploratory	*Descriptive*	*Causal*
Objective:	Discovery of ideas and insights.	Describe market characteristics or functions.	Determine cause and effect relationships.
Characteristics:	Flexible, versatile.	Marked by the prior formulation of specific hypotheses.	Manipulation of one or more independent variables.
	Often the front end of total research design.	Preplanned and structured design.	Control of other mediating variables.
Methods:	Expert surveys	Secondary data	Experiments
	Pilot surveys	Surveys	
	Secondary data	Panels	
	Qualitative research	Observational and other data	

ingenuity of the researcher plays a major role in exploratory research. Yet, the abilities of the researcher are not the sole determinants of good exploratory research. Exploratory research can greatly benefit from use of the following methods (see Table 3.2):

Survey of experts (discussed in chapter 2)
Pilot surveys (discussed in chapter 2)
Analysis of secondary data (discussed in chapter 4)
Qualitative research (discussed in chapter 5)

The use of exploratory research in defining the problem and developing an approach was discussed in chapter 2. The advantages and disadvantages of exploratory research are further discussed in chapter 4 (secondary data) and chapter 5 (qualitative research). To aid the reader in visualizing the applications of exploratory research, we now consider the department store patronage project, which might employ the following types of exploratory studies:

A review of academic and trade literature to identify the relevant demographic and psychographic factors that influence consumer patronage of department stores.

Interviews with retailing experts to determine trends, such as emergence of new types of outlets and shifts in consumer patronage patterns (e.g., shopping on the Internet).

A comparative analysis of the three best and three worst stores of the same chain to gain some idea of the factors that influence store performance.

Focus groups to determine the factors that consumers consider important in selecting department stores.

Further illustration of exploratory research is provided by the following example.

EXAMPLE

Focus on Small Business Leads to Large Gains for Microsoft

Microsoft®

Statistics from the U.S. Small Business Administration show that in 1997 small businesses generated 47 percent of all U.S. sales as well as contributed 50 percent of the private Gross Domestic Product. They also employed 53 percent of the U.S. workforce. Whereas most software manufacturers overlooked this potential market until recently, Microsoft Corporation created a marketing research group in 1995 just to study the needs of small businesses.

Microsoft conducted exploratory research. The marketing research group spent more than 25,000 hours of research to examine how small businesses can use technology to solve marketing, customer service, and growth problems. It began with exploratory research analyzing available secondary data, conducting in-depth one-on-one interviews, and small-scale pilot surveys. From this research Microsoft learned that, for the small business market, the focus should be on selling business solutions, not just selling technology. Small business owners desired integrated tools that were easy to learn and allowed access to the Internet. Research also showed that the market was a heterogeneous one whose members have differing needs. In order to meet these disparate needs, the research allowed Microsoft to consider different factors in reaching solutions for a small business. These factors include the PC–employee ratio, the amount of information processing the company does, and the computing expertise the company has.

Through exploratory research, Microsoft discovered insights about a market that had been virtually ignored before by software vendors. Additional descriptive research allowed

Microsoft to create a product specifically tailored for small businesses: Office 97, Small Business Edition. Microsoft still continues to develop solutions for the small business market through various services: a Web site just for small businesses; the Microsoft Small Business Council, which provides information to help small businesses use technology; the Microsoft Small Business Technology Partnership Board, an educational resource; the BackOffice Small Business Server; and a Small Business Edition of Microsoft Works. Through these efforts, Microsoft hopes to land more small business customers and remain the leader to this market segment whose potential and needs were identified through extensive market research.[6] ■

Note that Microsoft did not rely *exclusively* on exploratory research. Once new positioning ideas were identified, they were further tested by descriptive research in the form of customer surveys. This example points to the importance of descriptive research in obtaining more conclusive findings.

DESCRIPTIVE RESEARCH

As the name implies, the major objective of **descriptive research** is to describe something—usually market characteristics or functions (see Table 3.2). Descriptive research is conducted for the following reasons:

Descriptive Research A type of conclusive research which has as its major objective the description of something—usually market characteristics or functions.

1. To describe the characteristics of relevant groups, such as consumers, salespeople, organizations, or market areas. For example, we could develop a profile of the "heavy users" (frequent shoppers) of prestigious department stores such as Saks Fifth Avenue and Neiman Marcus.
2. To estimate the percentage of units in a specified population exhibiting a certain behavior; for example, the percentage of heavy users of prestigious department stores who also patronize discount department stores.
3. To determine the perceptions of product characteristics. For example, how do households perceive the various department stores in terms of salient factors of the choice criteria?
4. To determine the degree to which marketing variables are associated. For example, to what extent is shopping at department stores related to eating out?
5. To make specific predictions. For example, what will be the retail sales of Neiman Marcus (specific store) for fashion clothing (specific product category) in the Dallas area (specific region)?

Both examples at the beginning of the chapter (women's golf apparel and customer value) employed descriptive research. These examples show that descriptive research assumes that the researcher has much prior knowledge about the problem situation.[7] In fact, a major difference between exploratory and descriptive research is that descriptive research is characterized by the prior formulation of specific hypotheses. Thus, the information needed is clearly defined. As a result, descriptive research is preplanned and structured. It is typically based on large representative samples. A formal research design specifies the methods for selecting the sources of information and for collecting data from those sources. A descriptive design requires a clear specification of the who, what, when, where, why, and way (the six Ws) of the research. (It is interesting to note that news reporters use a similar formula for describing a situation.) We illustrate this in the context of the department store patronage project.

These, and other similar questions, should be asked until the information to be obtained has been clearly defined.

In summary, descriptive research, in contrast to exploratory research, is marked by a clear statement of the problem, specific hypotheses, and detailed information needs. The survey conducted in the department store patronage project, which involved personal interviews, is an example of descriptive research. Other examples of descriptive studies are:

- Market studies, which describe the size of the market, buying power of the consumers, availability of distributors, and consumer profiles.
- Market share studies, which determine the proportion of total sales received by a company and its competitors.

DEPARTMENT STORE PATRONAGE PROJECT

The Six Ws

1. *Who*: Who should be considered a patron of a particular department store? Some of the possibilities are:
   a. Anyone who enters the department store, whether or not she or he purchases anything
   b. Anyone who purchases anything from the store
   c. Anyone who makes purchases at the department store at least once a month
   d. The person in the household most responsible for department store shopping
2. *What*: What information should be obtained from the respondents? A wide variety of information could be obtained, including:
   a. Frequency with which different department stores are patronized for specific product categories
   b. Evaluation of the various department stores in terms of the salient choice criteria
   c. Information pertaining to specific hypotheses to be tested
   d. Psychographics and lifestyles, media consumption habits, and demographics
3. *When*: When should the information be obtained from the respondents? The available options include:
   a. Before shopping
   b. While shopping
   c. Immediately after shopping
   d. Sometime after shopping to allow time for evaluation of their shopping experience
4. *Where*: Where should the respondents be contacted to obtain the required information? Possibilities include contacting the respondents:
   a. In the store
   b. Outside the store but in the shopping mall
   c. In the parking lot
   d. At home
5. *Why*: Why are we obtaining information from the respondents? Why is the marketing research project being conducted? Possible reasons could be to:
   a. Improve the image of the sponsoring store
   b. Improve patronage and market share
   c. Change the product mix
   d. Develop a suitable promotional campaign
   e. Decide on the location of a new store
6. *Way*: In what way are we going to obtain information from the respondents? The possible ways could be:
   a. Observe respondents' behavior
   b. Personal interviews
   c. Telephone interviews
   d. Mail interviews

- Sales analysis studies, which describe sales by geographic region, product line, type and size of the account.
- Image studies, which determine consumer perceptions of the firm and its products.
- Product usage studies, which describe consumption patterns.
- Distribution studies, which determine traffic flow patterns and the number and location of distributors.
- Pricing studies, which describe the range and frequency of price changes and probable consumer response to proposed price changes.
- Advertising studies, which describe media consumption habits and audience profiles for specific television programs and magazines.

These examples demonstrate the range and diversity of descriptive research studies. A vast majority of marketing research studies involve descriptive research, which incorporates the following major methods:

Secondary data (discussed in chapter 4).
Surveys (chapter 6).
Panels (chapters 4 and 6).
Observational and other data (chapter 6).

Although the methods shown in Table 3.2 are typical, it should be noted that the researcher is not limited to these methods. For example, surveys can involve the use of exploratory (open-ended) questions, or causal studies (experiments) are sometimes administered by surveys. Descriptive research using the methods of Table 3.2 can be further classified into cross-sectional and longitudinal research (Figure 3.1).

Cross-Sectional Designs

The cross-sectional study is the most frequently used descriptive design in marketing research. **Cross-sectional designs** involve the collection of information from any given sample of population elements only once. They may be either single cross-sectional or multiple cross-sectional (Figure 3.1). In **single cross-sectional designs** only one sample of respondents is drawn from the target population, and information is obtained from this sample only once. These designs are also called sample survey research designs. In **multiple cross-sectional designs**, there are two or more samples of respondents, and information from each sample is obtained only once. Often, information from different samples is obtained at different times. The following examples illustrate single and multiple cross-sectional designs.

Cross-Sectional Design A type of research design involving the collection of information from any given sample of population elements only once.

Single Cross-Sectional Design A cross-sectional design in which one sample of respondents is drawn from the target population and information is obtained from this sample once.

Multiple Cross-Sectional Design A cross-sectional design in which there are two or more samples of respondents, and information from each sample is obtained only once.

EXAMPLE

Cross-Sectional Design Reveals Attitude toward Direct Mail Is Less Cross

The Equifax/Harris Survey is an annual telephone survey with a sample of 1,000 randomly chosen adults aged 18 and older. It deals with privacy issues in marketing and marketing research. A multiple cross-sectional design is followed and a different sample of 1,000 respondents is chosen each year.

The multiple cross-sectional design enables a comparison of the aggregate results over the years. For example, the 1996 survey found that public attitudes toward direct mail appear to be warming. In 1996, 37 percent of the respondents said that they regard mail offers as a nuisance, down from 47 percent in 1994. At the same time, 43 percent said they rarely use mail offers but don't have a problem with them, an 8 percent increase from 1994 (35 percent). In 1996, 12 percent regarded mail offers as a useful opportunity, up 2 percent from 1994. The percent who consider mail offers an invasion of privacy remained stable, at 8 percent.

These positive changes in attitudes toward mail offers is promising for catalog retailers such as L. L. Bean and other direct marketers who offer their products by mail.[8] ■

In this example, the aggregate percentages from 1996 could be compared with the corresponding percentages for 1994 to determine the shift in attitudes toward direct mail. Multiple cross-sectional designs allow comparisons at the aggregate level but not at the individual respondent level. Because a different sample is taken each time a survey is conducted, there is no way to compare the measures on an individual respondent across surveys. A type of multiple cross-sectional design of special interest is cohort analysis.

Cohort Analysis A multiple cross-sectional design consisting of a series of surveys conducted at appropriate time intervals. The cohort refers to the group of respondents who experience the same event within the same time interval.

Cohort Analysis. **Cohort analysis** consists of a series of surveys conducted at appropriate time intervals, where the cohort serves as the basic unit of analysis. A cohort is a group of respondents who experience the same event within the same time interval.[9] For example, a birth (or age) cohort is a group of people who were born during the same time interval, such as 1951–1960. The term *cohort analysis* refers to any study in which there are measures of some characteristics of one or more cohorts at two or more points in time.

It is unlikely that any of the individuals studied at time 1 will also be in the sample at time 2. For example, the age cohort of people between 8 and 19 years was selected and their soft drink consumption was examined every 10 years for 30 years. In other words, every 10 years a different sample of respondents was drawn from the population of those who were then between 8 and 19 years old. This sample was drawn independently of any previous sample drawn in this study from the population of 8 to 19 years. Obviously, people who were selected once were unlikely to be included again in the same age cohort (8 to 19 years), as these people would be much older at the time of subsequent sampling. This study showed that this cohort had increased consumption of soft drinks over time. Similar findings were obtained for other age cohorts (20–29, 30–39, 40–49, and 50+). Further, the soft drink consumption of each cohort did not decrease as the cohort aged. These results are presented in Table 3.3, in which the consumption of the various age cohorts over time can be determined by reading down the diagonal. These findings contradicted the common belief that the consumption of soft drinks will decline with the graying of America. This common but erroneous belief was based on single cross-sectional studies. Note that if any column of Table 3.3 is viewed in isolation, as a single cross-sectional study (reading down the column), the consumption of soft drinks declines with age, fostering the erroneous belief.[10]

Cohort analysis is also used to predict changes in voter opinions during a political campaign. Well-known marketing researchers such as Louis Harris or George Gallup, who

TABLE 3.3

CONSUMPTION OF SOFT DRINKS BY VARIOUS AGE COHORTS (Percentage Consuming on a Typical Day)

Age	*1950*	*1960*	*1969*	*1979*	
8–19	52.9	62.6	73.2	81.0	
20–29	45.2	60.7	76.0	75.8	C8
30–39	33.9	46.6	67.7	71.4	C7
40–49	23.2	40.8	58.6	67.8	C6
50+	18.1	28.8	50.0	51.9	C5
		C1	C2	C3	C4

C1: cohort born prior to 1900
C2: cohort born 1901–10
C3: cohort born 1911–20
C4: cohort born 1921–30
C5: cohort born 1931–40
C6: cohort born 1941–49
C7: cohort born 1950–59
C8: cohort born 1960–69

specialize in political opinion research, periodically question cohorts of voters (people with similar voting patterns during a given interval) about their voting preferences to predict election results. Thus, cohort analysis is an important cross-sectional design. The other type of descriptive design is longitudinal design.

Longitudinal Designs

In **longitudinal designs**, a fixed sample (or samples) of population elements is measured repeatedly. A longitudinal design differs from a cross-sectional design in that the sample or samples remain the same over time. In other words, the same respondents are studied over time. In contrast to the typical cross-sectional design, that gives a snapshot of the variables of interest at a single point in time, a longitudinal study provides a series of pictures that give an in-depth view of the situation and the changes that take place over time. For example, the question, "How did the American people rate the performance of Bill Clinton immediately after his second term?" would be addressed using a cross-sectional design. However, a longitudinal design would be used to address the question, "How did the American people change their view of Clinton's performance during his presidency?"

Longitudinal Design A type of research design involving a fixed sample of population elements, which is measured repeatedly. The sample remains the same over time, thus providing a series of pictures that, when viewed together, offer a vivid illustration of the situation and the changes that are taking place.

Often, the term *panel* is used interchangeably with the term *longitudinal design.* A **panel** consists of a sample of respondents, generally households, that have agreed to provide information at specified intervals over an extended period. Panels are maintained by syndicated firms, and panel members are compensated for their participation with gifts, coupons, information, or cash. Panels are discussed further in chapter 4 and an example of a mail panel recruitment letter is shown here.

Panel A sample of respondents who have agreed to provide information at specified intervals over an extended period.

The following example illustrates how a panel design can be used to understand and monitor changes in attitudes.

CONSUMER MAIL PANEL

P.O. Box 4602 North Suburban, IL 60197-4602

CMP

WHAT IS CONSUMER MAIL PANEL?

Consumer Mail Panel, a facility of Market Facts, is more than thirty years old and is nationally recognized as a reliable and accurate means of learning consumer reactions and attitudes. It was established to give people like you the chance to say what you think, with privacy, about the products you buy. And, it provides the opportunity for your opinions to be heard by the people who make these products.

Members are asked to express their opinions about products and services they use. Their opinions about different things are asked on a questionnaire sent through the mail. From time to time, a product to try may be sent.

WHAT DOES IT COST?

Nothing at all. Postage is paid both ways on everything. You are never asked to buy anything.

All information received is absolutely confidential. Answers become a part of general statistics. The questionnaires ask for your frank opinions just as they occur to you. Households of all sizes, including persons living alone, are equally important. I may be interested in the opinions of the whole family. Occasionally, I have some questions about gasoline or tires on the family car, or I may ask what the children think of products they use.

TO BECOME A MEMBER OF CONSUMER MAIL PANEL . . .

Just answer all the questions on the enclosed questionnaire. I am looking for representatives of every kind of household in the country; that is, members of all ages and all income categories.

After completing my questionnaire, please use the postage paid envelope to return it to me. That is all there is to it.

Does it sound to you as though Consumer Mail Panel might be interesting? Members tell me it's fun -- and I think you'll find it fun too. I hope to hear from you soon.

If you have any questions, please call 1-800-745-4267.

Cordially,

Marie Brighton

Marie Brighton
for Consumer Mail Panel

P.S. If you are already a member of Consumer Mail Panel, or if for some reason you are not in a position to join now, please pass along the questionnaire and return envelope to any friend, neighbor or relative you feel might enjoy panel membership.

A mail panel recruitment letter.

EXAMPLE

The National Football League Is Tickled Pink

Longitudinal monitoring of changes in women's attitudes via a panel will be crucial for NFL to maintain the loyalty of women who are 50 percent of the fans.

Recently, the National Football League (NFL) discovered that 50 percent of its fans were women. It gave the company a new problem: How can NFL satisfy women's needs given that it assumed in the past that the fans were mainly men?

An exploratory research design would be a good way to understand more about these unexpected new consumers and clients. Exploratory research would help in identifying the factors that influence women's attitudes toward the NFL, football games, and merchandising products.

Once these factors are known, descriptive research should be undertaken to measure women's attitudes. The league also needs to know in the years to come if its new policies and its new products have satisfied women and to measure changes in women's attitudes over time. This requires a longitudinal design implemented by using a mail panel. The panel members could be rewarded with coupons or NFL-licensed products and tickets to NFL games.

NFL merchandising is a whopping $3 billion a year business, of which women account for half the spending. The NFL is expanding its line of women's apparel, including sports bras, sleepwear, jewelry, as well as home goods (sheets, pillows, and so on). Continuous monitoring of the trends and changes in women's attitudes via a panel will be the key to maintaining the loyalty of these newly found friends.[11] ■

Data obtained from panels not only provide information on market shares based on an extended period of time but these data also allow the researcher to examine changes in market share over time.[12] As the following section explains, these changes cannot be determined from cross-sectional data.

Relative Advantages and Disadvantages of Longitudinal and Cross-Sectional Designs

The relative advantages and disadvantages of longitudinal versus cross-sectional designs are summarized in Table 3.4. A major advantage of longitudinal design over the cross-sectional design is the ability to detect change as a result of repeated measurement of the same variables on the same sample.

Tables 3.5 and 3.6 demonstrate how cross-sectional data can mislead researchers about changes over time. The cross-sectional data reported in Table 3.5 reveal that the purchases of Brands A, B, and C remain the same in time periods 1 and 2. In each survey, 20 percent of the respondents purchase Brand A, 30 percent Brand B, and 50 percent Brand C. The longitudinal data presented in Table 3.6 show that substantial change, in the form of brand-switching, occurred in the study period. For example, only 50 percent (100/200) of the respondents who purchased Brand A in period 1 also purchased it in period 2. The corresponding repeat purchase figures for Brands B and C are, respectively, 33.3 percent (100/300) and 55 percent (275/500). Hence, during this interval Brand C experienced the greatest loyalty and Brand B the least. Table 3.6 provides valuable information on brand loyalty and brand switching. (Such a table is called a turnover table or a brand-switching matrix.[13])

Longitudinal data enable researchers to examine changes in the behavior of individual units and to link behavioral changes to marketing variables, such as changes in advertising, packaging, pricing, and distribution. Because the same units are measured repeatedly, variations caused by changes in the sample are eliminated and even small changes are apparent.

Another advantage of panels is that relatively large amounts of data can be collected. Panel members are usually compensated for their participation, so they are willing to participate in lengthy and demanding interviews. Yet another advantage is that panel data can be more accurate than cross-sectional data. A typical cross-sectional survey requires the respondent to recall past purchases and behavior; these data can be inaccurate because of memory lapses. Panel data, which relies on continuous recording of purchases in a diary,

TABLE 3.4

RELATIVE ADVANTAGES AND DISADVANTAGES OF LONGITUDINAL AND CROSS-SECTIONAL DESIGNS

Evaluation Criteria	*Cross-Sectional Design*	*Longitudinal Design*
Detecting change	–	+
Large amount of data collection	–	+
Accuracy	–	+
Representative sampling	+	–
Response bias	+	–

Note: + indicates a relative advantage over the other design; whereas – indicates a relative disadvantage.

TABLE 3.5

CROSS-SECTIONAL DATA MAY NOT SHOW CHANGE

Brand Purchased	*Time Period*	
	Period 1 Survey	*Period 2 Survey*
Brand A	200	200
Brand B	300	300
Brand C	500	500
	1,000	1,000

places less reliance on the respondent's memory. A comparison of panel and cross-sectional survey estimates of retail sales indicates that panel data give more accurate estimates.[14]

The main disadvantage of panels is that they may not be representative. Nonrepresentativeness may arise because of:

1. *Refusal to cooperate*. Many individuals or households do not wish to be bothered with the panel operation and refuse to participate. Consumer panels requiring members to keep a record of purchases have a cooperation rate of 60 percent or less.
2. *Mortality*. Panel members who agree to participate may subsequently drop out because they move away or lose interest. Mortality or attrition rates can be as high as 20 percent per year.[15]
3. *Payment*. Payment may cause certain types of people to be attracted, making the group unrepresentative of the population.

Another disadvantage of panels is response bias. New panel members are often biased in their initial responses. They tend to increase the behavior being measured, such as food purchasing. This bias decreases as the respondent overcomes the novelty of being on the panel, so it can be reduced by initially excluding the data of new members. Seasoned panel members may also give biased responses because they believe they are experts or want to look good or give the "right" answer. Bias also results from boredom, fatigue, and incomplete diary entries.[16]

CAUSAL RESEARCH

Causal Research A type of conclusive research in which the major objective is to obtain evidence regarding cause-and-effect (causal) relationships.

Causal research is used to obtain evidence of cause-and-effect (causal) relationships (see Table 3.2). Marketing managers continually make decisions based on assumed causal relationships. These assumptions may not be justified, and the validity of the causal relationships should be examined via formal research.[17] For example, the common assumption that a decrease in price will lead to increased sales and market share does not hold in certain competitive environments. Causal research is appropriate for the following purposes:

TABLE 3.6

LONGITUDINAL DATA MAY SHOW SUBSTANTIAL CHANGE

	Brand Purchased in Period 2			
Brand Purchased in Period 1	*Brand A*	*Brand B*	*Brand C*	
Brand A	100	50	50	200
Brand B	25	100	175	300
Brand C	75	150	275	500
	200	300	500	1,000

1. To understand which variables are the cause (independent variables) and which variables are the effect (dependent variables) of a phenomenon.
2. To determine the nature of the relationship between the causal variables and the effect to be predicted.

Like descriptive research, causal research requires a planned and structured design. Although descriptive research can determine the degree of association between variables, it is not appropriate for examining causal relationships. Such an examination requires a causal design, in which the causal or independent variables are manipulated in a relatively controlled environment. A relatively controlled environment is one in which the other variables that may affect the dependent variable are controlled or checked as much as possible. The effect of this manipulation on one or more dependent variables is then measured to infer causality. The main method of causal research is experimentation.[18]

Due to their complexity and importance, causal designs and experimental research are discussed in a separate chapter (chapter 7). However, we give some examples here. In the context of the department store patronage project, a researcher wishes to determine whether the presence and helpfulness of salespeople (causal variable) will influence the sales of housewares (effect variable). A causal design could be formulated in which two groups of otherwise comparable housewares departments of a particular chain are selected. For four weeks, trained salespeople are stationed in one group of housewares departments but not in the other. Sales are monitored for both groups, while controlling for other variables. A comparison of sales for the two groups will reveal the effect of salespeople on housewares sales in department stores. Alternatively, instead of selecting two groups of stores, the researcher might select only one set of department stores and carry out this manipulation for two comparable time periods: salespeople are present in one time period and absent in the other. As another example, consider the following:

EXAMPLE

Advertising Your Way to Profits

A causal study was undertaken to measure the effect of business-to-business advertising on the sales of a variety of products as well as to evaluate the effects of ad frequency schedules and varying media weight. The study involved a participating manufacturer, the publishers of the magazines used in the study, and a tightly controlled stratification of the magazine's circulation into three cells, which were to receive light, medium, and heavy levels of advertising. Four products in the growth stage of the product life cycle were chosen for advertisement. To obtain clear sales data on these products, distribution channel restrictions were necessary, so that sales could be linked to the balanced advertising cells. After the four products and the participating magazines had been selected, the advertising cells and levels for each product were defined. At the conclusion of the one-year study, findings supported the hypothesis that more advertising caused an increase in sales. The study also concluded that if a product is sold through dealers, both dealers and end users should be targeted for ads. Further, increased advertising frequency can increase sales leads and result in higher profits.[19] ■

In this experiment the causal (independent) variable was advertising, which was manipulated to have three levels: light, medium, and heavy. The effect (dependent) variable was sales, and the influence of distribution on sales had to be controlled. Although the preceding example distinguished causal research from other types of research, causal research should not be viewed in isolation. Rather, the exploratory, descriptive, and causal designs often complement each other.

RELATIONSHIPS AMONG EXPLORATORY, DESCRIPTIVE, AND CAUSAL RESEARCH

We have described exploratory, descriptive, and causal research as major classifications of research designs, but the distinctions among these classifications are not absolute. A given marketing research project may involve more than one type of research design and thus serve several purposes.[20] Which combination of research designs to employ depends on the nature of the problem. We offer the following general guidelines for choosing research designs:

1. When little is known about the problem situation, it is desirable to begin with exploratory research. Exploratory research is appropriate when the problem needs to be defined more precisely, alternative courses of action identified, research questions or hypotheses developed, and key variables isolated and classified as dependent or independent.
2. Exploratory research is the initial step in the overall research design framework. It should, in most instances, be followed by descriptive or causal research (see Research in Practice 3.1).[21] For example, hypotheses developed via exploratory research should be statistically tested using descriptive or causal research.

RESEARCH IN PRACTICE 3.1

NASCAR Tries to Shed Redneck Image

The National Association of Stock Car Auto Racing (NASCAR) in the past has appealed to Southerners with lower incomes that work in laborer-type jobs. NASCAR, in an attempt to increase its audience, chose to make over its stereotyped image and used exploratory and descriptive research to generate ideas for reaching a more affluent market.

NASCAR conducted exploratory research to identify ways to penetrate the nonrace market, reach younger fans, and build its brand image across the nation. Extensive focus groups revealed that (1) NASCAR had a rural sports image, (2) this image was not necessarily negative, and (3) companies that supported sports were viewed positively.

Descriptive research was conducted to define the market characteristics of the viewer and to quantify the findings of focus groups. Survey research showed that 29 percent of fans had income over $50,000 and 27 percent worked as a professional or manager. Additionally, 73 percent had a positive rural sports image of NASCAR, and 71 percent of fans purchased products of companies that support the sport. NASCAR, of course, sought to increase these percentages and developed marketing plans that would build on the image of NASCAR as a rural sport by emphasizing that most of America is suburbs and small towns. NASCAR moved to reach all of America, not just the traditional Southern market.

Exploratory research followed by descriptive research helped the National Association of Stock Car Auto Racing (NASCAR) to shed its redneck image.

DEPARTMENT STORE PATRONAGE PROJECT

Exploring and Describing Store Patronage

In the store patronage project, exploratory research, including secondary data analysis and qualitative research, was first conducted to define the problem and develop a suitable approach. This was followed by a descriptive study consisting of a survey in which a questionnaire was constructed and administered by personal interviews.

Suppose the patronage study was to be repeated after two years to determine if any changes had taken place. At that point, exploratory research would probably be unnecessary and the research design could begin with descriptive research.

Assume that the survey is repeated two years later and some unexpected findings are obtained. Management wonders why the store's ratings on in-store service have declined when the sales staff has increased. Exploratory research in the form of focus groups might be undertaken to probe the unexpected findings. The focus groups may reveal that while the salespeople are easy to find, they are not perceived to be friendly or helpful. This may suggest the need for further training of the sales staff.

3. It is not necessary to begin every research design with exploratory research. It depends on the precision with which the problem has been defined and the researcher's degree of certainty about the approach to the problem. A research design could well begin with descriptive or causal research. To illustrate, a consumer satisfaction survey conducted annually need not begin with nor include an exploratory phase.
4. Although exploratory research is generally the initial step, it need not be. Exploratory research may follow descriptive or causal research. For example, descriptive or causal research results in findings that are hard for managers to interpret. Exploratory research may provide more insights to help understand these findings.

The relationship between exploratory, descriptive, and causal research is further illustrated by the department store patronage project.

This example involves the use of exploratory and descriptive research but not causal research. This reflects the fact that exploratory and descriptive research are frequently used in commercial marketing research but causal research is not as popular. However, it is possible to combine exploratory, descriptive, and causal research as demonstrated by Citigroup (Research in Practice 3.2).[22]

Regardless of the kind of research design employed, the researcher should attempt to minimize the potential sources of error.

POTENTIAL SOURCES OF ERROR

Several potential sources of error can affect a research design. A good research design attempts to control the various sources of error. These errors are discussed in great detail in subsequent chapters, but it is pertinent at this stage to give brief descriptions.

The **total error** is the variation between the true mean value in the population of the variable of interest and the observed mean value obtained in the marketing research project. As shown in Figure 3.2, total error is composed of random sampling error and nonsampling error.

Total Error The variation between the true mean value in the population of the variable of interest and the observed mean value obtained in the marketing research project.

Random Sampling Error

Random sampling error occurs because the particular sample selected is an imperfect representation of the population of interest. Random sampling error is the variation between the true mean value for the population and the true mean value for the original sample. Random sampling error is discussed further in chapters 11 and 12.

Random Sampling Error The error occurs because the particular sample selected is an imperfect representation of the population of interest. It may be defined as the variation between the true mean value for the sample and the true mean value of the population.

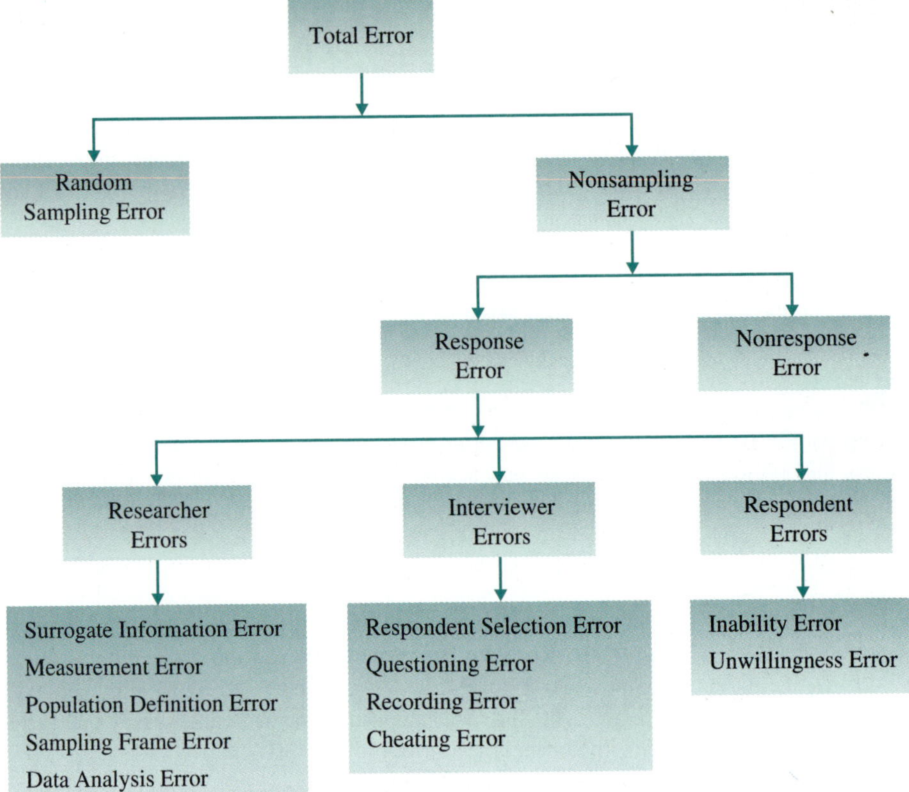

Figure 3.2
Potential Sources of Error in Research Designs

RESEARCH IN PRACTICE 3.2

Citigroup Banks on Exploratory, Descriptive, and Causal Research

Marketing Research at Citigroup is typical in that it is used to measure consumer awareness of products, monitor their satisfaction and attitudes associated with the product, track product usage, and diagnose problems as they occur. To accomplish these tasks Citigroup makes extensive use of exploratory, descriptive, and causal research.

Often it is advantageous to offer special financial packages to specific groups of customers. In this case, a financial package is being designed for senior citizens. The following seven-step process was taken by marketing research to help in the design.

1. A task force was created to better define the market parameters to include all the needs of the many Citigroup branches. A final decision was made to include Americans 55 years of age or older, retired, and in the upper half of the financial strata of that market.
2. Exploratory research in the form of secondary data analysis of the mature or older market was then performed and a study of competitive products was conducted. Exploratory qualitative research involving focus groups was also carried out in order to determine the needs and desires of the market and the level of satisfaction with the current products. In the case of senior citizens, a great deal of diversity was found in the market. This was determined to be due to such factors as affluence, relative age, and the absence or presence of a spouse.
3. The next stage of research was brainstorming. This involved the formation of many different financial packages targeted for the target market. In this case, a total of 10 ideas were generated.
4. The feasibility of the 10 ideas generated in step 3 were then tested. They were tested on the basis of whether they were possible in relation to the business. The following list of questions was used as a series of hurdles that the ideas had to pass to continue on to the next step.

(Continued)

RESEARCH IN PRACTICE 3.2

- Can the idea be explained in a manner that the target market will easily understand it?
- Does the idea fit into the overall strategy of Citigroup?
- Is there an available description of a specific target market for the proposed product?
- Does the research conducted so far indicate a potential match for target market needs and is the idea perceived to have appeal to this market?
- Is there a feasible outline of the tactics and strategies for implementing the program?
- Have the financial impact and cost of the program been thoroughly evaluated and determined to be in line with company practices?

In this study, only one idea generated from the brainstorming session made it past all the listed hurdles and on to step 5.

5. A creative workplan was then generated. This plan was to emphasize the competitive advantage of the proposed product as well as better delineate the specific features of the product.
6. The previous exploratory research was followed up with descriptive research in the form of mall-intercept surveys of people in the target market range. The survey showed that the list of special features was too long and it was decided to drop the features more commonly offered by competitors.
7. Finally, the product was test marketed in six of the Citigroup branches within the target market. Test marketing is a form of causal research. Given successful test marketing results, the product is introduced nationally.

Banks undertake exploratory, descriptive, and causal research to understand the financial services needs of consumers.

Nonsampling Error Nonsampling errors are errors that can be attributed to sources other than sampling and that can be random or nonrandom.

Nonresponse Error A type of nonsampling error that occurs when some of the respondents included in the sample do not respond. This error may be defined as the variation between the true mean value of the variable in the original sample and the true mean value in the net sample.

Response Error A type of nonsampling error arising from respondents who do respond but give inaccurate answers, or whose answers are misrecorded or misanalyzed. It may be defined as the variation between the true mean value of the variable in the net sample and the observed mean value obtained in the marketing research project.

Nonsampling Error

Nonsampling errors can be attributed to sources other than sampling, and they may be random or nonrandom. They result from a variety of reasons, including errors in problem definition, approach, scales, questionnaire design, interviewing methods, and data preparation and analysis. Nonsampling errors consist of nonresponse errors and response errors.

Nonresponse Error. **Nonresponse error** arises when some of the respondents included in the sample do not respond. The primary causes of nonresponse are refusals and not-at-homes (see chapter 12). Nonresponse will cause the net or resulting sample to be different in size or composition from the original sample. Nonresponse error is defined as the variation between the true mean value of the variable in the original sample and the true mean value in the net sample.

Response Error. **Response error** arises when respondents give inaccurate answers or their answers are misrecorded or misanalyzed. Response error is defined as the variation between the true mean value of the variable in the net sample and the observed mean value obtained in the marketing research project. Response errors can be made by researchers, interviewers, or respondents.[23]

Errors made by the researcher include surrogate information, measurement, population definition, sampling frame, and data analysis errors.

Surrogate information error may be defined as the variation between the information needed for the marketing research problem and the information sought by the researcher. For example, instead of obtaining information on consumer choice of a new brand (needed for the marketing research problem), the researcher obtains information on consumer preferences because the choice process cannot be easily observed.

Measurement error may be defined as the variation between the information sought and information generated by the measurement process employed by the researcher. While seeking to measure consumer preferences, the researcher employs a scale that measures perceptions rather than preferences.

Population definition error may be defined as the variation between the actual population relevant to the problem at hand and the population as defined by the researcher. The problem of appropriately defining the population may be far from trivial, as illustrated by the case of affluent households.

EXAMPLE

How Affluent Is Affluent?

In a recent study, the population of U.S. affluent households was defined in four ways: (1) households with income of $50,000 or more; (2) the top 20 percent of households, as measured by income; (3) households with net worth over $250,000; and (4) households with spendable discretionary income 30 percent higher than that of comparable households. The number and characteristics of the affluent households varied depending on the definition, underscoring the need to avoid population definition error.[24] ■

As may be surmised, the results of this study would have varied markedly depending on the way the population of affluent households was defined.

Sampling frame error may be defined as the variation between the population defined by the researcher and the population as implied by the sampling frame (list) used. For example a telephone directory used to generate a list of telephone numbers does not accurately represent the population of potential consumers because there are unlisted, disconnected, and new numbers in service that are not listed in the directory.

Data analysis error encompasses errors that occur while raw data from questionnaires are transformed into research findings. For example, an inappropriate statistical procedure is used resulting in incorrect interpretation and findings.

Response errors made by the interviewer include respondent selection, questioning, recording, and cheating errors.

Respondent selection error occurs when interviewers select respondents other than those specified by the sampling design or in a manner inconsistent with the sampling design. For example, in a readership survey, a nonreader is selected for the interview but classified as a reader of the *Wall Street Journal* in the 15 to 19 years category in order to meet a difficult quota requirement.

Questioning error denotes errors made in asking questions of the respondents or in not probing when more information is needed. For example, while asking questions an interviewer does not use the exact wording given in the questionnaire.

Recording error arises due to errors in hearing, interpreting, and recording the answers given by the respondents. For example, a respondent indicates a neutral response (undecided) but the interviewer misinterprets that to mean a positive response (would buy the new brand).

Cheating error arises when the interviewer fabricates answers to a part or whole of the interview. For example, an interviewer does not ask the sensitive questions related to respondent's debt but later fills in the answers based on personal assessment.

Response errors made by the respondent are comprised of inability and unwillingness errors.

Inability error results from the respondent's inability to provide accurate answers. Respondents may provide inaccurate answers because of unfamiliarity, fatigue, boredom, faulty recall, question format, question content, and other factors. For example, a respondent cannot recall the brand of yogurt purchased four weeks ago.

Unwillingness error arises from the respondent's unwillingness to provide accurate information. Respondents may intentionally misreport their answers because of a desire to provide socially acceptable answers, avoid embarrassment, or please the interviewer. For example, a respondent intentionally misreports reading *Time* magazine in order to impress the interviewer.

These sources of error are discussed in more detail in subsequent chapters; what is important here is that there are many sources of error. In formulating a research design, the researcher should attempt to minimize the total error not just a particular source. This admonition is warranted by the general tendency among students and unsophisticated researchers to control sampling error with large samples. Increasing the sample size does decrease sampling error, but it may also increase nonsampling error by increasing interviewer errors.

Nonsampling error is likely to be more problematic than sampling error. Sampling error can be calculated, whereas many forms of nonsampling error defy estimation. Moreover, nonsampling error has been found to be the major contributor to total error, whereas random sampling error is relatively small in magnitude.[25] The point is that total error is important. A particular type of error is important only in that it contributes to total error.

Sometimes, researchers deliberately increase a particular type of error to decrease the total error by reducing other errors. For example, suppose a mail survey is being conducted to determine consumer preferences for purchasing fashion clothing from department stores. A large sample size has been selected to reduce sampling error. A response rate of 30 percent may be expected. Given the limited budget for the project, the selection of a large sample size does not allow for follow-up mailings. However, past experience indicates that the response rate could be increased to 45 percent with one follow-up and to 55 percent with two follow-up mailings. Given the subject of the survey, nonrespondents are likely to differ from respondents in terms of salient variables. Hence, it may be desirable to reduce the sample size so that money is available for follow-up mailings. Although decreasing the sample size will increase random sampling error, the two follow-up mailings will more than offset this loss by decreasing nonresponse error.

BUDGETING AND SCHEDULING THE PROJECT

Budgeting and Scheduling
Management tools needed to help ensure that the marketing research project is completed within the available resources.

Critical Path Method
Management technique of dividing a research project into component activities, determining the sequence of these components, and the total time each activity will require.

Program Evaluation and Review Technique (PERT)
A more sophisticated critical path method that accounts for the uncertainty in project completion times.

Graphical Evaluation and Review Technique (GERT)
A sophisticated critical path method that accounts for both the completion probabilities and the activity costs.

Once a research design, appropriately controlling the total error, has been specified, the budgeting and scheduling decisions should be made. **Budgeting and scheduling** help to ensure that the marketing research project is completed within the available resources—financial, time, human resources, and other. By specifying the time parameters within which each task should be completed and the costs of each task, the research project can be effectively managed. A useful approach for managing a project is the **critical path method** (CPM), which involves dividing the research project into component activities, determining the sequence of these activities, and estimating the total time required for each activity. These activities and time estimates are diagrammed in the form of a network flow chart. The critical path, the series of activities whose delay will hold up the project, can then be identified.

An advanced version of CPM is the **program evaluation and review technique (PERT)**, which is a probability-based scheduling approach that recognizes and measures the uncertainty of the project completion times.[26] An even more advanced scheduling technique is the **graphical evaluation and review technique (GERT)**, in which both the completion probabilities and the activity costs can be built into a network representation.

MARKETING RESEARCH PROPOSAL

Marketing Research Proposal
The official layout of the planned marketing research activity for management. It describes the research problem, the approach, the research design, data collection methods, data analysis methods, and reporting methods.

Once the research design has been formulated and budgeting and scheduling of the project accomplished, a written research proposal should be prepared. The **marketing research proposal** contains the essence of the project and serves as a contract between the researcher and management. The research proposal covers all phases of the marketing research process. It describes the research problem, the approach, the research design, and how the data will be collected, analyzed, and reported. It gives a cost estimate and a time schedule for completing the project. The format of a research proposal may vary considerably, but most proposals address all the steps of the marketing research process and contain the following elements.

1. *Executive summary*. The proposal should begin with a summary of the major points from each of the other sections, presenting an overview of the entire proposal.
2. *Background*. The background to the problem, including the environmental context, should be discussed.
3. *Problem definition/objectives of the research*. Normally, a statement of the problem, including the specific components, should be presented. If this statement has not been developed (as in the case of problem identification research), the objectives of the marketing research project should be clearly specified.
4. *Approach to the problem*. At a minimum, a review of the relevant academic and trade literature should be presented, along with some kind of an analytical model. If research questions, hypotheses, and factors influencing the research design have been identified, then these should be included in the proposal.
5. *Research design*. The research design adopted, whether exploratory, descriptive, or causal, should be specified. Information should be provided on the following components: (1) kind of information to be obtained, (2) method of administering the questionnaire (mail, telephone, or personal interviews), (3) scaling techniques, (4) nature of the questionnaire (type of questions asked, length, average interviewing time), and (5) sampling plan and sample size.
6. *Field work/data collection*. The proposal should discuss how the data will be collected and who will collect it. If the field work is to be subcontracted to another supplier, this should be stated. Control mechanisms to ensure the quality of data collected should be described.

7. *Data analysis*. The kind of data analysis that will be conducted (simple cross-tabulations, univariate analysis, multivariate analysis) and how the results will be interpreted should be described.
8. *Reporting*. The proposal should specify whether intermediate reports will be presented and at what stages, what will be the form of the final report, and whether a formal presentation of the results will be made.
9. *Cost and time*. The cost of the project and a time schedule, broken down by phases, should be presented. A CPM or PERT chart might be included. In large projects, a payment schedule is also worked out in advance.
10. *Appendices*. Any statistical or other information that is of interest to only a few people should be contained in appendices.

Preparing a research proposal has several advantages. It ensures that the researcher and management agree about the nature of the project and helps sell the project to management. As preparation of the proposal entails planning, it helps the researcher conceptualize and execute the marketing research project.

INTERNATIONAL MARKETING RESEARCH

In conducting international marketing research, the researcher must realize that given the environmental differences (see chapter 23), the research design appropriate for one country may not be suitable in another. Consider the problem of determining household attitudes toward major appliances in the United States and in Saudi Arabia. While conducting exploratory research in the United States, it is appropriate to conduct focus groups jointly with male and female heads of households. However, it would be inappropriate to conduct such focus groups in Saudi Arabia. Given the traditional culture, the wives are unlikely to participate freely in the presence of their husbands. It would be more useful to conduct one-on-one depth interviews with both male and female heads of households being included in the sample.

EXAMPLE

Chinese Sport a Favorable Attitude toward Sporting Goods

A marketing research study was performed to gain insight and understanding into the behavior of consumers in China in relation to sports and sporting goods. The research design included both exploratory and conclusive research. Exploratory research was necessary to gain an understanding of the social, cultural, economic, and legal environment of China. The researcher utilized both secondary data and one-on-one depth interviews with retail outlet managers to gather this information.

For the conclusive research, a single cross-sectional design was used. A survey was developed and 4,000 questionnaires were distributed to respondents in 10 cities in China. Of these, 53.9 percent were completed and returned. A single cross-sectional design was appropriate because the researcher wanted to gain an understanding of the current state of consumers' attitudes, motivations, and behaviors in relation to sporting goods.

The study results were very interesting. Some of the results were as follows:

- Shoes were rated the favorite sporting good item by respondents.
- Quality, style, and price were the most important factors in choosing a product.
- Respondents exhibited brand recognition for Adidas, Nike, Asics, and Reebok.
- Most respondents said they spent less than the equivalent of 40 American dollars per year on sporting goods. Income levels in the survey ranged from approximately $173 U.S. to $863 U.S. per month.
- Most respondents said they believe advertisements "rarely" or "occasionally."

Some specific social, cultural, and environmental trends were also identified. For instance, China is becoming more fitness-conscious. China is also becoming a more casual society, which is leading to the use of sporting goods for facilitation of the casual lifestyle. Also, Chinese shop a lot on Sundays. In addition, in China the wife in the family makes purchase decisions. These are all characteristics of the Chinese norms and lifestyles that would impact the marketing of sporting goods in China.

This information would be very useful to any sporting goods manufacturer that is considering entering the Chinese market. Manufacturers already supplying sporting goods to China could use this information to improve their marketing strategies.[27] ■

In many countries, particularly developing countries, consumer panels have not been developed, making it difficult to conduct descriptive longitudinal research. Likewise, in many countries the marketing support infrastructure, that is, retailing, wholesaling, advertising, and promotional infrastructure is lacking, making it infeasible to implement a causal design involving a field experiment. In formulating a research design, the researcher must expend considerable effort to ensure the equivalence and comparability of secondary and primary data obtained from different countries. In the context of collecting primary data, qualitative research, survey methods, scaling techniques, questionnaire design, and sampling considerations are particularly important. These topics are discussed in more detail in subsequent chapters.

ETHICS IN MARKETING RESEARCH

During the research design stage, not only are the concerns of the researcher and the client involved, but the rights of the respondents also must be respected. Although there usually isn't any direct contact between the respondent and the other stakeholders (client and researcher) during research design, this is the stage when decisions, such as using hidden video or audio tape recorders, with ethical ramifications are made.

The basic question of the type of research design to be adopted (i.e., descriptive or causal, cross-sectional or longitudinal) has ethical implications. For example, when studying brand switching in toothpaste purchases, a longitudinal design is the only accurate way to assess changes in an individual respondent's brand choice. A research firm that has not conducted many longitudinal studies may try to justify the use of a cross-sectional design. Is this ethical?

The researchers must ensure that the research design utilized will provide the information needed to address the marketing research problem that has been identified. The client should have the integrity not to misrepresent the project and should describe the constraints under which the researcher must operate and not make unreasonable demands. Longitudinal research takes time. Descriptive research might require interviewing customers. If time is an issue, or if customer contact has to be restricted, the client should make these constraints known at the start of the project. Finally, the client should not take undue advantage of the research firm to solicit unfair concessions for the current project by making false promises of future research contracts.

EXAMPLE

When Ethical Becomes Unethical

Ethical dilemmas may arise due to the strong desire of marketing research firms to become suppliers to large business firms who are heavy users of marketing research. Take for example, VISA, United Airlines, Coca-Cola, or Procter & Gamble. Such firms have large marketing research budgets and regularly hire external marketing research suppliers. These large clients can bargain the price for the current study or demand unreasonable concessions in the research design (e.g., the examination of additional variables; more focus groups; a larger, more targeted sample for the survey; or additional data analyses) by suggesting the potential for the marketing research firm to become a regular supplier. This may be considered "ethical business," but it becomes unethical when there is no intention to follow up with a larger study or to use the research firm in the future.[28] ■

Equally important, the responsibilities to the respondents must not be overlooked. The researcher should design the study so as not to violate the respondents' right to safety, right to privacy, or right to choose. Furthermore, the client must not abuse power to jeopardize the anonymity of the respondents. These respondent-related issues are discussed in more detail in the chapters 4, 5, 6, and 7.

INTERNET AND COMPUTER APPLICATIONS

The Internet can facilitate the implementation of different types of research designs.

FOCUS ON Burke

Burke starts the process of formulating a research design with a listing of the key information that the client needs. This is not a small task. Burke tries to clarify what information is critical and what is "nice to know," that is, what information is "report card" and what is needed to allow a specific action. For example, in a study for a local Blood Bank a question was asked "How convenient was the Blood Bank location?" This is a "report card" question. Thirty percent of the respondents said the location was inconvenient. What does management do? The question certainly doesn't imply any action. Some members of management jumped to the conclusion that this meant the Blood Bank was too far from the normal driving range of donors and a more suburban center should be considered. Follow-up research found that this wasn't at all the case. Those reporting that the Blood Bank location was inconvenient were those who had trouble finding a parking place when they donated. The proper action was improving the parking, not creating a new donation center. To ensure the usefulness of the information collected, Burke addresses the question of "What are we going to do with what we measure?"

Once this has been done, Burke asks a series of questions: Who has the information? Do they really know the information? Are they willing to share the information? These are key questions in defining the relevant population for the study. The definition must be tight enough that any number of judges when evaluating a respondent would all agree as to whether the respondent is legitimately in the population or not. Another key question in formulating the research design is, "Will the respondents understand the measurement methods such that they can share the information accurately and reliably?" It is important that the researcher and the respondent use the same language. In the Blood Bank project the word "convenient" was used. Is this defined the same way by all respondents and by the researcher? If you are going to ask a series of attribute ratings, are you sure that you are including the attributes the respondents really use and in the words they will understand?

Burke conducts exploratory, descriptive, and causal research. Generally, some combination of these basic designs is used in a particular study. When a new project is undertaken for a client, exploratory research is generally the first phase. This involves extensive analysis of available secondary data and some form of qualitative research, with focus groups being the most popular. The purpose of exploratory research is to understand the environmental context of the problem, particularly the underlying decision making process of the consumers or the customers with respect to the client's products. In the Blood Bank project, secondary data were analyzed and focus groups conducted to answer questions such as, "What factors do people consider in deciding to donate blood? What are the major motivations for donating blood? What are people's attitudes toward donating blood?" Exploratory research is in most instances followed by descriptive research, or sometimes by causal research if that is appropriate. In the Blood Bank project, exploratory research was followed by a single cross-sectional survey. The survey shed further light and quantified the findings of exploratory research. If unexpected or ambiguous findings are generated at the second phase, further exploratory or descriptive research may be undertaken, as in the Blood Bank project.

Exploratory Research

During the exploratory phase of the research, forums, chat rooms, or newsgroups can be used to generally discuss a topic with anyone who visits the chat room. Newsgroups focus on a particular topic and function like bulletin boards. Internet users "stop by" a newsgroup to read messages left by others, and to post their own responses or comments. Internet browsers such as Netscape Navigator or Microsoft Internet Explorer come with newsgroup readers. To find a particular newsgroup, open your newsreader program and search for the topic of interest. Newsgroups or chat rooms could be used to set up more formal focus groups with experts or individuals representing the target audience in order to obtain initial information on a subject. In chapter 5 we discuss the use of the Internet for conducting focus groups in more detail.

List servers could also be used to obtain the initial information needed to begin research design. List servers make interactive discussion possible for special interest groups, user groups, customer service forums, and so on, using e-mail. Messages sent to the list server are forwarded to all subscribers of that list server. Broad or specific questions could be asked of list server subscribers. The questions might not constitute a specifically developed survey, and the members of the list servers might not all represent the target audience precisely, but if the list servers are chosen based on their relationship to the area being researched, they should provide a means of quickly receiving responses that can begin to clarify the research area. Such responses would feed into more conclusive research. More information on list servers including a listing of e-mail addresses can be obtained at www.cuenet.com/ml.html.

Conclusive Research

Many descriptive studies utilize secondary data, the methodology of which we describe in chapter 4; surveys, which are discussed in chapter 6; and panels, which are discussed in chapters 4 and 6. The use of Internet for causal research designs is discussed in chapter 7. The Internet, in its capacity as a source of information, can be useful in uncovering secondary data and collecting primary data needed in conclusive research, as illustrated by Greenfield Online Research Center, Inc. (Research in Practice 3.3.)

RESEARCH IN PRACTICE 3.3

The Green Field of Online Research

Greenfield Online Research Center, Inc. (www.greenfieldonline.com), based in Westport, Connecticut, is a subsidiary of the Greenfield Consulting Group. The Online Research Center conducts focus groups, surveys, and polls over the Internet. The company has built up a "panel" of close to 200,000 Internet users, from which it draws survey samples. The samples may be used for descriptive research designs such as single or multiple cross-sectional designs, as well as longitudinal designs. Causal designs can also be implemented. Respondents may also be chosen from the registered Internet users.

Internet users wishing to take part in surveys and other projects begin by registering on-line at Greenfield's Web site. The registration consists of a "sign-up survey" that asks for e-mail address, type of computer used, personal interests, and information about the respondent's household. Once an Internet user is registered, Greenfield Online matches the user with research studies that are well suited to his or her interests.

Incentives to take part in focus groups or special surveys are offered by the companies whose products or services are being researched. This incentive is often cash or valuable prizes. Incentives are also offered to Internet users to encourage them to register with Greenfield's Internet panel. New registrants automatically qualify for prizes that are awarded in monthly drawings.

In addition to Internet applications, computers can also help control total error. By using computers, researchers can see how the various sources of error will affect the results and what levels of errors might be acceptable. It is relatively easy to estimate random sampling error when probability sampling schemes are used. Estimating the impact of various nonsampling errors, however, is much more problematic. Simulation can be conducted to determine how the distributions and levels of various nonsampling errors will affect final results.[29] This would indicate the acceptable levels of error, and the research design could be adjusted to contain these errors within the acceptable limits. The simulations provide only an indication, and considerable judgment is needed on the part of the researcher. Software such as Monte Carlo Simulations (MCS) by Actuarial Micro Software is useful for these purposes.

SUMMARY

A research design is a framework or blueprint for conducting the marketing research project. It specifies the details of how the project should be conducted. Research designs may be broadly classified as exploratory or conclusive. The primary purpose of exploratory research is to provide insights into the problem. Conclusive research is conducted to test specific hypotheses and examine specific relationships. The findings from conclusive research are used as input into managerial decision making. Conclusive research may be either descriptive or causal.

The major objective of descriptive research is to describe market characteristics or functions. A descriptive design requires a clear specification of the who, what, when, where, why, and way of the research. Descriptive research can be further classified into cross-sectional and longitudinal research. Cross-sectional designs involve the collection of information from a sample of population elements at a single point in time. In contrast, in longitudinal designs repeated measurements are taken on a fixed sample. Causal research is designed for the primary purpose of obtaining evidence about cause-and-effect (causal) relationships.

A research design consists of six components. Error can be associated with any of these components. The total error is composed of random sampling error and nonsampling error. Nonsampling error consists of nonresponse and response errors. Response error encompasses errors made by researchers, interviewers, and respondents. A written marketing research proposal including all the elements of the marketing research process should be prepared. In formulating a research design when conducting international marketing research, considerable effort is required to ensure the equivalence and comparability of secondary and primary data obtained from different countries. In terms of ethical issues, the researchers must ensure that the research design utilized will provide the information sought, and that the information sought is the information needed by the client. The client should have the integrity not to misrepresent the project and should describe the situation that the researcher must operate within and not make unreasonable demands. Every precaution should be taken to insure the respondents' or subjects' right to safety, right to privacy, or right to choose. The Internet and computers can be employed to aid the process of formulating a research design.

KEY TERMS AND CONCEPTS

research design
exploratory research
conclusive research
descriptive research
cross-sectional design
single cross-sectional design
multiple cross-sectional design
cohort analysis
longitudinal design
panel
causal research
total error
random sampling error
nonsampling error
nonresponse error
response error
surrogate information error
measurement error
population definition error
sampling frame error
data analysis error
respondent selection error

questioning error
recording error
cheating error
inability error
unwillingness error
budgeting and scheduling
critical path method (CPM)
program evaluation and review technique (PERT)
graphical evaluation and review technique (GERT)
marketing research proposal

ACRONYMS

The components of a research design may be summarized by the acronym DESIGN:

D ata analysis plan
E xploratory, descriptive, causal design
S caling and measurement
I nterviewing forms, questionnaire design
G enerate the information needed
N Sample size and plan

EXERCISES

Questions

1. Define research design in your own words.
2. How does formulating a research design differ from developing an approach to a problem?
3. Differentiate between exploratory and conclusive research.
4. What are the major purposes for which descriptive research is conducted?
5. List the six Ws of descriptive research and give an example of each.
6. Compare and contrast cross-sectional and longitudinal designs.
7. Describe cohort analysis. Why is it of special interest?
8. Discuss the advantages and disadvantages of panels.
9. What is a causal research design? What is its purpose?
10. What is the relationship between exploratory, descriptive, and causal research?
11. List the major components of a research design.
12. What potential sources of error can affect a research design?
13. Why is it important to minimize total error rather than any particular source of error?

Problems

1. Sweet Cookies is planning to launch a new line of cookies and wants to assess the market size. The cookies have a mixed chocolate-pineapple flavor and will be targeted at the premium end of the market. Discuss the six Ws of a descriptive research design that may be adopted.
2. Express each of the following types of error as an equation:
   a. Total error
   b. Random sampling error
   c. Nonresponse error
   d. Response error
3. Welcome Inc. is a chain of fast food restaurants located in major metropolitan areas in the South. Sales have been growing very slowly for the last two years. Management has decided to add some new items to the menu, but first they want to know more about their customers and their preferences.
   a. List two hypotheses.
   b. What kind of research design is appropriate? Why?

INTERNET AND COMPUTER EXERCISES

1. Visit the Greenfield Online Research Center (see Research in Practice 3.3).
   a. What surveys are currently being conducted by Greenfield?
   b. How are the respondents being recruited for these surveys?
   c. Discuss the different types of error likely to arise given the way the respondents are being recruited.
2. Visit the Web page of three of the marketing research firms listed in Research in Practice 1.3. What types of research designs have been implemented recently by these firms?
3. Obtain one of the CPM/PERT programs. Using this program, develop a schedule for a research design identified in one of the previous exercises.
4. You are conducting an image study for Carnival Cruise Lines. As part of exploratory research, analyze the messages posted to the newsgroup rec.travel.cruises to determine the factors that consumers use in evaluating cruise companies.

Chapter 4

"Secondary Data can be an immediate and cost-effective means to gaining valuable insight into research issues; provided that the information comes from reliable and timely sources."

Sandy Bautista, manager, Corporate Information Center, Burke, Inc.

Exploratory Research Design: Secondary Data

OBJECTIVES

After reading this chapter, the student should be able to

1. define the nature and scope of secondary data and distinguish secondary data from primary data
2. analyze the advantages and disadvantages of secondary data and their uses in the various steps of the marketing research process
3. evaluate secondary data using the criteria of specifications, error, currency, objectives, nature, and dependability
4. describe, in detail, the different sources of secondary data including internal sources and external sources in the form of published materials, computerized databases, and syndicated services
5. discuss in detail the syndicated sources of secondary data including household/consumer data obtained via surveys, mail diary panels, and electronic scanner services, as well as institutional data related to retailers, wholesalers, and industrial/service firms
6. explain the need to use multiple sources of secondary data and describe single-source data
7. discuss applications of secondary data in computer mapping
8. identify and evaluate the sources of secondary data useful in international marketing research
9. understand the ethical issues involved in the use of secondary data
10. discuss the use of Internet and computers in researching secondary data

OVERVIEW

As mentioned in the previous chapters, analysis of secondary data helps define the marketing research problem and develop an approach (chapter 2). Also, before the research design for collecting primary data is formulated (chapter 3), the researcher should analyze the relevant secondary data. In some projects, particularly those with limited budgets, research may be largely confined to the analysis of secondary data, as some routine problems may be addressed based only on secondary data. This chapter discusses the distinction between primary and secondary data. The advantages and disadvantages of secondary data are considered and criteria for evaluating secondary data are presented, along with a classification of secondary data. Internal secondary data are described and major sources of external secondary data, such as published materials, on-line and off-line databases, and syndicated services, are also discussed. We consider applications of secondary data in computer mapping. The sources of secondary data useful in international marketing research are discussed. Several ethical issues that arise in the use of secondary data are identified. Finally, we discuss the use of Internet and computers in identifying and analyzing secondary data.[1]

We begin by citing several examples to give you the flavor of secondary data.

EXAMPLE

Secondary Data: It's in the Bag

To strengthen its link with its customers, Samsonite Corporation uses a toll-free number Consumer Link program as well as an in-house consumer database. Both are part of an effort to build stronger consumer relationships, increase satisfaction, establish a "travel expert" image for Samsonite, and help sell products directly to consumers.

Information from consumers comes from consumer response cards and the toll-free number used to elicit information calls from potential customers. This information becomes a part of the internal database and provides Samsonite with a great deal of planning data. By analyzing purchasers of specific types of luggage, Samsonite is better able to plan for future product offerings. By analyzing the response data, the company can plan new products and research product modifications. Research can also be done to estimate customer satisfaction with existing products by performing quarterly studies of past customers utilizing the database information. Samsonite used this type of study to determine a repurchase intent in the mid-1990s for new owners of the Piggyback Carry-On.[2] ■

EXAMPLE

Boston Market Comes to Town

Intelligent use of secondary data has enabled Boston Market to become a leader in the home meal replacement (HMR) market.

According to secondary data, home meal replacement (HMR) will be the family dining business of the next century. HMR is portable, high-quality food that's meant for take-out, and it is the fastest-growing and most significant opportunity in food industry today. NPD Group (a research firm based in Washington, NY) recently reported that in 1996 for the first time ever, American restaurants sold more meals to take out than to be eaten on-premise (with take-out accounting for 51 percent of restaurant transactions). A study by the Food Marketing Institute last year reported 38 percent of consumers say they eat meals at home that were prepared away from home "fairly often." Another recent study by consultants McKinsey & Co. projected that between 1998 and 2005, virtually all growth in food sales will come from food service, defined as food prepared at least partially away from home. Estimates of total HMR market size, as well as future potential, vary widely. Numbers ranging from $25 billion to $100 billion have been given. It is the most important trend to hit the food industry since the advent of frozen food.

Most industry experts say the trend started when Boston Market came to town, attracting consumers with promises of food just like Mom used to make. Boston Market is now the HMR leader. The company constantly monitors HMR-related data available from secondary sources and uses them as inputs into its research and marketing programs.[3] ■

EXAMPLE

High Touch Goes High Tech

The U.S. Department of Labor says that the average age of the American workforce will increase from 35 to 39 by the year 2000. This is in part the result of the maturation of the "baby bust" generation (those born between 1965 and 1976), which will cause a decline in the number of young (age 16–24) workers available to fill entry-level positions.[4] This potential shortage of young workers has caused many marketers, such as fast food restaurants, to formulate aggressive programs to recruit and keep workers. ■

EXAMPLE

Top Five Hits under the Convenience Label

A report by the National Association of Convenience Stores shows that the top five items in planned purchases (non-impulse buying) from convenience stores are (1) soft drinks, (2) tobacco products, (3) gasoline, (4) dairy products (milk, eggs, margarine), and (5) reading material. This information can be valuable to convenience stores in determining their product mix. It is also useful to marketers of these products in designing sales promotional activities such as sampling, coupons, and point-of-sale displays.[5] ■

EXAMPLE

J. D. Power Powers Research on Electric Vehicles

Syndicated sources are companies that collect and sell common pools of data designed to serve information needs shared by a number of clients. One such syndicated source is J. D. Power and Associates. A recent J. D. Power study was the first independently funded survey of Southern California's potential electric vehicle (EV) buyers, who have been exposed to promotion and advertising of EVs. Twenty-five percent of the respondents to the study said they would consider buying or leasing an EV. Consumers cited the key factors they consider in the purchase of a gasoline-powered vehicle as the same ones they would consider in the purchase of an EV. The study listed the top 10 requirements for an EV purchase. It also indicates that the true success of EVs will be based on their performance as vehicles, rather than their image as environmentally friendly. Indeed, the research established that consumers might be willing to eschew the benefits of pure EVs and zero emissions in return for other benefits offered by natural gas vehicles, hybrid EVs, and fuel-cell vehicles.

Every significant automobile company in the world is working on highly advanced EV technologies. General Motors is marketing the EV1. The secondary data produced by the J. D. Power and Associates study can be used to help GM better understand potential EV buyers. GM can also build on this study by initiating a research design that has been shaped by this secondary data. GM knows the requirements for an EV purchase. GM now needs to gather primary data so it can design features for the EV2, its new electric vehicle, that will meet the needs of potential buyers.[6] ■

As these examples illustrate, internal database (Samsonite), research and consulting firms (NPD Group, McKinsey & Co.), government departments (U.S. Department of Labor), industry associations (National Association of Convenience Stores), and syndicated firms (J. D. Power) are only a few of the sources from which secondary data may be obtained. The nature and role of secondary data become clear when we understand the distinction between primary and secondary data.

PRIMARY VERSUS SECONDARY DATA

Primary Data Data originated by the researcher for the specific purpose of addressing the research problem.

Secondary Data Data collected for some purpose other than the problem at hand.

Primary data are originated by a researcher for the specific purpose of addressing the problem at hand. The collection of primary data involves all six steps of the marketing research process (chapter 1). Obtaining primary data can be expensive and time consuming. The department store patronage project cited in chapter 1 is an example of primary data collection.

Secondary data have already been collected for purposes other than the problem at hand. These data can be located quickly and inexpensively. In the department store patronage project, secondary data on the criteria used by households to select department stores were obtained from marketing journals (*Journal of Retailing*, *Journal of Marketing*, *Journal of the Academy of Marketing Science*, and *Journal of Marketing Research*). Several other examples of secondary data were provided in the preceding section. The differences between primary and secondary data are summarized in Table 4.1. As compared to primary data, secondary data are collected rapidly and easily, at a relatively low cost, and in a short time.

These differences between primary and secondary data lead to some distinct advantages and uses of secondary data.

ADVANTAGES AND USES OF SECONDARY DATA

As can be seen from the foregoing discussion, secondary data offer several advantages over primary data. Secondary data are easily accessible, relatively inexpensive, and quickly obtained. Some secondary data, such as those provided by the U.S. Bureau of the Census, are available on topics for which it would not be feasible for a firm to collect primary data. While it is rare for secondary data to provide all the answers to a nonroutine research problem, such data can be useful in a variety of ways.[7] Secondary data can help you:

TABLE 4.1

A COMPARISON OF PRIMARY AND SECONDARY DATA

	Primary Data	*Secondary Data*
Collection purpose	For the problem at hand	For other problems
Collection process	Very involved	Rapid and easy
Collection cost	High	Relatively low
Collection time	Long	Short

1. Identify the problem
2. Better define the problem
3. Develop an approach to the problem
4. Formulate an appropriate research design (for example, by identifying the key variables)
5. Answer certain research questions and test some hypotheses
6. Interpret primary data more insightfully

Given these advantages and uses of secondary data, we state the following general rule:

> Examination of available secondary data is a prerequisite to the collection of primary data. Start with secondary data. Proceed to primary data only when the secondary data sources have been exhausted or yield marginal returns.

The rich dividends obtained by following this rule are illustrated in the several examples we have given in the introduction. These examples show that analysis of secondary data can provide valuable insights and lay the foundation for conducting primary data. However, the researcher should be cautious in using secondary data, because they have some limitations and disadvantages.

DISADVANTAGES OF SECONDARY DATA

Because secondary data have been collected for purposes other than the problem at hand, their usefulness to the current problem may be limited in several important ways, including relevance and accuracy. The objectives, nature, and methods used to collect the secondary data may not be appropriate to the present situation. Also, secondary data may not be accurate, or they may not be completely current or dependable. Before using secondary data, it is important to evaluate them on these factors. These factors are discussed in more detail in the following section.

CRITERIA FOR EVALUATING SECONDARY DATA

The quality of secondary data should be routinely evaluated, using the criteria of Table 4.2 discussed in the following sections.

Specifications: Methodology Used to Collect the Data

The specifications or the methodology used to collect the data should be critically examined to identify possible sources of bias. Such methodological considerations include size and nature of the sample, response rate and quality, questionnaire design and administration, procedures used for field work, and data analysis and reporting procedures. These checks provide information on the reliability and validity of the data and help determine whether they can be generalized to the problem at hand. The reliability and validity can be further ascertained by an examination of the error, currency, objectives, nature, and dependability associated with the secondary data.

EXAMPLE

Nielsen Media Research

There is controversy in Miami. WTVJ-TV, an NBC affiliate, uses the syndicated services of Nielsen Media Research to determine ratings and media buys. The television station feels that the data have been skewed and the methodology used was flawed. Specifically, they claim that Nielsen is putting too many meters into the homes of families that only speak Spanish, which is underestimating the station's ratings.

TABLE 4.2

CRITERIA FOR EVALUATING SECONDARY DATA

Criteria	*Issues*	*Remarks*
Specifications and methodology	Data collection method Response rate Quality of data Sampling technique Sample size Questionnaire design Field work Data analysis	Data should be reliable, valid, and generalizable to the problem at hand.
Error and accuracy	Examine errors in approach, research design, sampling, data collection, data analysis, reporting.	Assess accuracy by comparing data from different sources.
Currency	Time lag between collection and publication Frequency of updates	Census data are periodically updated by syndicated firms.
Objective	Why were the data collected?	The objective will determine the relevance of data.
Nature	Definition of key variables Units of measurement Categories used Relationships examined	Reconfigure the data to increase their usefulness, if possible.
Dependability	Expertise, credibility, reputation and trustworthiness of the source.	Data should be obtained from an original rather than an acquired source.

The problem is that the station is an English-speaking one. By placing more meters in homes that do not speak English, the information is not representative of Miami community or the station's viewers. Also, since many decisions are made from the information provided by Nielsen—such as programming, advertising, and media buys—it is important that the station have accurate and reliable information about the market.

Although many support the actions of Nielsen and feel that the data do represent the community, it still raises a very important question. Can a company be confident that the information it receives is generated using appropriate methodology?[8] ■

Error: Accuracy of the Data

The researcher must determine whether the data are accurate enough for the purposes of the present study. Secondary data can have a number of sources of error, or inaccuracy, including errors in the approach, research design, sampling, data collection, analysis, and reporting stages of the project. Moreover, it is difficult to evaluate the accuracy of secondary data, because the researcher did not participate in the research. One approach is to find multiple sources of data and compare them using standard statistical procedures.

The accuracy of secondary data can vary, particularly if they relate to phenomena that are subject to change. Moreover, data obtained from different sources may not agree. In these cases, the researcher should verify the accuracy of secondary data by conducting pilot studies or by other appropriate methods. Often, by exercising creativity, this can be done without much expense or effort.

Currency: When the Data Were Collected

Secondary data may not be current, and the time lag between data collection and publication may be long, as in the case with much census data. Moreover, the data may not be updated frequently enough for the purpose of the problem at hand. Marketing research requires current data; therefore the value of secondary data is diminished as they become dated. For instance, although the 1990 *Census of Population* data are comprehensive, they may not be applicable to a metropolitan area whose population has changed rapidly during the last two years. Likewise, in the department store patronage project, the 1980 *Census of Population* data had to be updated to reflect demographic changes that had subsequently taken place. Fortunately, several marketing research firms update census data periodically and make the current information available on a syndicated basis.

Objective: The Purpose for Which the Data Were Collected

Data are invariably collected with some objective in mind, and a fundamental question to ask is, "Why were the data collected in the first place?" The objective for collecting data will ultimately determine the purpose for which that information is relevant and useful. Data collected with a specific objective in mind may not be appropriate in another situation. As explained in more detail later in the chapter, scanner **volume tracking data** are collected with the objective of examining aggregate movement of brands, including shifts in market shares. Such data on sales of orange juice, for example, would be of limited value in a study aimed at understanding how households select specific brands.

Volume Tracking Data
Scanner data that provides information on purchases by brand, size, price, and flavor, or formulation.

Nature: The Content of the Data

The nature, or content, of the data should be examined with special attention to the definition of key variables, the units of measurement, categories used, and the relationships examined. If the key variables have not been defined or are defined in a manner inconsistent with the researcher's definition, then the usefulness of the data is limited. Consider, for example, secondary data on consumer preferences for TV programs. To use this information, it is important to know how preference for programs was defined. Was it defined in terms of the program watched most often, the one considered most needed, most enjoyable, most informative, or the program of greatest service to the community?

Likewise, secondary data may be measured in units that may not be appropriate for the current problem. For example, income may be measured by individual, family, household, or spending unit, and could be gross or net after taxes and deductions. Income may be classified into categories that are different from research needs. If the researcher is interested in high-income consumers with gross annual household incomes of over $90,000, secondary data with income categories of less than $15,000, $15,001–$35,000, $35,001–$50,000, and more than $50,000 will not be of much use. Determining the measurement of variables such as income may be a complex task. Finally, the relationships examined should be taken into account in evaluating the nature of data. If, for example, actual behavior is of interest, then data inferring behavior from self-reported attitudinal information may have limited usefulness. Sometimes it is possible to reconfigure the available data, for example convert the units of measurement, so that the resulting data are more useful to the problem at hand.

Dependability: How Dependable Are the Data?

An overall indication of the dependability of data may be obtained by examining the expertise, credibility, reputation, and trustworthiness of the source. This information can be obtained by checking with others who have used the information provided by the source. Data published to promote sales, to advance specific interests, or to carry on propaganda should be viewed with suspicion. The same may be said of data published anonymously or in a form which attempts to hide the details of the data collection methodology and

problems. This information can be used to help guide corporate marketing decisions and provide insight to individual stores that may not have the technology or expertise to complete their own market research. By using the data warehouse, customer profiles are developed, analyzing what and when purchases are made including the percentage of customers eating in, going through the drive-through, and requesting home delivery.

By understanding consumer behavior, KFC could greatly improve the profitability and customer satisfaction within its individual franchisees. For example, the database is used to forecast sales by hour, day of the week, and by time of year based on stored historical data within the warehouse and economic trends in the geographic area. These forecasts are used to maximize the efficiency of employee scheduling and minimize food inventory. Thus, by using database marketing techniques, KFC helps franchisees anticipate customer needs, improve service, customer satisfaction, and maximize efficiency and profitability.[11] ■

PUBLISHED EXTERNAL SECONDARY SOURCES

Sources of published external secondary data include federal, state, and local governments, nonprofit organizations (e.g., Chambers of Commerce), trade associations and professional organizations, commercial publishers, investment brokerage firms, and professional marketing research firms. In fact, so much data are available that the researcher can be overwhelmed. Therefore, it is important to classify published sources (see Figure 4.2.). Published external sources may be broadly classified as general business data or government data. General business sources comprise guides, directories, indexes, and statistical data. Government sources may be broadly categorized as census data and other publications.[12]

General Business Data

Businesses publish a lot of information in the form of books, periodicals, journals, newspapers, magazines, reports, and trade literature. This information can be located by using guides, directories, and indexes. Sources are also available for identifying statistical data.

Guides. Guides are an excellent source of standard or recurring information. A guide may help identify other important sources of directories, trade associations, and trade publications. Guides are one of the first sources a researcher should consult. Some of the most useful are the *American Marketing Association Bibliography Series, Business Information Sources, Data Sources for Business and Market Analysis*, and *Encyclopedia of Business Information Sources*.

Figure 4.2
A Classification of Published Secondary Sources

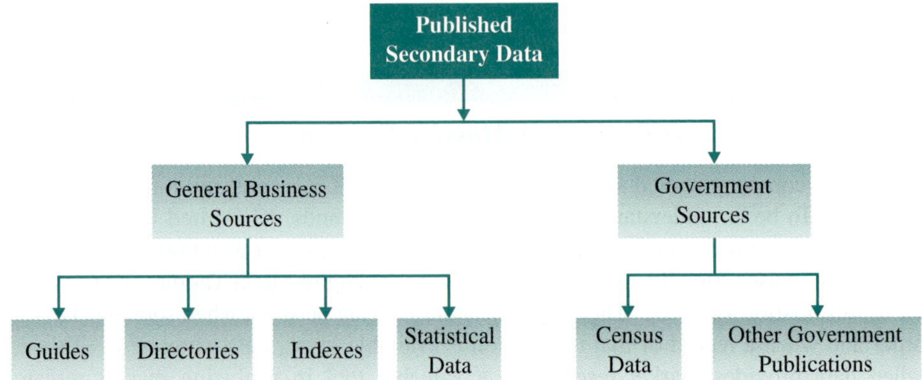

DEPARTMENT STORE PATRONAGE PROJECT

Data Search

In addition to reviewing the theoretical literature, as discussed in chapter 2, it was also necessary to identify the nonacademic sources of secondary data related to the factors considered in selecting department stores and other aspects of store patronage. *Business Periodical Index*, the *Wall Street Journal Index*, and the *New York Times Index* were used to generate a list of relevant articles that had appeared in the last five years. *Business Periodical Index* classifies articles by specific industries and firms, making it easy to locate articles of interest. Several articles obtained in this manner proved useful. One pointed to the tendency of people to combine shopping with eating out. Therefore, as discussed in chapter 2, a specific research question was framed to investigate this behavior.

Directories. Directories are helpful for identifying individuals or organizations that collect specific data. Some of the important directories include *Directories in Print, Consultants and Consulting Organizations Directory, Encyclopedia of Associations, FINDEX: The Directory of Market Research Reports, Studies and Surveys*, and *Research Services Directory*.

Indexes. It is possible to locate information on a particular topic in several different publications by using an index. Indexes can, therefore, increase the efficiency of the search process. Several were used in the department store project.

As illustrated by this example, indexes greatly facilitate a directed search of the relevant literature. Several indexes are available for both academic and business sources. Some of the more useful business indexes are *Business Periodical Index, Business Index, Predicasts F & S Index: United States, Social Sciences Citation Index*, and the *Wall Street Journal Index*.

Nongovernment Statistical Data. Published statistical data are of great interest to researchers. Graphic and statistical analyses can be performed on these data to draw important insights. Important sources of nongovernment statistical data include *A Guide to Consumer Markets, Predicasts Forecasts, Sales and Marketing Management Survey of Buying Power, Standard & Poor's Statistical Service*, and *Standard Rate and Data Service*.

Government Sources

The U.S. government also produces large amounts of secondary data. Its publications may be divided into census data and other publications.[13]

Census Data. The U.S. Bureau of the Census is the world's largest source of statistical data. Its monthly catalog lists and describes its various publications.[14] More convenient, however, is the *Guide to Economic Census*. The quality of census data is high and the data are often extremely detailed. Furthermore, one can purchase computer tapes or diskettes from the U.S. Bureau of the Census for a nominal fee and recast this information in a desired format.[15] Many private sources update the census data at a detailed geographic level for the between-census years.[16] Important census data include *Census of Housing, Census of Manufacturers, Census of Population, Census of Retail Trade, Census of Service Industries*, and *Census of Wholesale Trade*.

EXAMPLE

The Changing Color of the American Marketplace

The 1990 U.S. Census revealed that 25 percent of the American population was either African American, Hispanic, or Asian American. While the nonminority population will grow roughly 3 percent by the year 2000, ethnic populations will skyrocket from 14 percent to 52 percent over the same time frame. Such a dramatic difference in growth seriously changes the retailing landscape. Marketing groups must embrace these trends and determine how to best configure their marketing mix to meet the needs of these varying cultures. Their inclusion in the research process and marketing plans will be crucial to the long-term success of many organizations. Maintaining a close eye on the U.S. Census data and understanding that the African American, Asian American, and Hispanic markets are not only different markets but also different cultures, each with vastly different histories, will fuel America's growth into the next century.[17]

Other Government Publications. The federal government collects and publishes a great deal of statistical data in addition to the Census. The more useful publications are *Business America, Business Conditions Digest, Business Statistics, Index to Publications, Statistical Abstract of the United States*, and *Survey of Current Business*.

COMPUTERIZED DATABASES

Most published information is also available in the form of computerized databases. Computerized databases contain information that has been made available in computer-readable form for electronic distribution. In the 1980s and 1990s, the number of databases, as well as the vendors providing these services, has grown enormously. Computerized databases offer a number of advantages over printed data including:[18]

1. The data are current and up-to-date, as publishers and data compilers are now using computers as the primary production technology.
2. The search process is more comprehensive, quicker, and simpler. On-line vendors provide ready access to hundreds of databases. Moreover, this information can be accessed instantaneously, and the search process is simplified as the vendors provide uniform search protocols and commands for accessing the database.
3. The cost of accessing these databases is low, because information can be transferred at high speed.
4. It is convenient to access these data using a personal computer fitted with an appropriate communication device, such as a modem or a communication network.

On-Line Databases Databases, stored in computers, that require a telecommunications network to access.

Internet Databases Internet databases can be accessed, searched, and analyzed on the Internet. It is also possible to download data from the Internet and store it in the computer or an auxiliary storage device.

Off-Line Databases Databases that are available on diskette or CD-ROM.

While computerized database information can be helpful, it is vast and can be confusing. Thus, a classification of computerized databases is helpful.

Classification of Computerized Databases

Computerized databases may be classified as on-line, Internet, or off-line, as shown in Figure 4.3. **On-line databases** consist of a central data bank that is accessed with a computer (or dumb terminal) via a telecommunications network. **Internet databases** can be accessed, searched, and analyzed on the Internet. It is also possible to download data from the Internet and store it in the computer or an auxiliary storage device.[19] **Off-line databases** make the information available on diskettes and CD-ROM disks. Thus, off-line databases can be accessed at the user's location without the use of an external telecommunications network.[20] For example, the U.S. Bureau of the Census makes computer data files available on CD-ROM disks. These disks contain detailed information organized by census track or

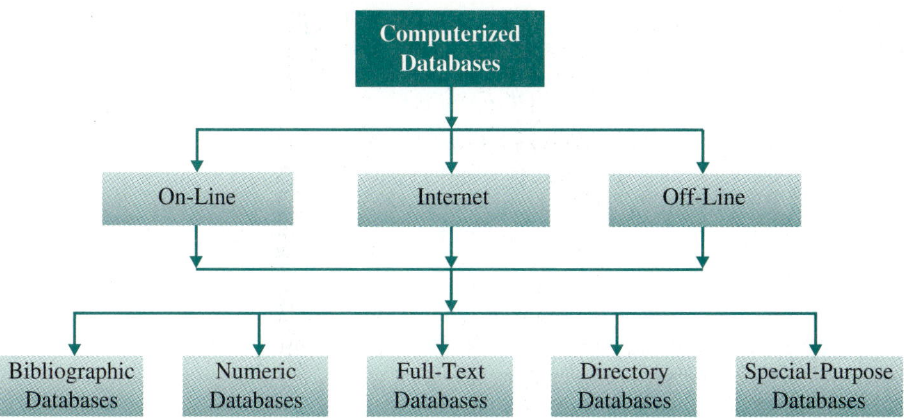

Figure 4.3
A Classification of Computerized Databases

Zip code. In the department store patronage project, this type of information was used in sample selection.[21] As indicated by Research in Practice 4.2, several vendors are providing data in various forms.[22]

On-line, Internet, and off-line databases may be further classified as bibliographic, numeric, full-text, directory, or special-purpose databases. **Bibliographic databases** are composed of citations to articles in journals, magazines, newspapers, marketing research studies, technical reports, government documents, and the like.[23] They often provide summaries or abstracts of the material cited. Examples of bibliographic databases include ABI/Inform and the Predicasts Terminal System. Another bibliographic database, Management Contents, provided by the Dialog Corporation, was used to enhance the literature search in the department store patronage project.

Bibliographic Databases Databases composed of citations to articles in journals, magazines, newspapers, marketing research studies, technical reports, government documents, and the like. They often provide summaries or abstracts of the material cited.

Numeric Databases. contain numerical and statistical information. For example, some numeric databases provide time series data (data arranged in relation to time) about the economy and specific industries produced by vendors such as Boeing Computer Services Co., Data Resources, Evans Economics, and the Office of Economic Coordination and Development. Census-based numeric databases that use the 1980 and 1990 census of population and housing with proprietary updating to provide data at the census tract and zip code level are also available. Vendors providing these databases include the U.S. Bureau of the Census, Donnelley Marketing Information Services, CACI, Inc., and National Decision Systems.

Numeric Databases Numeric databases contain numerical and statistical information that may be important sources of secondary data.

Full-Text Databases. contain the complete text of the source documents of the database. Vu/Text Information Systems, Inc., provides electronic full-text delivery and search capabilities for a number of newspapers (e.g., *Washington Post, Boston Globe, Miami Herald*).

Full-Text Databases Databases containing the complete text of source documents of the database.

RESEARCH IN PRACTICE 4.2

American Business Information: Here, There, and Everywhere

American Business Information, Inc., markets subsets of its data in a number of forms, including the professional on-line services (LEXIS-NEXIS and DIALOG), the general on-line services (CompuServe and Microsoft Network), the Internet (LookupUSA), and on CD-ROM. The underlying database, on which all these products are based, contains information on 110 million residential listings and 11 million business listings. ABI also assigns credit scores to company listings. The ABI database most business researchers are familiar with are the *American Business Directory* and the *Canadian Business Directory*.

Mead Data Central, through its NEXIS service, provides full-text access to hundreds of business databases, including selected newspapers, periodicals, company annual reports, and investment firm reports.

Directory Databases Directory databases provide information on individuals, organizations, and services.

Directory Databases. provide information on individuals, organizations, and services. Economic Information Systems, Inc., through its database, EIS Nonmanufacturing Establishments, provides information on location, headquarters, name, percent of industry sales, industry classification, and employment size class, for about 200,000 nonmanufacturing establishments that employ 20 or more people. As another example, the national electronic Yellow Pages directories of manufacturers, wholesalers, retailers, professionals, and service organizations provide the names, addresses and Standard Industrial Classification numbers of numerous organizations.

Special-Purpose Databases Databases that contain information of a specific nature, e.g., data on a specialized industry.

Finally, there are **special-purpose databases**. For example, the Profit Impact of Market Strategies (PIMS) database is an ongoing database of research and analysis on business strategy compiled by the Strategic Planning Institute in Cambridge, Massachusetts. This database comprises more than 250 companies, which provide data on over 2,000 businesses.[24] Virtually all libraries of major universities maintain computerized databases of management and related literature, which students can access free of charge.

Computerized databases are numerous and varied, and their sheer number can be overwhelming. Locating a particular database may seem difficult. How, then, do you locate specific bibliographic, numeric, full-text, directory, or special-purpose databases? Directories of databases provide the needed help.[25]

Directories of Databases

There are numerous sources of information on databases. Perhaps the best way to obtain information about databases is to consult a directory. *Gale Directory of Databases* by Gale Research, Inc., is published every six months. Volume I covers on-line databases and volume 2 covers CD-ROMs and other off-line databases. Some of the other useful directories that are periodically updated are:

- *Directory of On-Line Databases*
  Santa Monica, CA: Cuadra Associates, Inc.
- *Encyclopedia of Information System and Services*
  Detroit: Gale Research Company
- *Information Industry Marketplace*
  New York: R. R. Bowker

SYNDICATED SOURCES OF SECONDARY DATA

Syndicated Services Information services offered by marketing research organizations that provide information from a common database to different firms that subscribe to their services.

In addition to published data or data available in the form of computerized databases, syndicated sources constitute the other major source of external secondary data. **Syndicated services**, also referred to as syndicated sources, are companies that collect and sell common pools of data designed to serve information needs shared by a number of clients (see chapter 1). These data are not collected for the purpose of marketing research problems, but the data and reports supplied to client companies can be personalized to fit specific needs. For example, reports could be organized on the basis of the clients' sales territories or product lines. Using syndicated services is frequently less expensive than collecting primary data. Figure 4.4 presents a classification of syndicated sources. Syndicated sources can be classified based on the unit of measurement (household/consumers or institutions). Household/consumer data may be obtained from surveys, diary panels, or electronic scanner services. Information obtained through surveys consists of values and lifestyles, advertising evaluation, or general information related to preferences, purchase, consumption

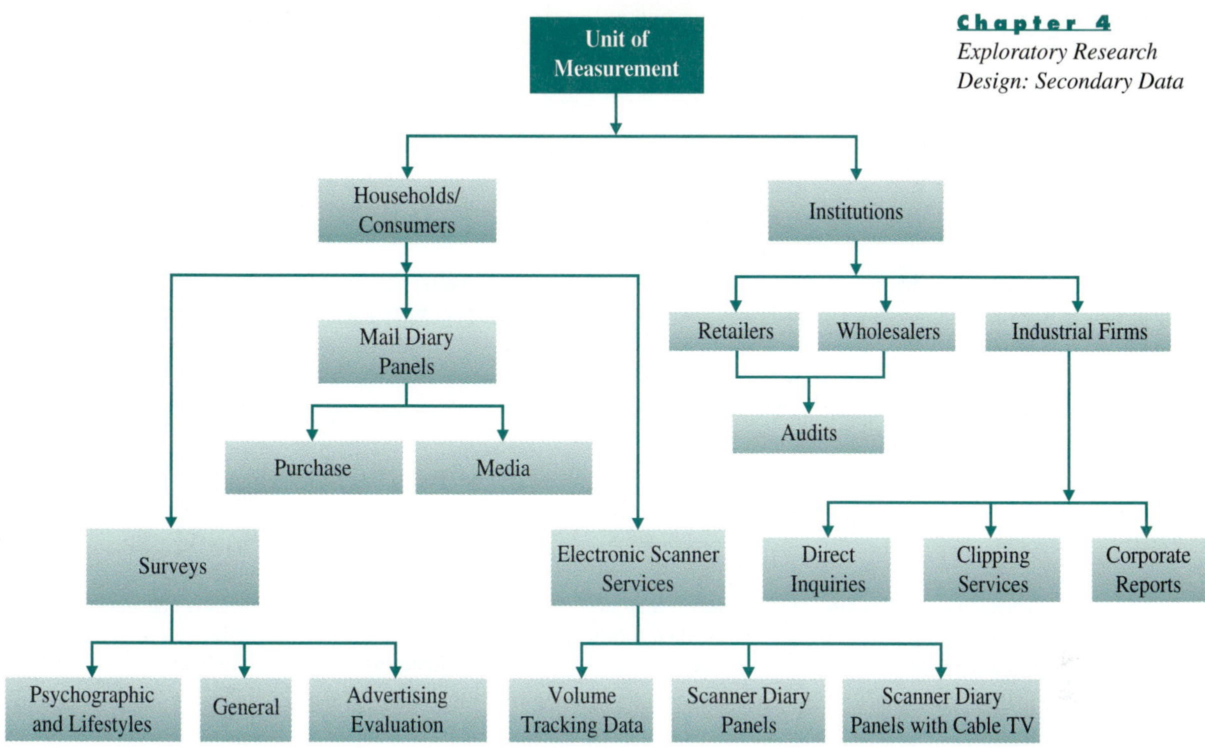

Figure 4.4
A Classification of Syndicated Services

and other aspects of behavior. Diary panels emphasize information on purchases or media consumption. Electronic scanner services might provide scanner data only, scanner data linked to diary panels, or scanner data linked to diary panels and (cable) TV. When institutions are the unit of measurement, the data may be obtained from retailers, wholesalers, or industrial firms. An overview of the various syndicated sources is given in Table 4.3. Each of these sources will be discussed.

SYNDICATED DATA FROM HOUSEHOLDS

Surveys

Various services regularly conduct **surveys**, which involve interviews with a large number of respondents using a predesigned questionnaire. Surveys may be broadly classified on the basis of their content as psychographics and lifestyles, advertising evaluation, or general surveys.

Surveys Interviews with a large number of respondents using a predesigned questionnaire.

Psychographics and Lifestyles. **Psychographics** refer to the psychological profiles of individuals and to psychologically based measures of lifestyle. **Lifestyles** refer to the distinctive modes of living of a society or some of its segments. Together, these measures are generally referred to as Activities, Interest, and Opinions, or simply AIOs. The Yankelovich Monitor provides an application.

Psychographics Quantified psychological profiles of individuals.

Lifestyles A lifestyle may be defined as a distinctive pattern of living that is described by the activities people engage in, the interests they have, and the opinions they hold of themselves and the world around them (AIOs).

EXAMPLE

Campbell Makes Sure AIOs Are in Its Alphabet Soup

Yankelovich Partners, Inc., provides the Yankelovich Monitor, a survey that contains data on lifestyles and social trends. The survey is conducted at the same time each year among a nationally projectable sample of 2,500 adults, 16 years of age or older, including a special

TABLE 4.3

OVERVIEW OF SYNDICATED SERVICES

Type	*Characteristics*	*Advantages*	*Disadvantages*	*Uses*
Surveys	Surveys conducted at regular intervals	Most flexible way of obtaining data; information on underlying motives	Interviewer errors; respondent errors	Market segmentation, advertising theme selection, and advertising effectiveness
Diary Purchase Panels	Households provide specific information regularly over an extended period of time; respondents asked to record specific behaviors as they occur	Recorded purchase behavior can be linked to the demographic/ psychographic characteristics	Lack of representativeness; response bias; maturation	Forecasting sales, market share, and trends; establishing consumer profiles, brand loyalty and switching; evaluating test markets, advertising, and distribution
Diary Media Panels	Electronic devices automatically recording behavior, supplemented by a diary	Same as diary purchase panel	Same as diary purchase panel	Establishing advertising rates; selecting media program or air time; establishing viewer profiles
Scanner Volume Tracking Data	Household purchases are recorded through electronic scanners in supermarkets	Data reflect actual purchases; timely data less expensive	Data may not be representative; errors in recording purchases; difficult to link purchases to elements of marketing mix other than price	Price tracking, modeling, effectiveness of in-store promotion
Scanner Diary Panels with Cable TV	Scanner panels of households that subscribe to cable TV	Data reflect actual purchases; sample control; ability to link panel data to household characteristics	Data may not be representative; quality of data limited	Promotional mix analyses, copy testing, new-product testing, positioning
Audit Services	Verification of product movement by examining physical records or performing inventory analysis	Relatively precise information at the retail and wholesale levels	Coverage may be incomplete; matching of data on competitive activity may be difficult	Measurement of consumer sales and market share, competitive activity, analyzing distribution patterns: tracking of new products
Industrial Product Syndicated Services	Data banks on industrial establishments created through direct inquiries of companies, clipping services, and corporate reports	Important source of information on industrial firms, particularly useful in initial phases of the projects	Data is lacking in terms of content, quantity, and quality	Determining market potential by geographic area, defining sales territories, allocating advertising budget

sample of 300 college students living on campus. The sample is based on the most recent census data. All interviews are conducted in person at the respondent's home and take approximately 2.5 hours to complete. Advertising agencies use the Yankelovich Monitor to discern changes in lifestyles and design advertising themes that reflect these trends. For example, a Campbell Soup campaign that shows a husband fixing soup was designed when a significant trend toward reversal of traditional roles was discovered.[26] ■

Another example is the DDB Needham Life Style Study, which has been tracking consumer attitudes and behaviors for a number of years.[27] The Stanford Research Institute conducts an annual survey of consumers that is used to classify persons into VALS-2 (Values and

Lifestyles) types for segmentation purposes.[28] Information on specific aspects of consumers' lifestyles is also available. Audits and Surveys, Inc., conducts an annual survey of 5,000 consumers who participate in leisure sports and recreational activities.

Advertising Evaluation. The purpose of advertising evaluation surveys is to assess the effectiveness of advertising using print and broadcast media. Two well-known surveys are the Gallup and Robinson Magazine Impact Studies and Starch Readership Survey. The following example shows how Starch is used.

EXAMPLE

Starch Stiffens Ad Effectiveness Evaluations

Starch provides evaluation for most consumer magazines and selected business and industrial publications. This assessment can be provided for individual advertisements as well as for campaigns over time. As a measure of an advertisement's effectiveness, Starch classifies magazine readership into three groups: those who (1) remember seeing a particular advertisement ("noted"), (2) associate the sponsor's name with the advertisement ("seen-associated"), and (3) read half of its copy ("read most"). Such results are particularly important to heavy advertisers, such as Procter & Gamble, General Motors, Sears, PepsiCo, Eastman Kodak, and McDonald's, who are greatly concerned about how well their advertising dollars are spent.[29] ■

Evaluation of effectiveness is even more critical in the case of TV advertising. Television commercials are evaluated using either the recruited audience method or the in-home viewing method. In the former method, respondents are recruited and brought to a central viewing facility, such as a theater or mobile viewing laboratory. The respondents view the commercials and provide data regarding knowledge, attitudes, and preferences related to the product being advertised and the commercial itself. McCollum/Spielman Company Audience Studies (ASI), Burgoyne, Inc., PACE (Personation and Communication Effectiveness), and Tele-Research, Inc., are among the syndicated services that use this method.

In the in-home viewing method, consumers evaluate commercials at home in their normal viewing environment. New commercials can be pretested at the network level or in local markets. A survey of viewers is then conducted to assess the effectiveness of the commercials. The services that use this method include AdTel, Ltd., Television Testing Company, ARS Division, Research Systems, Inc., and Audience Studies/Com. Lab, Inc.

General Surveys. Surveys are also conducted for a variety of other purposes, including examination of purchase and consumption behavior. The Gallup Organization, Inc., surveys 15,000 households annually about their purchase of consumer products. The National Menu Census conducted by Marketing Research Corporation of America asks about consumption of food products in the home. Data are provided about meals, snack items, take-out foods, and so forth. Trendex, Inc., surveys 15,000 households quarterly about ownership and acquisition of consumer durables. These surveys can be customized to suit the needs of specific clients as the following example shows.

EXAMPLE

Customization via Syndication

Roper Reports, prepared by the Roper Organization, is a syndicated service offering customization. This service provides public opinion and behavior concerning a broad range of social, economic, and political issues, as well as various kinds of products and lifestyles.

The data are collected every five weeks through personal interviews with a national sample of 2,000 adults aged 18 or older. In addition to the standard questions, a tack-on custom question service is also available to clients. The Roper Organization claims that this service offers a unique combination of frequency, speed of report delivery, quality, low cost, large sample size, and extensive demographic breaks.[30] ■

Uses of Surveys. Because of their wide variety, survey data have numerous uses. They can be used for market segmentation, as with psychographics and lifestyles data, and for establishing consumer profiles. Surveys are also useful for determining product image, measurement and positioning, and conducting price perception analysis. Other notable uses include advertising theme selection and evaluation of advertising effectiveness.

Advantages and Disadvantages of Surveys. Surveys are the most flexible means of obtaining data from respondents. The researcher can focus on only a certain segment of the population—for example, teenagers, owners of vacation homes, or homemakers between age 30 and 40. Surveys are the primary means of obtaining information about consumers' motives, attitudes, and preferences. A variety of questions can be asked, and visual aids, packages, products, or other props can be used during the interviews. Properly analyzed, survey data can be manipulated in many ways so that the researcher can look at intergroup differences, examine the effects of independent variables such as age or income, or even predict future behavior.

On the other hand, survey data may be limited in several significant ways. The researcher has to rely primarily on the respondents' self-reports. There is a gap between what people say and what they actually do. Errors may occur because respondents remember incorrectly or give socially desirable responses. Furthermore, samples may be biased, questions poorly phrased, interviewers not properly instructed or supervised, and results misinterpreted.

Diary Panels

Often, survey data can be complemented with data obtained from diary panels. Panels were discussed in chapter 3 in the context of longitudinal research designs. Diary panels are samples of respondents who provide specified information at regular intervals over an extended period of time. These respondents may be organizations, households, or individuals, although household diary panels are most common. The distinguishing feature of diary panels is that the respondents record specific behaviors as they occur in a diary. Typically, the diary is returned to the research organization every one to four weeks. Panel members are compensated for their participation with gifts, coupons, information, or cash. Based on the content of information recorded, diary panels can be classified as diary purchase panels or diary media panels.

Diary Purchase Panels A data gathering technique in which respondents record their purchases in a diary.

Diary Purchase Panels. In **diary purchase panels**, respondents record their purchases of a variety of different products, as in the National Purchase Diary Panel.

EXAMPLE

Information in These Diaries Is No Secret

The National Purchase Diary Panel (NPD) maintains the largest diary panel in the United States. More than 14,500 households use preprinted diaries to record their monthly purchases in about 50 product categories. Respondents provide detailed information regarding the brand and amount purchased, price paid, whether any special deals were involved, the store where purchased, and intended use. The total panel includes 29 miniature panels, each representative of a local market. The composition of the panel is representative of the

U.S. population as a whole. Information provided by the National Purchase Diary Panel is used by soft drink firms such as the Coca-Cola Company to determine brand loyalty and brand switching and to profile heavy users of various brands.[31] ■

Other organizations that maintain diary purchase panels include National Family Opinion (NFO) and Market Research Corporation of America (MRCA). These organizations also maintain special purpose diary panels. For example, NFO has a beverages panel consisting of 12,000 households that provide quarterly information on beverage consumption. MRCA's Funds panel reports information on the day-to-day financial decisions of America's most active retail consumers of financial services. The Funds panel is based on a national sample selected to represent households with annual incomes above $25,000, with a special concentration in the $75,000-and-up category.

For respondents with access, the diaries can also be maintained on the Internet. The usage and maintenance of the diaries on the Internet can provide the marketer with a rich and easily accessible source of reliable information. The respondents have to fill in the diaries in a timely manner, thereby enhancing accuracy. Further, more information can be gathered from the respondents due to the ease of use of the Internet as a medium of quick and easy information exchange.

Diary Media Panels. In **diary media panels**, electronic devices automatically record viewing behavior, thus supplementing a diary. Perhaps the most familiar diary media panel is Nielsen Television Index (NTI).

Diary Media Panels A data-gathering technique comprising samples of respondents whose television viewing behavior is automatically recorded by electronic devices, supplementing the purchase information recorded in a diary.

The NTI consists of a representative sample of approximately 5,000 households. Each of these households has an electronic device, called a storage instantaneous audimeter, attached to its television sets. The audimeter continuously monitors television viewing behavior, including at what times the set is turned on, what channels are viewed, and for how long. These data are stored in the audimeter and transmitted via telephone lines to a central computer. The data collected by the audimeter are supplemented with diary panel records, called audilogs. The audilog contains information on who was watching each program, so that audience size and demographic characteristics can be calculated.

Using these data, Nielsen estimates the number and percentage of all TV households viewing a given show. Its popular report, issued biweekly, is available to clients within two

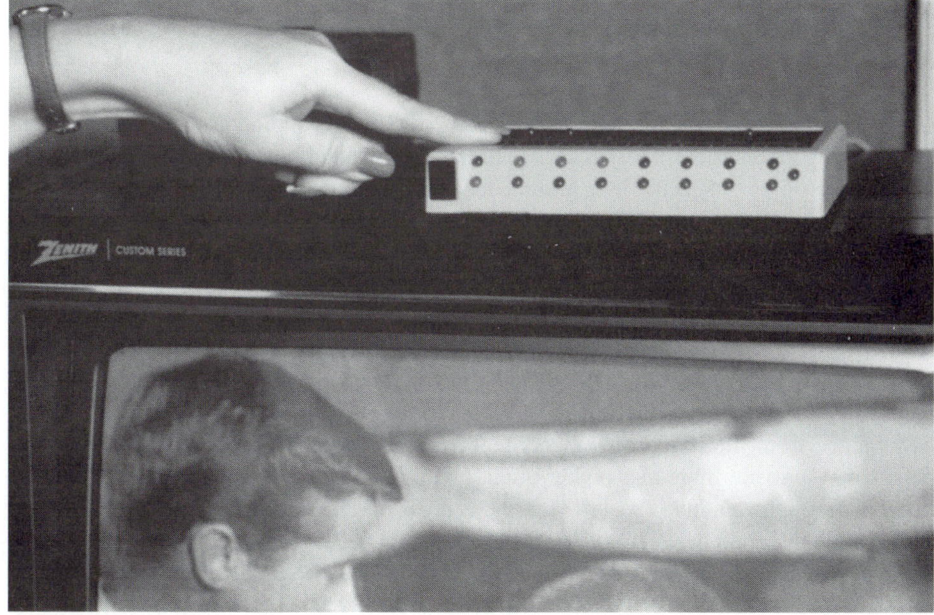

A Nielsen Audimeter, which continuously monitors television viewing behavior.

weeks after a measurement period. For those requiring information more frequently, Nielsen installs a terminal in the client's office that permits receipt of national household ratings within 24 hours of a broadcast. This information is also disaggregated by 10 demographic and socioeconomic characteristics, such as household income, education of head of house, occupation of head of house, household size, age of children, age of women, and geographical location. The NTI is useful to firms such as AT&T, Kellogg Company, J. C. Penney, Pillsbury, and Unilever in selecting specific TV programs on which to air their commercials.[32]

EXAMPLE

Nielsen Entering the "Commercial" Market

For decades, television networks have relied on Nielsen Media Research to determine the top-rated programs. Now Nielsen is preparing to introduce a new syndicated service in conjunction with the coming of the digital television age—commercial ratings. Currently, it has the technology to determine how many people are watching a channel minute-by-minute, but it is so expensive that only one network has ever requested the service.

The new service will be more accessible because of technology that will encode invisible signals into TV programs and commercials. Networks such as CBS will be able to determine if their current assumptions about channel surfing and viewer attention spans are correct. David Poltrack, head of research for CBS, estimates that only 5 percent of viewers change channels during a commercial break within a program. However, the networks believe that many more people change stations during the break between programs. This assumption has led NBC to move seamlessly from one program to the next, without a commercial break.

However, the best use of Nielsen's new technology may be with the advertisers themselves. Instead of dumping the ratings for thousands of commercials into the hands of networks, if Nielsen can provide advertisers with secondary data indicating when and where their advertising dollars can be most effective, advertisers will certainly pay for the information![33] ■

In addition to the Nielsen Television Index, other services provide diary media panels. Arbitron maintains local and regional radio and TV diary panels.[34] In the ScanAmerica people-meter ratings system, continuous detailed measures of television set tuning for every set in the home, including normal on-air programming, cable, and VCR usage, are collected automatically by an electronic meter.

Uses of Diary Panels. Diary purchase panels provide information useful for forecasting sales, estimating market shares, assessing brand loyalty and brand switching behavior, establishing profiles of specific user groups, measuring promotional effectiveness, and conducting controlled store tests. Diary media panels yield information helpful for establishing advertising rates by radio and TV networks, selecting appropriate programming, and profiling viewer or listener subgroups. Advertisers, media planners, and buyers find panel information to be particularly useful.

Advantages and Disadvantages of Diary Panels. As compared to sample surveys, diary panels offer certain distinct advantages.[35] Panels can provide longitudinal data (data can be obtained from the same respondents repeatedly). People who are willing to serve on panels may provide more and higher-quality data than sample respondents. In purchase diary panels, information is recorded at the time of purchase, eliminating recall errors.[36] Information recorded by electronic devices is accurate because it eliminates human errors.

The disadvantages of diary panels include lack of representativeness, maturation, and response biases. Most diary panels are not representative of the U.S. population. They underrepresent certain groups such as minorities and those with low education levels. This problem is further compounded by refusal to respond and attrition of panel members. Over time maturation sets in, and the panel members must be replaced (see chapter 7). Response biases may occur, because simply being on the panel may alter behavior. Purchase or media data are entered by hand, so recording errors are also possible (see chapter 3).

Electronic Scanner Services

Although information provided by surveys and diary panels is useful, electronic scanner services are becoming increasingly popular. **Scanner data** reflect some of the latest technological developments in the marketing research industry. Scanner data are collected by passing merchandise over a laser scanner, which optically reads the bar-coded description printed on the merchandise. This code is then linked to the current price held in the computer memory and used to prepare a sales slip. Information printed on the sales slip includes descriptions as well as prices of all items purchased. Check-out scanners, which are now used in many retail stores, are revolutionizing packaged goods marketing research.

Scanner Data Data obtained by passing merchandise over a laser scanner, which reads the UPC code from the packages.

Three types of scanner data are available: volume tracking data, scanner diary panels, and scanner diary panels with cable TV. **Volume tracking data** provide information on purchases by brand, size, price, and flavor or formulation, based on sales data collected from the check-out scanner tapes. This information is collected nationally from a sample of supermarkets with electronic scanners. Scanner services providing volume tracking data include National Scan Track (A. C. Nielsen), NABSCAN (The Newspaper Advertising Bureau), and TRIM (Tele-Research, Inc.).[37] In **scanner diary panels**, each household member is given an identification card that looks like a credit card. Panel members present the identification card at the check-out counter each time they shop. The checker keys in the identification numbers, and each item of that customer's order. The information is stored by day of week and time of day.[38]

Volume Tracking Data Scanner data that provides information on purchases by brand, size, price, and flavor, or formulation.

Scanner Diary Panels Scanner data collected from panel members identified by an identification card allowing each panel member's purchases to be stored with respect to the individual shopper.

An even more advanced use of scanning, **scanner diary panels with cable TV**, combines diary panels with new technologies developed by the cable TV industry. Households on these panels subscribe to one of the cable TV systems in their market. By means of a cable TV "split," the researcher targets different commercials into the homes of the panel members. For example, half the households might see test commercial A during the 6:00 P.M. newscast while the other half see test commercial B. These panels allow researchers to conduct fairly controlled experiments in a relatively natural environment.[39]

Scanner Diary Panels with Cable TV The combination of a scanner diary panel with manipulations of the advertising that is being broadcast by cable television companies.

EXAMPLE

Using Total TV Households for Testing Total Advertising

Testsight (ERIM, A.C. Nielsen) allows transmission of advertising into participating households without the use of a cable TV system. Because the panels can be selected from all available TV households, not just those with cable TV, the bias of cable-only testing is eliminated. Using this type of system, General Mills can test which one of four test commercials for Total cereal results in the highest sales. Four groups of panel members are selected, and each receives a different test commercial. These households are monitored via scanner data to determine which group purchased the most Total cereal. ■

This example shows how scanner services incorporate advanced marketing research technology, which results in some advantages over survey and diary panel data.

Uses of Scanner Data. Scanner data are useful for a variety of purposes.[40] National volume tracking data can be used for tracking sales, prices, distribution, modeling, and analyzing early warning signals. Scanner diary panels with cable TV can be used for testing new products, repositioning products, analyzing promotional mix, and making advertising decisions, including budget, copy and media, and pricing. These panels provide marketing researchers with a unique controlled environment for the manipulation of marketing variables.

Advantages and Disadvantages of Scanner Data. Scanner data have an obvious advantage over surveys and diary panels, in that they reflect purchasing behavior not subject to interviewing, recording, memory, or expert biases. The record of purchases obtained by scanners is complete and unbiased by price sensitivity, as the panelist is not required to be overly conscious of price levels and changes. Another advantage is that in-store variables such as pricing, promotions, and displays are part of the data set. The data are also likely to be current and can be obtained quickly. Finally, scanner panels with cable TV provide a highly controlled testing environment.

A major weakness of scanner data is lack of representativeness. National volume tracking data may not be projectable on to the total population, because not all outlets have scanners. Likewise, scanners have limited geographical dispersion and coverage.

The quality of scanner data may be limited by several factors. Not all products can be scanned. For example, a clerk may use the register to ring up a heavy item to avoid lifting it. If an item does not scan on the first try, the clerk may key in the price and ignore the bar code. Sometimes a consumer purchases many flavors of the same item, but the clerk scans only one package and then rings in the number of purchases. Thus, the transaction is inaccurately recorded. With respect to scanner panels, the available technology permits the monitoring of only one TV set per household. Hence, there is a built-in bias if the household has a second or third TV set. Also, the system provides information on TV sets in use rather than actual viewing behavior. Although scanner data provide behavioral and sales information, they do not provide information on underlying attitudes, preferences, and reasons for specific choices.

SYNDICATED DATA FROM INSTITUTIONS

Retailer and Wholesaler Audits

As Figure 4.4 shows, syndicated data are available for retailers and wholesalers as well as industrial firms. The most popular means of obtaining data from retailers and wholesalers is an audit. An **audit** is a formal examination and verification of product movement carried out by examining physical records or analyzing inventory. Retailers and wholesalers who participate in the audit receive basic reports and cash payments from the audit service. Audit data focus on the products or services sold through the outlets or the characteristics of the outlets themselves, as illustrated by the following example.

Audit A data collection process derived from physical records or performing inventory analysis. Data are collected personally by the researcher or by representatives of the researcher and the data are based on counts usually of physical objects other than people.

Retailing Auditing for Retailing Information

The largest retail audit service for consumer packaged goods is the Nielsen Retail Index. This index involves a biweekly store audit of supermarkets, drugstores, and mass merchandisers. Nielsen makes over 76,000 separate audits annually in over 11,350 different retail outlets.

Another major service is Audits and Surveys' National Total Market Audit, which uses different product categories than does the Nielsen service. Retail audit data can be useful to consumer product firms. For example, Colgate Palmolive is contemplating the introduction of a new toothpaste brand. A retail audit can help determine the size of the total market and distribution of sales by type of outlet and by different regions.[41]

Wholesale audit services, the counterpart of retail audits, monitor warehouse withdrawals. Participating operators, which include supermarket chains, wholesalers, and frozen food warehouses, typically account for over 80 percent of the volume in the area.

Uses of Audit Data. The uses of retail and wholesale audit data include (1) determining the size of the total market and the distribution of sales by type of outlet, region, or city; (2) assessing brand shares and competitive activity; (3) identifying shelf space allocation and inventory problems; (4) analyzing distribution problems; (5) developing sales potentials and forecasts; and (6) developing and monitoring promotional allocations based on sales volume. Thus, audit data were particularly helpful in obtaining information on the environmental context of the problem in the department store patronage project.

Advantages and Disadvantages of Audit Data. Audits provide relatively accurate information on the movement of many different products at the wholesale and retail levels. Furthermore, this information can be broken down by a number of important variables, such as brand, type of outlet, and size of market.

However, audits have limited coverage. Not all markets or operators are included. Also, audit information may not be timely or current, particularly compared to scanner data. Typically, there is a two-month gap between the completion of the audit cycle and the publication of reports. Another disadvantage is that, unlike scanner data, audit data cannot be linked to consumer characteristics. In fact, there may even be a problem in relating audit data to advertising expenditures and other marketing efforts. Some of these limitations are overcome in computerized audit panels, such as ELCAP.

EXAMPLE

Hats Off to ELCAP

Elrick & Lavidge has developed ELCAP, a computerized audit panel, for the highly volatile consumer electronics industry. It allows manufacturers and retailers to track consumer acceptance of new features and new technology, strengths and weaknesses in the distribution system, trends in retail pricing, and sales of the competition. The panel consists of about 1,000 retail stores that sell consumer electronic products, including department stores, discount stores, specialty stores, stores selling major home appliances, and superstores.

Data are collected and tabulated electronically from the computerized sales records of each participating retailer. This data collection method is not prone to errors common to physical audits, such as failure to include all sales transactions, incorrect recording, or double counting.[42] ■

Industry Services

Industry services provide syndicated data about industrial firms, businesses, and other institutions. These data are collected by making direct inquiries, from clipping services and corporate reports. The range and sources of syndicated data available to industrial goods firms are more limited than those available to consumer goods firms. Services available include Dun and Bradstreet's Market Identifiers, *Fortune* magazine's Input/Output Matrix Reports, and McGraw-Hill's Dodge Reports.

EXAMPLE

Women Make the Cut but Not the Decisions

Trinet, Inc., and Dunn's Marketing Services are two U.S. companies that provide a database of in-depth information on businesses. Trinet provides three basic information services: a database of 7 million U.S. business locations, application services, and business-to-business telemarketing services. Recently, Trinet conducted a telephone survey of 100,000 U.S.

EXERCISES

Questions

1. What are the differences between primary and secondary data?
2. Why is it important to obtain secondary data before primary data?
3. Differentiate between internal and external secondary data.
4. List the various sources of published secondary data.
5. What are the different forms of computerized databases?
6. What are the advantages of computerized databases?
7. List and describe the various syndicated sources of secondary data.
8. What is the nature of information collected by surveys?
9. How can surveys be classified?
10. Explain what a diary panel is. What is the difference between diary purchase panels and diary media panels?
11. What are the relative advantages of diary panels over surveys?
12. What kinds of data can be gathered through electronic scanner services?
13. Describe the uses of scanner data.
14. What is an audit? Discuss the uses, advantages, and disadvantages of audits.
15. Describe the information provided by industrial services.
16. Why is it desirable to use multiple sources of secondary data?
17. What are the advantages of secondary data?
18. What are the disadvantages of secondary data?
19. What are the criteria to be used when evaluating secondary data?

Problems

1. Obtain automobile industry sales and sales of major automobile manufacturers for the last five years from secondary sources. (Hint: See chapter 22, Table 22.1.)
2. Select an industry. Using secondary sources, obtain industry sales and the sales of the major firms in that industry for the past year. Estimate the market shares of each major firm. From another source, obtain information on the market shares of these same firms. Do the two estimates agree?

INTERNET AND COMPUTER EXERCISES

1. Conduct an on-line data search to obtain background information on an industry of your choice (e.g., sporting goods or home health care). Your search should encompass both qualitative and quantitative information.
2. Visit the Web site of a company of your choice. Suppose the management decision problem facing this company was to expand its share of the market. Obtain as much secondary data from the Web site of this company and other sources on the Internet as are relevant to this problem.
3. Visit the Web site of the U.S. Bureau of Census (see one of the URLs given in the book). Write a report about the secondary data available from the bureau which would be useful to a fast food firm such as McDonald's for the purpose of formulating domestic marketing strategy.
4. Visit www.census.gov/statab. Use state rankings and vital statistics to identify the top six states for marketing products to the elderly.
5. For the Department Store Patronage Project, Sears would like you to summarize the retail sales in the United States by visiting www.census.gov/ftp/pub/indicator/www/indicat.html.
6. Visit www.npd.com and write a description of the panel maintained by NPD.
7. Visit www.acnielsen.com and write a report about the various services offered by A.C. Nielsen.

Chapter 5

Exploratory Research Design: Qualitative Research

"Qualitative research provides the fundamental understanding of peoples' language, perceptions, and values. Qualitative most often provides the understanding that allows us to decide on the information we must have to solve the research problem and how to properly interpret that information."

Carol Raffel, vice president, qualitative services, Burke, Inc.

OBJECTIVES

After reading this chapter, the student should be able to

1. explain the difference between qualitative and quantitative research in terms of the objectives, sampling, data collection and analysis, and outcomes
2. understand the various forms of qualitative research including direct procedures such as focus groups and depth interviews, and indirect methods such as projective techniques
3. describe focus groups in detail with emphasis on planning and conducting focus groups, and their advantages, disadvantages, and applications
4. describe depth interview techniques in detail, citing their advantages, disadvantages, and applications
5. explain projective techniques in detail and compare association, completion, construction, and expressive techniques
6. discuss the considerations involved in conducting qualitative research in an international setting
7. understand the ethical issues involved in conducting qualitative research
8. Discuss the use of the Internet and computers in obtaining and analyzing qualitative data

OVERVIEW

Like secondary data analysis (see chapter 4), qualitative research is a major methodology used in exploratory research (chapter 3). Researchers undertake qualitative research to define the problem or develop an approach (chapter 2). In developing an approach, qualitative research is often used for generating hypotheses and identifying variables that should be included in the research. In cases in which conclusive or quantitative research is not done, qualitative research and secondary data make up the major part of the research project. In this chapter we discuss the differences between qualitative and quantitative research and the role of each in the marketing research project. We present a classification of qualitative research and cover the major techniques—focus groups and depth interviews—in detail. We also consider the indirect procedures called projective techniques with emphasis on association, completion, construction, and expressive techniques. The considerations involved in conducting qualitative research when researching international markets are discussed. Several ethical issues that arise in qualitative research are identified. The chapter concludes with a discussion of the use of the Internet and computers in qualitative research. The following examples give a flavor of qualitative research and its applications in marketing research.

EXAMPLE

"Show-and-Tell" Focus Groups Tell "Baby-Boomer" Values

Baby boomers are a large consumer target for many products and "show-and-tell" focus groups are providing needed insight into the values these boomers hold close to their heart.

The show-and-tell focus groups work this way: Participants are asked to bring in three or four items that represent their ideal environment. The items can be pictures or objects, it does not matter as long as the participants are able to explain why they chose the items and how they fit into their ideal environment. A few examples might be: A man brings in a good luck fishing lure that his father gave to him as a present, or an elementary teacher brings a manuscript of the book she has finally begun to write. Group discussion is then centered around these items. What qualitative research has uncovered about the baby boomers can be described in these five specific themes:

1. Quality family life is a major concern. The ability to have a positive impact on the lives of their children is extremely important, as is a tight-knit family unit that is supportive of each other.
2. Long-term friendships help round out their identity outside of the workplace and home. Keeping in touch with friends is an integral element of the boomer lifestyle.
3. Taking the time to get away from the hassles of everyday life in the form of "getaway vacations" with family and friends helps to maintain firm understanding of what is important in life and recharge dying batteries.
4. Spiritual and physical fitness are important in leading a full, well-balanced life.
5. No such thing as a midlife crisis. Life is too short to dwell on successes or failures.

This type of research is invaluable in designing advertising and promotional campaigns. It provides the necessary foundation for appealing to those values that are most important to the boomers and to those values that are most likely to stimulate their buying behavior.[1] ■

EXAMPLE

Feelings, Nothing More Than Feelings

Qualitative research in the form of focus groups and individual depth interviews is used to discover what sensory feelings are important to customers. Such feelings cannot be uncovered by quantitative research. Depth interviews are conducted one on one and allow extensive probing of each respondent. Thus, it is possible to uncover underlying feelings (as well as values, beliefs, and attitudes). Several examples show how identifying consumers' sensory feelings is crucial in designing products.

- Ford: Ford decided to redesign one of its Taurus models. They remodeled the dashboard buttons, the rear fenders, and other parts. They decided to change the door latches. However, there was a problem with the sound the door made when it closed. It sounded weird. The latch made two thumps, which gave the impression to the user that something was going wrong even if there was no problem at all. Although consumers might not be aware of this perception, they are very sensitive to sounds a car makes.

- Whirlpool: Whereas one might think that the perfect product would not make any noise, the case of Whirlpool denies it. Whirlpool launched a new refrigerator, a quieter one. However, customers called the company to complain about "the softer, water-gurgling sounds" of the model. People had the impression that the new refrigerator was the noisiest they had ever heard although it was objectively the quietest ever manufactured.
- IBM: IBM focused on a new button in the middle of the keyboard that was to replace the mouse. Because people spend hours working on a computer, comfort for the finger used to touch the button was crucial. It took IBM nine years to "create the perfect cushion for a finger."
- Estée Lauder: The cosmetic industry provides a lot of examples of qualitative research because cosmetic products are viewed intimately by women. For example, Estée Lauder changed the shape of its blue compact so it appeals more to the customer. The shape was redesigned by rounding the edges to make it softer and thus create a link with the round shape of a woman's body.[2] ■

These examples illustrate the rich insights into the underlying behavior of consumers that can be obtained by using qualitative procedures.

PRIMARY DATA: QUALITATIVE VERSUS QUANTITATIVE RESEARCH

As was explained in chapter 4, primary data are originated by the researcher for the specific purpose of addressing the problem at hand. Primary data may be qualitative or quantitative in nature, as shown in Figure 5.1. The distinction between qualitative and quantitative research closely parallels the distinction between exploratory and conclusive research discussed in chapter 3. The differences between the two research methodologies are summarized in Table 5.1.[3] **Qualitative research** provides insights and understanding

Qualitative Research An unstructured, exploratory research methodology based on small samples that provides insights and understanding of the problem setting.

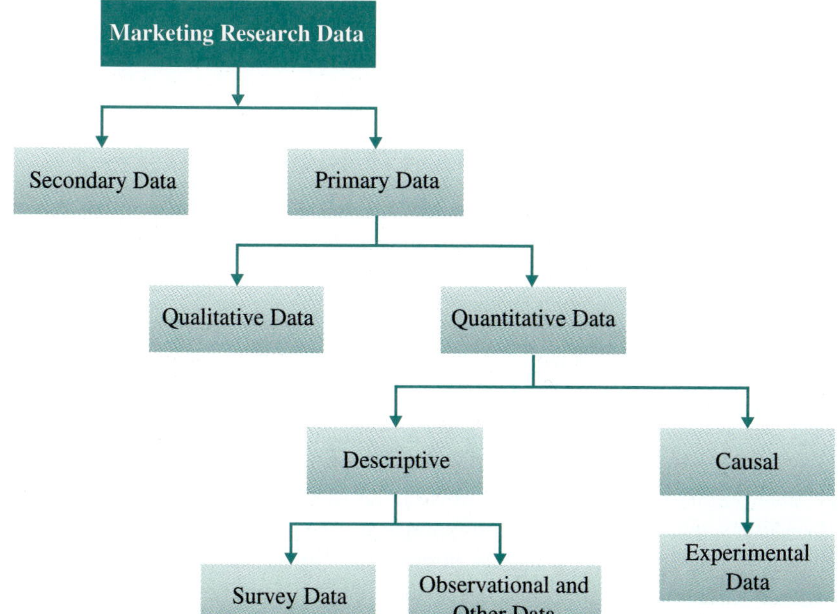

Figure 5.1
A Classification of Marketing Research Data

TABLE 5.1

QUALITATIVE VERSUS QUANTITATIVE RESEARCH

	Qualitative Research	*Quantitative Research*
Objective	To gain a qualitative understanding of the underlying reasons and motivations	To quantify the data and generalize the results from the sample to the population of interest
Sample	Small number of non-representative cases	Large number of representative cases
Data collection	Unstructured	Structured
Data analysis	Nonstatistical	Statistical
Outcome	Develop an initial understanding	Recommend a final course of action

Reprinted with permission from *Marketing News*, published by the American Marketing Association, Tom Murphy, 31 (7) (March 31, 1997): 18.

Quantitative Research
A research methodology that seeks to quantify the data and, typically, applies some form of statistical analysis.

of the problem setting, whereas **quantitative research** seeks to quantify the data and, typically, applies some form of statistical analysis. Whenever a new marketing research problem is being addressed, quantitative research must be preceded by appropriate qualitative research. Sometimes qualitative research is undertaken to explain the findings obtained from quantitative research. However, the findings of qualitative research are misused when they are regarded as conclusive and are used to make generalizations to the population of interest.[4] It is a sound principle of marketing research to view qualitative and quantitative research as complementary, rather than in competition with each other.[5]

The story goes that Alfred Politz, a strong proponent of quantitative research, and Ernest Dichter, a strong proponent of qualitative research, were having their usual debate about the merits of the two methods. Politz stressed the importance of large-scale, projectable samples. Dichter answered, "But, Alfred, 10 thousand times nothing is still nothing!" As Dichter argued, mere quantification, when the underlying behavior of interest is not well understood, will not lead to meaningful results.[6]

RATIONALE FOR USING QUALITATIVE RESEARCH

There are several reasons to use qualitative research. It is not always possible, or desirable, to use fully structured or formal methods to obtain information from respondents (see chapter 3). People may be unwilling or unable to answer certain questions. People are unwilling to give truthful answers to questions that invade their privacy, embarrass them, or have a negative impact on their ego or status. Examples of such sensitive questions include: "Have you recently purchased sanitary napkins? Drugs for nervous tension? Pills for anxiety?" Second, people may be unable to provide accurate answers to questions that tap their subconscious. The values, emotional drives, and motivations residing at the subconscious level are disguised from the outer world by rationalization and other ego defenses. For example, a person may have purchased an expensive sports car to overcome feelings of inferiority. However, if asked, "Why did you purchase this sports car?" he may say, "I got a great deal," "My old car was falling apart," or "I need to impress my customers and clients." In such cases, the desired information can be best obtained through qualitative research by using one or more of the procedures described in the following section.[7]

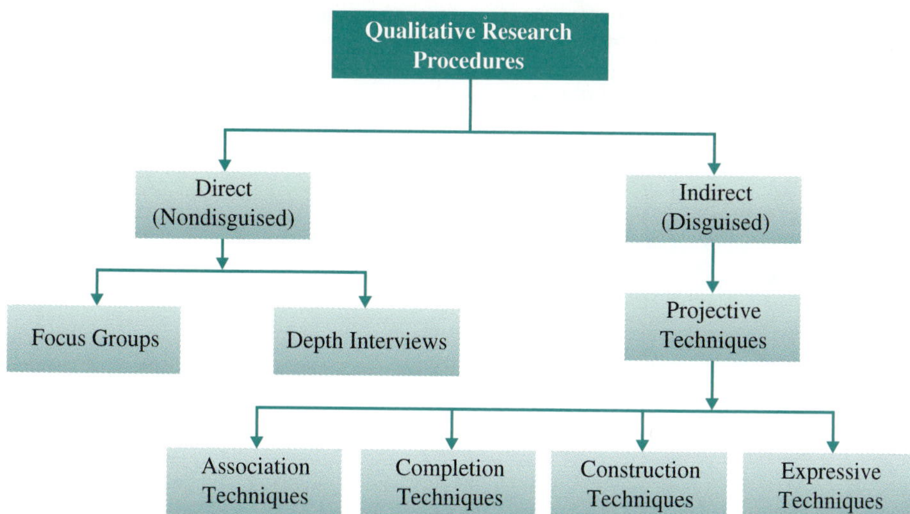

Figure 5.2
A Classification of Qualitative Research Procedures

A CLASSIFICATION OF QUALITATIVE RESEARCH PROCEDURES

A classification of qualitative research procedures is presented in Figure 5.2. These procedures are classified as either direct or indirect, based on whether the true purpose of the project is known to the respondents. A **direct approach** is not disguised. The purpose of the project is disclosed to the respondents or is otherwise obvious to them from the questions asked. Focus groups and depth interviews are the major direct techniques. In contrast, research that takes an **indirect approach** disguises the true purpose of the project. Projective techniques, the commonly used indirect techniques, consist of association, completion, construction, and expressive techniques. Each of these techniques is discussed in detail, beginning with focus groups.

Direct Approach One type of qualitative research in which the purposes of the project are disclosed to the respondent or are obvious given the nature of the interview.

Indirect Approach A type of qualitative research in which the purposes of the project are disguised from the respondents.

FOCUS GROUP INTERVIEWS

A **focus group** is an interview conducted by a trained moderator in a nonstructured and natural manner with a small group of respondents. The moderator leads the discussion. The main purpose of focus groups is to gain insights by listening to a group of people from the appropriate target market talk about issues of interest to the researcher. The

Focus Group An interview conducted in an unstructured and natural manner by a trained moderator among a small group of respondents.

A typical focus group session.

RESEARCH IN PRACTICE 5.1

Samples Costs of a Focus Group

Item	*Cost*
Developing outline and screening participants	$ 250
Moderator's fee	500
Facility rental, recruiting	800
Food	100
Respondent incentives ($30 × 10 people)	300
Analysis and report	500
	$2,450
Extras:	
Videotaping	350
Travel costs for moderator and observers	1,200
TOTAL	$4,000

value of the technique lies in the unexpected findings often obtained from a free-flowing group discussion.

Focus groups are the most important qualitative research procedure. They are so popular that many marketing research practitioners consider this technique synonymous with qualitative research.[8] Several hundred facilities around the country now conduct focus groups several times a week, and, as shown in Research in Practice 5.1, the typical focus group costs the client about $4,000. This adds up to a lot of money—more than $390 million a year.[9] Given their importance and popularity, we describe the salient characteristics of focus groups in detail.

Characteristics

The major characteristics of a focus group are summarized in Table 5.2. A focus group generally includes 8 to 12 members. Groups of fewer than 8 are unlikely to generate the momentum and group dynamics necessary for a successful session. Likewise, groups of more than 12 may be too crowded and may not be conducive to a cohesive and natural discussion.[10]

A focus group should be homogeneous in terms of demographic and socioeconomic characteristics. Commonalty among group members avoids interactions and conflicts among group members on side issues.[11] Thus, a women's group should not combine married homemakers with small children, young unmarried working women, and elderly divorced or widowed women because their lifestyles are substantially different. Moreover, the participants should be carefully screened to meet certain criteria. The participants

TABLE 5.2

CHARACTERISTICS OF FOCUS GROUPS

Group size	8–12
Group composition	Homogeneous; respondents prescreened
Physical setting	Relaxed, informal atmosphere
Time duration	1–3 hours
Recording	Use of audiocassettes and videotapes
Moderator	Observational, interpersonal, and communication skills of the moderator

must have had adequate experience with the object or issue being discussed. People who have already participated in numerous focus groups should not be included. These so-called professional respondents are atypical, and their participation leads to serious validity problems.[12]

The physical setting for the focus group is also important. A relaxed, informal atmosphere encourages spontaneous comments. Light refreshments should be served before the session and made available throughout. Although a focus group may last from one to three hours, a duration of one and one-half to two hours is typical. This period of time is needed to establish rapport with the participants and explore, in depth, their beliefs, feelings, ideas, attitudes, and insights regarding the topics of concern. Focus group interviews are invariably recorded, often on videotape, for subsequent replay, transcription, and analysis. Videotaping has the advantage of recording facial expressions and body movements, but it can increase the costs significantly. Frequently, clients observe the session from an adjacent room using a one-way mirror. Video transmission technology enables the clients to observe focus group sessions live from a remote location. For example, Stamford, Connecticut–based Focus Vision Network, Inc., offers such a videoconferencing system.

The moderator plays a key role in the success of a focus group. The moderator must establish rapport with the participants, keep the discussion moving forward, and probe the respondents to elicit insights. In addition, the moderator may have a central role in the analysis and interpretation of the data. Therefore, the moderator should possess skill, experience, knowledge of the discussion topic, and an understanding of the nature of group dynamics. The key qualifications of the moderator are summarized in Research in Practice 5.2.[13]

Planning and Conducting Focus Groups

The procedure for planning and conducting focus groups is described in Figure 5.3. Planning begins with an examination of the objectives of the marketing research project. In most instances, the problem has been defined by this stage, and if so, the general statement as well as the specific components of the problem should be carefully studied. Given the problem definition, the objectives of the qualitative research should be clearly specified, as illustrated by the department store patronage project.

RESEARCH IN PRACTICE 5.2

Key Qualifications of Focus Group Moderators

1. *Kindness with firmness.* The moderator must combine a disciplined detachment with empathy in order to generate the necessary interaction.
2. *Permissiveness.* The moderator must be permissive yet alert to signs that the group's cordiality or purpose is disintegrating.
3. *Involvement.* The moderator must encourage and stimulate intense personal involvement.
4. *Incomplete understanding.* The moderator must encourage respondents to be more specific about generalized comments by exhibiting incomplete understanding.
5. *Encouragement.* The moderator must encourage unresponsive members to participate.
6. *Flexibility.* The moderator must be able to improvise and alter the planned outline amid the distractions of the group process.
7. *Sensitivity.* The moderator must be sensitive enough to guide the group discussion at an intellectual as well as emotional level.

DEPARTMENT STORE PATRONAGE PROJECT

Qualitative Research Objectives

In the department store study, the objectives of qualitative research were as follows:

1. Identify the relevant factors (choice criteria) used by households in selecting department stores.
2. Identify what consumers consider to be competing stores for specific product categories.
3. Identify the psychological characteristics of consumers that are likely to influence store patronage behavior.
4. Identify any other aspects of consumer choice behavior that may be relevant to store patronage.

Note that these objectives are closely tied to the components of the department store problem defined in chapter 2. The objectives must be specified before conducting any qualitative research, whether focus groups, depth interviews, or projective techniques.

The next step is to develop a detailed list of objectives for the focus group. This may take the form of a list of questions the researcher would like answered. Then a questionnaire to screen potential participants is prepared. Typical information obtained from the

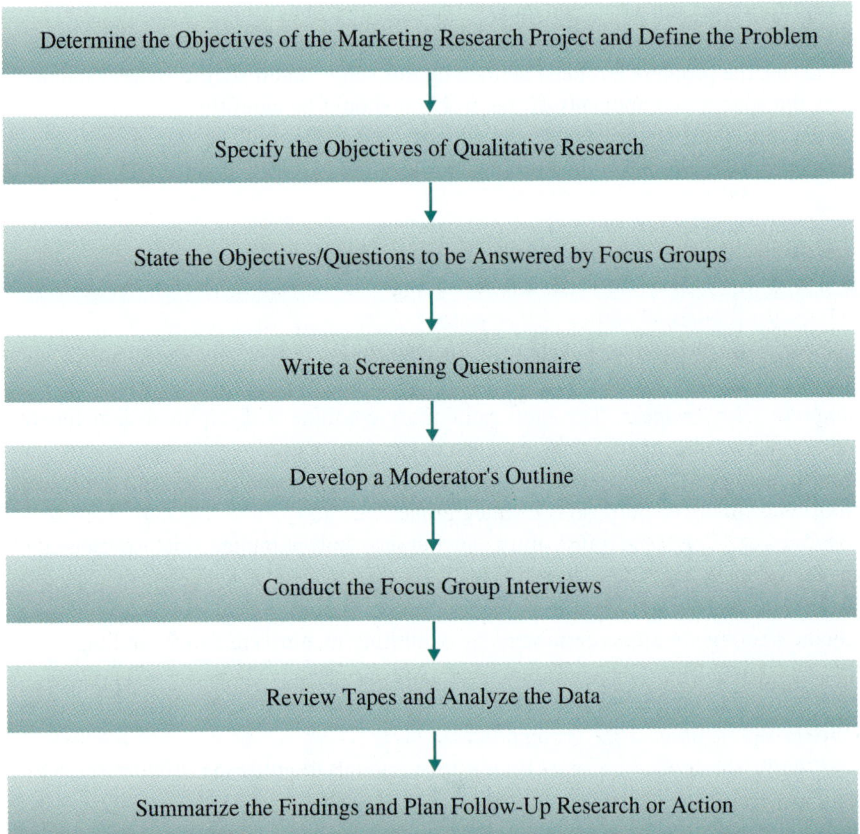

Figure 5.3
Procedure for Planning and Conducting Focus Groups

The moderator must encourage and stimulate intense personal involvement of the focus group members.

questionnaire includes product familiarity and knowledge, usage behavior, attitudes toward and previous participation in focus groups, and standard demographic characteristics.

A detailed moderator's outline for use during the focus group interview should be constructed. This involves extensive discussions among the researcher, client, and moderator. Because the moderator must be able to pursue important ideas when they are mentioned by participants, the moderator must understand the client's business, focus group objectives, and how the findings will be used. Use of a moderator's outline reduces some of the reliability problems inherent in focus groups, such as those caused by different moderators not covering the same content areas in comparable ways. Given its importance, we illustrate how a moderator's outline should be constructed using the department store example and the procedure developed by Arbor, Inc.[14]

As can be seen, theory (chapter 2) played an important role in developing the moderator's outline in the department store project. After a detailed outline is formulated, participants are recruited and the focus group interview conducted. During the interview, the moderator must (1) establish rapport with the group; (2) state the rules of group interaction; (3) set objectives; (4) probe the respondents and provoke intense discussion in the relevant areas; and (5) attempt to summarize the group's response to determine the extent of agreement.

Following the group discussion, either the moderator or an analyst reviews and analyzes the results. The analyst not only reports specific comments and findings but also looks for consistent responses, new ideas, concerns suggested by facial expressions and body language, and other hypotheses that may or may not have received confirmation from all of the participants.

Because the number of participants is small, frequencies and percentages are not usually reported in a focus group summary. Instead, reports typically include expressions such as "most participants thought" or "participants were divided on this issue." Meticulous documentation and interpretation of the session lays the groundwork for the final step: taking action. This usually means doing additional research.

The number of focus groups that should be conducted on a single subject depends on (1) the nature of the issue, (2) the number of distinct market segments, (3) the number of new ideas generated by each successive group, and (4) time and cost. Resources permitting, one should conduct additional discussion groups until the moderator can anticipate what will be said. This usually happens after three or four groups are conducted on the same topic.[15] It is recommended that at least two groups be conducted.[16] Properly conducted focus groups can generate important hypotheses that can serve as a basis for conducting quantitative research as the following example indicates.

DEPARTMENT STORE PATRONAGE PROJECT

The Moderator's Outline

Eighteen information requirements derived from attitude theory serve as the basis for developing the focus group moderator's guide. This example lists one of the several specific questions to be used for each information requirement.

1. Definition of significant classes of the attitude object. "What kinds of department stores are there?"
2. Brand awareness. "Which department stores are you familiar with?"
3. Evaluation of attitude objects. "Which department store is best, worst, and why?"
4. Situational contexts/relevant others. "How, when, and where do you shop for general merchandise?"
5. Weights of situational contexts/relevant others. "When shopping in department stores for a gift, what is important?"
6. Evaluation of each attitude object in each situational context/relevant others. "Which department stores do you prefer when shopping for a gift, and why?"
7. Attributes of the attitude object for each situational context. "When you think about shopping, what features of the department store come to mind?"
8. Associations among attributes. "If a department store has liberal return policies, will it be more or less likely to offer high quality products?"
9. Dimensions, level, and range of attributes. "When you say you want a high-quality product, what do you mean by 'high-quality'?"
10. Threshold of satisfaction. "What would be the features of a department store you consider satisfactory for shopping?"
11. Beliefs and opinions of brands on attributes, dimensions, and threshold of satisfaction. "Are discount department stores good enough for you to consider patronizing?"
12. Latitude of acceptance of beliefs and opinions. "Would you believe me if I said that the quality of the salespeople ultimately determines the image of a department store?"
13. Evaluation of attributes (salience). "For which of these things that you say you want in your department store would you be willing to pay more?"
14. Determination of values. "How would you characterize someone who is a good shopper?"
15. Hierarchy of values. "Would you rather be a good shopper or have more money to spend?"
16. Saliency of relationships between attributes and values. "You say you like a store that offers good value for money. What does that affect, your finances, your reputation as a shopper, or something else?"
17. Attribute salience and latitude of acceptance as related to values. "How much do you think convenience of shopping can really affect your lifestyle?"
18. Category importance as related to value system. "How much time in an average month do you spend in department stores?"

EXAMPLE

Focus Groups Make the Introduction of Plymouth Breeze "a Breeze"

Before the Plymouth Breeze was introduced in 1996, extensive focus groups were conducted among the target customers: young people between 20 and 40, especially women. This qualitative research helped the company better understand the psychographic profiles of individuals and their lifestyles, their activities, interests, and opinions. The research revealed that during this period of life people experience dramatic changes (graduation, career, wedding, family), and that their purchasing criteria change with those different stages of life. In particular, focus groups helped to generate several hypotheses including:

H1: As people's lifestyles and needs change, so does their preferences for cars.
H2: As people make more money, they are willing to pay a higher price for cars.
H3: People have negative perceptions of the sales pressure involved in the car buying process.

These hypotheses were verified by survey research and formed the basis for launching the Plymouth Breeze. Single and young families are the target customers of the new car. The Breeze complements perfectly the existing product range. It enables:

- a linear progression of vehicles that complements the lifestyles needs and changes as found in the focus groups. Neon, a subcompact car, is aimed at young people that have just graduated from school or started working. On the other hand, Voyager is a family car. Research showed that 45 percent of subcompact car buyers purchased a compact car after, and compact car buyers eventually purchased minivans. As a result, Plymouth's product range was missing a compact car, and Breeze filled this gap.
- a linear progression of price that corresponds to the evolution in financial possibilities of the target customers.
- a consistent image that corresponds to the tastes of the target market.

To address the issue of sales pressure, Plymouth opened Plymouth Place, some 1,000 square-feet showrooms in regional shopping malls, where people can get information on Plymouth without sales pressure, because no sales can be done in those showrooms. The company also created a Plymouth Place Web to respond to the openness of customers to shop at home (also identified by focus groups). This new strategy is working. On the two test markets, Plymouth sales have increased by 16 percent and 36 percent.[17] ■

Other Variations in Focus Groups

Focus groups can use several variations of the standard procedure. These include:

Two-way focus group. This allows one target group to listen to and learn from a related group. In one application, physicians viewed a focus group of arthritis patients discussing the treatment they desired. A focus group of these physicians was then held to determine their reactions.
Dual-moderator group. This is a focus group interview conducted by two moderators. One moderator is responsible for the smooth flow of the session, and the other ensures that specific issues are discussed.
Dueling-moderator group. Here also there are two moderators, but they deliberately take opposite positions on the issues to be discussed. This allows the researcher to explore both sides of controversial issues.
Respondent-moderator group. In this type of focus group, the moderator asks selected participants to play the role of moderator temporarily to improve group dynamics.
Client-participant groups. Client personnel are identified and made part of the discussion group. Their primary role is to offer clarifications that will make the group process more effective.
Mini groups. These groups consist of a moderator and only four or five respondents. They are used when the issues of interest require more extensive probing than is possible in the standard group of 8 to 12.
Telesession groups. Focus group sessions by phone using the conference call technique.[18]

Telesession Groups A focus group technique using a telecommunications network.

On-line focus groups are emerging as an important form of focus groups and are discussed in detail in the section on the Internet and computer applications. We conclude our section on focus groups with a discussion of the advantages and disadvantages.

Advantages and Disadvantages of Focus Groups

Focus groups offer several advantages over other data collection techniques. These may be summarized by the 10 Ss:[19]

1. *Synergism.* Putting a group of people together will produce a wider range of information, insight, and ideas than will individual responses secured privately.
2. *Snowballing.* A bandwagon effect often operates in a group interview, in that one person's comment triggers a chain reaction from the other participants.
3. *Stimulation.* Usually after a brief introductory period, the respondents want to express their ideas and expose their feelings as the general level of excitement over the topic increases in the group.
4. *Security.* Because the participants' feelings are similar to those of other group members, they feel comfortable and are therefore willing to express their ideas and feelings.
5. *Spontaneity.* Since participants are not required to answer specific questions, their responses can be spontaneous and unconventional and should therefore provide an accurate idea of their views.
6. *Serendipity.* Ideas are more likely to arise out of the blue in a group than in an individual interview.
7. *Specialization.* Because a number of participants are involved simultaneously, use of a highly trained, but expensive, interviewer is justified.
8. *Scientific scrutiny.* The group interview allows close scrutiny of the data collection process, in that observers can witness the session and it can be recorded for later analysis.
9. *Structure.* The group interview allows for flexibility in the topics covered and the depth with which they are treated.
10. *Speed.* Because a number of individuals are being interviewed at the same time, data collection and analysis proceed relatively quickly.

The disadvantages of focus groups may be summarized by the five Ms:

1. *Misuse.* Focus groups can be misused and abused by considering the results as conclusive rather than exploratory.
2. *Misjudge.* Focus group results can be more easily misjudged than the results of other data collection techniques. Focus groups are particularly susceptible to client and researcher biases.
3. *Moderation.* Focus groups are difficult to moderate. Moderators with all the desirable skills (see Research in Practice 5.2) are rare. The quality of the results depends heavily on the skills of the moderator.
4. *Messy.* The unstructured nature of the responses makes coding, analysis, and interpretation difficult. Focus group data tend to be messy.
5. *Misrepresentation.* Focus group results are not representative of the general population and are not projectable. Consequently, focus group results should not be the sole basis for decision making as the following example illustrates.

EXAMPLE

Projecting the Unprojectable Projects Loss

A sophisticated insurance direct marketer conducted focus groups. The results were translated into clear-cut mail order marketing strategies. However, every single conclusion that grew out of the research flopped. What happened? The insurance company made the mistake of trying to project the unprojectable.[20] ■

This example illustrates a misuse and misrepresentation of focus groups. However, when properly conducted and used, focus groups have numerous applications.

Applications of Focus Groups

Focus groups are being used extensively for profit, nonprofit, and all types of organizations.[21] They can be used in almost any situation requiring some preliminary understanding and insights, as illustrated in Research in Practice 5.3.[22] We will discuss some substantive and methodological applications that represent the wide range of use of this technique. Focus groups can be used to address substantive issues such as:

1. Understanding consumers' perceptions, preferences, and behavior concerning a product category.
2. Obtaining impressions of new product concepts.
3. Generating new ideas about older products.
4. Developing creative concepts and copy material for advertisements.
5. Securing price impressions.
6. Obtaining preliminary consumer reaction to specific marketing programs.

The methodological applications of focus groups include:

1. Defining a problem more precisely.
2. Generating alternative courses of action.
3. Developing an approach to a problem.
4. Obtaining information helpful in structuring consumer questionnaires.
5. Generating hypotheses that can be tested quantitatively.
6. Interpreting previously obtained quantitative results.

DEPTH INTERVIEWS

Depth interviews are another method of obtaining qualitative data. Here we describe the general procedure for conducting depth interviews and then illustrate some specific techniques. The advantages, disadvantages, and applications of depth interviews are also discussed.

Depth Interview An unstructured, direct, personal interview in which a single respondent is probed by a highly skilled interviewer to uncover underlying motivations, beliefs, attitudes, and feelings on a topic.

RESEARCH IN PRACTICE 5.3

The Regal Use of Focus Groups at GM

The Buick division of General Motors used focus groups and survey research to help develop the Regal two-door, six-passenger coupe. Five years before the introduction, Buick held 20 focus groups across the country to determine what features customers wanted in a car. These focus groups told GM that customers wanted a real back seat, at least 20 miles per gallon, and 0 to 60 miles per hour acceleration in 11 seconds or less. They wanted a stylish car, but they didn't want it to look like it had landed from outer space.

Based on the focus group results, which were confirmed in subsequent research, the Buick engineers created clay models of the car and mock-ups of the interior. The company then went back to another set of focus groups of target buyers. These respondents didn't like the oversized bumpers and the severe slope of the hood, but liked the four-wheel disk brakes and independent suspension.

Focus groups also helped refine the advertising campaign for the Regal. Participants were asked which competing cars most resembled the Buick in image and features. The answer was Oldsmobile, a sister GM division. In an effort to differentiate the two, Buick was repositioned above Oldsmobile by focusing on speed, comfort, and luxury features. The tag line for the 1998 Regal, "Official Car of the Supercharged Family," was based on focus group findings. This repositioning has greatly aided the sales of Buick Regal.

Characteristics

Like focus groups, depth interviews are an unstructured and direct way of obtaining information; unlike focus groups, depth interviews are conducted one on one. A depth interview is an unstructured, direct, personal interview in which a single respondent is probed by a highly skilled interviewer to uncover underlying motivations, beliefs, attitudes, and feelings on a topic.[23]

A depth interview may take from 30 minutes to more than one hour. To illustrate the technique in the context of the department store example, the interviewer begins by asking a general question such as, "How do you feel about shopping at department stores?" The interviewer then encourages the subject to talk freely about his or her attitudes toward department stores. After asking the initial question, the interviewer uses an unstructured format. The subsequent direction of the interview is determined by the respondent's initial reply, the interviewer's probes for elaboration, and the respondent's answers. Suppose the respondent replies to the initial question by saying, "Shopping isn't fun anymore." The interviewer might then pose a question such as "Why isn't it fun anymore?" If the answer is not very revealing ("Fun has just disappeared from shopping"), the interviewer may ask a probing question, such as "Why was it fun before and what has changed?"

Although the interviewer attempts to follow a rough outline, the specific wording of the questions and the order in which they are asked is influenced by the subject's replies. Probing is of critical importance in obtaining meaningful responses and uncovering hidden issues. Probing is done by asking questions such as "Why do you say that?" "That's interesting, can you tell me more?" or "Would you like to add anything else?"[24] Probing is further discussed in chapter 13 on field work. The value of information uncovered by probing is shown in the following example.

EXAMPLE

Probing for Intelligence

Qualitative research techniques such as depth interviews have played a major role in the design of credit card features.

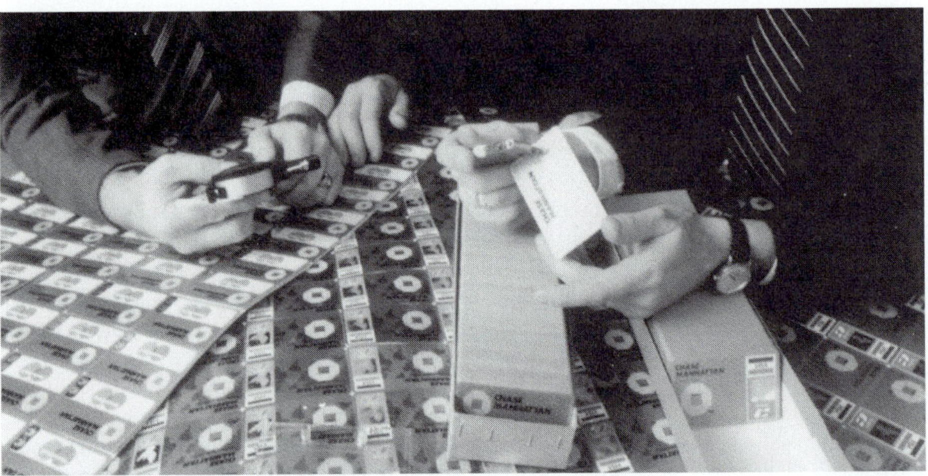

In a study designed to come up with new credit card features, respondents merely listed features of existing credit cards when questioned in a structured way. Then depth interviews were employed to probe the respondents. For example, the interviewer asked respondents to ask themselves, "What is important to me? What problems do I have? How do I wish I could live? What is my ideal world?" As a result of this method, consumers relayed information they had previously been unaware of, and several new credit card features surfaced. For instance, the study uncovered the need for an "intelligent" credit card that could perform tasks such as keeping track of credit card and bank balances, investments, and emergency telephone numbers.[25] ■

As this example indicates, probing effectively uncovers hidden information. Probing is an integral part of depth interviews and is used in all the depth interviewing techniques.

Techniques

Three depth-interviewing techniques that have recently gained popularity are laddering, hidden issue questioning, and symbolic analysis. In **laddering**, the line of questioning proceeds from product characteristics to user characteristics. This technique allows the researcher to discover the different meanings assigned by one consumer to an object or issue. In **hidden issue questioning**, the focus is not on socially shared values but rather on personal "sore spots"; not on general lifestyles but on deeply felt personal concerns. **Symbolic analysis** attempts to analyze the symbolic meaning of objects by comparing them with their opposites. To learn what something is, the researcher attempts to learn what it is not. The logical opposites of a product investigated are nonusage of the product, attributes of an imaginary "nonproduct," and opposite types of products. The three techniques are illustrated with the following example.

Laddering A technique for conducting depth interviews in which a line of questioning proceeds from product characteristics to user characteristics.

Hidden Issue Questioning A type of depth interview that attempts to locate personal sore spots related to deeply felt personal concerns.

Symbolic Analysis A technique for conducting depth interviews in which the symbolic meaning of objects is analyzed by comparing them with their opposites.

EXAMPLE

Hidden Issues and Hidden Dimensions in Air Travel

In this study the researcher was investigating attitudes toward airlines among male middle managers.

LADDERING.
Each airline attribute, such as wide-body aircrafts, was probed to determine why it was important (I can get more work done), and then that reason was probed (I accomplish more), and so on (I feel good about myself). Laddering indicated that managers preferred advanced seat reservation, wide-body aircraft, and first-class cabin seating that resulted in greater physical comfort. This enabled them to get more work done while on the flight, leading to a sense of accomplishment and higher self-esteem. This technique showed that an advertising campaign, such as the old United Airlines campaign of "You're the Boss," that bolsters the self-esteem of the managers is worthy of consideration.

HIDDEN ISSUE QUESTIONING.
Respondents were questioned about fantasies, work lives, and social lives to identify hidden life issues. The answers indicated that glamorous, historical, elite, "masculine-camaraderie," competitive activities—such as Grand Prix car racing, fencing, and World War II airplane dog fighting—were of personal interest to the managers. These interests could be tapped with an advertising campaign such as the one by Lufthansa German Airlines featuring a World War I–type "Red Baron" spokesperson. That campaign communicated the aggressiveness, high status, and competitive heritage of the airline.

SYMBOLIC ANALYSIS.
Questions asked included "What would it be like if you could no longer use airplanes?" Responses such as, "Without planes, I would have to rely on letters and long-distance calls" were received. This suggests that what airlines sell to the managers is face-to-face communication. Thus, an effective ad might be one that guarantees that the airline will do the same thing for a manager as Federal Express does for a package.

Information revealed by these techniques can be used to effectively position an airline and to design appropriate advertising and communication strategies.[26] ■

The interviewer's role is critical to the success of the depth interview. The interviewer should (1) avoid appearing superior and put the respondent at ease; (2) be detached and objective, yet personable; (3) ask questions in an informative manner; (4) not accept brief "yes" or "no" answers; and (5) probe the respondent.

Advantages and Disadvantages of Depth Interviews

Depth interviews can uncover greater depth of insights than can focus groups. Also, depth interviews attribute the responses directly to the respondent, unlike focus groups, in which it is often difficult to determine which respondent made a particular response. Depth interviews result in free exchange of information that may not be possible in focus groups because there is no social pressure to conform to group response.

Depth interviews suffer from many of the disadvantages of focus groups and often to a greater extent. Skilled interviewers capable of conducting depth interviews are expensive and difficult to find. The lack of structure makes the results susceptible to the interviewer's influence, and the quality and completeness of the results depend heavily on the interviewer's skills. The data obtained are difficult to analyze and interpret, and the services of skilled psychologists are typically required for this purpose. The length of the interview combined with high costs means that the number of depth interviews in a project will be small. Despite these disadvantages, depth interviews do have some applications.

Applications of Depth Interviews

As with focus groups, the primary use of depth interviews is for exploratory research to gain insights and understanding. However, unlike focus groups, depth interviews are used infrequently in marketing research. Nevertheless, depth interviews can be effectively employed in special problem situations, such as those requiring the following:[27]

1. Detailed probing of the respondent (automobile purchase)
2. Discussion of confidential, sensitive, or embarrassing topics (personal finances, loose dentures)
3. Situations in which strong social norms exist and the respondent may be easily swayed by group response (attitude of college students toward sports)
4. Detailed understanding of complicated behavior (department store shopping)
5. Interviews with professional people (industrial marketing research)
6. Interviews with competitors, who are unlikely to reveal the information in a group setting (travel agents' perceptions of airline package travel programs)
7. Situations in which the product consumption experience is sensory in nature, affecting mood states and emotions (perfumes, bath soap)

The following example illustrates a case in which depth interviews were particularly helpful.

EXAMPLE

Soaps Look for a Fresh Way to Work Consumers into a Lather

In studies of bath soaps, respondents invariably say that a good soap makes them feel "clean and fresh" after a shower. However, they often have difficulty explaining what exactly that means. Copywriters trying to find a new way to talk about freshness in their advertising do not find such data helpful. Hence, the respondents were probed via depth interviews about all the things "clean and fresh" meant to them: the times they felt this way, their mental pictures, the moods and feelings connected with it, what music and colors come to mind, and even what fantasies it evoked.

Escape from ordinary life was one of the main themes that emerged from the depth interviews—getting away from the cramped, rushed city to being free, relaxed, unhindered, and surrounded by nature in the country. The words and images sparked by this theme offered new ideas for creative advertising resulting in a successful campaign that was refreshingly different from the competition.[28] ■

This example illustrates the value of depth interviews in uncovering the hidden responses that underlie the clichés elicited in ordinary questioning.

PROJECTIVE TECHNIQUES

Both focus groups and depth interviews are direct approaches in which the true purpose of the research is disclosed to the respondents or is otherwise obvious to them. Projective techniques are different in that they attempt to disguise the purpose of the research. A **projective technique** is an unstructured, indirect form of questioning that encourages respondents to project their underlying motivations, beliefs, attitudes, or feelings regarding the issues of concern.[29] In projective techniques, respondents are asked to interpret the behavior of others rather than describe their own behavior. In interpreting the behavior of others, respondents indirectly project their own motivations, beliefs, attitudes, or feelings into the situation. Thus, the respondent's attitudes are uncovered by analyzing their responses to scenarios that are deliberately unstructured, vague, and ambiguous. The more ambiguous the situation, the more respondents project their emotions, needs, motives, attitudes, and values, as demonstrated by work in clinical psychology on which projective techniques are based.[30] As in psychology, these techniques are classified as association, completion, construction, and expressive. Each of these classifications is discussed.[31]

Projective Technique An unstructured and indirect form of questioning that encourages the respondents to project their underlying motivations, beliefs, attitudes, or feelings regarding the issues of concern.

Association Techniques

In **association techniques**, an individual is presented with a stimulus and asked to respond with the first thing that comes to mind. **Word association** is the best known of these techniques. In word association, respondents are presented with a list of words, one at a time, and asked to respond to each with the first word that comes to mind. The words of interest, called *test words*, are interspersed throughout the list, which also contains some neutral, or filler, words to disguise the purpose of the study. For example, in the department store study, some of the test words might be "location," "parking," "shopping," "quality," and "price." The subject's response to each word is recorded verbatim and responses are timed so that respondents who hesitate or reason out (defined as taking longer than three seconds to reply) can be identified. The interviewer, not the respondent, records the responses. This controls for the time required for the respondent to write the response.

Association Techniques A type of projective technique in which the respondent is presented with a stimulus and asked to respond with the first thing that comes to mind.

Word Association A projective technique in which respondents are presented with a list of words, one at a time. After each word, they are asked to give the first word that comes to mind.

The underlying assumption of this technique is that association allows respondents to reveal their inner feelings about the topic of interest. Responses are analyzed by calculating (1) the frequency with which any word is given as a response; (2) the amount of time that elapses before a response is given; and (3) the number of respondents who do not respond at all to a test word within a reasonable period of time. Those who do not respond at all are judged to have an emotional involvement so high that it blocks a response. It is often possible to classify the associations as favorable, unfavorable, or neutral. An individual's pattern of responses and the details of the response are used to determine the person's underlying attitudes or feelings on the topic of interest, as shown in the following example.

EXAMPLE

Dealing with Dirt

Word association was used to study women's attitudes toward detergents. Below is a list of stimulus words used and the responses of two women of similar age and household status. The set of responses are quite different, suggesting that the women differ in personality and in their attitudes toward housekeeping. Mrs. M's associations suggest that she is resigned to dirt. She sees dirt as inevitable and does not want to do much about it. She does not do hard cleaning, nor does she get pleasure from her family. Mrs. C sees dirt too, but is energetic, factual-minded, and less emotional. She is actively ready to combat dirt and uses soap and water as her weapons.[32]

Procter & Gamble has positioned different detergent brands for different attitudinal segments, as revealed by word association.

Stimulus	*Mrs. M*	*Mrs. C*
washday	everyday	ironing
fresh	and sweet	clean
pure	air	soiled
scrub	does not; husband does	clean
filth	this neighborhood	dirt
bubbles	bath	soap and water
family	squabbles	children
towels	dirty	wash

These findings suggest that the market for detergents could be segmented on the basis of attitudes. Firms (such as Procter & Gamble) that market several different brands of detergents (Tide, Cheer, Gain, Bold, etc.) could benefit from positioning different brands for different attitudinal segments. ■

There are several variations to the standard word association procedure illustrated here. Respondents might be asked to give the first two, three, or four words that come to mind rather than just the first word. This technique can also be used in controlled tests, as contrasted with free association. In controlled tests, respondents might be asked "What department stores come to mind first when I mention high-quality merchandise?" More detailed information can be obtained from completion techniques, which are a natural extension of association techniques.

Completion Techniques

In **completion techniques**, the respondent is asked to complete an incomplete stimulus situation. Common completion techniques in marketing research are sentence completion and story completion.

Completion Technique A projective technique that requires the respondent to complete an incomplete stimulus situation.

Sentence Completion. **Sentence completion** is similar to word association. Respondents are given incomplete sentences and asked to complete them. Generally, they are asked to use the first word or phrase that comes to mind, as illustrated in the department store patronage project.

The example in the department store patronage project illustrates one advantage of sentence completion over word association: respondents can be provided with a more directed stimulus. Sentence completion can provide more information about the subjects' feelings than word association. However, sentence completion is not as disguised, and many respondents may be able to guess the purpose of the study. A variation of sentence completion is paragraph completion, in which the respondent completes a paragraph beginning with the stimulus phrase. An expanded version of sentence completion and paragraph completion is story completion.

Sentence Completion A projective technique in which respondents are presented with a number of incomplete sentences and asked to complete them.

Story Completion. In **story completion**, respondents are given part of a story—enough to direct attention to a particular topic but not to hint at the ending. They are required to give the conclusion in their own words, as in the example on page 164.

The respondent's completion of this story will reveal the relative value he or she places on the time spent selecting merchandise and the emotional investment he or she makes in the shopping.

Story Completion A projective technique in which the respondents are provided with part of a story and required to give the conclusion in their own words.

Construction Techniques

Construction techniques are closely related to completion techniques. Construction techniques require the respondent to construct a response in the form of a story, dialogue, or description. In a construction technique, the researcher provides less initial structure to the respondent than in a completion technique. The two main construction techniques are (1) picture response, and (2) cartoons.

Construction Technique A projective technique in which the respondent is required to construct a response in the form of a story, dialogue, or description.

DEPARTMENT STORE PATRONAGE PROJECT

Sentence Completion

In the context of the store patronage study, the following incomplete sentences may be used.

A person who shops at Sears is

____

A person who receives a gift certificate good for Sak's Fifth Avenue would be

____

J. C. Penney is most liked by

____

When I think of shopping in a department store, I

____

DEPARTMENT STORE PATRONAGE PROJECT

Role Playing

Respondents are asked to play the role of a manager handling consumer complaints. How the role players handle the complaints reveals their feelings and attitudes toward store managers. Respondents who treat complaining customers with respect and courtesy indicate that they, as customers, expect these attitudes from the store management.

Third-Person Technique
A projective technique in which the respondent is presented with a verbal or visual situation and asked to relate the beliefs and attitudes of a third person to the situation.

Third-Person Technique. In **third-person technique**, the respondent is presented with a verbal or visual situation and the respondent is asked to relate the beliefs and attitudes of a third person rather than directly expressing personal beliefs and attitudes. This third person might be a friend, a neighbor, a colleague, or a "typical" person. Again, the researcher assumes that the respondent will reveal personal beliefs and attitudes while describing the reactions of a third party. Asking the individual to respond in the third person reduces the social pressure to give an acceptable answer, as the following example shows.

EXAMPLE

What Will the Neighbors Say?

A study was performed for a commercial airline to understand why some people do not fly. When the respondents were asked "Are you afraid to fly?" very few people said yes. The major reasons given for not flying were cost, inconvenience, and delays caused by bad weather. However, it was suspected that the answers were heavily influenced by the need to give socially acceptable responses. Therefore, a follow-up study was done. In the second study, the respondents were asked "Do you think your neighbor is afraid to fly?" The answers indicated that most of the "neighbors" who traveled by some other means of transportation were afraid to fly.[35] ■

Note that asking the question in the first person ("Are you afraid to fly?") did not elicit the true response. Phrasing the same question in the third person ("Do you think your neighbor is afraid to fly?") lowered the respondent's defenses and resulted in truthful answers. In a popular version of the third-person technique, the researcher presents the respondent with a description of a shopping list and asks for a characterization of the purchaser.[36]

We conclude our discussion of projective techniques by describing their advantages, disadvantages, and applications.

Advantages and Disadvantages of Projective Techniques

Projective techniques have a major advantage over unstructured direct techniques (focus groups and depth interviews): They may elicit responses that subjects would be unwilling or unable to give if they knew the purpose of the study. At times, in direct questioning, the respondent may intentionally or unintentionally misunderstand, misinterpret, or mislead the researcher. In these cases, projective techniques can increase the validity of responses by disguising the purpose. This is particularly true when the issues to be addressed are personal, sensitive, or subject to strong social norms. Projective techniques are also helpful when underlying motivations, beliefs, and attitudes are operating at a subconscious level.[37]

Projective techniques suffer from many of the disadvantages of unstructured direct techniques, but to a greater extent. These techniques generally require personal interviews

TABLE 5.3

A COMPARISON OF FOCUS GROUPS, DEPTH INTERVIEWS, AND PROJECTIVE TECHNIQUES

Criteria	*Focus Groups*	*Depth Interviews*	*Projective Techniques*
Degree of structure	Relatively high	Relatively medium	Relatively low
Probing of individual respondents	Low	High	Medium
Moderator bias	Relatively medium	Relatively high	Low to high
Interpretation bias	Relatively low	Relatively medium	Relatively high
Uncovering subconscious information	Low	Medium to high	High
Discovering innovative information	High	Medium	Low
Obtaining sensitive information	Low	Medium	High
Involve unusual behavior/questioning	No	To a limited extent	Yes
Overall usefulness	Highly useful	Useful	Somewhat useful

with highly trained interviewers. Skilled interpreters are also required to analyze the responses. Hence, they tend to be expensive. Furthermore, there is a serious risk of interpretation bias. With the exception of word association, all techniques are open ended, making the analysis and interpretation difficult and subjective.

Some projective techniques, such as role playing, require respondents to engage in unusual behavior. In such cases the researcher may assume that respondents who agree to participate are themselves unusual in some way and therefore not representative of the population of interest. As a result, it is desirable to compare findings generated by projective techniques with the findings of the other techniques that permit a more representative sample. Table 5.3 gives a relative comparison of focus groups, depth interviews, and projective techniques.

Applications of Projective Techniques

Projective techniques are used less frequently than are unstructured direct methods (focus groups and depth interviews). A possible exception may be word association, which is used commonly to test brand names and occasionally to measure attitudes about particular products, brands, packages, or advertisements. As the examples have shown, projective techniques can be used in a variety of situations. The usefulness of these techniques is enhanced when the following guidelines are observed.

1. Projective techniques should be used when the required information cannot be accurately obtained by direct methods.
2. Projective techniques should be used for exploratory research to gain initial insights and understanding.
3. Given their complexity, projective techniques should not be used naively.

Given these guidelines, projective techniques, along with other qualitative techniques, can yield valuable information.

INTERNATIONAL MARKETING RESEARCH

Because the researcher is often not familiar with the foreign product market to be examined, qualitative research is crucial in international marketing research. In the initial stages of cross-national research, qualitative research can provide insights into the problem and help in developing an approach by generating relevant research questions and hypotheses, models, and characteristics that influence the research design. Thus, qualitative research may reveal the differences between the foreign and domestic markets. Focus groups can be used in many settings, particularly in industrialized countries. The moderator should not only be trained in focus group methodology but should also be familiar with the language, culture, and patterns of social interaction prevailing in that country. The focus group findings should be derived not only from the verbal contents but also from nonverbal cues such as voice intonations, inflections, expressions, and gestures.[38] The size of the focus group could also vary. For example, in Asia seven respondents produce the highest level of interaction among group members. In some countries, such as in the Middle or Far East, people are hesitant to discuss their feelings in a group setting. In other countries such as Japan, people think it is impolite to disagree publicly with others. In these cases, depth interviews should be used. Moreover, qualitative data that are generated should be interpreted in the context of the culture. The following example highlights the importance of cultural differences in qualitative research.

EXAMPLE

Bugs Bug British

Culture is a very important determinant of how qualitative research, such as focus groups, should be conducted. In focus group discussions in Britain, it is not easy to make a homemaker admit she has cockroaches. To do this, the moderator must reassure her that everyone else has the problem too. In France, just the opposite occurs: The respondents start to chatter away about cockroaches within seconds of sitting down. These cultural attitudes greatly influence which qualitative research techniques should be used, how they should be implemented, and how the data should be interpreted. [39] ■

The use of projective techniques in international marketing research should be carefully considered. Association techniques (word association), completion techniques (sentence completion, story completion), and expressive techniques (role playing, third-person technique) involve the use of verbal cues. Construction techniques (picture response and cartoon tests) employ nonverbal stimuli (pictures). Whether verbal or nonverbal stimuli are used, the equivalence of meaning across the cultures should be established. This can be a difficult task if the sociocultural environments in which the research is conducted vary greatly. Establishing the equivalence of pictures can be particularly problematic. Line drawings are subject to fewer problems of interpretation than are photographs. However, techniques employing verbal cues, such as word association, can be applied with greater ease, as illustrated in the following.

EXAMPLE

Whirlpool Whirls Qualitative Research Around the World

Whirlpool has become a giant in the appliance world, currently doing business in every corner of the world including the United States and Canada and expanding markets in Asia, Europe, and Latin America. Whirlpool produces products under 12 brand names in over 140 countries.

How does Whirlpool intend to prosper in these very diverse markets? Whirlpool has heavily invested in cross-cultural market research. Through the expertise of local staff members, qualitative research in the form of focus groups, depth interviews, and various forms of projective techniques is undertaken around the world. In refrigerator research in Europe, Whirlpool found that British consumers want strong construction, French consumers want fresh fruit and vegetables, and the Spanish want fresh meat. For ovens, the research revealed that Italians want child-proof features and the Spanish favor accurate timers. Overall, Germans were the only group concerned about environmental features. In Latin America gas ranges are favored because of high electricity prices. Whirlpool strives to understand cultural factors so that they can take advantage of growing markets. For example, Latin America's economy is expected to grow at over 5 percent annually in the next decade. Whirlpool is well educated on their different consumers from their global qualitative research and well equipped to compete in a global market.[40] ■

The usual limitations of qualitative techniques also apply in the international context, perhaps to a greater extent. It is often difficult to find trained moderators and interviewers overseas. The development of appropriate coding, analysis, and interpretation procedures poses additional difficulties.

ETHICS IN MARKETING RESEARCH

When conducting qualitative research, ethical issues related to the respondents and the general public are of primary concern. These issues include disguising the purpose of the research and the use of deceptive procedures, videotaping and recording the proceedings, comfort level of the respondents, and misusing the findings of qualitative research.[41]

All indirect procedures require disguising the purpose of the research, at least to some extent. Often, a cover story is used to camouflage the true purpose. This can not only violate the respondents' right to know but also result in psychological harm. For example, respondents may be upset if, after responding to a series of completion techniques, they discovered that the object of the study was the color of the can of a new orange drink, when they believed they had been recruited to participate in a study on nutrition. To minimize such negative effects, the respondents should be informed up front that the true purpose of the research is being disguised so as not to bias the responses. After completing the research tasks, debriefing sessions should be held in which the respondents are informed about the true purpose and given opportunities to make comments or ask questions. Deceptive procedures that violate respondents' right to privacy and informed consent should be avoided; for example, allowing clients to observe focus groups or in-depth interviews by introducing them as colleagues helping with the project.

Videotaping or recording the focus group or the depth interview without the prior knowledge or consent of the participants raises ethical concerns. Ethical guidelines suggest that respondents should be informed and their consent obtained prior to the start of the proceedings, preferably at the time of recruitment. Furthermore, at the end of the meeting, participants should be asked to sign a written statement conveying their explicit permission to use the recording. This statement should disclose the true purpose of the research and all people who will have access to the recording. Participants should be given an opportunity to refuse signing. The tapes should be edited to completely omit the identity and comments of the respondents who have refused.

Another concern that needs to be addressed is the comfort level of the respondents. During qualitative research, particularly in depth interviews, respondents should not be pushed beyond a point so as to make them uncomfortable. If a respondent does not wish to answer more questions on a particular topic, the interviewer should not aggressively probe further. A final issue relates to the general public and deals with the ethics of using qualitative research results for questionable purposes, as in the political campaigns profiled below.

EXAMPLE

Focus (Groups) on Mudslinging in Presidential Campaigns

The ethics of negative or "attack" ads has been under debate for some time. However, the focus has shifted from the ads themselves to the ethics of employing marketing research techniques to design the ad message. Nowhere, perhaps, is this phenomenon more prevalent than in political "mudslinging" campaigns. In particular, the 1988 George Bush campaign against Michael Dukakis has been cited. In designing negative ads about Dukakis, the Bush campaign leaders tested negative information about Dukakis in focus groups. The idea was to develop some insight into how the American public would react if this negative information were released in the form of advertisements. Negative issues that elicited very negative emotions from the focus groups were chosen to be incorporated into Bush's political advertising. The result? Painted ". . . as an ineffectual, weak, liberal, do-gooder lacking in common sense . . . ," Dukakis lost the election by a wide margin. Similar (mis)use of qualitative research was observed in the 1992 and 1996 presidential elections, which Bill Clinton won in part by negatively attacking the Republicans.[42] ■

INTERNET AND COMPUTER APPLICATIONS

The use of forums, newsgroups, and chat rooms to conduct exploratory research was discussed in chapter 3. Here we discuss the use of the Internet for conducting focus groups, depth interviews, and projective techniques.[43]

The Internet and Focus Group Interviews

On-line focus group participation is by invitation only. The respondents are prerecruited, generally from an on-line list of people who have expressed an interest in participating. A screening questionnaire is administered on-line to qualify the respondents. Those who qualify are invited to participate in a focus group. They receive a time, a URL, a room name, and a password via e-mail. Generally, four to six people participate in the on-line group. There are fewer people in an on-line focus group than in a face-to-face meeting because too many voices can confuse the discussion.

Before the focus group begins, participants receive information about the focus group that covers such things as how to express emotions when typing. Electronic emotion indicators are produced using keyboard characters and are standard in their use on the Internet. For example, :-) and :-(are examples of smiling and sad faces, respectively. The emotions are usually inserted in the text at the point in which the emotion is meant. Emotions can also be expressed by using a different font or color. There is a wide range of emotions to choose, such as: I'm frowning, I'm laughing to myself, I'm embarrassed, I'm mad now, I'm responding passionately now, etc. This is then followed by the response. The participants can also preview information about the focus group topic by visiting a Web site and reading information or downloading and viewing an actual TV ad on PCs. Then, just before the focus group begins, participants visit a Web site where they log on and get some last-minute instructions.

When it is time for the group, they move into a Web-based chat room. They go to the focus group location (URL) and click on the "Enter Focus Room" item. To enter, they must supply the room name, user name, and password that was e-mailed to them earlier. In the chat room, the moderator and the participants type to each other in real time. The general practice is for the moderators always to pose their questions in all capital letters and the respondents are asked to use upper- and lowercase. The respondents are also asked always to start their response with the question number, so the moderator can quickly tie the response to the proper question. This makes it fast and easy to transcribe a focus group session. The group interaction lasts for about an hour. A raw transcript is available as soon as the group is completed, and a formatted transcript is available within 48 hours. The whole process is much faster than is the traditional method.

Advantages

People from all over the country or even the world can participate, and the client can observe the group from the convenience of the home or office. Geographical constraints are removed and time constraints are eased. Unlike traditional focus groups, there is the unique opportunity to re-contact group participants at a later date, to either revisit issues, or introduce them to modifications in material presented in the original focus group. The Internet enables the researcher to reach segments that are usually hard to survey: doctors, lawyers, professional people; working mothers; and others who lead busy lives and are not interested in taking part in traditional focus groups.

Moderators may also be able to carry on side conversations with individual respondents, probing deeper into interesting areas. People are generally less inhibited in their responses and are more likely to fully express their thoughts on-line. A lot of on-line focus groups go well past their allotted time because so many responses are expressed. Finally, as there is no travel, videotaping, or facilities to arrange, the cost is much lower than traditional focus groups. Firms are able to keep costs between one-fifth and one-half the cost of traditional focus groups.

Disadvantages

Only people that have and know how to use a computer can be surveyed on-line. Because the name of an individual on the Internet is often private, actually verifying that a respondent is a member of a target group is difficult. This is illustrated in a cartoon in *The New Yorker*, in which two dogs are seated at a computer and one says to the other "On the Internet, nobody knows you are a dog"! To overcome this limitation, other traditional methods such as telephone calls are used for recruitment and verification of respondents.

Another factor that must be considered is the lack of general control over the respondents' environment and their potential exposure to distracting external stimuli. Because on-line focus groups could potentially have respondents scattered all over the world, the researchers and moderator(s) have no idea what else the respondents might be doing while participating in the group. Only audio and visual stimuli can be tested. Products can not be touched (e.g., clothing) or smelled (e.g., perfumes).

Uses

There are instances in which traditional focus groups will continue to be preferred. For instance, you really can't explore highly emotional issues or subject matters on-line. Because the reach for on-line focus groups is currently limited to people with Internet access, on-line focus groups are not appropriate for every research situation. However, they are very suitable for companies who use the Internet to sell products or services and want to either gain market share or gather intelligence. Another potential use for on-line focus groups or surveys are corporations who want to gather feedback on workplace issues such as downsizing, job changes, and diversity. Employees can be referred to a Web site where they can participate anonymously in discussions with management. Companies such as CyberDialogue (www.cyberdialogue.com) specialize in on-line focus groups, e-mail surveys, and Web surveys.

EXAMPLE

Consumer Response to HEAT.net Heats Up Due to On-Line Qualitative Research

Sega of America is the arm of Tokyo, Japan–based Sega Enterises Ltd., and is responsible for the development, marketing, and distribution of Sega video game systems and video games in the Americas. In 1996, Sega launched HEAT.net, an on-line gaming service that allows subscribers to play PC games against each other over the Internet. At that time, many competitors, including Microsoft and AOL, already had fully developed sites. Sega needed to determine how to add value to HEAT.net and convince gamers to play on their site instead of the competitors.

King, Brown & Partners (KB&P), Inc., one of the leading providers of strategic market research for the development of commercial Web sites, assisted Sega through a multiphased project using both on-line and in-person research methodologies. KB&P conducted on-line focus group interviews to identify key issues in consumers' minds. First, they prescreened Internet users to identify respondents who were predisposed to playing games on the

FOCUS ON Burke

The dominant use of qualitative research conducted by Burke worldwide is through focus groups. In using focus groups, two very practical issues have to be addressed. The first results from the question most clients ask: "How many groups should we do and where should they be?" The second is of prime importance to the researcher but almost never voiced by the client: "How can the client be a contributing participant to focus group–based research?"

Number and Location

For most groups the question of number and location is really one of definition of the populations of interest. Are there different market segments that should be explored in different groups? Shouldn't those who are likely "very knowledgeable" be separated from the "less knowledgeable" to avoid dominance? Should groups be conducted in different regions where the level of market development is different? These decisions can only be made with secondary research or internal data to help support a position. The only clear rule of thumb is that if Burke decides on a particular composition of groups by character or location, at least two focus groups are done for each composition. The reasoning behind this is that each of these groups has its own dynamic and a second, confirmatory group will help ensure that conclusions are not drawn prematurely from one group's composition and group dynamic.

One of the largest casual-dining restaurant chains in the United States wanted to determine what types of desserts are "irresistible" to customers. The company hoped to boost sales by fine-tuning its dessert menu.

Burke conducted a series of 10 focus groups split among four constituencies or segments:

1. People who usually order dessert when eating at a casual dining restaurant
2. The company's own customers who usually order dessert
3. The company's own customers who rarely order dessert
4. The company's servers

Participants discussed what types of desserts they like, how many desserts should be offered on a restaurant menu, and how desserts should be "presented" by servers to entice people to order one. In each group the Burke moderator read descriptions of more than 25 different desserts and showed photos of more than 50 desserts. The moderator asked participants to evaluate the overall appeal of each dessert. Burke used this exercise to identify irresistible desserts that appealed to a broad range of customers. The restaurant chain used this qualitative information to improve its dessert menu.

The Client as a Contributor to the Process

Burke takes great pains in properly training its clients in the evaluation of focus groups. When a group of managers sits behind a one-way glass observing a focus group, they have to be coached in what to do and what not to do. The first thing they are told to avoid is counting responses and thinking in terms of quantitative results. The issue is not how many people say something, but whether general agreement among the group seems apparent or if there are divergent opinions. Any "count" can be a function of a forceful person in the group, social compliance, or any number of other reasons. This issue is the variety of responses and their nature, not the counts.

Burke coaches client Observers to listen to all opinions and not just to those that supports a preconceived position. Every time a position is heard, immediate attention should be paid to both the physical reaction of others in the group and to any indication of contrary opinions. Too often a person hears a comment that supports a previously held position and immediately turns to others in the room to discuss how this comment is "so relevant" and then misses all of the continuing dialogue that offers differing opinions and positions.

If the researcher doesn't manage the observation process correctly, the observing managers will often walk away from the session having already drawn their own conclusions and not fully understanding what actually happened. The final report will typically be ignored under these circumstances. Moreover, Burke focuses on managing the total communication process, not just the groups.

Internet. Qualified respondents were re-contacted via e-mail and paid an incentive to participate. On-line depth interviews were conducted to uncover underlying attitudes and feelings about Web site games. From this qualitative research and multiphase follow-up research, Sega had detailed information on who the appropriate target market was for the site, the types of games they wanted to play, the value-added services they wanted to use, and their expectations for short- and long-term capabilities of the site.

Based on these research findings, Sega of America launched a new premium on-line channel in January 1997 for Sega Saturn Net Link that combines up-to-the minute, localized information on news, weather, sports, TV programming, entertainment, and many other consumer-interest topics all in one location, which adds a tremendous value to net users who play games on the Internet. Subsequently, Sega on-line gaming service generated thousands of new subscribers.[44] ■

In a similar manner, depth interviews can be conducted over the Internet, with the interviewer and the respondent at separate locations. Virtually all the projective techniques that we have discussed can be implemented over the Internet. Picture response techniques are being used effectively by various companies and market researchers; for instance, Coca-Cola can provide a picture and ask the respondents to write a story about it. The demographic data of the person coupled with the story can provide valuable insights into the psychographics and the consumption pattern of the respondent.

Microcomputers and mainframes can be used to select and screen respondents in qualitative research. A computerized system can maintain and manage respondent files, storing information on a large number of demographic and other characteristics for each respondent. Thus respondents who meet stated criteria can be easily and quickly identified, and recruiting forms, confirmation letters, and sign-in sheets can be automatically generated. A problem common to all qualitative research techniques is the coding and analysis of responses to open-ended questions. Microcomputers and mainframes are increasingly being utilized for this purpose. With artificial intelligence programs such as CATPAC from Terra Research and Computing of Royal Oak, Michigan, the difficulties of qualitative data analysis can be reduced dramatically.

SUMMARY

Qualitative and quantitative research should be viewed as complementary. Qualitative research methods may be direct or indirect. In direct methods respondents are able to discern the true purpose of the research, whereas indirect methods disguise the purpose of the research. The major direct methods are focus groups and depth interviews. Focus groups are conducted in a group setting, whereas depth interviews are done one on one. Focus group interviews are the most widely used qualitative research technique.

The indirect techniques are called projective techniques because they aim to project the respondent's motivations, beliefs, attitudes, and feelings onto ambiguous situations. The projective techniques may be classified as association (word association), completion (sentence completion, story completion), construction (picture response, cartoon tests), and expressive (role playing, third-person) techniques. Projective techniques are particularly useful when respondents are unwilling or unable to provide the required information by direct methods.

Qualitative research can reveal the salient differences between the domestic and foreign markets. Whether focus groups or depth interviews should be conducted and how the findings should be interpreted depends heavily on cultural factors. When conducting qualitative research, the researcher and the client must respect the respondents. This should include protecting the anonymity of respondents, honoring all statements and promises used to ensure participation, and conducting research in a way not to embarrass or harm the respondents. Focus groups, depth interviews, and projective techniques can also be conducted on-line. Microcomputers and mainframes can be used to select and screen respondents and to code and analyze qualitative data.

KEY TERMS AND CONCEPTS

qualitative research
quantitative research
direct approach
indirect approach
focus group
telesessions
depth interview
laddering
hidden issue questioning
symbolic analysis
projective technique
association techniques
word association
completion techniques
sentence completion
story completion
construction techniques
picture response techniques
cartoon tests
expressive techniques
role playing
third-person technique

ACRONYMS

The key characteristics of a focus group may be described by the acronym FOCUS GROUPS:

F ocused (on a particular topic)
O utline prepared for discussion
C haracteristics of the moderator
U nstructured
S ize: 8–12
G roup composition: homogeneous
R ecorded: audiocassettes and videotapes
O bservation: one-way mirror
U ndisguised
P hysical setting: relaxed
S everal sessions needed: 1–3 hours each

The main features of a depth interview may be summarized by the acronym DEPTH:

D epth of coverage
E ach respondent individually interviewed
P robe the respondent
T alented interviewer required
H idden motives may be uncovered

The main characteristics of projective techniques may be described by the acronym PROJECTIVE:

P roject underlying motivations, beliefs, attitudes
R elationship: association techniques
O vercome respondent's unwillingness or inability to answer
J udgment required in interpretation of responses
E xpressive techniques
C onstruction, completion techniques
T hematic: Themes are elicited
I ndirect
V ague situations are used as stimuli
E xploratory in nature

EXERCISES

Questions

1. What are the primary differences between qualitative and quantitative research techniques?
2. What is qualitative research and how is it conducted?
3. Differentiate between direct and indirect qualitative research. Give an example of each.
4. Why is the focus group the most popular qualitative research technique?
5. Why is the focus group moderator so important in obtaining quality results?
6. What are some key qualifications of focus group moderators?
7. Why should one safeguard against professional respondents?
8. Give two ways in which focus groups can be misused.
9. What is the difference between a "dual-moderator" and a "dueling-moderator" group?
10. What are telesession groups?
11. What is a depth interview? Under what circumstances is it preferable to focus groups?
12. What are the major advantages of depth interviews?

13. What are projective techniques? What are the four types of projective techniques?
14. Describe the word association technique. Give an example of a situation in which this technique is especially useful.
15. When should projective techniques be employed?
16. What ethical considerations are involved in conducting qualitative research?

Problems

1. Following the methods outlined in the text, develop a plan for conducting a focus group to determine consumers' attitudes toward, and preferences for, imported automobiles. Specify the objectives of the focus group, write a screening questionnaire, and develop a moderator's outline.
2. Suppose Baskin Robbins wants to know why some people do not eat ice cream regularly. Develop a cartoon test for this purpose.

INTERNET AND COMPUTER EXERCISES

1. The Coca-Cola Company has asked you to conduct Internet focus groups with heavy consumers of soft drinks. Explain how you would identify and recruit such respondents.
2. Could a depth interview be conducted via the Internet? What are the advantages and disadvantages of this procedure over conventional depth interviews?
3. Visit the Web site of Qualitative Research Consultants Association (www.qrca.org). Write a report about the current state-of-the-art in qualitative research.
4. *Tennis* magazine would like to recruit participants for online focus groups. How would you make use of a newsgroup (Usenet: rec.sport.tennis) to recruit participants?
5. Obtain the CATPAC program discussed in the text. Use it to analyze the data from a depth interview that you have conducted with a fellow student (as the respondent) to determine attitude toward sports.

Chapter 6

"The key to good descriptive research is knowing exactly what you want to measure and selecting a survey method in which every respondent is willing to cooperate and capable of giving you complete and accurate information efficiently."

Joe Ottaviani, senior vice president, general manager, Burke, Inc.

Descriptive Research Design: Survey and Observation

OBJECTIVES

After reading this chapter, the student should be able to

1. discuss and classify survey methods available to marketing researchers and describe the various telephone, personal, and mail interviewing methods
2. identify the criteria for evaluating survey methods, compare the different methods, and evaluate which is best suited for a particular research project
3. explain and classify the different observation methods used by marketing researchers and describe personal observation, mechanical observation, audit, content analysis, and trace analysis
4. identify the criteria for evaluating observation methods, compare the different methods, and evaluate which, if any, is suited for a particular research project
5. describe the relative advantages and disadvantages of observational methods and compare them to survey methods
6. discuss the considerations involved in implementing surveys and observation methods in an international setting
7. understand the ethical issues involved in conducting survey and observation research
8. discuss the use of the Internet and computers in surveys and observation methods

OVERVIEW

In previous chapters we have explained that once the marketing research problem has been defined (step 1 of the marketing research process) and an appropriate approach developed (step 2), the researcher is in a position to formulate the research design (step 3). As was discussed in chapter 3, the major types of research designs are exploratory and conclusive. Exploratory designs employ secondary data analysis (chapter 4) and qualitative research (chapter 5) as the major methodologies. Conclusive research designs may be classified as causal or descriptive. Causal designs will be explained in chapter 7.

In this chapter we focus on the major methods employed in descriptive research designs: survey and observation. As was explained in chapter 3, descriptive research has as its major objective the description of something—usually market characteristics or functions. Survey, or communication, methods may be classified by mode of administration as traditional telephone interviews, computer-assisted telephone interviews, personal in-home interviews, mall-intercept interviews, computer-assisted personal interviews, mail interviews, mail panels, e-mail surveys, and Internet (or Web) surveys. We describe each of these methods and present a comparative evaluation of all the survey methods. Next, we consider the major observational methods: personal observation, mechanical observation, audit, content analysis, and trace analysis. The relative advantages and disadvantages of observation over survey methods are discussed. The considerations involved in conducting survey and observation research when researching international markets are discussed. Several ethical issues that arise in survey research and observation methods are identified. The chapter concludes with a discussion of the use of microcomputers and mainframes in survey and observation research. To begin our discussion, here are some examples of these methods.

EXAMPLE

Exploring the Internet with Microsoft Explorer

When Netscape introduced its Navigator Internet browser, the Web as we now know it became a reality. Microsoft did not initially consider the Web in its efforts to become and stay the world's leading software manufacturer. Microsoft soon found itself lagging as users were flocking to use the new entity called the World Wide Web. To catch up, Microsoft began developing its own browser, but the early versions were clearly inferior to Netscape's Navigator. Microsoft began gaining ground as the quality of its Internet Explorer browser improved.

After introducing Internet Explorer 4.0, Microsoft used Roper Starch Worldwide (RSW) to conduct market research to determine market penetration. Roper Starch Worldwide began its research by using random telephone interviews. By using a longitudinal design, RSW screened the same households for Internet use over a two-week period. After this period, it was found that Explorer was used in 40 percent of browsing cases. The telephone survey also helped Microsoft to understand better the users' needs and preferences for software used to access the Web.

In addition to telephone surveys, Microsoft also posts surveys on its Web site. Internet users are recruited by posting notices at popular sites and inviting browsers to participate. These surveys provide further insights into the Web browsing behavior of users and their preferences for different features of software used to explore the Web. These insights have helped in continually improving the Internet Explorer and expanding its share of the browser market.[1] ■

EXAMPLE

Mall Intercept, Frankly Speaking

Carousel Snack Bars of Minnesota, Inc., is a restaurant chain. Its 325 food outlets—also known as Hot Dogs & More, The Great Hot Dog Experience, The Great Hamburger Experience, Carousel Pizza, and Frankly Speaking—are located in major shopping malls nationwide. The chain's customers are 35 percent mall employees, 50 percent middle-age shoppers, and 15 percent teens and senior citizens. Carousel conducts mall-intercept interviews regularly to test new-product introductions. Customers in shopping malls are questioned about their food preferences. The interviews help the restaurants find out what foods are appealing to customers and what new types of food they would like to see on the menu. These interviews also indicate how the consumers perceive the restaurants' service, responsiveness, cleanliness, menu variety, value, and price. This research effort has paid rich dividends and helped the company to launch several new products. The successful introduction of Carousel's International Sausages is but one example of the fruits of this research.[2] ■

EXAMPLE

Marketing Research: The Japanese Way

Japanese companies rely heavily on personal observation to obtain information. When Canon Cameras was losing market share to Minolta in the United States, Canon decided that its distributor, Bell & Howell, was not giving adequate support. However, Canon did not use data from a broad survey of consumers or retailers to make this decision. Instead, it sent three managers to the United States to look into the problem.

Canon's head of the team, Tatehiro Tsuruta, spent almost six weeks in America. On entering a camera store, he would pretend to be a customer. He would note how the cameras were displayed and how the clerks served customers. He observed that the dealers were not enthusiastic about Canon. He also observed that it would not be advantageous for Canon to use drugstores and other discount outlets. This led Canon to open its own sales subsidiary resulting in increased sales and market share.[3] ■

Telephone, Internet, and mall-intercept interviews, as well as other survey methods, are becoming increasingly popular. Observation methods are employed less frequently, but they too have important uses in marketing research.

SURVEY METHODS

Survey Method A structured questionnaire given to a sample of a population and designed to elicit specific information from respondents.

Structured Data Collection Use of a formal questionnaire that presents questions in a prearranged order.

Fixed-Alternative Questions Questions that require respondents to choose from a set of predetermined answers.

The **survey method** of obtaining information is based on the questioning of respondents. Respondents are asked a variety of questions regarding their behavior, intentions, attitudes, awareness, motivations, and demographic and lifestyle characteristics. These questions may be asked verbally, in writing, or via computer, and the responses may be obtained in any of these forms. Typically, the questioning is structured, meaning some standardization is imposed on the data collection process. In **structured data collection**, a formal questionnaire is prepared and the questions are asked in a prearranged order; thus the process is also direct. Whether research is classified as direct or indirect is based on whether the true purpose is known to the respondents. As explained in chapter 5, a direct approach is nondisguised, in that the purpose of the project is disclosed to the respondents or is otherwise obvious to them from the questions asked.

The structured direct survey, the most popular data collection method, involves administering a questionnaire. In a typical questionnaire, most questions are **fixed-alternative questions**, which require the respondent to select from a predetermined set of responses. Consider, for example, the following question designed to measure attitude toward department stores:

	Disagree				*Agree*
Shopping in department stores is fun.	1	2	3	4	5

The survey method has several advantages. First, the questionnaire is simple to administer. Second, the data obtained are reliable because the responses are limited to the alternatives stated. The use of fixed-response questions reduces the variability in the results that may be caused by differences in interviewers. Finally, coding, analysis, and interpretation of data are relatively simple.[4]

Disadvantages are that respondents may be unable or unwilling to provide the desired information. For example, consider questions about motivational factors. Respondents may not be consciously aware of their motives for choosing specific brands or shopping at specific department stores. Therefore, they may be unable to provide accurate answers to questions about their motives. Respondents may be unwilling to respond if the information requested is sensitive or personal. Also, structured questions and fixed-response alternatives may result in loss of validity for certain types of data such as beliefs and feelings. Finally, wording questions properly is not easy (see chapter 10 on questionnaire design). Yet, despite these disadvantages, the survey approach is by far the most common method of primary data collection in marketing research. Research in Practice 6.1 illustrates this method.[5]

Survey methods can be classified based on the mode used to administer the questionnaire. These classification schemes help distinguish among survey methods.

SURVEY METHODS CLASSIFIED BY MODE OF ADMINISTRATION

Survey questionnaires may be administered in four major modes: (1) telephone interviews, (2) personal interviews, (3) mail interviews, and (4) electronic (see Figure 6.1). Telephone interviews may be further classified as traditional telephone interviews or computer-assisted telephone interviews (CATI). Personal interviews may be conducted in-home, as mall-intercept interviews, or as computer-assisted personal interviews (CAPI). The third major method, mail interviews, take the form of ordinary mail surveys or surveys conducted using mail panels. Finally, electronic interviews can be conducted via e-mail or administered on the Internet. Of these methods, telephone interviews are the most popular, followed by personal interviews, and mail surveys. The use of electronic methods, especially Internet surveys, is growing at a fast pace. We now describe each of these methods.

Telephone Methods

Traditional Telephone Interviews. Traditional telephone interviews involve phoning a sample of respondents and asking them a series of questions. The interviewer uses a paper questionnaire and records the responses with a pencil. Low-priced WATS (wide-area telephone service) lines have made nationwide telephone interviewing from a central location practical. With the popularity of WATS lines, the use of local telephone interviewing has decreased in recent years.[6]

Computer-Assisted Telephone Interviewing. Computer-assisted telephone interviewing from a central location is now more popular than the traditional telephone method. Computer-assisted telephone interviewing (CATI) uses a computerized questionnaire administered to respondents

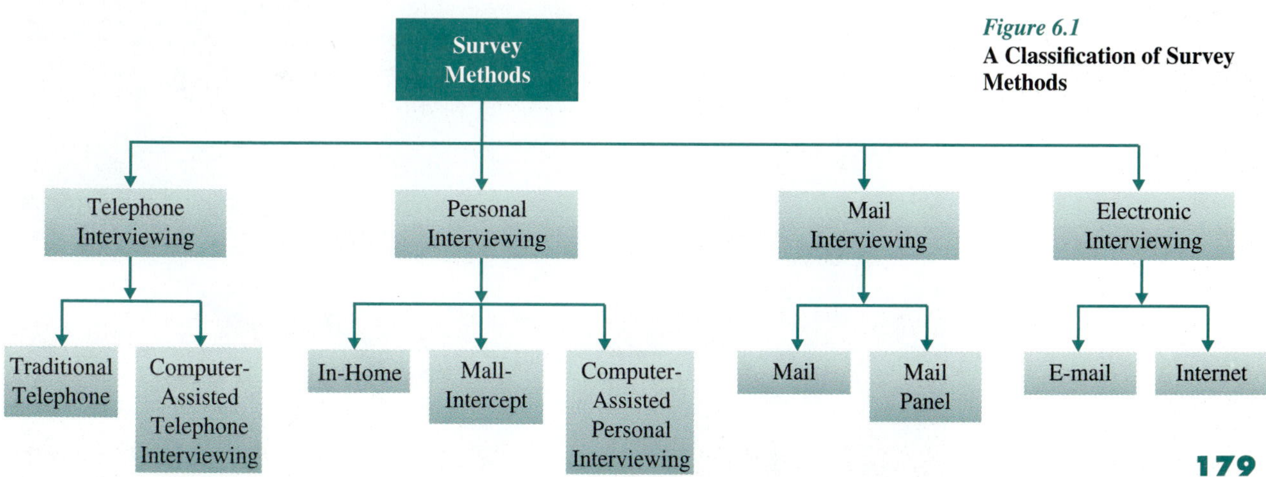

Figure 6.1
A Classification of Survey Methods

RESEARCH IN PRACTICE 6.1

Survey Research Is in the Cards for DEC

Digital Equipment Corporation (DEC) has made a conscious effort to shift from a product-driven focus to a more market- and consumer-driven focus. The product focus is not unusual in companies manufacturing high-tech products. There is a serious need for market research in these high-tech companies as they direct their products to the market. Still, market research in this arena is difficult. It is complicated by the rapid change of technology as well as the sheer size of the application market. Often the technology will be employed in many different industries. This holds true for the computer market in which DEC is a key player. Computers are bought by individuals in every walk of life as well as businesses in every market imaginable. The breadth of the market makes useful market research a formidable task.

However, this is the task being undertaken at DEC in their Corporate Marketing Services (CMS) Division. "Digital's Corporate Marketing Services Division has been a core element in the company's transition to a market-driven strategy." CMS is coordinating the company's strategy to redefine their product from simply "computers" to a broader view of "business solutions." CMS has employed many research techniques to gain a better understanding of the "business solutions" market. Both primary and secondary research data are used. Primary data are obtained through the use of phone and mail surveys as well as seminars and focus groups. Phone surveys have been used to define customer needs and to direct products to the customers more effectively. Mail surveys have been used to study customer purchasing habits as well as future purchasing plans. Seminars are held to gain feedback on the long-term production plans at DEC. Finally, focus groups are used to determine whether the chosen strategy is a good one and one that will effectively manage and make use of the market's potential.

Without CMS and marketing research, DEC would be facing the unknowns of their technology as well as the market. This combination of obstacles would have made the transition from a product focused to a market/consumer focused company an impossibility. This emphasis on survey research has continued even after the acquisition of DEC by Compaq Computer Corporation in 1998.

over the telephone. A computerized questionnaire may be generated using a mainframe computer, a minicomputer, or a personal computer. The interviewer sits in front of a cathode-ray tube (CRT) terminal and wears a mini-headset. The CRT replaces a paper-and-pencil questionnaire and the mini-headset substitutes for a telephone. On command, the computer dials the telephone number to be called. When contact is made, the interviewer reads questions posed on the CRT screen and records the respondent's answers directly into the computer.

In computer-assisted telephone interviewing, the computer systematically guides the interviewer.

The computer systematically guides the interviewer. Only one question at a time appears on the CRT screen. The computer checks the responses for appropriateness and consistency. It uses the responses as they are obtained to personalize the questionnaire. The data collection flows naturally and smoothly. Interviewing time is reduced, data quality is enhanced, and the laborious steps in the data collection process, coding questionnaires, and entering the data into the computer, are eliminated. Because the responses are entered directly into the computer, interim and update reports on data collection or results can be provided almost instantaneously. The following example shows how CATI helps ensure a representative sample.[7]

EXAMPLE

There's No Place Like Home

Marriott's Courtyard hotels are designed for and by business travelers (main customer base). When Courtyard wanted to understand its customers' needs and preferences, it hired the marketing research firm of D. K. Shifflet & Associates in September 1996. The research firm conducted a computer-assisted telephone survey with 300 business travelers who had taken at least six business-related trips in the previous year. The survey found that:

- 58 percent bring a laptop computer (70 percent of those people have games on their computer)
- 7 percent bring a teddy bear or another stuffed animal
- most business travelers bring photos of their families or pets (to feel connected to home)
- most business travelers check both their office voice mail and their home answering machines regularly (three times a day for more than 40 percent)
- they like to have time to relax

A more recent survey of 395 business travelers using CATI conducted by CLT Research Associates and Marriott Lodging International found that 62 percent of U.S. business travelers pack personal computers, 28 percent carry portable phones, and 24 percent bring pagers.

Armed with this information, Courtyard has made several changes in its marketing approach. The hotels now try to replicate the features of business travelers' homes and offices, with services such as voice mail, and fax and computer data ports. They also offer a Web site designed for business travelers looking for information on the hotels and promotions. In addition, Courtyard hotels provide quiet lounges to relax. The lounges usually are not playing music or blaring a television across the room; instead most are quiet enough to allow business travelers to read a book or hold a quiet conversation. By simply meeting the needs identified through telephone surveys, Courtyard has seen an increase in satisfied business travelers staying with this market leader.[8] ■

Personal Methods

Personal interviewing methods may be categorized as in-home, mall-intercept, or computer assisted.

Personal In-Home Interviews. In personal in-home interviews, respondents are interviewed in person in their homes. The interviewer's task is to contact the respondents, ask the questions, and record the responses. In recent years, personal in-home interviews have declined due to high cost. Nevertheless, they are still used, particularly by syndicated firms, such as the Roper Organization (see chapter 4).[9]

EXAMPLE

Limobus: A Limo or a Bus Ride into American Homes

The Roper Organization's omnibus panel, Limobus, conducts personal in-home interviews with 2,000 adult Americans every month and makes the results available four weeks after the survey. The sample size and composition of the panel for a specific project are tailored to the client's needs: All or some of the panel members may be asked questions of interest to a specific client. Limobus can be used for checking advertising and brand awareness, conducting pre- and postcampaign measurements, checking ad impact, recall, and communication, assessing brand penetration, testing new or altered packaging, evaluating new product performance, and other marketing research problems.[10] ■

While personal in-home interviews are declining, mall-intercepts are on the rise.

Mall-Intercept Personal Interviews. In mall-intercept personal interviews, mall shoppers are intercepted and brought to test facilities in the malls. The interviewer then administers a questionnaire as in the in-home personal survey. The advantage of mall-intercept interviews is that it is more efficient for the respondent to come to the interviewer than for the interviewer to go to the respondent.[11] This method has become increasingly popular and there are several hundred permanent mall research facilities in the United States. As the following example shows, mall intercepts are especially appropriate when the respondents need to see, handle, or consume the product before they can provide meaningful information.

EXAMPLE

Mall-Intercept Interviews Give Birth to Infant Apparel

Soft Care Apparel, Inc., manufacturer of Curity children's wear, is the largest soft-goods manufacturer of infant apparel in the United States. Soft Care uses mall-intercept interviews to evaluate its new products. The company hires an independent research firm that tests the company's new designs against its current designs and the designs of its competition, simulating a marketplace situation. The company's product managers often go to test malls to receive firsthand feedback from potential customers. Several products—including printed crib sheets, comforters, and coordinated bedding—have been successfully designed and introduced using information obtained from mall-intercept interviews.[12] ■

A mall intercept interview in progress.

Computer-Assisted Personal Interviewing (CAPI). In computer-assisted personal interviewing (CAPI), the third form of personal interviewing, the respondent sits in front of a computer terminal and answers a questionnaire on the CRT screen by using the keyboard, a mouse, or touch screen. There are several user-friendly electronic packages that design questions which are easy for the respondent to understand. Help screens and courteous error messages are also provided. The colorful screens and on- and off-screen stimuli add to the respondent's interest and involvement in the task. This method has been classified as a personal interview technique because an interviewer is usually present to serve as a host or hostess, and to guide the respondent as needed.

CAPI has been used to collect data at shopping malls, product clinics, conferences, and trade shows. However, you may wonder, how does CAPI compare with the traditional method of conducting personal interviews, using paper-and-pencil questionnaires? The experience of the First National Bank of Chicago provides some insight.[13]

EXAMPLE

Banking on Computers Creates Interest

The First National Bank of Chicago compared CAPI with interviewer-assisted paper-and-pencil questionnaires. It was found that computer questionnaires took longer to complete, although the respondents underestimated the time they spent at the CRT. Respondents found the computer-assisted surveys more interesting and expressed more positive predispositions toward them. Greater variance and less-inhibited answers were obtained with CAPI. Computer-assisted interviews resulted, in certain instances, in 33 to 40 percent cost savings over interviewer-assisted paper-and-pencil questionnaires. Therefore, the First National Bank of Chicago has continued to use CAPI in many of its ongoing research programs.[14] ■

Mail Methods

Mail Interviews. In the traditional mail interview, questionnaires are mailed to preselected potential respondents. A typical mail interview package consists of the outgoing envelope, cover letter, questionnaire, return envelope, and possibly an incentive.[15] The respondents complete and return the questionnaires. There is no verbal interaction between the researcher and the respondent.[16]

However, before data collection can begin, the respondents need to be at least broadly identified. Therefore, the first step is to obtain a valid mailing list. Mailing lists can be compiled from telephone directories, customer rosters or association membership rolls, or purchased from publication subscription lists or commercial mailing list companies. Research in Practice 6.2 (found on page 191) illustrates the variety of mailing lists offered by one firm, the approximate number of names per list, and the respective prices.[17] Regardless of its source, a mailing list should be current and closely related to the population of interest. The researcher must also make decisions about the various elements of the mail interview package (see Table 6.1). Mail surveys are used for a variety of purposes.

Mail Panels. Mail panels were introduced in chapters 3 and 4. A **mail panel** consists of a large, nationally representative sample of households that has agreed to participate in periodic mail questionnaires, product tests, and telephone surveys. The household members are compensated with various incentives. Some marketing research organizations that maintain mail panels include National Family Opinion, Market Fact's Consumer Mail Panel, Marketing and Research Counselors' National Neighborhood Panel, and Home Testing Institute. Mail panels can be used to obtain information repeatedly from the same respondents. Thus, they can be used to implement a longitudinal design. Several magazines, such as *Seventeen*, maintain their own panels, as illustrated by the following example.[18]

Mail Panels A large and nationally representative sample of households that has agreed to periodically participate in mail questionnaires, product tests, and telephone surveys.

TABLE 6.1

SOME DECISIONS RELATED TO THE MAIL INTERVIEW PACKAGE

Outgoing Envelope			
Outgoing envelope: size, color, return address			
Postage	Method of addressing		
Cover Letter			
Sponsorship	Type of appeal	Postscript	
Personalization	Signature		
Questionnaire			
Length	Size	Layout	Format
Content	Reproduction	Color	Respondent anonymity
Return Envelope			
Type of envelope	Postage		
Incentives			
Monetary versus nonmonetary		Prepaid versus promised amount	

A mail questionnaire with return envelope.

PART II

PLEASE INDICATE YOUR SATISFACTION WITH:

PLEASE CIRCLE YOUR RESPONSE.

	VERY SATIS-FIED	SATIS-FIED	NEU-TRAL	DIS-SATIS-FIED	VERY DIS-SATIS-FIED
1. THE QUALITY OF YOUR EQUIPMENT	1	2	3	4	5
2. THE RESPONSE TIME TO YOUR CALL	1	2	3	4	5
3. THE QUALITY OF SERVICE PERFORMED	1	2	3	4	5
4. THE COURTESY OF MY SERVICE PERSON	1	2	3	4	5
5. MEETING OUR SERVICE COMMITMENTS TO YOU	1	2	3	4	5
6. MY OVERALL SERVICE	1	2	3	4	5

TEAR HERE

NO POSTAGE NECESSARY IF MAILED IN THE UNITED STATES

BUSINESS REPLY CARD

FIRST CLASS PERMIT NO 832 ATLANTA, GA

POSTAGE WILL BE PAID BY ADDRESSEE

ELRICK AND LAVIDGE, INC.
P.O. Box 4402
Atlanta, GA 30302

EXAMPLE

Mail Targets Female

Several magazines such as *Seventeen* maintain their own consumer panels for conducting surveys.

Seventeen magazine conducted a study to determine the shopping habits of its readers. Questionnaires were mailed to 2,000 members of *Seventeen*'s Consumer Panel, representing a cross-section of the female 13–21 market. Of these, 1,315 were returned, for a completion rate of 65.8 percent. The results were balanced by age and geographic area to census data so that they reflect all females age 13–21 in the United States. Some of the major findings were:

- nine out of ten shopped at a large mall
- almost two thirds shopped in a small shopping center
- over half shopped at a single standing store

The magazine used these results to target advertisers and obtain higher advertising revenues. Several marketers—such as clothing, cosmetics, and personal care brands—target females in this age group. *Seventeen* magazine uses its mail panel to conduct periodic surveys to stay in touch with its target market. As a result, *Seventeen* is the number one magazine in the teenage market with 1.6 million subscribers.[19] ■

Electronic Methods

E-Mail Interviews. To conduct an e-mail survey, a list of e-mail addresses is obtained. The survey is written within the body of the e-mail message and sent to respondents. E-mail surveys use pure text (ASCII) to represent questionnaires, and can be received and responded to by anyone with an e-mail address, whether or not they have access to the Web. Respondents type the answers to either closed-ended or open-ended questions at designated places, and click on "reply." Responses are data entered and tabulated. Note that data entry is typically required before any statistical analysis can be conducted.

E-mail surveys have several limitations. Given the technical limitations of most e-mail systems, questionnaires cannot utilize programmed skip patterns, logic checks, or randomization. The limited intelligence of ASCII text cannot keep a respondent from, say, choosing both "yes" and "no" to a question where only one response is meaningful. Skipping instructions (e.g., "If the answer to question 5 is yes, go to question 9") must appear explicitly, just as on paper. These factors can reduce the quality of data from an e-mail survey and can require postsurvey data cleaning. Another limitation is that some e-mail software products limit the length of the body of an e-mail message.[20]

EXAMPLE

An E-Mail Survey

Here's a sample:

To: respondent@xyz.com
From: survey@analysis.net
Subject: Employee survey

Hello,

We have been commissioned by Jane Smith of the Human Resources department to conduct a survey of XYZ company employees. The results will be used o give senior management a better understanding of what issues are important to employees.

Please be assured that ALL responses to ALL questions will be held completely confidential by Analysis.Net. We will provide only summarized or anonymous comments in our final report. For each of the following questions, please place your answer in the appropriate [ ] box, like this: [x] or this: [3]

---

1. How long have you been working at XYZ company? [ ] years.

---

2. Overall, would you say you are very satisfied, satisfied, neutral, dissatisfied, or very dissatisfied with your job at XYZ company?

[ ] very satisfied
[ ] satisfied
[ ] neutral
[ ] dissatisfied
[ ] very dissatisfied

---

3. What would you say is the biggest challenge facing XYZ company today?
[ ]

Note that we are able to collect comments as well as numeric or "multiple-choice" responses. ■

Hypertext Markup Language Hypertext markup language (HTML) is the language of the Web.

Internet Interviews. In contrast to e-mail surveys, Internet or Web surveys use **hypertext markup language** (HTML), the language of the Web, and are posted on a Web site. Respondents may be recruited on-line from potential respondent databases maintained by the marketing research firm or they can be recruited by conventional methods (mail, telephone). Respondents are asked to go to a particular Web location to complete the survey. Many times, respondents are not recruited but those who happen to be visiting the Web site on which the survey is posted (or other popular Web sites) are invited to participate in the survey. Either all or every *i*th Web site visitor is allowed to participate. Web surveys offer several advantages over e-mail surveys. It is possible in HTML, but not in ASCII text, to construct buttons, check boxes, and data entry fields that prevent respondents from selecting more than one response where only one is intended, or from otherwise typing where no response is required. Skip patterns can be programmed and performed automatically as in CATI or CAPI. It is possible to validate responses as they are entered. Finally, additional survey stimuli such as graphs, images, animations, and links to other Web pages may be integrated into or around the survey. The responses are collected in an adjoining database. The data require some processing before they can be tabulated or used in a statistical package. All these factors contribute to higher quality data.

EXAMPLE

AmeriPoll: Polling America's Pulse

Maritz gathers a variety of information on its AmeriPoll survey Web page (www.maritz.com/mmri/apoll/) from users of the World Wide Web. AmeriPoll is an on-line panel of volunteer respondents recruited from other Web sites using banner advertisements. The on-line survey is an extension of the Maritz AmeriPoll telephone panel. When users visit the AmeriPoll home page, they are asked to register. Maritz gathers basic demographic information from respondents and adds them to a database of panel members. Panel members are then able to complete an on-line survey. Maritz notifies panel members by e-mail when new surveys are ready.

Panel members are encouraged to participate by the offer of a prize drawing. Prizes are awarded randomly after each survey.

After each survey is completed, Maritz compiles and analyzes the results and posts them on their Web page. Results can be searched by date or topic. Topics cover a broad range, including fashion, travel, government, education, shopping, food, and cars. These surveys are useful to marketing researchers as well as managers. ■

Remember, however, that not all survey methods are appropriate in a given situation. Therefore, the researcher should conduct a comparative evaluation to determine which methods are appropriate.

A COMPARATIVE EVALUATION OF SURVEY METHODS

Table 6.2 compares the different survey methods across a variety of factors. For any particular research project, the relative importance attached to these factors will vary. These factors consist of flexibility of data collection, diversity of questions, use of physical stimuli, sample control, control of the data collection environment, control of field force, quantity of data, response rate, perceived anonymity, social desirability, obtaining sensitive information, potential for interviewer bias, speed, and cost.

Flexibility of Data Collection

The flexibility of data collection is determined primarily by the extent to which the respondent can interact with the interviewer and the survey questionnaire. The personal interview, whether conducted in-home or as mall-intercept interview, allows the highest flexibility of data collection. Because the respondent and the interviewer meet face to face, the interviewer can administer complex questionnaires, explain and clarify difficult questions, and even utilize unstructured techniques.

The traditional telephone interview, by contrast, allows only moderate flexibility, because it is more difficult to use unstructured techniques, ask complex questions, or obtain in-depth answers to open-ended questions over the telephone. CATI, CAPI, and Internet surveys allow somewhat greater flexibility because the questionnaire is administered in an

TABLE 6.2

A COMPARATIVE EVALUATION OF SURVEY METHODS

Criteria	*Telephone CATI*	*In-Home Interviews*	*Mall-Intercept Interviews*	*CAPI*	*Mail Surveys*	*Mail Panels*	*E-mail*	*Internet/ Web*
Flexibility of data collection	Moderate to high	High	High	Moderate to high	Low	Low	Low	Moderate to high
Diversity of questions	Low	High	High	High	Moderate	Moderate	Moderate	Moderate to high
Use of physical stimuli	Low	Moderate to high	High	High	Moderate	Moderate	Low	Moderate
Sample Control	Moderate to high	Potentially high	Moderate	Moderate	Low	Moderate to high	Low	Low to moderate
Control of data collection environment	Moderate	Moderate to high	High	High	Low	Low	Low	Low
Control of field force	Moderate	Low	Moderate	Moderate	High	High	High	High
Quantity of data	Low	High	Moderate	Moderate	Moderate	High	Moderate	Moderate
Response rate	Moderate	High	High	High	Low	Moderate	Low	Very low
Perceived anonymity of the respondent	Moderate	Low	Low	Low	High	High	Moderate	High
Social desirability	Moderate	High	High	Moderate to High	Low	Low	Moderate	Low
Obtaining sensitive information	High	Low	Low	Low to moderate	High	Moderate to high	Moderate	High
Potential for interviewer bias	Moderate	High	High	Low	None	None	None	None
Speed	High	Moderate	Moderate to high	Moderate to high	Low	Low to moderate	High	Very high
Cost	Moderate	High	Moderate to high	Moderate to high	Low	Low to moderate	Low	Low

interactive mode. The researcher can use various question formats, personalize the questionnaire, and handle complex skip patterns (directions for skipping questions in the questionnaire based on the subject's responses). Because these modes do not allow for interaction between the interviewer and the respondent, mail surveys, mail panels, and e-mail surveys have low flexibility.

An often-overlooked benefit of Internet survey research is the ease with which an Internet survey can be quickly modified. For example, early data returns may suggest additional questions that should be asked. Changing or adding questions on the fly would be nearly impossible with a mail questionnaire and difficult with personal or telephone questionnaires, but can be achieved in a matter of minutes with some Internet survey systems.

Diversity of Questions

The diversity of questions that can be asked in a survey depends on the degree of interaction the respondent has with the interviewer and the questionnaire, as well as the respondent's ability to actually see the questions. A wide variety of questions can be asked in a personal interview because the respondents can see the questionnaire and an interviewer is present to clarify ambiguities. Thus in-home, mall-intercept, and CAPI methods allow for diversity. In Internet surveys, multimedia capabilities can be utilized and so the ability to ask a diversity of questions is moderate to high, despite the absence of an interviewer. In mail surveys, mail panels, and e-mail surveys, less diversity is possible. In traditional telephone interviews and CATI, the respondent cannot see the questions while answering and this limits the diversity of questions. For example, in a telephone interview or CATI, one could not ask respondents to rank 15 brands of automobiles in terms of preference.

Use of Physical Stimuli

Often it is helpful or necessary to use physical stimuli such as the product, a product prototype, commercials, or promotional displays during the interview. For the most basic example, a taste test involves tasting the product. In other cases photographs, maps, or other audiovisual cues are helpful. In these cases, personal interviews conducted at central locations (mall-intercept and CAPI) are preferable to in-home interviews. Mail surveys and mail panels are moderate on this dimension, because sometimes it is possible to mail the facilitating aids or even product samples. Internet surveys are also moderately suitable. Because they are Web-based, the questionnaires can include multimedia elements such as prototype Web pages and advertisements. The use of physical stimuli is limited in traditional telephone interviews and CATI, as well as in e-mail surveys.

Sample Control

Sample Control The ability of the survey mode to reach the units specified in the sample effectively and efficiently.

Sample control is the ability of the survey mode to reach the units (e.g., individuals, households) specified in the sample effectively and efficiently.[21] At least in principle, in-home personal interviews offer the best sample control. It is possible to control which sampling units are interviewed, who is interviewed, the degree of participation of other members of the household, and many other aspects of data collection. In practice, to achieve a high degree of control the in-home researcher has to overcome several problems. It is difficult to find respondents at home during the day as most people work outside the home. Also, for safety reasons, interviewers are reluctant to venture into certain neighborhoods and people have become cautious of responding to strangers at their door.

Mall-intercept interviews allow only a moderate degree of sample control. While the interviewer has control over which respondents to intercept, the choice is limited to mall shoppers and frequent shoppers have a greater probability of being included. Also, potential respondents can intentionally avoid or initiate contact with the interviewer. Compared to mall intercepts, CAPI offers slightly better control, as sampling quotas can be set and respondents randomized automatically.

Sampling Frame A representation of the elements of the target population. It consists of a list or set of directions for identifying the target population.

Moderate to high sampling control can be achieved with traditional telephone interviews and CATI. Telephones offer access to geographically dispersed respondents and hard-to-reach areas. These procedures depend on a **sampling frame**—a list of population units with their telephone numbers.[22] The sampling frames normally used are telephone directories, but telephone directories are limited in that (1) not everyone has a phone, (2) some people have unlisted numbers, and (3) directories do not reflect new phones in service or recently disconnected phones. While the telephone has achieved an almost total penetration of households in the U.S., there are some variations by region and within regions. The percentage of households with unlisted numbers is about 31 percent and varies considerably by geographical region. In large metropolitan areas it may be as high as

60 percent.[23] The total of unpublished numbers and new phones in service since the directory was published can account for as much as 40 percent of total telephone households in some metropolitan areas.[24]

Random Digit Dialing
A technique used to overcome the bias of unpublished and recent telephone numbers, by selecting all telephone number digits at random.

The **random digit dialing (RDD)** technique is used to overcome the bias of unpublished and recent numbers. RDD consists of selecting all 10 (area code, prefix or exchange, suffix) telephone number digits at random. While this approach gives all households with telephones an approximately equal chance of being included in the sample, it suffers from limitations. It is costly and time consuming to implement, because not all possible telephone numbers are in service: although there are 10 billion possible telephone numbers, there are only about 100 million actual household telephone numbers. Also, RDD does not distinguish between telephone numbers of interest and those that are not (in a consumer survey, for example, business and government numbers are not of interest). There are several variations of RDD that reduce wasted effort. One variation, randomly selects a working exchange and adds a block of four-digit random numbers. In **random digit directory designs** a sample of numbers is drawn from the directory. These numbers are modified to allow unpublished numbers a chance of being included in the sample. The popular approaches for modification of numbers include (1) adding a constant to the last digit, (2) randomizing the last *r* digits, and (3) a two-stage procedure. These procedures are described and illustrated in Figure 6.2. Of these three methods, adding a constant to the last digit, particularly plus-one sampling, results in high contact rates and representative samples.[25]

Random-Digit Directory Designs (RDD) A research design for telephone surveys in which a sample of numbers is drawn from the telephone directory and modified to allow unpublished numbers a chance of being included in the sample.

Mail surveys require a list of addresses of individuals or households eligible for inclusion in the sample. Mail surveys can reach geographically dispersed respondents and hard-to-reach areas.[26] However, mailing lists are sometimes unavailable, outdated, or incomplete. Typically, telephone and street directories are used for a listing of the general population. Problems with these types of lists have been discussed already. As illustrated in Research in Practice 6.2, catalogs of mailing lists contain thousands of lists that can be purchased.[27]

Figure 6.2
Random Digit Directory Designs

Addition of a Constant to the Last Digit

An integer between 1 and 9 is added to the telephone number selected from the directory. In plus-one sampling the number added to the last digit is one.

Number selected from directory: 953-3004 (exchange-block). Add one to the last digit to form 953-3005. This is the number to be included in the sample.

Randomization on the r Last Digits

Replace the r ($r = 2$, 3, or 4) last digits with an equal number of randomly selected digits.

Number selected from directory: 881-1124. Replace the last four digits of block with randomly selected numbers 5, 2, 8, and 6 to form 881-5286.

Two-Stage Procedure

The first stage consists of selecting an exchange and telephone number from the directory. In the second stage, the last three-digits of the selected number are replaced with a three-digit random number between 000 and 999.

Cluster 1

Selected exchange: 636
Selected number: 636-3230
Replace the last three digits (230) with randomly selected 389 to form 636-3389.
Repeat this process until the desired number of telephone numbers from this cluster is obtained.

RESEARCH IN PRACTICE 6.2

Sample Mailing Lists

List Title	*Number on List*	*Price**
Advertising Agencies (major)	3,817	$45/M
Banks, Branches	30,299	$85/M
Boat Owners	4,289,601	$50/M
Chambers of Commerce	6,959	$45/M
Personal Computer Owners	4,721,987	Inquire
Families	76,000,000	Inquire
Hardware Wholesalers	8,501	$45/M
Magazines, Consumer	4,119	$45/M
Photographic, Portrait	36,491	$45/M
Sales Executives	200,259	$55/M
Wives of Professional Men	1,663,614	$60/M
YMCAs	1,007	$85

* Price shown is per 1,000 names (/M), except where noted.
Source: Best Mailing Lists, Inc., Catalog 1999 (800-692-2378)

Another factor outside the researcher's control is whether the questionnaire is answered and who answers it. Some subjects refuse to respond because of lack of interest or motivation; others cannot respond because they are illiterate.[28] For these reasons, the degree of sample control in mail surveys is low.[29]

Mail panels, on the other hand, provide moderate to high control over the sample. They provide samples matched to U.S. Bureau of the Census statistics on key demographic variables. It is also possible to identify specific user groups within a panel and to direct the survey to households with specific characteristics. Specific members of households in the panel can be questioned. Finally, low-incidence groups, groups that occur infrequently in the population, can be reached with panels, but there is a question of the extent to which a panel can be considered to be representative of the entire population.

Not all populations are candidates for Internet survey research. The general consumer population is often a poor fit, because fewer than 30 percent of U.S. households regularly use Internet services. Although the respondents can be screened to meet qualifying criteria and quotas imposed, the ability to meet quotas is limited by the number and characteristics of respondents who visit the Web site. However, there are some exceptions to this broad statement. For example, computer products purchasers and users of Internet services are both ideal populations. Business and professional users of Internet services are also an excellent population to reach with Internet surveys. Over 90 percent of businesses are currently estimated to have Internet connections. However, it can be difficult to prevent respondents from completing the Internet survey multiple times. Thus, sample control is low to moderate for Internet surveys. E-mail surveys suffer from many of the limitations of mail surveys and thus offer low sample control.

Control of the Data Collection Environment

The degree of control a researcher has over the environment in which the respondent answers the questionnaire is another factor that differentiates the various survey modes. Personal interviews conducted at central locations (mall-intercept and CAPI) offer the greatest degree of environmental control. For example, the researcher can set up a special facility for demonstrating the product. In-home personal interviews offer moderate to high control because the interviewer is present. Traditional telephone and CATI offer moderate control. The interviewer cannot see the environment in which the interview is being conducted, but he or she can sense the background conditions and encourage the respondent to be attentive and involved. In mail surveys, panels, e-mail, and Internet surveys, the researcher has little control over the environment.

Control of Field Force

Field Force The field force is the interviewers and the supervisors involved in data collection.

The **field force** consists of interviewers and supervisors involved in data collection. Because they require no such personnel, mail surveys, mail panels, e-mail, and Internet surveys eliminate field force problems. Traditional telephone interviews, CATI, mall-intercept, and CAPI all offer moderate degrees of control because the interviews are conducted at a central location, making supervision relatively simple. In-home personal interviews are problematic in this respect. Since many interviewers work in many different locations, continual supervision is impractical.[30]

Quantity of Data

In-home personal interviews allow the researcher to collect large amounts of data. The social relationship between the interviewer and the respondent, as well as the home environment, motivate the respondent to spend more time in the interview. Less effort is required of the respondent in a personal interview than in a telephone or mail interview. The interviewer records answers to open-ended questions and provides visual aids to help with lengthy and complex scales. Some personal interviews last as long as 75 minutes. In contrast to in-home interviews, mall-intercept and CAPI provide only moderate amounts of data. Because these interviews are conducted in shopping malls and other central locations, the respondents' time is more limited. Typically, the interview time is 30 minutes or less. For example, in recent mall-intercept interviews conducted by General Foods, the interview time was limited to 25 minutes.[31]

Mail surveys also yield moderate amounts of data. Fairly long questionnaires can be used, because short questionnaires have not been shown to generate higher response rates than long ones. The same is true for e-mail and Internet surveys, although the Internet is a better medium in this respect. Mail panels, on the other hand, can generate large amounts of data because of the special relationship between the panel members and the sponsoring organization. For example, the author has used the Market Facts panel to administer a questionnaire that took two hours to complete.

Traditional telephone interviews and CATI result in the most limited quantities of data. They tend to be shorter than other surveys, because respondents can easily terminate the telephone conversation at their own discretion. These interviews commonly last about 15 minutes, although longer interviews may be conducted when the subject matter is of interest to the respondents.[32] Studies indicate that respondents tend to underestimate the length of telephone interviews by as much as 50 percent. This suggests that telephone interviews may be conducted for a longer duration than is currently the practice.

Response Rate

Response Rate The percentage of the total attempted interviews that are completed.

Survey **response rate** is broadly defined as the percentage of the total attempted interviews that are completed. Personal, in-home, mall-intercept, and computer-assisted interviews yield the highest response rate (typically more than 80 percent). Problems caused by not-at-homes can often be resolved by calling back at different times. Telephone interviews, traditional and CATI, yield response rates between 60 and 80 percent. These modes also suffer from not-at-homes or no-answers. Higher response rates are obtained by callbacks. Many telephone surveys attempt to call back at least three times.

Mail surveys have poor response rates. In a mail survey of randomly selected respondents, without any pre- or postmailing contact, the response rate is typically less than 15 percent. Such low response rate can lead to serious bias (nonresponse bias) because whether a person responds to a mail survey is related to his or her interest in the topic. The magnitude of **nonresponse bias** increases as the response rate decreases. However, use of appropriate response-inducement procedures can increase the response rate in mail surveys to 80 percent or more. Response rates in mail panels are typically in the 70 to 80 percent range, because of assured respondent cooperation.

Nonresponse Bias When actual respondents differ from those who refuse to participate.

Internet surveys have the poorest response rates, even lower than e-mail surveys. This is due to the fact that some respondents may have access to e-mail but not to the Web, and accessing the Web requires more effort and skill. Furthermore, respondents generally need to be connected to the Internet while completing a Web survey; they may not be off-line, as with an e-mail survey. If the respondents are prerecruited, they have to log on to a Web site. Many are unwilling to undertake this effort.

A comprehensive review of the literature covering 497 response rates in 93 journal articles found weighted average response rates of 81.7, 72.3, and 47.3 percent for, respectively, personal, telephone, and mail surveys.[33] The same review also found that response rates increase with

- Either prepaid or promised monetary incentives
- Increase in the amount of monetary incentive
- Nonmonetary premiums and rewards (pens, pencils, books)
- Preliminary notification
- Foot-in-the door techniques. These are multiple-request strategies. The first request is relatively small, and all or most people agree to comply. The small request is followed by a larger request, called the **critical request**, which is actually the target behavior.
- Personalization (sending letters addressed to specific individuals)
- Follow-up letters.

Critical Request The target behavior that is being researched.

A further discussion of improving response rates is found in chapter 12.

Perceived Anonymity

Perceived anonymity refers to the respondents' perceptions that their identities will not be discerned by the interviewer or the researcher. Perceived anonymity of the respondent is high in mail surveys, mail panels, and Internet surveys because there is no contact with an interviewer while responding. It is low in personal interviews (in-home, mall-intercept, and computer-assisted) due to face-to-face contact with the interviewer. Traditional telephone interviews and CATI fall in the middle. It is also moderate with e-mail—while there is no contact with the interviewer, respondents know that their names can be located on the return e-mail.

Perceived Anonymity The respondent's perceptions that their identities will not be discerned by the interviewer or the researcher.

Social Desirability/Sensitive Information

Social desirability is the tendency of the respondents to give answers that are socially acceptable, whether or not they are true. As mail surveys, mail panels, and Internet surveys do not involve any social interaction between the interviewer and the respondent, they are least susceptible to social desirability. Evidence suggests that such methods are good for obtaining sensitive information such as that related to financial or personal behavior. Traditional telephone interviews and CATI are moderately good at avoiding socially desirable responses. They are good for obtaining sensitive information, as the respondents have the perception that they are not committing to anything in writing over the telephone.[34] E-mail is only moderately good for controlling social desirability and obtaining sensitive information, given the respondents' awareness that their names can be located on the return e-mail.

Social Desirability The tendency of the respondents to give answers that may not be accurate but may be desirable from a social standpoint.

Personal interviews, whether in-home, mall-intercept, or computer-assisted, are limited in this respect, although the problem is somewhat mitigated in the case of computer-assisted interviews.[35]

Potential for Interviewer Bias

An interviewer can bias the results of a survey by the manner in which he or she (1) selects respondents (interviewing somebody else when required to interview the male head of household), (2) asks research questions (omitting questions), and (3) records answers (incorrectly or incompletely). The extent of the interviewer's role determines the potential for bias.[36] In-home and mall-intercept personal interviews are highly susceptible to interviewer bias. Traditional telephone interviews and CATI are less susceptible, although the potential is still there. For example, with inflection and tone of voice, interviewers can convey their own attitudes and thereby suggest answers. Computer-assisted interviews have a low potential for bias. Mail surveys, mail panels, e-mail, and Internet surveys are free of it.

Speed

First, there is the speed with which a questionnaire can be created, distributed to respondents, and the data returned. Because printing, mailing and data keying delays are eliminated, data can be in hand within hours of writing an Internet questionnaire. Data are obtained in electronic form, so statistical analysis software can be programmed to process standard questionnaires and return statistical summaries and charts automatically. Thus, the Internet is by far the fastest method of obtaining data from a large number of respondents. The e-mail survey is also fast, although slower than Internet since greater time is needed to compile an e-mail list and data entry is also required.

Traditional telephone interviews and CATI are also fast ways of obtaining information. When a central telephone facility is used, several hundred telephone interviews can be done per day. Data for even large national surveys can be collected in two weeks or less. Next in speed are mall-intercept and computer-assisted interviews, which reach potential respondents in central locations. In-home personal interviews are slower, because there is dead time between interviews while the interviewer travels to the next respondent. To expedite data collection, interviews can be conducted in different markets or regions simultaneously. Mail surveys are typically the slowest. It usually takes several weeks to receive completed questionnaires; follow-up mailings take even longer. Mail panels are faster than mail surveys, because little follow-up is required.

Cost

For large samples, the cost of Internet surveys is the lowest. Printing, mailing, keying, and interviewer costs are eliminated, and the incremental costs per respondent are typically low, so studies with large numbers of respondents can be done at substantial savings compared to mail, telephone, or personal surveys. Personal interviews tend to be the most expensive mode of data collection per completed response. In general, Internet, e-mail, mail surveys, mail panel, traditional telephone, CATI, CAPI, mall-intercept, and personal in-home interviews require progressively larger field staff and greater supervision and control. Hence, the cost increases in this order. However, relative costs depend on the subject of inquiry and the procedures adopted.[37]

SELECTION OF SURVEY METHOD(S)

As is evident from Table 6.2 and the preceding discussion, no survey method is superior in all situations. Depending on factors such as information requirements, budgetary constraints (time and money), and respondent characteristics, none, one, two, or even all methods may

DEPARTMENT STORE PATRONAGE PROJECT

Personal In-Home Interviews

In the department store project, personal in-home interviews were utilized for a number of reasons. Many diverse questions were asked. Some questions were complex and a relatively large amount of data had to be collected. The information obtained was not sensitive or threatening. Trained students were used as interviewers, thereby reducing the cost. Another critical consideration was that the personal interviews could be conducted without subcontracting the data collection to a field service organization.

Telephone methods were not appropriate because of the complexity of the questions and amount of data needed. Mall-intercept and CAPI were not appropriate either, because so much data were needed. The use of a central location facility would have necessitated subcontracting with a field service organization. Mail surveys were ruled out due to low response rate and complexity of the information needed. Mail panels were inappropriate given the complexity of information needed; also a self-administered questionnaire was not considered to be appropriate. The electronic methods were not chosen as few people in the target market had access to e-mail or the Internet when the survey was conducted.

be appropriate.[38] Remember that the various data collection modes are not mutually exclusive. Rather, they can be employed in a complementary fashion to build on each other's strengths and compensate for each other's weaknesses. The researcher can employ these methods in combination and develop creative methods. To illustrate, in a classic project, interviewers distributed the product, self-administered questionnaires, and return envelopes to respondents. Traditional telephone interviews were used for follow-up. Combining the data collection modes resulted in telephone cooperation from 97 percent of the respondents. Furthermore, 82 percent of the questionnaires were returned by mail.[39] In the introduction we illustrated how Microsoft successfully combined telephone and Internet interviewing. The following examples illustrate the selection of survey modes.

EXAMPLE

New-Product Development at Oscar Mayer Uses Old but Proven Methods

New-product development at Oscar Mayer starts by using fact-based data and prior research to form questions such as:

Who is your target buyer?
What product are they currently using?
What is their big problem with it?
How will you solve this problem?

Once these questions are considered, a prototype of the new-product idea is formed and tested in focus groups. The feedback from these groups allows the inventors to make adjustments to their products and in essence fine-tune the idea. Next, quantitative testing is used in the form of questionnaires mailed to households. Mail survey is used because it enables Oscar Mayer to collect the required quantity of data at a very low cost and eliminates the potential for interviewer bias. The major drawback of low response rates is overcome

Focus groups, mail surveys, and central location surveys have enabled Oscar Mayer to develop several successful products.

by offering suitable incentives. Once information is received from these consumers the data are compared to the normative database of prior research for evaluation. Once evaluated, the information is used to create options for the product in areas such as composition, packaging, size, or shape. These various designs are tested at the marketing research facility by bringing in approximately 200 target market consumers to give their opinions and rate the product variations. Central location interviewing at the marketing research facility is chosen because the "use of physical stimuli" criterion dominates, and it is necessary for the respondents to see, handle, and even taste the product. The information obtained at this stage is used to help choose between the possible product configurations.[40] ■

OBSERVATION METHODS

Observation The recording of behavioral patterns of people, objects, and events in a systematic manner to obtain information about the phenomenon of interest.

Observation methods are the second type of methodology used in descriptive research. **Observation** involves recording the behavioral patterns of people, objects, and events in a systematic manner to obtain information about the phenomenon of interest. The observer does not question or communicate with the people being observed. Information may be recorded as the events occur or from records of past events. Observational methods may be structured or unstructured, direct or indirect. Furthermore, observation may be conducted in a natural or contrived environment.[41]

Structured versus Unstructured Observation

Structured Observation Observation techniques in which the researcher clearly defines the behaviors to be observed and the methods by which they will be measured.

Unstructured Observation Observation that involves a researcher monitoring all relevant phenomenon, without specifying the details in advance.

For **structured observation**, the researcher specifies in detail what is to be observed and how the measurements are to be recorded—for example, an auditor performing inventory analysis in a store. This reduces the potential for observer bias and enhances the reliability of the data. Structured observation is appropriate when the marketing research problem has been clearly defined and the information needed has been specified. In these circumstances, the details of the phenomenon to be observed can be clearly identified. Structured observation is suitable for use in conclusive research.

In **unstructured observation** the observer monitors all aspects of the phenomenon that seem relevant to the problem at hand—for example, observing children playing with new toys. This form of observation is appropriate when the problem has yet to be formulated precisely and flexibility is needed in observation to identify key components of the problem and to develop hypotheses. In unstructured observation, potential for observer bias is high. For this reason, the observation findings should be treated as hypotheses to be tested rather than as conclusive findings. Thus, unstructured observation is most appropriate for exploratory research.

Disguised versus Undisguised Observation

In disguised observation, the respondents are unaware that they are being observed. Disguise enables respondents to behave naturally; people tend to behave differently when they know they are being observed. Disguise may be accomplished by using one-way mirrors, hidden cameras, or inconspicuous mechanical devices. Observers may be disguised as shoppers or sales clerks or in other appropriate roles.

In undisguised observation, the respondents are aware that they are under observation. For example, they may be aware of the presence of the observer. Researchers disagree on how much effect the presence of an observer has on behavior. One viewpoint is that the observer effect is minor and short-lived.[42] The other position is that the observer can seriously bias the behavior patterns.[43]

Natural versus Contrived Observation

Natural observation involves observing behavior as it takes places in the environment. For example, one could observe the behavior of respondents eating fast food in Burger King. In **contrived observation**, respondents' behavior is observed in an artificial environment, such as a test kitchen.

Natural Observation Observing behavior as it takes place in the environment.

Contrived Observation The behavior is observed in an artificial environment.

The advantage of natural observation is that the observed phenomenon will more accurately reflect the true phenomenon. The disadvantages are the cost of waiting for the phenomenon to occur and the difficulty of measuring the phenomenon in a natural setting.

OBSERVATION METHODS CLASSIFIED BY MODE OF ADMINISTRATION

As shown in Figure 6.3, observation methods may be classified by mode of administration as personal observation, mechanical observation, audit, content analysis, and trace analysis.

Personal Observation

In **personal observation**, a researcher observes actual behavior as it occurs. The observer does not attempt to control or manipulate the phenomenon being observed. The observer merely records what takes place in a natural (e.g., a store) or a contrived environment (e.g., a research facility). For example, a researcher might record traffic counts and observe traffic flows in a department store. This information could aid in designing store layout and determining location of individual departments, shelf locations, and merchandise displays. As another example consider the following.

Personal Observation An observational research strategy in which human observers record the phenomenon being observed as it occurs.

Research in Practice 6.3 shows how one Japanese company used personal observation to make an important marketing decision.[44]

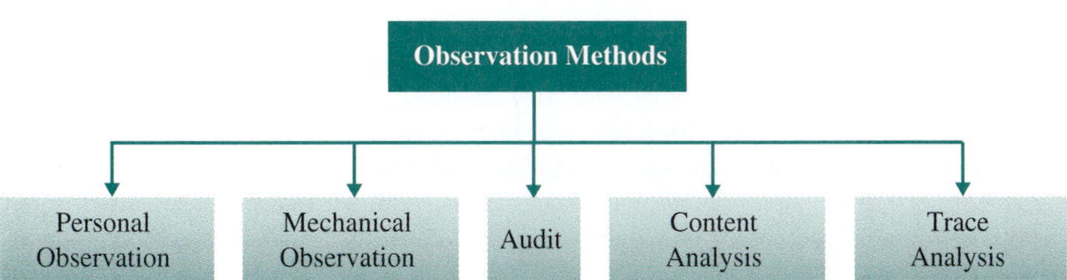

Figure 6.3
A Classification of Observation Methods

DEPARTMENT STORE PATRONAGE PROJECT

Personal Observation

In the department store project, license plate surveys could be used to establish the primary trading area of a shopping mall. These surveys help marketers determine where their customers live. In a license plate survey, observers record the license plate numbers of the automobiles in a parking lot. These numbers are fed into a computer and paired with automobile registration data. This results in a map of customers located by census tract or zip codes. Such a map, along with other demographic data, can help a department store chain determine new locations, decide on billboard space, and target direct marketing efforts. License plate surveys cost less ($5,000 to $25,000) and are believed to be quicker and more reliable than direct communication methods such as interviews with shoppers.

Mechanical Observation

Mechanical Observation An observational research strategy in which mechanical devices, rather than human observers, record the phenomenon being observed.

In **mechanical observation**, mechanical devices, rather than human observers, record the phenomenon being observed. These devices may or may not require the respondents' direct participation. They are used for continuously recording ongoing behavior for later analysis.

Of the mechanical devices that do not require respondents' direct participation, the A. C. Nielsen audimeter is best known. The audimeter is attached to a television set to continually record what channel the set is tuned to. Recently, "people meters" have been introduced. People meters attempt to measure not only the channels to which a set is tuned but also who is watching.[45] Other common examples include turnstiles that record the number of people entering or leaving a building, and traffic counters placed across streets to determine the number of vehicles passing certain locations. On-site cameras (still, motion picture, or video) are increasingly used by retailers to assess package designs, floor displays, and traffic flow patterns. Technological advances such as the universal product code (UPC)

RESEARCH IN PRACTICE 6.3

Building Accord according to Personal Observation

Honda Motor Co. had a lot of complaints on their sporty, restyled Accord (not big enough for U.S. drivers, not stylish enough for the Japanese drivers). Afraid to lose its market, Honda sent teams to visit U.S. families and observe how they used their Honda Accords. By personal observation, the teams found out that the Americans like lots of compartments for storing maps and change. The teams also actually took U.S. road trips in Accord and in Ford Taurus and Toyota Camry as its rivals in midsize car. The results of this observation study were used to design a new 1998 Accord for U.S. drivers. This car has 101.7 cubic feet for passenger space compared to 101.5 cubic feet for Ford Taurus and 97.9 cubic feet for Toyota Camry. Moreover, Accord also delivered higher customer value by cutting the price. With these changes, Honda executives are expecting to increase U.S. sales to total of 1 million units by the year 2000.

Using the results of personal observation studies, Honda customizes the Accord to world markets. U.S. Accord is designed as a family car by providing extra headroom and a roomy interior to keep up with the demands of its aging baby-boomers customers, whereas Japanese Accord is designed as a compact, sporty car loaded with high-tech gizmos aimed at young professionals. It is also smaller to adjust to narrower roads in Japan. Honda also paid attention to its European market. The 1998 Accord for European version was a short, narrow body customized to tiny streets in Europe but not losing its stiff and sporty ride aimed at the Old World drivers.

have made a major impact on mechanical observation. The UPC system together with optical scanners, allow for mechanized information collection regarding consumer purchases by product category, brand, store type, price, and quantity (see chapter 4).

In contrast, many mechanical observation devices do require respondent involvement. These mechanical devices may be classified into five groups (1) eye-tracking monitors, (2) pupilometers, (3) psychogalvanometers, (4) voice pitch analyzers, and (5) devices measuring response latency. Eye-tracking equipment, such as oculometers, eye cameras, or eye view minuters, records the gaze movements of the eye. These devices can be used to determine how a respondent reads an advertisement or views a TV commercial and for how long the respondent looks at various parts of the stimulus. Such information is directly relevant to assessing advertising effectiveness. The pupilometer measures changes in the diameter of the pupils of the respondent's eyes. Respondents are asked to look at a screen on which an advertisement or other stimulus is projected. Image brightness and distance from the respondents' eyes are held constant. Changes in pupil size are interpreted as changes in cognitive (thinking) activity resulting from exposure to the stimulus. The underlying assumption is that increased pupil size reflects interest and positive attitudes toward the stimulus.[46]

Psychogalvanometer An instrument that measures a respondent's galvanic skin response.

Galvanic Skin Response Changes in the electrical resistance of the skin that relate to a respondent's affective state.

The **psychogalvanometer** measures **galvanic skin response** (GSR) or changes in the electrical resistance of the skin.[47] The respondent is fitted with small electrodes that monitor electrical resistance and is shown stimuli such as advertisements, packages, and slogans. The theory behind this device is that physiological changes, such as increased perspiration, accompany emotional reactions. Excitement leads to increased perspiration, which increases the electrical resistance of the skin. From the strength of the response, the researcher infers the respondent's interest level and attitudes toward the stimuli.

Voice Pitch Analysis Measurement of emotional reactions through changes in the respondent's voice.

Voice pitch analysis measures emotional reactions through changes in the respondent's voice. Changes in the relative vibration frequency of the human voice that accompany emotional reaction are measured with audio-adapted computer equipment.[48]

Response Latency The amount of time it takes to respond to a question.

Response latency is the time a respondent takes before answering a question. It is used as a measure of the relative preference for various alternatives.[49] Response time is thought to be directly related to uncertainty. Therefore, the longer a respondent takes to choose between two alternatives, the closer the alternatives are in terms of preference. On the other hand, if the respondent makes a quick decision, one alternative is clearly preferred. With the increased popularity of computer-assisted data collection, response latency can be recorded accurately and without the respondent's awareness.

Use of eye-tracking monitors, pupilometers, psychogalvanometers, and voice pitch analyzers assumes that physiological reactions are associated with specific cognitive and affective responses. This has yet to be clearly demonstrated.[50] Furthermore, calibration of these devices to measure physiological arousal is difficult, and they are expensive to use. Another limitation is that respondents are placed in an artificial environment and know that they are being observed. Despite these limitations, such devices can be useful as illustrated by the NutraSweet Company.

EXAMPLE

All Packages Are Not Created Equal

The NutraSweet Co., maker of Equal sugar substitute, wanted to reposition the product to compete with sugar and market it as a natural, more healthful replacement for use in foods. To achieve this objective, a new package was created for Equal. Nova Research, Inc., was commissioned to undertake research to test several new package designs. The study conducted involved a sample of 1,121 female heads-of-household between ages 21 and 59 who sweetened food and beverages on a regular basis.

Respondents participated in a shelf visibility test in which eye-tracking equipment was used to measure speed of registration of the product category, brand identity, and key packaging elements for the Equal designs and competitive products within the array. The shelf visibility test uses an electronically timed shutter to control how long the respondents view a particular stimulus. In this case, respondents saw slides of grocery shelves stocked with variously arranged packages of Equal, competing sugar substitutes, and regular sugar. The slides included a mass display and a close-up of each Equal test package.

This research enabled Nova to select the best package for Equal. The package design that was selected was the one that scored fastest in speed of recognition. It also attained a high level of brand recognition and shelf visibility. The new package strengthened the sales of Equal, which is the category leader with 49.8 percent of the sugar substitute market.[51] ■

Audit

Pantry Audit A type of audit in which the researcher inventories the brands, quantities, and package sizes of products in a consumer's home.

In an audit, the researcher collects data by examining physical records or performing inventory analysis. Audits have two distinguishing features. First, data are collected personally by the researcher. Second, the data are based on counts, usually of physical objects. Retail and wholesale audits conducted by marketing research suppliers were discussed in the context of secondary data (see chapter 4). Here we focus on the role of audits in collecting primary data. In this respect, an important audit conducted at the consumer level, generally in conjunction with one of the survey methods, is the pantry audit. In a **pantry audit**, the researcher takes an inventory of brands, quantities, and package sizes in a consumer's home, perhaps in the course of a personal interview. Pantry audits greatly reduce the problem of untruthfulness or other forms of response bias. However, obtaining permission to examine consumers' pantries can be difficult, and the field work is expensive. Furthermore, the brands in the pantry do not necessarily reflect the most preferred brands or the brands purchased most often. For these reasons, audits are most common at the retail and wholesale level, as the following example illustrates.

EXAMPLE

The Product Pipeline

An important marketing research task is finding out where the product is in the long pipeline from manufacturer to consumer. This was a problem in the personal computer industry. No one was quite sure which computers people were actually buying and which were piling up in inventory. The movement of PCs through the various distribution channels could not be tracked accurately from the available data. To remedy this situation, the A. C. Nielsen Company arranged with major computer chains to send in teams of auditors to take physical inventory and determine what people were buying. The audit provided information on the retail sales of the various brands of personal computers and their movement in the distribution channels.[52] ■

Content Analysis

Content Analysis The objective, systematic, and quantitative description of the manifest content of a communication.

Content analysis is an appropriate method when the phenomenon to be observed is communication, rather than behavior or physical objects. It is defined as the objective, systematic, and quantitative description of the manifest content of a communication.[53] It includes observation as well as analysis. The unit of analysis may be words (different words or types of words in the message), characters (individuals or objects), themes (propositions), space and time measures (length or duration of the message), or topics (subject of the message). Analytical categories for classifying the units are developed and the communication is broken down according to prescribed rules. Marketing research applications involve observing and analyzing the content or message of advertisements, newspaper articles, television and radio programs, and so on. For example, the frequency of appearance of blacks, women, and members of other minority groups in mass media has been studied using content analysis. In the department store patronage project, content analysis may be used to analyze magazine advertisements of the sponsoring and competing stores to compare their projected images. Content analysis has also been used in cross-cultural advertising research, as in the following example.

EXAMPLE

Cross-Cultural Content Makes Ad Agencies Content

Content analysis was used to compare the information content in American and Japanese magazine advertising. Six categories of magazines (general, women's, men's, professional, sports, and entertainment) were chosen from each country. All advertisements were sampled from issues of these magazines pertaining to the same time period. This resulted in a total of 1,440 advertisements: 832 from American magazines and 608 from Japanese magazines. Three judges independently noted whether each advertisement was informative or uninformative, which criteria for information content were satisfied by the advertisement, the size of the ad, and the product category being advertised. Japanese magazine advertising was found to be consistently more informative than U.S. magazine advertising. For example, more than 85 percent of the Japanese ads analyzed satisfied at least one criterion for information content and thus were perceived to be informative, compared to only 75 percent of the American ads. Likewise, Japanese ads had an average of 1.7 information cues per ad, compared to 1.3 cues per ad for the American ads. This information is useful for multinational companies and advertising agencies including Saatchi & Saatchi Worldwide, McCann Erickson Worldwide, BBDO Worldwide, and others with global operations conducting cross-cultural advertising campaigns.[54] ■

Content analysis can involve tedious coding and analysis. However, microcomputers and mainframes can be used to facilitate coding and analysis. The manifest content of the object can be computer coded. The observed frequencies of category codes can be aggregated and compared on the criteria of interest using computers. Although content analysis has not been widely used in marketing research, the technique offers great potential. For example, it could be profitably employed in the analysis of open-ended questions.

Trace Analysis

Trace Analysis An approach in which data collection is based on physical traces, or evidence, of past behavior.

An observation method that can be inexpensive if used creatively is trace analysis. In **trace analysis**, data collection is based on physical traces, or evidence, of past behavior. These traces may be left intentionally or unintentionally by the respondents. To illustrate, in the context of the department store patronage project, store charge card slips are traces that can be analyzed to examine shoppers' store credit usage behavior. Several other innovative applications of trace analysis have been made in marketing research.

- The selective erosion of tiles in a museum indexed by the replacement rate was used to determine the relative popularity of exhibits.
- The number of different fingerprints on a page was used to gauge the readership of various advertisements in a magazine.
- The position of the radio dials in cars brought in for service was used to estimate share of listening audience of various radio stations. Advertisers used the estimates to decide on which stations to advertise.
- The age and condition of cars in a parking lot were used to assess the affluence of customers.
- The magazines people donated to charity were used to determine people's favorite magazines.
- Internet visitors leave traces that can be analyzed to examine browsing and usage behavior, as in the following example.

EXAMPLE

Have a Cookie

Many users do not realize it, but they have been served a cookie or two while on the Internet. A "cookie" is not a culinary delight in this case. It is a sophisticated means by which a Web site can collect information on visitors. Often this process takes place without the knowledge of the Web surfer.

The cookie is a group of letters and numbers stored in a Web surfer's browser that identify the user. Companies and individuals that host Web sites use cookies to collect marketing research information on visitors. Cookies follow the traveler through the Web site and record the pages accessed by the visitor, and the number of minutes spent on each page. Your name, address, phone number, and access site can be collected by the cookie and saved into a database if the visitor enters any information. In essence, the cookie collects data on the user during every visit to the site.

Hotwired's *Packet* uses cookies to collect information about site traffic. The information helps marketing personnel at the electronic and print magazine to collect demographics on the reader. Also, the company can monitor "hits" on particular topics and gain valuable feedback on user interest. Data collection is based on visitor behavior. This disguised technique enables Hotwired to monitor use patterns and to eliminate socially acceptable response bias. Information collected in this manner has been used to modify editorial content and format to make the magazine more appealing.[55] ■

Although trace analysis has been creatively applied, it has limitations. Often the data are incomplete and several assumptions have to be made in order to analyze them. Current evidence indicates that it should be used only when no other approach is possible. Moreover, ethical issues, such as the use of cookies, should be duly addressed.

A COMPARATIVE EVALUATION OF OBSERVATION METHODS

A comparative evaluation of the observation methods is given in Table 6.3. The different observation methods are evaluated in terms of the degree of structure, degree of disguise, ability to observe in a natural setting, observation bias, measurement and analysis bias, and additional general factors.

Structure relates to the specification of what is to be observed and how the measurements are to be recorded. As can be seen from Table 6.3, personal observation is low, trace analysis is medium, and audit and content analysis are high on the degree of structure. Mechanical observation can vary widely from low to high depending on the methods used. Methods such as optical scanners are very structured in that the characteristics to be measured; for instance, characteristics of items purchased scanned in supermarket check-outs are precisely defined. Thus, these methods are high in the degree of structure. In contrast, mechanical methods, such as use of hidden cameras to observe children at play with toys, tend to be unstructured.

The degree of disguise is low in audits as it is difficult to conceal the identity of auditors. Personal observation offers a medium degree of disguise as there are limitations on the extent to which the observer can be disguised as a shopper, sales clerk, employee, etc. Trace analysis and content analysis offer a high degree of disguise as the data are collected after the phenomenon to be observed has taken place. Some mechanical observations such as hidden cameras offer excellent disguise, whereas the use of others, such as psychogalvanometers, is very difficult to disguise.

The ability to observe in a natural setting is low in trace analysis because the observation takes place after the behavior has occurred. It is medium in the case of content analysis because the communication being analyzed is only a limited representation of the natural

TABLE 6.3

A COMPARATIVE EVALUATION OF OBSERVATION METHODS

Criteria	*Personal Observation*	*Mechanical Observation*	*Audit*	*Content Analysis*	*Trace Analysis*
Degree of structure	Low	Low to High	High	High	Medium
Degree of disguise	Medium	Low to High	Low	High	High
Ability to observe in natural setting	High	Low to High	High	Medium	Low
Observation bias	High	Low	Low	Medium	Medium
Analysis bias	High	Low to Medium	Low	Low	Medium
General remarks	Most flexible	Can be intrusive	Expensive	Limited to communications	Method of last resort

phenomenon. Personal observation and audits are excellent on this score as human observers can observe people or objects in a variety of natural settings. Mechanical observation methods vary from low (e.g., psychogalvanometers) to high (e.g., turnstiles).

Observation bias is low in the case of mechanical observation because a human observer is not involved. It is also low for audits. Although the auditors are humans, the observation usually takes place on objects and the characteristics to be observed are well defined leading to low observation bias. Observation bias is medium for trace analysis and content analysis. In both these methods, human observers are involved and the characteristics to be observed are not that well defined. However, the observers typically do not interact with human respondents during the observation process, thus lessening the degree of bias. It is high for personal observation due to the use of human observers who interact with the phenomenon being observed.

Data analysis bias is low for audits and content analysis because the variables are precisely defined, the data are quantitative, and statistical analysis is conducted. Trace analysis has a medium degree of bias because the definition of variables is not very precise. Mechanical observation methods can have a low (e.g., scanner data) to medium (e.g., hidden camera) degree of analysis bias. Unlike personal observation, the bias in mechanical observation is limited to the medium level due to improved measurement and classification, the phenomenon to be observed can be recorded continuously using mechanical devices.

In addition, personal observation is the most flexible as human observers can observe a wide variety of phenomena in a wide variety of settings. Some mechanical observation methods such as psychogalvanometers can be very intrusive leading to artificiality and bias. Audits using human auditors tend to be expensive. Content analysis is well suited for and limited to the observation of communications. As mentioned earlier, trace analysis is a method of last resort. The application of these criteria will lead to the identification of an appropriate method, if observation is at all suitable in the given situation.

A COMPARISON OF SURVEY AND OBSERVATION METHODS

Few marketing research projects rely solely on observational methods to obtain primary data.[56] This implies that observational methods have some major disadvantages as compared to survey methods. Yet these methods offer some advantages that make their use in conjunction with survey methods quite fruitful.

Relative Advantages of Observation

The greatest advantage of observational methods is that they permit measurement of actual behavior rather than reports of intended or preferred behavior. There is no reporting bias, and potential bias caused by the interviewer and the interviewing process is eliminated or reduced. Certain types of data can be collected only by observation. These include behavior patterns of which the respondent is unaware or is unable to communicate. For example, information on babies' toy preferences is best obtained by observing babies at play. Moreover, if the observed phenomenon occurs frequently or is of short duration, observational methods may cost less and be faster than survey methods.

Relative Disadvantages of Observation

The most serious disadvantage of observation is that the reasons for the observed behavior may not be determined because little is known about the underlying motives, beliefs, attitudes, and preferences. For example, people observed buying a brand of cereal may or may not like it themselves. They may be purchasing that brand for someone else in the household. Another limitation of observation is that selective perception (bias in the researcher's perception) can bias the data. In addition, observational data is often time consuming and expensive and it is difficult to observe certain forms of behavior such as personal activities. Finally, in some cases the use of observational methods may be unethical, as in monitoring the behavior of people without their knowledge or consent.

To sum up, observation has the potential to provide valuable information when properly used. From a practical standpoint, it is best to view observation as a complement to survey methods, rather than as being in competition with them. The following example illustrates this point.

EXAMPLE

Stores Plan on Unplanned Purchases

Point-of-Purchase Advertising Institute, Inc. (POPAI) recently conducted a study to determine the purchasing behavior of grocery shoppers. Consumers were surveyed as they began their shopping trips and questioned on their intended purchases. At the check-out counter, their actual purchases were recorded with UPC scanners. These observational data were then compared with their intended purchases. It was found that 81 percent of all brand (e.g., Lipton tea) purchases were unplanned and the result of in-store decisions, a substantial increase from 64.8 percent a decade ago. Unplanned product (e.g., tea) purchases also were up; 60.4 percent of all items bought were classified as unplanned purchases. Shoppers are not committed to their shopping list when they enter the store. Moreover, brand decisions often are made at point-of-purchase. Thus marketers of grocery products can greatly benefit from in-store advertising, point-of-purchase displays, and other in-store promotions.[57] ■

INTERNATIONAL MARKETING RESEARCH

Selection of appropriate interviewing methods is much more difficult because of the challenges of conducting research in foreign countries. Given the differences in the economic, structural, informational and technological, and sociocultural environments, the feasibility and popularity of the different interviewing methods vary widely. In the United States and Canada, the telephone has achieved almost total penetration of households. As a result, telephone interviewing is the dominant mode of questionnaire administration. The same situation exists in some European countries such as Sweden. However, in many other European countries, telephone penetration is still not complete. In developing countries only very few households have telephones.

In-home personal interviews are the dominant mode of collecting survey data in many European countries such as Switzerland, newly industrialized countries (NICs), and developing countries. While mall intercepts are being conducted in some European countries, such as Sweden, they are not popular in Europe or developing countries. In contrast, central location/street interviews constitute the dominant method of collecting survey data in France and the Netherlands.

Because of low cost, mail interviews continue to be used in most developed countries where literacy is high and the postal system is well developed: United States, Canada, Denmark, Finland, Iceland, Norway, Sweden, and the Netherlands, for example. In Africa, Asia, and South America, however, the use of mail surveys and mail panels is low because of wider illiteracy and the large proportion of population living in rural areas. Mail panels are extensively used only in a few countries outside the United States, such as Canada, the United Kingdom, France, West Germany, and the Netherlands. However, the use of panels may increase with the advent of new technology. Likewise, although a Web site can be accessed from anywhere in the world, access to the Web or e-mail is limited in many countries, particularly developing countries. Hence, the use of electronic surveys is not feasible, especially for interviewing households. The different methods of survey administration are discussed in more detail in chapter 23.

Selection of Survey Methods

No questionnaire administration method is superior in all situations. Table 6.4 presents a comparative evaluation of the major modes of collecting quantitative data in the context of international marketing research. In this table, the survey methods are discussed only under the broad headings of telephone, personal, mail, and electronic interviews. The use of CATI, CAPI, and mail panels depends heavily on the state of technological development in the country. Likewise, the use of mall-intercept interviewing is contingent on the dominance of shopping malls in the retailing environment. The same is true for e-mail and Internet surveys, which rely on access to computers and the Internet. The major methods of interviewing should be carefully evaluated on the criteria given in Table 6.4, as shown.

Another very important consideration in selecting the methods of administering questionnaires is to ensure equivalence and comparability across countries. Different methods may have different reliabilities in different countries. In collecting data from different countries, it is desirable to use survey methods with equivalent levels of reliability, rather than the same method, as illustrated in the following example.[58]

EXAMPLE

Using Dominant Survey Methods to Gain Dominant Market Share

Reebok International Ltd., with a 16 percent share of the athletic shoe market in the United States, is seeking to expand in Europe. Europe is a market with vast potential for sales of sneakers amounting to $7 billion in 1998. Rather than strictly compete with Nike, Adidas, and Puma in Europe for the athletic market, Reebok would like to institute strong marketing programs to sell street sneakers to the European masses. A survey of consumer preferences for sneakers is to be undertaken in three countries: Sweden, France, and Switzerland. Comparability of results can best be achieved by using the dominant mode of interviewing in each country: telephone interviews in Sweden, central location/street interviews in France, and in-home personal interviews in Switzerland.[59] ■

TABLE 6.4

A COMPARATIVE EVALUATION OF SURVEY METHODS FOR INTERNATIONAL MARKETING RESEARCH

Criteria	*Telephone*	*Personal*	*Mail*	*Electronic*
High sample control	+	+	–	–
Difficulty in locating respondents at home	+	–	+	+
Inaccessibility of homes	+	–	+	+
Unavailability of a large pool of trained interviewers	+	–	+	+
Large population in rural areas	–	+	–	–
Unavailability of maps	+	–	+	+
Unavailability of current telephone directory	–	+	–	+
Unavailability of mailing lists	+	+	–	+
Low penetration of telephones	–	+	+	–
Lack of an efficient postal system	+	+	–	+
Low level of literacy	–	+	–	–
Face-to-face communication culture	–	+	–	–
Poor access to computers and Internet	+	+	+	–

Note: A + denotes an advantage, and a – denotes a disadvantage.

As in the case of surveys, the selection of an appropriate observation method in international marketing research should also take into account the differences in the economic, structural, informational and technological, and sociocultural environment.

ETHICS IN MARKETING RESEARCH

The unethical use of survey research as a guise for selling or fund raising was discussed in chapter 1. Another ethical issue that is salient in survey and observation research is respondents' anonymity. Researchers have an obligation to not disclose respondents' names to outside parties including the client. This is all the more critical if the respondents were promised anonymity in order to obtain their participation. The client is not entitled to the names of respondents. Only when respondents are notified in advance and their consent is obtained prior to administering the survey can their names be disclosed to the client. Even in such situations, the researcher should have the assurance that the client will not use respondents' names in sales efforts or misuse them in other ways.

EXAMPLE

The Signal Is Busy for Telephone Research

The Council for Marketing and Opinion Research (CMOR) recently identified the "major threats to research vitality." At the top of the list was telephone research due to concern over proposed legislation. About half of the states have introduced bills to regulate unsolicited telephone calls and the remaining are considering similar legislation. A California law, designed to limit eavesdropping, makes it illegal to listen in on an extension, and this might limit supervisory monitoring of telephone interviewers.

Another issue facing the marketing research industry is image as the general public does not distinguish between telephone research and telemarketing. This identity crisis is exacerbated by the action of some firms to commit "sugging and frugging," industry terms for selling or fund raising under the guise of a survey (discussed in chapter 1).

All these barriers have raised the cost of telephone research and make it difficult for researchers to obtain representative samples. A study by Walker Research revealed that the refusal rate in telephone interviews doubled in just 10 years to about 30 percent due to annoyance with unsolicited calls and concern about privacy.

The CMOR is fighting back and has hired the Washington law firm of Covington and Burling to lobby Congress and coordinate state-level lobbying. Another action under consideration is a "seal of approval" from the CMOR to raise the public's image perceptions of responsible research firms. The battle to save telephone research must be waged; all it takes is a phone call.[60] ■

Researchers should not place respondents in stressful situations. Disclaimers such as "there are no right or wrong answers, we are only interested in your opinion" can relieve much of the stress inherent in a survey.

Often the behavior of people is observed without their knowledge because informing the respondents may alter their behavior.[61] However, this can violate the respondents' privacy. One guideline is that people should not be observed for research in situations in which they would not expect to be observed by the public. However, observing people in public places such as a mall or a grocery store is appropriate if certain procedures are followed. Notices should be posted in these areas stating that they are under observation for marketing research purposes. After the data have been collected, the researcher should obtain the necessary permission from the respondents. If any of the respondents refuse to grant permission, the observation records pertaining to them should be destroyed. These guidelines should also be applied when using cookies on the Internet.[62]

INTERNET AND COMPUTER APPLICATIONS

The use of the Internet and computers has been discussed throughout the chapter. Internet surveys are gaining in popularity. One reason is that the cost in most cases is less than phone and mail surveys or personal interviews. Also, the Internet survey is not as intrusive as the phone call in the middle of dinner. The on-line survey can be completed in one's own time and place. Quick response time is another advantage cited by those producing on-line surveys. Greenfield Online Research Center cited a case in which they placed a survey on-line "Friday and had 2,400 completed forms on Monday morning." Greenfield has a panel of nearly 200,000 people via the Internet. Thus the speed of response is a definite advantage of on-line market research.

Another advantage of Internet market research is the ability to target specific populations. For example, the purchasers of a specific model home office product, purchased over a specific time interval, were needed to conduct some market research. Several months of traditional research were conducted via telephone and several thousands of dollars were spent to land a very few individuals. Then using the Internet, hundreds of potential candidates were found in only a few weeks at very little cost in comparison. Thus on-line market research aids those researchers attempting to find specific target markets.

There are limitations to electronic surveys. The Internet or e-mail users are not representative of the general population. Burke Marketing Research is trying to improve the randomness of those participating in on-line surveys by designing suitable Internet sampling programs. Other limitations of such market research is the verification of who is actually responding to the survey. The absence of a human facilitator to motivate participants, security, and privacy are also areas of concern. The research company can receive "flames," messages from recipients who consider receiving an on-line survey as an invasion of their privacy.

One company, Decisive Technology Corporation, created two software tools to help users create and analyze e-mail and Web-based surveys. One product, Decisive Survey, retails for $799, and allows users to create, administer, and analyze Web-based and e-mail surveys. Their other product, Decisive Feedback, retails for $249, and is used for e-mail surveys only. Both products currently run exclusively on Windows platforms, from Windows 3.1 to Windows NT. The software is a forms-based tool that gives the users a graphical way to design surveys. Once the completed surveys are returned, the software then allows the easy porting of data to databases and statistical software such as SAS and SPSS. Previously, marketing research companies would use text-based surveys for the Internet. However, this meant that the data had to be rekeyed once it was returned. Decisive Survey and Decisive Feedback allow for automatic tabulation and graphical outputs such as pie and line charts. The system also allows for the full range of responses, such as choose one, choose all that apply, and fill in the blank.[63]

EXAMPLE

On-Line Survey Leads to the Development of OnCart Site

Prior to developing their OnCart site (www.kroger.com), which enables customers to buy their groceries over the Internet and have them delivered at home, Kroger conducted research to identify the market potential for on-line shopping. They posted a survey on the Internet. This allowed them to target the Internet users instead of calling random households to find ones that use the Internet on a regular basis. It also allowed them to target their questions specifically to the motivations of the on-line shoppers and nonshoppers. Other information obtained through the survey was Internet usage, products purchased, security concerns, and convenience issues.

Through this survey, Kroger was able to determine the interest for on-line grocery shopping that helped them develop the OnCart site. In addition, they received valuable information about the individuals who shop over the Internet and the general characteristics of this market. The information helped Kroger create effective ways to advertise this new service in order to reach a broad group of Internet users that may be interested in on-line grocery shopping. ■

The Web can be a very good source for observation and can provide valuable information. The observations can be made in variety of ways. The primary observations can be made by the number of times the Web page is visited, the time spent on the page can also be measured by advanced techniques of starting the timer when the person visiting the page clicks on a certain icon and stopping the timer when he or she clicks on the next button. Further, various other links can be provided by the researcher on the Web page, and it can be observed as to which links are accessed more often. This will provide the researcher with important information about the information needs of the individuals and also of the interests of the target segment. The analysis of the links from which the company site is being approached by the individuals will provide the market researcher the important information regarding the consumers' related interests, and an in-depth analysis of the link sites will provide information on advertising, competitors, consumers, target market demographics, and psychographics.

The use of microcomputers and mainframes has already been discussed in the context of CATI, CAPI, content analysis, audits, and trace analysis. Software for implementing these and other survey and observation methods is available. Computer-automated telephone surveys (CATS) systems are capable of dialing and interviewing respondents without any human intervention, other than the digital recording of questions to be asked during the phone survey. A handheld computer can replace paper questionnaires used in personal interviewing with the use of the SidePad utility and the ABase programming language from

FOCUS ON Burke

Burke uses all the major interviewing methods (telephone, mail, personal, and electronic). The use of multiple methods is illustrated in customer satisfaction research. Burke generally uses telephone interviews, mail surveys, or a combination of the two to collect customer satisfaction data. Telephone interviews are most appropriate when:

- Customers must be screened to identify the person best qualified to answer the questions.
- The project requires fast turnaround.
- The questionnaire has complex skip patterns or a number of open-ended questions.
- The number of customers eligible to participate in the survey is relatively small.

Burke operates three data collection centers with a total of 250 CATI stations.

Mail surveys tend to cost less than do telephone surveys and are therefore most appropriate for large-scale projects. For example, Burke uses mail surveys to collect data from customers of a nationwide fast food restaurant chain.

Interactive voice recognition systems have gained popularity in recent years. Burke uses this technology for a large financial institution. Both customers and employees use their touch tone phone to key in answers to Burke's satisfaction questions.

In a typical customer satisfaction study, Burke's client provides the list of customer names, addresses, and phone numbers. Client-supplied lists are particularly common for business-to-business studies. Clients generally ask Burke to interview current customers, though it is not unusual to interview former customers.

Mall-intercept surveys are also conducted frequently, when it is advantageous to administer the questionnaire using personal interviewing. For this purpose, Burke has contacts with a network of more than 200 mall agencies. Opinion One is a specialized mall-intercept survey offered by Burke. It is computer administered (CAPI) using a fully interactive multimedia platform designed to collect data based on a variety of visual and audio stimuli. All the mall locations offering Opinion One are electronically linked to ensure fast transmission of data to and from Burke's Cincinnati headquarters.

For the Internet, Burke has designed WEBNOSTICS, a survey that is administered at the client's Web site to every *n*th visitor to obtain a systematic evaluation of the Web site. The Secure Surfer Index is an Internet survey that evaluates the impact of the client's Web site on the commitment and loyalty of Web visitors. As people visit the client's Web site, they are randomly presented with a link to the Burke Secure Surfer Index questions. If they do not want to participate, they press the "decline" button and continue surfing unhindered. If they agree to participate, they press the "accept" button and are tracked from the exact location and subdirectory of the client's Web site.

The bulk of worldwide research is done by face-to-face interviews and self-administered interviews. The United States and Canada are the only countries with high levels of telephone interviewing. Among Burke's international affiliates, Sweden is the third highest at about 18 percent of interviews conducted by telephone. Therefore, while conducting international marketing research, Burke designs surveys so that they may be administered by different modes in different countries.

Burke conducted a study for a software vendor in 14 countries. The range of feasible data collection methods included telephone, mail, face to face, and fax. A major consideration for research design was creating questions that could be legitimately administered using any of these methods and produce comparable results. Burke's procedure is to involve a research professional in each country to give a perspective on how the data could best be collected in their country and how the questions should be modified for their country. At this point, key budget and timing decisions have to be made as a change of data collection method to allow greater comparability across countries can seriously affect the cost and time of completion of the study. These are the types of decisions and trade-offs that only experienced professionals in the different cultures can manage. By building expertise in different survey methods at a global level, Burke has the resources to select the survey method that is best suited for a given study in a specific country, and which will result in data comparable to those collected in other countries in which different survey methods may be used.

Advanced Data Research, Inc. (ADR) of Bloomfield Hills, Michigan. Using pen-based computing technology, this system uses the display memory as a software keypad. DOS-based PC survey software (such as Ci2, Ci3, or ACA being run simultaneously with the SidePad utility) accepts the touch of the screen as a key stroke on a keyboard. A variety of software is also available for conducting mail surveys. Conquest Direct Express by Donnelley Marketing Information Services defines market areas and obtains counts and consumer lists for only those households or individuals in the block group or enumeration districts, census tracts, or zip codes in a desired area (geometric or geographic).

SUMMARY

The two basic means of obtaining primary quantitative data in descriptive research are survey and observation. Survey involves the direct questioning of respondents, while observation entails recording respondent behavior.

Surveys involve the administration of a questionnaire and may be classified, based on the method or mode of administration, as (1) traditional telephone interviews, (2) CATI, (3) in-home personal interviews, (4) mall-intercept interviews, (5) CAPI, (6) mail surveys, (7) mail panels, (8) e-mail surveys, and (9) Internet surveys. Of these methods, traditional telephone interviews and CATI are the most popular. However, each method has some general advantages and disadvantages. The various methods may be compared in terms of flexibility of data collection, diversity of questions, use of physical stimuli, sample control, control of the data collection environment, control of field force, quantity of data, social desirability, obtaining sensitive information, potential for interviewer bias, response rate, perceived anonymity, speed, and cost. Although these data collection methods are usually thought of as distinct and competitive, they should not be considered mutually exclusive. It is possible to employ them productively in combination.

Observational methods may be classified as structured or unstructured, disguised or undisguised, and natural or contrived. The major methods are personal observation, mechanical observation, audit, content analysis, and trace analysis. As compared to surveys, the relative advantages of observational methods are (1) they permit measurement of actual behavior, (2) there is no reporting bias, and (3) there is less potential for interviewer bias. Also, certain types of data can be obtained best, or only, by observation. The relative disadvantages of observation are (1) very little can be inferred about motives, beliefs, attitudes and preferences, (2) potential for observer bias, (3) most methods are time consuming and expensive, (4) it is difficult to observe some forms of behavior, and (5) potential for being unethical. Observation is rarely used as the sole method of obtaining primary data, but it can be usefully employed in conjunction with survey methods.

In collecting data from different countries, it is desirable to use survey methods with equivalent levels of reliability, rather than the same method. Respondents' anonymity should be protected and their names should not be turned over to the clients. People should not be observed without consent for research in situations in which they would not expect to be observed by the public. The Internet and computers are used extensively in survey research. They also facilitate observation methods, particularly content analysis, audits, and trace analysis.

KEY TERMS AND CONCEPTS

survey method
structured data collection
fixed-alternative questions
mail panel
hypertext markup language
sample control
sampling frame
random digit dialing (rdd)
random digit directory designs
field force
response rate
nonresponse bias
critical request
perceived anonymity
social desirability
observation
structured observation
unstructured observation
natural observation
contrived observation

personal observation
mechanical observation
psychogalvanometer
galvanic skin response
voice pitch analysis
response latency
pantry audit
content analysis
trace analysis

ACRONYMS

The classification of survey methods by mode of administration may be described by the acronym METHODS:

M ail panels
E lectronic methods: e-mail and Internet surveys
T elephone interviews
H ome (in-home personal) interviewing
O n-site mall interviews
D irect mail interviews
S oftware for CATI and CAPI

In using observational methods, you must WATCH the respondents' behavior. These methods may be described by the acronym WATCH:

W alkie-talkie: mechanical observation
A udit
T race analysis
C ontent analysis
H uman (personal) observation

EXERCISES

Questions

1. Explain briefly how the topics covered in this chapter fit into the framework of the marketing research process.
2. What are the advantages and disadvantages of the structured direct survey method?
3. Name the major modes for obtaining information via a survey.
4. What are the relevant factors for evaluating which survey method is best suited to a particular domestic research project?
5. What would be the most appropriate survey method for a project in which control of field force and cost are critical factors?
6. Name the types of mechanical observation and explain how they work.
7. Explain how content analysis could be employed in the analysis of open-ended questions. Comment on the relative advantages and disadvantages of using such a method.
8. Why is trace analysis used as a last resort?
9. What are the relative advantages and disadvantages of observation?
10. What are the relevant factors for evaluating which survey method is best for an international marketing research project?

Problems

1. Describe a marketing research problem in which both survey and observation methods could be used for obtaining the information needed.
2. Collect 30 advertisements featuring women from recent issues of popular magazines. Do a content analysis of these ads to examine the different roles in which women are portrayed in advertising.
3. The campus food service would like to determine how many people eat in the student cafeteria. List the survey method that could be used to obtain this information. Which method is best?

INTERNET AND COMPUTER EXERCISES

1. Ask your instructor or other faculty members if you could serve as a respondent in a computer-assisted personal interview. Then answer the same questionnaire in a pencil-and-paper format. Compare the two experiences.
2. Use simple spreadsheet software, such as Lotus 1-2-3 or Excel or any appropriate microcomputer or mainframe program, to conduct the content analysis described in problem 2 above.
3. Locate an Internet survey for which you would qualify as a respondent. Answer this survey. How would you evaluate this survey based on the criteria factors of Table 6.2?
4. Locate an Internet survey. Examine the content of the questionnaire carefully. What are relative advantages and disadvantages of administering the same survey using CATI or mall-intercept interviewing?
5. Design an e-mail survey to measure students' attitudes toward credit cards. E-mail the survey to 10 students. Summarize, in a qualitative way, the responses received. Are student attitudes toward credit cards positive or negative?
6. Visit the Gallup organization's Web site at www.gallup.com. What survey methods have been used by Gallup in some of the recent surveys posted at this site? Why were these survey methods selected?

Chapter 7

"Our experiments can not prove causality. They can, however, go a long way toward eliminating all the possible causes other than the ones we are interested in."

Michael Baumgardner, president, Burke, Inc.

Causal Research Design: Experimentation

OBJECTIVES

After reading this chapter, the student should be able to

1. explain the concept of causality as defined in marketing research and distinguish between the ordinary meaning and the scientific meaning of causality
2. define and differentiate the two types of validity: internal and external
3. discuss the various extraneous variables that can affect the validity of results obtained through experimentation and explain how the researcher can control extraneous variables
4. describe and evaluate experimental designs and the differences among preexperimental, true experimental, quasi-experimental, and statistical designs
5. compare and contrast the use of laboratory versus field experimentation and experimental versus nonexperimental designs in marketing research
6. describe test marketing and its various forms: standard test market, controlled test market, and simulated test market
7. understand why the internal and external validity of field experiments conducted overseas is generally lower than in the United States
8. describe the ethical issues involved in conducting causal research and the role of debriefing in addressing some of these issues
9. discuss the use of the Internet and computers in causal research

OVERVIEW

We introduced causal designs in chapter 3, where we discussed their relationship to exploratory and descriptive designs, and defined experimentation as the primary method employed in causal designs. This chapter explores the concept of causality further. We identify the necessary conditions for causality, examine the role of validity in experimentation, and consider the extraneous variables and procedures for controlling them. We present a classification of experimental designs and consider specific designs, along with the relative merits of laboratory and field experiments. An application in the area of test marketing is discussed in detail. The considerations involved in conducting experimental research for international markets are discussed. Several ethical issues that arise in experimentation are identified. The chapter concludes with a discussion of the use of the Internet and computers in causal research. We begin with some examples.

EXAMPLE

It's in the Bag

LeSportsac, Inc., filed a suit against Kmart Corp. after Kmart introduced a "di Paris sac" line of bags, which LeSportsac claimed looked like its bags. According to LeSportsac, Kmart led consumers to believe that they were purchasing LeSportsac bags when they were not. To prove its point, LeSportsac undertook marketing research.

Two groups of women were selected in a field experiment. One group was shown two LeSportsac lightweight soft-sided bags from which all tags were removed and all words and designs were reprinted within the distinctive LeSportsac ovals. The second group of women were shown two "di Paris sac" bags with the brand name visible and bearing the tags and labels these bags carry in Kmart stores. Information was obtained from both groups of women to learn whether or not they perceived a single company or source and/or brand identification of masked bags, what identifications they make, if any, and the reasons they give for doing so.

The sample consisted of 200 women in each group selected by personal-intercept interviews conducted in central locations in Chicago, Los Angeles, and New York. Rather than utilizing a probability sample, the respondents were selected in accordance with age quotas.

The study indicated that many consumers could not distinguish the origin of the two makes of bags, supporting the position of LeSportsac. The field experiment helped LeSportsac convince the court of appeals to affirm the issuance of a preliminary injunction against Kmart. Kmart agreed to stop selling its "di Paris sac."[1] ■

EXAMPLE

POP Buys

Drugstores such as Eckerd are increasingly experimenting with in-store advertising and other in-store promotions.

Eckerd Drug Co. conducted an experiment to examine the effectiveness of in-store radio advertisements to induce point-of-purchase (POP) buys. Twenty statistically compatible stores were selected based on store size, geographical location, traffic flow count, and age. Half of these were randomly selected as test stores, while the other half served as control stores. The test stores aired the radio advertisements, while the control stores' POP radio systems were removed. Tracking data in the form of unit sales and dollar volume was obtained for seven days before the experiment, during the course of the four-week experiment, and seven days after the experiment. The products monitored varied from inexpensive items to small kitchen appliances. Results indicated that sales of the advertised products in the test stores at least doubled. Based on this evidence, Eckerd concluded that in-store radio advertising was highly effective in inducing POP buys and decided to continue it.[2] ■

CONCEPT OF CAUSALITY

Causality When the occurrence of *X* increases the probability of the occurrence of *Y*.

Experimentation is commonly used to infer causal relationships. The concept of **causality** requires some explanation. The scientific concept of causality is complex. "Causality" means something very different to the average person on the street than it does to a scientist.[3] A statement such as "*X* causes *Y*" will have the following meanings to an ordinary person and to a scientist.

Ordinary Meaning	*Scientific Meaning*
X is the only cause of *Y*.	*X* is only one of a number of possible causes of *Y*.
X must always lead to *Y* (*X* is a deterministic cause of *Y*).	The occurrence of *X* makes the occurrence of *Y* more probable (*X* is a probabilistic cause of *Y*).
It is possible to prove that *X* is a cause of *Y*.	We can never prove that *X* is a cause of *Y*. At best, we can infer that *X* is a cause of *Y*.

The scientific meaning of causality is more appropriate to marketing research than is the everyday meaning. Marketing effects are caused by multiple variables and the relationship between cause and effect tends to be probabilistic. Moreover, we can never *prove* causality (i.e., demonstrate it conclusively); we can only *infer* a cause-and-effect relationship. In other words, it is possible that the true causal relation, if one exists, may not have been identified. We further clarify the concept of causality by discussing the conditions for causality.

CONDITIONS FOR CAUSALITY

Before making causal inferences, or assuming causality, three conditions must be satisfied. These are (1) concomitant variation, (2) time order of occurrence of variables, and (3) elimination of other possible causal factors. These conditions are necessary but not sufficient to demonstrate causality. No one of these three conditions nor all three conditions combined can demonstrate decisively that a causal relationship exists.[4] These conditions are explained in more detail in the following sections.

Concomitant Variation

Concomitant Variation A condition for inferring causality that requires that the extent to which a cause, *X*, and an effect, *Y*, occur together or vary together is predicted by the hypothesis under consideration.

Concomitant variation is the extent to which a cause, *X*, and an effect, *Y*, occur together or vary together in the way predicted by the hypothesis under consideration. Evidence pertaining to concomitant variation can be obtained in a qualitative or quantitative manner.

For example, in the qualitative case, the management of a department store believes that sales are highly dependent on the quality of in-store service. This hypothesis could be examined by assessing concomitant variation. Here, the causal factor *X* is in-store service, and the effect factor *Y* is sales. A concomitant variation supporting the hypothesis would imply that stores with satisfactory in-store service would also have satisfactory sales. Likewise, stores with unsatisfactory service would exhibit unsatisfactory sales. If, on the other hand, the opposite pattern were found, we would conclude that the hypothesis was untenable.

For a quantitative example, consider a random survey of 1,000 respondents regarding purchase of fashion clothing from department stores. This survey yields the data in Table 7.1. The respondents have been classified into high and low education groups based on a median or even split. This table suggests that the purchase of fashion clothing is influenced

TABLE 7.1

EVIDENCE OF CONCOMITANT VARIATION BETWEEN PURCHASE OF FASHION CLOTHING AND EDUCATION

		Purchase of Fashion Clothing, Y		
		High	*Low*	
Education, X	High	363 (73%)	137 (27%)	500 (100%)
	Low	322 (64%)	178 (36%)	500 (100%)

by education level. Respondents with high education are likely to purchase more fashion clothing. Seventy-three percent of the respondents with high education have a high purchase level, whereas only 64 percent of those with low education have a high purchase level. Furthermore, this is based on a relatively large sample of 1,000 people.

Based on this evidence, can we conclude that high education causes high purchase of fashion clothing? Certainly not! All that can be said is that association makes the hypothesis more tenable; it does not prove it. What about the effect of other possible causal factors such as income? Fashion clothing is expensive, so people with higher incomes can buy more of it. Table 7.2 shows the relationship between purchase of fashion clothing and education for different income segments. This is equivalent to holding the effect of income constant. Here again, the sample has been split at the median to produce high- and low-income groups of equal size. Table 7.2 shows that the difference in purchase of fashion clothing between high and low education respondents has been reduced considerably. This suggests that the association indicated by Table 7.1 may be spurious.

We could give you similar examples to show why the absence of initial evidence of concomitant variation does not imply that there is no causation. It is possible that considering a third variable may reveal an association that was originally obscure. The time order of the occurrence of variables provides additional insights into causality.

Time Order of Occurrence of Variables

The time order of occurrence condition states that the causing event must occur either before or simultaneously with the effect; it cannot occur afterwards. By definition, an effect cannot be produced by an event that occurs after the effect has taken place. However, it is possible for each event in a relationship to be both a cause and an effect of the other event.

TABLE 7.2

PURCHASE OF FASHION CLOTHING BY INCOME AND EDUCATION

		Low Income Purchase		
		High	*Low*	
Education	High	122 (61%)	78 (39%)	200 (100%)
	Low	171 (57%)	129 (43%)	300 (100%)

		High Income Purchase		
		High	*Low*	
Education	High	241 (80%)	59 (20%)	300
	Low	151 (76%)	49 (24%)	200

In other words, a variable can be both a cause and an effect in the same causal relationship. To illustrate, customers who shop frequently in a department store are more likely to have the credit card for that store. Also, customers who have the credit card for a department store are likely to shop there frequently.

Consider the in-store service and sales of a department store. If in-store service is the cause of sales, then improvements in service must be made before, or at least simultaneously with, an increase in sales. These improvements might consist of training or hiring more sales personnel. Then, in subsequent months, the sales of the department store should increase. Alternatively, the sales might increase simultaneously with the training or hiring of additional sales personnel. On the other hand, suppose a store experienced an appreciable increase in sales and then decided to use some of that money to retrain its sales personnel, leading to an improvement in service. In this case, in-store service cannot be a cause of increased sales. Rather, just the opposite hypothesis might be plausible.

Absence of Other Possible Causal Factors

The absence of other possible causal factors means that the factor or variable being investigated should be the only possible causal explanation. Better in-store service may be a cause of increased sales if we can be sure that changes in all other factors affecting sales, pricing, advertising, level of distribution, product quality, competition, and so on, were held constant or otherwise controlled.

In an after-the-fact examination of a situation, we can never confidently rule out all other causal factors. In contrast, with experimental designs, it is possible to control for some of the other causal factors. It is also possible to balance the effects of some of the uncontrolled variables so that only random variations resulting from these uncontrolled variables will be measured. These aspects are discussed in more detail later in this chapter. The difficulty of establishing a causal relationship is illustrated by the following example.

EXAMPLE

Which Comes First?

Recent statistical data show that consumers increasingly make buying decisions in the store while they are shopping. Some studies indicate that as much as 80 percent of buying decisions are made at point-of-purchase (POP). POP buying decisions have increased concurrently with increased advertising efforts in the stores. These include radio advertisements, ads on shopping carts and grocery bags, ceiling signs, and shelf displays. It is difficult to ascertain from these data whether the increased POP decision making is the result of increased advertising efforts in the store, or whether the increase in store advertising results from attempts to capture changing consumer attitudes toward purchasing and to capture sales from the increase in POP decision making. It is also possible that both variables may be both causes and effects in this relationship.[5] ■

If, as the preceding example indicates, it is difficult to establish cause and effect relationships, what is the role of evidence obtained in experimentation?

Role of Evidence

Evidence of concomitant variation, time order of occurrence of variables, and elimination of other possible causal factors, even if combined, still does not demonstrate conclusively that a causal relationship exists. However, if all the evidence is strong and consistent, it may be reasonable to conclude that there is a causal relationship. Accumulated evidence from several investigations increases our confidence that a causal relationship exists. Confidence is further enhanced if the evidence is interpreted in light of intimate conceptual knowledge of the problem situation. Controlled experiments can provide strong evidence on all three conditions.

DEFINITIONS AND CONCEPTS

In this section we define some basic concepts and illustrate them using examples, including the LeSportsac and Eckerd examples given at the beginning of this chapter.

Independent Variables. **Independent variables** are variables or alternatives that are manipulated (i.e., the levels of these variables are changed by the researcher) and whose effects are measured and compared. These variables, also known as *treatments*, may include price levels, package designs, and advertising themes. In the two examples given at the beginning of this chapter, the treatments consisted of LeSportsac versus the "di Paris sac" bags in the first example and in-store radio advertising (present versus absent) in the second.

Independent Variables Variables that are manipulated by the researcher and whose effects are measured and compared.

Test Units. **Test units** are individuals, organizations, or other entities whose response to the independent variables or treatments is being examined. Test units may include consumers, stores, or geographic areas. The test units were women in the LeSportsac case and stores in the Eckerd example.

Test Units Individuals, organizations, or other entities whose response to independent variables or treatments is being studied.

Dependent Variables. **Dependent variables** are the variables that measure the effect of the independent variables on the test units. These variables may include sales, profits, and market shares. The dependent variable was brand or source identification in the LeSportsac example and sales in the Eckerd example.

Dependent Variables Variables that measure the effect of the independent variables on the test units.

Extraneous Variables. **Extraneous variables** are all variables other than the independent variables that affect the response of the test units. These variables can confound the dependent variable measures in a way that weakens or invalidates the results of the experiment. Extraneous variables include store size, store location, and competitive effort. In the Eckerd example, store size, geographical location, traffic flow count, and age of the stores were extraneous variables that had to be controlled.

Extraneous Variables Variables, other than the independent variables, which influence the response of the test units.

Experiment. An **experiment** is formed when the researcher manipulates one or more independent variables and measures their effect on one or more dependent variables, while controlling for the effect of extraneous variables.[6] Both the LeSportsac and Eckerd research projects qualify as experiments based on this definition.

Experiment The process of manipulating one or more independent variables and measuring their effect on one or more dependent variables, while controlling for the extraneous variables.

Experimental Design. An **experimental design** is a set of procedures specifying (1) the test units and how these units are to be divided into homogeneous subsamples, (2) what independent variables or treatments are to be manipulated, (3) what dependent variables are to be measured, and (4) how the extraneous variables are to be controlled.[7]

As a further illustration of these definitions, consider the following example.

Experimental Design The set of experimental procedures specifying (1) the test units and sampling procedures, (2) independent variables, (3) dependent variables, and (4) how to control the extraneous variables.

EXAMPLE

Taking Coupons at Face Value

An experiment was conducted to test the effects of the face value of coupons on the likelihood of coupon redemption, controlling for the frequency of brand usage. Personal interviews were conducted in greater New York with 280 shoppers who were entering or leaving a supermarket. Subjects were randomly assigned to two treatment groups, one offered 15¢ coupons and the other 50¢ coupons for four products: Tide detergent, Kellogg's corn flakes, Aim toothpaste, and Joy liquid detergent. During the interviews, the respondents answered questions about which brands they used and how likely they were to cash coupons of the given face value the next time they shopped. An interesting finding was that higher face value coupons produced higher likelihood of redemption among infrequent or nonbuyers of the promoted brand but had little effect on regular buyers.[8] ■

Marketers use coupons of varying face value to induce purchase.

In the preceding experiment, the independent variable that was manipulated was the value of the coupon (15¢ versus 50¢). The dependent variable was the likelihood of cashing the coupon. The extraneous variable that was controlled was brand usage. The test units were individual shoppers. The experimental design required the random assignment of test units (shoppers) to treatment groups (15¢ coupon or 50¢ coupon).

DEFINITION OF SYMBOLS

To facilitate our discussion of extraneous variables and specific experimental designs, we define a set of symbols which are now commonly used in marketing research.

X = the exposure of a group to an independent variable, treatment or event, the effects of which are to be determined.

O = the process of observation or measurement of the dependent variable on the test units or group of units.

R = the random assignment of test units or groups to separate treatments.

In addition, the following conventions are adopted:

- Movement from left to right indicates movement through time.
- Horizontal alignment of symbols implies that all those symbols refer to a specific treatment group.
- Vertical alignment of symbols implies that those symbols refer to activities or events that occur simultaneously.

For example, the symbolic arrangement

$$X \quad O_1 \quad O_2$$

means that a given group of test units was exposed to the treatment variable (X) and the response was measured at two different points in time O_1 and O_2.

Likewise, the symbolic arrangement

$$\begin{array}{ccc} R & X_1 & O_1 \\ R & X_2 & O_2 \end{array}$$

means that two groups of test units were randomly assigned to two different treatment groups at the same time, and the dependent variable was measured in the two groups simultaneously.

VALIDITY IN EXPERIMENTATION

When conducting an experiment, a researcher has two goals: (1) Draw valid conclusions about the effects of independent variables on the study group, and (2) make valid generalizations to a larger population of interest. The first goal concerns internal validity; the second, external validity.[9]

Internal Validity

Internal validity refers to whether the manipulation of the independent variables or treatments actually caused the observed effects on the dependent variables. Thus, internal validity refers to whether the observed effects on the test units could have been caused by variables other than the treatment. If the observed effects are influenced or confounded by extraneous variables, it is difficult to draw valid inferences about the causal relationship between the independent and dependent variables. Internal validity is the basic minimum that must be present in an experiment before any conclusion about treatment effects can be made. Without internal validity, the experimental results are confounded. Control of extraneous variables is a necessary condition for establishing internal validity.

Internal Validity A measure of accuracy of an experiment. It measures if the manipulation of the independent variables, or treatments, actually caused the effects on the dependent variable(s).

External Validity

External validity refers to whether the cause-and-effect relationships found in the experiment can be generalized. In other words, can the results be generalized beyond the experimental situation, and if so, to what populations, settings, times, independent variables, and dependent variables can the results be projected?[10] Threats to external validity arise when the specific set of experimental conditions do not realistically take into account the interactions of other relevant variables in the real world.

External Validity A determination of whether the cause-and-effect relationships found in the experiment can be generalized.

It is desirable to have an experimental design which has both internal and external validity, but in applied marketing research often we have to trade one type of validity for another.[11] To control for extraneous variables, a researcher may conduct an experiment in an artificial environment. This enhances internal validity, but it may limit the generalizability of the results, thereby reducing external validity. For example, fast food chains test customers' preferences for new formulations of menu items in test kitchens. Can the effects measured in this environment be generalized to fast food outlets? (Further discussion of the influence of artificiality on external validity may be found in the section of this chapter on laboratory versus field experimentation.) In spite of these deterrents to external validity, if an experiment lacks internal validity, it may not be meaningful to generalize the results. Factors that threaten internal validity may also threaten external validity; the most serious of these factors is extraneous variables.

EXTRANEOUS VARIABLES

The need to control extraneous variables to establish internal and external validity has already been discussed. In this section we classify extraneous variables in the following categories: history, maturation, testing, instrumentation, statistical regression, selection bias, and mortality.

History

History Specific events that are external to the experiment but occur at the same time as the experiment.

Contrary to what the name implies, **history** (H) does not refer to the occurrence of events before the experiment. Rather, history refers to specific events that are external to the experiment but occur at the same time as the experiment. These events may affect the dependent variable. Consider the following experiment

$$O_1 \quad X_1 \quad O_2$$

where O_1 and O_2 are measures of sales of a department store chain in a specific region, and X_1 represents a new promotional campaign. The difference $(O_2 - O_1)$ is the treatment effect. Suppose the experiment revealed that there was no difference between O_2 and O_1. Can we then conclude that the promotional campaign was ineffective? Certainly not! The promotional campaign (X_1) is not the only possible explanation of the difference between O_2 and O_1. The campaign might well have been effective. What if general economic conditions declined during the experiment, and the local area was particularly hard hit by layoffs and plant closings (history)? Conversely, even if there was some difference between O_2 and O_1, it may be incorrect to conclude that the campaign was effective if history was not controlled, because the experimental effects might have been confounded by history. The longer the time interval between observations, the greater the possibility that history will confound an experiment of this type.[12]

Maturation

Maturation An extraneous variable attributable to changes in the test units themselves that occur with the passage of time.

Maturation (MA) is similar to history except that it refers to changes in the test units themselves. These changes are not caused by the impact of independent variables or treatments but occur with the passage of time. In an experiment involving people, maturation takes place as people become older, more experienced, tired, bored, or uninterested. Tracking and market studies that span several months are vulnerable to maturation because it is difficult to know how respondents are changing over time.

Maturation effects also extend to test units other than people. For example, stores change over time in terms of physical layout, decor, traffic, and composition.

Testing Effects

Testing Effects Effects caused by the process of experimentation.

Testing effects are caused by the process of experimentation. Typically, these are the effects on the experiment of taking a measure on the dependent variable before and after the presentation of the treatment. There are two kinds of testing effects: (1) main testing effect (MT), and (2) interactive testing effect (IT).

Main Testing Effect An effect of testing that occurs when a prior observation affects a later observation.

The **main testing effect** (MT) occurs when a prior observation affects a later observation. Consider an experiment to measure the effect of advertising on attitudes toward a certain brand. The respondents are given a pretreatment questionnaire measuring background information and attitude toward the brand. They are then exposed to the test commercial embedded in an appropriate program. After viewing the commercial, the respondents again answer a questionnaire measuring, among other things, attitude toward the brand. Suppose that there is no difference between the pre- and posttreatment attitudes. Can we conclude that the commercial was ineffective? An alternative explanation might be that the respondents tried to maintain consistency between their pre- and posttreatment attitudes. As a result of the main testing effect, posttreatment attitudes were influenced more by pretreatment attitudes than by the treatment itself. The main testing effect may also be reactive, causing the respondents to change their attitudes simply because these attitudes have been measured. The main testing effect compromises the internal validity of the experiment.

Interactive Testing Effect An effect in which a prior measurement affects the test unit's response to the independent variable.

In the **interactive testing effect** (IT), a prior measurement affects the test unit's response to the independent variable. Continuing with our advertising experiment, when people are asked to indicate their attitudes toward a brand, they become aware of that brand. They are sensitized to that brand and become more likely to pay attention to the test commercial than are people who were not included in the experiment. The measured effects are then not generalizable to the population; therefore, the interactive testing effects influence the experiment's external validity.

Instrumentation

Instrumentation (*I*) refers to changes in the measuring instrument, in the observers or in the scores themselves. Sometimes, measuring instruments are modified during the course of an experiment. In the advertising experiment, if a newly designed questionnaire were used to measure the posttreatment attitudes, this could lead to variations in the responses obtained. Consider an experiment in which dollar sales are being measured before and after exposure to an in-store display (treatment). If there is a nonexperimental price change between O_1 and O_2, this results in a change in instrumentation because dollar sales will be measured using different unit prices. In this case, the treatment effect $(O_2 - O_1)$ could be attributed to a change in instrumentation.

Instrumentation An extraneous variable involving changes in the measuring instrument or in the observers or scores themselves.

As shown above, instrumentation effects are likely when interviewers make pre- and posttreatment measurements. The effectiveness of interviewers can be different at different times.

Statistical Regression

Statistical regression effects (*SR*) occur when test units with extreme scores move closer to the average score during the course of the experiment. In the advertising experiment, suppose that some respondents had either very favorable or very unfavorable attitudes. On posttreatment measurement, their attitudes might have moved toward the average. People's attitudes change continuously. People with extreme attitudes have more room for change, so variation is more likely. This has a confounding effect on the experimental results, because the observed effect (change in attitude) may be attributable to statistical regression rather than to the treatment (test commercial).

Statistical Regression An extraneous variable that occurs when test units with extreme scores move closer to the average score during the course of the experiment.

Selection Bias

Selection bias (*SB*) refers to the improper assignment of test units to treatment conditions. This bias occurs when selection or assignment of test units results in treatment groups that differ on the dependent variable before the exposure to the treatment condition. If test units self-select their own groups or are assigned to groups on the basis of the researchers' judgment, selection bias is possible. For example, consider a merchandising experiment in which two different merchandising displays (old and new) are assigned to different department stores. The stores in the two groups may not be equivalent to begin with. They may vary with respect to a key characteristic, such as store size. Store size is likely to affect sales regardless of which merchandising display was assigned to a store.

Selection Bias An extraneous variable attributable to the improper assignment of test units to treatment conditions.

Mortality

Mortality (*MO*) refers to the loss of test units while the experiment is in progress. This happens for many reasons, such as test units refusing to continue in the experiment. Mortality confounds results because it is difficult to determine if the lost test units would respond in the same manner to the treatments as those that remain. Consider again the merchandising display experiment. Suppose that during the course of the experiment three stores in the new display treatment condition drop out. The researcher could not determine whether the average sales for the new display stores would have been higher or lower if these three stores had continued in the experiment.

Mortality An extraneous variable attributable to the loss of test units while the experiment is in progress.

The various categories of extraneous variables are not mutually exclusive. They can occur jointly and also interact with each other. To illustrate, testing—maturation—mortality refers to a situation in which, because of pretreatment measurement, the respondents' beliefs and attitudes change over time, and there is a differential loss of respondents from the various treatment groups.

CONTROLLING EXTRANEOUS VARIABLES

Confounding Variables Synonymous with extraneous variables. Used to illustrate that extraneous variables can confound the results by influencing the dependent variable.

Extraneous variables represent alternative explanations of experimental results. They pose a serious threat to the internal and external validity of an experiment. Unless they are controlled for, they affect the dependent variable and thus confound the results. For this reason, they are also called **confounding variables**. There are four ways of controlling extraneous variables: randomization, matching, statistical control, and design control.

Randomization

Randomization One method of controlling extraneous variables involving randomly assigning test units to experimental groups by using random numbers. Treatment conditions are also randomly assigned to experimental groups.

Randomization refers to the random assignment of test units to experimental groups by using random numbers. Treatment conditions are also randomly assigned to experimental groups. For example, respondents are randomly assigned to one of three experimental groups. One of the three versions of a test commercial, selected at random, is administered to each group. As a result of random assignment, extraneous factors can be represented equally in each treatment condition. Randomization is the preferred procedure for ensuring the prior equality of experimental groups.[13] However, randomization may not be effective when the sample size is small because randomization merely produces groups that are equal on average. It is possible, though, to check whether randomization has been effective by measuring the possible extraneous variables and comparing them across the experimental groups.

Matching

Matching One method of controlling extraneous variables that involves matching test units on a set of key background variables before assigning them to the treatment conditions.

Matching involves comparing test units on a set of key background variables before assigning them to the treatment conditions. In the merchandising display experiment, stores could be matched on the basis of annual sales, size, or location. Then one store from each matched pair would be assigned to each experimental group.

Matching has two drawbacks. First, test units can be matched on only a few characteristics, so the test units may be similar on the variables selected but unequal on others. Second, if the matched characteristics are irrelevant to the dependent variable, then the matching effort has been futile.[14]

Statistical Control

Statistical Control One method of controlling extraneous variables by measuring the extraneous variables and adjusting for their effects through statistical methods.

Statistical control involves measuring the extraneous variables and adjusting for their effects through statistical analysis. This was illustrated in Table 7.2, which examined the relationship (association) between purchase of fashion clothing and education, controlling for the effect of income. More advanced statistical procedures, such as analysis of covariance (ANCOVA), are also available. In ANCOVA, the effects of the extraneous variable on the dependent variable are removed by an adjustment of the dependent variable's mean value within each treatment condition. ANCOVA is discussed in more detail in chapter 16.

Design Control

Design Control One method of controlling extraneous variables that involves using specific experimental designs.

Design control involves the use of experiments designed to control specific extraneous variables. The types of controls made possible by suitably designing the experiment are illustrated in the following example.

EXAMPLE

Experimenting with New Products

Controlled distribution electronic test markets are used increasingly to conduct experimental research on new products. This method makes it possible to control for several extraneous factors that affect new product performance and manipulate the variables of interest. It is possible to ensure that a new product (1) obtains the right level of store acceptance and all commodity volume distribution, (2) is positioned in the correct aisle in each store, (3) receives the right number of facings on the shelf, (4) has the correct everyday price, (5) never has out-of-stock problems, and (6) obtains the planned level of trade promotion, display, and price features on the desired time schedule. Thus, a high degree of internal validity can be obtained.[15] ■

Test marketing is considered in more detail later in this chapter, but the preceding example shows that controlled distribution electronic test markets can be effective in controlling for specific extraneous variables. Extraneous variables can also be controlled by adopting specific experimental designs, as described in the next section.

Preexperimental Designs Designs that do not control for extraneous factors by randomization.

A CLASSIFICATION OF EXPERIMENTAL DESIGNS

True Experimental Designs Experimental designs distinguished by the fact that the researcher can randomly assign test units to experimental groups and also randomly assign treatments to experimental groups.

Quasi-Experimental Designs Designs that apply part of the procedures of true experimentation, but lack full experimental control.

Statistical Design Designs that allow for the statistical control and analysis of external variables.

Experimental designs may be classified as preexperimental, true experimental, quasi-experimental, and statistical (Figure 7.1). **Preexperimental designs** do not employ randomization procedures to control for extraneous factors. Examples of these designs include the one-shot case study, the one-group pretest-posttest design, and the static group. In **true experimental designs**, the researcher can randomly assign test units to experimental groups and treatments to experimental groups. Included in this category are the pretest-posttest control group design, the posttest-only control group design, and the Solomon four-group design. **Quasi-experimental designs** result when the researcher is unable to achieve full manipulation of scheduling or allocation of treatments to test units but can still apply part of the apparatus of true experimentation. Two such designs are time series and multiple time series designs. A **statistical design** is a series of basic experiments that allows for statistical control and analysis of external variables. The basic designs used in statistical designs include preexperimental, true experimental, and quasi-experimental. Statistical designs are classified on the basis of their characteristics and use. The important

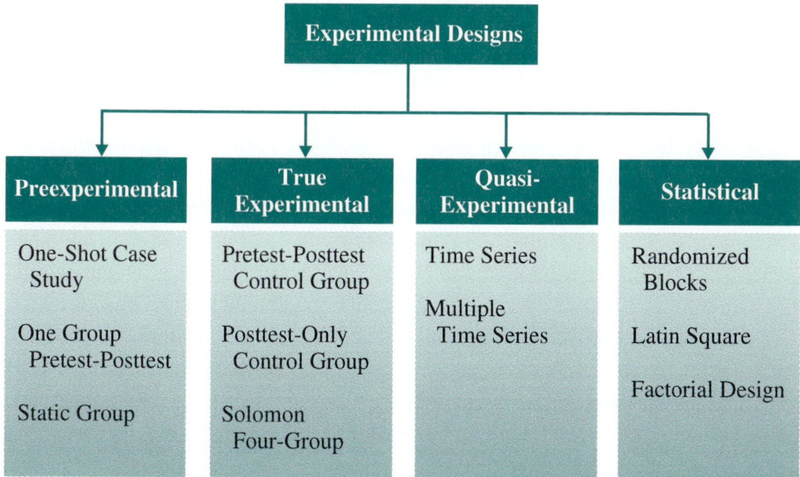

Figure 7.1
A Classification of Experimental Designs

statistical designs include randomized block design, Latin square design, and factorial designs. These designs are illustrated in the context of measuring the effectiveness of a test commercial for a department store. [16]

We begin our discussion with the first type, preexperimental designs.

PREEXPERIMENTAL DESIGNS

These designs are characterized by an absence of randomization. Three specific designs are described: the one-shot case study, the one-group pretest-posttest design, and the static group.

One-Shot Case Study

One-Shot Case Study A preexperimental design in which a single group of test units is exposed to a treatment X, and then a single measurement on the dependent variable is taken.

Also known as the after-only design, the **one-shot case study** may be symbolically represented as

$$X \qquad O_1$$

A single group of test units is exposed to a treatment X, and then a single measurement on the dependent variable is taken (O_1). There is no random assignment of test units. Note that the symbol R is not used, because the test units are self-selected or selected arbitrarily by the researcher.

The danger of drawing valid conclusions from experiments of this type can easily be seen. It does not provide a basis of comparing the level of O_1 to what would happen when X was absent. Also, the level of O_1 might be affected by many extraneous variables including history, maturation, selection, and mortality. Lack of control for these extraneous variables undermines the internal validity. For these reasons, the one-shot case study is more appropriate for exploratory than for conclusive research.

One-Group Pretest-Posttest Design

One-Group Pretest-Posttest Design A preexperimental design in which a group of test units is measured twice.

The **one-group pretest-posttest design** may be symbolized as

$$O_1 \qquad X \qquad O_2$$

In this design, a group of test units is measured twice. There is no control group. First, a pretreatment measure is taken (O_1) then the group is exposed to the treatment (X). Finally, a posttreatment measure is taken (O_2). The treatment effect is computed as $O_2 - O_1$, but the validity of this conclusion is questionable as extraneous variables are largely uncontrolled.

DEPARTMENT STORE PATRONAGE PROJECT

One-Shot Case Study

A one-shot case study to measure the effectiveness of a test commercial for a department store would be conducted as follows. Telephone interviews are conducted with a national sample of respondents who report watching a particular TV program the previous night. The program selected is the one that contains the test commercial (X). The dependent variables (Os) are unaided and aided recall. First, unaided recall is measured by asking the respondents whether they recall seeing a commercial for the product category of interest. If they recall the test commercial, details about commercial content and execution are elicited. Respondents who do not recall the test commercial are asked about it specifically (aided recall). The results of aided and unaided recall are compared to norm scores to develop an index for interpreting the scores.

DEPARTMENT STORE PATRONAGE PROJECT

One-Group Pretest-Posttest Design

A one-group pretest-posttest design to measure the effectiveness of a test commercial for a department store would be implemented as follows. Respondents are recruited to central theater locations in different test cities. At the central location, respondents are first administered a personal interview to measure, among other things, attitudes towards the brand (O_1). Then they watch a TV program containing the test commercial (X). After viewing the TV program, the respondents are again administered a personal interview to measure attitudes toward the brand (O_2). The effectiveness of the test commercial is measured as $O_2 - O_1$.

History, maturation, testing (both main and interactive testing effects), instrumentation, selection, mortality, and regression could possibly be present. The department store patronage project shows how this design is used.

Static Group Design

Static Group
A preexperimental design in which there are two groups: the experimental group (EG), which is exposed to the treatment, and the control group (CG). Measurements on both groups are made only after the treatment, and test units are not assigned at random.

The **static group** is a two-group experimental design. One group, called the *experimental group* (EG), is exposed to the treatment, and the other, called the *control group* (CG), is not. Measurements on both groups are made only after the treatment, and test units are not assigned at random. This design may be symbolically described as:

$$\begin{array}{lll} \text{EG:} & X & O_1 \\ \text{CG:} & & O_2 \end{array}$$

The treatment effect would be measured as $O_1 - O_2$. Note that this difference could also be attributed to at least two extraneous variables (selection and mortality). Because test units are not randomly assigned, the two groups (EG and CG) may differ before the treatment, and selection bias may be present. There may also be mortality effects, as more test units may withdraw from the experimental group than from the control group. This would be particularly likely to happen if the treatment was unpleasant.

In practice, a control group is sometimes defined as the group that receives current levels of marketing activity, rather than a group that receives no treatment at all. The control group is defined this way because it is difficult to reduce current marketing activities such as advertising and personal selling to zero. We illustrate the static group and several other designs in the context of the department store patronage project.

DEPARTMENT STORE PATRONAGE PROJECT

Static Group

A static group comparison to measure the effectiveness of a test commercial for a department store would be conducted as follows. Two groups of respondents would be recruited on the basis of convenience. Only the experimental group would be exposed to the TV program containing the test commercial. Then, attitudes toward the department store of both the experimental and control group respondents would be measured. The effectiveness of the test commercial would be measured as $O_1 - O_2$.

QUASI-EXPERIMENTAL DESIGNS

A quasi-experimental design results under the following conditions. First, the researcher can control when measurements are taken and on whom they are taken. Second, the researcher lacks control over the scheduling of the treatments and also is unable to expose test units to the treatments randomly.[18] Quasi-experimental designs are useful when true experimentation cannot be used, and because they are quicker and less expensive. However, because full experimental control is lacking, the researcher must take into account the specific variables that are not controlled. Popular forms of quasi-experimental designs are time series and multiple time series designs.

Time Series Design

Time Series Design A quasi-experimental design that involves periodic measurements on the dependent variable for a group of test units. Then, the treatment is administered by the researcher or occurs naturally. After the treatment, periodic measurements are continued in order to determine the treatment effect.

The **time series design** involves a series of periodic measurements on the dependent variable for a group of test units. The treatment is then administered by the researcher or occurs naturally. After the treatment, periodic measurements are continued to determine the treatment effect. A time series experiment may be symbolized as:

$$O_1\ O_2\ O_3\ O_4\ O_5\ X\ O_6\ O_7\ O_8\ O_9\ O_{10}$$

This is a quasi-experiment, because there is no randomization of test units to treatments, and the timing of treatment presentation, as well as which test units are exposed to the treatment, may not be within the researcher's control.

Taking a series of measurements before and after the treatment provides at least partial control for several extraneous variables. Maturation is at least partially controlled, because it would not affect O_5 and O_6 alone but would also influence other observations. By similar reasoning, main testing effect, instrumentation, and statistical regression are controlled as well. If the test units are selected randomly or by matching, selection bias can be reduced. Mortality may pose a problem, but it can be largely controlled by paying a premium or offering other incentives to respondents.

The major weakness of the time series design is the failure to control history. Another limitation is that the experiment may be affected by the interactive testing effect because multiple measurements are being made on the test units. Nevertheless, time series designs are useful, as illustrated by this example. The effectiveness of a test commercial (*X*) may be examined by broadcasting the commercial a predetermined number of times and examining the data from a preexisting test panel. Although the marketer can control the scheduling of the test commercial, it is uncertain when or whether the panel members are exposed to it. The panel members' purchases before, during, and after the campaign are examined to determine whether the test commercial has a short-term effect, a long-term effect, or no effect.

Multiple Time Series Design

Multiple Time Series Design A time series design that includes another group of test units to serve as a control group.

The **multiple time series design** is similar to the time series design except that another group of test units is added to serve as a control group. Symbolically, this design may be described as:

$$\text{EG}: O_1\ O_2\ O_3\ O_4\ O_5\ X\ O_6\ O_7\ O_8\ O_9\ O_{10}$$
$$\text{CG}: O_1\ O_2\ O_3\ O_4\ O_5\quad O_6\ O_7\ O_8\ O_9\ O_{10}$$

If the control group is carefully selected, this design can be an improvement over the simple time series experiment. The improvement lies in the ability to test the treatment effect twice: against the pretreatment measurements in the experimental group and against the control group. To use the multiple time series design to assess the effectiveness of a commercial, the test panel example would be modified as follows: the test commercial would be shown in only a few of the test cities. Panel members in these cities would comprise the experimental group. Panel members in cities in which the commercial was not shown would constitute the control group. Another application of multiple time series design is the ADTEL split-cable TV advertising field experiment.

EXAMPLE

Splitting Commercials Shows Their Strength

A multiple time series design was used to examine the build-up effect of increased advertising. The data were obtained from Burke Marketing Services, Inc., from an ADTEL split-cable TV advertising field experiment. In the split-cable system, one group of households was assigned to the experimental panel and an equivalent group to the control panel. The two groups were matched on demographic variables. Data were collected for 76 weeks. Both panels received the same level of advertising for the first 52 weeks for the brand in question. For the next 24 weeks, the experimental panel was exposed to twice as much advertising as the control panel. The results indicated that the build-up effect of advertising was immediate with a duration of the order of the purchase cycle. Information of this type can be useful in selecting advertising timing patterns (allocating a set of advertising exposures over a specified period to obtain maximum impact).[19] ■

In concluding our discussion of preexperimental, true experimental, and quasi-experimental designs, we summarize in Table 7.3 the potential sources of invalidity that may affect each of these designs. In this table, a minus sign indicates a definite weakness,

TABLE 7.3

SOURCES OF INVALIDITY OF EXPERIMENTAL DESIGNS

	Source of Invalidity							
	Internal							*External*
Design	History	Maturation	Testing	Instrumentation	Regression	Selection	Mortality	Interaction of testing and *X*
Preexperimental designs:								
One-shot case study X O	–	–				–	–	
One-group pretest-posttest design O X O	–	–	–	–	?			–
Static group comparison X O O	+	?	+	+	+	–	–	
True experimental designs:								
Pretest-posttest control R O X O R O O	+	+	+	+	+	+	+	–
Posttest-only control group design R X O R O	+	+	+	+	+	+	+	+
Quasi-experimental designs:								
Time series O O O X O O O	–	+	+	?	+	+	+	–
Multiple time series O O O X O O O O O O O O O	+	+	+	+	+	+	+	–

a plus sign indicates that the factor is controlled, a question mark denotes a possible source of concern, and a blank means that the factor is not relevant. It should be remembered that potential sources of invalidity are not the same as actual errors.

STATISTICAL DESIGNS

Statistical designs consist of a series of basic experiments that allow for statistical control and analysis of external variables. In other words, several basic experiments are conducted simultaneously. Thus, statistical designs are influenced by the same sources of invalidity that affect the basic designs being used. Statistical designs offer the following advantages:

1. The effects of more than one independent variable can be measured.
2. Specific extraneous variables can be statistically controlled.
3. Economical designs can be formulated when each test unit is measured more than once.

The most common statistical designs are the randomized block design, the Latin square design, and the factorial design.

Randomized Block Design

Randomized Block Design A statistical design in which the test units are blocked on the basis of an external variable to ensure that the various experimental and control groups are matched closely on that variable.

A **randomized block design** is useful when there is only one major external variable, such as sales, store size, or income of the respondent, that might influence the dependent variable. The test units are blocked, or grouped, on the basis of the external variable. The researcher must be able to identify and measure the blocking variable. By blocking, the researcher ensures that the various experimental and control groups are matched closely on the external variable.

DEPARTMENT STORE PATRONAGE PROJECT

Randomized Block Design

Let us extend the department store test commercial example to measure the impact of humor on the effectiveness of advertising. Three test commercials, A, B, and C, have, respectively, no humor, some humor, and high humor. Which of these would be the most effective? Management feels that the respondents' evaluation of the commercials will be influenced by the extent of their store patronage, so store patronage is identified as the blocking variable and the randomly selected respondents are classified into four blocks (heavy, medium, light, or nonpatrons of the department store). Respondents from each block are randomly assigned to the treatment groups (test commercials A, B, and C). The results reveal that the some humor commercial (B) was most effective overall (see Table 7.4).[20]

TABLE 7.4

AN EXAMPLE OF A RANDOMIZED BLOCK DESIGN

			Treatment Groups	
Block Number	*Store Patronage*	*Commercial A*	*Commercial B*	*Commercial C*
1	Heavy			
2	Medium			
3	Low			
4	None			

As this example illustrates, in most marketing research situations, external variables—such as sales, store size, store type, location, income, occupation, and social class of the respondent—can influence the dependent variable. Therefore, generally speaking, randomized block designs are more useful than completely random designs. Their main limitation is that the researcher can control for only one external variable. When more than one variable must be controlled, the researcher must use Latin square or factorial designs.

Latin Square Design

Latin Square Design A statistical design that allows for the statistical control of two noninteracting external variables in addition to the manipulation of the independent variable.

A **Latin square design** allows the researcher to statistically control two noninteracting external variables as well as to manipulate the independent variable. Each external or blocking variable is divided into an equal number of blocks or levels. The independent variable is also divided into the same number of levels. A Latin square is conceptualized as a table (see Table 7.5), with the rows and the columns representing the blocks in the two external variables. The levels of the independent variable are then assigned to the cells in the table. The assignment rule is that each level of the independent variable should appear only once in each row and each column, as shown in Table 7.5.

While Latin square designs are popular in marketing research, they are not without limitations. They require equal numbers of rows, columns, and treatment levels, which is sometimes problematic. Note that in the above example, the low and nonpatrons had to be combined to satisfy this requirement. Also, only two external variables can be controlled simultaneously. An additional variable can be controlled with an expansion of this design into a Graeco-Latin square. Finally, Latin squares do not allow the researcher to examine interactions of the external variables with each other or with the independent variable. To examine interactions, factorial designs should be used.

Factorial Design

Factorial Design A statistical experimental design that is used to measure the effects of two or more independent variables at various levels and to allow for interactions between variables.

A **factorial design** is used to measure the effects of two or more independent variables at various levels. Unlike the randomized block design and the Latin square, factorial designs allow for interactions between variables.[21] An interaction is said to take place when the simultaneous effect of two or more variables is different from the sum of their separate effects. For example, an individual's favorite drink might be coffee and her favorite temperature level might be cold, but this individual might not prefer cold coffee, leading to an interaction.

A factorial design may also be conceptualized as a table. In a two-factor design, each level of one variable represents a row and each level of another variable represents a column. Multidimensional tables can be used for three or more factors. Factorial designs involve a cell for every possible combination of treatment variables. Suppose that in the previous

TABLE 7.5

AN EXAMPLE OF LATIN SQUARE DESIGN

	Interest in the Store		
Store Patronage	*High*	*Medium*	*Low*
High	B	A	C
Medium	C	B	A
Low and none	A	C	B

Note: A, B, and C denote the three test commercials, which have, respectively, no humor, some humor, and high humor.

DEPARTMENT STORE PATRONAGE PROJECT

Latin Square

To illustrate the Latin square design, suppose that in the previous example, in addition to controlling for store patronage, the researcher also wanted to control for interest in the store (defined as high, medium, or low). To implement a Latin square design, store patronage would also have to be blocked at three rather than four levels (e.g., by combining the low and nonpatrons into a single block). Assignments of the three test commercials could then be made as shown in Table 7.5. Note that each of the commercials, A, B, and C, appears once, and only once, in each row and each column.

example, in addition to examining the effect of humor, the researcher was also interested in simultaneously examining the effect of amount of store information. Further, the amount of store information was also varied at three levels (high, medium, and low). As shown in Table 7.6, this would require $3 \times 3 = 9$ cells. The respondents would be randomly selected and randomly assigned to the nine cells. Respondents in each cell would receive a specific treatment combination. For example, respondents in the upper left-hand corner cell would view a commercial that had no humor and low store information. The results revealed a significant interaction between the two factors or variables. Respondents with low amount of store information preferred the high humor commercial (C). However, those with a high amount of store information preferred the no humor commercial (A). Note that although Table 7.6 may appear somewhat similar to Table 7.4, the random assignment of respondents and data analysis are very different for the randomized block design and the factorial design.[22]

Another example of a factorial design follows.

EXAMPLE

Price and Information Are for the Dogs

Burke Marketing Services, Inc., conducted an experiment to determine the effect of price and competitive set information on purchase intentions with respect to a new dog food. A two-factor design was used. Price was manipulated to have four levels: one discount ($1.07), two parity ($1.27; $1.47), and one premium ($1.67). Competitive set information was varied at two levels: whether information on competitive brands was provided or not. Approximately 240 respondents were randomly assigned to one of eight (4×2) treatment conditions. Respondents were asked to indicate their purchase intent for the new product on a five-point scale. The results indicated that neither price nor competitive set information had a significant effect on purchase intentions.[23] ■

TABLE 7.6

AN EXAMPLE OF A FACTORIAL DESIGN

Amount of Store Information	*Amount of Humor*		
	No Humor	*Medium Humor*	*High Humor*
Low			
Medium			
High			

The main disadvantage of a factorial design is that the number of treatment combinations increases multiplicatively with an increase in the number of variables or levels. In the Burke Marketing Services example, if the price had been manipulated at six levels (e.g., $0.99, $1.07, $1.27, $1.47, $1.67, and $1.99) and competitive information at three levels (no information, partial information, full information), the number of cells would have jumped from 8 to 18. All the treatment combinations are required if all the main effects and interactions are to be measured. If the researcher is interested in only a few of the interactions or main effects, fractional factorial designs may be used. As their name implies, these designs consist of only a fraction or portion of the corresponding full factorial design.

LABORATORY VERSUS FIELD EXPERIMENTS

Experiments may be conducted in a laboratory or field environment. A laboratory environment is an artificial one, which the researcher constructs with the desired conditions specific to the experiment. The term **field environment** is synonymous with actual market conditions. Our experiment to measure the effectiveness of a test commercial could be conducted in a **laboratory environment** by showing the test commercial embedded in a TV program to respondents in a test theater. The same experiment could also be conducted in a field environment by running the test commercial on actual TV stations. The differences between the two environments are summarized in Table 7.7.

Field Environment An experimental location set in actual market conditions.

Laboratory Environment An artificial setting for experimentation in which the researcher constructs the desired conditions.

Laboratory experiments have the following advantages over field experiments: The laboratory environment offers a high degree of control because it isolates the experiment in a carefully monitored environment. Therefore, the effects of history can be minimized. A laboratory experiment also tends to produce the same results if repeated with similar subjects, leading to high internal validity. Laboratory experiments tend to use a small number of test units, last for a shorter time, be more restricted geographically, and are easier to conduct than field experiments. Hence, they are generally less expensive as well.

As compared to field experiments, laboratory experiments suffer from the following main disadvantages: The artificiality of the environment may cause reactive error, in that the respondents react to the situation itself, rather than to the independent variable.[24] Also, the environment may cause **demand artifacts**, a phenomenon in which the respondents attempt to guess the purpose of the experiment and respond accordingly. For example, while viewing the test commercial the respondents may recall pretreatment questions about the brand and guess that the commercial is trying to change their attitudes toward the brand.[25] Finally, laboratory experiments are likely to have lower external validity than field experiments. Because a laboratory experiment is conducted in an artificial environment, the ability to generalize the results to the real world may be diminished.

Demand Artifacts Responses given because the respondents attempt to guess the purpose of the experiment and respond accordingly.

TABLE 7.7

LABORATORY VERSUS FIELD EXPERIMENTS

Factor	*Laboratory*	*Field*
Environment	Artificial	Realistic
Control	High	Low
Reactive error	High	Low
Demand artifacts	High	Low
Internal validity	High	Low
External validity	Low	High
Time	Short	Long
Number of units	Small	Large
Ease of implementation	High	Low
Cost	Low	High

It has been argued that artificiality or lack of realism in a laboratory experiment need not lead to lower external validity. However, one must be aware of the aspects of the laboratory experiment that differ from the situation to which generalizations are to be made. External validity will be reduced only if these aspects interface with the independent variables explicitly manipulated in the experiment, as is often the case in applied marketing research. However, another consideration is that laboratory experiments allow for more complex designs than do field experiments. Hence, the researcher can control for more factors or variables in the laboratory setting, which increases external validity.[26]

The researcher must consider all these factors when deciding whether to conduct laboratory or field experiments. Field experiments are less common in marketing research than are laboratory experiments, although laboratory and field experiments play complementary roles.[27]

EXPERIMENTAL VERSUS NONEXPERIMENTAL DESIGNS

In chapter 3 we discussed three types of research designs: exploratory, descriptive, and causal. Of these, only causal designs are truly appropriate for inferring cause-and-effect relationships. Although descriptive survey data are often used to provide evidence of "causal" relationships, these studies do not meet all the conditions required for causality. For example, it is difficult in descriptive studies to establish the prior equivalence of the respondent groups with respect to both the independent and dependent variables. On the other hand, an experiment can establish this equivalence by random assignment of test units to groups. In descriptive research it is also difficult to establish time order of occurrence of variables. However, in an experiment, the researcher controls the timing of the measurements and the introduction of the treatment. Finally, descriptive research offers little control over other possible causal factors.

We do not wish to undermine the importance of descriptive research designs in marketing research. As we mentioned in chapter 3, descriptive research constitutes the most popular research design in marketing research, and we do not want to imply that it should never be used to examine causal relationships. Indeed, some authors have suggested procedures for drawing causal inferences from descriptive (nonexperimental) data.[28] Rather, our intent is to alert the reader to the limitations of descriptive research for examining causal relationships. Likewise, we also want to make the reader aware of the limitations of experimentation.[29]

LIMITATIONS OF EXPERIMENTATION

Experimentation is becoming increasingly important in marketing research, but there are limitations of time, cost, and administration of an experiment.

Time. Experiments can be time consuming, particularly if the researcher is interested in measuring the long-term effects of the treatment, such as the effectiveness of an advertising campaign. Experiments should last long enough so that the posttreatment measurements include most or all the effects of the independent variables.

Cost. Experiments are often expensive. The requirements of experimental group, control group, and multiple measurements significantly add to the cost of research.

Administration. Experiments can be difficult to administer. It may be impossible to control for the effects of the extraneous variables, particularly in a field environment. Field experiments often interfere with a company's ongoing operations, and obtaining cooperation from the retailers, wholesalers, and others involved may be difficult. Finally, competitors may deliberately contaminate the results of a field experiment.

APPLICATION: TEST MARKETING

Test marketing, also called *market testing*, is an application of a controlled experiment, done in limited but carefully selected parts of the marketplace called **test markets**. It involves a replication of a planned national marketing program in the test markets. Often, the marketing mix variables (independent variables) are varied in test marketing and the sales (dependent variable) are monitored so that an appropriate national marketing strategy can be identified. The two major objectives of test marketing are (1) to determine market acceptance of the product, and (2) to test alternative levels of marketing mix variables. Test marketing procedures may be classified as standard test markets, controlled and minimarket tests, and simulated test marketing.

Standard Test Market

In a **standard test market**, test markets are selected and the product is sold through regular distribution channels. Typically, the company's own sales force is responsible for distributing the product. Sales personnel stock the shelves, restock, and take inventory at regular intervals. One or more combinations of marketing mix variables (product, price, distribution, and promotional levels) are employed.

Designing a standard test market involves deciding what criteria are to be used for selecting test markets, how many test markets to use, and the duration of the test. Test markets must be carefully selected. The criteria for selection of test markets is described in Research in Practice 7.1. A list of commonly used test markets is given in Research in Practice 7.2.[30] In general, the more test markets that can be used, the better. If resources are limited, at least two test markets should be used for each program variation to be tested. However, where external validity is important, at least four test markets should be used.

The duration of the test depends on the repurchase cycle for the product, the probability of competitive response, cost considerations, the initial consumer response, and company philosophy. The test should last long enough for repurchase activity to be observed. This indicates the long-term impact of the product. If competitive reaction to the test is anticipated, the duration should be short. The cost of the test is also an important factor. The longer a test, the more it costs, and at some point the value of additional information is outweighed by the cost to collect it. Recent evidence suggests that tests of new brands should run for at least 10 months. An empirical analysis found that the final test market share was reached in 10 months 85 percent of the time and in 12 months 95 percent of the time. Test marketing can be very beneficial to a product's successful introduction, as the following example demonstrates.[31]

Test Marketing An application of a controlled experiment done in limited, but carefully selected, test markets. It involves a replication of the planned national marketing program for a product in the test markets.

Test Market A carefully selected part of the marketplace that is particularly suitable for test marketing.

Standard Test Market A test market in which the product is sold through regular distribution channels. For example, no special considerations are given to products simply because they are being test marketed.

RESEARCH IN PRACTICE 7.1

Criteria for the Selection of Test Markets

Test markets should have the following qualities.

1. Be large enough to produce meaningful projections: They should contain at least 2 percent of the potential actual population
2. Be representative demographically
3. Be representative with respect to product consumption behavior
4. Be representative with respect to media usage
5. Be representative with respect to competition
6. Be relatively isolated in terms of media and physical distribution
7. Have normal historical development in the product class
8. Have marketing research and auditing services available
9. Not be overtested

EXAMPLE

Test Marketing: Wow!

Test marketing played a crucial role in Frito-Lay's decision to launch nationally, the "WOW!" line of Ruffles, Lays, and Doritos chips, all made with Olestra.

Olestra, marketed under the name Olean, developed and researched by Procter & Gamble over 25 years at a cost of more than $200 million, is a kind of cooking oil that adds zero calories and no fat to the snacks people love. During April 22 to June 21, 1996, Frito-Lay's Max chips with Olean were test marketed in three cities in 31 supermarkets. Researchers collected sales data and customer reports of any effects they associated with eating Frito-Lay's Max chips. The key findings were encouraging: (1) Sales exceeded expectations. Both the initial purchase and repurchase rates were very high; (2) most people responded

RESEARCH IN PRACTICE 7.2

Dancer Fitzgerald Sample's List of Recommended Test Markets

Albany-Schenectady-Troy, NY
Knoxville, TN
Boise, ID
Lexington, KY
Buffalo, NY
Little Rock, AR
Cedar Rapids-Waterloo, IA
Louisville, KY
Charlotte, NC
Minneapolis, MN
Cincinnati, OH
Nashville, TN
Cleveland, OH
Oklahoma City, OK
Colorado Springs-Pueblo, CO
Omaha, NE
Columbus, OH
Orlando-Daytona Beach, FL
Des Moines, IA
Phoenix, AZ
Erie, PA
Pittsburgh, PA
Evansville, IN
Portland, OR
Fargo, ND
Roanoke-Lynchburg, VA
Fort Wayne, IN
Rochester, NY
Green Bay, WI
Sacramento-Stockton, CA
Greensboro-High Point, NC
St. Louis, MO
Greenville-Spartanburg, SC
Salt Lake City, UT
Grand Rapids-Battle Creek, MI
Seattle-Tacoma, WA
Kansas City, MO
Wichita-Hutchinson, KA

positively that snacks made with Olean offered a good way to reduce fat in their diets; and (3) the reporting rate of any side effects was lower than the small reporting rate anticipated prior to FDA approval.

Because the initial findings were encouraging, Procter & Gamble decided to expand the test marketing to Indianapolis, Indiana, in February 1997. The product in these test market was changed in packaging design, price, and the name became WOW! which better described the product with its great taste and fat/calorie reduced attributes. The test market results were again positive. Based on favorable results, the decision was made in February 1998 to launch nationally Frito-Lay's "WOW!" line of Ruffles, Lays, and Doritos chips, all made with Olestra.[32] ■

A standard test market constitutes a one-shot case study. In addition to the problems associated with this design, test marketing faces two unique problems. First, competitors often take actions such as increasing their promotional efforts to contaminate the test marketing program. When Procter & Gamble test marketed its hand-and-body lotion, Wondra, the market leader, Cheeseborough Ponds, started a competitive buy-one-get-one-free promotion for its flagship brand, Vaseline Intensive Care Lotion. This encouraged consumers to stock up on Vaseline Intensive Care lotion and as a result, Wondra did poorly in the test market. In spite of this, Procter & Gamble launched the Wondra line nationally. Ponds again countered with the same promotional strategy. Today, Wondra has about 4 percent of the market and Vaseline Intensive Care has 22 percent.[33]

Another problem is that while a firm's test marketing is in progress, competitors have an opportunity to beat it to the national market.[34] Hills Bros. High Yield Coffee was test marketed and introduced nationally, but only after Procter & Gamble introduced Folger's Flakes. Procter & Gamble skipped test marketing Folger's Flakes and beat Hills Bros. to the national market. Procter & Gamble also launched Ivory shampoo without test marketing.[35]

Sometimes it is not feasible to implement a standard test market using the company's personnel. Instead, the company must seek help from an outside supplier, in which case the controlled test market may be an attractive option.

Controlled Test Market

In a **controlled test market**, the entire test marketing program is conducted by an outside research company. The research company guarantees distribution of the product in retail outlets that represent a predetermined percentage of the market. It handles warehousing and field sales operations, such as shelf-stocking, selling, and inventory control. The controlled test market includes both minimarket (or forced distribution) tests and the smaller controlled store panels. This service is provided by a number of research firms, including Audits & Surveys; Burgoyne, Inc.; Dancer, Fitzgerald, and Sample; and A. C. Nielsen.

Controlled Test Market A test marketing program conducted by an outside research company in field experimentation. The research company guarantees distribution of the product in retail outlets that represent a predetermined percentage of the market.

Simulated Test Market

Also called a laboratory test or test market simulation, a **simulated test market** yields mathematical estimates of market share based on initial reaction of consumers to a new product. The procedure works as follows. Typically, respondents are intercepted in high-traffic locations, such as shopping malls, and prescreened for product usage. The selected individuals are exposed to the proposed new-product concept and given an opportunity to buy the new product in a real-life or laboratory environment. Those who purchase the new product are interviewed about their evaluation of the product and repeat purchase intentions. The trial and repeat-purchase estimates so generated are combined with data on proposed promotion and distribution levels to project a share of the market.[36]

Simulated Test Market A quasi-test market in which respondents are preselected; then they are interviewed and observed on their purchases and attitudes toward the product.

Simulated test markets can be conducted in 16 weeks or less. The information they generate is confidential and the competition cannot get hold of it. They are also relatively inexpensive. A standard test market can cost as much as $1 million, but simulated test markets cost less than 10 percent as much. The major firms supplying this service are Management Decision Systems, Elrick & Lavidge, Burke Marketing Services, and Yankelovich Partners, Inc. Simulated test markets are becoming increasingly popular.[37]

DETERMINING A TEST MARKETING STRATEGY

The first decision to be made is whether or not to test market the proposed new product, or whatever element of the marketing program that is under consideration. This decision must take into account the competitive environment, the sociocultural environment, particularly consumer preferences and past behaviors, the need to keep the firm's marketing efforts secret, and the overall marketing strategy of the firm, as shown in Figure 7.2. If the marketing research already undertaken to develop the new product provides compelling positive evidence, or if factors such as preempting competitive moves dominate, the new product may well be introduced nationally without test marketing. If, however, the decision is to conduct test marketing, simulated test marketing may be conducted first, followed by controlled test market, followed by standard test market, leading to national introduction if the results are positive. Of course, very positive results at any stage may directly lead to national introduction, circumventing subsequent testing.

INTERNATIONAL MARKETING RESEARCH

If field experiments are difficult to conduct in the United States, the challenge they pose is greatly increased in the international arena. In many countries, the marketing, economic, structural, information, and technological environment (see chapter 23) is not developed to the extent that it is in the United States. For example, in many countries the TV stations are owned and operated by the government with severe restrictions on television advertising. This makes field experiments manipulating advertising levels extremely difficult. Consider for example M&M/Mars, which has set up massive manufacturing facilities in Russia and advertises its candy bars on television. Yet, the sales potential has not been realized. Is Mars advertising too much, too little, or just right? The answer could be determined by conducting

Figure 7.2
Selecting a Test-Marketing Strategy

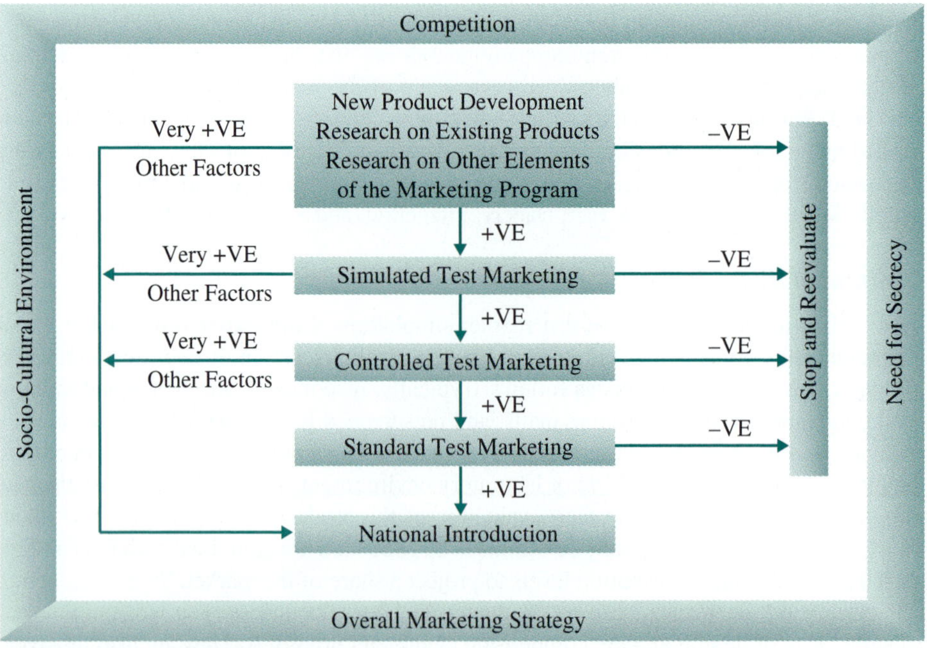

+VE = Positive –VE = Negative

a field experiment that manipulated the level of advertising, but such causal research is not feasible given the tight control of the Russian government on television stations.

Likewise, the lack of major supermarkets in the Baltic states makes it difficult for Procter & Gamble to conduct field experiments to determine the effect of in-store promotions on the sales of its detergents. In some countries in Asia, Africa, and South America, a majority of the population lives in small towns and villages. Yet, basic infrastructure such as roads, transportation, and warehouse facilities are lacking, making it difficult to achieve desired levels of distribution. Even when experiments are designed, it is difficult to control for the time order of occurrence of variables and the absence of other possible causal factors, two of the necessary conditions for causality. Because the researcher has far less control over the environment, control of extraneous variables is particularly problematic. Furthermore, it may not be possible to address this problem by adopting the most appropriate experimental design as environmental constraints may make that design infeasible.

Thus, the internal and external validity of field experiments conducted overseas is generally lower than in the United States. While pointing to the difficulties of conducting field experiments in other countries, we do not wish to imply that such causal research cannot or should not be conducted. Some form of test marketing is generally possible, as the following example indicates.

EXAMPLE

Flawless Quality and Exclusivity at $87,000 a Piece

Post-communist Eastern Europe has its problems. Eastern Germany's sky-high wage costs have continued to hamper recovery. One worker in four cannot find work. Six of ten companies in former East Germany lose money and 8,000 failed in 1995, which was double the number the previous year. Among this chaos, however, are a few rising stars. Watchmaker Lange Uhren has succeeded in the struggling economy of this German region. The reason is their market savvy.

Simulated test marketing was done in the United States, Japan, and France to determine an effective positioning and pricing strategy for the watches. In each country, the price and the positioning strategy were varied and consumer response assessed. The results, which were similar across countries, indicated that a prestige positioning with a premium price would be most effective. The eastern Germany area was well known for superior craftsmanship prior to the rise of communism. Lange Uhren used a well-trained workforce and the new marketing platform to rekindle this tradition. The new positioning strategy is based on flawless quality and exclusivity, which are portrayed uniquely in each cultural context. The watches are sold by only 22 retailers worldwide for as much as $87,000 each. The strategy has been successful. Watch sales increased 30 percent to $18.5 million in 1997.[38] ■

ETHICS IN MARKETING RESEARCH

It is often necessary to disguise the purpose of the experiment in order to produce valid results. Consider, for example, a project conducted to determine the effectiveness of television commercials for Total cereal. The respondents are recruited and brought to a central facility. They are told that they would be watching a television program on nutrition and then would be asked some questions. Interspersed in the program is the commercial for Total cereal (test commercial) as well as commercials for some other products (filler commercials). After viewing the program and the commercials, the respondents are administered a questionnaire. The questionnaire obtains evaluations on the program content, the test commercial, and some of the filler commercials. Note, the evaluations of the program content and the filler commercials are not of interest but are obtained to reinforce the nature of the disguise. If the respondents knew the true purpose was to determine the effectiveness of Total commercial, their responses might be biased.

Disguising the purpose of the research should be done in a manner that does not violate the rights of the respondents. One way to handle this ethical dilemma is to inform the respondents, at the beginning, that the experiment has been disguised. They should also be given a description of the research task and told that they can leave the experiment at any time. After the data have been collected, the true purpose of the study and the nature of the disguise should be fully explained to the respondents and they should be given an opportunity to withdraw their information. The procedure is called **debriefing**. Disclosure in this way does not bias the results. There is evidence indicating that data collected from subjects informed of the disguise and those not informed is similar.[39] Debriefing can alleviate stress and make the experiment a learning experience for the respondents. However, if not properly handled, debriefing itself can be stressful. In the Total cereal example, respondents may find it disheartening that they spent their time on a trivial task—evaluating a cereal commercial. The researcher should anticipate and address this issue in the debriefing session.

Debriefing After a disguised experiment, informing test subjects what the experiment was about and how the experimental manipulations were performed.

One further ethical concern is the responsibility of the researcher to use an appropriate experimental design for the problem so as to control errors caused by extraneous variables. As the following example illustrates, determining the most appropriate experimental design for the problem requires not only an initial evaluation but also continuous monitoring.

EXAMPLE

Correcting Errors Early: A Stitch in Time Saves Nine

A marketing research firm specializing in advertising research is examining the effectiveness of a television commercial for Nike athletic shoes. A one-group pretest-posttest design is used. Attitudes held by the respondents toward Nike athletic shoes are obtained prior to their being exposed to a sports program and several commercials, including the one for Nike. Attitudes are measured after viewing the program and the commercials. Initial evaluation based on a small sample found the one-group pretest-posttest design adopted in this study to be susceptible to demand artifacts: respondents attempt to guess the purpose of the experiment and respond accordingly. Because time and financial constraints make redesigning the study difficult at best, the research continues without correction. Continuing a research project after knowing errors were made in the early stages is not ethical behavior. Experimental design problems should be disclosed immediately to the client. Decisions whether to redesign or accept the flaw should be made jointly.[40] ■

INTERNET AND COMPUTER APPLICATIONS

The Internet can also be a useful vehicle for conducting causal research. Different experimental treatments can be displayed at different Web sites. Respondents can then be recruited to visit these sites and respond to a questionnaire that obtains information on the dependent and extraneous variables. Thus, the Internet can provide a mechanism for controlled experimentation, although in a laboratory type of environment.

Let us continue with the example of testing advertising effectiveness considered in this chapter. Different advertisements or commercials can be posted at different Web sites. Matched or randomly selected respondents can be recruited to visit these sites, with each group visiting only one site. If any pretreatment measures have to be obtained, the respondents answer a questionnaire posted on the site. Then they are exposed to a particular advertisement or a commercial at that site. After viewing the advertisement or commercial, the respondents answer additional questions providing posttreatment measures. Control groups can also be implemented in a similar way. Thus, all types of experimental designs that we have considered can be implemented in this manner.

This approach is being implemented on the Internet in different ways. One market research firm offers rewards for those willing to evaluate advertisements by enrolling in their "frequent browser" program known as Goldmail. The individuals are then sent advertisements (which they can choose to read or not) and to answer a few questions. The advertisers are only charged for those ads that are viewed. CyberGold, Inc., is reported to have a similar on-line interactive service. Another approach is that taken by Interactive Imaginations. They provide riddles, trivia questions, and crossword games. The games can only be accessed after viewing advertisements, evaluating them, and providing personal information. Those playing have opportunities to win prizes such as cruises, cars, and even cash. Similar experimental designs can be adopted for determining the effectiveness of other marketing programs, as in the following example.

EXAMPLE

Internet Experimentation: A Noble Effort

Experimental research can help Barnes & Noble to determine the optimal value of Internet coupons in its effort to get on-line customers to visit its stores.

Barnes & Noble has recently launched an Internet couponing service with Interactive Coupon Network. The goal of Internet couponing was to establish complementary promotional programs, reach more consumers, and gain additional data about these consumers. Barnes & Noble wanted to link on-line customers to the ones actually getting to their stores. What should be the face value of these coupons? An experimental design can be adopted in which coupons of different face values can be offered to different Internet users and the results monitored to determine the optimal value.[41] ■

To complement the Internet, microcomputers and mainframe software can be used in the design and analysis of experiments. The comprehensive statistical analysis software package Minitab can be used to design experiments. Although similar in use to SPSS, SAS, or BMDP, Minitab includes functions and documentation specifically for industrial-quality control work in which factorial designs are encountered. For example, researchers for a destination-type specialty retail outlet, such as Niketown, might want to investigate some of the interactions of independent variables, such as elements of store atmospherics in one section of their store. The dependent variable in this experiment would be the subjects' rating of the store section for browsing. Three factors would be included in this $2 \times 2 \times 2$ study. Assuming two lighting levels (i.e., low or medium), two sound types (i.e., outdoor stadium noise or indoor arena noise), and two olfactory stimuli (i.e., hot chocolate or hot popcorn smell), the best combinations of store atmospherics can be examined.

FOCUS ON Burke

Burke has the capability to implement a variety of experimental designs, including those discussed in this chapter. Due consideration is given to factors that will affect internal and external validity. However, from a practical standpoint, Burke has to give careful consideration to cost and efficiency. To illustrate, Burke had to design a very simple experiment with two factors in order to examine the potential of a premixed liquid cake mix. Basically, consumers pour the mix from a carton into a pan and put it in the oven. Historically, products from the refrigerator case are judged "fresher" by respondents than products found on the grocery shelf. Also, there has been some resistance (among people who are heavy users of cake mix) to such low involvement with the final product. It seems psychologically more appealing to have added something to the mix as opposed to just dumping it in a pan. To examine these premises, the new liquid cake mix was tested with two factors:

Refrigeration (Refrig): refrigeration required versus no refrigeration required
Ingredients: Eggs must be added by the baker versus no ingredients added

The simplest design, requiring the fewest assumptions, would call for selecting four random samples and giving each sample group a different cake mix as illustrated below. This, however, was the most expensive design. With a sample size of 100 people per group, we would need 400 people. This was also a statistically inefficient design.

	Refrig	*No Refrig*
Eggs	Random group 1	Random group 3
No eggs	Random group 2	Random group 4

An alternative design was used with only two random samples. Each sample got two different storage methods but the same ingredients.

	Refrig	*No Refrig*
Eggs	Random group 1	Random group 1
No eggs	Random group 2	Random group 2

The implications of this design are twofold:

I. We use fewer respondents (two groups instead of four).
II. The differences are estimated more efficiently.
- **A.** Eggs versus no eggs is based on two random samples. This has about the same sensitivity as the design with four random samples. The differences between mixes with eggs and mixes without eggs are measured between two random samples.
- **B.** Refrigeration versus no refrigeration is based on differences within respondents. As each respondent saw a mix with refrigeration and a mix without refrigeration, this difference is measured without the random effects of differences between people. This leads to a more sensitive measure for this effect.

Thus, the major benefits of Burke's approach to experimental design is that it saves money and it enables the researcher to make sensitive measures on the most important factor. Of course, Burke has to make sure that the respondents are capable of handling the experimental task—handling two types of cake mix rather than one. Also, the design should not negatively affect the internal validity of the experiment.

Burke occasionally uses an experimental design to determine the order in which respondents evaluate stimuli such as products or concepts. For example, a leading manufacturer of juice drinks asked Burke to measure the appeal of five different juice blends. Burke recommended a sip test conducted in shopping malls. To avoid sensory overload, respondents were asked to evaluate only three of the five products. Burke used an experimental design to determine how the products should be grouped. Each product was evaluated an equal number of times in the first, second, and third positions. Each product was positioned an equal number of times before and after each of the other four products. This design helped minimize order bias.

SUMMARY

The scientific notion of causality implies that we can never prove that *X* causes *Y*. At best, we can only infer that *X* is one of the causes of *Y* in that it makes the occurrence of *Y* probable. Three conditions must be satisfied before causal inferences can be made: (1) concomitant variation, which implies that *X* and *Y* must vary together in a hypothesized way; (2) time order of occurrence of variables, which implies that *X* must precede *Y*; and (3) elimination of other possible causal factors, which implies that competing explanations must be ruled out. Experiments provide the most convincing evidence of all three conditions. An experiment is formed when one or more independent variables are manipulated or controlled by the researcher, and their effect on one or more dependent variables is measured.

In designing an experiment it is important to consider internal and external validity. Internal validity refers to whether the manipulation of the independent variables actually caused the effects on the dependent variables. External validity refers to the generalizability of experimental results. For the experiment to be valid the researcher must control the threats imposed by extraneous variables, such as history, maturation, testing (main and interactive testing effects), instrumentation, statistical regression, selection bias, and mortality. There are four ways of controlling extraneous variables: randomization, matching, statistical control, and design control.

Experimental designs may be classified as preexperimental, true experimental, quasi-experimental, and statistical. An experiment may be conducted in a laboratory environment or under actual market conditions in a real-life setting. Only causal designs encompassing experimentation are appropriate for inferring cause-and-effect relationships.

Although experiments have limitations in terms of time, cost, and administration, they are becoming increasingly popular in marketing. Test marketing is an important application of experimental design.

The internal and external validity of field experiments conducted overseas is generally lower than in the United States. The level of development in many countries is lower and the researcher lacks control over many of the marketing variables. The ethical issues involved in conducting causal research include disguising the purpose of the experiment. Debriefing can be used to address some of these issues. The Internet and computers are very useful in the design and implementation of experiments.

KEY TERMS AND CONCEPTS

causality
concomitant variation
independent variables
test units
dependent variables
extraneous variables
experiment
experimental design
internal validity
external validity
extraneous variables
history
maturation
testing effects
main testing effect
interactive testing effect
instrumentation
statistical regression
selection bias
mortality
confounding variables
randomization
matching
statistical control
design control
preexperimental designs
true experimental designs
quasi-experimental designs
statistical design
one-shot case study
one-group pretest-posttest design
static group
pretest-posttest control group design
posttest-only control group design
time series design
multiple time series design
randomized block design
Latin square design
factorial design
field environment
laboratory environment
demand artifacts

are void of any meaning other than order (see the following example). For these reasons, in addition to the counting operation allowable for nominal scale data, ordinal scales permit the use of statistics based on centiles. It is meaningful to calculate percentile, quartile, median (chapter 15), rank-order correlation (chapter 17), or other summary statistics from ordinal data.

As a further illustration, *Fortune* magazine uses ordinal scaling to determine the world's most admired companies (Research in Practice 8.1).[6]

Interval Scale

Interval Scale A scale in which the numbers are used to rate objects such that numerically equal distances on the scale represent equal distances in the characteristic being measured.

In an **interval scale**, numerically equal distances on the scale represent equal values in the characteristic being measured. An interval scale contains all the information of an ordinal scale, but it also allows you to compare the differences between objects. The difference between any two scale values is identical to the difference between any other two adjacent values of an interval scale. There is a constant or equal interval between scale values. The difference between 1 and 2 is the same as the difference between 2 and 3, which is the same as the difference between 5 and 6. A common example in everyday life is a temperature scale. In marketing research, attitudinal data obtained from rating scales are often treated as interval data.[7]

In an interval scale, the location of the zero point is not fixed. Both the zero point and the units of measurement are arbitrary. Hence, any positive linear transformation of the form $y = a + bx$ will preserve the properties of the scale. Here, x is the original scale value, y is the transformed scale value, b is a positive constant, and a is any constant. Therefore, two interval scales that rate objects A, B, C, and D as 1, 2, 3, and 4, or as 22, 24, 26, and 28 are equivalent. Note that the latter scale can be derived from the former by using $a = 20$

RESEARCH IN PRACTICE 8.1

The World's Most Admired Companies

The value of the World's Most Admired Companies rankings, as with *Fortune*'s list of America's most admired, lies in the ranking's having been bestowed by the people who are closest to the action: senior executives and outside directors in each industry, and financial analysts who are in a position to study and compare the competitors in each field. *Fortune* asked them to rate international companies on the eight criteria used to rank America's most admired: innovativeness, overall quality of management, value as a long-term investment, responsibility to the community and the environment, ability to attract and keep talented people, quality of products or services, financial soundness, and wise use of corporate assets. *Fortune* then added a ninth category to reflect the international scope of this new listing: a company's effectiveness in doing business globally. A company's overall ranking is based on the average of the scores of all nine attributes. Here is the honor roll for selected industries:

Industry	*Top Ranked Company*
Aerospace	Boeing
Airlines	British Airways
Beverages	Coca-Cola
Electrical Equipment	General Electric
Food	General Mills
Motor Vehicles	Toyota Motor
Petroleum Refining	Royal Dutch/Shell Group
Pharmaceuticals	Pfizer
Soaps, Cosmetics	Procter & Gamble
Telecommunications	SBC Communications

DEPARTMENT STORE PATRONAGE PROJECT

Interval Scale

In Table 8.2, a respondent's preferences for the 10 stores are expressed on a seven-point rating scale. We can see that although Sears received a preference rating of 6 and Wal-Mart a rating of 2, this does not mean that Sears is preferred three times as much as Wal-Mart. When the ratings are transformed to an equivalent 11 to 17 scale, the ratings for these stores become 16 and 12, and the ratio is no longer 3 to 1. In contrast, the ratios of preference differences are identical on the two scales. The ratio of the preference difference between J.C. Penney and Wal-Mart to the preference difference between Neiman Marcus and Wal-Mart is 5 to 3 on both the scales.

and $b = 2$ in the transforming equation. Because the zero point is not fixed, it is not meaningful to take ratios of scale values. As can be seen, the ratio of D to B values changes from 2:1 to become 7:6 when the scale is transformed. Yet, ratios of differences between scale values are permissible. In this process, the constants a and b in the transforming equation drop out in the computations. The ratio of the difference between D and B to the difference between C and B is 2:1 in both the scales.

Statistical techniques that may be used on interval scale data include all of those that can be applied to nominal and ordinal data in addition to the arithmetic mean, standard deviation (chapter 15), product-moment correlations (chapter 17), and other statistics commonly used in marketing research. However, certain specialized statistics such as geometric mean, harmonic mean, and coefficient of variation are not meaningful on interval scale data. The department store example gives a further illustration of an interval scale.

Ratio Scale

A **ratio scale** possesses all the properties of the nominal, ordinal, and interval scales, and, in addition, an absolute zero point. Thus, in ratio scales we can identify or classify objects, rank the objects, and compare intervals or differences. It is also meaningful to compute ratios of scale values. Not only is the difference between 2 and 5 the same as the difference between 14 and 17, but also 14 is seven times as large as 2 in an absolute sense. Common examples of ratio scales include height, weight, age, and money. In marketing, sales, costs, market share, and number of customers are variables measured on a ratio scale.

Ratio Scale The highest scale. It allows the researcher to identify or classify objects, rank order the objects, and compare intervals or differences. It is also meaningful to compute ratios of scale values.

Ratio scales allow only proportionate transformations of the form $y = bx$, where b is a positive constant. One cannot add an arbitrary constant, as in the case of an interval scale. An example of this transformation is provided by the conversion of yards to feet ($b = 3$). The comparisons between the objects are identical whether made in yards or feet.

DEPARTMENT STORE PATRONAGE PROJECT

Ratio Scale

In the ratio scale illustrated in Table 8.2, a respondent is asked to indicate the dollar amounts spent in each of the 10 stores during the last two months. Note that because this respondent spent \$200 in Macy's and only \$10 in Wal-Mart, this person spent 20 times as much in Macy's as in Wal-Mart. Also, the zero point is fixed; 0 means that the respondent did not spend anything at that store. Multiplying these numbers by 100 to convert dollars to cents results in an equivalent scale.

All statistical techniques can be applied to ratio data. These include specialized statistics such as geometric mean, harmonic mean, and coefficient of variation. The ratio scale is further illustrated in the context of the department store example.

The four primary scales discussed here do not exhaust the measurement level categories. It is possible to construct a nominal scale that provides partial information on order (the partially ordered scale). Likewise, an ordinal scale can convey partial information on distance, as in the case of an ordered metric scale. A discussion of these scales is beyond the scope of this text.[8]

A COMPARISON OF SCALING TECHNIQUES

Comparative Scales One of two types of scaling techniques in which there is direct comparison of stimulus objects with one another.

The scaling techniques commonly employed in marketing research can be classified into comparative and noncomparative scales (see Figure 8.2). **Comparative scales** involve the direct comparison of stimulus objects. For example, respondents might be asked whether they prefer Coke or Pepsi. Comparative scale data must be interpreted in relative terms and have only ordinal or rank-order properties. For this reason, comparative scaling is also referred to as nonmetric scaling. As shown in Figure 8.2, comparative scales include paired comparisons, rank order, constant sum scales, Q-Sort, and other procedures.

The major benefit of comparative scaling is that small differences between stimulus objects can be detected. As they compare the stimulus objects, respondents are forced to choose between them. In addition, respondents approach the rating task from the same known reference points. Consequently, comparative scales are easily understood and can be applied easily. Other advantages of these scales are that they involve fewer theoretical assumptions, and they also tend to reduce halo or carryover effects from one judgment to another. The major disadvantages of comparative scales include the ordinal nature of the data and the inability to generalize beyond the stimulus objects scaled. For instance, to compare RC Cola to Coke and Pepsi, the researcher would have to do a new study. These disadvantages are substantially overcome by the noncomparative scaling techniques.

Noncomparative Scales One of two types of scaling techniques in which each stimulus object is scaled independently of the other objects in the stimulus set.

In **noncomparative scales**, also referred to as monadic or metric scales, each object is scaled independently of the others in the stimulus set. The resulting data are generally assumed to be interval or ratio scaled.[9] For example, respondents may be asked to evaluate Coke on a 1 to 6 preference scale (1 = not at all preferred; 6 = greatly preferred). Similar

Figure 8.2
A Classification of Scaling Techniques

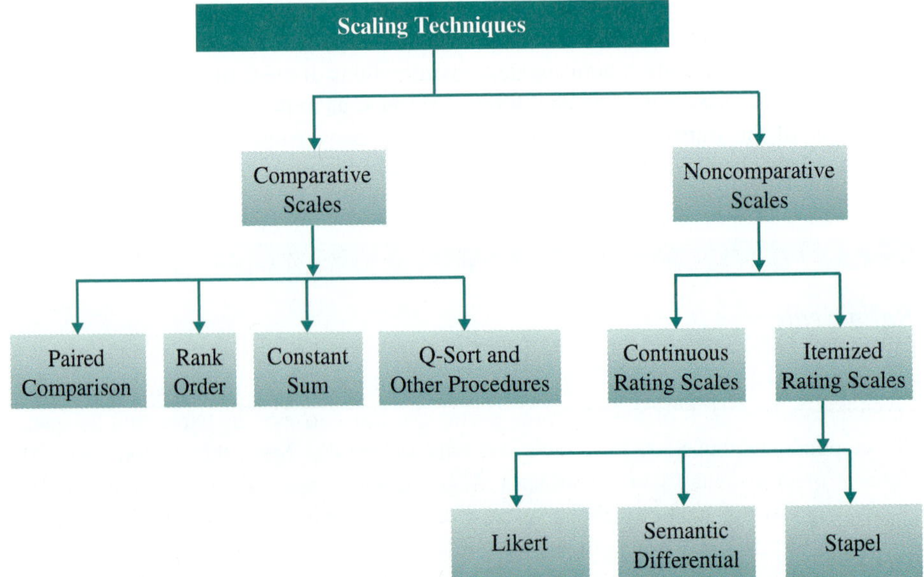

evaluations would be obtained for Pepsi and RC Cola. As can be seen in Figure 8.2, noncomparative scales can be continuous rating or itemized rating scales. The itemized rating scales can be further classified as Likert, semantic differential, or Stapel scales. Noncomparative scaling is the most widely used scaling technique in marketing research. Given its importance, chapter 9 is devoted to noncomparative scaling. The rest of this chapter focuses on comparative scaling techniques.

COMPARATIVE SCALING TECHNIQUES

Paired Comparison Scaling

As its name implies, in **paired comparison scaling** a respondent is presented with two objects and asked to select one according to some criterion.[10] The data obtained are ordinal in nature. A respondent may state that she shops at J.C. Penney more than Sears, likes Total cereal better than Kellogg's Product 19, or likes Crest more than Colgate. Paired comparison scales are frequently used when the stimulus objects are physical products. Coca-Cola is reported to have conducted more than 190,000 paired comparisons before introducing New Coke.[11] Paired comparison scaling is the most widely used comparative scaling technique.

Paired Comparison Scaling
A comparative scaling technique in which a respondent is presented with two objects at a time and asked to select one object in the pair according to some criterion. The data obtained are ordinal in nature.

Figure 8.3 shows paired comparison data obtained to assess a respondent's shampoo preferences. As can be seen, this respondent made 10 comparisons to evaluate 5 brands. In general, with n brands, $[n(n-1)/2]$ paired comparisons include all possible pairings of objects.[12]

Paired comparison data can be analyzed in several ways.[13] The researcher can calculate the percentage of respondents who prefer one stimulus over another by summing the matrices of Figure 8.3 for all the respondents, dividing the sum by the number of respondents, and multiplying by 100. Simultaneous evaluation of all the stimulus objects is also possible. Under the assumption of transitivity, it is possible to convert paired comparison data to a rank order. **Transitivity of preference** implies that if brand A is preferred to B, and brand B is preferred to C, then brand A is preferred to C. To arrive at a rank order, the researcher determines the number of times each brand is preferred by summing the column entries in Figure 8.3. Therefore, this respondent's order of preference, from most to the least preferred, is Head and Shoulders, Jhirmack, Finesse, Pert, and Vidal Sassoon. It is also possible to derive an interval scale from paired comparison data using the Thurstone case V procedure. Refer to the appropriate literature for a discussion of this procedure.[14]

Transitivity of Preference
An assumption made in order to convert paired comparison data to rank-order data. It implies that if brand A is preferred to brand B and brand B is preferred to brand C, then brand A is preferred to brand C.

Figure 8.3
Obtaining Shampoo Preferences Using Paired Comparisons

Instruction

We are going to present you with 10 pairs of shampoo brands. For each pair, please indicate which one of the two brands of shampoo in the pair you would prefer for personal use.

Recording Form

	Jhirmack	Finesse	Vidal Sassoon	Head and Shoulders	Pert
Jhirmack		0	0	1	0
Finesse	1[a]		0	1	0
Vidal Sassoon	1	1		1	1
Head and Shoulders	0	0	0		0
Pert	1	1	0	1	
Number of times preferred[b]	3	2	0	4	1

[a]1 means that the brand in that column was preferred over the brand in the corresponding row. 0 means that the row brand was preferred over the column brand.
[b]The number of times a brand was preferred is obtained by summing the 1s in each column.

Several modifications of the paired comparison technique have been suggested. One involves the inclusion of a neutral/no difference/no opinion response. Another extension is graded paired comparisons. In this method, respondents are asked which brand in the pair is preferred and how much it is preferred. The degree of preference may be expressed by how much more the respondent is willing to pay for the preferred brand. The resulting scale is a dollar metric scale. Another modification of paired comparison scaling is widely used in obtaining similarity judgments in multidimensional scaling (see chapter 21).

Paired comparison scaling is useful when the number of brands is limited, because it requires direct comparison and overt choice. However, with a large number of brands, the number of comparisons becomes unwieldy. Other disadvantages are that violations of the assumption of transitivity may occur, and the order in which the objects are presented may bias the results. Paired comparisons bear little resemblance to the marketplace situation, which involves selection from multiple alternatives. Also respondents may prefer one object over certain others, but they may not like it in an absolute sense. Research in Practice 8.2 provides further insights into paired comparison scaling.[15]

Rank-Order Scaling

Rank-Order Scaling
A comparative scaling technique in which respondents are presented with several objects simultaneously and asked to order or rank them according to some criterion.

After paired comparisons, the most popular comparative scaling technique is rank-order scaling. In **rank-order scaling** respondents are presented with several objects simultaneously and asked to order or rank them according to some criterion. For example, respondents may be asked to rank brands of toothpaste according to overall preference. As shown in Figure 8.4, these rankings are typically obtained by asking the respondents to assign a rank of 1 to the most preferred brand, 2 to the second most preferred, and so on, until a rank of n is assigned to the least preferred brand. Like paired comparison, this approach is also comparative in nature, and it is possible that the respondent may dislike the brand ranked 1 in an absolute sense. Furthermore, rank-order scaling also results in ordinal data. See Table 8.2, which uses rank-order scaling to derive an ordinal scale.

Rank-order scaling is commonly used to measure preferences for brands as well as attributes. Rank-order data are frequently obtained from respondents in conjoint analysis (see

Figure 8.4
Preference for Toothpaste Brands Using Rank-Order Scaling

Instructions
Rank the various brands of toothpaste in order of preference. Begin by picking out the one brand that you like most and assign it a number 1.
Then find the second most preferred brand and assign it a number 2.
Continue this procedure until you have ranked all the brands of toothpaste in order of preference. The least preferred brand should be assigned a rank of 10.
No two brands should receive the same rank number.
The criterion of preference is entirely up to you. There is no right or wrong answer. Just try to be consistent.

Brand	*Rank Order*
1. Crest	———
2. Colgate	———
3. Aim	———
4. Gleem	———
5. Macleans	———
6. Ultra Brite	———
7. Close Up	———
8. Pepsodent	———
9. Plus White	———
10. Stripe	———

RESEARCH IN PRACTICE 8.2

Paired Comparison Scaling

The most common method of taste testing is paired comparison. The consumer is asked to sample two different products and select the one with the most appealing taste. The test is done in private, either in homes or other predetermined sites. A minimum of 1,000 responses is considered an adequate sample.

A blind taste test for a soft drink, for which imagery, self-perception, and brand reputation are very important factors in the consumer's purchasing decision, may not be a good indicator of performance in the marketplace. The introduction of New Coke illustrates this point. New Coke was heavily favored in blind paired comparison taste tests, but its introduction was less than successful, in large part because image plays a major role in the purchase of soft drinks.

A paired comparison taste test.

chapter 21), because rank-order scaling forces the respondent to discriminate among the stimulus objects. Moreover, as compared to paired comparisons, this type of scaling process more closely resembles the shopping environment. It also takes less time and eliminates intransitive responses. If there are n stimulus objects, only $(n - 1)$ scaling decisions need be made in rank-order scaling. However, in paired comparison scaling, $[n(n - 1)/2]$ decisions are required. Another advantage is that most respondents easily understand the instructions for ranking. The major disadvantage is that this technique produces only ordinal data.

Finally, under the assumption of transitivity, rank-order data can be converted to equivalent paired comparison data, and vice versa. This point was illustrated by Figure 8.3. Hence, it is possible to derive an interval scale from rankings using the Thurstone case V procedure. Other approaches for deriving interval scales from rankings have also been suggested.[16]

Constant Sum Scaling

In **constant sum scaling**, respondents allocate a constant sum of units, such as points, dollars, or chips, among a set of stimulus objects with respect to some criterion. As shown in Figure 8.5, respondents may be asked to allocate 100 points to attributes of a bathing soap in a way that reflect the importance they attach to each attribute. If an attribute is unimportant, the respondent assigns it zero points. If an attribute is twice as important as some other attribute, it receives twice as many points. The sum of all the points is 100. Hence, the name of the scale.

Constant Sum Scaling
A comparative scaling technique in which respondents are required to allocate a constant sum of units such as points, dollars, chits, stickers, or chips among a set of stimulus objects with respect to some criterion.

The attributes are scaled by counting the points assigned to each one by all the respondents and dividing by the number of respondents. These results are presented for three groups, or segments, of respondents in Figure 8.5. Segment I attaches overwhelming importance to price. Segment II considers basic cleaning power to be of prime importance. Segment III values lather, fragrance, moisturizing, and cleaning power. Such information cannot be obtained from rank-order data unless they are transformed into interval data. Note that the constant sum also has an absolute zero—10 points are twice as many as 5 points, and the difference between 5 and 2 points is the same as the difference between 57 and 54 points. For this reason, constant sum scale data are sometimes treated as metric. Although this may be appropriate in the limited context of the stimuli scaled, these results are not generalizable to other stimuli not included in the study. Hence, strictly speaking, the constant sum should be considered an ordinal scale because of its comparative nature and the resulting lack of generalizability. It can be seen that the allocation of points in Figure 8.5 is influenced by the specific attributes included in the evaluation task.

The main advantage of the constant sum scale is that it allows for fine discrimination among stimulus objects without requiring too much time. However, it has two primary disadvantages. Respondents may allocate more or fewer units than those specified. For example, a respondent may allocate 108 or 94 points. The researcher must modify such data in some way or eliminate this respondent from analysis. Another potential problem is rounding error if too few units are used. On the other hand, the use of a large number of units may be too taxing on the respondent and cause confusion and fatigue.

Q-Sort and Other Procedures

Q-Sort Scaling A comparative scaling technique that uses a rank-order procedure to sort objects based on similarity with respect to some criterion.

Q-Sort scaling was developed to discriminate among a relatively large number of objects quickly. This technique uses a rank-order procedure in which objects are sorted into piles based on similarity with respect to some criterion. For example, respondents are given 100 attitude statements on individual cards and asked to place them into 11 piles, ranging from "most highly agreed with" to "least highly agreed with." The number of objects to be sorted should not be less than 60 nor more than 140; 60 to 90 objects is a reasonable range. The number of objects to be placed in each pile is prespecified, often to result in a roughly normal distribution of objects over the whole set.

Figure 8.5
Importance of Bathing Soap Attributes Using a Constant Sum Scale

Instructions

Below are eight attributes of bathing soaps. Please allocate 100 points among the attributes so that your allocation reflects the relative importance you attach to each attribute. The more points an attribute receives, the more important the attribute is. If an attribute is not at all important, assign it zero points. If an attribute is twice as important as some other attribute, it should receive twice as many points.

Forms

	Average Responses of Three Segments		
Attribute	*Segment I*	*Segment II*	*Segment III*
1. Mildness	8	2	4
2. Lather	2	4	17
3. Shrinkage	3	9	7
4. Price	53	17	9
5. Fragrance	9	0	19
6. Packaging	7	5	9
7. Moisturizing	5	3	20
8. Cleaning Power	13	60	15
Sum	100	100	100

Use of constant sum scaling to determine the relative importance of bathing soap attributes has enabled Irish Spring to develop a superior product.

Another comparative scaling technique is magnitude estimation.[17] In this technique numbers are assigned to objects such that ratios between the assigned numbers reflect ratios on the specified criterion. For example, respondents may be asked to indicate whether they agree or disagree with each of a series of statements measuring attitude toward department stores. Then they assign a number between 0 to 100 to each statement to indicate the intensity of their agreement or disagreement. Providing this type of number imposes a cognitive burden on the respondents. Finally, mention must be made of Guttman scaling, or scalogram analysis, which is a procedure for determining whether a set of objects can be ordered into an internally consistent, unidimensional scale.

VERBAL PROTOCOLS

An approach that is particularly useful for measuring cognitive responses or thought processes consists of **verbal protocols**. Respondents are asked to "think out loud" and verbalize anything going through their heads as they make a decision or perform a task. The researcher says, "If you think anything, say it aloud, no matter how trivial the thought may be." Even with such explicit instruction, the respondent may be silent. At these times, the researcher will say, "Remember to say aloud everything you are thinking." Everything that the respondent says is tape recorded. This record of the respondent's verbalized thought processes is referred to as a protocol.[18]

Verbal Protocol A technique used to understand respondents' cognitive responses or thought processes by having them think aloud while completing a task or making a decision.

Protocols have been used to measure consumers' cognitive responses in actual shopping trips as well as in simulated shopping environments. An interviewer accompanies the respondent and holds a microphone into which the respondent talks. Protocols, thus collected, have been used to determine the attributes and cues used in making purchase decisions, product usage behavior, and the impact of the shopping environment on consumer decisions. Protocol analysis has also been employed to measure consumer response to advertising. Immediately after seeing an ad, the respondent is asked to list all the thoughts that came to mind while he or she watched the ad. The respondent is given a limited amount of time to list the thoughts so as to minimize the probability of collecting thoughts generated after, rather than during, the message. After the protocol has been collected, the individual's thoughts or cognitive responses are coded into three categories:[19]

Category	*Definition*	*Example*
Support argument	Support the claim made by the message	"Diet Coke tastes great."
Counter argument	Refute the claim made by the message	"Diet Coke has an aftertaste."
Source derogation	Negative opinion about the source of the message	"Coca-Cola is not an honest company."

Protocols are, typically, incomplete. The respondent has many thoughts that she or he cannot or will not verbalize. The researcher must take the incomplete record and infer from it a measure of the underlying cognitive response.

INTERNATIONAL MARKETING RESEARCH

In the four primary scales, the level of measurement increases from nominal to ordinal to interval to ratio scale. This increase in measurement level is obtained at the cost of complexity. From the view point of the respondents, nominal scales are the simplest to use whereas the ratio scales are the most complex. Respondents in many developed countries, due to higher education and consumer sophistication levels, are quite used to providing responses on interval and ratio scales. However, it has been argued that opinion formation may not be well crystallized in some developing countries. Hence, these respondents experience difficulty in expressing the gradation required by interval and ratio scales. Preferences can, therefore, be best measured by using ordinal scales. In particular, the use of binary scales (e.g., preferred/not preferred), the simplest type of ordinal scale, has been recommended.[20] For example, while measuring preferences for jeans in the United States, Levi Strauss & Co. could ask consumers to rate their preferences for wearing jeans on specified occasions using a seven-point interval scale. However, consumers in Papua New Guinea could be shown a pair of jeans and simply asked whether or not they would prefer to wear it for a specific occasion (e.g., when shopping, working, relaxing on a holiday, etc.). The advantage of selecting the primary scales to match the profile of the target respondents is well illustrated by the Japanese survey of automobile preferences in Europe.

EXAMPLE

Car War—Japan Making a Spearhead

For the first time, European journalists had given their car-of-the-year award to a Japanese model—Nissan's new British-made Micra, a $10,000 subcompact. This came as a big blow to the European automakers who have been trying to keep the Japanese onslaught at bay. "They will change the competitive balance," warns Bruce Blythe, Ford of Europe, Inc.'s head of business strategy. How did the Japanese do it?

Nissan conducted a survey of European consumers' preferences for automobiles, using interval scales to capture the magnitude of the preference differences. The use of interval scales enabled Nissan to compare the differences between automobile features and determine which features were preferred. The findings revealed distinct consumer preferences. So the Japanese made inroads by transplants in production and building technical centers in Europe to customize to local styling tastes and preferences. By 1998 the Japanese were producing about one million cars a year in Europe, 75 percent of them in Britain. The Japanese are taking away share from Renault in the French, Italian, and Spanish markets. The European automakers need to be on guard against such fierce competition.[21] ■

It should also be noted that comparative scales, except for paired comparisons, require comparisons of multiple stimulus objects and are, therefore, taxing on the respondents. In contrast, in noncomparative scales, each object is scaled independently of others in the stimulus set—that is, objects are scaled one at a time. Hence, noncomparative scales are simpler to administer and more appropriate in cultures in which the respondents are less educated or unfamiliar with marketing research.

ETHICS IN MARKETING RESEARCH

The researcher has the responsibility to use the appropriate type of scales to get the data needed to answer the research questions and test the hypotheses. For example, a newspaper such as the *Wall Street Journal* wants information on the personality profiles of its readers and nonreaders. Information on the personality characteristics might be obtained best by giving respondents (readers and nonreaders) several cards, each listing one personality characteristic. The respondents are asked to sort the cards and to rank order the personality characteristics; listing, in order, those they believe describe their personality best first and those which do not describe themselves last. This process will provide rich insight into the personality characteristics by allowing respondents to compare and shuffle the personality cards. However, the resulting data are ordinal and cannot be easily used in multivariate analysis. To examine differences in the personality characteristics of readers and nonreaders and relate them to marketing strategy variables, interval scale data are needed. It is the obligation of the researcher to obtain the data that are most appropriate given the research questions, as the following example illustrates.

EXAMPLE

Scaling Ethical Dilemmas

In a study designed to measure ethical judgments of marketing researchers, scale items from a previously developed and tested scale were used. After a pretest was conducted on a convenience sample of 65 marketing professionals, however, it became apparent that some original scale items were worded in a way that did not reflect current usage. Therefore, these items were updated. For example, an item that was gender specific, such as, "He pointed out that . . ." was altered to read "The project manager pointed out that . . . " Subjects were requested to show their approval or disapproval of the stated action (item) of a marketing research director with regard to specific scenarios. Realizing that a binary or dichotomous scale would be too restrictive, approval or disapproval was indicated by having respondents supply interval level data via five-point scales with descriptive anchors of 1 = disapprove, 2 = disapprove somewhat, 3 = neither approve nor disapprove, 4 = approve somewhat, and 5 = approve. In this way, scaling dilemmas were resolved.[22] ■

After the data have been collected, they should be analyzed correctly. If nominal scaled data are gathered, then statistics permissible for nominal scaled data must be used. Likewise, when ordinal scaled data are collected, statistical procedures developed for use with interval or ratio data should not be used. Conclusions based on the misuse of statistics are misleading. Using the personality example above, if it were decided to gather data by the rank-order technique described, ordinal data would be collected. If after collection the client wishes to know how the readers and the nonreaders differed, the researcher should treat these data correctly and use nonmetric techniques for analysis (discussed in chapter 15). When the researcher lacks the expertise to identify and use the appropriate statistical techniques, help should be sought from other sources, for example, from statisticians.

INTERNET AND COMPUTER APPLICATIONS

All the primary scales of measurement that we have considered can be implemented on the Internet. The same is true for the commonly used comparative scales. Paired comparisons involving verbal, visual, or auditory comparisons can be implemented with ease. However, taste, smell, and touch comparisons are difficult to implement. It may also be difficult to implement specialized scales such as the Q-Sort. The process of implementing comparative scales may be facilitated by searching the Internet for similar scales that have been implemented by other researchers.

EXAMPLE

Primary Scales of Measurement Help Domino's to Become a Primary Competitor

Domino's Pizza builds Web sites to communicate its image and give information on its products. It also sees its Web site as a medium to collect information on customers and

FOCUS ON Burke

Given the diverse nature of projects conducted by Burke, it employs all the four basic types of scales. Nominal scales are employed to denote subjects, brands, stores, advertisements, and virtually any type of marketing stimuli. Rank-order scales are used to rank new-product names, packages, competing brands, and other choice alternatives in terms of preference and purchase intent. Most of the projects will employ some form of interval scale measurement. For example, customer satisfaction is measured on a four-point scale (1 = very dissatisfied, 2 = somewhat dissatisfied, 3 = somewhat satisfied, and 4 = very satisfied). Ratio scales are also used to measure sales potential, sales, and market share. An illustration of the use of a ratio scale is provided by the Burke Integrated Concept Evaluation System (ICES). The ICES evaluates new product concepts by estimating for each concept a potential score in terms of the number of units of that product (concept) that could be sold per 100 households. This measure, called the Concept Potential Score (CPS), constitutes a ratio scale. Based on the CPS, concepts with the greatest potential can be identified.

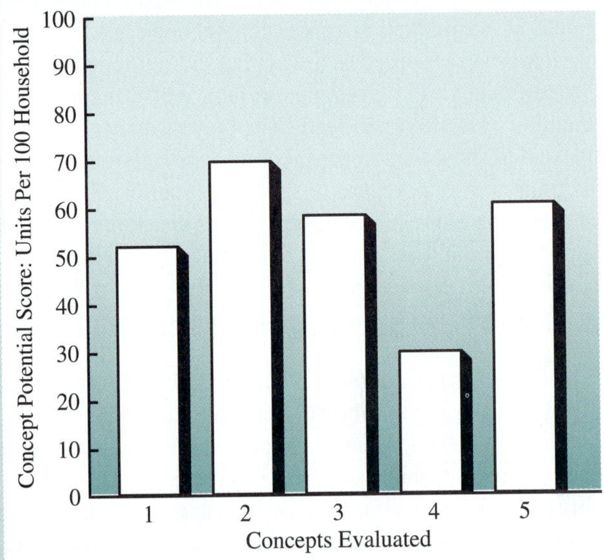

A major dog food manufacturer had identified 13 new-product opportunities and needed to find a way to set priorities for product development. Burke's ICES was chosen for its ability to efficiently screen multiple concepts and estimate sales potential using the concept potential score (CPS). Based on the CPS, several high-potential products were accelerated, a few low-potential ideas were shelved, and the remaining were scheduled for subsequent development. ICES helped this manufacturer solve its immediate problem of setting priorities, but the real value became evident when concept and product testing as well as in-market sales performance validated these early screening results. In addition, this manufacturer has established a database of concept screening results against which to compare future waves of ICES tested concepts.

Finally, Burke is very cautious about using comparative scales. To illustrate Burke's concerns, imagine this scenario in which the category manager reports to the president of the company:

Category Manager: "We had 100 people try our two product concepts and 70 percent said that they preferred concept A! Let's start production."
President, after a moment's thought, asks: "Do you think anyone will buy this new product?"
Category Manager: "We didn't ask that, but 70 percent prefer A over B!"
President: "Is it possible that A is the best of two bad products … the king of the pigs?"

This conversation could continue but it points out why Burke is very careful with comparative scales. When you ask respondents to compare, rank order, allocate points, or state a relative preference, you are asking for their judgments internal to the set of objects. You have little or no measurement that has validity external to the set.

therefore conduct marketing research. Although no pizza is sold on-line, the company has one national Web site (www.dominos.com) and Web sites for each of its local subsidiaries.

On the Gainesville Web site, the customer is asked to fill in a comment form. This posted survey, which is different on each Domino's Pizza's Web site, helps the local team to understand its customers' needs better, and better service them. Different scales are utilized to obtain the following information.

- Name, phone number, and (e-mail) address (nominal scale)
- Impressions on the service offered by Domino's Pizza as a whole (interval scale)
- Assessments on the products and price (interval scale)
- Preference for pizza restaurants in the local area (ordinal scale)
- Customer satisfaction (interval scale)
- Amount spent on pizza and fast foods (ratio scale)

This enables the company to set up a database of clients for target marketing and to know what to improve in its marketing mix (product/price/delivery). It also enables Domino's to measure customer satisfaction and to gather data for various purposes, by linking customer satisfaction to salaries, for example.[23] ■

Database managers allow researchers to develop and test several different scales to determine their appropriateness for a particular application. For example, the author has developed and tested ordinal, interval, and ratio scale configurations using dBASE. Database managers are also available for mainframes, which handle larger amounts of data faster. Several off-the-shelf packages are also available. Microcomputers have been used to administer paired comparison scales in taste tests. Several programs are available for designing and administering paired comparison scales. EZPAIR by Barry Cohen can design paired comparison scales and paired comparison product tests using statistical quality control techniques. It allows testing to end early, without compromising test reliability, if one product is clearly winning.

SUMMARY

Measurement is the assignment of numbers or other symbols to characteristics of objects according to set rules. Scaling involves the generation of a continuum on which measured objects are located. The four primary scales of measurement are nominal, ordinal, interval, and ratio. Of these, the nominal scale is the most basic in that the numbers are used only for identifying or classifying objects. In the ordinal scale, the next higher-level scale, the numbers indicate the relative position of the objects but not the magnitude of difference between them. The interval scale permits a comparison of the differences between the objects. However, as it has an arbitrary zero point, it is not meaningful to calculate ratios of scale values on an interval scale. The highest level of measurement is represented by the ratio scale in which the zero point is fixed. The researcher can compute ratios of scale values using this scale. The ratio scale incorporates all the properties of the lower-level scales.

Scaling techniques can be classified as comparative or noncomparative. Comparative scaling involves a direct comparison of stimulus objects. Comparative scales include paired comparisons, rank-order, constant sum, and the Q-Sort. The data obtained by these procedures have only ordinal properties. Verbal protocols, in which the respondent is instructed to think out loud, can be used for measuring cognitive responses.

Respondents in many developed countries, due to higher education and consumer sophistication levels, are quite used to providing responses on interval and ratio scales. However, in developing countries, preferences can be measured best by using ordinal scales. Ethical considerations require that the appropriate type of scale be used in order to get the data needed to answer the research questions and test the hypotheses. The Internet, as well as several specialized computer programs, are available to implement the different types of scales.

KEY TERMS AND CONCEPTS

measurement
scaling
nominal scale
ordinal scale
interval scale
ratio scale
comparative scales
noncomparative scales
paired comparison scaling
transitivity of preference
rank-order scaling
constant sum scaling
Q-Sort scaling
verbal protocols

ACRONYMS

The four primary types of scales may be described by the acronym FOUR:

F igurative: nominal scale
O rdinal scale
U nconstrained zero point: interval scale
R atio scale

The different comparative and noncomparative scales may be represented by the acronym SCALES:

S emantic differential scale
C onstant sum scale
A rranged in order: rank-order scale
L ikert scale
E ngaged: paired comparison scale
S tapel scale

EXERCISES

Questions

1. What is measurement?
2. What are the primary scales of measurement?
3. Describe the differences between a nominal and an ordinal scale.
4. What are the implications of having an arbitrary zero point in an interval scale?
5. What are the advantages of a ratio scale over an interval scale? Are these advantages significant?
6. What is a comparative rating scale?
7. What is a paired comparison?
8. What are the advantages and disadvantages of paired comparison scaling?
9. Describe the constant sum scale. How is it different from the other comparative rating scales?
10. Describe the Q-Sort methodology.
11. What is a verbal protocol? How are verbal protocols used?

Problems

1. Identify the type of scale (nominal, ordinal, interval, or ratio) being used in each of the following. Please explain your reasoning.
   a. I like to solve crossword puzzles.
   Disagree   Agree
   1   2   3   4   5
   b. How old are you? __________
   c. Please rank the following activities in terms of your preference by assigning ranks 1 to 5.
   i. Reading magazines _____
   ii. Watching television _____
   iii. Dating _____
   iv. Shopping _____
   v. Eating out _____
   d. What is your Social Security number?
   _____-_____-_____
   e. On an average week day, how much time do you spend doing your homework and class assignments?
   i. Less than 15 minutes _____
   ii. 15 to 30 minutes _____
   iii. 31 to 60 minutes _____
   iv. 61 to 120 minutes _____
   v. More than 120 minutes _____
   f. How much money did you spend last month on entertainment? _____
2. Suppose each of the questions a through f above were administered to 100 respondents. Identify the kind of analysis that should be done for each question to summarize the results.

INTERNET AND COMPUTER EXERCISES

1. Visit the Web sites of two marketing research firms conducting surveys. Analyze one survey of each firm to critically evaluate the primary type of scales being used.
2. Surf the Net to find two examples of each of the four primary types of scales. Write a report describing the context in which these scales are being used.
3. Search the Internet to identify the top five selling automobile brands during the last calendar year. Rank-order these brands according to sales.
4. Target and Wal-Mart are two of the stores considered in the department store patronage project. Develop a series of paired comparison scales comparing these two stores on store image characteristics. Identify the relevant store image characteristics by visiting the Web sites of these two stores (www.targetstores.com, www.wal-mart.com). How do the store image characteristics that you have identified compare to those used in the department store patronage project (see chapter 2, section on relevant characteristics)?

Chapter 9

"The purpose of a scale is to allow us to represent respondents with the highest possible accuracy and reliability. We can't have one without the other and still believe in our data."

Bart Gamble,
senior account executive,
client services,
Burke, Inc.

Measurement and Scaling: Noncomparative Scaling Techniques

OBJECTIVES

After reading this chapter, the student should be able to

1. describe the noncomparative scaling techniques; distinguish between continuous and itemized rating scales; and explain Likert, semantic differential, and Stapel scales
2. discuss the decisions involved in constructing itemized rating scales with respect to the number of scale categories, balanced versus unbalanced scales, odd or even number of categories, forced versus nonforced choice, degree of verbal description, and the physical form of the scale
3. discuss the criteria used for scale evaluation and explain how to assess reliability, validity, and generalizability
4. discuss the considerations involved in implementing noncomparative scales in an international setting
5. understand the ethical issues involved in developing noncomparative scales
6. discuss the use of the Internet and computers in implementing continuous and itemized rating scales

OVERVIEW

As discussed in chapter 8, scaling techniques are classified as comparative or noncomparative. The comparative techniques—of paired comparison, rank-order, constant sum, and Q-Sort scaling—were discussed in the last chapter. The subject of this chapter is noncomparative techniques, which comprise continuous and itemized rating scales. We discuss the popular itemized rating scales, the Likert, semantic differential, and Stapel scales, as well as the construction of multiitem rating scales. We show how scaling techniques should be evaluated in terms of reliability and validity and consider how the researcher selects a particular scaling technique. Mathematically derived scales are also presented. The considerations involved in implementing noncomparative scales when researching international markets are discussed. Several ethical issues that arise in rating scale construction are identified. The chapter concludes with a discussion of the use of the Internet and computers in developing continuous and itemized rating scales. We begin with some examples of noncomparative scaling techniques.

EXAMPLE

Scaling Emotional Peaks

PEAC Media Research, a Toronto-based company, has developed a Program Evaluation Analysis Computer to aid in recording the emotions of focus group members. This computer is a handheld device with a row of buttons or a dial that registers responses ranging from negative to neutral to positive. Respondents press the appropriate buttons as they watch a commercial. This device allows for continuous and unbiased recording of emotional responses by the members of the focus group. It was recently used to measure response to a series of commercials for McDonald's, and the researchers found that daughters and their mothers responded differently to different images in the commercials. Since McDonald's attempts to design "slice of life" commercials that appeal to all segments, the researchers used PEAC to determine which aspects of the commercials appealed to which segments. Commercials with the greatest emotional appeal across segments were selected for the campaign.[1] ■

EXAMPLE

New York City Transit

The New York City Transit (NYCT) does not have a wholly captive audience as some people believe. Many people do not use the mass transit system when they have a choice. A much-needed rate hike brought fears that more people would avoid taking the bus or subway. Therefore, research was undertaken to uncover ways to increase ridership.

In a telephone survey, respondents were asked to rate different aspects of the transit system using five-point Likert scales. Likert scales were chosen as they are easy to administer over the telephone and the respondents merely indicate their degree of (dis)agreement (1 = strongly disagree, 5 = strongly agree).

The results showed that personal safety was the major concern on subways. New Yorkers were afraid to use a subway station in their own neighborhoods. The factor that contributed most to riders' fears was lack of a way to contact someone in case of trouble. NYCT was able to respond to riders' concerns by increasing police presence, having a more visible NYCT staff, increasing lighting, repositioning walls, columns, and stairways for better visibility throughout the stations.

Telephone surveys also revealed that cleanliness of subway stations and subway cars are related to the perception of crime. In response, NYCT concentrated on ways to maintain a cleaner appearance. Action was also taken to reduce the number of homeless people and panhandlers in subway entrances and stations. They were asked to leave, and sometimes transportation to shelters was provided.

Results of marketing research efforts have helped NYCT improve perceptions surrounding the system. Increased ridership levels over a five-year period were also attributed to these efforts.[2] ■

EXAMPLE

Supermarkets

It is not a matter of luck. Rather, superior products and services designed to meet customer needs have enabled supermarkets like Lucky to score high quality ratings.

In a survey of the services industry conducted by the Gallup Organization, participants were asked to rate services on a 10-point Likert-type scale, with 1 signifying low quality and 10 signifying very high quality. Over half the respondents gave supermarkets a rating of 8 or better. Restaurants and banks were also well regarded. Hotels, department stores, insurance companies, auto repair companies, and airlines ended up in the middle. Toward the bottom of the scale were local government, public transportation, and real estate. Therefore, to engender public goodwill and patronage, local governments, public transportation authorities, and real estate agencies need to improve their services and communicate the improvements to their constituents and customers.[3] ■

The PEAC example illustrated a continuous rating scale used to measure emotion, and the NYCT and Gallup surveys used itemized rating scales to measure perceptions. Both are examples of noncomparative scaling techniques.

Noncomparative Scale One of two types of scaling techniques in which each stimulus object is scaled independently of the other objects in the stimulus set.

NONCOMPARATIVE SCALING TECHNIQUES

Respondents using a **noncomparative scale** employ whatever rating standard seems appropriate to them. They do not compare the object being rated either to another object or to some specified standard, such as "your ideal brand." They evaluate only one object at a time, and for this reason noncomparative scales are often referred to as *monadic scales*. Noncomparative techniques consist of continuous and itemized rating scales, which are described in Table 9.1 and discussed in the following sections.

Continuous Rating Scale Also referred to as graphic rating scale, this measurement scale has the respondents rate the objects by placing a mark at the appropriate position on a line that runs from one extreme of the criterion variable to the other. The form may vary considerably.

CONTINUOUS RATING SCALE

In a **continuous rating scale**, also referred to as a *graphic rating scale*, respondents rate the objects by placing a mark at the appropriate position on a line that runs from one extreme of the criterion variable to the other. Thus, the respondents are not restricted to se-

TABLE 9.1

BASIC NONCOMPARATIVE SCALES

Scale	*Basic Characteristics*	*Examples*	*Advantages*	*Disadvantages*
Continuous rating scale	Place a mark on a continuous line	Reaction to TV commercials	Easy to construct	Scoring can be cumbersome unless computerized
Itemized Rating Scales				
Likert scale	Degree of agreement on a 1 (strongly disagree) to 5 (strongly agree) scale	Measurement of attitudes	Easy to construct, administer, and understand	More time consuming
Semantic differential	Seven-point scale with bipolar labels	Brand, product, and company images	Versatile	Controversy as to whether the data are interval
Stapel scale	Unipolar 10-point scale, −5 to +5, without a neutral point (zero)	Measurement of attitudes and images	Easy to construct; administered over telephone	Confusing and difficult to apply

lecting from marks previously set by the researcher. The form of the continuous scale may vary considerably. For example, the line may be vertical or horizontal; scale points, in the form of numbers or brief descriptions, may be provided; and if provided, the scale points may be few or many. Three versions of a continuous rating scale are illustrated below.

Once the respondent has provided the ratings, the researcher divides the line into as many categories as desired and assigns scores based on the categories into which the ratings fall. In the department store project example, the respondent exhibits an unfavorable attitude toward Sears. These scores are typically treated as interval data.

DEPARTMENT STORE PATRONAGE PROJECT

Continuous Rating Scales

How would you rate Sears as a department store?

Version 1

Probably the worst - - - - - - -I - Probably the best

Version 2

Probably the worst - - - - - - -I - Probably the best

0 10 20 30 40 50 60 70 80 90 100

Version 3

Very bad | Neither good nor bad | Very good

Probably the worst - - - - - - -I - Probably the best

0 10 20 30 40 50 60 70 80 90 100

RESEARCH IN PRACTICE 9.1

RATE: Rapid Analysis and Testing Environment

A relatively new research tool, the perception analyzer, provides continuous measurement of "gut reaction." A group of up to 400 respondents is presented with TV or radio spots or advertising copy. The measuring device consists of a dial that contains a 100-point range. Each participant is given a dial and instructed to continuously record his or her reaction to the material being tested. As the respondents turn the dials, the information is fed to a computer, which tabulates second-by-second response profiles. As the results are recorded by the computer, they are superimposed on a video screen, enabling the researcher to view the respondents' scores immediately. The responses are also stored in a permanent data file for use in further analysis. The response scores can be broken down by categories, such as age, income, sex, or product usage.

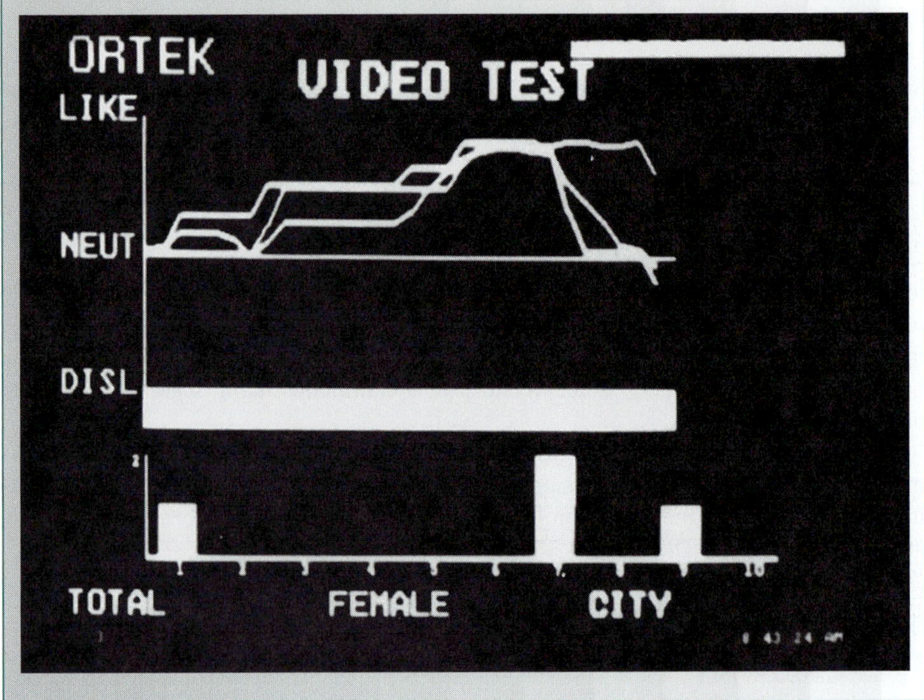

Systems such as RATE from ORTEK enable the continuous measurement of reactions to a company video, commercial, or any audio/visual material.

The advantage of continuous scales is that they are easy to construct.[4] However, scoring is cumbersome and unreliable. Moreover, continuous scales provide little new information. Hence, their use in marketing research has been limited. Recently, however, with the increased popularity of computer-assisted personal interviewing and other technologies, their use is becoming more frequent, as illustrated by Research in Practice 9.1.[5]

ITEMIZED RATING SCALES

Itemized Rating Scale
A measurement scale having numbers and/or brief descriptions associated with each category. The categories are ordered in terms of scale position.

In an **itemized rating scale**, the respondents are provided with a scale that has a number or brief description associated with each category. The categories are ordered in terms of scale position; and the respondents are required to select the specified category that best describes the object being rated. Itemized rating scales are widely used in marketing research and form the basic components of more complex scales, such as multiitem rating scales. We first describe the commonly used itemized rating scales, the Likert, semantic differential, and Stapel scales, and then examine the major issues surrounding the use of itemized rating scales.

Likert Scale

Named after its developer, Rensis Likert, the **Likert scale** is a widely used rating scale that requires the respondents to indicate a degree of agreement or disagreement with each of a series of statements about the stimulus objects.[6] Typically, each scale item has five response categories, ranging from "strongly disagree" to "strongly agree." We illustrate with a Likert scale for evaluating attitudes toward Sears in the context of the department store patronage project.

Likert Scale A measurement scale with five response categories ranging from "strongly disagree" to "strongly agree", which requires the respondents to indicate a degree of agreement or disagreement with each of a series of statements related to the stimulus objects.

To conduct the analysis, each statement is assigned a numerical score, ranging either from −2 to +2 or 1 to 5. The analysis can be conducted on an item-by-item basis (profile analysis), or a total (summated) score can be calculated for each respondent by summing across items. Suppose the Likert scale in the department store example was used to measure attitudes toward Sears as well as J. C. Penney. Profile analysis would involve comparing the two stores in terms of the average respondent ratings for each item, such as quality of merchandise, in-store service, and brand mix. The summated approach is most frequently used, and as a result the Likert scale is also referred to as a *summated scale*.[7] In this approach to determine the total score for each respondent on each store, it is important to use a consistent scoring procedure so that a high (or low) score consistently reflects a favorable response. This requires that the categories assigned to the negative statements by the respondents be scored by reversing the scale. Note that for a negative statement, an agreement reflects an unfavorable response, whereas for a positive statement, agreement represents a favorable response. Accordingly, a "strongly agree" response to a favorable statement and a "strongly disagree" response to an unfavorable statement would both receive scores of five.[8] In the scale shown above, if a higher score is to denote a more

DEPARTMENT STORE PATRONAGE PROJECT

Likert Scale

Instructions

Listed below are different opinions about Sears. Please indicate how strongly you agree or disagree with each by using the following scale:

1 = Strongly disagree
2 = Disagree
3 = Neither agree nor disagree
4 = Agree
5 = Strongly agree

	Strongly Disagree	*Disagree*	*Neither Agree nor Disagree*	*Agree*	*Strongly Agree*
1. Sears sells high-quality merchandise.	1	2X	3	4	5
2. Sears has poor in-store service.	1	2X	3	4	5
3. I like to shop at Sears.	1	2	3X	4	5
4. Sears does not offer a good mix of different brands within a product category.	1	2	3	4X	5
5. The credit policies at Sears are terrible.	1	2	3	4X	5
6. Sears is where America shops.	1X	2	3	4	5
7. I do not like the advertising done by Sears.	1	2	3	4X	5
8. Sears sells a wide variety of merchandise.	1	2	3	4X	5
9. Sears charges fair prices.	1	2X	3	4	5

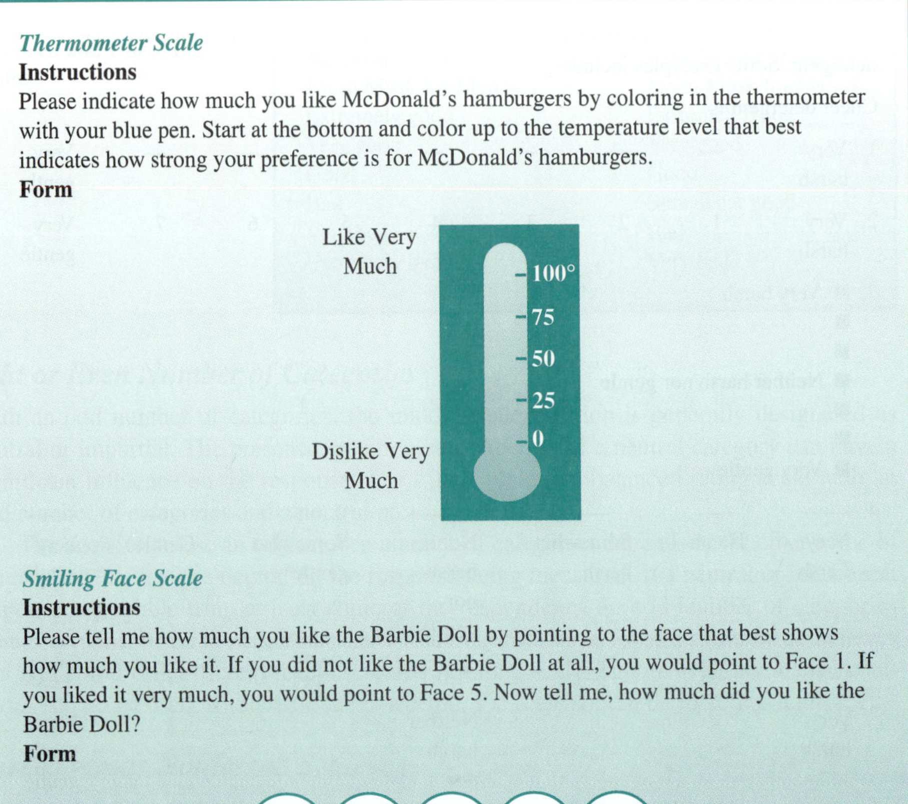

Figure 9.3
Some Unique Rating Chart Configurations

MULTIITEM SCALES

The development of multiitem rating scales requires considerable technical expertise.[24] Figure 9.4 is a framework for constructing multiitem scales. The characteristic to be measured is frequently called a *construct*. Scale development begins with an underlying theory of the construct being measured. A theory is necessary not only for constructing the scale but also for interpreting the resulting scores. The next step is to generate an initial pool of scale items. Typically, this is done based on theory, analysis of secondary data, and qualitative research. From this pool, a reduced set of potential scale items is generated by the judgment of the researcher and other knowledgeable individuals. Some qualitative criterion is adopted to aid their judgment. The reduced set of items is still too large to constitute a scale. Thus, further reduction is achieved in a quantitative manner.

Data are collected on the reduced set of potential scale items from a large pretest sample of respondents. The data are analyzed using techniques such as correlations, factor analysis, cluster analysis, discriminant analysis, and statistical tests discussed later in this book. As a result of these statistical analyses, several more items are eliminated, resulting in a purified scale. The purified scale is evaluated for reliability and validity by collecting more data from a different sample (see the following section). On the basis of these assessments, a final set of scale items is selected. As can be seen from Figure 9.4, the scale development process is an iterative one with several feedback loops.[25]

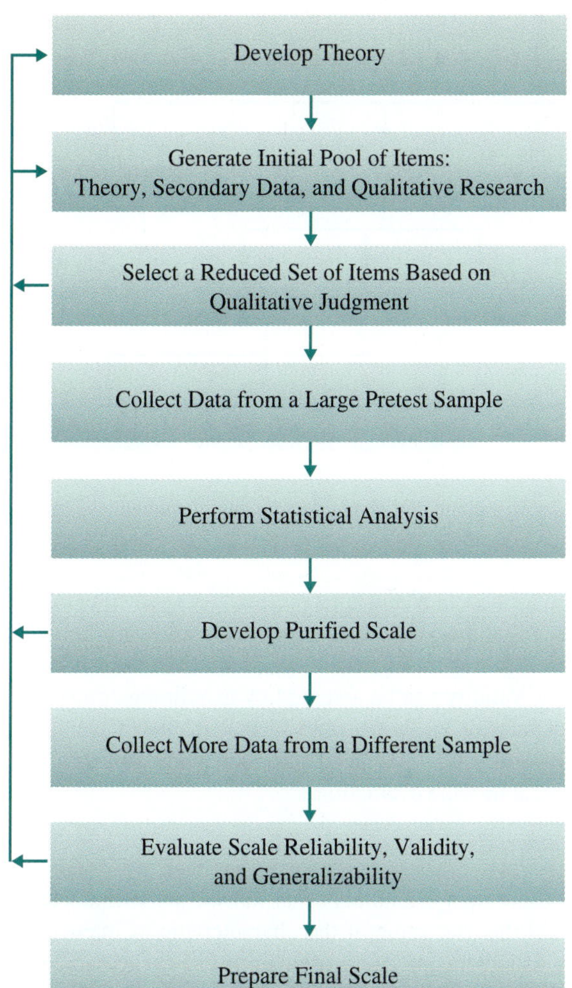

Figure 9.4
Development of a Multiitem Scale

An example of a scale developed for use in industrial marketing research is given below.

EXAMPLE

Measuring Technical Sophistication with a Technically Sophisticated Scale

The following multiitem scale measures the technical sophistication of a product line.[26]

1. Technical	1	2	3	4	5	6	7	Nontechnical
2. Low engineering content	1	2	3	4	5	6	7	High engineering content
3. Fast changing	1	2	3	4	5	6	7	Slowly changing
4. Unsophisticated	1	2	3	4	5	6	7	Sophisticated
5. Commodity	1	2	3	4	5	6	7	Customized
6. Unique	1	2	3	4	5	6	7	Common
7. Complex	1	2	3	4	5	6	7	Simple

Items 1, 3, 6, and 7 are reversed in scoring. This scale can be used in industrial marketing to measure the technical sophistication of a customer's product line and suggest changes to improve technical quality. ■

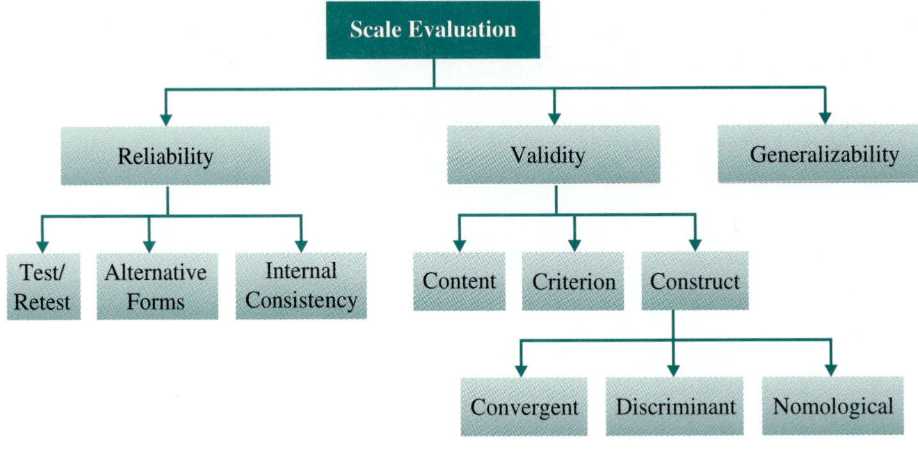

Figure 9.5
Scale Evaluation

Scale Evaluation

A multiitem scale should be evaluated for accuracy and applicability.[27] As shown in Figure 9.5, this involves an assessment of the reliability, validity, and generalizability of the scale. Approaches to assessing reliability include test-retest reliability, alternative-forms reliability, and internal consistency reliability. Validity can be assessed by examining content validity, criterion validity, and construct validity.

Before we can examine reliability and validity we need an understanding of measurement accuracy, because it is fundamental to scale evaluation.

Measurement Accuracy

Measurement Error The variation in the information sought by the researcher and the information generated by the measurement process employed.

True Score Model A mathematical model that provides a framework for understanding the accuracy of measurement.

As was mentioned in chapter 8, a measurement is a number that reflects some characteristic of an object. A measurement is not the true value of the characteristic of interest but rather an observation of it. A variety of factors can cause **measurement error**, which results in the measurement or observed score being different from the true score of the characteristic being measured (see Figure 9.6). The **true score model** provides a framework for understanding the accuracy of measurement. According to this model,

$$X_O = X_T + X_S + X_R$$

where

X_O = the observed score or measurement

X_T = the true score of the characteristic

X_S = systematic error

X_R = random error

Systematic Error Systematic error affects the measurement in a constant way and represents stable factors that affect the observed score in the same way each time the measurement is made.

Random Error Measurement error that arises from random changes or differences in respondents or measurement situations.

Note that the total measurement error includes the systematic error, X_S, and the random error, X_R. **Systematic error** affects the measurement in a constant way. It represents stable factors that affect the observed score in the same way each time the measurement is made: for example, mechanical factors (see Figure 9.6). **Random error**, on the other hand, is not constant. It represents transient factors that affect the observed score in different ways each time the measurement is made, such as transient personal or situational factors. The distinction between systematic and random error is crucial to our understanding of reliability and validity.

1. Other relatively stable characteristics of the individual that influence the test score, such as intelligence, social desirability, and education.
2. Short-term or transient personal factors, such as health, emotions, fatigue.
3. Situational factors, such as the presence of other people, noise, and distractions.
4. Sampling of items included in the scale: addition or deletion of or changes in the scale items.
5. Lack of clarity of the scale, in the instructions or the items themselves.
6. Mechanical factors, such as poor printing, overcrowding of items in the questionnaire, and poor design.
7. Administration of the scale, such as differences among interviewers.
8. Analysis factors, such as differences in scoring and statistical analysis.

Figure 9.6
Potential Sources of Error in Measurement

Reliability

Reliability refers to the extent to which a scale produces consistent results if measurements are made repeatedly.[28] Systematic sources of error do not have an adverse impact on reliability, because they affect the measurement in a constant way and do not lead to inconsistency. In contrast, random error produces inconsistency, leading to lower reliability. Reliability can be defined as the extent to which measures are free from random error, X_R. If $X_R = 0$, the measure is perfectly reliable.

Reliability The extent to which a scale produces consistent results if repeated measurements are made on the characteristic.

Reliability is assessed by determining the proportion of systematic variation in a scale. This is done by determining the association between scores obtained from different administrations of the scale. If the association is high, the scale yields consistent results and is therefore reliable. Approaches for assessing reliability include the test-retest, alternative-forms, and internal consistency methods.

Test-Retest Reliability. In **test-retest reliability**, respondents are administered identical sets of scale items at two different times under as nearly equivalent conditions as possible. The time interval between tests or administrations is, typically, two to four weeks. The degree of similarity between the two measurements is determined by computing a correlation coefficient (see chapter 17). The higher the correlation coefficient, the greater the reliability.

Test-Retest Reliability An approach for assessing reliability in which respondents are administered identical sets of scale items at two different times under as nearly equivalent conditions as possible.

There are several problems associated with the test-retest approach to determining reliability. First, it is sensitive to the time interval between testing. Other things being equal, the longer the time interval, the lower the reliability. Second, the initial measurement may alter the characteristic being measured. For example, measuring respondents' attitudes toward low-fat milk may cause them to become more health-conscious and develop a more positive attitude toward low-fat milk. Third, it may be impossible to make repeated measurements (for example, the research topic may be the respondent's initial reaction to a new product). Fourth, the first measurement may have a carryover effect to the second or subsequent measurements. Respondents may attempt to remember answers they gave the first time. Fifth, the characteristic being measured may change between measurements. For example, favorable information about an object between measurements may make a respondent's attitude more positive. Finally, the test-retest reliability coefficient can be inflated by the correlation of each item with itself. These correlations tend to be higher than correlations between different scale items across administrations. Hence, it is possible to have high test-retest correlations because of the high correlations between the same scale items measured at different times even though the correlations between different scale items are quite low. Because of these problems, a test-retest approach is best applied in conjunction with other approaches, such as alternative-forms.[29]

Alternative-Forms Reliability. In **alternative-forms reliability**, two equivalent forms of the scale are constructed. The same respondents are measured at two different times, usually two to four weeks apart. The scores from the administrations of the alternative scale forms are correlated to assess reliability.[30]

There are two major problems with this approach. First, it is time consuming and expensive to construct an equivalent form of the scale. Second, it is difficult to construct two equivalent forms of a scale. The two forms should be equivalent with respect to content. In a strict sense, this requires that the alternative sets of scale items should have the same means, variances, and intercorrelations. Even if these conditions are satisfied, the two forms may not be equivalent in content. Thus, a low correlation may reflect either an unreliable scale or nonequivalent forms.

Alternative-Forms Reliability An approach for assessing reliability that requires two equivalent forms of the scale to be constructed and then the same respondents are measured at two different times.

Internal Consistency Reliability An approach for assessing the internal consistency of the set of items, when several items are summated in order to form a total score for the scale.

Split-Half Reliability A form of internal consistency reliability in which the items constituting the scale are divided into two halves and the resulting half scores are correlated.

Coefficient Alpha A measure of internal consistency reliability, which is the average of all possible split-half coefficients resulting from different splittings of the scale items.

Internal Consistency Reliability. **Internal consistency reliability** is used to assess the reliability of a summated scale in which several items are summed to form a total score. In a scale of this type, each item measures some aspect of the construct measured by the entire scale, and the items should be consistent in what they indicate about the characteristic. This measure of reliability focuses on the internal consistency of the set of items forming the scale.

The simplest measure of internal consistency is **split-half reliability**. The items on the scale are divided into two halves and the resulting half scores are correlated. High correlations between the halves indicate high internal consistency. The scale items can be split into halves based on odd- and even-numbered items or randomly. The problem is that the results will depend on how the scale items are split. A popular approach to overcoming this problem is to use the coefficient alpha.

The **coefficient alpha**, or *Cronbach's alpha*, is the average of all possible split-half coefficients resulting from different ways of splitting the scale items. This coefficient varies from 0 to 1, and a value of 0.6 or less generally indicates unsatisfactory internal consistency reliability. An important property of coefficient alpha is that its value tends to increase with an increase in the number of scale items. Therefore, coefficient alpha may be artificially, and inappropriately, inflated by including several redundant scale items.[31] Another coefficient that can be employed in conjunction with coefficient alpha is coefficient beta. Coefficient beta assists in determining whether the averaging process used in calculating coefficient alpha is masking any inconsistent items.

Some multiitem scales include several sets of items designed to measure different aspects of a multidimensional construct. For example, store image is a multidimensional construct that includes quality of merchandise, variety and assortment of merchandise, returns and adjustment policy, service of store personnel, prices, convenience of location, layout of the store, and credit and billing policies. Hence, a scale designed to measure store image would contain items measuring each of these dimensions. Because these dimensions are somewhat independent, a measure of internal consistency computed across dimensions would be inappropriate. However, if several items are used to measure each dimension, internal consistency reliability can be computed for each dimension, as in the Beaumont emotion battery.

EXAMPLE

Emotionally Charged Battery

The Beaumont emotion battery has been developed by the Beaumont Organization, Ltd., to measure emotional response to advertising. Respondents rate the advertisement or commercial to which they are exposed across a battery of items that tap eight primary emotions: acceptance, fear, surprise, sadness, disgust, anger, anticipation, and joy. The internal consistency reliability of this battery, measured in terms of Cronbach's alpha, has been determined for each primary emotion. For the emotions listed, these reliability coefficients are 0.73, 0.66, 0.63, 0.75, 0.72, 0.81, 0.79, and 0.85. These results indicate satisfactory internal consistency reliability for the Beaumont emotion battery.[32] ■

Validity

The **validity** of a scale may be defined as the extent to which differences in observed scale scores reflect true differences among objects on the characteristic being measured, rather than systematic or random error. Perfect validity requires that there be no measurement error ($X_O = X_T$, $X_R = 0$, $X_S = 0$). Researchers may assess content validity, criterion validity, or construct validity.[33]

Validity The extent to which differences in observed scale scores reflect true differences among objects on the characteristic being measured, rather than systematic or random errors.

Content Validity. **Content validity**, sometimes called *face validity*, is a subjective but systematic evaluation of how well the content of a scale represents the measurement task at hand. The researcher or someone else examines whether the scale items adequately cover the entire domain of the construct being measured. Thus, a scale designed to measure store image would be considered inadequate if it omitted any of the major dimensions (quality, variety, and assortment of merchandise, etc.). Given its subjective nature, content validity alone is not a sufficient measure of the validity of a scale, yet it aids in a commonsense interpretation of the scale scores. A more formal evaluation can be obtained by examining criterion validity.

Content Validity A type of validity, sometimes called *face validity*, consisting of a subjective but systematic evaluation of the representativeness of the content of a scale for the measuring task at hand.

Criterion Validity. **Criterion validity** reflects whether a scale performs as expected in relation to other variables selected (criterion variables) as meaningful criteria. Criterion variables may include demographic and psychographic characteristics, attitudinal and behavioral measures, or scores obtained from other scales. Based on the time period involved, criterion validity can take two forms; concurrent and predictive validity.

Criterion Validity A type of validity that examines whether the measurement scale performs as expected in relation to other variables selected as meaningful criteria.

Concurrent validity is assessed when the data on the scale being evaluated and on the criterion variables are collected at the same time. To assess concurrent validity, a researcher may develop short forms of standard personality instruments, such as the Beaumont emotion battery. The original instruments and the short versions would be administered simultaneously to a group of respondents and the results compared. To assess predictive validity, the researcher collects data on the scale at one point in time and data on the criterion variables at a future time. For example, attitudes toward cereal brands could be used to predict future purchases of cereals by members of a scanner panel. Attitudinal data are obtained from the panel members, and then their future purchases are tracked with scanner data. The predicted and actual purchases are compared to assess the predictive validity of the attitudinal scale.

Construct Validity A type of validity that addresses the question of what construct or characteristic the scale is measuring. An attempt is made to answer theoretical questions of why a scale works and what deductions can be made concerning the theory underlying the scale.

Construct Validity. **Construct validity** addresses the question of what construct or characteristic the scale is, in fact, measuring. When assessing construct validity, the researcher attempts to answer theoretical questions about why the scale works and what deductions can be made concerning the underlying theory. Thus, construct validity requires a sound theory of the nature of the construct being measured and how it relates to other constructs. Construct validity is the most sophisticated and difficult type of validity to establish. As Figure 9.5 shows, construct validity includes convergent, discriminant, and nomological validity.

Convergent validity is the extent to which the scale correlates positively with other measures of the same construct. It is not necessary that all these measures be obtained by using conventional scaling techniques. **Discriminant validity** is the extent to which a measure does not correlate with other constructs from which it is supposed to differ. It involves demonstrating a lack of correlation among differing constructs. **Nomological validity** is the extent to which the scale correlates in theoretically predicted ways with measures of different but related constructs. A theoretical model is formulated that leads to

Convergent Validity A measure of construct validity that measures the extent to which the scale correlates positively with other measures of the same construct.

Discriminant Validity A type of construct validity that assesses the extent to which a measure does not correlate with other constructs from which it is supposed to differ.

Nomological Validity A type of validity that assesses the relationship between theoretical constructs. It seeks to confirm significant correlations between the constructs as predicted by a theory.

further deductions, tests, and inferences. Gradually, a nomological net is built in which several constructs are systematically interrelated. We illustrate construct validity in the context of a multiitem scale designed to measure self concept.[34]

EXAMPLE

To Thine Own Self Be True

The following findings would provide evidence of construct validity for a multiitem scale to measure self-concept.

- High correlations with other scales designed to measure self-concepts and with reported classifications by friends (convergent validity).
- Low correlations with unrelated constructs of brand loyalty and variety seeking (discriminant validity).
- Brands that are congruent with the individual's self-concept are more preferred, as postulated by the theory (nomological validity).
- A high level of reliability. ■

Notice that a high level of reliability was included as an evidence of construct validity in this example. This illustrates the relationship between reliability and validity.

Relationship between Reliability and Validity

The relationship between reliability and validity can be understood in terms of the true score model. If a measure is perfectly valid, it is also perfectly reliable. In this case $X_O = X_T$, $X_R = 0$, and $X_S = 0$. Thus, perfect validity implies perfect reliability. If a measure is unreliable, it cannot be perfectly valid, because at a minimum $X_O = X_T + X_R$. Furthermore, systematic error may also be present, that is, $X_S \neq 0$. Thus, unreliability implies invalidity. If a measure is perfectly reliable, it may or may not be perfectly valid, because systematic error may still be present ($X_O = X_T + X_S$). While lack of reliability constitutes negative evidence for validity, reliability does not in itself imply validity. Reliability is a necessary, but not sufficient, condition for validity.

Generalizability

Generalizability The degree to which a study based on a sample applies to the population as a whole.

Generalizability refers to the extent to which one can generalize from the observations at hand to a universe of generalizations. The set of all conditions of measurement over which the investigator wishes to generalize is the universe of generalization. These conditions may include items, interviewers, situations of observation, etc. A researcher may wish to generalize a scale developed for use in personal interviews to other modes of data collection, such as mail and telephone interviews. Likewise, one may wish to generalize from a sample of items to the universe of items, from a sample of times of measurement to the universe of times of measurement, from a sample of observers to a universe of observers, and so on.[35]

In generalizability studies, measurement procedures are designed to investigate the universes of interest by sampling conditions of measurement from each of them. For each universe of interest, an aspect of measurement called a *facet* is included in the study. Traditional reliability methods can be viewed as single-facet generalizability studies. A test-retest correlation is concerned with whether scores obtained from a measurement scale are generalizable to the universe of scores across all times of possible measurement. Even if the test-retest correlation is high, nothing can be said about the generalizability of the scale to other universes. To generalize to other universes, generalizability theory procedures must be employed.

CHOOSING A SCALING TECHNIQUE

In addition to theoretical considerations and evaluation of reliability and validity, certain practical factors should be considered in selecting scaling techniques for a particular marketing research problem.[36] These include the level of information (nominal, ordinal, interval, or ratio) desired, the capabilities of the respondents, the characteristics of the stimulus objects, method of administration, the context, and cost.

As a general rule, using the scaling technique that will yield the highest level of information feasible in a given situation will permit the use of the greatest variety of statistical analyses. Also, regardless of the type of scale used, whenever feasible, several scale items should measure the characteristic of interest. This provides more accurate measurement than a single item scale. In many situations it is desirable to use more than one scaling technique or to obtain additional measures using mathematically derived scales.

MATHEMATICALLY DERIVED SCALES

All the scaling techniques discussed in this chapter require the respondents to evaluate directly various characteristics of the stimulus objects. In contrast, mathematical scaling techniques allow researchers to infer respondents' evaluations of characteristics of stimulus objects. These evaluations are inferred from the respondents' overall judgments of the objects. Two popular mathematically derived scaling techniques are multidimensional scaling and conjoint analysis. These techniques are discussed in detail in chapter 21.

INTERNATIONAL MARKETING RESEARCH

In designing the scale or response format, one should take into account respondents' educational or literacy levels.[37] One approach is to develop scales that are pan-cultural, or free of cultural biases. Of the scaling techniques we have considered, the semantic differential scale may be said to be pan-cultural. It has been tested in a number of countries and has consistently produced similar results.

EXAMPLE

Copying the Name Xerox

Semantic differential scales have been used to measure the image of Xerox and its competitors in Russia.

Xerox was a name well received in the former Soviet Union since the 1960s. In fact, the act of copying documents was called *Xeroxing*, a term coined after the name of the company. It was a brand name people equated with quality. However, with the disintegration of Soviet Union into the Commonwealth of Independent States, sales of Xerox started to fall. Management initially attributed this to strong competition from companies such as Canon, Ricoh Co., Mitsubishi Electric Corp., and Minolta Camera Co. First attempts at making the product more competitive did not help. Subsequently, marketing research was undertaken to measure the image of Xerox and its competitors. Semantic differential scales were used, as this type of scale is considered pan-cultural. The bipolar labels used were carefully tested to ensure that they had the intended meaning in the Russian context.

The results of the study revealed that the real problem was a growing negative perception of Russian customers toward Xerox products. What could have gone wrong? The problem was not with Xerox, but with several independent producers of copying machines that had illegally infringed on Xerox trademark rights. With the disintegration of Soviet Union, the protection of these trademarks was unclear and trademark infringement kept growing. As a result, customers developed the notion that Xerox Company sold low-quality products. Among other courses of action, Xerox ran a corporate campaign on the national Russian TV and radio networks as well as in local print media. The campaign emphasized Xerox's leadership position in the commonwealth countries where quality demands were very high. This was a definite step in removing some misconceptions of Russian consumers toward Xerox. Xerox also registered its trademark separately in each republic.[38] ■

While the semantic differential worked well in the Russian context, an alternative approach is to develop scales that use a self-defined cultural norm as a base referent. For example, respondents may be required to indicate their own anchor point and position relative to a culture-specific stimulus set. This approach is useful for measuring attitudes that are defined relative to cultural norms (e.g., attitude toward marital roles). In developing response formats, verbal rating scales appear to be the most suitable. Even less-educated respondents can readily understand and respond to verbal scales. Special attention should be devoted to determining equivalent verbal descriptors in different languages and cultures. The end points of the scale are particularly prone to different interpretations. In some cultures "1" may be interpreted as best, whereas in others it may be interpreted as worst, regardless of how it is scaled. It is important that the scale end points and the verbal descriptors be employed in a manner consistent with the culture.

Finally, in international marketing research it is critical to establish the equivalence of scales and measures used to obtain data from different countries. This topic is complex and is discussed in some detail in chapter 23.

ETHICS IN MARKETING RESEARCH

The researcher has the ethical responsibility to use scales that have reasonable reliability, validity, and generalizability. The findings generated by scales that are unreliable, invalid, or not generalizable to the target population are questionable at best and raise serious ethical issues as the client is entitled to research conducted in a competent manner. Moreover, the researcher should not bias the scales so as to slant the findings in any particular direction. This is easy to do by either biasing the wording of the statements (Likert-type scales), the scale descriptors, or aspects of the scales. Consider the use of scale descriptors. The descriptors used to frame a scale can be chosen to bias results in a desired direction, for example, generate a positive view of the client's brand or a negative view of a competitor's brand. To project the client's brand favorably, respondents are asked to indicate their opinion of the brand on several attributes using seven-point scales anchored by the descriptors "extremely poor" to "good". In such a case, respondents are reluctant to rate the product extremely poorly. In fact, respondents who believe the product to be only mediocre will end up responding favorably. Try this yourself. How would you rate BMW automobiles on the following attributes?

Reliability:	Horrible	1	2	3	4	5	6	7	Good
Performance:	Very poor	1	2	3	4	5	6	7	Good
Quality:	One of the worst	1	2	3	4	5	6	7	Good
Prestige:	Very low	1	2	3	4	5	6	7	Good

Did you find yourself rating BMW cars positively? Using this same technique, it is possible to negatively bias evaluations of competitors' brands by providing a mildly negative descriptor (somewhat poor) against a strong positive descriptor (extremely good).

Thus, we see how important it is to use balanced scales with comparable positive and negative descriptors. When this guideline is violated, responses are biased and should be interpreted accordingly. The researcher has a responsibility to both the client and respondents to ensure the applicability and usefulness of the scale, as we see in the following example.

EXAMPLE

An Ethical Scale for Measuring Ethics

Although everyone knows ethics are important, how do you go about measuring ethical evaluations of marketing activities? To answer this question, one set of researchers turned to concepts of moral philosophy (see chapter 24) to develop a scale for measuring ethical evaluations. Twenty-nine seven-point bipolar scales, developed from moral philosophy and ranging from fair to unfair and efficient to inefficient resulted. Tests of these scales, through their use in evaluating various ethical scenarios, indicated that the reliabilities for these scales (measured via Cronbach's alpha) were high, and validity measures indicated a strong degree of construct validity. Accordingly, this scale has been useful in a variety of contexts for investigating ethical issues in marketing.[39] ■

INTERNET AND COMPUTER APPLICATIONS

Continuous rating scales may be easily implemented on the Internet. The cursor can be moved on the screen in a continuous fashion to select the exact position on the scale that best describes the respondent's evaluation. Moreover, the scale values can be automatically scored by the computer, thus increasing the speed and accuracy of processing the data.

Similarly, it is also easy to implement all of the three itemized rating scales on the Internet. Moreover, using the Internet one can search for and locate similar scales used by other researchers. It is also possible that other researchers have reported reliability and validity assessments for multiitem scales. Before generating new scales, a researcher should first examine similar scales used by other researchers and use them if they meet the measurement objectives. The Office of Scales Research at Southern Illinois University-Carbondale, best known for the production of the *Marketing Scales Handbook*, has posted its technical reports on the Internet (www.siu.edu/departments/coba/mktg/osr).

EXAMPLE

HERMES On-line Security and Privacy Survey

The University of Michigan Business School's HERMES research project addresses the issue of Web users' concern for security and privacy through the use of a Web survey.

The survey asks several questions regarding an individual's opinion of risk associated with on-line transactions. Each question allows the respondent to respond on a scale of 1 to 7 through the use of a pull-down menu. After each section of the questionnaire is complete, the respondent is prompted to submit their responses.

Despite some other limitations, the use of a seven-point scale has been effective in capturing respondents' attitude toward on-line transactions including risk perceptions. ■

Microcomputers are useful for developing and testing continuous and itemized rating scales, particularly multiitem scales. EZWRITER—a module of the computer-assisted telephone interviewing system C-SURVENT—uses a series of menu-driven screens to

FOCUS ON Burke

Burke tailors each study to address the client's needs, and thus the use of scales varies considerably. The different forms of scales discussed in this chapter are used, although Likert-type scales are the most popular. For its branded products, Burke generally adheres to a standard protocol and the same set of scales are used across clients. Consider the scales designed to measure the percentage of "secure" customers and to provide a strategic blueprint that highlights improvement priorities. Burke's protocol uses the following three criterion measures to create a composite measure known as the Secure Customer Index™:

Overall Satisfaction

4 = Very satisfied
3 = Somewhat satisfied
2 = Somewhat dissatisfied
1 = Very dissatisfied

Willingness to Recommend

5 = Definitely would recommend
4 = Probably would recommend
3 = Might or might not recommend
2 = Probably would not recommend
1 = Definitely would not recommend

Likelihood to Use Again

5 = Definitely will use again
4 = Probably will use again
3 = Might or might not use again
2 = Probably will not use again
1 = Definitely will not use again

The Secure Customer Index™ is the percentage of customers who are "very satisfied" *and* "definitely would recommend" *and* "definitely will use the client's product or service again."

(Continued)

guide the market researcher through the scale development process. EZWRITER by Computers for Marketing Corporation (CfMC) of San Francisco can customize scales for printed questionnaires or for use by telephone interviewers at computer screens in a fraction of the time this would take without automation. Other specialized programs are also available for constructing itemized rating scales. ATTITUDE SCALES by Persimmon Software constructs a variety of rating scales for measuring attitudes in marketing and opinion research. Several of the questionnaire design packages, discussed in chapter 10, can construct comparative and noncomparative scales.

SUMMARY

In noncomparative scaling, each object is scaled independently of the other objects in the stimulus set. The resulting data are generally assumed to be interval or ratio scaled. Noncomparative rating scales can be either continuous or itemized. The itemized rating scales are further classified as Likert, semantic differential, or Stapel scales. When using noncomparative itemized rating scales, the researcher must decide on the number of scale categories,

FOCUS ON Burke *(Continued)*

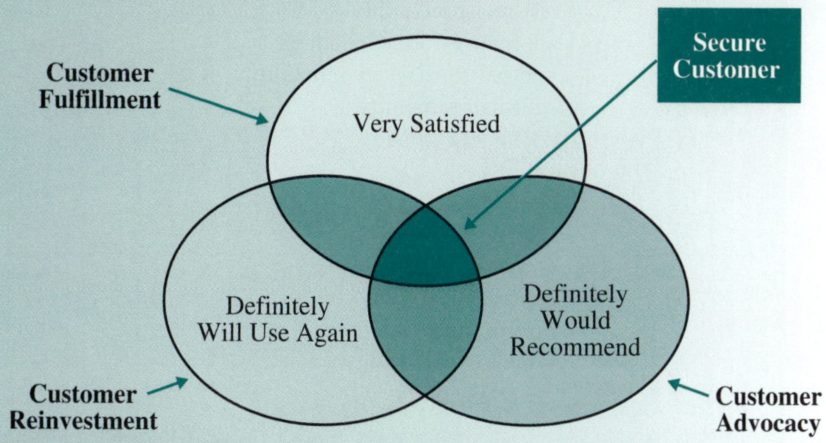

Burke has found that the Secure Customer Index™ is more discriminating than an overall satisfaction question alone. Burke has also documented a strong correlation between the Secure Customer Index™ and actual performance measures such as margin, market share, and customer retention rates. For example, in a study among commercial purchasers of computer hardware and software, Burke found that retention rates increased as the level of customer "security" increased:

Level of Security	*Retention Rate*
Secure	88%
Still favorable	57%
Indifferent	30%
Dissatisfied	25%

In addition to the Secure Customer Index™, Burke generally collects ratings on a battery of attributes. Again, Likert-type scales are used. Burke analyzes the data to determine which attributes "drive" customer security, thus identifying attributes the client should target for improvements.

balanced versus unbalanced scales, odd or even number of categories, forced versus nonforced scales, nature and degree of verbal description, and the physical form or configuration.

Multiitem scales consist of a number of rating scale items. These scales should be evaluated in terms of reliability and validity. Reliability refers to the extent to which a scale produces consistent results if repeated measurements are made. Approaches to assessing reliability include test-retest, alternative-forms, and internal consistency. Validity, or accuracy of measurement, may be assessed by evaluating content validity, criterion validity, and construct validity.

The choice of particular scaling techniques in a given situation should be based on theoretical and practical considerations. As a general rule, the scaling technique used should be the one that will yield the highest level of information feasible. Also, multiple measures should be obtained.

In international marketing research, special attention should be devoted to determining equivalent verbal descriptors in different languages and cultures. The researcher has a responsibility to both the client and respondents to ensure the applicability and usefulness of the scales. The Internet and computers are useful for developing and testing continuous and itemized rating scales, particularly multiitem scales.

KEY TERMS AND CONCEPTS

noncomparative scale
continuous rating scale
itemized rating scale
Likert scale
semantic differential
stapel scale
balanced scale
forced rating scales
measurement error
true score model
systematic error
random error
reliability
test-retest reliability
alternative-forms reliability
internal consistency reliability
split-half reliability
coefficient alpha
validity
content validity
criterion validity
construct validity
convergent validity
discriminant validity
nomological validity
generalizability

ACRONYMS

The rating scale decisions may be described by the acronym RATING:

R esponse option: forced versus. nonforced
A ttractive versus unattractive number of categories; balanced versus unbalanced
T otal number of categories
I mpartial or neutral category; odd versus even number of categories
N ature and degree of verbal description
G raphics: physical form and configuration

EXERCISES

Questions

1. What is a semantic differential scale? For what purposes is this scale used?
2. Describe the Likert scale.
3. What are the differences between the Stapel scale and the semantic differential? Which scale is more popular?
4. What are the major decisions involved in constructing an itemized rating scale?
5. How many scale categories should be used in an itemized rating scale? Why?
6. What is the difference between balanced and unbalanced scales?
7. Should an odd or even number of categories be used in an itemized rating scale?
8. What is the difference between forced and nonforced scales?
9. How does the nature and degree of verbal description affect the response to itemized rating scales?
10. What are multiitem scales?
11. Describe the true score model.
12. What is reliability?
13. What are the differences between test-retest and alternative-forms reliability?
14. Describe the notion of internal consistency reliability.
15. What is validity?
16. What is criterion validity? How is it assessed?
17. How would you assess the construct validity of a multiitem scale?
18. What is the relationship between reliability and validity?
19. How would you select a particular scaling technique?

Problems

1. Develop a Likert, semantic differential, and a Stapel scale for measuring store loyalty.
2. Develop a multiitem scale to measure students' attitudes toward internationalization of the management curriculum. How would you assess the reliability and validity of this scale?
3. Develop a Likert scale for measuring the attitude of students toward the Internet as a source of general information. Administer your scale to a small sample of ten students and refine it.
4. The following scale was used in a recent study to measure attitude toward new technology. Please tell me how much you agree or disagree with the following statements as they describe how you view new technology. Use a scale of 1 to 5, where 1 = strongly disagree and 5 = strongly agree.

I'm a person who avoids new technology.

I'm a technology buff who keeps up with the latest equipment.

I take a "wait-and-see" approach to new technology until it is proven.

I'm the kind of person friends turn to for advice on buying new technology.

a. How would you score this scale to measure attitude toward new technology?

b. Develop an equivalent semantic differential scale to measure attitude toward new technology.

c. Develop an equivalent Stapel scale to measure attitude toward new technology.

d. Which scale form is most suited for a telephone survey?

INTERNET AND COMPUTER EXERCISES

1. Design Likert scales to measure the usefulness of Ford Motor Company's Web site. Visit the site at www.ford.com and rate it on the scales that you have developed.
2. Design semantic differential scales to measure the perception of FedEx overnight delivery service and compare it to that offered by UPS. Relevant information may be obtained by visiting the Web sites of these two companies (www.fedex.com, www.ups.com)
3. Visit the Office of Scales Research Web site (www.siu.edu/departments/coba/mktg/osr). Identify one application of the Likert scale and one application of the semantic differential. Write a report describing the context in which these scales have been used.
4. Visit the Web sites of two marketing research firms conducting surveys. Analyze one survey of each firm to critically evaluate the itemized rating scales being used.
5. Surf the Net to find two examples each of Likert, semantic differential, and Stapel scales. Write a report describing the context in which these scales are being used.

Chapter 10

"A good questionnaire must engage the respondent and stimulate their interest in providing complete and accurate answers. It must do this while creating a common understanding of both the questions and answers among all respondents."

Bobbi Brantley,
training manager,
research services,
Burke, Inc.

Questionnaire and Form Design

OBJECTIVES

After reading this chapter, the student should be able to

1. explain the purpose of a questionnaire and its objectives of asking questions that the respondents can and will answer, encouraging respondents, and minimizing response error
2. describe the process of designing a questionnaire, the steps involved, and the guidelines that must be followed at each step
3. discuss the observational form of data collection and specify the who, what, when, where, why, and way of behavior to be observed
4. discuss the considerations involved in designing questionnaires for international marketing research
5. understand the ethical issues involved in questionnaire design
6. discuss the use of the Internet and computers in designing questionnaires

OVERVIEW

Questionnaire or form design is an important step in formulating a research design. Once the researcher has specified the nature of research design (chapters 3 through 7), and determined the scaling procedures (chapters 8 and 9), he or she can develop a questionnaire or an observational form. This chapter discusses the importance of questionnaires and observational forms. Next, we describe the objectives of a questionnaire and the steps involved in designing questionnaires. We provide several guidelines for developing sound questionnaires. We also consider the design of observation forms. The considerations involved in designing questionnaires when conducting international marketing research are discussed. Several ethical issues that arise in questionnaire design are identified. The chapter concludes with a discussion of the use of the Internet and computers in designing questionnaires.

We begin with an example to introduce questionnaire design and show the types of information that can be obtained from a questionnaire.

EXAMPLE

Driving at Seventeen

Seventeen magazine carefully designed a self-administered questionnaire to obtain information on the driving habits of females age 15–21. Questions were asked about driver's license status, number of miles driven in the past week, reasons for using a car, specific car driven, how the car was acquired, cost of a new car, method of new-car purchase, most important reasons for selecting a new car, make of car owned, information sources most important in new car selection, reasons for preferring an American-made or foreign car, and degree of interest in seeing car ads in *Seventeen*. Different question formats and scaling techniques were employed. The questionnaire was mailed to 2,150 members of *Seventeen*'s Consumer Panel. A total of 1,143 returns was received representing a response rate of 53.2 percent. Some of the major findings of the survey were:

- The average distance driven in the past week was 123 miles.
- The most important reasons for selecting a new car were styling and features, price, and gas mileage.
- Among drivers who owned their own cars, two-thirds owned a domestic model. One-fifth owned a Chevrolet; almost one-fifth owned a Ford.

Seventeen used this information to solicit advertising from major automobile companies and to plan articles that would appeal to readers.[1] ■

QUESTIONNAIRES AND OBSERVATION FORMS

As was discussed in chapter 5, survey and observation are the two basic methods for obtaining quantitative primary data in descriptive research. Both these methods require some procedure for standardizing the data collection process so that the data obtained are internally consistent and can be analyzed in a uniform and coherent manner. If 40 different interviewers conduct personal interviews or make observations in different parts of the country, the data they collect will not be comparable unless they follow specific guidelines and ask questions and record answers in a standard way. A standardized questionnaire or form will ensure comparability of the data, increase speed and accuracy of recording, and facilitate data processing.

Questionnaire Definition

A **questionnaire**, whether it is called a schedule, interview form, or measuring instrument, is a formalized set of questions for obtaining information from respondents. Typically, a questionnaire is only one element of a data collection package that might also include (1) field work procedures, such as instructions for selecting, approaching, and questioning respondents (see chapter 13); (2) some reward, gift, or payment offered to respondents; and (3) communication aids such as maps, pictures, advertisements, and products (as in personal interviews) and return envelopes (in mail surveys). Regardless of the form of administration, a questionnaire is characterized by some specific objectives.

Questionnaire A structured technique for data collection consisting of a series of questions, written or verbal, to which a respondent replies.

Objectives of a Questionnaire

Any questionnaire has three specific objectives. First, it must translate the information needed into a set of specific questions that the respondents can and will answer. Developing questions that respondents can and will answer and that will yield the desired information is difficult. Two apparently similar ways of posing a question may yield different information. Hence, this objective is a challenge.

Second, a questionnaire must uplift, motivate, and encourage the respondent to become involved in the interview, to cooperate, and to complete the interview. Incomplete interviews have limited usefulness at best. In designing a questionnaire, the researcher should strive to minimize respondent fatigue, boredom, and effort to minimize incompleteness and nonresponse.

Third, a questionnaire should minimize response error. The potential sources of error in research designs were discussed in chapter 3, where response error was defined as the error that arises when respondents give inaccurate answers or their answers are misrecorded or misanalyzed. A questionnaire can be a major source of response error. Minimizing this error is an important objective of questionnaire design. Research in Practice 10.1 illustrates how questionnaires can be designed to achieve these objectives.[2]

RESEARCH IN PRACTICE 10.1

Youth Research Achieves Questionnaire Objectives

Youth Research (YR) of Brookfield, Connecticut, conducts an omnibus survey of children every quarter. Typically, YR interviews 150 boys and girls between ages 6 and 8, along with 150 boys and girls between ages 9 and 12. YR uses mall intercepts of mothers in malls to recruit for its one-on-one interviews that last eight minutes. The study obtains children's views on favorite snack foods, television shows, commercials, radio stations, magazines, buzzwords, and movies.

YR intentionally keeps its questionnaire to eight minutes because of attention span limits of children. YR president Karen Forcade notes that some clients attempt to meet all of their research objectives with one study, instead of iteratively surveying, fine-tuning objectives, and resurveying. In doing so, these clients overlook attention limits of young respondents when developing questionnaires. "The questionnaires keep going through the approval process and people keep adding questions, 'Well let's ask this question, let's add that question, and why don't we talk about this also'," Forcade said. "And so you end up keeping children 25 minutes in a central location study and they get kind of itchy." The response error increases and the quality of data suffers.

Forcade notes other lessons from interviewing children. When asking questions, interviewers should define the context to which the question refers. "It involves getting them to focus on things, putting them in a situation so that they can identify with it," Forcade said. "For example, when asking about their radio listening habits we said, 'What about when you're in Mom's car, do you listen to radio?' rather than, 'How often do you listen to radio? More than once a day, once a day, more than once a week?' Those are kind of big questions for little children."

Questionnaires designed by Youth Research to obtain children's views on favorite snack foods, television shows, commercials, radio stations, magazines, buzzwords, and movies attempt to minimize response error.

QUESTIONNAIRE DESIGN PROCESS

The great weakness of questionnaire design is lack of theory. Because there are no scientific principles that guarantee an optimal or ideal questionnaire, questionnaire design is a skill acquired through experience. It is an art rather than a science. Stanley Payne's *The Art of Asking Questions*, published in 1951, is still a basic work in the field.[3] This section presents guidelines useful to beginning researchers in designing questionnaires. Although these rules can help you avoid major mistakes, the fine-tuning of a questionnaire comes from the creativity of a skilled researcher.

Questionnaire design will be presented as a series of steps (see Figure 10.1). We will present guidelines for each step. Although shown sequentially in Figure 10.1, these steps are interrelated and the development of a questionnaire will involve some iteration and looping. For example, the researcher may discover that respondents misunderstand all the possible wordings of a question. This may require a loop back to the earlier step of deciding on the question structure.[4]

SPECIFY THE INFORMATION NEEDED

The first step in questionnaire design is to specify the information needed. This is also the first step in the research design process. Note that as the research project progresses, the information needed becomes more and more clearly defined. It is helpful to review components of the problem and the approach, particularly the research questions, hypotheses, and characteristics that influence the research design. To further ensure that the information obtained fully addresses all the components of the problem, the researcher should prepare a set

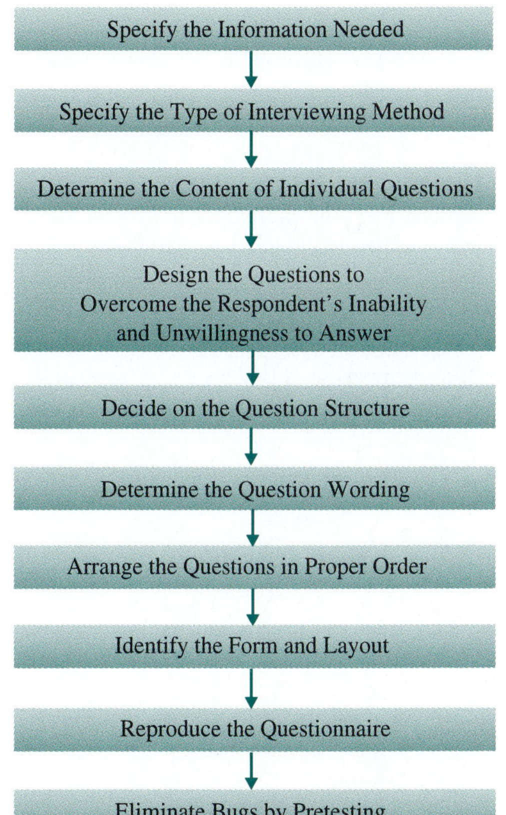

Figure 10.1
Questionnaire Design Process

of dummy tables. A dummy table is a blank table used to catalog data. It describes how the analysis will be structured once the data have been collected.

It is also important to have a clear idea of the target population. The characteristics of the respondent group have a great influence on questionnaire design. Questions that are appropriate for college students may not be appropriate for housewives. Understanding is related to respondent socioeconomic characteristics.[5] Furthermore, poor understanding is associated with a high incidence of uncertain or no opinion responses. The more diversified the respondent group, the more difficult it is to design a single questionnaire that is appropriate for the entire group.

TYPE OF INTERVIEWING METHOD

An appreciation of how the type of interviewing method influences questionnaire design can be obtained by considering how the questionnaire is administered under each method (see chapter 6). In personal interviews, respondents see the questionnaire and interact face-to-face with the interviewer. Thus lengthy, complex, and varied questions can be asked. In telephone interviews, the respondents interact with the interviewer, but they do not see the questionnaire. This limits the type of questions that can be asked to short and simple ones (see the department store patronage project). Mail questionnaires are self-administered, so the questions must be simple and detailed instructions must be provided. In computer-assisted interviewing (CAPI and CATI), complex skip patterns and randomization of questions to eliminate order bias can be easily accommodated. Internet questionnaires share many of the characteristics of CAPI, but e-mail questionnaires have to be simpler. Questionnaires designed for personal and telephone interviews should be written in a conversational style.[6]

DEPARTMENT STORE PATRONAGE PROJECT

Effect of Interviewing Method on Questionnaire Design

Mail Questionnaire

Please rank the following department stores in order of your preference to shop at these stores. Begin by picking out the one store that you like most and assign it a number 1. Then find the second most preferred department store and assign it a number 2. Continue this procedure until you have ranked all the stores in order of preference. The least preferred store should be assigned a rank of 10.

No two stores should receive the same rank number.

The criterion of preference is entirely up to you. There is no right or wrong answer. Just try to be consistent.

Store	*Rank Order*
1. Lord & Taylor	________
2. Macy's	________
3. Kmart	________
4. Rich's	________
5. J.C. Penney	________
6. Neiman-Marcus	________
7. Target	________
8. Saks Fifth Avenue	________
9. Sears	________
10. Wal-Mart	________

(Continued)

DEPARTMENT STORE PATRONAGE PROJECT *(Continued)*

Telephone Questionnaire

I will read to you the names of some department stores. Please rate them in terms of your preference to shop at these stores. Use a 10-point scale, where 1 denotes not so preferred and 10 denotes greatly preferred. Numbers between 1 and 10 reflect intermediate degrees of preference. Again, please remember that the higher the number, the greater the degree of preference. Now, please tell me your preference to shop at ... (**Read one store at a time**)

Store	*Not So Preferred*							*Greatly Preferred*		
1. Lord & Taylor	1	2	3	4	5	6	7	8	9	10
2. Macy's	1	2	3	4	5	6	7	8	9	10
3. Kmart	1	2	3	4	5	6	7	8	9	10
4. Rich's	1	2	3	4	5	6	7	8	9	10
5. J.C. Penney	1	2	3	4	5	6	7	8	9	10
6. Neiman Marcus	1	2	3	4	5	6	7	8	9	10
7. Target	1	2	3	4	5	6	7	8	9	10
8. Saks Fifth Avenue	1	2	3	4	5	6	7	8	9	10
9. Sears	1	2	3	4	5	6	7	8	9	10
10. Wal-Mart	1	2	3	4	5	6	7	8	9	10

Personal Questionnaire

(Hand department store cards to the respondent.) Here is a set of department store names, each written on a separate card. Please examine these cards carefully. **(Give respondent time.)** Now, please examine these cards again and pull out the card that has the name of the store you like the most, that is, your most-preferred store for shopping. **(Record the store name and keep this card with you.)** Now, please examine the remaining nine cards. Of these remaining nine stores, what is your most-preferred store for shopping? **(Repeat this procedure sequentially until the respondent has only one card left.)**

<None>

1.	*1*	
2.	*2*	
3.	*3*	
4.	*4*	
5.	*5*	
6.	*6*	
7.	*7*	
8.	*8*	
9.	*9*	
10.	*10*	

This question for e-mail and Internet questionnaires will be very similar to that for the mail questionnaire; in all these methods, the questionnaire is self-administered by the respondent.

In the department store project example, ranking 10 stores is too complex a task to be administered over the telephone. Instead, the simpler rating task, in which the stores are rated one at a time, is selected to measure preferences. Note the use of cards to facilitate the ranking task in the personal interview. Interviewer instructions (typed in **bold** letters) are much more extensive in the personal interview. Another difference is that the respondent records the ranks in mail and electronic surveys, whereas the interviewer records the store names in the personal interview. The type of interviewing method also influences the content of individual questions.

INDIVIDUAL QUESTION CONTENT

Once the information needed is specified and the type of interviewing method decided, the next step is to determine individual question content: what to include in individual questions.

Is the Question Necessary?

Every question in a questionnaire should contribute to the information needed or should serve some specific purpose. If there is no satisfactory use for the data resulting from a question, that question should be eliminated.

In certain situations, however, questions may be asked that are not directly related to the information that is needed. It is useful to ask some neutral questions at the beginning of the questionnaire to establish involvement and rapport, particularly when the topic of the questionnaire is sensitive or controversial. Sometimes filler questions are asked to disguise the purpose or sponsorship of the project. Rather than limiting the questions to the brand of interest, questions about competing brands may also be included to disguise the sponsorship. For example, a survey on personal computers sponsored by IBM may also include filler questions related to Dell, Compaq, and Apple. Questions unrelated to the immediate problem may sometimes be included to generate client support for the project. At times, certain questions may be duplicated for the purpose of assessing reliability or validity.[7]

Are Several Questions Needed Instead of One?

Once we have ascertained that a question is necessary, we must make sure that it is sufficient to get the desired information. Sometimes, several questions are needed to obtain the required information in an unambiguous manner. Consider the question,

"Do you think Coca-Cola is a tasty and refreshing soft drink?" (Incorrect)

A "yes" answer will presumably be clear, but what if the answer is "no"? Does this mean that the respondent thinks that Coca-Cola is not tasty, that it is not refreshing, or that it is neither tasty nor refreshing? Such a question is called a **double-barreled question**, because two or more questions are combined into one. To obtain the required information, two distinct questions should be asked:

Double-Barreled Question
A single question that attempts to cover two issues. Such questions can be confusing to respondents and result in ambiguous responses.

"Do you think Coca-Cola is a tasty soft drink?" and
"Do you think Coca-Cola is a refreshing soft drink?" (Correct)

Another example of multiple questions embedded in a single question is the "why" question. In the context of the department store study, consider the question,

"Why do you shop at Nike Town?" (Incorrect)

The possible answers may include "it is more conveniently located than other stores," and "it was recommended by my best friend." Each of these answers relates to a different question embedded in the "why" question. The first answer tells what the respondent likes about Nike Town as compared to other stores, and the second answer reveals how the respondent learned about Nike Town. The two answers are not comparable and any one answer may not be sufficient. Complete information may be obtained by asking two separate questions:

"What do you like about Nike Town as compared to other stores?" and
"How did you first happen to shop in Nike Town?" (Correct)

A question such as "What do you like about Nike Town as compared to other stores?" will reveal several positive features of Nike Town.

Most "why" questions about the use of a product or choice alternative involve two aspects: (1) attributes of the product, and (2) influences leading to knowledge of it.[8]

OVERCOMING INABILITY TO ANSWER

Researchers should not assume that respondents can provide accurate or reasonable answers to all questions. The researcher should attempt to overcome the respondents' inability to answer. Certain factors limit the respondents' ability to provide the desired information. The respondents may not be informed, may not remember, or may be unable to articulate certain types of responses.

Is the Respondent Informed?

Respondents are often asked about topics on which they are not informed. A husband may not be informed about monthly expenses for groceries and department store purchases if it is the wife who makes these purchases, and vice versa. Research has shown that respondents will often answer questions even though they are uninformed, as the following example shows.

EXAMPLE

Unknown Answers

In one study, respondents were asked to express their degree of agreement or disagreement with the following statement: "The National Bureau of Consumer Complaints provides an effective means for consumers who have purchased a defective product to obtain relief." As many as 96.1 percent of the lawyers and 95 percent of the general public who responded expressed an opinion. Even with a "don't know" option in the response set, 51.9 percent of the lawyers and 75.0 percent of the public still expressed an opinion about the National Bureau of Consumer Complaints. Why should these high response rates be problematic? There is no such entity as the National Bureau of Consumer Complaints![9] ■

Filter Questions An initial question in a questionnaire that screens potential respondents to ensure they meet the requirements of the sample.

In situations in which not all respondents are likely to be informed about the topic of interest, **filter questions** that measure familiarity, product use, and past experience should be asked before questions about the topics themselves.[10] Filter questions enable the researcher to filter out respondents who are not adequately informed.

Do you think that patriotic Americans should buy imported automobiles when that would put American labor out of work?
_____ Yes
_____ No
_____ Don't know (Incorrect)

This question would lead most respondents to a "no" answer. After all, how can patriotic Americans put American labor out of work? Therefore, this question would not help determine the preferences of Americans for imported versus domestic automobiles. A better question would be:

Do you think that Americans should buy imported automobiles?
_____ Yes
_____ No
_____ Don't know (Correct)

Bias may also arise when respondents are given clues about the sponsor of the project. Respondents tend to respond favorably toward the sponsor. The question, "Is Colgate your favorite toothpaste?" is likely to bias the responses in favor of Colgate. A more unbiased way of obtaining this information would be to ask, "What is your favorite toothpaste brand?" Likewise, the mention of a prestigious or nonprestigious name can bias the response, as in, "Do you agree with the American Dental Association that Colgate is effective in preventing cavities?" An unbiased question would be to ask, "Is Colgate effective in preventing cavities?"[34]

Avoid Implicit Alternatives

Implicit Alternative
An alternative that is not explicitly expressed.

An alternative that is not explicitly expressed in the options is an **implicit alternative**. Making an implied alternative explicit may increase the percentage of people selecting that alternative, as in the two following questions.

1. Do you like to fly when traveling short distances? (Incorrect)
2. Do you like to fly when traveling short distances, or would you rather drive? (Correct)

In the first question, the alternative of driving is only implicit, but in the second question it is explicit. The first question is likely to yield a greater preference for flying than the second question.

Questions with implicit alternatives should be avoided unless there are specific reasons for including them.[35] When the alternatives are close in preference or large in number, the alternatives at the end of the list have a greater chance of being selected. To overcome this bias, the split ballot technique should be used to rotate the order in which the alternatives appear.

Avoid Implicit Assumptions

Questions should not be worded so that the answer is dependent on implicit assumptions about what will happen as a consequence. Implicit assumptions are assumptions that are not stated in the question, as in the following example.[36]

1. Are you in favor of a balanced budget? (Incorrect)
2. Are you in favor of a balanced budget if it would result in an increase in the personal income tax? (Correct)

Implicit in question 1 are the consequences that will arise as a result of a balanced budget. There might be a cut in defense expenditures, an increase in personal income tax, cuts in social programs, and so on. Question 2 is a better way to word this question. Question 1's failure to make its assumptions explicit would result in overestimating the respondents' support for a balanced budget.

Avoid Generalizations and Estimates

Questions should be specific, not general. Moreover, questions should be worded so that the respondent does not have to make generalizations or compute estimates. Suppose we were interested in households' annual per capita expenditure on groceries. If we asked respondents

> "What is the annual per capita expenditure on groceries in your household?" (Incorrect)

they would first have to determine the annual expenditure on groceries by multiplying the monthly expenditure on groceries by 12 or the weekly expenditure by 52. Then they would have to divide the annual amount by the number of persons in the household. Most respondents would be unwilling or unable to perform these calculations. A better way of obtaining the required information would be to ask the respondents two simple questions:

> "What is the monthly (or weekly) expenditure on groceries in your household?" and
> "How many members are there in your household?" (Correct)

The researcher can then perform the necessary calculations.

Dual Statements: Positive and Negative

Many questions, particularly those measuring attitudes and lifestyles, are worded as statements to which respondents indicate their degree of agreement or disagreement. Evidence indicates that the response obtained is influenced by the directionality of the statements: whether they are stated positively or negatively. In these cases, it is better to use dual statements, some of which are positive and the others are negative. Two different questionnaires could be prepared. One questionnaire would contain half negative and half positive statements in an interspersed way. The direction of these statements would be reversed in the other questionnaire. An example of dual statements was provided in the summated Likert scale in chapter 9 designed to measure attitudes toward Sears.

DETERMINING THE ORDER OF QUESTIONS

Opening Questions

The opening questions can be crucial in gaining the confidence and cooperation of respondents. The opening questions should be interesting, simple, and nonthreatening. Questions that ask respondents for their opinions can be good opening questions, because most people like to express their opinions. Sometimes such questions are asked even though they are unrelated to the research problem and their responses are not analyzed.[37] The American Chicle Youth Poll is a good example.

EXAMPLE

Opening Opinion Question Opens the Door to Cooperation

The American Chicle Youth Poll was commissioned by the American Chicle Group, Warner-Lambert Company, and conducted by the Roper Organization, Inc. A nationwide cross-section of 1,000 American young people, aged 8 to 17 and attending school, was interviewed. The questionnaire contained a simple opening question asking opinion about living in the local town or city.

To begin with, I'd like to know, how much do you like living in this (town/city)? Would you say you like it *a lot*, *a little*, or *not too much*?

A lot _____
A little _____
Not too much _____
Don't know _____ ■

Placement of branching questions is important and the following guidelines should be followed: (1) the question being branched (the one to which the respondent is being directed) should be placed as close as possible to the question causing the branching, and (2) the branching questions should be ordered so that the respondents cannot anticipate what additional information will be required. Otherwise the respondents may discover that they can avoid detailed questions by giving certain answers to branching questions. For example, the respondents should first be asked if they have seen any of the listed commercials before they are asked to evaluate commercials. Otherwise, the respondents will quickly discover that stating they have seen a commercial leads to detailed questions about that commercial and that they can avoid detailed questions by stating that they have not seen the commercial.

FORM AND LAYOUT

The format, spacing, and positioning of questions can have a significant effect on the results. This is particularly important for self-administered questionnaires. Experiments on mail questionnaires for the 1980 census revealed that questions at the top of the page received more attention than those placed at the bottom. Instructions printed in red made little difference except that they made the questionnaire appear more complicated to the respondents.

It is a good practice to divide a questionnaire into several parts. Several parts may be needed for questions pertaining to the basic information.

The questions in each part should be numbered, particularly when branching questions are used. Numbering of questions also makes the coding of responses easier. Preferably, the questionnaires should be precoded. In **precoding**, the codes to enter in the computer are printed on the questionnaire. Typically, the code identifies the line number and the column numbers in which a particular response will be entered. Research in Practice 10.2 gives an example of a precoded questionnaire. To conserve space, only part of the questionnaire is reproduced. Note that when CATI or CAPI are used, the precoding is built into the software. Coding of questionnaires is explained in more detail in chapter 14 on data preparation.

Precoding In questionnaire design, assigning a code to every conceivable response before data collection.

The questionnaires themselves should be numbered serially. This facilitates the control of questionnaires in the field as well as the coding and analysis. Numbering makes it easy to account for the questionnaires and to determine if any have been lost. A possible exception to this rule is mail questionnaires. If these are numbered, respondents assume that a given number identifies a particular respondent. Some respondents may refuse to participate or answer differently under these conditions. However, recent research suggests that this loss of anonymity has little, if any, influence on the results.[40]

DEPARTMENT STORE PATRONAGE PROJECT

Form and Layout

In the department store project, the questionnaire was divided into several parts. Part A contained the qualifying question, information on familiarity, frequency of shopping, evaluation of the 10 stores on each of the 8 factors of the choice criteria, and preference ratings for the 10 stores. Part B contained questions on the relative importance attached to each factor of the choice criteria and the preference rankings of the 10 stores. Part C obtained information on lifestyles. Finally, part D obtained standard demographic and identification information. Identification information was obtained along with classification information, rather than in a separate part, so as to minimize its prominence. Dividing the questionnaire into parts in this manner provided natural transitions. It also alerted the interviewer and the respondent that, as each part began, a different kind of information was being solicited.

RESEARCH IN PRACTICE 10.2

Example of a Precoded Survey

THE AMERICAN LAWYER
A Confidential Survey of Our Subscribers

(5-1)

(Please ignore the numbers alongside the answers. They are only to help us in data processing.)

1. Considering all the times you pick it up, about how much time, in total, do you spend in reading or looking through a typical issue of *The American Lawyer*?

(6)

Less than 30 minutes . . . .❑-1	1 ½ hours to 1 hour 59 minutes . . . . .❑-4
30 to 59 minutes . . . .❑-2	2 hours to 2 hours 59 minutes . . . . . .❑-5
1 hour to 1 hour 29 minutes . . . .❑-3	3 hours or more . . . .❑-6

2. After you have finished reading an issue of *The American Lawyer*, what do you usually do with it?

(7)

Save entire issue for firm library . . . . ❑-1	Place in a waiting room/ public area . . . .❑-5
Save entire issue for home use . . . . . ❑-2	Discard it . . . .❑-6
Pass it along (route it) to others in my company . . . .❑-3	Other____________________ ❑-7 (Please specify)
Clip and save items of interest . . . . . . ❑-4	

3. Not including yourself, how many other people, on the average, would you estimate read or look through your personal copy (not the office copy) of *The American Lawyer*?

(8)

Number of additional readers per copy:

One . . . .❑-1	Five . . . .❑-5	10 to 14 . . . .❑-9
Two . . . .❑-2	Six . . . .❑-6	15 or more . . . .❑-x
Three . . . .❑-3	Seven . . . .❑-7	None . . . .❑-0
Four . . . .❑-4	8 to 9 . . . .❑-8	

REPRODUCTION OF THE QUESTIONNAIRE

How a questionnaire is reproduced for administration can influence the results. For example, if the questionnaire is reproduced on poor-quality paper or is otherwise shabby in appearance, the respondents will think the project is unimportant and the quality of response will be adversely affected. Therefore, the questionnaire should be reproduced on good-quality paper and have a professional appearance.

When a printed questionnaire runs to several pages, it should take the form of a booklet rather than a number of sheets of paper clipped or stapled together. Booklets are easier for the interviewer and the respondents to handle and do not come apart with use as do clipped and stapled papers. They allow the use of a double-page format for questions and look professional.

Each question should be reproduced on a single page (or double-page spread). A researcher should avoid splitting a question or its response categories. Split questions can mislead the interviewer or the respondent into thinking that the question has ended at the end of a page. This will result in answers based on incomplete questions.

Vertical response columns should be used for individual questions. It is easier for interviewers and respondents to read down a single column rather than sideways across several columns. Sideways formatting and splitting, done frequently to conserve space, should be avoided. This problem can be observed in *The American Lawyer* questionnaire (Research in Practice 10.2). Consider the following example.

What was the approximate gross income of your household from all sources, before taxes, in the past year?
__ Under $20,000 __$20,000 to $39,999 __ $40,000 to $59,999
__ $60,000 to $79,999 __$80,000 to $99,999 __ $100,000 and over (Incorrect)

These response categories should be listed in a single column, rather than in a sideways format, as shown.[41] In the income question, the respondent may be confused and wonder whether a blank line should be used for the response category before it or for the one after it. The correct format for listing the categories would be as follows:

__ Under $20,000
__ $20,000 to $39,999
__ $40,000 to $59,999
__ $60,000 to $79,999
__ $80,000 to $99,999
__ $100,000 and over (Correct)

Grids are useful when there are a number of related questions that use the same set of response categories, as in the American Chicle Youth Poll.

EXAMPLE

Opinion Grid

In the American Chicle Youth Poll, a grid format was employed for some of the questions.

Now here is a list (HAND RESPONDENT CARD), and for each item I'd like you to tell me how old you feel people should be before they make their own decisions on those things. First regarding, (*read each item*), how old do you think people should be to make their own decisions? (ASK ABOUT EACH ITEM)

	14 and under	15	16	17	18	19	20	21	Over 21	Don't know
Choosing their own clothes	❑	❑	❑	❑	❑	❑	❑	❑	❑	❑
Getting married	❑	❑	❑	❑	❑	❑	❑	❑	❑	❑
Deciding whether to quit school	❑	❑	❑	❑	❑	❑	❑	❑	❑	❑
Staying out at night as late as they want	❑	❑	❑	❑	❑	❑	❑	❑	❑	❑ ■

The tendency to crowd questions together to make the questionnaire look shorter should be avoided. Overcrowded questions with little blank space between them can lead to errors in data collection and yield shorter and less informative replies. Moreover, overcrowding gives the impression that the questionnaire is complex and can result in lower cooperation and completion rates. Although shorter questionnaires are more desirable than longer ones, the reduction in size should not be obtained at the expense of crowding.

Directions or instructions for individual questions should be placed as close to the questions as possible. Instructions relating to how the question should be administered or answered by the respondent should be placed just before the question. Instructions concerning how the answer should be recorded or how the probing should be done should be placed after the question (for more information on probing and other interviewing procedures, see chapter 13). It is a common practice to distinguish instructions from questions by using distinctive type (such as capital letters).

Color does not influence response rates to questionnaires, but it can be employed advantageously in some respects. For instance, color coding is useful for branching questions. The next question to which the respondent is directed is printed in a color that matches the space in which the answer to the branching question was recorded. Surveys directed at different respondent groups can be reproduced on different colored paper. In a mail survey conducted for a major telecommunications firm, the business questionnaire was printed on white paper, whereas the household questionnaire was printed on yellow paper.

The questionnaire should be reproduced in such a way that it is easy to read and answer. The type should be large and clear. Reading the questionnaire should not impose a strain.

New technologies allow researchers to obtain better print quality and simultaneously reduce costs. One effort along these lines resulted in a lowering of printing costs from $1,150 to $214.[42]

PRETESTING

Pretesting refers to the testing of the questionnaire on a small sample of respondents in order to identify and eliminate potential problems.[43] Even the best questionnaire can be improved by pretesting. As a general rule, a questionnaire should not be used in the field survey without adequate pretesting. A pretest should be extensive.[44] All aspects of the questionnaire should be tested, including question content, wording, sequence, form and layout, question difficulty, and instructions. The respondents in the pretest should be similar to those who will be included in the actual survey in terms of background characteristics, familiarity with the topic, and attitudes and behaviors of interest.[45] In other words, respondents for the pretest and for the actual survey should be drawn from the same population.

Pretesting The testing of the questionnaire on a small sample of respondents for the purpose of identifying and eliminating potential problems.

Pretests are best done by personal interviews, even if the actual survey is to be conducted by mail, telephone, or electronic methods, because interviewers can observe respondents' reactions and attitudes. After the necessary changes have been made, another pretest can be conducted by mail, telephone, or electronic methods, if those methods are to be used in the actual survey. The latter pretests should reveal problems peculiar to the interviewing method. To the extent possible, a pretest should involve administering the questionnaire in an environment and context similar to that of the actual survey.

A variety of interviewers should be used for pretests. The project director, the researcher who developed the questionnaire, and other key members of the research team should conduct some pretest interviews. This will give them a good feel for potential problems and the nature of the expected data. Most of the pretest interviews, however, should be conducted by regular interviewers. It is good practice to employ both experienced and new interviewers. The experienced interviewers can easily perceive uneasiness, confusion, and resistance in the respondents. New interviewers can help the researcher identify interviewer-related problems. Ordinarily the pretest sample size is small, varying from 15 to 30 respondents for the initial testing, depending on the heterogeneity of the target population. The sample size can increase substantially if the pretesting involves several stages.

Protocol analysis and debriefing are two commonly used procedures in pretesting. In protocol analysis, the respondent is asked to "think aloud" while answering the questionnaire, as explained in chapter 8. Typically, the respondent's remarks are tape-recorded and analyzed to determine the reactions invoked by different parts of the questionnaire. Debriefing occurs after the questionnaire has been completed. Respondents are told that the questionnaire they just completed was a pretest and the objectives of pretesting are described to them. They are then asked to describe the meaning of each question, explain their answers, and to state any problems they encountered while answering the questionnaire.

Editing involves correcting the questionnaire for the problems identified during pretesting. After each significant revision of the questionnaire, another pretest should be conducted using a different sample of respondents. Sound pretesting involves several stages. One pretest is a bare minimum. Pretesting should be continued until no further changes are needed.

Finally, the responses obtained from the pretest should be coded and analyzed. The analysis of pretest responses can serve as a check on the adequacy of the problem definition and the data and analysis required to obtain the necessary information. The dummy tables prepared before developing the questionnaire will point to the need for the various sets of data. If the response to a question cannot be related to one of the preplanned dummy tables, either those data are superfluous, or some relevant analysis has not been foreseen. If part of a dummy table remains empty, a necessary question may have been omitted. Analysis of pretest data helps to ensure that all data collected will be utilized and that the questionnaire will obtain all the necessary data.[46]

Table 10.1 summarizes the questionnaire design process in the form of a checklist.

TABLE 10.1

QUESTIONNAIRE DESIGN CHECKLIST

Step 1 Specify the Information Needed

1. Ensure that the information obtained fully addresses all the components of the problem. Review components of the problem and the approach, particularly the research questions, hypotheses, and characteristics that influence the research design.
2. Prepare a set of dummy tables.
3. Have a clear idea of the target population.

Step 2 Type of Interviewing Method

1. Review the type of interviewing method determined based on considerations discussed in chapter 6.

Step 3 Individual Question Content

1. Is the question necessary?
2. Are several questions needed instead of one to obtain the required information in an unambiguous manner?
3. Do not use double-barreled questions.

Step 4 Overcoming Inability and Unwillingness to Answer

1. Is the respondent informed?
2. If respondents are not likely to be informed, filter questions that measure familiarity, product use, and past experience should be asked before questions about the topics themselves.
3. Can the respondent remember?
4. Avoid errors of omission, telescoping, and creation.
5. Questions that do not provide the respondent with cues can underestimate the actual occurrence of an event.
6. Can the respondent articulate?
7. Minimize the effort required of the respondents.
8. Is the context in which the questions are asked appropriate?
9. Make the request for information seem legitimate.
10. If the information is sensitive:
    a. Place sensitive topics at the end of the questionnaire.
    b. Preface the question with a statement that the behavior of interest is common.
    c. Ask the question using the third-person technique.
    d. Hide the question in a group of other questions that respondents are willing to answer.
    e. Provide response categories rather than asking for specific figures.
    f. Use randomized techniques, if appropriate.

Step 5 Choosing Question Structure

1. Open-ended questions are useful in exploratory research and as opening questions.
2. Use structured questions whenever possible.

(Continued)

3. In multiple-choice questions, the response alternatives should include the set of all possible choices and should be mutually exclusive.
4. In a dichotomous question, if a substantial proportion of the respondents can be expected to be neutral, include a neutral alternative.
5. Consider the use of the split ballot technique to reduce order bias in dichotomous and multiple-choice questions.
6. If the response alternatives are numerous, consider using more than one question to reduce the information processing demands on the respondents.

Step 6 Choosing Question Wording

1. Define the issue in terms of who, what, when, where, why, and way (the six Ws).
2. Use ordinary words. Words should match the vocabulary level of the respondents.
3. Avoid ambiguous words: *usually, normally, frequently, often, regularly, occasionally, sometimes,* etc.
4. Avoid leading questions that clue the respondent to what the answer should be.
5. Avoid implicit alternatives that are not explicitly expressed in the options.
6. Avoid implicit assumptions.
7. Respondent should not have to make generalizations or compute estimates.
8. Use positive and negative statements.

Step 7 Determine the Order of Questions

1. The opening questions should be interesting, simple, and nonthreatening.
2. Qualifying questions should serve as the opening questions.
3. Basic information should be obtained first, followed by classification, and, finally, identification information.
4. Difficult, sensitive, or complex questions should be placed late in the sequence.
5. General questions should precede the specific questions.
6. Questions should be asked in a logical order.
7. Branching questions should be designed carefully to cover all possible contingencies.
8. The question being branched should be placed as close as possible to the question causing the branching, and the branching questions should be ordered so that the respondents cannot anticipate what additional information will be required.

Step 8 Form and Layout

1. Divide a questionnaire into several parts.
2. Questions in each part should be numbered.
3. The questionnaire should be precoded.
4. The questionnaires themselves should be numbered serially.

Step 9 Reproduction of the Questionnaire

1. The questionnaire should have a professional appearance.
2. Booklet format should be used for long questionnaires.
3. Each question should be reproduced on a single page (or double-page spread).
4. Vertical response columns should be used.
5. Grids are useful when there are a number of related questions that use the same set of response categories.
6. The tendency to crowd questions to make the questionnaire look shorter should be avoided.
7. Directions or instructions for individual questions should be placed as close to the questions as possible.

Step 10 Pretesting

1. Always pretest.
2. All aspects of the questionnaire should be tested, including question content, wording, sequence, form and layout, question difficulty, and instructions.
3. The respondents in the pretest should be similar to those who will be included in the actual survey.
4. Begin the pretest by using personal interviews.
5. Pretest should also be conducted by mail, telephone, or electronically, if those methods are to be used in the actual survey.
6. A variety of interviewers should be used for pretests.
7. The pretest sample size is small, varying from 15 to 30 respondents for the initial testing.
8. Use protocol analysis and debriefing to identify problems.
9. After each significant revision of the questionnaire, another pretest should be conducted, using a different sample of respondents.
10. The responses obtained from the pretest should be coded and analyzed.

OBSERVATIONAL FORMS

Forms for recording observational data are easier to construct than are questionnaires. The researcher need not be concerned with the psychological impact of the questions and the way they are asked. The researcher need only develop a form that identifies the required information clearly, makes it easy for the field worker to record the information accurately, and simplifies the coding, entry, and analysis of data.

Observational forms should specify the who, what, when, where, why, and way of behavior to be observed. In the department store patronage project, an observational form for the study of purchases would include space for all of this information.

The form and layout as well as the reproduction of observational forms should follow the same guidelines discussed for questionnaires. A well-designed form permits field workers to record individual observations but not to summarize observations, as that would lead to error. Finally, as with questionnaires, observational forms require adequate pretesting.

INTERNATIONAL MARKETING RESEARCH

The questionnaire or research instrument should be adapted to the specific cultural environment. This requires careful attention to each step of the questionnaire design process. The information needed should be clearly specified. It is important to take into account any differences in underlying consumer behavior, decision-making process, psychographic, lifestyle, and demographic variables. In the context of demographic characteristics, information on marital status, education, household size, occupation, income, and dwelling unit may have to be specified differently for different countries, as these variables may not be directly comparable across countries. For example, household definition and size varies greatly, given the extended family structure in some countries and the practice of two or even three families living under the same roof.

Although personal interviewing is the dominant survey method in international marketing research, different interviewing methods may be used in different countries. Hence, the questionnaire may have to be suitable for administration by more than one method. For ease of comprehension and translation, it is desirable to have two or more simple questions rather than a single complex question. In overcoming the inability to answer, the variability in the extent to which respondents in different cultures are informed about the subject matter of the survey should be taken into account.

The use of unstructured or open-ended questions may be desirable if the researcher lacks knowledge about the determinants of response in other countries. Unstructured questions also reduce cultural bias, because they do not impose any response alternatives. However, unstructured questions are more affected by differences in educational levels

DEPARTMENT STORE PATRONAGE PROJECT

Observation

Who: Purchasers, browsers, males, females, parents with children, children alone.
What: Products/brands considered, products/brands purchased, size, price of package inspected, influence of children or other family members.
When: Day, hour, date of observation.
Where: Inside the store, check-out counter, or type of department within the store.
Why: Influence of price, brand name, package size, promotion, or family members on the purchase.
Way: Personal observer disguised as sales clerk, undisguised personal observer, hidden camera, or obtrusive mechanical device.

than structured questions. They should be used with caution in countries with high illiteracy rates. When appropriately used, unstructured questions can provide rich insights, as in the research S. C. Johnson and Co. conducted in Japan.

EXAMPLE

Johnson Solidifies the Japanese Oil Solidifier Market

S. C. Johnson has succeeded in cracking the market in Japan despite rumors of difficulties in working with the Japanese. Johnson derives about 60 percent of its $3 billion–plus worldwide sales from overseas. Asia-Pacific is the fastest growing region, and Japanese sales have grown to over $500 million in 1998. The secret behind this success is that Johnson directed efforts studying the market and conducted extensive consumer research.

In a questionnaire designed to investigate Tempura oil, several unstructured or open-ended questions were used. The use of open-ended questions was justified as (1) the response options to these questions could not be easily predetermined, (2) Japanese women are educated and would therefore have no difficulty in responding, and (3) the questionnaire would be administered by the interviewers in in-home interviews. The kind of unstructured questions included in the questionnaire were: What problems do you experience in using oil for cooking Tempura in the home? What can manufacturers do to address these problems?

The unstructured questions resulted in several useful findings. For example, it was identified that disposing of hot oil used for Tempura was a problem for Japanese households. It not only clogged the plumbing but also polluted Japan's river's and streams. Furthermore, disposing Tempura oil as a solid waste would be greatly preferred by the Japanese. Based on the findings, the company developed a new product, Tempura Oil Solidifier, which has the capability to dispose oil as a solid waste.

As another example, Johnson also developed a special formula of grout cleaner to remove mildew by following a similar process. Both these products are being launched in other countries as well. Japan offers a conducive environment for new products since Japanese consumers are very innovative and always willing to try something new. "Japan is probably a close second (to the United States) in developing our products," says Mr. Carpenter, President-CEO of S. C. Johnson.[47] ■

As in the preceding example, the questionnaire may have to be translated for administration in different cultures. The researcher must ensure that the questionnaires in different languages are equivalent. The special procedures designed for this purpose are discussed in chapter 23.

Pretesting of the questionnaire is complicated in international research, because the linguistic equivalence must be pretested. Two sets of pretests are recommended. The translated questionnaire should be pretested on monolingual subjects in their native language. The original and translated versions should also be administered to bilingual subjects. The pretest data from administration of the questionnaire in different countries or cultures should be analyzed and the pattern of responses compared to detect any cultural biases.

ETHICS IN MARKETING RESEARCH

Several ethical issues related to the researcher-respondent relationship and the researcher-client relationship may have to be addressed in questionnaire design. Of particular concern are using overly long questionnaires, asking sensitive questions, combining questions of more than one client in the same questionnaire or survey (piggybacking), and deliberately biasing the questionnaire.

Respondents are volunteering their time and should not be overburdened by soliciting too much information. The researcher should avoid overly long questionnaires. An overly long questionnaire may vary in length or completion time depending on variables such as topic of the survey, the effort required, the number of open-ended questions, the frequency of use of complex scales, and the method of administration. According to the guidelines of the Professional Marketing Research Society of Canada, with the exception of in-home personal interviews, questionnaires that take more than 30 minutes to complete are generally considered "overly long." Personal in-home interviews can take up to 60 minutes without overloading the respondents. Overly long questionnaires are burdensome on the respondents and adversely affect the quality of responses. Similarly, questions that are confusing, difficult, improperly worded, or exceed the respondent's ability, should be avoided.

Sensitive questions deserve special attention. On one hand, candid and honest responses are needed to generate meaningful findings. On the other hand, the researcher should not invade respondents' privacy or cause them undue stress. The guidelines we have given in this chapter should be followed. To minimize discomfort, it should be made clear at the beginning of the interview that respondents are not obligated to answer any question that makes them uncomfortable.[48]

An important researcher-client issue is piggybacking, which occurs when a questionnaire contains questions pertaining to more than one client. This is often done in omnibus panels (see chapters 3 and 4), which different clients can use to field their questions. Piggybacking can substantially reduce costs and can be a good way for clients to collect primary data they would not be able to afford otherwise. In these cases, all clients must be aware of and consent to the arrangement. Unfortunately, piggybacking is sometimes used without the client's knowledge for the sole purpose of increasing the research firm's profit. This is unethical.

Finally, the researcher has the ethical responsibility of designing the questionnaire so as to obtain the required information in an unbiased manner. Deliberately biasing the questionnaire in a desired direction—for example, by asking leading questions—cannot be condoned. In deciding the question structure, the most appropriate, rather than the most convenient, option should be adopted, as illustrated by the next example. Also, the questionnaire should be thoroughly pretested before field work begins, or an ethical breach has occurred.

EXAMPLE

Questioning International Marketing Ethics

In designing a questionnaire, open-ended questions may be most appropriate if the response categories are not known. In a study designed to identify ethical problems in international marketing, series of open-ended questions were used. The objective of the survey was to elicit the three most frequently encountered ethical problems, in order of priority, to Australian firms that engage in international marketing activities. After reviewing the results, the researcher tabulated and categorized them into 10 categories that occurred most often: traditional small-scale bribery; large-scale bribery; gifts, favors, and entertainment; pricing; inappropriate products or technology; tax evasion practices; illegal or immoral activities; questionable commissions to channel members; cultural differences, and involvement in political affairs. The sheer number of categories indicates that international marketing ethics should probably be questioned more closely! The use of structured questions in this case, although more convenient, would have been inappropriate, raising ethical concerns.[49] ■

INTERNET AND COMPUTER APPLICATIONS

The questionnaire design process outlined in this chapter also applies to Internet questionnaires. Several firms, such as Decisive Technology (www.decisive.com/), supply software and services for designing Internet or Web questionnaires. Internet questionnaires share many of the features of CAPI questionnaires. The questionnaire can be designed using a wide variety of stimuli such as graphics, pictures, advertisements, animations, sound clips,

FOCUS ON Burke

In developing a questionnaire, Burke ensures that it will obtain all the information specified by the marketing research problem. Certain procedures are followed to achieve this end.

I. Develop a flow chart of the information required based on the marketing research problem (see Figure 10.2)
   A. Once the entire sequence of information is laid out, the interrelationships should become clear.
   B. Match up the actual data you would expect to collect from the questionnaire against the information needs listed in the flow chart.
   C. Be specific in the objective for each area of information and data. You should be able to write an objective for each area so specifically that it guides your construction of the questions.

II. At this stage, put on your "critic's" hat and go back over the flow chart and ask:
   A. Do I need to know it and know exactly what I am going to do with it, or
   B. It would be nice to know it but I don't have to have it.

You will constantly run into the situation in which the client says, "Since we have the respondent's attention this is a great opportunity to ask ____________________!" Burke argues strongly against adding "nice to know" questions.

Once the need for a question is established, Burke decided on the structure. A majority of the questions are structured questions employing multiple-choices or scales. The use of unstructured questions is limited, especially in surveys administered to a large number of respondents. Considerable attention is devoted to choosing question wording. The goal is to frame questions that are simple, precise, will be understood by all respondents in the manner intended by the researcher, and will elicit accurate and unbiased responses. In deciding on the order, screening questions meant to qualify the respondents are asked first, and the demographic and personal information is obtained last. In between are questions related to the marketing research problem, arranged in a logical order. The form and layout is such that a questionnaire is often divided into parts, with each part containing questions about a specific topic. Consider the WEBNOSTICS survey questionnaire designed to assess the tactical performance of a Web site. The type of information obtained, and the order in which it is obtained, is as follows:

- Content of the Web site (informative, relevant, entertaining)
- Technical performance (time to download Web pages, use of plug-ins)
- Design/layout (cool, easy to navigate, intuitive, quality of graphics)
- Downloads (usefulness, speed, reliability, updated often)
- Links (suitability, were links explored, incoming hits)
- Purchasing (security, ease of transactions, price, quality)
- Advertising (appeal, were "click me" ads clicked?)
- Chats/threaded newsgroups (relevance, frequency of use)
- Games/contests (interest, prizes, frequency of participation)
- Privacy (trustworthiness of site, personal information requests)

Note that privacy, being a sensitive issue, is asked last.

Finally, Burke is very particular about pretesting. Every questionnaire is thoroughly pretested using the same respondents and interviewing procedures that will be used in the actual survey. If problems are discovered, the questionnaire will undergo another wave of pretesting. Superior questionnaire design has enabled Burke to generate valuable findings for its clients.

---

and full-motion video. Moreover, the researcher can control the amount of time that the stimuli are available to the respondents, and the number of times a respondent can access each stimulus. This greatly increases the range and complexity of questionnaires that can be administered over the Internet. As in the case of CATI and CAPI, complicated skip patterns can be programmed into the questionnaire. The questions can be personalized and answers to previous questions can be inserted into subsequent questions. The various types of scales, such as the ordinal ranking scale, Likert scale, semantic differential scale, and Stapel scale can be utilized. See, for example, www.CustomerSat.com/amd.htm.

EXAMPLE

SurveySite for Web Site Evaluation

On-line marketers and Web site designers are increasingly concerned with what design features and experiences make visitors return to a site. An equally important concern is knowing what features and experiences are *undesirable* so that they avoid including them in their site. SurveySite, an on-line marketing research company, conducted an extensive study to address these questions.

It recruited 87 American and Canadian Web sites to participate in the study. Each site was equipped with a feedback icon so visitors could participate in a standardized survey that asked evaluative questions about the visit. The questionnaire consisted of 12 questions that fell into two broad areas: design/technical evaluation and emotional experience during the site visit. The design/technical questions were asked first in a logical order. All the questions but one were asked using seven-point rating scales. The other question was open-ended and asked respondents what factors were most important in their decisions to return or not return to the site. The questionnaire had been extensively pretested before it was used in the study.

The results of the survey found that content was the most important factor in determining whether or not a site would receive repeat visitors. Correspondingly, "frivolous content" was the most-cited reason for not returning to a site. The second most important factor in determining the repeat visit rate was whether or not the respondent found the visit enjoyable. Enjoyment may mean that visitors found the information they were looking for. Next, quality of the organization of the site and its degree of uniqueness also influence repeat visit rates. Based on the results of this survey, marketers and site designers should consider content, layout, and uniqueness when developing Web sites. Doing so will help improve the number of repeat visitors to their site.[50] ■

Many questionnaire design packages are available, especially for microcomputers. Some of the well-known packages are the Ci2 and Ci3 systems. Another recent release, SURVEYOR, by Computers for Marketing Corporation, can also create, test, and prepare questionnaires and pass the completed questionnaires to compatible interviewing systems for the field work. SURVEYPRO by Apian Software of Menlo Park, California, brings ease-of-use and desktop publishing capabilities to printed questionnaire design.

SUMMARY

To collect quantitative primary data, a researcher must design a questionnaire or an observation form. A questionnaire has three objectives. It must translate the information needed into a set of specific questions the respondents can and will answer. It must motivate respondents to complete the interview. It must also minimize response error.

Designing a questionnaire is an art rather than a science. The process begins by specifying (1) the information needed and (2) the type of interviewing method. The next step (3) is to decide on the content of individual questions.

The question should overcome the respondents' inability to answer (4). Respondents may be unable to answer if they are not informed, cannot remember, or cannot articulate the response. The unwillingness of the respondents to answer must also be overcome (5). Respondents may be unwilling to answer if the question requires too much effort, is asked in a situation or context deemed inappropriate, does not serve a legitimate purpose, or solicits sensitive information. Then comes the decision regarding the question structure (6). Questions can be unstructured (open-ended) or structured to a varying degree. Structured questions include multiple-choice, dichotomous questions, and scales.

Determining the wording of each question (7) involves defining the issue, using ordinary words, using unambiguous words, and using dual statements. The researcher should avoid leading questions, implicit alternatives, implicit assumptions, and generalizations and estimates. Once the questions have been worded, the order in which they will appear in the questionnaire must be decided (8). Special consideration should be given to opening questions, type of information, difficult questions, and the effect on subsequent questions. The questions should be arranged in a logical order.

The stage is now set for determining the form and layout of the questions (9). Several factors are important in reproducing the questionnaire (10). These include appearance, use of booklets, fitting entire question on a page, response category format, avoiding overcrowding, placement of directions, color coding, easy to read format, and cost. Last but not least is pretesting (11). Important issues are the extent of pretesting, nature of respondents, type of interviewing method, type of interviewers, sample size, protocol analysis and debriefing, and editing and analysis.

The design of observational forms requires explicit decisions about what is to be observed and how that behavior is to be recorded. It is useful to specify the who, what, when, where, why, and way of the behavior to be observed.

The questionnaire or research instrument should be adapted to the specific cultural environment. Also, the questionnaire may have to be suitable for administration by more than one method as different interviewing methods may be used in different countries. For ease of comprehension and translation, it is desirable to have simple rather than complex questions. The Internet and computers can greatly assist the researcher in designing sound questionnaires and observational forms.

KEY TERMS AND CONCEPTS

questionnaire
double-barreled question
filter questions
telescoping
unstructured questions
structured questions
order or position bias
dichotomous question
leading question
implicit alternative
classification information
identification information
funnel approach
branching questions
precoding
pretesting

ACRONYMS

The objectives and steps involved in developing a questionnaire may be defined by the acronym QUESTIONNAIRE:

Objectives and Steps

Q uestions that respondents can answer
U plift the respondent
E rror elimination
S pecify the information needed
T ype of interviewing method
I ndividual question content
O vercoming inability and unwillingness to answer
N onstructured versus structured questions
N onbiased question wording
A rrange the questions in proper order
I dentify form and layout
R eproduction of the questionnaire
E liminate bugs by pretesting

The guidelines for question wording may be summarized by the acronym WORDING:

W ho, what, when, where, why, and way
O rdinary words
R *egularly, normally, usually,* etc., should be avoided
D ual statements (positive and negative)
I mplicit alternatives and assumptions should be avoided
N onleading and nonbiasing questions
G eneralizations and estimates should be avoided

The guidelines for deciding on the order of questions may be summarized by the acronym ORDER:

O pening questions: simple
R udimentary or basic information should be obtained first
D ifficult questions toward the end
E xamine the influence on subsequent questions
R eview the sequence to ensure a logical order

The guidelines for reproducing a questionnaire may be summarized by the acronym REPRODUCE:

R esponse category format
E ntire question on a page
P rofessional appearance
R educe costs
O vercrowding should be avoided
D irections or instructions
U se of booklets
C olor coding
E asy to read

The guidelines for pretesting a questionnaire may be summarized by the acronym PRETEST:

P rotocol analysis and debriefing
R espondents from the same population
E xtent: extensive
T ype of interviewing method
E diting and analysis
S ample size: 15 to 30 per iteration
T ype of interviewers

EXERCISES

Questions

1. What is the purpose of questionnaires and observation forms?
2. Explain how the mode of administration affects questionnaire design.
3. How would you determine whether a specific question should be included in a questionnaire?
4. What is a double-barreled question?
5. What are the reasons that respondents are unable to answer the question asked?
6. Explain the errors of omission, telescoping, and creation. What can be done to reduce such errors?
7. Explain the concepts of aided and unaided recall.
8. What are the reasons that respondents are unwilling to answer specific questions?
9. What can a researcher do to make the request for information seem legitimate?
10. Explain the use of randomized techniques in obtaining sensitive information.
11. What are the advantages and disadvantages of unstructured questions?
12. What are the issues involved in designing multiple-choice questions?
13. What are the guidelines available for deciding on question wording?
14. What is a leading question? Give an example.
15. What is the proper order for questions intended to obtain basic, classification, and identification information?
16. What guidelines are available for deciding on the form and layout of a questionnaire?
17. Describe the issues involved in pretesting a questionnaire.
18. What are the major decisions involved in designing observational forms?

Problems

1. Develop three double-barreled questions related to flying and to passengers' airline preferences. Also, develop corrected versions of each question.
2. List at least 10 ambiguous words that should not be used in framing questions.
3. Do the following questions define the issue? Why or why not?
   a. What is your favorite brand of toothpaste?
   b. How often do you go on a vacation?
   c. Do you consume orange juice?
   1. Yes 2. No
4. Design an open-ended question to determine whether households engage in gardening. Also develop a multiple-choice and a dichotomous question to obtain the same information. Which form is the most desirable?
5. Formulate five questions that ask respondents to provide generalizations or estimates.
6. Develop a series of questions for determining the proportion of households with children under age 10 in which child abuse takes place. Use the randomized response technique.
7. A new graduate hired by the marketing research department of a major telephone company is asked to prepare a questionnaire to determine household preferences for telephone calling cards. The questionnaire is to be administered in mall intercept interviews. Using the principles of questionnaire design, critically evaluate this questionnaire.

HOUSEHOLD TELEPHONE CALLING CARD SURVEY

1. Your name? ___________________________
2. Age _________________
3. Marital status _______________
4. Income __________________
5. Which, if any, of the following telephone calling cards do you have?
   1. ____ AT&T 2. ____ MCI
   3. ____ US Sprint 4. ____ Others
6. How frequently do you use a telephone calling card?

   Infrequently Very Frequently

   1 2 3 4 5 6 7
7. What do you think of the telephone calling card offered by AT&T?

   ____
8. Suppose your household were to select a telephone calling card. Please rate the importance of the following factors in selecting a card.

	Not Important				Very Important
a. Cost per call	1	2	3	4	5
b. Ease of use	1	2	3	4	5
c. Local and long distance charges included in the same bill	1	2	3	4	5
d. Rebates and discounts on calls	1	2	3	4	5
e. Quality of telephone service	1	2	3	4	5
f. Quality of customer service	1	2	3	4	5

9. How important is it for a telephone company to offer a calling card?

   Not important Very Important

   1 2 3 4 5 6 7
10. Do you have children living at home? _______________

Thank You For Your Help.

INTERNET AND COMPUTER EXERCISES

1. IBM would like to conduct an Internet survey to determine the image of IBM PCs and the images of its major competitors (Compaq, Dell, and Hewlett Packard). Develop such a questionnaire. Relevant information may be obtained by visiting the Web sites of these companies (www.ibm.com, www.compaq.com, www.dell.com, www.hp.com).
2. Develop a questionnaire for measuring preferences for sneakers using an electronic questionnaire design package such as the Ci3 System. Using a microcomputer, administer this questionnaire to 10 students.
3. Develop the questionnaire for problem 7 using an electronic questionnaire design package. Compare your experiences in designing this questionnaire electronically and manually.
4. Visit the Web site of one of the on-line marketing research firms (e.g., Greenfield Online Research Center, Inc. at www.greenfieldonline.com). Locate a survey being currently administered at this site. Critically analyze the questionnaire using the principles discussed in this chapter.

Chapter 11

"It is almost impossible to do a complete census of most populations. A properly designed sample is more efficiently managed, has less potential for bias (than a failed census), and can provide the level of information necessary for most objectives."

Linda Klump, vice president, client services, Burke, Inc.

Sampling: Design and Procedures

OBJECTIVES

After reading this chapter, the student should be able to

1. differentiate a sample from a census and identify the conditions that favor the use of a sample versus a census
2. discuss the sampling design process: defining the target population, determining the sampling frame, selecting sampling technique(s), determining sample size, and executing the sampling process
3. classify sampling techniques as nonprobability and probability sampling techniques
4. describe the nonprobability sampling techniques of convenience, judgmental, quota, and snowball sampling
5. describe the probability sampling techniques of simple random, systematic, stratified, and cluster sampling
6. identify the conditions that favor the use of nonprobability sampling versus probability sampling
7. understand the sampling design process and the use of sampling techniques in international marketing research
8. identify the ethical issues related to the sampling design process and the use of appropriate sampling techniques
9. explain the use of the Internet and computers in sampling design

OVERVIEW

Sampling is one of the components of a research design. The formulation of the research design is the third step of the marketing research process. At this stage, the information needed to address the marketing research problem has been identified and the nature of the research design (exploratory, descriptive, or causal) has been determined (chapters 3 through 7). Furthermore, the scaling and measurement procedures have been specified (chapters 8 and 9), and the questionnaire has been designed (chapter 10). The next step is to design suitable sampling procedures. Sampling design involves several basic questions:

(1) Should a sample be taken? (2) If so, what process should be followed? (3) What kind of sample should be taken? (4) How large should it be? and (5) What can be done to control and adjust for nonresponse errors?

This chapter introduces the fundamental concepts of sampling and the qualitative considerations necessary to answer these questions. We address the question of whether or not to sample and describe the steps involved in sampling. Next, we present nonprobability and probability sampling techniques. We discuss the use of sampling techniques in international marketing research, identify the relevant ethical issues, and describe the use of the Internet and computers for sampling. Statistical determination of sample size, and the causes for, control of, and adjustments for nonresponse error are discussed in chapter 12.

We begin with the following examples, which illustrate the usefulness of sampling.

EXAMPLE

Sampling the MTV Generation

MTV Networks, which includes MTV, Nickelodeon, and VH1, have earned big profits for parent Viacom in the last two years. The company has used a free-flowing corporate culture, a "slacker" turned CEO, and a group of powerful brands to grow profits by 25 percent annually during the 1990s. The days were not always so rosy for the network, however. Market research by MTV spotted trouble in the 18- to 24-year-old group that has helped to give MTV its hip image. The channel had fading hits such as *Beavis & Butt-head* and *The Real World*. Ratings began to slip as users complained that there was no longer music on MTV.

Telephone surveys were conducted with the 18- to 24-year-old group. The sample was selected by picking households based on computerized random digit dialing. If the household had 18- to 24-year-olds, one person was selected using the next-birthday method: The interviewer asked which of the eligible persons in the household had the next birthday and included that person in the sample. The results of this survey showed that MTV needed a makeover. As a result, MTV launched music hours shown live from Times Square. New shows such as the animated *Daria* were created. The *Video Music Awards* were revamped. VeeJays became more authentic, and not TV-pretty. The objective was to give MTV a cleaner, more pensive image to keep its viewers happy. The 18 to 24 crowd is important to the network because it is this group that younger teens and the 25 to 35 crowd looks to for image and style ideas.

Stagnant Nielsen ratings and upset advertisers suddenly got a wake-up call. In 1997, MTV Networks delivered close to $625 million in earnings, roughly 32 percent of Viacom's estimated earnings before interest, taxes, depreciation, and amortization. Viacom's $513 million purchase of MTV in 1986 is now worth about $9 billion. Market research based on appropriate sampling procedures has helped the company to better understand its target customer and it has reaped financial rewards in the process.[1] ■

EXAMPLE

A Sampler on Sampling

The American Chicle Youth Poll, conducted by the Roper Organization for the American Chicle Group of Warner-Lambert Co., is the most comprehensive and systematic study of children and teens: their hopes and worries, their families and schools, and their opinions on a broad range of issues.

The survey consisted of personal in-home interviews with a nationwide cross-section of 1,000 American young people aged 8 to 17 who were attending school. The sample was representative of the population of 8- to 17-year-olds attending school in the continental United States. A three-stage, stratified probability sampling technique was used to select interviewing locations:

1. After all the counties in the nation had been stratified by population size within each geographic region, 100 counties were selected at random, proportionate to the general population.
2. Cities and towns within the sample counties were drawn at random, proportionate to the general population.
3. Where census tract statistics within cities and towns were available, tracts were selected at random, proportionate to the general population. Where no statistics were available, rural route segments were drawn at random.

Interviewers were then given starting points within the census tract or rural route segment. Quotas were imposed for sex and age levels of respondents to ensure proper representation of each group in the sample. The assigned quotas resulted in the correct number of males and females aged 8 to 12 and 13 to 17, but small imbalances were found when the sample was examined more minutely. For example, there were too few 8- to 10-year-olds and too many 11- and 12-year-olds. To overcome this imbalance, the sample was weighted to achieve the correct proportions of males and females in each age category (8 to 10, 11 and 12, 13 and 14, and 15 to 17).[2] ■

This example illustrates the various aspects of sampling design: defining the target population (American young people aged 8 to 17 who are attending school), determining the sampling frame (list of all the counties in United States and cities and towns within counties), selecting a sampling technique (three-stage, stratified probability sampling), determining sample size (1,000), and executing the sampling process (steps 1, 2, and 3, and interviewer instructions). Before we discuss these aspects of sampling in detail, we will address the question of whether the researcher should sample or take a census.

SAMPLE OR CENSUS

Population The aggregate of all the elements, sharing some common set of characteristics, comprising the universe for the purpose of the marketing research problem.

Census A complete enumeration of the elements of a population or study objects.

Sample A subgroup of the elements of the population selected for participation in the study.

The objective of most marketing research projects is to obtain information about the characteristics or parameters of a population. A **population** is the aggregate of all the elements that share some common set of characteristics, and that comprise the universe for the purpose of the marketing research problem. The population parameters are typically numbers, such as the proportion of consumers who are loyal to a particular brand of toothpaste. Information about population parameters may be obtained by taking a census or a sample. A **census** involves a complete enumeration of the elements of a population. The population parameters can be calculated directly in a straightforward way after the census is enumerated. A **sample**, on the other hand, is a subgroup of the population selected for participation in the study. Sample characteristics, called statistics, are then used to make inferences about the population parameters. The inferences that link sample characteristics and population parameters are estimation procedures and tests of hypotheses. These inference procedures are considered later in chapters 15 to 21.

Table 11.1 summarizes the conditions favoring the use of a sample versus a census. Budget and time limits are obvious constraints favoring the use of a sample. A census is both costly and time consuming to conduct. A census is unrealistic if the population is large, as it is for most consumer products. In the case of many industrial products, however, the population is small making a census feasible as well as desirable. For example, in investigating the use of certain machine tools by U.S. automobile manufacturers, a census would be preferred to a sample. Another reason for preferring a census in this case is that variance in the characteristic of interest is large. For example, machine tool usage by Ford will vary greatly from the usage by Honda. Small population sizes as well as high variance in the characteristic to be measured favor a census.

If the cost of sampling errors is high (e.g., if the sample omitted a major manufacturer such as Ford, the results could be misleading), a census, which eliminates such errors, is

TABLE 11.1

SAMPLE VERSUS CENSUS

	Conditions Favoring the Use of	
	Sample	*Census*
1. Budget	Small	Large
2. Time available	Short	Long
3. Population size	Large	Small
4. Variance in the characteristic	Small	Large
5. Cost of sampling errors	Low	High
6. Cost of nonsampling errors	High	Low
7. Nature of measurement	Destructive	Nondestructive
8. Attention to individual cases	Yes	No

desirable. The high cost of nonsampling errors, on the other hand, would favor sampling. A census can greatly increase nonsampling error to the point that these errors exceed the sampling errors of a sample. Nonsampling errors are found to be the major contributor to total error, whereas random sampling errors have been relatively small in magnitude (see chapter 3).[3] Hence, in most cases, accuracy considerations would favor a sample over a census. This is one of the reasons that the U. S. Bureau of the Census checks the accuracy of various censuses by conducting sample surveys.[4] However, it is not always possible to reduce nonsampling error sufficiently to compensate for sampling error, as in the case of a study involving U.S. automobile manufacturers.

A sample may be preferred if the measurement process results in the destruction or contamination of the elements sampled. For example, product usage tests result in the consumption of the product. Therefore, taking a census in a study that requires households to use a new brand of photographic film would not be feasible. Sampling may also be necessary to focus attention on individual cases, as in the case of depth interviews. Finally, other pragmatic considerations, such as the need to keep the study secret, may favor a sample over a census.

THE SAMPLING DESIGN PROCESS

The sampling design process includes five steps which are shown sequentially in Figure 11.1. These steps are closely interrelated and relevant to all aspects of the marketing research project, from problem definition to the presentation of the results. Therefore, sample design decisions should be integrated with all other decisions in a research project.[5]

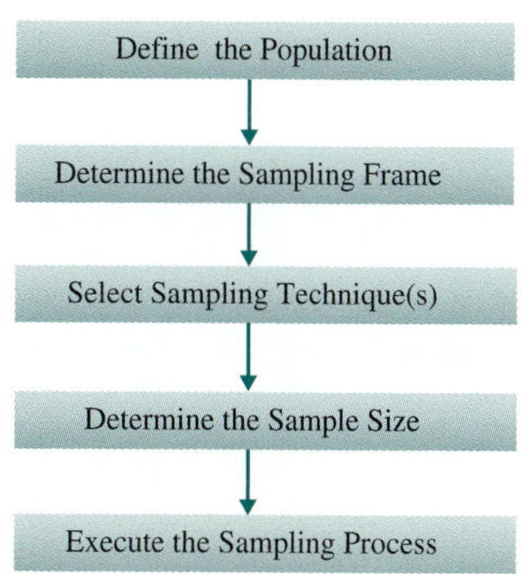

Figure 11.1
The Sampling Design Process

Define the Target Population

Target Population The collection of elements or objects that possess the information sought by the researcher and about which inferences are to be made.

Element Objects that possess the information sought by the researcher and about which inferences are to be made.

Sampling Unit The basic unit containing the elements of the population to be sampled.

Sampling design begins by specifying the **target population**. The target population is the collection of elements or objects that possess the information sought by the researcher and about which inferences are to be made. The target population must be defined precisely. Imprecise definition of the target population will result in research that is ineffective at best and misleading at worst. Defining the target population involves translating the problem definition into a precise statement of who should and should not be included in the sample.

The target population should be defined in terms of elements, sampling units, extent, and time. An **element** is the object about which or from which the information is desired. In survey research, the element is usually the respondent. A **sampling unit** is an element, or a unit containing the element, that is available for selection at some stage of the sampling process. Suppose that Revlon wanted to assess consumer response to a new line of lipsticks and wanted to sample females over 18 years of age. It may be possible to sample females over 18 directly, in which case a sampling unit would be the same as an element. Alternatively, the sampling unit might be households. In the latter case, households would be sampled and all females over 18 in each selected household would be interviewed. Here, the sampling unit and the population element are different. Extent refers to the geographical boundaries, and the time factor is the time period under consideration. We use the department store patronage project to illustrate.

Defining the target population may not be as easy as it was in this example. Consider a marketing research project assessing consumer response to a new brand of men's cologne. Who should be included in the target population? All men? Men who have used a cologne during the last month? Men 17 or older? Because some women buy colognes for their husbands, should females be included? These and similar questions must be resolved before the target population can be appropriately defined.[6]

Determine the Sampling Frame

Sampling Frame A representation of the elements of the target population. It consists of a list or set of directions for identifying the target population.

A **sampling frame** is a representation of the elements of the target population. It consists of a list or set of directions for identifying the target population. Examples of a sampling frame include the telephone book, an association directory listing the firms in an industry, a mailing list purchased from a commercial organization, a city directory, or a map.[7] If a list cannot be compiled then at least some directions for identifying the target population should be specified, such as random digit dialing procedures in telephone surveys (see chapter 6).

Often it is possible to compile or obtain a list of population elements, but the list may omit some elements of the population or include other elements that do not belong. Therefore the use of a list will lead to sampling frame error, which was discussed in chapter 3.[8]

DEPARTMENT STORE PATRONAGE PROJECT

Target Population

The target population for the department store patronage project could be defined as follows:

Elements: male or female head of the household responsible for most of the shopping at department stores.
Sampling units: households
Extent: metropolitan Atlanta
Time: 1999

In some instances the discrepancy between the population and the sampling frame is small enough to ignore. However, in most cases, the researcher should recognize and treat the sampling frame error. This can be done in at least three ways. One approach is to redefine the population in terms of the sampling frame. If the telephone book is used as a sampling frame, the population of households could be redefined as those with a correct listing in the telephone book in a given area. Although this approach is simplistic, it does prevent the researcher from being misled about the actual population being investigated.[9]

Another way is to account for sampling frame error by screening the respondents in the data collection phase. The respondents could be screened with respect to demographic characteristics, familiarity, product usage, and other characteristics to ensure that they satisfy the criteria for the target population. Screening can eliminate inappropriate elements contained in the sampling frame, but it cannot account for elements that have been omitted.

Yet another approach is to adjust the data collected by a weighting scheme to counterbalance the sampling frame error. This is discussed in chapter 12 and also in chapter 14. Regardless of which approach is adopted, it is important to recognize any sampling frame error that exists, so that inappropriate population inferences can be avoided.

Select a Sampling Technique

Selecting a sampling technique involves several decisions of a broader nature. The researcher must decide whether to use a Bayesian or traditional sampling approach, to sample with or without replacement, and to use nonprobability or probability sampling.

In the **Bayesian approach** the elements are selected sequentially. After each element is added to the sample, the data are collected, sample statistics computed, and sampling costs determined. The Bayesian approach explicitly incorporates prior information about population parameters as well as the costs and probabilities associated with making wrong decisions. This approach is theoretically appealing. Yet, it is not used widely in marketing research because much of the required information on costs and probabilities is not available. In the traditional sampling approach, the entire sample is selected before data collection begins. Because the traditional approach is most commonly used, this is the approach assumed in the following sections.

Bayesian Approach A selection method whereby the elements are selected sequentially. The Bayesian approach explicitly incorporates prior information about population parameters as well as the costs and probabilities associated with making wrong decisions.

In **sampling with replacement**, an element is selected from the sampling frame and appropriate data obtained. Then the element is placed back in the sampling frame. As a result, it is possible for an element to be included in the sample more than once. In **sampling without replacement**, once an element is selected for inclusion in the sample, it is removed from the sampling frame and, therefore, cannot be selected again. The calculation of statistics is done somewhat differently for the two approaches, but statistical inference is not very different if the sampling frame is large relative to the ultimate sample size. Thus the distinction is important only when the sampling frame is small compared to the sample size.

Sampling with Replacement A sampling technique in which an element can be included in the sample more than once.

Sampling without Replacement A sampling technique in which an element cannot be included in the sample more than once.

The most important decision about the choice of sampling technique is whether to use probability or nonprobability sampling. Given its importance, the issues involved in this decision are discussed in great detail in this chapter.

If the sampling unit is different from the element, it is necessary to specify precisely how the elements within the sampling unit should be selected. In in-home personal interviews and telephone interviews, merely specifying the address or the telephone number may not be sufficient. For example, should the person answering the doorbell or the telephone be interviewed, or someone else in the household? Often, more than one person in a household may qualify. For example, both the male and female heads of household may be eligible to participate in a study examining family leisure time activities. When a probability sampling technique is being employed, a random selection must be made from all the eligible persons in each household. A simple procedure for random selection is the next-birthday method. The interviewer asks which of the eligible persons in the household has the next birthday and includes that person in the sample.

Other Probability Sampling Techniques

In addition to the four basic probability sampling techniques, there are a variety of other sampling techniques. Most of these may be viewed as extensions of the basic techniques and were developed to address complex sampling problems. Two techniques with some relevance to marketing research are sequential sampling and double sampling.

Sequential Sampling A probability sampling technique in which the population elements are sampled sequentially, data collection and analysis are done at each stage, and a decision is made as to whether additional population elements should be sampled.

In **sequential sampling**, the population elements are sampled sequentially, data collection and analysis are done at each stage, and a decision is made as to whether additional population elements should be sampled. The sample size is not known in advance, but a decision rule is stated before sampling begins. At each stage, this rule indicates whether sampling should be continued or whether enough information has been obtained. Sequential sampling has been used to determine preferences for two competing alternatives. In one study, respondents were asked which of two alternatives they preferred, and sampling was terminated when sufficient evidence was accumulated to validate a preference. It has also been used to establish the price differential between a standard model and a deluxe model of a consumer durable.[26]

Double Sampling A sampling technique in which certain population elements are sampled twice.

In **double sampling**, also called two-phase sampling, certain population elements are sampled twice. In the first phase, a sample is selected and some information is collected from all the elements in the sample. In the second phase, a subsample is drawn from the original sample and additional information is obtained from the elements in the subsample. The process may be extended to three or more phases, and the different phases may take place simultaneously or at different times. Double sampling can be useful when no sampling frame is readily available for selecting final sampling units but when the elements of the frame are known to be contained within a broader sampling frame. For example, a researcher wants to select households in a given city that consume apple juice. The households of interest are contained within the set of all households, but the researcher does not know which they are. In applying double sampling, the researcher would obtain a sampling frame of all households in the first phase. This would be constructed from the city directory or purchased. Then a sample of households would be drawn, using systematic random sampling to determine the amount of apple juice consumed. In the second phase, households that consume apple juice would be selected and stratified according to the amount of apple juice consumed. Then a stratified random sample would be drawn and detailed questions regarding apple juice consumption asked.[27]

Choosing Nonprobability versus Probability Sampling

The choice between nonprobability and probability samples should be based on considerations such as the nature of the research, relative magnitude of nonsampling versus sampling errors, variability in the population, as well as statistical and operational considerations (see Table 11.4). For example, in exploratory research the findings are treated as preliminary and the use of probability sampling may not be warranted. On the other hand, in conclusive research in which the researcher wishes to use the results to estimate overall market shares or the size of the total market, probability sampling is favored. Probability samples allow statistical projection of the results to a target population.

For some research problems, highly accurate estimates of population characteristics are required. In these situations, the elimination of selection bias and the ability to calculate sampling error make probability sampling desirable. However, probability sampling will not always result in more accurate results. If nonsampling errors are likely to be an important factor, then nonprobability sampling may be preferable, as the use of judgment may allow greater control over the sampling process.

Another consideration is the homogeneity of the population with respect to the variables of interest. A more heterogeneous population would favor probability sampling,

TABLE 11.4

CHOOSING NONPROBABILITY VERSUS PROBABILITY SAMPLING

	Conditions Favoring the Use of	
Factors	*Nonprobability Sampling*	*Probability Sampling*
Nature of research	Exploratory	Conclusive
Relative magnitude of sampling and nonsampling errors	Nonsampling errors are larger	Sampling errors are larger
Variability in the population	Homogeneous (low)	Heterogeneous (high)
Statistical considerations	Unfavorable	Favorable
Operational considerations	Favorable	Unfavorable

because it would be more important to secure a representative sample. Probability sampling is preferable from a statistical viewpoint, as it is the basis of most common statistical techniques.

However, probability sampling is sophisticated and requires statistically trained researchers. It generally costs more and takes longer than does nonprobability sampling. In many marketing research projects, it is difficult to justify the additional time and expense. Therefore, in practice, the objectives of the study dictate which sampling method will be used.

Uses of Nonprobability and Probability Sampling

Nonprobability sampling is used in concept tests, package tests, name tests, and copy tests, for which projections to the populations are usually not needed. In such studies, interest centers on the proportion of the sample that gives various responses or expresses various attitudes. Samples for these studies can be drawn using methods such as mall-intercept quota sampling. On the other hand, probability sampling is used when there is a need for highly accurate estimates of market share or sales volume for the entire market. National market tracking studies, which provide information on product category and brand usage rates, as well as psychographic and demographic profiles of users, use probability sampling. Studies that use probability sampling generally employ telephone interviews. Stratified and systematic sampling are combined with some form of random digit dialing to select the respondents.

International Marketing Research

Implementing the sampling design process in international marketing research is seldom an easy task. Several factors should be considered in defining the target population. The relevant element (respondent) may differ from country to country. In the United States, children play an important role in the purchase of children's cereals. However, in countries with authoritarian child-rearing practices, the mother may be the relevant element. Women play a key role in the purchase of automobiles and other durables in the United States; in male-dominated societies, such as in the Middle East, such decisions are made by men. Accessibility also varies across countries. In Mexico, upper class houses cannot be entered by strangers because of boundary walls and servants. Additionally, dwelling units may be unnumbered and streets unidentified, making it difficult to locate designated households.[28]

Developing an appropriate sampling frame is also a difficult task. In many countries, particularly in developing countries, reliable information about the target population may not be available from secondary sources. Government data may be unavailable or highly biased. Population lists may not be available commercially. The time and money required to compile these lists may be prohibitive. For example, in Saudi Arabia, there is no officially recognized census of population; no elections, and hence no voter registration records; and no accurate maps of population centers. In this situation, the interviewers could be instructed to begin at specified starting points and to sample every *n*th dwelling, until the specified number of units has been sampled.

Given the lack of suitable sampling frames, the inaccessibility of certain respondents, such as women in some cultures, and the dominance of personal interviewing, probability sampling techniques are uncommon in international marketing research. Quota sampling has been used widely in the developed and developing countries in both consumer and industrial surveys. Snowball sampling is also appealing when the characteristic of interest is rare in the target population or when respondents are hard to reach. For example, it has been suggested that in Saudi Arabia graduate students be employed to hand-deliver questionnaires to relatives and friends. These initial respondents can be asked for referrals to other potential respondents, and so on. This approach would result in a large sample size and a high response rate.

Sampling techniques and procedures vary in accuracy, reliability, and cost from country to country. If the same sampling procedures are used in each country, the results may not be comparable.[29] To achieve comparability in sample composition and representativeness, it may be desirable to use different sampling techniques in different countries, as the following example illustrates.

EXAMPLE

Achieving Sample Comparability through Diversity

Research in the United States has shown that most consumers feel that a purchase is accompanied by a degree of risk when they must choose among alternative brands. A study was conducted to compare the U.S. results with those from Mexico, the Netherlands, Turkey, Thailand, and Saudi Arabia. The targeted respondent in each culture was an upper-middle-income woman residing in a major city. However, differences in sampling occurred across the countries. In the United States, random sampling from the telephone directory was used. In Mexico, judgmental sampling was used by having experts identify neighborhoods in which the target respondents lived; homes were then randomly selected for personal interviews. In Thailand, judgmental sampling was also used, but the survey took place in major urban centers and a store-intercept technique was used to select respondents. Finally, in Saudi Arabia, convenience sampling employing the snowball procedure was used, because there were no lists from which sampling frames could be drawn and social customs prohibited spontaneous personal interviews. Thus, comparability in sample composition and representativeness was achieved by using different sampling procedures in different countries.[30] ■

Ethics in Marketing Research

The researcher has several ethical responsibilities to both the client and the respondents in the sampling process. Pertaining to the client, the researcher must develop a sampling design that is appropriate for controlling the sampling and nonsampling errors (see chapter 3). When appropriate, probability sampling should be used. When nonprobability sampling is used, effort should be made to obtain a representative sample. It is unethical and misleading to treat nonprobability samples as probability samples and to project the results to a target population. As the following example demonstrates, appropriate definition of the population and the sampling frame, and application of the correct sampling techniques are essential if the research is to be conducted and the findings used ethically.

EXAMPLE

Systematic Sampling Reveals Systematic Gender Differences in Ethical Judgments

In an attempt to explore differences in research ethics judgments between male and female marketing professionals, data were obtained from 420 respondents. The population was defined as marketing professionals, and the sampling frame was the American Marketing Association directory. The respondents were selected based on a systematic sampling plan from the directory. Attempts were made to overcome nonresponse by not only mailing a cover letter and a stamped preaddressed return envelope along with the questionnaire, but also by promising to provide each respondent with a copy of the research study results. Results of the survey showed that female marketing professionals, in general, demonstrated higher levels of research ethical judgments than their male counterparts.[31] ■

Researchers must be sensitive to preserving the anonymity of the respondents when conducting business-to-business research, employee research, and other projects in which the population size is small. When the population size is small, it is easier to discern the identities of the respondents than when the samples are drawn from a large population. Sampling details that are too revealing or verbatim quotations in reports to the client can compromise the anonymity of the respondents. In such situations, the researcher has the ethical obligation to protect the identities of the respondents, even if it means limiting the level of sampling detail that is reported to the client and other parties.

INTERNET AND COMPUTER APPLICATIONS

Sampling potential respondents who are surfing the Internet is meaningful if the sample generated is representative of the target population. More and more industries are meeting this criterion. In software, computers, networking, technical publishing, semiconductors, and graduate education, it is rapidly becoming feasible to use the Internet for sampling respondents for quantitative research, such as surveys. For internal customer surveys, where the client's employees share a corporate e-mail system, an "intranet" survey is practical even if workers have no access to the external Internet. However, sampling on the Internet is not yet practical for many noncomputer-oriented consumer products.

To avoid sampling errors, the researcher must be able to control the pool from which the respondents are selected. Also, it must be ensured that the respondents do not respond multiple times ("stuff the ballot box"). These requirements are met by e-mail surveys, in which the researcher selects specific respondents. Furthermore, the surveys can be encoded to match the returned surveys with their corresponding outbound e-mailings. This can also be accomplished with Web surveys by e-mailing invitations to selected respondents and asking them to visit the Web site on which the survey is posted. In this case, the survey is posted in a hidden location on the Web, which is protected by a password. Hence, non-invited Web surfers are unable to access it.

Nonprobability as well as probability sampling techniques can be implemented on the Internet. Moreover, the respondents can be prerecruited or tapped on-line. Tapping visitors to a Web site is an example of convenience sampling. Based on the researcher's judgment, certain qualifying criteria can be introduced to prescreen the respondents. Even quotas can be imposed. However, the extent to which the quotas will be met is limited by the number as well as the characteristics of the visitors to the site.

Likewise, simple random sampling is commonly used. To prevent gathering information from the same professional respondents (here, *professional* means that respondents make a lot of on-line surveys to get points), and so not to have a nonrepresentative sample, some companies, such as MBinteractive, use a "click-stream intercept," in which it randomly

FOCUS ON Burke

Burke makes use of a variety of sampling techniques depending on the nature and objectives of the project. Of the nonprobability sampling techniques, quota sampling is used most often, primarily in conjunction with mall-intercept interviews, such as Opinion One surveys (see "Focus on Burke" in chapter 6). In these projects, the interest is mainly in the relative evaluation of stimuli (e.g., different advertisements) rather than in projecting the results to the population. When the projections are of interest, as in estimating sales and market shares of specific brands, probability techniques are used to select the sample. Simple random sampling is used to select respondents from a mailing list and for generating telephone numbers for CATI surveys using modified forms of random digit dialing. Burke has developed efficient procedures for eliminating nonproductive telephone numbers generated in this manner (e.g., eliminating nonworking numbers, duplicates, business numbers from household surveys). Systematic sampling has been used to select respondents for Internet surveys. Burke's Webnostics surveys assessing the tactical performance of a Web site make use of the randomized *n*th (*i*th in terms of the terminology used in this book) visitor methodology to sample Internet respondents. For every *n*th (*i*th) visitor to the client's Web site, a frame pops into view on the visitor's browser, requesting participation in a survey and offering incentives to do so. As is the case with physical world research, the Web visitor has the opportunity to decline participation. By using systematic sampling, Burke is able to avoid respondent self-selection bias, which plagues a simple "click me" button placed on a site to collect on-line information.

Another probability sampling that Burke uses widely is stratified sampling. In several projects, the population is stratified by demographic or other variables to ensure that certain segments are included in the sample and to increase precision. A key issue that Burke faces in such projects is whether to select proportionate or disproportionate stratified sampling. Burke recently conducted a project for a company that had developed an annuity investment product targeted to women. The client had decided to stratify the women using two variables: age (under 35 years old, and 35 and over) and marital status (never married, and ever married). The client's original specification called for 100 respondents in each of the four resulting strata. By looking at Census data, Burke found these groups to be distributed in the population as:

Women 15 to 34 and never married:	10.4%
Women 35 plus and never married:	3.4%
Women 15 to 34 and ever married:	22.3%
Women 35 plus and ever married:	64.0%

Clearly the cost of finding a sample of 35-plus and never married would be considerable given the very low incidence of such women in the population (3.4 percent). Secondly, the weighting considerations for analyzing the data would be very complicating (see chapter 14). Without going into statistical details, it is sufficient to say that this degree of weighting would seriously increase the variance of the final estimate compared to a proportionately selected representative sample. Therefore, Burke recommended to the client that proportionate stratified sampling be used, because the client was interested in making projections to the overall women's market, not to any specific segments. Burke is very sensitive to the client's needs. Suppose, in this case the client considered the 3.4 percent of 35-plus and never married women as an important niche market for which separate estimates were needed. In that case, the client's need would have taken priority over cost savings and the negative consequences of extreme weighting, and Burke would have gone along with the client's original specification. In sum, Burke adopts a sampling design that is in the best interest of the client.

samples on-line users, and gives them the opportunity to participate or decline. It reported a 75 percent cooperation rate (compared to a response rate of 60 percent over the telephone). Various other forms of probability sampling can be implemented, some techniques such as systematic random sampling with relative ease.

EXAMPLE

Random Sampling and Pop-Up Surveys

SurveySite is a full-service research firm based out of Ontario, Canada (www.surveysite.com). SurveySite's mission is to provide "leading-edge and innovative Web site evaluation systems and market research to the Internet community." Its goal is to be the "undisputed leader in quality Web site research and visitor analysis."

One research program SurveySite offers is the "Pop-Up Survey." The product counts the number of people that visit a Web site and selects visitors at a predetermined interval. For example, every 100th person to click on a client's Web site is selected, based on systematic random sampling. When this happens, a small Java script pops up. The script requests the user to complete a short on-line survey. If the visitor clicks "No," the Java script disappears and the person continues browsing. If the visitor clicks "Yes," a client-designed survey appears.

The advantage to this "pop-up" model is that it significantly increases the user response rate. The typical survey method offers a banner that asks visitors to take the survey. The banners, however, tend to have a very poor response rate. In general the rate is about 0.02 percent or 1 of every 500 visitors. The SurveySite "pop-up" dramatically improves the response rate, and data collection time is reduced from weeks to days.

As a result, SurveySite's Internet research strategy has helped the Internet research firm to land corporate clients such as Timex, Delta Hotels, Toronto-Dominion Bank, Kellogg's, and Canadian Tire.[32] ■

Microcomputers and mainframes can make the sampling design process more effective and efficient. Computers can be used for specifying the sampling frame, because they can handle lists of population elements as well as geographical maps. Microcomputers and mainframes may be employed to select the sample needed, using either nonprobability or probability techniques. Once the sampling frame has been determined, simulations can be used to generate random numbers and select the sample directly from the database. Software such as SPSS, SAS, or BMDP (microcomputer and mainframe packages), Minitab, or Excel can be used for this purpose. Specialized programs, such as Genesys sampling systems for telephone interviewing, provide the market researcher the power to compose an accurate random digit dialing (RDD) sample, while avoiding the waste of dialing nonproductive numbers during surveys.

SUMMARY

Information about the characteristics of a population may be obtained by conducting either a sample or a census. Budget and time limits, large population size, and small variance in the characteristic of interest favor the use of a sample. Sampling is also preferred when the cost of sampling error is low, the cost of nonsampling error is high, the nature of measurement is destructive, and attention must be focused on individual cases. The opposite set of conditions favor the use of a census.

Sampling design begins by defining the target population in terms of elements, sampling units, extent, and time. Then the sampling frame should be determined. A sampling frame is a representation of the elements of the target population. It consists of a list of directions for identifying the target population. At this stage, it is important to recognize any sampling frame errors that may exist. The next step involves selecting a sampling technique and determining the sample size. In addition to quantitative analysis, several qualitative considerations should be taken into account in determining the sample size. Finally, execution of the sampling process requires detailed specifications for each step in the sampling process.

Sampling techniques may be classified as nonprobability and probability techniques. Nonprobability sampling techniques rely on the researcher's judgment. Consequently, they do not permit an objective evaluation of the precision of the sample results, and the estimates obtained are not statistically projectable to the population. The commonly used nonprobability sampling techniques include convenience sampling, judgmental sampling, quota sampling, and snowball sampling.

In probability sampling techniques, sampling units are selected by chance. Each sampling unit has a nonzero chance of being selected and the researcher can prespecify every potential sample of a given size that could be drawn from the population, as well as the probability of selecting each sample. It is also possible to determine the precision of the sample estimates and inferences and make projections to the target population. Probability sampling techniques include simple random sampling, systematic sampling, stratified sampling, cluster sampling, sequential sampling, and double sampling. The choice between probability and nonprobability sampling should be based on the nature of the research, degree of error tolerance, relative magnitude of sampling and nonsampling errors, variability in the population, and statistical and operational considerations.

When conducting international marketing research it is desirable to achieve comparability in sample composition and representativeness even though this may require the use of different sampling techniques in different countries. It is unethical and misleading to treat nonprobability samples as probability samples and project the results to a target population. The Internet and computers can be used to make the sampling design process more effective and efficient.

KEY TERMS AND CONCEPTS

population
census
sample
target population
element
sampling unit
sampling frame
Bayesian approach
sampling with replacement
sampling without replacement
sample size
nonprobability sampling
probability sampling
convenience sampling
judgmental sampling
quota sampling
snowball sampling
simple random sampling
systematic sampling
stratified sampling
cluster sampling
area sampling
probability proportionate to size
sequential sampling
double sampling

ACRONYMS

The sampling design process and the steps involved may be represented by the acronym SAMPLE:

S ampling design process
A mount: sample size determination
M ethod: sampling technique selection
P opulation definition
L ist: sampling frame determination
E xecution of the sampling process

EXERCISES

Questions

1. What is the major difference between a sample and a census?
2. Under what conditions would a sample be preferable to a census? A census preferable to a sample?
3. Describe the sampling design process.
4. How should the target population be defined?
5. What is a sampling unit? How is it different from the population element?
6. What qualitative factors should be considered in determining the sample size?
7. What are incidence rates? How do they affect the sample size?

8. How do probability sampling techniques differ from nonprobability sampling techniques?
9. What is the least expensive and least time-consuming of all sampling techniques? What are the major limitations of this technique?
10. What is the major difference between judgmental and convenience sampling?
11. What is the relationship between quota sampling and judgmental sampling?
12. What are the distinguishing features of simple random sampling?
13. Describe the procedure for selecting a systematic random sample.
14. Describe stratified sampling. What are the criteria for the selection of stratification variables?
15. What are the differences between proportionate and disproportionate stratified sampling?
16. Describe the cluster sampling procedure. What is the key distinction between cluster sampling and stratified sampling?
17. What factors should be considered in choosing between probability and nonprobability sampling?

Problems

1. Define the appropriate target population and the sampling frame in each of the following situations:
   a. The manufacturer of a new cereal brand wants to conduct in-home product usage tests in Chicago.
   b. A national chain store wants to determine the shopping behavior of customers who have its store charge card.
   c. A local TV station wants to determine households' viewing habits and programming preferences.
   d. The local chapter of the American Marketing Association wants to test the effectiveness of its new member drive in Atlanta.
2. A manufacturer would like to survey users to determine the demand potential for a new power press. The new press has a capacity of 500 tons and costs $225,000. It is used for forming products from lightweight and heavyweight steel and can be used by automobile, construction equipment, and major appliance manufacturers.
   a. Identify the population and sampling frame that could be used.
   b. Describe how a simple random sample can be drawn using the identified sampling frame.
   c. Could a stratified sample be used? If so, how?
   d. Could a cluster sample be used? If so, how?
   e. Which sampling technique would you recommend? Why?

INTERNET AND COMPUTER EXERCISES

1. Procter & Gamble would like to conduct a survey of consumer preferences for toothpaste brands in Los Angeles. Stratified random sampling will be used. Visit www.city.net to identify information relevant in determining income and age strata.
2. Using software such as Genesys, generate a random digit telephone sample of 1,000 people in your metropolitan area.
3. Using a microcomputer or mainframe program, generate a set of 1,000 random numbers for selecting a simple random sample.
4. Visit the SurveySite Web site (www.surverysite.com). Examine the Internet surveys being conducted. Write a report about the sampling plans being used.

Chapter 12

"The size of the sample you ultimately take will depend on your budget, the economic importance of the decisions, and the variability in the population. Two of the three are managerial issues for you to determine; only the third (variability) is outside your control."

Brenda Landy, senior account executive, client services, Burke, Inc.

Sampling: Final and Initial Sample Size Determination

OBJECTIVES

After reading this chapter, the student should be able to

1. define key concepts and symbols pertinent to sampling
2. understand the concepts of the sampling distribution, statistical inference, and standard error
3. discuss the statistical approach to determining sample size based on simple random sampling and the construction of confidence intervals
4. derive the formulas to statistically determine the sample size for estimating means and proportions
5. discuss the nonresponse issues in sampling and the procedures for improving response rates and adjusting for nonresponse
6. understand the difficulty of statistically determining the sample size in international marketing research
7. identify the ethical issues related to sample size determination, particularly the estimation of population variance
8. explain the use of the Internet and computers in statistically determining the sample size

OVERVIEW

In chapter 11, we considered the role of sampling in research design formulation, described the sampling process, and presented the various nonprobability and probability sampling techniques. This chapter focuses on the determination of sample size in simple random sampling. We define various concepts and symbols and discuss the properties of the sampling distribution. Additionally, we describe statistical approaches to sample size determination based on confidence intervals. We present the formulas for calculating the sample size with these approaches and illustrate their use. We briefly discuss the extension to determining sample size in other probability sampling designs. The sample size determined statistically is the final or net sample size; that is, it represents the completed number of interviews or observations. However, to obtain this final sample size, a much larger number of potential respondents have to be contacted initially. We describe the adjustments that need to be made to the statistically determined sample size to account for incidence and completion rates and calculate the initial sample size. We also cover the nonresponse issues in sampling, with a focus on improving response rates and adjusting for nonresponse. We discuss the difficulty of statistically determining the sample size in international marketing research, identify the relevant ethical issues, and explain the role of the Internet and computers in sampling.

Statistical determination of sample size requires knowledge of the normal distribution and the use of normal probability tables. The normal distribution is bell-shaped and symmetrical. Its mean, median, and mode are identical (see chapter 15). Information on the normal distribution and the use of normal probability tables is presented in the appendix to this chapter. The following examples illustrate the statistical aspects of sampling.

EXAMPLE

Bicycling *Reduces Accidents Due to Error*

Like the cyclists who read it, *Bicycling* attempted to limit the error due to chance (sampling) factors.

The sample size in *Bicycling* magazine's survey of U.S. retail bicycle stores was influenced by statistical considerations. The allowance for sampling error was limited to 5 percentage points.

The table that follows was used to determine the allowances that should be made for sampling error. The computed confidence intervals took into account the effect of the sample design on sampling error. These intervals indicate the range (plus or minus the figure shown) within which the results of repeated samplings in the same time period could be expected to vary, 95 percent of the time, assuming that the sample procedure, survey execution, and questionnaire used were the same.[1]

RECOMMENDED ALLOWANCE FOR SAMPLING ERROR OF A PERCENTAGE

In Percentage Points (at .95 Confidence Level for a Sample Size of 456)

Percentage near 10	3
Percentage near 20	4
Percentage near 30	4
Percentage near 40	5
Percentage near 50	5
Percentage near 60	5
Percentage near 70	4
Percentage near 80	4
Percentage near 90	3

The table should be used as follows: If a reported percentage is 43, look at the row labeled "percentages near 40." The number in this row is 5, which means that the 43 percent obtained in the sample is subject to a sampling error of plus or minus 5 percentage points. Another way of saying this is that very probably (95 times out of 100) the average of repeated samplings would be somewhere between 38 percent and 48 percent, with the most likely figure being 43 percent. ■

EXAMPLE

Kodak Fun Saver Sports Camera: The Camera That Can Take a Punch

The Eastman Kodak Co. was considering what changes should be made to improve its disposable waterproof camera so that it could be used in other outdoor sports such as hiking, biking, beach volleyball, etc. To find out customer preferences and needs, personal interviews were conducted in the United States and Germany. Systematic random sampling was used and the final sample size was 400 in each country. The sample size was statistically determined so as to keep the margin of error on percentage estimates to less than 5 percent at a high level of confidence (95 percent confidence level).

The results showed that customers wanted cameras that could take a punch, so Kodak replaced the plastic of its underwater camera with a tough rubber "wet suit" that is easy to grip with one hand. It also designed an oversize film-advance knob with a large shutter button, which can be used when the consumers are wearing gloves. The result? The redesigned Kodak Fun Saver Sports Camera won gold awards in 1997.[2] ■

These examples illustrate the importance of calculating confidence intervals to estimate the effect of sampling errors.

DEFINITIONS AND SYMBOLS

Confidence intervals and other statistical concepts that play a central role in sample size determination are defined in the following list.

Parameter. A **parameter** is a summary description of a fixed characteristic or measure of the target population. A parameter denotes the true value that would be obtained if a census rather than a sample was undertaken.

Statistic. A **statistic** is a summary description of a characteristic or measure of the sample. The sample statistic is used as an estimate of the population parameter.

Finite population correction. The **finite population correction** (fpc) is a correction for overestimation of the variance of a population parameter, e.g., a mean or proportion, when the sample size is 10 percent or more of the population size.

Precision level. When estimating a population parameter by using a sample statistic, the **precision level** is the desired size of the estimating interval. This is the maximum permissible difference between the sample statistic and the population parameter.

Confidence interval. The **confidence interval** is the range into which the true population parameter will fall, assuming a given level of confidence.

Confidence level. The **confidence level** is the probability that a confidence interval will include the population parameter.

The symbols used in statistical notation for describing population and sample characteristics are summarized in Table 12.1.

THE SAMPLING DISTRIBUTION

Sampling Distribution The distribution of the values of a sample statistic computed for each possible sample that could be drawn from the target population under a specified sampling plan.

The **sampling distribution** is the distribution of the values of a sample statistic computed for each possible sample that could be drawn from the target population under a specified sampling plan.[3] Suppose a simple random sample of 5 hospitals is to be drawn from a

TABLE 12.1

SYMBOLS FOR POPULATION AND SAMPLE VARIABLES

Variable	*Population*	*Sample*
Mean	μ	$\bar{X}$
Proportion	π	p
Variance	σ^2	s^2
Standard deviation	σ	s
Size	N	n
Standard error of the mean	$\sigma_{\bar{x}}$	$S_{\bar{x}}$
Standard error of the proportion	σ_p	S_p
Standardized variate (z)	$\frac{X - \mu}{\sigma}$	$\frac{X - \bar{X}}{S}$
Coefficient of variation (C)	$\frac{\sigma}{\mu}$	$\frac{S}{\bar{X}}$

population of 20 hospitals. There are $(20 \times 19 \times 18 \times 17 \times 16)/(1 \times 2 \times 3 \times 4 \times 5)$, or 15,504 different samples of size 5 that can be drawn. The relative frequency distribution of the values of the mean of these 15,504 different samples would specify the sampling distribution of the mean.

An important task in marketing research is to calculate statistics, such as the sample mean and sample proportion, and use them to estimate the corresponding true population values. This process of generalizing the sample results to the population results is referred to as **statistical inference**. In practice, a single sample of predetermined size is selected and the sample statistics (such as mean and proportion) are computed. Hypothetically, in order to estimate the population parameter from the sample statistic, every possible sample that could have been drawn should be examined. If all possible samples were actually to be drawn, the distribution of the statistic would be the sampling distribution. Although in practice only one sample is actually drawn, the concept of a sampling distribution is still relevant. It enables us to use probability theory to make inferences about the population values.

Statistical Inference The process of generalizing the sample results to the population results.

The important properties of the sampling distribution of the mean, and the corresponding properties for the proportion, for large samples (30 or more) are as follows:

1. The sampling distribution of the mean is a normal distribution (see appendix 12A). Strictly speaking, the sampling distribution of a proportion is a binomial. However, for large samples ($n = 30$ or more), it can be approximated by the normal distribution.
2. The mean of the sampling distribution of the mean $\left(\bar{X} = \left(\sum_{i=1}^{n} X_i\right)/n\right)$ or of the proportion (p) equals the corresponding population parameter value, μ or π, respectively.
3. The standard deviation is called the **standard error** of the mean or the proportion to indicate that it refers to a sampling distribution of the mean or the proportion, and not to a sample or a population. The formulas are:

Standard Error The standard deviation of the sampling distribution of the mean or proportion.

Mean	Proportion
$\sigma_{\bar{x}} = \frac{\sigma}{\sqrt{n}}$	$\sigma_p = \sqrt{\frac{\pi(1-\pi)}{n}}$

4. Often the population standard deviation, σ, is not known. In these cases, it can be estimated from the sample by using the following formula:

$$s = \sqrt{\frac{\sum_{i=1}^{n} (X_i - \bar{X})^2}{n - 1}} \quad \text{or } s = \sqrt{\frac{\sum_{i=1}^{n} X_i^2 - \frac{\left(\sum_{i=1}^{n} X_i\right)^2}{n}}{n - 1}}$$

In cases where σ is estimated by s, the standard error of the mean becomes

$$\text{est. } \sigma_{\bar{X}} = \frac{s}{\sqrt{n}}$$

where "est." denotes that s has been used as an estimate of σ.

Assuming no measurement error, the reliability of an estimate of a population parameter can be assessed in terms of its standard error.

5. Likewise, the standard error of the proportion can be estimated by using the sample proportion p as an estimator of the population proportion, π, as:

$$\text{est. } s_p = \sqrt{\frac{p\,(1 - p)}{n}}$$

z **Value** The number of standard errors a point is away from the mean.

6. The area under the sampling distribution between any two points can be calculated in terms of ***z* values**. The z value for a point is the number of standard errors a point is away from the mean. The z values may be computed as follows:

$$z = \frac{\bar{X} - \mu}{\sigma_{\bar{X}}}$$

For example, the areas under one side of the curve between the mean and points that have z values of 1.0, 2.0, and 3.0 are, respectively, .3413, .4772, and .4986. (See Table 2 in the Appendix of Statistical Tables.) In the case of proportion, the computation of z values is similar.

7. When the sample size is 10 percent or more of the population size, the standard error formulas will overestimate the standard deviation of the population mean or proportion. Hence, these should be adjusted by a finite population correction factor defined by:

$$\sqrt{\frac{N - n}{N - 1}}$$

In this case

$$\sigma_{\bar{x}} = \frac{\sigma}{\sqrt{n}}\sqrt{\frac{N - n}{N - 1}}$$

STATISTICAL APPROACHES TO DETERMINING SAMPLE SIZE

Several qualitative factors should also be taken into consideration when determining the sample size (see chapter 11). These include the importance of the decision, the nature of the research, the number of variables, the nature of the analysis, sample sizes used in similar studies, incidence rates, completion rates, and resource constraints. The statistically determined sample size is the net or final sample size—the sample remaining after eliminating potential respondents who do not qualify or who do not complete the interview. Depending on incidence and completion rates, the size of the initial sample may have to be much larger. In commercial marketing research, limits on time, money, and expert resources can exert an overriding influence on sample size determination. In the department store patronage project, the sample size was determined based on these considerations.

The statistical approach to determining sample size that we consider is based on traditional statistical inference.[4] In this approach the precision level is specified in advance. This approach is based on the construction of confidence intervals around sample means or proportions.

THE CONFIDENCE INTERVAL APPROACH

The confidence interval approach to sample size determination is based on the construction of confidence intervals around the sample means or proportions using the standard error formula. As an example, suppose that a researcher has taken a simple random sample of 300 households to estimate the monthly expenses on department store shopping and found that the mean household monthly expense for the sample is \$182. Past studies indicate that the population standard deviation σ can be assumed to be \$55.

We want to find an interval within which a fixed proportion of the sample means would fall. Suppose we want to determine an interval around the population mean that will include 95 percent of the sample means, based on samples of 300 households. The 95 percent could be divided into two equal parts, half below and half above the mean, as shown in Figure 12.1. Calculation of the confidence interval involves determining a distance below ($\bar{X}_L$) and above ($\bar{X}_U$) the population mean ($\bar{X}$), which contains a specified area of the normal curve.

The z values corresponding to $\bar{X}_L$ and $\bar{X}_U$ may be calculated as

$$z_L = \frac{\bar{X}_L - \mu}{\sigma_{\bar{x}}}$$

$$z_U = \frac{\bar{X}_U - \mu}{\sigma_{\bar{x}}}$$

where $z_L = -z$ and $z_U = +z$. Therefore, the lower value of $\bar{X}$ is

$$\bar{X}_L = \mu - z\sigma_{\bar{x}}$$

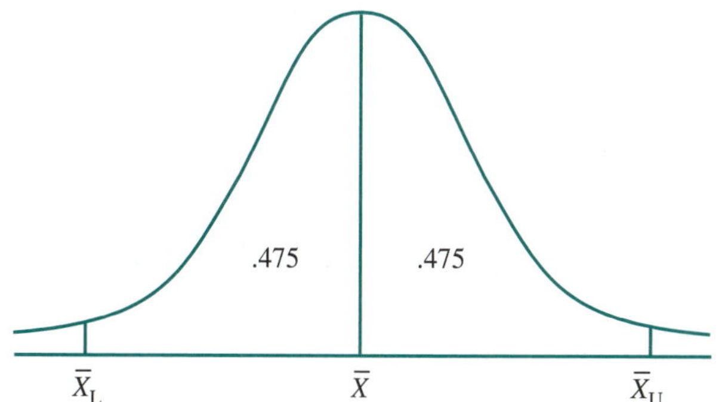

Figure 12.1
95% Confidence Interval

and the upper value of $\bar{X}$ is

$$\bar{X}_U = \mu + z\sigma_{\bar{x}}$$

Note that μ is estimated by $\bar{X}$. The confidence interval is given by

$$\bar{X} \pm z\sigma_{\bar{x}}$$

We can now set a 95% confidence interval around the sample mean of \$182. As a first step, we compute the standard error of the mean:

$$\sigma_{\bar{x}} = \frac{\sigma}{\sqrt{n}} = \frac{55}{\sqrt{300}} = 3.18$$

From Table 2 in the Appendix of Statistical Tables, it can be seen that the central 95 percent of the normal distribution lies within ±1.96 z values. The 95% confidence interval is given by

$$\bar{X} \pm 1.96\ \sigma_{\bar{x}}$$

$$= 182.00 \pm 1.96\ (3.18)$$

$$= 182.00 \pm 6.23$$

Thus the 95% confidence interval ranges from \$175.77 to \$188.23. The probability of finding the true population mean to be within \$175.77 and \$188.23 is 95 percent.

Sample Size Determination: Means

The approach used here to construct a confidence interval can be adapted to determine the sample size that will result in a desired confidence interval.[5] Suppose the researcher wants to estimate the monthly household expense on department store shopping more

Estimating monthly household expenses on department store shopping can be done only with a certain degree of confidence.

precisely so that the estimate will be within ±\$5.00 of the true population value. What should be the size of the sample? The following steps, summarized in Table 12.2, will lead to an answer.

1. Specify the level of precision. This is the maximum permissible difference (D) between the sample mean and the population mean. In our example, $D = \pm\$5.00$.
2. Specify the level of confidence. Suppose that a 95 percent confidence level is desired.
3. Determine the z value associated with the confidence level using Table 2 in the Appendix of Statistical Tables. For a 95 percent confidence level, the probability that the population mean will fall outside one end of the interval is 0.025 (0.05/2). The associated z value is 1.96.
4. Determine the standard deviation of the population. The standard deviation of the population may be known from secondary sources. If not, it might be estimated by conducting a pilot study. Alternatively, it might be estimated on the basis of the researcher's judgment. For example, the range of a normally distributed variable is approximately equal to plus or minus three standard deviations, and one can thus estimate the standard deviation by dividing the range by six. The researcher can often estimate the range based on knowledge of the phenomenon.
5. Determine the sample size using the formula for the standard error of the mean.

$$z = \frac{\bar{X} - \mu}{\sigma_{\bar{x}}}$$

TABLE 12.2

SAMPLE SIZE DETERMINATION FOR MEANS AND PROPORTIONS

Steps	*Means*	*Proportions*
1. Specify the level of precision.	$D = \pm\$5.00$	$D = p - \pi = \pm.05$
2. Specify the confidence level (CL).	CL = 95%	CL = 95%
3. Determine the z value associated with the CL.	z value is 1.96.	z value is 1.96.
4. Determine the standard deviation of the population.	Estimate σ: $\sigma = 55$	Estimate π: $\pi = 0.64$
5. Determine the sample size using the formula for the standard error.	$n = \frac{\sigma^2 z^2}{D^2}$ $n = \frac{55^2(1.96)^2}{5^2}$ $= 465$	$n = \frac{\pi(1-\pi)z^2}{D^2}$ $n = \frac{.64(1-.64)(1.96)^2}{(.05)^2}$ $= 355$
6. If the sample size represents 10 percent of the population, apply the finite population correction (fpc).	$n_c = \frac{nN}{N+n-1}$	$n_c = \frac{nN}{N+n-1}$
7. If necessary, reestimate the confidence interval by employing s to estimate σ.	$= \bar{X} \pm z s_{\bar{x}}$	$p \pm z s_p$
8. If precision is specified in relative rather than absolute terms, then use these equations to determine the sample size.	$D = R\mu$ $n = \frac{C^2 z^2}{R^2}$	$D = R\pi$ $n = \frac{z^2(1-\pi)}{R^2\pi}$

$$= \frac{D}{\sigma_{\bar{x}}}$$

or $$\sigma_{\bar{x}} = \frac{D}{z}$$

or $$\frac{\sigma}{\sqrt{n}} = \frac{D}{z}$$

or $$n = \frac{\sigma^2 z^2}{D^2}$$

In our example,

$$n = \frac{55^2(1.96)^2}{5^2}$$

$$= 464.83$$

$$= 465 \text{ (rounded to the next higher integer)}$$

It can be seen from the formula for sample size that sample size increases with an increase in the population variability, degree of confidence, and the precision level required of the estimate. Because the sample size is directly proportional to σ^2, the larger the population variability, the larger the sample size. Likewise, a higher degree of confidence implies a larger value of z, and thus a larger sample size. Both σ^2 and z appear in the numerator. Greater precision means a smaller value of D, and thus a larger sample size because D appears in the denominator.

6. If the resulting sample size represents 10 percent or more of the population, the finite population correction (fpc) should be applied. The required sample size should then be calculated from the formula

$$n_c = \frac{nN}{N + n - 1}$$

where

$$n = \text{sample size without fpc}$$

$$n_c = \text{sample size with fpc}$$

7. If the population standard deviation, σ, is unknown and an estimate is used, it should be reestimated once the sample has been drawn. The sample standard deviation, s, is used as an estimate of σ. A revised confidence interval should then be calculated to determine the precision level actually obtained.

   Suppose that the value of 55.00 used for σ was an estimate because the true value was unknown. A sample of $n = 465$ is drawn, and these observations generate a mean $\bar{X}$ of 180.00 and a sample standard deviation s of 50.00. The revised confidence interval then is

$$= \bar{X} \pm z s_{\bar{x}}$$

$$= 180.00 \pm 1.96 \frac{50.0}{\sqrt{465}}$$

$$= 180.00 \pm 4.55$$

or

$$175.45 \leq \mu \leq 184.55$$

Note that the confidence interval obtained is narrower than planned, because the population standard deviation was overestimated, as judged by the sample standard deviation.

8. In some cases, precision is specified in relative rather than absolute terms. In other words, it may be specified that the estimate be within plus or minus R percentage points of the mean. Symbolically,

$$D = R\mu$$

In these cases, the sample size may be determined by

$$n = \frac{\sigma^2 z^2}{D^2}$$

$$= \frac{C^2 z^2}{R^2}$$

where the coefficient of variation $C = (\sigma/\mu)$ would have to be estimated.

The population size, N, does not directly affect the size of the sample, except when the finite population correction factor has to be applied. This may be counterintuitive, but on reflection it makes sense. For example, if all the population elements are identical on the characteristics of interest, then a sample size of one will be sufficient to estimate the mean perfectly. This is true whether there are 50, 500, 5,000, or 50,000 elements in the population. What directly affects the sample size is the variability of the characteristic in the population. This variability enters into the sample size calculation by way of population variance σ^2 or sample variance s^2.

Sample Size Determination: Proportions

If the statistic of interest is a proportion, rather than a mean, the approach to sample size determination is similar. Suppose that the researcher is interested in estimating the proportion of households possessing a department store credit card. The following steps should be followed.[6]

1. Specify the level of precision. Suppose the desired precision is such that the allowable interval is set as $D = p - \pi = \pm.05$.
2. Specify the level of confidence. Suppose that a 95 percent confidence level is desired.
3. Determine the z value associated with the confidence level. As explained in the case of estimating the mean, this will be $z = 1.96$.
4. Estimate the population proportion π. As explained earlier, the population proportion may be estimated from secondary sources, from a pilot study, or based on the judgment of the researcher. Suppose that based on secondary data the researcher estimates that 64 percent of the households in the target population possess a department store credit card. Hence, $\pi = .64$.

5. Determine the sample size using the formula for the standard error of the proportion.

$$\sigma_p = \frac{p - \pi}{z}$$

$$= \frac{D}{z}$$

$$= \sqrt{\frac{\pi(1 - \pi)}{n}}$$

or

$$n = \frac{\pi(1 - \pi)z^2}{D^2}$$

In our example,

$$n = \frac{.64(1 - .64)(1.96)^2}{(.05)^2}$$

$$= 354.04$$

$$= 355 \text{ (rounded to the next higher integer)}$$

6. If the resulting sample size represents 10 percent or more of the population, the finite population correction (fpc) should be applied. The required sample size should then be calculated from the formula:

$$n_c = \frac{nN}{N + n - 1}$$

where

$$n = \text{sample size without fpc}$$

$$n_c = \text{sample size with fpc}$$

7. If the estimate of π turns out to be poor, the confidence interval will be more or less precise than desired. Suppose that after the sample has been taken, the proportion p is calculated to have a value of .55. The confidence interval is then reestimated by employing s_p to estimate the unknown σ_p as

$$p \pm zs_p$$

where

$$s_p = \sqrt{\frac{p(1 - p)}{n}}$$

In our example,

$$s_p = \sqrt{\frac{.55\,(1 - .55)}{355}}$$

$$= .0264$$

The confidence interval, then, is

$$= .55 \pm 1.96\ (.0264) = .55 \pm .052$$

which is wider than that specified. This could be attributed to the fact that the sample standard deviation based on $p = .55$ was larger than the estimate of the population standard deviation based on $\pi = .64$.

If a wider interval than specified is unacceptable, the sample size can be determined to reflect the maximum possible variation in the population. This occurs when the product $\pi(1 - \pi)$ is the greatest, which happens when π is set at .5. This result can also be seen intuitively. Because one-half the population has one value of the characteristic and the other half the other value, more evidence would be required to obtain a valid inference than if the situation was more clear-cut and the majority had one particular value. In our example, this leads to a sample size of

$$n = \frac{.5(.5)(1.96)^2}{(.05)^2}$$

$$= 384.16$$

$$= 385 \text{ (rounded to the next higher integer)}$$

8. Sometimes, precision is specified in relative rather than absolute terms. In other words, it may be specified that the estimate be within plus or minus R percentage points of the population proportion. Symbolically,

$$D = R\pi$$

In such a case, the sample size may be determined by

$$n = \frac{z^2(1 - \pi)}{R^2\pi}$$

MULTIPLE CHARACTERISTICS AND PARAMETERS

In the preceding examples we focused on the estimation of a single parameter. In commercial marketing research several characteristics, not just one, are of interest in any project. The researcher is required to estimate several parameters, not just one. The calculation of sample size in these cases should be based on a consideration of all the parameters that must be estimated, as illustrated in the department store example.

So far, the discussion of sample size determination has been based on the methods of traditional statistical inference and has assumed simple random sampling. Next, we discuss the determination of sample size when other sampling techniques are used.

DEPARTMENT STORE PATRONAGE PROJECT

Sample Size Estimation

Suppose that in addition to the mean household monthly expenses on department store shopping, it was decided to estimate the mean household monthly expense on clothes and on gifts. The sample sizes needed to estimate each of the three mean monthly expenses are given in Table 12.3 and are 465 for department store shopping, 246 for clothes, and 217 for gifts. If all the three variables were equally important, the most conservative approach would be to select the largest value of $n = 465$ to determine the sample size. This will lead to each variable being estimated at least as precisely as specified. However, if the researcher was most concerned with the mean household monthly expense on clothes, a sample size of $n = 246$ could be selected.

OTHER PROBABILITY SAMPLING TECHNIQUES

The determination of sample size for other probability sampling techniques is based on the same underlying principles. The researcher must specify the level of precision and the degree of confidence and estimate the sampling distribution of the test statistic.

In simple random sampling, cost does not enter directly into the calculation of sample size. However, in the case of stratified or cluster sampling, cost has an important influence. The cost per observation varies by strata or cluster, and the researcher needs some initial estimates of these costs. In addition, the researcher must take into account within-strata variability or within- and between-cluster variability. Once the overall sample size is determined, the sample is apportioned among strata or clusters. This increases the complexity of the sample size formulas. The interested reader is referred to standard works on sampling theory for more information.[7] In general, to provide the same reliability as simple random sampling, sample sizes are the same for systematic sampling, smaller for stratified sampling, and larger for cluster sampling.

ADJUSTING THE STATISTICALLY DETERMINED SAMPLE SIZE

The sample size determined statistically represents the final or net sample size that must be achieved in order to ensure that the parameters are estimated with the desired degree of precision and the given level of confidence. In surveys this represents the number of interviews that must be completed. In order to achieve this final sample size, a much greater number of

TABLE 12.3

SAMPLE SIZE FOR ESTIMATING MULTIPLE PARAMETERS

	Variable		
	Mean Household Monthly Expense on:		
	Department Store Shopping	Clothes	Gifts
Confidence level	95%	95%	95%
z value	1.96	1.96	1.96
Precision level (D)	\$5	\$5	\$4
Standard deviation of the population (σ)	\$55	\$40	\$30
Required sample size (n)	465	246	217

potential respondents have to be contacted. In other words, initial sample size has to be much larger because typically the incidence rates and completion rates are less than 100 percent.[8]

Incidence rate refers to the rate of occurrence or the percentage of persons eligible to participate in the study. Incidence rate determines how many contacts need to be screened for a given sample size requirement. Suppose a study of floor cleaners calls for a sample of female heads of households aged 25 to 55. Of the women between the ages of 20 and 60 who might reasonably be approached to see if they qualify, approximately 75 percent are heads of households between 25 and 55. This means that, on average, 1.33 women would be approached to obtain one qualified respondent. Additional criteria for qualifying respondents (for example, product usage behavior) will further increase the number of contacts. Suppose that an added eligibility requirement is that the women should have used a floor cleaner during the last two months. It is estimated that 60 percent of the women contacted would meet this criterion. Then the incidence rate is $.75 \times .60 = .45$. Thus, the final sample size will have to be increased by a factor of (1/.45) or 2.22.

Incidence Rate The rate of occurrence of persons eligible to participate in the study, expressed as a percentage.

Similarly, the determination of sample size must take into account anticipated refusals by people who qualify. The **completion rate** denotes the percentage of qualified respondents who complete the interview. If, for example, the researcher expects an interview completion rate of 80 percent of eligible respondents, the number of contacts should be increased by a factor of 1.25. The incidence rate and the completion rate together imply that the number of potential respondents contacted, that is, the initial sample size, should be 2.22×1.25 or 2.77 times the sample size required. In general, if there are c qualifying factors with an incidence of $Q_1, Q_2, Q_3, \ldots Q_c$, each expressed as a proportion,

Completion Rate The percentage of qualified respondents who complete the interview. It enables researchers to take into account anticipated refusals by people who qualify.

$$\text{Incidence rate} = Q_1 \times Q_2 \times Q_3 \ldots \times Q_c$$

$$\text{Initial sample size} = \frac{\text{final sample size}}{\text{incidence rate} \times \text{completion rate}}$$

The number of units that will have to be sampled will be determined by the initial sample size. Often, as in the symphony example, a number of variables are used for qualifying potential respondents, thereby decreasing the incidence rate.

EXAMPLE

Tuning Up a Symphony Sample

The Jacksonville Symphony Orchestra tuned up the right sample by appropriately screening the respondents.

A telephone survey was conducted to determine the consumer's awareness of and attitudes toward the Jacksonville Symphony Orchestra. The screening qualifications for a respondent included in the survey were (1) has lived in the Jacksonville area for more than one year; (2) 25 years old or older; (3) listens to classical or pop music; and (4) attends live performances of classical or pop music. These qualifying criteria decreased the incidence rate to less than 15 percent, leading to a substantial increase in the number of contacts. While having four qualifying factors resulted in a highly targeted or tuned sample, it also made the interviewing process inefficient.[9]

Completion rates are affected by nonresponse. Hence, nonresponse issues deserve attention.

NONRESPONSE ISSUES IN SAMPLING

The two major nonresponse issues in sampling are improving response rates and adjusting for nonresponse. Nonresponse error arises when some of the potential respondents included in the sample do not respond (see chapter 3). This is one of the most significant problems in survey research. Nonrespondents differ from respondents in terms of demographic, psychographic, personality, attitudinal, motivational, and behavioral variables.[10] For a given study, if the nonrespondents differ from the respondents on the characteristics of interest, the sample estimates will be seriously biased. Higher response rates, in general, imply lower rates of nonresponse bias, yet response rate may not be an adequate indicator of nonresponse bias. Response rates themselves do not indicate whether the respondents are representative of the original sample.[11] Increasing the response rate may not reduce nonresponse bias if the additional respondents do not differ from those who have already responded but do differ from those who still do not respond. As low response rates increase the probability of nonresponse bias, an attempt should be made to improve the response rate.[12]

Improving the Response Rates

The primary causes of low response rates are refusals and not at homes as shown in Figure 12.2.

Figure 12.2
Improving Response Rates

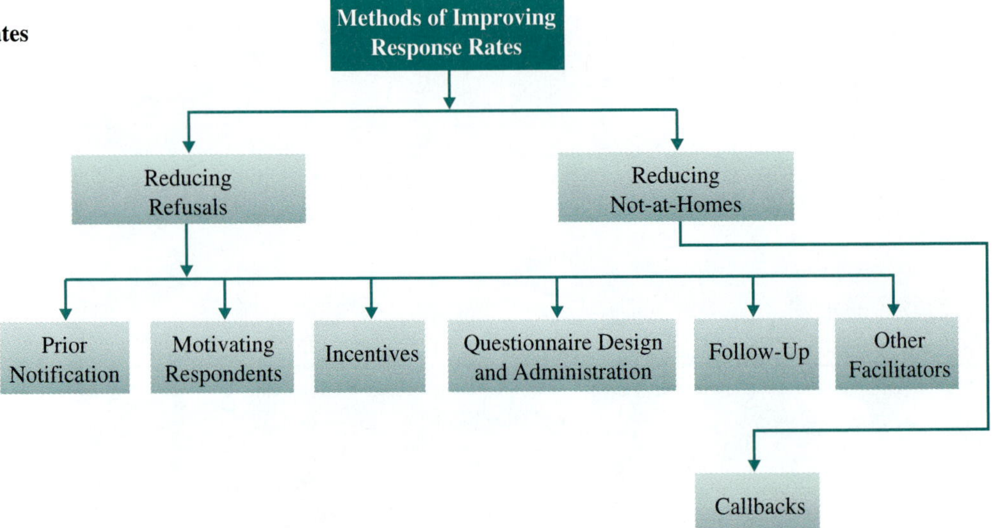

Refusals. Refusals, which result from the unwillingness or inability of people included in the sample to participate, result in lower response rates and increased potential for nonresponse bias. Refusal rates, the percentage of contacted respondents who refuse to participate, range from 0 to 50 percent in telephone surveys. Refusal rates for mall-intercept interviews and mail interviews are progressively higher, and they are highest of all for Internet surveys. Most refusals occur immediately after the interviewer's opening remarks or when the potential respondent first opens the mail package. In a national telephone survey, 40 percent of those contacted refused at the introduction stage, but only 6 percent refused during the interview. The following example gives further information on refusals, terminations, and completed interviews.

EXAMPLE

Reasons for Refusal

In a study investigating the refusal problem in telephone surveys, telephone interviews were conducted with responders and nonresponders to a previous survey, using quotas of 100 for each subsample. The results are presented in the following.[13]

REFUSALS, TERMINATIONS, AND COMPLETED INTERVIEWS

Property	*Total Sample*	*Responders*	*Nonresponders*
Number of refusals (1)	224	31	193
Number of terminations (2)	100	33	67
Number of completed interviews (3)	203	102	101
Total number of contacts (1 + 2 + 3)[a]	527	166	361
Refusal rate (1/[1 + 2 + 3])[b]	42.5%	18.7%	53.5%
Termination rate (2/[1 + 2 + 3])	19.0%	19.9%	18.5%
Completion rate (3/[1 + 2 + 3])[b]	38.5%	61.4%	28.0%

[a] A total of 1,388 attempts was required to make these contacts: The 166 responder contacts required 406 attempts (with one callback per respondent), and the 361 nonresponder contacts required 982 attempts (with two callbacks per respondent). The sampling frame contained 965 phone numbers—313 responders and 652 nonresponders.
[b] Responder/nonresponder differences were significant at $\alpha = .05$ (two-tail test).

The study found that people who are likely to participate in a telephone survey (responders) differ from those who are likely to refuse (nonresponders) in the following ways: (1) confidence in survey research, (2) confidence in the research organization, (3) demographic characteristics, and (4) beliefs and attitudes about telephone surveys. ■

Given the differences between responders and nonresponders that this study demonstrated, researchers should attempt to lower refusal rates. This can be done by prior notification, motivating the respondents, incentives, good questionnaire design and administration, and follow-up.

Prior notification. Potential respondents are sent a letter notifying them of the imminent mail, telephone, personal, or electronic survey. Prior notification increases response rates for samples of the general public because it reduces surprise and uncertainty and creates a more cooperative atmosphere.[14]

Motivating the respondents. Potential respondents can be motivated to participate in the survey by increasing their interest and involvement. Two of the ways this can be done are the foot-in-the-door and door-in-the-face strategies. Both strategies attempt to obtain participation through the use of sequential requests. As explained briefly in chapter 6, in the foot-in-the-door strategy the interviewer starts with a relatively small request, such as "Will you please take five minutes to answer five questions," to which a large majority of people will comply. The small request is followed by a larger request, the critical request, that solicits participation in the survey or experiment. The rationale is that compliance with an initial request should increase the chances of compliance with the subsequent request. The door-in-the-face is the reverse strategy. The initial request is relatively large and a majority of people refuse to comply. The large request is followed by a smaller request, the critical request, soliciting participation in the survey. The underlying reasoning is that the concession offered by the subsequent critical request should increase the chances of compliance. Foot-in-the-door is more effective than door-in-the-face.[15]

Incentives. Response rates can be increased by offering monetary as well as nonmonetary incentives to potential respondents. Monetary incentives can be prepaid or promised. The prepaid incentive is included with the survey or questionnaire. The promised incentive is sent to only those respondents who complete the survey. The most commonly used nonmonetary incentives are premiums and rewards, such as pens, pencils, books, and offers of survey results.[16]

Prepaid incentives have been shown to increase response rates to a greater extent than promised incentives. The amount of incentive can vary from 10 cents to $50 or more. The amount of incentive has a positive relationship with response rate, but the cost of large monetary incentives may outweigh the value of additional information obtained.

Questionnaire design and administration. A well-designed questionnaire can decrease the overall refusal rate as well as refusals to specific questions (see chapter 10). Likewise, the skill used to administer the questionnaire in telephone and personal interviews can increase the response rate. Trained interviewers are skilled in refusal conversion or persuasion. They do not accept a "no" response without an additional plea. The additional plea might emphasize the brevity of the questionnaire or importance of the respondent's opinion. Skilled interviewers can decrease refusals by about 7 percent on average. Interviewing procedures are discussed in more detail in chapter 13.

Follow-up. Follow-up, or contacting the nonrespondents periodically after the initial contact, is particularly effective in decreasing refusals in mail surveys. The researcher might send a postcard or letter to remind nonrespondents to complete and return the questionnaire. Two or three mailings are needed, in addition to the original one. With proper follow-up, the response rate in mail surveys can be increased to 80 percent or more. Follow-ups can also be done by telephone, telegraph, e-mail, or personal contacts.

Other facilitators. Personalization, or sending letters addressed to specific individuals, is effective in increasing response rates.[17] Research in Practice 12.1 illustrates the procedure employed by Arbitron to increase its response rate.[18]

RESEARCH IN PRACTICE 12.1

Arbitron Responds to Low Response Rates

Arbitron, a major marketing research supplier, was trying to improve response rates in order to get more meaningful results from its surveys. Arbitron created a special cross-functional team of employees to work on the response rate problem. Their method was named the "breakthrough method," and the whole Arbitron system concerning the response rates was put in question and changed. The team suggested six major strategies for improving response rates:

1. Maximize the effectiveness of placement/follow-up calls
2. Make materials more appealing and easy to complete
3. Increase Arbitron name awareness
4. Improve survey participant rewards
5. Optimize the arrival of respondent materials
6. Increase usability of returned diaries

Eighty initiatives were launched to implement these six strategies. As a result, response rates improved significantly. However, in spite of those encouraging results, people at Arbitron remain very cautious. They know that they are not done yet and that it is an everyday fight to keep those response rates high.

Not-at-Homes. The second major cause of low response rates is not-at-homes. In telephone and in-home personal interviews, low response rates can result if the potential respondents are not at home when contact is attempted. A study analyzing 182 commercial telephone surveys involving a total sample of over one million consumers revealed that a large percentage of potential respondents was never contacted. The median noncontact rate was 40 percent. In nearly 40 percent of the surveys, only a single attempt was made to contact potential respondents. The results of 259,088 first-call attempts using the sophisticated random digit dialing M/A/R/C Telno System show that less than 10 percent of the calls resulted in completed interviews, and 14.3 percent of those contacted refused to participate.[19]

The likelihood that potential respondents will not be at home varies with several factors. People with small children are more likely to be at home than are single or divorced people. Consumers are more likely to be at home on weekends than on weekdays, and in the evening as opposed to during the afternoon. Prenotification and appointments increase the likelihood that the respondent will be at home when contact is attempted.

The percentage of not-at-homes can be substantially reduced by employing a series of callbacks, or periodic follow-up attempts to contact nonrespondents. The decision about the number of callbacks should weigh the benefits of reducing nonresponse bias against the additional costs. As callbacks are completed, the callback respondents should be compared to those who have already responded to determine the usefulness of making further callbacks. In most consumer surveys, three to four callbacks may be desirable. Whereas the first call yields the most responses, the second and third calls have higher response per call. It is important that callbacks be made and controlled according to a prescribed plan.

Adjusting for Nonresponse

High response rates decrease the probability that nonresponse bias is substantial. Nonresponse rates should always be reported and, whenever possible, the effects of nonresponse should be estimated. This can be done by linking the nonresponse rate to estimated differences between respondents and nonrespondents. Information on differences between the two groups may be obtained from the sample itself. For example, differences found through callbacks could be extrapolated, or a concentrated follow-up could be conducted on a subsample of the nonrespondents. Alternatively, it may be possible to estimate these differences from other sources.[20] To illustrate, in a survey of owners of major appliances, demographic and other information may be obtained for respondents and nonrespondents from the warranty cards. For a mail panel, a wide variety of information is available for both groups from syndicate organizations. If the sample is supposed to be representative of the general population, then comparisons can be made with census figures. Even if it is not feasible to estimate the effects of nonresponse, some adjustments should still be made during data analysis and interpretation.[21] The strategies available to adjust for nonresponse error include subsampling of nonrespondents, replacement, substitution, subjective estimates, trend analysis, simple weighting, and imputation.

Subsampling of Nonrespondents. Subsampling of nonrespondents, particularly in the case of mail surveys, can be effective in adjusting for nonresponse bias. In this technique, the researcher contacts a subsample of the nonrespondents, usually by means of telephone or personal interviews. This often results in a high response rate within that subsample. The values obtained for the subsample are then projected to all the nonrespondents, and the survey results are adjusted to account for nonresponse. This method can estimate the effect of nonresponse on the characteristic of interest.

Replacement. In replacement, the nonrespondents in the current survey are replaced with nonrespondents from an earlier, similar survey. The researcher attempts to contact these nonrespondents from the earlier survey and administer the current survey questionnaire to them, possibly by offering a suitable incentive. It is important that the nature of nonresponse in the current survey be similar to that of the earlier survey. The two surveys should use similar kinds of respondents, and the time interval between them should be short. As an example, if the department store survey is being repeated one year later, the nonrespondents in the present survey may be replaced by the nonrespondents in the original survey.

Substitution A procedure that substitutes for nonrespondents other elements from the sampling frame that are expected to respond.

Substitution. In **substitution**, the researcher substitutes for nonrespondents other elements from the sampling frame that are expected to respond. The sampling frame is divided into subgroups that are internally homogeneous in terms of respondent characteristics but heterogeneous in terms of response rates. These subgroups are then used to identify substitutes who are similar to particular nonrespondents but dissimilar to respondents already in the sample. Note that this approach would not reduce nonresponse bias if the substitutes are similar to respondents already in the sample. Research in Practice 12.2 illustrates the use of this method.[22]

Subjective Estimates. When it is no longer feasible to increase the response rate by subsampling, replacement, or substitution, it may be possible to arrive at subjective estimates of the nature and effect of nonresponse bias. This involves evaluating the likely effects of nonresponse based on experience and available information. For example, married adults with young children are more likely to be at home than single or divorced adults, or married adults with no children. This information provides a basis for evaluating the effects of nonresponse due to not-at-homes in personal or telephone surveys.

Trend Analysis A method of adjusting for nonresponse in which the researcher tries to discern a trend between early and late respondents. This trend is projected to nonrespondents to estimate their characteristic of interest.

Trend Analysis. **Trend analysis** is an attempt to discern a trend between early and late respondents. This trend is projected to nonrespondents to estimate where they stand on the characteristic of interest. For example, Table 12.4 presents the results of several waves of a mail survey. The characteristic of interest is dollars spent on shopping in department stores during the last two months. The known value of the characteristic for the total sample is given at the bottom of the table. The value for each successive wave of respondents becomes closer to the value for nonrespondents. For example, those responding to the second mailing spent 79 percent of the amount spent by those who responded to the first mailing. Those responding to the third mailing spent 85 percent of the amount spent by those who responded to the second mailing. Continuing this trend, one might estimate that those who did not respond spent 91 percent [85 + (85 – 79)] of the amount spent by those who

RESEARCH IN PRACTICE 12.2

Exit Polling of Voters

Warren Mitofsky, executive director of Voter Research & Surveys (VRS), states that planning exit interviews for a presidential election begins two years before the big day. The New York City-based staff of 22 grows to 60 during an election year; on election day, it blossoms to 6,000 workers who conduct exit interviews at 1,500 polling places.

The VRS workers give voters a list of about 25 questions. Certain issues are well-known determinants of a voter's choice, whereas other questions deal with last-minute events such as political scandal. The questionnaires are written at the last possible moment. The questionnaire is designed to determine not only who people voted for but on what basis.

Uncooperative voters are a problem for exit polling. VRS workers are told to record a basic demographic profile for noncompliers. From this demographic data, a voter profile is developed to replace the uncooperative voter using the method of substitution. Age, sex, race, and residence are strong indicators of how Americans vote. For example, younger voters are more likely to be swayed by moral issues whereas older voters are more likely to consider a candidate's personal qualities. Thus, VRS substitutes for nonrespondents other potential respondents who are similar in age, sex, race, and residence. The broad coverage of exit interviews and the substitution technique for noncompliant voters allow VRS to obtain margins of error close to 3 to 4 percent.

TABLE 12.4

USE OF TREND ANALYSIS IN ADJUSTING FOR NONRESPONSE

	Percentage Response	*Average Dollar Expenditure*	*Percentage of Previous Wave's Response*
First mailing	12	412	—
Second mailing	18	325	79
Third mailing	13	277	85
Nonresponse	(57)	(230)	91
Total	100	275	

responded to the third mailing. This results in an estimate of $252 (277 × .91) spent by nonrespondents, and an estimate of $288 for the average amount spent in shopping at department stores during the last two months for the overall sample. Note that the actual amount spent by the nonrespondents was $230 rather than the $252, and the actual sample average was $275 rather than the $288 estimated by trend analysis. Although the trend estimates are wrong, the error is smaller than the error that would have resulted from ignoring the nonrespondents. Had the nonrespondents been ignored, the average amount spent would have been estimated at $335 for the sample.

Weighting. **Weighting** attempts to account for nonresponse by assigning differential weights to the data depending on the response rates.[23] For example, in a survey on personal computers, the sample was stratified according to income. The response rates were 85, 70, and 40 percent, respectively, for the high-, medium-, and low-income groups. In analyzing the data, these subgroups are assigned weights inversely proportional to their response rates. That is, the weights assigned would be (100/85), (100/70), and (100/40), respectively, for the high-, medium-, and low-income groups. Although weighting can correct for the differential effects of nonresponse, it destroys the self-weighting nature of the sampling design and can introduce complications. Weighting is further discussed in chapter 14 on data preparation.

Weighting Statistical procedure that attempts to account for nonresponse by assigning differential weights to the data depending on the response rates.

Imputation. **Imputation** involves imputing, or assigning, the characteristic of interest to the nonrespondents based on the similarity of the variables available for both nonrespondents and respondents.[24] For example, a respondent who does not report brand usage may be imputed the usage of a respondent with similar demographic characteristics. Often there is a high correlation between the characteristic of interest and some other variables. In such cases, this correlation can be used to predict the value of the characteristic for the nonrespondents (see chapter 17).

Imputation A method to adjust for nonresponse by assigning the characteristic of interest to the nonrespondents based on the similarity of the variables available for both nonrespondents and respondents.

INTERNATIONAL MARKETING RESEARCH

In conducting marketing research in foreign countries, it may be difficult to estimate sample size statistically as estimates of the population variance may be unavailable. Hence, the sample size is often determined by qualitative considerations, as discussed in chapter 11: (1) the importance of the decision, (2) the nature of the research, (3) the number of variables, (4) the nature of the analysis, (5) sample sizes used in similar studies, (6) incidence rates, (7) completion rates, and (8) resource constraints. If statistical estimation of sample size is at all attempted, it should be realized that the estimates of the population variance may vary from country to country. For example, in measuring consumer preferences a greater degree of heterogeneity may be encountered in countries in which consumer preferences are not that well developed. Thus, it may be a mistake to assume that the population variance is the same or to use the same sample size in different countries.

For millions of Chinese, travel is a relatively new experience and Chinese preferences for air travel are likely to exhibit much more variability as compared with preferences of Americans.

EXAMPLE

The Chinese Take to the Sky

The airline industry seems to have a strong and promising market potential in China. The airline market in China is growing rapidly. With billions of dollars spent, China is trying to satisfy surging demand and to catch up with the rest of the world. The domestic airline traffic is growing as much as 30 percent a year. Strong economic growth, surging foreign trade, and a revival in tourism as the memory of Tiananmen Square recedes have helped to fuel the boom. China is making rapid progress in increasing its fleet and training pilots. In 1984, the country had only 15 commercial aircraft—mostly outdated Soviet-made models. The fleet is now more than 30 times as big with aircraft from Boeing, McDonnell Douglas, and Airbus. The Civil Aviation Administration of China (which used to be known as "Chinese Airlines Always Cancel") has granted much flexibility to the individual airlines. Yet, for millions of Chinese, air travel is a relatively new experience and many more millions have never flown. Chinese preferences for air travel are likely to exhibit much more variability as compared to Americans. In a survey by Delta Airlines to compare the attitude toward air travel in China and the United States, the sample size of the Chinese survey would have to be larger than the U.S. survey in order for the two survey estimates to have comparable precision.[25] ■

ETHICS IN MARKETING RESEARCH

The statistical determination of sample size is usually objective, but nonetheless, it is susceptible to ethical concerns. As can be seen from the formula, the sample size is dependent on the standard deviation of the variable, and there is no way of precisely knowing the standard deviation until the data have been collected. An estimate of the standard deviation is used to calculate the sample size. This estimate is based on secondary data, judgment, or a small pilot study. By inflating the standard deviation, it is possible to increase the sample size and thus the project revenue for the research firm. Using the sample size formula it can be seen that increasing the standard deviation by 20 percent, for example, will increase the sample size by 44 percent. It is clearly unethical to inflate the standard deviation, and thereby increase the sample size, simply to enhance the revenue of the marketing research firm.

Ethical dilemmas can arise even when the standard deviation is estimated honestly. Often, the standard deviation in the actual study is different from that estimated at the outset. When the standard deviation is larger than the initial estimate, the confidence interval will also be larger than desired. In such a situation, the researcher has the responsibility to discuss this with the client and jointly decide on a course of action. The ethical ramifications of miscommunicating the confidence intervals of survey estimates based on statistical samples are underscored in political polling.

EXAMPLE

Surveys Serve Up Elections

The dissemination of some survey results has been strongly criticized as manipulative and unethical. In particular, the ethics of releasing political poll results before and during the election have been questioned. Opponents of such surveys claim that the general public is misled by these results. First, before the election, voters are influenced by whom the polls predict will win. If they see that the candidate they favor is trailing, they may decide not to vote; they assume that there is no way their candidate can win. The attempt to predict the election results while the election is in progress has come under even harsher criticism. Opponents of this practice feel that this predisposes voters to vote for the projected winner for their state or that it may discourage voters from voting, even though the polls have not closed in their state, because the media projects that there is already a winner. Furthermore, not only are the effects of these projections questionable, but frequently the accuracy of the projections is questionable as well. Although voters may be told a candidate has a certain percentage of the votes within ±1 percent, the confidence interval may be much larger, depending on the sample size.[26] ■

Researchers also have the ethical responsibility to investigate the possibility of nonresponse bias, and make a reasonable effort to adjust for nonresponse. The methodology adopted and the extent of nonresponse bias found should be clearly communicated.

INTERNET AND COMPUTER APPLICATIONS

The Internet has information available on calculating sample size or determining the margin of error for a given sample size. Discovery Research Group has the sample size calculator shown here, which can be found at www.drgutah.com. Research in Practice 12.3 illustrates how the sample size is determined in Internet surveys.

RESEARCH IN PRACTICE 12.3

Opinion Place *Bases Its Opinions on 1,000 Respondents*

Marketing research firms are now turning to the Web to conduct on-line research. Recently, four leading market research companies (ASI Market Research, Custom Research Inc., M/A/R/C Research, and Roper Starch Worldwide) partnered with Digital Marketing Services (DMS), Dallas, to conduct custom research on America Online (AOL).

DMS and AOL will conduct on-line surveys on AOL's *Opinion Place*, with an average base of 1,000 respondents per survey. This sample size was determined based on statistical considerations as well as sample sizes used in similar research conducted by traditional methods. AOL will give rewards points (which can be traded in for prizes) to respondents. Users will not have to submit their e-mail addresses. The surveys will help measure response to advertiser's on-line campaigns. The primary objective of this research is to gauge consumers' attitudes and other subjective information that can help media buyers plan their campaigns.

An advantage of on-line surveys is that researchers are sure to reach their target (sample control), and that the surveys are quicker than traditional surveys like mall-intercepts or home interviews. They also are cheaper (DMS charges $20,000 for an on-line survey, whereas it costs between $30,000 and $40,000 to conduct a mall-intercept survey of 1,000 respondents).

EXAMPLE

Sample Size Calculator

Directions:
Read sample size across top row (1).
Move down to percent affirmative replies (2).
Where the column and the row intersect indicates the range of error (percent plus or minus).

(1) → (2)	100	200	300	400	500	600	800	1,000	1,200	1,500	2,000	2,500	3,000	4,000	5,000
5% or 95%	4.4	3.1	2.5	2.2	2.0	1.8	1.5	1.4	1.3	1.1	.96	.87	.79	.69	.62
10% or 90%	6.0	4.3	3.5	3.0	2.7	2.5	2.1	1.9	1.7	1.6	1.3	1.2	1.1	.95	.85
15% or 85%	7.1	5.1	4.1	3.6	3.2	2.9	2.5	2.3	2.1	1.9	1.6	1.4	1.3	1.1	1.0
20% or 80%	8.0	5.7	4.6	4.0	3.6	3.3	2.8	2.5	2.3	2.1	1.8	1.6	1.4	1.3	1.1
25% or 75%	8.7	6.1	5.0	4.3	3.9	3.6	3.0	2.8	2.5	2.3	1.9	1.7	1.6	1.4	1.2
30% or 70%	9.2	6.5	5.3	4.6	4.1	3.8	3.2	2.9	2.7	2.4	2.0	1.8	1.7	1.4	1.3
35% or 65%	9.5	6.8	5.5	4.8	4.3	3.9	3.3	3.1	2.8	2.5	2.1	1.9	1.7	1.5	1.4
40% or 60%	9.8	7.0	5.7	4.9	4.4	4.0	3.4	3.1	2.8	2.5	2.2	2.0	1.8	1.5	1.4
45% or 55%	9.9	7.0	5.8	5.0	4.5	4.1	3.5	3.2	2.9	2.6	2.2	2.0	1.8	1.6	1.4
50%	10.0	7.1	5.8	5.0	4.5	4.1	3.5	3.2	2.9	2.6	2.2	2.0	1.8	1.6	1.4

This calculator can be used to either determine the range of error for percentage estimates given the sample size, or for determining the sample size for a given range of error (precision level). Thus, when a sample size of 500 is used, error for a percentage estimate near 5 percent (or 95 percent) is ±2 percent, and that for an estimate near 20 percent (or 80 percent) is ±3.6 percent. On the other hand, if the researcher wanted to determine what sample size is required to estimate a percentage near 50 percent within ±5 percent, the answer is 400. ■

FOCUS ON Burke

Before recommending an appropriate sample size, Burke considers the following factors:

- What is the size of the "universe"? That is, how many customers qualify to participate in the study? The size of the universe is not a consideration when the population is known to be large, as in the case of households or consumers. However, this becomes an important factor when the universe is small as in some business-to-business and industrial marketing situations.
- How much precision does the client need? The more precision required, the larger the sample size must be.
- Will any subgroups be analyzed? If so, the sample size must be adequate to draw reliable conclusions for each subgroup.
- How often does the client want to collect data? Since customers may object to participating in repeat studies, clients sometimes have to limit the number of customers Burke can interview in each wave.
- What is the client's budget?

When statistically determining the sample size, Burke uses the approaches discussed in this chapter for means and proportions. Estimates of the population standard deviation needed to calculate sample size are based on similar studies conducted by Burke in the past.

The chamber of commerce for a large city in the southeastern United States asked Burke to conduct a quality-of-life survey among residents of the 10-county metropolitan area. The chamber asked Burke to recommend the appropriate sample size based on the following three criteria:

- The chamber wanted to analyze data for the area as a whole and for each of the 10 individual counties.
- The chamber wanted to be 90 percent confident that the opinions expressed by the residents in the sample represented the views of all residents.
- The chamber would tolerate an error range of no more than 5 percent around the sample proportion.

Burke used these criteria to recommend a sample size of 270 per county. This sample size was statistically determined using the formula for proportions with $\pi = .5$, $D = .05$, and $z = 1.645$. Burke could say with 90 percent certainty that, in theory, the survey results for each county represented the views of all residents in the county within plus or minus 5 percentage points.

Burke calculates the initial incidence rate based on past studies conducted by Burke or other secondary sources. Burke has found that completion rate for telephone interviews is about 25 percent and so it uses the following formula to estimate how many telephone numbers may be required to complete the interviewing quota (final sample size): (quota ÷ estimated incidence) × 4. To complete a quota of 1,000 at an incidence of 37 percent, Burke would start with about 10,800 telephone numbers.

Burke offers monetary incentives in many business-to-business studies. Incentives may range from $10 to as much as $100, depending on what the respondent's job entails, whether there is a "gatekeeper" to screen calls, and how long the interview takes to complete. For example, a 20-minute interview with a cardiologist may require a $100 incentive.

Burke rarely offers incentives for consumers to complete telephone interviews. Exceptions are sometimes made when the interview is long (45 minutes or longer) or the incidence is low (5 percent or less). Burke may offer incentives for consumers prerecruited by phone to complete a follow-up survey by phone or mail. For example, a regional telecommunications company asked Burke to collect evaluations of several new products and services that the company had developed for residential customers. Burke screened people by phone to recruit qualified respondents for a follow-up mail survey. To encourage participation, Burke used a sweepstakes, entering the names of participants in a drawing for several high-ticket items. Burke also enclosed a $2 bill in the package of materials mailed to respondents.

When Burke conducts "blind" mail surveys (i.e., without prerecruiting respondents by phone), incentives are almost mandatory to achieve an acceptable response rate. When one of the largest banks in the United States asked Burke to conduct a mail survey among account holders, Burke used a $2 bill, enclosed with the eight-page questionnaire, to achieve a response rate of about 60 percent. Mall intercepts generally require a monetary incentive only when the interview length exceeds 20 minutes or the incidence drops below 20 percent. Incentives for mall intercepts typically range from $2 to $5.

Improving Response Rates

Although very low, response rates to Internet surveys can be increased by making the surveys easy to access and complete in multiple sessions if necessary. Because the length of a survey on the Internet is hidden from respondents, they are less inclined to not respond due to survey length. The inclusion of electronic skip patterns in the questionnaire design also help promote higher response rates by making it easier for the respondent to maneuver through the survey. Internet surveys can also use attractive design and plug-ins such as music and video to make the process of responding more interesting.

For electronic mail surveys, prior e-mails, sent by the sponsor to announce the survey, are strongly suggested by many of the Internet marketing research firms. These firms also send reminder e-mails to nonrespondents a few days after the initial survey has been sent. Another way to motivate respondents to complete surveys is to tell them if the results will be used to enhance service.

Another motivator is to provide incentives for completion of surveys. One respondent to a Research Info Chat Board request on how to recruit respondents for Web-based interviewing noted that he had participated in a survey because he would be entered into a cash drawing for participating. Another technique cited was to give points redeemable for merchandise or discounts to survey respondents. To visit the Research Info chat room to find other responses on how to recruit respondents for Web-based research, explore the site called www.researchinfo.com.

Microcomputers and mainframes can determine the sample size for various sampling techniques. For simple applications, appropriate sample size formulas can be entered using spreadsheet programs. The researcher specifies the desired precision level, confidence level, and population variance, and the program determines the appropriate sample size for the study. By incorporating the cost of each sampling unit, the sample size can be adjusted based on budget considerations. Standard Error by Bardsley & Haslacher, Inc., uses spreadsheets to calculate mean standard errors and 95% confidence intervals and can be used for computing sample sizes. Statchek by Detail Technologies, Inc., calculates confidence intervals and can be used to determine sample sizes. Several marketing research firms supply sample design software and services including statistical determination of sample sizes and estimation of sample statistics. Survey Sampling, Inc., has a line of sampling products. Their Contact and Cooperation Rate Adjustment software statistically adjusts sample sizes by taking into account the expected incidence and completion rates.

SUMMARY

The statistical approaches to determining sample size are based on confidence intervals. These approaches may involve the estimation of the mean or proportion. When estimating the mean, determination of sample size using the confidence interval approach requires the specification of precision level, confidence level, and population standard deviation. In the case of proportion, the precision level, confidence level, and an estimate of the population proportion must be specified. The sample size determined statistically represents the final or net sample size that must be achieved. In order to achieve this final sample size, a much greater number of potential respondents have to be contacted to account for reduction in response due to incidence rates and completion rates.

Nonresponse error arises when some of the potential respondents included in the sample do not respond. The primary causes of low response rates are refusals and not-at-homes. Refusal rates may be reduced by prior notification, motivating the respondents, incentives, proper questionnaire design and administration, and follow-up. The percentage of not-at-homes can be substantially reduced by callbacks. Adjustments for nonresponse can be made by subsampling nonrespondents, replacement, substitution, subjective estimates, trend analysis, simple weighting, and imputation.

The statistical estimation of sample size is even more complicated in international marketing research as the population variance may differ from one country to the next. The preliminary estimation of population variance for the purpose of determining the sample size also has ethical ramifications. The Internet and computers can assist in determining the sample size and adjusting it to account for expected incidence and completion rates.

KEY TERMS AND CONCEPTS

parameter
statistic
finite population correction
precision level
confidence interval
confidence level
sampling distribution
statistical inference
standard error
z value
incidence rate
completion rate
substitution
trend analysis
weighting
imputation
normal distribution

ACRONYMS

The statistical considerations involved in determining the sample size may be summarized by the acronym SIZE:

S ampling distribution
I nterval (confidence)
Z value
E stimation of population standard deviation

EXERCISES

Questions

1. Define the sampling distribution.
2. What is the standard error of the mean?
3. Define finite population correction.
4. Define a confidence interval.
5. What is the procedure for constructing a confidence interval around a mean?
6. Describe the difference between absolute precision and relative precision when estimating a population mean.
7. How do the degree of confidence and the degree of precision differ?
8. Describe the procedure for determining the sample size necessary to estimate a population mean, given the degree of precision and confidence and a known population variance. After the sample is selected, how is the confidence interval generated?
9. Describe the procedure for determining the sample size necessary to estimate a population mean, given the degree of precision and confidence but where the population variance is unknown. After the sample is selected, how is the confidence interval generated?
10. How is the sample size affected when the absolute precision with which a population mean is estimated is doubled?
11. How is the sample size affected when the degree of confidence with which a population mean is estimated is increased from 95 percent to 99 percent?
12. Define what is meant by absolute precision and relative precision when estimating a population proportion.
13. Describe the procedure for determining the sample size necessary to estimate a population proportion given the degree of precision and confidence. After the sample is selected, how is the confidence interval generated?
14. How can the researcher ensure that the generated confidence interval will be no larger than the desired interval when estimating a population proportion?
15. When several parameters are being estimated, what is the procedure for determining the sample size?
16. Define incidence rate and completion rate. How do these rates affect the determination of the final sample size?
17. What strategies are available for adjusting for nonresponse?

Problems

1. Using Table 2 of the Appendix of Statistical Tables, calculate the probability that:
   a. z is less than 1.48.
   b. z is greater than 1.90.

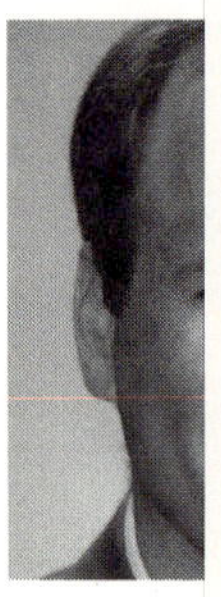

Charles D
Vice Presi

Mr. Eden
in Burke's
service of
responsib
consulting
refine stu
coordinat
managing
required t
projects.
years at E
conducte
broad rar

to capitalize on the widespread interest in extended-stay rooms. In 1997, Holiday Inn was considering a new extension, Staybridge Suites by Holiday Inn, specifically designed for this market.

Hotels are attempting to segment the market and offer enhanced services to attract customers. For a hotel to be successful in attracting customers, it must be the "host with the most."

Questions

1. Identify some possible sources of secondary data for the hotel industry. What type of data are available on the Internet?
2. The hotel industry has faced the troublesome problem of differentiation. Hampton Inns would like to undertake marketing research to determine how it can differentiate itself from its competitors. What research design would you recommend?
3. What information is needed for Hampton Inns to develop a program to differentiate itself from competition?
4. Design a questionnaire to obtain the relevant information.
5. What research design would be appropriate for monitoring consumers' changing needs and preferences for hotels?
6. Marriott would like to know what is the best way to segment the hotel market. What type of research design would you recommend and why?

References

Anthony Marshall, "Seniors Have Big Travel Budgets but Need Accommodation," *Hotel & Motel Management* 212 (6) (April 7, 1997): 17.

Nicole Harris, "Sleepless Nights at Holiday Inn," *Businessweek* (November 3, 1997): 66–7.

Michael Malley, "Hospitality's New Homemakers Finding Niche," *Hotel & Motel Management* 212 (18) (October 20, 1997): 18.

"Marriott Joins Midpriced Extended Stay War," *Lodging Hospitality* 53 (4) (April 1997): 10.

2.3 Candy Is Dandy for Hershey

The battle was on! Hershey and Mars, the two candy giants, dueling over the number one spot in the $7-billion-a-year candy industry. Hershey lost its throne in the early 1970s, and it took the company time to get back into the competitive arena. By 1985, however, Mars and Hershey were the manufacturers of the top 10 candy bars, and together they shared 70 percent of the market. Cadbury held about 9 percent of the market and Nestle only 6 percent. Then in 1988, Hershey acquired Cadbury, and its share jumped from 36 percent to 44 percent of the candy market. The addition of brands such as Cadbury Dairy Milk Chocolate, Peter Paul Mounds, Almond Joy, and York Peppermint Pattie enabled Hershey to regain its throne in the candy market. The late 1980s and early 1990s saw the introduction of products such as Hershey's Kisses with Almonds, Hugs, Hugs with Almonds, Amazin' Fruit Gummy Bears, and the Cookies 'n' Mint Chocolate bar. In 1994, Hershey Food Corp. celebrated its 100th year in business. In 1996, Hershey addressed its lack of strong showing products in the nonchocolate sector of the industry by acquiring Leaf North American brand, which produces strong sellers such as Jolly Rancher and Good & Plenty. Also in 1996, Hershey unveiled its low-fat Sweet Escapes line, which brought in over $100 million in 1997. The decisions over the past 100 years have been both diverse and profitable. (See Tables 1 and 2.)

One of the factors that was in Hershey's favor in the battle with M&M/Mars was its excellent marketing research department. Hershey's research showed that the typical consumer viewed candy as a luxury good or as a self-indulgence. Because of these attitudes and beliefs, 70 percent of all candy sales were attributed to impulse buying. Candy customers also tended to be fickle, rarely purchasing the same candy bar twice in a row. A consumer's age was also shown to influence buying habits. Surveys indicated that of consumers in the 18 to 34 age group, 60 percent indulged themselves at least once a week, and 55 percent of all the candy items sold were consumed by people over 18. However, of consumers in the 35 to 64 age group, only 6 percent indulged themselves at least once a week.

Market research also informed Hershey that the population was getting older. In the 1970s and early 1980s, young people from age 13 to the late 20s was the dominant age group. In the 1990s it is becoming the 35 to 50 age group. For this reason, the candy industry decided to move upscale to attract the baby-boom adults. By the year 2000, the median age for Americans will be 40. The National

TABLE 1

HERSHEY'S TIME LINE

1895	First Hershey's Chocolate Bar is sold.
1907	Hershey's Kisses are introduced.
1908	Hershey's Milk Chocolate Bar with Almonds is introduced.
1911	Sales reach $5 million.
1925	Mr. Goodbar chocolate bar is introduced.
1938	The Hershey's Krakel bar is introduced.
1939	Hershey's Miniatures are introduced.
1945	Milton Hershey dies at the age of 88.
1963	Reese Candy Co., producer of Reese's Peanut Butter Cups, is purchased.
1966	Hershey purchases San Giorgio Macaroni Co.
1968	Hershey Chocolate Corp. changes its name to Hershey Food Corp.
1977	Y & S Candies, Inc., manufacturer of licorice and licorice-type products such as Twizzlers and Nibs, is purchased.
1986	Luden's and 5th Avenue trademarks are added through acquisition of the Dietrich Corporations confectionery operations.
1988	Hershey Foods Corp. acquires Peter Paul/Cadbury U.S. confectionery operations. Brands acquired include Peter Paul Mounds and Almond Joy bars and York Peppermint Patties.
1990	Hershey's Kisses with Almonds are introduced.
1991	Fluid milk plant used to produce a chocolate drink is purchased.
1992	Hershey's Cookies 'n' Mint bar and Amazin' Fruit Gummy Bears are introduced.
1993	Hershey's Hugs and Hershey's Hugs with Almonds are introduced.
1994	Hershey's Nuggets chocolates and Reese's Peanut Butter Puffs brand cereal are introduced.
1996	Hershey launches the Sweet Escapes low-fat chocolate line. Hershey acquires Leaf North American brand to strengthen its non-chocolate line.

Confectioners Association believes that as Americans get older, they tend to favor the better things in life. Among these better things are quality confections. A multiple cross-sectional analysis of consumption patterns revealed that adults were consuming an ever-increasing percentage of candy (Table 3). The adult market has therefore proven to be increasingly lucrative.

TABLE 2

TOP 10 CHOCOLATE BRANDS

Rank	*Brand*	*Share(%)*
1	Snickers	10.2
2	Reese's	9.33
3	M&M Peanut	6.31
4	M&M Plain	5.26
5	Kit Kat	4.97
6	Butterfinger	4.71
7	Hershey Almond	3.39
8	Crunch	3.33
9	Milky Way	3.25
10	Hershey Milk	2.91

Hershey successfully launched its adult-oriented Golden chocolate line and subsequently introduced Grand Slam, a combination of caramel, peanuts, and crisp rice that was targeted at the 18 to 34 age group. Hershey's Solitaire and Life Saver's Fruit Juice flavors had also increased in popularity in the adult market. In 1989, Hershey introduced Solitaire, premium chocolate with almonds and toffee chips. It was Hershey's first new milk chocolate bar since the classic Hershey's milk chocolate bar nearly a century ago.

Additionally, to gain market share, Hershey decided to become a fearless product innovator. For adults, Hershey introduced Skor, a chocolate-covered toffee bar, and Five, a chocolate-covered wafer and peanut-cream bar, which did well in the test market. Bar None, introduced in 1988, exceeded expectations. Golden Almond Nuggets and Symphony also were released nationally. Earlier, Hershey had introduced its 2.2-ounce bars, followed by Big Blocks, which were 50 percent larger than ordinary Hershey bars. This trend continued with the launching of 3.2-ounce bars—premium bars such as Golden Almond and Golden Pecan. In 1990, Hershey was again successful with the introduction of Kisses with Almonds. In 1993, the Kisses line extension continued with Hugs and Hugs

TABLE 4

MINORITY MARKETS

	Male Fragrance Users	*Popular Male Fragrances*	*Popular Female Fragrances*
Black	73%	Old Spice, Brut	Tatiana, Giorgio
Hispanic	62%	Eau Savage	Jean Naté

focus. Because the 1990s was the era of developing a positive image for the female, some believe that the next decades will be the era of developing a positive image for the male.

Another segment that perfume manufacturers cannot afford to overlook is the older American. By the year 2000, one-third of the population will be over 50. In the past, advertisers have tended to gear their products toward the 18-to-49-year-olds. Venetia Hands of Ogilvy and Mather has suggested that the older segment should be broken into two more segments; the Luckies, 50 to 64, and the Savvies, 64 and up. The Luckies are less price sensitive than the Savvies.

To turn lagging sales around, fragrance marketers are looking at both purchase patterns and the products themselves. Some fragrance marketers are taking the initiative in first trying to help department stores, their mainstay prestige fragrance retailers, compete with the host of alternate fragrance retailers. With many fragrances closely tied into department store distribution, in the minds of consumers, shifting to other venues is not practical. For example, some manufacturers, such as Aramis, are attempting to help department stores compete on some point of difference from alternative fragrance retailers—such as promotion and customer services—because they cannot compete on price. Marketers are also trying to increase consumer usage for the fragrances. Approximately 76 percent of the 20 to 30 age group wears a fragrance only three or four times a week. "You need to get more people wearing fragrance on a daily basis," says David Nap, vice president of marketing at Aramis. Attracting new customers is also key to improving sales for the industry. For now, new-product entries are still the way to earn new business. Marketers have increasingly learned the importance of marketing research. The keys to success have been in defining the market, truly understanding the consumers' preferences, creating a brand that consistently meets these expectations, and communicating these brand attributes to the consumer. Beyond discerning the popular trends, it is important to match the brand image to the fragrance. Even the most brilliant fragrance will not sell if it does not meet the perceptions of the brands' traits. Consumer testing, used to make sure that the product meets its image, has become increasingly vital to the industry.

Today's consumers have diverse lifestyles and the goal for fragrance marketers is to meet these very different needs. One important trend is consumer interest in the inner-directed search for peace and relief from stress. Comforting home scents such as vanilla, chocolate, and coffee are becoming popular. The healthy lifestyle trend is still popular and scents such as flowers and fruits, which connote health and vitality, are also popular. Meanwhile, consumers are showing a renewed interest in glamour and dressing up for a night or the evening. To accommodate these differing lifestyles, consumers are looking for fragrances that can accommodate the look or feel of a particular day or evening. Brands that can offer a gentle attitude combined with an elegant luxury and can successfully communicate and deliver on a popular image will be popular. It is up to marketers to meet consumer expectation if they wish to revitalize sales in the next millennium and mask the bitter taste of competition with the sweet smell of success.

Questions

1. Identify some possible sources of secondary data for the fragrance industry. What sources can be located on the Internet and how should an Internet search be conducted?
2. Discuss the kind of market research fragrance manufacturers could conduct to determine if there is a demand for a new fragrance.
3. Once an audience for a new fragrance has been targeted, what kind of information is needed about their attitudes, preferences, purchase intentions, behaviors, motivations, psychographics, and demographics?
4. Which techniques would you recommend for collecting the information needed above? Discuss.
5. Design appropriate scales for obtaining the information identified above.
6. For a marketing research project aimed at assessing the demand for a new fragrance, a junior analyst designed the enclosed questionnaire (Exhibit 1). Is this a well-designed questionnaire? If not, how could it be improved?

References

Sue G. Phillips, "Separating the Winners from the Losers: How to Create a Winner in Today's Fragrance Marathon," *Drug & Cosmetic Industry* 161 (3) (September 1997): 40–8.

Michael Sweeney, "Fragrances for the Millennium and Beyond," *Drug & Cosmetic Industry* 160 (6) (June 1997): 42–6.

Pat Sloan and Aminda Heckman, "Fickle Mass Market Turns Cold Shoulder to Scents," *Advertising Age* 67 (40) (September 30, 1996): S12.

Exhibit 1
New Fragrance Survey

Please fill out the following survey, answering the questions as accurately as possible.

PART I

1. What is your sex?
_____Male _____Female

2. What age group are you in?
_____18–24 _____25–29 _____30–34 _____35–44 _____45 and over

3. What category of annual income do you fit into?
_____0–$15,000 _____$15,000–$25,000 _____$25,000–$35,000 _____$35,000–$45,000 _____$45,000 and above

4. What is your marital status?
_____Married _____Single

5. If you are married, how many children do you have?
_____one _____two _____three _____four or more

6. How often do you go to the mall?
_____once a week (or more) _____once a month _____once every 6 months _____once a year

7. If you shop at department stores, which one do you frequent?
_____Macy's _____J. C. Penney _____Sears _____Sak's Fifth Avenue/Neiman-Marcus

PART II

8. I usually buy my fragrances in a department store.

1	2	3	4	5
Strongly agree	Agree	Don't know	Disagree	Strongly disagree

9. I usually buy my fragrances in a drugstore.

1	2	3	4	5
Strongly agree	Agree	Don't know	Disagree	Strongly disagree

10. I only buy one brand of fragrance.

1	2	3	4	5
Strongly agree	Agree	Don't know	Disagree	Strongly disagree

11. Department store fragrances are worth the extra cost.

1	2	3	4	5
Strongly agree	Agree	Don't know	Disagree	Strongly disagree

12. Free gift packages are a definite incentive to buy a fragrance product.

1	2	3	4	5
Strongly agree	Agree	Don't know	Disagree	Strongly disagree

13. Celebrity endorsement of a fragrance gives it more appeal.

1	2	3	4	5
Strongly agree	Agree	Don't know	Disagree	Strongly disagree

14. Fragrances endorsed by celebrities are higher in quality.

1	2	3	4	5
Strongly agree	Agree	Don't know	Disagree	Strongly disagree

15. I would be interested in a new fragrance.

1	2	3	4	5
Strongly agree	Agree	Don't know	Disagree	Strongly disagree

16. I frequently try new fragrances.

1	2	3	4	5
Strongly agree	Agree	Don't know	Disagree	Strongly disagree

PART III

17. ***How often do you buy fragrances?***

____

18. ***What is your favorite fragrance?***

____

19. ***What are the qualities you look for in a fragrance?***

____

20. ***Are you happy with the fragrances currently on the market?***

____

Thank you for your time. Your assistance will help us in better meeting your fragrance needs.

2.5 Is Super Bowl Advertising Super Effective?

About 140 million Americans and 600 million total global viewers tune in to Super Bowl Sunday making the event one of the largest occasion for home entertainment. Advertising time during the Super Bowl is limited and priced at a premium. The fight for the prime spots starts months in advance of the actual air time. Large companies with the most money to spend, jockey to obtain the most highly visible air times. In 1993 the cost for a 30-second time slot was a high $850,000, but by 1997 the cost had shot to $1.2 million for the same short time frame. In 1998, a 30-second spot during the Super Bowl cost $1.3 million. Despite the exorbitant cost, all spots for 1998's Super Bowl XXXII were sold, with marketers likely expecting big returns on their investment. For instance, M&M/Mars used its slot to launch a campaign that was planned to last for the next few months. Despite a virtually guaranteed audience in the hundreds of millions, a number of marketers are questioning whether Super Bowl advertising is worth the price.

For many advertisers who bought time slots in previous games, the answer was a resounding no. Nissan, Porsche, Fila, and MCI passed on the chance to advertise during the game. According to marketing consultant Jack Trout, the increasing rates made buying Super Bowl ad time difficult to justify. Nissan marketing chief Brad Bradshaw stated that although the company had intended to advertise during the game, it came to the conclusion that the resources could be better used to sell its vehicles in other ways.

In addition to the cost factor, many question what effect does advertising actually have on the audience. The purpose of an advertisement is to increase customer awareness for a particular brand. For Super Bowl ads, however, the brand name often becomes secondary to the commercial itself in terms of viewer attention. Super Bowl ads have become events in and of themselves, with each firm trying to put out the next earth-shattering commercial that will stir talk about the commercial itself. Ever since Apple computer's classic "1984" ad, firms have been trying to top previous year's ads. Ad agencies and clients often seem to shoot for ads that are extraordinary for the sake of creativity, rather than their intended purpose, with many attention-getting promotions not translating into product purchases. It is questionable whether brand name is retained, and so despite having an incredible commercial many advertisers' ad dollars possibly go into just providing new fodder for water cooler conversation for the week instead of forming a lasting brand image in the minds of consumers. Without new research into the effectiveness of Super Bowl advertising and its effect on consumers, many advertisers may be better off avoiding buying Super Bowl ad time and abandoning the world's biggest television audience.

Some advertisers such as Purina Cat Chow are taking a slightly different approach by purchasing airtime on the show directly following the Super Bowl. They obtain airtime at one-sixth of the cost during the game, and they believe that they retain approximately 40 percent of the audience.

Which advertiser is getting the biggest bang for the bucks? M&M/Mars or Purina Cat Chow? Without systematic marketing research aimed at measuring Super Bowl advertising effectiveness, questions such as these go unanswered.

Questions

1. What kind of research design would you recommend for determining the effectiveness of M&M/Mars's advertising during the Super Bowl?
2. If the research design involves a survey of households, which survey method would you recommend and why?
3. What kind of measures and scales will you employ in your survey?
4. Can the observation method be used to determine the effectiveness of M&M/Mars' advertising during the Super Bowl? If so, which observation method would you recommend and why?
5. Which syndicated services discussed in the book can provide useful information?

References

"Super Promos: Many Promotions Center on the Super Bowl, Which is Watched by 140 Mil Americans and 600 Mil Other People around the World," *Promo* 11 (2), (January 1998): 32.

"More Bang for the Super Bowl Bucks: The Cost of Advertising During the Super Bowl Rose to $1.3 Mil for a 30-second Spot, but Many Advertisers Were Still Willing to Meet the Cost, Especially If They Could Extend Their Visibility Beyond the Commercial," *Business Week* (February 2, 1998): 70.

"Super Bowl Ad Roster Missing Some Veterans: A Number of Past Super Bowl Advertisers Will Not Be Seen During the Broadcast of the 1998 Game," *USA Today* 16 (82) (January 9, 1998): 3B.

Part III

Data Collection, Preparation, and Analysis

This part presents a practical and managerially oriented discussion of field work, the fourth step in the marketing research process. We offer several guidelines for interviewer training, supervision, and conducting interviews. When the field work is complete, the researcher moves on to data preparation and analysis, the fifth step of the marketing research process. In this step we emphasize the importance and discuss the process of preparing data to make them suitable for analysis. Then we describe the various data analysis techniques. We cover not only the basic techniques of frequency distribution, cross-tabulation, and hypothesis testing, but also the commonly used multivariate techniques of analysis of variance and regression. Finally, we describe the more advanced techniques: discriminant, factor, and cluster analysis, as well as multidimensional scaling and conjoint analysis. In the discussion of each statistical technique, the emphasis is on explaining the procedure, interpreting the results, and managerial implications, rather than on statistical elegance. Three of the cases with statistical data sets provide ample opportunities to practice these techniques. Four additional cases with data sets are found in the supplement entitled Exercises in Marketing Research. *(See Instructor's Manual or visit the Web site).*

Chapter 13

Field Work

"No matter how well you design the research process, the persons actually doing the work have control of the quality. The key to good field work is founded in careful selection, thorough training, and continuous evaluation . . . always with an eye to quality."

Karen Cravens, vice president, data collection, Burke, Inc.

OBJECTIVES

After reading this chapter, the student should be able to

1. describe the field work process and explain the selection, training, and supervision of field workers, the validation of field work, and the evaluation of field workers
2. discuss the training of field workers in making the initial contact, asking the questions, probing, recording the answers, and terminating the interview
3. discuss the supervision of field workers in terms of quality control and editing, sampling control, control of cheating, and central office control
4. describe the evaluation of field workers in areas of cost and time, response rates, quality of interviewing, and the quality of data
5. explain the issues related to field work in conducting international marketing research
6. discuss the ethical aspects of field work
7. illustrate the use of the Internet and computers in field work

OVERVIEW

Field work is the fourth step in the marketing research process. It follows problem definition and development of the approach (chapter 2), and formulation of the research design (chapters 3 through 12). During this phase the field workers make contact with the respondents, administer the questionnaires or observation forms, record the data, and turn in the completed forms for processing. A personal interviewer administering questionnaires door-to-door, an interviewer intercepting shoppers in a mall, a telephone interviewer calling from a central location, a worker mailing questionnaires from an office, an observer counting customers in a particular section of a store, and others involved in data collection and supervision of the process are all field workers.

This chapter describes the nature of field work and the general field work/data collection process. This process involves the selection, training, and supervision of field workers, the validation of field work, and the evaluation of field workers. We briefly discuss field

DEPARTMENT STORE PATRONAGE PROJECT

Field Work

In the department store patronage project, in-home personal interviews were conducted by interviewers who were graduate and undergraduate students enrolled in marketing research courses taught by the author. The field workers' training included having each interviewer (1) act as a respondent and self-administer the questionnaire, and (2) administer the questionnaire to a few other students not involved in the project (dummy respondents). Detailed guidelines for interviewing were developed and provided to each interviewer. The supervision of interviewers was carried out by graduate students who monitored the field work activities on a day-to-day basis. All the respondents were called back to verify that the interviewer had actually administered the questionnaire to them and to thank them for participating in the survey. A 100 percent validation check was performed. All the field workers, interviewers, and supervisors were evaluated by the author.

work in the context of international marketing research, identify the relevant ethical issues, and explain the role of the Internet and computers. To begin, we present brief examples that highlight the nature of field work.

EXAMPLE

Narrowing the Field of Refusals

Efforts by the Your Opinion Counts™ Committee aimed at reducing refusal rates are really making the opinions of people count.

LEGITIMATE MARKETING AND OPINION RESEARCHERS PRACTICE *RESPECT*

We will:

- Contact you between the hours of 9:00 a.m. and 9:00 p.m.
- Give you our name and company
- Tell you the nature of the survey
- Respect your time
- Keep your individual answers confidential

We will not:

- Try to sell you anything
- Ask you for money
- Sell your name or telephone number to any other company
- Mislead you about the length of the survey

We want to hear from you...

CMOR
Council for Marketing and Opinion Research
170 North Country Road • Port Jefferson, New York 11777
Phone: (516) 928-6206 • Fax: (516) 928-6041
1-800-887-CMOR (2667) Please call during business hours.

Printed on recycled paper

Recently the "Your Opinion Counts" (YOC) National Steering Committee conducted a benchmark study to determine the level and nature of respondent refusal rates in consumer surveys. The overall refusal rate was found to be 38 percent. Initial refusal amounted to almost 90 percent of total refusals. Several guidelines offered by the YOC Committee for reducing refusal rates relate to field work:

- Interviewer training programs should be routinely administered so that field workers will be effective in their jobs.
- Courtesy should be exercised when deciding what hours of the day to call respondents. YOC recommends calling between 9 A.M. and 9 P.M.
- If mall respondents indicate the time is not convenient, an appointment should be made to conduct the interview later.
- The subject matter should be disclosed to the respondents if this can be done without biasing the data. The more information people are given, the less reason they have to be suspicious.
- Field workers should make the interviews as pleasant and appealing as possible.[1] ■

THE NATURE OF FIELD WORK

Marketing research data are rarely collected by the persons who design the research. Researchers have two major options for collecting their data: They can develop their own organizations or they can contract with a field work agency. In either case, data collection involves the use of some kind of field force. The field force may operate either in the field (personal in-home, mall-intercept, computer-assisted personal interviewing, and observation) or from an office (telephone, mail, e-mail, and Internet surveys). The field workers who collect the data typically have little research background or training. Ethical concerns are particularly germane to field work. Although there is ample opportunity for violation of ethical standards, clients need not be overly concerned when dealing with reputable field work agencies. Michael Redington, senior vice president for corporate development at Marketing and Research Counselors, is an aggressive advocate of field quality. His evaluation of the quality of field work in the marketing research industry is as follows: "I was very pleased to help shoot down the myth that data collection is characterized by a bunch of people out there attempting to bend the rules, to rip you off, and to cheat on interviews. There are a lot of people on the client side who believe just that. Quite frankly, we were out trying to find it, but we didn't. That was a revelation to us. We were afraid that there were more unethical practices in the field than there really were."[2] The quality of field work is high because the field work/data collection process is streamlined and well controlled, as discussed in the following section.

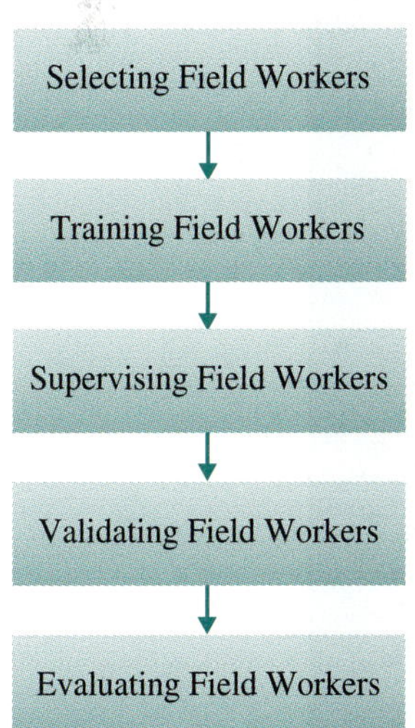

Figure 13.1
Field Work/Data Collection Process

FIELD WORK/DATA COLLECTION PROCESS

All field work involves the selection, training, and supervision of persons who collect data.[3] The validation of field work and the evaluation of field workers are also parts of the process. Figure 13.1 represents a general framework for the field work/data collection process. As we describe a general process, it should be recognized that the nature of field work varies with the mode of data collection, and the relative emphasis on the different steps will be different for telephone, personal, mail, and electronic interviews.

SELECTION OF FIELD WORKERS

The first step in the field work process is the selection of field workers. The researcher should: (1) develop job specifications for the project, taking into account the mode of data collection; (2) decide what characteristics the field workers should have; and (3) recruit

DEPARTMENT STORE PATRONAGE PROJECT

Initial Contact Statement

Hello, my name is ________________. I represent the marketing department of Georgia Tech. We are conducting a survey about household preferences for department stores. You are one of the select group of respondents who have been scientifically selected to participate in this survey. We value your opinion highly and would like to ask you a few questions.[11]

Note that the interviewer did not specifically ask the respondent's permission. Questions that directly ask permission, such as, "May I have some of your valuable time?" or "Would you like to answer a few questions?" should be avoided. Interviewers should be also instructed on handling objections and refusals. For example, if the respondent says, "This is not a convenient time for me," the interviewer should respond, "What would be a more convenient time for you? I will call back then." If the foot-in-the-door or door-in-the-face techniques discussed in chapter 12 are being employed, interviewers should be trained accordingly.

Asking the Questions

Even a slight change in the wording, sequence, or manner in which a question is asked can distort its meaning and bias the response. Asking questions is an art. Training in asking questions can yield high dividends in eliminating potential sources of bias. Changing the phrasing or order of questions during the interview can make significant differences in the response obtained. "While we could be faulted for not writing as perfect a questionnaire as we possibly could, still it must be asked in the exact way it was written. It's a challenge for us to try to get the interviewers more conversational, but despite this the field force absolutely must ask questions as they are written."[12] The following are guidelines for asking questions.[13]

1. Be thoroughly familiar with the questionnaire.
2. Ask the questions in the order in which they appear in the questionnaire.
3. Use the exact wording given in the questionnaire.
4. Read each question slowly.
5. Repeat questions that are not understood.
6. Ask every applicable question.
7. Follow instructions, skip patterns, probing carefully.

Probing

Probing A motivational technique used when asking survey questions to induce the respondents to enlarge on, clarify, or explain their answers and to help the respondents to focus on the specific content of the interview.

Probing is intended to motivate respondents to enlarge on, clarify, or explain their answers. Probing also helps respondents focus on the specific content of the interview and provide only relevant information. Probing should not introduce any bias. Listed below are some commonly used probing techniques.[14]

1. *Repeating the question.* Repeating the question in the same words can be effective in eliciting a response.
2. *Repeating the respondent's reply.* Respondents can be stimulated to provide further comments by repeating, verbatim, their replies. This can be done as the interviewer records the replies.
3. *Using a pause or silent probe.* A silent probe, or an expectant pause or look, can cue the respondent to provide a more complete response. However, the silence should not become embarrassing.

4. *Boosting or reassuring the respondent.* If the respondent hesitates, the interviewer should reassure the respondent with comments such as, "There are no right or wrong answers. We are just trying to get your opinions." If the respondent needs an explanation of a word or phrase, the interviewer should not offer an interpretation. Rather, the responsibility for the interpretation should be returned to the respondent. This can be done with a comment such as, "Just whatever it means to you."
5. *Eliciting clarification.* The respondent's motivation to cooperate with the interviewer and provide complete answers can be aroused with a question such as, "I don't quite understand what you mean by that—could you please tell me a little more?"
6. *Using objective/neutral questions or comments.* Research in Practice 13.1 provides several examples of the common questions or comments used as probes.[15] Corresponding abbreviations are also provided. The interviewer should record the abbreviations on the questionnaire in parentheses next to the question asked.

Recording the Answers

Although recording respondent answers seems simple, several mistakes are common.[16] All interviewers should use the same format and conventions to record the interviews and edit completed interviews. The rules for recording answers to structured questions vary with each specific questionnaire, but the general rule is to check the box that reflects the respondent's answer. The general rule for recording answers to unstructured questions is to record the responses verbatim. The *Interviewer's Manual* of the Survey Research Center provides the following specific guidelines for recording answers to unstructured questions.

1. Record responses during the interview.
2. Use the respondent's own words.
3. Do not summarize or paraphrase the respondent's answers.
4. Include everything that pertains to the question objectives.
5. Include all probes and comments.
6. Repeat the response as it is written down.

Terminating the Interview

The interview should not be closed before all the information is obtained. Any spontaneous comments the respondent offers after all the formal questions have been asked should be recorded. The interviewer should answer the respondent's questions about the

RESEARCH IN PRACTICE 13.1

Commonly Used Probes and Abbreviations

Standard Interviewer's Probe	Abbreviation
Any other reason?	(AO?)
Any others?	(Other?)
Anything else?	(AE or Else?)
Could you tell me more about your thinking on that?	(Tell more)
How do you mean?	(How mean?)
Repeat question.	(RQ)
What do you mean?	(What mean?)
Which would be closer to the way you feel?	(Which closer?)
Why do you feel that way?	(Why?)
Would you tell me what you have in mind?	(What in mind?)

RESEARCH IN PRACTICE 13.2

Guidelines on Interviewer Training: The Council of American Survey Research Organizations

Training should be conducted under the direction of supervisory personnel and should cover the following:

1. The research process—how a study is developed, implemented, and reported.
2. The importance of the interviewers to this process—the need for honesty, objectivity, organizational skills, and professionalism.
3. Confidentiality of the respondent and client.
4. Familiarity with market research terminology.
5. The importance of following the exact wording and recording responses verbatim.
6. The purpose and use of probing and clarifying techniques.
7. The reason for and use of classification and respondent information questions.
8. A review of samples of instructions and questionnaires.
9. The importance of the respondent's positive feelings about survey research.

No person should work as an interviewer unless that person has been trained in the general interviewing techniques as outlined above.

project. The respondent should be left with a positive feeling about the interview. It is important to thank the respondent and express appreciation.

The Council of American Survey Research Organizations' guidelines on interviewer training are given in Research in Practice 13.2.

SUPERVISION OF FIELD WORKERS

Supervision of field workers means making sure that they are following the procedures and techniques in which they were trained. Supervision involves quality control and editing, sampling control, control of cheating, and central office control.

Quality Control and Editing

Quality control of field workers requires checking to see if the field procedures are being properly implemented.[17] If any problems are detected, the supervisor should discuss them with the field workers and provide additional training if necessary. To understand the interviewers' problems, the supervisors should also do some interviewing. Supervisors should collect questionnaires and other forms, and edit them daily. They should examine the questionnaires to make sure all appropriate questions have been completed, unsatisfactory or incomplete answers have not been accepted, and the writing is legible.

Supervisors should also keep a record of hours worked and expenses. This will allow a determination of the cost per completed interview, whether the job is moving on schedule, and if any interviewers are having problems.

Sampling Control

Sampling Control An aspect of supervision that ensures that the interviewers strictly follow the sampling plan rather than select sampling units based on convenience or accessibility.

An important aspect of supervision is **sampling control**, which attempts to ensure that the interviewers are strictly following the sampling plan rather than selecting sampling units based on convenience or accessibility. Interviewers tend to avoid dwellings or sampling units that they perceive as difficult or undesirable. If the sampling unit is not at home, the interviewers may be tempted to substitute the next available unit rather than call back. Interviewers sometimes stretch the requirements of quota samples. For example, a 58-year-old person may be placed in the 46-to-55 age category and interviewed to fulfill quota requirements.

To control these problems, supervisors should keep daily records of the number of calls made, number of not-at-homes, number of refusals, number of completed interviews for each interviewer, and the total for all interviewers under their control.

Control of Cheating

Cheating involves falsifying part of a question or the entire questionnaire. An interviewer may falsify part of an answer to make it acceptable or may fake answers. The most blatant form of cheating occurs when the interviewer falsifies the entire questionnaire, merely filling in fake answers without contacting the respondent. Cheating can be minimized through proper training, supervision, and validation of field work.[18]

Central Office Control

Supervisors provide quality and cost-control information to the central office so that a total progress report can be maintained. In addition to the controls initiated in the field, other controls may be added at the central office to identify potential problems. Central office control includes tabulation of quota variables, important demographic characteristics, and answers to key variables. Research in Practice 13.3 provides guidelines for supervision from the Council of American Survey Research Organizations.

RESEARCH IN PRACTICE 13.3

Guidelines on Supervision: The Council of American Survey Research Organizations

All research projects should be properly supervised. It is the responsibility of the data collection agency to:

1. Properly supervise interviewers.
2. See that an agreed upon proportion of interviewers' telephone calls are monitored.
3. Be available to report on the status of the project daily to the project director, unless otherwise instructed.
4. Keep all studies, materials, and findings confidential.
5. Notify concerned parties if the anticipated schedule is not likely to be met.
6. Attend all interviewer briefings.
7. Keep current and accurate records of the interviewing progress.
8. Make sure interviewers have all materials in time.
9. Edit each questionnaire.
10. Provide consistent and positive feedback to interviewers.
11. Not falsify any work.

CATI Systems enable on-line supervisors to monitor the screen as well as the conversation.

VALIDATION OF FIELD WORK

Validation of field work means verifying that the field workers are submitting authentic interviews. To validate the study, the supervisors call 10 to 25 percent of the respondents to inquire whether the field workers actually conducted the interviews. The supervisors ask about the length and quality of the interview, reaction to the interviewer, and basic demographic data. The demographic information is cross-checked against the information reported by the interviewers on the questionnaires.

EVALUATION OF FIELD WORKERS

It is important to evaluate field workers to provide them with feedback on their performance as well as to identify the better field workers and build a better, high-quality field force. The evaluation criteria should be clearly communicated to the field workers during their training. The evaluation of field workers should be based on the criteria of cost and time, response rates, quality of interviewing, and quality of data.[19]

Cost and Time

The interviewers can be compared in terms of the total cost (salary and expenses) per completed interview. If the costs differ by city size, comparisons should be made only among field workers working in comparable cities. The field workers should also be evaluated on how they spend their time. Time should be broken down into categories such as actual interviewing, travel, and administration.

Response Rates

It is important to monitor response rates on a timely basis so that corrective action can be taken if these rates are too low.[20] Supervisors can help interviewers with an inordinate number of refusals by listening to the introductions they use and providing immediate feedback. When all the interviews are over, different field workers' percentage of refusals can be compared to identify the better ones.

Quality of Interviewing

To evaluate interviewers on the quality of interviewing, the supervisor must directly observe the interviewing process. The supervisor can do this in person, or the field worker can tape record the interview. The quality of interviewing should be evaluated in terms of (1) the appropriateness of the introduction, (2) the precision with which the field worker asks questions, (3) the ability to probe in an unbiased manner, (4) the ability to ask sensitive questions, (5) interpersonal skills displayed during the interview, and (6) the manner in which the interview is terminated.

Quality of Data

The completed questionnaires of each interviewer should be evaluated for the quality of data. Some indicators of quality data are (1) the recorded data are legible, (2) all instructions, including skip patterns, are followed, (3) the answers to unstructured questions are recorded verbatim, (4) the answers to unstructured questions are meaningful and complete enough to be coded, and (5) item nonresponse occurs infrequently.

Guidelines on interviewing from the Council of American Survey Research Organizations are given in Research in Practice 13.4.

INTERNATIONAL MARKETING RESEARCH

The selection, training, supervision, and evaluation of field workers is critical in international marketing research. Local field work agencies are unavailable in many countries. Therefore, it may be necessary to recruit and train local field workers or import trained foreign workers.

RESEARCH IN PRACTICE 13.4

Guidelines on Interviewing: The Council of American Survey Research Organizations

Each interviewer is to follow these techniques for good interviewing:

1. Provide his or her full name, if asked by the respondent, as well as a phone number for the research firm.
2. Read each question exactly as written. Report any problems to the supervisor as soon as possible.
3. Read the questions in the order indicated on the questionnaire, following the proper skip sequences.
4. Clarify any question by the respondent in a neutral way.
5. Not mislead respondents as to the length of the interview.
6. Not reveal the identity of the ultimate client unless instructed to do so.
7. Keep a tally on each terminated interview and the reason for each termination.
8. Remain neutral in interviewing. Do not indicate agreement or disagreement with the respondent.
9. Speak slowly and distinctly so that words will be understood.
10. Record all replies verbatim, not paraphrased.
11. Avoid unnecessary conversations with the respondent.
12. Probe and clarify for additional comments on all open end questions, unless otherwise instructed. Probe and clarify in a neutral way.
13. Write neatly and legibly.
14. Check all work for thoroughness before turning in to the supervisor.
15. When terminating a respondent, do so in a neutral way such as, "Thank you," or "Our quota has already been filled in this area, but thank you anyway."
16. Keep all studies, materials, and findings confidential.
17. Not falsify any interviews or any answers to any question.
18. Thank the respondent for participating in the study.

The use of local field workers is desirable, as they are familiar with the local language and culture. They can thus create an appropriate climate for the interview and be sensitive to the concerns of the respondents. Extensive training may be required and close supervision may be necessary. As observed in many countries, interviewers tend to help the respondent with the answers and select household or sampling units based on personal considerations rather than the sampling plan. Finally, interviewer cheating may be more of a problem in many foreign countries than in the United States, given the lower work ethics. Validation of field work is critical. Proper application of field work procedures can greatly reduce these difficulties and result in consistent and useful findings, as the following example demonstrates.

EXAMPLE

Americanism Unites Europeans

An image study conducted by Research International, a U.K. market research company, showed that despite unification of the European market, European consumers still increasingly favor U.S. products. It is expected that Americanism will unite the consumers in Europe. The survey was conducted in Germany, the United Kingdom, Italy, and the Netherlands. In each country, local interviewers and supervisors were used as it was felt they would be able to identify better with the respondents. However, the field workers were trained extensively and supervised closely in order to ensure quality results and minimize the variability in country to country results due to differences in interviewing procedures.

A total of 6,724 personal interviews were conducted. Some of the findings were that Europeans gave U.S products high marks for being innovative and some countries also regarded them as fashionable and of high quality. Interestingly, France considered as anti-American, also emerged as pro-American. Among the 1,034 French consumers surveyed, 40 percent considered U.S. products fashionable and 38 percent believed they were innovative, whereas 15 percent said U.S. products were of high quality. In addition, when asked what nationality they preferred for a new company in their area, a U.S. company was the first choice. These findings were comparable and consistent across the four countries. A key to the discovery of these findings was the use of local field workers and extensive training and supervision, which resulted in high quality data.

This study is very useful for marketers to drum up and overplay the American brand name in the European market. "Rather than trying to hide the fact that they are American, we think companies ought to stress or try to exploit their American heritage," says Eric Salama, director of European operations for the Henley Center, the U.K. economic forecasting consultancy.[21] ■

ETHICS IN MARKETING RESEARCH

The data, whether collected by the internal marketing research department or by an external field work agency, should be obtained by following high ethical standards. The researchers and field workers should make the respondents feel comfortable by addressing their apprehensions. One way in which the comfort level of the respondents can be increased is by providing them with adequate information about the research firm, the project, addressing their questions, and clearly stating the responsibilities and expectations of the field workers and the respondents at the start of the interview. Moreover, the respondents should be told that they are not obligated to answer questions that make them uncomfortable, and that they can terminate the interview at any point should they experience discomfort. The researcher and field workers have an ethical responsibility to respect the respondents' privacy, feelings, and dignity."[22] Moreover, the respondents should be left with a positive and pleasant experience. This will enhance goodwill and future cooperation from respondents.

The researchers and the field work agencies are also responsible to the clients for following the accepted procedures for the selection, training, supervision, validation, and evaluation of field workers. They must ensure the integrity of the data collection process. The field work procedures should be carefully documented and made available to the clients. Appropriate actions by researchers and field work agencies can go a long way in addressing ethical concerns associated with field work, as illustrated by the following example.

EXAMPLE

Sophisticated Data Research Is Sophisticated in Its Field Work

Information provided while responding to an 800 number, using a credit card, or purchasing a product is often used to compile lists of customers and potential customers? These lists are rarely sold to telemarketing and direct marketing organizations. The public perception is different, however, and many people feel that marketers and marketing researchers misuse the information they collect. This misperception is giving marketing research a negative image.

In an effort to fight back, many marketing researchers and field work agencies are addressing these issues head-on at the start of the interview. For example, when contacting potential respondents, Sophisticated Data Research (SDR) of Atlanta provides them with information about the firm (SDR) and the marketing research project. The respondents are assured that SDR operates within a code of ethics. Some marketing research firms and field work agencies provide potential respondents with toll free numbers, which can be

FOCUS ON Burke

Burke makes sure that the interviewers assigned to each and every project have the proper training, motivation, supervision, and evaluation to make the research effective and efficient. How does it manage this process? The first step is to have good managers. Burke recruits to its management trainee program from the ranks of successful interviewers and universities. The employment of new recruits starts with a 6- to 12-month training program depending on background and rate of completing 24 two- to three-hour training modules and supervised (under a senior data collection manager) implementation of what they have learned. The focus is on data collection standard operating procedures. Additionally, the manager trainees are cross-trained in:

- Customer service procedures
- Sample management procedures and systems
- Human Resources management
- Interaction Management (employee relations, evaluation procedures, conflict resolution, etc.)

Burke's data collection area has full-time human resource professionals assigned to maintain the recruiting and training activities both for management and interviewers. To maintain a highly professional interviewing staff, Burke recruits from three basic target populations: college students, second income workers, and career interviewers. It uses a variety of media to reach these people:

- Advertising (newspaper and radio)
- Recruiting fairs/job expos/open houses
- Strong internal referral program
- College campuses
- Temporary staff services

Burke has adopted rigorous procedures for the selection and training of its field workers. As part of the initial screening the applicants are given simple literacy and numeracy tests. It is sad to say that a very high proportion of the applicants either fail these tests or pass marginally. In Burke's training process attention is given to improving these skills. At an early stage the applicants are put in to a group discussion session and observed in this exercise to determine their ability to listen and react logically and coherently to what they hear. After passing these checks, the final hiring decision is based on:

- Practice dialing under close supervision
- Listening and evaluation by supervisors
- Classroom drills and discussions of effective interviewing
- Ability to read and sound conversational
- Apparent professionalism
- Skill at implementing standard procedures and guidelines

The interviewers attend workshops on:

- Handling respondent refusals and interview terminations
- Efficiency in the interviewing process
- Vocalization workshop (enunciation, pronunciation, etc.)
- Typing skills
- Customer satisfaction training (interviewing as an identified representative of an organization)

To ensure the integrity of data collection for each project, Burke continually monitors for quality and consistency across interviewers through:

- Daily listening and evaluating on every project, every interviewer
- Standardized reports generated by the CATI system
- Interview length by interviewer
- Termination rate by interviewer
- Dialing disposition by interviewer
- On-line time, open-end detail report
- Senior management involvement through open monitoring program in which managers listen at random to interviewers.

called to obtain more information or verify the information given by the field workers. Such actions make the respondents more comfortable and informed, and result in higher-quality data for the clients.[23] ■

INTERNET AND COMPUTER APPLICATIONS

Regardless of which method is used for interviewing (telephone, personal, mail, or electronic), the Internet can play a valuable role in all the phases of field work: selection, training, supervision, validation, and evaluation of field workers. As far as selection is concerned, interviewers can be located, interviewed, and hired by using the Internet. This process can be initiated, for example, by posting job vacancies notices for interviewers at the company Web site, bulletin boards, and other suitable locations. While this would confine the search to only Internet-savvy interviewers, this may well be a qualification to look for in the current marketing research environment.

Similarly, the Internet with its multimedia capabilities can be a good supplementary tool for training the field workers in all aspects of interviewing. Training in this manner can complement personal training programs and add value to the process. Supervision is enhanced by facilitating communication between the supervisors and the interviewers via e-mail and secured chatrooms. Central office control can be strengthened by posting progress reports, quality, and cost-control information on a secured location at a Web site, so that it is easily available to all the relevant parties.

Validation of field work, especially for personal and telephone interviews, can be easily accomplished for those respondents who have an e-mail address or access to the Internet. These respondents can be sent a short verification survey by e-mail or asked to visit a Web site where the survey is posted. Finally, the evaluation criteria can be communicated to the field workers during the training stage by using the Internet, and performance feedback can also be provided to them by using this medium.

Microcomputers and mainframes, such as the Ci3 System by Sawtooth Software, Inc., can be used in field work for respondent selection, interviewer planning, supervision, and control. Ci3 CATI's ability to guide the interview process makes it a valuable asset in marketing research. Computers can also be used to manage mailing lists. For example, the mailing lists can be sorted according to zip codes, geographical regions, or other prespecified characteristics. Computers can also electronically monitor mail survey nonresponse. Computers can generate accurate and timely reports for supervision and control purposes. These include quota reports, **call disposition** reports, incidence reports, top-line reports of respondent data, and interviewer productivity reports. Automatic reporting enhances supervision and control and increases the overall quality of data collection. Because less time is spent compiling reports, more time can be spent on data interpretation and on supervision.

Call Disposition Call disposition records the outcome of an interview call.

SUMMARY

Researchers have two major options for collecting data: developing their own organizations or contracting with field work agencies. In either case, data collection involves the use of a field force. Field workers should be healthy, outgoing, communicative, pleasant, educated, and experienced. They should be trained in important aspects of field work, including making the initial contact, asking the questions, probing, recording the answers, and terminating the interview. Supervision of field workers involves quality control and editing, sampling control, control of cheating, and central office control. Validation of field work can be accomplished by calling 10 to 25 percent of those who have been identified as interviewees and inquiring whether the interviews took place. Field workers should be evaluated on the basis of cost and time, response rates, quality of interviewing, and quality of data collection.

The selection, training, supervision, and evaluation of field workers is even more critical in international marketing research as local field work agencies are not available in many countries. Ethical issues include making the respondents feel comfortable in the data collection process so that their experience is positive. Every effort must be undertaken to ensure that the data are of high quality. The Internet and computers can greatly facilitate and improve the quality of field work.

KEY TERMS AND CONCEPTS

probing
sampling control
call disposition

ACRONYMS

In the field work/data collection process, the organization VESTS in the field workers:

V alidation of field work
E valuation of field workers
S election of field workers
T raining of field workers
S upervision of field workers

The areas in which field workers should be trained may be summarized by the acronym TRAIN:

T erminating the interview
R ecording the answers
A sking the questions
I nitial contact development
N osy behavior: probing

EXERCISES

Questions

1. What options are available to researchers for collecting data?
2. Describe the field work/data collection process.
3. What qualifications should field workers possess?
4. What are the guidelines for asking questions?
5. What is probing?
6. How should the answers to unstructured questions be recorded?
7. How should the field worker terminate the interview?
8. What aspects are involved in the supervision of field workers?
9. How can respondent selection problems be controlled?
10. What is validation of field work? How is this done?
11. Describe the criteria that should be used for evaluating field workers.
12. Describe the major sources of error related to field work.

Problems

1. Write some interviewer instructions for in-home personal interviews to be conducted by students.
2. Comment on the following field situations, making recommendations for corrective action.
   a. One of the interviewers has an excessive rate of refusals in in-home personal interviewing.
   b. In a CATI situation, many phone numbers are giving a busy signal during the first dialing attempt.
   c. An interviewer reports that, at the end of the interviews, many respondents asked if they had answered the questions correctly.
   d. While validating the field work, a respondent reports that she cannot remember being interviewed over the telephone, but the interviewer insists that the interview was conducted.

INTERNET AND COMPUTER EXERCISES

1. Visit the Web sites of some marketing research suppliers. Make a report of all the material related to field work that is posted on these sites.
2. Visit the Marketing Research Association Web site (www.mra-net.org) and examine the ethical codes relating to data collection. Write a brief report.
3. Using PERT/CPM software such as MacProject, Timeline, Harvard Project Manager, Microsoft Project, or Category PERTmaster, develop a field work schedule for conducting a national survey of consumer preferences for fast foods involving 2,500 mall-intercept interviews in Los Angeles, Salt Lake City, Dallas, St. Louis, Milwaukee, New Orleans, Cincinnati, Orlando, Atlanta, New York City, and Boston.

Chapter 14

"No matter how often you hear 'garbage in . . . garbage out,' this must be your mantra when working with data."

Donna Closterman, senior vice president, administration, Burke, Inc.

Data Preparation

OBJECTIVES

After reading this chapter, the student should be able to

1. discuss the nature and scope of data preparation and the data preparation process
2. explain questionnaire checking and editing, and treatment of unsatisfactory responses by returning to the field, assigning missing values, and discarding unsatisfactory responses
3. describe the guidelines for coding questionnaires including the coding of structured and unstructured questions
4. discuss the data-cleaning process and the methods used to treat missing responses: substitution of a neutral value, imputed response, casewise deletion, and pairwise deletion
5. state the reasons for and methods of statistically adjusting data: weighting, variable respecification, and scale transformation
6. describe the procedure for selecting a data analysis strategy and the factors influencing the process
7. classify statistical techniques and give a detailed classification of univariate techniques as well as a classification of multivariate techniques
8. understand the intracultural, pan-cultural, and cross-cultural approaches to data analysis in international marketing research
9. identify the ethical issues related to data processing, particularly the discarding of unsatisfactory responses, violation of the assumptions underlying the data analysis techniques, and evaluation and interpretation of results
10. explain the use of the Internet and computers in data preparation and analysis

OVERVIEW

After the research problem has been defined and a suitable approach developed (chapter 2), an appropriate research design formulated (chapters 3 to 12) and the field work conducted (chapter 13), the researcher can move on to data preparation and analysis, the fifth step of the marketing research process. Before the raw data contained in the questionnaires can be subjected to statistical analysis, they must be converted into a form suitable for analysis. The quality of statistical results depends on the care exercised in the data preparation phase. Paying inadequate attention to data preparation can seriously compromise statistical results, leading to biased findings and incorrect interpretation.

This chapter describes the data collection process, which begins with checking the questionnaires for completeness. Then, we discuss the editing of data and provide guidelines for handling illegible, incomplete, inconsistent, ambiguous, or otherwise unsatisfactory responses. We also describe coding, transcribing, and data cleaning, emphasizing the treatment of missing responses and statistical adjustment of data. We discuss the selection of a data analysis strategy and classify statistical techniques. The intracultural, pancultural, and cross-cultural approaches to data analysis in international marketing research are explained. The ethical issues related to data processing are identified with emphasis on discarding unsatisfactory responses, violation of the assumptions underlying the data analysis techniques, and evaluation and interpretation of results. Finally, we explain the use of the Internet and computers in data preparation and analysis.

We begin with some examples of data preparation.

EXAMPLE

Custom Cleaning

According to Joann Harristhal of Custom Research, Inc., completed questionnaires from the field often have many small errors because of the inconsistent quality of interviewing. For example, qualifying responses are not circled or skip patterns are not followed accurately.

DEPARTMENT STORE PATRONAGE PROJECT

Data Preparation

In the department store patronage project, the data were obtained by in-home personal interviews. The questionnaires were edited by the supervisors as they were being turned in by the interviewers. The questionnaires were checked for incomplete, inconsistent, and ambiguous responses. Questionnaires with unsatisfactory responses were returned to the field, and the interviewers were asked to recontact the respondents to obtain the required information. Nine questionnaires were discarded because the proportion of unsatisfactory responses was large. This resulted in a final sample size of 271.

A code book was developed for coding the questionnaires. Coding was relatively simple because there were no open-ended questions. The data were transcribed onto a computer tape via key-punching. About 25 percent of the data were verified for key punching errors. The data were cleaned by identifying out-of-range and logically inconsistent responses. Most of the rating information was obtained using 6-point scales, so responses of 0, 7, and 8 were considered out of range, and a code of 9 was assigned to missing responses.

Any missing responses were treated by casewise deletion, in which respondents with any missing values were dropped from the analysis. Casewise deletion was selected because the number of cases (respondents) with missing values was small and the sample size was sufficiently large. In statistically adjusting the data, dummy variables were created for the categorical variables. New variables that were composites of original variables were also created. For example, the familiarity ratings of the ten department stores were summed to create a familiarity index. Finally, a data analysis strategy was developed.

These small errors can be costly. When responses from such questionnaires are put into a computer, Custom Research runs a cleaning program that checks for completeness and logic. Discrepancies are identified on a computer printout, which is checked by the tabulation supervisors. Once the errors are identified, appropriate corrective action is taken before data analysis is carried out. Custom Research has found that this procedure substantially increases the quality of statistical results.[1] ■

The department store example describes the various phases of the data preparation process. Note that the process is initiated while the field work is still in progress. The Custom Research example describes the importance of cleaning data, and identifying and correcting errors before the data are analyzed. A systematic description of the data preparation process follows.

THE DATA PREPARATION PROCESS

The data preparation process is shown in Figure 14.1. The entire process is guided by the preliminary plan of data analysis that was formulated in the research design phase (chapter 3). The first step is to check for acceptable questionnaires. This is followed by editing, coding, and transcribing the data. The data are cleaned and a treatment for missing responses prescribed. Often, statistical adjustment of the data may be necessary to make them representative of the population of interest. The researcher should then select an appropriate data analysis strategy. The final data analysis strategy differs from the preliminary plan of data analysis due to the information and insights gained since the preliminary plan was formulated. Data preparation should begin as soon as the first batch of questionnaires is received from the field, while the field work is still going on. Thus, if any problems are detected, the field work can be modified to incorporate corrective action.

Figure 14.1
Data Preparation Process

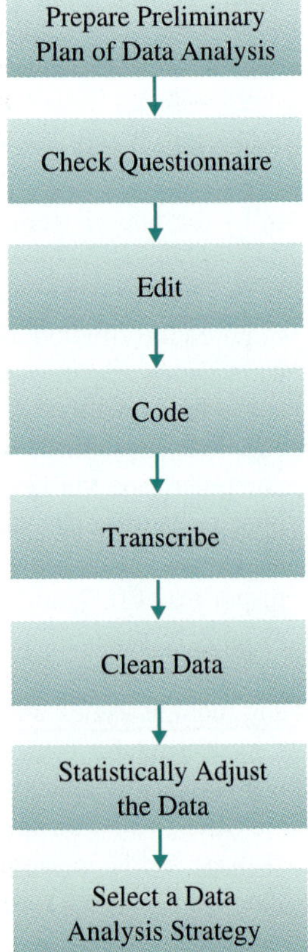

QUESTIONNAIRE CHECKING

The initial step in questionnaire checking involves a check of all questionnaires for completeness and interviewing quality. Often these checks are made while field work is still underway. If the field work was contracted to a data collection agency, the researcher should make an independent check after it is over. A questionnaire returned from the field may be unacceptable for several reasons:

1. Parts of the questionnaire may be incomplete.
2. The pattern of responses may indicate that the respondent did not understand or follow the instructions. For example, skip patterns may not have been followed.
3. The responses show little variance. For example, a respondent has checked only 4s on a series of 7-point rating scales.
4. The returned questionnaire is physically incomplete—one or more pages is missing.
5. The questionnaire is received after the preestablished cutoff date.
6. The questionnaire is answered by someone who does not qualify for participation.

If quotas or cell group sizes have been imposed, the acceptable questionnaires should be classified and counted accordingly. Any problems in meeting the sampling requirements should be identified and corrective action taken, such as conducting additional interviews in the underrepresented cells, before the data are edited.

EDITING

Editing is the review of the questionnaires with the objective of increasing accuracy and precision. It consists of screening questionnaires to identify illegible, incomplete, inconsistent, or ambiguous responses.

Editing A review of the questionnaires with the objective of increasing accuracy and precision.

Responses may be illegible if they have been poorly recorded. This is particularly common in questionnaires with a large number of unstructured questions. The data must be legible if they are to be properly coded. Likewise, questionnaires may be incomplete to varying degrees. A few or many questions may be unanswered.

At this stage, the researcher makes a preliminary check for consistency. Certain obvious inconsistencies can be easily detected. For example, a respondent reports an annual income of less than $20,000 yet indicates frequent shopping at prestigious department stores such as Saks Fifth Avenue and Neiman-Marcus.

Responses to unstructured questions may be ambiguous and difficult to interpret clearly. The answer may be abbreviated, or some ambiguous words may have been used. For structured questions, more than one response may be marked for a question designed to elicit a single response. Suppose a respondent circles 2 and 3 on a 5-point rating scale. Does this mean that 2.5 was intended? To complicate matters further, the coding procedure may allow for only a single digit response.

Treatment of Unsatisfactory Responses

Unsatisfactory responses are commonly handled by returning to the field to get better data, assigning missing values, and discarding unsatisfactory respondents.

Returning to the Field. The questionnaires with unsatisfactory responses may be returned to the field, where the interviewers recontact the respondents. This approach is particularly attractive for business and industrial marketing surveys, in which the sample sizes are small and the respondents are easily identifiable. However, the data obtained the second time may be different from those obtained during the original survey. These differences may be attributed to changes over time or differences in the mode of questionnaire administration (e.g., telephone versus in-person interview).

Assigning Missing Values. If returning the questionnaires to the field is not feasible, the editor may assign missing values to unsatisfactory responses. This approach may be desirable if (1) the number of respondents with unsatisfactory responses is small, (2) the proportion of unsatisfactory responses for each of these respondents is small, or (3) the variables with unsatisfactory responses are not the key variables.

Discarding Unsatisfactory Respondents. In this approach, the respondents with unsatisfactory responses are simply discarded. This approach may have merit when (1) the proportion of unsatisfactory respondents is small (less than 10 percent), (2) the sample size is large, (3) the unsatisfactory respondents do not differ from satisfactory respondents in obvious ways (e.g., demographics, product usage characteristics), (4) the proportion of unsatisfactory responses for each of these respondents is large, or (5) responses on key variables are missing. However, unsatisfactory respondents may differ from satisfactory respondents in systematic ways and the decision to designate a respondent as unsatisfactory may be subjective. Both these factors bias the results. If the researcher decides to discard unsatisfactory respondents, the procedure adopted to identify these respondents and their number should be reported, as in the following example.

EXAMPLE

Declaring Discards

In a cross-cultural survey of marketing managers from English-speaking African countries, questionnaires were mailed to 565 firms. A total of 192 completed questionnaires were returned, of which four were discarded because respondents suggested that they were not in charge of overall marketing decisions. The decision to discard the four questionnaires was based on the consideration that the sample size was sufficiently large and the proportion of unsatisfactory respondents was small.[2] ■

CODING

Coding The assignment of a code to represent a specific response to a specific question along with the data record and column position that code will occupy.

Coding means assigning a code, usually a number, to each possible response to each question. The code includes an indication of the column position (field) and data record it will occupy. For example, sex of respondents may be coded as 1 for females and 2 for males. A field represents a single item of data, such as sex of the respondent. A record consists of related fields, such as sex, marital status, age, household size, occupation, etc. All the demographic and personality characteristics of a respondent may be contained in a single record. Normally, each record has 80 columns, although this is not a requirement. A number of records may be used for each respondent.

The data (all the records) for all the respondents are stored in a computer file, as illustrated in Table 14.1. In this table, the columns represent the fields and the rows the records. Table 14.1 presents coded data for part of the first record for respondents in the department store patronage project. These data have been coded according to the coding scheme specified in Figure 14.2. Columns 1–3 represent a single field and contain the respondent numbers coded 001 to 271. Column 4 contains the record number. This column has a value of 1 for all the rows as only the first record of the respondents is displayed. Columns 5–6 contain the project code, which is 31. The next two columns, 7–8, display the interviewer code, which varies from 01 to 55, as 55 interviewers were used. Columns 26–35, each one representing a field, contain familiarity ratings for the 10 stores, with values ranging from 1 to 6. Finally, column 77 represents the rating of store 10 on prices. Note that columns 78 to 80 are blank. There are ten records for each respondent. There are 2,710 rows, indicating that data for 271 respondents are stored in this file.

TABLE 14.1

ILLUSTRATIVE COMPUTER FILE: DEPARTMENT STORE PATRONAGE PROJECT

			Fields				
			Column Numbers				
RECORDS	*1–3*	*4*	*5–6*	*7–8*	. . .	*26 . . . 35*	*77*
Record #1	001	1	31	01		6544234553	5
Record #11	002	1	31	01		5564435433	4
Record #21	003	1	31	01		4655243324	4
Record #31	004	1	31	01		5463244645	6
Record #2701	271	1	31	55		6652354435	5

Figure 14.2
Codebook Excerpt Showing Information for the First Record: Department Store Patronage Project

Column Number	*Variable Number*	*Variable Name*	*Question Number*	*Coding Instructions*
1–3	1	Respondent ID		001 to 890 add leading zeros as necessary
4	2	Record number		1 (same for all respondents)
5–6	3	Project code		31 (same for all respondents)
7–8	4	Interview code		As coded on the questionnaire
9–14	5	Date code		As coded on the questionnaire
15–20	6	Time code		As coded on the questionnaire
21–22	7	Validation code		As coded on the questionnaire
23–24		Blank		Leave these columns blank
25	8	Who shops	I	Male head = 1 Female head = 2 Other = 3 **Input the number circled** Missing values = 9
26	9	Familiarity with store 1	IIa	For question II parts a through j, **input the number circled**
27	10	Familiarity with store 2	IIb	Not so familiar = 1 Very familiar = 6 Missing values = 9
28	11	Familiarity with store 3	IIc	
35	18	Familiarity with store 10	IIj	
36	19	Frequency : store 1	IIIa	For question III parts a through j, **input the number circled**
37	20	Frequency : store 2	IIIb	Not at all = 1 Very frequently = 6 Missing values = 9
45	28	Frequency : store 10	IIIj	
46–47		Blank		Leave these columns blank
48	29	Rating of store 1 on quality	IVa	For store IV through XI, **input the number circled**
57	38	Rating of store 10 on quality	IVa	
58	39	Ratings of store 1 on variety	IVb	
67	48	Rating of store 10 on variety	IVb	
68	49	Rating of store 1 on prices	IVc	
77	58	Rating of store 10 on prices	IVc	
78–80		Blank		Leave these columns blank

If the questionnaire contains only structured questions or very few unstructured questions, it is precoded. This means that codes are assigned before field work is conducted. If the questionnaire contains unstructured questions, codes are assigned after the questionnaires have been returned from the field (postcoding).[3] Precoding was briefly discussed in chapter 10 on questionnaire design; further guidelines are provided below.[4]

Coding Questions

Fixed Field Code A code in which the number of records for each respondent is the same, and the same data appear in the same columns for all respondents.

The respondent code and the record number should appear on each record in the data. The following additional codes should be included for each respondent: project code, interviewer code, date and time codes, and validation code. **Fixed field codes**, in which the number of records for each respondent is the same and the same data appear in the same column(s) for all respondents, are highly desirable. If possible, standard codes should be used for missing data. For example, a code of 9 could be used for a single column variable, 99 for a double-column variable, and so on. The missing value codes should be distinct from the codes assigned to the legitimate responses.

Coding of structured questions is relatively simple, because the response options are predetermined. The researcher assigns a code for each response to each question and specifies the appropriate record and columns in which the response codes are to appear. For example,

Do you have a currently valid passport?
1. Yes 2. No (2/54)

For this question, a "Yes" response is coded 1 and a "No" response 2. The numbers in parentheses indicate that the code assigned will appear on the second record for this respondent in column 54. Because only one response is allowed, and there are only two possible responses (1 or 2), a single column is sufficient. In general, a single column is sufficient to code a structured question with a single response if there are fewer than nine possible responses.

In questions that permit a large number of responses, each possible response option should be assigned a separate column. Such questions include those about brand ownership or usage, magazine readership, and television viewing. For example,

Which accounts do you* now *have at this bank? ("X" as many as apply)

		Record #9
Regular savings account	❑	(62)
Regular checking account	❑	(63)
Mortgage	❑	(64)
NOW account	❑	(65)
Club account (Christmas, etc.)	❑	(66)
Line of credit	❑	(67)
Term savings account (time deposits, etc.)	❑	(68)
Savings bank life insurance	❑	(69)
Home improvement loan	❑	(70)
Auto loan	❑	(71)
Other services	❑	(72)

In this example, suppose a respondent checked regular savings, regular checking, and term savings accounts. On record #9, a 1 will be entered in the column numbers 62, 63, and 68. All the other columns (64, 65, 66, 67, 69, 70, 71, and 72) will receive a 0.

The coding of unstructured or open-ended questions is more complex. Respondents' verbatim responses are recorded on the questionnaire. Codes are then developed and assigned to these responses. Sometimes, based on previous projects or theoretical considerations, the researcher can develop the codes before beginning field work. Usually, this must wait until the completed questionnaires are received. Then the researcher lists 50 to 100 responses to an unstructured question to identify the categories suitable for coding. Once codes are developed the coders should be trained to assign the correct codes to the verbatim responses. The following guidelines are suggested for coding unstructured questions and questionnaires in general.[5]

Category codes should be mutually exclusive and collectively exhaustive. Categories are mutually exclusive if each response fits into one and only one category code. Categories should not overlap. Categories are collectively exhaustive if every response fits into one of the assigned category codes. This can be achieved by adding an additional category code of "other" or "none of the above." However, only a few (10 percent or less) of the responses should fall into this category. The vast majority of the responses should be classified into meaningful categories.

Category codes should be assigned for critical issues even if no one has mentioned them. It may be important to know that no one has mentioned a particular response. For example, the management of a major consumer goods company was concerned about the packaging for a new brand of bath soap. Hence, packaging was included as a separate category in coding responses to the question, "What do you like least about this bath soap?"

Data should be coded to retain as much detail as possible. For example, if data on the exact number of trips made on commercial airlines by business travelers have been obtained, they should be coded as such, rather than grouped into two category codes of "infrequent fliers" and "frequent fliers." Obtaining information on the exact number of trips allows the researcher to later define categories of business travelers in several different ways. If the categories were predefined, the subsequent analysis of data would be limited by those categories.

Codebook

A **codebook** contains coding instructions and the necessary information about variables in the data set. A codebook guides the coders in their work and helps the researcher to properly identify and locate the variables. Even if the questionnaire has been precoded, it is helpful to prepare a formal codebook. A codebook generally contains the following information: (1) column number, (2) record number, (3) variable number, (4) variable name, (5) question number, and (6) instructions for coding. Figure 14.2 is an excerpt from a coding book developed for the department store patronage project.

Codebook A book containing coding instructions and the necessary information about variables in the data set.

Coding Questionnaires

Figure 14.3 is an example of questionnaire coding, showing the coding of part of the questionnaire used in the department store patronage project. This questionnaire was precoded. The respondent code and the record number appear on each record in the data. The first record contains the additional codes: project code, interviewer code, date and time codes, and validation code. It is a good practice to insert blanks between parts. Sometimes, instead of writing the codes on the questionnaire, the codes are written on special 80-column paper called coding sheets.

TRANSCRIBING

Transcribing data involves transferring the coded data from the questionnaires or coding sheets onto disks or magnetic tapes or directly into computers by key-punching. If the data have been collected via CATI or CAPI, this step is unnecessary as the data are entered directly into the computer as they are collected. Besides key-punching, the data can be transferred by using mark sense forms, optical scanning, or computerized sensory analysis (see Figure 14.4). Mark sense forms require responses to be recorded with a special pencil in a predesignated area coded for that response. The data can then be read by a machine. Optical scanning involves direct machine reading of the codes and simultaneous transcription. A familiar example of optical scanning is the transcription of UPC (universal product

Figure 14.3
Example of Questionnaire Coding Showing Coding of Demographic Data

Finally, in this part of the questionnaire we would like to ask you some background information for classification purposes.

PART D **Record #7**

1. This questionnaire was answered by (29)
  1. ______ Primarily the male head of household
  2. ______ Primarily the female head of household
  3. ______ Jointly by the male and female heads of household

2. Marital Status (30)
  1. ______ Married
  2. ______ Never Married
  3. ______ Divorced/Separated/Widowed

3. What is the total number of family members living at home? ______ (31–32)

4. Number of children living at home:
  a. Under six years ______ (33)
  b. Over six years ______ (34)

5. Number of children not living at home ______ (35)

6. Number of years of formal education which you (and your spouse, if applicable) have completed. (please circle)

	High School	College Undergraduate	Graduate	
a. You	8 or less 9 10 11 12	13 14 15 16	17 18 19 20 21 22 or more	(36–37)
b. Spouse	8 or less 9 10 11 12	13 14 15 16	17 18 19 20 21 22 or more	(38–39)

7. a. Your age: ______ (40–41)
  b. Age of spouse (if applicable) ______ (42–43)

8. If employed please indicate your household's occupations by checking the appropriate category.

	44 Male Head	45 Female Head
1. Professional and technical	______	______
2. Managers and administrators	______	______
3. Sales workers	______	______
4. Clerical and kindred workers	______	______
5. Craftsman/operative/laborers	______	______
6. Homemakers	______	______
7. Others (please specify)	______	______
8. Not applicable	______	______

9. Is your place of residence presently owned by household? (46)
  1. Owned ______
  2. Rented ______

10. How many years have you been residing in the greater Atlanta area?
  ______ years. (47–48)

11. What is the approximate combined annual income of your household before taxes? Please check. (49–50)

01. Less than $10,000 ______	**08.** $40,000 to 44,999 ______
02. $10,000 to 14,999 ______	**09.** $45,000 to 49,999 ______
03. $15,000 to 19,999 ______	**10.** $50,000 to 54,999 ______
04. $20,000 to 24,999 ______	**11.** $55,000 to 59,999 ______
05. $25,000 to 29,999 ______	**12.** $60,000 to 69,999 ______
06. $30,000 to 34,999 ______	**13.** $70,000 to 89,999 ______
07. $35,000 to 39,999 ______	**14.** $90,000 and over ______

Note: Columns 1–3 of this record contain the respondent ID, column 4 the record number (7), columns 5 and 6 are blank. Columns 7 through 27 contain information from part C, and column 28 is blank. Thus, information on Part D is coded beginning with column number 29.

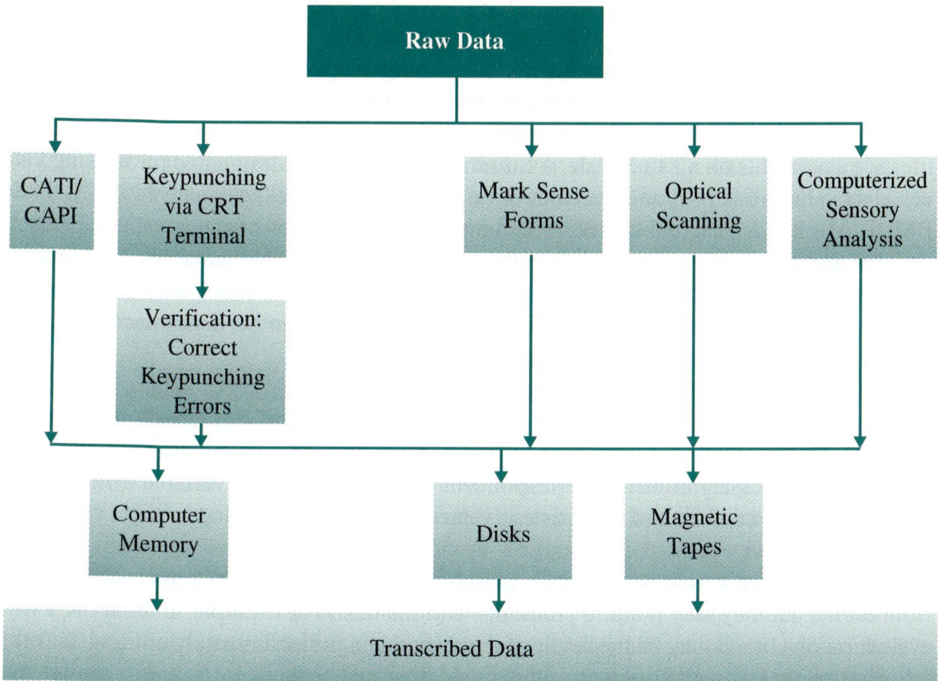

Figure 14.4
Data Transcription

code) data at supermarket checkout counters. Technological advances have resulted in computerized sensory analysis systems, which automate the data collection process. The questions appear on a computerized gridpad, and responses are recorded directly into the computer using a sensing device.

If key-punching is used, errors can occur, and it is necessary to verify the data set, or at least a portion of it, for key-punching errors. A verifier machine and a second operator are utilized for data verification. The second operator repunches the data from the coded questionnaires. The transcribed data from the two operators are compared record by record. Any discrepancy between the two sets of transcribed data is investigated to identify and correct for key-punching errors. Verification of the entire data set will double the time and cost of data transcription. Given the time and cost constraints, as well as the fact that experienced keypunch operators are quite accurate, it is sufficient to verify only 25 to 50 percent of the data.

When CATI or CAPI are employed, data are verified as they are collected. In the case of inadmissible responses, the computer will prompt the interviewer or respondent. In case of admissible responses, the interviewer or the respondent can see the recorded response on the screen and verify it before proceeding.

The selection of a data transcription method is guided by the type of interviewing method used and the availability of equipment. If CATI or CAPI are used, the data are entered directly into the computer. Key-punching via CRT terminal is most frequently used for ordinary telephone, in-home, mall-intercept, and mail interviews. However, the use of computerized sensory analysis systems in personal interviews is increasing with the increasing use of gridpads and handheld computers. Optical scanning can be used in structured and repetitive surveys and mark sense forms are used in special cases.[6]

DATA CLEANING

Data Cleaning Thorough and extensive checks for consistency and treatment of missing responses.

Data cleaning includes consistency checks and treatment of missing responses. While preliminary consistency checks have been made during editing, the checks at this stage are more thorough and extensive, because they are made by computer.

(intracultural analysis), and (3) across countries or cultural units: pan-cultural or cross-cultural analysis. Several ethical issues are related to data processing particularly the discarding of unsatisfactory responses, violation of the assumptions underlying the data analysis techniques, and evaluation and interpretation of results. The Internet and computers play a significant role in data preparation and analysis.

KEY TERMS AND CONCEPTS

editing
coding
fixed field codes
codebook
data cleaning
consistency checks
missing responses
casewise deletion
pairwise deletion
weighting
variable respecification
dummy variables
scale transformation
standardization
univariate techniques
multivariate techniques
metric data
nonmetric data
dependence techniques
interdependence techniques
intracultural analysis
pan-cultural analysis
cross-cultural analysis

ACRONYMS

The data preparation process may be summarized by the acronym DATA PREP:

D ata cleaning
A djusting the data statistically
T ranscribing
A nalysis strategy

P ost–field work questionnaire checking
R ecording numerical or alphanumerical values: coding
E diting
P reliminary plan of data analysis

EXERCISES

Questions

1. Describe the data preparation process.
2. What activities are involved in the preliminary checking of questionnaires that have been returned from the field?
3. What is meant by editing a questionnaire?
4. How are unsatisfactory responses discovered in editing treated?
5. What is the difference between precoding and postcoding?
6. Describe the guidelines for the coding of unstructured questions.
7. What does transcribing the data involve?
8. What kinds of consistency checks are made in cleaning the data?
9. How are missing data treated?
10. What kinds of statistical adjustments are sometimes made to the data?
11. Describe the weighting process. What are the reasons for weighting?
12. What are dummy variables? Why are such variables created?
13. Explain why scale transformations are made.
14. Which scale transformation procedure is most commonly used? Briefly describe this procedure.
15. What considerations are involved in selecting a data analysis strategy?

Problems

1. Develop dummy variable coding schemes for the following variables.
   - Sex
   - Marital status consisting of the following four categories: never married, now married, divorced, other (separated, widowed, etc.)
   - Frequency of international travel, measured as:

a. Do not travel abroad
b. Travel abroad 1 or 2 times a year
c. Travel abroad 3 to 5 times a year
d. Travel abroad 6 to 8 times a year
e. Travel abroad more than 8 times a year

2. Shown below is part of a questionnaire used to determine consumer preferences for cameras. Set up a coding scheme for these three questions.

9. Please rate the importance of the following features you would consider when shopping for a new camera.

	Not so important				*Very important*
a. DX film speed setting	1	2	3	4	5
b. Auto-film advance	1	2	3	4	5
c. Autofocus	1	2	3	4	5
d. Autoloading	1	2	3	4	5

10. If you were to buy a new camera, which of the following outlets would you visit? Please check as many as apply.
a. ____ Drugstore
b. ____ Camera store
c. ____ Discount/mass merchandiser
d. ____ Supermarket
e. ____ Other

11. Where do you get most of your photo processing done? Please check only one option.
a. ____ Drugstore
b. ____ Mini labs
c. ____ Camera stores
d. ____ Discount/mass merchandiser
e. ____ Supermarkets
f. ____ Mail order
g. ____ Kiosk/other

INTERNET AND COMPUTER EXERCISES

1. Explain how you would make consistency checks for the questionnaire given in problem 2 above using SPSS, SAS, BMDP, Minitab, or Excel.
2. Use an electronic questionnaire design and administration package such as Ci3 to program the camera preference questionnaire given in problem 2. Add one or two questions of your own. Administer the questionnaire to five students and prepare the data for analysis. Does computer administration of the questionnaire facilitate data preparation?

Chapter 15

"Cross-tabulations and frequency distributions are the fundamental building blocks of analysis. They offer a simple and quick look at the data. This simplicity is both a virtue and a problem. They are a great starting point but not sufficient, in most cases, for a complete analysis."

Betty Fraley,
vice president,
account management,
Burke, Inc.

Frequency Distribution, Cross-Tabulation, and Hypothesis Testing

OBJECTIVES

At the end of this chapter, the student should be able to

1. describe the significance of preliminary data analysis and the insights that can be obtained from such an analysis
2. discuss data analysis associated with frequencies including measures of location, measures of variability, and measures of shape
3. explain data analysis associated with cross-tabulations and the associated statistics: chi-square, phi coefficient, contingency coefficient, Cramer's V, and lambda coefficient
4. describe data analysis associated with parametric hypothesis testing for one sample, two independent samples, and paired samples
5. understand data analysis associated with nonparametric hypothesis testing for one sample, two independent samples, and paired samples

OVERVIEW

Once the data have been prepared for analysis (chapter 14), the researcher should conduct some basic analysis. This chapter describes basic data analysis including frequency distribution, cross-tabulation, and hypothesis testing. First, we describe the frequency distribution and explain how it provides both an indication of the number of out-of-range, missing, or extreme values as well as insights into the central tendency, variability, and shape of the underlying distribution. Next, we introduce hypothesis testing by describing the general procedure. Hypothesis testing procedures are classified as tests of associations or tests of differences. We consider the use of cross-tabulation for understanding the associations between variables taken two or three at a time. Although the nature of the association can be observed from tables, statistics are available for examining the significance and strength of the association. Finally, we present tests for examining hypotheses related to differences based on one or two samples.

Many commercial marketing research projects do not go beyond basic data analysis. These findings are often displayed using tables and graphs, as discussed further in chapter 22.

DEPARTMENT STORE PATRONAGE PROJECT

Basic Data Analysis

In the department store patronage project, basic data analysis formed the foundation for conducting subsequent multivariate analysis. Data analysis began by obtaining a frequency distribution and descriptive statistics for each variable. In addition to identifying possible problems with the data (see chapter 14), this information provided a good feel for the data and insights into how specific variables should be treated in subsequent analyses. For example, should some variables be treated as categorical, and, if so, how many categories should there be? Several two- and three-variable cross-tabulations were also conducted to identify associations in the data. The effects of variables with two categories on the metric dependent variables of interest were examined by means of *t* tests and other hypotheses testing procedures.

The findings of basic analysis are valuable in their own right, but they also provide guidance for conducting multivariate analysis. The insights gained from the basic analysis are also invaluable in interpreting the results obtained from more sophisticated statistical techniques. To provide the reader with a flavor of these techniques, we illustrate the use of cross-tabulation, chi-square analysis, and hypothesis testing.

EXAMPLE

Commercial Battle of the Sexes

Cross-tabulation and chi-square analysis reveal that in the United States men appear in commercials for products used by either sex.

A comparison of television advertising in Australia, Mexico, and the United States focused on the analysis of sex roles in advertising. Results showed differences in the portrayal of the sexes in different countries. Australian advertisements revealed somewhat fewer, and Mexican advertisements slightly more, sex-role differences than did U.S. advertisements. Cross-tabulation and chi-square analysis provided the following information for Mexico.

Product Advertised Used by	*Persons Appearing in the Ad (%):* Women	Men
Females	25.0	4.0
Males	6.8	11.8
Either	68.2	84.2
	$\chi^2 = 19.73, p \leq .001$	

These results indicate that in Mexican commercials, women appeared in commercials for products used by women or by either sex but rarely in commercials for men's products. Men appeared in commercials for products used by either sex. These differences were also found in the U.S. ads, although to a lesser extent, but were not found in Australian ads.[1] ■

EXAMPLE

Catalogs Are Risky Business

Catalog shopping is perceived more risky than shopping at retail stores as revealed by paired *t* tests.

Twelve product categories were examined to compare catalog to store shopping. The hypothesis—that there is no significant difference in the overall amount of risk perceived when buying products by catalog compared to buying the same products in a retail store—was rejected. The hypothesis was tested by computing 12 (one for each product) paired-observations *t* tests. Mean scores for overall perceived risk for some of the products in both buying situations are presented in the following table, with higher scores indicating greater risk.

MEAN SCORES OF OVERALL PERCEIVED RISK FOR PRODUCTS BY PURCHASE MODE

	Overall Perceived Risk	
Product	*Catalog*	*Retail Store*
Stereo hi-fi	48.89	41.98*
Record albums	32.65	28.74*
Dress shoes	58.60	50.80*
13-inch color TV	48.53	40.91*
Athletic socks	35.22	30.22*
Pocket calculator	49.62	42.00*
35 mm camera	48.13	39.52*
Perfume	34.85	29.79*

* Significant at .01 level

As can be seen, a significantly ($p < .01$) higher overall amount of perceived risk was attached to products purchased by catalog as compared to those purchased from a retail store.[2] ■

The department store example illustrates the role of basic data analysis used in conjunction with multivariate procedures, whereas the other two examples show how such analysis can be useful in its own right. The cross-tabulation and chi-square analysis in the international television advertising example, and the paired t tests in the catalog shopping example, enabled us to draw specific conclusions from the data. These and other concepts discussed in this chapter are illustrated in the context of explaining Internet usage for personal (nonprofessional) reasons. Table 15.1 contains data for 30 respondents giving the sex (1 = male, 2 = female), familiarity with the Internet (1 = very unfamiliar, 7 = very familiar), Internet usage in hours per week, attitude toward Internet and toward technology, both measured on a seven-point scale (1 = very unfavorable, 7 = very favorable), whether the respondents has done shopping or banking on the Internet (1 = yes, 2 = no). As a first step in the analysis, it is often useful to examine the frequency distributions of the relevant variables.

TABLE 15.1

INTERNET USAGE DATA

Respondent Number	*Sex*	*Familiarity*	*Internet Usage*	*Attitude toward Internet*	*Attitude toward Technology*	*Usage of Internet for Shopping*	*Usage of Internet for Banking*
1	1.00	7.00	14.00	7.00	6.00	1.00	1.00
2	2.00	2.00	2.00	3.00	3.00	2.00	2.00
3	2.00	3.00	3.00	4.00	3.00	1.00	2.00
4	2.00	3.00	3.00	7.00	5.00	1.00	2.00
5	1.00	7.00	13.00	7.00	7.00	1.00	1.00
6	2.00	4.00	6.00	5.00	4.00	1.00	2.00
7	2.00	2.00	2.00	4.00	5.00	2.00	2.00
8	2.00	3.00	6.00	5.00	4.00	2.00	2.00
9	2.00	3.00	6.00	6.00	4.00	1.00	2.00
10	1.00	9.00	15.00	7.00	6.00	1.00	2.00
11	2.00	4.00	3.00	4.00	3.00	2.00	2.00
12	2.00	5.00	4.00	6.00	4.00	2.00	2.00
13	1.00	6.00	9.00	6.00	5.00	2.00	1.00
14	1.00	6.00	8.00	3.00	2.00	2.00	2.00
15	1.00	6.00	5.00	5.00	4.00	1.00	2.00
16	2.00	4.00	3.00	4.00	3.00	2.00	2.00
17	1.00	6.00	9.00	5.00	3.00	1.00	1.00
18	1.00	4.00	4.00	5.00	4.00	1.00	2.00
19	1.00	7.00	14.00	6.00	6.00	1.00	1.00
20	2.00	6.00	6.00	6.00	4.00	2.00	2.00
21	1.00	6.00	9.00	4.00	2.00	2.00	2.00
22	1.00	5.00	5.00	5.00	4.00	2.00	1.00
23	2.00	3.00	2.00	4.00	2.00	2.00	2.00
24	1.00	7.00	15.00	6.00	6.00	1.00	1.00
25	2.00	6.00	6.00	5.00	3.00	1.00	2.00
26	1.00	6.00	13.00	6.00	6.00	1.00	1.00
27	2.00	5.00	4.00	5.00	5.00	1.00	1.00
28	2.00	4.00	2.00	3.00	2.00	2.00	2.00
29	1.00	4.00	4.00	5.00	3.00	1.00	2.00
30	1.00	3.00	3.00	7.00	5.00	1.00	2.00

FREQUENCY DISTRIBUTION

Marketing researchers often need to answer questions about a single variable. For example:

- How many users of the brand may be characterized as brand loyal?
- What percentage of the market consists of heavy users, medium users, light users, and nonusers?
- How many customers are very familiar with a new-product offering? How many are familiar, somewhat familiar, and unfamiliar with the brand? What is the mean familiarity rating? Is there much variance in the extent to which customers are familiar with the new product?
- What is the income distribution of brand users? Is this distribution skewed toward low-income brackets?

Frequency Distribution A mathematical distribution whose objective is to obtain a count of the number of responses associated with different values of one variable and to express these counts in percentage terms.

The answers to these kinds of questions can be determined by examining frequency distributions. In a **frequency distribution**, one variable is considered at a time. The objective is to obtain a count of the number of responses associated with different values of the variable. The relative occurrence, or frequency, of different values of the variable is expressed in percentages. A frequency distribution for a variable produces a table of frequency counts, percentages, and cumulative percentages for all the values associated with that variable.

Table 15.2 gives the frequency distribution of familiarity with the Internet. In the table, the first column contains the labels assigned to the different categories of the variable, and the second column indicates the codes assigned to each value. Note that a code of 9 has been assigned to missing values. The third column gives the number of respondents checking each value. For example, three respondents checked value 5, indicating that they were somewhat familiar with the Internet. The fourth column displays the percentage of respondents checking each value. The next column shows percentages calculated by excluding the cases with missing values. If there are no missing values, columns 4 and 5 are identical. The last column represents cumulative percentages after adjusting for missing cases. As can be seen, of the 30 respondents who participated in the survey, 10.0 percent checked value 5. If the one respondent with a missing value is excluded, this percentage changes to 10.3. The cumulative percentage corresponding to the value of 5 is 58.6. In other words, 58.6 percent of the respondents with valid responses indicated a familiarity value of 5 or less.

A frequency distribution helps determine the extent of item nonresponse (1 respondent out of 30 in Table 15.2). It also indicates the extent of illegitimate responses. Values of 0 and 8 would be illegitimate responses, or errors. The cases with these values could be

TABLE 15.2

FREQUENCY DISTRIBUTION OF FAMILIARITY WITH THE INTERNET

Value Label	*Value*	*Frequency (N)*	*Percentage*	*Valid Percentage*	*Cumulative Percentage*
Not so familiar	1	0	0.0	0.0	0.0
	2	2	6.7	6.9	6.9
	3	6	20.0	20.7	27.6
	4	6	20.0	20.7	48.3
	5	3	10.0	10.3	58.6
	6	8	26.7	27.6	86.2
Very familiar	7	4	13.3	13.8	100.0
	9	1	3.3	Missing	
	TOTAL	30	100.0	100.0	

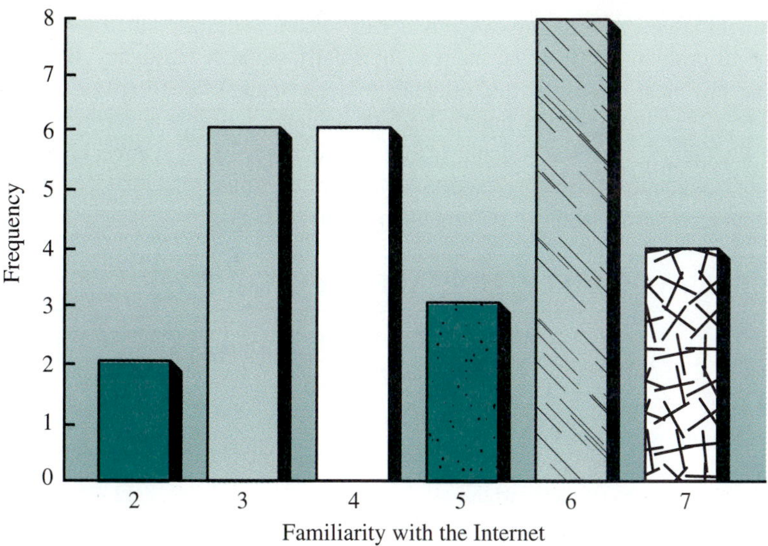

Figure 15.1
Frequency Histogram

identified and corrective action taken. The presence of outliers or cases with extreme values can also be detected. In the case of a frequency distribution of household size, a few isolated families with household sizes of 9 or more might be considered outliers. A frequency distribution also indicates the shape of the empirical distribution of the variable. The frequency data may be used to construct a *histogram*, or a vertical bar chart in which the values of the variable are portrayed along the *X* axis and the absolute or relative frequencies of the values are placed along the *Y* axis. Figure 15.1 is a histogram of the frequency data in Table 15.2. From the histogram, one could examine whether the observed distribution is consistent with an expected or assumed distribution. For further illustration, consider the following example.

EXAMPLE

Advertising's Ethical Dilemmas

A frequency distribution of responses can help determine the ethical problems faced most often by advertising agency executives.

In a survey of ethical issues, advertising executives were asked to describe the most difficult ethical or moral problem confronting them in their daily work. A frequency distribution indicated that the most often reported ethical problem was (1) "treating our clients fairly," followed by (2) creating honest, nonmisleading, socially desirable advertisements; (3) considering whether to represent clients whose product/services are unhealthy, unneeded, useless, or unethical; (4) treating suppliers, vendors, and media fairly; (5) treating employees and managers fairly; and (6) treating other agencies fairly.[3]

ETHICAL PROBLEMS OF ADVERTISING AGENCY EXECUTIVES

	Responses	
Problem	*Number*	*Percent*
1. Treating clients fairly	80	28
2. Creating honest, nonmisleading, socially desirable advertisements	66	24
3. Considering whether to represent clients whose products/services are unhealthy, unneeded, useless, or unethical	34	12
4. Treating suppliers, vendors, and media fairly	25	9
5. Treating employees and managers fairly	15	5
6. Treating other agencies fairly	7	3
7. Other	11	4
8. None	43	15
TOTAL	281	100% ■

Note that the numbers and percentages in the preceding example indicate the extent of the various ethical problems. Since numbers are involved, a frequency distribution can be used to calculate descriptive or summary statistics. We discuss some of the statistics associated with frequency distribution in the next section.

STATISTICS ASSOCIATED WITH FREQUENCY DISTRIBUTION

As illustrated in the previous section, a frequency distribution is a convenient way of looking at different values of a variable. A frequency table is easy to read and provides basic information, but sometimes this information may be too detailed and the researcher must summarize it by the use of descriptive statistics.[4] The most commonly used statistics associated with frequencies are measures of location (mean, mode, and median), measures of variability (range, interquartile range, standard deviation, and coefficient of variation), and measures of shape (skewness and kurtosis).[5]

Measures of Location

Measures of Location A statistic that describes a location within a data set. Measures of central tendency describe the center of the distribution.

The **measures of location** that we discuss are measures of central tendency because they tend to describe the center of the distribution. If the entire sample is changed by adding a fixed constant to each observation, then the mean, mode, and median change by the same fixed amount.

Mean The average; that value obtained by summing all elements in a set and dividing by the number of elements.

Mean. The **mean**, or average value, is the most commonly used measure of central tendency. It is used to estimate the mean when the data have been collected using an interval or ratio scale. The data should display some central tendency, with most of the responses distributed around the mean.

The mean, $\bar{X}$, is given by

$$\bar{X} = \sum_{i=1}^{n} X_i / n$$

where,

X_i = observed values of the variable X
n = number of observations (sample size)

Generally, the mean is a robust measure and does not change markedly as data values are added or deleted. For the frequencies given in Table 15.2, the mean value is calculated as follows:

$$\bar{X} = \frac{(2 \times 2 + 6 \times 3 + 6 \times 4 + 3 \times 5 + 8 \times 6 + 4 \times 7)}{29}$$

$$= \frac{(4 + 18 + 24 + 15 + 48 + 28)}{29}$$

$$= 137/29$$

$$= 4.724$$

Mode. The **mode** is the value that occurs most frequently. It represents the highest peak of the distribution. The mode is a good measure of location when the variable is inherently categorical or has otherwise been grouped into categories. The mode in Table 15.2 is 6.000.

Mode A measure of central tendency given as the value that occurs the most in a sample distribution.

Median. The **median** of a sample is the middle value when the data are arranged in ascending or descending order. If the number of data points is even, the median is usually estimated as the midpoint between the two middle values—by adding the two middle values and dividing their sum by 2. The median is the 50th percentile. The median is an appropriate measure of central tendency for ordinal data. In Table 15.2, the median is 5.000.

Median A measure of central tendency, given as the value above which half of the values fall and below which half of the values fall.

As can be seen from Table 15.2, the three measures of central tendency for this distribution are different (mean = 4.724, mode = 6.000, median = 5.000). This is not surprising, because each measure defines central tendency in a different way. So which measure should be used? If the variable is measured on a nominal scale, the mode should be used. If the variable is measured on an ordinal scale, the median is appropriate. If the variable is measured on an interval or ratio scale, the mode is a poor measure of central tendency. This can be seen from Table 15.2. Although the modal value of 6.000 has the highest frequency, it represents only 27.6 percent of the sample. In general, for interval or ratio data, the median is a better measure of central tendency, although it too ignores available information about the variable. The actual values of the variable above and below the median are ignored. The mean is the most appropriate measure of central tendency for interval or ratio data. The mean makes use of all the information available because all of the values are used in computing it. However, the mean is sensitive to extremely small or extremely large values (outliers). When there are outliers in the data, the mean is not a good measure of central tendency and it is useful to consider both the mean and the median.

Measures of Variability

The **measures of variability**, which are calculated on interval or ratio data, include the range, interquartile range, variance or standard deviation, and coefficient of variation.

Measures of Variability A statistic that indicates the distribution's dispersion.

Range The difference between the largest and smallest values of a distribution.

Interquartile Range The range of a distribution encompassing the middle 50 percent of the observations.

Variance The mean squared deviation of all the values from the mean.

Standard Deviation The square root of the variance.

Range. The **range** measures the spread of the data. It is simply the difference between the largest and smallest values in the sample. As such, the range is directly affected by outliers.

$$\text{range} = X_{\text{largest}} - X_{\text{smallest}}$$

If all the values in the data are multiplied by a constant, the range is multiplied by the same constant. The range in Table 15.2 is 7 − 2 = 5.000.

Interquartile Range. The **interquartile range** is the difference between the 75th and 25th percentile. For a set of data points arranged in order of magnitude, the pth percentile is the value that has p percent of the data points below it and $(100 - p)$ percent above it. If all the data points are multiplied by a constant, the interquartile range is multiplied by the same constant. The interquartile range in Table 15.2 is 6 − 3 = 3.000.

Variance and Standard Deviation. The difference between the mean and an observed value is called the deviation from the mean. The **variance** is the mean squared deviation from the mean. The variance can never be negative. When the data points are clustered around the mean, the variance is small. When the data points are scattered, the variance is large. If all the data values are multiplied by a constant, the variance is multiplied by the square of the constant. The **standard deviation** is the square root of the variance. Thus, the standard deviation is expressed in the same units as the data, rather than in squared units.

The standard deviation of a sample, s_x, is calculated as:

$$s_x = \sqrt{\sum_{i=1}^{n} \frac{(X_i - \bar{X})^2}{n - 1}}$$

We divide by $n - 1$ instead of n because the sample is drawn from a population and we are trying to determine how much the responses vary from the mean of the entire population. However, the population mean is unknown; therefore the sample mean is used instead. The use of the sample mean makes the sample seem less variable than it really is. By dividing by $n - 1$, instead of n, we compensate for the smaller variability observed in the sample. For the data given in Table 15.2, the variance is calculated as follows:

$$s_x^2 = \frac{\{2 \times (2 - 4.724)^2 + 6 \times (3 - 4.724)^2 + 6 \times (4 - 4.724)^2 + 3 \times (5 - 4.724)^2 + 8 \times (6 - 4.724)^2 + 4 \times (7 - 4.724)^2\}}{28}$$

$$= \frac{\{14.840 + 17.833 + 3.145 + 0.229 + 13.025 + 20.721\}}{28}$$

$$= \frac{69.793}{28}$$

$$= 2.493$$

The standard deviation, therefore, is calculated as:

$$s_x = \sqrt{2.493}$$

$$= 1.579$$

Coefficient of Variation. The **coefficient of variation** is the ratio of the standard deviation to the mean expressed as a percentage, and it is a unitless measure of relative variability. The coefficient of variation, *CV*, is expressed as:

Coefficient of Variation A useful expression in sampling theory for the standard deviation as a percentage of the mean.

$$CV = s_x/\bar{X}$$

The coefficient of variation is meaningful only if the variable is measured on a ratio scale. It remains unchanged if all the data values are multiplied by a constant. Because familiarity with the Internet is not measured on a ratio scale, it is not meaningful to calculate the coefficient of variation for the data in Table 15.2.

Measures of Shape

In addition to measures of variability, measures of shape are also useful in understanding the nature of the distribution. The shape of a distribution is assessed by examining skewness and kurtosis.

Skewness. Distributions can be either symmetric or skewed. In a symmetric distribution, the values on either side of the center of the distribution are the same, and the mean, mode, and median are equal. The positive and corresponding negative deviations from the mean are also equal. In a skewed distribution, the positive and negative deviations from the mean are unequal. **Skewness** is the tendency of the deviations from the mean to be larger in one direction than in the other. It can be thought of as the tendency for one tail of the distribution to be heavier than the other (see Figure 15.2). The skewness value for the data of Table 15.2 is – 0.094, indicating a slight negative skew.

Skewness A characteristic of a distribution that assesses its symmetry about the mean.

Figure 15.2
Skewness of a Distribution

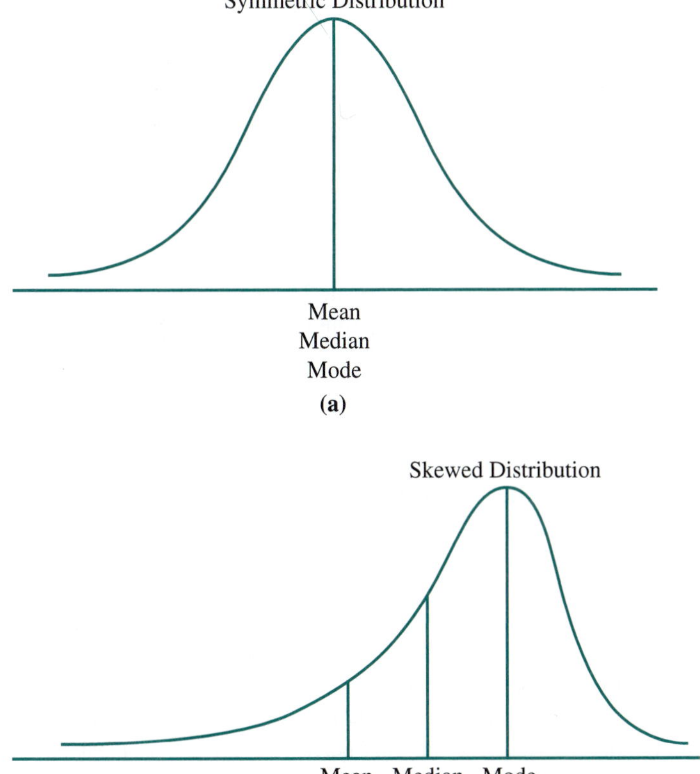

Kurtosis A measure of the relative peakedness of the curve defined by the frequency distribution.

Kurtosis. **Kurtosis** is a measure of the relative peakedness or flatness of the curve defined by the frequency distribution. The kurtosis of a normal distribution is zero. If the kurtosis is positive, then the distribution is more peaked than a normal distribution. A negative value means that the distribution is flatter than a normal distribution. The value of this statistic for Table 15.2 is −1.261, indicating that the distribution is flatter than a normal distribution.

INTRODUCTION TO HYPOTHESIS TESTING

This section provides an introduction to hypothesis testing. Basic analysis invariably involves some hypothesis testing. Examples of hypotheses generated in marketing research abound:

- The department store is being patronized by more than 10 percent of the households.
- The heavy and light users of a brand differ in terms of psychographic characteristics.
- One hotel has a more upscale image than its close competitor.
- Familiarity with a restaurant results in greater preference for that restaurant.

Chapter 12 covered the concepts of the sampling distribution, standard error of the mean or the proportion, and the confidence interval.[6] All these concepts are relevant to hypothesis testing and should be reviewed. Now, we describe a general procedure for hypothesis testing that can be applied to test hypotheses about a wide range of parameters.

A GENERAL PROCEDURE FOR HYPOTHESIS TESTING

The following steps are involved in hypothesis testing (Figure 15.3).

1. Formulate the null hypothesis H_0 *and the alternative hypothesis* H_1.
2. Select an appropriate statistical technique and the corresponding test statistic.
3. Choose the level of significance, α.
4. Determine the sample size and collect the data. Calculate the value of the test statistic.
5. Determine the probability associated with the test statistic under the null hypothesis, using the sampling distribution of the test statistic. Alternatively, determine the critical values associated with the test statistic that divide the rejection and nonrejection region.
6. Compare the probability associated with the test statistic with the level of significance specified. Alternatively, determine whether the test statistic has fallen into the rejection or the nonrejection region.
7. Make the statistical decision to reject or not reject the null hypothesis.
8. Express the statistical decision in terms of the marketing research problem.

Step 1: Formulating the Hypothesis

Null Hypothesis A statement in which no difference or effect is expected. If the null hypothesis is not rejected, no changes will be made.

Alternative Hypothesis A statement that some difference or effect is expected. Accepting the alternative hypothesis will lead to changes in opinions or actions.

The first step is to formulate the null and alternative hypothesis. A **null hypothesis** is a statement of the status quo, one of no difference or no effect. If the null hypothesis is not rejected, no changes will be made. An **alternative hypothesis** is one in which some difference or effect is expected. Accepting the alternative hypothesis will lead to changes in opinions or actions. Thus, the alternative hypothesis is the opposite of the null hypothesis.

The null hypothesis is always the hypothesis that is tested. The null hypothesis refers to a specified value of the population parameter (e.g., μ, σ, π), not a sample statistic (e.g., $\bar{X}$). A null hypothesis may be rejected, but it can never be accepted based on a single test. A statistical test can have one of two outcomes: (1) The null hypothesis is rejected and the alternative hypothesis accepted, or (2) the null hypothesis is not rejected based on the evidence. However, it would be incorrect to conclude that because the null hypothesis is not rejected, it can be accepted as valid. In classical hypothesis testing, there is no way to determine whether the null hypothesis is true.

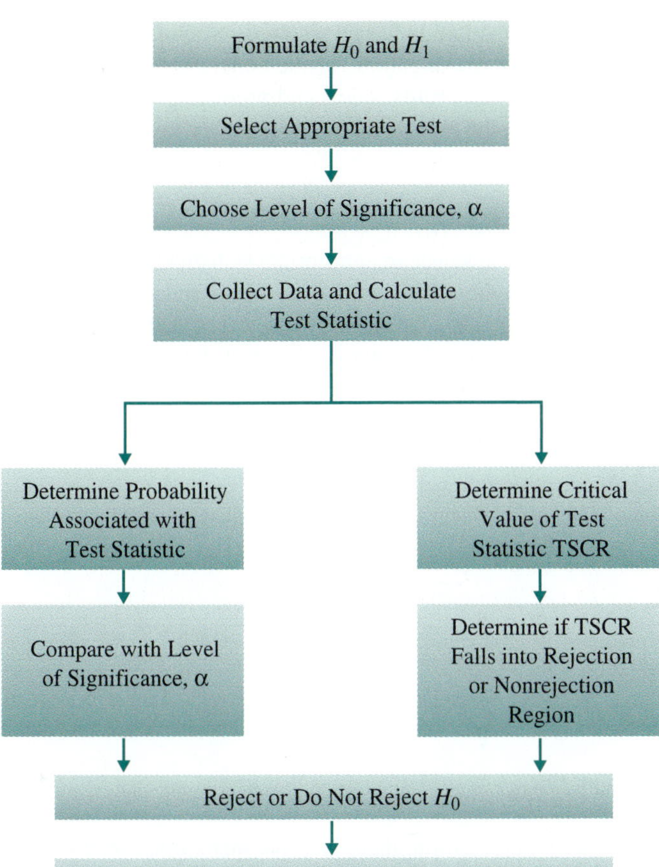

Figure 15.3
A General Procedure for Hypothesis Testing

In marketing research, the null hypothesis is formulated in such a way that its rejection leads to the acceptance of the desired conclusion. The alternative hypothesis represents the conclusion for which evidence is sought. For example, a major department store is considering the introduction of an Internet shopping service. The new service will be introduced if more than 40 percent of the Internet users shop via the Internet. The appropriate way to formulate the hypotheses:

$$H_0\colon \pi \leq .40$$
$$H_1\colon \pi > .40$$

If the null hypothesis H_0 is rejected, then the alternative hypothesis H_1 will be accepted and the new Internet shopping service introduced. On the other hand, if H_0 is not rejected, then the new service should not be introduced unless additional evidence is obtained.

The test of the null hypothesis is a **one-tailed test**, because the alternative hypothesis is expressed directionally: The proportion of Internet users who use the Internet for shopping is greater than 0.40. On the other hand, suppose the researcher wanted to determine whether the proportion of Internet users who shop via the Internet is different from 40 percent. Then a **two-tailed test** would be required, and the hypotheses would be expressed as:

One-tailed test A test of the null hypothesis in which the alternative hypothesis is expressed directionally.

Two-tailed test A test of the null hypothesis in which the alternative hypothesis is not expressed directionally.

$$H_0\colon \pi = .400$$
$$H_1\colon \pi \neq .400$$

In commercial marketing research, the one-tailed test is used more often than a two-tailed test. Typically, there is some preferred direction for the conclusion for which evidence is sought. For example, the higher the profits, sales, and product quality, the better. The one-tailed test is more powerful than the two-tailed test. The power of a statistical test is discussed further in step 3.

Step 2: Selecting an Appropriate Test

Test statistic A measure of how close the sample has come to the null hypothesis. It often follows a well-known distribution, such as the normal, *t*, or chi-square distribution.

To test the null hypothesis, it is necessary to select an appropriate statistical technique. The researcher should take into consideration how the test statistic is computed and the sampling distribution that the sample statistic (e.g., the mean) follows. The **test statistic** measures how close the sample has come to the null hypothesis. The test statistic often follows a well-known distribution, such as the normal, *t*, or chi-square distribution. Guidelines for selecting an appropriate test or statistical technique are discussed later in this chapter. In our example, the z statistic, which follows the standard normal distribution, would be appropriate. This statistic would be computed as follows:

$$z = \frac{p - \pi}{\sigma_p}$$

where

$$\sigma_p = \sqrt{\frac{\pi(1 - \pi)}{n}}$$

Step 3: Choosing Level of Significance

Whenever we draw inferences about a population, there is a risk that an incorrect conclusion will be reached. Two types of error can occur:

Type I error Also known as *alpha error*, occurs when the sample results lead to the rejection of a null hypothesis that is in fact true.

Level of significance The probability of making a type I error.

Error. **Type I error** occurs when the sample results lead to the rejection of the null hypothesis when it is in fact true. In our example, a type I error would occur if we concluded, based on the sample data, that the proportion of customers preferring the new service plan was greater than .40, when in fact it was less than or equal to .40. The probability of type I error (α) is also called the **level of significance**. The type I error is controlled by establishing the tolerable level of risk of rejecting a true null hypothesis. The selection of a particular risk level should depend on the cost of making a type I error.

Type II error Also known as beta error, occurs when the sample results lead to nonrejection of a null hypothesis that is in fact false.

Type II Error. **Type II error** occurs when, based on the sample results, the null hypothesis is not rejected when it is in fact false. In our example, the type II error would occur if we concluded, based on sample data, that the proportion of customers preferring the new service plan was less than or equal to .40 when, in fact, it was greater than .40. The probability of type II error is denoted by β. Unlike α, which is specified by the researcher, the magnitude of β depends on the actual value of the population parameter (proportion). The probability of type I error (α) and the probability of type II error (β) are shown in Figure 15.4. The complement ($1 - \beta$) of the probability of a type II error is called the power of a statistical test.

Power of a test The probability of rejecting the null hypothesis when it is in fact false and should be rejected.

Power of a Test. The **power of a test** is the probability ($1 - \beta$) of rejecting the null hypothesis when it is false and should be rejected. Although β is unknown, it is related to α. An extremely low value of α (e.g., = .001) will result in intolerably high β errors. So it is necessary to balance the two types of errors. As a compromise, α is often set at .05; sometimes it is .01; other values of α are rare. The level of α along with the sample size will determine the level of β for a particular research design. The risk of both α and β can be controlled by increasing the sample size. For a given level of α, increasing the sample size will decrease β, thereby increasing the power of the test.

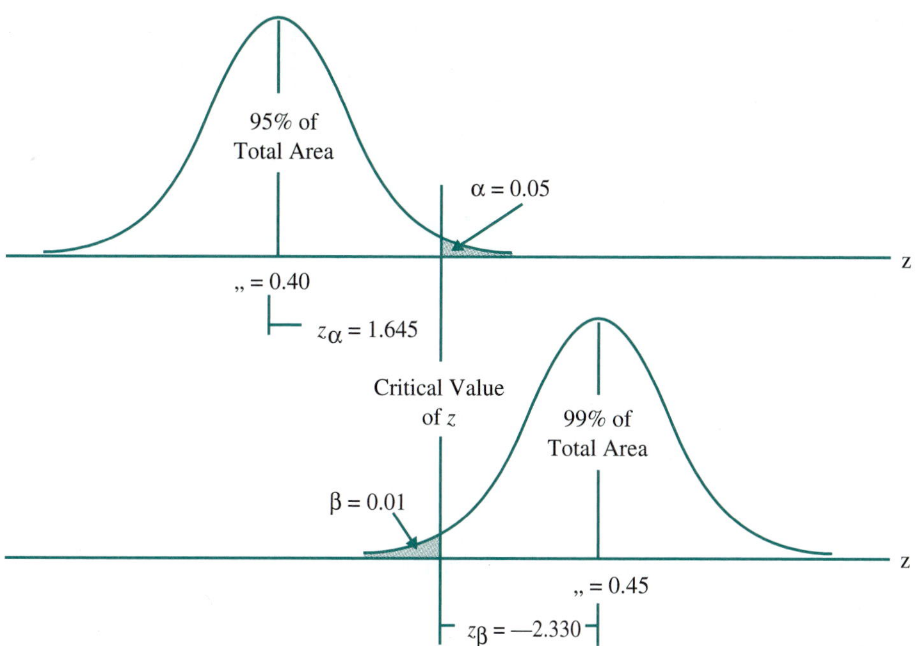

Figure 15.4
Type I Error (α) and Type II Error (β)

Step 4: Data Collection

Sample size is determined after taking into account the desired α and β errors and other qualitative considerations, such as budget constraints. Then the required data are collected and the value of the test statistic computed. In our example, 30 users were surveyed and 17 indicated that they used the Internet for shopping. Thus the value of the sample proportion is $\hat{p}$ = 17/30 = 0.567.

The value of $\sigma_{\hat{p}}$ can be determined as follows:

$$\sigma_{\hat{p}} = \sqrt{\frac{\pi(1 - \pi)}{n}}$$

$$= \sqrt{\frac{(.40)(.6)}{30}}$$

$$= .089$$

The test statistic z can be calculated as follows:

$$z = \frac{\hat{p} - \pi}{\sigma_{\hat{p}}}$$

$$= \frac{.567 - .40}{.089}$$

$$= 1.88$$

Step 5: Determining the Probability (Critical Value)

Using standard normal tables (Table 2 of the statistical appendix), the probability of obtaining a z value of 1.88 can be calculated (see Figure 15.5). The shaded area between $-\infty$ and 1.88 is .9699. Therefore, the area to the right of $z = 1.88$ is 1.0000 – 0.9699 = .0301.

Figure 15.5
Probability of z with a One-Tailed Test

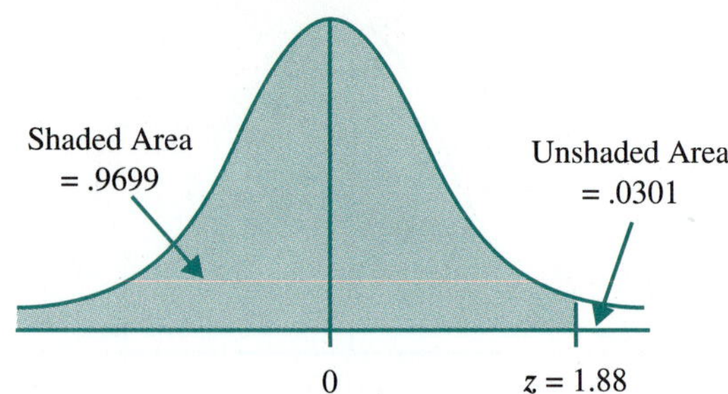

Alternatively, the critical value of z, which will give an area to the right side of the critical value of .05, is between 1.64 and 1.65 and equals 1.645. Note, that in determining the critical value of the test statistic, the area to the right of the critical value is either α or $\alpha/2$. It is α for a one-tailed test and $\alpha/2$ for a two-tailed test.

Steps 6 and 7: Comparing the Probability (Critical Value) and Making the Decision

The probability associated with the calculated or observed value of the test statistic is .0301. This is the probability of getting a p value of 0.567 when $\hat{p} = .40$. This is less than the level of significance of .05. Hence, the null hypothesis is rejected. Alternatively, the calculated value of the test statistic $z = 1.88$ lies in the rejection region, beyond the value of 1.645. Again, the same conclusion to reject the null hypothesis is reached. Note that the two ways of testing the null hypothesis are equivalent but mathematically opposite in the direction of comparison. If the probability associated with the calculated or observed value of the test statistic (TS_{CAL}) is *less than* the level of significance (α), the null hypothesis is rejected. However, if the calculated value of the test statistic is *greater than* the critical value of the test statistic (TS_{CR}), the null hypothesis is rejected. The reason for this sign shift is that the larger the value of TS_{CAL}, the smaller the probability of obtaining a more extreme value of the test statistic under the null hypothesis. This sign shift can be easily seen:

$$\text{if probability of } TS_{CAL} < \text{significance level } (\alpha)\text{, then reject } H_0,$$

but

$$\text{if } TS_{CAL} > TS_{CR}\text{, then reject } H_0.$$

Step 8: Marketing Research Conclusion

The conclusion reached by hypothesis testing must be expressed in terms of the marketing research problem. In our example, we conclude that there is evidence that the proportion of Internet users who shop via the Internet is significantly greater than .40. Hence, the recommendation to the department store would be to introduce the new Internet shopping service.

As can be seen from Figure 15.6, hypotheses testing can be related to either an examination of associations or an examination of differences. In tests of associations the null hypothesis is that there is no association between the variables (H_0: . . . is NOT related to . . .). In tests of differences the null hypothesis is that there is no difference (H_0: . . . is NOT different from . . .). Tests of differences could relate to distributions, means, proportions, medians, or rankings. First, we discuss hypotheses related to associations in the context of cross-tabulations.

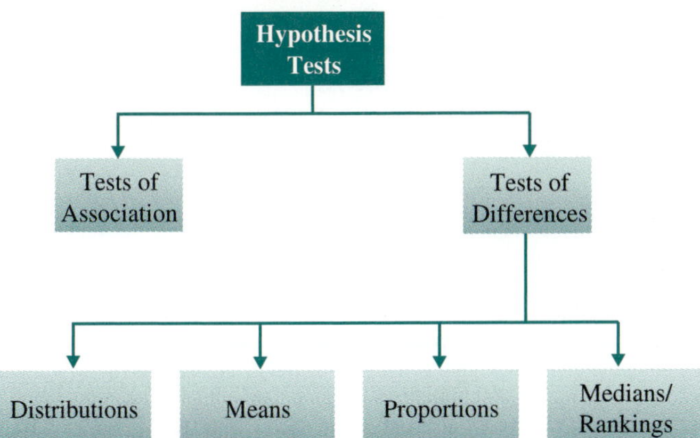

Figure 15.6
A Broad Classification of Hypothesis Tests

CROSS-TABULATIONS

Although answers to questions related to a single variable are interesting, they often raise additional questions about how to link that variable to other variables. To introduce the frequency distribution, we posed several representative marketing research questions. For each of these, a researcher might pose additional questions to relate these variables to other variables. For example:

- How many brand loyal users are males?
- Is product use (measured in terms of heavy users, medium users, light users, and nonusers) related to interest in outdoor activities (high, medium, and low)?
- Is familiarity with a new product related to age and education levels?
- Is product ownership related to income (high, medium, and low)?

The answers to such questions can be determined by examining cross-tabulations. Whereas a frequency distribution describes one variable at a time, a **cross-tabulation** describes two or more variables simultaneously. A cross-tabulation is the merging of the frequency distribution of two or more variables in a single table. It helps us to understand how one variable such as brand loyalty relates to another variable such as sex. Cross-tabulation results in tables that reflect the joint distribution of two or more variables with a limited number of categories or distinct values. The categories of one variable are cross-classified with the categories of one or more other variables. Thus, the frequency distribution of one variable is subdivided according to the values or categories of the other variables.

Cross-Tabulation A statistical technique that describes two or more variables simultaneously and results in tables that reflect the joint distribution of two or more variables with a limited number of categories or distinct values.

Suppose we are interested in determining whether Internet usage is related to sex. For the purpose of cross-tabulation, respondents are classified as light or heavy users. Those reporting five hours or less usage are classified as light users and the remaining are heavy users. The cross-tabulation is shown in Table 15.3. A cross-tabulation includes a cell for every combination of the categories of the two variables. The number in each cell shows how many respondents gave that combination of responses. In Table 15.3, 10 respondents were females who reported light Internet usage. The marginal totals in this table indicate that of the 30 respondents with valid responses on both the variables, 15 reported light usage and 15 were heavy users. In terms of sex, 15 respondents were females and 15 were males. Note that this information could have been obtained from a separate frequency distribution for each variable. In general, the margins of a cross-tabulation show the same information as the frequency tables for each of the variables. Cross-tabulation tables are also called **contingency tables**. The data are considered to be qualitative or categorical data, because each variable is assumed to have only a nominal scale.[7]

Contingency Table A cross-tabulation table. It contains a cell for every combination of categories of the two variables.

TABLE 15.3

SEX AND INTERNET USAGE

	Sex		
Internet Usage	*Male*	*Female*	*Row Total*
Light (1)	5	10	15
Heavy (2)	10	5	15
Column Total	15	15	

Cross-tabulation is widely used in commercial marketing research, because (1) cross-tabulation analysis and results can be easily interpreted and understood by managers who are not statistically oriented; (2) the clarity of interpretation provides a stronger link between research results and managerial action; (3) a series of cross-tabulations may provide greater insights into a complex phenomenon than would a single multivariate analysis; (4) cross-tabulation may alleviate the problem of sparse cells, which could be serious in discrete multivariate analysis; and (5) cross-tabulation analysis is simple to conduct and appealing to less sophisticated researchers.[8] We will discuss cross-tabulation for two and three variables.

Two Variables

Cross-tabulation with two variables is also known as bivariate cross-tabulation. Consider again the cross-classification of Internet usage with sex given in Table 15.3. Is usage related to sex? It appears to be from Table 15.3. We see that disproportionately more of the respondents who are males are heavy Internet users as compared to females. Computation of percentages can provide more insights.

Because two variables have been cross-classified, percentages could be computed either columnwise, based on column totals (Table 15.4), or rowwise, based on row totals (Table 15.5). Which of these tables is more useful? The answer depends on which variable will be considered as the independent variable and which as the dependent variable.[9] The general rule is to compute the percentages in the direction of the independent variable, across the dependent variable. In our analysis, sex may be considered as the independent variable, and Internet usage as the dependent variable, and the correct way of calculating percentages is as shown in Table 15.4. Note that while 66.7 percent of the males are heavy users, only 33.3 percent of females fall into this category. This seems to indicate that males are more likely to be heavy users of the Internet as compared to females.

Note that computing percentages in the direction of the dependent variable across the independent variable, as shown in Table 15.5, is not meaningful in this case. Table 15.5 implies that heavy Internet usage *causes* people to be males. This latter finding is implausible. It is possible, however, that the association between Internet usage and sex is mediated

TABLE 15.4

SEX BY INTERNET USAGE

	Sex	
Internet Usage	*Male*	*Female*
Light	33.3%	66.7%
Heavy	66.7%	33.3%
Column Total	100.0%	100.0%

TABLE 15.5

SEX BY INTERNET USAGE

	Internet Usage		
Sex	*Light*	*Heavy*	*Total*
Male	33.3%	66.7%	100.0%
Female	66.7%	33.3%	100.0%

by a third variable, such as age or income. This kind of possibility points to the need to examine the effect of a third variable.

Three Variables

Often the introduction of a third variable clarifies the initial association (or lack of it) observed between two variables. As shown in Figure 15.7, the introduction of a third variable can result in four possibilities:

1. It can refine the association observed between the two original variables.
2. It can indicate no association between the two variables, although an association was initially observed. In other words, the third variable indicates that the initial association between the two variables was spurious.
3. It can reveal some association between the two variables, although no association was initially observed. In this case, the third variable reveals a suppressed association between the first two variables.
4. It can indicate no change in the initial association.[10]

These cases are explained with examples based on a sample of 1,000 respondents. Although these examples are contrived to illustrate specific cases, such cases are not uncommon in commercial marketing research.

Refine an Initial Relationship. An examination of the relationship between the purchase of fashion clothing and marital status resulted in the data reported in Table 15.6. The respondents were classified into either high or low categories based on their purchase of fashion clothing. Marital status was also measured in terms of two categories: currently

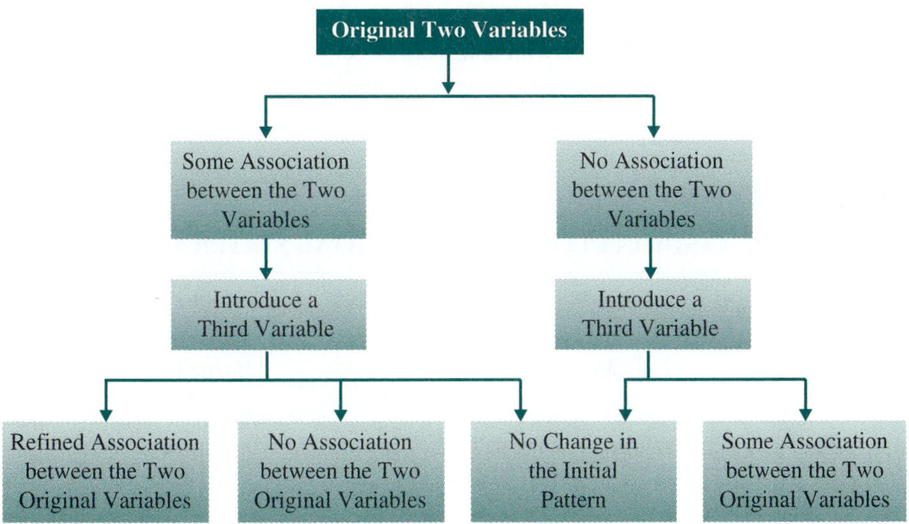

Figure 15.7
The Introduction of a Third Variable in Cross-Tabulation

TABLE 15.6

PURCHASE OF FASHION CLOTHING BY MARITAL STATUS

Purchase of Fashion Clothing	*Current Marital Status*	
	Married	*Unmarried*
High	31%	52%
Low	69%	48%
Column total	100%	100%
Number of respondents	700	300

married or unmarried. As can be seen from Table 15.6, 52 percent of unmarried respondents fell in the high-purchase category, as opposed to 31 percent of the married respondents. Before concluding that unmarried respondents purchase more fashion clothing than those who are married, a third variable, the buyer's sex, was introduced into the analysis.

The buyer's sex was selected as the third variable based on past research. The relationship between purchase of fashion clothing and marital status was reexamined in light of the third variable, as shown in Table 15.7. In the case of females, 60 percent of the unmarried fall in the high-purchase category, as compared to 25 percent of those who are married. On the other hand, the percentages are much closer for males, with 40 percent of the unmarried and 35 percent of the married falling in the high-purchase category. Hence, the introduction of sex (third variable) has refined the relationship between marital status and purchase of fashion clothing (original variables). Unmarried respondents are more likely to fall in the high-purchase category than are married ones, and this effect is much more pronounced for females than for males.

Initial Relationship Was Spurious. A researcher working for an advertising agency promoting a line of automobiles costing more than $30,000 was attempting to explain the ownership of expensive automobiles (see Table 15.8). The table shows that 32 percent of those with college degrees own an expensive automobile, as compared to 21 percent of those without college degrees. The researcher was tempted to conclude that education influenced ownership of expensive automobiles. Realizing that income may also be a factor, the researcher decided to reexamine the relationship between education and ownership of expensive automobiles in light of income level. This resulted in Table 15.9. Note that the percentages of those with and without college degrees who own expensive automobiles are the same for each of the income groups. When the data for the high-income

TABLE 15.7

PURCHASE OF FASHION CLOTHING BY MARITAL STATUS AND SEX

	Sex			
Purchase of Fashion Clothing	*Male Marital Status*		*Female Marital Status*	
	Married	*Unmarried*	*Married*	*Unmarried*
High	35%	40%	25%	60%
Low	65%	60%	75%	40%
Column total	100%	100%	100%	100%
Number of respondents	400	120	300	180

TABLE 15.8

OWNERSHIP OF EXPENSIVE AUTOMOBILES BY EDUCATION LEVEL

Own Expensive Automobile	*Education*	
	College Degree	*No College Degree*
Yes	32%	21%
No	68%	79%
Column total	100%	100%
Number of respondents	250	750

TABLE 15.9

OWNERSHIP OF EXPENSIVE AUTOMOBILES BY EDUCATION AND INCOME LEVELS

Own Expensive Automobile	*Income*			
	Low-Income Education		*High-Income Education*	
	College Degree	*No College Degree*	*College Degree*	*No College Degree*
Yes	20%	20%	40%	40%
No	80%	80%	60%	60%
Column totals	100%	100%	100%	100%
Number of respondents	100	700	150	50

and low-income groups are examined separately, the association between education and ownership of expensive automobiles disappears, indicating that the initial relationship observed between these two variables was spurious.

Reveal Suppressed Association. A researcher suspected desire to travel abroad may be influenced by age. However, a cross-tabulation of the two variables produced the results in Table 15.10, indicating no association. When sex was introduced as the third variable, Table 15.11 was obtained. Among men, 60 percent of those under 45 indicated a desire to travel abroad, as compared to 40 percent of those 45 or older. The pattern was reversed for women, where 35 percent of those under 45 indicated a desire to travel abroad as opposed to 65 percent of those 45 or older. Because the association between desire to travel abroad

TABLE 15.10

DESIRE TO TRAVEL ABROAD BY AGE

Desire to Travel Abroad	*Age*	
	Less than 45	*45 or More*
Yes	50%	50%
No	50%	50%
Column total	100%	100%
Number of respondents	500	500

TABLE 15.11

DESIRE TO TRAVEL ABROAD BY AGE AND SEX

	Sex			
Desire to Travel	*Male Age*		*Female Age*	
Abroad	*< 45*	*≥45*	*< 45*	*≥45*
Yes	60%	40%	35%	65%
No	40%	60%	65%	35%
Column total	100%	100%	100%	100%
Number of respondents	300	300	200	200

and age runs in opposite directions for males and females, the relationship between these two variables is masked when the data are aggregated across sex as in Table 15.10. But when the effect of sex is controlled, as in Table 15.11, the suppressed association between preference and age is revealed for the separate categories of males and females.

No Change in Initial Relationship. In some cases the introduction of the third variable does not change the initial relationship observed, regardless of whether the original variables were associated. This suggests that the third variable does not influence the relationship between the first two. Consider the cross-tabulation of family size and the tendency to eat out frequently in fast food restaurants as shown in Table 15.12. The respondents were classified into small and large family size categories based on a median split of the distribution, with 500 respondents in each category. No association is observed. The respondents were further classified into high- or low-income groups based on a median split. When income was introduced as a third variable in the analysis, Table 15.13 was obtained. Again, no association was observed.

General Comments on Cross-Tabulation

More than three variables can be cross-tabulated, but the interpretation is quite complex. Also, because the number of cells increases multiplicatively, maintaining an adequate number of respondents or cases in each cell can be problematic. As a general rule, there should be at least five expected observations in each cell for the statistics computed to be reliable. Thus, cross-tabulation is an inefficient way of examining relationships when there are several variables. Note that cross-tabulation examines *association* between variables, not *causation*. To examine causation, the causal research design framework should be adopted (see chapter 7).

TABLE 15.12

EATING FREQUENTLY IN FAST FOOD RESTAURANTS BY FAMILY SIZE

Eat Frequently in Fast Food	***Family Size***	
Restaurants	*Small*	*Large*
Yes	65%	65%
No	35%	35%
Column total	100%	100%
Number of respondents	500	500

TABLE 15.13

EATING FREQUENTLY IN FAST FOOD RESTAURANTS BY FAMILY SIZE AND INCOME

Eat Frequently in Fast Food Restaurants	***Income***			
	Low-Income Family Size		*High-Income Family Size*	
	Small	*Large*	*Small*	*Large*
Yes	65%	65%	65%	65%
No	35%	35%	35%	35%
Column total	100%	100%	100%	100%
Number of respondents	250	250	250	250

STATISTICS ASSOCIATED WITH CROSS-TABULATION

We will discuss the statistics commonly used for assessing the statistical significance and strength of association of cross-tabulated variables. The statistical significance of the observed association is commonly measured by the chi-square statistic. The strength of association, or degree of association, is important from a practical or substantive perspective. Generally, the strength of association is of interest only if the association is statistically significant. The strength of the association can be measured by the phi correlation coefficient, the contingency coefficient, Cramer's *V*, and the lambda coefficient. These statistics are described in detail.

Chi-Square

Chi-square Statistic The statistic used to test the statistical significance of the observed association in a cross-tabulation. It assists us in determining whether a systematic association exists between the two variables.

The **chi-square statistic** (χ^2) is used to test the statistical significance of the observed association in a cross-tabulation. It assists us in determining whether a systematic association exists between the two variables. The null hypothesis, H_0, is that there is no association between the variables. The test is conducted by computing the cell frequencies that would be expected if no association were present between the variables, given the existing row and column totals. These expected cell frequencies, denoted f_e, are then compared to the actual observed frequencies, f_o, found in the cross-tabulation to calculate the chi-square statistic. The greater the discrepancies between the expected and actual frequencies, the larger the value of the statistic. Assume that a cross-tabulation has r rows and c columns and a random sample of n observations. Then the expected frequency for each cell can be calculated by using a simple formula:

$$f_e = \frac{n_r n_c}{n}$$

where

n_r = total number in the row
n_c = total number in the column
n = total sample size

For the data in Table 15.3, the expected frequencies for the cells, going from left to right and from top to bottom, are:

$$\frac{15 \times 15}{30} = 7.50 \qquad \frac{15 \times 15}{30} = 7.50$$

$$s_{\bar{X}} = \frac{1.579}{\sqrt{29}} = \frac{1.579}{5.385} = .293$$

$$t = \frac{(4.724 - 4.0)}{.293} = \frac{.724}{.293} = 2.471$$

The degrees of freedom for the t statistic to test hypothesis about one mean are $n - 1$. In this case, $n - 1 = 29 - 1$ or 28. From Table 4 in the statistical appendix, the probability of getting a more extreme value than 2.471 is less than .05. (Alternatively, the critical t value for 28 degrees of freedom and a significance level of .05 is 1.7011, which is less than the calculated value.) Hence, the null hypothesis is rejected. The familiarity level does exceed 4.0.

z test A univariate hypothesis test using the standard normal distribution.

Note that if the population standard deviation was assumed to be known as 1.5, rather than estimated from the sample, a **z test** would be appropriate. In this case the value of the z statistic would be:

$$z = (\bar{X} - \mu)/\sigma_{\bar{X}}$$

where

$$\sigma_{\bar{X}} = \frac{1.5}{\sqrt{29}} = \frac{1.5}{5.385} = .279$$

and

$$z = \frac{(4.724 - 4.0)}{.279} = \frac{.724}{.279} = 2.595$$

From Table 2 in the statistical appendix, the probability of getting a more extreme value of z than 2.595 is less than .05. (Alternatively, the critical z value for a one-tailed test and a significance level of .05 is 1.645, which is less than the calculated value.) Therefore, the null hypothesis is rejected, reaching the same conclusion arrived at earlier by the t test.

The procedure for testing a null hypothesis with respect to a proportion was illustrated earlier in this chapter when we introduced hypothesis testing.

Two Independent Samples

Several hypotheses in marketing relate to parameters from two different populations: for example, the users and nonusers of a brand differ in terms of their perceptions of the brand, the high-income consumers spend more on entertainment than do low-income consumers, or the proportion of brand loyal users in segment 1 is more than the proportion in segment 2. Samples drawn randomly from different populations are termed **independent samples**. As in the case for one sample, the hypotheses could relate to means or proportions.

Independent Samples Two samples that are not experimentally related. The measurement of one sample has no effect on the values of the second sample.

Means. In the case of means for two independent samples, the hypotheses take the following form.

$$H_0: \mu_1 = \mu_2$$
$$H_1: \mu_1 \neq \mu_2$$

The two populations are sampled and the means and variances computed based on samples of sizes n_1 and n_2. If both populations are found to have the same variance, a pooled variance estimate is computed from the two sample variances as follows:

$$s^2 = \frac{\sum_{i=1}^{n_1} (X_{i_1} - \bar{X}_1)^2 + \sum_{i=1}^{n_2} (X_{i_2} - \bar{X}_2)^2}{}$$

The standard deviation of the test statistic can be estimated as:

$$s_{\bar{X}_1 - \bar{X}_2} = \sqrt{s^2\left(\frac{1}{n_1} + \frac{1}{n_2}\right)}$$

The appropriate value of t can be calculated as:

$$t = \frac{(\bar{X}_1 - \bar{X}_2) - (\mu_1 - \mu_2)}{s_{\bar{X}_1 - \bar{X}_2}}$$

The degrees of freedom in this case are $(n_1 + n_2 - 2)$.

If the two populations have unequal variances, an exact t cannot be computed for the difference in sample means. Instead, an approximation to t is computed. The number of degrees of freedom in this case is usually not an integer, but a reasonably accurate probability can be obtained by rounding to the nearest integer.[17]

An ***F* test** of sample variance may be performed if it is not known whether the two populations have equal variance. In this case the hypotheses are:

***F* test** A statistical test of the equality of the variances of two populations.

$$H_0: \sigma_1^2 = \sigma_2^2$$
$$H_1: \sigma_1^2 \neq \sigma_2^2$$

The ***F* statistic** is computed from the sample variances as follows:

***F* statistic** The F statistic is computed as the ratio of two sample variances.

$$F_{(n_1 - 1), (n_2 - 1)} = \frac{s_1^2}{s_2^2}$$

where

n_1 = size of sample 1
n_2 = size of sample 2
$n_1 - 1$ = degrees of freedom for sample 1
$n_2 - 1$ = degrees of freedom for sample 2
s_1^2 = sample variance for sample 1
s_2^2 = sample variance for sample 2

As can be seen, the critical value of the ***F* distribution** depends on two sets of degrees of freedom—those in the numerator and those in the denominator. The critical values of F for various degrees of freedom for the numerator and denominator are given in Table 5 of the statistical appendix. If the probability of F is greater than the significance level α, H_0 is not rejected, and t based on the pooled variance estimate can be used. On the other hand, if the probability of F is less than or equal to α, H_0 is rejected and t based on a separate variance estimate is used.

***F* distribution** A frequency distribution that depends on two sets of degrees of freedom—the degrees of freedom in the numerator and the degrees of freedom in the denominator.

Using the data of Table 15.1, suppose we wanted to determine whether Internet usage was different for males as compared to females. A two-independent-samples t test was conducted. The results are presented in Table 15.14. Note that the F test of sample variances has a probability that is less than .05. Accordingly, H_0 is rejected, and the t test based on the "Equal variances not assumed" should be used. The t value is –4.492, and with 18.014 degrees of freedom this gives a probability of .000, which is less than the significance level of

TABLE 15.14

TWO INDEPENDENT SAMPLES *t* TEST

	Summary Statistics		
	Number of Cases	*Mean*	*Standard Deviation*
Male	15	9.333	1.137
Female	15	3.867	0.435

F Test for Equality of Variances	
F Value	*Two-Tail Probability*
15.507	.000

t Test					
Equal Variances Assumed			*Equal Variances Not Assumed*		
t Value	Degrees of Freedom	Two-Tail Probability	*t* Value	Degrees of Freedom	Two-Tail Probability
–4.492	28	.000	–4.492	18.014	.000

.05. Therefore, the null hypothesis of equal means is rejected. Since the mean usage for males (sex = 1) is 9.333 and that for females (sex = 2) is 3.867, males use the Internet to a significantly greater extent than do females. We also show the *t* test assuming equal variances as most computer programs automatically conduct the *t* test both ways. As an application of *t* test, consider the following example.

EXAMPLE

Stores Seek to Suit Elderly to a "t"

A study based on a national sample of 789 respondents who were 65 or older attempted to determine the effect of lack of mobility on patronage behavior. A major research question related to the differences in the physical requirements of dependent and self-reliant elderly persons. That is, did the two groups require different things to get to the store or after they arrived at the store? A more detailed analysis of the physical requirements conducted by two independent sample *t* tests (shown in the table) indicated that dependent elderly persons are more likely to look for stores that offer home delivery and phone orders, and stores to which they have transportation. They are also more likely to look for a variety of stores located close together.[18] ■

DIFFERENCES IN PHYSICAL REQUIREMENTS BETWEEN DEPENDENT AND SELF-RELIANT ELDERLY

	MEAN[a]		
Physical Requirement Items	*Self-reliant*	*Dependent*	*t Test Probability*
Delivery to home	1.787	2.000	.023
Phone in order	2.030	2.335	.003
Transportation to store	2.188	3.098	.000
Convenient parking	4.001	4.095	.305
Location close to home	3.177	3.325	.137
Variety of stores close together	3.456	3.681	.023

[a]Measured on a five-point scale from not important (1) to very important (5).

In this example, we tested the difference between means. A similar test is available for testing the difference between proportions for two independent samples.

Proportions. The case involving proportions for two independent samples is also illustrated using the data of Table 15.1 which gives the number of males and females who use the Internet for shopping. Is the proportion of respondents using the Internet for shopping the same for males and females? The null and alternative hypotheses are:

$$H_0: \pi_1 = \pi_2$$
$$H_1: \pi_1 \neq \pi_2$$

A z test is used as in testing the proportion for one sample. However, in this case the test statistic is given by:

$$z = \frac{P_1 - P_2}{s_{\bar{P}_1 - \bar{P}_2}}$$

In the test statistic, the numerator is the difference between the proportions in the two samples, P_1 and P_2. The denominator is the standard error of the difference in the two proportions and is given by

$$s_{\bar{P}_1 - \bar{P}_2} = \sqrt{P(1 - P)\left[\frac{1}{n_1} + \frac{1}{n_2}\right]}$$

where

$$P = \frac{n_1 P_1 + n_2 P_2}{n_1 + n_2}$$

A significance level of $\alpha = .05$ is selected. Given the data of Table 15.15 the test statistic can be calculated as:

$$P_1 - P_2 = (11/15) - (6/15)$$
$$= .733 - .400 = .333$$

$$P = \frac{(15 \times .733 + 15 \times .400)}{(15 + 15)} = .567$$

$$s_{\bar{P}_1 - \bar{P}_1} = \sqrt{.567 \times .433\left[\frac{1}{15} + \frac{1}{15}\right]} = .181$$

$$z = \frac{.333}{.181} = 1.84$$

Given a two-tailed test, the area to the right of the critical value is $\alpha / 2$ or .025. Hence, the critical value of the test statistic is 1.96. Since, the calculated value is less than the critical value, the null hypothesis can not be rejected. Thus, the proportion of users (.733) for males and (.400) for females is not significantly different for the two samples. Note that while the difference is substantial, it is not statistically significant due to the small sample sizes (15 in each group).

Paired Samples In hypothesis testing, the observations are paired so that the two sets of observations relate to the same respondents.

Paired samples t test A test for differences in the means of paired samples.

Paired Samples

In many marketing research applications, the observations for the two groups are not selected from independent samples. Rather, the observations relate to **paired samples** in that the two sets of observations relate to the same respondents. A sample of respondents may rate two competing brands, indicate the relative importance of two attributes of a product, or evaluate a brand at two different times. The difference in these cases is examined by a **paired samples *t* test**. To compute t for paired samples, the paired difference variable, denoted by D, is formed and its mean and variance calculated. Then the t statistic is computed. The degrees of freedom are $n - 1$, where n is the number of pairs. The relevant formulas are:

$$H_0\colon \mu_D = 0$$
$$H_1\colon \mu_D \neq 0$$

$$t_{n-1} = \frac{\bar{D} - \mu_D}{\frac{s_D}{\sqrt{n}}}$$

where

$$\bar{D} = \frac{\sum_{i=1}^{n} D_i}{}$$

$$s_D = \sqrt{\frac{\sum_{i=1}^{n} (D_i - \bar{D})^2}{}}$$

In Internet usage example (Table 15.1), a paired t test could be used to determine if the respondents differed in their attitude toward the Internet and attitude toward technology. The resulting output is shown in Table 15.15. The mean attitude toward the Internet is 5.167 and that toward technology is 4.10. The mean difference between the variables is 1.067, with a standard deviation of .828 and a standard error of .1511. This results in a t value of (1.067/.1511) = 7.06, with 30 – 1 = 29 degrees of freedom and a probability of less than .001. Therefore, the respondents have a more favorable attitude toward the Internet than toward technology in general. Another application is provided in the context of determining the relative effectiveness of 15-second versus 30-second television commercials.

TABLE 15.15

PAIRED SAMPLES *t* TEST

Variable	*Number of Cases*	*Mean*	*Standard Deviation*	*Standard Error*
Internet attitude	30	5.167	1.234	.225
Technology attitude	30	4.100	1.398	.255

Difference = Internet – Technology

Difference Mean	*Standard Deviation*	*Standard Error*	*Correlation*	*Two-Tailed Probability*	*t Value*	*Degrees of Freedom*	*Two-Tailed Probability*
1.067	.828	.1511	.809	.000	7.059	29	.000

EXAMPLE

Seconds Count

A survey of 83 media directors of the largest Canadian advertising agencies was conducted to determine the relative effectiveness of 15-second versus 30-second commercial advertisements. Using a five-point rating scale (1 being excellent and 5 being poor), respondents rated 15- and 30-second commercials for brand awareness, main idea recall, persuasion, and ability to tell an emotional story. The table indicates that 30-second commercials were rated more favorably on all the dimensions. Paired t tests indicated that these differences were significant, and the 15-second commercials were evaluated as less effective.[19]

MEAN RATING OF 15- AND 30-SECOND COMMERCIALS ON THE FOUR COMMUNICATION VARIABLES

Brand Awareness		*Main Idea Recall*		*Persuasion*		*Ability to Tell Emotional Story*	
15	*30*	*15*	*30*	*15*	*30*	*15*	*30*
2.5	1.9	2.7	2.0	3.7	2.1	4.3	1.9 ■

The difference in proportions for paired samples can be tested by using the McNemar test or the chi-square test, as explained in the following section on nonparametric tests.

NONPARAMETRIC TESTS

Nonparametric tests are used when the independent variables are nonmetric. Similar to parametric tests, nonparametric tests are available for testing variables from one sample, two independent samples, or two related samples.

One Sample

Sometimes the researcher wants to test whether the observations for a particular variable could reasonably have come from a particular distribution, such as the normal, uniform, or Poisson distribution. Knowledge of the distribution is necessary for finding probabilities corresponding to known values of the variable or variable values corresponding to known probabilities (see Appendix 12A). The **Kolmogorov-Smirnov** (K-S) **one-sample test** is one such goodness-of-fit test. The K-S compares the cumulative distribution function for a variable with a specified distribution. A_i denotes the cumulative relative frequency for each category of the theoretical (assumed) distribution, and O_i the comparable value of the sample frequency. The K-S test is based on the maximum value of the absolute difference between A_i and O_i. The test statistic is

Kolmogorov-Smirnov one-sample test A one-sample nonparametric goodness-of-fit test that compares the cumulative distribution function for a variable with a specified distribution.

$$K = \text{Max} \mid A_i - O_i \mid$$

The decision to reject the null hypothesis is based on the value of K. The larger the K is, the more confidence we have that H_0 is false. For $\alpha = .05$, the critical value of K for large samples (over 35) is given by $1.36/\sqrt{n}$.[20] Alternatively, K can be transformed into a normally distributed z statistic and its associated probability determined.

In the context of the Internet usage example, suppose we wanted to test whether the distribution of Internet usage was normal. A K-S one-sample test is conducted, yielding the data shown in Table 15.16. The largest absolute difference between the observed and normal distribution was $K = .222$. Although our sample size is only 30 (less than 35), we can use the approximate formula, and the critical value for K is $1.36/\sqrt{30} = .248$. Since the calculated value of K is smaller than the critical value, the null hypothesis cannot be rejected. Alternatively, Table 15.16 indicates that the probability of observing a K value of .222, as determined by the normalized z statistic, is .103. Since this is more than the significance level of .05, the null hypothesis can not be rejected, leading to the same conclusion. Hence, the distribution of Internet usage does not deviate significantly from the normal distribution.

As mentioned earlier, the chi-square test can also be performed on a single variable from one sample. In this context, the chi-square serves as a goodness-of-fit test. It tests whether a significant difference exists between the observed number of cases in each category and the expected number. Other one sample nonparametric tests include the runs test and the binomial test. The **runs test** is a test of randomness for the dichotomous variables. This test is conducted by determining whether the order or sequence in which observations are obtained is random. The **binomial test** is also a goodness-of-fit test for dichotomous variables. It tests the goodness of fit of the observed number of observations in each category to the number expected under a specified binomial distribution. For more information on these tests, refer to standard statistical literature.[21]

Runs test A test of randomness for a dichotomous variable.

Binomial Test A goodness-of-fit statistical test for dichotomous variables. It tests the goodness of fit of the observed number of observations in each category to the number expected under a specified binomial distribution.

Two Independent Samples

When the difference in the location of two populations is to be compared based on observations from two independent samples, and the variable is measured on an ordinal scale, the **Mann-Whitney *U* test** can be used.[22] This test corresponds to the two independent samples t test, for interval scale variables, when the variances of the two populations are assumed equal.

Mann-Whitney U test A statistical test for a variable measured on an ordinal scale comparing the difference in the location of two populations based on observations from two independent samples.

In the Mann-Whitney U test, the two samples are combined and the cases are ranked in order of increasing size. The test statistic, U, is computed as the number of times a score from sample or group 1 precedes a score from group 2. If the samples are from the same population, the distribution of scores from the two groups in the rank list should be random. An extreme value of U would indicate a nonrandom pattern pointing to the inequality of the two groups. For samples of less than 30, the exact significance level for U is computed. For larger samples, U is transformed into a normally distributed z statistic. This z can be corrected for ties within ranks.

We examine again the difference in the Internet usage of males and females. This time, though, the Mann-Whitney U test is used. The results are given in Table 15.17. Again, a significant difference is found between the two groups, corroborating the results of the two independent samples t test reported earlier. Since the ranks are assigned from the smallest observation to the largest, the higher mean rank (20.93) of males indicates that they use the Internet to a greater extent than females (mean rank = 10.07).

Researchers often wish to test for a significant difference in proportions obtained from two independent samples. As an alternative to the parametric z test considered earlier, one could also use the cross-tabulation procedure to conduct a chi-square test.[23] In this case,

TABLE 15.16

K-S ONE-SAMPLE TEST FOR NORMALITY FOR INTERNET USAGE

Test Distribution—Normal	
Mean:	6.600
Standard Deviation:	4.296
Cases:	30

Most Extreme Differences				
Absolute	Positive	Negative	K-S z	Two-Tailed p
.222	.222	–.142	1.217	.103

TABLE 15.17

MANN-WHITNEY *U* TEST
MANN-WHITNEY *U*–WILCOXON RANK SUM *W* TEST
INTERNET USAGE BY SEX

Sex	*Mean Rank*	*Cases*
Male	20.93	15
Female	10.07	15
Total		30

U	*W*	*z*	*Corrected for Ties Two-Tailed p*
31.000	151.000	−3.406	.001

Note
U = Mann-Whitney test statistic
W = Wilcoxon *W* Statistic
z = *U* transformed into a normally distributed *z* statistic.

we will have a 2 × 2 table. One variable will be used to denote the sample, and will assume the value 1 for sample 1 and the value of 2 for sample 2. The other variable will be the binary variable of interest.

Two other independent-samples nonparametric tests are the median test and Kolmogorov-Smirnov test. The **two-sample median test** determines whether the two groups are drawn from populations with the same median. It is not as powerful as the Mann-Whitney *U* test because it merely uses the location of each observation relative to the median, and not the rank, of each observation. The **Kolmogorov-Smirnov two-sample test** examines whether the two distributions are the same. It takes into account any differences between the two distributions, including the median, dispersion, and skewness, as illustrated by the following example.

Two-sample median test Nonparametric test statistic that determines whether two groups are drawn from populations with the same median. This test is not as powerful as the Mann-Whitney *U*.

Kolmogorov-Smirnov two-sample test Nonparametric test statistic that determines whether two distributions are the same. It takes into account any differences in the two distributions including median, dispersion, and skewness.

EXAMPLE

Directors Change Direction

How do marketing research directors and users in Fortune 500 manufacturing firms perceive the role of marketing research in initiating changes in marketing strategy formulation? It was found that the marketing research directors were more strongly in favor of initiating changes in strategy and less in favor of holding back than were users of marketing research. The percentage responses to one of the items, "Initiate change in the marketing strategy of the firm whenever possible," are given below. Using the Kolmogorov-Smirnov (K-S) test, these differences of role definition were statistically significant at the .05 level, as shown in the table.[24]

THE ROLE OF MARKETING RESEARCH IN STRATEGY FORMULATION

		Responses (%)				
Sample	*n*	*Absolutely Must*	*Preferably Should*	*May or May Not*	*Preferably Should Not*	*Absolutely Must Not*
D	77	7	26	43	19	5
U	68	2	15	32	35	16
K-S significance = .05						

**D* = Directors, *U* = users ■

In this example, the marketing research directors and users comprised two independent samples. However, the samples are not always independent. In the case of paired samples, a different set of tests should be used.

Paired Samples

Wilcoxon matched-pairs signed-ranks test A nonparametric test that analyzes the differences between the paired observations, taking into account the magnitude of the differences.

An important nonparametric test for examining differences in the location of two populations based on paired observations is the **Wilcoxon matched-pairs signed-ranks test**. This test analyzes the differences between the paired observations, taking into account the magnitude of the differences. It computes the differences between the pairs of variables and ranks the absolute differences. The next step is to sum the positive and negative ranks. The test statistic, z, is computed from the positive and negative rank sums. Under the null hypothesis of no difference, z is a standard normal variate with mean 0 and variance 1 for large samples. This test corresponds to the paired t test considered earlier.[25]

The example considered for the paired t test, whether the respondents differed in terms of attitude toward the Internet and attitude toward technology, is considered again. Suppose we assume that both these variables are measured on ordinal rather than interval scales. Accordingly, we use the Wilcoxon test. The results are shown in Table 15.18. Again, a significant difference is found in the variables, and the results are in accordance with the conclusion reached by the paired t test. There are 23 negative differences (attitude toward technology is less favorable than is attitude toward Internet). The mean rank of these negative differences is 12.72. On the other hand, there is only 1 positive difference (attitude toward technology is more favorable than attitude toward Internet). The mean rank of this difference is 7.50. There are 6 ties, or observations with the same value for both variables. These numbers indicate that the attitude toward the Internet is more favorable than toward technology. Furthermore, the probability associated with the z statistic is less than .05, indicating that the difference is indeed significant.

Sign Test A nonparametric test for examining differences in the location of two populations, based on paired observations, which only compares the signs of the differences between pairs of variables without taking into account the magnitude of the differences.

Another paired sample nonparametric test is the **sign test**.[26] This test is not as powerful as the Wilcoxon matched-pairs signed-ranks test as it only compares the signs of the differences between pairs of variables without taking into account the magnitude of the differences. In the special case of a binary variable where the researcher wishes to test differences in proportions, the McNemar test can be used. Alternatively, the chi-square test can also be used for binary variables. The various parametric and nonparametric tests for differences are summarized in Table 15.19. The tests in Table 15.19 can be easily related to those in Figure 15.9. Table 15.19 classifies the tests in more detail as parametric tests (based on metric data) are classified separately for means and proportions. Likewise, nonparametric tests (based on nonmetric data) are classified separately for distributions and rankings/medians. Research in Practice 15.1 illustrates the use of hypothesis testing in international branding strategy, while Research in Practice 15.2 cites the use of descriptive statistics in research on ethics.

TABLE 15.18

WILCOXON MATCHED-PAIRS SIGNED-RANKS TEST

	Internet with Technology	
(Technology–Internet)	*Cases*	*Mean Rank*
–Ranks	23	12.72
+Ranks	1	7.50
Ties	6	
Total	30	
$z = -4.207$		Two-Tailed $p = .0000$

TABLE 15.19

A SUMMARY OF HYPOTHESIS TESTS RELATED TO DIFFERENCES

Sample	*Application*	*Level of Scaling*	*Test/Comments*
One Sample			
One sample	Distributions	Nonmetric	K-S and chi-square for goodness of fit Runs test for randomness Binomial test for goodness of fit for dichotomous variables
One sample	Means	Metric	t test, if variance is unknown z test, if variance is known
One sample	Proportions	Metric	z test
Two Independent Samples			
Two independent samples	Distributions	Nonmetric	K-S two-sample test for examining the equivalence of two distributions
Two independent samples	Means	Metric	Two-group t test F test for equality of variances
Two independent samples	Proportions	Metric Nonmetric	z test Chi-square test
Two independent samples	Rankings/Medians	Nonmetric	Mann-Whitney U test is more powerful than the median test
Paired Samples			
Paired samples	Means	Metric	Paired t test
Paired samples	Proportions	Nonmetric	McNemar test for binary variables. Chi-square test
Paired samples	Rankings/Medians	Nonmetric	Wilcoxon matched-pairs signed-ranks test is more powerful than the sign test

INTERNET AND COMPUTER APPLICATIONS

All three standard statistical packages (SPSS, SAS, and BMDP) have similar programs in their microcomputer and mainframe versions for computing frequency distributions, cross-tabulations and testing hypotheses. The major programs for frequency distribution are FREQUENCIES (SPSS), UNIVARIATE (SAS), and 2D (BMDP). Other programs provide only the frequency distribution (FREQ in SAS, 4D in BMDP) or only some of the associated statistics (Exhibit 15.1).[27] In Minitab, the main function is Stats>Descriptive Statistics. The output values include the mean, median, standard deviation, minimum, maximum, and quartiles. Histogram in a bar chart or graph can be produced from the Graph>Histogram selection. Several of the spreadsheets can also be used to obtain frequencies and descriptive statistics. In Excel, the Tools>Data Analysis function computes the descriptive statistics. The output produces the mean, standard error, median, mode, standard deviation, variance, kurtosis, skewness, range, minimum, maximum, sum, count, and confidence level. Frequencies can be selected under the histogram function. A histogram can be produced in bar format.

The major cross-tabulation programs are CROSSTABS (SPSS), FREQ (SAS), and 4F (BMDP). All these programs will display the cross-classification tables and provide cell counts, row and column percentages, the chi-square test for significance, and all the measures of the strength of the association that have been discussed. In addition, the TABULATE (SAS) program can be used for obtaining cell counts and row and column percentages, although it does not provide any of the associated statistics. In Minitab, cross-tabulations (cross tabs) and chi-square are under the Stats>Tables function. Each of these

RESEARCH IN PRACTICE 15.1

International Brand Equity—The Name of the Game

In the 1990s, the trend is toward global marketing. How can marketers market a brand abroad in the midst of diverse historical and cultural differences? According to Bob Kroll, the former president of Del Monte International, uniform packaging may be an asset, yet catering to individual countries' culinary taste preferences is more important. One recent survey on international product marketing makes this clear. Marketing executives now believe it's best to think globally but act locally. Respondents included 100 brand and product managers and marketing people from some of the nation's largest food, pharmaceutical, and personal product companies. Thirty-nine percent said that it would not be a good idea to use uniform packaging in foreign markets whereas 38 percent were in favor of it. Those in favor of regionally targeted packaging, however, mentioned the desirability of maintaining as much brand equity and package consistency as possible from market to market. But they also believed it was necessary to tailor the package to fit the linguistic and regulatory needs of different markets. Based on this finding, a suitable research question can be: Do consumers in different countries prefer to buy global name brands with different packaging customized to suit their local needs? Based on this research question, one can frame a hypothesis that, other things being constant, standardized branding with customized packaging for a well-established name brand will result in greater market share. The hypotheses may be formulated as follows:

> H_0: Standardized branding with customized packaging for a well-established name brand will not lead to greater market share in the international market.
> H_1: Other factors remaining equal, standardized branding with customized packaging for a well-established name brand will lead to greater market share in the international market.

To test the null hypothesis, a well-established brand such as Colgate toothpaste, which has followed a mixed strategy, can be selected. The market share in countries with standardized branding and standardized packaging can be compared with market share in countries with standardized branding and customized packaging, after controlling for the effect of other factors. A two independent samples t test can be used.[28]

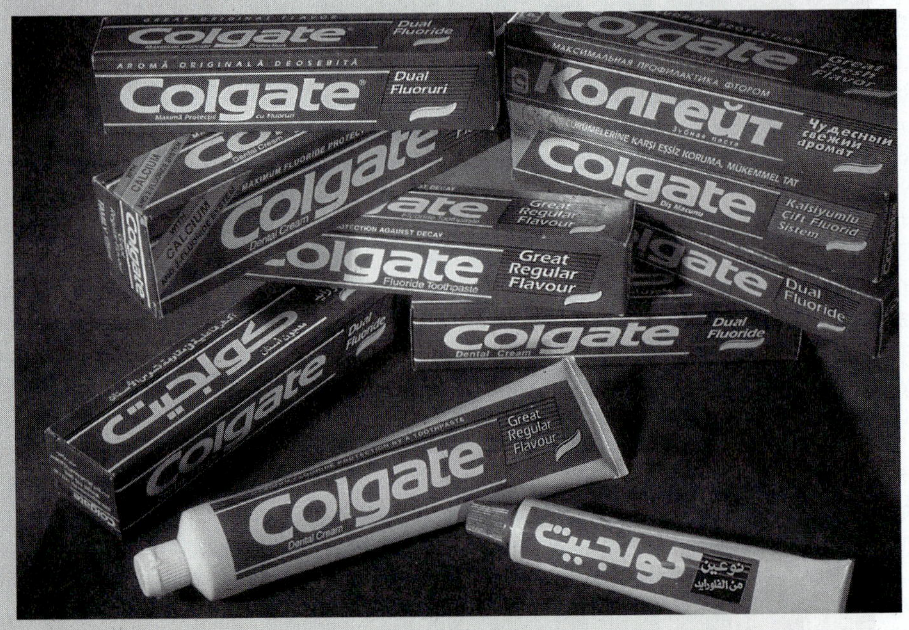

Colgate toothpaste has followed a mixed strategy of standardized branding with customized packaging in some foreign markets. A two independent samples t test can be used to assess the effectiveness of this strategy.

RESEARCH IN PRACTICE 15.2

Statistics Describe Distrust

Descriptive statistics indicate that the public perception of ethics in business, and thus ethics in marketing, are poor. In a poll conducted by *Business Week*, 46 percent of those surveyed said that the ethical standards of business executives are only fair. A *Time* magazine survey revealed that 76 percent of Americans felt that business managers (and thus researchers) lacked ethics and this lack contributes to the decline of moral standards in the United States. However, the general public is not alone in its disparagement of business ethics. In a Touche Ross survey of businesspersons, results showed that the general feeling was that ethics were a serious concern and media portrayal of the lack of ethics in business has not been exaggerated.[29]

features must be selected separately under the Tables function. The Data>Pivot Table function performs crosstabs in Excel. To do additional analysis or customize data, select a different summary function such as max, min, average, or standard deviation. In addition, a custom calculation can be selected to calculate based on other cells in the data plane. ChiTest can be accessed under the Insert>Function>Statistical>ChiTest function.

Exhibit 15.1
Computer Programs for Frequencies

SPSS
The main program in SPSS is FREQUENCIES. It produces a table of frequency counts, percentages, and cumulative percentages for the values of each variable. It gives all of the associated statistics except for the coefficient of variation. If the data are interval scaled and only the summary statistics are desired, the DESCRIPTIVES procedure can be used. All of the statistics computed by DESCRIPTIVES are available in FREQUENCIES. However, DESCRIPTIVES is more efficient because it does not sort values into a frequency table. An additional program, MEANS, computes means and standard deviations for a dependent variable over subgroups of cases defined by independent variables.

SAS
The main program in SAS is UNIVARIATE. In addition to providing a frequency table, this program provides all of the associated statistics. Another procedure available is FREQ. For one-way frequency distribution, FREQ does not provide any associated statistics. If only summary statistics are desired, procedures such as MEANS, SUMMARY, and TABULATE can be used. It should be noted that FREQ is not available as an independent program in the microcomputer version.

BMDP
The main procedure in BMDP is 2D, which gives the frequency distribution and all the associated statistics except for the coefficient of variation. 1D provides the summary statistics for interval data but does not give the frequency distribution. 4D gives a frequency distribution for numeric and nonnumeric data but does not compute the summary statistics.

Minitab
The main function is Stats>Descriptive Statistics. The output values include the mean, median, mode, standard deviation, minimum, maximum, and quartiles. Histogram in a bar chart or graph can be produced from the Graph>Histogram selection.

Excel
The Tools>Data Analysis function computes the descriptive statistics. The output produces the mean, standard error, median, mode, standard deviation, variance, kurtosis, skewness, range, minimum, maximum, sum, count, and confidence level. Frequencies can be selected under the histogram function. A histogram can be produced in bar format.

FOCUS ON Burke

The basic tool used by most researchers to examine their data is the cross-tabulation. It affords a quick look at the distribution of responses and may show any data problems. However, it can be misleading unless care is taken.

Burke completed a study that caused great concern for the client. The results from the Burke tables were very different from previous results from another research company. We use contrived data to illustrate the situation (the actual data are proprietary). This study was conducted among small businesses (fewer than 20 employees) concerning their use of temporary worker ("temp") agencies. A sample of 100 businesses with one employee was taken as well as a sample of 100 businesses with from 2 to 19 employees. The following tabulation was created.

This was the type of table the client was accustomed to seeing. Do you believe that 52 percent of businesses used temporary assistance agencies? The Burke Corporate Information Center had census records that show that in the population there are 9.2 million one-person businesses and only 2.5 million business with from 2 to 20 employees (from county business patterns). The weighted total column should look like the table below:

		Number of Full-Time t Employees		
		=1	*2 to 19*	*Total*
	Base	100	100	200
	Yes	40	65	105
Used Temps?		40%	65%	52%
		60	35	95
	No	60%	35%	48%

- A representative sample would have had 157 businesses with 1 employee and 43 with 2 to 20 employees.
- The weights are then 1.57 and .43 to create the total column.

The proper table would be as follows:

		Number of Full-Time Employees		*Weighed*
		=1	*2 to 19*	*Total*
	Base	100	100	200
	Yes	40	65	91
Used Temps?		40%	65%	45%
		60	35	109
	No	60%	35%	55%

% sampled population = 1 emp. is .79
% sampled population = 2 to 20 emp. is .21

Now the client is told that 45 percent rather than 52 percent of companies with fewer than 20 employees use temporary employee agencies. This may not sound like a big change, but when the client saw the proper table, they realized that all of their historical trending had to be reconstructed. Never construct total column in tabulations without considering the true distribution in the population.

The major program for conducting *t* tests in SPSS is T-TEST. This program can be used to conduct *t* tests on independent as well as paired samples. All the nonparametric tests that we have discussed can be conducted by using the NPAR TESTS program. In SAS, the program T-TEST can be used. The nonparametric tests may be conducted by using NPAR1WAY. This program will conduct the two independent samples tests (Mann-Whitney, median, and K-S) as well as the Wilcoxon test for paired samples. The parametric *t* tests in BMDP may be conducted by using the 3D program and the nonparametric tests by using 3S. Parametric tests available in Minitab in descriptive stat function are *z* test means, *t* test for means, and two-sample *t* test. The nonparametric tests can be accessed under the Stat>Time Series function. The output includes the one-sample sign, one-sample Wilcoxon, Mann Whitney, Kruskal-Wallis, median test, Friedman, runs test, and pairwise differences. The available parametric tests in Excel and other spreadsheets include the *t* test: paired samples for means, *t* test: two independent samples assuming equal variances, *t* test: two independent samples assuming unequal variances, *z* test: two samples for means, and *F* test for variances of two samples. Non parametric tests are not available.

SUMMARY

Basic data analysis provides valuable insights and guides the rest of the data analysis as well as the interpretation of the results. A frequency distribution should be obtained for each variable in the data. This analysis produces a table of frequency counts, percentages, and cumulative percentages for all the values associated with that variable. It indicates the extent of out-of-range, missing, or extreme values. The mean, mode, and median of a frequency distribution are measures of central tendency. The variability of the distribution is described by the range, the variance or standard deviation, coefficient of variation, and interquartile range. Skewness and kurtosis provide an idea of the shape of the distribution.

Cross-tabulations are tables that reflect the joint distribution of two or more variables. In cross-tabulation, the percentages can be computed either columnwise, based on column totals, or rowwise, based on row totals. The general rule is to compute the percentages in the direction of the independent variable, across the dependent variable. Often the introduction of a third variable can provide additional insights. The chi-square statistic provides a test of the statistical significance of the observed association in a cross-tabulation. The phi coefficient, contingency coefficient, Cramer's *V*, and the lambda coefficient provide measures of the strength of association between the variables.

Parametric and nonparametric tests are available for testing hypotheses related to differences. In the parametric case, the *t* test is used to examine hypotheses related to the population mean. Different forms of the *t* test are suitable for testing hypotheses based on one sample, two independent samples, or paired samples. In the nonparametric case, popular one-sample tests include the Kolmogorov-Smirnov, chi-square, runs test, and the binomial test. For two independent nonparametric samples, the Mann-Whitney *U* test, median test, and the Kolmogorov-Smirnov test can be used. For paired samples, the Wilcoxon matched-pairs signed-ranks test and the sign test are useful for examining hypotheses related to measures of location.

KEY TERMS AND CONCEPTS

frequency distribution
measures of location
mean
mode
median
measures of variability
range
interquartile range
variance
standard deviation
coefficient of variation
skewness
kurtosis
null hypothesis
alternative hypothesis
one-tailed test
two-tailed test
test statistic
type I error
level of significance
type II error
power of a test
cross-tabulation
contingency table

chi-square statistic
chi-square distribution
phi coefficient
contingency coefficient
Cramer's *V*
asymmetric lambda
symmetric lambda
tau *b*
tau *c*
gamma
parametric tests
nonparametric tests
t test
t statistic
t distribution
z test
independent samples
F test
F statistic
F distribution
paired samples
paired samples *t* test
Kolmogorov-Smirnov one-sample test
runs test
binomial test
Mann-Whitney *U* test
two-sample median test
Kolmogorov-Smirnov two-sample test
Wilcoxon matched-pairs signed-ranks test
sign test

ACRONYMS

The statistics associated with frequencies may be summarized by the acronym FREQUENCIES:

F latness or peakedness: kurtosis
R ange
E stimate of location: mean
Q uotients: percentages
U ndulation: variance
E stimate of location: mode
N umbers or counts
C oefficient of variation
I nterquartile range
E stimate of location: median
S kewness

The salient characteristics of cross-tabulations may be summarized by the acronym C TABULATIONS:

C ube: chi-square, contingency coefficient, and Cramer's *V*

T wo by two table statistic: phi coefficient
A dditional insights or refinements provided by third variable
B ased on cell count of at least five
U nchanged association with third variable introduction
L ambda coefficient
A ssociation and not causation is measured
T wo- and three-variable cases
I nitial relationship may be spurious
O ver three variables poses problems
N umbers and percentages
S uppressed association may be revealed

EXERCISES

Questions

1. Describe the procedure for computing frequencies.
2. What measures of location are commonly computed?
3. Define the interquartile range. What does it measure?
4. What is meant by the coefficient of variation?
5. How is the relative flatness or peakedness of a distribution measured?
6. What is a skewed distribution? What does it mean?
7. What is the major difference between cross-tabulation and frequency distribution?
8. What is the general rule for computing percentages in cross-tabulation?
9. Define a spurious correlation.
10. What is meant by a suppressed association? How is it revealed?
11. Discuss the reasons for the frequent use of cross-tabulations. What are some of its limitations?
12. Present a classification of hypothesis testing procedures.
13. Describe the general procedure for conducting a *t* test.
14. What is the major difference between parametric and nonparametric tests?
15. Which nonparametric tests are the counterparts of the two independent samples *t* test for parametric data?
16. Which nonparametric tests are the counterparts of the paired samples *t* test for parametric data?

Problems

1. In each of the following situations, indicate the statistical analysis you would conduct and the appropriate test or test statistic that should be used.

a. Consumer preferences for Camay bar soap were obtained on an 11-point Likert scale. The same consumers were then shown a commercial about Camay. After the commercial, preferences for Camay were again measured. Has the commercial been successful in inducing a change in preferences?
b. Does the preference for Camay bar soap follow a normal distribution?
c. Respondents in a survey of 1,000 households were classified as heavy, medium, light, or nonusers of ice cream. They were also classified as being in high-, medium-, or low-income categories. Is the consumption of ice cream related to income level?
d. In a survey using a representative sample of 2,000 households from the Market Facts consumer mail panel, the respondents were asked to rank 10 department stores, including Sears, in order of preference. The sample was divided into small and large households based on a median split of the household size. Does preference for shopping at Sears vary by household size?

2. The current advertising campaign for a major soft drink brand would be changed if less than 30 percent of the consumers like it.
   a. Formulate the null and alternative hypotheses.
   b. Discuss the type I and type II errors that could occur in hypothesis testing.
   c. Which statistical test would you use? Why?
   d. A random sample of 300 consumers was surveyed, and 84 respondents indicated that they liked the campaign. Should the campaign be changed? Why?
3. A major department store chain is having an end-of-season sale on refrigerators. The number of refrigerators sold during this sale at a sample of 10 stores was:
   80 110 0 40 70 80 100 50 80 30
   a. Is there evidence that an average of more than 50 refrigerators per store were sold during this sale? Use $\alpha = .05$.
   b. What assumption is necessary to perform this test?

INTERNET AND COMPUTER EXERCISES

1. Use one of the statistical packages (SPSS, SAS, BMDP, Minitab, or Excel) to conduct the statistical test for problem 3.

Chapter 16

"Analysis of variance is a necessity in the researcher's tool kit. It is a straightforward way to look at differences between groups of responses measured on interval or ratio scales."

Tammy Wise, vice president, client services, Burke Inc.

Analysis of Variance and Covariance

OBJECTIVES

After reading this chapter, the student should be able to

1. discuss the scope of the analysis of variance (ANOVA) technique and its relationship to *t* test and regression
2. describe one-way analysis of variance including decomposition of the total variation, measurement of effects, significance testing, and interpretation of results
3. describe *n*-way analysis of variance and the testing of the significance of the overall effect, the interaction effect, and the main effect of each factor
4. describe analysis of covariance and show how it accounts for the influence of uncontrolled independent variables
5. explain key factors pertaining to the interpretation of results with emphasis on interactions, relative importance of factors, and multiple comparisons
6. discuss specialized ANOVA techniques applicable to marketing, such as repeated measures ANOVA, nonmetric analysis of variance, and multivariate analysis of variance (MANOVA)

OVERVIEW

In chapter 15 we examined tests of differences between two means or two medians. In this chapter we discuss procedures for examining differences between more than two means or medians. These procedures are called *analysis of variance* and *analysis of covariance*. Although these procedures have traditionally been used for analyzing experimental data, they are also useful for analyzing survey or observational data.

We describe the analysis of variance and covariance procedures and discuss their relationship to other techniques. Then we describe one-way analysis of variance, the simplest of these procedures, followed by *n*-way analysis of variance and analysis of covariance. Special attention is given to issues in interpretation of results as they relate to interactions, relative importance of factors, and multiple comparisons. Some specialized topics, such as

DEPARTMENT STORE PATRONAGE PROJECT

Analysis of Variance

In the department store patronage project, several independent variables were examined as categorical variables having more than two categories. For example, familiarity with the department stores considered was respecified as high, medium, or low. The effects of these independent variables on metric dependent variables were examined using analysis of variance procedures. Several useful insights were obtained, which guided subsequent data analysis and interpretation. For example, a three-category respecification of familiarity produced results that were not significant, whereas treating familiarity as a binary variable (high or low) produced significant results. This, along with the frequency distribution, indicated that treating familiarity as having only two categories was most appropriate.

repeated measures analysis of variance, nonmetric analysis of variance, and multivariate analysis of variance are briefly discussed. We begin with some examples illustrating the applications of analysis of variance.

EXAMPLE

Electronic Shopping Risks

Analysis of variance was used to test differences in preferences for electronic shopping for products with different economic and social risks. In a 2×2 design, economic risk and social risk were varied at two levels each (high, low). Preference for electronic shopping served as the dependent variable. The results indicated a significant interaction of social risk with economic risk. Electronic shopping was not perceived favorably for high social risk products (e.g., fashion clothing), regardless of the level of economic product risk, but it was preferred for low economic risk products over high economic risk products when the level of social risk was low.[1] ■

EXAMPLE

Antacids Are Treatments for ANOVA

The role of verbal content and relative newness of a brand in determining the effectiveness of a comparative advertising format for over-the-counter antacids was investigated. The measure of attitude toward the sponsoring brand was the dependent variable. Three factors, advertising format (AF), verbal content (VC), and relative newness (RN), each manipulated at two levels, were the independent variables.

Advertising format was either noncomparative or comparative. In the comparative format, well-known national brands (Rolaids and Tums) were used for comparison. Relative newness was manipulated by changing the brand's sponsor. Alka-Seltzer was the sponsor in the well-established brand treatment, whereas Acid-Off was the sponsor in the new-brand condition. The name "Acid-Off" was chosen based on a pretest. Verbal content was manipulated to reflect factual or evaluative content in an ad.

The subjects were recruited at a shopping mall and randomly assigned to the treatment by an interviewer who was blind to the purpose of the study. A total of 207 responses were collected, 200 of which were usable. Twenty-five subjects were assigned to each of the eight ($2 \times 2 \times 2$) treatments.

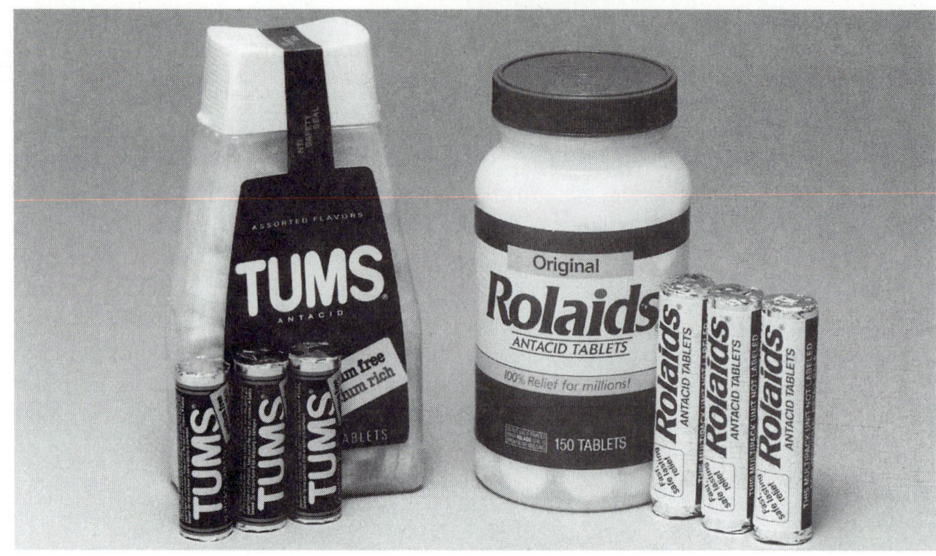

Analysis of variance revealed that comparative advertising emphasizing factual information is best suited for launching a new brand of antacids.

A three-way analysis of variance was performed, with attitude as the dependent variable. The overall results were significant. The three-way interaction was also significant. The only two-way interaction that was significant was between ad format and relative newness. A major conclusion from these results was that a comparative format that emphasized factual information was best suited for launching a new brand.[2] ■

In the department store example, when familiarity had three categories, the *t* test was not appropriate to examine the overall difference in category means, so analysis of variance was used instead. The electronic shopping study involved a comparison of means when there were two factors (independent variables), each of which was varied at two levels. The more complex comparative advertising study involved three factors, each with two levels. In the latter two examples, *t* tests were not appropriate, because the effect of each factor was not independent of the effect of other factors (in other words, interactions were significant). Analysis of variance provided meaningful conclusions in these studies. The relationship of analysis of variance to the *t* test and other techniques is considered in the next section.

RELATIONSHIP AMONG TECHNIQUES

Analysis of Variance (ANOVA) A statistical technique for examining the differences among means for two or more populations.

Factor Categorical independent variables. The independent variables must be all categorical (nonmetric) to use ANOVA.

Treatment In ANOVA, a particular combination of factor levels or categories.

One-way Analysis of Variance An ANOVA technique in which there is only one factor.

Analysis of variance and analysis of covariance are used for examining the differences in the mean values of the dependent variable associated with the effect of the controlled independent variables, after taking into account the influence of the uncontrolled independent variables. Essentially, **analysis of variance (ANOVA)** is used as a test of means for two or more populations. The null hypothesis, typically, is that all means are equal. For example, suppose the researcher was interested in examining whether heavy, medium, light, and nonusers of cereals differed in their preference for Total cereal, measured on a nine-point Likert scale. The null hypothesis that the four groups were not different in preference for Total could be tested using analysis of variance.

In its simplest form, analysis of variance must have a dependent variable (preference for Total cereal) that is metric (measured using an interval or ratio scale). There must also be one or more independent variables (product use: heavy, medium, light, and nonusers). The independent variables must be all categorical (nonmetric). Categorical independent variables are also called **factors**. A particular combination of factor levels, or categories, is called a **treatment**. **One-way analysis of variance** involves only one categorical variable, or a single factor. The differences in preference of heavy, medium, light, and nonusers would be examined by one-way ANOVA. In one-way analysis of variance, a treatment is the same as a factor level (medium users constitute a treatment). If two or more factors are involved, the analysis is termed ***n*-way analysis of variance**. (If, in addition to product use, the researcher also wanted to examine the preference for Total cereal of customers who are loyal and those who are not, an *n*-way analysis of variance would be conducted.)

n-way Analysis of Variance An ANOVA model in which two or more factors are involved.

If the set of independent variables consists of both categorical and metric variables, the technique is called **analysis of covariance (ANCOVA)**. For example, analysis of covariance would be required if the researcher wanted to examine the preference of product use groups and loyalty groups taking into account the respondents' attitudes toward nutrition and the importance they attached to breakfast as a meal. The latter two variables would be measured on nine-point Likert scales. In this case, the categorical independent variables (product use and brand loyalty) are still referred to as factors, whereas the metric independent variables (attitude toward nutrition and importance attached to breakfast) are referred to as **covariates**.

Analysis of Covariance (ANCOVA) An advanced analysis of variance procedure in which the effects of one or more metric-scaled extraneous variables are removed from the dependent variable before conducting the ANOVA.

Covariate A metric independent variable used in ANCOVA.

The relationship of analysis of variance to *t* tests and other techniques, such as regression (see chapter 17), is shown in Figure 16.1. All of these techniques involve a metric dependent variable. ANOVA and ANCOVA can include more than one independent variable (product use, brand loyalty, attitude, importance). Furthermore, at least one of the independent variables must be categorical, and the categorical variables may have more than two categories (in our example, product use has four categories). A *t* test, on the other hand, involves a single, binary independent variable. For example, the difference in the preferences of loyal and nonloyal respondents could be tested by conducting a *t* test. Regression analysis, like ANOVA and ANCOVA, can also involve more than one independent variable. However, all the independent variables are generally interval scaled, although binary or categorical variables can be accommodated using dummy variables. For example, the relationship between preference for Total cereal, attitude toward nutrition, and importance attached to breakfast could be examined via regression analysis.

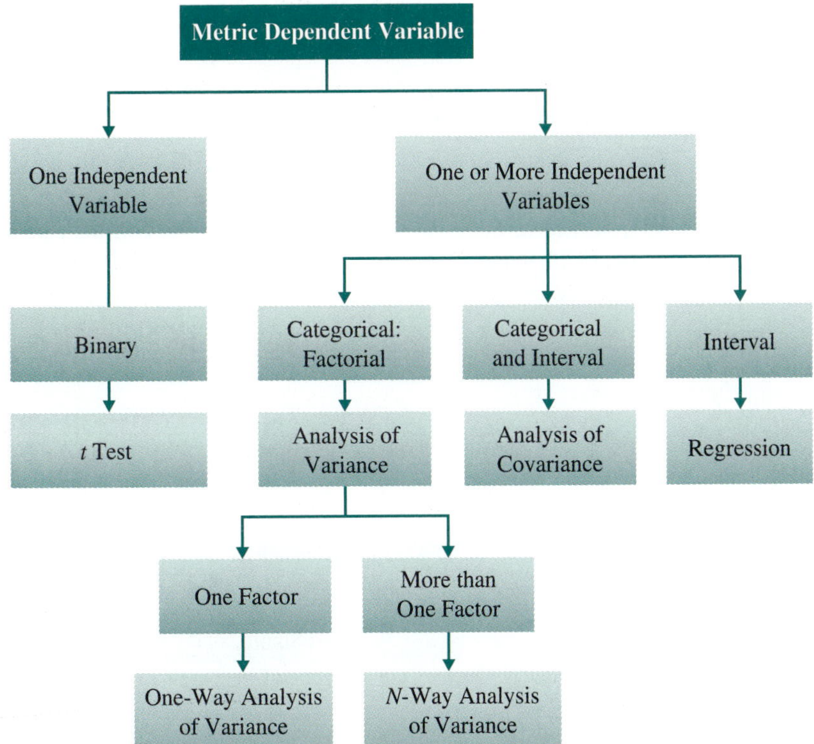

Figure 16.1
Relationship between *t* Test, Analysis of Variance, Analysis of Covariance, and Regression

ONE-WAY ANALYSIS OF VARIANCE

Marketing researchers are often interested in examining the differences in the mean values of the dependent variable for several categories of a single independent variable or factor. For example:

- Do the various segments differ in terms of their volume of product consumption?
- Do the brand evaluations of groups exposed to different commercials vary?
- Do retailers, wholesalers, and agents differ in their attitudes toward the firm's distribution policies?
- How do consumers' intentions to buy the brand vary with different price levels?
- What is the effect of consumers' familiarity with the store (measured as high, medium, and low) on preference for the store?

The answer to these and similar questions can be determined by conducting one-way analysis of variance. Before describing the procedure, we define the important statistics associated with one-way analysis of variance.[3]

STATISTICS ASSOCIATED WITH ONE-WAY ANALYSIS OF VARIANCE

eta^2 (η^2). The strength of the effects of X (independent variable or factor) on Y (dependent variable) are measured by **eta^2** (η^2). The value of η^2 varies between 0 and 1.

F *statistic.* The null hypothesis that the category means are equal in the population is tested by an ***F* statistic** based on the ratio of mean square related to X and mean square related to error.

Mean square. This is the sum of squares divided by the appropriate degrees of freedom.

$SS_{between}$. Also denoted as SS_x, this is the variation in Y related to the variation in the means of the categories of X. This represents variation between the categories of X, or the portion of the sum of squares in Y related to X.

SS_{within}. Also referred to as SS_{error}, this is the variation in Y due to the variation within each of the categories of X. This variation is not accounted for by X.

SS_y. This is the total variation in Y.

CONDUCTING ONE-WAY ANALYSIS OF VARIANCE

The procedure for conducting one-way analysis of variance is described in Figure 16.2. It involves identifying the dependent and independent variables, decomposing the total variation, measuring effects, significance testing, and interpreting results. We consider these steps in detail and illustrate them with some applications.

Figure 16.2
Conducting One-Way ANOVA

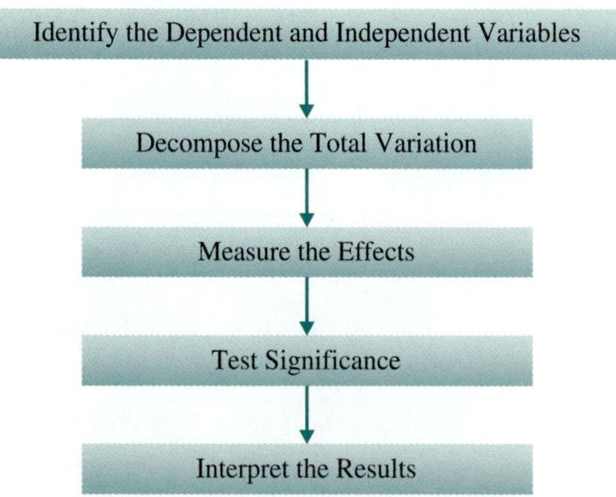

Identification of the Dependent and Independent Variables

The dependent variable is denoted by Y and the independent variable by X. X is a categorical variable having c categories. There are n observations on Y for each category of X, as shown in Table 16.1. As can be seen, the sample size in each category of X is n, and the total sample size $N = n \times c$. The sample sizes in the categories of X (the group sizes) are assumed to be equal for the sake of simplicity, but this is not a requirement.

Decomposition of the Total Variation

In examining the differences among means, one-way analysis of variance involves the **decomposition of the total variation** observed in the dependent variable. This variation is measured by the sums of squares corrected for the mean (SS). Analysis of variance is so named because it examines the variability or variation in the sample (dependent variable) and, based on the variability, determines whether there is reason to believe that the population means differ.

Decomposition of the Total Variation In one-way ANOVA, separation of the variation observed in the dependent variable into the variation due to the independent variables plus the variation due to error.

The total variation in Y, denoted by SS_y, can be decomposed into two components:

$$SS_y = SS_{between} + SS_{within}$$

where the subscripts *between* and *within* refer to the categories of X. $SS_{between}$ is the variation in Y related to the variation in the means of the categories of X. It represents variation between the categories of X. In other words, $SS_{between}$ is the portion of the sum of squares in Y related to the independent variable or factor X. For this reason, $SS_{between}$ is also denoted as SS_x. SS_{within} is the variation in Y related to the variation within each category of X. SS_{within} is not accounted for by X. Therefore it is referred to as SS_{error}. The total variation in Y may be decomposed as

$$SS_y = SS_x + SS_{error}$$

where

$$SS_y = \sum_{i=1}^{N} (Y_i - \bar{Y})^2$$

TABLE 16.1

DECOMPOSITION OF THE TOTAL VARIATION: ONE-WAY ANOVA

	Independent Variable			*X*			
			Categories			*Total Sample*	
	X_1	X_2	X_3	. . .	X_c		
	Y_1	Y_1	Y_1		Y_1	Y_1	
Within Category Variation $= SS_{within}$	Y_2	Y_2	Y_2		Y_2	Y_2	**Total Variation** $= SS_y$
	•					•	
	•					•	
	•					•	
	Y_n	Y_n	Y_n		Y_n	Y_N	
Category Mean	$\bar{Y}_1$	$\bar{Y}_2$	$\bar{Y}_3$		$\bar{Y}_c$	$\bar{Y}$	

Between Category Variation $= SS_{between}$

$$SS_x = \sum_{j=1}^{c} n\,(\overline{Y}_j - \overline{Y})^2$$

$$SS_{error} = \sum_{j}^{c} \sum_{i}^{n} (Y_{ij} - \overline{Y}_j)^2$$

Y_i = individual observation
$\overline{Y}_j$ = mean for category j
$\overline{Y}$ = mean over the whole sample, or grand mean
Y_{ij} = ith observation in the jth category

The logic of decomposing the total variation in Y, SS_y, into $SS_{between}$ and SS_{within} in order to examine differences in group means can be intuitively understood. Recall from chapter 15 that if the variation of the variable in the population was known or estimated, one could estimate how much the sample mean should vary because of random variation alone. In analysis of variance, there are several different groups (e.g., heavy, medium, light, and nonusers). If the null hypothesis is true and all the groups have the same mean in the population, one can estimate how much the sample means should vary because of sampling (random) variations alone. If the observed variation in the sample means is more than what would be expected by sampling variation, it is reasonable to conclude that this extra variability is related to differences in group means in the population.

In analysis of variance, we estimate two measures of variation: within groups (SS_{within}) and between groups ($SS_{between}$). Within-group variation is a measure of how much the observations, Y values, within a group vary. This is used to estimate the variance within a group in the population. It is assumed that all the groups have the same variation in the population. However, because it is not known that all the groups have the same mean, we cannot calculate the variance of all the observations together. The variance for each of the groups must be calculated individually, and these are combined into an "average" or "overall" variance. Likewise, another estimate of the variance of the Y values may be obtained by examining the variation between the means. (This process is the reverse of determining the variation in the means, given the population variances.) If the population mean is the same in all the groups, then the variation in the sample means and the sizes of the sample groups can be used to estimate the variance of Y. The reasonableness of this estimate of the Y variance depends on whether the null hypothesis is true. If the null hypothesis is true and the population means are equal, the variance estimate based on between-group variation is correct. On the other hand, if the groups have different means in the population, the variance estimate based on between-group variation will be too large. Thus, by comparing the Y variance estimates based on between-group and within-group variation, we can test the null hypothesis.[4] Decomposition of the total variation in this manner also enables us to measure the effects of X on Y.

Measurement of Effects

The effects of X on Y are measured by SS_x. Because SS_x is related to the variation in the means of the categories of X, the relative magnitude of SS_x increases as the differences among the means of Y in the categories of X increase. The relative magnitude of SS_x also increases as the variations in Y within the categories of X decrease. The strength of the effects of X on Y are measured as follows:

$$\eta^2 = \frac{SS_x}{SS_y} = \frac{(SS_y - SS_{error})}{SS_y}$$

The value of η^2 varies between 0 and 1. It assumes a value of 0 when all the category means are equal, indicating that X has no effect of X on Y. The value of η^2 will be 1 when there is no variability within each category of X but there is some variability between categories. Thus, η^2 is a measure of the variation in Y that is explained by the independent variable X. Not only can we measure the effects of X on Y, but we can also test for their significance.

Significance Testing

In one-way analysis of variance, the interest lies in testing the null hypothesis that the category means are equal in the population.[5] In other words,

$$H_0\text{: } \mu_1 = \mu_2 = \mu_3 = \ldots = \mu_c$$

Under the null hypothesis, SS_x and SS_{error} come from the same source of variation. In such a case, the estimate of the population variance of Y can be based on either between-category variation or within-category variation. In other words, the estimate of the population variance of Y,

$$S_y^2 = \frac{SS_x}{(c - 1)}$$

$$= \text{mean square due to } X$$

$$= MS_x$$

or

$$S_y^2 = \frac{SS_{error}}{(N - c)}$$

$$= \text{mean square due to error}$$

$$= MS_{error}$$

The null hypothesis may be tested by the F statistic based on the ratio between these two estimates:

$$F = \frac{SS_x/(c - 1)}{SS_{error}/(N - c)} = \frac{MS_x}{MS_{error}}$$

This statistic follows the F distribution, with $(c - 1)$ and $(N - c)$ degrees of freedom (df). A table of the F distribution is given as Table 5 in the statistical appendix at the end of the book. As mentioned in chapter 15, the F distribution is a probability distribution of the ratios of sample variances. It is characterized by degrees of freedom for the numerator and degrees of freedom for the denominator.[6]

Interpretation of Results

If the null hypothesis of equal category means is not rejected, then the independent variable does not have a significant effect on the dependent variable. On the other hand, if the null hypothesis is rejected, then the effect of the independent variable is significant. In other words, the mean value of the dependent variable will be different for different categories of the independent variable. A comparison of the category mean values will indicate the nature of the effect of the independent variable. Other salient issues in the interpretation of results, such as examination of differences among specific means, are discussed later. We illustrate the application of the one-way ANOVA and other related techniques.

Illustrative Data. We illustrate the concepts discussed in this chapter using the data presented in Table 16.2. These data were generated by an experiment in which a major department store chain wanted to examine the effect of the level of in-store promotion and store-wide coupon on sales. In-store promotion was varied at three levels: high (1), medium (2), and low (3). Couponing was manipulated at two levels. Either a $20 store-wide coupon was distributed to potential shoppers (denoted by 1) or it was not (denoted by 2 in Table 16.2). In-store promotion and coupon were crossed resulting in a 3×2 design with six cells. Thirty stores were randomly selected, and five stores were randomly assigned to each treatment condition as shown in Table 16.2. The experiment ran for two months. Sales in each store were measured, normalized to account for extraneous factors (store size, traffic, etc.) and converted to a 1-to-10 scale. In addition, a qualitative assessment was made of the relative affluence of the clientele of each store, again using a 1-to-10 scale. In these scales, higher numbers denote higher sales or more affluent clientele. The data generated are presented in Table 16.2.

TABLE 16.2

COUPON LEVEL, IN-STORE PROMOTION, STORE SALES, AND CLIENTELE RATING

Store Number	*Coupon Level*	*In-Store Promotion*	*Sales*	*Clientele Rating*
1	1.00	1.00	10.00	9.00
2	1.00	1.00	9.00	10.00
3	1.00	1.00	10.00	8.00
4	1.00	1.00	8.00	4.00
5	1.00	1.00	9.00	6.00
6	1.00	2.00	8.00	8.00
7	1.00	2.00	8.00	4.00
8	1.00	2.00	7.00	10.00
9	1.00	2.00	9.00	6.00
10	1.00	2.00	6.00	9.00
11	1.00	3.00	5.00	8.00
12	1.00	3.00	7.00	9.00
13	1.00	3.00	6.00	6.00
14	1.00	3.00	4.00	10.00
15	1.00	3.00	5.00	4.00
16	2.00	1.00	8.00	10.00
17	2.00	1.00	9.00	6.00
18	2.00	1.00	7.00	8.00
19	2.00	1.00	7.00	4.00
20	2.00	1.00	6.00	9.00
21	2.00	2.00	4.00	6.00
22	2.00	2.00	5.00	8.00
23	2.00	2.00	5.00	10.00
24	2.00	2.00	6.00	4.00
25	2.00	2.00	4.00	9.00
26	2.00	3.00	2.00	4.00
27	2.00	3.00	3.00	6.00
28	2.00	3.00	2.00	10.00
29	2.00	3.00	1.00	9.00
30	2.00	3.00	2.00	8.00

ILLUSTRATIVE APPLICATIONS OF ONE-WAY ANALYSIS OF VARIANCE

We illustrate one-way ANOVA first with an example showing calculations done by hand and then using computer analysis. Suppose that only one factor, namely in-store promotion was manipulated, that is, let us ignore couponing for the purpose of this illustration. The department store is attempting to determine the effect of in-store promotion (X) on sales (Y). For the purpose of illustrating hand calculations, the data of Table 16.2 are transformed in Table 16.3 to show the store (Y_{ij}) for each level of promotion. The null hypothesis is that the category means are equal: H_0: $\mu_1 = \mu_2 = \mu_3$.

To test the null hypothesis, the various sums of squares are computed as follows:

$$\begin{aligned}SS_y = {} & (10 - 6.067)^2 + (9 - 6.067)^2 + (10 - 6.067)^2 + (8 - 6.067)^2 + (9 - 6.067)^2\\ & + (8 - 6.067)^2 + (9 - 6.067)^2 + (7 - 6.067)^2 + (7 - 6.067)^2 + (6 - 6.067)^2\\ & + (8 - 6.067)^2 + (8 - 6.067)^2 + (7 - 6.067)^2 + (9 - 6.067)^2 + (6 - 6.067)^2\\ & + (4 - 6.067)^2 + (5 - 6.067)^2 + (5 - 6.067)^2 + (6 - 6.067)^2 + (4 - 6.067)^2\\ & + (5 - 6.067)^2 + (7 - 6.067)^2 + (6 - 6.067)^2 + (4 - 6.067)^2 + (5 - 6.067)^2\\ & + (2 - 6.067)^2 + (3 - 6.067)^2 + (2 - 6.067)^2 + (1 - 6.067)^2 + (2 - 6.067)^2\end{aligned}$$

$$\begin{aligned}= {} & (3.933)^2 + (2.933)^2 + (3.933)^2 + (1.933)^2 + (2.933)^2\\ & + (1.933)^2 + (2.933)^2 + (.933)^2 + (.933)^2 + (-.067)^2\\ & + (1.933)^2 + (1.933)^2 + (.933)^2 + (2.933)^2 + (-.067)^2\\ & + (-2.067)^2 + (-1.067)^2 + (-1.067)^2 + (-.067)^2 + (-2.067)^2\\ & + (-1.067)^2 + (.933)^2 + (-.067)^2 + (-2.067)^2 + (-1.067)^2\\ & + (-4.067)^2 + (-3.067)^2 + (-4.067)^2 + (-5.067)^2 + (-4.067)^2\\ = {} & 185.867\end{aligned}$$

$$\begin{aligned}SS_x &= 10(8.3 - 6.067)^2 + 10(6.2 - 6.067)^2 + 10(3.7 - 6.067)^2\\ &= 10(2.233)^2 + 10(.133)^2 + 10(-2.367)^2\\ &= 106.067\end{aligned}$$

$$\begin{aligned}SS_{error} = {} & (10 - 8.3)^2 + (9 - 8.3)^2 + (10 - 8.3)^2 + (8 - 8.3)^2 + (9 - 8.3)^2\\ & + (8 - 8.3)^2 + (9 - 8.3)^2 + (7 - 8.3)^2 + (7 - 8.3)^2 + (6 - 8.3)^2\\ & + (8 - 6.2)^2 + (8 - 6.2)^2 + (7 - 6.2)^2 + (9 - 6.2)^2 + (6 - 6.2)^2\\ & + (4 - 6.2)^2 + (5 - 6.2)^2 + (5 - 6.2)^2 + (6 - 6.2)^2 + (4 - 6.2)^2\\ & + (5 - 3.7)^2 + (7 - 3.7)^2 + (6 - 3.7)^2 + (4 - 3.7)^2 + (5 - 3.7)^2\\ & + (2 - 3.7)^2 + (3 - 3.7)^2 + (2 - 3.7)^2 + (1 - 3.7)^2 + (2 - 3.7)^2\end{aligned}$$

$$\begin{aligned}= {} & (1.7)^2 + (.7)^2 + (1.7)^2 + (-.3)^2 + (.7)^2\\ & + (-.3)^2 + (.7)^2 + (-1.3)^2 + (-1.3)^2 + (-2.3)^2\\ & + (1.8)^2 + (1.8)^2 + (.8)^2 + (2.8)^2 + (-.2)^2\\ & + (-2.2)^2 + (-1.2)^2 + (-1.2)^2 + (-.2)^2 + (-2.2)^2\\ & + (1.3)^2 + (3.3)^2 + (2.3)^2 + (.3)^2 + (1.3)^2\\ & + (-1.7)^2 + (-.7)^2 + (-1.7)^2 + (-2.7)^2 + (-1.7)^2\\ = {} & 79.80\end{aligned}$$

TABLE 16.3

EFFECT OF IN-STORE PROMOTION ON SALES

		Level of In-Store Promotion	
Number	*High*	*Medium*	*Low*
		Normalized Sales	
1	10	8	5
2	9	8	7
3	10	7	6
4	8	9	4
5	9	6	5
6	8	4	2
7	9	5	3
8	7	5	2
9	7	6	1
10	6	4	2
Column totals	83	62	37
Category means: $\bar{Y}_j$	$\frac{83}{10}$	$\frac{62}{10}$	$\frac{37}{10}$
	= 8.3	= 6.2	= 3.7
Grand mean, $\bar{Y}$	$= \frac{(83 + 62 + 37)}{30} = 6.067$		

It can be verified that

$$SS_y = SS_x + SS_{error}$$

as follows:

$$185.867 = 106.067 + 79.80$$

The strength of the effects of *X* on *Y* are measured as follows:

$$\eta^2 = \frac{SS_x}{SS_y}$$

$$= \frac{106.067}{185.867}$$

$$= .571$$

In other words, 57.1 percent of the variation in sales (*Y*) is accounted for by in-store promotion (*X*), indicating a modest effect. The null hypothesis may now be tested.

$$F = \frac{SS_x/(c - 1)}{SS_{error}/(N - c)} = \frac{MS_x}{MS_{error}}$$

$$= \frac{106.067/(3 - 1)}{79.800/(30 - 3)}$$

$$= 17.944$$

TABLE 16.4

**ONE-WAY ANOVA:
EFFECT OF IN-STORE PROMOTION ON STORE SALES**

Source of Variation	*Sum of Squares*	*df*	*Mean Square*	*F Ratio*	*F Probability*
Between groups (in-store promotion)	106.067	2	53.033	17.944	.000
Within groups (error)	79.800	27	2.956		
Total	185.867	29	6.409		

Cell Means

Level of In-store Promotion	*Count*	*Mean*
High (1)	10	8.300
Medium (2)	10	6.200
Low (3)	10	3.700
Total	30	6.067

From Table 5 in the statistical appendix we see that for 2 and 27 degrees of freedom, the critical value of F is 3.35 for $\alpha = .05$. Because the calculated value of F is greater than the critical value, we reject the null hypothesis. We conclude that the population means for the three levels of in-store promotion are indeed different. The relative magnitudes of the means for the three categories indicate that a high level of in-store promotion leads to significantly higher sales.

We now illustrate the analysis of variance procedure using a computer program. The results of conducting the same analysis by computer are presented in Table 16.4. The value of SS_x denoted by main effects is 106.067 with 2 df; that of SS_{error} is denoted by residual is 79.80 with 27 df. Therefore, $MS_x = 106.067/2 = 53.033$, and $MS_{error} = 79.80/27 = 2.956$. The value of $F = 53.033/2.956 = 17.944$ with 2 and 27 degrees of freedom, resulting in a probability of .000. Since the associated probability is less than the significance level of .05, the null hypothesis of equal population means is rejected. Alternatively, it can be seen from Table 5 in the statistical appendix that the critical value of F for 2 and 27 degrees of freedom is 3.35. Since the calculated value of F (17.944) is larger than the critical value, the null hypothesis is rejected. As can be seen from Table 16.4, the sample means, with values of 8.3, 6.2, and 3.7, are quite different.

The procedure for conducting one-way analysis of variance and the illustrative application help us understand the assumptions involved.

ASSUMPTIONS IN ANALYSIS OF VARIANCE

The salient assumptions in analysis of variance can be summarized as follows.

1. Ordinarily, the categories of the independent variable are assumed to be fixed. Inferences are made only to the specific categories considered. This is referred to as the *fixed-effects model*. Other models are also available. In the *random-effects model*, the categories or treatments are considered to be random samples from a universe of treatments. Inferences are made to other categories not examined in the analysis. A *mixed-effects model* results if some treatments are considered fixed and others random.[7]

2. The error term is normally distributed, with a zero mean and a constant variance. The error is not related to any of the categories of X. Modest departures from these assumptions do not seriously affect the validity of the analysis. Furthermore, the data can be transformed to satisfy the assumption of normality or equal variances.
3. The error terms are uncorrelated. If the error terms are correlated (that is, the observations are not independent), the F ratio can be seriously distorted.

In many data analysis situations, these assumptions are reasonably met. Analysis of variance is therefore a common procedure, as illustrated by the following example.

EXAMPLE

Videologs Put Marketers in the Picture

One-way analysis of variance shows that the videolog and catalog are complementary sales tools aimed at the shop-at-home market.

Although the videolog, a shop-at-home video catalog, is still in its infancy, many direct marketers have shown an interest in its use. Companies such as Spiegel and Neiman Marcus either plan to offer or already have offered video catalogs to consumers.

A study was designed to investigate the effectiveness of videolog retailing as a form of direct marketing. Subjects were randomly assigned to one of three treatments: (a) videolog only, (b) both videolog and catalog, or (c) catalog only. The dependent variables of interest, consisting of attitudes and opinions, were (1) assessments of product (clothing) attributes, (2) assessments of the videolog/catalog sponsoring company, (3) assessments of price information, and (4) intentions to purchase.

One-way analysis of variance was conducted separately for each dependent variable. The results showed that respondents exposed to the videolog, or videolog and catalog, perceived the clothing more positively than did those exposed only to the catalog. Although the videolog-only treatment enhanced perceptions of the sponsoring company, the results were not as striking as were those for clothing perceptions. No significant differences were found in price perceptions and intentions to purchase. Yet the mean number of items respondents said they were likely to purchase was greater for those viewing both the videolog and catalog than those seeing just the videolog or the catalog.

Although this study was an exploratory effort, the positive results found in assessments of clothing seen in the videolog suggest that this is an area that may have potential for direct marketers.[8] ■

N-WAY ANALYSIS OF VARIANCE

In marketing research, one is often concerned with the effect of more than one factor at a time.[9] For example:

- How do the consumers' intentions to buy a brand vary with different levels of price and different levels of distribution?
- How do advertising levels (high, medium, and low) interact with price levels (high, medium, and low) to influence a brand's sale?
- Do educational levels (less than high school, high school graduate, some college, and college graduate) and age (less than 35, 35–55, more than 55) affect consumption of a brand?
- What is the effect of consumers' familiarity with a department store (high, medium, and low) and store image (positive, neutral, and negative) on preference for the store?

In determining such effects, *n*-way analysis of variance can be used. A major advantage of this technique is that it enables the researcher to examine interactions between the factors. **Interactions** occur when the effects of one factor on the dependent variable depend on the level (category) of the other factors. The procedure for conducting *n*-way analysis of variance is similar to that for one-way analysis of variance. The statistics associated with *n*-way analysis of variance are also defined similarly. Consider the simple case of two factors X_1 and X_2 having categories c_1 and c_2. The total variation in this case is partitioned as follows:

Interaction When assessing the relationship between two variables, an interaction occurs if the effect of X_1 depends on the level of X_2, and vice versa.

$$SS_{total} = SS \text{ due to } X_1 + SS \text{ due to } X_2 + SS \text{ due to interaction of } X_1 \text{ and } X_2 + SS_{within}$$

or

$$SS_y = SS_{x_1} + SS_{x_2} + SS_{x_1x_2} + SS_{error}$$

A larger effect of X_1 will be reflected in a greater mean difference in the levels of X_1 and a larger SS_{x1}. The same is true for the effect of X_2. The larger the interaction between X_1 and X_2, the larger $SS_{x_1x_2}$ will be. On the other hand, if X_1 and X_2 are independent, the value of $SS_{x_1x_2}$ will be close to zero.[10]

The strength of the joint effect of two factors, called the overall effect, or **multiple** η^2, is measured as follows:

Multiple η^2 The strength of the joint effect of two (or more) factors, or the overall effect.

$$\text{multiple } \eta^2 = \frac{(SS_{x_1} + SS_{x_2} + SS_{x_1x_2})}{SS_y}$$

Significance of the Overall Effect A test that some differences exist between some of the treatment groups.

The **significance of the overall effect** may be tested by an F test, as follows:

$$F = \frac{(SS_{x1} + SS_{x2} + SS_{x1x2})/\text{df}_n}{SS_{error}/\text{df}_d}$$

$$= \frac{SS_{x1,\, x2,x1x2}/\text{df}_n}{SS_{error}/\text{df}_d}$$

$$= \frac{MS_{x1,\, x2,x1x2}}{MS_{error}}$$

where

$$\begin{aligned}
\text{df}_n &= \text{degrees of freedom for the numerator} \\
&= (c_1 - 1) + (c_2 - 1) + (c_1 - 1)(c_2 - 1) \\
&= c_1c_2 - 1 \\
\text{df}_d &= \text{degrees of freedom for the denominator} \\
&= N - c_1c_2 \\
MS &= \text{mean square}
\end{aligned}$$

Significance of the Interaction Effect A test of the significance of the interaction between two or more independent variables.

If the overall effect is significant, the next step is to examine the **significance of the interaction effect.**[11] Under the null hypothesis of no interaction, the appropriate F test is:

$$F = \frac{SS_{x1x2}/\text{df}_n}{SS_{error}/\text{df}_d}$$

$$= \frac{MS_{x1x2}}{MS_{error}}$$

where

$$\begin{aligned}
\text{df}_n &= (c_1 - 1)(c_2 - 1) \\
\text{df}_d &= N - c_1c_2
\end{aligned}$$

If the interaction effect is found to be significant, then the effect of X_1 depends on the level of X_2 and vice versa. Because the effect of one factor is not uniform, but varies with the level of the other factor, it is not generally meaningful to test the significance of the main effects. However, it is meaningful to test the significance of the main effect of each factor if the interaction effect is not significant.[12]

Significance of the Main Effect of Each Factor A test of the significance of the main effect for each individual factor.

The **significance of the main effect of each factor** may be tested as follows for X_1:

$$F = \frac{SS_{x1}/\text{df}_n}{SS_{error}/\text{df}_d}$$

$$= \frac{MS_{x1}}{MS_{error}}$$

where

$$\begin{aligned}
\text{df}_n &= c_1 - 1 \\
\text{df}_d &= N - c_1c_2
\end{aligned}$$

The foregoing analysis assumes that the design was orthogonal, or balanced (the number of cases in each cell was the same). If the cell size varies, the analysis becomes more complex. The following application illustrates n-way analysis of variance.

Illustrative Application of* N-*Way Analysis of Variance. Returning to the data of Table 16.2, let us now examine the effect of the level of in-store promotion and couponing on store sales. The results of running a 3 × 2 ANOVA on the computer are presented in Table 16.5. For the main effect of level of promotion, the sum of squares SS_{xp}, degrees of freedom, and mean square MS_{xp} are the same as earlier determined in Table 16.4. The sum of squares for couponing $SS_{xc} = 53.333$ with 1 df, resulting in an identical value for the mean square MS_{xc}. The combined main effect is determined by adding the sum of squares due to the two main effect ($SS_{xp} + SS_{xc} = 106.067 + 53.333 = 159.400$) as well as adding the degrees of freedom ($2 + 1 = 3$). For the promotion and coupon interaction effect, the sum of squares $SS_{xpxc} = 3.267$ with $(3 - 1) \times (2 - 1) = 2$ degrees of freedom, resulting in $MS_{xpxc} = 3.267/2 = 1.633$. For the overall (model) effect, the sum of squares is the sum of squares for promotion main effect, coupon main effect, and interaction effect $= 106.067 + 53.333 + 3.267 = 162.667$ with $2 + 1 + 2 = 5$ degrees of freedom, resulting in a mean square of $162.667/5 = 32.533$. Note, however, the error statistics are now different than in Table 16.4. This is due to the fact that we now have two factors instead of one. $SS_{error} = 23.2$ with $(30 - 3 \times 2)$ or 24 degrees of freedom resulting in $MS_{error} = 23.2/24 = .967$.

TABLE 16.5

TWO-WAY ANALYSIS OF VARIANCE

Source of Variation	*Sum of Squares*	*df*	*Mean Square*	*F*	*Significance of F*	ω^2
Main effects						
In-store promotion	106.067	2	53.033	54.862	.000	.557
Coupon	53.333	1	53.333	55.172	.000	.280
Combined	159.400	3	53.133	54.966	.000	
Two-way interaction	3.267	2	1.633	1.690	.206	
Model	162.667	5	32.533	33.655	.000	
Residual (error)	23.200	24	0.967			
Total	185.867	29	6.409			

Cell Means

In-Store Promotion	*Coupon*	*Count*	*Mean*
High	Yes	5	9.200
High	No	5	7.400
Medium	Yes	5	7.600
Medium	No	5	4.800
Low	Yes	5	5.400
Low	No	5	2.000

Factor Level Means

Promotion	*Coupon*	*Count*	*Mean*
High		10	8.300
Medium		10	6.200
Low		10	3.700
	Yes	15	7.400
	No	15	4.733
Grand Mean		30	6.067

The test statistic for the significance of the overall effect is

$$F = \left(\frac{32.533}{.967}\right)$$

$$= 33.655$$

with 5 and 24 degrees of freedom, which is significant at the .05 level.

The test statistic for the significance of the interaction effect is

$$F = \left(\frac{1.633}{.967}\right)$$

$$= 1.690$$

with 2 and 24 degrees of freedom, which is not significant at the .05 level.

As the interaction effect is not significant, the significance of the main effects can be evaluated. The test statistic for the significance of the main effect of promotion is

$$F = \left(\frac{53.033}{.967}\right)$$

$$= 54.862$$

with 2 and 24 degrees of freedom, which is significant at the .05 level.

The test statistic for the significance of the main effect of coupon is

$$F = \left(\frac{53.333}{.967}\right)$$

$$= 55.172$$

with 1 and 24 degrees of freedom, which is significant at the .05 level. Thus, higher level of promotion results in higher sales. The distribution of a storewide coupon results in higher sales. The effect of each is independent of the other.

The following example illustrates the use of n-way analysis.

EXAMPLE

Country Affects TV Reception

A study examined the impact of country affiliation on the credibility of product-attribute claims for televisions. The dependent variables were the following product-attribute claims: good sound, reliability, crisp-clear picture, and stylish design. The independent variables that were manipulated included price, country affiliation, and store distribution. A 2 × 2 × 2 between-subjects design was used. Two levels of price, $349.95 (low) and $449.95 (high), two levels of country affiliation, Korea and the United States, and two levels of store distribution, Hudson's and without Hudson's, were specified.

Data were collected from two suburban malls in a large midwestern city. Thirty respondents were randomly assigned to each of the eight treatment cells for a total of 240 subjects. Table 1 presents the results for manipulations that had significant effects on each of the dependent variables.

TABLE 1

ANALYSES FOR SIGNIFICANT MANIPULATIONS

Effect	*Dependent Variable*	*Univariate F*	*df*	p
Country × price	Good sound	7.57	1,232	.006
Country × price	Reliability	6.57	1,232	.011
Country × distribution	Crisp-clear picture	6.17	1,232	.014
Country × distribution	Reliability	6.57	1,232	.011
Country × distribution	Stylish design	10.31	1,232	.002

The directions of country-by-distribution interaction effects for the three dependent variables are shown in Table 2. While the credibility ratings for the crisp-clear picture, reliability, and stylish design claims are improved by distributing the Korean-made TV set through Hudson's, rather than some other distributor, the same is not true of a U.S.-made set. Similarly, the directions of country-by-price interaction effects for the two dependent variables are shown in Table 3. At $449.95, the credibility ratings for the "good sound" and "reliability" claims are higher for the U.S.-made TV set than for its Korean counterpart, but there is little difference related to country affiliation when the product is priced at $349.95.

TABLE 2

COUNTRY-BY-DISTRIBUTION INTERACTION MEANS

Country × Distribution	*Crisp-Clear Picture*	*Reliability*	*Stylish Design*
Korea			
Hudson's	3.67	3.42	3.82
Without Hudson's	3.18	2.88	3.15
U.S.			
Hudson's	3.60	3.47	3.53
Without Hudson's	3.77	3.65	3.75

TABLE 3

COUNTRY-BY-PRICE INTERACTION MEANS

Country × Price	*Good Sound*	*Reliability*
$349.95		
Korea	3.75	3.40
U.S.	3.53	3.45
$449.95		
Korea	3.15	2.90
U.S.	3.73	3.67

This study demonstrates that credibility of attribute claims, for products traditionally exported to the United States by a company in a newly industrialized country, can be significantly improved if the same company distributes the product through a prestigious U.S. retailer and considers making manufacturing investments in the United States. Specifically, three product-attribute claims (crisp-clear picture, reliability, and stylish design) are perceived as more credible when the televisions are made in Korea if they are also distributed through a prestigious U.S. retailer. Also, the "good sound" and "reliability" claims for televisions are perceived to be more credible for a U.S-made set sold at a higher price, possibly offsetting the potential disadvantage of higher manufacturing costs in the United States.[13] ■

ANALYSIS OF COVARIANCE

When examining the differences in the mean values of the dependent variable related to the effect of the controlled independent variables, it is often necessary to take into account the influence of uncontrolled independent variables. For example:

- In determining how consumers' intentions to buy a brand vary with different levels of price, attitude toward the brand may have to be taken into consideration.
- In determining how different groups exposed to different commercials evaluate a brand, it may be necessary to control for prior knowledge.
- In determining how different price levels will affect a household's cereal consumption, it may be essential to take household size into account.

In such cases, analysis of covariance should be used. Analysis of covariance includes at least one categorical independent variable and at least one interval or metric independent variable. The categorical independent variable is called a *factor*, whereas the metric independent variable is called a *covariate*. The most common use of the covariate is to remove extraneous variation from the dependent variable, because the effects of the factors are of major concern. The variation in the dependent variable due to the covariates is removed by an adjustment of the dependent variable's mean value within each treatment condition. An analysis of variance is then performed on the adjusted scores.[14] The significance of the combined effect of the covariates, as well as the effect of each covariate, is tested by using the appropriate F tests. The coefficients for the covariates provide insights into the effect that the covariates exert on the dependent variable. Analysis of covariance is most useful when the covariate is linearly related to the dependent variable and is not related to the factors.[15]

We again use the data of Table 16.2 to illustrate analysis of covariance. Suppose that we wanted to determine the effect of in-store promotion and couponing on sales while controlling for the affluence of clientele. It is felt that the affluence of the clientele may also have an effect on sales of the department store. The dependent variable consists of store sales. As before, promotion has three levels and couponing has two. Clientele measured on an interval scale serves as the covariate. The results are shown in Table 16.6. As can be seen, the sum of squares attributable to the covariate is very small (.838) with 1 df resulting

TABLE 16.6

ANALYSIS OF COVARIANCE

Source of Variation	*Sum of Squares*	*df*	*Mean Square*	*F*	*Significance of F*
Covariates					
Clientele	.838	1	.838	.862	.363
Main effects					
Promotion	106.067	2	53.033	54.546	.000
Coupon	53.333	1	53.333	54.855	.000
Combined	159.400	3	53.133	54.649	.000
Two-way interaction					
Promotion*coupon	3.267	2	1.633	1.680	.208
Model	163.505	6	27.251	28.028	.000
Residual (error)	22.362	23	.972		
Total	185.867	29	6.409		
Covariate	Raw Coefficient				
Clientele	–.078				

in an identical value for the mean square. The associated F value is .838/.972 = .862, with 1 and 23 degrees of freedom, which is not significant at the .05 level. Thus, the conclusion is that the affluence of the clientele does not have an effect on the sales of the department store. If the effect of the covariate is significant, the sign of the raw coefficient can be used to interpret the direction of the effect on the dependent variable.

ISSUES IN INTERPRETATION

Important issues involved in the interpretation of ANOVA results include interactions, relative importance of factors, and multiple comparisons.

Interactions

The different interactions that can arise when conducting ANOVA on two or more factors are shown in Figure 16.3. One outcome is that ANOVA may indicate that there are no interactions (the interaction effects are not found to be significant). The other possibility is that the interaction is significant. An *interaction effect* occurs when the effect of an independent variable on a dependent variable is different for different categories or levels of another independent variable. The interaction may be ordinal or disordinal. In **ordinal interaction**, the rank order of the effects related to one factor does not change across the levels of the second factor. **Disordinal interaction**, on the other hand, involves a change in the rank order of the effects of one factor across the levels of another. If the interaction is disordinal, it could be of a noncrossover or crossover type.[16]

Ordinal Interaction An interaction where the rank order of the effects attributable to one factor does not change across the levels of the second factor.

Disordinal Interaction The change in the rank order of the effects of one factor across the levels of another.

These interaction cases are displayed in Figure 16.4, which assumes that there are two factors, X_1 with three levels (X_{11}, X_{12}, and X_{13}), and X_2 with two levels (X_{21} and X_{22}). Case 1 depicts no interaction. The effects of X_1 on Y are parallel over the two levels of X_2. There is some departure from parallelism, but this is not beyond what might be expected from chance. Parallelism implies that the net effect of X_{22} over X_{21} is the same across the three levels of X_1. In the absence of interaction, the joint effect of X_1 and X_2 is simply the sum of their individual main effects.

Case 2 depicts an ordinal interaction. The line segments depicting the effects of X_1 and X_2 are not parallel. The difference between X_{22} and X_{21} increases as we move from X_{11} to X_{12} and from X_{12} to X_{13}, but the rank order of the effects of X_1 is the same over the two levels of X_2. This rank order, in ascending order, is X_{11}, X_{12}, X_{13}, and it remains the same for X_{21} and X_{22}.

Disordinal interaction of a noncrossover type is displayed by case 3. The lowest effect of X_1 at level X_{21} occurs at X_{11}, and the rank order of effects is X_{11}, X_{12}, and X_{13}. However,

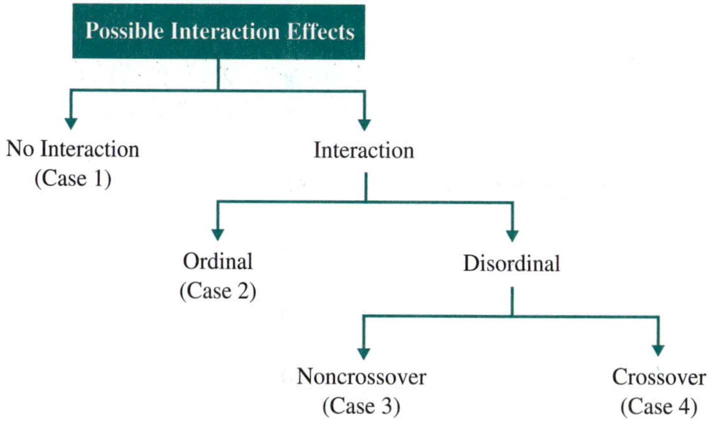

Figure 16.3
A Classification of Interaction Effects

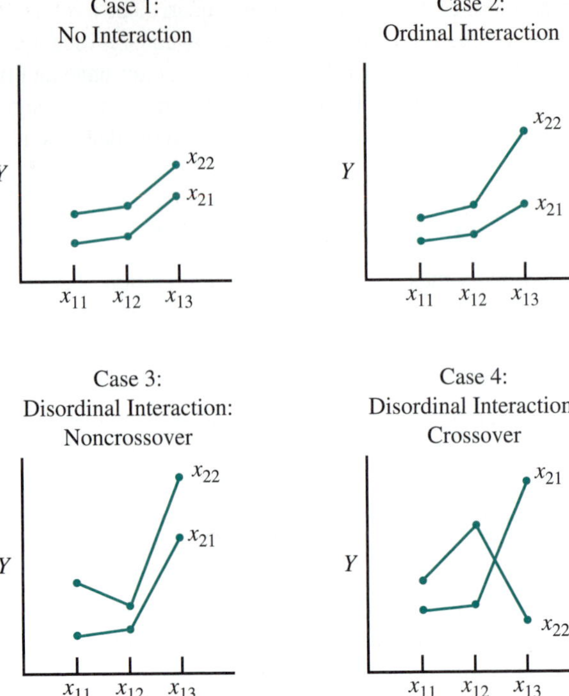

Figure 16.4
Patterns of Interaction

at level X_{22}, the lowest effect of X_1 occurs at X_{12}, and the rank order is changed to X_{12}, X_{11}, X_{13}. Because it involves a change in rank order, disordinal interaction is stronger than ordinal interaction.

In disordinal interactions of a crossover type, the line segments cross each other, as shown by case 4 in Figure 16.4. In this case, the relative effect of the levels of one factor changes with the levels of the other. Note that X_{22} has a greater effect than X_{21} when the levels of X_1 are X_{11} and X_{12}. When the level of X_1 is X_{13}, the situation is reversed, and X_{21} has a greater effect than X_{22}. (Note that in cases 1, 2, and 3, X_{22} had a greater impact than X_{21} across all three levels of X_1.) Hence, disordinal interactions of a crossover type represent the strongest interactions.[17]

RELATIVE IMPORTANCE OF FACTORS

Experimental designs are usually balanced, in that each cell contains the same number of respondents. This results in an orthogonal design in which the factors are uncorrelated. Hence, it is possible to determine unambiguously the relative importance of each factor in explaining the variation in the dependent variable.[18] The most commonly used measure in ANOVA is **omega squared**, ω^2. This measure indicates what proportion of the variation in the dependent variable is related to a particular independent variable or factor. The relative contribution of a factor X is calculated as follows:[19]

Omega Squared (ω^2)
A measure indicating the proportion of the variation in the dependent variable explained by a particular independent variable or factor.

$$\omega_x^2 = \frac{SS_x - (\mathrm{df}_x \times MS_{error})}{SS_{total} + MS_{error}}$$

Normally, ω^2 is interpreted only for statistically significant effects.[20] In Table 16.5, ω^2 associated with the level of instore promotion is calculated as follows:

$$\omega_p^2 = \frac{106.067 - (2 \times .967)}{185.867 + .967}$$

$$= \frac{104.133}{186.834}$$

$$= .557$$

Note, in Table 16.5, that

$$SS_{\text{total}} = 106.067 + 53.333 + 3.267 + 23.2$$
$$= 185.867$$

Likewise, the ω^2associated with couponing is

$$\omega_c^2 = \frac{53.333 - (1 \times .967)}{185.867 + .967}$$

$$= \frac{52.366}{186.834}$$

$$= .280$$

As a guide to interpreting ω^2, a large experimental effect produces an ω^2 of .15 or greater, a medium effect produces an index of around .06, and a small effect produces an index of .01.[21] In Table 16.5, while the effect of promotion and couponing are both large, the effect of promotion is much larger.

Multiple Comparisons

The ANOVA F test examines only the overall difference in means. If the null hypothesis of equal means is rejected, we can only conclude that not all of the group means are equal. However, only some of the means may be statistically different, and we may wish to examine differences among specific means. This can be done by specifying appropriate **contrasts**, or comparisons used to determine which of the means are statistically different. Contrasts may be a priori or a posteriori. **A priori contrasts** are determined before conducting the analysis, based on the researcher's theoretical framework. Generally, a priori contrasts are used in lieu of the ANOVA F test. The contrasts selected are orthogonal (they are independent in a statistical sense).

A posteriori contrasts are made after the analysis. These are generally **multiple comparison tests**. They enable the researcher to construct generalized confidence intervals that can be used to make pairwise comparisons of all treatment means. These tests, listed in order of decreasing power, include least significant difference, Duncan's multiple range test, Student-Newman-Keuls, Tukey's alternate procedure, honestly significant difference, modified least significant difference, and Scheffe's test. Of these tests, least significant difference is the most powerful, Scheffe's the most conservative. For further discussion on a priori and a posteriori contrasts, refer to the literature.[22]

Our discussion so far has assumed that each subject is exposed to only one treatment or experimental condition. Sometimes subjects are exposed to more than one experimental condition, in which case repeated measures ANOVA should be used.

Contrasts In ANOVA, a method of examining differences among two or more means of the treatment groups.

A Priori Contrasts Contrasts that are determined before conducting the analysis, based on the researcher's theoretical framework.

A Posteriori Contrasts Contrasts made after the analysis. These are generally multiple comparison tests.

Multiple Comparison Test A posteriori contrasts that enable the researcher to construct generalized confidence intervals that can be used to make pairwise comparisons of all treatment means.

REPEATED MEASURES ANOVA

Repeated Measures Analysis of Variance An ANOVA technique used when respondents are exposed to more than one treatment condition and repeated measurements are obtained.

In marketing research there are often large differences in the background and individual characteristics of respondents. If this source of variability can be separated from treatment effects (effects of the independent variable) and experimental error, then the sensitivity of the experiment can be enhanced. One way of controlling the differences between subjects is by observing each subject under each experimental condition (see Table 16.7). In this sense, each subject serves as its own control. For example, in a survey attempting to determine differences in evaluations of various airlines, each respondent evaluates all the major competing airlines. Since repeated measurements are obtained from each respondent, this design is referred to as within-subjects design or **repeated measures analysis of variance**. This differs from the assumption we made in our earlier discussion that each respondent is exposed to only one treatment condition, also referred to as between-subjects design.[23] Repeated measures analysis of variance may be thought of as an extension of the paired samples t test to the case of more than two related samples.

In the case of a single factor with repeated measures, the total variation, with nc-1 degrees of freedom, may be split into between-people variation and within-people variation.

$$SS_{total} = SS_{between\ people} + SS_{within\ people}$$

The between-people variation, which is related to the differences between the means of people, has $n - 1$ degrees of freedom. The within-people variation has $n(c - 1)$ degrees of freedom. The within-people variation may, in turn, be divided into two different sources of variation. One source is related to the differences between treatment means, and the second consists of residual or error variation. The degrees of freedom corresponding to the treatment variation are $c - 1$, and that corresponding to residual variation are $(c - 1)(n - 1)$. Thus,

$$SS_{within\ people} = SS_x + SS_{error}$$

TABLE 16.7

DECOMPOSITION OF THE TOTAL VARIATION: REPEATED MEASURES ANOVA

	Subject No.	*Independent Variable*		*Categories*		*X*	*Total Sample*	
		X_1	X_2	X_3	. . .	X_c		
Between People Variation $= SS_{between\ people}$	1	Y_{11}	Y_{12}	Y_{13}		Y_{1c}	Y_1	**Total Variation** $= SS_y$
	2	Y_{21}	Y_{22}	Y_{23}		Y_{2c}	Y_2	
		•					•	
		•					•	
		•					•	
	n	Y_{n1}	Y_{n2}	Y_{n3}		Y_{nc}	Y_N	
Category Mean		$\bar{Y}_1$	$\bar{Y}_2$	$\bar{Y}_3$		$\bar{Y}_c$	$\bar{Y}$	

Within-People Variation $= SS_{within\ people}$

A test of the null hypothesis of equal means may now be constructed in the usual way:

$$F = \frac{SS_x/(c-1)}{SS_{error}/(n-1)\,(c-1)} = \frac{MS_x}{MS_{error}}$$

So far we have assumed that the dependent variable is measured on an interval or ratio scale. If the dependent variable is nonmetric, however, a different procedure should be used.

NONMETRIC ANALYSIS OF VARIANCE

Nonmetric analysis of variance examines the difference in the central tendencies of more than two groups when the dependent variable is measured on an ordinal scale. One such procedure is the ***k*-sample median test**. As its name implies, this is an extension of the median test for two groups, which was considered in chapter 15. The null hypothesis is that the medians of the k populations are equal. The test involves the computation of a common median over the k samples. Then a $2 \times k$ table of cell counts based on cases above or below the common median is generated. A chi-square statistic is computed. The significance of the chi-square implies a rejection of the null hypothesis.

Nonmetric Analysis of Variance An ANOVA technique for examining the difference in the central tendencies of more than two groups when the dependent variable is measured on an ordinal scale.

k-sample Median Test Nonparametric test that is used to examine differences among more than two groups when the dependent variable is measured on an ordinal scale.

A more powerful test is the **Kruskal-Wallis one-way analysis of variance**. This is an extension of the Mann-Whitney test (chapter 15). This test also examines the difference in medians. The null hypothesis is the same as in the k-sample median test, but the testing procedure is different. All cases from the k groups are ordered in a single ranking. If the k populations are the same, the groups should be similar in terms of ranks within each group. The rank sum is calculated for each group. From these, the Kruskal-Wallis H statistic, which has a chi-square distribution, is computed.

Kruskal-Wallis One-Way Analysis of Variance A nonmetric ANOVA test that uses the rank value of each case, not merely its location relative to the median.

The Kruskal-Wallis test is more powerful than the k-sample median test because it uses the rank value of each case, not merely its location relative to the median. However, if there are a large number of tied rankings in the data, the k-sample median test may be a better choice.

Nonmetric analysis of variance is not popular in commercial marketing research. Another procedure that is also only rarely used is multivariate analysis of variance.

MULTIVARIATE ANALYSIS OF VARIANCE

Multivariate analysis of variance (MANOVA) is similar to analysis of variance (ANOVA), except that instead of one metric dependent variable we have two or more. The objective is the same, as MANOVA is also concerned with examining differences between groups. Whereas ANOVA examines group differences on a single dependent variable, MANOVA examines group differences across multiple dependent variables simultaneously. In ANOVA, the null hypothesis is that the means of the dependent variable are equal across the groups. In MANOVA, the null hypothesis is that the vector of means on multiple dependent variables are equal across groups. Multivariate analysis of variance is appropriate when there are two or more dependent variables that are correlated. If there are multiple dependent variables that are uncorrelated or orthogonal, ANOVA on each of the dependent variables is more appropriate than MANOVA.[24]

Multivariate Analysis of Variance (MANOVA) An ANOVA technique using two or more metric dependent variables.

As an example, suppose that four groups, each consisting of 100 randomly selected individuals, were exposed to four different commercials about Tide detergent. After seeing the commercial, each individual provided ratings on preference for Tide, preference for Procter & Gamble (the company marketing Tide), and preference for the commercial itself. Because these three preference variables are correlated, multivariate analysis of variance

RESEARCH IN PRACTICE 16.1

The Commonality of Unethical Research Practices Worldwide

A study examined marketing professionals' perceptions of the commonality of unethical marketing research practices on a cross-national basis. The sample of marketing professionals was drawn from Australia, Canada, Great Britain, and the United States.

Respondents' evaluations were analyzed using computer programs for MANOVA and ANOVA. Country of respondent comprised the predictor variable in the analysis, and 15 commonality evaluations served as the criterion variables. The F values from the ANOVA analyses indicated that only two of the 15 commonality evaluations achieved significance ($p < .05$ or better). Further, the MANOVA F value was not statistically significant, implying the lack of overall differences in commonality evaluations across respondents of the four countries. Therefore, it was concluded that marketing professionals in the four countries evince similar perceptions of the commonality of unethical research practices. This finding is not surprising, given research evidence that organizations in the four countries reflect similar corporate cultures.[25]

should be conducted to determine which commercial is the most effective (produced the highest preference across the three preference variables). Research in Practice 16.1 illustrates the application of ANOVA and MANOVA in international marketing research whereas Research in Practice 16.2 shows an application of these techniques in examining ethics in marketing research.

INTERNET AND COMPUTER APPLICATIONS

The three computer packages, SPSS, SAS, and BMDP, have programs for conducting analysis of variance and covariance available for the microcomputer and mainframe versions. In addition to the basic analysis that we have considered, these programs can also perform more complex analysis. Minitab and Excel also offer some programs. Exhibit 16.1 contains a description of the relevant programs. Refer to the user manuals for these packages for more details.[26]

RESEARCH IN PRACTICE 16.2

"MAN"OVA Demonstrates that Man is Different from Woman

In order to investigate differences between research ethics judgments in men and women, the statistical techniques of MANOVA and ANOVA were used. Respondents were asked to indicate their degree of approval with regard to a series of scenarios involving decisions of an ethical nature. These evaluations served as the dependent variable in the analysis, whereas sex of the respondent served as the independent variable. MANOVA was used for multivariate analysis and its resultant F value was significant at the $p < .001$ level—indicating that there was an "overall" difference between males and females in research ethics judgments. Univariate analysis was conducted via ANOVA, and F values indicated that three items were the greatest contributors to the overall gender difference in ethical evaluations: the use of ultraviolet ink to precode a mail questionnaire, the use of an ad that encourages consumer misuse of a product, and unwillingness by researcher to offer data help to an inner-city advisory group.[27]

Exhibit 16.1
Computer Programs for Anova and Ancova

Given the importance of analysis of variance and covariance, several programs are available in each package.

SPSS

One-way ANOVA can be efficiently performed using the program ONEWAY. This program also allows the user to test a priori and a posteriori contrasts, which cannot be done in other SPSS programs. For performing *n*-way analysis of variance, the program ANOVA can be used. Although covariates can be specified, ANOVA does not perform a full analysis of covariance. For comprehensive analysis of variance or analysis of covariance, including repeated measures and multiple dependent measures, the MANOVA procedure is recommended. For nonmetric analysis of variance, including the *k*-sample median test and Kruskal-Wallis one-way analysis of variance, the program NPAR TESTS should be used.

SAS

The main program for performing analysis of variance in the case of a balanced design is ANOVA. This program can handle data from a wide variety of experimental designs, including multivariate analysis of variance and repeated measures. Both a priori and a posteriori contrasts can be tested. For unbalanced designs, the more general GLM procedure can be used. This program performs analysis of variance, analysis of covariance, repeated-measures analysis of variance, and multivariate analysis of variance. It also allows the testing of a priori and a posteriori contrasts. Whereas GLM can also be used for analyzing balanced designs, it is not as efficient as ANOVA for such models. The VARCOMP procedure computes variance components. For nonmetric analysis of variance, the NPAR1WAY procedure can be used. For constructing designs and randomized plans, the PLAN procedure can be used.

BMDP

For one-way analysis of variance, the program P1V can be used. It also performs analysis of covariance and can test user specified contrasts of group means. The more general model, however, is P2V, which performs analysis of variance and covariance for a wide variety of fixed-effects models. It can handle repeated measures and balanced as well as unbalanced designs. P4V, a more advanced program, can perform multivariate analysis of variance and covariance, including analysis of complex experimental designs. Another specialized program is P3V, which uses the maximum-likelihood approach for analyzing fixed- and random-coefficients models. It allows for balanced as well as unbalanced designs. P8V is a general model that performs an analysis of variance for any complete design with equal cell sizes, including some complex designs. Nonparametric analysis of variance can be performed using P3S. Finally, P7D, in addition to providing histograms, can perform a one-way analysis of variance.

Minitab

Analysis of variance and covariance can be accessed from the Stats>ANOVA function. This function performs one way ANOVA, one-way unstacked ANOVA, two-way ANOVA, analysis of means, balanced ANOVA, analysis of covariance, general linear model, main effects plot, interactions plot, and residual plots. In order to compute the mean and standard deviation, the crosstab function must be used. To obtain F and p values, use the balanced ANOVA.

Excel

Both a one-way ANOVA and two-way ANOVA can be performed under the Tools>Data Analysis function. The two-way ANOVA has the features of a two-factor with replication and a two-factor without replication. The two factor with replication includes more than one sample for each group of data, while the two factor without replication does not include more than one sampling per group.

FOCUS ON Burke

Often problems for which ANOVA would be used have predictor variables that are correlated. This mandates great care in interpreting the results. Although the overall significance test for the model is unaffected, the manner in which you look at the contribution of the individual predictors will be impacted. Analysis of a Burke study in which the two categorical predictor variables were correlated illustrates this point with this small data set (the real data are proprietary).

Purchase Intent	*Performance Rating*	*Gender*
2.00	1.00	.00
4.00	2.00	1.00
6.00	3.00	1.00
4.00	4.00	.00
5.00	5.00	.00
6.00	6.00	1.00
2.00	1.00	.00
3.00	2.00	.00
4.00	3.00	.00
5.00	4.00	1.00
6.00	5.00	1.00
8.00	6.00	1.00

As the two predictors are somewhat correlated ($r^2 = .24$), the interpretation of the contribution of each predictor becomes an issue of concern.

The first ANOVA table shows the sum of squares running the model under the assumptions that the sums of squares for each predictor should be adjusted for the presence of the other predictor (i.e., as if each had been entered second).

The second ANOVA table shows the result run hierarchically with Rating first to "enter."

The third ANOVA table shows the result run hierarchically with Gender first to "enter."

ANOVA[a, b]

			Unique Method				
			Sum of Squares	*df*	*Mean Square*	*F*	*Significance*
PI	Main Effects	(Combined)	32.542	6	5.424	11.418	.009
		RATING	13.792	5	2.758	5.807	.038
		GENDER	3.125	1	3.125	6.579	.050
	Model		32.542	6	5.424	11.418	.009
	Residual		2.375	5	.475		
	Total		34.917	11	3.174		

a. PI by RATING, GENDER
b. All effects entered simultaneously

(Continued)

SUMMARY

In ANOVA and ANCOVA, the dependent variable is metric and the independent variables are all categorical, or combinations of categorical and metric variables. One-way ANOVA involves a single independent categorical variable. Interest lies in testing the null hypothesis that the category means are equal in the population.

ANOVA[a]

			Hierarchical Method				
			Sum of Squares	df	Mean Square	F	Significance
PI	Main Effects	(Combined)	32.542	6	5.424	11.418	.009
		RATING	29.417	5	5.883	12.386	.008
		GENDER	3.125	1	3.125	6.579	.050
	Model		32.542	6	5.424	11.418	.009
	Residual		2.375	5	.475		
	Total		34.917	11	3.174		

a. PI by RATING, GENDER

ANOVA[a]

			Hierarchical Method				
			Sum of Squares	df	Mean Square	F	Significance
PI	Main Effects	(Combined)	32.542	6	5.424	11.418	.009
		GENDER	18.750	1	18.750	39.474	.002
		RATING	13.792	5	2.758	5.807	.038
	Model		32.542	6	5.424	11.418	.009
	Residual		2.375	5	.475		
	Total		34.917	11	3.174		

a. PI by GENDER, RATING

Summarizing the results:

Sum of Squares	*Regression*	*Hierarchical Rating First*	*Gender First*
Rating	13.792	29.417	18.750
Gender	3.125	3.125	13.792
Total of predictors	16.917	32.542	32.542
Total explained	32.542	32.542	32.542

Now the issue is obvious, what portion of the sum of squares does each predictor explain? As the predictors are correlated, the hierarchical approach shows the sum of squares for the predictors entered in a specified order. The unique solution shows the explained sum of squares for each predictor as if it had been entered second (that is why it doesn't add up to the proper total . . . both predictors can't be entered second). The three solutions give a complete picture of the contribution of each variable if it was the only predictor and what its marginal contribution would be as the second predictor.

The total variation in the dependent variable is decomposed into two components: variation related to the independent variable and variation related to error. The variation is measured in terms of the sums of squares corrected for the mean (*SS*). The mean square is obtained by dividing the *SS* by the corresponding degrees of freedom (df). The null hypothesis of equal means is tested by an *F* statistic, which is the ratio of the mean square related to the independent variable to the mean square related to error.

N-way analysis of variance involves the simultaneous examination of two or more categorical independent variables. A major advantage is that the interactions between the independent variables can be examined. The significance of the overall effect, interaction terms, and main effects of individual factors is examined by appropriate *F* tests. It is meaningful to test the significance of main effects only if the corresponding interaction terms are not significant.

ANCOVA includes at least one categorical independent variable and at least one interval or metric independent variable. The metric independent variable, or covariate, is commonly used to remove extraneous variation from the dependent variable.

When analysis of variance is conducted on two or more factors, interactions can arise. An interaction occurs when the effect of an independent variable on a dependent variable is different for different categories or levels of another independent variable. If the interaction is significant, it may be ordinal or disordinal. Disordinal interaction may be of a noncrossover or crossover type. In balanced designs, the relative importance of factors in explaining the variation in the dependent variable is measured by omega squared (ω^2). Multiple comparisons in the form of a priori or a posteriori contrasts can be used for examining differences among specific means.

In repeated measures analysis of variance, observations on each subject are obtained under each treatment condition. This design is useful for controlling for the differences in subjects that exist prior to the experiment. Nonmetric analysis of variance involves examining the differences in the central tendencies of two or more groups when the dependent variable is measured on an ordinal scale. Multivariate analysis of variance (MANOVA) involves two or more metric dependent variables.

KEY TERMS AND CONCEPTS

analysis of variance (ANOVA)
factor
treatment
one-way analysis of variance
n-way analysis of variance
analysis of covariance (ANCOVA)
covariate
eta^2 (η^2)
F statistic
mean square
$SS_{between}$ (SS_x)
SS_{within} (SS_{error})
SS_y
decomposition of the total variation
interaction
multiple η^2
significance of the overall effect
significance of the interaction effect
significance of the main effect of each factor
ordinal interaction
disordinal interaction
omega squared $(\omega)^2$
contrasts
a priori contrasts
a posteriori contrasts
multiple comparison tests
repeated measures analysis of variance
nonmetric analysis of variance
k-sample median test
Kruskal-Wallis one-way analysis of variance
multivariate analysis of variance (MANOVA)

ACRONYMS

The major characteristics of analysis of variance may be described by the acronym ANOVA:

A nalysis of total variation
N ormally distributed errors, which are uncorrelated
O ne or more categorical independent variables with fixed categories
V ariance is assumed to be constant
A single dependent variable which is metric

The major characteristics of analysis of covariance may be summarized by the acronym ANCOVA:

A nalysis of total variation
N ormally distributed errors, which are uncorrelated
C ovariates: one or more metric independent variables
O ne or more categorical independent variables with fixed categories
V ariance is assumed to be constant
A single dependent variable that is metric

EXERCISES

Questions

1. Discuss the similarities and differences between analysis of variance and analysis of covariance.
2. What is the relationship between analysis of variance and the *t* test?
3. What is total variation? How is it decomposed in a one-way analysis of variance?
4. What is the null hypothesis in one-way ANOVA? What basic statistic is used to test the null hypothesis in one-way ANOVA? How is this statistic computed?
5. How does *n*-way analysis of variance differ from the one-way procedure?
6. How is the total variation decomposed in *n*-way analysis of variance?
7. What is the most common use of the covariate in ANCOVA?
8. Define an interaction.
9. What is the difference between ordinal and disordinal interaction?
10. How is the relative importance of factors measured in a balanced design?
11. What is an a priori contrast?
12. What is the most powerful test for making a posteriori contrasts? Which test is the most conservative?
13. What is meant by repeated measures ANOVA? Describe the decomposition of variation in repeated measures ANOVA.
14. What are the differences between metric and nonmetric analyses of variance?
15. Describe two tests used for examining differences in central tendencies in nonmetric ANOVA.
16. What is multivariate analysis of variance? When is it appropriate?

Problems

1. After receiving some complaints from the readers, your campus newspaper decides to redesign its front page. Two new formats, B and C, were developed and tested against the current format, A. A total of 75 students were randomly selected, and 25 students were randomly assigned to each of three format conditions. The students were asked to evaluate the effectiveness of the format on a 11-point scale (1 = poor, 11 = excellent).
   a. State the null hypothesis.
   b. What statistical test should you use?
   c. What are the degrees of freedom that are associated with the test statistic?
2. A marketing researcher wants to test the hypothesis that, in the population, there is no difference in the importance attached to shopping by consumers living in the northern, southern, eastern, and western United States. A study is conducted and analysis of variance is used to analyze the data. The results obtained are presented in the following table.

Source	*df*	*Sum of Squares*	*Mean F Squares*	*F Ratio*	*Probability*
Between groups	3	70.212	23.404	1.12	.3
Within groups	996	20,812.416	20.896		

   a. Is there sufficient evidence to reject the null hypothesis?
   b. What conclusion can be drawn from the table?
   c. If the average importance was computed for each group, would you expect the sample means to be similar or different?
   d. What was the total sample size in this study?
3. In a pilot study examining the effectiveness of three commercials (A, B, and C), 10 consumers were assigned to view each commercial and rate it on a nine-point Likert scale. The data obtained are shown in the table.
   a. Calculate the category means and the grand mean.
   b. Calculate SS_y, SS_x, and SS_{error}.
   c. Calculate η^2.
   d. Calculate the value of F.
   e. Are the three commercials equally effective?

	Commercial	
A	*B*	*C*
4	7	8
5	4	7
3	6	7
4	5	6
3	4	8
4	6	7
4	5	8
3	5	8
5	4	5
5	4	6

4. An experiment tested the effects of package design and shelf display on the likelihood of purchase of Product 19 cereal. Package design and shelf display were varied at two levels each, resulting in a 2 × 2 design. Purchase likelihood was measured on a seven-point scale. The results are partially described in the following table.

    a. Complete the table by calculating the mean square, F, significance of F, and ω^2 values.
    b. How should the main effects be interpreted?

Source of Variation	*Sum of Squares*	*df*	*Mean Square*	*F*	*Significance of F*	ω^2
Package design	68.76	1				
Shelf display	320.19	1				
Two-way interaction	55.05	1				
Residual error	176.00	40				

INTERNET AND COMPUTER EXERCISES

1. Using the appropriate microcomputer and mainframe programs in the package of your choice (SPSS, SAS, BMDP, Minitab, or Excel), analyze the data of Table 16.2. Conduct one-way ANOVA, two-way ANOVA, and analysis of covariance. Compare your results with those given in the book.
2. Using an appropriate computer program, analyze the data of problem 3.

Chapter 17

Correlation and Regression

"For a researcher, correlation is the most convenient and understandable way to look at the association between two metric variables. When extended to multiple regression, the relationship between one variable and several others becomes more understandable."

Sarah Evans, senior marketing research analyst, Burke, Inc.

OBJECTIVES

After reading this chapter, the student should be able to

1. discuss the concepts of product moment correlation, partial correlation, and part correlation and show how they provide a foundation for regression analysis
2. explain the nature and methods of bivariate regression analysis and describe the general model, estimation of parameters, standardized regression coefficient, significance testing, prediction accuracy, residual analysis, and model cross-validation
3. explain the nature and methods of multiple regression analysis and the meaning of partial regression coefficients
4. describe specialized techniques used in multiple regression analysis, particularly stepwise regression, regression with dummy variables, and analysis of variance and covariance with regression
5. discuss nonmetric correlation and measures such as Spearman's rho and Kendall's tau

OVERVIEW

Chapter 16 examined the relationship among the *t* test, analysis of variance and covariance, and regression. This chapter describes regression analysis, which is widely used for explaining variation in market share, sales, brand preference, and other marketing results in terms of marketing management variables such as advertising, price, distribution, and product quality. However, before discussing regression, we describe the concepts of product moment correlation and partial correlation coefficient, which lay the conceptual foundation for regression analysis.

In introducing regression analysis, we discuss the simple bivariate case first. We describe estimation, standardization of the regression coefficients, and testing and examination of the strength and significance of association between variables, prediction accuracy, and the assumptions underlying the regression model. Next, we discuss the multiple regression model, emphasizing the interpretation of parameters, strength of association, significance tests, and examination of residuals.

DEPARTMENT STORE PATRONAGE PROJECT

Multiple Regression

In the department store patronage project, multiple regression analysis was used to develop a model that explained store preference in terms of respondents' evaluations of the store on the eight choice criteria. The dependent variable was preference for each store. The independent variables were the evaluations of each store on quality of merchandise, variety and assortment of merchandise, returns and adjustment policy, service of store personnel, prices, convenience of location, layout of store, and credit and billing policies. The results indicated that all the factors of the choice criteria, except service of store personnel, were significant in explaining store preference. The coefficients of all the variables were positive, indicating that higher evaluations on each of the significant factors led to higher preference for that store. The model had a good fit and good ability to predict store preference.

We next cover topics of special interest in regression analysis, such as stepwise regression, multicollinearity, relative importance of predictor variables, and cross-validation. We describe regression with dummy variables and the use of this procedure to conduct analysis of variance and covariance. We begin with some examples illustrating applications of regression analysis.

EXAMPLE

Regression Rings the Right Bell for Avon

Good products, well-trained sales reps, and sophisticated regression models have opened the doors for Avon, enabling it to penetrate the cosmetics market.

Avon Products, Inc., was having significant problems with the sales staff. The company's business, dependent on sales representatives, was facing a shortage of sales reps without much hope of getting new ones. Regression models, operating on PCs, were developed to reveal the possible variables that were fueling this situation. The models revealed that the most significant variable was the level of the appointment fee that reps pay for materials. With data to back up its actions, the company lowered the fee. This resulted in an improvement in the recruitment and retention of sales reps.[1] ■

EXAMPLE

Retailing Revolution

Many retailing experts suggest that electronic shopping will be the next revolution in retailing. A research project investigating this trend looked for correlates of consumers' preferences for electronic shopping services via home videotex (computerized in-home shopping services). The explanation of consumers' preferences was sought in psychographic, demographic, and communication variables suggested in the literature. The study was conducted in south Florida where Viewtron, a videotex service, has been offered since 1983. Viewtron, a subsidiary of Knight-Ridder Corporation, spent millions on advertising in the area. All the respondents were familiar with the concept of computerized shopping from home.

Multiple regression was used to analyze the data. The overall multiple regression model was significant at .05 level. Univariate *t* tests indicated that the following variables in the model were significant at .05 level or better: price orientation, sex, age, occupation, ethnicity, and education. None of the three communication variables (mass media, word-of-mouth, and publicity) was significantly related to consumer preference, the dependent variable.

The results suggest that electronic shopping is preferred by white females who are older, better educated, working in supervisory or higher-level occupations, and who are price-oriented shoppers. Information of this type is valuable in targeting marketing effort to electronic shoppers.[2] ■

These examples illustrate some of the uses of regression analysis in determining which independent variables explain a significant variation in the dependent variable of interest, the structure and form of the relationship, the strength of the relationship, and predicted values of the dependent variable. Fundamental to regression analysis is an understanding of the product moment correlation.

PRODUCT MOMENT CORRELATION

In marketing research we are often interested in summarizing the strength of association between two metric variables, as in the following situations:

- How strongly are sales related to advertising expenditures?
- Is there an association between market share and size of the sales force?
- Are consumers' perceptions of quality related to their perceptions of prices?

Product Moment Correlation, r
A statistic summarizing the strength of association between two metric variables.

In situations like these, the **product moment correlation, *r***, is the most widely used statistic, summarizing the strength of association between two metric (interval or ratio scaled) variables, say *X* and *Y*. It is an index used to determine whether a linear or straight-line relationship exists between *X* and *Y*. It indicates the degree to which the variation in one variable, *X*, is related to the variation in another variable, *Y*. Because it was originally proposed by Karl Pearson, it is also known as the *Pearson correlation coefficient*. It is also referred to as *simple correlation*, *bivariate correlation*, or merely the *correlation coefficient*. From a sample of *n* observations, *X* and *Y*, the product moment correlation, *r*, can be calculated as

$$r = \frac{\sum_{i=1}^{n} (X_i - \overline{X})(Y_i - \overline{Y})}{\sqrt{\sum_{i=1}^{n} (X_i - \overline{X})^2 \sum_{i=1}^{n} (Y_i - \overline{Y})^2}}$$

Division of the numerator and denominator by $(n - 1)$ gives

$$r = \frac{\sum_{i=1}^{n} \frac{(X_i - \overline{X})(Y_i - \overline{Y})}{n - 1}}{}$$

$$= \frac{COV_{xy}}{S_x S_y}$$

TABLE 17.1

EXPLAINING ATTITUDE TOWARD THE CITY OF RESIDENCE

Respondent Number	*Attitude Toward the City*	*Duration of Residence*	*Importance Attached to Weather*
1	6	10	3
2	9	12	11
3	8	12	4
4	3	4	1
5	10	12	11
6	4	6	1
7	5	8	7
8	2	2	4
9	11	18	8
10	9	9	10
11	10	17	8
12	2	2	5

Covariance A systematic relationship between two variables in which a change in one implies a corresponding change in the other (COV_{xy}).

In these equations, $\overline{X}$ and $\overline{Y}$ denote the sample means and S_x and S_y the standard deviations. COV_{xy}, the **covariance** between X and Y, measures the extent to which X and Y are related. The covariance may be either positive or negative. Division by S_xS_y achieves standardization, so that r varies between −1.0 and +1.0. Note that the correlation coefficient is an absolute number and is not expressed in any unit of measurement. The correlation coefficient between two variables will be the same regardless of their underlying units of measurement.

As an example, suppose a researcher wants to explain attitudes toward a respondent's city of residence in terms of duration of residence in the city. The attitude is measured on a 11-point scale (1 = do not like the city, 11 = very much like the city), and the duration of residence is measured in terms of the number of years the respondent has lived in the city. In a pretest of 12 respondents, the data shown in Table 17.1 are obtained.

The correlation coefficient may be calculated as follows:

$$\overline{X} = \frac{(10 + 12 + 12 + 4 + 12 + 6 + 8 + 2 + 18 + 9 + 17 + 2)}{12}$$
$$= 9.333$$

$$\overline{Y} = \frac{(6 + 9 + 8 + 3 + 10 + 4 + 5 + 2 + 11 + 9 + 10 + 2)}{12}$$
$$= 6.583$$

$$\begin{aligned}\sum_{i=1}^{n}(X_i - \overline{X})(Y_i - \overline{Y}) &= (10 - 9.33)(6 - 6.58) + (12 - 9.33)(9 - 6.58) \\ &+ (12 - 9.33)(8 - 6.58) + (4 - 9.33)(3 - 6.58) \\ &+ (12 - 9.33)(10 - 6.58) + (6 - 9.33)(4 - 6.58) \\ &+ (8 - 9.33)(5 - 6.58) + (2 - 9.33)(2 - 6.58) \\ &+ (18 - 9.33)(11 - 6.58) + (9 - 9.33)(9 - 6.58) \\ &+ (17 - 9.33)(10 - 6.58) + (2 - 9.33)(2 - 6.58)\end{aligned}$$

$$= -.3886 + 6.4614 + 3.7914 + 19.0814$$
$$+ 9.1314 + 8.5914 + 2.1014 + 33.5714$$
$$+ 38.3214 - .7986 + 26.2314 + 33.5714$$
$$= 179.6668$$

$$\sum_{i=1}^{n} (X_i - \overline{X})^2 = (10 - 9.33)^2 + (12 - 9.33)^2 + (12 - 9.33)^2 + (4 - 9.33)^2$$
$$+ (12 - 9.33)^2 + (6 - 9.33)^2 + (8 - 9.33)^2 + (2 - 9.33)^2$$
$$+ (18 - 9.33)^2 + (9 - 9.33)^2 + (17 - 9.33)^2 + (2 - 9.33)^2$$
$$= .4489 + 7.1289 + 7.1289 + 28.4089$$
$$+ 7.1289 + 11.0889 + 1.7689 + 53.7289$$
$$+ 75.1689 + .1089 + 58.8289 + 53.7289$$
$$= 304.6668$$

$$\sum_{i=1}^{n} (Y_i - \overline{Y})^2 = (6 - 6.58)^2 + (9 - 6.58)^2 + (8 - 6.58)^2 + (3 - 6.58)^2$$
$$+ (10 - 6.58)^2 + (4 - 6.58)^2 + (5 - 6.58)^2 + (2 - 6.58)^2$$
$$+ (11 - 6.58)^2 + (9 - 6.58)^2 + (10 - 6.58)^2 + (2 - 6.58)^2$$
$$= .3364 + 5.8564 + 2.0164 + 12.8164$$
$$+ 11.6964 + 6.6564 + 2.4964 + 20.9764$$
$$+ 19.5364 + 5.8564 + 11.6964 + 20.9764$$
$$= 120.9168$$

Thus,

$$r = \frac{179.6668}{\sqrt{(304.6668)(120.9168)}}$$

$$= .9361$$

In this example, $r = .9361$, a value close to 1.0. This means that respondents' duration of residence in the city is strongly associated with their attitude toward the city. Furthermore, the positive sign of r implies a positive relationship; the longer the duration of residence, the more favorable the attitude and vice versa.

Because r indicates the degree to which variation in one variable is related to variation in another, it can also be expressed in terms of the decomposition of the total variation (see chapter 16). In other words,

$$r^2 = \frac{\text{explained variation}}{\text{total variation}}$$

$$= \frac{SS_x}{SS_y}$$

$$= \frac{\text{total variation} - \text{error variation}}{\text{total variation}}$$

$$= \frac{SS_y - SS_{error}}{SS_y}$$

Hence, r^2 measures the proportion of variation in one variable that is explained by the other. Both r and r^2 are symmetric measures of association. In other words, the correlation of X with Y is the same as the correlation of Y with X. It does not matter which variable is considered to be the dependent variable and which the independent. The product moment coefficient measures the strength of the linear relationship and is not designed to measure nonlinear relationships. Thus $r = 0$ merely indicates that there is no linear relationship between X and Y. It does not mean that X and Y are unrelated. There could well be a nonlinear relationship between them, which would not be captured by r (see Figure 17.1).

When it is computed for a population rather than a sample, the product moment correlation is denoted by ρ, the Greek letter rho. The coefficient r is an estimator of ρ. Note that the calculation of r assumes that X and Y are metric variables whose distributions have the same shape. If these assumptions are not met, r is deflated and underestimates ρ. In marketing research, data obtained by using rating scales with a small number of categories may not be strictly interval. This tends to deflate r, resulting in an underestimation of ρ.[3]

The statistical significance of the relationship between two variables measured by using r can be conveniently tested. The hypotheses are

$$H_0: \rho = 0$$
$$H_1: \rho \neq 0$$

The test statistic is

$$t = r\left[\frac{n - 2}{1 - r^2}\right]^{1/2}$$

which has a t distribution with $n - 2$ degrees of freedom.[4] For the correlation coefficient calculated based on the data given in Table 17.1,

$$t = .9361\left[\frac{12 - 2}{1 - (.9361)^2}\right]^{1/2}$$

$$= 8.414$$

and the degrees of freedom $= 12 - 2 = 10$. From the t distribution table (Table 4 in the statistical appendix), the critical value of t for a two-tailed test and $\alpha = .05$ is 2.228. Hence, the null hypothesis of no relationship between X and Y is rejected. This, along with the positive sign of r, indicates that attitude toward the city is positively related to the duration of residence in the city. Moreover, the high value of r indicates that this relationship is strong.

In conducting multivariate data analysis, it is often useful to examine the simple correlation between each pair of variables. These results are presented in the form of a correlation matrix, which indicates the coefficient of correlation between each pair of variables. Usually, only the lower triangular portion of the matrix is considered. The diagonal elements all equal

Figure 17.1
A Nonlinear Relationship for Which $r = 0$

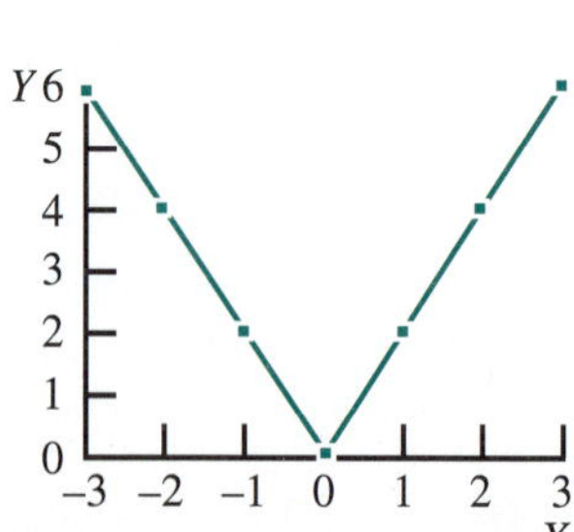

1.00, as a variable correlates perfectly with itself. The upper triangular portion of the matrix is a mirror image of the lower triangular portion, because r is a symmetric measure of association. The form of a correlation matrix for five variables, V_1 through V_5, is as follows.

	V_1	V_2	V_3	V_4	V_5
V_1					
V_2	.5				
V_3	.3	.4			
V_4	.1	.3	.6		
V_5	.2	.5	.3	.7	

Although a matrix of simple correlations provides insights into pairwise associations, sometimes researchers want to examine the association between two variables after controlling for one or more other variables. In the latter case, partial correlation should be estimated.

PARTIAL CORRELATION

Whereas the product moment or simple correlation is a measure of association describing the linear association between two variables, a **partial correlation coefficient** measures the association between two variables after controlling for or adjusting for the effects of one or more additional variables. This statistic is used to answer the following questions:

Partial Correlation Coefficient
A measure of the association between two variables after controlling or adjusting for the effects of one or more additional variables.

- How strongly are sales related to advertising expenditures when the effect of price is controlled?
- Is there an association between market share and size of the sales force after adjusting for the effect of sales promotion?
- Are consumers' perceptions of quality related to their perceptions of prices when the effect of brand image is controlled?

As in these situations, suppose one wanted to calculate the association between X and Y after controlling for a third variable, Z. Conceptually, one would first remove the effect of Z from X. To do this one would predict the values of X based on a knowledge of Z by using the product moment correlation between X and Z, r_{xz}. The predicted value of X is then subtracted from the actual value of X to construct an adjusted value of X. In a similar manner, the values of Y are adjusted to remove the effects of Z. The product moment correlation between the adjusted values of X and the adjusted values of Y is the partial correlation coefficient between X and Y, after controlling for the effect of Z, and is denoted by $r_{xy.z}$. Statistically, since the simple correlation between two variables completely describes the linear relationship between them, the partial correlation coefficient can be calculated by a knowledge of the simple correlations alone, without using individual observations.

$$r_{xy.z} = \frac{r_{xy} - (r_{xz})(r_{yz})}{\sqrt{1 - r_{xz}^2}\sqrt{1 - r_{yz}^2}}$$

To continue our example, suppose the researcher wanted to calculate the association between attitude toward the city, Y, and duration of residence, X_1, after controlling for a third variable, importance attached to weather, X_2. These data are presented in Table 17.1. The simple correlations between the variables are

$$r_{yx_1} = .9361 \qquad r_{yx_2} = .7334 \qquad r_{x_1x_2} = .5495$$

The required partial correlation can be calculated as follows:

$$r_{yx_1.x_2} = \frac{.9361 - (.5495)(.7334)}{\sqrt{1 - (.5495)^2}\sqrt{1 - (.7334)^2}}$$

$$= .9386$$

As can be seen, controlling for the effect of importance attached to weather has little effect on the association between attitude toward the city and duration of residence.

Partial correlations have an *order* associated with them. The order indicates how many variables are being adjusted or controlled for. The simple correlation coefficient, r, has a zero order, as it does not control for any additional variables while measuring the association between two variables. The coefficient $r_{xy.z}$ is a first-order partial correlation coefficient, as it controls for the effect of one additional variable, Z. A second-order partial correlation coefficient controls for the effects of two variables, a third-order for the effects of three variables, and so on. The higher order partial correlations are calculated similarly. The $(n + 1)$th-order partial coefficient may be calculated by replacing the simple correlation coefficients on the right side of the preceding equation with the nth-order partial coefficients.

Partial correlations can be helpful for detecting spurious relationships (see chapter 15). The relationship between X and Y is spurious if it is solely due to the fact that X is associated with Z, which is indeed the true predictor of Y. In this case, the correlation between X and Y disappears when the effect of Z is controlled. Consider a case in which consumption of a cereal brand (C) is positively associated with income (I), with $r_{ci} = .28$. Because this brand was popularly priced, income was not expected to be a significant factor. Therefore, the researcher suspected that this relationship was spurious. The sample results also indicated that income is positively associated with household size (H), $r_{hi} = .48$, and that household size is associated with cereal consumption, $r_{ch} = .56$. These figures seem to indicate that the real predictor of cereal consumption is not income but household size. To test this assertion, the first-order partial correlation between cereal consumption and income is calculated, controlling for the effect of household size. The reader can verify that this partial correlation, $r_{ci.h}$, is .02, and the initial correlation between cereal consumption and income vanishes when the household size was controlled. Therefore, the correlation between income and cereal consumption is spurious. The special case when a partial correlation is larger than its respective zero-order correlation involves a supressor effect (see chapter 15).[5]

Part Correlation Coefficient
A measure of the correlation between Y and X when the linear effects of the other independent variables have been removed from X (but not from Y).

Another correlation coefficient of interest is the **part correlation coefficient**. This coefficient represents the correlation between Y and X when the linear effects of the other independent variables have been removed from X but not from Y. The part correlation coefficient, $r_{y(x.z)}$ is calculated as follows:

$$r_{y(x.z)} = \frac{r_{xy} - r_{yz}r_{xz}}{\sqrt{1 - r_{xz}^2}}$$

The part correlation between attitude toward the city and the duration of residence, when the linear effects of the importance attached to weather have been removed from the duration of residence, can be calculated as

$$r_{y(x_1.x_2)} = \frac{.9361 - (.5495)(.7334)}{\sqrt{1 - (.5495)^2}}$$

$$= .63806$$

The partial correlation coefficient is generally viewed as more important than the part correlation coefficient. The product moment correlation, partial correlation, and the part correlation coefficient all assume that the data are interval or ratio scaled. If the data do not meet these requirements, the researcher should consider the use of nonmetric correlation.

EXAMPLE

Selling Ads to Home Shoppers

Advertisements play a very important role in forming attitudes/preferences for brands. In general, it has been found that for low-involvement products, attitude toward the advertisement mediates brand cognition (beliefs about the brand) and attitude toward the brand. What would happen to the effect of this mediating variable when products are purchased through a home shopping network? Home Shopping Budapest in Hungary conducted research to assess the impact of advertisements toward purchase. A survey was conducted in which several measures were taken such as attitude toward the product, attitude toward the brand, attitude toward the ad characteristics, brand cognitions, and so on. It was hypothesized that in the home shopping network, advertisements largely determined attitude toward the brand. In order to find the degree of association of attitude toward the ad with both attitude toward the brand and brand cognition, a partial correlation coefficient could be computed. The partial correlation would be calculated between attitude toward the brand and brand cognitions after controlling for the effects of attitude toward the ad on the two variables. If attitude toward the ad is significantly high, then the partial correlation coefficient should be significantly less than the product moment correlation between brand cognition and attitude toward the brand. Research was conducted that supported this hypothesis. Then, Saatchi & Saatchi designed the ads aired on Home Shopping Budapest to generate positive attitude toward the advertising and this turned out to be a major competitive weapon for the network.[6] ■

NONMETRIC CORRELATION

At times the researcher may have to compute the correlation coefficient between two variables that are nonmetric. It may be recalled that nonmetric variables do not have interval or ratio scale properties and do not assume a normal distribution. If the nonmetric variables are ordinal and numeric, Spearman's rho, ρ_s, and Kendall's tau, τ, are two measures of **nonmetric correlation** that can be used to examine the correlation between them. Both these measures use rankings rather than the absolute values of the variables and the basic concepts underlying them are quite similar. Both vary from −1.0 to +1.0 (see chapter 15).

Nonmetric Correlation
A correlation measure for two nonmetric variables, which relies on rankings to compute the correlation.

In the absence of ties, Spearman's ρ_s yields a closer approximation to the Pearson product moment correlation coefficient, ρ, than Kendall's τ. In these cases, the absolute magnitude of τ tends to be smaller than Pearson's ρ. On the other hand, when the data contain a large number of tied ranks, Kendall's τ seems more appropriate. As a rule of thumb, Kendall's τ is to be preferred when a large number of cases fall into a relatively small number of categories (thereby leading to a large number of ties). Conversely, the use of Spearman's ρ_s is preferable when we have a relatively larger number of categories (thereby having fewer ties).[7]

The product moment as well as the partial and part correlation coefficients provide a conceptual foundation for bivariate as well as multiple regression analysis.

Regression Analysis
A statistical procedure for analyzing associative relationships between a metric dependent variable and one or more independent variables.

REGRESSION ANALYSIS

Regression analysis is a powerful and flexible procedure for analyzing associative relationships between a metric dependent variable and one or more independent variables. It can be used to

1. Determine whether the independent variables explain a significant variation in the dependent variable: whether a relationship exists.
2. Determine how much of the variation in the dependent variable can be explained by the independent variables: strength of the relationship.
3. Determine the structure or form of the relationship: the mathematical equation relating the independent and dependent variables.
4. Predict the values of the dependent variable.
5. Control for other independent variables when evaluating the contributions of a specific variable or set of variables.

Although the independent variables may explain the variation in the dependent variable, this does not necessarily imply causation. The use of the terms *dependent* or *criterion* variables and *independent* or *predictor* variables in regression analysis arises from the mathematical relationship between the variables. These terms do not imply that the criterion variable is dependent on the independent variables in a causal sense. Regression analysis is concerned with the nature and degree of association between variables and does not imply or assume any causality. Bivariate regression is discussed first, followed by multiple regression.

BIVARIATE REGRESSION

Bivariate Regression
A procedure for deriving a mathematical relationship, in the form of an equation, between a single metric dependent variable and a single metric independent variable.

Bivariate regression is a procedure for deriving a mathematical relationship, in the form of an equation, between a single metric dependent or criterion variable and a single metric independent or predictor variable. The analysis is similar in many ways to determining the simple correlation between two variables. However, because an equation has to be derived, one variable must be identified as the dependent and the other as the independent variable. The examples given earlier in the context of simple correlation can be translated into the regression context.

- Can variation in sales be explained in terms of variation in advertising expenditures? What is the structure and form of this relationship, and can it be modeled mathematically by an equation describing a straight line?
- Can the variation in market share be accounted for by the size of the sales force?
- Are consumers' perceptions of quality determined by their perceptions of price?

Before discussing the procedure for conducting bivariate regression, we define some important statistics.

STATISTICS ASSOCIATED WITH BIVARIATE REGRESSION ANALYSIS

The following statistics and statistical terms are associated with bivariate regression analysis.

Bivariate Regression Model. The basic regression equation is $Y_i = \beta_0 + \beta_1 X_i + e_i$, where Y = dependent or criterion variable, X = independent or predictor variable, β_0 = intercept of the line, β_1 = slope of the line, and e_i is the error term associated with the ith observation.

Coefficient of Determination. The strength of association is measured by the coefficient of determination, r^2. It varies between 0 and 1 and signifies the proportion of the total variation in Y that is accounted for by the variation in X.

Estimated or Predicted Value. The estimated or predicted value of Y_i is $\hat{Y}_i = a + bx$, where $\hat{Y}_i$ is the predicted value of Y_i, and a and b are estimators of β_0 and β_1, respectively.

Regression Coefficient. The estimated parameter b is usually referred to as the nonstandardized regression coefficient.

Scattergram. A scatter diagram, or scattergram, is a plot of the values of two variables for all the cases or observations.

Standard Error of Estimate. This statistic, SEE, is the standard deviation of the actual Y values from the predicted $\hat{Y}$ values.

Standard Error. The standard deviation of b, SE_b, is called the standard error.

Standardized Regression Coefficient. Also termed the *beta coefficient* or *beta weight*, this is the slope obtained by the regression of Y on X when the data are standardized.

Sum of Squared Errors. The distances of all the points from the regression line are squared and added together to arrive at the sum of squared errors, which is a measure of total error, Σe_j^2.

t *Statistic.* A t statistic with $n - 2$ degrees of freedom can be used to test the null hypothesis that no linear relationship exists between X and Y, or H_0: $\beta_1 = 0$, where $t = \frac{b}{SE_b}$.

CONDUCTING BIVARIATE REGRESSION ANALYSIS

The steps involved in conducting bivariate regression analysis are described in Figure 17.2. Suppose the researcher wants to explain attitudes toward the city of residence in terms of the duration of residence (see Table 17.1). In deriving such relationships, it is often useful to first examine a scatter diagram.

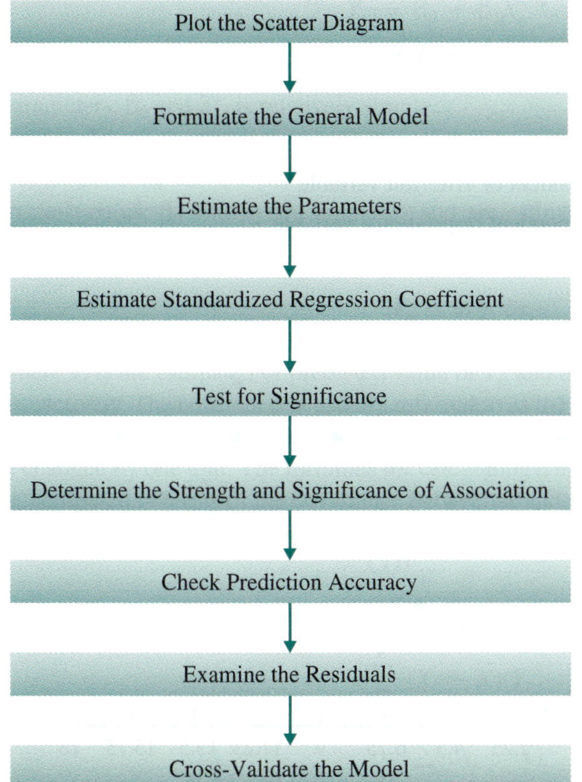

Figure 17.2
Conducting Bivariate Regression Analysis

$$= \frac{\sum_{i=1}^{n} X_i Y_i - n\overline{X}\overline{Y}}{\sum_{i=1}^{n} X_i^2 - n\overline{X}^2}$$

The intercept, a, may then be calculated using

$$a = \overline{Y} - b\overline{X}$$

For the data in Table 17.1, the estimation of parameters may be illustrated as follows:

$$\begin{aligned}\sum_{i=1}^{12} X_i Y_i &= (10)(6) + (12)(9) + (12)(8) + (4)(3) + (12)(10) + (6)(4) \\ &\quad + (8)(5) + (2)(2) + (18)(11) + (9)(9) + (17)(10) + (2)(2) \\ &= 917\end{aligned}$$

$$\begin{aligned}\sum_{i=1}^{12} X_i^2 &= 10^2 + 12^2 + 12^2 + 4^2 + 12^2 + 6^2 \\ &\quad + 8^2 + 2^2 + 18^2 + 9^2 + 17^2 + 2^2 \\ &= 1{,}350\end{aligned}$$

It may be recalled from earlier calculations of the simple correlation that

$$\begin{aligned}\overline{X} &= 9.333 \\ \overline{Y} &= 6.583\end{aligned}$$

Given $n = 12$, b can be calculated as

$$\begin{aligned}b &= \frac{917 - (12)(9.333)(6.583)}{1350 - (12)(9.333)^2} \\ &= .5897\end{aligned}$$

$$\begin{aligned}a &= \overline{Y} - b\overline{X} \\ &= 6.583 - (.5897)(9.333) \\ &= 1.0793\end{aligned}$$

Note that these coefficients have been estimated on the raw (untransformed) data. Should standardization of the data be considered desirable, the calculation of the standardized coefficients is also straightforward.

Standardized Regression Coefficient

Standardization is the process by which the raw data are transformed into new variables, which have a mean of 0 and a variance of 1 (chapter 14). When the data are standardized, the intercept assumes a value of 0. The term *beta coefficient* or *beta weight* is used to denote the standardized regression coefficient. In this case, the slope obtained by the regression of Y on X, B_{yx}, is the same as the slope obtained by the regression of X on Y, B_{xy}. Moreover, each of these regression coefficients is equal to the simple correlation between X and Y.

$$B_{yx} = B_{xy} = r_{xy}$$

There is a simple relationship between the standardized and nonstandardized regression coefficients:

$$B_{yx} = b_{yx}\left(\frac{S_x}{S_y}\right)$$

For the regression results given in Table 17.2, the value of the beta coefficient is estimated as .9361.

Once the parameters have been estimated, they can be tested for significance.

Significance Testing

The statistical significance of the linear relationship between X and Y may be tested by examining the hypotheses:

$$H_0\text{: } \beta_1 = 0$$
$$H_1\text{: } \beta_1 \neq 0$$

The null hypothesis implies that there is no linear relationship between X and Y. The alternative hypothesis is that there is a relationship, positive or negative, between X and Y. Typically, a two-tailed test is done. A t statistic with $n - 2$ degrees of freedom can be used, where

$$t = \frac{b}{SE_b}$$

SE_b denotes the standard deviation of b and is called the *standard error*.[10] The t distribution was discussed in chapter 15.

Using a computer program, the regression of attitude on duration of residence, using the data shown in Table 17.1, yielded the results shown in Table 17.2. The intercept, a, equals 1.0793, and the slope, b, equals .5897. Therefore, the estimated equation is

$$\text{Attitude } (\hat{Y}) = 1.0793 + .5897 \text{ (duration of residence)}$$

TABLE 17.2

BIVARIATE REGRESSION

Multiple R	.93608
R^2	.87624
Adjusted R^2	.86387
Standard error	1.22329

Analysis of Variance

	df	*Sum of Squares*	*Mean Square*
Regression	1	105.95222	105.95222
Residual	10	14.96444	1.49644
$F = 70.80266$	Significance of $F = .0000$		

Variables in the Equation

Variable	*b*	*SE_b*	*Beta (β)*	*T*	*Significance of T*
Duration	.58972	.07008	.93608	8.414	.0000
(Constant)	1.07932	.74335		1.452	.1772

The standard error or standard deviation of b is estimated as .07008, and the value of the t statistic, $t = .5897/.0701 = 8.414$, with $n - 2 = 10$ degrees of freedom. From Table 4 in the statistical appendix, we see that the critical value of t with 10 degrees of freedom and $\alpha = .05$ is 2.228 for a two-tailed test. Because the calculated value of t is larger than the critical value, the null hypothesis is rejected. Hence, there is a significant linear relationship between attitude toward the city and duration of residence in the city. The positive sign of the slope coefficient indicates that this relationship is positive. In other words, those who have resided in the city for a longer time have more positive attitudes toward the city.

Strength and Significance of Association

A related inference involves determining the strength and significance of the association between Y and X. The strength of association is measured by the coefficient of determination, r^2. In bivariate regression, r^2 is the square of the simple correlation coefficient obtained by correlating the two variables. The coefficient r^2 varies between 0 and 1. It signifies the proportion of the total variation in Y that is accounted for by the variation in X. The decomposition of the total variation in Y is similar to that for analysis of variance (chapter 16). As shown in Figure 17.5, the total variation, SS_y, may be decomposed into the variation accounted for by the regression line, SS_{reg}, and the error or residual variation, SS_{error} or SS_{res}, as follows:

$$SS_y = SS_{reg} + SS_{res}$$

where

$$SS_y = \sum_{i=1}^{n} (Y_i - \bar{Y})^2$$

$$SS_{reg} = \sum_{i=1}^{n} (\hat{Y}_i - \bar{Y})^2$$

$$SS_{res} = \sum_{i=1}^{n} (Y_i - \hat{Y}_i)^2$$

The strength of association may then be calculated as follows:

$$r^2 = \frac{SS_{reg}}{SS_y}$$

$$= \frac{SS_y - SS_{res}}{SS_y}$$

To illustrate the calculations of r^2, let us consider again the effect of the duration of residence on attitude toward the city. It may be recalled from earlier calculations of the simple correlation coefficient that

$$SS_y = \sum_{i=1}^{n} (Y_i - \bar{Y})^2$$

$$= 120.9168$$

The predicted values ($\hat{Y}$) can be calculated using the regression equation

$$\text{attitude } (\hat{Y}) = 1.0793 + .5897 \text{ (duration of residence)}$$

For the first observation in Table 17.1, this value is

$$(\hat{Y}) = 1.0793 + .5897 \times 10 = 6.9763$$

For each successive observation, the predicted values are, in order: 8.1557, 8.1557, 3.4381, 8.1557, 4.6175, 5.7969, 2.2587, 11.6939, 6.3866, 11.1042, 2.2587. Therefore,

$$\begin{aligned} SS_{reg} = \sum_{i=1}^{n} (\hat{Y}_i - \overline{Y})^2 &= (6.9763 - 6.5833)^2 + (8.1557 - 6.5833)^2 \\ &+ (8.1557 - 6.5833)^2 + (3.4381 - 6.5833)^2 \\ &+ (8.1557 - 6.5833)^2 + (4.6175 - 6.5833)^2 \\ &+ (5.7969 - 6.5833)^2 + (2.2587 - 6.5833)^2 \\ &+ (11.6939 - 6.5833)^2 + (6.3866 - 6.5833)^2 \\ &+ (11.1042 - 6.5833)^2 + (2.2587 - 6.5833)^2 \\ &= .1544 + 2.4724 + 2.4724 + 9.8922 + 2.4724 \\ &+ 3.8643 + .6184 + 18.7021 + 26.1182 \\ &+ .0387 + 20.4385 + 18.7021 \\ &= 105.9522 \end{aligned}$$

$$\begin{aligned} SS_{res} = \sum_{i=1}^{n} (Y_i - \hat{Y}_i)^2 &= (6 - 6.9763)^2 + (9 - 8.1557)^2 + (8 - 8.1557)^2 \\ &+ (3 - 3.4381)^2 + (10 - 8.1557)^2 + (4 - 4.6175)^2 \\ &+ (5 - 5.7969)^2 + (2 - 2.2587)^2 + (11 - 11.6939)^2 \\ &+ (9 - 6.3866)^2 + (10 - 11.1042)^2 + (2 - 2.2587)^2 \\ &= 14.9644 \end{aligned}$$

It can be seen that $SS_y = SS_{reg} + SS_{res}$. Furthermore,

$$\begin{aligned} r^2 &= \frac{SS_{reg}}{SS_y} \\ &= \frac{105.9524}{120.9168} \\ &= .8762 \end{aligned}$$

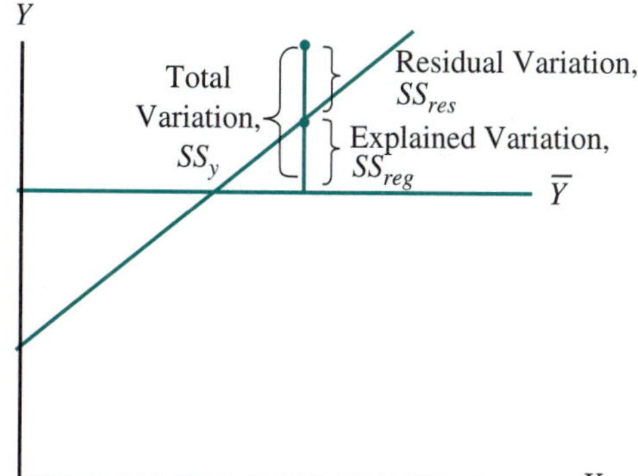

Figure 17.5
Decomposition of the Total Variation in Bivariate Regression

Another equivalent test for examining the significance of the linear relationship between X and Y (significance of b) is the test for the significance of the coefficient of determination. The hypotheses in this case are

$$H_0: R^2_{pop} = 0$$
$$H_1: R^2_{pop} > 0$$

The appropriate test statistic is the F statistic:

$$F = \frac{SS_{reg}}{SS_{res}/(n-2)}$$

which has an F distribution with 1 and $n - 2$ degrees of freedom. The F test is a generalized form of the t test (see chapter 15). If a random variable is t distributed with n degrees of freedom, then t^2 is F distributed with 1 and n degrees of freedom. Hence, the F test for testing the significance of the coefficient of determination is equivalent to testing the following hypotheses:

$$H_0: \beta_1 = 0$$
$$H_1: \beta_1 \neq 0$$

or

$$H_0: \rho = 0$$
$$H_1: \rho \neq 0$$

From Table 17.2, it can be seen that:

$$r^2 = \frac{105.9522}{(105.9522 + 14.9644)}$$

$$= .8762$$

Which is the same as the value calculated earlier. The value of the F statistic is:

$$F = \frac{105.9522}{(14.9644/10)}$$

$$= 70.8027$$

with 1 and 10 degrees of freedom. The calculated F statistic exceeds the critical value of 4.96 determined from Table 5 in the statistical appendix. Therefore, the relationship is significant at $\alpha = .05$, corroborating the results of the t test. If the relationship between X and Y is significant, it is meaningful to predict the values of Y based on the values of X and to estimate prediction accuracy.

Prediction Accuracy

To estimate the accuracy of predicted values, $\hat{Y}$, it is useful to calculate the standard error of estimate, SEE. This statistic is the standard deviation of the actual Y values from the predicted $\hat{Y}$ values.

$$\text{SEE} = \sqrt{}$$

$$\sqrt{\frac{SS_{res}}{n - 2}} \qquad \text{SEE} =$$

or more generally, if there are k independent variables,

$$\text{SEE} = \sqrt{\frac{SS_{res}}{n - k - 1}}$$

SEE may be interpreted as a kind of average residual or average error in predicting Y from the regression equation.[11]

Two cases of prediction may arise. The researcher may want to predict the mean value of Y for all the cases with a given value of X, say X_0, or predict the value of Y for a single case. In both situations, the predicted value is the same and is given by $\hat{Y}$, where

$$\hat{Y} = a + bX_0$$

However, the standard error is different in the two situations, although in both situations it is a function of SEE. For large samples, the standard error for predicting mean value of Y is SEE/$\sqrt{n}$, and for predicting individual Y values it is SEE. Hence, the construction of confidence intervals (see chapter 12) for the predicted value varies, depending on whether the mean value or the value for a single observation is being predicted.

For the data given in Table 17.2, the SEE is estimated as follows:

$$\text{SEE} = \sqrt{\frac{14.9644}{(12 - 2)}}$$

$$= 1.22329$$

The final two steps in conducting bivariate regression, namely examination of residuals and model cross-validation, are considered later, and we now turn to the assumptions underlying the regression model.

Assumptions

The regression model makes a number of assumptions in estimating the parameters and in significance testing, as shown in Figure 17.4:

1. The error term is normally distributed. For each fixed value of X, the distribution of Y is normal.[12]
2. The means of all these normal distributions of Y, given X, lie on a straight line with slope b.
3. The mean of the error term is 0.
4. The variance of the error term is constant. This variance does not depend on the values assumed by X.
5. The error terms are uncorrelated. In other words, the observations have been drawn independently.

Insights into the extent to which these assumptions have been met can be gained by an examination of residuals, which is covered in the next section on multiple regression.[13]

MULTIPLE REGRESSION

Multiple Regression A statistical technique that simultaneously develops a mathematical relationship between two or more independent variables and an interval-scaled dependent variable.

Multiple regression involves a single dependent variable and two or more independent variables. The questions raised in the context of bivariate regression can also be answered via multiple regression by considering additional independent variables:

- Can variation in sales be explained in terms of variation in advertising expenditures, prices, and level of distribution?
- Can variation in market shares be accounted for by the size of the sales force, advertising expenditures, and sales promotion budgets?
- Are consumers' perceptions of quality determined by their perceptions of prices, brand image, and brand attributes?

Additional questions can also be answered by multiple regression:

- How much of the variation in sales can be explained by advertising expenditures, prices, and level of distribution?
- What is the contribution of advertising expenditures in explaining the variation in sales when the levels of prices and distribution are controlled?
- What levels of sales may be expected given the levels of advertising expenditures, prices, and level of distribution?

EXAMPLE

Global Brands—Local Ads

Europeans welcome brands from other countries, but when it comes to advertising, they prefer the home-grown variety. A survey done by Yankelovich and Partners and its affiliates finds that most European consumers' favorite commercials are for local brands even though they are more than likely to buy foreign brands. Respondents in France, Germany, and the United Kingdom named Coca-Cola as the most often purchased soft drink. However, the French selected the famous award-winning spot for France's Perrier bottled water as their favorite commercial. Similarly, in Germany, the favorite advertising was for a German brand of nonalcoholic beer, Clausthaler. However, in the United Kingdom, Coca-Cola was the favorite soft drink and also the favorite advertising. In the light of such findings, the important question is—does advertising help? Does it help increase the purchase probability of the brand or does it merely maintain the brand recognition rate high. One way of finding out is by running a regression in which the dependent variable is the likelihood of brand purchase and the independent variables are brand attribute evaluations and advertising evaluations. Separate models with and without advertising can be run to assess any significant difference in the contribution. Individual *t* tests could also be examined to find out the significant contribution of both the brand attributes and advertising. The results will indicate the degree to which advertising plays an important part on brand purchase decisions.[14] ■

Multiple Regression Model An equation used to explain the results of multiple regression analysis.

The general form of the **multiple regression model** is as follows:

$$Y = \beta_0 + \beta_1 X_1 + \beta_2 X_2 + \beta_3 X_3 + \ldots + \beta_k X_k + e$$

which is estimated by the following equation:

$$\hat{Y} = a + b_1 X_1 + b_2 X_2 + b_3 X_3 + \ldots + b_k X_k$$

As before, the coefficient a represents the intercept, but the bs are now the partial regression coefficients. The least-squares criterion estimates the parameters in such a way as to minimize the total error, SS_{res}. This process also maximizes the correlation between the actual values of Y and the predicted values $\hat{Y}$. All the assumptions made in bivariate regression also apply in multiple regression. We define some associated statistics and then describe the procedure for multiple regression analysis.[15]

STATISTICS ASSOCIATED WITH MULTIPLE REGRESSION

Most of the statistics and statistical terms described under bivariate regression also apply to multiple regression. In addition, the following statistics are used:

Adjusted R^2. R^2, coefficient of multiple determination, is adjusted for the number of independent variables and the sample size to account for the diminishing returns. After the first few variables, the additional independent variables do not make much contribution.

Coefficient of Multiple Determination. The strength of association in multiple regression is measured by the square of the multiple correlation coefficient, R^2, which is also called the *coefficient of multiple determination.*

F *Test.* The F test is used to test the null hypothesis that the coefficient of multiple determination in the population, R^2_{pop}, is zero. This is equivalent to testing the null hypothesis H_0: $\beta_1 = \beta_2 = \beta_3 = \ldots = \beta_k = 0$. The test statistic has an F distribution with k and $(n - k - 1)$ degrees of freedom.

Partial* F *Test. The significance of a partial regression coefficient, β_i, of X_i may be tested using an incremental F statistic. The incremental F statistic is based on the increment in the explained sum of squares resulting from the addition of the independent variable X_i to the regression equation after all the other independent variables have been included.

Partial Regression Coefficient. The partial regression coefficient, b_1, denotes the change in the predicted value, $\hat{Y}$, per unit change in X_1 when the other independent variables, X_2 to X_k, are held constant.

CONDUCTING MULTIPLE REGRESSION ANALYSIS

The steps involved in conducting multiple regression analysis are similar to those for bivariate regression analysis. The discussion focuses on partial regression coefficients, strength of association, significance testing, and examination of residuals.

Partial Regression Coefficients

To understand the meaning of a partial regression coefficient, let us consider a case in which there are two independent variables, so that

$$\hat{Y} = a + b_1X_1 + b_2X_2$$

First, note that the relative magnitude of the partial regression coefficient of an independent variable is, in general, different from that of its bivariate regression coefficient. In other words, the partial regression coefficient, b_1, will be different from the regression coefficient, b, obtained by regressing Y on only X_1. This happens because X_1 and X_2 are usually correlated. In bivariate regression, X_2 was not considered, and any variation in Y that was shared by X_1 and X_2 was attributed to X_1. However, in the case of multiple independent variables, this is no longer true.

The interpretation of the partial regression coefficient, b_1, is that it represents the expected change in Y when X_1 is changed by one unit but X_2 is held constant or otherwise controlled. Likewise, b_2 represents the expected change in Y for a unit change in X_2, when X_1 is held constant. Thus calling b_1 and b_2 partial regression coefficients is appropriate. It can also be seen that the combined effects of X_1 and X_2 on Y are additive. In other words, if X_1 and X_2 are each changed by one unit, the expected change in Y would be $(b_1 + b_2)$.

Conceptually, the relationship between the bivariate regression coefficient and the partial regression coefficient can be illustrated as follows. Suppose one was to remove the effect of X_2 from X_1. This could be done by running a regression of X_1 on X_2. In other words, one would estimate the equation $\hat{X}_1 = a + bX_2$ and calculate the residual $X_r = (X_1 - \hat{X}_1)$. The partial regression coefficient, b_1, is then equal to the bivariate regression coefficient, b, obtained from the equation $\hat{Y} = a + bX_r$. In other words, the partial regression coefficient, b_1, is equal to the regression coefficient, b, between Y and the residuals of X_1 from which the effect of X_2 has been removed. The partial coefficient, b_2, can also be interpreted along similar lines.

Extension to the case of k variables is straightforward. The partial regression coefficient, b_1, represents the expected change in Y when X_1 is changed by one unit and X_2 through X_k are held constant. It can also be interpreted as the bivariate regression coefficient, b, for the regression of Y on the residuals of X_1, when the effect of X_2 through X_k has been removed from X_1.

The beta coefficients are the partial regression coefficients obtained when all the variables $(Y, X_1, X_2, \ldots X_k)$ have been standardized to a mean of 0 and a variance of 1 before estimating the regression equation. The relationship of the standardized to the nonstandardized coefficients remains the same as before:

$$B_1 = b_1 \left(\frac{S_{x1}}{S_y} \right)$$

$$\cdot$$

$$\cdot$$

$$B_k = b_k \left(\frac{S_{xk}}{S_y} \right)$$

The intercept and the partial regression coefficients are estimated by solving a system of simultaneous equations derived by differentiating and equating the partial derivatives to 0. Because these coefficients are automatically estimated by the various computer programs, we will not present the details. Yet it is worth noting that the equations cannot be solved if (1) the sample size, n, is smaller than or equal to the number of independent variables, k; or (2) one independent variable is perfectly correlated with another.

Suppose that in explaining the attitude toward the city, we now introduce a second variable, importance attached to the weather. The data for the 12 pretest respondents on attitude toward the city, duration of residence, and importance attached to the weather are given in Table 17.1. The results of multiple regression analysis are depicted in Table 17.3. The partial regression coefficient for duration (X_1) is now .4811, different from what it was in the bivariate case. The corresponding beta coefficient is .7636. The partial regression coefficient for importance attached to weather (X_2) is .2887, with a beta coefficient of .3138. The estimated regression equation is

$$(\hat{Y}) = .33732 + .48108X_1 + .28865X_2$$

or

$$\text{attitude} = .33732 + .48108\ (\text{duration}) + .28865\ (\text{importance})$$

TABLE 17.3

MULTIPLE REGRESSION

Multiple R	.97210
R^2	.94498
Adjusted R^2	.93276
Standard error	.85974

Analysis of Variance

	df	*Sum of Squares*	*Mean Square*
Regression	2	114.26425	57.13213
Residual	9	6.65241	.73916
$F = 77.29364$	Significance of $F = .0000$		

Variables in the Equation

Variable	*b*	SE_b	*Beta* (β)	*T*	*Significance of T*
Impor	.28865	.08608	.31382	3.353	.0085
Duration	.48108	.05895	.76363	8.160	.0000
(Constant)	.33732	.56736		.595	.5668

This equation can be used for a variety of purposes, including predicting attitudes toward the city, given a knowledge of the respondents' duration of residence in the city and the importance they attach to weather.

Strength of Association

The strength of the relationship stipulated by the regression equation can be determined by using appropriate measures of association. The total variation is decomposed as in the bivariate case

$$SS_y = SS_{reg} + SS_{res}$$

where

$$SS_y = \sum_{i=1}^{n} (Y_i - \bar{Y})^2$$

$$SS_{reg} = \sum_{i=1}^{n} (\hat{Y}_i - \bar{Y})^2$$

$$SS_{res} = \sum_{i=1}^{n} (Y_i - \hat{Y}_i)^2$$

The strength of association is measured by the square of the multiple correlation coefficient, R^2, which is also called the *coefficient of multiple determination.*

$$R^2 = \frac{SS_{reg}}{SS_y}$$

The multiple correlation coefficient, R, can also be viewed as the simple correlation coefficient, r, between Y and $\hat{Y}$. Several points about the characteristics of R^2 are worth noting. The coefficient of multiple determination, R^2, cannot be less than the highest bivariate, r^2, of any individual independent variable with the dependent variable. R^2 will be larger when the correlations between the independent variables are low. If the independent variables are statistically independent (uncorrelated), then R^2 will be the sum of bivariate r^2 of each independent variable with the dependent variable. R^2 cannot decrease as more independent variables are added to the regression equation. Yet diminishing returns set in, so that after the first few variables, the additional independent variables do not make much of a contribution.[16] For this reason, R^2 is adjusted for the number of independent variables and the sample size by using the following formula:

$$\text{adjusted } R^2 = R^2 - \frac{k(1 - R^2)}{n - k - 1}$$

For the regression results given in Table 17.3, the value of R^2 is

$$R^2 = \frac{114.2643}{(114.2643 + 6.6524)}$$

$$= .9450$$

This is higher than the r^2 value of .8762 obtained in the bivariate case. The r^2 in the bivariate case is the square of the simple (product moment) correlation between attitude toward the city and duration of residence. The R^2 obtained in multiple regression is also higher than the square of the simple correlation between attitude and importance attached to weather (which can be estimated as .5379). The adjusted R^2 is estimated as

$$\text{adjusted } R^2 = \frac{.9450 - 2(1.0 - .9450)}{(12 - 2 - 1)}$$

$$= .9328$$

Note that the value of adjusted R^2 is close to R^2 and both are higher than r^2 for the bivariate case. This suggests that the addition of the second independent variable, importance attached to weather, makes a contribution in explaining the variation in attitude toward the city.

Significance Testing

Significance testing involves testing the significance of the overall regression equation as well as specific partial regression coefficients. The null hypothesis for the overall test is that the coefficient of multiple determination in the population, $R^2{}_{pop}$, is zero.

$$H_0: R^2{}_{pop} = 0$$

This is equivalent to the following null hypothesis:

$$H_0: \beta_1 = \beta_2 = \beta_3 = \ldots = \beta_k = 0$$

The overall test can be conducted by using an F statistic

$$F = \frac{SS_{reg}/k}{SS_{res}/(n - k - 1)}$$

$$= \frac{R^2/k}{(1 - R^2)/(n - k - 1)}$$

which has an F distribution with k and $(n - k - 1)$ degrees of freedom.[17] For the multiple regression results given in Table 17.3,

$$F = \frac{114.2643/2}{6.6524/9} = 77.2944$$

which is significant at $\alpha = .05$.

If the overall null hypothesis is rejected, one or more population partial regression coefficients have a value different from 0. To determine which specific coefficients (β_is) are nonzero, additional tests are necessary. Testing for the significance of the β_is can be done in a manner similar to that in the bivariate case by using t tests. The significance of the partial coefficient for importance attached to weather may be tested by the following equation:

$$t = \frac{b}{SE_b}$$

$$= \frac{.2887}{.08608}$$

$$= 3.353$$

which has a t distribution with $n - k - 1$ degrees of freedom. This coefficient is significant at $\alpha = .05$. The significance of the coefficient for duration of residence is tested in a similar way and found to be significant. Therefore, both the duration of residence and importance attached to weather are important in explaining attitude toward the city.

Some computer programs provide an equivalent F test, often called the partial F test. This involves a decomposition of the total regression sum of squares, SS_{reg}, into components related to each independent variable. In the standard approach, this is done by assuming that each independent variable has been added to the regression equation after all the other independent variables have been included. The increment in the explained sum of squares, resulting from the addition of an independent variable, X_i, is the component of the variation attributed to that variable and is denoted by SS_{xi}.[18] The significance of the partial regression coefficient for this variable, β_i, is tested using an incremental F statistic:

$$F = \frac{SS_{Xi}/1}{SS_{res}/(n - k - 1)}$$

which has an F distribution with 1 and $(n - k - 1)$ degrees of freedom.

While high R^2 and significant partial regression coefficients are comforting, the efficacy of the regression model should be evaluated further by an examination of the residuals.

Examination of Residuals

A **residual** is the difference between the observed value of Y_i and the value predicted by the regression equation $\hat{Y}_i$. Residuals are used in the calculation of several statistics associated with regression. In addition, scattergrams of the residuals, in which the residuals are plotted against the predicted values, $\hat{Y}_i$, time, or predictor variables, provide useful insights in examining the appropriateness of the underlying assumptions and regression model fitted.[19]

Residual The difference between the observed value of Y_i and the value predicted by the regression equation $\hat{Y}_i$.

The assumption of a normally distributed error term can be examined by constructing a histogram of the residuals. A visual check reveals whether the distribution is normal. Additional evidence can be obtained by determining the percentages of residuals falling within ±1 SE or ±2 SE. These percentages can be compared with what would be expected under the normal distribution (68 percent and 95 percent, respectively). More formal assessment can be made by running the K-S one-sample test.

FOCUS ON Burke

We are often faced with the situation in which we must mix dummy variables and interval-scaled variables in the same analysis. This presents us with an interesting way to present the results and raises issues of interpretation. We illustrate this from a project conducted by Burke but we will use a very simple data set. The respondents were asked how many credit cards they had in their possession at the time of the interview and to rate "the value of credit" to their lifestyle (on a scale ranging from essential to maintaining our lifestyle to not at all needed to maintain our lifestyle). The dummy variable D indicates that the respondent lives in a rural area (1) or an urban area (0).

Number of Credit Cards	*Rating on Value of Credit*	*Location of Respondent*
y	x_1	d_1
2	1	1
4	2	1
6	3	1
4	4	0
5	5	0
6	6	0
2	1	1
3	2	1
4	3	1
5	4	0
6	5	0
8	6	0

The regression model was constructed and the criteria for inclusion of a variable was the 90 percent confidence level. Portions of the output from multiple regression follows:

MODEL SUMMARY[c]

					Change Statistics				
Model	*R*	*R Square*	*Adjusted R Square*	*Std. Error of the Estimate*	*R Square Change*	*F Change*	*df1*	*df2*	*Significance F Change*
1	.872[a]	.761	.737	.9131	.761	31.876	1	10	.000
2	.915[b]	.837	.800	.7964	.075	4.146	1	9	.072

a. Predictors: (Constant),VALUE
b. Predictors: (Constant), VALUE, LOCATION
c. Dependent Variable: CARDS

COEFFICIENTS[a]

		Unstandardized Coefficients		*Standardized Coefficients*			*95% Confidence Interval for B*		*Correlations*		
Model		*B*	*Std. Error*	*Beta*	*t*	*Significance*	*Lower Bound*	*Upper Bound*	*Zero-order*	*Partial*	*Part*
1	(Constant)	1.533	.601		2.551	.029	.194	2.873			
	VALUE	.871	.154	.872	5.646	.000	.528	1.215	.872	.872	.872
2	(Constant)	−1.208	1.445		−.836	.425	−4.477	2.060			
	VALUE	1.375	.282	1.377	4.883	.001	.738	2.012	.872	.852	.658
	LOCATION	1.958	.962	.574	2.036	.072	−.217	4.134	−.635	.562	.274

a. Dependent Variable: CARDS

(Continued)

FOCUS ON Burke *(Continued)*

EXCLUDED VARIABLES[b]

Model		Beta In	t	Sig.	Partial Correlation	Collinearity Statistics Tolerance
1	LOCATION	.574[a]	2.036	.072	.562	.229

a. Predictors in the Model: (Constant), VALUE
b. Dependent Variable: CARDS

In the preceding model we found:

$$Y = -1.2083 + 1.375(X_1) + 1.9583\,(D_1)$$

Recall that D_1 was simply a zero or one code and if $D_1 = 0$ the respondent lived in a city. If $D_1 = 1$ the respondent lived in a rural area. You could write the model as two models. For those respondents living in a city, there is no contribution to Y from the dummy code.

$$\text{City model} \quad Y = -1.2083 + 1.375(X_1)$$

For every respondent living in a rural area the contribution to Y was 1.9583. Therefore for these respondents, this is a constant value and can be added to the overall model constant of −1.2081 (e.g. −1.2083 + 1.9583 = .75). Now we have a separate model for rural respondents.

$$\text{Rural model} \quad Y = .7500 + 1.375(X_1)$$

One way to look at the difference between these two constant terms (the difference is, of course, the regression coefficient for D_1) is that it reflects the average difference between the rural respondents and the urban respondents holding the rating of credit constant.

What are the management implications of this? By modeling with a dummy variable as illustrated, you have made the assumption that the relationship between the number of credit cards and rating of credit is a constant for both urban and rural respondents. This can be tested by simply running a separate regression between rating of credit and number of credit cards by type of respondent. The two models can be then tested for different slopes. If the slopes aren't different then the one overall model

$$Y = -1.2083 + 1.375(X_1) + 1.9583(D_1)$$

could be used.

If the slopes are not the same, different models should be constructed for rural and urban respondents.

SUMMARY

The product moment correlation coefficient, r, measures the linear association between two metric (interval or ratio scaled) variables. Its square, r^2, measures the proportion of variation in one variable explained by the other. The partial correlation coefficient measures the association between two variables after controlling, or adjusting for, the effects of one or more additional variables. The order of a partial correlation indicates how many variables are being adjusted or controlled. Partial correlations can be very helpful for detecting spurious relationships.

$$PD = 23.4 + .003INC$$

The coefficient of the *INC* variable is reported as significant.

a. Does this relationship seem plausible? Is it possible to have a coefficient that is small in magnitude and yet significant?

b. From the information given, can you tell how good the estimated model is?

c. What are the expected expenditures on prepared dinners of a family earning $30,000?

d. If a family earning $40,000 spent $130 annually on prepared dinners, what is the residual?

e. What is the meaning of a negative residual?

INTERNET AND COMPUTER EXERCISES

1. Use an appropriate microcomputer or mainframe program (SPSS, SAS, BMDP, Minitab, or Excel) to analyze the data for:

a. Problem 1

b. Problem 2

Chapter 18

Discriminant Analysis

"Often you have measured different groups of respondents on many metric variables. Discriminant analysis is a useful way to answer the questions . . . are the groups different? . . . On what variables are they most different? . . . Can I predict which group a person belongs to using these variables?"

Andy Kennelly, senior marketing research analyst, Burke, Inc.

OBJECTIVES

After reading this chapter, the student should be able to

1. describe the concept of discriminant analysis, its objectives, and its applications in marketing research
2. outline the procedures for conducting discriminant analysis including the formulation of the problem, estimation of the discriminant function coefficients, determination of significance, interpretation, and validation
3. discuss multiple discriminant analysis and the distinction between two-group and multiple discriminant analysis
4. explain stepwise discriminant analysis and describe the Mahalanobis procedure

OVERVIEW

This chapter discusses the technique of discriminant analysis. We begin by examining the relationship of this procedure to regression analysis (chapter 17) and analysis of variance (chapter 16). We present a model and describe the general procedure for conducting discriminant analysis, with emphasis on formulation, estimation, determination of significance, interpretation, and validation of the results. The procedure is illustrated with an example of two-group discriminant analysis, followed by an example of multiple (three-group) discriminant analysis. The stepwise discriminant analysis procedure is also covered.

We begin with examples illustrating the applications of two-group and multiple discriminant analysis.

EXAMPLE

Rebate Redeemers

A study of 294 consumers was undertaken to determine the correlates of rebate proneness, or the characteristics of consumers who respond favorably to rebate promotions. The predictor variables were four factors related to household shopping attitudes and behaviors,

Multiple discriminant analysis shows that rebate-sensitive consumers associate less effort with fulfilling the requirements of the rebate purchase and they are willing to accept a relatively smaller refund than other customers.

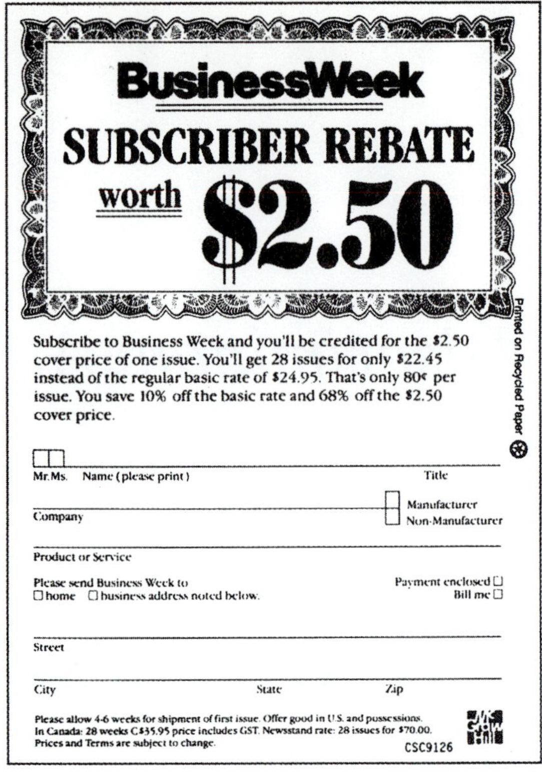
BusinessWeek

SUBSCRIBER REBATE

worth $2.50

Subscribe to Business Week and you'll be credited for the $2.50 cover price of one issue. You'll get 28 issues for only $22.45 instead of the regular basic rate of $24.95. That's only 80¢ per issue. You save 10% off the basic rate and 68% off the $2.50 cover price.

☐☐ Mr. Ms. Name (please print) Title

Company ☐ Manufacturer ☐ Non-Manufacturer

Product or Service

Please send Business Week to ☐ home ☐ business address noted below.

Payment enclosed ☐
Bill me ☐

Street

City State Zip

Please allow 4-6 weeks for shipment of first issue. Offer good in U.S. and possessions.
In Canada: 28 weeks C$35.95 price includes GST. Newsstand rate: 28 issues for $70.00.
Prices and Terms are subject to change.

CSC9126

Printed on Recycled Paper

and selected demographic characteristics (sex, age, and income). The dependent variable was the respondent's degree of rebate proneness, of which three levels were identified. Respondents who reported no rebate-triggered purchases during the past 12 months were classified as nonusers; those who reported one or two such purchases as light users; and those with more than two purchases, frequent users of rebates. Multiple discriminant analysis was used to analyze the data.

Two primary findings emerged. First, consumers' perception of the effort/value relationship was the most effective variable in discriminating among frequent, light, and nonusers of rebate offers. Clearly, rebate-sensitive consumers associate less effort with fulfilling the requirements of the rebate purchase, and they are willing to accept a relatively smaller refund than other customers. Second, consumers who are aware of the regular prices of products so that they recognize bargains, are more likely than others to respond to rebate offers.[1] ■

DEPARTMENT STORE PATRONAGE PROJECT

Two-Group Discriminant Analysis

In the department store patronage project, two-group discriminant analysis was used to examine whether those respondents who were familiar with the stores, versus those who were unfamiliar, attached different relative importance to the eight factors of the choice criteria. The dependent variable was the two familiarity groups, and the independent variables were the importance attached to the eight factors of the choice criteria. The overall discriminant function was significant, indicating significant differences between the two groups. The results indicated that, as compared to the unfamiliar respondents, the familiar respondents attached greater relative importance to quality of merchandise, return and adjustment policy, service of store personnel, and credit and billing policies.

In the department store example, there were two groups of respondents (familiar and unfamiliar), whereas the rebate proneness example examined three groups (nonusers, light users, and frequent users of rebates). In both studies, significant intergroup differences were found using multiple predictor variables. An examination of differences across groups lies at the heart of the basic concept of discriminant analysis.

BASIC CONCEPT

Discriminant analysis is a technique for analyzing data when the criterion or dependent variable is categorical and the predictor or independent variables are interval in nature.[2] For example, the dependent variable may be the choice of a brand of personal computer (brand A, B, or C) and the independent variables may be ratings of attributes of PCs on a seven-point Likert scale. The objectives of discriminant analysis are as follows:

Discriminant Analysis A technique for analyzing marketing research data when the criterion or dependent variable is categorical and the predictor or independent variables are interval in nature.

1. Development of **discriminant functions**, or linear combinations of the predictor or independent variables, that will best discriminate between the categories of the criterion or dependent variable (groups)
2. Examination of whether significant differences exist among the groups, in terms of the predictor variables
3. Determination of which predictor variables contribute to most of the intergroup differences
4. Classification of cases to one of the groups based on the values of the predictor variables
5. Evaluation of the accuracy of classification

Discriminant Function The linear combination of independent variables developed by discriminant analysis that will best discriminate between the categories of the dependent variable.

Discriminant analysis techniques are described by the number of categories possessed by the criterion variable. When the criterion variable has two categories, the technique is known as **two-group discriminant analysis**. When three or more categories are involved, the technique is referred to as **multiple discriminant analysis**. The main distinction is that, in the two-group case, it is possible to derive only one discriminant function. In multiple discriminant analysis more than one function may be computed.[3]

Two-Group Discriminant Analysis Discriminant analysis technique in which the criterion variable has two categories.

Multiple Discriminant Analysis Discriminant analysis technique in which the criterion variable involves three or more categories.

Examples of discriminant analysis abound in marketing research. This technique can be used to answer questions such as:[4]

- In terms of demographic characteristics, how do customers who exhibit store loyalty differ from those who do not?
- Do heavy, medium, and light users of soft drinks differ in terms of their consumption of frozen foods?
- What psychographic characteristics help differentiate between price-sensitive and non–price-sensitive buyers of groceries?
- Do the various market segments differ in their media consumption habits?
- In terms of lifestyles, what are the differences between heavy patrons of regional department store chains and patrons of national chains?
- What are the distinguishing characteristics of consumers who respond to direct mail solicitations?

RELATIONSHIP TO REGRESSION AND ANOVA

The relationship among discriminant analysis, analysis of variance (ANOVA), and regression analysis is shown in Table 18.1. We explain this relationship with an example in which the researcher is attempting to explain the amount of life insurance purchased in terms of age and income. All three procedures involve a single criterion or dependent variable and multiple predictor or independent variables. However, the nature of these variables differ. In analysis of variance and regression analysis, the dependent variable is

TABLE 18.1

SIMILARITIES AND DIFFERENCES AMONG ANOVA, REGRESSION, AND DISCRIMINANT ANALYSIS

	ANOVA	*Regression*	*Discriminant Analysis*
Similarities			
Number of dependent variables	One	One	One
Number of independent variables	Multiple	Multiple	Multiple
Differences			
Nature of the dependent variable	Metric	Metric	Categorical
Nature of the independent variables	Categorical	Metric	Metric

metric or interval scaled (amount of life insurance purchased in dollars), whereas in discriminant analysis it is categorical (amount of life insurance purchased classified as high, medium, or low). The independent variables are categorical in the case of analysis of variance (age and income are each classified as high, medium, or low) but metric in the case of regression and discriminant analysis (age in years and income in dollars, i.e., both measured on a ratio scale).

Two-group discriminant analysis, in which the dependent variable has only two categories, is closely related to multiple regression analysis. In this case, multiple regression, in which the dependent variable is coded as a 0 or 1 dummy variable, results in partial regression coefficients that are proportional to discriminant function coefficients (see the following section on the discriminant analysis model).

DISCRIMINANT ANALYSIS MODEL

Discriminant Analysis Model The statistical model on which discriminant analysis is based.

The **discriminant analysis model** involves linear combinations of the following form:

$$D = b_0 + b_1X_1 + b_2X_2 + b_3X_3 + \ldots + b_kX_k$$

where

D = discriminant score
b = discriminant coefficient or weight
X = predictor or independent variable

The coefficients or weights (b) are estimated so that the groups differ as much as possible on the values of the discriminant function. This occurs when the ratio of between-group sum of squares to within-group sum of squares for the discriminant scores is at a maximum. Any other linear combination of the predictors will result in a smaller ratio. The technical details of estimation are described in appendix 18A. Several statistics are associated with discriminant analysis.

STATISTICS ASSOCIATED WITH DISCRIMINANT ANALYSIS

The important statistics associated with discriminant analysis include the following.

Canonical correlation. Canonical correlation measures the extent of association between the discriminant scores and the groups. It is a measure of association between the single discriminant function and the set of dummy variables that define the group membership.

Centroid. The centroid is the mean values for the discriminant scores for a particular group. There are as many centroids as there are groups, as there is one for each group. The means for a group on all the functions are the *group centroids*.

Classification matrix. Sometimes also called *confusion* or *prediction matrix*, the classification matrix contains the number of correctly classified and misclassified cases. The correctly classified cases appear on the diagonal, because the predicted and actual groups are the same. The off-diagonal elements represent cases that have been incorrectly classified. The sum of the diagonal elements divided by the total number of cases represents the *hit ratio*.

Discriminant function coefficients. The discriminant function coefficients (unstandardized) are the multipliers of variables, when the variables are in the original units of measurement.

Discriminant scores. The unstandardized coefficients are multiplied by the values of the variables. These products are summed and added to the constant term to obtain the discriminant scores.

Eigenvalue. For each discriminant function, the eigenvalue is the ratio of between-group to within-group sums of squares. Large eigenvalues imply superior functions.

F values and their significance. These are calculated from a one-way ANOVA, with the grouping variable serving as the categorical independent variable. Each predictor, in turn, serves as the metric dependent variable in the ANOVA.

Group means and group standard deviations. These are computed for each predictor for each group.

Pooled within-group correlation matrix. The pooled within-group correlation matrix is computed by averaging the separate covariance matrices for all the groups.

Standardized discriminant function coefficients. The discriminant function coefficients used as the multipliers when the variables have been standardized to a mean of 0 and a variance of 1.

Structure correlations. Also referred to as *discriminant loadings*, the structure correlations represent the simple correlations between the predictors and the discriminant function.

Total correlation matrix. If the cases are treated as if they were from a single sample and the correlations computed, a total correlation matrix is obtained.

Wilks's λ. Sometimes also called the *U* statistic, Wilks's λ for each predictor is the ratio of the within-group sum of squares to the total sum of squares. Its value varies between 0 and 1. Large values of λ (near 1) indicate that group means do not seem to be different. Small values of λ (near 0) indicate that the group means seem to be different.

The assumptions in discriminant analysis are that each of the groups is a sample from a multivariate normal population and all of the populations have the same covariance matrix. The role of these assumptions and the statistics just described can be better understood by examining the procedure for conducting discriminant analysis.

CONDUCTING DISCRIMINANT ANALYSIS

The steps involved in conducting discriminant analysis consist of formulation, estimation, determination of significance, interpretation, and validation (see Figure 18.1). These steps are discussed and illustrated within the context of two-group discriminant analysis. Discriminant analysis with more than two groups is discussed later in this chapter.

Figure 18.1
Conducting Discriminant Analysis

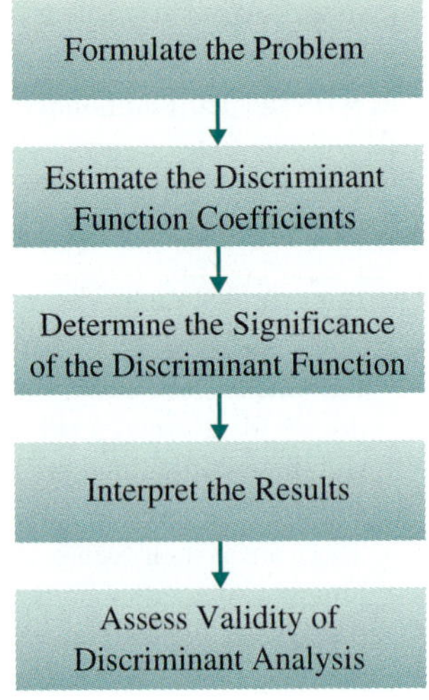

Formulate the Problem

The first step in discriminant analysis is to formulate the problem by identifying the objectives, the criterion variable, and the independent variables. The criterion variable must consist of two or more mutually exclusive and collectively exhaustive categories. When the dependent variable is interval or ratio scaled, it must first be converted into categories. For example, attitude toward the brand, measured on a seven-point scale, could be categorized as unfavorable (1, 2, 3), neutral (4) or favorable (5, 6, 7). Alternatively, one could plot the distribution of the dependent variable and form groups of equal size by determining the appropriate cutoff points for each category. The predictor variables should be selected based on a theoretical model or previous research, or, in the case of exploratory research, the experience of the researcher should guide their selection.

Analysis Sample Part of the total sample that is used for estimation of the discriminant function.

Validation Sample That part of the total sample used to check the results of the estimation sample.

The next step is to divide the sample into two parts. One part of the sample, called the *estimation* or **analysis sample**, is used for estimation of the discriminant function. The other part, called the *holdout* or **validation sample**, is reserved for validating the discriminant function. When the sample is large enough, it can be split in half. One half serves as the analysis sample, and the other is used for validation. The role of the halves is then interchanged and the analysis is repeated. This is called double cross-validation and is similar to the procedure discussed in regression analysis (chapter 17).

Often the distribution of the number of cases in the analysis and validation samples follows the distribution in the total sample. For instance, if the total sample contained 50 percent loyal and 50 percent nonloyal consumers, then the analysis and validation samples would each contain 50 percent loyal and 50 percent nonloyal consumers. On the other hand, if the sample contained 25 percent loyal and 75 percent nonloyal consumers, the analysis and validation samples would be selected to reflect the same distribution (25 percent versus 75 percent).

Finally, it has been suggested that the validation of the discriminant function should be conducted repeatedly. Each time, the sample should be split into different analysis and validation parts. The discriminant function should be estimated, and the validation analysis carried out. Thus, the validation assessment is based on a number of trials. More rigorous methods have also been suggested.[5]

To better illustrate two-group discriminant analysis let us look at an example. Suppose we want to determine the salient characteristics of families that have visited a vacation resort during the last two years. Data were obtained from a pretest sample of 42 households. Of these, 30 households shown in Table 18.2 were included in the analysis sample and the remaining 12 shown in Table 18.3 were part of the validation sample. The households that visited a resort during the last two years are coded as 1; those that did not, as 2 (visit). Both the analysis and validation samples were balanced in terms of visit. As can be seen, the analysis sample contains 15 households in each category whereas the validation sample has 6 in each category. Data were also obtained on annual family income (income), attitude toward travel (travel, measured on a nine-point scale), importance attached to family vacation (vacation, measured on a nine-point scale), household size (hsize), and age of the head of the household (age).

Estimate the Discriminant Function Coefficients

Once the analysis sample has been identified, as in Table 18.2, we can estimate the discriminant function coefficients. Two broad approaches are available. The **direct method** involves estimating the discriminant function so that all the predictors are included simultaneously. In this case, each independent variable is included, regardless of its discriminating power. This method is appropriate when, based on previous research or a theoretical

Direct Method An approach to discriminant analysis that involves estimating the discriminant function so that all the predictors are included simultaneously.

TABLE 18.2

INFORMATION ON RESORT VISITS: ANALYSIS SAMPLE

Number	*Resort Visit*	*Annual Family Income ($000)*	*Attitude Toward Travel*	*Importance Attached to Family Vacation*	*Household Size*	*Age of Head of Household*	*Amount Spent on Family Vacation*
1	1	50.2	5	8	3	43	M (2)
2	1	70.3	6	7	4	61	H (3)
3	1	62.9	7	5	6	52	H (3)
4	1	48.5	7	5	5	36	L (1)
5	1	52.7	6	6	4	55	H (3)
6	1	75.0	8	7	5	68	H (3)
7	1	46.2	5	3	3	62	M (2)
8	1	57.0	2	4	6	51	M (2)
9	1	64.1	7	5	4	57	H (3)
10	1	68.1	7	6	5	45	H (3)
11	1	73.4	6	7	5	44	H (3)
12	1	71.9	5	8	4	64	H (3)
13	1	56.2	1	8	6	54	M (2)
14	1	49.3	4	2	3	56	H (3)
15	1	62.0	5	6	2	58	H (3)
16	2	32.1	5	4	3	58	L (1)
17	2	36.2	4	3	2	55	L (1)
18	2	43.2	2	5	2	57	M (2)
19	2	50.4	5	2	4	37	M (2)
20	2	44.1	6	6	3	42	M (2)
21	2	38.3	6	6	2	45	L (1)
22	2	55.0	1	2	2	57	M (2)
23	2	46.1	3	5	3	51	L (1)
24	2	35.0	6	4	5	64	L (1)
25	2	37.3	2	7	4	54	L (1)
26	2	41.8	5	1	3	56	M (2)
27	2	57.0	8	3	2	36	M (2)
28	2	33.4	6	8	2	50	L (1)
29	2	37.5	3	2	3	48	L (1)
30	2	41.3	3	3	2	42	L (1)

TABLE 18.3

INFORMATION ON RESORT VISITS: HOLDOUT SAMPLE

Number	*Resort Visit*	*Annual Family Income ($000)*	*Attitude Toward Travel*	*Importance Attached to Family Vacation*	*Household Size*	*Age of Head of Household*	*Amount Spent on Family Vacation*
1	1	50.8	4	7	3	45	M (2)
2	1	63.6	7	4	7	55	H (3)
3	1	54.0	6	7	4	58	M (2)
4	1	45.0	5	4	3	60	M (2)
5	1	68.0	6	6	6	46	H (3)
6	1	62.1	5	6	3	56	H (3)
7	2	35.0	4	3	4	54	L (1)
8	2	49.6	5	3	5	39	L (1)
9	2	39.4	6	5	3	44	H (3)
10	2	37.0	2	6	5	51	L (1)
11	2	54.5	7	3	3	37	M (2)
12	2	38.2	2	2	3	49	L (1)

Stepwise Discriminant Analysis Discriminant analysis in which the predictors are entered sequentially based on their ability to discriminate between the groups.

model, the researcher wants the discrimination to be based on all the predictors. An alternative approach is the stepwise method. In **stepwise discriminant analysis**, the predictor variables are entered sequentially, based on their ability to discriminate among groups. This method, described in more detail later, is appropriate when the researcher wants to select a subset of the predictors for inclusion in the discriminant function.

The results of running two-group discriminant analysis on the data of Table 18.2 using a popular computer program are presented in Table 18.4. Some intuitive feel for the results may be obtained by examining the group means and standard deviations. It appears that the two groups are more widely separated in terms of income than other variables. There appears to be more of a separation on the importance attached to the family vacation than on attitude toward travel. The difference between the two groups on age of the head of the household is small, and the standard deviation of this variable is large.

Two-group discriminant analysis can be used to determine the salient characteristics of families that have visited a vacation resort.

The pooled within-groups correlation matrix indicates low correlations between the predictors. Multicollinearity is unlikely to be a problem. The significance of the univariate F ratios indicates that when the predictors are considered individually, only income, importance of vacation, and household size significantly differentiate between those who visited a resort and those who did not.

Because there are two groups, only one discriminant function is estimated. The eigenvalue associated with this function is 1.7862, and it accounts for 100 percent of the explained variance. The canonical correlation associated with this function is .8007. The square of this correlation, $(.8007)^2 = .64$, indicates that 64 percent of the variance in the dependent variable (visit) is explained or accounted for by this model. The next step is to determine the significance of the discriminant function.

Determine the Significance of the Discriminant Function

It would not be meaningful to interpret the analysis if the discriminant functions estimated were not statistically significant. The null hypothesis that, in the population, the means of all discriminant functions in all groups are equal can be statistically tested. In SPSS this test is based on Wilks's λ. If several functions are tested simultaneously (as in the case of multiple discriminant analysis), the Wilks's λ statistic is the product of the univariate λ for each function. The significance level is estimated based on a chi-square transformation of the statistic. In testing for significance in the vacation resort example (see Table 18.4), it may be noted that the Wilks's λ associated with the function is .3589, which transforms to a chi-square of 26.13 with 5 degrees of freedom. This is significant beyond the .05 level. In SAS an approximate F statistic, based on an approximation to the distribution of the likelihood ratio, is calculated. In BMDP, the test of the null hypothesis is based on an F transformation of Wilks's λ. A test of significance is not available in Minitab. If the null hypothesis is rejected, indicating significant discrimination, one can proceed to interpret the results.[6]

Interpret the Results

The interpretation of the discriminant weights, or coefficients, is similar to that in multiple regression analysis. The value of the coefficient for a particular predictor depends on the other predictors included in the discriminant function. The signs of the coefficients are arbitrary, but they indicate which variable values result in large and small function values and associate them with particular groups.

Given the multicollinearity in the predictor variables, there is no unambiguous measure of the relative importance of the predictors in discriminating between the groups.[7] With this caveat in mind, we can obtain some idea of the relative importance of the variables by examining the absolute magnitude of the standardized discriminant function coefficients. Generally, predictors with relatively large standardized coefficients contribute more to the discriminating power of the function, as compared with predictors with smaller coefficients.

Some idea of the relative importance of the predictors can also be obtained by examining the structure correlations, also called *canonical loadings* or *discriminant loadings*. These simple correlations between each predictor and the discriminant function represent the variance that the predictor shares with the function. Like the standardized coefficients, these correlations must also be interpreted with caution.

An examination of the standardized discriminant function coefficients for the vacation resort example is instructive. Given the low intercorrelations between the predictors, one might cautiously use the magnitudes of the standardized coefficients to suggest that income is the most important predictor in discriminating between the groups, followed by household size and importance attached to the family vacation. The same observation is obtained from examination of the structure correlations. These simple correlations between the predictors and the discriminant function are listed in order of magnitude.

TABLE 18.4

RESULTS OF TWO-GROUP DISCRIMINANT ANALYSIS

Group Means

Visit	*Income*	*Travel*	*Vacation*	*Hsize*	*Age*
1	60.52000	5.40000	5.80000	4.33333	53.73333
2	41.91333	4.33333	4.06667	2.80000	50.13333
Total	51.21667	4.86667	4.93333	3.56667	51.93333

Group Standard Deviations

1	9.83065	1.91982	1.82052	1.23443	8.77062
2	7.55115	1.95180	2.05171	.94112	8.27101
Total	12.79523	1.97804	2.09981	1.33089	8.57395

Pooled Within-Groups Correlation Matrix

	Income	*Travel*	*Vacation*	*Hsize*	*Age*
Income	1.00000				
Travel	.19745	1.00000			
Vacation	.09148	.08434	1.00000		
Hsize	.08887	−.01681	.07046	1.00000	
Age	−.01431	−.19709	.01742	−.04301	1.00000

Wilks's λ (*U* statistic) and univariate *F* ratio with 1 and 28 degrees of freedom

Variable	***Wilks's λ***	***F***	***Significance***
Income	.45310	33.80	.0000
Travel	.92479	2.277	.1425
Vacation	.82377	5.990	.0209
Hsize	.65672	14.64	.0007
Age	.95441	1.338	.2572

Canonical Discriminant Functions

Function	*Eigenvalue*	*Percent of Variance*	*Cumulative Percent*	*Canonical Correlation*		*After Function*	*Wilks's λ*	*Chi-square*	*df*	*Significance*
					:	0	.3589	26.130	5	.0001
1*	1.7862	100.00	100.00	.8007	:					

* marks the 1 canonical discriminant functions remaining in the analysis.

Standard Canonical Discriminant Function Coefficients

	Func 1
Income	.74301
Travel	.09611
Vacation	.23329
Hsize	.46911
Age	.20922

Structure Matrix:

Pooled within-groups correlations between discriminating variables and canonical discriminant functions (variables ordered by size of correlation within function)

	Func 1
Income	.82202
Hsize	.54096
Vacation	.34607
Travel	.21337
Age	.16354

(Continued)

TABLE 18.4 *(Continued)*

Unstandardized Canonical Discriminant Function Coefficients

	Func 1
Income	.8476710E-01
Travel	.4964455E-01
Vacation	.1202813
Hsize	.4273893
Age	.2454380E-01
(constant)	−7.975476

Canonical Discriminant Functions Evaluated at Group Means (Group Centroids)

Group	*Func 1*
1	1.29118
2	−1.29118

Classification Results for Cases Selected for Use in Analysis

			Predicted	*Group Membership*
	Actual Group	*Number of Cases*	*1*	*2*
Group	1	15	12	3
			80.0%	20.0%
Group	2	15	0	15
			.0%	100.0%

Percent of grouped cases correctly classified: 90.00%

Classification Results for Cases Not Selected for Use in the Analysis (Holdout Sample)

			Predicted	*Group Membership*
	Actual Group	*Number of Cases*	*1*	*2*
Group	1	6	4	2
			66.7%	33.3%
Group	2	6	0	6
			.0%	100.0%

Percent of grouped cases correctly classified: 83.33%.

The unstandardized discriminant function coefficients are also given. These can be applied to the raw values of the variables in the holdout set for classification purposes. The group centroids, giving the value of the discriminant function evaluated at the group means, are also shown. Group 1, those who have visited a resort, has a positive value, whereas Group 2 has an equal negative value. The signs of the coefficients associated with all the predictors are positive. This suggests that higher family income, household size, importance attached to family vacation, attitude toward travel, and age are more likely to result in the family visiting the resort. It would be reasonable to develop a profile of the two groups in terms of the three predictors that seem to be the most important: income, household size, and importance of vacation. The values of these three variables for the two groups are given at the beginning of Table 18.4.

The determination of relative importance of the predictors is further illustrated by the following example.

EXAMPLE

Satisfied Salespeople Stay

Discriminant analysis was used to determine what factors explained the differences between salespeople who left a large computer manufacturing company and those who stayed. The independent variables were company rating, job security, seven job satisfaction dimensions, four role-conflict dimensions, four role-ambiguity dimensions, and nine measures of sales performance. The dependent variable was the dichotomy between those who stayed and those who left. The canonical correlation, an index of discrimination ($R = .4572$), was significant (Wilks's $\lambda = .7909$, $F(26,173) = 1.7588$, $p = .0180$). This result indicated that the variables discriminated between those who left and those who stayed.

The results from simultaneously entering all variables in discriminant analysis are presented in the table. The rank order of importance, as determined by the relative magnitude of the canonical loadings, is presented in the first column. Satisfaction with the job and promotional opportunities were the two most important discriminators, followed by job security. Those who stayed in the company found the job to be more exciting, satisfying, challenging, and interesting than those who left.[8]

DISCRIMINANT ANALYSIS RESULTS

Variable	*Coefficients*	*Standardized Coefficients*	*Canonical Loadings*
1. Work[a]	.0903	.3910	.5446
2. Promotion[a]	.0288	.1515	.5044
3. Job security	.1567	.1384	.4958
4. Customer relations[b]	.0086	.1751	.4906
5. Company rating	.4059	.3240	.4824
6. Working with others [b]	.0018	.0365	.4651
7. Overall performance [b]	−.0148	−.3252	.4518
8. Time–terrritory management[b]	.0126	.2899	.4496
9. Sales produced[b]	.0059	.1404	.4484
10. Presentation skill[b]	.0118	.2526	.4387
11. Technical information[b]	.0003	.0065	.4173
12. Pay–benefits[a]	.0600	.1843	.3788
13. Quota achieved[b]	.0035	.2915	.3780
14. Management[a]	.0014	.0138	.3571
15. Information collection[b]	−.0146	−.3327	.3326
16. Family[c]	−.0684	−.3408	−.3221
17. Sales manager[a]	−.0121	−.1102	.2909
18. Coworker[a]	.0225	.0893	.2671
19. Customer[c]	−.0625	−.2797	−.2602
20. Family[d]	.0473	.1970	.2180
21. Job[d]	.1378	.5312	.2119
22. Job[c]	.0410	.5475	−.1029
23. Customer[d]	−.0060	−.0255	.1004
24. Sales Manager[c]	−.0365	−.2406	−.0499
25. Sales Manager[d]	−.0606	−.3333	.0467
26. Customer[a]	−.0338	−.1488	.0192

Note: Rank order of importance is based on the magnitude of the canonical loadings.
[a]Satisfaction
[b]Performance
[c]Ambiguity
[d]Conflict ■

Characteristic Profile An aid to interpreting discriminant analysis results by describing each group in terms of the group means for the predictor variables.

Note that in this example promotion was identified as the second most important variable based on the canonical loadings. However, it is not the second most important variable based on the absolute magnitude of the standardized discriminant function coefficients. This anomaly results from multicollinearity.

Another aid to interpreting discriminant analysis results is to develop a **characteristic profile** for each group by describing each group in terms of the group means for the predictor variables. If the important predictors have been identified, then a comparison of the group means on these variables can assist in understanding the intergroup differences. However, before any findings can be interpreted with confidence, it is necessary to validate the results.

Assess Validity of Discriminant Analysis

As explained earlier, the data are randomly divided into two subsamples. One, the analysis sample, is used for estimating the discriminant function; the validation sample is used for developing the classification matrix. The discriminant weights, estimated by using the analysis sample, are multiplied by the values of the predictor variables in the holdout sample to generate discriminant scores for the cases in the holdout sample. The cases are then assigned to groups based on their discriminant scores and an appropriate decision rule. For example, in two-group discriminant analysis, a case will be assigned to the group whose centroid is the closest. The **hit ratio**, or the percentage of cases correctly classified, can then be determined by summing the diagonal elements and dividing by the total number of cases.[9]

Hit Ratio The percentage of cases correctly classified by the discriminant analysis.

It is helpful to compare the percentage of cases correctly classified by discriminant analysis to the percentage that would be obtained by chance. When the groups are equal in size, the percentage of chance classification is 1 divided by the number of groups. How much improvement should be expected over chance? No general guidelines are available, although some authors have suggested that classification accuracy achieved by discriminant analysis should be at least 25 percent greater than that obtained by chance.[10]

Most discriminant analysis programs also estimate a classification matrix based on the analysis sample. Because they capitalize on chance variation in the data, such results are invariably better than the classification obtained on the holdout sample.[11]

Table 18.4, of the vacation resort example, also shows the classification results based on the analysis sample. The hit ratio, or the percentage of cases correctly classified, is $(12 + 15)/30 = .90$, or 90 percent. One might suspect that this hit ratio is artificially inflated, as the data used for estimation was also used for validation. Conducting classification analysis on an independent holdout set of data results in the classification matrix with a slightly lower hit ratio of $(4 + 6)/12 = .833$, or 83.3 percent (see Table 18.4). Given two groups of equal size, by chance one would expect a hit ratio of $1/2 = .50$, or 50 percent. Hence, the improvement over chance is more than 25 percent, and the validity of the discriminant analysis is judged as satisfactory.

Another application of two-group discriminant analysis is provided by the following example.

EXAMPLE

Home Bodies and Couch Potatoes

Two-group discriminant analysis was used to assess the strength of each of five dimensions used in classifying individuals as TV users or nonusers. The procedure was appropriate for this use because of the nature of the predefined categorical groups (users and nonusers) and the interval scales used to generate individual factor scores.

Two equal groups of 185 elderly consumers, users and nonusers (total $n = 370$), were created. The discriminant equation for the analysis was estimated by using a subsample of 142 respondents from the sample of 370. Of the remaining respondents, 198 were used as a validation subsample in a cross-validation of the equation. Thirty respondents were excluded from the analysis because of missing discriminant values.

The canonical correlation for the discriminant function was .4291, significant at the $p < .0001$ level. The eigenvalue was .2257. The table summarizes the standardized canonical discriminant coefficients. A substantial portion of the variance is explained by the discriminant function. In addition, as the table shows, the home-orientation dimension made a fairly strong contribution to classifying individuals as users or nonusers of television. Morale, security and health, and respect also contributed significantly. The social factor appeared to make little contribution.

The cross-validation procedure using the discriminant function from the analysis sample gave support to the contention that the dimensions aided researchers in discriminating between users and nonusers of television. As the table shows, the discriminant function was successful in classifying 75.76 percent of the cases. This suggests that consideration of the identified dimensions will help marketers understand the elderly market.[12]

SUMMARY OF DISCRIMINANT ANALYSIS

Standard Canonical Discriminant Function Coefficients

Morale	.27798
Security and health	.39850
Home orientation	.77496
Respect	.32069
Social	–.01996

Classification Results for Cases Selected for Use in the Analysis

Actual Group	Number of Cases	Predicted Group Membership: Nonusers	Users
TV nonusers	77	56	21
		72.7%	27.3%
TV users	65	24	41
		36.9%	63.1%

Percent of grouped cases correctly classified: 68.31%.

Classification Results for Cases Used for Cross-Validation

Actual Group	Number of Cases	Predicted Group Membership: Nonusers	Users
TV nonusers	108	85	23
		78.7%	21.3%
TV users	90	25	65
		27.8%	72.2%

Percent of grouped cases correctly classified: 75.76%. ■

The extension from two-group discriminant analysis to multiple discriminant analysis involves similar steps and is illustrated with an application.

MULTIPLE DISCRIMINANT ANALYSIS

Formulate the Problem

The data presented in Tables 18.2 and 18.3 can also be used to illustrate three-group discriminant analysis. In the last column of these tables, the households are classified into three categories, based on the amount spent on family vacation (high, medium, or low). Ten households fall in each category. The question of interest is whether the households that spend high, medium, or low amounts on their vacations (amount) can be differentiated in terms of annual family income (income), attitude toward travel (travel), importance attached to family vacation (vacation), household size (hsize), and age of the head of household (age).[13]

Estimate the Discriminant Function Coefficients

Table 18.5 presents the results of estimating three-group discriminant analysis. An examination of group means indicates that income appears to separate the groups more widely than any other variable. There is some separation on travel and vacation. Groups 1 and 2 are very close in terms of household size and age. Age has a large standard deviation relative to the separation between the groups. The pooled within-groups correlation matrix indicates some correlation of vacation and household size with income. Age has some negative correlation with travel. Yet, these correlations are on the lower side indicating that although multicollinearity may be of some concern, it is not likely to be a serious problem. The significance attached to the univariate F ratios indicates that when the predictors are considered individually, only income and travel are significant in differentiating between the two groups.

In multiple discriminant analysis, if there are G groups, $G - 1$ discriminant functions can be estimated if the number of predictors is larger than this quantity. In general, with G groups and k predictors, it is possible to estimate up to the smaller of $G - 1$, or k, discriminant functions. The first function has the highest ratio of between-groups to within-groups sum of squares. The second function, uncorrelated with the first, has the second highest ratio, and so on. However, not all the functions may be statistically significant.

Since there are three groups, a maximum of two functions can be extracted. The eigenvalue associated with the first function is 3.8190, and this function accounts for 93.93 percent of the explained variance.

Because the eigenvalue is large, the first function is likely to be superior. The second function has a small eigenvalue of .2469 and accounts for only 6.07 percent of the explained variance.

Determine the Significance of the Discriminant Function

To test the null hypothesis of equal group centroids, both the functions must be considered simultaneously. It is possible to test the means of the functions successively by first testing all means simultaneously. Then one function is excluded at a time, and the means of the remaining functions are tested at each step. In Table 18.5, the 0 below "After Function" indicates that no functions have been removed. The value of Wilks's λ is .1644. This transforms to a chi-square of 44.831, with 10 degrees of freedom, which is significant beyond the .05 level. Thus, the two functions together significantly discriminate among the three groups. However, when the first function is removed, the Wilks's λ associated with the second function is .8020, which is not significant at the .05 level. Therefore, the second function does not contribute significantly to group differences.

Interpret the Results

The interpretation of the results is aided by an examination of the standardized discriminant function coefficients, the structure correlations, and certain plots. The standardized coefficients indicate a large coefficient for income on function 1; whereas function 2 has relatively larger coefficients for travel, vacation, and age. A similar conclusion is reached by an examination of the structure matrix (see Table 18.5). To help interpret the functions, variables with large coefficients for a particular function are grouped together. These groupings are shown with asterisks. Thus income and household size have asterisks for function 1 because these variables have coefficients which are larger for function 1 than for function 2. These variables are associated primarily with function 1. On the other hand, travel, vacation, and age are predominantly associated with function 2, as indicated by the asterisks.

Figure 18.2 is a scattergram plot of all the groups on function 1 and function 2. It can be seen that group 3 has the highest value on function 1, group 1 the lowest. Because function 1 is primarily associated with income and household size, one would expect the three groups to be ordered on these two variables. Those with higher incomes and higher household size are likely to spend large amounts of money on vacations. Conversely, those with low incomes and smaller household size are likely to spend small amounts on vacations. This interpretation is further strengthened by an examination of group means on income and household size.

TABLE 18.5

RESULTS OF THREE-GROUP DISCRIMINANT ANALYSIS

Group Means

Amount	*Income*	*Travel*	*Vacation*	*Hsize*	*Age*
1	38.57000	4.50000	4.70000	3.10000	50.30000
2	50.11000	4.00000	4.20000	3.40000	49.50000
3	64.97000	6.10000	5.90000	4.20000	56.00000
Total	51.21667	4.86667	4.93333	3.56667	51.93333
Group Standard Deviations					
1	5.29718	1.71594	1.88856	1.19722	8.09732
2	6.00231	2.35702	2.48551	1.50555	9.25263
3	8.61434	1.19722	1.66333	1.13529	7.60117
Total	12.79523	1.97804	2.09981	1.33089	8.57395

Pooled Within-Groups Correlation Matrix

	Income	*Travel*	*Vacation*	*Hsize*	*Age*
Income	1.00000				
Travel	.05120	1.00000			
Vacation	.30681	.03588	1.00000		
Hsize	.38050	.00474	.22080	1.00000	
Age	−.20939	−.34022	−.01326	−.02512	1.00000

Wilks's λ (*U* statistic) and univariate *F* ratio with 2 and 27 degrees of freedom.

Variable	*Wilks's λ*	*F*	*Significance*
Income	.26215	38.00	.0000
Travel	.78790	3.634	.0400
Vacation	.88060	1.830	.1797
Hsize	.87411	1.944	.1626
Age	.88214	1.804	.1840

Canonical Discriminant Functions

Function	*Eigenvalue*	*Percent of Variance*	*Cumulative Percentage*	*Canonical Correlation*		*After Function*	*Wilks's λ*	*Chi-square*	*df*	*Significance*
					:	0	.1664	44.831	10	.00
1*	3.8190	93.93	93.93	.8902	:	1	.8020	5.517	4	.24
2*	.2469	6.07	100.00	.4450	:					

* marks the two canonical discriminant functions remaining in the analysis.

Standardized Canonical Discriminant Function Coefficients

	Func 1	*Func 2*
Income	1.04740	−.42076
Travel	.33991	.76851
Vacation	−.14198	.53354
Hsize	−.16317	.12932
Age	.49474	.52447

Structure Matrix:

Pooled within-groups correlations between discriminating variables and canonical discriminant functions (variables ordered by size of correlation within function)

	Func 1	*Func 2*
Income	.85556*	−.27833
Hsize	.19319*	.07749
Vacation	.21935	.58829*
Travel	.14899	.45362*
Age	.16576	.34079*

(Continued)

TABLE 18.5 *(Continued)*

Unstandardized Canonical Discriminant Function Coefficients

	Func 1	*Func 2*
Income	.1542658	−.6197148E-01
Travel	.1867977	.4223430
Vacation	−.6952264E-01	.2612652
Hsize	−.1265334	.1002796
Age	.5928055E-01	.6284206E-01
(constant)	−11.09442	−3.791600

Canonical Discriminant Functions Evaluated at Group Means (Group Centroids)

Group	*Func 1*	*Func 2*
1	−2.04100	.41847
2	−.40479	−.65867
3	2.44578	.24020

Classification Results:

	Actual Group	*Number of Cases*	*Predicted Group Membership* 1	2	3
Group	1	10	9	1	0
			90.0%	10.0%	.0%
Group	2	10	1	9	0
			10.0%	90.0%	.0%
Group	3	10	0	2	8
			.0%	20.0%	80.0%

Percent of grouped cases correctly classified: 86.67%

Classification Results for Cases not Selected for Use in the Analysis

	Actual Group	*Number of Cases*	*Predicted Group Membership* 1	2	3
Group	1	4	3	1	0
			75.0%	25.0%	.0%
Group	2	4	0	3	1
			.0%	75.0%	25.0%
Group	3	4	1	0	3
			25.0%	.0%	75.0%

Percent of grouped cases correctly classified: 75.00%

Figure 18.2 further indicates that function 2 tends to separate group 1 (highest value) and group 2 (lowest value). This function is primarily associated with travel, vacation, and age. Given the positive correlations of these variables with function 2 in the structure matrix, we expect to find group 1 to be higher than group 2 in terms of travel, vacation, and age. This is indeed true for travel and vacation, as indicated by the group means of these variables. If families in group 1 have more favorable attitudes toward travel and attach more importance to family vacation than do group 2, why do they spend less? Perhaps they would like to spend more on vacations but cannot afford it because they have low incomes.

Territorial Map A tool for assessing discriminant analysis results by plotting the group membership of each case on a graph.

A similar interpretation is obtained by examining a **territorial map**, as shown in Figure 18.3. In a territorial map, each group centroid is indicated by an asterisk. The group boundaries are shown by numbers corresponding to the groups. Thus, group 1 centroid is bounded by 1s; group 2 centroid by 2s; and group 3 centroid by 3s.

Figure 18.2
All-Groups Scattergram

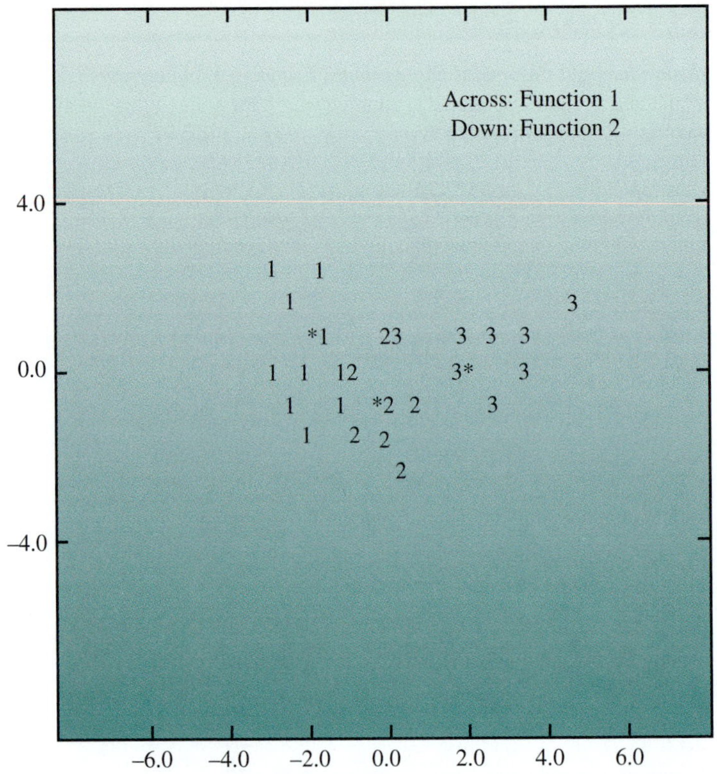
Across: Function 1
Down: Function 2
4.0
0.0
–4.0
–6.0
–4.0
–2.0
0.0
2.0
4.0
6.0

*indicates a group centroid

Figure 18.3
Territorial Map

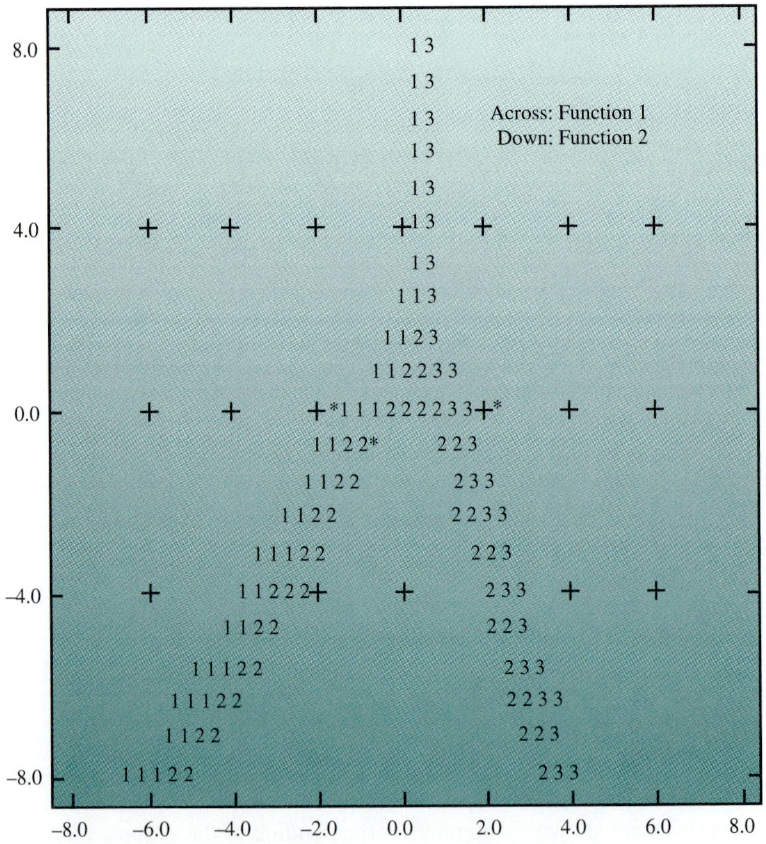
Across: Function 1
Down: Function 2
8.0
4.0
0.0
–4.0
–8.0
–8.0
–6.0
–4.0
–2.0
0.0
2.0
4.0
6.0
8.0

*indicates a group centroid

Assess Validity of Discriminant Analysis

The classification results based on the analysis sample indicate that (9 + 9 + 8)/ 30 = 86.67 percent of the cases are correctly classified. When the classification analysis is conducted on the independent holdout sample of Table 18.3, a slightly lower hit ratio of 83.3 percent is obtained. Given three groups of equal size, by chance alone one would expect a hit ratio of 1/3 = .333 or 33.3 percent. The improvement over chance is 50 percent, indicating at least satisfactory validity.[14]

Further illustration of multiple group discriminant analysis is provided by the following example.

EXAMPLE

The Home Is Where the Patient's Heart Is

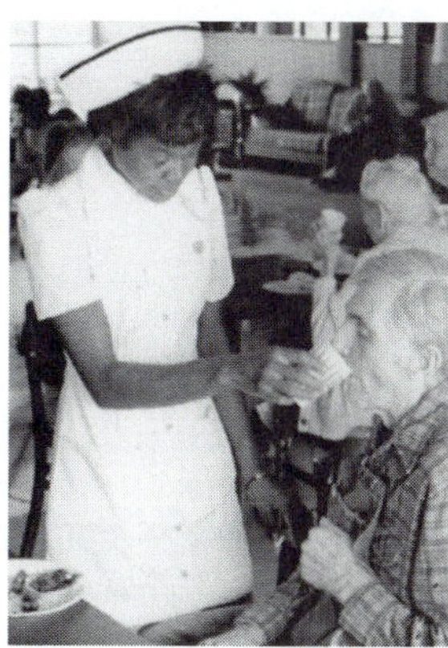

Multiple discriminant analysis shows that nursing homes are perceived unfavorably on the dimensions of personalized care, quality of medical care, and value.

Consumers were surveyed to determine their attitudes toward four systems of health care delivery (home health care, hospitals, nursing homes, and outpatient clinics) along 10 attributes. A total of 102 responses were obtained, and the results were analyzed using multiple discriminant analysis (Table 1). Three discriminant functions were identified. Chi-square tests performed on the results indicated that all three discriminant functions were significant at the .01 level. The first function accounted for 63 percent of the total discriminative power, and the remaining two functions contributed 29.4 percent and 7.6 percent, respectively.

Table 1 gives the standardized discriminant function coefficients of the 10 variables in the discriminant equations. Coefficients ranged in value from −1 to +1. In determining the ability of each attribute to classify the delivery system, absolute values were used. In the first discriminant function, the two variables with the largest coefficients were comfort (.53) and privacy (.40). Because both related to personal attention and care, the first dimension was labeled "personalized care." In the second function, the two variables with the largest coefficients were quality of medical care (.67) and likelihood of faster recovery (.32). Hence, this dimension was labeled "quality of medical care." In the third discriminant function, the most significant attributes were sanitation (−.70) and expense (.52). Because these two attributes represent value and price, the third discriminant function was labeled "value."

The four group centroids are shown in Table 2. This table shows that home health care was evaluated most favorably along the dimension of personalized care, and hospitals least favorably. Along the dimension of quality of medical care, there was a substantial separation between nursing homes and the other three systems. Also, home health care received higher evaluations on the quality of medical care than did outpatient clinics. Outpatient clinics, on the other hand, were judged to offer the best value.

Classification analysis of the 102 responses, reported in Table 3, showed correct classifications ranging from 86 percent for hospitals to 68 percent for outpatient clinics. The misclassifications for hospitals were 6 percent each to nursing homes and outpatient clinics, and 2 percent to home health care. Nursing homes showed misclassifications of 9 percent to hospitals, 10 percent to outpatient clinics, and 3 percent to home health care. For outpatient clinics, 9 percent misclassifications were made to hospitals, 13 percent to nursing homes, and 10 percent to home health care. For home health care the misclassifications were 5 percent to hospitals, 4 percent to nursing homes, and 13 percent to outpatient clinics. The results demonstrated that the discriminant functions were fairly accurate in predicting group membership.[15]

TABLE 1

STANDARDIZED DISCRIMINANT FUNCTION COEFFICIENTS

	Discriminant Function		
Variable	*1*	*2*	*3*
Safe	−.20	−.04	.15
Convenient	.08	.08	.07
Chance of medical complications[a]	−.27	.10	.16
Expensive[a]	.30	−.28	.52
Comfortable	.53	.27	−.19
Sanitary	−.27	−.14	−.70
Best medical care	−.25	.67	−.10
Privacy	.40	.08	.49
Faster recovery	.30	.32	−.15
Staffed with best medical personnel	−.17	−.03	.18
Percentage of explained variance	63.0	29.4	7.6
Chi-square	663.3[b]	289.2[b]	70.1[b]

[a]These two items were worded negatively on the questionnaire. They were reverse-coded for purposes of data analysis.
[b]$p < .01$.

TABLE 2

CENTROIDS OF HEALTH CARE SYSTEMS IN DISCRIMINANT SPACE

	Discriminant Function		
System	*1*	*2*	*3*
Hospital	−1.66	.97	−.08
Nursing home	−.60	−1.36	−.27
Outpatient clinic	.54	−.13	.77
Home health care	1.77	.50	−.39

TABLE 3

CLASSIFICATION TABLE

	Classification (percent)			
System	*Hospital*	*Nursing Home*	*Outpatient Clinic*	*Home Health Care*
Hospital	86	6	6	2
Nursing home	9	78	10	3
Outpatient clinic	9	13	68	10
Home health care	5	4	13	78

STEPWISE DISCRIMINANT ANALYSIS

Stepwise discriminant analysis is analogous to stepwise multiple regression (see chapter 17) in that the predictors are entered sequentially based on their ability to discriminate between the groups. An *F* ratio is calculated for each predictor by conducting a univariate analysis of variance in which the groups are treated as the categorical variable and the predictor as the criterion variable. The predictor with the highest *F* ratio is the first to be selected for inclusion in the discriminant function, if it meets certain significance and tolerance criteria. A second predictor is added based on the highest adjusted or partial *F* ratio, taking into account the predictor already selected.

Each predictor selected is tested for retention based on its association with other predictors selected. The process of selection and retention is continued until all predictors meeting the significance criteria for inclusion and retention have been entered in the discriminant function. Several statistics are computed at each stage. In addition, at the conclusion, a summary of the predictors entered or removed is provided. The standard output associated with the direct method is also available from the stepwise procedure.

The selection of the stepwise procedure is based on the optimizing criterion adopted. The **Mahalanobis procedure** is based on maximizing a generalized measure of the distance between the two closest groups. This procedure allows marketing researchers to make maximal use of the available information.[16]

Mahalanobis Procedure
A stepwise procedure used in discriminant analysis to maximize a generalized measure of the distance between the two closest groups.

The Mahalanobis method was used to conduct a two-group stepwise discriminant analysis on the data pertaining to the visit variable in Tables 18.2 and 18.3. The first predictor variable to be selected was income, followed by household size and then vacation. The order in which the variables were selected also indicates their importance in discriminating between the groups. This was further corroborated by an examination of the standardized discriminant function coefficients and the structure correlation coefficients. Note that the findings of the stepwise analysis agree with the conclusions reported earlier by the direct method.

Research in Practice 18.1 gives an application of discriminant analysis in international marketing research[17] whereas Research in Practice 18.2 presents an application in ethics.[18]

RESEARCH IN PRACTICE 18.1

Satisfactory Results of Satisfaction Programs in Europe

These days more and more computer companies are emphasizing customer service programs rather than computer features and capabilities. Hewlett-Packard learned this lesson while doing business in Europe. Research conducted on the European market revealed that there was a difference in emphasis on service requirements across age segments. Focus groups revealed that customers above 40 years of age had a hard time with the technical aspects of the computer and greatly required the customer service programs. On the other hand, young customers appreciated the technical aspects of the product that added to their satisfaction. Further research in the form of a large single cross-sectional survey was done to uncover the factors leading to differences in the two segments. A two-group discriminant analysis was conducted with satisfied and dissatisfied customers as the two groups and several independent variables such as technical information, ease of operation, variety and scope of customer service programs, and so on. Results confirmed the fact that the variety and scope of customer satisfaction programs was indeed a strong differentiating factor. This was a crucial finding because Hewlett-Packard could handle dissatisfied customers better by focusing more on customer services than on technical details. Consequently, Hewlett-Packard successfully started three programs on customer satisfaction—customer feedback, customer satisfaction surveys, and total quality control. This effort resulted in increased customer satisfaction.

RESEARCH IN PRACTICE 18.2

Discriminant Analysis Discriminates Ethical and Unethical Firms

In order to identify the important variables that predict ethical and unethical behavior, discriminant analysis was used. Prior research suggested that the variables that impact ethical decisions are attitudes, leadership, the presence or absence of ethical codes of conduct, and the organization's size.

To determine which of these variables are the best predictors of ethical behavior, 149 firms were surveyed and asked to indicate how their firm operates in 18 different ethical situations. Of these 18 situations, 9 related to marketing activities. These activities included using misleading sales presentations, accepting gifts for preferential treatment, pricing below out-of-pocket expenses, and the like. Based on these 9 issues, the respondent firms were classified into two groups: "never practice" and "practice."

An examination of the variables that influenced classification indicated that attitudes and a company's size were the best predictors of ethical behavior. Evidently, smaller firms tend to demonstrate more ethical behavior on marketing issues.

FOCUS ON Burke

As with multiple regression, the primary uses of discriminant analysis are prediction and determining relative importance of predictor variables. The key difference between these two techniques is the multiple regression requirement of an interval or ratio-dependent variable, whereas discriminant analysis uses a dichotomous or categorical dependent variable. Whereas multiple regression might be used to predict degree of purchase interest, discriminant analysis would be used if one only wanted to predict group membership of purchasers versus nonpurchasers.

One of the issues for researchers to consider is the use of "natural groups" versus "created groups." For example, if you ask the age of respondents, you often collect the data in categories rather than measure the actual years of age. When you do this, the categories you used have determined the outcome of an analysis where the categories are to be used as the dependent variable. By pooling people into arbitrary age groups you may obscure the differences between these people. Looking at the data in the most granular form allows you to make judgments about creating larger groups of respondents based on any particular measurement. In another situation, you may also collect data on whether the person lives in a single family residence, an apartment, or condominium. As nominal categories these are relatively "natural," it would be difficult to find categories describing the residence that were more interval in quality. Having confidence in the meaning of the groups allows further confidence in the validity of the conclusions.

In a Burke study, the following classification matrix resulted from a study of brand usage. Each respondent was asked if they had tried a certain brand. The discrimination was attempted based on the respondents' ratings of benefits desired in a product in this category. Every respondent was screened to be a category user. In the sample, 30 percent (60) had not tried the brand and 70 percent (202) had tried the brand. It is generally expected when the groups are disproportionate in the population that the larger group will be predicted better than the smaller group. One way to think of this is that if random choice is used you would correctly classify a brand trier 49 percent of the time (.7 * .7) and a non-trier 9 percent of the time (.3 * .3) and people would be misclassified 42 percent of the time (.3 * .7 + .7 * .3). This model classified the smaller group (brand nontriers) less accurately than brand triers, but it was better than what one would expect from random chance.

The cross-validation option in SPSS was used. In this option, the discriminant model is reestimated as many times as there are respondents in the sample. Each reestimated model leaves out one respondent and the model is used to predict for that respondent. When a large hold-out sample is not possible, this gives a sense of the robustness of the estimate using each respondent, in turn, as a hold-out. In this situation the cross-validation produced almost the same level of

(Continued)

INTERNET AND COMPUTER APPLICATIONS

In the mainframe version of SPSS, the DISCRIMINANT procedure is used for conducting discriminant analysis. This is a general program that can be used for two-group or multiple discriminant analysis. Furthermore, the direct or the stepwise method can be adopted. A similar program, DSCRIMINANT, is available in SPSS/PC+.

In SAS the DISCRIM procedure can be used for performing two-group or multiple discriminant analysis. If the assumption of a multivariate normal distribution cannot be met, the NEIGHBOR procedure can be used. In this procedure, a nonparametric nearest neighbor rule is used for classifying the observations. CANDISC performs canonical discriminant analysis and is related to principal component analysis and canonical correlation. The STEPDISC procedure can be used for performing stepwise discriminant analysis. The mainframe and microcomputer versions are similar, except that the program NEIGHBOR is not available on the microcomputer version.

In BMDP the P7M program can be used to perform stepwise discriminant analysis. It does not print the standardized discriminant function coefficients. The program P7M is available in both mainframe and microcomputer versions.[19]

FOCUS ON Burke *(Continued)*

accuracy as the total model. Note that the cross-validation produced more errors in predicting to the smaller group.

The typical output sometimes doesn't lend itself to the alternative ways management may want to interpret the model in light of its intended use. For example, management asks, "If you were to predict that a respondent was a nontrier, what is the estimated likelihood that you are correct?" In this situation (using the cross-validation results), Burke would say, "We would expect to predict a respondent to be nontrier about 18 percent of the time [(33 + 15)/262 = .18]. When we do this we would expect to be correct approximately 69 percent of the time (33/48 = .69). The standard output is not laid out to allow management to immediately see this answer. Again, referring to random chance, Burke would tell management "Random selection would estimate about 30 percent to be nontriers and be correct only 43 percent of the time when this happens" (that is, proportion of sample randomly estimated to be nontriers is .3 * .7 + .3 * .3 = .30; proportion correctly predicted .3 * .3/.3 * .7 = 43%). Just looking at the percent correctly classified does not tell the whole story.

CLASSIFICATION RESULTS

		Have Tried Brand	*Predicted Group Membership* *No*	*Yes*	*Total*
Original	Count	no	35	25	60
		yes	15	187	202
	%	no	58.3	41.7	100.0
		yes	7.4	92.6	100.0
Cross-validated[a]	Count	no	33	27	60
		yes	15	187	202
	%	no	55.0	45.0	100.0
		yes	7.4	92.6	100.0

a. Cross-validation is done only for those cases in the analysis. In cross-validation, each case is classified by the functions derived from all cases other than that case.
b. 84.7% of original grouped cases correctly classified.
c. 84.0% of cross-validated grouped cases correctly classified.

In Minitab, discriminant analysis can be conducted using the Stats>Multivariate>Discriminate Analysis function. It computes both linear and quadratic discriminant analysis in the classification of observations into two or more groups. Discriminant analysis is not available in Excel (version 7.0 for the PC).

SUMMARY

Discriminant analysis is useful for analyzing data when the criterion or dependent variable is categorical and the predictor or independent variables are interval scaled. When the criterion variable has two categories, the technique is known as two-group discriminant analysis. Multiple discriminant analysis refers to the case when three or more categories are involved.

Conducting discriminant analysis is a five-step procedure. First, formulating the discriminant problem requires identification of the objectives and the criterion and predictor variables. The sample is divided into two parts. One part, the analysis sample, is used to estimate the discriminant function. The other part, the holdout sample, is reserved for validation. Estimation, the second step, involves developing a linear combination of the predictors, called discriminant functions, so that the groups differ as much as possible on the predictor values.

Determination of statistical significance is the third step. It involves testing the null hypothesis that, in the population, the means of all discriminant functions in all groups are equal. If the null hypothesis is rejected, it is meaningful to interpret the results.

The fourth step, the interpretation of discriminant weights or coefficients, is similar to that in multiple regression analysis. Given the multicollinearity in the predictor variables, there is no unambiguous measure of the relative importance of the predictors in discriminating between the groups. However, some idea of the relative importance of the variables may be obtained by examining the absolute magnitude of the standardized discriminant function coefficients and by examining the structure correlations or discriminant loadings. These simple correlations between each predictor and the discriminant function represent the variance that the predictor shares with the function. Another aid to interpreting discriminant analysis results is to develop a characteristic profile for each group, based on the group means for the predictor variables.

Validation, the fifth step, involves developing the classification matrix. The discriminant weights estimated by using the analysis sample are multiplied by the values of the predictor variables in the hold-out sample to generate discriminant scores for the cases in the hold-out sample. The cases are then assigned to groups based on their discriminant scores and an appropriate decision rule. The percentage of cases correctly classified is determined and compared to the rate that would be expected by chance classification.

Two broad approaches are available for estimating the coefficients. The direct method involves estimating the discriminant function so that all the predictors are included simultaneously. An alternative is the stepwise method, in which the predictor variables are entered sequentially, based on their ability to discriminate among groups.

In multiple discriminant analysis, if there are G groups and k predictors, it is possible to estimate up to the smaller of $G - 1$, or k, discriminant functions. The first function has the highest ratio of between-group to within-group sums of squares. The second function, uncorrelated with the first, has the second highest ratio, and so on.

KEY TERMS AND CONCEPTS

discriminant analysis
discriminant function
two-group discriminant analysis
multiple discriminant analysis
discriminant analysis model
canonical correlation
centroid
classification matrix
discriminant function coefficients
discriminant scores
eigenvalue
F values and their significance
grouped means
group standard deviations
pooled within-group correlation matrix
standardized discriminant function coefficients

structure correlations
total correlation matrix
Wilks's λ
analysis sample
validation sample
direct method
stepwise discriminant analysis
characteristic profile
hit ratio
territorial map
Mahalanobis procedure

ACRONYMS

The steps involved and some key concepts in discriminant analysis may be summarized by the acronym DISCRIMINANT:

D ependent variable: categorical
I ndependent variable: metric
S tructure correlations or discriminant loadings
C alculation of the discriminant function
R elative importance of predictors: ambiguous
I nterpretation: scattergram and territorial map
M eans and standard deviations for groups
I nference: determination of significance
N umber of functions possible: minimum $(G-1, k)$
A ssociation: canonical correlation
N umber 1 function has highest eigenvalue
T esting for validity: classification analysis

EXERCISES

Questions

1. What are the objectives of discriminant analysis?
2. What is the main distinction between two-group and multiple discriminant analysis?
3. Describe the relationship of discriminant analysis to regression and ANOVA.
4. What are the steps involved in conducting discriminant analysis?
5. How should the total sample be split for estimation and validation purposes?
6. What is Wilks's λ? For what purpose is it used?
7. Define discriminant scores.
8. Explain what is meant by an eigenvalue.
9. What is a classification matrix?
10. Explain the concept of structure correlations.
11. How is the statistical significance of discriminant analysis determined?
12. Describe a common procedure for determining the validity of discriminant analysis.
13. When the groups are of equal size, how is the accuracy of chance classification determined?
14. How does the stepwise discriminant procedure differ from the direct method?

Problems

1. In investigating the differences between heavy and light or nonusers of frozen foods, it was found that the two largest standardized discriminant function coefficients were .97 for convenience orientation and .61 for income. Is it correct to conclude that convenience orientation is more important than income when each variable is considered by itself?
2. Given the following information, calculate the discriminant score for each respondent. The value of the constant is 2.04

Unstandardized Discriminant Function Coefficients

Age	.38
Income	.44
Risk taking	−.39
Optimistic	1.26

Respondent ID	*Age*	*Income*	*Risk Taking*	*Optimistic*
0246	36	43.7	21	65
1337	44	62.5	28	56
2375	57	33.5	25	40
2454	63	38.7	16	36

INTERNET AND COMPUTER EXERCISES

1. Conduct a two-group discriminant analysis on the data given in Tables 18.2 and 18.3 using the SPSS, SAS, BMDP, and Minitab packages (microcomputer or mainframe). Compare the output from all the packages. Discuss the similarities and differences.
2. Conduct a three-group stepwise discriminant analysis on the data given in Tables 18.2 and 18.3 using the SPSS, SAS, BMDP, or Minitab package. Compare the results to those given in Table 18.5 for three-group discriminant analysis.

APPENDIX 18A

Estimation of Discriminant Function Coefficients

Suppose there are G groups, $i = 1, 2, 3, \ldots, G$, each containing n_i observations on K independent variables, X_1, $X_2, \ldots, X_k$. The following notations are used.

N = total sample size

$= \sum_{i=1}^{G} n_i$

W_i = matrix of mean corrected sum of squares and cross-products for the ith group

W = matrix of pooled within-groups mean corrected sum of squares and cross-products

B = matrix of between-groups mean corrected sum of squares and cross-products

T = matrix of total mean corrected sum of squares and cross-products for all the N observations ($= W + B$)

$\overline{X}_i$ = vector of means of observations in the ith group

$\overline{X}$ = vector of grand means for all the N observations

λ = ratio of between-groups to within-groups sums of squares

b = vector of discriminant coefficients or weights

Then,

$$T = \sum_{i=1}^{G} \sum_{j=1}^{n_i} (X_{ij} - \overline{X})(X_{ij} - \overline{X})'$$

$$W_i = \sum_{j=1}^{n_i} (X_{ij} - \overline{X}_i)(X_{ij} - \overline{X}_i)'$$

$$W = W_1 + W_2 + W_3 + \ldots + W_G$$

$$B = T - W$$

Define the linear composite $D = b'_1X$. Then, with reference to D, the between-groups and within-groups sums of squares are, respectively, given by b'_1Bb and b'_1Wb. In order to maximally discriminate the groups, the discriminant functions are estimated to maximize the between-group variability. The coefficients b are calculated to maximize λ, by solving

$$\text{Max } \lambda = \frac{b'Bb}{b'Wb}$$

Taking the partial derivative with respect to λ and setting it equal to zero, with some simplification, yields:

$$(B - \lambda W)b = 0$$

To solve for b, it is more convenient to premultiply by W^{-1} and solve the following characteristic equation:

$$(W^{-1}B - \lambda I)b = 0$$

The maximum value of λ is the largest eigenvalue of the matrix $W^{-1}B$, and b is the associated eigenvector. The elements of b are the discriminant coefficients, or weights, associated with the first discriminant function. In general, it is possible to estimate up to the smaller of $G - 1$ or k discriminant functions, each with its associated eigenvalue. The discriminant functions are estimated sequentially. In other words, the first discriminant function exhausts most of the between-group variability. The second function maximizes the between-group variation that was not explained by the first one, and so on.

Chapter 19

Factor Analysis

"Often among the many variables you measure, a few are more related to each other than they are to others. Factor analysis allows us to look at these groups of variables that tend to be related to each other and estimate what underlying reasons might cause these variables to be more highly correlated with each other."

Jeff Miller,
vice president,
consulting and analytical,
Burke, Inc.

OBJECTIVES

After reading this chapter, the student should be able to

1. describe the concept of factor analysis and explain how it is different from analysis of variance, multiple regression, and discriminant analysis
2. discuss the procedure for conducting factor analysis including problem formulation, construction of the correlation matrix, selection of an appropriate method, determination of the number of factors, rotation, and interpretation of factors
3. understand the distinction between principal component factor analysis and common factor analysis methods
4. explain the selection of surrogate variables and their application with emphasis on their use in subsequent analysis
5. describe the procedure for determining the fit of a factor analysis model using the observed and the reproduced correlations

OVERVIEW

In analysis of variance (chapter 16), regression (chapter 17), and discriminant analysis (chapter 18), one of the variables is clearly identified as the dependent variable. We now turn to a procedure, factor analysis, in which variables are not classified as independent or dependent. Instead, the whole set of interdependent relationships among variables is examined. This chapter discusses the basic concept of factor analysis and gives an exposition of the factor model. We describe the steps in factor analysis and illustrate them in the context of principal components analysis. Next, we present an application of common factor analysis. To begin, we provide some examples to illustrate the usefulness of factor analysis.

DEPARTMENT STORE PATRONAGE PROJECT

Factor Analysis

The respondents' ratings of 21 lifestyle statements were factor analyzed to determine the underlying lifestyle factors. Seven factors emerged: bank card versus store card preference, credit proneness, credit avoidance, leisure time orientation, credit card favorableness, credit convenience, and credit card cost-consciousness. These factors, along with the demographic characteristics, were used to profile the segments formed as a result of clustering.

EXAMPLE

Factor Analysis Earns Interest at Banks

How do consumers evaluate banks? Respondents in a survey were asked to rate the importance of 15 bank attributes. A five-point scale ranging from not important to very important was employed. These data were analyzed via principal components analysis.

A four-factor solution resulted, with the factors being labeled as traditional services, convenience, visibility, and competence. Traditional services included interest rates on loans, reputation in the community, low rates for checking, friendly and personalized service, easy to read monthly statements, and obtainability of loans. Convenience comprised convenient branch location, convenient ATM locations, speed of service, and convenient banking hours. The visibility factor included recommendations from friends and relatives, attractiveness of the physical structure, community involvement, and obtainability of loans. Competence consisted of employee competence and availability of auxiliary banking services. It was concluded that consumers evaluated banks using the four basic factors of traditional services, convenience, visibility, and competence.[1] ■

BASIC CONCEPT

Factor Analysis A class of procedures primarily used for data reduction and summarization.

Factor analysis is a general name denoting a class of procedures primarily used for data reduction and summarization. In marketing research, there may be a large number of variables, most of which are correlated and which must be reduced to a manageable level. Relationships among sets of many interrelated variables are examined and represented in terms of a few underlying factors. For example, store image may be measured by asking respondents to evaluate stores on a series of items on a semantic differential scale. These item evaluations may then be analyzed to determine the factors underlying store image.

In analysis of variance, multiple regression, and discriminant analysis, one variable is considered as the dependent or criterion variable, and the others as independent or predictor variables. However, no such distinction is made in factor analysis. Rather, factor analysis is an **interdependence technique** in that an entire set of interdependent relationships is examined.[2]

Interdependence Technique Multivariate statistical technique in which the whole set of interdependent relationships is examined.

Factor An underlying dimension that explains the correlations among a set of variables.

Factor analysis is used in the following circumstances:

1. To identify underlying dimensions, or **factors**, that explain the correlations among a set of variables. For example, a set of lifestyle statements may be used to measure the psychographic profiles of consumers. These statements may then be factor analyzed to identify the underlying psychographic factors, as illustrated in the department store example.[3]
2. To identify a new, smaller set of uncorrelated variables to replace the original set of correlated variables in subsequent multivariate analysis (regression or discriminant analysis).

For example, the psychographic factors identified may be used as independent variables in explaining the differences between loyal and nonloyal consumers.

3. To identify a smaller set of salient variables from a larger set for use in subsequent multivariate analysis. For example, a few of the original lifestyle statements that correlate highly with the identified factors may be used as independent variables to explain the differences between the loyal and nonloyal users.

Factor analysis has numerous applications in marketing research. For example:

- It can be used in market segmentation for identifying the underlying variables on which to group the customers. New-car buyers might be grouped based on the relative emphasis they place on economy, convenience, performance, comfort, and luxury. This might result in five segments: economy seekers, convenience seekers, performance seekers, comfort seekers, and luxury seekers.
- In product research, factor analysis can be employed to determine the brand attributes that influence consumer choice. Toothpaste brands might be evaluated in terms of protection against cavities, whiteness of teeth, taste, fresh breath, and price.
- In advertising studies, factor analysis can be used to understand the media consumption habits of the target market. The users of frozen foods may be heavy viewers of cable TV, see a lot of movies, and listen to country music.
- In pricing studies, it can be used to identify the characteristics of price-sensitive consumers. For example, these consumers might be methodical, economy minded, and home centered.

FACTOR ANALYSIS MODEL

Mathematically, factor analysis is somewhat similar to multiple regression analysis, in that each variable is expressed as a linear combination of underlying factors. The amount of variance a variable shares with all other variables included in the analysis is referred to as *communality*. The covariation among the variables is described in terms of a small number of common factors plus a unique factor for each variable. These factors are not overtly observed. If the variables are standardized, the factor model may be represented as:

$$X_i = A_{i1}F_1 + A_{i2}F_2 + A_{i3}F_3 + \ldots + A_{im}F_m + V_iU_i$$

where

X_i = ith standardized variable
A_{ij} = standardized multiple regression coefficient of variable i on common factor j
F = common factor
V_i = standardized regression coefficient of variable i on unique factor i
U_i = the unique factor for variable i
m = number of common factors

The unique factors are uncorrelated with each other and with the common factors.[4] The common factors themselves can be expressed as linear combinations of the observed variables.

$$F_i = W_{i1}X_1 + W_{i2}X_2 + W_{i3}X_3 + \ldots + W_{ik}X_k$$

where

F_i = estimate of ith factor
W_i = weight or factor score coefficient
k = number of variables

It is possible to select weights or factor score coefficients so that the first factor explains the largest portion of the total variance. Then a second set of weights can be selected, so that the second factor accounts for most of the residual variance, subject to being uncorrelated with the first factor. This same principle could be applied to selecting additional weights for the additional factors. Thus, the factors can be estimated so that their factor scores, unlike the values of the original variables, are not correlated. Furthermore, the first factor accounts for the highest variance in the data, the second factor the second highest, and so on. A technical treatment of the factor analysis model is presented in appendix 19A. Several statistics are associated with factor analysis.

STATISTICS ASSOCIATED WITH FACTOR ANALYSIS

The key statistics associated with factor analysis are as follows:

Bartlett's test of sphericity. A test statistic used to examine the hypothesis that the variables are uncorrelated in the population. In other words, the population correlation matrix is an identity matrix; each variable correlates perfectly with itself ($r = 1$) but has no correlation with the other variables ($r = 0$).

Correlation matrix. A lower triangle matrix showing the simple correlations, r, between all possible pairs of variables included in the analysis. The diagonal elements, which are all 1, are usually omitted.

Communality. The amount of variance a variable shares with all the other variables being considered. This is also the proportion of variance explained by the common factors.

Eigenvalue. Represents the total variance explained by each factor.

Factor loadings. Simple correlations between the variables and the factors.

Factor loading plot. A plot of the original variables using the factor loadings as coordinates.

Factor matrix. Contains the factor loadings of all the variables on all the factors extracted.

Factor scores. Composite scores estimated for each respondent on the derived factors.

Kaiser-Meyer-Olkin (KMO) measure of sampling adequacy. An index used to examine the appropriateness of factor analysis. High values (between .5 and 1.0) indicate factor analysis is appropriate. Values below .5 imply that factor analysis may not be appropriate.

Percentage of variance. The percentage of the total variance attributed to each factor.

Residuals. The differences between the observed correlations, as given in the input correlation matrix, and the reproduced correlations, as estimated from the factor matrix.

Scree plot. A plot of the eigenvalues against the number of factors in order of extraction.

We describe the uses of these statistics in the next section, in the context of the procedure for conducting factor analysis.

CONDUCTING FACTOR ANALYSIS

The steps involved in conducting factor analysis are illustrated in Figure 19.1. The first step is to formulate the factor analysis problem and identify the variables to be factor analyzed. Then a correlation matrix of these variables is constructed and a method of factor analysis selected. The researcher decides on the number of factors to be extracted and the method of rotation. Next, the rotated factors should be interpreted. Depending on the objectives, the factor scores may be calculated, or surrogate variables selected, to represent the factors in subsequent multivariate analysis. Finally, the fit of the factor analysis model is determined. We discuss these steps in more detail in the following sections.[5]

Formulate the Problem

Formulating the problem involves several tasks. First, the objectives of factor analysis should be identified. The variables to be included in the factor analysis should be specified based on past research, theory, and judgment of the researcher. It is important that the

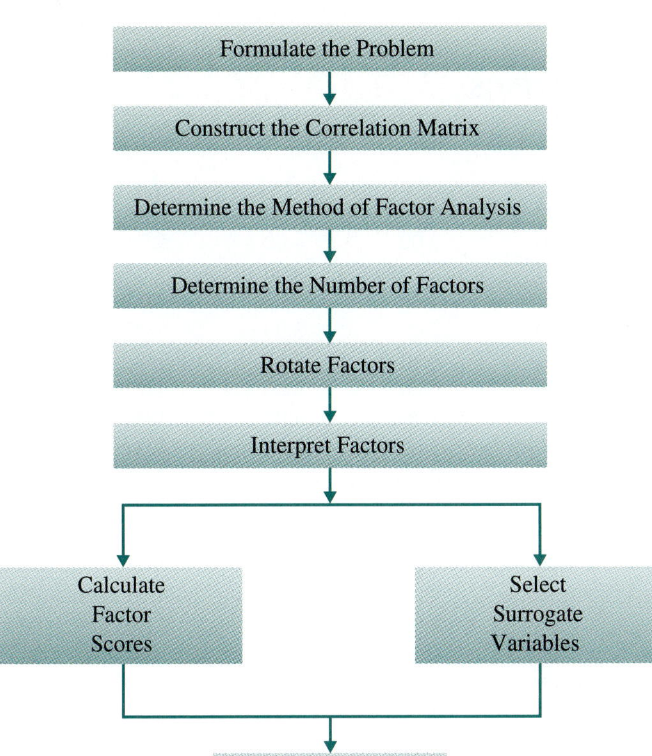

Figure 19.1
Conducting Factor Analysis

variables be appropriately measured on an interval or ratio scale. An appropriate sample size should be used. As a rough guideline, there should be at least four or five times as many observations (sample size) as there are variables.[6] In many marketing research situations, the sample size is small, and this ratio is considerably lower. In these cases, the results should be interpreted cautiously.

To illustrate factor analysis, suppose the researcher wants to determine the underlying benefits consumers seek from the purchase of a toothpaste. A pretest sample of 30 respondents was interviewed using mall-intercept interviewing. The respondents were asked to indicate their degree of agreement with the following statements using a seven-point scale (1 = strongly disagree, 7 = strongly agree):

V_1: It is important to buy a toothpaste that prevents cavities.
V_2: I like a toothpaste that gives shiny teeth.
V_3: A toothpaste should strengthen your gums.
V_4: I prefer a toothpaste that freshens breath.
V_5: Prevention of tooth decay is not an important benefit offered by a toothpaste.
V_6: The most important consideration in buying a toothpaste is attractive teeth.

The data obtained are given in Table 19.1. A correlation matrix was constructed based on these ratings data. This construction process is discussed in the next section.

Construct the Correlation Matrix

The analytical process is based on a matrix of correlations between the variables. Valuable insights can be gained from an examination of this matrix. For the factor analysis to be appropriate, the variables must be correlated. In practice, this is usually the case. If the correlations between all the variables are small, factor analysis may not be appropriate. We

TABLE 19.1

TOOTHPASTE ATTRIBUTE RATINGS

Respondent Number	V_1	V_2	V_3	V_4	V_5	V_6
1	7.00	3.00	6.00	4.00	2.00	4.00
2	1.00	3.00	2.00	4.00	5.00	4.00
3	6.00	2.00	7.00	4.00	1.00	3.00
4	4.00	5.00	4.00	6.00	2.00	5.00
5	1.00	2.00	2.00	3.00	6.00	2.00
6	6.00	3.00	6.00	4.00	2.00	4.00
7	5.00	3.00	6.00	3.00	4.00	3.00
8	6.00	4.00	7.00	4.00	1.00	4.00
9	3.00	4.00	2.00	3.00	6.00	3.00
10	2.00	6.00	2.00	6.00	7.00	6.00
11	6.00	4.00	7.00	3.00	2.00	3.00
12	2.00	3.00	1.00	4.00	5.00	4.00
13	7.00	2.00	6.00	4.00	1.00	3.00
14	4.00	6.00	4.00	5.00	3.00	6.00
15	1.00	3.00	2.00	2.00	6.00	4.00
16	6.00	4.00	6.00	3.00	3.00	4.00
17	5.00	3.00	6.00	3.00	3.00	4.00
18	7.00	3.00	7.00	4.00	1.00	4.00
19	2.00	4.00	3.00	3.00	6.00	3.00
20	3.00	5.00	3.00	6.00	4.00	6.00
21	1.00	3.00	2.00	3.00	5.00	3.00
22	5.00	4.00	5.00	4.00	2.00	4.00
23	2.00	2.00	1.00	5.00	4.00	4.00
24	4.00	6.00	4.00	6.00	4.00	7.00
25	6.00	5.00	4.00	2.00	1.00	4.00
26	3.00	5.00	4.00	6.00	4.00	7.00
27	4.00	4.00	7.00	2.00	2.00	5.00
28	3.00	7.00	2.00	6.00	4.00	3.00
29	4.00	6.00	3.00	7.00	2.00	7.00
30	2.00	3.00	2.00	4.00	7.00	2.00

would also expect that variables that are highly correlated with each other would also highly correlate with the same factor or factors.

Formal statistics are available for testing the appropriateness of the factor model. Bartlett's test of sphericity can be used to test the null hypothesis that the variables are uncorrelated in the population: In other words, the population correlation matrix is an identity matrix. In an identity matrix, all the diagonal terms are 1, and all off-diagonal terms are 0. The test statistic for sphericity is based on a chi-square transformation of the determinant of the correlation matrix. A large value of the test statistic will favor the rejection of the null hypothesis. If this hypothesis cannot be rejected, then the appropriateness of factor analysis should be questioned. Another useful statistic is the Kaiser-Meyer-Olkin (KMO) measure of sampling adequacy. This index compares the magnitudes of the observed correlation coefficients to the magnitudes of the partial correlation coefficients. Small values of the KMO statistic indicate that the correlations between pairs of variables cannot be explained by other variables and that factor analysis may not be appropriate.

The correlation matrix, constructed from the data obtained to understand toothpaste benefits, is shown in Table 19.2. There are relatively high correlations among V_1 (prevention of cavities), V_3 (strong gums), and V_5 (prevention of tooth decay). We would expect

TABLE 19.2

CORRELATION MATRIX

Variables	V_1	V_2	V_3	V_4	V_5	V_6
V_1	1.00					
V_2	–.053	1.00				
V_3	.873	–.155	1.00			
V_4	–.086	.572	–.248	1.00		
V_5	–.858	.020	–.778	–.007	1.00	
V_6	.004	.640	–.018	.640	–.136	1.00

these variables to correlate with the same set of factors. Likewise, there are relatively high correlations among V_2 (shiny teeth), V_4 (fresh breath), and V_6 (attractive teeth). These variables may also be expected to correlate with the same factors.[7]

The results of factor analysis are given in Table 19.3. The null hypothesis, that the population correlation matrix is an identity matrix, is rejected by the Bartlett's test of sphericity. The approximate chi-square statistic is 111.314 with 15 degrees of freedom which is significant at the .05 level. The value of the KMO statistic (.660) is also large, (> .5). Thus factor analysis may be considered an appropriate technique for analyzing the correlation matrix of Table 19.2.

Determine the Method of Factor Analysis

Once it has been determined that factor analysis is an appropriate technique for analyzing the data, an appropriate method must be selected. The approach used to derive the weights or factor score coefficients differentiates the various methods of factor analysis. The two basic approaches are principal components analysis and common factor analysis. In **principal components analysis**, the total variance in the data is considered. The diagonal of the correlation matrix consists of unities, and full variance is brought into the factor matrix. Principal components analysis is recommended when the primary concern is to determine the minimum number of factors that will account for maximum variance in the data for use in subsequent multivariate analysis. The factors are called *principal components*.

Principal Components Analysis An approach to factor analysis that considers the total variance in the data.

In **common factor analysis**, the factors are estimated based only on the common variance. Communalities are inserted in the diagonal of the correlation matrix. This method is appropriate when the primary concern is to identify the underlying dimensions and the common variance is of interest. This method is also known as *principal axis factoring*.

Common Factor Analysis An approach to factor analysis that estimates the factors based only on the common variance.

Other approaches for estimating the common factors are also available. These include the methods of unweighted least squares, generalized least squares, maximum likelihood, alpha method, and image factoring. These methods are complex and are not recommended for inexperienced users.[8]

Table 19.3 shows the application of principal components analysis to the toothpaste example. Under "Communalities," "Initial" column, it can be seen that the communality for each variable, V_1 to V_6, is 1.0 as unities were inserted in the diagonal of the correlation matrix. The table labeled "Initial Eigenvalues" gives the eigenvalues. The eigenvalues for the factors are, as expected, in decreasing order of magnitude as we go from factor 1 to factor 6. The eigenvalue for a factor indicates the total variance attributed to that factor. The total variance accounted for by all the six factors is 6.00, which is equal to the number of variables. Factor 1 accounts for a variance of 2.731, which is (2.731/6) or 45.52 percent of the total variance. Likewise, the second factor accounts for (2.218/6) or 36.97 percent of the total variance, and the first two factors combined account for 82.49 percent of the total variance. Several considerations are involved in determining the number of factors that should be used in the analysis.

TABLE 19.3

RESULTS OF PRINCIPAL COMPONENTS ANALYSIS

Bartlett test of sphericity
Approximate chi-square = 111.314, df = 15, significance = .00000
Kaiser-Meyer-Olkin measure of sampling adequacy = .660

Communalities

Variable	*Initial*	*Extraction*
V_1	1.000	.926
V_2	1.000	.723
V_3	1.000	.894
V_4	1.000	.739
V_5	1.000	.878
V_6	1.000	.790

Initial Eigenvalues

Factor	*Eigenvalue*	*Percentage of Variance*	*Cumulative Percent*
1	2.731	45.520	45.520
2	2.218	36.969	82.488
3	.442	7.360	89.848
4	.341	5.688	95.536
5	.183	3.044	98.580
6	.085	1.420	100.000

Extraction Sums of Squared Loadings

Factor	*Eigenvalue*	*Percentage of Variance*	*Cumulative Percent*
1	2.731	45.520	45.520
2	2.218	36.969	82.488

Factor Matrix

	Factor 1	*Factor 2*
V_1	.928	.253
V_2	–.301	.795
V_3	.936	.131
V_4	–.342	.789
V_5	–.869	–.351
V_6	–.177	.871

Rotation Sums of Squared Loadings

Factor	*Eigenvalue*	*Percentage of Variance*	*Cumulative Percent*
1	2.688	44.802	44.802
2	2.261	37.687	82.488

Rotated Factor Matrix

	Factor 1	*Factor 2*
V_1	.962	–.027
V_2	–.057	.848
V_3	.934	–.146
V_4	–.098	.854
V_5	–.933	–.084
V_6	.083	.885

Factor Score Coefficient Matrix

	Factor 1	*Factor 2*
V_1	.358	.011
V_2	–.001	.375
V_3	.345	–.043
V_4	–.017	.377
V_5	–.350	–.059
V_6	.052	.395

(Continued)

TABLE 19.3 *(Continued)*

Reproduced Correlation Matrix

	V_1	V_2	V_3	V_4	V_5	V_6
V_1	.926*	.024	−.029	.031	.038	−.053
V_2	−.078	.723*	.022	−.158	.038	−.105
V_3	.902	−.177	.894*	−.031	.081	.033
V_4	−.117	.730	−.217	.739*	−.027	−.107
V_5	−.895	−.018	−.859	.020	.878*	.016
V_6	.057	.746	−.051	.748	−.152	.790*

*The lower-left triangle contains the reproduced correlation matrix; the diagonal, the communalities; the upper-right triangle, the residuals between the observed correlations and the reproduced correlations.

Determine the Number of Factors

It is possible to compute as many principal components as there are variables, but in doing so, no parsimony is gained. In order to summarize the information contained in the original variables, a smaller number of factors should be extracted. The question is, how many? Several procedures have been suggested for determining the number of factors. These include a priori determination and approaches based on eigenvalues, scree plot, percentage of variance accounted for, split-half reliability, and significance tests.

A Priori *Determination.* Sometimes, because of prior knowledge, the researcher knows how many factors to expect and thus can specify the number of factors to be extracted beforehand. The extraction of factors ceases when the desired number of factors have been extracted. Most computer programs allow the user to specify the number of factors, allowing for an easy implementation of this approach.

Determination Based on Eigenvalues. In this approach, only factors with eigenvalues greater than 1.0 are retained; the other factors are not included in the model. An eigenvalue represents the amount of variance associated with the factor. Hence, only factors with a variance greater than 1.0 are included. Factors with variance less than 1.0 are no better than a single variable, because, due to standardization, each variable has a variance of 1.0. If the number of variables is less than 20, this approach will result in a conservative number of factors.

Determination Based on Scree Plot. A *scree plot* is a plot of the eigenvalues against the number of factors in order of extraction. The shape of the plot is used to determine the number of factors. Typically, the plot has a distinct break between the steep slope of factors, with large eigenvalues and a gradual trailing off associated with the rest of the factors. This gradual trailing off is referred to as the *scree*. Experimental evidence indicates that the point at which the scree begins denotes the true number of factors. Generally, the number of factors determined by a scree plot will be one or a few more than that determined by the eigenvalue criterion.

Determination Based on Percentage of Variance. In this approach the number of factors extracted is determined so that the cumulative percentage of variance extracted by the factors reaches a satisfactory level. What level of variance is satisfactory depends upon the problem. However, it is recommended that the factors extracted should account for at least 60 percent of the variance.

Determination Based on Split-Half Reliability. The sample is split in half and factor analysis is performed on each half. Only factors with high correspondence of factor loadings across the two subsamples are retained.

Determination Based on Significance Tests. It is possible to determine the statistical significance of the separate eigenvalues and retain only those factors that are statistically significant. A drawback is that with large samples (size greater than 200), many factors are likely to be statistically significant, although from a practical viewpoint many of these account for only a small proportion of the total variance.

In Table 19.3, we see that the eigenvalue greater than 1.0 (default option) results in two factors being extracted. Our a priori knowledge tells us that toothpaste is bought for two major reasons. The scree plot associated with this analysis is given in Figure 19.2. From the scree plot, a distinct break occurs at three factors. Finally, from the cumulative percentage of variance accounted for, we see that the first two factors account for 82.49 percent of the variance, and that the gain achieved in going to three factors is marginal. Furthermore, split-half reliability also indicates that two factors are appropriate. Thus, two factors appear to be reasonable in this situation.

The second column under "Communalities" in Table 19.3 gives relevant information after the desired number of factors have been extracted. The communalities for the variables under "Extraction" are different from those under "Initial" because all of the variances associated with the variables are not explained unless all the factors are retained. The "Extraction Sums of Squared Loadings" give the variances associated with the factors that are retained. Note that these are the same as those under "Initial Eigenvalues." This is always the case in principal components analysis. The percentage variance accounted by a factor is determined by dividing the associated eigenvalue with the total number of factors (or variables) and multiplying by 100. Thus, the first factor accounts for $(2.731/6) \times 100$ or 45.52 percent of the variance of the six variables. Likewise, the second factor accounts for $(2.218/6) \times 100$ or 36.969 percent of the variance. Interpretation of the solution is often enhanced by a rotation of the factors.

Rotate Factors

An important output from factor analysis is the factor matrix, also called the *factor pattern matrix*. The factor matrix contains the coefficients used to express the standardized variables in terms of the factors. These coefficients, the *factor loadings*, represent the correlations between the factors and the variables. A coefficient with a large absolute value indicates that the factor and the variable are closely related. The coefficients of the factor matrix can be used to interpret the factors.

Figure 19.2
Scree Plot

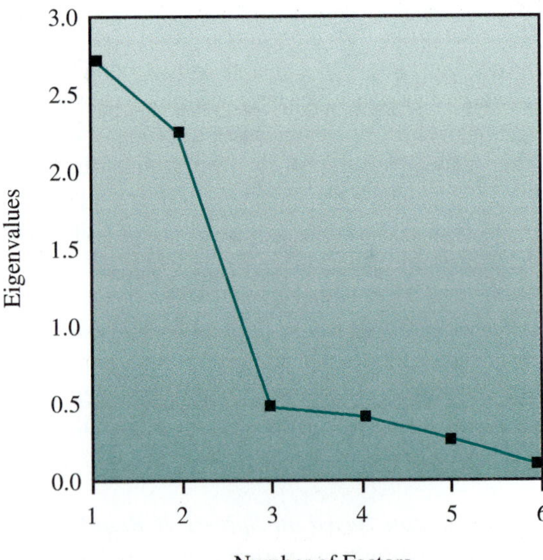

Although the initial or unrotated factor matrix indicates the relationship between the factors and individual variables, it seldom results in factors that can be interpreted, because the factors are correlated with many variables. For example, in Table 19.3, factor 1 is at least somewhat correlated with five of the six variables (absolute value of factor loading greater than 0.3). How should this factor be interpreted? In such a complex matrix it is difficult to interpret the factors. Therefore, through rotation the factor matrix is transformed into a simpler one that is easier to interpret.

In rotating the factors, we would like each factor to have nonzero, or significant, loadings or coefficients for only some of the variables. Likewise, we would like each variable to have nonzero or significant loadings with only a few factors, if possible with only one. If several factors have high loadings with the same variable, it is difficult to interpret them. Rotation does not affect the communalities and the percentage of total variance explained. However, the percentage of variance accounted for by each factor does change. This is seen in Table 19.3. The variance explained by the individual factors is redistributed by rotation. Hence different methods of rotation may result in the identification of different factors.

The rotation is called **orthogonal rotation** if the axes are maintained at right angles. The most commonly used method for rotation is the **varimax procedure**. This is an orthogonal method of rotation that minimizes the number of variables with high loadings on a factor, thereby enhancing the interpretability of the factors.[9] Orthogonal rotation results in factors that are uncorrelated. The rotation is called **oblique rotation** when the axes are not maintained at right angles, and the factors are correlated. Sometimes, allowing for correlations among factors can simplify the factor pattern matrix. Oblique rotation should be used when factors in the population are likely to be strongly correlated.

Orthogonal Rotation Rotation of factors in which the axes are maintained at right angles.

Varimax Procedure An orthogonal method of factor rotation that minimizes the number of variables with high loadings on a factor, thereby enhancing the interpretability of the factors.

Oblique Rotation Rotation of factors when the axes are not maintained at right angles.

In Table 19.3, by comparing the varimax rotated factor matrix with the unrotated matrix (entitled *factor matrix*), we can see how rotation achieves simplicity and enhances interpretability. Whereas five variables correlated with factor 1 in the unrotated matrix, only variables V_1, V_3, and V_5 correlate with factor 1 after rotation. The remaining variables, V_2, V_4 and V_6, correlate highly with factor 2. Furthermore, no variable correlates highly with both the factors. The rotated factor matrix forms the basis for interpretation of the factors.

Interpret Factors

Interpretation is facilitated by identifying the variables that have large loadings on the same factor. That factor can then be interpreted in terms of the variables that load high on it. Another useful aid in interpretation is to plot the variables, using the factor loadings as coordinates. Variables at the end of an axis are those which have high loadings on only that factor, and hence describe the factor. Variables near the origin have small loadings on both the factors. Variables that are not near any of the axes are related to both the factors. If a factor cannot be clearly defined in terms of the original variables, it should be labeled as an undefined or a general factor.

In the rotated factor matrix of Table 19.3, factor 1 has high coefficients for variables V_1 (prevention of cavities), V_3 (strong gums), and a negative coefficient for V_5 (prevention of tooth decay is not important). Therefore, this factor may be labeled a health benefit factor. Note that a negative coefficient for a negative variable (V_5) leads to a positive interpretation that prevention of tooth decay is important. Factor 2 is highly related with variables V_2 (shiny teeth), V_4 (fresh breath), and V_6 (attractive teeth). Thus factor 2 may be labeled a social benefit factor. A plot of the factor loadings, given in Figure 19.3, confirms this interpretation. Variables V_1, V_3, and V_5 (denoted by 1, 3, and 5 respectively) are at the end of the horizontal axis (factor 1), with V_5 at the end opposite to V_1 and V_3, whereas variables V_2, V_4, and V_6 (denoted by 2, 4, and 6) are at the end of the vertical axis (factor 2). One could summarize the data by stating that consumers appear to seek two major kinds of benefits from a toothpaste: health benefits and social benefits.

Figure 19.3
Factor Loading Plot

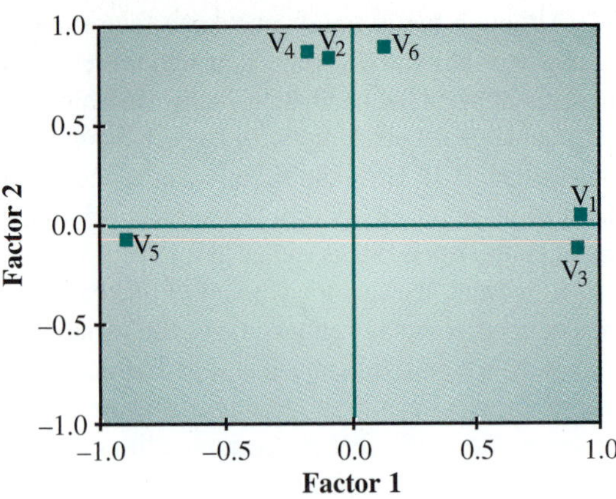

Calculate Factor Scores

Factor Scores Composite scores estimated for each respondent on the derived factors.

Following interpretation, factor scores can be calculated, if necessary. Factor analysis has its own stand-alone value. However, if the goal of factor analysis is to reduce the original set of variables to a smaller set of composite variables (factors) for use in subsequent multivariate analysis, it is useful to compute factor scores for each respondent. A factor is simply a linear combination of the original variables. The **factor scores** for the *i*th factor may be estimated as follows:

$$F_i = W_{i1}X_1 + W_{i2}X_2 + W_{i3}X_3 + \ldots + W_{ik}X_k$$

These symbols were defined earlier in the chapter.

The weights or factor score coefficients used to combine the standardized variables are obtained from the factor score coefficient matrix. Most computer programs allow you to request factor scores. Only in the case of principal components analysis is it possible to compute exact factor scores. Moreover, in principal component analysis these scores are uncorrelated. In common factor analysis, estimates of these scores are obtained, and there is no guarantee that the factors will be uncorrelated with each other. The factor scores can be used instead of the original variables in subsequent multivariate analysis. For example, using the factor score coefficient matrix in Table 19.3, one could compute two factor scores for each respondent. The standardized variable values would be multiplied by the corresponding factor score coefficients to obtain the factor scores.

Select Surrogate Variables

Surrogate Variables A subset of original variables selected for use in subsequent analysis.

Sometimes, instead of computing factor scores, the researcher wishes to select surrogate variables. Selection of substitute, or **surrogate variables**, involves singling out some of the original variables for use in subsequent analysis. This allows the researcher to conduct subsequent analysis and interpret the results in terms of original variables rather than factor scores. By examining the factor matrix, one could select for each factor the variable with the highest loading on that factor. That variable could then be used as a surrogate variable for the associated factor. This process works well if one factor loading for a variable is clearly higher than all other factor loadings. However, the choice is not as easy if two or more variables have similarly high loadings. In such a case, the choice between these variables should be based on theoretical and measurement considerations. For example, theory may suggest that a variable with a slightly lower loading is more important than one with a slightly higher loading. Likewise, if a variable has a slightly lower loading but has been measured more precisely, it should be selected as the surrogate variable. In Table 19.3, the variables V_1, V_3, and V_5 all have high loadings on factor 1, and all are fairly close in magnitude, although V_1 has relatively the highest loading and would therefore be a likely candidate. However, if prior knowledge suggests that prevention of tooth decay is a very important benefit, V_5 would be selected as the surrogate for factor 1. Also, the choice of a surrogate for factor 2 is not straightforward. Variables V_2, V_4, and V_6 all have comparable high loadings on this factor. If prior knowledge suggests that attractive teeth is the most important social benefit sought from a toothpaste, the researcher would select V_6.

Determine the Model Fit

The final step in factor analysis is to determine the model fit. A basic assumption underlying factor analysis is that the observed correlation between variables can be attributed to common factors. Hence, the correlations between the variables can be deduced or reproduced from the estimated correlations between the variables and the factors. The differences between the observed correlations (as given in the input correlation matrix) and the reproduced correlations (as estimated from the factor matrix) can be examined to determine model fit. These differences are called *residuals*. If there are many large residuals, the factor model does not provide a good fit to the data and the model should be reconsidered. In Table 19.3, we see that only five residuals are larger than .05, indicating an acceptable model fit.

The following example further illustrates principal components factoring in the context of trade promotion.

EXAMPLE

Manufacturing Promotion Components

Item importance is the most important factor influencing the retailer's promotion support decision.

The objective of this study was to develop a rather comprehensive inventory of manufacturer-controlled trade promotion variables and to demonstrate that an association exists between these variables and the retailer's promotion support decision. Retailer or trade support was defined operationally as the trade buyer's attitude toward the promotion.

Factor analysis was performed on the explanatory variables with the primary goal of data reduction. The principal components method, using varimax rotation, reduced the 30 explanatory variables to 8 factors having eigenvalues greater than 1.0. For the purpose of interpretation, each factor comprised variables that loaded .40 or higher on that factor. In two instances, in which variables loaded .40 or above on two factors, each variable was assigned to the factor where it had the highest loading. Only one variable, "ease of handling/stocking at retail," did not load at least .40 on any factor. In all, the 8 factors explained 62 percent of

TABLE 1

FACTORS INFLUENCING TRADE PROMOTIONAL SUPPORT

Factor	*Factor Interpretation (% variance explained)*	*Loading*	*Variables Included in the Factor*
F_1	Item importance (16.3%)	.77	Item is significant enough to warrant promotion
		.75	Category responds well to promotion
		.66	Closest trade competitor is likely to promote item
		.64	Importance of promoted product category
		.59	Item regular (nondeal) sales volume
		.57	Deal meshes with trade promotional requirements
F_2	Promotion elasticity (9.3%)		Buyer's estimate of sales increase on the basis of:
		.86	Price reduction and display
		.82	Display only
		.80	Price reduction only
		.70	Price reduction, display, and advertising
F_3	Manufacturer brand support (8.2%)		Manufacturer's brand support in form of:
		.85	Coupons
		.81	Radio and television advertising
		.80	Newspaper advertising
		.75	Point-of-purchase promotion (e.g., display)
F_4	Manufacturer reputation (7.3%)	.72	Manufacturer's overall reputation
		.72	Manufacturer cooperates in meeting trade's promotional needs
		.64	Manufacturer cooperates on emergency orders, backhaul, etc.
		.55	Quality of sales presentation
		.51	Manufacturer's overall product quality
F_5	Promotion wearout (6.4%)	.93	Product category is overpromoted
		.93	Item is overpromoted
F_6	Sales velocity (5.4%)	−.81	Brand market share rank[a]
		.69	Item regular sales volume[a]
		.46	Item regular sales volume
F_7	Item profitability (4.5%)	.79	Item regular gross margin
		.72	Item regular gross margin[a]
		.49	Reasonableness of deal performance requirements
F_8	Incentive amount (4.2%)	.83	Absolute amount of deal allowances
		.81	Deal allowances as percent of regular trade cost[a]
		.49	Absolute amount of deal allowances[a]

[a]Denotes objective (archival) measure

the total variance. Interpretation of the factor loading matrix was straightforward. Table 1 lists the factors in the order in which they were extracted.

Stepwise discriminant analysis was conducted to determine which, if any, of the eight factors predicted trade support to a statistically significant degree. The factor scores for the eight factors were the explanatory variables. The dependent variable consisted of the retail buyer's overall rating of the deal (rating), which was collapsed into a three-group (low, medium, and high) measure of trade support. The results of the discriminant analyses are shown in Table 2. All eight entered the discriminant functions. Goodness-of-fit measures indicated that, as a group, the eight factors discriminated between high, medium, and low levels of trade support. Multivariate *F* ratios, indicating the degree of discrimination between each pair of groups, were significant at $p < .001$. Correct classification into high, medium, and low categories was achieved for 65 percent of the cases. The order of entry into discriminant analysis was used to determine the relative importance of factors as trade support influencers, as shown in Table 3.[10]

TABLE 2

DISCRIMINANT ANALYSIS RESULTS: ANALYSIS ON RATING AND PERFORM ($n = 564$)

		Standardized Discriminant Coefficients Analysis of Rating	
Factor		*Function 1*	*Function 2*
F_1	Item importance	.861	−.253
F_2	Promotion elasticity	.081	.398
F_3	Manufacturer brand support	.127	−.036
F_4	Manufacturer reputation	.394	.014
F_5	Promotion wearout	−.207	.380
F_6	Sales velocity	.033	−.665
F_7	Item profitability	.614	.357
F_8	Incentive amount	.461	.254
	Wilks's λ (for each factor)	All significant at $p < .001$	
	Multivariate *F* ratios	All significant at $p < .001$	
	Percentage of cases correctly classified	65% correct ($t = 14.4$, $p < .001$)	

TABLE 3

RELATIVE IMPORTANCE OF TRADE SUPPORT INFLUENCERS (AS INDICATED BY ORDER OF ENTRY INTO THE DISCRIMINANT ANALYSIS)

Analysis of Rating	
Order of Entry	*Factor Name*
1	Item importance
2	Item profitability
3	Incentive amount
4	Manufacturer reputation
5	Promotion wearout
6	Sales velocity
7	Promotion elasticity
8	Manufacturer brand support ■

In the next section we describe common factor analysis and provide applications of this method.

TABLE 19.4

RESULTS OF COMMON FACTOR ANALYSIS

Bartlett test of sphericity
Approximate chi-square = 111.314, df = 15, significance = .00000
Kaiser-Meyer-Olkin measure of sampling adequacy = .660

Communalities

Variable	*Initial*	*Extraction*
V_1	.859	.928
V_2	.480	.562
V_3	.814	.836
V_4	.543	.600
V_5	.763	.789
V_6	.587	.723

Initial Eigenvalues

Factor	*Eigenvalue*	*Percentage of Variance*	*Cumulative Percentage*
1	2.731	45.520	45.520
2	2.218	36.969	82.488
3	.442	7.360	89.848
4	.341	5.688	95.536
5	.183	3.044	98.580
6	.085	1.420	100.000

Extraction Sums of Squared Loadings

Factor	*Eigenvalue*	*Percentage of Variance*	*Cumulative Percentage*
1	2.570	42.837	42.837
2	1.868	31.126	73.964

Factor Matrix

	Factor 1	*Factor 2*
V_1	.949	.168
V_2	–.206	.720
V_3	.914	.038
V_4	–.246	.734
V_5	–.850	–.259
V_6	–.101	.844

Rotation Sums of Squared Loadings

Factor	*Eigenvalue*	*Percentage of Variance*	*Cumulative Percentage*
1	2.541	42.343	42.343
2	1.897	31.621	73.964

Rotated Factor Matrix

	Factor 1	*Factor 2*
V_1	.963	–.030
V_2	–.054	.747
V_3	.902	–.150
V_4	–.090	.769
V_5	–.885	–.079
V_6	.075	.847

Factor Score Coefficient Matrix

	Factor 1	*Factor 2*
V_1	.628	.101
V_2	–.024	.253
V_3	.217	–.169
V_4	–.023	.271
V_5	–.166	–.059
V_6	.083	.500

(Continued)

TABLE 19.4 *(Continued)*

Reproduced Correlation Matrix

	V_1	V_2	V_3	V_4	V_5	V_6
V_1	.928*	.022	−.000	.024	−.008	−.042
V_2	−.075	.562*	.006	−.008	.031	.012
V_3	.873	−.161	.836*	−.051	.008	.042
V_4	−.110	.580	−.197	.600*	−.025	−.004
V_5	−.850	−.012	−.786	.019	.789*	−.003
V_6	.046	.629	−.060	.645	−.133	.723*

*The lower-left triangle contains the reproduced correlation matrix; the diagonal, the communalities; the upper-right triangle, the residuals between the observed correlations and the reproduced correlations.

APPLICATIONS OF COMMON FACTOR ANALYSIS

The data of Table 19.1 were analyzed using the common factor analysis model. Instead of using unities in the diagonal, the communalities were inserted. The output, shown in Table 19.4, is similar to the output from principal components analysis presented in Table 19.3. Under "Communalities" under the "Initial" column, the communalities for the variables are no longer 1.0. Based on the eigenvalue criterion, again two factors are extracted. The variances, after extracting the factors, are different from the initial eigenvalues. The first factor accounts for 42.84 percent of the variance, while the second accounts for 31.13 percent, in each case a little less than what was observed in principal components analysis.

The values in the unrotated factor pattern matrix of Table 19.4 are a little different from those in Table 19.3, although the pattern of the coefficients is similar. Sometimes, however, the pattern of loadings for common factor analysis is different than that for principal components analysis, with some variables loading on different factors. The rotated factor matrix has the same pattern as that in Table 19.3, leading to a similar interpretation of the factors.

We end with another application of common factor analysis, in the context of consumer perceptions of rebates.

EXAMPLE

"Common" Rebate Perceptions

Rebates are effective in obtaining new users, brand switching, and repeat purchases among current users. A study was undertaken to determine the factors underlying consumer perception of rebates. A set of 24 items measuring consumer perceptions of rebates was constructed. Respondents were asked to express their degree of agreement with these items on five-point Likert scales. The data were collected by a one-stage area telephone survey conducted in the Memphis metropolitan area. A total of 303 usable questionnaires were obtained.

Three factors characterizing consumers' perceptions of rebates are efforts associated with rebate redemption, faith in the rebate system, and manufacturers' motives for offering rebates.

The 24 items measuring perceptions of rebates were analyzed using common factor analysis. The initial factor solution did not reveal a simple structure of underlying rebate perceptions. Therefore, items that had low loadings were deleted from the scale, and the factor analysis was performed on the remaining items. This second solution yielded three interpretable factors. The factor loadings are presented in the table below. The three factors contained four, four, and three items, respectively, as shown by the underlined factor loadings. Factor 1 seemed to capture the consumers' perceptions of the efforts and difficulties associated with rebate redemption (efforts). Factor 2 was defined as a representation of consumers' faith in the rebate system (faith). Factor 3 represented consumers' perceptions of the manufacturers' motives for offering rebates (motives). The loadings of items on their respective factor ranged from .527 to .744.[11]

FACTOR ANALYSIS OF PERCEPTIONS OF REBATES

	Factor Loading		
Scale Items[a]	*Factor 1*	*Factor 2*	*Factor 3*
Manufacturers make the rebate process too complicated.	.194	.671	−.127
Mail-in rebates are not worth the trouble involved.	−.031	.612	.352
It takes too long to receive the rebate check from the manufacturer.	.013	.718	.051
Manufacturers could do more to make rebates easier to use.	.205	.616	.173
Manufacturers offer rebates because consumers want them.[b]	.660	.172	.101
Today's manufacturers take real interest in consumer welfare.[b]	.569	.203	.334
Consumer benefit is usually the primary consideration in rebate offers.[b]	.660	.002	.318
In general, manufacturers are sincere in their rebate offers to consumers.[b]	.716	.047	−.033
Manufacturers offer rebates to get consumers to buy something they don't really need.	.099	.156	.744
Manufacturers use rebate offers to induce consumers to buy slow-moving items.	.090	.027	.702
Rebate offers require you to buy more of a product than you need.	.230	.066	.527
Eigenvalues	2.030	1.344	1.062
Percentage of explained variance	27.500	12.2	9.700

[a]The response categories for all items were: strongly agree (1), agree (2), neither agree nor disagree (3), disagree (4), strongly disagree (5), and don't know (6). "Don't know" responses were excluded from data analysis.
[b]The scores of these items were reversed. ■

Note that in this example when the initial factor solution was not interpretable, items that had low loadings were deleted and the factor analysis was performed on the remaining items. If the number of variables is large (greater than 15), principal components analysis and common factor analysis result in similar solutions. However, principal components analysis is less prone to misinterpretation and is recommended for the nonexpert user. Research in Practice 19.1 illustrates an application of principal components analysis in international marketing research,[12] whereas Research in Practice 19.2 presents an application in the area of ethics.[13]

RESEARCH IN PRACTICE 19.1

Driving Nuts for Beetles

Generally, with time, consumer needs and tastes change. Consumer preferences for automobiles need to be continually tracked to identify changing demands and specifications. However, there is one car that is quite an exception—the Volkswagen Beetle. More than 21 million have been built since the car was introduced in 1938. Surveys have been conducted in different countries to determine the reasons people purchase Beetles. Principal components analyses of the variables measuring the reasons for owning Beetles have consistently revealed one dominant factor—fanatical loyalty. This noisy and cramped "bug" has inspired devotion in drivers. Now old bugs are being sought everywhere. "The Japanese are going absolutely nuts for Beetles," says Jack Finn, a recycler of old Beetles in West Palm Beach, Florida. Because of faithful loyalty for the "bug," VW has repositioned the beetle as a new shiny VW Passat, a premium quality car which gives an image of sophistication and class as opposed to the old one which symbolized a low-priced brand.

RESEARCH IN PRACTICE 19.2

Factors Predicting Unethical Marketing Research Practices

In order to identify organizational variables that are determinants of the incidence of unethical marketing research practices, 420 marketing professionals were surveyed. These marketing professionals were asked to provide responses on several scales, and to provide evaluations of incidence of 15 research practices that have been found to pose research ethics problems.

One of these scales included 11 items pertaining to the extent ethical problems plagued the organization, and what top management's actions were toward ethical situations. A principal components analysis with varimax rotation indicated that the data could be represented by two factors. These two factors were then used in a multiple regression along with four other predictor variables. They were found to be the two best predictors of unethical marketing research practices.

Factor Analysis of Ethical Problems and Top Management Action Scales

	Extent of Ethical Problems within the Organization (Factor 1)	*Top Management Actions on Ethics (Factor 2)*
1. Successful executives in my company make rivals look bad in the eyes of important people in my company.	.66	
2. Peer executives in my company often engage in behaviors that I consider to be unethical.	.68	
3. There are many opportunities for peer executives in my company to engage in unethical behaviors.	.43	
4. Successful executives in my company take credit for the ideas and accomplishment of others.	.81	
5. In order to succeed in my company, one must often compromise one's ethics.	.66	
6. Successful executives in my company are generally more unethical than unsuccessful executives.	.64	
7. Successful executives in my company look for a "scapegoat" when they feel they may be associated with failure.	.78	
8. Successful executives in my company withhold information that is detrimental to their self-interest.	.68	
9. Top management in my company has let it be known in no uncertain terms that unethical behaviors will not be tolerated.		.73
10. If an executive in my company is discovered to have engaged in unethical behavior that results primarily in personal gain (rather than corporate gain), he/she will be promptly reprimanded.		.80
11. If an executive in my company is discovered to have engaged in an unethical behavior that results primarily in corporate gain (rather than personal gain), he/she will be promptly reprimanded.		.78
Eigenvalue	5.06	1.17
Percentage of variance explained	46%	11%
Coefficient alpha	.87	.75

To simplify the table, only varimax-rotated loading of .40 or greater are reported.
Each was rated on a five-point scale with 1 = strongly agree and 5 = strongly disagree.

FOCUS ON Burke

Burke states its goal in using factor analysis in one word . . . simplify! In a typical interview Burke asks many questions and groups of these questions are highly correlated with each other. Whether factor analysis is used for clarifying which questions tend to measure the same basic concepts or to aid in using the question responses as predictors in regression, Burke has to be careful in interpreting the results.

A recent project conducted by Burke involved 16 questions (variables). The correlation matrix was subjected to principal components analysis. Five factors or components were retained. The varimax rotated solution shows that component 5 is essentially a "one-question" component (we have omitted loadings less than .4 to make the picture clearer). Note the questions that load on the first rotated component.

ROTATED COMPONENT MATRIX[a]

	Component				
	1	*2*	*3*	*4*	*5*
V01		−.649			
V02	.460			.720	
V03					.873
V04	.553	.675			
V05			.840		
V06			.683		
V07			.857		
V08				.881	
V09	.898				
V10	.472				
V11		.697			
V12	.826				
V13	.764				
V14	.701				
V15		.860			
V16	.578	.617			

Extraction Method: Principal Component Analysis.
Rotation Method: Varimax with Kaiser Normalization.
[a]Rotation converged in 6 iterations.

As a "one-question" component is not very parsimonious, we will find a four-component solution. Note that V10 now appears to be somewhat related to variables 2, 8, and 14, although it was previously somewhat more related to the questions in component 1. V14 now appears to be less related to component 1 than seen in the first (five-component) solution. The structure of components 2 and 3 remain very stable in the two solutions. This leads to several practical considerations:

(Continued)

INTERNET AND COMPUTER APPLICATIONS

Computer programs are available to implement both the approaches: principal components analysis and common factor analysis. The mainframe and microcomputer programs are similar for SPSS, SAS, and BMDP. In the SPSS packages, the program FACTOR may be used for principal components analysis as well as for common factor analysis. Some other methods of factor analysis are also available and factor scores are calculated.

In the SAS system, the program PRINCOMP performs principal components analysis and calculates principal component scores. To perform common factor analysis, the

1. Not all questions will necessarily be correlated enough with other questions to form a component. When this happens, it is often the case that the question is ambiguous or one in which everyone seems to give the same answer with only random variation among the responses. Take a look at the question and see if the question was a "good one."
2. The questions loading together can change when you rotate a different number of components. Look to the most stable ones for your interpretation of the results. Even a high loading on a component doesn't mean that it will be a relationship that holds up under a different rotation (look at V14 on the first, five-component, solution).
3. As a last point, the questions that load together are a result of the relative size, not the absolute size, of the correlations between the questions. You could divide all the correlations in this matrix by 10 and the same questions would load on the same components after rotation . . . the loadings would just be smaller. You must not assume that because questions load together on a component that they have a strong relationship. The strength of relationship is indicated by how much of the variance in the original variable is captured in the factor.

ROTATED COMPONENT MATRIX[a]

	Component			
	1	*2*	*3*	*4*
V01		−.651		
V02				.813
V03				
V04	.516	.662		
V05			.837	
V06			.672	
V07			.843	
V08				.817
V09	.870			
V10				.436
V11		.679		
V12	.734			
V13	.810			
V14	.589			.438
V15		.860		
V16	.550	.604		

Extraction Method: Principal Component Analysis.
Rotation Method: Varimax with Kaiser Normalization.
[a]Rotation converged in 5 iterations.

program FACTOR can be used. The FACTOR program also performs principal components analysis. In the BMDP package, principal components analysis and common factor analysis can be performed with the 4M program.[14]

In Minitab, factor analysis can be accessed using Multivariate>Factor analysis. Principal components or maximum likelihood can be used to determine the initial factor extraction. If maximum likelihood is used, specify the number of factors to extract. If a number is not specified with a principal component extraction, the program will set it equal to a number of variables in the data set. Factor analysis is not available in Excel (version 7.0 for the PC).

SUMMARY

Factor analysis is a class of procedures used for reducing and summarizing data. Each variable is expressed as a linear combination of the underlying factors. Likewise, the factors themselves can be expressed as linear combinations of the observed variables. The factors are extracted in such a way that the first factor accounts for the highest variance in the data, the second the next highest, and so on. Additionally, it is possible to extract the factors so that the factors are uncorrelated, as in principal components analysis.

In formulating the factor analysis problem, the variables to be included in the analysis should be specified based on past research, theory, and the judgment of the researcher. These variables should be measured on an interval or ratio scale. Factor analysis is based on a matrix of correlation between the variables. The appropriateness of the correlation matrix for factor analysis can be statistically tested.

The two basic approaches to factor analysis are principal components analysis and common factor analysis. In principal components analysis, the total variance in the data is considered. Principal components analysis is recommended when the researcher's primary concern is to determine the minimum number of factors that will account for maximum variance in the data for use in subsequent multivariate analysis. In common factor analysis, the factors are estimated based only on the common variance. This method is appropriate when the primary concern is to identify the underlying dimensions, and when the common variance is of interest. This method is also known as principal axis factoring.

The number of factors that should be extracted can be determined a priori or based on eigenvalues, scree plots, percentage of variance, split-half reliability, or significance tests. Although the initial or unrotated factor matrix indicates the relationship between the factors and individual variables, it seldom results in factors that can be interpreted, because the factors are correlated with many variables. Therefore, rotation is used to transform the factor matrix into a simpler one that is easier to interpret. The most commonly used method of rotation is the varimax procedure, which results in orthogonal factors. If the factors are highly correlated in the population, oblique rotation can be used. The rotated factor matrix forms the basis for interpreting the factors.

Factor scores can be computed for each respondent. Alternatively, surrogate variables may be selected by examining the factor matrix and selecting for each factor a variable with the highest or near-highest loading. The differences between the observed correlations and the reproduced correlations, as estimated from the factor matrix, can be examined to determine model fit.

KEY TERMS AND CONCEPTS

factor analysis
interdependence technique
factor
Bartlett's test of sphericity
correlation matrix
communality
eigenvalue
factor loadings
factor loading plot
factor matrix
factor scores
Kaiser-Meyer-Olkin (KMO) measure of sampling adequacy
percentage of variance
residuals
scree plot
principal components analysis
common factor analysis
orthogonal rotation
varimax procedure
oblique rotation
factor scores

ACRONYMS

The steps involved in conducting factor analysis may be summarized by the acronym FACTOR STEP:

F ormulate the problem
A priori or otherwise determine the number of factors
C orrelation matrix
T est for the appropriateness of factor analysis
O bserve the rotated factor matrix: interpretation of factors
R otation

S urrogate variable
T esting for model fit
E stimate the factor scores
P rincipal components or common factor analysis

EXERCISES

Questions

1. How is factor analysis different from multiple regression and discriminant analysis?
2. What are the major uses of factor analysis?
3. Describe the factor analysis model.
4. What hypothesis is examined by Bartlett's test of sphericity? For what purpose is this test used?
5. What is meant by the term "communality of a variable"?
6. Briefly define the following: eigenvalue, factor loadings, factor matrix, and factor scores.
7. For what purpose is the Kaiser-Meyer-Olkin measure of sampling adequacy used?
8. What is the major difference between principal components analysis and common factor analysis?
9. Explain how eigenvalues are used to determine the number of factors.
10. What is a scree plot? For what purpose is it used?
11. Why is it useful to rotate the factors? Which is the most common method of rotation?
12. What guidelines are available for interpreting the factors?
13. When is it useful to calculate factor scores?
14. What are surrogate variables? How are they determined?
15. How is the fit of the factor analysis model examined?

Problems

1. Complete the following portion of an output from principal component analysis:

Variable	*Communality*	*Factor*	*Eigenvalue*	*Percentage of Variance*
V_1	1.01	1	3.25	
V_2	1.02	2	1.78	
V_3	1.03	3	1.23	
V_4	1.04	4	.78	
V_5	1.05	5	.35	
V_6	1.06	6	.30	
V_7	1.07	7	.19	
V_8	1.08	8	.12	

2. Draw a scree plot based on the data given in problem 1.
3. How many factors should be extracted in problem 1? Explain your reasoning.

INTERNET AND COMPUTER EXERCISES

1. In a study of the relationship between household behavior and shopping behavior, data on the following lifestyle statements were obtained on a seven-point scale (1= disagree, 7 = agree):

V_1	I would rather spend a quiet evening at home than go out to a party.
V_2	I always check prices, even on small items.
V_3	Magazines are more interesting than movies.
V_4	I won't buy products advertised on billboards.
V_5	I am a homebody.
V_6	I save and cash coupons.
V_7	Companies waste a lot of money advertising.

The data obtained from a pretest sample of 25 respondents are in the following table.

a. Analyze this data using principal components analysis, using the varimax rotation procedure.
b. Interpret the factors extracted.
c. Calculate factor scores for each respondent.
d. If surrogate variables were to be selected, which ones would you select?
e. Examine the model fit.
f. Analyze the data using common factor analysis, and answer questions b through e.

No.	V_1	V_2	V_3	V_4	V_5	V_6	V_7
1	6	2	7	6	5	3	5
2	5	7	5	6	6	6	4
3	5	3	4	5	6	6	7
4	3	2	2	5	1	3	2
5	4	2	3	2	2	1	3
6	2	6	2	4	3	7	5
7	1	3	3	6	2	5	7
8	3	5	1	4	2	5	6
9	7	3	6	3	5	2	4
10	6	3	3	4	4	6	5
11	6	6	2	6	4	4	7
12	3	2	2	7	6	1	6
13	5	7	6	2	2	6	1
14	6	3	5	5	7	2	3
15	3	2	4	3	2	6	5
16	2	7	5	1	4	5	2
17	3	2	2	7	2	4	6
18	6	4	5	4	7	3	3
19	7	2	6	2	5	2	1
20	5	6	6	3	4	5	3
21	2	3	3	2	1	2	6
22	3	4	2	1	4	3	6
23	2	6	3	2	1	5	3
24	6	5	7	4	5	7	2
25	7	6	5	4	6	5	3

Fundamental Equations of Factor Analysis

In the factor analysis model, hypothetical components are derived that account for the linear relationship between observed variables.[1] The factor analysis model requires that the relationships between observed variables be linear and that the variables have nonzero correlations between them. The derived hypothetical components have the following properties:

1. They form a linearly independent set of variables. No hypothetical component is derivable from the other hypothetical components as a linear combination of them.
2. The hypothetical components' variables can be divided into two basic kinds of components: common factors and unique factors. These two components can be distinguished in terms of the patterns of weights in the linear equations, which derive the observed variables from the hypothetical components' variables. A common factor has more than one variable with a nonzero weight or factor loading associated with the factor. A unique factor has only one variable with a nonzero weight associated with the factor. Hence, only one variable depends on a unique factor.
3. Common factors are always assumed to be uncorrelated with the unique factors. Unique factors are also usually assumed to be mutually uncorrelated, but common factors may or may not be correlated with each other.
4. Generally, it is assumed that there are fewer common factors than there are observed variables. However, the number of unique factors is usually assumed to be equal to the number of observed variables.

The following notations are used.

$\boldsymbol{X}$ = An $n \times 1$ random vector of observed random variables $X_1, X_2, X_3, \ldots X_n$.

It is assumed that

$$E(\boldsymbol{X}) = 0 \text{ and}$$
$$E(\boldsymbol{XX'}) = \boldsymbol{R}_{xx}\text{, a correlation matrix with unities in the main diagonal.}$$

$\boldsymbol{F}$ = An $m \times 1$ vector of m common factors, $F_1, F_2, \ldots, F_m$.

[1]The material in this appendix has been drawn from Stanley A. Muliak, *The Foundations of Factor Analysis* (New York: McGraw-Hill, 1972).

It is assumed that

$$E(\boldsymbol{F}) = 0 \text{ and}$$
$$E(\boldsymbol{FF'}) = \boldsymbol{R}_{ff}\text{, a correlation matrix.}$$

$\boldsymbol{U}$ = An $n \times 1$ random vector of the n unique factors variables, $U_1, U_2, \ldots, U_n$.

It is assumed that

$$E(\boldsymbol{U}) = 0\text{, and}$$
$$E(\boldsymbol{UU'}) = \boldsymbol{I}.$$

The unique factors are normalized to have unit variances and are mutually uncorrelated.

$\boldsymbol{A}$ = An $n \times m$ matrix of coefficients called the factor pattern matrix.

$\boldsymbol{V}$ = An $n \times n$ diagonal matrix of coefficients for the unique factors.

The observed variables, which are the coordinates of X, are weighted combinations of the common factors and the unique factors. The fundamental equation of factor analysis can then be written as:

$$\boldsymbol{X} = \boldsymbol{AF} + \boldsymbol{VU}$$

The correlations between variables in terms of the factors may be derived as follows:

$$\begin{aligned}\boldsymbol{R}_{xx} &= E(\boldsymbol{XX'})\\ &= E\{(\boldsymbol{AF}+\boldsymbol{VU})(\boldsymbol{AF}+\boldsymbol{VU})'\}\\ &= E\{(\boldsymbol{AF}+\boldsymbol{VU})(\boldsymbol{F'A'}+\boldsymbol{U'V'})\}\\ &= E(\boldsymbol{AFF'A'}+\boldsymbol{AFU'V'}+\boldsymbol{VUF'A'}+\boldsymbol{VUU'V'})\\ &= \boldsymbol{AR}_{ff}\boldsymbol{A'}+\boldsymbol{AR}_{fu}\boldsymbol{V'}+\boldsymbol{VR}_{uf}\boldsymbol{A'}+\boldsymbol{V}^2\end{aligned}$$

Given that the common factors are uncorrelated with the unique factors, we have:

$$\boldsymbol{R}_{fu} = \boldsymbol{R}_{uf}' = 0.$$

Hence,

$$\boldsymbol{R}_{xx} = \boldsymbol{AR}_{ff}\boldsymbol{A'} + \boldsymbol{V}^2$$

Suppose we subtract the matrix of unique factor variance, $\boldsymbol{V}^2$, from both sides. We then obtain:

$$\boldsymbol{R}_{xx} - \boldsymbol{V}^2 = \boldsymbol{A}\boldsymbol{R}_{ff}\boldsymbol{A}'$$

$\boldsymbol{R}_{xx}$ is dependent only on the common factor variables, and the correlations among the variables are related only to the common factors. Let $\boldsymbol{R}_c = \boldsymbol{R}_{xx} - \boldsymbol{V}^2$ be the reduced correlation matrix.

We have already defined the factor pattern matrix $\boldsymbol{A}$. The coefficients of the factor pattern matrix are weights assigned to the common factors when the observed variables are expressed as linear combinations of the common and unique factors. We now define the factor structure matrix. The coefficients of the factor structure matrix are the covariances between the observed variables and the factors. The factor structure matrix is helpful in the interpretation of factors as it shows which variables are similar to a common factor variable. The factor structure matrix, $\boldsymbol{A}_s$, is defined as:

$$\begin{aligned}\boldsymbol{A}_s &= E(\boldsymbol{X}\boldsymbol{F}') \\ &= E[(\boldsymbol{A}\boldsymbol{F} + \boldsymbol{V}\boldsymbol{U})\boldsymbol{F}'] \\ &= \boldsymbol{A}\boldsymbol{R}_{ff} + \boldsymbol{V}\boldsymbol{R}_{uf} \\ &= \boldsymbol{A}\boldsymbol{R}_{ff}\end{aligned}$$

Thus, the factor structure matrix is equivalent to the factor pattern matrix $\boldsymbol{A}$ multiplied by the matrix of covariances among the factors $\boldsymbol{R}_{ff}$. Substituting $\boldsymbol{A}_s$ for $\boldsymbol{A}\boldsymbol{R}_{ff}$, the reduced correlation matrix becomes the product of factor structure and the factor pattern matrix.

$$\begin{aligned}\boldsymbol{R}_c &= \boldsymbol{A}\boldsymbol{R}_{ff}\boldsymbol{A}' \\ &= \boldsymbol{A}_s\boldsymbol{A}'\end{aligned}$$

Chapter 20

"We all believe that every population is made up of distinct segments. If we have measured the right variables, cluster analysis helps us to see if groups exist that are more like each other than they are like members of other groups."

Tom Myers, senior consultant, Burke Customer Satisfaction Associates

Cluster Analysis

OBJECTIVES

After reading this chapter, the student should be able to

1. describe the basic concept and scope of cluster analysis and its importance in marketing research
2. discuss the statistics associated with cluster analysis
3. explain the procedure for conducting cluster analysis including formulating the problem, selecting a distance measure, selecting a clustering procedure, deciding on the number of clusters, interpreting and profiling clusters
4. describe the purpose and methods for evaluating the quality of clustering results and assessing reliability and validity
5. discuss the applications of nonhierarchical clustering and clustering of variables

OVERVIEW

Like factor analysis (chapter 19), cluster analysis examines an entire set of interdependent relationships. Cluster analysis makes no distinction between dependent and independent variables. Rather, interdependent relationships between the whole set of variables are examined. The primary objective of cluster analysis is to classify objects into relatively homogenous groups based on the set of variables considered. Objects in a group are relatively similar in terms of these variables and different from objects in other groups. When used in this manner, cluster analysis is the obverse of factor analysis, in that it reduces the number of objects, not the number of variables, by grouping them into a much smaller number of clusters.

This chapter describes the basic concept of cluster analysis. The steps involved in conducting cluster analysis are discussed and illustrated in the context of hierarchical clustering by using a popular computer program. Then an application of nonhierarchical clustering is presented, followed by a discussion of clustering of variables. We begin with two examples.

DEPARTMENT STORE PATRONAGE PROJECT

Cluster Analysis

Respondents were clustered on the basis of self-reported importance attached to each factor of the choice criteria utilized in selecting a department store. The results indicated that respondents could be clustered into four segments. Differences among the segments were statistically tested. Thus, each segment contained respondents who were relatively homogenous with respect to their choice criteria. The store choice model was then estimated separately for each segment. This procedure resulted in choice models that better represented the underlying choice process of respondents in specific segments.

EXAMPLE

Ice Cream Shops for "Hot" Regions

Haagen-Dazs increased its penetration by identifying geodemographic clusters offering potential for increased ice cream sales.

Haagen-Dazs Shoppe Co., with more than 300 retail ice cream shops throughout the United States, was interested in expanding its customer base. The objective was to identify potential consumer segments that could generate additional sales. Geodemography, a method of clustering consumers based on geographic, demographic, and lifestyle characteristics, was employed for this purpose. Primary research was conducted to develop demographic and psychographic profiles of Haagen-Dazs Shoppe users, including frequency of purchase, time of the day they came in, day of the week, and other product use variables. The addresses and zip codes of the respondents were also obtained. The respondents were then assigned to 40 geodemographic clusters based on the clustering procedure developed by Claritas. For each geodemographic cluster, the profile of Haagen-Dazs customers was compared to the cluster profile to determine the degree of penetration. Using this information, Haagen-Dazs was also able to identify several potential customer groups from which to attract traffic.[1] ■

The Haagen-Dazs example illustrates the use of clustering to arrive at homogenous segments for the purpose of formulating specific marketing strategies. In the department store example, clustering was used to group respondents for subsequent multivariate analysis.

BASIC CONCEPT

Cluster analysis is a class of techniques used to classify objects or cases into relatively homogenous groups called *clusters*. Objects in each cluster tend to be similar to each other and dissimilar to objects in the other clusters. Cluster analysis is also called *classification analysis*, or *numerical taxonomy*.[2] We will be concerned with clustering procedures that assign each object to one and only one cluster.[3] Figure 20.1 shows an ideal clustering situation, in which the clusters are distinctly separated on two variables: quality-consciousness (variable 1) and price-sensitivity (variable 2). Note that each consumer falls into one cluster and there are no overlapping areas. Figure 20.2, on the other hand, presents a clustering situation that is more likely to be encountered in practice. In Figure 20.2, the boundaries for some of the clusters are not clear-cut, and the classification of some consumers is not obvious, as many of them could be grouped into one cluster or another.

Both cluster analysis and discriminant analysis are concerned with classification. However, discriminant analysis requires prior knowledge of the cluster or group membership for each object or case included, to develop the classification rule. In contrast, in cluster analysis there is no a priori information about the group or cluster membership for any of the objects. Groups or clusters are suggested by the data, not defined a priori.[4]

Figure 20.1
An Ideal Clustering Situation

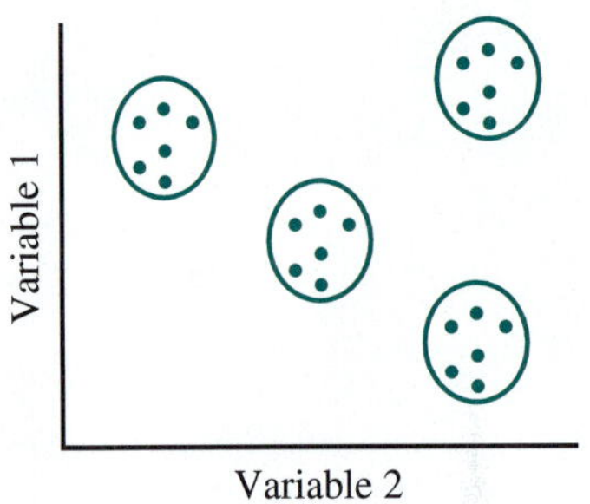

Figure 20.2
A Practical Clustering Situation

Cluster analysis has been used in marketing for a variety of purposes, including the following:[5]

- *Segmenting the market*: For example, consumers may be clustered on the basis of benefits sought from the purchase of a product. Each cluster would consist of consumers who are relatively homogenous in terms of the benefits they seek.[6] This approach is called *benefit segmentation*. We illustrate it with the following example.

EXAMPLE

The Vacationing Demanders, Educationalists, and Escapists

Cluster analysis has revealed distinct market segments of international vacationers.

In a study examining decision-making patterns among international vacationers, 260 respondents provided information on six psychographic orientations: psychological, educational, social, relaxational, physiological, and aesthetic. Cluster analysis was used to group respondents into psychographic segments. The results suggested that there were three meaningful segments based on these lifestyles. The first segment (53 percent) consisted of individuals who were high on nearly all lifestyle scales. This group was called the "demanders." The second group (20 percent) was high on the educational scale and was named the "educationalists." The last group (26 percent) was high on relaxation and low on social scales and was named the "escapists." Specific marketing strategies were formulated to attract vacationers in each segment.[7] ■

- *Understanding buyer behaviors*: Cluster analysis can be used to identify homogenous groups of buyers. Then the buying behavior of each group may be examined separately, as in the Department Store Patronage Project, in which respondents were clustered on the basis of self-reported importance attached to each factor of the choice criteria utilized in selecting a department store. Cluster analysis has also been used to identify the kinds of strategies automobile purchasers use to obtain external information.
- *Identifying new-product opportunities*: By clustering brands and products, competitive sets within the market can be determined. Brands in the same cluster compete more

fiercely with each other than with brands in other clusters. A firm can examine its current offerings compared to those of its competitors to identify potential new-product opportunities.

- *Selecting test markets*: By grouping cities into homogenous clusters, it is possible to select comparable cities to test various marketing strategies.
- *Reducing data*: Cluster analysis can be used as a general data reduction tool to develop clusters or subgroups of data that are more managable than individual observations. Subsequent multivariate analysis is conducted on the clusters rather than on the individual observations. For example, to describe differences in consumers' product usage behavior, the consumers may first be clustered into groups. The differences among the groups may then be examined using multiple discriminant analysis.

STATISTICS ASSOCIATED WITH CLUSTER ANALYSIS

Before discussing the statistics associated with cluster analysis, it should be mentioned that most clustering methods are relatively simple procedures that are not supported by an extensive body of statistical reasoning. Rather, most clustering methods are heuristics, which are based on algorithms. Thus cluster analysis contrasts sharply with analysis of variance, regression, discriminant analysis, and factor analysis, which are based on an extensive body of statistical reasoning. Although many clustering methods have important statistical properties, the fundamental simplicity of these methods needs to be recognized.[8] The following statistics and concepts are associated with cluster analysis.

Agglomeration schedule. Gives information on the objects or cases being combined at each stage of a hierarchical clustering process.
Cluster centroid. The mean values of the variables for all the cases or objects in a particular cluster.
Cluster centers. The initial starting points in nonhierarchical clustering. Clusters are built around these centers or *seeds*.
Cluster membership. Indicates the cluster to which each object or case belongs.
Dendrogram. Also called a *tree graph*, a graphical device for displaying clustering results. Vertical lines represent clusters that are joined together. The position of the line on the scale indicates the distances at which clusters were joined. The dendrogram is read from left to right. (Figure 20.8 is a dendrogram.)
Distances between cluster centers. Indicate how separated the individual pairs of clusters are. Clusters that are widely separated are distinct, and therefore desirable.
Icicle diagram. An icicle diagram is a graphical display of clustering results, so-called because it resembles a row of icicles hanging from the eaves of a house. The columns correspond to the objects being clustered, and the rows correspond to the number of clusters. An icicle diagram is read from bottom to top. (Figure 20.7 is an icicle diagram.)
Similarity/distance coefficient matrix. A similarity/distance coefficient matrix is a lower-triangle matrix containing pairwise distances between objects or cases.

CONDUCTING CLUSTER ANALYSIS

The steps involved in conducting cluster analysis are listed in Figure 20.3. The first step is to formulate the clustering problem by defining the variables on which the clustering will be based. Then an appropriate distance measure must be selected. The distance measure determines how similar or dissimilar the objects being clustered are. Several clustering procedures have been developed, and the researcher should select one that is appropriate for the problem at hand. Deciding on the number of clusters requires judgment on the part of the researcher. The derived clusters should be interpreted in terms of the variables used to cluster them and profiled in terms of additional salient variables. Finally, the researcher must assess the validity of the clustering process.

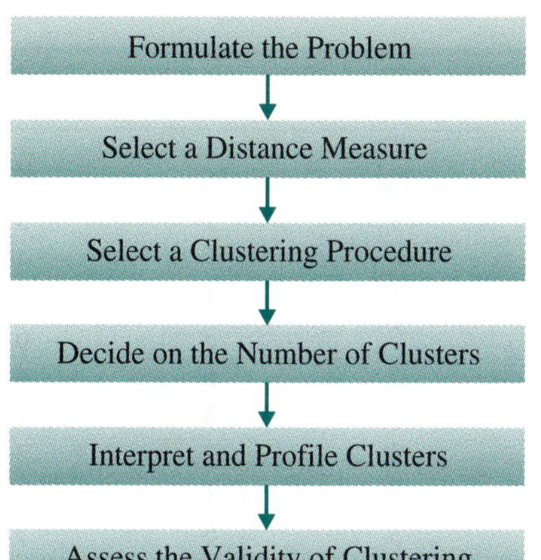

Figure 20.3
Conducting Cluster Analysis

Formulate the Problem

Perhaps the most important part of formulating the clustering problem is selecting the variables on which the clustering is based. Inclusion of even one or two irrelevant variables may distort an otherwise useful clustering solution. Basically, the set of variables selected should describe the similarity between objects in terms that are relevant to the marketing research problem. The variables should be selected based on past research, theory, or a consideration of the hypotheses being tested. In exploratory research, the researcher should exercise judgment and intuition.

To illustrate, we consider a clustering of consumers based on attitudes toward shopping. Based on past research, six attitudinal variables were identified. Consumers were asked to express their degree of agreement with the following statements on a seven-point scale (1 = disagree, 7 = agree):

V_1: Shopping is fun.
V_2: Shopping is bad for your budget.
V_3: I combine shopping with eating out.
V_4: I try to get the best buys while shopping.
V_5: I don't care about shopping.
V_6: You can save a lot of money by comparing prices.

Data obtained from a pretest sample of 20 respondents are shown in Table 20.1. Note that, in practice, clustering is done on much larger samples of 100 or more. A small sample size has been used to illustrate the clustering process.

Select a Distance or Similarity Measure

Because the objective of clustering is to group similar objects together, some measure is needed to assess how similar or different the objects are. The most common approach is to measure similarity in terms of distance between pairs of objects. Objects with smaller distances between them are more similar to each other than are those at larger distances. There are several ways to compute the distance between two objects.[9]

The most commonly used measure of similarity is the euclidean distance or its square.[10] The **euclidean distance** is the square root of the sum of the squared differences in values for each variable. Other distance measures are also available. The *city-block* or *Manhattan distance* between two objects is the sum of the absolute differences in values for each variable. The *Chebychev distance* between two objects is the maximum absolute difference in values for any variable. For our example, we will use the squared euclidean distance.

Euclidean Distance The square root of the sum of the squared differences in values for each variable.

If the variables are measured in vastly different units, the clustering solution will be influenced by the units of measurement. In a supermarket shopping study, attitudinal

Figure 20.5
Linkage Methods of Clustering

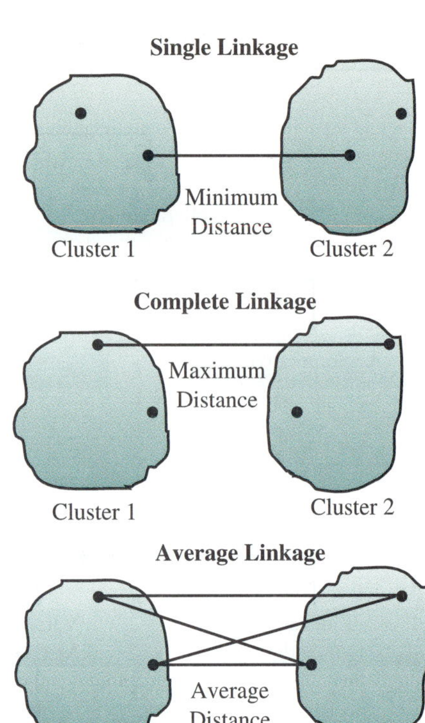

Parallel Threshold Method Nonhierarchical clustering method that specifies several cluster centers at once. All objects that are within a prespecified threshold value from the center are grouped together.

Optimizing Partitioning Method Nonhierarchical clustering method that allows for later reassignment of objects to clusters to optimize an overall criterion.

grouped together. Then a new cluster center or seed is selected, and the process is repeated for the unclustered points. Once an object is clustered with a seed, it is no longer considered for clustering with subsequent seeds. The **parallel threshold method** operates similarly, except that several cluster centers are selected simultaneously and objects within the threshold level are grouped with the nearest center. The **optimizing partitioning method** differs from the two threshold procedures in that objects can later be reassigned to clusters to optimize an overall criterion, such as average within-cluster distance for a given number of clusters.

Figure 20.6
Other Agglomerative Clustering Methods

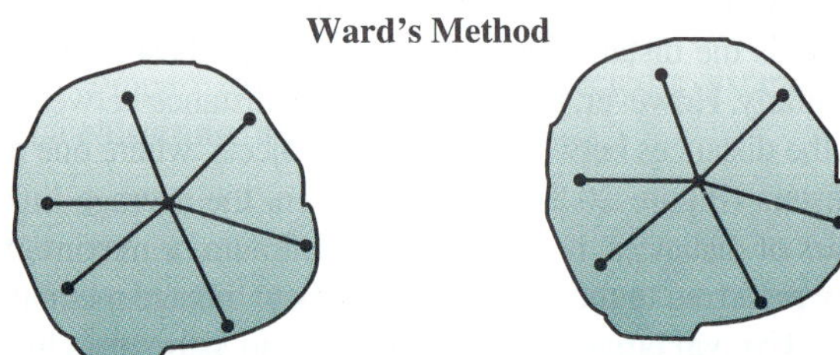

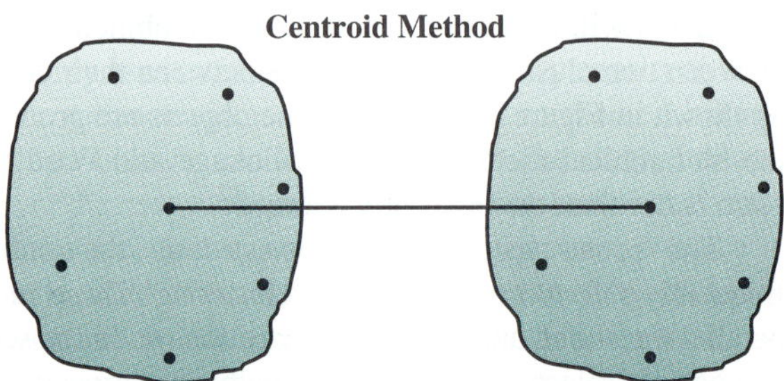

Two major disadvantages of the nonhierarchical procedures are that the number of clusters must be prespecified and the selection of cluster centers is arbitrary. Furthermore, the clustering results may depend on how the centers are selected. Many nonhierarchical programs select the first k (k = number of clusters) cases without missing values as initial cluster centers. Thus, the clustering results may depend on the order of observations in the data. Yet nonhierarchical clustering is faster than hierarchical methods and has merit when the number of objects or observations is large. It has been suggested that the hierarchical and nonhierarchical methods be used in tandem. First, an initial clustering solution is obtained using a hierarchical procedure, such as average linkage or Ward's. The number of clusters and cluster centroids so obtained are used as inputs to the optimizing partitioning method.[13]

Choice of a clustering method and choice of a distance measure are interrelated. For example, squared euclidean distances should be used with the Ward's and centroid methods. Several nonhierarchical procedures also use squared euclidean distances.

We will use the Ward's procedure to illustrate hierarchical clustering. The output obtained by clustering the data of Table 20.1 is given in Table 20.2. Useful information is contained in the agglomeration schedule, which shows the number of cases or clusters being combined at each stage. The first line represents stage 1, with 19 clusters. Respondents 14 and 16 are combined at this stage, as shown in the columns labeled "Clusters Combined." The squared euclidean distance between these two respondents is given under the column labeled "Coefficient." The column entitled "Stage Cluster First Appears" indicates the stage at which a cluster is first formed. To illustrate, an entry of 1 at stage 7 indicates that respondent 14 was first grouped at stage 1. The last column, "Next Stage," indicates the stage at which another case (respondent) or cluster is combined with this one. Because the number in the first line of the last column is 7, we see that at stage 7, respondent 10 is combined with 14 and 16 to form a single cluster. Similarly, the second line represents stage 2 with 18 clusters. In stage 2, respondents 2 and 13 are grouped together.

Another important part of the output is contained in the icicle plot given in Figure 20.7. The columns correspond to the objects being clustered, in this case respondents labeled 1 through 20. The rows correspond to the number of clusters. This figure is read from bottom to top. At first, all cases are considered as individual clusters. Because there are 20 respondents, there are 20 initial clusters. At the first step, the two closest objects are combined, resulting in 19 clusters. The last line of Figure 20.7 shows these 19 clusters. The two cases, respondents 14 and 16, that have been combined at this stage have no blank (white) space separating them. Row number 18 corresponds to the next stage, with 18 clusters. At this stage, respondents 2 and 13 are grouped together. Thus, at this stage there are 18 clusters; 16 of them consist of individual respondents, and two contain two respondents each. Each subsequent step leads to the formation of a new cluster in one of three ways: (1) two individual cases are grouped together, (2) a case is joined to an already existing cluster, or (3) two clusters are grouped together.

Another graphic device that is useful in displaying clustering results is the dendrogram (see Figure 20.8). The dendrogram is read from left to right. Vertical lines represent clusters that are joined together. The position of the line on the scale indicates the distances at which clusters were joined. Because many of the distances in the early stages are of similar magnitude, it is difficult to tell the sequence in which some of the early clusters are formed. However, it is clear that in the last two stages, the distances at which the clusters are being combined are large. This information is useful in deciding on the number of clusters (see next section).

It is also possible to obtain information on cluster membership of cases if the number of clusters is specified. Although this information can be discerned from the icicle plot, a tabular display is helpful. Table 20.2 contains the cluster membership for the cases, depending on whether the final solution contains two, three, or four clusters. Information of this type can be obtained for any number of clusters and is useful for deciding on the number of clusters.

a predominance of British companies in the two least successful clusters. Apparently Japanese companies do not deploy strategies that are unique to them; rather, more of them pursue strategies that work effectively in the British market.

The findings indicate that there are generic strategies that describe successful companies irrespective of their industry. Three successful strategies can be identified. The first is the Quality Marketeers strategy. These companies have strengths in marketing and research and development. They concentrate their technical developments on achieving high quality rather than pure innovation. These companies are characterized by entrepreneurial organizations, long-range planning, and well-communicated sense of mission. The second generic strategy is that of the Innovators who are weaker on advanced research and development but are entrepreneurial and driven by a quest for innovation. The last successful group is the Mature Marketeers, who are highly profit oriented and have in-depth marketing skills. All three appear to consist of highly marketing-oriented businesses.[15] ■

APPLICATIONS OF NONHIERARCHICAL CLUSTERING

We illustrate the nonhierarchical procedure using the data in Table 20.1 and an optimizing partitioning method. Based on the results of hierarchical clustering, a three-cluster solution was prespecified. The results are presented in Table 20.4. The initial cluster centers are the values of the first three cases. The classification cluster centers are interim centers used for the assignment of cases. Each case is assigned to the nearest classification cluster center. The classification centers are updated until the stopping criteria are reached. The final cluster centers represent the variable means for the cases in the final clusters.

Table 20.4 also displays cluster membership and the distance between each case and its classification center. Note that the cluster memberships given in Table 20.2 (hierarchical clustering) and Table 20.4 (nonhierarchical clustering) are identical. (Cluster 1 of Table 20.2 is labeled cluster 3 in Table 20.4, and cluster 3 of Table 20.2 is labeled cluster 1 in Table 20.4.) The distances between the final cluster centers indicate that the pairs of

TABLE 20.4

RESULTS OF NONHIERARCHICAL CLUSTERING

Initial Cluster Centers

Cluster	V_1	V_2	V_3	V_4
1	4.0000	6.0000	3.0000	7.0000
2	2.0000	3.0000	2.0000	4.0000
3	7.0000	2.0000	6.0000	4.0000

Cluster	V_5	V_6
1	2.0000	7.0000
2	7.0000	2.0000
3	1.0000	3.0000

Classification Cluster Centers

Cluster	V_1	V_2	V_3	V_4
1	3.8135	5.8992	3.2522	6.4891
2	1.8507	3.0234	1.8327	3.7864
3	6.3558	2.8356	6.1576	3.6736

Cluster	V_5	V_6
1	2.5149	6.6957
2	6.4436	2.5056
3	1.3047	3.2010

(Continued)

TABLE 20.4

Case Listing of Cluster Membership

Case ID	*Cluster*	*Distance*
1	3	1.780
2	2	2.254
3	3	1.174
4	1	1.882
5	2	2.525
6	3	2.340
7	3	1.862
8	3	1.410
9	2	1.843
10	1	2.112
11	2	1.923
12	3	2.400
13	2	3.382
14	1	1.772
15	3	3.605
16	1	2.137
17	3	3.760
18	1	4.421
19	1	0.853
20	2	0.813

Final Cluster Centers

Cluster	V_1	V_2	V_3	V_4
1	3.5000	5.8333	3.3333	6.0000
2	1.6667	3.0000	1.8333	3.5000
3	5.7500	3.6250	6.0000	3.1250

Cluster	V_5	V_6
1	3.5000	6.0000
2	5.5000	3.3333
3	1.7500	3.8750

Distances between Final Cluster Centers

Cluster	*1*	*2*	*3*
1	0.0000		
2	5.5678	0.0000	
3	5.7353	6.9944	0.0000

Analysis of Variance

Variable	*Cluster MS*	*df*	*Error MS*	*df*	*F*	*p*
V_1	29.1083	2	0.6078	17.0	47.8879	.000
V_2	13.5458	2	0.6299	17.0	21.5047	.000
V_3	31.3917	2	0.8333	17.0	37.6700	.000
V_4	15.7125	2	0.7279	17.0	21.5848	.000
V_5	24.1500	2	0.7353	17.0	32.8440	.000
V_6	12.1708	2	1.0711	17.0	11.3632	.001

Number of Cases in each Cluster

Cluster	*Unweighted Cases*	*Weighted Cases*
1	6.0	6.0
2	6.0	6.0
3	8.0	8.0
Missing	0.0	
Total	20.0	20.0

clusters are well separated. The univariate F test for each clustering variable is presented. These F tests are only descriptive. The cases or objects are systematically assigned to clusters to maximize differences on the clustering variables, so the resulting probabilities should not be interpreted as testing the null hypothesis of no differences among clusters.

The following example of hospital choice further illustrates nonhierarchical clustering.

EXAMPLE

Segmentation with Surgical Precision

Cluster analysis was used to classify consumers who preferred hospitals for inpatient care as old-fashioned, affluent, value-conscious, or professional want-it-alls.

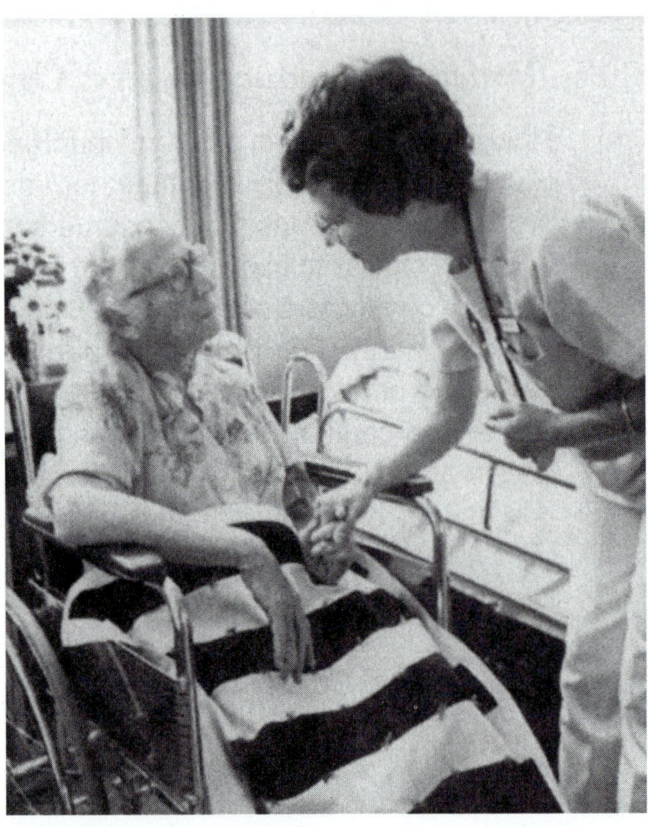

Cluster analysis was used to classify respondents who preferred hospitals for in-patient care to identify hospital preference segments. The clustering was based on the reasons respondents gave for preferring a hospital. The demographic profiles of the grouped respondents were compared to learn whether the segments could be identified efficiently.

Quick Cluster (SPSS), a minimum variance clustering method, was used for grouping the respondents based on their answers to the hospital preference items. The squared euclidean distances between all clustering variables were minimized. Because different individuals perceive scales of importance differently, each individual's ratings were normalized before clustering. The results indicated that the respondents could best be classified into four clusters. The cross-validation procedure for cluster analysis was run twice, on halves of the total sample.

As expected, the four groups differed substantially by their distributions and average responses to the reasons for their hospital preferences. The names assigned to the four groups reflected the demographic characteristics and reasons for hospital preferences: Old-Fashioned, Affluent, Value-Conscious, and Professional Want-It-Alls.[16] ■

CLUSTERING VARIABLES

Sometimes cluster analysis is used for clustering variables to identify homogenous groups. In this instance, the units used for analysis are the variables, and the distance measures are computed for all pairs of variables. For example, the correlation coefficient, either the absolute value or with the sign, can be used as a measure of similarity (the opposite of distance) between variables.

Hierarchical clustering of variables can aid in the identification of unique variables, or variables that make a unique contribution to the data. Clustering can also be used to reduce the number of variables. Associated with each cluster is a linear combination of the variables in the cluster, called the *cluster component.* A large set of variables can often be replaced by the set of cluster components with little loss of information. However, a given number of cluster components does not generally explain as much variance as the same number of principal components. Why, then, should the clustering of variables be used? Cluster components are usually easier to interpret than the principal components, even if the latter are rotated.[17] We illustrate the clustering of variables with an example from advertising research.

EXAMPLE

Feelings—Nothing More Than Feelings

A study was conducted to identify feelings that are provoked by advertising. A total of 655 feelings were reduced to a set of 180 that were judged by respondents to be most likely to be stimulated by advertising. This group was clustered on the basis of judgments of similarity between feelings resulting in 31 feeling clusters. These were divided into 16 positive and 15 negative clusters.[18]

Positive Feelings	*Negative Feelings*
1. Playful/childish	1. Fear
2. Friendly	2. Bad/sick
3. Humorous	3. Confused
4. Delighted	4. Indifferent
5. Interested	5. Bored
6. Strong/confident	6. Sad
7. Warm/tender	7. Anxious
8. Relaxed	8. Helpless/timid
9. Energetic/impulsive	9. Ugly/stupid
10. Eager/excited	10. Pity/deceived
11. Contemplative	11. Mad
12. Pride	12. Disagreeable
13. Persuaded/expectant	13. Disgusted
14. Vigorous/challenged	14. Irritated
15. Amazed	15. Moody/frustrated
16. Set/informed	

Thus, 655 feeling responses to advertising were reduced to a core set of 31 feelings. As such, advertisers now have a managable set of feelings for understanding and measuring emotional responses to advertising. When measured, these feelings can provide information on a commercial's ability to persuade the target consumers. ■

Cluster analysis, particularly clustering of objects, is also frequently used in international marketing research (Research in Practice 20.1[19]) and could also be useful in researching ethical evaluations (Research in Practice 20.2[20]).

RESEARCH IN PRACTICE 20.1

Perceived Product Parity—Once Rarity—Now Reality

How do consumers in different countries perceive brands in different product categories? Surprisingly, the answer is that the product perception parity rate is quite high. Perceived product parity means that consumers perceive all/most of the brands in a product category as similar to each other or at par. A new study by BBDO Worldwide shows that two-thirds of consumers surveyed in 28 countries considered brands in 13 product categories to be at parity. The product categories ranged from airlines to credit cards to coffee. Perceived parity averaged 63 percent for all categories in all countries. The Japanese have the highest perception of parity across all product categories at 99 percent and Colombians the lowest at 28 percent. Viewed by product category, credit cards have the highest parity perception at 76 percent and cigarettes the lowest at 52 percent.

BBDO clustered the countries based on product parity perceptions to arrive at clusters that exhibited similar levels and patterns of parity perceptions. The highest perception parity figure came from France and from Asia/Pacific region (83 percent), which included countries of Australia, Japan, Malaysia, and South Korea,. It is no surprise that France was in this list because for most products the French use highly visual advertising that is feelings oriented. The next cluster was U.S.-influenced markets (65 percent), which included Argentina, Canada, Hong Kong, Kuwait, Mexico, Singapore, and the United States. The third cluster, primarily European countries (60 percent), included Austria, Belgium, Denmark, Italy, the Netherlands, South Africa, Spain, the United Kingdom, and Germany.

What all this means is that in order to differentiate the product/brand, advertising can not just focus on product performance, but also must relate the product to the person's life in an important way. Also, much greater marketing effort will be required in the Asia/Pacific region and in France in order to differentiate the brand from competition and establish a unique image. A big factor in this growing parity is of course the emergence of the global market.

RESEARCH IN PRACTICE 20.2

Clustering Marketing Professionals Based on Ethical Evaluations

Cluster analysis can be used to explain differences in ethical perceptions by using a large multi-item, multidimensional scale developed to measure how ethical different situations are. One such scale was developed by Reidenbach and Robin. This scale has 29 items, which compose five dimensions, that measure how a respondent judges a certain action. For example, a given respondent will read about a marketing researcher that has provided proprietary information of one of his clients to a second client. The respondent is then asked to complete the 29-item ethics scale. For example, to indicate if this action is:

Just	:___:___:___:___:___:___:___:	Unjust
Traditionally acceptable	:___:___:___:___:___:___:___:	Unacceptable
Violates	:___:___:___:___:___:___:___:	Does not violate an unwritten contract

This scale could be administered to a sample of marketing professionals. By clustering respondents based on these 29 items, two important questions should be investigated. First, how do the clusters differ with respect to the five ethical dimensions; in this case, Justice, Relativist, Egoism, Utilitarianism, Deontology (see chapter 24). Second, what types of firms compose each cluster? The clusters could be described in terms of industry classification (SIC), firm size, and firm profitability. Answers to these two questions should provide insight into what type of firms use what dimensions to evaluate ethical situations. For instance, do large firms fall into a different cluster than do small firms? Do more-profitable firms perceive questionable situations more acceptable than less-profitable firms?

INTERNET AND COMPUTER APPLICATIONS

In SPSS the main program for hierarchical clustering of objects or cases is CLUSTER. Different distance measures can be computed, and all the hierarchical clustering procedures discussed here are available. For nonhierarchical clustering, the QUICK CLUSTER program can be used. This program is particularly helpful for clustering a large number of cases. All the default options will result in a *k*-means clustering. To cluster variables, the distance measures should be computed across variables using the PROXIMITIES program. This proximity matrix can be read into CLUSTER to obtain a grouping of the variables.

In SAS, the CLUSTER program can be used for the hierarchical clustering of cases or objects. All the clustering procedures discussed here are available, as well as some additional ones. Nonhierarchical clustering of cases or objects can be accomplished using FASTCLUS. For clustering of variables, the VARCLUS program can be used. Dendrograms are not automatically computed but can be obtained using the TREE program.

In the BMDP package, the main program for the clustering of cases using the hierarchical procedures is 2M. This program allows the use of several distance measures, but it permits the use of only single linkage, centroid, or *k* nearest neighbor clustering procedures. For nonhierarchical clustering, the KM program can be used for performing *k*-means clustering of cases. Clustering of variables can be done using the 1M program. It permits the use of single linkage, complete linkage, and average linkage procedures. A special program, 3M, is available for constructing block clusters for categorical data. Subsets of cases are grouped into clusters that are alike for subsets of variables.[21]

In Minitab, cluster analysis can be accessed in the Multivariate>Cluster observation function. Also available are Clustering of Variables and Cluster *K*-Means. Cluster analysis is not available in Excel (version 7.0 for the PC).

SUMMARY

Cluster analysis is used for classifying objects or cases, and sometimes variables, into relatively homogenous groups. The groups or clusters are suggested by the data and are not defined a priori.

The variables on which the clustering is done should be selected based on past research, theory, the hypotheses being tested, or the judgment of the researcher. An appropriate measure of distance or similarity should be selected. The most commonly used measure is the euclidean distance or its square.

Clustering procedures may be hierarchical or nonhierarchical. Hierarchical clustering is characterized by the development of a hierarchy or tree-like structure. Hierarchical methods can be agglomerative or divisive. Agglomerative methods consist of linkage methods, variance methods, and centroid methods. Linkage methods comprise single linkage, complete linkage, and average linkage. A commonly used variance method is Ward's procedure. The nonhierarchical methods are frequently referred to as *k*-means clustering. These methods can be classified as sequential threshold, parallel threshold, and optimizing partitioning. Hierarchical and nonhierarchical methods can be used in tandem. The choice of a clustering procedure and the choice of a distance measure are interrelated.

The number of clusters may be based on theoretical, conceptual, or practical considerations. In hierarchical clustering, the distances at which the clusters are being combined is an important criterion. The relative sizes of the clusters should be meaningful. The clusters should be interpreted in terms of cluster centroids. Often it is helpful to profile the clusters in terms of variables that were not used for clustering. The reliability and validity of the clustering solutions may be assessed in different ways.

FOCUS ON Burke

When Burke presents the results of a cluster analysis to a client the three big questions to be answered are:

1. What do the clusters tell me about my market?
2. What variables drive the clustering?
3. How different are the clusters?

What Do the Clusters Tell Me About My Market?

To answer this question, Burke typically uses respondent data that was not included in the clustering procedure. For example, we might find four clusters of respondents based on their evaluations of product benefits. We also collected data on past purchase behavior and purchase intention for a new concept. If the clusters do not show any managerially significant differences on these behavioral and intentions measures, then it will be hard to justify to management that the clusters are useful. Because the purpose of clustering is to create groups that are as much alike as possible, there is no guarantee that they will be different in any way that has external value. We can't simply accept that because the clusters were created that they are really different.

What Variables Drive the Clustering?

If we use several variables to create the clustering, we have to be very careful that we don't create an implicit weighting system. For example, in a project for an automobile company, 20 questions about the benefits desired in a new automobile were proposed for use in clustering respondents. It was immediately clear that seven of the questions directly or indirectly were related to economy, eight of the questions were related to image, three questions were related to price/value, and two questions reflected speed/acceleration. Of course, a factor analysis was helpful in making these observations. You could predict that the questions that would impact the clustering the most would lead management to conclude "the clusters of respondents seem to heavily reflect economy and image." You would be amazed if this did not happen. When you calculate euclidean distance to examine the differences between respondents, the sum of squares would include 15 from economy and image with only 5 from either price/value or speed/acceleration. If these are all on comparable scales, the latter two categories have little opportunity to overcome the strength of

(Continued)

KEY TERMS AND CONCEPTS

agglomeration schedule
cluster centroid
cluster centers
dendrogram
distances between cluster centers
icicle diagram
similarity/distance coefficient matrix
euclidean distance
hierarchical clustering
agglomerative clustering
divisive clustering
linkage methods
single linkage
complete linkage
average linkage
variance methods
Ward's procedure
centroid method
nonhierarchical clustering
sequential threshold method
parallel threshold method
optimizing partitioning method

FOCUS ON Burke *(Continued)*

the first two categories. It would be more reasonable to pare down the number of questions to come as close as possible to having the same number reflecting highly correlated groups of questions. If you don't do this, the number of questions you ask about a topic has the potential to have a stronger influence on your results than the topic itself.

How Different Are the Clusters?

In the first topic above, the notion of determining if the clusters are useful because of differences among external variables was discussed. We also need to examine if the clusters are actually "different" based on the variables used to create the clusters. You can put your data in a clustering algorithm and, if you tell it to stop at two clusters, you will have two clusters because of the nature of the process, not necessarily because of the logic or structure of differences that exist in the population. It becomes important to look at the clusters and see if the differences are of a magnitude and stability to evoke confidence.

1. It is not likely that the clusters will be different on all the questions you used as input for the clustering process. Although statistical procedures are not really valid when applied to systematically created clusters, they do offer insight as to how the clusters are formed. One-way ANOVA tells you if the individual questions are different across the clusters based on a statistic that would be appropriate for a probability sample (of course that is not what you have . . . but it is a useful "index"). Using discriminant analysis is even more appealing as it will show which of the questions would be potential discriminators between groups taking into account the colinearity between these predictors.
2. Managerial significance is a different issue. Suppose your clusters appear to be different on these statistical indices (ANOVA and discriminant analysis). That doesn't mean that the differences are large enough to be seen as useful by management. For example, a question for which the clusters are "different" was a rating of economy and yet 90 percent of the ratings ranged between 6 and 9 on a 10-point scale. You would need additional supporting evidence to be able to support this as a meaningful difference to management. The ratings show different in degree of "positiveness" and not different in that some are high and some are low. This is a difficult issue and there is no cookbook answer for it. You have to be comfortable that you can interpret these numeric differences into meaningful management decisions.

ACRONYMS

The steps involved and the salient concepts in clustering may be summarized by the acronym CLUSTERING:

C entroid methods
L inkage methods
U nderlying problem: selection of clustering variables
S imilarity or distance measures
T ype of clustering method: hierarchical versus nonhierarchical
E rror sums of squares or variance methods
R eliability and validity assessment
I nterpreting and profiling clusters
N umber of clusters
G raphical aids: dendrogram and icicle plot

EXERCISES

Questions

1. Discuss the similarity and difference between cluster analysis and discriminant analysis.
2. What are some of the uses of cluster analysis in marketing?
3. Briefly define the following terms: dendrogram, icicle plot, agglomeration schedule, and cluster membership.
4. What is the most commonly used measure of similarity in cluster analysis?
5. Present a classification of clustering procedures.
6. Why is the average linkage method usually preferred to single linkage and complete linkage?
7. What are the two major disadvantages of nonhierarchical clustering procedures?
8. What guidelines are available for deciding on the number of clusters?
9. What is involved in the interpretation of clusters?
10. What are some of the additional variables used for profiling the clusters?
11. Describe some procedures available for assessing the quality of clustering solutions.
12. How is cluster analysis used to group variables?

Problems

1. Are the following statements true or false?
   - **a.** Hierarchical and nonhierarchical clustering methods always produce different results.
   - **b.** One should always standardize data before performing cluster analysis.
   - **c.** Small-distance coefficients in the agglomeration schedule imply that dissimilar cases are being merged.
   - **d.** It does not matter which distance measure you use; the clustering solutions are essentially the same.
   - **e.** It is advisable to analyze the same data set using different clustering procedures.

INTERNET AND COMPUTER EXERCISES

1. Analyze the data in Table 20.1 using the following methods: (a) single linkage, (b) complete linkage, and (c) method of centroid. Use SPSS, SAS, BMDP or Minitab. Compare your results with those given in Table 20.2.

Chapter 21

Multidimensional Scaling and Conjoint Analysis

"Often, relationships are easier to see if you can draw a picture or create a chart that illustrates the relationships . . . and that is the goal of multidimensional scaling. Conjoint analysis, on the other hand, helps us profile which attributes contribute most heavily to a person's choice among a variety of offerings made up of different combinations of these attributes."

Michael Baumgardner, president, Burke, Inc.

OBJECTIVES

After reading this chapter, the student should be able to

1. discuss the basic concept and scope of multidimensional scaling (MDS) in marketing research and describe its various applications
2. describe the steps involved in multidimensional scaling of perception data including formulating the problem, obtaining input data, selecting an MDS procedure, deciding on the number of dimensions, labeling the dimensions and interpreting the configuration, and assessing reliability and validity
3. explain the multidimensional scaling of preference data and distinguish between internal and external analysis of preferences
4. explain correspondence analysis and discuss its advantages and disadvantages
5. understand the relationship between MDS, discriminant analysis, and factor analysis
6. discuss the basic concepts of conjoint analysis and contrast it with MDS and discuss its various applications
7. describe the procedure for conducting conjoint analysis including formulating the problem, constructing the stimuli, deciding the form of input data, selecting a conjoint analysis procedure, interpreting the results, and assessing reliability and validity
8. define the concept of hybrid conjoint analysis and explain how it simplifies the data collection task

OVERVIEW

This final chapter on data analysis presents two related techniques for analyzing consumer perceptions and preferences: multidimensional scaling (MDS) and conjoint analysis. We outline and illustrate the steps involved in conducting MDS and discuss the relationships among MDS, factor analysis, and discriminant analysis. Then we describe conjoint analysis and present a step-by-step procedure for conducting it. We also provide brief coverage of hybrid conjoint models.

We begin with examples illustrating MDS and conjoint analysis.

DEPARTMENT STORE PATRONAGE PROJECT

Multidimensional Scaling

Respondents' evaluations of the 10 stores on each of the 8 factors of the choice criteria were used to derive similarity measures between the stores. Euclidean distances were calculated between each pair of stores. These data were analyzed using multidimensional scaling to obtain spatial maps that represented the respondents' perceptions of the 10 stores. In one such map, the dimensions were identified as prestigious versus discount stores and local versus national store chains. Stores that competed directly with each other (e.g., Saks Fifth Avenue and Neiman Marcus) were located close together in the perceptual space. These perceptual maps were used to gain insights into the competitive positioning of the ten department stores.

EXAMPLE

Colas Collide

MDS has been used to understand consumers' perceptions of soft drinks and the competitive structure of the soft drink market.

In a survey, respondents were asked to rank-order all the possible pairs of 10 brands of soft drinks in terms of their similarity. These data were analyzed via multidimensional scaling and resulted in the following spatial representation of soft drinks.

From other information obtained in the questionnaire, the horizontal axis was labeled as "cola flavor." Tab was perceived to be the most cola-flavored and 7-Up the least cola-flavored. The vertical axis was labeled as "Dietness," with Tab being perceived to be the most

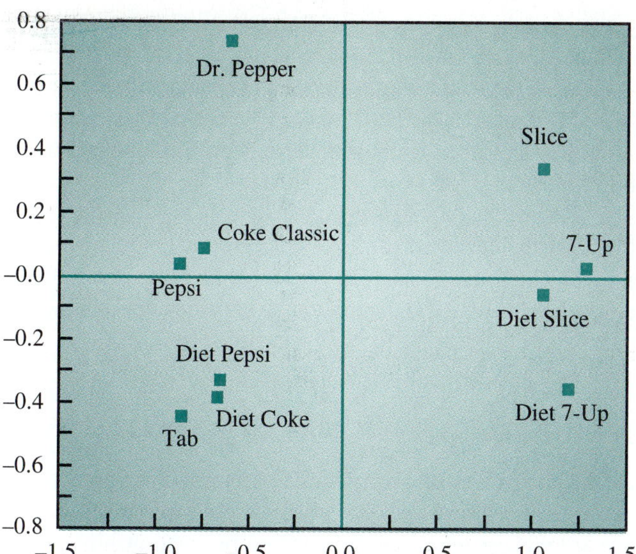

dietetic and Dr. Pepper the most nondietetic. Note that Pepsi and Coke Classic were perceived to be very similar as indicated by their closeness in the perceptual map. Close similarity was also perceived between 7-Up and Slice, Diet 7-Up and Diet Slice, and Tab, Diet Coke and Diet Pepsi. Note that Dr. Pepper is perceived to be relatively dissimilar to the other brands. Such MDS maps are very useful in understanding the competitive structure of the soft drink market.[1] ■

EXAMPLE

Complete Credit Card Features Identified by Conjoint Analysis

The Complete MasterCard—a "cobranded" card with Ameritech, one of the seven regional Bell telephone companies—resulted from the adroit use of focus group research and conjoint analysis research. The Complete MasterCard became available recently to Ameritech's 10 million residential customers in Illinois, Indiana, Michigan, Ohio, and Wisconsin.

"With the increased competition in the calling card market, we needed to offer our customers the convenience of a multipurpose card in order to meet their expectations," Rich Bialek, director of Ameritech's credit card services said. "We wanted market research to help us determine what mix of features would make our card most appealing to customers."

In the first round of eight focus group sessions with users of both credit cards and calling cards, Kennedy Research, Inc., of Grand Rapids, Michigan, focused on the acceptance and expectations for the concept of a credit card with a calling card feature. In the second round of focus groups, Kennedy researchers probed to identify a new card's features to be studied in the subsequent conjoint analysis phase.

During the conjoint analysis study, Kennedy recruited 500 Ameritech customers—about 100 in each of the 5 states served—to participate in a self-administered, computerized questionnaire taking 30 minutes. Kennedy included 15 features of a credit and calling card, such as annual fee (four options), interest rate (three options), and card name (seven options). All questions gave the respondents two choices. For example, "What is more important—a card with no annual fee or a card that offers a variable interest rate?"

"By the time participants went through a series of 50 or so questions, they weren't sure what they wanted, " Jamal Din, Kennedy's conjoint designer, said. "The computer was able to assign relative values to the various features, based on each individual's answers, and then design the one card that would most likely be irresistible to that individual."

As a result of the study, the card received the name "Ameritech Complete MasterCard." The card featured no annual fee, and an annual automatic rebate of 10 percent—paid by the sponsoring bank—on most local and long-distance calls made with the card. In addition, the card included a tiered interest rate with a 25-day grace period. The usefulness of conjoint analysis in designing the Ameritech Complete MasterCard is demonstrated by the gratifying customer response to the card.[2] ■

The first two examples illustrate the derivation and use of perceptual maps, which lie at the heart of MDS. The Ameritech Complete MasterCard example involves trade-offs respondents make while evaluating alternatives. The conjoint analysis procedure is based on these trade-offs.

BASIC CONCEPTS IN MULTIDIMENSIONAL SCALING (MDS)

Multidimensional Scaling (MDS) A class of procedures for representing perceptions and preferences of respondents spatially by means of a visual display.

Multidimensional scaling (MDS) is a class of procedures for representing perceptions and preferences of respondents spatially by means of a visual display. Perceived or psychological relationships among stimuli are represented as geometric relationships among points in a multidimensional space. These geometric representations are often called *spatial maps*. The axes of the spatial map are assumed to denote the psychological basis or underlying dimensions respondents use to form perceptions and preferences for stimuli.[3] MDS has been used in marketing to identify:

1. The number and nature of dimensions consumers use to perceive different brands in the marketplace
2. The positioning of current brands on these dimensions
3. The positioning of consumers' ideal brand on these dimensions

Information provided by MDS has been used for a variety of marketing applications, including:

- *Image measurement.* Comparing the customers' and noncustomers' perceptions of the firm with the firm's perceptions of itself.
- *Market segmentation.* To position brands and consumers in the same space and thus identify groups of consumers with relatively homogenous perceptions.
- *New product development.* To look for gaps in the spatial map, which indicate potential opportunities for positioning new products. Also, to evaluate new product concepts and existing brands on a test basis to determine how consumers perceive the new concepts. The proportion of preferences for each new product is one indicator of its success.
- *Assessing advertising effectiveness.* Spatial maps can be used to determine whether advertising has been successful in achieving the desired brand positioning.
- *Pricing analysis.* Spatial maps developed with and without pricing information can be compared to determine the impact of pricing.
- *Channel decisions.* Judgments on compatibility of brands with different retail outlets could lead to spatial maps useful for making channel decisions.
- *Attitude scale construction.* MDS techniques can be used to develop the appropriate dimensionality and configuration of the attitude space.

STATISTICS AND TERMS ASSOCIATED WITH MDS

The important statistics and terms associated with MDS include the following:

Similarity judgments. Ratings on all possible pairs of brands or other stimuli in terms of their similarity using a Likert-type scale.

Preference rankings. Rank orderings of the brands or other stimuli from the most preferred to the least preferred. They are normally obtained from the respondents.
Stress. This is a lack-of-fit measure; higher values of stress indicate poorer fits.
R-*square.* *R*-square is a squared correlation index that indicates the proportion of variance of the optimally scaled data that can be accounted for by the MDS procedure. This is a goodness-of-fit measure.
Spatial map. Perceived relationships among brands or other stimuli represented as geometric relationships among points in a multidimensional space.
Coordinates. Indicate the positioning of a brand or a stimulus in a spatial map.
Unfolding. The representation of both brands and respondents as points in the same space.

CONDUCTING MULTIDIMENSIONAL SCALING

Figure 21.1 shows the steps in MDS. The researcher must formulate the MDS problem carefully because a variety of data may be used as input into MDS. The researcher must also determine an appropriate form in which data should be obtained and select an MDS procedure for analyzing the data. An important aspect of the solution involves determining the number of dimensions for the spatial map. Also, the axes of the map should be labeled and the derived configuration interpreted. Finally, the researcher must assess the quality of the results obtained.[4] We describe each of these steps, beginning with problem formulation.

Formulate the Problem

Formulating the problem requires that the researcher specify the purpose for which the MDS results would be used and select the brands or other stimuli to be included in the analysis. The number of brands or stimuli selected and the specific brands included determines the nature of the resulting dimensions and configurations. At a minimum, eight brands or stimuli should be included so as to obtain a well-defined spatial map. Including more than 25 brands is likely to be cumbersome and may result in respondent fatigue.

The decision regarding which specific brands or stimuli to include should be made carefully. Suppose a researcher is interested in obtaining consumer perceptions of automobiles. If luxury automobiles are not included in the stimulus set, this dimension may not emerge in the results. The choice of the number and specific brands or stimuli to be

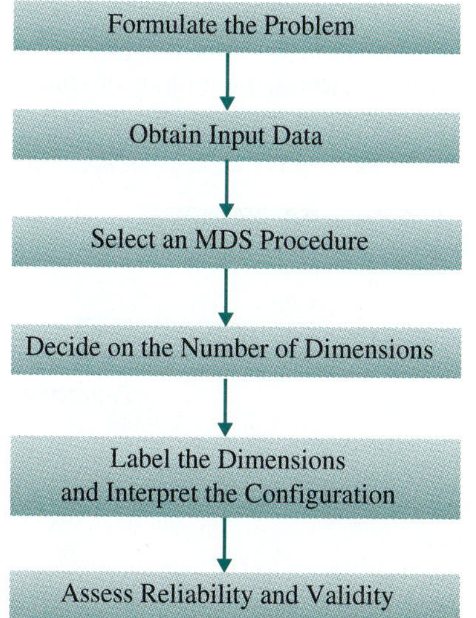

Figure 21.1
Conducting Multidimensional Scaling

included should be based on the statement of the marketing research problem, theory, and the judgment of the researcher.

Multidimensional scaling will be illustrated in the context of obtaining a spatial map for 10 toothpaste brands. These brands are Aqua-Fresh, Crest, Colgate, Aim, Gleem, Macleans, Ultra Brite, Close-Up, Pepsodent, and Dentagard. The next question, then, is how to obtain data on these 10 brands.

Obtain Input Data

As shown in Figure 21.2, input data obtained from the respondents may be related to perceptions or preferences. Perception data, which may be direct or derived, is discussed first.

Perception Data: Direct Approaches. In direct approaches to gathering perception data, the respondents are asked to judge how similar or dissimilar the various brands or stimuli are, using their own criteria. Respondents are often required to rate all possible pairs of brands or stimuli in terms of similarity on a Likert scale. These data are referred to as similarity judgments. For example, similarity judgments on all the possible pairs of toothpaste brands may be obtained in the following manner:

	Very Dissimilar						*Very Similar*
Crest versus Colgate	1	2	3	4	5	6	7
Aqua-Fresh versus Crest	1	2	3	4	5	6	7
Crest versus Aim	1	2	3	4	5	6	7
.							
.							
.							
Colgate versus Aqua-Fresh	1	2	3	4	5	6	7

The number of pairs to be evaluated is $n(n - 1)/2$, where n is the number of stimuli. Other procedures are also available. Respondents could be asked to rank-order all the possible pairs from the most similar to the least similar. In another method, the respondent rank-orders the brands in terms of their similarity to an anchor brand. Each brand, in turn, serves as the anchor.

In our example, the direct approach was adopted. Subjects were asked to provide similarity judgments for all 45 ($10 \times 9/2$) pairs of toothpaste brands, using a seven-point scale. The data obtained from one respondent are given in Table 21.1.[5]

Derived Approaches In MDS, attribute-based approaches to collecting perception data requiring the respondents to rate the stimuli on the identified attributes using semantic differential or Likert scales.

Perception Data: Derived Approaches. **Derived approaches** to collecting perception data are attribute-based approaches requiring the respondents to rate the brands or stimuli

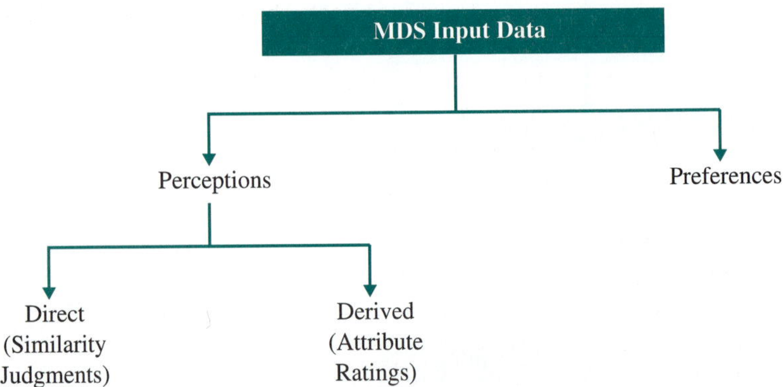

Figure 21.2
Input Data for Multidimensional Scaling

TABLE 21.1

SIMILARITY RATINGS OF TOOTHPASTE BRANDS

	Aqua-Fresh	*Crest*	*Colgate*	*Aim*	*Gleem*	*Macleans*	*Ultra Bright*	*Close-Up*	*Pepsodent*	*Dentagard*
Aqua-Fresh										
Crest	5									
Colgate	6	7								
Aim	4	6	6							
Gleem	2	3	4	5						
Macleans	3	3	4	4	5					
Ultra Brite	2	2	2	3	5	5				
Close-Up	2	2	2	2	6	5	6			
Pepsodent	2	2	2	2	6	6	7	6		
Dentagard	1	2	4	2	4	3	3	4	3	

on the identified attributes using semantic differential or Likert scales. For example, the different brands of toothpaste may be rated on attributes like these:

Whitens teeth	__ __ __ __ __ __ __ __ __ __	Does not whiten teeth
Prevents tooth decay	__ __ __ __ __ __ __ __ __ __	Does not prevent tooth decay
.		
.		
.		
.		
Pleasant tasting	__ __ __ __ __ __ __ __ __ __	Unpleasant tasting

Sometimes an ideal brand is also included in the stimulus set. The respondents are asked to evaluate their hypothetical ideal brand on the same set of attributes. If attribute ratings are obtained, a similarity measure (such as euclidean distance) is derived for each pair of brands.

Direct versus Derived Approaches. Direct approaches have the advantage that the researcher does not have to identify a set of salient attributes. Respondents make similarity judgments using their own criteria, as they would under normal circumstances. The disadvantages are that the criteria are influenced by the brands or stimuli being evaluated. If the various brands of automobiles being evaluated are in the same price range, then price will not emerge as an important factor. It may be difficult to determine before analysis if and how the individual respondents' judgments should be combined. Furthermore, it may be difficult to label the dimensions of the spatial map.

The advantage of the attribute-based approach is that it is easy to identify respondents with homogenous perceptions. The respondents can be clustered based on the attribute ratings. It is also easier to label the dimensions. A disadvantage is that the researcher must identify all the salient attributes—a difficult task. The spatial map obtained depends on the attributes identified.

The direct approaches are more frequently used than the attribute-based approaches. However, it may be best to use both these approaches in a complementary way. Direct similarity judgments may be used for obtaining the spatial map, and attribute ratings may be used as an aid to interpreting the dimensions of the perceptual map. Similar procedures are used for preference data.

Preference Data. Preference data order the brands or stimuli in terms of respondents' preference for some property. A common way in which such data are obtained is preference rankings. Respondents are required to rank the brands from the most preferred to the least preferred. Alternatively, respondents may be required to make paired comparisons and indicate which brand in a pair they prefer. Another method is to obtain preference ratings for the various brands. (The rank-order, paired comparison, and rating scales were discussed in chapters 8 and 9 on scaling techniques.) When spatial maps are based on preference data, distance implies differences in preference. The configuration derived from preference data may differ greatly from that obtained from similarity data. Two brands may be perceived as different in a similarity map yet similar in a preference map, and vice versa. For example, Crest and Pepsodent may be perceived by a group of respondents as very different brands and thus appear far apart on a perception map. However, these two brands may be about equally preferred and appear close together on a preference map. We will continue using the perception data obtained in the toothpaste example to illustrate the MDS procedure and then consider the scaling of preference data.

Select an MDS Procedure

Nonmetric MDS A type of multidimensional scaling that assumes the input data are ordinal.

Metric MDS A multidimensional scaling method that assumes input data are metric.

Selection of a specific MDS procedure depends on whether perception or preference data are being scaled, or whether the analysis requires both kinds of data. The nature of the input data is also a determining factor. **Nonmetric MDS** procedures assume that the input data are ordinal, but they result in metric output. The distances in the resulting spatial map may be assumed to be interval scaled. These procedures find, in a given dimensionality, a spatial map whose rank orders of estimated distances between brands or stimuli best preserve or reproduce the input rank orders. In contrast, **metric MDS** methods assume that input data are metric. As the output is also metric, a stronger relationship between the output and input data is maintained, and the metric (interval or ratio) qualities of the input data are preserved. The metric and nonmetric methods produce similar results.[6]

Another factor influencing the selection of a procedure is whether the MDS analysis will be conducted at the individual respondent level or at an aggregate level. In individual-level analysis, the data are analyzed separately for each respondent, resulting in a spatial map for each respondent. Although individual-level analysis is useful from a research perspective, it is not appealing from a managerial standpoint. Marketing strategies are typically formulated at the segment or aggregate level, rather than at the individual level. If aggregate-level analysis is conducted, some assumptions must be made in aggregating individual data. Typically, it is assumed that all respondents use the same dimensions to evaluate the brands or stimuli, but that different respondents weigh these common dimensions differentially.

The data of Table 21.1 were treated as rank-ordered and scaled using a nonmetric procedure. Because these data were provided by one respondent, an individual-level analysis was conducted. Spatial maps were obtained in one to four dimensions and then a decision on an appropriate number of dimensions was made. This decision is central to all MDS analyses; therefore, it is explored in greater detail in the following section.

Decide on the Number of Dimensions

The objective in MDS is to obtain a spatial map that best fits the input data in the smallest number of dimensions. However, spatial maps are computed in such a way that the fit improves as the number of dimensions increases. Therefore, a compromise has to be made. The fit of an MDS solution is commonly assessed by the stress measure. Stress is a lack-of-fit measure; higher values of stress indicate poorer fits. The following guidelines are suggested for determining the number of dimensions.

- *A priori knowledge*. Theory or past research may suggest a particular number of dimensions.

- *Interpretability of the spatial map.* Generally, it is difficult to interpret configurations or maps derived in more than three dimensions.
- ***Elbow criterion.*** A plot of stress versus dimensionality should be examined. The points in this plot usually form a convex pattern, as shown in Figure 21.3. The point at which an elbow or a sharp bend occurs indicates an appropriate number of dimensions. Increasing the number of dimensions beyond this point is usually not worth the improvement in fit.
- *Ease of use.* It is generally easier to work with two-dimensional maps or configurations than with those involving more dimensions.
- *Statistical approaches.* For the sophisticated user, statistical approaches are also available for determining the dimensionality.[7]

Elbow Criterion A plot of stress versus dimensionality used in MDS. The point at which an elbow or a sharp bend occurs indicates an appropriate dimensionality.

Based on the plot of stress versus dimensionality (Figure 21.3), interpretability of the spatial map, and ease of use criteria, it was decided to retain a two-dimensional solution. This is shown in Figure 21.4.

Label the Dimensions and Interpret the Configuration

Once a spatial map is developed, the dimensions must be labeled and the configuration interpreted. Labeling the dimensions requires subjective judgment on the part of the researcher. The following guidelines can assist in this task:

- Even if direct similarity judgments are obtained, ratings of the brands on researcher supplied attributes may still be collected. Using statistical methods such as regression, these attribute vectors may be fitted in the spatial map (see Figure 21.5). The axes may then be labeled for the attributes with which they are most closely aligned.
- After providing direct similarity or preference data, the respondents may be asked to indicate the criteria they used in making their evaluations. These criteria may then be subjectively related to the spatial map to label the dimensions.

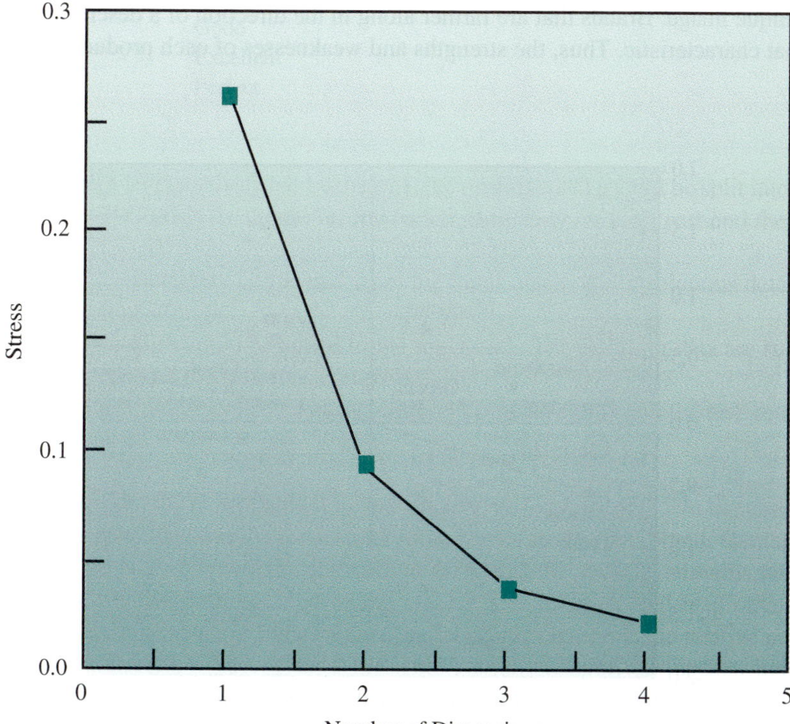

Figure 21.3
Plot of Stress versus Dimensionality

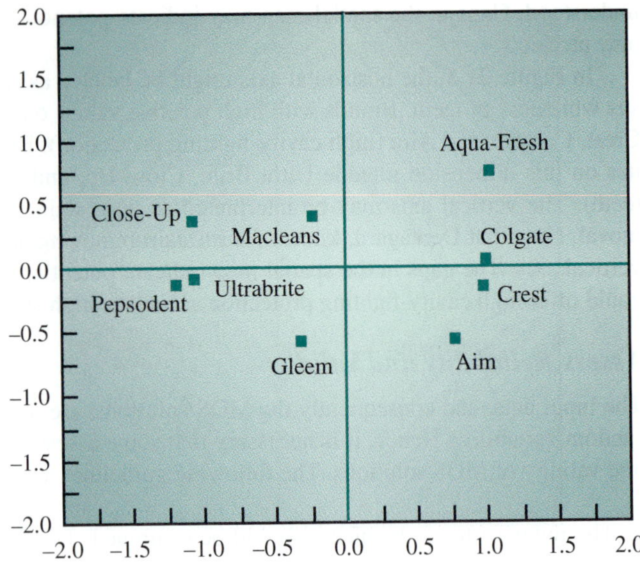

Figure 21.6
Assessment of Stability by Deleting One Brand

ASSUMPTIONS AND LIMITATIONS OF MDS

It is worthwhile to point out here some assumptions and limitations of MDS. It is assumed that the similarity of stimulus A to B is the same as the similarity of stimulus B to A. There are some instances in which this assumption may be violated. For example, Mexico is perceived as more similar to the United States than the United States is to Mexico. MDS assumes that the distance (similarity) between two stimuli is some function of their partial similarities on each of several perceptual dimensions. Not much research has been done to test this assumption. When a spatial map is obtained, it is assumed that interpoint distances are ratio scaled and that the axes of the map are multidimensional interval scaled. A limitation of MDS is that dimension interpretation relating physical changes in brands or stimuli to changes in the perceptual map is difficult at best. These limitations also apply to the scaling of preference data.

SCALING PREFERENCE DATA

Internal Analysis of Preferences A method of configuring a spatial map such that the spatial map represents both brands or stimuli and respondent points or vectors and is derived solely from the preference data.

External Analysis of Preferences A method of configuring a spatial map such that the ideal points or vectors based on preference data are fitted in a spatial map derived from perception data.

Analysis of preference data can be internal or external. In **internal analysis of preferences**, a spatial map representing both brands or stimuli and respondent points or vectors is derived solely from the preference data. Thus by collecting preference data, both brands and respondents can be represented in the same spatial map. In **external analysis of preferences**, the ideal points or vectors based on preference data are fitted in a spatial map derived from perception (e.g., similarities) data. In order to perform external analysis, both preference and perception data must be obtained. The representation of both brands and respondents as points in the same space, by using internal or external analysis, is referred to as *unfolding*.

External analysis is preferred in most situations.[11] In internal analysis, the differences in perceptions are confounded with differences in preferences. It is possible that the nature and relative importance of dimensions may vary between the perceptual space and the preference space. Two brands may be perceived to be similar (located close to each other in the perceptual space), yet one brand may be distinctly preferred over the other (i.e., the brands may be located apart in the preference space). These situations cannot be accounted for in internal analysis. In addition, internal analysis procedures are beset with computational difficulties.[12]

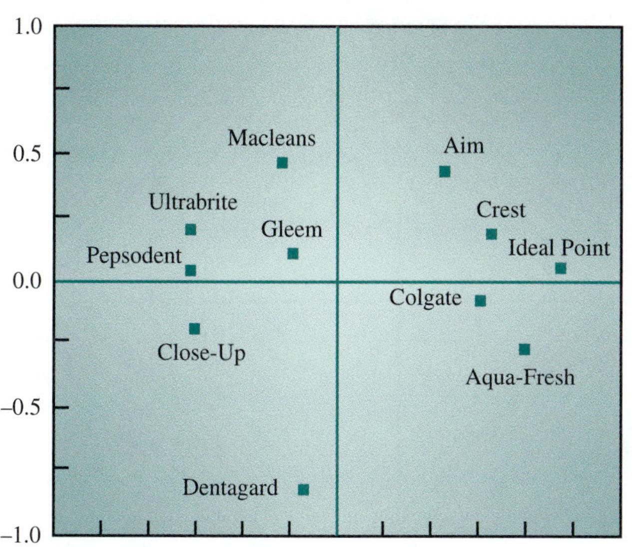

Figure 21.7
External Analysis of Preference Data

We illustrate external analysis by scaling the preferences of our respondent into his spatial map. The respondent ranked the brands in the following order of preference (most preferred first): Colgate, Crest, Aim, Aqua-Fresh, Gleem, Pepsodent, Ultra Brite, Macleans, Close-Up, and Dentagard. These preference rankings, along with the coordinates of the spatial map (Figure 21.5), were used as input into a preference scaling program to derive Figure 21.7. Notice the location of the ideal point. It is close to Colgate, Crest, Aim, and Aqua-Fresh, the four most-preferred brands, and far from Close-Up and Dentagard, the two least-preferred brands. If a new brand were to be located in this space, its distance from the ideal point, relative to the distances of other brands from the ideal point, would determine the degree of preference for this brand. Another application is provided by the following example.

EXAMPLE

Respondents Park in Different Spaces

An illustrative MDS map of selected automobile brands derived from similarity data is shown. In this spatial representation, each brand is identified by its distance from the other brands. The closer two brands are (e.g., Volkswagen and Dodge), the more similar they are perceived to be. The further apart two brands are (e.g., Volkswagen and Mercedes), the less similar they are perceived to be. Small distance (i.e., similarity) may also indicate competition. To illustrate, Honda competes closely with Toyota, but not with Continental or Porsche. The dimensions can be interpreted as economy/prestige versus sportiness/nonsportiness, and the position of each car on these dimensions can be determined.

The preference data consisted of a simple rank-order of the brands according to consumers' preferences. Respondents' ideal points are also located in the same spatial representation. Each ideal point represents the locus of preference of a particular respondent. Thus, respondent 1 (denoted by I1) prefers the sporty cars: Porsche, Jaguar, and Audi. Respondent 2 (denoted by I2) on the other hand, prefers luxury cars: Continental, Mercedes, Lexus, and Cadillac.

Such analysis can be done at the individual respondent level, enabling the researcher to segment the market according to similarities in the respondents' ideal points. Alternatively,

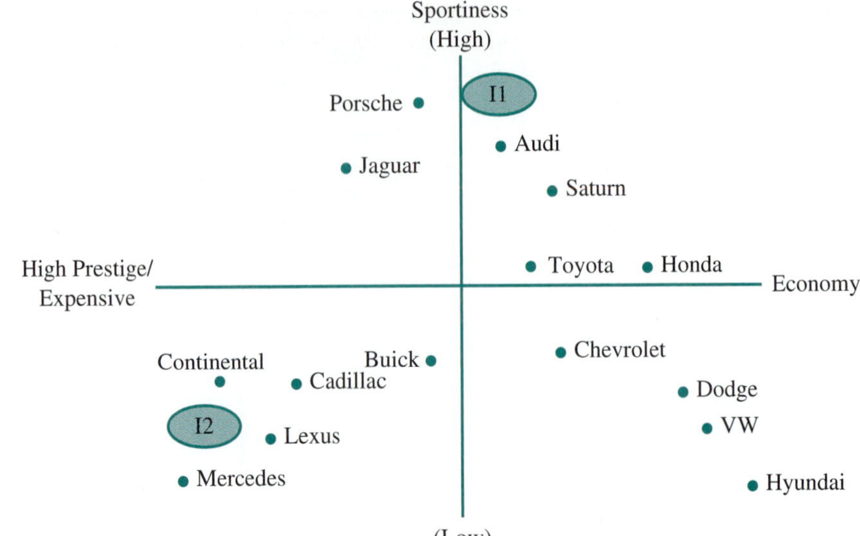

Joint Space Configuration of Automobile Brands and Consumer Preferences (illustrative output)

MDS has been used to identify consumers who prefer sporty cars, like Corvettes.

the respondents can be clustered based on their similarity with respect to the original preference ranking and ideal points established for each segment.[13] ■

Although so far we have considered only quantitative data, qualitative data can also be mapped using procedures such as correspondence analysis.

CORRESPONDENCE ANALYSIS

Correspondence Analysis An MDS technique for scaling qualitative data that scales the rows and columns of the input contingency table in corresponding units so that each can be displayed in the same low-dimensional space.

Correspondence analysis is an MDS technique for scaling qualitative data in marketing research. The input data are in the form of a contingency table indicating a qualitative association between the rows and columns. Correspondence analysis scales the rows and columns in corresponding units so that each can be displayed graphically in the same low-dimensional space. These spatial maps provide insights into (1) similarities and differences within the rows with respect to a given column category, (2) similarities and differences within the column categories with respect to a given row category, and (3) relationship among the rows and columns.[14]

The interpretation of results in correspondence analysis is similar to that in principal components analysis (chapter 19), given the similarity of the algorithms. Correspondence analysis results in the grouping of categories (activities, brands, or other stimuli) found within the contingency table, just as principal components analysis involves the grouping of the independent variables. The results are interpreted in terms of proximities among the rows and columns of the contingency table. Categories that are closer together are more similar in underlying structure.[15]

The advantage of correspondence analysis, as compared to other multidimensional scaling techniques, is that it reduces the data collection demands imposed on the respondents, because only binary or categorical data are obtained. The respondents are merely asked to check which attributes apply to each of several brands. The input data are the number of "yes" responses for each brand on each attribute. The brands and the attributes are then displayed in the same multidimensional space. The disadvantage is that between-set (i.e., between-column and -row) distances cannot be meaningfully interpreted. Correspondence analysis is an exploratory data analysis technique that is not suitable for hypothesis testing.[16]

MDS, including correspondence analysis, is not the only procedure available for obtaining perceptual maps. Two other techniques that we have discussed before, discriminant analysis (chapter 18) and factor analysis (chapter 19), can also be used for this purpose.

RELATIONSHIP AMONG MDS, FACTOR ANALYSIS, AND DISCRIMINANT ANALYSIS

If the attribute-based approaches are used to obtain input data, spatial maps can also be obtained by using factor or discriminant analysis. In this approach, each respondent rates n brands on m attributes. By factor analyzing the data, one could derive for each respondent n factor scores for each factor, one for each brand. By plotting brand scores on the factors, a spatial map could be obtained for each respondent. If an aggregate map is desired, the factor score for each brand for each factor can be averaged across respondents. The dimensions would be labeled by examining the factor loadings, which are estimates of the correlations between attribute ratings and underlying factors.[17]

The goal of discriminant analysis is to select the linear combinations of attributes that best discriminate between the brands or stimuli. To develop spatial maps by means of discriminant analysis, the dependent variable is the brand rated and the independent or predictor variables are the attribute ratings. A spatial map can be obtained by plotting the discriminant scores for the brands. The discriminant scores are the ratings on the perceptual dimensions, based on the attributes that best distinguish the brands. The dimensions can be labeled by examining the discriminant weights, or the weightings of attributes that make up a discriminant function or dimension.[18]

BASIC CONCEPTS IN CONJOINT ANALYSIS

Conjoint analysis attempts to determine the relative importance consumers attach to salient attributes and the utilities they attach to the levels of attributes.[19] This information is derived from consumers' evaluations of brands, or brand profiles composed of these attributes and their levels. The respondents are presented with stimuli that consist of combinations of attribute levels. They are asked to evaluate these stimuli in terms of their desirability. Conjoint procedures attempt to assign values to the levels of each attribute, so that the resulting values or utilities attached to the stimuli match, as closely as possible, the input evaluations provided by the respondents. The underlying assumption is that any set of stimuli, such as products, brands, or stores, is evaluated as a bundle of attributes.[20]

Conjoint Analysis A technique that attempts to determine the relative importance consumers attach to salient attributes and the utilities they attach to the levels of attributes.

Like multidimensional scaling, conjoint analysis relies on respondents' subjective evaluations. However, in MDS the stimuli are products or brands. In conjoint analysis, the stimuli are combinations of attribute levels determined by the researcher. The goal in MDS is to develop a spatial map depicting the stimuli in a multidimensional perceptual or preference space. Conjoint analysis, on the other hand, seeks to develop the part-worth or utility functions describing the utility consumers attach to the levels of each attribute. The two techniques are complementary.[21]

Conjoint analysis has been used in marketing for a variety of purposes, including:

- Determining the relative importance of attributes in the consumer choice process. A standard output from conjoint analysis consists of derived relative importance weights for all the attributes used to construct the stimuli used in the evaluation task. The relative importance weights indicate which attributes are important in influencing consumer choice.
- Estimating market share of brands that differ in attribute levels. The utilities derived from conjoint analysis can be used as input into a choice simulator to determine the share of choices, and hence the market share, of different brands.
- Determining the composition of the most-preferred brand. The brand features can be varied in terms of attribute levels and the corresponding utilities determined. The brand features that yield the highest utility indicate the composition of the most-preferred brand.
- Segmenting the market based on similarity of preferences for attribute levels. The part-worth functions derived for the attributes may be used as a basis for clustering respondents to arrive at homogenous preference segments.[22]

Applications of conjoint analysis have been made in consumer goods, industrial goods, financial and other services. Moreover, these applications have spanned all areas of marketing. A recent survey of conjoint analysis reported applications in the areas of new-product/concept identification, competitive analysis, pricing, market segmentation, advertising, and distribution.[23]

STATISTICS AND TERMS ASSOCIATED WITH CONJOINT ANALYSIS

The important statistics and terms associated with conjoint analysis include:

Part-worth functions. Also called *utility functions,* these describe the utility consumers attach to the levels of each attribute.

Relative importance weights. Indicate which attributes are important in influencing consumer choice. These weights are estimated.

Attribute levels. Denote the values assumed by the attributes.

Full profiles. Full profiles or complete profiles of brands are constructed in terms of all the attributes by using the attribute levels specified by the design.

Pairwise tables. The respondents evaluate two attributes at a time until all the required pairs of attributes have been evaluated.

Cyclical designs. Designs employed to reduce the number of paired comparisons.

Fractional factorial designs. Designs employed to reduce the number of stimulus profiles to be evaluated in the full-profile approach.

Orthogonal arrays. A special class of fractional designs that enable the efficient estimation of all main effects.

Internal validity. This involves correlations of the predicted evaluations for the holdout or validation stimuli with those obtained from the respondents.

CONDUCTING CONJOINT ANALYSIS

Figure 21.8 lists the steps in conjoint analysis. Formulating the problem involves identifying the salient attributes and their levels. These attributes and levels are used for constructing the stimuli to be used in a conjoint evaluation task. The respondents rate or rank the

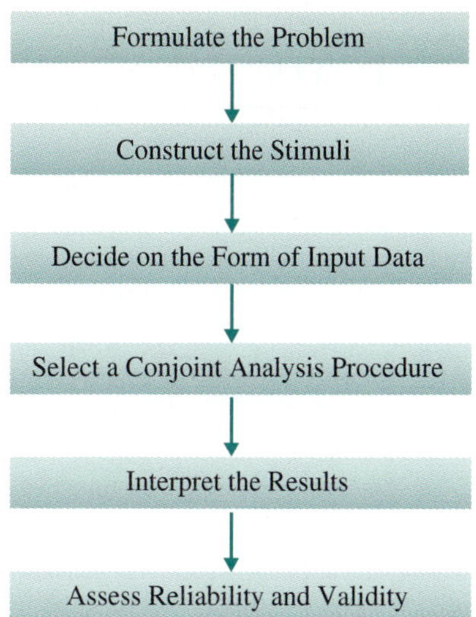

Figure 21.8
Conducting Conjoint Analysis

stimuli using a suitable scale and the data obtained are analyzed. The results are interpreted and their reliability and validity assessed. We now describe each of the steps of conjoint analysis in detail.

Formulate the Problem

In formulating the conjoint analysis problem, the researcher must identify the attributes and attribute levels to be used in constructing the stimuli. Attribute levels denote the values assumed by the attributes. From a theoretical standpoint, the attributes selected should be salient in influencing consumer preference and choice. For example, in the choice of an automobile brand, price, gas mileage, interior space, and so forth should be included. From a managerial perspective, the attributes and their levels should be actionable. To tell a manager that consumers prefer a sporty car to one that is conservative looking is not helpful, unless sportiness and conservativeness are defined in terms of attributes over which a manager has control. The attributes can be identified through discussions with management and industry experts, analysis of secondary data, qualitative research, and pilot surveys. A typical conjoint analysis study involves six or seven attributes.

Once the salient attributes have been identified, their appropriate levels should be selected. The number of attribute levels determines the number of parameters that will be estimated and also influences the number of stimuli that will be evaluated by the respondents. To minimize the respondent evaluation task and yet estimate the parameters with reasonable accuracy, it is desirable to restrict the number of attribute levels. The utility or part-worth function for the levels of an attribute may be nonlinear. For example, a consumer may prefer a medium-sized car to either a small or large one. Likewise, the utility for price may be nonlinear. The loss of utility in going from a low price to a medium price may be much smaller than the loss in utility in going from a medium to a high price. In these cases, at least three levels should be used. Some attributes, though, may naturally occur in binary form (two levels): a car does or does not have a sunroof.

The attribute levels selected will affect the consumer evaluations. If the price of an automobile brand is varied at $10,000, $12,000, and $14,000, price will be relatively unimportant. On the other hand, if the price is varied at $10,000, $20,000, and $30,000, it will be an important factor. Hence, the researcher should take into account the attribute levels prevalent in the marketplace and the objectives of the study. Using attribute levels that are beyond the range reflected in the marketplace will decrease the believability of the

TABLE 21.2

SNEAKER ATTRIBUTES AND LEVELS

	Level	
Attribute	*Number*	*Description*
Sole	3	Rubber
	2	Polyurethane
	1	Plastic
Upper	3	Leather
	2	Canvas
	1	Nylon
Price	3	$30.00
	2	$60.00
	1	$90.00

evaluation task, but it will increase the accuracy with which the parameters are estimated. The general guideline is to select attribute levels so that the ranges are somewhat greater than that prevalent in the market place but not so large as to adversely impact the believability of the evaluation task.

We illustrate the conjoint methodology by considering the problem of how students evaluate sneakers. Qualitative research identified three attributes as salient: the sole, the upper, and the price.[24] Each was defined in terms of three levels, as shown in Table 21.2. These attributes and their levels were used for constructing the conjoint analysis stimuli. It has been argued that pictorial stimuli should be used when consumers' marketplace choices are strongly guided by the product's styling, such that the choices are heavily based on an inspection of actual products or pictures of products.[25]

Construct the Stimuli

Two broad approaches are available for constructing conjoint analysis stimuli: the pairwise approach and the full-profile procedure. In the pairwise approach, also called *two-factor evaluations*, the respondents evaluate two attributes at a time until all the possible pairs of attributes have been evaluated. This approach is illustrated in the context of the sneaker example in Figure 21.9. For each pair, respondents evaluate all the combinations of levels of both the attributes, which are presented in a matrix. In the full-profile approach, also called *multiple-factor evaluations*, full or complete profiles of brands are constructed for all the attributes. Typically, each profile is described on a separate index card. This approach is illustrated in the context of the sneaker example in Table 21.3.

It is not necessary to evaluate all the possible combinations, nor is it feasible in all cases. In the pairwise approach, it is possible to reduce the number of paired comparisons

TABLE 21.3

FULL-PROFILE APPROACH TO COLLECTING CONJOINT DATA

Example of a Sneaker Product Profile	
Sole	Made of rubber
Upper	Made of nylon
Price	$30.00

Sneaker manufacturers like Reebok have made use of conjoint analysis to develop sneakers with appealing features.

by using cyclical designs. Likewise, in the full-profile approach the number of stimulus profiles can be greatly reduced by means of fractional factorial designs. A special class of fractional designs, called *orthogonal arrays*, allow for the efficient estimation of all main effects. Orthogonal arrays permit the measurement of all main effects of interest on an uncorrelated basis. These designs assume that all interactions are negligible. Orthogonal arrays are constructed from basic full factorial designs by substituting a new factor for

Upper \ **Sole**	Rubber	Polyurethane	Plastic
Leather			
Canvas			
Nylon			

Price \ **Sole**	Rubber	Polyurethane	Plastic
$30.00			
$60.00			
$90.00			

Upper \ **Price**	$30.00	$60.00	$90.00
Leather			
Canvas			
Nylon			

Figure 21.9
Pairwise Approach to Collecting Conjoint Data

selected interaction effects that are presumed to be negligible.[26] Generally, two sets of data are obtained. One, the *estimation set*, is used to calculate the part-worth functions for the attribute levels. The other, the *holdout set*, is used to assess reliability and validity.

The advantage of the pairwise approach is that it is easier for the respondents to provide these judgments. However, its relative disadvantage is that it requires more evaluations than does the full-profile approach. Also, the evaluation task may be unrealistic when only two attributes are being evaluated simultaneously. Studies comparing the two approaches indicate that both methods yield comparable utilities, yet the full-profile approach is more commonly used.

The sneaker example follows the full-profile approach. Given three attributes, defined at three levels each, a total of $3 \times 3 \times 3 = 27$ profiles can be constructed. To reduce the respondent evaluation task, a fractional factorial design was employed, and a set of nine profiles was constructed to constitute the estimation stimuli set (see Table 21.4). Another set of nine stimuli was constructed for validation purposes. Input data were obtained for both the estimation and validation stimuli. However, before the data could be obtained, it was necessary to decide on the form of the input data. [27]

Decide on the Form of Input Data

As in the case of MDS, conjoint analysis input data can be either nonmetric or metric. For nonmetric data, the respondents are typically required to provide rank-order evaluations. For the pairwise approach, respondents rank all the cells of each matrix in terms of their desirability. For the full-profile approach, they rank all the stimulus profiles. Rankings involve relative evaluations of the attribute levels. Proponents of ranking data believe that such data accurately reflect the behavior of consumers in the marketplace.

In the metric form, the respondents provide ratings, rather than rankings. In this case, the judgments are typically made independently. Advocates of rating data believe that they are more convenient for the respondents and easier to analyze than rankings. In recent years, the use of ratings has become increasingly common.

In conjoint analysis, the dependent variable is usually preference or intention to buy. In other words, respondents provide ratings or rankings in terms of their preference or intentions to buy. However, the conjoint methodology is flexible and can accommodate a range of other dependent variables, including actual purchase or choice.

In evaluating sneaker profiles, respondents were required to provide preference ratings for the sneakers described by the nine profiles in the estimation set. These ratings were obtained using a nine-point Likert scale (1 = not preferred, 9 = greatly preferred). Ratings obtained from one respondent are shown in Table 21.4.

Select a Conjoint Analysis Procedure

Conjoint Analysis Model The mathematical model expressing the fundamental relationship between attributes and utility in conjoint analysis.

The basic **conjoint analysis model** may be represented by the following formula:[28]

$$U(X) = \sum_{i=1}^{m} \sum_{j=1}^{k_i} \alpha_{ij} x_{ij}$$

where

$U(X)$ = overall utility of an alternative

α_{ij} = the part-worth contribution or utility associated with the jth level ($j, j = 1, 2, \ldots k_i$) of the ith attribute ($i, i = 1, 2, \ldots m$)

k_i = number of levels of attribute i

m = number of attributes

xy = 1 of the ith level of the ith attribute is present

= 0 otherwise

TABLE 21.4

SNEAKER PROFILES AND THEIR RATINGS

	Attribute Levels[a]			
Profile Number	*Sole*	*Upper*	*Price*	*Preference Rating*
1	1	1	1	9
2	1	2	2	7
3	1	3	3	5
4	2	1	2	6
5	2	2	3	5
6	2	3	1	6
7	3	1	3	5
8	3	2	1	7
9	3	3	2	6

[a]The attribute levels correspond to those in Table 21.2.

The importance of an attribute, I_i, is defined in terms of the range of the part-worths, α_{ij}, across the levels of that attribute:

$$I_i = \{\max(\alpha_{ij}) - \min(\alpha_{ij})\}, \text{ for each } i$$

The attribute's importance is normalized to ascertain its importance relative to other attributes, W_i:

$$W_i = \frac{I_i}{\sum_{i=1}^{m} I_i}$$

So that $\sum_{i=1}^{m} W_i = 1$

Several different procedures are available for estimating the basic model. The simplest, and one which is gaining in popularity, is dummy variable regression (see chapter 17). In this case, the predictor variables consist of dummy variables for the attribute levels. If an attribute has k_i levels, it is coded in terms of $k_i - 1$ dummy variables (see chapter 14). If metric data are obtained, the ratings, assumed to be interval scaled, form the dependent variable. If the data are nonmetric, the rankings may be converted to 0 or 1 by making paired comparisons between brands. In this case, the predictor variables represent the differences in the attribute levels of the brands being compared. Other procedures that are appropriate for nonmetric data include LINMAP, MONANOVA, and the LOGIT model.[29]

The researcher must also decide whether the data will be analyzed at the individual respondent or the aggregate level. At the individual level, the data of each respondent are analyzed separately. If an aggregate-level analysis is to be conducted, some procedure for grouping the respondents must be devised. One common approach is first to estimate individual-level part-worth or utility functions. The respondents are then clustered on the basis of the similarity of their part-worths. Aggregate analysis is then conducted for each cluster.[30] An appropriate model for estimating the parameters should be specified.[31]

TABLE 21.5

SNEAKER DATA CODED FOR DUMMY VARIABLE REGRESSION

Preference Ratings	*Attributes*					
	Sole		*Upper*		*Price*	
Y	X_1	X_2	X_3	X_4	X_5	X_6
9	1	0	1	0	1	0
7	1	0	0	1	0	1
5	1	0	0	0	0	0
6	0	1	1	0	0	1
5	0	1	0	1	0	0
6	0	1	0	0	1	0
5	0	0	1	0	0	0
7	0	0	0	1	1	0
6	0	0	0	0	0	1

The data reported in Table 21.4 were analyzed using ordinary least squares (OLS) regression with dummy variables. The dependent variable was the preference ratings. The independent variables or predictors were six dummy variables, two for each variable. The transformed data are shown in Table 21.5. Because the data pertain to a single respondent, an individual-level analysis was conducted. The part-worth or utility functions estimated for each attribute, as well as the relative importance of the attributes, are given in Table 21.6.[32]

The model estimated may be represented as:

$$U = b_0 + b_1X_1 + b_2X_2 + b_3X_3 + b_4X_4 + b_5X_5 + b_6X_6$$

where

X_1, X_2 = dummy variables representing sole
X_3, X_4 = dummy variables representing upper
X_5, X_6 = dummy variables representing price

For sole, the attribute levels were coded as follows:

TABLE 21.6

RESULTS OF CONJOINT ANALYSIS

	Level			
Attribute	*Number*	*Description*	*Utility*	*Importance*
Sole	3	Rubber	.778	
	2	Polyurethane	−.556	
	1	Plastic	−.222	.286
Upper	3	Leather	.445	
	2	Canvas	.111	
	1	Nylon	−.556	.214
Price	3	\$30.00	1.111	
	2	\$60.00	.111	
	1	\$90.00	−1.222	.500

	X_1	X_2
Level 1	1	0
Level 2	0	1
Level 3	0	0

The levels of the other attributes were coded similarly. The parameters were estimated as follows:

$$b_0 = 4.222$$
$$b_1 = 1.000$$
$$b_2 = -.333$$
$$b_3 = 1.000$$
$$b_4 = .667$$
$$b_5 = 2.333$$
$$b_6 = 1.333$$

Given the dummy variable coding, in which level 3 is the base level, the coefficients may be related to the part-worths. As explained in chapter 17, each dummy variable coefficient represents the difference in the part-worth for that level minus the part-worth for the base level. For sole, we have the following:

$$\alpha_{11} - \alpha_{13} = b_1$$
$$\alpha_{12} - \alpha_{13} = b_2$$

To solve for the part-worths, an additional constraint is necessary. The part-worths are estimated on an interval scale, so the origin is arbitrary. Therefore, the additional constraint which is imposed is of the form:

$$\alpha_{11} + \alpha_{12} + \alpha_{13} = 0$$

These equations for the first attribute, sole, are:

$$\alpha_{11} - \alpha_{13} = 1.000$$
$$\alpha_{12} - \alpha_{13} = -.333$$
$$\alpha_{11} + \alpha_{12} + \alpha_{13} = 0$$

Solving these equations, we get,

$$\alpha_{11} = .778$$
$$\alpha_{12} = -.556$$
$$\alpha_{13} = -.222$$

The part-worths for other attributes reported in Table 21.6 can be estimated similarly. For upper we have:

$$\alpha_{21} - \alpha_{23} = b_3$$
$$\alpha_{22} - \alpha_{23} = b_4$$
$$\alpha_{21} + \alpha_{22} + \alpha_{23} = 0$$

For the third attribute, price, we have:

$$\alpha_{31} - \alpha_{33} = b_5$$
$$\alpha_{32} - \alpha_{33} = b_6$$
$$\alpha_{31} + \alpha_{32} + \alpha_{33} = 0$$

The relative importance weights were calculated based on ranges of part-worths, as follows:

$$\begin{aligned}\text{sum of ranges of part-worths} &= [.778 - (-.556)] + [.445 - (-.556)] \\ &\quad + [1.111 - (-1.222)] \\ &= 4.668\end{aligned}$$

$$\text{relative importance of sole} = \frac{[.778 - (-.556)]}{4.668} = \frac{1.334}{4.668} = .286$$

$$\text{relative importance of upper} = \frac{[.445 - (-.556)]}{4.668} = \frac{1.001}{4.668} = .214$$

$$\text{relative importance of price} = \frac{[1.111 - (-1.222)]}{4.668} = \frac{2.333}{4.668} = .500$$

The estimation of the part-worths and the relative importance weights provides the basis for interpreting the results.

Interpret the Results

For interpreting the results, it is helpful to plot the part-worth functions. The part-worth function values for each attribute given in Table 21.6 are graphed in Figure 21.10. As can be seen from Table 21.6 and Figure 21.10, this respondent has the greatest preference for a rubber sole when evaluating sneakers. Second preference is for a plastic sole, and a polyurethane sole is least preferred. A leather upper is most preferred, followed by canvas and nylon. As expected, a price of $30.00 has the highest utility and a price of $90.00 the lowest. The utility values reported in Table 21.6 have only interval scale properties, and their origin is arbitrary. In terms of relative importance of the attributes, we see that price is number one. Second most important is sole, followed closely by upper. Because price is by far the most important attribute for this respondent, this person could be labeled as price-sensitive.

Assess Reliability and Validity

Several procedures are available for assessing the reliability and validity of conjoint analysis results.[33]

- The goodness of fit of the estimated model should be evaluated. For example, if dummy variable regression is used, the value of R^2 will indicate the extent to which the model fits the data. Models with poor fit are suspect.
- Test–retest reliability can be assessed by obtaining a few replicated judgments later in data collection. In other words, at a later stage in the interview, the respondents are asked to evaluate certain selected stimuli again. The two values of these stimuli are then correlated to assess test–retest reliability.
- The evaluations for the hold-out or validation stimuli can be predicted by the estimated part-worth functions. The predicted evaluations can then be correlated with those obtained from the respondents to determine internal validity.
- If an aggregate-level analysis has been conducted, the estimation sample can be split in several ways and conjoint analysis conducted on each subsample. The results can be compared across subsamples to assess the stability of conjoint analysis solutions.

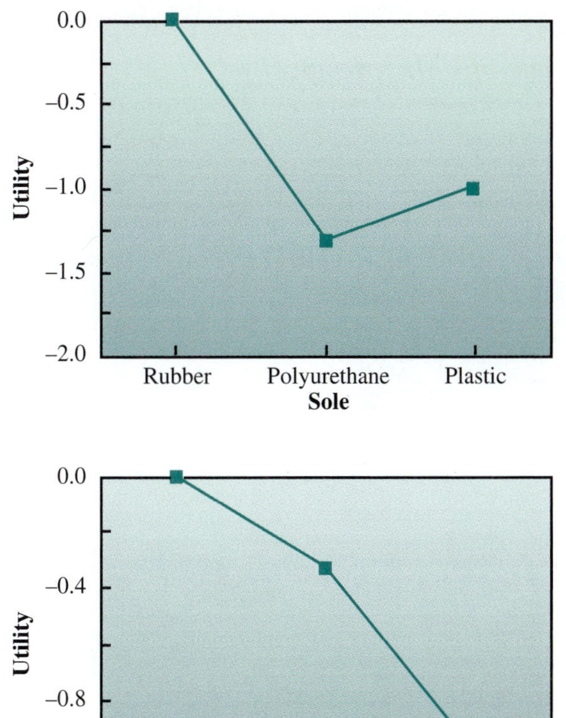

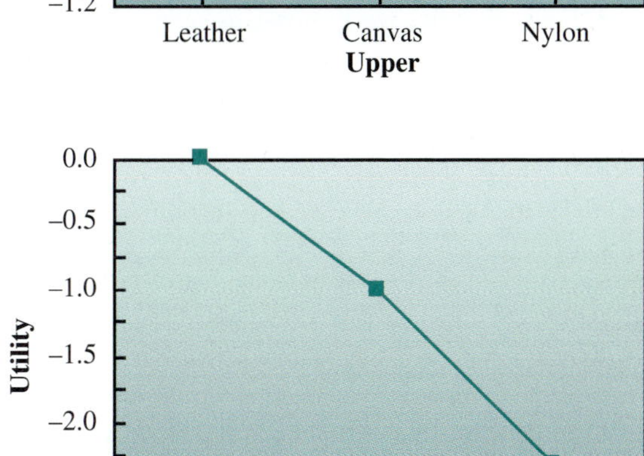

Figure 21.10
Part-Worth Functions

In running a regression analysis on the data of Table 21.5, an R^2 of .934 was obtained, indicating a good fit. The preference ratings for the nine validation profiles were predicted from the utilities reported in Table 21.6. These were correlated with the input ratings for these profiles obtained from the respondent. The correlation coefficient was .95, indicating a good predictive ability. This correlation coefficient is significant at $\alpha = .05$.

The following example further illustrates the conjoint analysis procedure.

EXAMPLE

Examining Microcomputer Trade-offs Microscopically

Consumers make trade-offs between various attributes when buying microcomputers.

Conjoint analysis was used to determine how consumers make trade-offs between various attributes when selecting microcomputers. Four attributes were chosen as salient. These attributes and their levels are:

Input Mode
- Keyboard
- Mouse

Display Monitor
- Normal resolution
- Extra High resolution

Screen Size
- 17-inch
- 13-inch

Price Level
- $1,000
- $1,500
- $2,000

All possible combinations of these attribute levels result in 24 ($2 \times 2 \times 2 \times 3$) profiles of microcomputers. One such profile is shown:

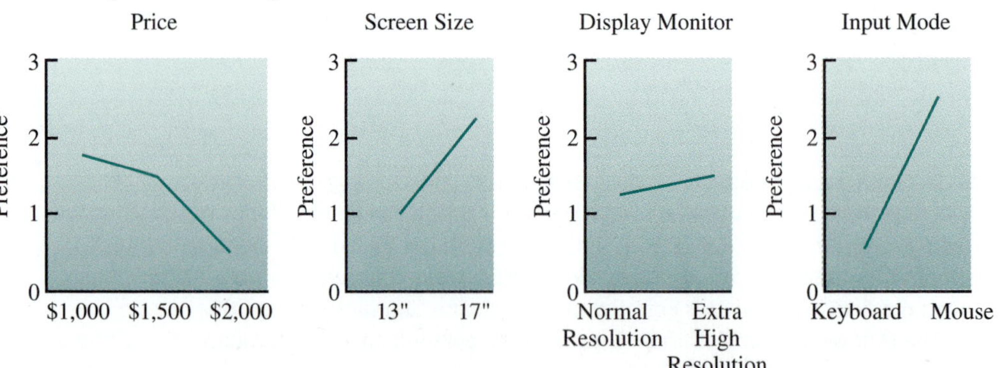

Input mode:	Mouse
Display monitor:	Normal Resolution
Screen size:	17-inch
Price level:	$1,500

Respondents rank-ordered these profiles in terms of preferences. The data for each respondent can be utilized to develop preference functions. The preference functions for one individual are illustrated.

Based on the derived part-worth or preference functions, the relative importance of the various attributes in determining these consumer preferences can be estimated by comparing part-worths as follows:

Relative importance

Evaluative Criteria	*Importance*
Input mode	45%
Display monitor	5%
Screen size	25%
Price level	25%

For this consumer, input mode is the most important feature and the mouse is the preferred option. Although price and screen size are also important, price becomes a factor only between $1,500 and $2,000. As expected, a 17-inch screen size is preferred. Whether the display monitor is normal or extra high resolution does not matter much. Information provided by the part-worth functions and relative importance weights can be used to cluster respondents to determine benefit segments for microcomputers.[34] ■

ASSUMPTIONS AND LIMITATIONS OF CONJOINT ANALYSIS

Although conjoint analysis is a popular technique, like MDS, it carries a number of assumptions and limitations. Conjoint analysis assumes that the important attributes of a product can be identified. Furthermore, it assumes that consumers evaluate the choice alternatives in terms of these attributes and make trade-offs. However, in situations in which image or brand name is important, consumers may not evaluate the brands or alternatives in terms of attributes. Even if consumers consider product attributes, the trade-off model may not be a good representation of the choice process. Another limitation is that data collection may be complex, particularly if a large number of attributes are involved and the model must be estimated at the individual level. This problem has been mitigated to some extent by procedures such as interactive or adaptive conjoint analysis and hybrid conjoint analysis. It should also be noted that the part-worth functions are not unique.

HYBRID CONJOINT ANALYSIS

Hybrid Conjoint Analysis
A form of conjoint analysis that can simplify the data collection task and estimate selected interactions as well as all main effects.

Hybrid conjoint analysis is an attempt to simplify the burdensome data collection task required in traditional conjoint analysis. Each respondent evaluates a large number of profiles, yet usually only simple part-worths, without any interaction effects, are estimated. In the simple part-worths or main effects model, the value of a combination is simply the sum of the separate main effects (simple part-worths). In actual practice, two attributes may interact, in the sense that the respondent may value the combination more than the average contribution of the separate parts. Hybrid models have been developed to serve two main purposes: (1) simplify the data collection task by imposing less of a burden on each respondent, and (2) permit the estimation of selected interactions (at the subgroup level) as well as all main (or simple) effects at the individual level.

In the hybrid approach, the respondents evaluate a limited number, generally no more than nine, conjoint stimuli, such as full profiles. These profiles are drawn from a large master design, and different respondents evaluate different sets of profiles, so that over a group of respondents all the profiles of interest are evaluated. In addition, respondents directly evaluate the relative importance of each attribute and desirability of the levels of each attribute. By combining the direct evaluations with those derived from the evaluations of the conjoint stimuli, it is possible to estimate a model at the aggregate level and still retain some individual differences.[35]

MDS and conjoint analysis are complementary techniques and may be used in combination, as the following example shows.

EXAMPLE

Weeding out the Competition

ICI Americas Agricultural Products didn't know whether it should lower the price of Fusilade, its herbicide. It knew it had developed a potent herbicide, but it wasn't sure the weed killer would survive in a price-conscious market. So a survey was designed to assess the relative importance of different attributes in selecting herbicides and measure and map perceptions of major herbicides on the same attributes. Personal interviews were conducted with 601 soybean and cotton farmers who had at least 200 acres dedicated to growing these crops and who had used herbicides during the past growing season. First, conjoint analysis was used to determine the relative importance of attributes farmers use when selecting herbicides. Then multidimensional scaling was used to map farmers' perceptions of herbicides. The study showed that price greatly influenced herbicide selections, and respondents were particularly sensitive when costs were more than $18 an acre. But price was not the only determinant. Farmers also considered how much weed control the herbicide provided. They were willing to pay higher prices to keep the pests off their land. The study showed that herbicides that failed to control even one of the four most common weeds would have to be very inexpensive to attain a reasonable market share. Fusilade promised good weed control. Furthermore, multidimensional scaling indicated that one of Fusilade's competitors was considered to be expensive. Hence, ICI kept its original pricing plan and did not lower the price of Fusilade.[36] ■

Both MDS and conjoint analysis are useful in conducting international marketing research as illustrated by Research in Practice 21.1[37] and 21.2.[38] Research in Practice 21.3 presents an application of MDS in researching ethical perceptions.[39]

INTERNET AND COMPUTER APPLICATIONS

Over the years, several computer programs have been developed for conducting MDS analysis using microcomputers and mainframes. The ALSCAL program, available in the mainframe versions of both SPSS and SAS, incorporates several different MDS models and can be used for conducting individual- or aggregate-level analysis. Other MDS programs are easily available and widely used. Most are available in both microcomputer and mainframe versions.

- MDSCAL 5M derives a spatial map of brands in a specified number of dimensions. Similarity data are used. A variety of input data formats and distance measures can be accommodated.
- KYST performs metric and nonmetric scaling and unfolding using similarity data.
- INDSCAL, denoting individual differences scaling, is useful for conducting MDS at the aggregate level. Similarity data are used as input.

RESEARCH IN PRACTICE 21.1

Herit-Age or Merit-Age in Europe?

European car manufacturers are increasingly focusing on an attribute that competitors will not be able to buy or build—it is heritage. For BMW, it is superior engineering. A. B. Volvo of Sweden has a reputation for safe cars. Italian Alfa Romeo rides on the laurels of engines that won numerous races. The French Renault has savoir-faire. On the other hand, Japanese cars are advanced technologically but they do not have class or heritage. For example, Lexus and Infiniti are high-performance cars, but they lack class. Philip Gamba, VP-marketing at Renault, believes Japanese brands lack the "French touch" of that automaker's design and credibility. These days Renault is building a car with a focus on comfort. BMW is trying to emphasize not the prestige of owning a luxury automobile but the "inner value" of its cars. To communicate value in cars is of growing importance. BMW has the edge of German heritage.

Because performance and heritage are important attributes or dimensions in automobile preferences of Europeans, the positioning of different European cars on these two dimensions is shown in the following diagram. Note that BMW has attained the best positioning on both these dimensions. Typical of most American and Japanese cars in the 1990s has been the emphasis on quality, reliability, and efficiency. However, to compete in the European market in the 21st century, Americans and Japanese are faced with the challenge of an added dimension—heritage. This calls for new marketing strategies by American and Japanese automakers.

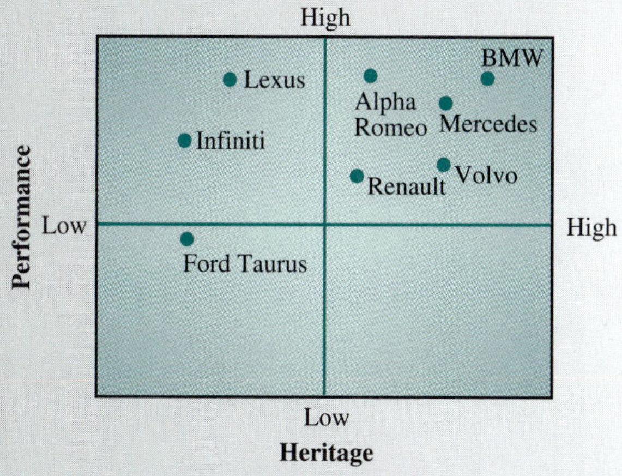

- MDPREF performs internal analysis of preference data. The program develops vector directions for preferences and the configuration of brands or stimuli in a common space.
- PREFMAP performs external analysis of preference data. This program uses a known spatial map of brands or stimuli to portray an individual's preference data. PREFMAP2 performs both internal and external analysis.
- PC-MDS contains a variety of multidimensional scaling algorithms, including factor analysis, discriminant analysis, and some other multivariate procedures. It is available for the IBM PC and compatibles.
- APM (adaptive perceptual mapping) is an adaptive scaling program, available for the microcomputer, that can handle up to 30 brands and 50 attributes. There is no limit on the number of respondents per study or the number of computers that can be used to collect the data.
- MAPWISE by Market Action Research Software, Inc., is perceptual mapping software for conducting correspondence analysis. CORRESPONDENCE ANALYSIS by the Beaumont Organization Ltd. conducts correspondence analysis, what-if simulations, and ideal-product analysis. Another program for correspondence analysis is SIMCA by Greenacre.

FOCUS ON Burke

A major role for Burke is advising clients in research design. Often clients will come to Burke with a request to execute the client's study design. It is our responsibility to advise the client if we see issues of application or interpretation. For example, in a full-profile conjoint for a cellular phone manufacturer the following design was specified by the client.

Factors: levels
Power: 3 watts or 6 watts
Weight: 10 ounce or 14 ounce
Battery Life: 30 minutes talk time; 1 hour talk time; 1.5 hours talk time, or 2 hours talk time
Brand: Brand A; Brand B
Price: Free with two-year subscription; \$100; \$200; or \$250 (if you buy the phone, you can use any service you desire)
Design Specifications: Full factorial = $2 \times 2 \times 4 \times 2 \times 4 = 128$ possible combinations

Because having a respondent evaluate 128 possible cellular phones was out of the question, a fractional factorial design (main effects only) using 16 profiles was selected. To see one of our objections to this design, a hypothetical respondent's answers are shown.
The 16 profiles are:

	Power	*Weight*	*Talk Time*	*Brand*	*Price*
Profile 1:	3 watts	10 ounce	30 minutes	Brand B	Free
Profile 2:	6 watts	10 ounce	30 minutes	Brand B	\$200
Profile 3:	6 watts	14 ounce	30 minutes	Brand A	\$250
Profile 4:	3 watts	14 ounce	30 minutes	Brand A	\$100
Profile 5:	6 watts	10 ounce	1 hour	Brand A	\$100
Profile 6:	3 watts	10 ounce	1 hour	Brand A	\$250
Profile 7:	3 watts	14 ounce	1 hour	Brand B	\$200
Profile 8:	6 watts	14 ounce	1 hour	Brand B	Free
Profile 9:	3 watts	14 ounce	1.5 hours	Brand A	\$200
Profile 10:	6 watts	14 ounce	1.5 hours	Brand A	Free
Profile 11:	6 watts	10 ounce	1.5 hours	Brand B	\$100
Profile 12:	3 watts	10 ounce	1.5 hours	Brand B	\$250
Profile 13:	6 watts	14 ounce	2.0 hours	Brand B	\$250
Profile 14:	3 watts	14 ounce	2.0 hours	Brand B	\$100
Profile 15:	3 watts	10 ounce	2.0 hours	Brand A	Free
Profile 16:	6 watts	10 ounce	2.0 hours	Brand A	\$200

(Continued)

If OLS regression is used as the estimation procedure in conjoint analysis, these programs are universally available. In particular, the microcomputer and mainframe versions of SAS, SPSS, BMDP, Minitab, and Excel have several regression programs. (These were discussed in chapter 17.) Several specialized programs are also available for conjoint analysis. MONANOVA (monotone analysis of variance) is a nonmetric procedure that uses full-profile data. For pairwise data, the TRADEOFF procedure can be used. TRADEOFF is also a nonmetric procedure that uses the rank ordering of preferences for attribute-level pairs. Both MONANOVA and TRADEOFF are available for the mainframe and microcomputers. Other popular programs include LINMAP and ACA (adaptive conjoint analysis). ACA focuses on the attributes and levels most relevant for each individual re-

FOCUS ON Burke *(Continued)*

One respondent's ratings on a 10 point purchase interest scale:

Profile 1: 2	Profile 9: 1
Profile 2: 5	Profile 10: 4
Profile 3: 1	Profile 11: 10
Profile 4: 1	Profile 12: 5
Profile 5: 5	Profile 13: 6
Profile 6: 1	Profile 14: 8
Profile 7: 3	Profile 15: 3
Profile 8: 6	Profile 16: 5

Subjecting this respondent's data to OLS regression, using the design matrix as predictor variables, the following results emerge.

Attribute	*Utility Value*	*Relative Importance*
Power		
3 watts	−1.12	
6 watts	1.12	18.8%
Weight		
10 ounce	0.375	
14 ounce	−0.375	6.0%
Battery Life		
30 minutes	−1.875	
1 hour	−0.375	
1.5 hours	0.875	
2.0 hours	1.375	27.1%
Brand		
A	1.5	
B	−1.5	25.0%
Price		
Free with/two-year subscription	−0.375	
$100	1.875	
$200	−0.625	
$250	−0.875	22.9%

Why would Burke question this design?

First, management wanted to understand the sensitivity to price. This model would assume that either both brands had the same price elasticity or management would gain the needed information from an "average" price elasticity for the two brands. When directly asked about this, the client had not considered that this "price sensitivity" may not actually fit either brand. Burke suggested a design that would examine the interaction between brand and price as this is a way to examine the price elasticity of a brand (not an average of brands).

spondent. PC-MDS also contains a program for conjoint analysis. Other useful programs include software by Bretton-Clark, including CONJOINT DESIGNER, CONJOINT ANALYZER, CONJOINT LINMAP, SIMGRAF, and BRIDGER. POSSE (product optimization and selected segmentation evaluation) by Robinson Associates, Inc., is a generalized system for optimizing product and service designs using hybrid conjoint analysis and experimental design methods. It uses consumer choice simulators, response surface modeling, and optimization procedures to develop optimal product configurations. Choice-based conjoint (CBC) and multimedia conjoint programs, which demonstrate product features rather than just describe them, are also available, for example from Sawtooth Technologies (www.sawtooth.com).

RESEARCH IN PRACTICE 21.2

Fabs' Fabulous Foamy Fight

Competition in the detergent market was brewing in Thailand. Superconcentrate detergent is fast becoming the prototype with a market share of over 50 percent in the detergent category by the end of 1998. Market potential research in Thailand indicated that superconcentrates would grow by about 40 percent a year. In addition, this category had already dominated other Asian markets such as Taiwan, Hong Kong, and Singapore. Consequently, Colgate entered this new line of competition with Fab Power Plus with the objective of capturing 4 percent market share. The main players in the market were Kao Corporation's Attack (14.6 percent), 2.8 percent by Lever Brothers' Breeze Ultra, 1.1 percent by Lion Corporation's Pao M. Wash and 0.4 percent by Lever's Omo. Based on qualitative research and secondary data, Colgate assessed the critical factors for the success of superconcentrates. Some of these factors were environmental appeal, hand-washing and machine-wash convenience, superior cleaning abilities, optimum level of suds for hand wash, and brand name. Market research also revealed that no brand had both hand- and machine-wash capabilities. Pao Hand Force was formulated as the hand-washing brand. Pao M. Wash was the machine-wash version. Lever's Breezematic was targeted for machine use. Therefore, a formula that had both hand- and machine-wash capability was desirable. A conjoint study was designed and these factors varied at either two or three levels. Preference ratings were gathered from respondents and part-worths for the factors estimated both at the individual and the group level. Results showed that the factor on hand–machine capability had a substantial contribution supporting earlier claims. Based on these findings, Fab Power Plus was successfully introduced as a brand with both hand- and machine-wash capabilities.

RESEARCH IN PRACTICE 21.3

Ethical Perceptions of Marketing Research Firms

In a refined scale to measure the degree a certain situation is ethical or unethical, three factors have been found to have acceptable validity and parsimony. Two of these dimensions are particularly interesting. These are a broad-based moral equity dimension (factor 1), and a relativistic dimension (factor 2). Using multidimensional scaling one can plot the perceived ethicalness of marketing research firms using these dimensions. For example, an MDS plot might look like this.

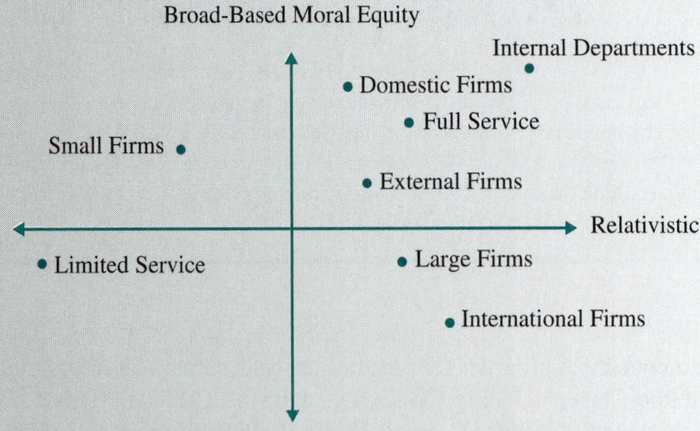

In this example, internal marketing research departments are perceived to be the most ethical on both dimensions. Large marketing research firms are perceived to be more ethical on the relativistic dimension, whereas small firms are more ethical on the moral equity factor. International marketing research firms are more ethical on relativistic terms, whereas the domestic firms are higher on the moral equity dimension. Finally, full-service firms are perceived to be more ethical on both the dimensions as compared to the limited-service firms.

SUMMARY

Multidimensional scaling is used for obtaining spatial representations of respondents' perceptions and preferences. Perceived or psychological relationships among stimuli are represented as geometric relationships among points in a multidimensional space. Formulating the MDS problem requires a specification of the brands or stimuli to be included. The number and nature of brands selected influences the resulting solution. Input data obtained from the respondents can be related to perceptions or preferences. Perception data can be direct or derived. The direct approaches are more common in marketing research.

The selection of an MDS procedure depends on the nature (metric or nonmetric) of the input data and whether perceptions or preferences are being scaled. Another determining factor is whether the analysis will be conducted at the individual or aggregate level. The decision about the number of dimensions in which to obtain a solution should be based on theory, interpretability, elbow criterion, and ease-of-use considerations. Labeling the dimensions is a difficult task that requires subjective judgment. Several guidelines are available for assessing the reliability and validity of MDS solutions. Preference data can be subjected to either internal or external analysis. If the input data are of a qualitative nature, they can be analyzed via correspondence analysis. If the attribute-based approaches are used to obtain input data, spatial maps can also be obtained by means of factor or discriminant analysis.

Conjoint analysis is based on the notion that the relative importance that consumers attach to salient attributes, and the utilities they attach to the levels of attributes, can be determined when consumers evaluate brand profiles that are constructed using these attributes and their levels. Formulating the problem requires an identification of the salient attributes and their levels. The pairwise and the full-profile approaches are commonly employed for constructing the stimuli. Statistical designs are available for reducing the number of stimuli in the evaluation task. The input data can be either nonmetric (rankings) or metric (ratings). Typically, the dependent variable is preference or intention to buy.

Although other procedures are available for analyzing conjoint analysis data, regression using dummy variables is becoming increasingly important. Interpretation of the results requires an examination of the part-worth functions and relative importance weights. Several procedures are available for assessing the reliability and validity of conjoint analysis results.

KEY TERMS AND CONCEPTS

multidimensional scaling (MDS)
similarity judgments
preference rankings
stress
R-square
spatial map
coordinates
unfolding
derived approaches
nonmetric MDS
metric MDS
elbow criterion
internal analysis of preferences
external analysis of preferences
correspondence analysis
conjoint analysis
part-worth functions
relative importance weights
attribute levels
full profiles
pairwise tables
cyclical designs
fractional factorial designs
orthogonal arrays
internal validity
conjoint analysis model
hybrid conjoint analysis

ACRONYMS

The steps involved in conducting multidimensional scaling may be represented by the acronym SCALING:

S timuli selection: problem formulation
C hoice of an MDS procedure
A ssessing reliability and validity
L abeling dimensions
I nput data: metric or nonmetric
N umber of dimensions
G eometric representation and interpretation

The steps involved in conducting conjoint analysis may be represented by the acronym ANALYSIS:

A ssessing reliability and validity
N umber and levels of attributes: problem formulation
A ttribute importance determination
L evel of analysis: individual versus aggregate
Y axis: utility values for attribute levels
S timuli construction: full-profile versus pairwise
I nput data: metric or nonmetric
S election of a conjoint procedure

EXERCISES

Questions

1. For what purposes are MDS procedures used?
2. What is meant by a spatial map?
3. Describe the steps involved in conducting MDS.
4. Describe the direct and derived approaches to obtaining MDS input data.
5. What factors influence the choice of an MDS procedure?
6. What guidelines are used for deciding on the number of dimensions in which to obtain an MDS solution?
7. Describe the ways in which the reliability and validity of MDS solutions can be assessed.
8. What is the difference between internal and external analysis of preference data?
9. Briefly describe correspondence analysis.
10. What is involved in formulating a conjoint analysis problem?
11. Describe the full-profile approach to constructing stimuli in conjoint analysis.
12. Describe the pairwise approach to constructing stimuli in conjoint analysis.
13. How can regression analysis be used for analyzing conjoint data?
14. Graphically illustrate what is meant by part-worth functions.
15. What procedures are available for assessing the reliability and validity of conjoint analysis results?
16. Briefly describe hybrid conjoint analysis.

Problems

1. Identify two marketing research problems in which MDS could be applied. Explain how you would apply MDS in these situations.
2. Identify two marketing research problems in which conjoint analysis could be applied. Explain how you would apply conjoint analysis in these situations.

INTERNET AND COMPUTER EXERCISES

1. Analyze the data of Table 21.1 using an appropriate MDS procedure. Compare your results to those given in the text.
2. Consider the following 12 brands of bar soap: Jergens, Dove, Zest, Dial, Camay, Ivory, Palmolive, Irish Spring, Lux, Safeguard, Tone, and Monchel. Form all the possible 66 pairs of these brands. Rate these pairs of brands in terms of similarity using a seven-point scale. Analyze the similarity judgments that you provided for the 12 bar soap brands. Use an appropriate MDS procedure, such as ALSCAL or KYST. Label the dimensions and interpret your own spatial map.
3. Construct the nine sneaker profiles given in Table 21.4. Rate these nine profiles in terms of your preference using a nine-point rating scale. Use OLS regression to develop part-worth functions for the three sneaker attributes, using the data you provided. How do your results compare with those reported in the text?

Professional Perspectives

3.1 Cross-Tabulation

Bob McDonald

Bob is vice president, Philadelphia client services. He joined Burke in 1973 and founded the company's Philadelphia-area client service office in 1976. He currently provides research design and analytic assistance to several client organizations and to Burke account representatives.

INTRODUCTION

Although a variety of sophisticated statistical techniques are available, virtually all surveys and tests will initially, and often exclusively, rely on the "counts" and percentages found in cross-tabulations. For example, when presented with test data of the nature of Table 1, management can readily interpret the results of this pairing of two television commercials in generating positive purchase intent:

	Commercial	
	"Warren's Tavern"	*"New Boston"*
Base—Viewers Per Ad	(200)%	(200)%
Positive Purchase Intent	46	67
Definitely Would Buy	18	31
Probably Would Buy	28	36

In the jargon of the trade, the headings are referred to as the "banner":

Commercial:

"Warren's Tavern" *"New Boston"*

The row captions are referred to as the "stubs":

Positive Purchase Intent
Definitely Would Buy
Probably Would Buy

The terminology is simple, but the design and presentation of cross-tabular data, however, is not always as simplistic as the above example suggests. Consider the following points:

BANNER DESIGN

- A total column may or may not be appropriate, based on the research design. Within an independent-cells test design in which the samples are not drawn proportionate to their presence in the population, an aggregated total (unless it is based on weighted columns) is clearly inappropriate.

■ The banner should generally avoid the presentation of highly intercorrelated variables which, unsurprisingly, yield highly redundant results. For example, in a child's snack product test conducted among a sample of mothers of children and/or teenagers, looking at the cross-tabulations shows greater purchase interest among younger moms, among moms of fewer children, among employed moms, and among single moms. The point, of course, is that virtually the same subgroup is being "read" four times, the proportional overlaps between the four classificatory segments being extensive. Although not technically "wrong," conclusions drawn from the correlated banner points could be misleading. A simple example shows:

	Number of children		
	1	*2*	*3*
	%	%	%
Positive purchase intent	90	80	60
base	120	100	80

It appears clear that positive purchase intent declines with the number of children in the household.

	Age of Mother	
	Under 25	*25 and Older*
Positive purchase intent	83%	74%
base	160	140

It is also clear that older mothers have a lower percentage of positive purchase intent.

	Age of Mother					
	Moms under 25 Number of Children:			*Moms 25 and Over Number of Children*		
	1	*2*	*3+*	*1*	*2*	*3+*
	%	%	%	%	%	%
Positive purchase intent	90	80	60	90	80	60
base	85	55	20	35	45	60

Now, with the "nested" tabulation, it is clear that the age of the mother isn't related to positive purchase intent, rather the distribution of mothers by number of children is very different for younger versus older moms.

RESPONSE CATEGORIES

In many surveys the number of categories in which a measurement is taken is decided by the researcher without evidence of the consequence of using the selected categorization. For example, respondent age might be initially tabbed via three, four, five, or more subgroups. As a rule of thumb, use the largest number of categories you can (or get exact data if possible). Subsequent analysis always presents the opportunity for "collapsing" to fewer groups. You can explore how the categories relate to other measures without concern that the categories you selected are artificially hiding relationships because they are too broad.

- Nature of the sample banner subgroups to be tested for statistically significant differences need be clearly recognized as either (1) completely independent groups (mutually exclusive), (2) completely matched (the same respondents), or (3) a partially overlapping mixture. Matched groups, of course, will often appear when, for example, two brands each with near 100 percent awareness are rated. Where broader variation is seen in brand awareness levels, the overlapping mixture result occurs: Some respondents rate brand A/not B, some rate brand B/not A, and some rate both. The point, of course, is simply that maximal precision of interpretation will depend on the application of the most appropriate test (or tests) as directed by the nature of the subgroups.
- A distinction should be made between statistical versus managerial significance. Strict and complete reliance on the presence or absence of statistically significant differences is not always desirable.

Statistical variations that do not "hang together" to cogently support the major results within the "story" are also not high priority with management; they do not enhance their decisions nor forward their careers. Conversely, differences and patterns (typically termed "directional") that do buttress the "story" but "miss" the 95 percent confidence levels may potentially be of high priority, and when omitted because the 95 percent bell was not rung represents a disservice to management.

STUB DESIGN

Because such a multitude of alternatives can not be assessed without excessive length, the following comments are offered to focus on only a few selected fundamental issues and basic decision themes in stub design.

- As elementary as it may seem, the order of presenting tables is not a given. The not uncommon practice of tables[1] being ordered to match the sequence in which the questions appear within the interview frequently has little to endorse it other than its being easier than developing a custom flow that reveals the story the data tells.
- Each table needs to be considered as to the most meaningful base that is to be employed. Most often, this will reflect the respondents that asked the particular question and, therefore, can easily vary between tables due to interview skip patterns. (An overall brand satisfaction question tabbed on total, that is, makes little sense when only one-third of the survey respondents have ever tried the brand.) Likewise, some tables will clearly be more informative with the base "floated" down to a particular subgroup from those asked.
- Ratios and percentage differences/changes need to be employed with caution and presented with appropriate caveats.
- Classic "conversion ratios," such as awareness-to-trial or trial-to-brand-used-most-often (BUMO), need to be carefully approached from two perspectives. First, if several brands are being profiled, the composition of awareness may differ substantively as to aware-tried versus aware-not tried ("Ford" versus "Rolls Royce"). Because triers have experience-based perceptions and non-triers respond only from imagery, interbrand (and intergroup) differences may be misleading. Secondly, attention must be focused on the appropriate sample size on which a ratio is calculated. If, for example, comparisons are being made across brands (or across waves of a tracking survey) for trial-to-BUMO levels, and if a given brand has only a 10 percent or 15 percent trial penetration, the total survey sample of 300 interviews is irrelevant to the statistical evaluation; the 30 or 45 triers is the rather shaky foundation for the ratio.

Conjoint has a wide variety of applications including the following examples:

- Identifying the product or service with the optimum combination of features
- Determining the relative contributions of each attribute and each attribute level to the overall evaluation of product/service
- Predicting market share among products/services with differing sets of features
- Measuring market opportunities for products not currently on the market
- Determining the profitability of possible products based on a comparison of feature costs to expected price and market share
- Understanding the potential for multiproduct or multibrand strategy, including an estimate of cannibalism
- Assessing the impact of deleting a product or brand from the market
- Determining how to change a current product to compete with new products entering the market
- Estimating the effect of eliminating some product features that are costly to provide but are of marginal value to customers
- Segmenting customers who place differing importance on features, possibly understanding the size of the segment who buys strictly on price or the size of the segment who buys strictly on brand

Irrespective of the approach you use to conjoint design and analysis, choosing the features and levels to include is of vital importance to the study's success. The tendency of new researchers is to want to include an overabundance of features thinking that the consumers are as involved in their category as they are. Humans tend to simplify decision processes, and as a result, including the five to eight most important features is generally sufficient to predict purchase interest. When selecting the final variables for inclusion in the conjoint, be sure to include only features that can add to or detract from overall choice, differentiate between products, be acted on, and be easily communicated.

Another issue for the new researcher is the tendency to overgeneralize the solution. If the change in levels of price tends to have a great impact on the preference for a product, one can not make the general statement that "price is the most important characteristic." What you have measured is that the change from one level of price to another among the prices you chose to test was more determinant of choice than a change from one level to another on other characteristics. You could have chosen price levels that were closer together and gotten a very different result. This somewhat subtle point is discussed in the Burke Viewpoint included in the conjoint analysis chapter.

Cases

3.1 Danger! Celebrity in Use

The theory behind the use of celebrities is that featuring stars in advertising has special cultural significance, borne from the unique way that they have constructed an image through various forms of media in the culture. In associating the star with the product, these special meanings are passed on to the products or brands. Celebrities have particular configurations of meanings that cannot be found elsewhere.

However, celebrities are expensive to use and there are hidden dangers. In 1996, it was estimated that about 20 percent of all advertising uses celebrities, and about 10 percent of the costs go toward celebrities' pay checks. In 1997, a then-21-year-old Tiger Woods was expected to command $1 billion from the golf pro's combined endorsements, including $12 million from the sum of his Nike and Titleist contracts. In addition to the exorbitant costs, there are risks and dangers associated with the use of celebrities in advertising. Pepsi signed up Madonna for several million dollars in order to feature her in their Pepsi campaign. The controversy over the religious imagery in her "Like a Prayer" video led to the threat of a consumer boycott, and Pepsi lost $10 million. Cybil Shepherd's ad for the beef industry flopped when she publicly admitted that she rarely ate red meat. These examples are only a few of the problems with celebrity endorsements. Unfortunately, there have always been hidden dangers when using celebrities as exemplified by the use of O. J. Simpson in Hertz advertising.

If so many dangers abound, why use celebrities? Many advertisers feel that celebrities make an advertisement more effective. PepsiCo's Pepsi Cola and Revlon, for example, have boosted their products' images and sales by using Cindy Crawford in commercials. The use of celebrities has been demonstrated to lead to higher recall of an advertisement. Further evidence supporting the use of celebrities includes research showing that for attractiveness-related products, physically attractive celebrities elicit high credibility and attitude ratings for an ad.

One researcher, Michael Kamins, employed marketing research techniques in order to explore the uses of celebrities in advertising more scientifically. Kamins states that three processes of social influence determine whether an individual will adopt the attitude an advertiser is trying to convey: compliance, identification, and internalization. Although the first of these factors is not relevant to Kamins's study, the last two hold considerable implications for celebrity advertising. Identification, whereby individuals try to imitate another person because they want to be like that person, is the most important factor determining a celebrity's influence in an advertisement. Internalization occurs when individuals imitate another because they perceive the other person to be sincere and to have values similar to their own.

Kamins inferred that if both identification and internalization could be achieved, the effectiveness of advertising would be increased. Therefore, he studied whether celebrities could increase the effectiveness of advertising through the identification component, and whether so-called truth in advertising (operationalized as two-sided advertising, or advertising that included both positive and negative aspects about a product) could increase effectiveness through internalization. Furthermore, he wondered whether combining these two approaches resulted in even greater effectiveness.

In order to research this, a 2×2 factorial design was adopted. Sidedness (one-sided versus two-sided) and type of spokesperson (celebrity versus noncelebrity) were the two factors. Seventy-seven executives enrolled in an executive MBA program were randomly assigned to four groups: one-sided/noncelebrity, one-sided/celebrity, two-sided/noncelebrity, and two-sided/celebrity. Four ads corresponding to these criteria were made up, and each member of each group evaluated the appropriate ad on the basis of four variables: expectancy-value brand attitude (A), global brand attitude (B), global attitude toward the ad (C), and purchase intention (D). Expectancy-value brand attitude represented the degree to which the subject believed the product possessed an attribute the ad claimed it had. Global brand attitude was a measure of how appealing the subjects found the product in the ad to be. Global attitude toward the ad was an evaluation of the ad's effectiveness. Purchase intention indicated how likely a subject was to purchase the product when an opportunity to do so came about.

Table 1 shows the mean (x) and standard deviation values (sd), along with the number of subjects (n), for each variable across each of the groups in Kamins's study. Note that the results from related groups can be combined to yield information on each of the four group characteristics (one-sided, two-sided, noncelebrity, and celebrity) separately. Table 2 contains the ANOVA results for the effect of the independent variables of sidedness (E) and type of spokesperson (S). These results provide valuable information about the effectiveness of celebrity spokespersons in advertisements.

Although the above research results are useful, they are also very specific. Celebrity advertising can be researched in other ways. For example, dead celebrities have been shown to be hip, hot, and safe. Although they are not cheap (advertisers do have to pay licensing fees to the celebrities' estates), they are safe, because they can't do anything unpredictable that might jeopardize a product's image or embarrass the sponsor. Abbott and Costello have been used to sell bran cereal, Humphrey Bogart to lend flair to cellular phones and Diet Coke, and Charlie Chaplin to push IBM personal computers. This just goes to show that while the celebrities themselves may be dead, their use as advertising spokespersons has a long life.

Questions

1. What kind of marketing research could businesses conduct to determine if their products would perform better with celebrity endorsements?
2. Discuss the role of MDS in the matching of a celebrity to the right product.

MEANS, STANDARD DEVIATIONS, AND NUMBER OF SUBJECTS

Experimental Condition		*Variable*			
		Expectancy-Value Brand Attitude (A)	*Global Brand Attitude (B)*	*Global Attitude toward the Ad (C)*	*Purchase Intention (D)*
	(x)	7.97	3.47	3.4	2.22
	(sd)	3.92	1.47	1.52	1.4
One-sided	(n)	38	40	40	40
	(x)	8.33	4.22	3.65	2.92
	(sd)	5.32	1.6	1.62	1.44
Two-sided	(n)	36	37	37	37
	(x)	8.04	3.5	3.65	2.55
	(sd)	4.73	1.55	1.46	1.38
Noncelebrity	(n)	38	40	40	40
	(x)	8.26	4.19	3.38	2.57
	(sd)	4.58	1.52	1.67	1.56
Celebrity	(n)	36	37	37	37
	(x)	7.89	3.45	3.55	2.4
	(sd)	4.48	1.57	1.39	1.5
One-sided noncelebrity	(n)	19	20	20	20
	(x)	8.04	3.5	3.25	2.05
	(sd)	3.4	1.4	1.65	1.32
One-sided celebrity	(n)	19	20	20	20
	(x)	8.18	3.55	3.75	2.7
	(sd)	5.09	1.57	1.55	1.26
Two-sided noncelebrity	(n)	19	20	20	20
	(x)	8.5	5	3.53	3.18
	(sd)	5.72	1.27	1.74	1.63
Two-sided celebrity	(n)	17	17	17	17

ANOVA RESULTS FOR THE DEPENDENT MEASURES

Variable	*Main Effect for Sidedness* (E)	*Main Effect for Spokesperson* (S)	*Interaction* (E × S)
Expectancy-value brand attitude (A)	$F = .013$	$F = .035$	$F = .003$
Global brand attitude (B)	$F = 10.876^a$	$F = 4.355^a$	$F = 4.233^a$
Global attitude toward the ad (C)	$F = .209$	$F = .276$	$F = .001$
Purchase intention (D)	$F = 4.845^a$	$F = .050$	$F = 1.868$

[a] indicates significance at $p \leq .05$.

3. Could conjoint analysis be used to determine whether celebrities should be used and, if so, which celebrity should be selected? How could it be used?
4. What kinds of precautions or pretesting should the researcher engage in to ensure that the celebrities and two-sided ads used in the experiment were appropriate? What complications or contaminations might be present in the experimental results if these precautions were not taken?
5. Based on the results presented, do two-sided ads have an advantage over one-sided ads? Celebrity ads over noncelebrity ads?
6. Which type of ad is the most effective? The least effective? (*Hint*: look at the ANOVA results.)
7. Is analysis of variance an appropriate technique to use to analyze the data obtained in this study? Why or why not?
8. Could regression analysis be used to analyze the data obtained in this research? If so, how?

References

Al Ries, "Count on Consumers to Follow the Leader," *Brandweek* 38 (25) (June 23, 1997): 18.

George Lazarus, "Tiger's Shooting for an Endorsement Record, Too," *Chicago Tribune* (May 5, 1997): 4, 6.

Michael A. Kamins, "Celebrity and Noncelebrity Advertising in a Two-Sided Context," *Journal of Advertising Research* (June–July 1989): 34–42.

Michael A. Kamins, "An Investigation into the 'Match-Up' Hypothesis in Celebrity Advertising: When Beauty May Be Only Skin Deep," *Journal of Advertising* 19 (1) (1990): 4–13.

M. Kamins, M. Brand, S. Hoeke, and J. Moe, "Two-Sided versus One-Sided Celebrity Endorsements: The Impact on Advertising Effectiveness and Credibility," *Journal of Advertising* 18 (2) (1989): 4–10.

3.2 The Demographic Discovery of the Decade

Many marketers are ill-positioned to take advantage of some of the most important consumer segment groups to rise in the next 20 years—senior citizens. Senior households were responsible for one of every four dollars spent by U.S. households in 1998 and that percentage is expected to grow in the new millennium. Senior citizens control more than $7 trillion of net worth, or over 77 percent of the country's financial assets and spend more than most of their younger counterparts in nearly all spending categories. Nonetheless, marketers continue to aim promotions at and cater to younger segments. As the members of the baby boom generation mature, marketers must realize that mature Americans will now become the largest spending group.

The mature market is divisible into four segments. There are the so-called older adults ranging from 55 to 64 years of age. The second market segment, the elderly, is made up of those aged 65 to 74. The aged, those from 75 to 84, and the very old, those 85 and over, constitute the other two segments. A closer look at the older adult group reveals that they are interested in maintaining a youthful appearance and are major targets for exercise equipment, health programs, diets, cosmetics, cosmetic surgery, sports clothing, designer wear, and a wide array of personal services that improve appearance. An increasing number of older adults opt for early retirement or move into new careers and part-time jobs. The elderly group comprises those who have been retired for some time.

They tend to take a keen interest in health and nutrition and to be concerned with diet, salt intake, cholesterol, fried foods, and calories. They often drink less alcohol than the younger population and are a good market for skin care products, prescriptions, vitamins and minerals, health and beauty aids, and medicines that ease pain and promote the performance of everyday activities. The aged group often has health and mobility problems and hence requires health care services and special care facilities. The very old need help in their day-to-day tasks. They find it difficult to get around and need regular medical and hospital care. Again, they represent a large market for health care facilities.

While the classification of the mature market into these four segments has been useful, another classification, and perhaps a better one for advertising purposes, is based on attitudes toward advertising. These segments could then be profiled in terms of psychographic variables. A major concern of advertisers targeting the aged consumer has been the way in which the older population utilizes and evaluates information from advertising to make purchasing decisions. One study by Davis and French explored aged consumers' use of advertising as a primary source of information in purchase decisions. The respondents were clustered based on attitudes toward advertising. Psychographic profiles were developed for each of the derived segments.

A database of annual lifestyle surveys was used to obtain a sample of 217 married female respondents age 60 and over who were not employed outside the home. Respondents were asked to rate their degree of agreement with each of the 200 AIO (activities, interests, opinions) statements on the survey. Respondents were also asked to rate four attitudinal statements measuring information usage and beliefs about advertising, as well as the credibility of the source of advertising. Identical information obtained from a previous study was used for replication purposes by Davis and French.

The data on the four statements (shown in Table 1) measuring attitudes toward advertising was analyzed using Ward's method of clustering. Three clusters—Engaged, Autonomous, and Receptive consumers—were identified. Mean scores for each cluster are presented in Table 1. To test stability, replication of the cluster analysis was undertaken using the data obtained in the previous study. Ward's method of clustering was used to analyze the data from the previous study. Again, three clusters were obtained. Cluster means on each of the clustering variables for the replication sample (previous study) are also shown in Table 1 obtained by Davis and French.

To determine the psychographic differences among the three clusters, two additional steps were taken. First, one-way ANOVA was carried out to determine the discriminating variables. The three segments formed the grouping or the independent variable, and each psychographic statement served as a dependent variable. Forty-one of the original 200 psychographic statements were found to be statistically significant. With the realization

CLUSTER VARIABLE SCORES BY SEGMENT

		Means	
Cluster Variable	*Segment*	*Study Sample*	*Replication*
Advertising insults my intelligence.	Engaged	5.24 (agree)	4.35 (agree)
	Autonomous	4.86 (agree)	5.01 (agree)
	Receptive	2.20 (disagree)	2.10 (disagree)
Information from advertising helps me make better buying decisions.	Engaged	4.69 (agree)	4.88 (agree)
	Autonomous	3.65 (agree)	3.30 (disagree)[a]
	Receptive	4.78 (agree)	4.18 (agree)
I often seek out the advice of friends regarding brands and products.	Engaged	4.55 (agree)	4.21 (agree)
	Autonomous	2.16 (disagree)	1.87 (disagree)
	Receptive	2.99 (disagree)	3.02 (disagree)
I don't believe a company's ad when it claims that test results show its product to be better than competitive products.	Engaged	4.78 (agree)	4.25 (agree)
	Autonomous	4.85 (agree)	5.00 (agree)
	Receptive	4.12 (agree)	4.94 (agree)

[a] 3.5 is the neutral point.

STUDY SAMPLE MEAN FACTOR SCORES BY CLUSTER

Factor	*Engaged*	*Autonomous*	*Receptive*
Factor 1	.45	−.11	−.21
I am interested in the cultures of other countries. (loading = .58966)	4.41	3.92	3.87
I get personal satisfaction from using cosmetics. (loading = .48283)	4.29	3.74	3.45
I enjoy looking through fashion magazines. (loading = .41592)	4.89	4.31	4.55
Factor 2	.29	−.32	.17
I like to bake. (loading = .70466)	5.49	4.75	5.19
I like to cook. (loading = .60793)	5.28	4.63	5.01
I always bake from scratch. (loading = .54404)	3.76	3.15	3.62
Factor 3	.28	−.26	.10
I try to select foods that are fortified with vitamins and minerals. (loading = .49480)	4.89	4.36	4.59
I try to buy a company's products if they support educational TV. (loading = .43730)	4.13	3.53	3.72
I am usually among the first to try new products. (loading = .42521)	3.47	2.81	3.19
Factor 4	.26	.14	−.36
Generally, manufacturers' warranties are not worth the paper they are printed on. (loading = .50313)	3.31	3.47	2.82
Most big companies are just out for themselves. (loading = .47638)	4.25	4.50	3.93
TV advertising is condescending toward women. (loading = .41031)	4.25	4.24	3.55

that some of these significant variables were probably measuring the same characteristics, a principal components factor analysis was carried out, with four factors (accounting for 60.3 percent of the variance) extracted in a varimax rotation. Factor scores were computed for each of the three segments by Davis and French, and Table 2 shows these scores, along with the variables that loaded highly on these factors and the variable means. This information can be used to provide psychographic profiles for each of the three segments identified in cluster analysis.

The results of this research and similar studies help marketers target the elderly, an especially promising group in light of the financial assets that they possess. By 2025, some 113 million Americans—about 40 percent of the population—will be over 50. Hence, the discovery of the mature market represents a golden opportunity for marketers to target an old segment in a new way.

Questions

1. Studies have found that the older, elderly, aged, and the very old segments of the mature market need good supporting health services and facilities. Describe in detail how health maintenance organizations (HMOs) can effectively determine the differences in the health care needs of these segments. What kind of information should be obtained? Which statistical techniques should be used to analyze the data?

respondents were obtained from the mailing lists of *Car and Driver, Business Week*, and *Inc*. magazines and they were telephoned at their homes by an independent surveying company. The statements used in the survey of 400 respondents are listed below:

1. I am in very good physical condition.
2. When I must choose between the two, I usually dress for fashion, not comfort.
3. I have more stylish clothes than most of my friends.
4. I want to look a little different from others.
5. Life is too short not to take some gambles.
6. I am not concerned about the ozone layer.
7. I think the government is doing too much to control pollution.
8. Basically, society today is fine.
9. I don't have time to volunteer for charities.
10. Our family is not too heavily in debt today.
11. I like to pay cash for everything I buy.
12. I pretty much spend for today and let tomorrow bring what it will.
13. I use credit cards because I can pay the bill off slowly.
14. I seldom use coupons when I shop.
15. Interest rates are low enough to allow me to buy what I want.
16. I have more self-confidence than most of my friends.
17. I like to be considered a leader.
18. Others often ask me to help them out of a jam.
19. Children are the most important thing in a marriage.
20. I would rather spend a quiet evening at home than go out to a party.
21. American-made cars can't compare with foreign-made cars.
22. The government should restrict imports of products from Japan.
23. Americans should always try to buy American products.
24. I would like to take a trip around the world.
25. I wish I could leave my present life and do something entirely different.
26. I am usually among the first to try new products.
27. I like to work hard and play hard.
28. Skeptical predictions are usually wrong.
29. I can do anything I set my mind to.
30. Five years from now, my income will be a lot higher than it is now.

In addition, the criterion variable, attitude toward Dodge Viper, was measured by asking each person to respond to the statement, "I would consider buying the Dodge Viper made by Chrysler." This statement was measured on the same nine-point scale as the 30 predictor statements.

The data for the case are provided on the disk as well as the Web site. In the enclosed data, the first variable represents attitude toward a Chrysler sportscar. The next 30 variables, in the order listed in the case, represent the ratings of the lifestyle statements. Each field occupies three columns.

Questions

The director of marketing for Chrysler is interested in knowing the psychological characteristics of Yuppies to configure the Dodge Viper program. You have been presented with the responses from the survey outlined above. Analyze the data according to the following guidelines:

1. *Frequency distribution*: Ensure that each variable is appropriate for analysis by running a frequency distribution for each variable.
2. *Regression*: Using a stepwise regression analysis, locate those variables that best explain the criterion variable. Evaluate the strength of the model and assess the impact of each variable included on the criterion variable.
3. *Factor analysis*: Determine the underlying psychological factors that characterize the respondents by means of factor analysis of all 30 independent variables. Use principle component extraction with varimax rotation for ease of interpretation. Save the factor scores and then regress them on the criterion variable, forcing all predictor variables to be included in the analysis. Evaluate the strength of this model and compare it with the initial regression. Use the factor scores to cluster the respondents into three groups. Discuss the significance of the groups based on the underlying factors. Repeat this cluster analysis for four groups.
4. *Cluster analysis*: Cluster the respondents on the original variables into three and four clusters. Which is a better model? Compare these cluster results with the cluster results on the factor scores. Which is easier to interpret, and which explains the data better?

Based on the analysis, prepare a report to management explaining the Yuppie consumer and offering recommendations on the design of the Dodge Viper. Your recommendations should aid Chrysler in achieving what they seek: an image for the Viper that is attractive to the Yuppie market and that helps them outperform the competition in the performance car market.

References

Steven Lipin and Brandon Mitchener, "Daimler–Chrysler Merger to Produce $3 Billion in Savings, Revenue Gains within 3 to 5 Years," *Wall Street Journal* (May 8, 1998): A10.

"Snakes Got Legs! The Newest Version of the Dodge Viper RT/10 Roadster Has Been Introduced," *AutoWeek* 47 (19) (May 12, 1997): 20.

"Chrysler's Next Snake? The Dodge Copperhead Is Discussed in Detail: Chrysler Is Positioning It as an Affordable Alternative to the Dodge Viper," *AutoWeek* 47 (5) (February 3, 1997): 17.

Note: This case was prepared for class discussion purposes only and does not represent the views of Chrysler or their affiliates. The problem scenario is hypothetical and the data provided are simulated.

Part IV

Communication, International and Ethical Dimensions with Applications

Communicating the research by preparing and presenting a formal report constitutes the sixth step in a marketing research project. With a practical orientation, we provide guidelines for writing reports and preparing tables and graphs and also discuss oral presentation of the report. We focus on the international and ethical dimensions of marketing research. Although both these topics have been discussed in the previous chapters, this part presents additional details. We present a conceptual framework for international marketing research and illustrate, in detail, how the environment prevailing in the countries, cultural units, or international markets being researched influences the way the marketing research process should be performed. In this part we also emphasize the necessity for ethics in marketing research and discuss some of the leading methods that aid managers and researchers alike in ethical decision making. A framework for ethics in marketing research is proposed. The way in which ethics influences each step of the marketing research process is discussed. In keeping with the rest of the book, our orientation continues to be applied and managerial. The professional perspectives provide additional applications in these areas.

Chapter 22

Report Preparation and Presentation

"If your report doesn't make the information easy to understand, believable, and actionable . . . it is likely that management won't value your work."

Nancy Bunn, director, corporate communications, Burke, Inc.

OBJECTIVES

After reading this chapter, the student should be able to

1. discuss the basic requirements of report preparation including report format, report writing, graphs, and tables
2. discuss the nature and scope of the oral presentation and describe the "Tell 'Em" and "KISS 'Em" principles
3. describe the approach to the marketing research report from the client's perspective and the guidelines for reading the research report
4. explain the reason for follow-up with the client and describe the assistance that should be given to the client and the evaluation of the research project
5. understand the report preparation and presentation process in international marketing research
6. identify the ethical issues related to the interpretation and reporting of the research process and findings to the client and the use of these results by the client
7. explain the use of the Internet and computers in report preparation and presentation

OVERVIEW

Report preparation and presentation constitutes the sixth and final step in a marketing research project. It follows problem definition, developing an approach, research design formulation, field work, and data preparation and analysis. This chapter describes the importance of this last step, as well as a process for report preparation and presentation. We provide guidelines for report preparation, including report writing and preparing tables and graphs. We discuss oral presentation of the report. Research follow-up, including assisting the client and evaluating the research process, is described. The special considerations for report preparation and presentation in international marketing research are discussed, and the relevant ethical issues identified. We conclude by explaining the role of the Internet and computers in report preparation and presentation.

We begin with some examples describing the nature and importance of report preparation and presentation.

DEPARTMENT STORE PATRONAGE PROJECT

Report Preparation and Presentation

The formal report was prepared for the client's vice president of marketing. The first volume, the main body of the report, had a title page, table of contents, executive summary, and details of problem definition, approach, research design, methodology used to analyze the data, results, limitations of the project, and conclusions and recommendations. Volume II contained a title page, list of figures, and all the figures and graphs. Finally, all the statistical details, including all the tables, were given in Volume III. The writing of the report was influenced by the style preferences of the vice president for marketing and other key executives. Volume I had a nontechnical orientation and was easy to follow. In addition to the written report, an oral presentation of the entire project was made to the top management. Several of the recommendations made to management in the report were eventually implemented.

EXAMPLE

Reporting the Friendly Skies

The task of marketing research is to assess information needs, to provide this information and to help the decision maker in making the right decision. That is what United Airlines, the Chicago-based airline company, has understood with its ongoing in-flight customer satisfaction tracking program. Each month, 192,000 passengers among 900 flights are selected and surveyed, using a four-page scannable form. The survey covers the satisfaction of passengers on both "on the ground services" (flight reservation, airport service) and "in the air services" (flight attendants, meal, aircraft). The forms are distributed early in the flight by the attendants, so that the passenger can take time to fill in the questionnaire.

Each month the internal department of marketing research of United issues a report, summarizing customer satisfaction. The report is also posted on the Internet and available on-line to United managers all over the world.

Because of the size of the sample (tripled since 1994), the data are very reliable (representative) and used by all departments of the company:

- the marketing department to make strategic planning, product positioning, and target marketing decisions.
- the finance department to measure the success of its product investments.
- the airport department to evaluate ground service, including speed and efficiency of check-in (service representatives, waiting lines).
- the executive management to evaluate the performance of United both internally achieving its goals, and externally compared to the competition.

The result of this high-range customer satisfaction survey is that all departments at United Airlines are customer oriented. This helps the company to differentiate itself in an environment in which all companies have the same schedules, the same service, and the same fare. For example, based on the survey results, United recognized that airline food is an important component of travelers' satisfaction and consequently improved its meal service. The company also established brand partnership with some well-known food companies such as Starbucks coffee and Godiva Chocolates and advertised that as one more reason to fly the friendly skies.[1] ■

The department store example illustrates how the main body of the report follows the format of the earlier steps of the marketing research process. The United Airlines example highlights the importance of regular reporting.

IMPORTANCE OF THE REPORT AND PRESENTATION

For the following reasons, the report and its presentation are important parts of the marketing research project:

1. They are the tangible products of the research effort. After the project is complete and management has made the decision, there is little documentary evidence of the project other than the written report. The report serves as a historical record of the project.
2. Management decisions are guided by the report and the presentation. If the first five steps in the project are carefully conducted but inadequate attention is paid to the sixth step, the value of the project to management will be greatly diminished.
3. The involvement of many marketing managers in the project is limited to the written report and the oral presentation. These managers evaluate the quality of the entire project on the quality of the report and presentation.
4. Management's decision to undertake marketing research in the future or to use the particular research supplier again will be influenced by the perceived usefulness of the report and the presentation.

THE REPORT PREPARATION AND PRESENTATION PROCESS

Figure 22.1 illustrates report preparation and presentation. The process begins by interpreting the results of data analysis in light of the marketing research problem, approach, research design, and field work. Instead of merely summarizing the statistical results, the

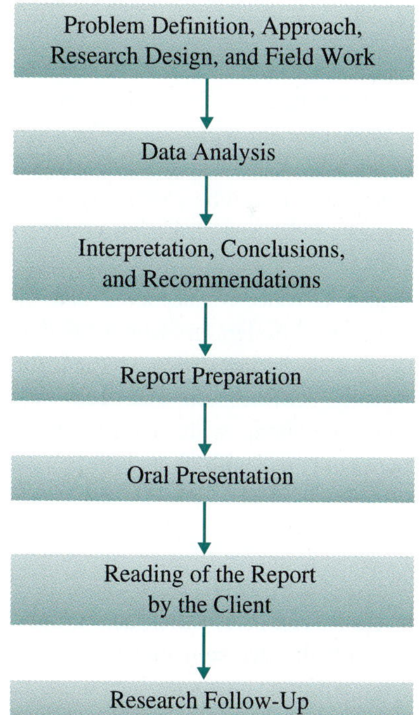

Figure 22.1
The Report Preparation and Presentation Process

researcher should present the findings in such a way that they can be used directly as input into decision making. Wherever appropriate, conclusions should be drawn and recommendations made. Recommendations should be actionable. Before writing the report, the researcher should discuss the major findings, conclusions, and recommendations with the key decision makers. These discussions play a major role in ensuring that the report meets the client's needs and is ultimately accepted. These discussions should confirm specific dates for the delivery of the written report and other data.

The entire marketing research project should be summarized in a single written report or in several reports addressed to different readers. Generally, an oral presentation supplements the written documents. The client should be given an opportunity to read the report. After that, the researcher should take necessary follow-up actions. The researcher should assist the client in understanding the report, implementing the findings, undertaking further research, and evaluating the research process in retrospect. The importance of the researcher's being intimately involved in the report preparation and presentation process is highlighted by the following example.

EXAMPLE

Focus Group Moderators' Ghostwriters Can Shortchange Clients

Thomas Greenbaum, president of a market research company focusing on qualitative research, notes a disturbing trend in recent years in the focus group service sector. Greenbaum of Groups Plus, Inc., of Wilton, Connecticut, asserts that some moderators of focus groups misrepresent their work to clients because their reports are actually written by ghostwriters who did not participate in the focus group sessions.

According to Greenbaum, perhaps more than half of moderators use ghostwriters to develop their reports for clients. Often, junior researchers learning the business, or part-time employees write these ghostwritten reports. Greenbaum criticizes such ghostwriting because the nonverbal reactions of focus group participants, or group synergy cannot always be accurately reported by those who merely listen to audio tapes, or view videotapes of focus group sessions. Greenbaum calls on moderators to be forthright with clients about the authorship of focus group reports, and calls on clients to be more demanding of their contracted research teams.

"Although some people in the industry defend ghostwriting by saying they always review the reports before they are sent to the client, or perhaps even write certain key sections, this practice must be looked at carefully by clients who use focus group research," Greenbaum said. "If the clients know in advance that their reports will be written by someone else, it is clearly less of a problem, but they still do not get the best effort from their research consultants."

In addition to the likelihood of degrading a report, Greenbaum observes that the ghostwriting system delays the submission of the final report. "Moderators who write their own reports try to complete them within a week or 10 days of the last group, so the information is still fresh in their minds when they do the writing," Greenbaum said. "However, most moderators (using ghostwriters) are not able to provide clients with final reports for three to four weeks after the last group, due to the process they use with ghostwriters."[2] ■

REPORT PREPARATION

Researchers differ in the way they prepare a research report. The personality, background, expertise, and responsibility of the researcher, along with the decision maker (DM) to whom the report is addressed, interact to give each report a unique character. Yet, there are guidelines for formatting and writing reports and designing tables and graphs.[3]

Report Format

Report formats are likely to vary with the researcher or the marketing research firm conducting the project, the client for whom the project is being conducted, and the nature of the project itself. Hence, the following is intended as a guideline from which the researcher can develop a format for the research project at hand. Most research reports include the following elements:

- **I.** Title page
- **II.** Letter of transmittal
- **III.** Letter of authorization
- **IV.** Table of contents
- **V.** List of tables
- **VI.** List of graphs
- **VII.** List of appendices
- **VIII.** List of exhibits
- **IX.** Executive summary
  - **a.** Major findings
  - **b.** Conclusions
  - **c.** Recommendations
- **X.** Problem definition
  - **a.** Background to the problem
  - **b.** Statement of the problem
- **XI.** Approach to the problem
- **XII.** Research design
  - **a.** Type of research design
  - **b.** Information needs
  - **c.** Data collection from secondary sources
  - **d.** Data collection from primary sources
  - **e.** Scaling techniques
  - **f.** Questionnaire development and pretesting
  - **g.** Sampling techniques
  - **h.** Field work
- **XIII.** Data analysis
  - **a.** Methodology
  - **b.** Plan of data analysis
- **XIV.** Results
- **XV.** Limitations and caveats
- **XVI.** Conclusions and recommendations
- **XVII.** Exhibits
  - **a.** Questionnaires and forms
  - **b.** Statistical output
  - **c.** Lists

This format closely follows the earlier steps of the marketing research process. The results may be presented in several chapters of the report. For example, in a national survey, data analysis may be conducted for the overall sample and then the data for each of the four geographic regions may be analyzed separately. If so, the results may be presented in five chapters instead of one.

Title Page. The title page should include the title of the report, information (name, address, and telephone) about the researcher or organization conducting the research, the name of the client for whom the report was prepared, and the date of release. The title should indicate the nature of the project, as illustrated in Research in Practice 22.1.

RESEARCH IN PRACTICE 22.1

Elrick & Lavidge Guidelines on the Title Page

- Use client language in title—avoid "research-eze"

  "Practices Followed in Selecting Long-Distance Carriers" better than: "Long-Distance Service Study"

  "Customers' Reactions to an Expanded Financial/Insurance Relationship" better than: "Relationship Study"

Letter of Transmittal. A formal report generally contains a letter of transmittal that delivers the report to the client and summarizes the researcher's overall experience with the project, without mentioning the findings. The letter should also identify the need for further action on the part of the client, such as implementation of the findings or further research that should be undertaken.

Letter of Authorization. A letter of authorization is written by the client to the researcher before work on the project begins. It authorizes the researcher to proceed with the project and specifies its scope and the terms of the contract. Often, it is sufficient to refer to the letter of authorization in the letter of transmittal. However, sometimes it is necessary to include a copy of the letter of authorization in the report.

Table of Contents. The table of contents should list the topics covered and the appropriate page numbers. In most reports, only the major headings and subheadings are included. The table of contents is followed by a list of tables, list of graphs, list of appendices, and list of exhibits.

Executive Summary. The executive summary is an extremely important part of the report, as this is often the only portion of the report that executives read. The summary should concisely describe the problem, approach, and research design that was adopted. A summary section should be devoted to the major results, conclusions, and recommendations. The executive summary should be written after the rest of the report.

Problem Definition. This section of the report gives the background to the problem, highlights the discussions with the decision makers and industry experts, discusses the secondary data analysis, the qualitative research that was conducted, and the factors that were considered. Moreover, it should contain a clear statement of the management decision problem and the marketing research problem (see chapter 2).

Approach to the Problem. This section should discuss the broad approach that was adopted in addressing the problem. This section should also contain a description of the theoretical foundations that guided the research, any analytical models formulated, research questions, hypotheses, and the factors that influenced the research design.

Research Design. The section on research design should specify the details of how the research was conducted (see chapters 3–13). This should include the nature of the research design adopted, information needed, data collection from secondary and primary sources, scaling techniques, questionnaire development and pretesting, sampling techniques, and field work. These topics should be presented in a nontechnical, easy-to-understand manner. The technical details should be included in an appendix. This section of the report should justify the specific methods selected.

Data Analysis. This section should describe the plan of data analysis and justify the data analysis strategy and techniques used. The techniques used for analysis should be described in simple, nontechnical terms.

Results. This section is normally the longest part of the report and may comprise several chapters. Often, the results are presented not only at the aggregate level but also at the subgroup (market segment, geographical area, etc.) level. The results should be organized in a coherent and logical way. For example, in a health care marketing survey of hospitals, the results were presented in four chapters. One chapter presented the overall results, another examined the differences between geographical regions, a third presented the differences between for-profit and nonprofit hospitals, and a fourth presented the differences according to bed capacity. The presentation of the results should be geared directly to the components of the marketing research problem and the information needs that were identified. The details should be presented in tables and graphs, with the main findings discussed in the text.

Limitations and Caveats. All marketing research projects have limitations caused by time, budget, and other organizational constraints. Furthermore, the research design adopted may be limited in terms of the various types of errors (see chapter 3), and some of these may be serious enough to warrant discussion. This section should be written with great care and a balanced perspective. On the one hand, the researcher must make sure that management does not overly rely on the results or use them for unintended purposes, such as projecting them to unintended populations. On the other hand, this section should not erode their confidence in the research or unduly minimize its importance.

Conclusions and Recommendations. Presenting a mere summary of the statistical results is not enough. The researcher should interpret the results in light of the problem being addressed to arrive at major conclusions. Based on the results and conclusions, the researcher may make recommendations to the decision makers. Sometimes marketing researchers are not asked to make recommendations because they research only one area but do not understand the bigger picture at the client firm. If recommendations are made, they should be feasible, practical, actionable, and directly usable as inputs into managerial decision making. Research in Practice 22.2 contains guidelines on conclusions and recommendations.

Report Writing

Readers. A report should be written for a specific reader or readers: the marketing managers who will use the results. The report should take into account the readers' technical sophistication and interest in the project, as well as the circumstances under which they will read the report and how they will use it.[4]

Technical terminology and jargon should be avoided. As expressed by one expert, "The readers of your reports are busy people; and very few of them can balance a research report, a cup of coffee, and a dictionary at one time."[5] Instead of technical terms such as maximum likelihood, heteroscedasticity, and nonparametric, use descriptive explanations. If some technical terms cannot be avoided, briefly define them in an appendix. When it comes to marketing research, people would rather live with a problem they cannot solve, than accept a solution they cannot understand.

Often the researcher must cater to the needs of several audiences with different levels of technical sophistication and interest in the project. Such conflicting needs may be met by including different sections in the report for different readers or preparing entirely separate reports.

RESEARCH IN PRACTICE 22.2

Elrick & Lavidge Guidelines on Conclusions and Recommendations

Conclusions

- Conclusions
  - Conclusions concerning, for example:
    - . . . customer behavior
    - . . . customer attitudes or perceptions
    - . . . the nature of the markets studied
  - Generally, in studies with samples designed to represent the market
  - Avoid interesting results that are not relevant to the conclusions
- May be in form of statement or paragraphs
- Use subheadings to identify conclusions covering different subjects or market segments

Recommendations

- Recommendations regarding actions that should be taken or considered in light of the research results:
  - Add/drop a product
  - What to say in advertising—advertising positioning
  - Market segments to select as primary targets
  - How to price product
  - Further research that should be considered
- Should be related to the stated purpose of the research
- Sometimes omitted—for instance,
  - Client staff members want to author the recommendations
  - Study designed merely to familiarize client with a market
- Most clients are interested in our suggestions, in spite of the fact that we may not be familiar with internal financial issues and other internal corporate factors

Easy to Follow. The report should be easy to follow.[6] It should be structured logically and written clearly. The material, particularly the body of the report, should be structured in a logical manner so that the reader can easily see the inherent connections and linkages. Headings should be used for main topics and subheadings for subtopics.

A logical organization also leads to a coherent report. Clarity can be enhanced by using well-constructed sentences that are short and to the point. The words used should express precisely what the researcher wants to communicate. Difficult words, slang, and clichés should be avoided. An excellent check on the clarity of a report is to have two or three people who are unfamiliar with the project read it and offer critical comments. Several revisions of the report may be needed before the final document emerges.

Presentable and Professional Appearance. The looks of a report are important. The report should be professionally reproduced with quality paper, typing, and binding. The typography should be varied. Variation in type size and skillful use of white space can greatly contribute to the appearance and readability of the report.

Objective. Objectivity is a virtue that should guide report writing. Researchers can become so fascinated with their project that they overlook their scientific role. The report should accurately present the methodology, results, and conclusions of the project, without slanting the findings to conform to the expectations of management. Decision makers are unlikely to receive with enthusiasm a report that reflects unfavorably on their judgment or actions. However, the researcher must have the courage to present and defend the results objectively. The rule is, "Tell it like it is."

Reinforce Text with Tables and Graphs. It is important to reinforce key information in the text with tables, graphs, pictures, maps, and other visual devices. Visual aids can greatly facilitate communication and add to the clarity and impact of the report. Guidelines for tabular and graphical presentation are discussed later.

Terse. A report should be terse and concise. Anything unnecessary should be omitted. If too much information is included, important points may be lost. Avoid lengthy discussions of common procedures. Yet, brevity should not be achieved at the expense of completeness.

Guidelines for Tables

Statistical tables are a vital part of the report and deserve special attention. We illustrate the guidelines for tables using the data for U.S. automobile sales reported in Table 22.1. The numbers in parentheses in the following paragraphs refer to the numbered sections of the table.

Title and Number. Every table should have a number (1a) and title (1b). The title should be brief yet clearly descriptive of the information provided. Arabic numbers are used to identify tables so that they can be referred in the text.[7]

Arrangement of Data Items. The arrangement of data items in a table should emphasize the most significant aspect of the data. Thus, when the data pertain to time, the items should be arranged by appropriate time period. When order of magnitude is most important, the data items should be arranged in that order (2a). If ease of locating items is critical, an alphabetical arrangement is most appropriate.

Basis of Measurement. The basis or unit of measurement should be clearly stated (3a).

Leaders, Rulings, Spaces. *Leaders*, dots or hyphens used to lead the eye horizontally, impart uniformity and improve readability (4a). Instead of ruling the table horizontally or vertically, white spaces (4b) are used to set off data items. Skipping lines after different sections of the data can also assist the eye. Horizontal rules (4c) are often used after the headings.

(1a)

TABLE 22.1

(1b) **U.S. AUTOMOTIVE SALES 1992–1996** (3a) (5a) (4c) (4a) (4b) (5b) (2a)

MFG	*1992*	*1993*	*Unit Sales* *1994*	*1995*	*1996*
GM	2,843,860	2,908,689	3,057,872	2,930,568	2,757,671
Ford	1,777,635	1,878,149	1,938,841	1,791,225	1,737,252
Chrysler.......	679,586	834,132	811,824	786,180	832,633
Toyota	760,159	741,826	765,143	793,974	793,592
Honda	768,845	716,440	762,242	740,487	786,154
Nissan	417,970	482,646	537,228	520,258	500,377
Other*	965,058	955,977	1,117,367	1,072,272	1,119,074
Total	8,213,113	8,517,859	8,990,517	8,634,964	8,526,753

(5c) *includes all other producers

(6a) *Source*: 1997 Ward's Automotive Yearbook, p. 19.

Explanations and Comments: Headings, Stubs, and Footnotes. Explanations and comments clarifying the table can be provided in the form of captions, stubs, and footnotes. Designations placed over the vertical columns are called headings (5a). Designations placed in the left-hand column are called stubs (5b). Information that cannot be incorporated in the table should be explained by footnotes (5c). Letters or symbols rather than numbers should be used for footnotes. The footnotes should come after the main table, but before the source note.

Sources of the Data. If the data contained in the table are secondary, the source of data should be cited (6a).

Guidelines for Graphs

As a general rule, graphic aids should be employed whenever practical. Graphical display of information can effectively complement the text and tables to enhance clarity of communication and impact.[8] As the saying goes, a picture is worth a thousand words. The guidelines for preparing graphs are similar to those for tables. Therefore, this section focuses on the different types of graphical aids.[9] We illustrate several of these using the U.S. automobile sales data from Table 22.1.

Geographic and Other Maps. Geographic and other maps, such as product positioning maps, can communicate relative location and other comparative information. Geographic maps can pertain to countries, states, counties, sales territories, and other divisions. For example, suppose the researcher wanted to present information on the relative number of Coca-Cola Company bottlers versus the bottlers for PepsiCo and other competitors for each state in the United States. This information could be effectively communicated in a map in which each state was divided into three areas, proportionate to the number of Coca-Cola, PepsiCo, and other bottlers, with each area in a different color. Chapter 21 showed examples of product-positioning maps.

Pie Chart A round chart divided into sections.

Round or Pie Charts. In a **pie chart**, the area of each section, as a percentage of the total area of the circle, reflects the percentage associated with the value of a specific variable. A pie chart is not useful for displaying relationships over time or relationships among several variables. As a general guideline, a pie chart should not require more than seven sections.[10] Figure 22.2 shows a pie chart for U.S. automobile sales.

Despite loss of sales and market share, General Motors remains the leader in automobiles with cars like Saturn.

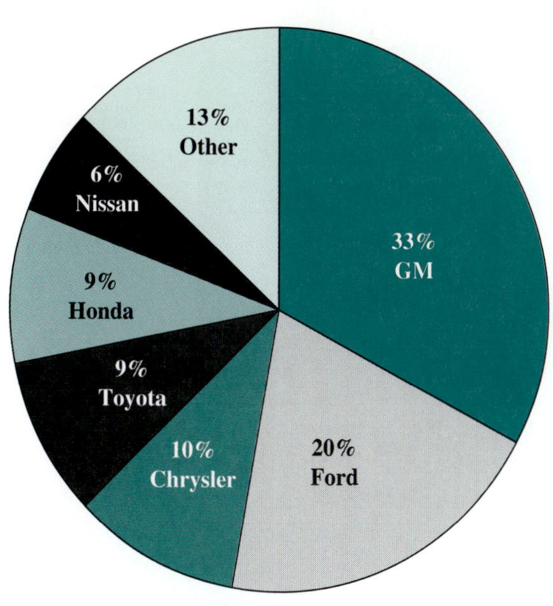

Figure 22.2
Pie Chart of 1996 U.S. Car Sales

Line Charts. A **line chart** connects a series of data points using continuous lines. This is an attractive way of illustrating trends and changes over time. Several series can be compared on the same chart, and forecasts, interpolations, and extrapolations can be shown. If several series are displayed simultaneously, each line should have a distinctive color or form (see Figure 22.3).[11]

A **stratum chart** is a set of line charts in which the data are successively aggregated over the series. Areas between the line charts display the magnitudes of the relevant variables (see Figure 22.4).

Line Chart A chart that connects a series of data points using continuous lines.

Stratum Chart A set of line charts in which the data are successively aggregated over the series. Areas between the line charts display the magnitudes of the relevant variables.

Pictographs. A **pictograph** uses small pictures or symbols to display the data. As Figure 22.5 shows, pictographs do not depict results precisely. Hence, caution should be exercised when using them.[12]

Pictograph A graphical depiction that makes use of small pictures or symbols to display the data.

Histograms and Bar Charts. A **bar chart** displays data in various bars that may be positioned horizontally or vertically. Bar charts can be used to present absolute and relative magnitudes, differences, and change. The **histogram** is a vertical bar chart in which the height of the bars represents the relative or cumulative frequency of occurrence of a specific variable (see Figure 22.6).

Bar Chart A chart that displays data in bars positioned horizontally or vertically.

Histogram A vertical bar chart in which the height of the bars represents the relative or cumulative frequency of occurrence.

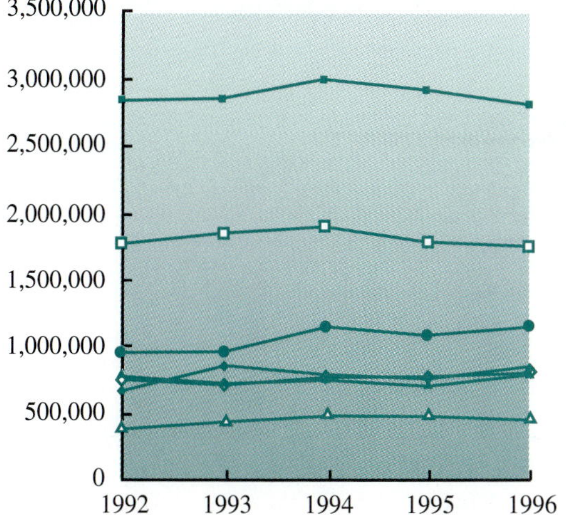

Figure 22.3
Line Chart of Total U.S. Car Sales

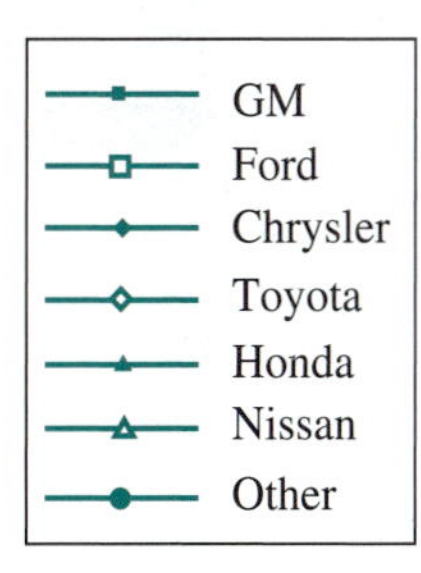

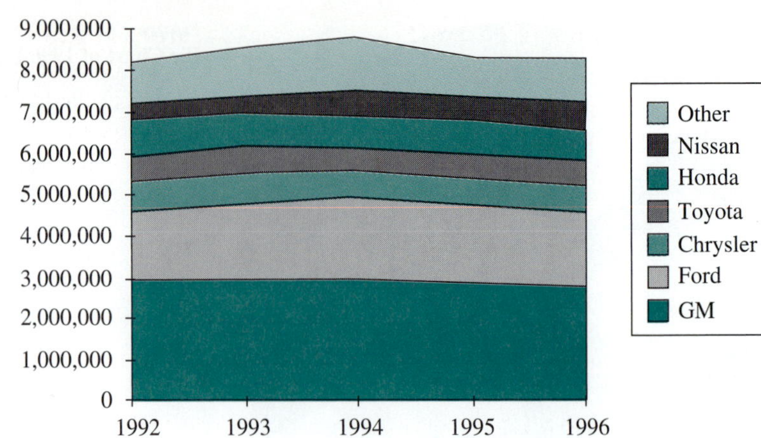

Figure 22.4
Stratum Chart of Total U.S. Car Sales

Figure 22.5
Pictograph for 1996 U.S. Car Sales

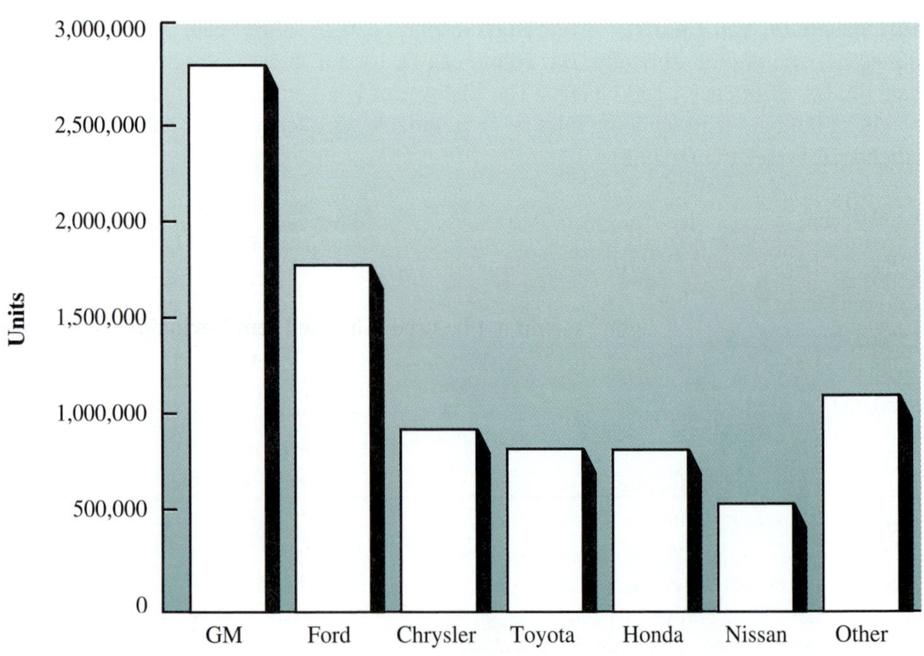

Figure 22.6
Histogram of 1996 U.S. Car Sales

Schematic Figures and Flow Charts. **Schematic figures** and **flow charts** take on a number of different forms. They can be used to display the steps or components of a process, as in Figure 22.1. Another useful form of these charts is classification diagrams. Examples of classification charts for classifying secondary data were provided in chapter 4 (Figures 4.1 to 4.4). An example of a flow chart for questionnaire design was given in chapter 10 (Figure 10.2).[13]

Burke gives its clients the best report graphics, bar none.

ORAL PRESENTATION

The entire marketing research project should be presented to the management of the client firm. This presentation will help management understand and accept the written report. Any preliminary questions the management may have can be addressed in the presentation. Because many executives form their first and lasting impressions about the project based on the presentation, its importance cannot be overemphasized.[14]

The key to an effective presentation is preparation. A written script or detailed outline should be prepared following the format of the written report. The presentation must be geared to the audience. For this purpose the researcher should determine their backgrounds, interests, and involvement in the project, as well as the extent to which they are likely to be affected by it. The presentation should be rehearsed several times before it is made to the management.

Visual aids, such as tables and graphs, should be displayed with a variety of media. Chalkboards or whiteboards enable the researcher to manipulate numbers. They are particularly useful in communicating answers to technical questions. While not as flexible, magnetic boards and felt boards allow for rapid presentation of previously prepared material. Flip charts are large pads of blank paper mounted on an easel, which can be used like a chalkboard or whiteboard. Visual aids are drawn on the pages in advance, and the speaker flips through the pages during the presentation. Overhead projectors can present simple charts as well as complex overlays produced by the successive additions of new images to the screen. Several computer programs are available for producing attractive overhead transparencies (acetate sheet). Color transparencies can also be prepared. Slides are useful for projecting photographs on the screen. Videotape equipment (VCRs) and large-screen projectors are particularly effective in presenting focus groups and other aspects of field work that are dynamic in nature. Computer projectors attached to personal computers, which project the monitor image onto a screen, may also be employed. They can be used for making computer-controlled presentations or for presenting technical information such as analytical models.

It is important to maintain eye contact and interact with the audience during the presentation. Sufficient opportunity should be provided for questions, both during and after the presentation.[15] The presentation should be made interesting and convincing with the use of appropriate stories, examples, experiences, and quotations. Filler words such as "uh," "y'know," and "all right," should not be used. The **"tell 'em" principle** is effective for structuring a presentation. This principle states: (1) tell 'em what you're going to tell 'em, (2) tell 'em, and (3) tell 'em what you've told 'em. Another useful guideline is the **"KISS 'em" principle**, which states: Keep It Simple and Straightforward (hence the acronym KISS).

Tell 'em Principle
An effective guideline for structuring a presentation. This principle states, (1) tell 'em what you're going to tell 'em, (2) tell 'em, and (3) tell 'em what you've told 'em.

KISS 'em Principle
A principle of report presentation that states, Keep It Simple and Straightforward.

Body language should be employed. Descriptive gestures are used to clarify or enhance verbal communication. Emphatic gestures are used to emphasize what is being said. Suggestive gestures are symbols of ideas and emotions. Prompting gestures are used to elicit a desired response from the audience. The speaker should vary the voice volume, pitch, quality, articulation, and rate while speaking. The presentation should terminate with a strong closing. To stress its importance, the presentation should be sponsored by a top-level manager in the client's organization, as in the following example.

EXAMPLE

Taking It to the Top

The importance of oral presentation cannot be overemphasized since many executives form their lasting impressions about the project based on it.

Elrick & Lavidge conducted a research project to measure the relative effectiveness of television, print, and radio as advertising media for a client firm. In addition, the effectiveness of 10 TV commercials, radio commercials, and print ads was assessed. Given the nature of the project, the oral presentation of the report was particularly important in communicating the findings. In addition to an overhead projector and slide projector, a VCR (for playing TV commercials), a tape recorder (for playing radio commercials), and a story board (for showing print ads) were utilized. The presentation was made to the client's top corporate officers, consisting of the president, all vice presidents, and all assistant vice presidents at one of their monthly meetings.[16] ■

After the presentation, key executives in the client firm should be given time to read the report in detail. Some guidelines are available for report reading.

READING THE RESEARCH REPORT

Guidelines for reading the report and evaluating the marketing research project have been developed by the Advertising Research Foundation.[17]

Addresses the Problem

The reader should pay attention to the problem being addressed and the relevant background information provided. The organization sponsoring the research, as well as the one conducting the research, should be noted. The report should not assume that the reader has prior knowledge of the problem situation; but should give all the relevant information. The reader should attempt to fully understand the environmental context, the management decision problem, and the marketing research problem.

Research Design

The reader should attempt to understand, at least in nontechnical terms, the research design procedures. Particular attention should be paid to the discussion of the information needs, data collection methods, scaling techniques, questionnaire design and pretesting, sampling techniques, and field work. Does the report justify the specific methods used? Reports which do not contain, or otherwise make available, methodological details should be viewed with caution.

Execution of the Research Procedures

The reader should pay special attention to the manner in which the research procedures were executed. The people working on the project should be well qualified and properly trained. Proper supervision and control procedures should be followed. This is particularly important with respect to data collection, data preparation, and statistical analysis.

Numbers and Statistics

Numbers and statistics reported in tables and graphs should be examined carefully by the reader. Inappropriate numbers and statistics can be highly misleading. Consider, for example, percentages based on small samples or means reported for ordinal data. Unfortunately, the occurrence of these types of misleading statistics in reports is not uncommon.

Interpretations and Conclusions

The findings should be reported in an objective and candid way. The interpretation of the basic results should be differentiated from the results per se. Any assumptions made in interpreting the results should be clearly identified. The limitations of the research should be discussed. Any conclusions or recommendations made without a specification of the underlying assumptions or limitations should be treated cautiously by the reader.

Generalizability

It is the responsibility of the researcher to provide evidence regarding the reliability, validity, and generalizability of the findings. The report should clearly identify the target population to which the findings apply. Factors that limit the generalizability of the findings, such as the nature and representativeness of the sample, mode and time of data collections, and various sources of error should be clearly identified. The reader should not attempt to generalize the findings of the report without explicit consideration of these factors.

Disclosure

Finally, the reader should carefully examine whether the spirit in which the report was written indicates an honest and complete disclosure of the research procedures and results. It is particularly important that procedures, for instance, those used for the treatment of missing values, weighting, etc., which call for subjective judgment on the part of the researcher, be made known. If any negative or unexpected findings were obtained, they should be reported. The reader should feel free to ask for any relevant information that is not contained in the report.

A careful reading of the report using these guidelines will help the client to effectively participate in research follow-up.

RESEARCH FOLLOW-UP

The researcher's task does not end with the oral presentation. Two other tasks remain. The researcher should help the client understand and implement the findings and take follow-up action. Secondly, while it is still fresh in the researcher's mind, the entire marketing research project should be evaluated.

Assisting the Client

After the client has read the report in detail, several questions may arise. Parts of the report, particularly those dealing with technical matters, may not be understood and the researcher should provide the help needed. Sometimes the researcher helps implement the findings. Often, the client retains the researcher to help with the selection of a new product or advertising agency, development of a pricing policy, market segmentation, or other marketing actions. An important reason for client follow-up is to discuss further research projects. For example, the researcher and management may agree to repeat the study after two years. Finally, the researcher should help the client firm make the information generated in the marketing research project a part of the firm's marketing (management) information system (MIS) or decision support system (DSS), as discussed in chapter 1.

Evaluation of the Research Project

Marketing research is scientific, but it also involves creativity, intuition, and expertise. Hence, every marketing research project provides an opportunity for learning and the researcher should critically evaluate the entire project to obtain new insights and knowledge. The key question to ask is, "Could this project have been conducted more effectively or efficiently?" This question, of course, raises several more specific questions. Could the problem have been defined differently so as to enhance the value of the project to the client or reduce the costs? Could a different approach have yielded better results? Was the research design that was used the best? How about the mode of data collection? Should mall intercepts have been used instead of telephone interviews? Was the sampling plan employed the most appropriate? Were the sources of possible design error correctly anticipated and kept under control, at least in a qualitative sense? If not, what changes could have been made? How could the selection, training, and supervision of field workers be altered to improve data collection? Was the data analysis strategy effective in yielding information useful for decision making? Were the conclusions and recommendations appropriate and useful to the client? Was the report adequately written and presented? Was the project completed within the time and budget allocated? If not, what went wrong? The insights gained from such an evaluation will benefit the researcher and the subsequent projects conducted.

INTERNATIONAL MARKETING RESEARCH

The guidelines presented earlier in the chapter apply to international marketing research, although report preparation may be complicated by the need to prepare reports for management in different countries and in different languages. In such a case, the researcher should prepare different versions of the report, each geared to specific readers. The different reports should be comparable, although the formats may differ. The guidelines for oral presentation are also similar to those given earlier, with the added proviso that the presenter should be sensitive to cultural norms. For example, making jokes, which is frequently done in the United States, is not appropriate in all cultures. Most marketing decisions are made from facts and figures arising out of marketing research. But, these figures have to pass the test and limits of logic, subjective experience, and gut feelings of decision makers. The subjective experience and gut feelings of managers could vary widely across countries necessitating that different recommendations be made for implementing the research findings in different countries. This is particularly important when making innovative or creative recommendations such as advertising campaigns.

EXAMPLE

Camry Chicken Fries Ford

The ad campaign designed for Toyota Camry in Australia was very different from the one in Japan. "Why did the chicken cross the road?" Toyota asks in a continuing series of TV commercials aired recently in Australia. The answer: "To sell more Toyota Camrys, of course." The spots showing an animated chicken trying to cross the road and getting its feathers blown off by a passing Camry were created by Saatchi & Saatchi Advertising. When Bob Miller, Toyota's general manager for marketing, tried to explain the ad to their counterpart in Japan, they thought he was insane. Maybe so, but the commercial did unbelievably well. Hoary old joke that it was, the gag helped Toyota topple Ford's dominance in Australia. As a continuing series, the next ad showed the featherless chicken sitting on a pile of eggs in the middle of the road and hatching chicks as the Camry speeds past. Although such use of humor would have been offensive to the Japanese, it elicited a favorable response from the Australians.[18] ■

ETHICS IN MARKETING RESEARCH

Report preparation and presentation involves many issues pertaining to research integrity. These issues include defining the marketing research problem to suit hidden agendas, compromising the research design, deliberately misusing statistics, falsifying figures, altering research results, misinterpreting the results with the objective of supporting a personal or corporate point of view, and withholding information.[19] A survey of 254 marketing researchers revealed that 33 percent of the respondents considered the most difficult ethical problems they face encompass issues of research integrity. The researcher must address these issues while preparing the report and presenting the findings. The dissemination of the marketing research results to the client, and other stakeholders as appropriate should be honest, accurate, and complete.

The researcher should be objective throughout all phases of the marketing research process. Some research procedures and analyses may not reveal anything new or significant. For example, the discriminant function may not classify better than chance (chapter 18). Ethical dilemmas can arise in these instances if the researcher nevertheless attempts to draw conclusions from such analyses. Such temptations must be resisted to avoid unethical conduct.

Likewise, clients also have the responsibility for complete and accurate disclosure of the research findings and are obligated to use the research results in an ethical manner. For example, the public can be disadvantaged by a client who distorts the research findings to develop a biased advertising campaign that makes brand claims that have not been substantiated by marketing research. Such activities are condemned by the code of ethics of the American Marketing Association and other professional research associations (see chapter 24).[20] Ethical issues also arise when client firms, such as tobacco companies, use marketing research findings to formulate questionable marketing programs.

EXAMPLE

Tobacco Industry Is "Smoking Gun"

Examination of secondary data sources uncovered the facts that tobacco smoking is responsible for 30 percent of all cancer deaths in the United States and is a leading cause of heart disease, along with being associated with problems such as colds, gastric ulcers, chronic bronchitis, emphysema, and other diseases. Do tobacco companies share an ethical responsibility for this situation? Is it ethical for these companies to employ marketing research to create glamorous images that have a strong appeal to the target market? It is estimated that advertising by the tobacco industry based on systematic research has a part in creating more than 3,000 teenage smokers each day in the United States. Advertising for Camel cigarettes through the Old Joe cartoon advertisements increased Camel's share of the illegal children's cigarette market segment from .5 percent to 32.8 percent—representing sales estimates at $476 million per year. These detrimental effects aren't limited to the United States. Not only is the tobacco industry enticing children to smoke, but it also targets other less-informed populations such as Third World countries as this is a way for tobacco companies to replace those smokers that quit or die.[21]

INTERNET AND COMPUTER APPLICATIONS

Marketing research reports are being published or posted directly to the Web. Normally, these reports are not located in publicly accessible areas but in locations protected by passwords or on corporate intranets. The various word-processing, spreadsheet, and presentation packages have the capability to produce material in a format that can be posted directly to the Web, thus facilitating the process.

There are a number of advantages to publishing marketing research reports on the Web. These reports can incorporate all kinds of multimedia presentations including, graphs, pictures, animation, audio, and full-motion video. The dissemination is immediate and the reports can be accessed by authorized persons on-line on a worldwide basis. These reports can be electronically searched to identify materials of specific interest. For example, a General Electric manager in Kuala Lumpur can electronically locate the portions of the report that pertain to Southeast Asia. Storage and future retrieval is efficient and effortless. It is easy to integrate these reports to become a part of the decision support system. The main disadvantage is that the readers may not have permanent access to the reports as the Web sites are changed periodically.

Originally, the main application of microcomputers was in word processing. However with great developments in processor and software technology, a variety of word processors and other tools have evolved that allow for professional preparation and presentation of marketing research reports at reasonable costs. For example, not only do word processors such as Microsoft Word and WordPerfect include a dictionary, thesaurus, and grammar checkers, they also have the ability to incorporate graphs, tables, and images created with other software such as spreadsheets, graphics packages, and image processing tools. For further flexibility in text and image layout design, page layout programs such as Quark Express and Pagemaker can be used.

Another important addition for reports and presentations is the inclusion of graphics. These can be in the form of clip art, scanned and manipulated images, and original graphics. Several companies offer a multitude of clip art images that are available for royalty-free distribution in reports. If, however, the images that need to be included in a report are not available as clip art, images can be scanned using a flatbed or slide scanner and an image modification package such as Adobe Photoshop or Aldus Photostyler.

A vast number of software programs are available for developing remarkable presentations with great ease. For example, Microsoft Powerpoint allows for the development of a slide show as a presentation. The development process is very simple, but the final product can be very intricate. In addition, some presentation programs also allow for the addition of sound and video clips for a more complete representation of data. With a little more effort, presentation software such as Director or Authorware can be used to fully animate a presentation.

The mainframe and microcomputer versions of the major statistical packages have reporting procedures. In SPSS, the program REPORT can be used to present results in the desired format. TABLE(S) is particularly suited for formatting data for an on-page presentation. In SAS, procedures such as PRINT, FORMS, CHARTS, PLOT, CALENDAR, and TIMEPLOT display information for reporting purposes. The PRINT paragraph in BMDP

FOCUS ON Burke

Burke's philosophy and procedures for report preparation are discussed in the professional perspectives. Therefore, this section focuses on the presentation.

Burke's guidelines for working with management place a great emphasis on the personal presentation as the most effective means of assuring that the research is understood, believed, and used. In some situations a personal presentation is not asked for . . . push hard to be "invited." Keep pushing every time the opportunity arises. Getting an invitation is the first step, next comes managing the presentation and the audience. Listed below are many of Burke's key items to remember.

1. The real decision makers may be above the level that commissioned your work. Push to go higher with your personal presentation. Anyone likely to use the information should be in the presentation.
2. Always believe that you are the catalyst that will make the data come alive. You are more important to the presentation and the findings than is a chart or picture.
3. Be willing to change your style. Many people are laid back or low key. It is said that many famous comedians are not at all funny off stage. Your role when giving the presentation is to be active, enthusiastic, and forceful. Maybe this is a "role" for you—but if you don't play the role, you won't be invited back.
4. Don't apologize to the audience or yourself: No one in the room knows the data and its meaning better than you do. At the moment of the presentation you are the critical element. Don't apologize for not knowing a particular answer. Don't apologize if the room is not comfortable. Don't apologize if a piece of equipment doesn't work. Don't apologize if you have a cold. Don't apologize for anything. Just get on with the presentation.
5. Research your audience. Talk to the people "hosting" the meeting. Who will be there? What are their roles? What stake do they have in the results? What can you find out about positions they might take on the research? Prepare for those positions. How much do they already know about the subject of the meeting? You don't want to bore them with information they already have. What are their styles? Is it a technical, detail-oriented group? Is it a generalist group, etc.?
6. Be prepared for skepticism. If you don't immediately have the answer, ask for a later meeting to discuss the issue and to determine how you and the questioner can arrive at an answer.
7. Don't stay on a topic more than five minutes unless your audience asks for you to do so with questions. The average attention span for a topic is about six minutes. After that time people will start looking at their papers, thinking about other issues and you will be losing them.
8. Be on time, start on time, and don't go beyond your allotted time. No matter how interested you are and how interested the audience is, unless the senior host specifically requests it, stop exactly on time!

allows control of the width of the output panel format of printed data and verbosity of output. The tables and graphs produced from these packages can be directly incorporated into the report. Minitab also has the capability to create graphs and charts and edit them for use in reports or professional presentations. Graphs can be created using Graph > Plot, or Graph > Chart, or Graph > Histogram. Editing can be done using Edit > Edit last command dialog. Excel has extensive charting capabilities and through Microsoft Office provides a direct link to Word, and Powerpoint for report preparation and presentation.

SUMMARY

Report preparation and presentation is the final step in the marketing research project. This process begins with interpretation of data analysis results and leads to conclusions and recommendations. Next, the formal report is written and an oral presentation made. After management has read the report, the researcher should conduct a follow-up, assisting management and undertaking a thorough evaluation of the marketing research project.

In international marketing research, report preparation may be complicated by the need to prepare reports for management in different countries and in different languages. Several ethical issues are pertinent, particularly those related to the interpretation and reporting of the research process and findings to the client and the use of these results by the client. The use of the Internet and computers can greatly facilitate report preparation and presentation.

KEY TERMS AND CONCEPTS

pie chart
line chart
stratum chart
pictograph
bar chart
histogram
"tell 'em" principle
"KISS 'em" principle

ACRONYMS

The guidelines for report writing may be expressed by the acronym REPORT:

R eaders: written for specific readers
E asy to follow
P resentable and professional appearance
O bjective
R einforce text with tables and graphs
T erse: concise, yet complete

The guidelines for constructing tables may be described by the acronym TABLES:

T itle and number
A rrangement of data items
B asis of measurement
L eaders, rulings, spaces
E xplanations and comments: headings, stubs, and footnotes
S ources of data

GRAPHS can be used as an acronym for guidelines for constructing graphs:

G eographic and other maps
R ound or pie chart
A ssembly or line charts
P ictographs
H istograms and bar charts
S chematic figures and flow charts

The guidelines for making a presentation can be summarized by the acronym PRESENTATION:

P reparation
R ehearse your presentation
E ye contact
S tories, experiences, examples, and quotations
E quipment: multimedia
N o filler words
T ell 'em principle
A udience analysis
T erminate with a strong closing
I nteract with the audience
O utline or script should be prepared
N umber one level manager should sponsor it

guidelines for reading and evaluating a report may be
d by the acronym READING:

ırch design
ution of the research procedures
esses the problem
losure
rpretation and conclusion
ıbers and statistics
eralizability

EXERCISES

Questions

1. Describe the process of report preparation.
2. Describe a commonly used format for writing marketing research reports.
3. Describe the following parts of a report: title page, table of contents, executive summary, problem definition, research design, data analysis, conclusions and recommendations.
4. Why is the "limitations and caveats" section included in the report?
5. Discuss the importance of objectivity in writing a marketing research report.
6. Describe the guidelines for report writing.
7. How should the data items be arranged in a table?
8. What is a pie chart? For what type of information is it suitable? For what type of information is it not suitable?

9. Describe a line chart. What kind of information is commonly displayed using such charts?
10. Describe the role of pictographs. What is the relationship between bar charts and histograms?
11. What is the purpose of an oral presentation? What guidelines should be followed in an oral presentation?
12. Describe the "tell 'em" and "KISS 'em" principles.
13. Describe the evaluation of a marketing research project in retrospect.

Problems

1. The following passage is taken from a marketing research report prepared for a group of printers and lithographers without much formal education who run a small family-owned business.

   To measure the image of the printing industry, two different scaling techniques were employed. The first was a series of semantic differential scales. The second consisted of a set of Likert scales. The use of two different techniques for measurement could be justified based on the need to assess the convergent validity of the findings. Data obtained using both these techniques were treated as interval scaled. Pearson product moment correlations were computed between the sets of ratings. The resulting correlations were high, indicating a high level of convergent validity.

   Rewrite this paragraph so that it is suitable for inclusion in the report.

2. Graphically illustrate the consumer decision-making process described in the following paragraph:

   The consumer first becomes aware of the need. Then the consumer simultaneously searches for information from several sources: retailers, advertising, word of mouth, and independent publications. After that a criterion is developed for evaluating the available brands in the marketplace. Based on this evaluation, the most preferred brand is selected.

INTERNET AND COMPUTER EXERCISES

1. For the data given in Table 22.1, use a graphics package or a spreadsheet, such as Excel, to construct the following graphs:
   - **a.** Pie chart
   - **b.** Line chart
   - **c.** Bar chart
2. Using one of the report-generation programs discussed in this chapter or a similar package, write a report explaining the data in and the charts constructed in exercise 1 of this section.
3. Visit www.gallup.com to identify a recent report prepared by this company. How does the format of this report compare to the one in the book?

Chapter 23

"In international research it is critical to take into account the environment and culture of the countries we are working in. This can mean not only adapting what we would normally do from our own perspective, but even going as far as to adapt our whole perspective."

Ian Jarvis, managing director, Infratest Burke

International Marketing Research

OBJECTIVES

After reading this chapter, the student should be able to

1. develop a framework for conducting international marketing research
2. explain in detail the marketing, governmental, legal, economic, structural, informational and technological, and sociocultural environmental factors and how they have an impact on international marketing research
3. describe the use of telephone, personal, and mail survey methods in different countries
4. discuss how to establish the equivalence of scales and measures including construct, operational, scalar, and linguistic equivalence
5. describe the processes of back translation and parallel translation in translating a questionnaire into a different language
6. discuss the ethical considerations in international marketing research
7. explain the use of the Internet and computers in international marketing research

OVERVIEW

This chapter discusses the environment in which international marketing research is conducted, focusing on the marketing, government, legal, economic, structural, informational and technological, and sociocultural environments.[1] Although discussions of how the six steps of the marketing research process should be implemented in an international setting were given in earlier chapters, here we present additional details on survey methods, scaling techniques, and questionnaire translation. The relevant ethical issues in international marketing research are identified and the use of the Internet and computers discussed. We begin with some examples illustrating the role of marketing research in international marketing.

EXAMPLE

Best in the West—and around the World

Best Western, with its more than 3,800 independently owned and operated hotels, is the world's largest chain in terms of number of hotels. As the following chart shows, business travelers make up 36 percent of the market, the largest single share. Best Western has found, through marketing research, that business travelers often resist trying less-expensive hotels and appreciate the security of a well-known brand. This information has helped the chain attract business travelers.

International marketing research has helped Best Western to become the world's largest hotel chain.

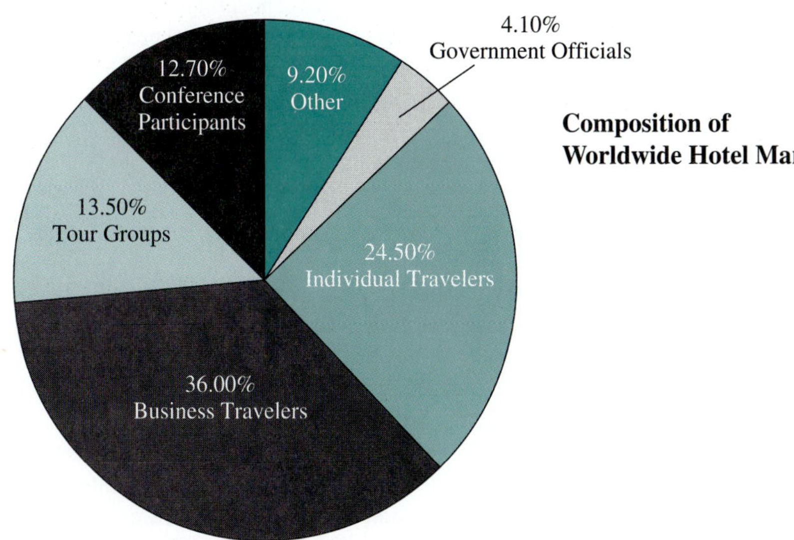

Composition of Worldwide Hotel Market

Through marketing research, Best Western has identified the sources of hotel business in different regions of the world and geared its marketing strategy accordingly (see the following table). For example, the chain emphasizes domestic business in North America, focuses on both domestic and international business in Europe, and emphasizes foreign business in the Far East, Australia, Africa, and the Middle East.[2]

SOURCES OF WORLDWIDE HOTEL BUSINESS BY REGION

Source of Hotel Business	*All Hotels Worldwide*	*Africa/Middle East*	*Asia/ Australia*	*North America*	*Europe*
Domestic	51.49%	26.89%	35.0%	77.49%	47.8%
Foreign	48.69%	73.29%	65.0%	22.6%	52.2%
Total	100 %	100 %	100 %	100 %	100 % ■

EXAMPLE

Blue Diamond Maintains Cutting Edge

One of the most successful U.S. advertising campaigns ever was "A can a week, that's all we ask" by Blue Diamond Growers. The goal was to change U.S. consumers' perception of almonds from a special-occasion treat to an everyday snack food. The domestic goal was reached, but the campaign was not used in other countries. Rather, through extensive marketing research, Blue Diamond tailored its message to each market it selected for a campaign.

Before entering a new foreign market, Blue Diamond conducts extensive secondary data analysis and even collects primary data. For example, before entering the Russian market, Blue Diamond learned that the former USSR was undertaking a plan to improve its citizens' diet. Blue Diamond commissioned a study of the nutritive qualities of almonds and found that almonds contain no cholesterol but provide as much protein per pound as cooked lean beef. By 1995, Russia was Blue Diamond's third-largest overseas customer. In India, where almonds are thought to be brain food and an aphrodisiac, Blue Diamond is considering the possibilities.[3] ■

Both these examples point to the fact that marketing research can contribute significantly to the formulation of successful international marketing strategies. The term *international marketing research* is used very broadly. It denotes research for true international products (international research), research carried out in a country other than the country of the research-commissioning organization (foreign research), research conducted in all important countries in which the company is represented (multinational research), and research conducted in/across different cultures (cross-cultural research).

MARKETING RESEARCH GOES INTERNATIONAL

In the 1990s revenue generated outside the United States has become important to the top market research firms in the United States. Several of the top 50 research firms in the United States reported revenue from work through subsidiaries, branch offices, and/or affiliates that are located outside the United States. This revenue amounted to approximately $2 billion or 40 percent of the top 50 firms' total revenue.[4]

Because overseas expansion is a hot topic in the 1990s, many marketers will begin to expand into the overseas market. This expansion is primarily due to economic integration and the lowering of trade barriers. Overseas expansion will mean increased opportunities for market research companies inside and outside of the United States. When consumers outside of the United States begin to spend their money, they give far greater attention to price and quality rather than to the product's country of origin. To many firms, regional markets represent the "international order of the day."[5]

As attractive as foreign markets are, companies must realize that setting up for operations in these markets does not guarantee success. Many economists warn that the economic conditions are, at best, sluggish. Others argue that it is unrealistic to expect aggressive consumerism in the near future even in markets with a taste for foreign concepts. The greatest problems that many firms will face in foreign markets is "red tape." Many governments have implemented laws and policies that will protect their countries' businesses.

Since the demise of the Cold War, the world's economy is no longer a simple three-way battle between the United States, Japan, and Germany. Stiffer competition will force many companies inside of the United States to try to gain competitive advantages outside of the United States. Three massive markets have developed since the end of the Cold War, some of which will require significant amounts of market research before entrance into that market can occur. The three markets are the Americas, Europe, and the Pacific Rim nations.

Since the passage of NAFTA, a veritable free market-revolution has begun to take place in Mexico. The passage of NAFTA created the world's largest market. This market is larger in terms of economics than is the European Community. In other Latin American countries, trade barriers are being reduced. Companies entering these changing markets will be forced to change the ways in which they do business. Quality standards will increase and prices will become more competitive due to greater selection. As product choices widen, consumer awareness and sophistication will increase. Latin Americans will become shoppers and companies can no longer hide behind the protective barriers of their countries, facing more competition due to the greater selection in the marketplace. As a result market researchers will be faced with two significant challenges. First, as manufacturing and markets assume a regional focus, service providers will be forced to do the same to achieve consistent results and quality. Researchers, both those internal to product operations and their outside suppliers, must follow this trend for a regional, quality approach. A top-down approach to marketing research will mean that company executives will become increasingly involved in marketing research. Secondly, marketing researchers must remain flexible to handle local conditions.[6] Appropriate methodologies will not be the same, as indicated by Research in Practice 23.1.[7]

With the number of U.S. products that are currently available in Europe, one can see that many manufacturers and researchers will not have to radically alter their marketing plans and objectives. The recently formed European Community (EC) is perhaps the source of the greatest economic potential in the world. The Western European market is roughly the size of the North American market, but the total size of the European market will increase due to the opening of the Eastern bloc area of Europe. However, companies must remain cognizant of the fact that there is a significantly lower level of disposable income in Eastern bloc countries. Therefore, they must find ways to cope with this particular problem. A particular opportunity that should be explored is the potential for small- and medium-sized companies to expand in the European market.

Many believe that the Pacific Rim is the fastest growing part of the world. This growth is paced by a rapid rate of investment and an abundance of trained human capital. Countries that are included in the Pacific Rim range from Australia to Indonesia to China. This region's

RESEARCH IN PRACTICE 23.1

Marketing Research Opportunities and Challenges of NAFTA

The North American Free Trade Agreement (NAFTA) presents U.S. market researchers with freer access to Mexican and Canadian markets. Yearly spending for market research services are estimated to be U.S. $55 million in Mexico, and U.S. $250 million in Canada. By comparison, the U.S.'s top 50 market research firms tallied revenues of $3 billion from domestic research in 1996.

In Mexico, a subsidiary of Nielsen Marketing Research is the dominant marketing research firm accounting for more than half of all revenues from market research. One of the first things U.S. researchers in Mexico must face is the unreliability of telephone and mail service for data collection. As an example, even household diary panel documents are dropped off and picked up to ensure delivery. Most data collection is done door-to-door in four of the largest cities, Matamoros, Monterrey, Guadalajara, and Mexico City—the world's second largest city (17 million) and home to one of five Mexicans. Despite its Hispanic culture, six million Native Americans of the more than 80 million Mexicans speak languages other than Spanish. Surveys typically bypass this segment of the population in much the same way that U.S. surveys fail to sample from the U.S. segment that speaks only Spanish.

Because of common language and long-standing ties between U.S. and Canadian research firms, a gauge of the Canadian research market is easier than that of Mexico. Annual revenues for Canadian research firms are about U.S. $250 million—about one-tenth the size of the U.S. market for research services (Canada's 25 million population stands in the same 1:10 proportion to the U.S. population of about 250 million). As in Mexico, and in the United States, Nielsen boasts the largest research operation with U.S. $44 million.

Although the Mexican research community formed a trade association in February 1993—*Associacion Mexicana de Agencias de Investigacion de Mercados y Opinion Publica* (AMAI)—two trade associations have existed in Canada since 1975: (1) the Professional Marketing Research Society (PMRS), and (2) the Canadian Association of Marketing Research Organizations (CAMRO). PMRS regional and national conferences provide a valuable means to become familiar with Canada's research practitioners, and to understand the special nuances of doing research in Canada.

Personal interviews are most suited for determining shopper preferences in Mexico.

average real economic growth is more than 5 percent per year and is expected to continue through the next decade. China is being called the next great Mecca for marketing research because it has a consumer population of over 1.2 billion. Recently Gallup announced the formation of Gallup China, the first foreign research firm in China. Gallup China will undoubtedly face many challenges such as rapidly increasing competition, governmental regulation, and the forming of bonds with the Chinese people in order to be able to conduct successful research. Chinese research firms have begun to form within China, and American companies have begun to form alliances with these companies in order to penetrate the Chinese market.[8] Certainly, international marketing research can be very complex. We present a framework for understanding and dealing with the complexities involved.

A FRAMEWORK FOR INTERNATIONAL MARKETING RESEARCH

Conducting international marketing research is much more complex than is domestic marketing research.[9] Although the six-step framework for domestic marketing research (chapter 1) is applicable, the environment prevailing in the countries, cultural units, or international markets being researched influences the way the six steps of the marketing research process should be performed. Figure 23.1 presents a framework for conducting international marketing research.

The Environment

The differences in the environments of countries, cultural units, or foreign markets should be considered while conducting international marketing research. These differences may arise in the marketing environment, government environment, legal environment, economic environment, structural environment, informational and technological environment, and sociocultural environment, as shown in Figure 23.1.

Marketing Environment

The role of marketing in economic development varies in different countries. For example, developing countries are frequently oriented toward production rather than marketing. Demand typically exceeds supply, and there is little concern about customer satisfaction, especially as the level of competition is low. In assessing the marketing environment, the researcher should consider the variety and assortment of products available, pricing policies, government control of media and the public's attitude toward advertising, the efficiency of the distribution system, the level of marketing effort undertaken, and the unsatisfied needs and behavior of consumers. For example, surveys conducted in the United States usually involve questions on the variety and selection of merchandise. These questions would be inappropriate in many countries, such as in Eastern Europe, which are characterized by shortage economies. Likewise, questions about pricing may have to incorporate bargaining as an integral part of the exchange process. Questions about promotion should be modified as well. Television advertising, an extremely important promotion vehicle in the United States, is restricted or prohibited in many countries in which TV stations are owned and operated by the government. Certain themes, words, and illustrations used in the United States are taboo in some countries. The types of retailers and intermediary institutions available and the services these institutions offer vary from country to country.

Government Environment

An additional relevant factor is the government environment. The type of government has a bearing on the emphasis on public policy, regulatory agencies, government incentives and penalties, and investment in government enterprises. Some governments, particularly

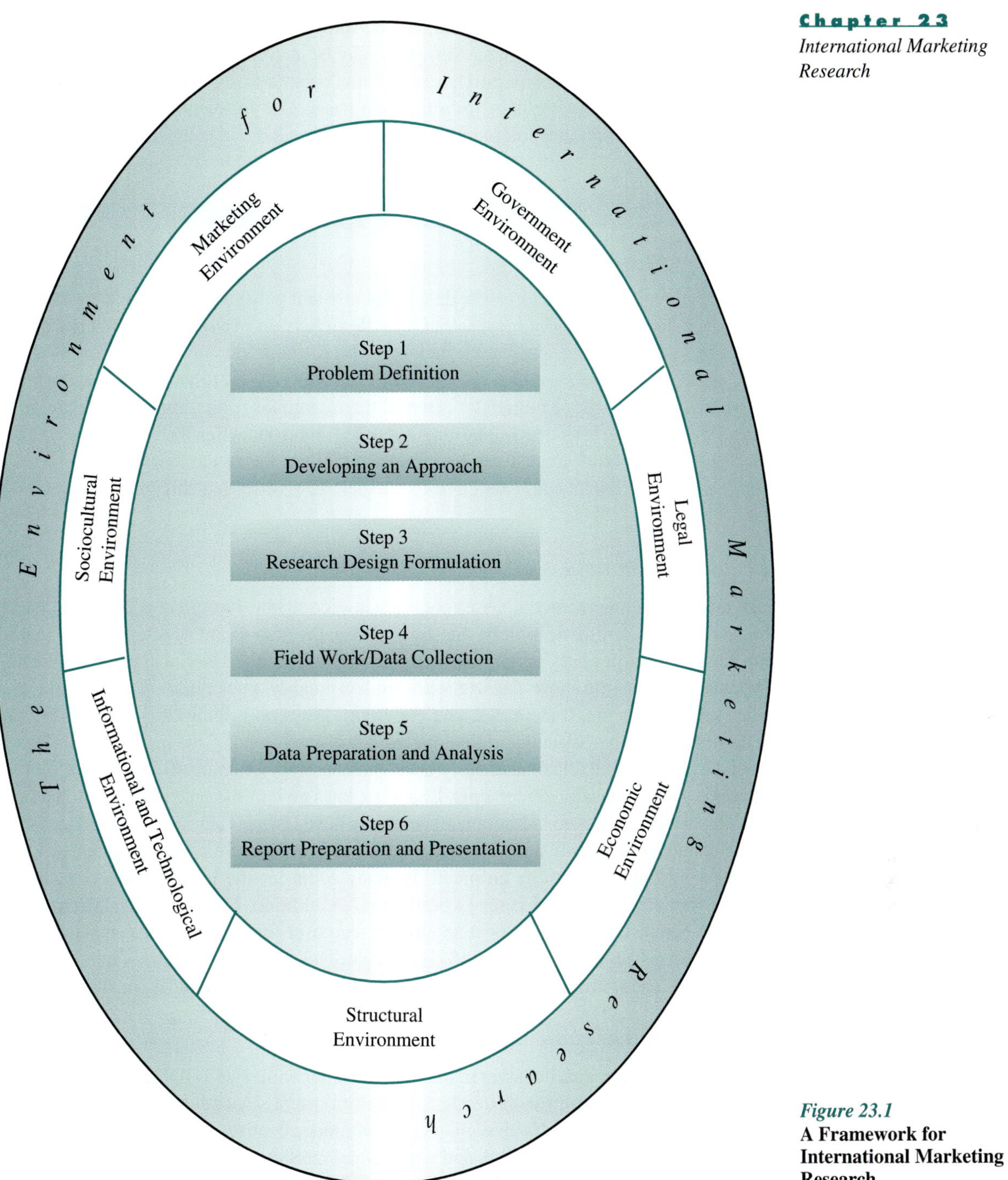

Figure 23.1
A Framework for International Marketing Research

in developing countries, do not encourage foreign competition. High tariff barriers create disincentives to the efficient use of marketing research approaches. Also, the role of government in setting market controls, developing infrastructure, and acting as an entrepreneur should be carefully assessed. The role of government is also crucial in many advanced countries, such as Germany and Japan, in which government has traditionally worked with industry toward a common national industrial policy. At the tactical level, the government determines tax structures, tariffs, and product safety rules and regulations and often imposes special rules and regulations on foreign multinationals and their marketing practices. In many countries, the government may be an important member of the distribution channel. The government purchases essential products on a large scale and then sells them to the consumers, perhaps on a rationed basis. The following example shows how government may influence international marketing research.

EXAMPLE

Red Tape in Red China

In international marketing research, data collection and politics may go hand-in-hand. One Western industrial marketing researcher on a short, hurried trip through China learned this fact when attempting to interview officials of the Chinese automobile industry. Although they agreed to an interview, the automobile executives refused to answer any questions of substance. Instead, they continually referred the researcher to the Ministry of Foreign Affairs (MFA) as the first step in learning about the industry. After the researcher met with the MFA, they would grant a detailed interview. When the researcher became somewhat frustrated, the Chinese auto executives gave their assurance that this process would only take a few days.[10] ■

Legal Environment

The legal environment encompasses common law, code law, foreign law, international law, transaction law, antitrust, bribery, and taxes. From the standpoint of international marketing research, particularly salient are laws related to the elements of the marketing mix. Product laws include those dealing with product quality, packaging, warranty and after-sales service, patents, trademarks, and copyright. Laws on pricing deal with price fixing, price discrimination, variable pricing, price controls, and retail price maintenance. Distribution laws relate to exclusive territory arrangements, type of channels, and cancellation of distributor or wholesaler agreements. Likewise, laws govern the type of promotional methods that can be employed. Although all countries have laws regulating marketing activities, some countries have only a few laws that are loosely enforced and others have many complicated laws that are strictly enforced. In many countries the legal channels are clogged and the settlement of court cases is prolonged. In addition, home-country laws may also apply to conducting business or marketing research in foreign countries. For example, a U.S. citizen is subject to certain U.S. laws regardless of the country in which business is being done. These laws relate to national security, antitrust, and ethical considerations.

Economic Environment

Economic environmental characteristics include economic size (GDP), level, source, and distribution of income, growth trends, and sectoral trends. A country's stage of economic development determines the size, the degree of modernization, and the standardization of its markets. Consumer, industrial, and commercial markets become more standardized and consumers' work, leisure, and lifestyles become more homogenized by economic development and advances in technology.

Structural Environment

Structural factors relate to transportation, communication, utilities, and infrastructure. For example, telephone usage in Europe is much lower than in the United States, and many households do without telephones. Mail service is inefficient in many developing countries. Personal contact with respondents is difficult, as city people work during the day and rural residents are inaccessible. Block statistics and maps are not available or can be obtained only with great difficulty. Many dwelling units are unidentified.

Differences in the marketing environment of countries should be considered when conducting international marketing research. Open-air markets like this one in Paris are quite common in France.

Informational and Technological Environment

Elements of the informational and technological environment include information and communication systems, computerization, use of electronic equipment, energy, production technology, science, and invention. For example, in India, South Korea, and many Latin American countries, advances in science and technology have not had a proportionate impact on the lifestyle of the common citizens. Computers and electronic information transfer have still to make an impact at the grass-roots level. Information handling and record keeping are performed in the traditional way. This, again, has an impact on the type of information that can be solicited from consumers, businesses, and other enterprises.

Sociocultural Environment

Sociocultural factors include values, literacy, language, religion, communication patterns, and family and social institutions. Relevant values and attitudes toward time, achievement, work, authority, wealth, scientific method, risk, innovation, change, and the Western world should be considered. The marketing research process should be modified so that it does not conflict with the cultural values. In many developing countries, 60 percent or more of the population is illiterate. In tradition-directed, less-developed societies, the ability of respondents to formulate opinions of their own seems to be all but absent; consequently, it is difficult to elicit information from these respondents. As a result, the sophisticated rating scales employed in the United States are not useful. Complexities are added by the fact that in a given nation or region there may be several distinct spoken languages and dialects.

A country with a homogenous family structure is likely to be more culturally homogenous than is a country with multiple family structures. For example, Japan is culturally more homogenous than either the United States or many African countries, which have many different kinds of family structures. The importance of designing products to be consistent with the sociocultural factors prevailing in a country is brought home by the success of BurgerLand in Saudi Arabia.

EXAMPLE

Arabian Appetites

Astute use of focus groups and depth interviews have helped BurgerLand to succeed in Saudi Arabia where the major hamburger chains have failed. By combining fast food experience with an understanding of the sociocultural environment in the Middle East, the owners of BurgerLand International hope to expand their operations throughout the Middle East. "Arabs like new things. Their life at home is often so restricted that when they have the chance to try new things, they're very much in favor of it," says a director of the company, Fuad El-Hibri. Special seating areas are provided for family groups. Arabs like children, and if the children like the restaurants then their parents may be attracted also. Although "the Saudi culture does not permit dating, the family section is also a place where brothers might wish to take their sisters and, possibly, meet other brothers with their sisters." Arabs also don't worry about calories, so "the heavier the food, the better," remarks El-Hibri.[11] ■

Each country's environment is unique, so international marketing research must take into consideration the environmental characteristics of the countries or foreign markets involved. The previous chapters, 1 through 22, included discussions of how the marketing research process can be adapted to international situations. In the following sections we provide additional details for implementing survey methods, scaling techniques, and questionnaire translation in international marketing research.[12]

SURVEY METHODS

The following sections discuss the major interviewing methods in light of the challenges of conducting research in foreign countries, especially Europe and developing countries.[13]

Telephone Interviewing and CATI

In the United States and Canada, the telephone has achieved almost total penetration of households. As a result, telephone interviewing is the dominant mode of questionnaire administration. The same situation exists in some of the European countries. In Sweden the number of telephones per 1,000 inhabitants exceeds 900, and in Stockholm the figure is even higher.[14] This along with the low cost has led to a sharp increase in the use of telephone interviews, which now account for 46 percent of the interviews conducted and constitute the dominant interviewing method. In other countries, such as the Netherlands, the number of telephone interviews exceeds the number of personal interviews.[15] Even in these countries, the sampling of respondents for telephone interviewing may pose serious problems. (See chapter 6 for a discussion of the issues related to the selection of probability samples in telephone interviewing.)

In many other European countries, telephone penetration is still not complete. Telephone penetration in Great Britain is only about 80 percent, and many practitioners are still skeptical of the value of telephone interviewing, especially for voting intention measurement.[16] In Finland, only 11.2 percent of interviews are administered over the telephone.[17] In Portugal telephone penetration is still low (33.6 percent), except in the Lisbon area (76 percent). For this reason, only 17 percent of interviews conducted are telephone interviews.

In Hong Kong, 96 percent of households (other than on outlying islands and on boats) can be contacted by telephone. With some persistence, evening telephone interviewing can successfully achieve interviews with 70 to 75 percent of selected respondents. Residents are uninhibited about using telephones and relaxed about telephone interviews. Yet, given the culture, this is not the most important mode of data collection.

In developing countries, only very few households have telephones. Telephone incidence is low in Africa. India is a predominantly rural society in which the penetration of telephones is less than 5 percent of households.[18] In Brazil the proportion of households with telephones is low (30 percent in large cities).[19] Even in countries such as Saudi

Arabia, in which telephone ownership is extensive, telephone directories tend to be incomplete and out-dated. In many developing countries, telephone interviewing may present additional problems. Daytime calls to households may be unproductive, as social customs may prohibit the housewife from talking with strangers. This situation can be somewhat alleviated by using female telephone interviewers, but the employment of women creates many obstacles in such countries. In many cultures face-to-face relationships are predominant. These factors severely limit the use of telephone interviewing.

Telephone interviews are most useful with relatively upscale consumers who are accustomed to business transactions by phone or consumers who can be reached by phone and can express themselves easily. With the decline of costs for international telephone calls, multicountry studies can be conducted from a single location.[20] This greatly reduces the time and costs associated with the organization and control of the research project in each country. Furthermore, international calls obtain a high response rate, and the results have been found to be stable (i.e., the same results are obtained from the first 100 interviews as from the next 200 or 500). It is necessary to find interviewers fluent in the relevant languages, but in most European countries this is not a problem.

Computer-assisted telephone interviewing (CATI) facilities are well developed in the United States and Canada and in some European countries, such as Germany. As the use of telephone interviewing is growing, they are becoming popular in other countries.[21]

In-Home Personal Interviews

In-home interviews require a large pool of qualified interviewers. Contractual arrangements with interviewers vary considerably. For example, in France, there are three categories of interviewers: interviewers with annual guarantee for a specified duration, interviewers with annual guarantee for an unspecified duration, and freelance interviewers with no salary guarantee. Overheads can also vary. In France, the employer and the interviewer must pay large social security contributions, in Belgium the interviewers are self-employed and pay their own social security contributions, whereas in the United Kingdom, although both the employer and the interviewer pay national insurance contributions, these tend to be small.

Due to high cost, the use of in-home personal interviews has declined in the United States and Canada, but this is the dominant mode of collecting survey data in many parts of Europe and the developing world. In-home personal interviewing is the dominant interviewing method in Switzerland.[22] In Portugal face-to-face interviews are 77 percent of the total interviews conducted. The majority of the surveys are done door-to-door, but some quick sociopolitical polls are carried out in the street. Likewise, in-home interviews are also popular in many Latin American countries.

EXAMPLE

Sweet Memories

In one of the research surveys conducted by Gallup Organization, the objective was to assess consumers' recall of different ads they had seen in the past month. In-home personal surveys were conducted by Gallup and its affiliates in the United States, Canada, Uruguay, Chile, Argentina, Brazil, Mexico, and Panama. In all, 7,498 people were surveyed. Unaided recall was used to get responses. Questions such as "What brands of soft drink advertisements seen in the past month first come to mind?" were asked. Results show that Coca-Cola ads are the choice of a new generation of both North and South Americans. Coca-Cola ads were among the top six ads mentioned in seven of the eight Western Hemisphere nations and were cited the most often in four countries. Ads of

International marketing research shows that Coca-Cola ads are the choice of a new generation of both North and South Americans.

archrival PepsiCola were named among the top six in four countries, and McDonald's Corporation appeared in the top six in two countries. However, none of these three made it to the top six in Brazil.[23] ■

Mall Intercept and CAPI

In North America many marketing research organizations have permanent facilities in malls equipped with interviewing rooms, kitchens, observation areas, and other devices. Mall intercepts constitute 15.2 percent of the interviews in Canada and 19 percent in the United States. Although mall intercepts are being conducted in some European countries, such as Sweden, they are not popular in Europe or developing countries.[24] In contrast, central location/street interviews constitute the dominant method of collecting survey data in France and the Netherlands.

However, some interesting developments with respect to computer-assisted personal interviewing (CAPI) are taking place in Europe. An interviewing program for the home computer has been developed in the Netherlands and used in panel studies and at central locations using CAPI.[25]

Mail Interviews

Because of relatively low cost, mail interviews continue to be used in most developed countries where literacy is high and the postal system is well developed. Mail interviews constitute 6.2 percent of the interviews in Canada and 7 percent in the United States.[26] In countries where the educational level of the population is extremely high (Denmark, Finland, Iceland, Norway, Sweden, and the Netherlands), mail interviews are common.[27] In Africa, Asia, and South America, however, the use of mail surveys and mail panels is low because of illiteracy and the large proportion of population living in rural areas. In Hong

Kong, mail surveys have been tried with varied success. Mail surveys are, typically, more effective in industrial international marketing research, although it is difficult to identify the appropriate respondent within each firm and to personalize the address. Nevertheless, mail surveys are used internationally, as illustrated by the following example.

EXAMPLE

Worldwide Achievers

Global Scan is a detailed survey conducted annually by Backer Spielvogel Bates to measure the attitudes and behaviors of 15,000 respondents in 14 countries. The questionnaire contains 120 attitudinal statements and is customized for each country by insertion of attitudes, lifestyles, and purchases (both product and brands).

The questionnaire is administered by mail, with local country offices responsible for distribution, meeting sampling requirements, and then transcribing the returned questionnaires to computer tape, which is shipped to the home office in New York. Global Scan averages a 50 percent response rate.

Based on the data, five lifestyle segments have emerged and have remained constant over time: Strivers, Achievers, Pressured, Adapters, and Traditionals. Thus marketers have a common set of attitudes and behaviors for defining consumers all over the world. For example, the similarities between Achievers in the United States, England, Australia, and Finland are greater than those between Achievers and Strivers in the United States. Global Scan collects detailed brand and category information on more than 1,000 products. Marketers can then use this information to develop specific strategies.[28] ■

Mail Panels

Mail panels are extensively used in the United Kingdom, France, West Germany, and the Netherlands. Mail and diary panels are also available in Finland, Sweden, Italy, Spain, and other European countries. Use of panels may increase with the advent of new technology. For example, in Germany, two agencies (A. C. Nielsen and GfK-Nurnberg) have installed fully electronic scanner test markets, based on the Behavior Scan model from the United States. Nielsen will use on-the-air television; GfK, cable. Panels of this kind have not yet been developed in Hong Kong and most of the developing countries.[29]

Electronic Surveys

In the United States and Canada, the use of e-mail and the Internet is growing by leaps and bounds. As such, the use of these methods for conducting surveys is growing not only with business and institutional respondents but also with households. Both these methods have become viable for conducting surveys related to a wide range of product categories and scenarios. The popularity of both e-mail and Internet surveys is also growing overseas. Both these types of surveys are increasingly being used in Western Europe where the access to the Internet is freely available. However, in some parts of Eastern Europe and in other developing countries, e-mail access is restricted and Internet availability is even poorer. Hence, these methods are not suitable for household surveys in these countries. However, surveys with business and institutional respondents may still be attempted, particularly using e-mail. E-mail surveys use pure text (ASCII) to represent questionnaires, and can be received and responded to by anyone with an e-mail address, whether or not they have access to the Internet. As we illustrate in the section on Internet and computer applications later in the chapter, multinational firms are using both the e-mail and the Internet to survey their employees worldwide.

The criteria for the selection of survey methods were discussed in chapter 6. As was discussed and illustrated in chapter 6, an important consideration in selecting the methods of administering questionnaires is to ensure equivalence and comparability across countries. Issues of equivalence are also salient in measurement and scaling.

MEASUREMENT AND SCALING

In international marketing research it is critical to establish the equivalence of scales and measures used to obtain data from different countries.[30] As illustrated in Figure 23.2, this requires examinations of construct equivalence, operational equivalence, scalar equivalence, and linguistic equivalence.[31]

Construct Equivalence A construct equivalence deals with the question of whether the marketing constructs have the same meaning and significance in different countries.

Construct equivalence deals with the question of whether the marketing constructs (for example, opinion leadership, variety seeking, brand loyalty) have the same meaning and significance in different countries. In many countries, the number of brands available in a given product category is limited. In some countries the dominant brands have become generic labels symbolizing the entire product category. Consequently, a different perspective on brand loyalty may have to be adopted in these countries.

Conceptual Equivalence A construct equivalence issue that deals specifically with whether the interpretation of brands, products, consumer behavior, and the marketing effort is the same in different countries.

Functional Equivalence A construct equivalence issue that deals specifically with whether a given concept or behavior serves the same role or function in different countries.

Category Equivalence A construct equivalence issue that deals specifically with whether the categories in which brands, products, and behavior are grouped is the same in different countries.

Construct equivalence comprises conceptual equivalence, functional equivalence, and category equivalence. **Conceptual equivalence** deals with the interpretation of brands, products, consumer behavior, and marketing effort. For example, promotional sales are an integral component of marketing efforts in the United States. On the other hand, in countries with shortage economies, where the market is dominated by the sellers, consumers view sales with suspicion, because they believe that the product being promoted is of poor quality. **Functional equivalence** examines whether a given concept or behavior serves the same role or function in different countries. For example, in many developing countries bicycles are predominantly a means of transportation rather than of recreation. Marketing research related to the use of bicycles in these countries must examine different motives, attitudes, behaviors, and even different competing products than such research would in the United States. **Category equivalence** refers to the category in which stimuli such as products, brands, and behaviors are grouped. In the United States, the category of the principal shopper may be defined as either the male or female head of household. This category may be inappropriate in countries where routine daily shopping is done by a domestic servant. Furthermore, the category "household" itself varies across countries.

Operational Equivalence A type of equivalence that measures how theoretical constructs are operationalized in different countries to measure marketing variables.

Item Equivalence A concept proposing that the same instrument should be used in different countries.

Operational equivalence concerns how theoretical constructs are operationalized to make measurements. In the United States leisure may be operationalized as playing golf, tennis, or other sports; watching television; or basking in the sun. This operationalization may not be relevant in countries where people do not play these sports or do not have round-the-clock TV transmission. Lying in the sun is not normal behavior in countries with hot climates. **Item equivalence**, which is closely connected to operational equivalence, presupposes both construct and operational equivalence. To establish item equivalence, the construct should be measured by the same instrument in different countries.

Scalar equivalence, also called *metric equivalence*, is established if the other types of equivalence have been attained. This involves demonstrating that two individuals from different countries with the same value on some variable, such as brand loyalty, will score at

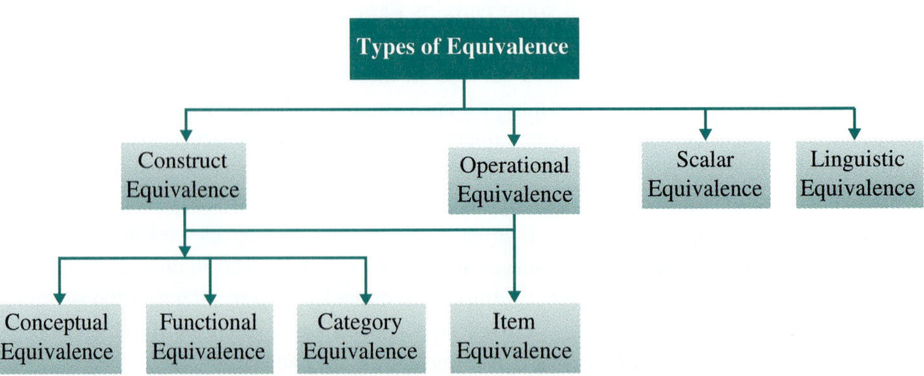

Figure 23.2
Scaling and Measurement Equivalence in International Marketing Research

the same level on the same test. Scalar equivalence has two aspects. The specific scale or scoring procedure used to establish the measure should be equivalent. The equivalence of response to a given measure in different countries should be considered. For example, do the scores on a purchase intent scale reflect similar likelihood of purchase in different countries? Finally, **linguistic equivalence** refers to both the spoken and the written language forms used in scales, questionnaires, and interviewing. The scales and other verbal stimuli should be translated so that they are readily understood by respondents in different countries and have equivalent meaning.[32]

Scalar Equivalence The demonstration that two individuals from different countries with the same value on some variable will score at the same level on the same test; also called *metric equivalence*.

QUESTIONNAIRE TRANSLATION

Linguistic Equivalence The equivalence of both spoken and written language forms used in scales and questionnaires.

The questions may have to be translated for administration in different cultures. Direct translation, in which a bilingual translator translates the questionnaire directly from a base language to the respondent's language, is frequently used. However, if the translator is not fluent in both languages and not familiar with both cultures, direct translation of certain words and phrases may be erroneous. Procedures such as back translation and parallel translation have been suggested to avoid these errors. In **back translation**, the questionnaire is translated from the base language by a bilingual speaker whose native language is the language into which the questionnaire is being translated. This version is then translated back into the original language by a bilingual whose native language is the initial or base language. Translation errors can then be identified. Several repeat translations and back translations may be necessary to develop equivalent questionnaires, and this process can be cumbersome and time-consuming.[33]

Back Translation A translation technique by which a translator whose native language is the one into which the questionnaire is being translated translates a questionnaire from the base language. This version is then translated back into the original language by someone else whose native language is the base language. Translation errors can then be identified.

An alternative procedure is **parallel translation**. A committee of translators, each of whom is fluent in at least two of the languages in which the questionnaire will be administered, discusses alternative versions of the questionnaire and makes modifications until consensus is reached. In countries where several languages are spoken, the questionnaire should be translated into the language of each respondent subgroup. It is important that any nonverbal stimuli (pictures and advertisements) also be "translated" using similar procedures. The following example underscores the importance of correct translation.

Parallel Translation A translation method in which a committee of translators, each of whom is fluent in at least two languages, discusses alternative versions of a questionnaire and makes modifications until consensus is reached.

EXAMPLE

Researchers Can't Get Self-Respect in Germany

A common questionnaire used to measure consumer values is the list of values (LOV). In North America, it has revealed nine basic value segments of consumers. The most widely held values of Americans are self-respect, security, and warm relationships with others. To conduct a comparative study in Germany, the LOV had to be translated into a German version (GLOV). Through the process of translation and back translation, a suitable form was created; however, some inconsistencies remained. For example, it was very difficult to translate the English concepts of "warm relationships with others" and "self-respect" into German. As a result, the data revealed that significantly fewer Germans than Americans hold these values as their most important. The researchers concluded that the imprecise translation was more responsible for these results than were actual differences in value orientations. The table shows the distribution of the top three values for each culture, with the rank in parentheses.[34]

Values	*Germany*		*United States*	
Self-respect	13%	(3)	21%	(1)
Security	24	(2)	21	(2)
Warm relationships	8	(4)	16	(3)
Sense of belonging	29	(1)	8	(7) ■

RESEARCH IN PRACTICE 23.2

Europeans Legislate Data Privacy

There is widespread implementation of data privacy laws in the European community nations. A prototype of European nations' data privacy laws is the United Kingdom's Data Protection Act (DPA), which embodies eight guidelines:

1. Personal data will be obtained and processed fairly and lawfully.
2. Personal data will be held only for specified and lawful purposes.
3. Personal data will not be used for any reason other than the specified purpose.
4. Personal data for specified purposes will not be excessive in amount.
5. Personal data will be accurate and will be kept current.
6. Personal data will not be kept longer than necessary for the specified purpose.
7. Users of personal data must provide nondelayed access to personal data (at no expense) when individuals make requests to examine their personal data over reasonable intervals. Where appropriate, data users must correct or erase erroneous data.
8. Data users must take appropriate security measures against unauthorized access, alteration, disclosure, destruction, or loss of personal data.

As can be seen, the guidelines of the British DPA are similar to those espoused by the domestic codes of ethics.

FOCUS ON Burke

Burke has had offices (either owned or licensed affiliates) in countries other than the United States for over 30 years. Among the many issues relative to conducting research across cultural boundaries (as well as political boundaries) addressed is the issue of creating a "common questionnaire" for different cultures.

Some researchers may initially approach a multicountry study as an issue of creating a questionnaire in their language and then working diligently to translate it accurately and with the proper tone, into the language of another culture. This is required and necessary but not sufficient in many situations, as illustrated by the following projects.

A non-U.S. telephone company had their questionnaire translated into English to be administered in the United States by Burke's data collection unit. Although the translation was very good, the questionnaire referred at many points to the U.S. National Telephone Company. The researcher hadn't done the simple secondary research to learn that the United States has hundreds of telephone companies and not a governmental national phone company, as was true in the researcher's country. Dumb you say? It happened.

A U.S. company wanted to do research on cooking chocolate in Mexico. The questionnaire was beautifully translated but failed to take into account the very different cooking behaviors and attitudes toward chocolate that were not typical of the United States. For example, cooking chocolate in Mexico may be sold in large, loosely wrapped bars. If these bars are not exuding beads of oil on their surface, many cooks think they are not "natural and pure." The U.S. researcher had never heard of this, didn't include this notion in the questionnaire, and completely missed why the product was not seen as acceptable.

The advice Burke gives to avoid such mistakes is, "Be concerned that you are asking about relevant issues in the culture before you worry about the translation!" The desire to have a common instrument can't blind you to asking about issues that are culturally relevant in each country. In most situations this requires local knowledge through local research professionals with access to secondary or primary research to aid in the "cultural translation" as well as the "language translation."

ETHICS IN MARKETING RESEARCH

Ethical responsibilities for marketing research conducted abroad are very similar to that conducted domestically. For each of the six stages of the marketing research design process the same four stakeholders (client, researcher, respondent, and public) must act honorably and respect their responsibilities to one another. As Research in Practice 23.2 indicates, the ethical constraints facing marketing researchers abroad are fairly similar to those at home.[35] For all the similarities, some ethical issues become more difficult. Conducting marketing research in a foreign country can easily become a political issue. Reseearchers must be careful to adopt the ethical guidelines of not only the domestic country but the host (foreign) country as well.

INTERNET AND COMPUTER APPLICATIONS

The Internet and computers can be extensively used in all phases of the international marketing research process. These uses parallel those discussed in the earlier chapters (1 through 22) and, hence, will not be repeated here. The fact that the Internet can be used to communicate with respondents anywhere in the world has given a new dimension to international marketing research. For example, the on-line survey overcomes geographic boundaries by soliciting responses from around the world. The on-line survey also takes advantage of one interviewer (the computer) that can present the same survey in several different translations, as illustrated in the case of Hewlett Packard.

EXAMPLE

Internet Surveys Pack Hewlett Packard's International Marketing Research Tool Box

Hewlett-Packard conducts on-line surveys to gather information about Internet users' perceptions about the Hewlett-Packard Web site. Because Hewlett-Packard customers are all over the world, the respondents get a choice of which language version of the surveys they wish to complete. Some other pages of the Hewlett-Packard Web site are also available in several different translations. This approach recognizes the need to adapt marketing research tools as well as marketing communications to a more global environment.

As an example of one of the multilanguage surveys, the Web site contained an eight-page chemical analysis survey that first allowed the respondent to choose from six languages to complete the survey. The survey itself asked the respondents if having on-line information available in a local language is an advantage.

Some parts of the survey were fixed-response alternative questions that asked the respondent to rate items on a scale of 1 to 5. This part of the survey was structured. There were other parts to the survey that were not as structured. For example, one objective of the survey was to determine how easy or difficult it is to find some information in the Hewlett-Packard chemical analysis site. In this part of the survey, respondents were asked to search out information about two particular areas: the product features and benefits of the Mass Spectrometer Model HP 5973 and the application notes for the Gas Chromatograph Model HP 6890. Once the respondents looked for the information, they were instructed to return to the survey and answer questions about how easy it was to find the information in the Web site.

Chapter 24

"Our value to those who use our information is based on trust. Without ethical conduct at every level and phase of our activity, we cannot earn nor maintain that trust."

Mike Kuhn, senior vice president, Burke Customer Satisfaction Associates

Ethics in Marketing Research

OBJECTIVES

After reading this chapter, the student should be able to

1. discuss the importance of ethics in the marketing research process and explain why ethical conduct is crucial to the survival of marketing research
2. describe the ethical vulnerability of the various stakeholders in the marketing research process: the public, respondents, clients, and marketing researchers
3. describe the ethical guidelines that have been proposed in the literature
4. understand how ethics provide an overall framework for the marketing research process and describe the various approaches to ethical decision making
5. explain how ethical issues impact each step of the marketing research process
6. understand the ethical issues in international marketing research
7. explain the ethical issues related to the use of the Internet and computers

OVERVIEW

Throughout the previous chapters we have identified specific ethical issues and discussed the importance of adhering to ethical practices at each step of the marketing research process. In this capstone chapter we begin by emphasizing the necessity for ethics in research and identifying the stakeholders in marketing research. We discuss some of the guidelines that aid managers and researchers alike in ethical decision making. A framework for ethics in marketing research is then proposed. The way in which ethics influence each step of the marketing research process is summarized. Finally, the ethical issues in international marketing research and the use of the Internet and computers are examined. To give the reader some exposure to ethical dilemmas in marketing research, we provide a few introductory examples.[1]

EXAMPLE

Earthquakes Shake Marketing Ethics

Research on cognitive heuristics (mental rules of thumb) has revealed that consumers frequently use the availability heuristic. Simply put, this means that the judged probability of an event is proportional to the ease of imaging that event. Marketers of life insurance have increased sales by providing consumers with vivid images of untimely death and grieving (and penurious) loved ones (i.e., "fear appeals") in advertising. These images increase anxiety and reinforce the necessity of protection. However, they portray that the occurrence of untimely death is more likely than it is in reality. Are such marketing practices ethical?[2] ■

EXAMPLE

When Is a Sale Not a Sale?

Marketing research revealed that advertising by May D&F was not misleading.

Special sales are common with retailers. But when is a sale not a sale? May D&F, a division of the May Department Stores which used to operate 12 department stores in Colorado, was forced to prove in court that its sale prices were actually sale prices. The ethical issue: If a price for an item is marked as "sale," does it have to be lower than the price of the item that is in effect most of the year?

May D&F had been accused by the Colorado attorney general's office of violating the Colorado Consumer Protection Act, specifically the section dealing with deceptive trade practices. Prices in the Home Store department were originally set at one price and then placed on sale. The attorney general objected because the original price was in effect for only 10 days every 6 months whereas a variety of sale prices existed over the remainder of the time. Consumers responding to advertising claims of sale prices of 30 percent off were likely to find the price they had seen the week before. May D&F's response to the attorney general was to research what constituted a sale price in the minds of consumers. Two surveys were conducted by May D&F's marketing research supplier. The first was a random sample of 500 Denver households by telephone that attempted to assess May D&F's reputation among retailers and some specific advertising practices. In the second survey, 331 individuals were surveyed in a number of malls in Denver. A series of yes/no questions were asked to show what the term "original price" meant to them and whether respondents' perceptions of the term were influenced by the amount of merchandise actually sold at that price.

The results of this research showed that consumers viewed May D&F as a store that had higher prices than competitors, good-quality products, and good service. Also, consumers believed May D&F's sale prices to be higher than those of other area merchants. Consumers went on to say that a 50 percent off sale at May D&F did not mean the price was lower than at other area retailers. It was also clear from the research that most Denver-area consumers feel that the most important thing to look for when trying to judge a price is to compare that price with other stores. Few felt that the store's own reference or original price held great importance for them. Taken collectively, the results of this survey could be interpreted to indicate that May D&F advertising is not misleading for households in the Denver metropolitan area.

May D&F used the research findings to counter claims made regarding its pricing and sale policies. The public seems to understand that a sale at one store may not mean prices lower than those available at other stores. On the other hand, May D&F did advertise a "sale price" that differed little from the price of the product for most of the year (sometimes the sale price was the price in effect most of the year). Clearly this is an accepted practice in retailing, but does that mean it is an ethical practice? It is also clear that the attorney general in this case perceived the practice to be not only unethical, but illegal.[3] ■

These two examples help illustrate why the consideration of ethical issues is important in marketing. If research is to be done well and to provide useful information for marketing decision making, it must be conducted within the bounds of ethical behavior.

IMPORTANCE OF ETHICS IN MARKETING RESEARCH

Ethics The process of evaluating and addressing whether a particular action is right or wrong, good or bad.

Ethics address whether a particular action is right or wrong, good or bad. The topic of ethics is extremely pertinent for marketing and for marketing research, due to the amount and variety of contact marketers have with the public. Of all the aspects of business, "marketing is closest to the public view and, consequently, is subject to considerable societal analysis and scrutiny."[4] This has created a perception that, within business, marketing is the area most prone to unethical practices. It is therefore imperative that marketers, and marketing researchers in particular, adhere to ethical practices because public perceptions of the field determine how and even whether marketing research can continue. Volunteer participants are the very heart of marketing research. Consumer research would practically cease to continue without the cooperation of the public from which the respondents in marketing research are drawn.

Even though the need for ethics is clear, the subject itself is somewhat complex. Although this complexity is due to a variety of factors, five major characteristics describing ethical decisions have been identified.[5] First, most ethical decisions have extended or long-term effects. Second, ethical decisions are rarely black and white; rather there are multiple alternatives that are acceptable to varying degrees. Third, these alternatives have both positive and negative outcomes, depending on the viewpoint of the evaluator. Fourth, what the positive or negative outcomes will be is always uncertain and unpredictable. Finally, most ethical decisions have personal implications. This may result in many types of costs: personal, social, financial, and so forth.[6]

Stakeholders Any group or individual who is, or can be, affected by the process under scrutiny. When that process is marketing research, there are four stakeholders: the public at large, the actual respondents used in a study, the client, and the researcher.

Identifying those affected by unethical marketing research practices, the stakeholders, enables us to be aware of some easily avoidable ethical pitfalls. The **stakeholder** concept is a method of looking at ethical relationships by identifying any group or individual who is, or can be, affected by the process under scrutiny. When that process is marketing research, there are four stakeholders: the public at large, the actual respondents used in a study, the client, and the researcher. Each of the four stakeholders are in some way vulnerable to the others. For the relationships to work ethically, each group has certain responsibilities and must be trusted to act honorably. Ethical dilemmas surrounding marketing research frequently revolve around the stakeholders' responsibilities.

STAKEHOLDERS IN MARKETING RESEARCH

We examine each of the marketing research stakeholders in turn. To identify ethical dilemmas, attention will be focused on instances in which each stakeholder is vulnerable to the others and where each can be harmed.

Public

With regard to the general public, ethical concerns revolve primarily around the methods of generating and reporting research results. The public often relies on marketing research for information on products. When this information is distorted, by either the marketing researcher or the client, the public is at a disadvantage. It is the joint responsibility of the researcher and the client to ensure that the research findings are being disseminated accurately. In particular, care should be taken by both the market researcher and the client to avoid incomplete reporting, misleading reporting, and biased research.[7]

Incomplete Reporting. As the name implies, whenever a client firm or researcher does not reveal the research results in their entirety, **incomplete reporting** has occurred. This unethical act is more likely to take place when a researcher uncovers negative information, which might not be favorably received by the client or the public at large.

Incomplete Reporting Whenever a client firm or researcher does not reveal the research results in their entirety.

Misleading Reporting. **Misleading reporting**, on the other hand, involves the distortion of information. Although the information presented to the public may not be falsified, it nevertheless leaves the public with an erroneous impression. For example, suppose a research project attempts to find out which brand of toothpaste is preferred by most dentists, and arrives at the following results: 90 percent of dentists surveyed express no preference, 5 percent prefer brand A, 3 percent brand B, and 2 percent prefer some brand other than A or B. It is misleading if the client firm, which manufactures brand A, claims in its advertising that more dentists prefer brand A than any other toothpaste. Not because it is necessarily untrue, but because it leaves the public with the inaccurate conclusion that *most* dentists prefer brand A, when this is clearly not the case. The overwhelming majority of the dentists do not have a preference for any brand.

Misleading Reporting The distortion of research information. By distortion, it is meant that although the information presented to the public is correct, it leaves the public with an erroneous impression.

Biased Research. **Biased research** occurs when the research process is performed improperly resulting in incorrect findings. Errors of this nature can occur when the problem is incorrectly defined, the approach or the research design is faulty, the scales are lacking in validity, the questionnaire is poorly designed or administered, the sample is inappropriately selected, improper statistical methods are employed, or any other type of failure to execute properly the steps in the marketing research process takes place. Examples might include leading the respondents to answer in a certain way during data collection, throwing out selected respondents to produce the desired result, or using a simple average when a weighted average would have been more appropriate. When the research is biased in this manner, the ultimate loser is the public. Anyone conducting and publishing market research results should treat the public honorably. Otherwise, the public's trust of marketing will be further eroded.

Biased Research Research that is performed in a nonobjective manner that results in misleading findings.

Respondent

Many would argue that it is perhaps the ethical concerns of the respondents that deserve the most attention. Without their involvement there could be little research. Therefore, it is to the marketing researcher's advantage to protect the respondents from unethical research practices. The ethical issues in the researcher-respondent relationship are highlighted in Table 24.1. Two of these deserve special attention: conducting a survey as a guise to sell products, and the invasion of the privacy of the respondent.

TABLE 24.1

ETHICAL CONCERNS IN THE RESEARCHER–RESPONDENT RELATIONSHIP

Deceptive Practices
- Unrealized promise of anonymity
- Falsified sponsor identification
- Selling under the guise of research
- Misrepresenting research procedures
  - Questionnaire or interview length
  - Possible follow-up contacts
  - Purpose of study
  - Uses made of results
  - Undelivered compensation (premiums, summaries, or results)

Invasion of Privacy
- Observation studies without informed consent
- Use of qualitative research techniques
- Merging data from several sources
- Overly personal questions and topics

Lack of Concern for Subjects or Respondents
- Contacting respondents at inconvenient times
- Incompetent or insensitive interviewers
- Failure to debrief after deception or disguise
- Research producing a depressing effect on respondents
- Too frequent use of public in research
- Nondisclosure of research procedures (length, follow-up, purpose, use)

Conducting a Survey to Sell Products. Unfortunately, respondents have been deliberately deceived by telemarketing masquerading as market research. Some unethical marketers have been known to tell respondents that they were conducting a survey as a lead-in to a sales presentation, or as an attempt to get information that could be used for sales leads or mailing lists. This practice, called **sugging** in trade language, is illegal as well as unethical. A similar practice, fund raising under the guise of research, is called **frugging** and is also unethical. These practices violate the respondents' trust and erode their willingness to support legitimate surveys.

Sugging The use of marketing research to deliberately disguise a sales effort.

Frugging The use of marketing research to deliberately disguise fund-raising activities.

Invasion of the Privacy of Respondents. The privacy of respondents is a legitimate right that must be protected. This means, among other things, that respondents who are promised anonymity or confidentiality must be provided just that. It also means that respondents should not be contacted at times that are inconvenient, such as late at night when most might be expected to be in bed, or during mealtimes, when they might be interrupted. Another concern is the prevalent practice of buying and selling mailing lists, especially those compiled through somewhat deceptive means, such as returned product warranty cards and frequent shopper programs.

EXAMPLE

Informed Consent and the Uninformed Respondents

A supermarket has instituted a frequent shoppers program by which shoppers can receive discounts on weekly specials by obtaining frequent shoppers cards. Each card has a UPC code that identifies the customer by name, address, and relevant demographic information

Some supermarket shoppers may be participating in a scanner panel without their knowledge or consent.

provided when applying for the card. This card is scanned before grocery products at check-out every time the customer shops. Thus, the customer's identity and actual purchases are recorded. The supermarket may sell this information to syndicated services. Marketers can purchase this information from the syndicated service companies and use it to determine the purchase habits of their consumers and target their marketing effort.

This example points to the principle of informed consent, which states that researchers should try to avoid both uninformed and misinformed participation by subjects in research. Shoppers in this example are participating in a scanner panel without their knowledge or consent. They were not informed that their purchases were going to be recorded and analyzed. Thus, the supermarket can be considered as invading the privacy of the consumer.[8] ■

Client

Given the complexity involved, it is not surprising that the ethical issues surrounding the researcher–client relationship are somewhat numerous (see Table 24.2).[9] Areas that deserve special attention from an ethical standpoint are: abuse of position arising from specialized knowledge, unnecessary research, an unqualified researcher, disclosure of identity, treating data as nonconfidential, and misleading presentation of data.

Abuse of Position. Because the marketing researcher, not the marketing manager, possesses the research expertise, the researcher has a responsibility not to take unfair advantage of this position. In other words, the researcher should make every effort to follow correct research procedures and adopt a suitable approach and research design. In short, the researcher must conduct quality research while respecting the clients' resources of time and money.

Unnecessary Research. The researcher has the ethical duty to not perform unnecessary research. Such situations may arise when the client wishes to conduct research that would serve no useful purpose, has already been done, or does not need to be carried out to the degree specified (e.g., primary research may not be necessary as secondary data provide the required information).

Unqualified Researcher. In some instances, the researcher may not have the necessary skills or technical expertise, or may not have the necessary resources to conduct the research. In these situations, the researcher should explain these limitations to the prospective client and refuse the project.

TABLE 24.2

ETHICAL CONCERNS IN THE RESEARCHER–CLIENT RELATIONSHIP

Abuse of Research Design, Methodology, or Results
- Conducting unnecessary research
- Researching wrong or irrelevant problems
- Using unwarranted shortcuts to secure contracts or save expenses
- Misrepresenting limitations of research design
- Inappropriate analytical techniques
- Lack of sufficient expertise to conduct required research
- Overly technical language in research report
- Overstating validity or reliability of conclusions

Researcher Abuse of the Researcher–Client Relationship
- Overbilling the project
- Failing to maintain client confidentiality
- Failing to avoid possible conflict of interest

Client Abuse of the Researcher–Client Relationship
- Inappropriate use of research proposals
- Disclosure or use of the researcher's specialized techniques and models
- Cancellation of project (or refusal to pay) without cause
- Conducting research solely to support a priori conclusions
- Failing to act on dangerous or damaging findings

Disclosure of Identity. A client firm has the right to expect that its identity will be protected before, during, and after the completion of the research project. The researcher is ethically bound to not reveal the client's identity to competitors, respondents, or any other firms or individuals without the express consent of the client.

Nonconfidential Data. The client has a right to expect that any data collected or results obtained will belong to the client firm and will be held in strict confidence by the researcher. Proprietary data should not be released to the competition and should not be reused in a subsequent research project for another firm, without the original firm's explicit knowledge and consent.

Misleading Presentations. The misleading presentation of research results can take on many forms, such as leading the client to believe that the results are more precise than they actually are. The researcher should avoid the use of unnecessarily technical terms that only serve to confuse or convey a false sense of complexity to the client. Further, the researcher should present numerical results only to the level of precision warranted by the study (e.g., if a numerical result is only accurate to the nearest $5, it should be reported as such and not be broken down into dollars and cents). Additionally, the researcher should not mislead the client by presenting incomplete research results or failing to provide the whole picture.

Researcher

The researcher (or the research firm) has the right to be treated ethically as well. Ethical treatment by clients involves several issues: improper solicitation of proposals, disclosure of proprietary techniques, and misrepresentation of findings (Table 24.2).[10]

Improper Solicitation. When a research firm submits a proposal to a prospective client, it should be confident that the client is seriously considering employing it to conduct the research project. Furthermore, should the potential client decide to employ another research firm, the client will not attempt to misuse the first proposal by turning it over to another firm for execution. The research proposal is the property of the research firm that developed it, unless it is paid for by the client.

Proprietary Techniques. A researcher also has the right to expect that any of its **proprietary techniques** will not be revealed by the client to other researchers or firms. The client firm should also refrain from using such techniques for their own future use—even if the technique was used in a project previously commissioned from the researcher in question—without the express permission of the researcher who developed the technique.

Proprietary Techniques
Research techniques that are considered intellectual property of a research firm.

The client has the responsibility to use marketing research findings in advertising and other marketing efforts in an ethical manner.

Misrepresentation of Findings. The client firm should not distort the research findings to their own benefit at the expense of the researcher's reputation. Returning to the earlier example of dentists' toothpaste preference, suppose that the researcher (say Burke Marketing Research) who conducted the study made it clear to the client firm that although more of those dentists that expressed a preference preferred brand A (5 percent), the majority of dentists did not express a preference (90 percent). It would be unethical for the client to distort this information and advertise that Burke Marketing Research found that more dentists prefer brand A than any other brand, without revealing that most dentists did not have a preference.

The researcher is also vulnerable to the unethical behaviors of the respondents. When respondents are recruited for a research project, the researcher assumes that they will provide truthful and well-thought-out responses. Respondents who fail to do so may be engaging in unethical behavior.

GUIDELINES FOR ETHICAL DECISION MAKING

Now that the stakeholders in marketing research have been identified and the more obvious ethical issues have been pointed out, we come to the more difficult task of ethical decision making. The very words "decision making" imply that a more complex process is at work, the boundaries are not well defined, and a clear-cut answer does not exist for every situation. So how do we approach such a monumental task?

One approach is to formulate some general guidelines for ethical behavior. To this purpose, the American Marketing Association (AMA) has developed a marketing research code of ethics given in Research in Practice 24.1.[11] Other associations have developed similar codes. Research in Practice 24.2 ranks the core moral values in the various associations' codes.[12] This code, along with an awareness of the stakeholders in marketing research, provides a good starting point for ethical decision making, but further guidelines are still needed.

A sound ethical framework, especially as it pertains to marketing research, has yet to be developed. Although various simplistic philosophies have been espoused, such as the golden rule, the utilitarian principle, Immanuel Kant's categorical imperative, the professional ethic, and the TV test, they are vague and not sufficiently rigorous to provide a solid basis for ethical decision making.[13] Therefore, in order to aid all types of businesspersons, including marketing researchers, checklists for ethical decision making have been developed in an attempt to improve the process. One such checklist is:

Laczniak's and Murphy's Ethical Decision Making Checklist:[14]

1. Does action A violate the law?
2. Does action A violate any moral obligations?
3. Does action A violate any special obligations stemming from the type of marketing organization in question (for example, the special duty of pharmaceutical firms to provide safe products)?
4. Is the intent of action A evil?
5. Are any major evils likely to result from or because of action A?
6. Is a satisfactory alternative B, which produces equal or more good with less evil than A, being knowingly rejected?
7. Does action A infringe on the inalienable liberties of the consumer?
8. Does action A leave another person or group less well off? Is this person or group already relatively underprivileged?

A more straightforward list of twelve questions to help clarify ethical problems was proposed by Laura Nash.[15]

RESEARCH IN PRACTICE 24.1

Code of Ethics of the American Marketing Association

The American Marketing Association, in furtherance of its central objective of the advancement of science in marketing and in recognition of its obligation to the public, has established these principles of ethical practice of marketing research for the guidance of its members.

For Research Users, Practitioners, and Interviewers:

1. No individual or organization will undertake any activity that is directly or indirectly represented to be marketing research but has as its real purpose the attempted sale of merchandise or services to some or all of the respondents interviewed in the course of the research.
2. If a respondent has been led to believe, directly or indirectly, that he is participating in a marketing research survey and that his anonymity will be protected, his name shall not be made known to anyone outside the research organization or research department, or used for other than research purposes.

For Research Practitioners:

1. There will be no intentional or deliberate misrepresentation of research methods or results. An adequate description of methods employed will be made available on request to the sponsor of the research. Evidence that fieldwork has been completed according to specifications will, on request, be made available to buyers of research.
2. The identity of the survey sponsor and/or the ultimate client for whom a survey is being done will be held in confidence at all times, unless this identity is to be revealed as part of the research design. Research information shall be held in confidence by the research organization or department and not used for personal gain or made available to any outside party unless the client specifically authorizes such release.
3. A research organization shall not undertake studies for competitive clients when such studies would jeopardize the confidential nature of client–agency relationships.

For Users of Marketing Research:

1. A user of research shall not knowingly disseminate conclusions from a given research project or service that are inconsistent with or not warranted by the data.
2. To the extent that a unique design involving techniques, approaches, or concepts not commonly available to research practitioners is used, a prospective user of research shall not solicit such a design from one practitioner and deliver it to another for execution without the approval of the design originator.

For Field Interviewers:

1. Research assignments and materials received, as well as information obtained from respondents, shall be held in confidence by the interviewer and revealed to no one except the research organization conducting the marketing study.
2. No information gained through a marketing research activity shall be used, directly or indirectly, for the personal gain or advantage of the interviewer.
3. Interviews shall be conducted in strict accordance with specifications and instructions received.
4. An interviewer shall not carry out two or more interviewing assignments simultaneously unless authorized by all contractors or employers concerned.

Members of the American Marketing Association will be expected to conduct themselves in accordance with provisions of this code in all of their marketing research activities.

1. Have you defined the problem accurately?
2. How would you define the problem if you stood on the other side of the fence?
3. How did this situation occur in the first place?
4. To whom and to what do you give your loyalty as a person and as a member of the corporation?
5. What is your intention in making this decision?
6. How does this intention compare with the probable results?
7. Who could your decision or action injure?
8. Can you discuss the problem with the affected parties before you make your decision?
9. Are you confident that your decision will be as valid over a long period of time as it seems now?
10. Could you disclose without qualm your decision or action to your boss, your CEO, the board of directors, your family, or society as a whole?
11. What is the symbolic potential of your action if understood? If misunderstood?
12. Under what conditions would you allow exceptions to your stand?

Even more simplistic are the six questions used in ethics training programs at the Center for Business Ethics at Bentley College.[16]

1. Is it right?
2. Is it fair?
3. Who gets hurt?
4. Would you be comfortable if the details of your decision were reported on the front page of your local newspaper?
5. What would you tell your child to do?
6. How does it feel?

Marketing researchers may find the Wade system of evaluating sources of information particularly useful (see Table 24.3).[17] These checklists are by no means completely exhaustive, nor are the questions in their entirety appropriate for every situation. They do, however, provide a set of external directions to guide marketing researchers and other decision makers through ethical dilemmas.

RESEARCH IN PRACTICE 24.2

CORE MORAL VALUES AS RANKED IN RESEARCH ASSOCIATIONS' CODES

			Associations		
Values*	*Advertising Research Foundation*	*American Marketing Association*	*Council of American Survey Research Organizations*	*Marketing Research Association*	*Qualitative Research Council of America*
Nondeception	1	1	2	2	
Keeping promises	2		1	1	2
Serving others		2*	3	3*	1
Not harming others				3*	3
Justice		2*			
Other values	3				

*Values are tied in ranking.

TABLE 24.3

THE WADE SYSTEM FOR JUDGING SOURCES OF INFORMATION

Ethical

1. Published material and public documents such as court records.
2. Disclosures made by competitors' employees, obtained without subterfuge.
3. Market surveys and consultants' reports.
4. Financial reports and brokers' research reports.
5. Trade fairs, exhibits, and competitors' brochures
6. Analysis of competitor's products.
7. Legitimate employment interviews with people who worked for competitor.

Arguably Unethical

8. Camouflaged questioning and "drawing out" of competitor's employees at technical meeting.
9. Direct observation under secret conditions.
10. False job interviews with a competitor's employee (i.e., without real intent to hire).
11. Hiring a professional investigator to obtain a specific piece of information.
12. Hiring an employee away from the competitor to get specific know-how.

Illegal

13. Trespassing on a competitor's property.
14. Bribing a competitor's supplier or employee.
15. "Planting" your agent on a competitor's payroll.
16. Eavesdropping on competitors (e.g., via wire-tapping).
17. Theft of drawings, samples, documents, and similar property.
18. Blackmail and extortion.

Note: The numbers in the list are ranked in descending degree of ethicality or legality.

AN ETHICAL FRAMEWORK

In an effort to move toward development of an ethical framework, we have developed an integrated model for ethical decision making in marketing research that takes into account the various ethical theories and perspectives (Figure 24.1). The integrated model also includes the various stakeholders of marketing research, i.e., the client, the researcher, the respondent, and the public.[18]

We begin with a description of the heart of the model (interior box, Figure 24.1). As in many other models, the process is activated when awareness of an ethical dilemma occurs. Then the ethical decision maker's stage of **cognitive moral development** (CMD) influences how the ethical issue will be dealt with. CMD theory postulates that in similar ethical dilemmas, different people make different decisions because they are in different stages of CMD.[19] One's moral development occurs through six stages, which can be simplified into three levels of two stages each. At the first level, preconventional morality, one is concerned with oneself and the external rewards or punishments that come about as a result of one's actions. The second level, conventional morality, moves beyond individual needs and permits one to make decisions based on society's or other significant reference group's expectations of what is right. Movement beyond individual and group expectations defines the third level, postconventional morality. Here rights that are beyond individual or group values and laws are used to make decisions.[20] Individuals advance through these stages toward a better understanding of moral obligations. Thus, people in stage six should demonstrate the ability to reason through moral dilemmas more effectively than individuals in stages one through five. How ethical situations are dealt with (individual, group, global) depends first on the level and stage of CMD that the decision maker has attained.

Cognitive Moral Development
Moral development occurs through three levels: (1) preconventional morality—concern with oneself and the external rewards or punishments, (2) conventional morality—society's or other significant reference group's expectations of what is right, and (3) postconventional morality—rights that are beyond individual or group values. Each level consists of two stages.

At this point the decision maker identifies a set of alternative solutions to the dilemma and evaluates each one on the various approaches: teleology (egoism and utilitarianism);

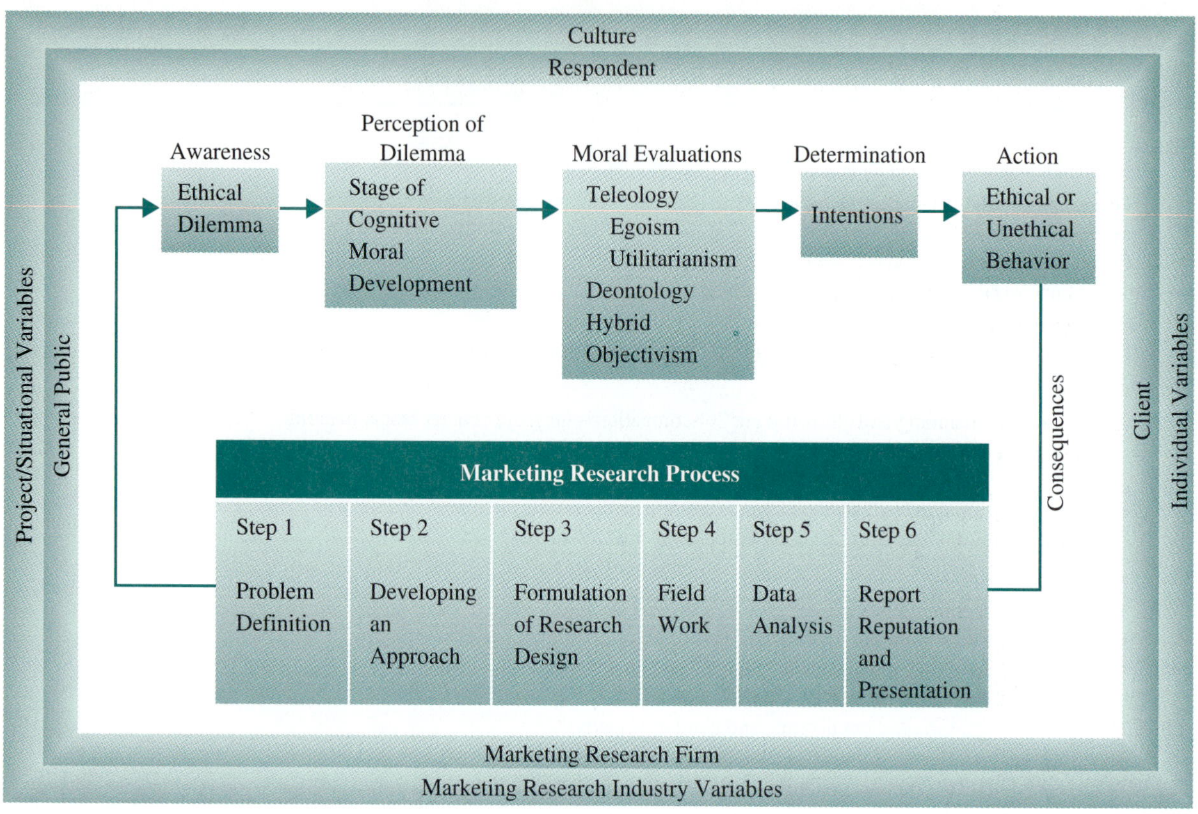

Figure 24.1
An Integrated Model for Ethical Decisions in Marketing Research

deontology (e.g., Kantian formalism); hybrid (i.e., combination of teleological and deontological views; e.g., Ross's prima facie framework); and objectivism.

Teleology

Teleology The degree of ethicalness depends on the outcomes or actions that result from the decisions. In other words, the end justifies the means.

Egoism An individualist perspective of teleology whereby one takes the actions that results in the greatest good for oneself (be it short- or long-term perspective).

Utilitarianism A global perspective of teleology that one should take the action that results in the maximization of good for all concerned, even though the goodness might not be equally distributed.

The teleological perspective is alsc known as a consequential theory. Broadly, **teleology** states that the evaluation of the degree of ethicalness depends on the outcomes or actions that result from the decisions. The objective is to select the outcome that results in the greatest good. In other words, the end justifies the means. More specifically, the teleological perspective can be further divided into egoism and utilitarianism. The difference is that whereas the egoist viewpoint focuses on the individual, the utilitarian considers all parties involved. **Egoism** means that one takes the actions that results in the greatest good for oneself (be it short- or long-term perspective). For instance, one decides to be nice to the boss (even though the boss is not nice), not necessarily because it brings immediate "good" or happiness to one, but because in the long run it is likely to lead to a promotion, which is a greater good than the more immediate good one would get from not being nice to the boss.

Utilitarianism suggests that one should take the action (i.e., make the decision) that results in the maximization of good for all concerned, even though the goodness might not be equally distributed. For example, if action A results in three units of good for person 1, four units of good for person 2, and three units of good for person 3; whereas action B results in nine units of good for person 1, two units of good for person 2, and no units for person 3, action A should be taken because it results in the greatest amount of good for all parties involved.[21]

A central question in teleology is, "Who decides what is good?" The answer to this question ultimately places the individual or people at the center of the moral universe.

Thus, the teleological perspective does not give adequate recognition to the laws of nature and God, which are needed to define moral behavior. The notion that an individual or people can act independent of these laws and of God invalidates the concept of good and evil.

Deontology

Contrary to the teleological approach, **deontology** is a nonconsequentialist approach.[22] It focuses on the intentions or the means behind the decision to pursue a particular alternative, rather than on the results of a decision (ends), to evaluate how an action stacks up ethically. The classical example of this school of thought is exemplified by **Kant's categorical imperative**, which states that the only ethical courses of action are those in which the action taken could serve as a universal law. In other words, what makes a decision right or ethical is that the decision maker would be willing to be so treated were the positions of the parties reversed. A recent study found that managers' decisions either to discipline or to reward the behavior of salespeople are guided primarily by the inherent rightness or wrongness of the salespeople's behaviors (deontological considerations) and only secondarily by the consequences of the behaviors on the organizations (teleological factors).[23]

Deontology A nonconsequentialist approach to ethical evaluation focusing on the intentions behind the decision to pursue a particular alternative, rather than on the results.

Kant's Categorical Imperative A deontological view that states that the only ethical courses of action are those in which the action taken could serve as a universal law.

Hybrid

Oddly enough, although it seems that teleology and deontology are diametrically opposed, some have argued that the true decision-making behavior of people encompasses some **hybrid** of both approaches. In other words, decision makers frequently focus on both the effects of carrying out the decision (means) as well as the result of the decision (end). For example, suppose that a research firm is approached by a client who wishes to test several TV commercials to determine which one is most effective for selling a new product. This product is a new brand of cigarette that touts as its primary benefit reduced tar (giving the impression that the new brand is "healthier" to smoke), but does not mention that medical tests have suggested that the cigarette is not "healthier," because the reduced tar content causes the smoker to draw more frequently and harder on the cigarette to get the flavor of a regular cigarette—and thus all the tar of a regular cigarette. Should the research firm engage in such a project?

Hybrid An approach that combines aspects of both teleology and deontology.

From the teleological perspective, it could be argued that engaging in such research would be ethical if it brings about the greatest good. The egoistic perspective would focus on the good for the research firm: It gains a new client. The utilitarian would consider the greatest good for all: the good resulting from the research firm is gaining a new client, the client finding the most effective way to advertise, and current smokers being made aware of a new brand of cigarette they may like better. The utilitarian perspective would argue that this is a greater good than any negative effects, such as new smokers may be cultivated and existing smokers are encouraged to endanger their health. From a strict deontological perspective this research is not ethical because it results in the deception of smokers and endangerment of their health, thus violating the rights of the individual through the imperative that it is wrong to endanger the health of people knowingly.

This leads to the observation that the world, and thus decisions, are not black and white and that they frequently involve trade-offs, which are accounted for in hybrid approaches such as **Ross's prima facie framework**, which notes that imperatives frequently conflict. To make decisions one has to prioritize or determine which imperative is more crucial or important.

Ross's Prima Facie Theory A hybrid view that notes that imperatives frequently conflict. To make decisions, one has to prioritize or determine which imperative is more crucial or important.

Objectivism

Objectivism holds that although ethics and completely ethical behavior are nice, for the most part they exist only in a perfect world. Ethics are determined by whatever is occurring in the real world. Thus, realizing that unethical behaviors exist, one should attempt to

Objectivism A view that instead of worrying about what ought to be, one should attempt to deal with or eliminate the unethical behaviors that do exist.

deal with or eliminate the unethical behaviors that do exist, rather than worry about what ought to be. One place to start is to attempt to lay down general guidelines for ethical behavior. To this purpose, the AMA and many other marketing organizations have developed marketing research codes of ethics. But even though this, along with an awareness of the stakeholders in marketing research, provides a good starting point for ethical decision making, further guidelines are still needed.

Once moral evaluations are made based on teleology, deontology, hybrid, or objectivism, next the intentions, or final decision by the decision maker with regard to which course of action to take, are made, followed by the action or behavior itself (Figure 24.1). Consequences of the action feed into the six steps of the marketing research process. It should be recognized that ethical dilemmas may be reflected throughout all six steps of the marketing research process, just a few steps, or even one step. In other words, the number of steps affected by the decision-making process depends on the nature of the ethical dilemma itself. Regardless of how many or how few of the steps are involved, once the consequences of the actions chosen reveal their effects on the marketing research process, the behavior is evaluated and the evaluation is stored to be retrieved and fed back into future decision-making activities. Ethics and the six steps of marketing research are discussed later in the chapter.

Now that the heart of the model has been described, we can move on to the next level outward: perspective. Here the model assumes particular significance for ethical decision making in marketing research because the perspective box allows the decision process to be considered from all angles, namely the viewpoints of the four stakeholders in marketing research: the public, the respondents, the client, and the researcher. (See the earlier discussion on each of these roles.)

The final, exterior box of the model includes the consideration of variables external to the decision maker, but essential in the decision-making process. These variables have an effect on the decision-making process in all the stakeholder roles in the marketing research process. Cultural variables may include the corporate culture of the client or the national culture of a respondent. These variables affect whether ethical dilemmas are perceived at all by these role players as well as their strategies for moral evaluations. Second, and somewhat related, are individual variables, namely knowledge, values, attitudes, intentions, ego strength, field dependence, and locus of control.

Situation/project variables include resources and constraints. Issues such as limited time or a limited budget may impose certain constraints on the project, introducing ethical dilemmas into the marketing research process. Marketing research industry variables such as what types of research practices are acceptable and what technologies are available also exert a significant impact on ethical decision making in marketing research.

ETHICS AND THE MARKETING RESEARCH PROCESS

Now that we are aware of the importance of ethics in marketing research, the major stakeholders in the research process, some checklists for ethical decision making, and a general framework within which to work, we can next turn specifically to ethics and the marketing research process. Although the examination of ethics pertaining to the marketing research process has been included within each individual chapter, each of the six steps of the marketing research process is briefly examined here.

The first step in the marketing research process is problem definition. This is a crucial step in the marketing research process, because a well-defined problem is necessary for the research to be carried out efficiently and effectively. Ethical issues in this stage might involve the researcher's deciding whether to proceed with the research project if in defining the problem it comes to light that research, or at least primary data collection, is not necessary. Ethical dilemmas may also be focused on whether the client chooses to disclose the true nature of the problem to the researcher, or withholds pertinent information. Step two is concerned with developing an approach to the problem. At this point, attention is focused on tasks such as developing models, research questions, and hypotheses. Here the researcher should be sure to treat preliminary findings as tentative and not as conclusive.

Research design is the third step in the marketing research process. This step encompasses everything from deciding on an exploratory, descriptive, or causal design to secondary data sources, qualitative techniques, measurement and scaling, questionnaire design, and sampling techniques. Because this includes many different activities, many ethical dilemmas can arise. Frequently occurring decisions might involve the researcher determining whether to inform respondents about the true purpose of the research up front rather than debriefing them or the misuse of focus groups due to the researcher treating the data as conclusive when they are not. The measurement of important variables is another challenging task.[24]

When conducting field work, the fourth step, field workers must make the respondents feel comfortable. They must not harass, badger, or grill any respondent. Also, validation checks should be conducted to ensure the quality of the data and the results made available to the client. Data analysis is the fifth step. Ethical issues that commonly arise here are throwing out data to produce desired results, altering the results or the analysis, or using statistical techniques that are inappropriate for the data. The final step in the marketing research process is report preparation and presentation. Here, ethical decisions may have to be made about the disclosure of the limitations of the project to the client, or avoiding misrepresentation of the findings.

INTERNATIONAL MARKETING RESEARCH

As more and more international marketing research is conducted due to the globalization of markets, new ethical issues must be addressed. Areas of concern include showing sensitivity to ethical differences among different cultures, determining whose ethical guidelines apply to what areas of marketing research, and taking into account inherent political and research integrity factors.[25]

Cultural Differences

Culture, philosophy, and morality determine what is considered acceptable behavior and thus have an impact on ethical conduct. It has been hypothesized that the degree of individualism or collectivism of a culture can influence ethical decision making. In support of this hypothesis, it was found that business practitioners in countries high on individualism (i.e., the United States or Canada) were more likely to consider themselves as a more important stakeholder than are owners/stockholders and other employees. In contrast, business practitioners in countries high on collectivism (i.e., Japan) were likely to consider the owners/stockholders and other employees as more important stakeholders than themselves.[26] Cultures can differ in other ways as well. Five major cultural dimensions have been identified and shown to influence ethical decision making individualism, power distance, masculinity, uncertainty avoidance, and Confucian dynamic.[27] Identifying how and why ethical concerns differ across cultures is important in overcoming ethical barriers to international trade, as illustrated by the following example.

EXAMPLE

Surveys Reveal Ethical Barriers to International Trade

Companies trying to crack international markets often find themselves in ethical dilemmas due to differences in culture. This problem can be most troublesome for smaller companies as ethical issues become another barrier these companies must overcome to be successful

Small businesses must overcome several ethical barriers when operating overseas.

overseas. Many small companies simply cannot afford another barrier and, as a result, decide against expanding overseas.

A recent study in the *Journal of Small Business Management* examined the most difficult ethical questions faced by small businesses operating overseas. A two-section mail questionnaire and follow-up phone survey named bribery, government intervention, customs clearance, questionable transfer of funds, and cultural differences as the top five ethical problems. The questionnaire asked respondents to identify those aspects of international marketing that posed the most difficult marketing problems. The questionnaire format allowed the respondents to identify up to three ethical problems and rate them according to frequency and the impact on the firm. Ethical problems were seen to negatively impact a small business's ability to compete effectively overseas. Additionally, these problems may not be evident before the decision to enter the market is made, resulting in time and money losses.[28] ■

Priority of Ethical Guidelines

The question of whose ethical guidelines should take precedence becomes relevant when conducting research in a foreign country. Should American researchers act ethically by their own guidelines, or by foreign guidelines, or by guidelines of both countries? A conservative approach would be to adhere to the ethical guidelines of both countries. One reason that American researchers must adhere to ethical guidelines established in the United States *and* those of the foreign country is that many foreign countries, particularly the developing nations, often have fewer ethical guidelines. The freedom these countries offer researchers can potentially be abused. For example, research firms may establish business in lesser developed countries with fewer ethical and legal restrictions just to conduct projects that would not be allowed in the United States. Adherence to domestic ethical guidelines can check such motives and the tendency to take advantage of the fewer ethical guidelines in some foreign countries. When the two sets of guidelines conflict, priority should be given to the foreign country guidelines. To illustrate, in the United States, teenagers' opinions are obtained for several products consumed by them (e.g., personal care items). In certain countries, however, interviewing teenagers may be considered fostering division in the family. Therefore, teenagers should not be interviewed when conducting research in these countries. Other situations of conflicting norms are not so easily resolved and general guidelines may not be available. If a broad set of guidelines are available, however, these should be applied to resolve the conflict. For example, ESOMAR, the European Society for Opinion and Marketing Research (www.esomar.nl), has a detailed and comprehensive code of ethical research behavior that could be used as guidelines for conducting research in Europe.

Political and Research Integrity Concerns

The main political and research integrity concerns that pertain to international marketing research include respecting the political concerns of the host country, respecting naive foreign respondents, and fully disclosing sensitive findings. From problem definition, which defines the choice of topic, to the reporting of findings and results, international marketing research may cause political concerns in the host country. For example, the topics of birth control, sex education, and religion are sensitive issues with political ramifications in Latin America. The researcher has a responsibility to address the political concerns of the foreign country and should be willing to make the necessary changes in the problem definition, approach, the research design, data collection, analysis, and reporting.

In contrast to the United States, respondents in many foreign countries are naive in that they are not familiar with the marketing research process. Researchers should not take advantage of them, for example by asking questions that are overly sensitive by local norms. Likewise, research integrity can be compromised when researchers are hesitant to disclose sensitive findings for fear that they will not be allowed to continue research in the foreign country. As more research involves people from differing cultural backgrounds, ethical concerns and the guidelines for addressing them will evolve.

INTERNET AND COMPUTER APPLICATIONS

Computer users increasingly believe that market research on the Internet that collects personal information about users without their consent is unethical. Often this is done by using cookies (see chapter 6). The cookie is a group of letters and numbers stored in a Web surfer's browser that identify the user. Companies and individuals that host Web sites use cookies to collect market research on visitors. Cookies follow the traveler through the Web site and record the pages accessed by the visitor, and the number of minutes spent on each page. The name, address, phone number, and access site can be collected by the cookie and saved into a database if the visitor enters any information. In essence, the cookie collects data on the user during every visit to the site.

EXAMPLE

Access Atlanta Will Access Cookies

Access Atlanta is a Web site collaboration between Cox Interactive Media's Atlanta studio, the *Atlanta Journal-Constitution*, WSB TV (Channel 2), and AM 750 WSB radio. The Web site is designed to give its browsers information on Atlanta such as news, weather, traffic updates, and sports. The site is designed to be interactive and promises to always be "new and provocative."

Although there is no fee to view various components of Access Atlanta, it places "cookies" on a viewer's computer, which allows Access Atlanta to recognize where an individual user has been. From these cookies, Access Atlanta can readily tell what pages on the site are of interest to each individual user and design banner ads based on the interests pursued by each user. There is an ethical issue because users don't know that market research is being conducted on them since users don't know which pages will award cookies. Access Atlanta states on its Web site that they will not share cookie information with anyone, but they still do not tell you which pages will place cookies on your computer. Thus, this practice raises ethical concerns. ■

FOCUS ON Burke

Burke's ethical guidelines are memorialized in its mission statement and through its statements of corporate commitments.

"We are committed to quality, honesty, and integrity in all endeavors."

This statement is the result of much discussion among Burke employees and management on how to express the company's intent. A simple statement that "we will behave ethically" was not seen as satisfactory. When dissected, this commitment is directly related to other commitments at Burke:

"We will hire and retain only the best people for all positions in the company." Part of the evaluation for "best people" will be honesty, integrity, and a commitment to quality.

"Employees will treat each other with respect and dignity, recognizing the worth, quality, and importance of each individual." Ethical behavior should be consistent with respect and dignity. Part of Burke's view of dignity is that it is inseparable for ethical behavior. Respect grows from ethical behavior and dies in the presence of unethical behavior.

"We will foster an environment where open communication exists among all employees." In the absence of rigid behavioral definitions of ethics, open communication allows both knowledge of intended behavior and discussion of this behavior to act as a strong moderating force. When communication is open and frequent among honest people, rigid "statutes of ethics" aren't needed.

Burke and most other research companies have to wrestle with the occasional demand that causes a struggle to define what is ethical. Burke tries to fall back on a simple benchmark for honesty and ethics: "Would you be willing to stand in front of any audience and say proudly that you did this?" If this test is not passed, then the action is reconsidered.

Another ethical issue is forcing cookies to enter Web site areas. Some Web sites will not allow access into areas without the use of cookies. In response to this invasion of privacy, some Internet users have begun to take evasive action, such as turning off recording files in their browsers or logging in under false identities. The task for marketers is to coax consumers into a "value exchange" by offering them something in return for access to personal information. By offering value exchange, Web sites entice consumers to volunteer personal information in order to receive something worthwhile in return.

Another ethical issue pertains to the use of Internet and computer software by researchers who do not have the appropriate knowledge or experience with the underlying methodologies and statistical techniques. In such cases there is a high potential for errors. Before using the Internet and computer technology, the researcher should be well trained so that no mistakes will be made. Where such expertise is lacking it should be made known to the client.

SUMMARY

Ethics must be a priority of marketing research. Marketing is highly visible to the public and it can be perceived as highly unethical. This general poor opinion can be detrimental to marketing research, which relies on the voluntary cooperation of the public.

When examining ethical issues, it is important to consider the rights and responsibilities of four stakeholders: the public, the respondents, the client, and the marketing researcher. All these stakeholders must act in the best interest of the marketing research project. When there are conflicts between what is best for the project and what is best for the stakeholders, ethical dilemmas arise.

Common ethical issues in marketing research can be identified by examining the ways each stakeholder can suffer because of undue advantages taken by the other three. The public can suffer because of incomplete reporting, misleading reporting, and biased research. Respondents volunteer their time and opinions which should not be abused. Specifically, surveys should not be used as a guise to sell products, and researchers should respect the privacy of the respondents. The researchers also have ethical responsibilities to the clients and should not abuse their positions, conduct unnecessary research, or undertake projects that they are not qualified to perform. The researchers are also obligated to maintain the confidentiality, to disclose all relevant information, and to analyze and interpret the data accurately. Finally, the researchers deserve to be treated ethically by the clients and the respondents. Clients should not solicit proposals that are not seriously being considered, should refrain from using proprietary techniques developed by the researcher without consent, and they should not misrepresent the research findings to the public. Likewise, respondents should take the interviewing seriously and give honest responses.

Several codes of conduct and ethical checklists have been developed. Their limitations motivate the development of an ethical framework. This framework describes an ethical decision as a process a stakeholder undergoes. Dilemmas are evaluated with respect to five approaches: teleology (egoism and utilitarianism), deontology, hybrid, and objectivism. Then, the consequences are evaluated with reference to the six stages of the marketing research process. The six-stage marketing research process can be a useful way of exploring the ethical problems faced in marketing research.

In international marketing research, additional issues must be addressed including ethical differences among different cultures, determining whose ethical guidelines apply to what areas of marketing research, and taking into account inherent political and research integrity concerns. Major ethical issues in Internet and computer usage include the use of cookies and technical expertise to properly execute the appropriate methodologies and statistical techniques.

KEY TERMS AND CONCEPTS

ethics
stakeholders
incomplete reporting
misleading reporting
biased research
sugging
frugging
proprietary techniques
cognitive moral development
teleology
egoism
utilitarianism
deontology
Kant's categorical imperative
hybrid approach
Ross's prima facie theory
objectivism

ACRONYMS

The steps of decision making and evaluations of the ethical framework can be summarized by the acronym ETHICS.

E thical dilemma is discovered, awareness
T heory of cognitive moral development indicates how the decision resolving the dilemma is made
H ybrid or another one of the approaches is used to evaluate the decision
I ntentions and subsequent actions are evaluated
C onsequences are evaluated
S takeholders' viewpoints are considered

EXERCISES

Questions

1. Why are ethics of particular importance to marketing researchers?
2. What are the five main characteristics describing ethical decisions?
3. Describe the idea of a stakeholder. Who are the four stakeholders of marketing research?
4. What responsibilities does the client have to the researcher, and conversely, what responsibilities does the researcher have to the client?
5. What responsibilities does the researcher have to the respondents, and conversely, what responsibilities do the respondents have to the researcher?
6. What responsibilities do the respondents have to the

client, and conversely, what responsibilities does the client have to the respondents?

7. Describe how the client can harm the public. How the researcher can harm the public. How the respondents can harm the public.
8. How are teleology and deontology different?
9. Describe the moral evaluations stage of the ethical framework.
10. What are the stages of cognitive moral development, and what do they entail?
11. What are the ethical considerations in the formulation of the research design stage of the marketing research process?
12. What are the ethical considerations in the data analysis stage of the marketing research process?

Problems

1. Identify a marketing research question that would require primary data gathering. Describe the ethical dilemmas you would face in gathering this data and how you would resolve them.
2. What unethical behaviors might describe a researcher who was solely trying to increase his billings? To answer this problem, identify at least one behavior for each of the six steps of the marketing research process.

INTERNET AND COMPUTER EXERCISES

1. Identify the ethical issues facing marketing researchers by visiting www.depaul.edu/ethics.
2. Prepare a code of ethics for marketing research firms by visiting www.cwru.edu/affil/www.ethics/texthome.html.
3. Do a search on the Internet to locate all the articles that have been published in the last three years related to Internet users' privacy and the use of cookies. Write a report on this topic.
4. Run factor analysis for the computer exercise in chapter 19. Eliminate at random several data values. Then run factor analysis eliminating missing values. How similar were the results to those produced with the entire data? What ethical issues does this analysis raise regarding the treatment of missing values?

Professional Perspective

4.1 Preparing and Presenting the Marketing Research Report

In report writing and presentation, we take all the art and all the science of marketing research and not only attempt to interpret what they really mean but also to communicate them to others outside our field of expertise—others who may be relying on this information to make decisions involving many millions of dollars.

Chapter 24 of this text is an excellent framework within which the student or professional practitioner of marketing research can find direction and guidance for writing and organizing effective reports and presentations. Often, there are pragmatic constraints that affect the final report. These constraints may be pressing, but it is possible to overcome them creatively and produce a report that is professional and meets the needs of the management. These constraints include time constraints, budget limitations, decentralized decision making, management indifference, and increasing scope and complexity of research projects. These constraints are discussed first. Then an example illustrates how these constraints can be accommodated without sacrificing the quality or usefulness of the report.

Michael R. Kuhn,
Senior Vice President, Burke Customer Satisfaction Associates

Michael Kuhn is the region manager for Burke Marketing Research's western business group and manages all Burke client service activities in Arizona, Colorado, northern California, and the Pacific Northwest. He has been a practitioner of marketing research since coming to Burke as a project manager in 1971. Mr. Kuhn has worked for clients in a wide variety of consumer packaged goods companies, high-technology and industrial manufacturing concerns, and the travel and leisure industry. He also serves as director of Burke's customer satisfaction and external quality control programs for clients in the western United States.

TIME CONSTRAINTS

In today's information age, we as information providers are often pressured to hurry up the results of a study and to minimize formality. The time window for decision making is becoming narrower and narrower. Management wants specific answers from the marketing research project, and it wants them quickly. The world's competitive environment very often leads management to move more quickly than any of us would like, imposing the risk of making decisions from inadequately analyzed and considered information.

BUDGET LIMITATIONS

This particular problem takes its toll in two areas. First, world competition and the recent wave of leveraged buyouts have put extreme pressure on corporations to be cost-conscious, and consequently to reduce the size of all corporate staff organizations, including marketing research staffs. Yet there remains as much pressure as ever to deliver actionable and timely results. Second, budgets available for marketing research projects have also come under close corporate scrutiny. In spite of the fact that most firms' market information needs are growing, the researcher is being asked to do more with the same budget or even with less. To balance these pressures there is a tendency to shortcut either the scope, the depth, or both, of the final report and presentation.

DECENTRALIZED DECISION MAKING

Many of our clients have undergone significant reorganizations during the past few years. The primary focus of the reorganization is to push decision making to the lowest possible line manager within an identifiable product, service, or business group. These line managers are interested primarily in the information that will answer their specific questions and help them move forward with a decision. Because they have responsibility for bottom line profit, these line managers often do not like the formal, corporate-appearing research report, and they question whether the money spent to produce such a report is worthwhile.

MANAGEMENT INDIFFERENCE

The "blood and toil" put into a formal research report sometimes goes unnoticed by management. To prevent this from happening, marketing researchers must make the information they deliver to managers easy to understand and digest, using a minimum of words and a maximum of charts, diagrams, and summary tables of relevant data. The goal is to make the report stand on its own and its worth self-evident.

INCREASING SCOPE AND COMPLEXITY OF RESEARCH PROJECTS

The old adage that says, "The more I know, the more I know that I don't know" is true. In the field of marketing research, the trend is to ask all the questions and get all the answers that one can possibly squeeze into a research study. The smarter managers become, the more questions they ask. Management, in an effort to get more bang for the buck, frequently tries to load several projects onto one study of the same respondent group. This often means that the researcher is tempted to short-cut the formal reporting and presentation process.

OVERCOMING THE CONSTRAINTS: AN EXAMPLE

Although these constraints can be pressing, researchers should resist the tendency to compromise the report preparation and presentation process. Often the researcher can creatively overcome the constraints without sacrificing the professional quality of the report and deliver the information in a form that can be used directly as input into decision making. An example from our experience is cited to illustrate this point.

Burke was asked to design and implement a customer satisfaction and problem tracking monitor for a major gasoline company. The client company operated retail service stations in 40 major markets and wanted a survey conducted among its retail service station customers in every market on a quarterly basis. To further complicate matters, the service stations themselves fell into six different ownership and service delivery configurations. Some were dealer owned, whereas others were managed by the company. Some offered gasoline only, but others had minimarkets or auto service bays. We had to run surveys in a total of 3,950 service stations in 40 markets and report to three levels of nonresearch management within two weeks of the close of each quarterly period.

We were charged with designing a reporting scheme that would satisfactorily communicate the results of the quarterly surveys. It was important to illustrate the progress made by our client's retail gasoline stations in improving customer satisfaction. These reports were to be used by three levels of management: service station owners/managers, field marketing representatives, and corporate managers in charge of the retail marketing operations. None were professional marketing researchers.

Given the constraints, it was necessary to create documents that could be understood and used by a service station manager as well as by a corporate officer. Our answer to this dilemma is shown in Figures 1 and 2. Data was downloaded directly into a Burke-designed automated chart-making system. The figures are two examples of the charts we designed to show results from the quarterly customer surveys. A short written introduction was also provided, explaining how to read the chart and interpret the information for decision making and program development. Corporate charts included summaries of this same information by region and for the total United States. From these charts, managers could read the following key performance information:

1. Incidence of problem occurrences this period
2. Performance trend, each problem, this period to past four periods
3. Performance relative to same period one year ago
4. Performance relative to group norms

CONCLUDING COMMENTS

Timing and cost considerations will continue to intensify, putting ever greater pressure on the marketing research professional to become more creative and efficient in delivering easy-to-understand and easy-to-digest research information. This information must be a tool that management can use with confidence to enhance the marketing and production decisions of the firm.

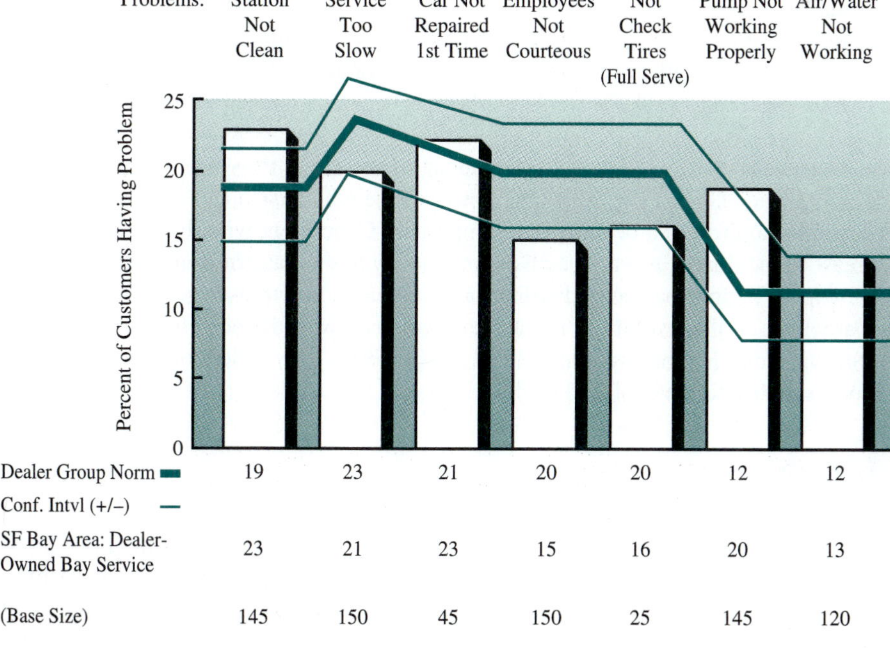

Figure 1
Problem Impact Analysis

Figure 2
Problem Trend Analysis

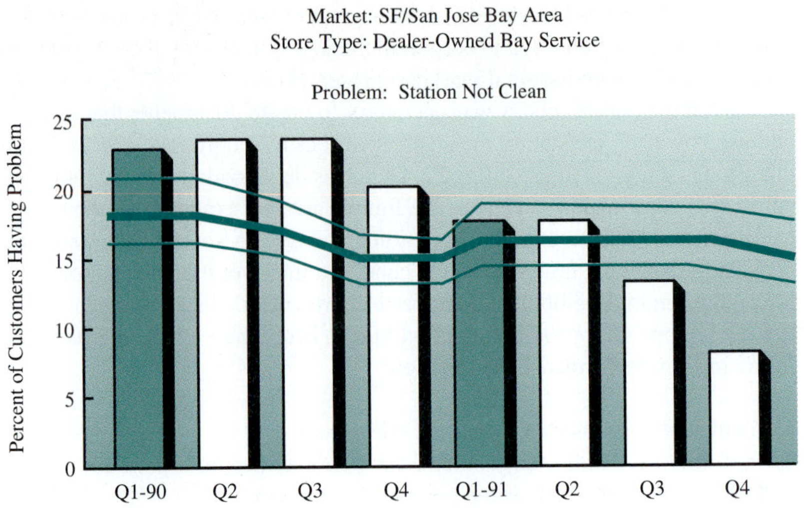

Market: SF/San Jose Bay Area
Store Type: Dealer-Owned Bay Service

Problem: Station Not Clean

Percent of Customers Having Problem

25
20
15
10
5
0

	Q1-90	Q2	Q3	Q4	Q1-91	Q2	Q3	Q4
Dealer Group Norm	19	18	17	16	18	18	18	16
Conf. Intvl (+/—)								
SF Bay Area: Dealer-Owned Bay Service	23	24	24	22	19	19	14	8
(Base Size)	145	150	145	142	125	137	144	139

4.2 International Research

Today, managers talk of international opportunity and the "global perspective." It is our task as researchers to define and build understanding of this global perspective such that our companies can act effectively in this broader marketplace. The 1990s were a critical time of transition. Until now, the world market has been dominated by North America and Western Europe. The bulk of research effort and monies have been spent within and between these two areas. By the early 2000s, about 40 percent of the world's population will reside in India and China. The economic power of the other Asian and Pacific Rim countries continues to grow and become more important. Concurrent with this development is an increase in the flow of research activity and money to the Eastern Hemisphere. Eventually we expect a more balanced distribution of research activities around the globe. To fully participate in this evolution, researchers are faced with the need to develop critical skills today. To develop these skills, a global perspective is truly called for. A few issues related to this globalization are listed below:

CULTURES

From cultural anthropology and sociology we learn that different societies have different ways of dealing with time, communication, information, authority, and conflict resolution (among many other things). These are not just academic curiosities; these are the building blocks for understanding how to do research in a culture other than your own. Numerous studies have shown that individuals, business organizations, and governmental organizations behave very differently across cultural types. If a study is designed to be "just right" to administer among a group of U.S. business people, it may not work in Brazil, for instance. The issue is not language, the issue is "the cultural mechanism" and how people perceive the questioner, the questions, and the context of the information. We may not be able to simply translate a questionnaire into another language and expect it to work.

Ron Tatham,

Chairman, Burke, Inc.

Dr. Tatham is chairman and CEO of Burke, Inc., one of the largest global research and consulting firms. In addition to the general management of Burke, Ron is involved in the development of research courses for the Training & Development Center at Burke. He is co-author of Multivariate Data Analysis *(Prentice Hall, 5th edition, 1994). He is a member of the Marketing Research Advisory Board at the University of Georgia and the MSMR Advisory Board at the University of Texas at Arlington.*

QUESTIONNAIRE

The preceding paragraph on culture warned you about the dangers (if not foolishness) of assuming that simply changing the language of a questionnaire allows you to use it in a different culture. When we use a structured questionnaire, we make the assumption that everyone understands the question as we understand it. We also assume that they see the range of answers the question either specifically states or suggests as the range of feasible answers. We further believe that the respondent is capable and willing to give accurate and reliable answers. These assumptions cannot be carried by a simple change in language. We have honed our skills, over the years, in our own cultures, to phrase a question "just right" to capture the sense and content of an issue. We move to a second culture and find that the sense and content of an issue are viewed very differently. The word structure in our native language doesn't exist in the language we are now to use. The willingness to reliably answer direct questions is far less in the second culture.

Rather than translating questionnaires you should work with research professionals who speak the language of the culture as their first language. You would discuss the purpose of the questions and the meanings you have intended. You would ask their help in creating questions in their language that have the same intent. Focus on translating meaning, not words.

To do the best research you can do, you must think of each new culture with a fresh viewpoint and reconcile yourself to the many occasions in which you simply can't have the same questionnaire across languages and cultures if you expect to do good work.

DATA COLLECTION

Among U.S. researchers, there has been a shift to more and more telephone data collection and a soon-to-be shift to Internet data collection. In other markets this has not been true. In Western Europe the dominant type of data collection is still face-to-face. In other parts of the world the data collection is 99 percent face-to-face. All researchers must know how to manage a process in which a wide variety of sampling and data collection methods must be understood and integrated to allow management to effectively use the data.

TIMING

People new to research are always surprised by the time factors in international research projects. It is not only the difficulty of working with professionals whose noon is your midnight, it is also the number of effective workdays. In Western Europe there are only about 50 days a year in which work can be conducted simultaneously in all countries. Due to religious holidays and governmental holidays, it is unlikely that you can schedule a study to be done at the same time in all countries. In Asia there are fewer concurrent workdays across countries. In all countries, the personal holiday schedules put limits on when you can do effective research. For example, you would not schedule a business-to-business study with senior managers to be done in many Western European countries in August. This is the primary month for personal holidays and many companies have only a skeleton crew of managers.

All of this impacts not only the execution of the study but the planning, getting bids, agreeing on changes, etc. The process gets longer unless you have the experience and working relationships with professional researchers across these countries to alleviate some of the problems.

Appendix

STATISTICAL TABLES

TABLE 1

SIMPLE RANDOM NUMBERS

Line/Col.	(1)	(2)	(3)	(4)	(5)	(6)	(7)	(8)	(9)	(10)	(11)	(12)	(13)	(14)
1	10480	15011	01536	02011	81647	91646	69179	14194	62590	36207	20969	99570	91291	90700
2	22368	46573	25595	85393	30995	89198	27982	53402	93965	34095	52666	19174	39615	99505
3	24130	48390	22527	97265	76393	64809	15179	24830	49340	32081	30680	19655	63348	58629
4	42167	93093	06243	61680	07856	16376	39440	53537	71341	57004	00849	74917	97758	16379
5	37570	39975	81837	16656	06121	91782	60468	81305	49684	60072	14110	06927	01263	54613
6	77921	06907	11008	42751	27756	53498	18602	70659	90655	15053	21916	81825	44394	42880
7	99562	72905	56420	69994	98872	31016	71194	18738	44013	48840	63213	21069	10634	12952
8	96301	91977	05463	07972	18876	20922	94595	56869	69014	60045	18425	84903	42508	32307
9	89579	14342	63661	10281	17453	18103	57740	84378	25331	12568	58678	44947	05585	56941
10	85475	36857	53342	53988	53060	59533	38867	62300	08158	17983	16439	11458	18593	64952
11	28918	69578	88231	33276	70997	79936	56865	05859	90106	31595	01547	85590	91610	78188
12	63553	40961	48235	03427	49626	69445	18663	72695	52180	20847	12234	90511	33703	90322
13	09429	93969	52636	92737	88974	33488	36320	17617	30015	08272	84115	27156	30613	74952
14	10365	61129	87529	85689	48237	52267	67689	93394	01511	26358	85104	20285	29975	89868
15	07119	97336	71048	08178	77233	13916	47564	81056	97735	85977	29372	74461	28551	90707
16	51085	12765	51821	51259	77452	16308	60756	92144	49442	53900	70960	63990	75601	40719
17	02368	21382	52404	60268	89368	19885	55322	44819	01188	65255	64835	44919	05944	55157
18	01011	54092	33362	94904	31273	04146	18594	29852	71685	85030	51132	01915	92747	64951
19	52162	53916	46369	58586	23216	14513	83149	98736	23495	64350	94738	17752	35156	35749
20	07056	97628	33787	09998	42698	06691	76988	13602	51851	46104	88916	19509	25625	58104
21	48663	91245	85828	14346	09172	30163	90229	04734	59193	22178	30421	61666	99904	32812
22	54164	58492	22421	74103	47070	25306	76468	26384	58151	06646	21524	15227	96909	44592
23	32639	32363	05597	24200	13363	38005	94342	28728	35806	06912	17012	64161	18296	22851
24	29334	27001	87637	87308	58731	00256	45834	15398	46557	41135	10307	07684	36188	18510
25	02488	33062	28834	07351	19731	92420	60952	61280	50001	67658	32586	86679	50720	94953
26	81525	72295	04839	96423	24878	82651	66566	14778	76797	14780	13300	87074	79666	95725
27	29676	20591	68086	26432	46901	20849	89768	81536	86645	12659	92259	57102	80428	25280
28	00742	57392	39064	66432	84673	40027	32832	61362	98947	96067	64760	64584	96096	98253
29	05366	04213	25669	26422	44407	44048	37937	63904	45766	66134	75470	66520	34693	90449
30	91921	26418	64117	94305	26766	25940	39972	22209	71500	64568	91402	42416	07844	69618
31	00582	04711	87917	77341	42206	35126	74087	99547	81817	42607	43808	76655	62028	76630
32	00725	69884	62797	56170	86324	88072	76222	36086	84637	93161	76038	65855	77919	88006
33	69011	65795	95876	55293	18988	27354	26575	08625	40801	59920	29841	80150	12777	48501
34	25976	57948	29888	88604	67917	48708	18912	82271	65424	69774	33611	54262	85963	03547
35	09763	83473	73577	12908	30883	18317	28290	35797	05998	41688	34952	37888	38917	88050

(Continued)

TABLE 1

(Continued)

Line/Col.	(1)	(2)	(3)	(4)	(5)	(6)	(7)	(8)	(9)	(10)	(11)	(12)	(13)	(14)
36	91567	42595	27958	30134	04024	86385	29880	99730	55536	84855	29088	09250	79656	73211
37	17955	56349	90999	49127	20044	59931	06115	20542	18059	02008	73708	83517	36103	42791
38	46503	18584	18845	49618	02304	51038	20655	58727	28168	15475	56942	53389	20562	87338
39	92157	89634	94824	78171	84610	82834	09922	25417	44137	48413	25555	21246	35509	20468
40	14577	62765	35605	81263	39667	47358	56873	56307	61607	49518	89656	20103	77490	18062
41	98427	07523	33362	64270	01638	92477	66969	98420	04880	45585	46565	04102	46880	45709
42	34914	63976	88720	82765	34476	17032	87589	40836	32427	70002	70663	88863	77775	69348
43	70060	28277	39475	46473	23219	53416	94970	25832	69975	94884	19661	72828	00102	66794
44	53976	54914	06990	67245	68350	82948	11398	42878	80287	88267	47363	46634	06541	97809
45	76072	29515	40980	07391	58745	25774	22987	80059	39911	96189	41151	14222	60697	59583
46	90725	52210	83974	29992	65831	38857	50490	83765	55657	14361	31720	57375	56228	41546
47	64364	67412	33339	31926	14883	24413	59744	92351	97473	89286	35931	04110	23726	51900
48	08962	00358	31662	25388	61642	34072	81249	35648	56891	69352	48373	45578	78547	81788
49	95012	68379	93526	70765	10592	04542	76463	54328	02349	17247	28865	14777	62730	92277
50	15664	10493	20492	38301	91132	21999	59516	81652	27195	48223	46751	22923	32261	85653
51	16408	81899	04153	53381	79401	21438	83035	92350	36693	31238	59649	91754	72772	02338
52	18629	81953	05520	91962	04739	13092	97662	24822	94730	06496	35090	04822	86774	98289
53	73115	35101	47498	87637	99016	71060	88824	71013	18735	20286	23153	72924	35165	43040
54	57491	16703	23167	49323	45021	33132	12544	41035	80780	45393	44812	12515	98931	91202
55	30405	83946	23792	14422	15059	45799	22716	19792	09983	74353	68668	30429	70735	25499
56	16631	35006	85900	98275	32388	52390	16815	69293	82732	38480	73817	32523	41961	44437
57	96773	20206	42559	78985	05300	22164	24369	54224	35083	19687	11052	91491	60383	19746
58	38935	64202	14349	82674	66523	44133	00697	35552	35970	19124	63318	29686	03387	59846
59	31624	76384	17403	53363	44167	64486	64758	75366	76554	31601	12614	33072	60332	92325
60	78919	19474	23632	27889	47914	02584	37680	20801	72152	39339	34806	08930	85001	87820
61	03931	33309	57047	74211	63445	17361	62825	39908	05607	91284	68833	25570	38818	46920
62	74426	33278	43972	10119	89917	15665	52872	73823	73144	88662	88970	74492	51805	99378
63	09066	00903	20795	95452	92648	45454	69552	88815	16553	51125	79375	97596	16296	66092
64	42238	12426	87025	14267	20979	04508	64535	31355	86064	29472	47689	05974	52468	16834
65	16153	08002	26504	41744	81959	65642	74240	56302	00033	67107	77510	70625	28725	34191
66	21457	40742	29820	96783	29400	21840	15035	34537	33310	06116	95240	15957	16572	06004
67	21581	57802	02050	89728	17937	37621	47075	42080	97403	48626	68995	43805	33386	21597
68	55612	78095	83197	33732	05810	24813	86902	60397	16489	03264	88525	42786	05269	92532
69	44657	66999	99324	51281	84463	60563	79312	93454	68876	25471	93911	25650	12682	73572
70	91340	84979	46949	81973	37949	61023	43997	15263	80644	43942	89203	71795	99533	50501
71	91227	21199	31935	27022	84067	05462	35216	14486	29891	68607	41867	14951	91696	85065
72	50001	38140	66321	19924	72163	09538	12151	06878	91903	18749	34405	56087	82790	70925
73	65390	05224	72958	28609	81406	39147	25549	48542	42627	45233	57202	94617	23772	07896
74	27504	96131	83944	41575	10573	03619	64482	73923	36152	05184	94142	25299	94387	34925
75	37169	94851	39117	89632	00959	16487	65536	49071	39782	17095	02330	74301	00275	48280
76	11508	70225	51111	38351	19444	66499	71945	05422	13442	78675	84031	66938	93654	59894
77	37449	30362	06694	54690	04052	53115	62757	95348	78662	11163	81651	50245	34971	52974
78	46515	70331	85922	38329	57015	15765	97161	17869	45349	61796	66345	81073	49106	79860
79	30986	81223	42416	58353	21532	30502	32305	86482	05174	07901	54339	58861	74818	46942
80	63798	64995	46583	09785	44160	78128	83991	42865	92520	83531	80377	35909	81250	54238
81	82486	84846	99254	67632	43218	50076	21361	64816	51202	88124	41870	52689	51275	83556
82	21885	32906	92431	09060	64297	51674	64126	62570	26123	05155	59194	52799	28225	85762
83	60336	98782	07408	53458	13564	59089	26445	29789	85205	41001	12535	12133	14645	23541

(Continued)

TABLE 1

(Continued)

Line/Col.	(1)	(2)	(3)	(4)	(5)	(6)	(7)	(8)	(9)	(10)	(11)	(12)	(13)	(14)
84	43937	46891	24010	25560	86355	33941	25786	54990	71899	15475	95434	98227	21824	19535
85	97656	63175	89303	16275	07100	92063	21942	18611	47348	20203	18534	03862	78095	50136
86	03299	01221	05418	38982	55758	92237	26759	86367	21216	98442	08303	56613	91511	75928
87	79626	06486	03574	17668	07785	76020	79924	25651	83325	88428	85076	72811	22717	50585
88	85636	68335	47539	03129	65651	11977	02510	26113	99447	68645	34327	15152	55230	93448
89	18039	14367	61337	06177	12143	46609	32989	74014	64708	00533	35398	58408	13261	47908
90	08362	15656	60627	36478	65648	16764	53412	09013	07832	41574	17639	82163	60859	75567
91	79556	29068	04142	16268	15387	12856	66227	38358	22478	73373	88732	09443	82558	05250
92	92608	82674	27072	32534	17075	27698	98204	63863	11951	34648	88022	56148	34925	57031
93	23982	25835	40055	67006	12293	02753	14827	23235	35071	99704	37543	11601	35503	85171
94	09915	96306	05908	97901	28395	14186	00821	80703	70426	75647	76310	88717	37890	40129
95	59037	33300	26695	62247	69927	76123	50842	43834	86654	70959	79725	93872	28117	19233
96	42488	78077	69882	61657	34136	79180	97526	43092	04098	73571	80799	76536	71255	64239
97	46764	86273	63003	93017	31204	36692	40202	35275	57306	55543	53203	18098	47625	88684
98	03237	45430	55417	63282	90816	17349	88298	90183	36600	78406	06216	95787	42579	90730
99	86591	81482	52667	61582	14972	90053	89534	76036	49199	43716	97548	04379	46370	28672
100	38534	01715	94964	87288	65680	43772	39560	12918	80537	62738	19636	51132	25739	56947

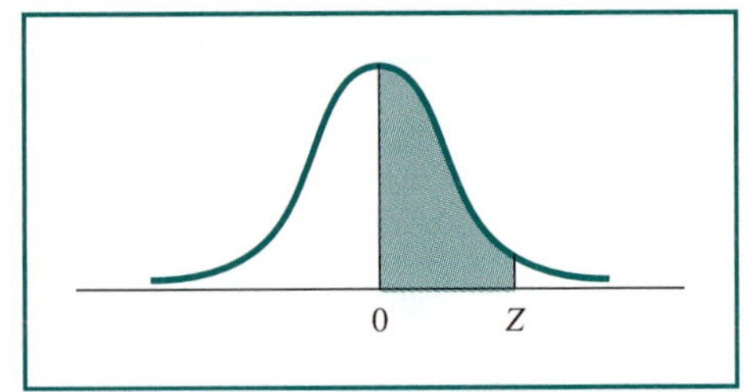

TABLE 2

AREA UNDER THE NORMAL CURVE

Z	.00	.01	.02	.03	.04	.05	.06	.07	.08	.09
0.0	.0000	.0040	.0080	.0120	.0160	.0199	.0239	.0279	.0319	.0359
0.1	.0398	.0438	.0478	.0517	.0557	.0596	.0636	.0675	.0714	.0753
0.2	.0793	.0832	.0871	.0910	.0948	.0987	.1026	.1064	.1103	.1141
0.3	.1179	.1217	.1255	.1293	.1331	.1368	.1406	.1443	.1480	.1517
0.4	.1554	.1591	.1628	.1664	.1700	.1736	.1772	.1808	.1844	.1879
0.5	.1915	.1950	.1985	.2019	.2054	.2088	.2123	.2157	.2190	.2224
0.6	.2257	.2291	.2324	.2357	.2389	.2422	.2454	.2486	.2518	.2549
0.7	.2580	.2612	.2642	.2673	.2704	.2734	.2764	.2794	.2823	.2852
0.8	.2881	.2910	.2939	.2967	.2995	.3023	.3051	.3078	.3106	.3133
0.9	.3159	.3186	.3212	.3238	.3264	.3289	.3315	.3340	.3365	.3389
1.0	.3413	.3438	.3461	.3485	.3508	.3531	.3554	.3577	.3599	.3621
1.1	.3643	.3665	.3686	.3708	.3729	.3749	.3770	.3790	.3810	.3830
1.2	.3849	.3869	.3888	.3907	.3925	.3944	.3962	.3980	.3997	.4015
1.3	.4032	.4049	.4066	.4082	.4099	.4115	.4131	.4147	.4162	.4177
1.4	.4192	.4207	.4222	.4236	.4251	.4265	.4279	.4292	.4306	.4319
1.5	.4332	.4345	.4357	.4370	.4382	.4394	.4406	.4418	.4429	.4441
1.6	.4452	.4463	.4474	.4484	.4495	.4505	.4515	.4525	.4535	.4545
1.7	.4554	.4564	.4573	.4582	.4591	.4599	.4608	.4616	.4625	.4633
1.8	.4641	.4649	.4656	.4664	.4671	.4678	.4686	.4693	.4699	.4706
1.9	.4713	.4719	.4726	.4732	.4738	.4744	.4750	.4756	.4761	.4767
2.0	.4772	.4778	.4783	.4788	.4793	.4798	.4803	.4808	.4812	.4817
2.1	.4821	.4826	.4830	.4834	.4838	.4842	.4846	.4850	.4854	.4857
2.2	.4861	.4864	.4868	.4871	.4875	.4878	.4881	.4884	.4887	.4890
2.3	.4893	.4896	.4898	.4901	.4904	.4906	.4909	.4911	.4913	.4916
2.4	.4918	.4920	.4922	.4925	.4927	.4929	.4931	.4932	.4934	.4936
2.5	.4938	.4940	.4941	.4943	.4945	.4946	.4948	.4949	.4951	.4952
2.6	.4953	.4955	.4956	.4957	.4959	.4960	.4961	.4962	.4963	.4964
2.7	.4965	.4966	.4967	.4968	.4969	.4970	.4971	.4972	.4973	.4974
2.8	.4974	.4975	.4976	.4977	.4977	.4978	.4979	.4979	.4980	.4981
2.9	.4981	.4982	.4982	.4983	.4984	.4984	.4985	.4985	.4986	.4986
3.0	.49865	.49869	.49874	.49878	.49882	.49886	.49889	.49893	.49897	.49900
3.1	.49903	.49906	.49910	.49913	.49916	.49918	.49921	.49924	.49926	.49929
3.2	.49931	.49934	.49936	.49938	.49940	.49942	.49944	.49946	.49948	.49950
3.3	.49952	.49953	.49955	.49957	.49958	.49960	.49961	.49962	.49964	.49965
3.4	.49966	.49968	.49969	.49970	.49971	.49972	.49973	.49974	.49975	.49976
3.5	.49977	.49978	.49978	.49979	.49980	.49981	.49981	.49982	.49983	.49983
3.6	.49984	.49985	.49985	.49986	.49986	.49987	.49987	.49988	.49988	.49989
3.7	.49989	.49990	.49990	.49990	.49991	.49991	.49992	.49992	.49992	.49992
3.8	.49993	.49993	.49993	.49994	.49994	.49994	.49994	.49995	.49995	.49995
3.9	.49995	.49995	.49996	.49996	.49996	.49996	.49996	.49996	.49997	.49997

Entry represents area under the standard normal distribution from the mean to *Z*

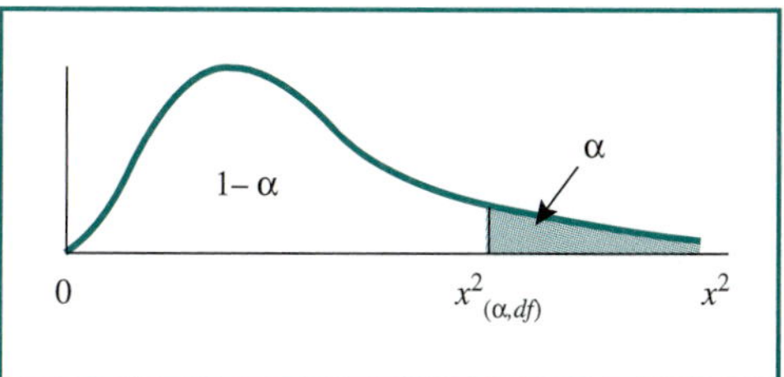

TABLE 3

CHI-SQUARE DISTRIBUTION

Degrees of Freedom	Upper Tail Areas (α)											
	.995	.99	.975	.95	.90	.75	.25	.10	.05	.025	.01	.005
1			0.001	0.004	0.016	0.102	1.323	2.706	3.841	5.024	6.635	7.879
2	0.010	0.020	0.051	0.103	0.211	0.575	2.773	4.605	5.991	7.378	9.210	10.597
3	0.072	0.115	0.216	0.352	0.584	1.213	4.108	6.251	7.815	9.348	11.345	12.838
4	0.207	0.297	0.484	0.711	1.064	1.923	5.385	7.779	9.488	11.143	13.277	14.860
5	0.412	0.554	0.831	1.145	1.610	2.675	6.626	9.236	11.071	12.833	15.086	16.750
6	0.676	0.872	1.237	1.635	2.204	3.455	7.841	10.645	12.592	14.449	16.812	18.548
7	0.989	1.239	1.690	2.167	2.833	4.255	9.037	12.017	14.067	16.013	18.475	20.278
8	1.344	1.646	2.180	2.733	3.490	5.071	10.219	13.362	15.507	17.535	20.090	21.955
9	1.735	2.088	2.700	3.325	4.168	5.899	11.389	14.684	16.919	19.023	21.666	23.589
10	2.156	2.558	3.247	3.940	4.865	6.737	12.549	15.987	18.307	20.483	23.209	25.188
11	2.603	3.053	3.816	4.575	5.578	7.584	13.701	17.275	19.675	21.920	24.725	26.757
12	3.074	3.571	4.404	5.226	6.304	8.438	14.845	18.549	21.026	23.337	26.217	28.299
13	3.565	4.107	5.009	5.892	7.042	9.299	15.984	19.812	22.362	24.736	27.688	29.819
14	4.075	4.660	5.629	6.571	7.790	10.165	17.117	21.064	23.685	26.119	29.141	31.319
15	4.601	5.229	6.262	7.261	8.547	11.037	18.245	22.307	24.996	27.488	30.578	32.801
16	5.142	5.812	6.908	7.962	9.312	11.912	19.369	23.542	26.296	28.845	32.000	34.267
17	5.697	6.408	7.564	8.672	10.085	12.792	20.489	24.769	27.587	30.191	33.409	35.718
18	6.265	7.015	8.231	9.390	10.865	13.675	21.605	25.989	28.869	31.526	34.805	37.156
19	6.844	7.633	8.907	10.117	11.651	14.562	22.718	27.204	30.144	32.852	36.191	38.582
20	7.434	8.260	9.591	10.851	12.443	15.452	23.828	28.412	31.410	34.170	37.566	39.997
21	8.034	8.897	10.283	11.591	13.240	16.344	24.935	29.615	32.671	35.479	38.932	41.401
22	8.643	9.542	10.982	12.338	14.042	17.240	26.039	30.813	33.924	36.781	40.289	42.796
23	9.260	10.196	11.689	13.091	14.848	18.137	27.141	32.007	35.172	38.076	41.638	44.181
24	9.886	10.856	12.401	13.848	15.659	19.037	28.241	33.196	36.415	39.364	42.980	45.559
25	10.520	11.524	13.120	14.611	16.473	19.939	29.339	34.382	37.652	40.646	44.314	46.928
26	11.160	12.198	13.844	15.379	17.292	20.843	30.435	35.563	38.885	41.923	45.642	48.290
27	11.808	12.879	14.573	16.151	18.114	21.749	31.528	36.741	40.113	43.194	46.963	49.645
28	12.461	13.565	15.308	16.928	18.939	22.657	32.620	37.916	41.337	44.461	48.278	50.993
29	13.121	14.257	16.047	17.708	19.768	23.567	33.711	39.087	42.557	45.722	49.588	52.336
30	13.787	14.954	16.791	18.493	20.599	24.478	34.800	40.256	43.773	46.979	50.892	53.672
31	14.458	15.655	17.539	19.281	21.434	25.390	35.887	41.422	44.985	48.232	52.191	55.003
32	15.134	16.362	18.291	20.072	22.271	26.304	36.973	42.585	46.194	49.480	53.486	56.328
33	15.815	17.074	19.047	20.867	23.110	27.219	38.058	43.745	47.400	50.725	54.776	57.648
34	16.501	17.789	19.806	21.664	23.952	28.136	39.141	44.903	48.602	51.966	56.061	58.964
35	17.192	18.509	20.569	22.465	24.797	29.054	40.223	46.059	49.802	53.203	57.342	60.275
36	17.887	19.233	21.336	23.269	25.643	29.973	41.304	47.212	50.998	54.437	58.619	61.581
37	18.586	19.960	22.106	24.075	26.492	30.893	42.383	48.363	52.192	55.668	59.892	62.883
38	19.289	20.691	22.878	24.884	27.343	31.815	43.462	49.513	53.384	56.896	61.162	64.181
39	19.996	21.426	23.654	25.695	28.196	32.737	44.539	50.660	54.572	58.120	62.428	65.476

(Continued)

TABLE 3

(Continued)

Degrees of Freedom	.995	.99	.975	.95	.90	.75	.25	.10	.05	.025	.01	.005
	Upper Tail Areas (α)											
40	20.707	22.164	24.433	26.509	29.051	33.660	45.616	51.805	55.758	59.342	63.691	66.766
41	21.421	22.906	25.215	27.326	29.907	34.585	46.692	52.949	56.942	60.561	64.950	68.053
42	22.138	23.650	25.999	28.144	30.765	35.510	47.766	54.090	58.124	61.777	66.206	69.336
43	22.859	24.398	26.785	28.965	31.625	36.436	48.840	55.230	59.304	62.990	67.459	70.616
44	23.584	25.148	27.575	29.787	32.487	37.363	49.913	56.369	60.481	64.201	68.710	71.893
45	24.311	25.901	28.366	30.612	33.350	38.291	50.985	57.505	61.656	65.410	69.957	73.166
46	25.041	26.657	29.160	31.439	34.215	39.220	52.056	58.641	62.830	66.617	71.201	74.437
47	25.775	27.416	29.956	32.268	35.081	40.149	53.127	59.774	64.001	67.821	72.443	75.704
48	26.511	28.177	30.755	33.098	35.949	41.079	54.196	60.907	65.171	69.023	73.683	76.969
49	27.249	28.941	31.555	33.930	36.818	42.010	55.265	62.038	66.339	70.222	74.919	78.231
50	27.991	29.707	32.357	34.764	37.689	42.942	56.334	63.167	67.505	71.420	76.154	79.490
51	28.735	30.475	33.162	35.600	38.560	43.874	57.401	64.295	68.669	72.616	77.386	80.747
52	29.481	31.246	33.968	36.437	39.433	44.808	58.468	65.422	69.832	73.810	78.616	82.001
53	30.230	32.018	34.776	37.276	40.308	45.741	59.534	66.548	70.993	75.002	79.843	83.253
54	30.981	32.793	35.586	38.116	41.183	46.676	60.600	67.673	72.153	76.192	81.069	84.502
55	31.735	33.570	36.398	38.958	42.060	47.610	61.665	68.796	73.311	77.380	82.292	85.749
56	32.490	34.350	37.212	39.801	42.937	48.546	62.729	69.919	74.468	78.567	83.513	86.994
57	33.248	35.131	38.027	40.646	43.816	49.482	63.793	71.040	75.624	79.752	84.733	88.236
58	34.008	35.913	38.844	41.492	44.696	50.419	64.857	72.160	76.778	80.936	85.950	89.477
59	34.770	36.698	39.662	42.339	45.577	51.356	65.919	73.279	77.931	82.117	87.166	90.715
60	35.534	37.485	40.482	43.188	46.459	52.294	66.981	74.397	79.082	83.298	88.379	91.952

For a particular number of degrees of freedom, entry represents the critical value of χ^2 corresponding to a specified upper tail area, α

For larger values of degrees of freedom (DF) the expression $z = \sqrt{2\chi^2} - \sqrt{2(DF) - 1}$ may be used and the resulting upper tail area can be obtained from the table of the standardized normal distribution.

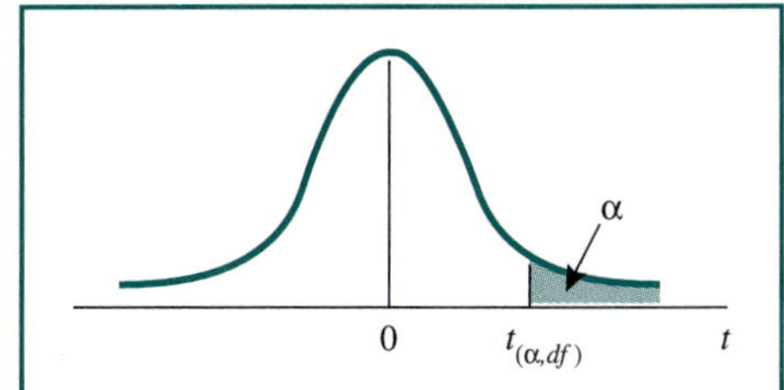

TABLE 4

t DISTRIBUTION

Degrees of Freedom	Upper Tail Areas .25	.10	.05	.025	.01	.005
1	1.0000	3.0777	6.3138	12.7062	31.8207	63.6574
2	0.8165	1.8856	2.9200	4.3027	6.9646	9.9248
3	0.7649	1.6377	2.3534	3.1824	4.5407	5.8409
4	0.7407	1.5332	2.1318	2.7764	3.7469	4.6041
5	0.7267	1.4759	2.0150	2.5706	3.3649	4.0322
6	0.7176	1.4398	1.9432	2.4469	3.1427	3.7074
7	0.7111	1.4149	1.8946	2.3646	2.9980	3.4995
8	0.7064	1.3968	1.8595	2.3060	2.8965	3.3554
9	0.7027	1.3830	1.8331	2.2622	2.8214	3.2498
10	0.6998	1.3722	1.8125	2.2281	2.7638	3.1693
11	0.6974	1.3634	1.7959	2.2010	2.7181	3.1058
12	0.6955	1.3562	1.7823	2.1788	2.6810	3.0545
13	0.6938	1.3502	1.7709	2.1604	2.6503	3.0123
14	0.6924	1.3450	1.7613	2.1448	2.6245	2.9768
15	0.6912	1.3406	1.7531	2.1315	2.6025	2.9467
16	0.6901	1.3368	1.7459	2.1199	2.5835	2.9208
17	0.6892	1.3334	1.7396	2.1098	2.5669	2.8982
18	0.6884	1.3304	1.7341	2.1009	2.5524	2.8784
19	0.6876	1.3277	1.7291	2.0930	2.5395	2.8609
20	0.6870	1.3253	1.7247	2.0860	2.5280	2.8453
21	0.6864	1.3232	1.7207	2.0796	2.5177	2.8314
22	0.6858	1.3212	1.7171	2.0739	2.5083	2.8188
23	0.6853	1.3195	1.7139	2.0687	2.4999	2.8073
24	0.6848	1.3178	1.7109	2.0639	2.4922	2.7969
25	0.6844	1.3163	1.7081	2.0595	2.4851	2.7874
26	0.6840	1.3150	1.7056	2.0555	2.4786	2.7787
27	0.6837	1.3137	1.7033	2.0518	2.4727	2.7707
28	0.6834	1.3125	1.7011	2.0484	2.4671	2.7633
29	0.6830	1.3114	1.6991	2.0452	2.4620	2.7564
30	0.6828	1.3104	1.6973	2.0423	2.4573	2.7500
31	0.6825	1.3095	1.6955	2.0395	2.4528	2.7440
32	0.6822	1.3086	1.6939	2.0369	2.4487	2.7385
33	0.6820	1.3077	1.6924	2.0345	2.4448	2.7333
34	0.6818	1.3070	1.6909	2.0322	2.4411	2.7284
35	0.6816	1.3062	1.6896	2.0301	2.4377	2.7238
36	0.6814	1.3055	1.6883	2.0281	2.4345	2.7195
37	0.6812	1.3049	1.6871	2.0262	2.4314	2.7154
38	0.6810	1.3042	1.6860	2.0244	2.4286	2.7116
39	0.6808	1.3036	1.6849	2.0227	2.4258	2.7079
40	0.6807	1.3031	1.6839	2.0211	2.4233	2.7045
41	0.6805	1.3025	1.6829	2.0195	2.4208	2.7012

(Continued)

TABLE 4

(Continued)

Degrees of Freedom	Upper Tail Areas .25	.10	.05	.025	.01	.005
42	0.6804	1.3020	1.6820	2.0181	2.4185	2.6981
43	0.6802	1.3016	1.6811	2.0167	2.4163	2.6951
44	0.6801	1.3011	1.6802	2.0154	2.4141	2.6923
45	0.6800	1.3006	1.6794	2.0141	2.4121	2.6896
46	0.6799	1.3002	1.6787	2.0129	2.4102	2.6870
47	0.6797	1.2998	1.6779	2.0117	2.4083	2.6846
48	0.6796	1.2994	1.6772	2.0106	2.4066	2.6822
49	0.6795	1.2991	1.6766	2.0096	2.4049	2.6800
50	0.6794	1.2987	1.6759	2.0086	2.4033	2.6778
51	0.6793	1.2984	1.6753	2.0076	2.4017	2.6757
52	0.6792	1.2980	1.6747	2.0066	2.4002	2.6737
53	0.6791	1.2977	1.6741	2.0057	2.3988	2.6718
54	0.6791	1.2974	1.6736	2.0049	2.3974	2.6700
55	0.6790	1.2971	1.6730	2.0040	2.3961	2.6682
56	0.6789	1.2969	1.6725	2.0032	2.3948	2.6665
57	0.6788	1.2966	1.6720	2.0025	2.3936	2.6649
58	0.6787	1.2963	1.6716	2.0017	2.3924	2.6633
59	0.6787	1.2961	1.6711	2.0010	2.3912	2.6618
60	0.6786	1.2958	1.6706	2.0003	2.3901	2.6603
61	0.6785	1.2956	1.6702	1.9996	2.3890	2.6589
62	0.6785	1.2954	1.6698	1.9990	2.3880	2.6575
63	0.6784	1.2951	1.6694	1.9983	2.3870	2.6561
64	0.6783	1.2949	1.6690	1.9977	2.3860	2.6549
65	0.6783	1.2947	1.6686	1.9971	2.3851	2.6536
66	0.6782	1.2945	1.6683	1.9966	2.3842	2.6524
67	0.6782	1.2943	1.6679	1.9960	2.3833	2.6512
68	0.6781	1.2941	1.6676	1.9955	2.3824	2.6501
69	0.6781	1.2939	1.6672	1.9949	2.3816	2.6490
70	0.6780	1.2938	1.6669	1.9944	2.3808	2.6479
71	0.6780	1.2936	1.6666	1.9939	2.3800	2.6469
72	0.6779	1.2934	1.6663	1.9935	2.3793	2.6459
73	0.6779	1.2933	1.6660	1.9930	2.3785	2.6449
74	0.6778	1.2931	1.6657	1.9925	2.3778	2.6439
75	0.6778	1.2929	1.6654	1.9921	2.3771	2.6430
76	0.6777	1.2928	1.6652	1.9917	2.3764	2.6421
77	0.6777	1.2926	1.6649	1.9913	2.3758	2.6412
78	0.6776	1.2925	1.6646	1.9908	2.3751	2.6403
79	0.6776	1.2924	1.6644	1.9905	2.3745	2.6395
80	0.6776	1.2922	1.6641	1.9901	2.3739	2.6387
81	0.6775	1.2921	1.6639	1.9897	2.3733	2.6379
82	0.6775	1.2920	1.6636	1.9893	2.3727	2.6371
83	0.6775	1.2918	1.6634	1.9890	2.3721	2.6364
84	0.6774	1.2917	1.6632	1.9886	2.3716	2.6356
85	0.6774	1.2916	1.6630	1.9883	2.3710	2.6349
86	0.6774	1.2915	1.6628	1.9879	2.3705	2.6342
87	0.6773	1.2914	1.6626	1.9876	2.3700	2.6335
88	0.6773	1.2912	1.6624	1.9873	2.3695	2.6329
89	0.6773	1.2911	1.6622	1.9870	2.3690	2.6322

(Continued)

TABLE 4

(Continued)

Degrees of Freedom	Upper Tail Areas .25	.10	.05	.025	.01	.005
90	0.6772	1.2910	1.6620	1.9867	2.3685	2.6316
91	0.6772	1.2909	1.6618	1.9864	2.3680	2.6309
92	0.6772	1.2908	1.6616	1.9861	2.3676	2.6303
93	0.6771	1.2907	1.6614	1.9858	2.3671	2.6297
94	0.6771	1.2906	1.6612	1.9855	2.3667	2.6291
95	0.6771	1.2905	1.6611	1.9853	2.3662	2.6286
96	0.6771	1.2904	1.6609	1.9850	2.3658	2.6280
97	0.6770	1.2903	1.6607	1.9847	2.3654	2.6275
98	0.6770	1.2902	1.6606	1.9845	2.3650	2.6269
99	0.6770	1.2902	1.6604	1.9842	2.3646	2.6264
100	0.6770	1.2901	1.6602	1.9840	2.3642	2.6259
110	0.6767	1.2893	1.6588	1.9818	2.3607	2.6213
120	0.6765	1.2886	1.6577	1.9799	2.3578	2.6174
130	0.6764	1.2881	1.6567	1.9784	2.3554	2.6142
140	0.6762	1.2876	1.6558	1.9771	2.3533	2.6114
150	0.6761	1.2872	1.6551	1.9759	2.3515	2.6090
∞	0.6745	1.2816	1.6449	1.9600	2.3263	2.5758

For a particular number of degrees of freedom, entry represents the critical value of t corresponding to a specified upper tail area α.

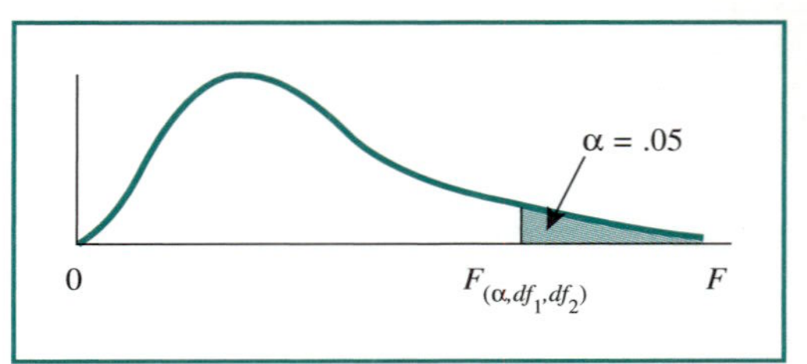

TABLE 5
F DISTRIBUTION

Denominator df_2	Numerator df_1 1	2	3	4	5	6	7	8	9	10	12	15	20	24	30	40	60	120	∞
1	161.4	199.5	215.7	224.6	230.2	234.0	236.8	238.9	240.5	241.9	243.9	245.9	248.0	249.1	250.1	251.1	252.2	253.3	254.3
2	18.51	19.00	19.16	19.25	19.30	19.33	19.35	19.37	19.38	19.40	19.41	19.43	19.45	19.45	19.46	19.47	19.48	19.49	19.50
3	10.13	9.55	9.28	9.12	9.01	8.94	8.89	8.85	8.81	8.79	8.74	8.70	8.66	8.64	8.62	8.59	8.57	8.55	8.53
4	7.71	6.94	6.59	6.39	6.26	6.16	6.09	6.04	6.00	5.96	5.91	5.86	5.80	5.77	5.75	5.72	5.69	5.66	5.63
5	6.61	5.79	5.41	5.19	5.05	4.95	4.88	4.82	4.77	4.74	4.68	4.62	4.56	4.53	4.50	4.46	4.43	4.40	4.36
6	5.99	5.14	4.76	4.53	4.39	4.28	4.21	4.15	4.10	4.06	4.00	3.94	3.87	3.84	3.81	3.77	3.74	3.70	3.67
7	5.59	4.74	4.35	4.12	3.97	3.87	3.79	3.73	3.68	3.64	3.57	3.51	3.44	3.41	3.38	3.34	3.30	3.27	3.23
8	5.32	4.46	4.07	3.84	3.69	3.58	3.50	3.44	3.39	3.35	3.28	3.22	3.15	3.12	3.08	3.04	3.01	2.97	2.93
9	5.12	4.26	3.86	3.63	3.48	3.37	3.29	3.23	3.18	3.14	3.07	3.01	2.94	2.90	2.86	2.83	2.79	2.75	2.71
10	4.96	4.10	3.71	3.48	3.33	3.22	3.14	3.07	3.02	2.98	2.91	2.85	2.77	2.74	2.70	2.66	2.62	2.58	2.54
11	4.84	3.98	3.59	3.36	3.20	3.09	3.01	2.95	2.90	2.85	2.79	2.72	2.65	2.61	2.57	2.53	2.49	2.45	2.40
12	4.75	3.89	3.49	3.26	3.11	3.00	2.91	2.85	2.80	2.75	2.69	2.62	2.54	2.51	2.47	2.43	2.38	2.34	2.30
13	4.67	3.81	3.41	3.18	3.03	2.92	2.83	2.77	2.71	2.67	2.60	2.53	2.46	2.42	2.38	2.34	2.30	2.25	2.21
14	4.60	3.74	3.34	3.11	2.96	2.85	2.76	2.70	2.65	2.60	2.53	2.46	2.39	2.35	2.31	2.27	2.22	2.18	2.13
15	4.54	3.68	3.29	3.06	2.90	2.79	2.71	2.64	2.59	2.54	2.48	2.40	2.33	2.29	2.25	2.20	2.16	2.11	2.07
16	4.49	3.63	3.24	3.01	2.85	2.74	2.66	2.59	2.54	2.49	2.42	2.35	2.28	2.24	2.19	2.15	2.11	2.06	2.01
17	4.45	3.59	3.20	2.96	2.81	2.70	2.61	2.55	2.49	2.45	2.38	2.31	2.23	2.19	2.15	2.10	2.06	2.01	1.96
18	4.41	3.55	3.16	2.93	2.77	2.66	2.58	2.51	2.46	2.41	2.34	2.27	2.19	2.15	2.11	2.06	2.02	1.97	1.92
19	4.38	3.52	3.13	2.90	2.74	2.63	2.54	2.48	2.42	2.38	2.31	2.23	2.16	2.11	2.07	2.03	1.98	1.93	1.88
20	4.35	3.49	3.10	2.87	2.71	2.60	2.51	2.45	2.39	2.35	2.28	2.20	2.12	2.08	2.04	1.99	1.95	1.90	1.84
21	4.32	3.47	3.07	2.84	2.68	2.57	2.49	2.42	2.37	2.32	2.25	2.18	2.10	2.05	2.01	1.96	1.92	1.87	1.81
22	4.30	3.44	3.05	2.82	2.66	2.55	2.46	2.40	2.34	2.30	2.23	2.15	2.07	2.03	1.98	1.94	1.89	1.84	1.78
23	4.28	3.42	3.03	2.80	2.64	2.53	2.44	2.37	2.32	2.27	2.20	2.13	2.05	2.01	1.96	1.91	1.86	1.81	1.76
24	4.26	3.40	3.01	2.78	2.62	2.51	2.42	2.36	2.30	2.25	2.18	2.11	2.03	1.98	1.94	1.89	1.84	1.79	1.73
25	4.24	3.39	2.99	2.76	2.60	2.49	2.40	2.34	2.28	2.24	2.16	2.09	2.01	1.96	1.92	1.87	1.82	1.77	1.71
26	4.23	3.37	2.98	2.74	2.59	2.47	2.39	2.32	2.27	2.22	2.15	2.07	1.99	1.95	1.90	1.85	1.80	1.75	1.69
27	4.21	3.35	2.96	2.73	2.57	2.46	2.37	2.31	2.25	2.20	2.13	2.06	1.97	1.93	1.88	1.84	1.79	1.73	1.67
28	4.20	3.34	2.95	2.71	2.56	2.45	2.36	2.29	2.24	2.19	2.12	2.04	1.96	1.91	1.87	1.82	1.77	1.71	1.65
29	4.18	3.33	2.93	2.70	2.55	2.43	2.35	2.28	2.22	2.18	2.10	2.03	1.94	1.90	1.85	1.81	1.75	1.70	1.64
30	4.17	3.32	2.92	2.69	2.53	2.42	2.33	2.27	2.21	2.16	2.09	2.01	1.93	1.89	1.84	1.79	1.74	1.68	1.62
40	4.08	3.23	2.84	2.61	2.45	2.34	2.25	2.18	2.12	2.08	2.00	1.92	1.84	1.79	1.74	1.69	1.64	1.58	1.51
60	4.00	3.15	2.76	2.53	2.37	2.25	2.17	2.10	2.04	1.99	1.92	1.84	1.75	1.70	1.65	1.59	1.53	1.47	1.39
120	3.92	3.07	2.68	2.45	2.29	2.17	2.09	2.02	1.96	1.91	1.83	1.75	1.66	1.61	1.55	1.50	1.43	1.35	1.25
∞	3.84	3.00	2.60	2.37	2.21	2.10	2.01	1.94	1.88	1.83	1.75	1.67	1.57	1.52	1.46	1.39	1.32	1.22	1.00

(Continued)

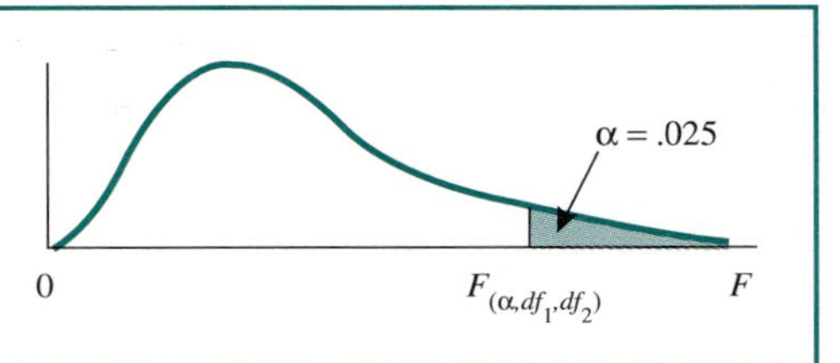

TABLE 5

(Continued)

Denominator df_2	Numerator df_1: 1	2	3	4	5	6	7	8	9	10	12	15	20	24	30	40	60	120	∞
1	647.8	799.5	864.2	899.6	921.8	937.1	948.2	956.7	963.3	968.6	976.7	984.9	993.1	997.2	1001	1006	1010	1014	1018
2	38.51	39.00	39.17	39.25	39.30	39.33	39.36	39.37	39.39	39.40	39.41	39.43	39.45	39.46	39.46	39.47	39.48	39.49	39.50
3	17.44	16.04	15.44	15.10	14.88	14.73	14.62	14.54	14.47	14.42	14.34	14.25	14.17	14.12	14.08	14.04	13.99	13.95	13.90
4	12.22	10.65	9.98	9.60	9.36	9.20	9.07	8.98	8.90	8.84	8.75	8.66	8.56	8.51	8.46	8.41	8.36	8.31	8.26
5	10.01	8.43	7.76	7.39	7.15	6.98	6.85	6.76	6.68	6.62	6.52	6.43	6.33	6.28	6.23	6.18	6.12	6.07	6.02
6	8.81	7.26	6.60	6.23	5.99	5.82	5.70	5.60	5.52	5.46	5.37	5.27	5.17	5.12	5.07	5.01	4.96	4.90	4.85
7	8.07	6.54	5.89	5.52	5.29	5.12	4.99	4.90	4.82	4.76	4.67	4.57	4.47	4.42	4.36	4.31	4.25	4.20	4.14
8	7.57	6.06	5.42	5.05	4.82	4.65	4.53	4.43	4.36	4.30	4.20	4.10	4.00	3.95	3.89	3.84	3.78	3.73	3.67
9	7.21	5.71	5.08	4.72	4.48	4.32	4.20	4.10	4.03	3.96	3.87	3.77	3.67	3.61	3.56	3.51	3.45	3.39	3.33
10	6.94	5.46	4.83	4.47	4.24	4.07	3.95	3.85	3.78	3.72	3.62	3.52	3.42	3.37	3.31	3.26	3.20	3.14	3.08
11	6.72	5.26	4.63	4.28	4.04	3.88	3.76	3.66	3.59	3.53	3.43	3.33	3.23	3.17	3.12	3.06	3.00	2.94	2.88
12	6.55	5.10	4.47	4.12	3.89	3.73	3.61	3.51	3.44	3.37	3.28	3.18	3.07	3.02	2.96	2.91	2.85	2.79	2.72
13	6.41	4.97	4.35	4.00	3.77	3.60	3.48	3.39	3.31	3.25	3.15	3.05	2.95	2.89	2.84	2.78	2.72	2.66	2.60
14	6.30	4.86	4.24	3.89	3.66	3.50	3.38	3.29	3.21	3.15	3.05	2.95	2.84	2.79	2.73	2.67	2.61	2.55	2.49
15	6.20	4.77	4.15	3.80	3.58	3.41	3.29	3.20	3.12	3.06	2.96	2.86	2.76	2.70	2.64	2.59	2.52	2.46	2.40
16	6.12	4.69	4.08	3.73	3.50	3.34	3.22	3.12	3.05	2.99	2.89	2.79	2.68	2.63	2.57	2.51	2.45	2.38	2.32
17	6.04	4.62	4.01	3.66	3.44	3.28	3.16	3.06	2.98	2.92	2.82	2.72	2.62	2.56	2.50	2.44	2.38	2.32	2.25
18	5.98	4.56	3.95	3.61	3.38	3.22	3.10	3.01	2.93	2.87	2.77	2.67	2.56	2.50	2.44	2.38	2.32	2.26	2.19
19	5.92	4.51	3.90	3.56	3.33	3.17	3.05	2.96	2.88	2.82	2.72	2.62	2.51	2.45	2.39	2.33	2.27	2.20	2.13
20	5.87	4.46	3.86	3.51	3.29	3.13	3.01	2.91	2.84	2.77	2.68	2.57	2.46	2.41	2.35	2.29	2.22	2.16	2.09
21	5.83	4.42	3.82	3.48	3.25	3.09	2.97	2.87	2.80	2.73	2.64	2.53	2.42	2.37	2.31	2.25	2.18	2.11	2.04
22	5.79	4.38	3.78	3.44	3.22	3.05	2.93	2.84	2.76	2.70	2.60	2.50	2.39	2.33	2.27	2.21	2.14	2.08	2.00
23	5.75	4.35	3.75	3.41	3.18	3.02	2.90	2.81	2.73	2.67	2.57	2.47	2.36	2.30	2.24	2.18	2.11	2.04	1.97
24	5.72	4.32	3.72	3.38	3.15	2.99	2.87	2.78	2.70	2.64	2.54	2.44	2.33	2.27	2.21	2.15	2.08	2.01	1.94
25	5.69	4.29	3.69	3.35	3.13	2.97	2.85	2.75	2.68	2.61	2.51	2.41	2.30	2.24	2.18	2.12	2.05	1.98	1.91
26	5.66	4.27	3.67	3.33	3.10	2.94	2.82	2.73	2.65	2.59	2.49	2.39	2.28	2.22	2.16	2.09	2.03	1.95	1.88
27	5.63	4.24	3.65	3.31	3.08	2.92	2.80	2.71	2.63	2.57	2.47	2.36	2.25	2.19	2.13	2.07	2.00	1.93	1.85
28	5.61	4.22	3.63	3.29	3.06	2.90	2.78	2.69	2.61	2.55	2.45	2.34	2.23	2.17	2.11	2.05	1.98	1.91	1.83
29	5.59	4.20	3.61	3.27	3.04	2.88	2.76	2.67	2.59	2.53	2.43	2.32	2.21	2.15	2.09	2.03	1.96	1.89	1.81
30	5.57	4.18	3.59	3.25	3.03	2.87	2.75	2.65	2.57	2.51	2.41	2.31	2.20	2.14	2.07	2.01	1.94	1.87	1.79
40	5.42	4.05	3.46	3.13	2.90	2.74	2.62	2.53	2.45	2.39	2.29	2.18	2.07	2.01	1.94	1.88	1.80	1.72	1.64
60	5.29	3.93	3.34	3.01	2.79	2.63	2.51	2.41	2.33	2.27	2.17	2.06	1.94	1.88	1.82	1.74	1.67	1.58	1.48
120	5.15	3.80	3.23	2.89	2.67	2.52	2.39	2.30	2.22	2.16	2.05	1.94	1.82	1.76	1.69	1.61	1.53	1.43	1.31
∞	5.02	3.69	3.12	2.79	2.57	2.41	2.29	2.19	2.11	2.05	1.94	1.83	1.71	1.64	1.57	1.48	1.39	1.27	1.00

(Conitnued)

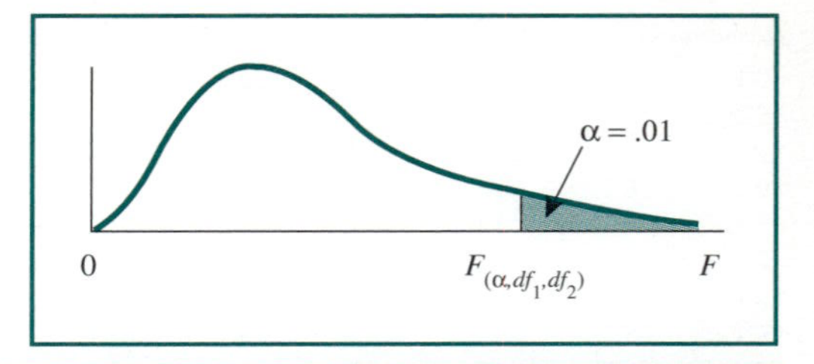

TABLE 5

(Continued)

Denominator df_2	Numerator df_1: 1	2	3	4	5	6	7	8	9	10	12	15	20	24	30	40	60	120	∞
1	4052	4999.5	5403	5625	5764	5859	5928	5982	6022	6056	6106	6157	6209	6235	6261	6287	6313	6339	6366
2	98.50	99.00	99.17	99.25	99.30	99.33	99.36	99.37	99.39	99.40	99.42	99.43	99.45	99.46	99.47	99.47	99.48	99.49	99.50
3	34.12	30.82	29.46	28.71	28.24	27.91	27.67	27.49	27.35	27.23	27.05	26.87	26.69	26.60	26.50	26.41	26.32	26.22	26.13
4	21.20	18.00	16.69	15.98	15.52	15.21	14.98	14.80	14.66	14.55	14.37	14.20	14.02	13.93	13.84	13.75	13.65	13.56	13.46
5	16.26	13.27	12.06	11.39	10.97	10.67	10.46	10.29	10.16	10.05	9.89	9.72	9.55	9.47	9.38	9.29	9.20	9.11	9.02
6	13.75	10.92	9.78	9.15	8.75	8.47	8.26	8.10	7.98	7.87	7.72	7.56	7.40	7.31	7.23	7.14	7.06	6.97	6.88
7	12.25	9.55	8.45	7.85	7.46	7.19	6.99	6.84	6.72	6.62	6.47	6.31	6.16	6.07	5.99	5.91	5.82	5.74	5.65
8	11.26	8.65	7.59	7.01	6.63	6.37	6.18	6.03	5.91	5.81	5.67	5.52	5.36	5.28	5.20	5.12	5.03	4.95	4.86
9	10.56	8.02	6.99	6.42	6.06	5.80	5.61	5.47	5.35	5.26	5.11	4.96	4.81	4.73	4.65	4.57	4.48	4.40	4.31
10	10.04	7.56	6.55	5.99	5.64	5.39	5.20	5.06	4.94	4.85	4.71	4.56	4.41	4.33	4.25	4.17	4.08	4.00	3.91
11	9.65	7.21	6.22	5.67	5.32	5.07	4.89	4.74	4.63	4.54	4.40	4.25	4.10	4.02	3.94	3.86	3.78	3.69	3.60
12	9.33	6.93	5.95	5.41	5.06	4.82	4.64	4.50	4.39	4.30	4.16	4.01	3.86	3.78	3.70	3.62	3.54	3.45	3.36
13	9.07	6.70	5.74	5.21	4.86	4.62	4.44	4.30	4.19	4.10	3.96	3.82	3.66	3.59	3.51	3.43	3.34	3.25	3.17
14	8.86	6.51	5.56	5.04	4.69	4.46	4.28	4.14	4.03	3.94	3.80	3.66	3.51	3.43	3.35	3.27	3.18	3.09	3.00
15	8.68	6.36	5.42	4.89	4.56	4.32	4.14	4.00	3.89	3.80	3.67	3.52	3.37	3.29	3.21	3.13	3.05	2.96	2.87
16	8.53	6.23	5.29	4.77	4.44	4.20	4.03	3.89	3.78	3.69	3.55	3.41	3.26	3.18	3.10	3.02	2.93	2.84	2.75
17	8.40	6.11	5.18	4.67	4.34	4.10	3.93	3.79	3.68	3.59	3.46	3.31	3.16	3.08	3.00	2.92	2.83	2.75	2.65
18	8.29	6.01	5.09	4.58	4.25	4.01	3.84	3.71	3.60	3.51	3.37	3.23	3.08	3.00	2.92	2.84	2.75	2.66	2.57
19	8.18	5.93	5.01	4.50	4.17	3.94	3.77	3.63	3.52	3.43	3.30	3.15	3.00	2.92	2.84	2.76	2.67	2.58	2.49
20	8.10	5.85	4.94	4.43	4.10	3.87	3.70	3.56	3.46	3.37	3.23	3.09	2.94	2.86	2.78	2.69	2.61	2.52	2.42
21	8.02	5.78	4.87	4.37	4.04	3.81	3.64	3.51	3.40	3.31	3.17	3.03	2.88	2.80	2.72	2.64	2.55	2.46	2.36
22	7.95	5.72	4.82	4.31	3.99	3.76	3.59	3.45	3.35	3.26	3.12	2.98	2.83	2.75	2.67	2.58	2.50	2.40	2.31
23	7.88	5.66	4.76	4.26	3.94	3.71	3.54	3.41	3.30	3.21	3.07	2.93	2.78	2.70	2.62	2.54	2.45	2.35	2.26
24	7.82	5.61	4.72	4.22	3.90	3.67	3.50	3.36	3.26	3.17	3.03	2.89	2.74	2.66	2.58	2.49	2.40	2.31	2.21
25	7.77	5.57	4.68	4.18	3.85	3.63	3.46	3.32	3.22	3.13	2.99	2.85	2.70	2.62	2.54	2.45	2.36	2.27	2.17
26	7.72	5.53	4.64	4.14	3.82	3.59	3.42	3.29	3.18	3.09	2.96	2.81	2.66	2.58	2.50	2.42	2.33	2.23	2.13
27	7.68	5.49	4.60	4.11	3.78	3.56	3.39	3.26	3.15	3.06	2.93	2.78	2.63	2.55	2.47	2.38	2.29	2.20	2.10
28	7.64	5.45	4.57	4.07	3.75	3.53	3.36	3.23	3.12	3.03	2.90	2.75	2.60	2.52	2.44	2.35	2.26	2.17	2.06
29	7.60	5.42	4.54	4.04	3.73	3.50	3.33	3.20	3.09	3.00	2.87	2.73	2.57	2.49	2.41	2.33	2.23	2.14	2.03
30	7.56	5.39	4.51	4.02	3.70	3.47	3.30	3.17	3.07	2.98	2.84	2.70	2.55	2.47	2.39	2.30	2.21	2.11	2.01
40	7.31	5.18	4.31	3.83	3.51	3.29	3.12	2.99	2.89	2.80	2.66	2.52	2.37	2.29	2.20	2.11	2.02	1.92	1.80
60	7.08	4.98	4.13	3.65	3.34	3.12	2.95	2.82	2.72	2.63	2.50	2.35	2.20	2.12	2.03	1.94	1.84	1.73	1.60
120	6.85	4.79	3.95	3.48	3.17	2.96	2.79	2.66	2.56	2.47	2.34	2.19	2.03	1.95	1.86	1.76	1.66	1.53	1.38
∞	6.63	4.61	3.78	3.32	3.02	2.80	2.64	2.51	2.41	2.32	2.18	2.04	1.88	1.79	1.70	1.59	1.47	1.32	1.00

For a particular combination of numerator and denominator degrees of freedom, entry represents the critical values of F corresponding to a specified upper tail area α.

Notes

Chapter 1

1. Wendy Marx, "More Companies Look to Redesigns to Drive Net Leads," *Business Marketing* 82(5) (June 1997): 27, 38; and Lotus Web site, www.lotus.com.
2. "Creative Marketing Puts Sandwich Chain On a Roll," *Franchising World* (September/October 1997): 14–15.
3. Leslie Goff, "The Webbing of the President: Populism or Propaganda," *Computerworld* 30(36) (September 2, 1996): 79–80; and Susan Garland, Richard Dunham, and Laura Zinn, "Polling for Policy, How Clinton Uses Whiz-Bang Marketing to Make Decisions," *Business Week* (February 22, 1993): 34–35.
4. Drew Winter, "Getting to Know the Customer's Customer," *Ward's Auto World* 33(8) (August 1997): 64; and Jeffrey Swaddling, "Beating the Odds," *Marketing Management* (Winter/Spring 1996): 20–33.
5. The M/A/R/C Group, "Survey of on-line grocery shoppers shows higher purchases, greater store loyalty are in the bag," Web site, www.marcgroup.com/html/5.14.97groc.html (May 14, 1997).
6. Bob Donath, "Lawyers Face Juries of Their Prospects," *Marketing News* 30(9) (April 22, 1996): 4; and Leslie M. Harris, "Expanding Horizons," *Marketing Research: A Magazine of Management & Applications* 8(2) (Summer 1996): 12.
7. "Back on track," *Marketing Technique Supplement* (September 25, 1997): 8.
8. For the strategic role of marketing research, see John Hagel III and Jeffrey F. Rayport, "The Coming Battle for Customer Information," *McKinsey Quarterly* 3 (1997): 64–76; "Understanding Your Shoppers," *Progressive Grocer* 75(5) (May 1996): 123.
9. For relationship among information processing, marketing decisions, and performance, see S. Altan Erdem and Cathy Owens Swift, "Items to Consider for Just-in-Time Use in Marketing Channels: Toward Development of a Decision Tool," *Industrial Marketing Management* 27(1) (January 1998): 21–29.
10. Andrew J Strenio Jr., "The Aspirin Wars," *Journal of Public Policy and Marketing* 15(2) (Fall 1996): 319–21.
11. For the role of marketing research in marketing management see Siva K. Balasubramanian, "The New Marketing Research Systems—How to Use Strategic Database Information for Better Marketing Decision," *Journal of the Academy of Marketing Science* 24(2) (Spring 1996): 179–81.
12. Ian P. Murphy, "Keynote Speaker Emphasizes Urgency of Strategic Research," *Marketing News* 31(1) (January 6, 1997): 6; and N. K. Malhotra, "Shifting Perspective on the Shifting Paradigm in Marketing Research," *Journal of the Academy of Marketing Science* 20 (Fall 1992): 379–87.
13. See Thomas T. Semon, "Marketing Research Needs Basic Research," *Marketing News* 28(6) (March 14, 1994): 12. The AMA definition is reported in "New Marketing Research Definition Approved," *Marketing News* 21 (January 2, 1987).
14. For a historical discussion and an assessment of marketing research see L. McTier Anderson, "Marketing Science: Where's the Beef?" *Business Horizons* 37 (January/February 1994): 8–16; Alvin J. Silk, "Marketing Science in a Changing Environment," *Journal of Marketing Research* 30 (November 1993): 401–404; and Frank M. Bass, "The Future of Research in Marketing: Marketing Science," *Journal of Marketing Research* 30 (February 1993): 1–6.
15. Jerry W. Thomas, "How, When, and Why to Do Market Research," *Nation's Restaurant News* 31(19) (May 12, 1997): 84, 136.
16. Barry de Ville, "Intelligent Tools for Marketing Research: Case-Based Reasoning," *Marketing Research: A Magazine of Management & Applications* 9(2) (Summer 1997): 38–40.
17. Ellen Neuborne, "MMM! Cereal for dinner," *Business Week* (November 24, 1997): 105–106.
18. Terrence V. O'Brien, Denise D. Schoenbachler, and Geoffrey L. Gordon, "Marketing Information Systems for Consumer Products Companies: A Management Overview," *Journal of Consumer Marketing* 12(5) (1995): 16–36.
19. R. P. Mohanty and S. G. Deshmukh, "Evolution of a Decision Support System for Human Resource Planning in a Petroleum Company," *International Journal of Production Economics* 51(3) (September 1997): 251–61.
20. Jae-Hyeon Ahn and Kazuo J. Ezawa, "Decision Support for Real-Time Telemarketing Operations Through Bayesian Network Learning," *Decision Support Systems* 21(1) (September 1997): 17–27.
21. Ian P. Murphy, "FedEx Practices What It Preaches About Segments," *Marketing News* 31(6) (March 17, 1997): 14; Linda Grant, "Why FedEx Is Flying High," *Fortune* 136(9) (November 10, 1997): 155–60; and Web site, www.fedex.com/acct_num.htm.
22. Judann Pollack, "Oscar Mayer Plans Taco Bell-Branded Lunchables Product," *Advertising Age* 68(29) (July 21, 1997): 3, 37; and Charlie Etmekjian and John Grede, "Marketing Research in a Team-Oriented Business: The Oscar Mayer Approach," *Marketing Research: A Magazine of Management & Applications* (December 1990): 6–12.
23. A complete listing and description of the individual firms in the marketing research industry is provided in *The GreenBook International Directory of Marketing Research*

Companies and Services (New York Chapter, American Marketing Association, annually). See the Web site, www.greenbook.org.
24. Jack Honomichl, "Honomichl 50: 1998 Business Report on the Marketing Research Industry," *Marketing News* 32(12) (June 8, 1998): H1, H21.
25. For a historical note and future directions in syndicated services see Cyndee Miller, "Small World After All," *Marketing News* 31(1) (January 6, 1997): 1, 22; Ira Teinowitz, "Nielsen Rates Expected to Rise," *Advertising Age* 67(4) (January 22, 1996): 37; and Mike Penford, "Continuous Research—Art Nielsen to A.D. 2000," *Journal of the Market Research Society* 36 (January 1994): 19–28.
26. Cyndee Miller, "Study: Firms Add Researchers but Continue to Outsource," *Marketing News* (June 9, 1997): 1, 7.
27. James H. Fouss, "Faster and Smarter," *Marketing Research: A Magazine of Management & Applications* 8(4) (Winter 1996): 16–17; and Thomas C. Kinnear and Ann R. Root, *1994 Survey of Marketing Research* (Chicago: American Marketing Association, 1995).
28. Richard Kitaeff, "Marketing Research Competencies," *Marketing Research: A Magazine of Management & Applications* 6(3) (Summer 1994): 40–41.
29. Ralph W. Giacobbe and Madhav N. Segal, "Rethinking Marketing Research Education: A Conceptual, Analytical, and Empirical Investigation," *Journal of Marketing Education* 16 (Spring 1994): 43–58.
30. Barbara Baumann, John Duncan, Stephen E. Forrer and Zandy Leibowitz, "Amoco Primes the Talent Pump," *Personnel Journal* 75(2) (February 1996): 79–84; "AMR Interviews Abdul Azhari, On Today and the Future of Marketing Research at a Major Corporation," *Applied Marketing Research* (Spring 1989): 3–8.
31. Chad Kaydo, "Marriott," *Sales & Marketing Management* 149(11) (October 1997): 61; Sanjit Sengupta, Robert E. Krapfel and Michael A. Pusateri, "The Marriott Experience," *Marketing Management* 6(2) (Summer 1997): 33.
32. Kenneth Wylie, "Research-Eager Marketers Driving New Globalization," *Advertising Age* 66(44) (October 30, 1995): 28–29; and E. H. Demby, "ESOMAR Urges Changes in Reporting Demographics, Issues Worldwide Report," *Marketing News* 24(1) (January 8, 1990): 24–5.
33. David Kilburn, "Thai Recipe for Haircare Growth," *Marketing Week* 20(2) (April 10, 1997).
34. Diane K. Bowers, "Sugging Banned, At Last," *Marketing Research: A Magazine of Management & Applications* 7(4) (Fall/Winter 1995): 40.
35. *WorldOpinion* (Winter 1998): 2, accessed on-line at www.worldopinion.com.
36. Barry De Ville, "Internet for Market Research," *Marketing Research: A Magazine of Management & Applications* 7(3) (Summer 1995): 36–38.
37. David A. Cohen, "Database of Marketing Research, Search Software, Version 1.0," *Journal of Marketing Research* 31(2) (May 1994): 316–17. Information about the software cited in this book, if not referenced, can be obtained from recent issues of *Marketing News* and *Marketing Research: A Magazine of Management & Applications*, published by the American Marketing Association, or from a software vendor directory.

Chapter 2

1. Reprinted with permission from *Marketing News*, published by the American Marketing Association, Ian Murphy, "Aided by Research, Harley Goes Whole Hog," *Marketing News* (December 2, 1996): 16–17.
2. Patrick Butler, "Marketing Problem: From Analysis to Decision," *Marketing Intelligence & Planning* 12(2) (1994): 4–12.
3. David Smith and Andy Dexter, "Quality in Marketing Research: Hard Frameworks for Soft Problems," *Journal of the Market Research Society* 36(2) (April 1994): 115–32.
4. Berend Wierenga and Gerrit H. van Bruggen, "The Integration of Marketing Problem Solving Modes and Marketing Management Support Systems," *Journal of Marketing* 61(3) (July 1997): 21–37.
5. Mary J. Cronin, "Using the Web to Push Key Data to Decision Makers," *Fortune* 36(6) (September 29, 1997): 254.
6. Merrilyn Astin Tarlton, "Quick Marketing Audit," *Law Practice Management* 23(6) (September 1997): 18, 63; and Leonard L. Berry, Jeffrey S. Conant, and A. Parasuraman, "A Framework for Conducting a Services Marketing Audit," *Journal of the Academy of Marketing Science* 19 (Summer 1991): 255–68.
7. Saviour L. S. Nwachukwu and Scott J. Vitell Jr., "The Influence of Corporate Culture on Managerial Ethical Judgments," *Journal of Business Ethics* 16(8) (June 1997): 757–76.
8. Ellen Neuborne and Stephanie Anderson Forest, "Look Who's Picking Levi's Pocket," *Business Week* (September 8, 1997): 68, 72.
9. Ruth Winett, "Guerilla Marketing Research Outsmarts the Competition," *Marketing News* 29(1) (January 2, 1995): 33; J. Scott Armstrong, "Prediction of Consumer Behavior by Experts and Novices," *Journal of Consumer Research* 18 (September 1991): 251–56.
10. *Consumers Digest* (January/February 1998): 11.
11. Ian P. Murphy, "Amtrak Enlists Customers' Help to Bring Service Up to Speed," *Marketing News* 27 (October 1997): 14, 47.
12. Dennis P. Slevin and Jeffrey G. Covin, "Strategy Formation Patterns, Performance, and the Significance of Context," *Journal of Management* 23(2) (1997): 189–209; Mary T. Curren, Valerie S. Folkes, and Joel H. Steckel, "Explanations for Successful and Unsuccessful Marketing Decisions: The Decision Maker's Perspective," *Journal of Marketing* 56(April 1992): 18–31.
13. Seth Mendelson, "You Can't Take It with You," *Discount Merchandiser* 37(11) (November 1997): 7; C. L. Jain, "Myths and Realities of Forecasting," *Journal of Business Forecasting* 9 (Fall 1990): 18–22.
14. Theresa Howard, "Pizza's 'Big Three' Hold the Gimmicks, Serve Simplicity," *Nation's Restaurant News* 31(2) (January 13, 1997): 16.
15. Lehman Benson III and Lee Roy Beach, "The Effect of Time Constraints on the Prechoice Screening of Decision Options," *Organizational Behavior & Human Decision Processes* 67(2) (August 1996): 222–28; and Ron Sanchez and D. Sudharshan, "Real-Time Market Research," *Marketing Intelligence and Planning* 11(1993): 29–38.

16. Based on a marketing research project conducted by the author. See also William Boulding, Ruskin Morgan, and Richard Staelin, "Pulling the Plug to Stop New Product Drain," *Journal of Marketing Research* 34(1) (February 1997): 164–76.
17. Adrian J. Slywotzky and Kevin Mundt, "Hold the Sugar," *Across the Board* 33(8) (September 1996): 39–43.
18. Stephen M. Heyl, "Decision Matrix Points the Way to Better Research ROI," *Marketing News* 31(19) (September 15, 1997): 18, 30.
19. Mark Adams, "Court Marshal," *Mediaweek* 6(12) (March 18, 1996): 22.
20. Phil Buchanan, "Putting Sales Theory into Practice," *US Banker* 107(9) (September 12, 1997): 112; Shelby D. Hunt, "For Reason and Realism in Marketing," *Journal of Marketing* 56 (April 1992): 89–102.
21. A positivist perspective on research is used here. Positivism encompasses logical positivism, logical empiricism, and all forms of falsificationism. This is the dominant perspective adopted in commercial marketing research. More recently, a relativist perspective has been offered. See, for example, Shelby D. Hunt, *Modern Marketing Theory* (Cincinnati: SouthWestern Publishing Co., 1991).
22. Mika Boedeker, "New-Type and Traditional Shoppers: A Comparison of Two Major Consumer Groups," *International Journal of Retail & Distribution Management* 23(3) (1995) 17–26; Naresh. K. Malhotra, "A Threshold Model of Store Choice," *Journal of Retailing* (Summer 1983): 3–21.
23. For an illustration of a graphical model of software piracy see Figure 1 of Moshe Givon, Vijay Mahajan, and Eitan Muller, "Software Piracy: Estimation of Lost Sales and the Impact on Software Diffusion," *Journal of Marketing* 59 (January 1995): 29–37.
24. Carol Krol, "Research Shifts to Gauging Actual Marketing Results," *Advertising Age* 68(32) (August 11, 1997): 10–11.
25. Gary L. Lilien and Arvind Rangaswamy, *Marketing Engineering* (Reading, MA: Addison Wesley Longman, 1998).
26. Jay Koblenz, "1997 Black Enterprise Auto Guide," *Black Enterprise* 27(9) (April 1997): 126–32.
27. For a recent example of hypotheses formulation see N. Craig Smith and Elizabeth Cooper-Martin, "Ethics and Target Marketing: The Role of Product Harm and Consumer Vulnerability," *Journal of Marketing* 61 (July 1997): 1–20.
28. For a recent example of model development and hypotheses formulation see Steven P. Brown, William L. Cron, and John W. Slocum Jr., "Effects of Goal-Directed Emotions on Salesperson Volitions, Behavior, and Performance: A Longitudinal Study," *Journal of Marketing* 61 (January 1997): 39–50.
29. The integrated role of theory, models, research questions, and hypotheses in marketing research can be seen in J. Brock Smith and Donald W. Barclay, *Journal of Marketing* 61 (January 1997): 3–21.
30. Philip A. Garton, "Store Loyal? A View of Differential Congruence," *International Journal of Retail & Distribution Management* 23(12) (1995): 29–35.
31. Athena Ehlert, "Holiday Fragrance Roundup," *Drug & Cosmetic Industry* 160(3) (March 1997): 22–8.
32. Reprinted with permission from *Marketing News*, published by the American Marketing Association, Karen Schwartz and Ian P. Murphy, "Marketers Improve Menus to Please Passengers," *Marketing News* 31(21) (October 13, 1997): 1, 10.
33. "ConAgra, Heinz Rule Mexican Frozens," *Frozen Food Age* 45(11) (June 1997): 16.
34. Christopher Orpen, "Developing International Marketing Strategies in Small Companies," *Journal of International Marketing & Marketing Research* 20(2) (June 1995): 89–96; Susan P. Douglas and C. Samuel Craig, *International Marketing Research* (Upper Saddle River, NJ: Prentice Hall, 1983).
35. Peter C. Du Bois, "International Trader: A Bear on Unilever Says Time Will Prove Him Right," *Barron's* 76(42) (October 14, 1996): MW8; David Kilburn, "Unilever Struggles with Surf in Japan," *Advertising Age* (May 6, 1991).
36. G. R. Laczniak and P. E. Murphy, *Ethical Marketing Decisions, The Higher Road* (Boston-Allyn and Bacon, 1993).

Chapter 3

1. Kim Steutermann Rogers, "In Focus: What the Female Consumer Thinks," *Sporting Goods Business* (September 22, 1997): 28.
2. Ian P. Murphy, "Study: Apparel Shopper's Pulse Has Quickened," *Marketing News* (April 14, 1997): 34.
3. Thomas T. Semon, "Marketing Research Needs Basic Research," *Marketing News* 28(6) (March 14, 1996): 12.
4. Hanjoon Lee, Jay D. Lindquist, and Frank Acito, "Managers' Evaluation of Research Design and Its Impact on the Use of Research: An Experimental Approach," *Journal of Business Research* 39(3) (July 1997): 231–40; R. Dale Wilson, "Research Design: Qualitative and Quantitative Approaches," *Journal of Marketing Research* 33(2) (May 1996): 252–55.
5. For an example of exploratory research, see Ajay Menon and Anil Menon, "Enviropreneurial Marketing Strategy: The Emergence of Corporate Environmentalism as Market Strategy," *Journal of Marketing* 61(1) (January 1997): 51–67.
6. Stuart Glascock, "Microsoft Attempts to Lure New Class of VARs," *Computer Reseller News* 751 (August 25, 1997): 315; Herman Mehling, "Zooming In on a Growing Market," *Computer Reseller News* 747 (July 28, 1997): 55–56; Microsoft's Web site: www.microsoft.com.
7. For an example of descriptive research see X. Michael Song and Mark E. Perry, "The Determinants of Japanese New Product Success," *Journal of Marketing Research* 34 (February 1997): 64–76.
8. "Private Opinion," *American Demographics* (Tools Supplement) (March 1997): 33–34.
9. Ranjita Misra and B. Panigrahi, "Changes in Attitudes toward Women: A Cohort Analysis," *International Journal of Sociology & Social Policy* 15(6) (1995): 1–20; Norval D. Glenn, *Cohort Analysis* (Beverly Hills: Sage Publications, 1981).
10. Joseph O. Rentz, Fred D. Reynolds, and Roy G. Stout, "Analyzing Changing Consumption Patterns with Cohort Analysis," *Journal of Marketing Research* 20 (February 1983): 12–20. See also see Joseph O. Rentz and Fred D. Reynolds, "Forecasting the Effects of an Aging Population

on Product Consumption: An Age-Period-Cohort Framework," *Journal of Marketing Research* (August 1991): 355–60.

11. John Davidson, "Football 101," *Working Woman* 22(10) (October 1997): 13–14.
12. For recent applications of panel data, see K. Sivakumar and S. P. Raj, "Quality Tier Competition: How Price Change Influences Brand Choice and Category Choice," *Journal of Marketing* 61(3) (July 1997): 71–84. For a basic treatment, see Gregory B. Markus, *Analyzing Panel Data* (Beverly Hills: Sage Publications, 1979).
13. Table 3.6 can also be viewed as a transition matrix. It depicts the brand-buying changes from period to period. Knowing the proportion of consumers who switch allows for early prediction of the ultimate success of a new product or change in market strategy.
14. R. Tim Coupe and Nnadi M. Onodu, "Evaluating the Impact of CASE: An Empirical Comparison of Retrospective and Cross-Sectional Survey Approaches," *European Journal of Information Systems* 6(1) (March 1997): 15–24; Seymour Sudman and Robert Ferber, *Consumer Panels* (Chicago: American Marketing Association, 1979), pp. 19–27.
15. G. J. Van Den Berg, M. Lindeboom, and G. Ridder, "Attrition in Longitudinal Panel Data and the Empirical Analysis of Dynamic Labour Market Behaviour," *Journal of Applied Econometrics* 9(4) (October–December 1994): 421–35; Russell S. Winer, "Attrition Bias in Econometric Models Estimated with Panel Data," *Journal of Marketing Research* 20 (May 1983): 177–86.
16. Laszlo Maytas and Patrick Sevestre, eds., *The Econometrics of Panel Data, A Handbook of the Theory with Applications* (Norwell, MA: Kluwer Academic Publishers, 1996).
17. John Hulland, Yiu Ho, and Shunyin Lam, "Use of Causal Models in Marketing Research: A Review," *International Journal of Research in Marketing* 13(2) (April 1996): 181–97.
18. For an application of causal research, see H. Rao Unnava, Robert E. Burnkrant, and Sunil Erevelles, "Effects of Presentation Order and Communication Modality on Recall and Attitude," *Journal of Consumer Research* 21 (December 1994): 481–90.
19. Jack Edmonston, "Targeted Magazines Key to Future Profits," *Advertising Age's Business Marketing* 81(10) (December 1996): 42; Michael J. Naples and Rolf M. Wulfsberg, "The Bottom Line: Does Industrial Advertising Sell?" *Journal of Advertising Research* (August–September, 1987): RC4–RC16.
20. See Doug Ayers, Robert Dahlstrom, and Steven J. Skinner, "An Exploratory Investigation of Organizational Antecedents to New Product Success," *Journal of Marketing Research* 34 (February 1997): 107–116.
21. Chad Rubel, "NASCAR Tries to Shed Redneck Image, Seeks Market in Suburbs," *Marketing News* 30(2) (January 15, 1997): 1, 15.
22. "The Best Emerging Market Banks in the World," *Global Finance* 11(5) (May 1997): 26–42; Sabra Brock, Sara Lipson, and Ron Levitt, "Trends in Marketing Research and Development at Citicorp/Citibank," *Marketing Research: A Magazine of Management and Applications* 1(4) (December 1989).
23. Solomon Dutka and Lester R. Frankel, "Measuring Response Error," *Journal of Advertising Research* 37(1) (January/February 1997): 33–9.
24. Rebecca P. Heath, "Life on Easy Street," *American Demographics* 19(4) (April 1997): 32–8; *Marketing News* (April 10, 1987): 3.
25. Margret R. Rollere, "Control Is Elusive in Research Design," *Marketing News* 31(19) (September 15, 1997): 17; Tom Corlett, "Sampling Errors in Practice," *Journal of Market Research Society* 38(4) (October 1996): 307–18.
26. Zedan Hatush and Martin Skitmore, "Assessment and Evaluation of Contractor Data Against Client Goals Using PERT Approach," *Construction Management & Economics* 15(4) (July 1997): 327–40.
27. Lizhong Geng, et al. "Sports Marketing Strategy: A Consumer Behavior Case Analysis in China." *Multinational Business Review* (Spring 1997): 147–54; Gallup Organization, "1997 Survey: The People's Republic of China. Consumers Attitudes & Lifestyle Trends," Web site: www.gallup.com/poll/special/china.html.
28. Betsy Peterson, "Ethics Revisited," *Marketing Research: A Magazine of Management & Applications* 8(4) (Winter 1996): 47–8.
29. John W. K. Leung and K. K. Lai, "A Structured Methodology to Build Discrete-Event Simulation Models," *Asia Pacific Journal of Operations Research* 14(1) (May 1997): 19–37; Naresh K. Malhotra, "An Approach to the Measurement of Consumer Preferences Using Limited Information," *Journal of Marketing Research* 23 (February 1986): 33–40; Naresh K. Malhotra, "Analyzing Marketing Research Data with Incomplete Information on the Dependent Variable," *Journal of Marketing Research* 24 (February 1987): 74–84.

Chapter 4

1. Gordon L. Patzer, *Using Secondary Data in Marketing Research* (Westport, CT: Greenwood Publishing Group, 1995); David W. Stewart, *Secondary Research: Information Sources and Methods* (Beverly Hills: Sage Publications, 1984): 23–33.
2. Rebecca A. Fannin, "Samsonite, with TBWA, Readies Global Push," *Advertising Age* 68(8) (February 24, 1997): 4; Robert Bengen, "Teamwork: It's in the Bag," *Marketing Research: A Magazine of Management and Applications* 5 (Winter 1993): 30–3.
3. Cyndee Miller, "It's Not Take-Out, It's Now Home Meal Replacement," *Marketing News* (June 9, 1997): 2; Carol Casper, "Some Place Like Home," *Restaurant Business* 96(15) (August 1, 1997): 63–8.
4. Ron Stodghill, "The Coming Job Bottleneck," *Business Week* (March 24, 1997): 184–5.
5. "C-Store Retailers Push Growth with Dollars, New Profit Centers," *NPN: National Petroleum News* 88(11) (October 1996): S3–S40.
6. Ann Chambers, "25% of Drivers Would Consider Buying an EV," *Power Engineering* 101(9) (September 1997): 10.
7. For a recent application of secondary data, see Michael R. Czinkota and Ilkka A. Ronkainen, "Market Research for Your Export Operations: Part I—Using Secondary Sources of Research," *International Trade Forum* 3 (1994): 22–33;

Dipak Jain, Vijay Mahajan, and Eitan Muller, "Innovation Diffusion in the Presence of Supply Restrictions," *Marketing Science* (Winter 1991): 83–90.

8. Claude Brodesser, "Nielsen under Fire on Hispanic Sample," *Mediaweek* (July 21, 1997): 15.
9. Peter Keating, "The Best Airlines to Fly Today," *Money* (November 1997): 118–28.
10. Judy Foster Davis, "Maintaining Customer Relationships through Effective Database Marketing: A Perspective for Small Retailers," *Journal of Marketing Theory and Practice* 5(2) (Spring 1997): 31–42.
11. "The Colonel's Bold Campaign," *Chain Store Age* (June 1997): A12–A13.
12. Ruth A. Pagell, "Market Research in the U.S.—Part I: Industry, Market, and Advertising Sources," *Business Information Review* 11(4) (April 1995): 54–70.
13. www.census.gov. See also James H. Andrews, "Countdown to the Census," *Planning* 62(12) (December 1996): 4–7.
14. Ruth A. Pagell, "Market Research in the U.S.—Part 4. Data from the Census of Population and Housing," *Business Information Review* 13(1) (March 1996): 49–56.
15. "Frequently Asked Questions about Census 2000," *Indiana Business Review* 72(8) (Summer 1997): 10.
16. "Claritas Has Household Data," *Insurance Systems Bulletin* 12(4) (October 1996): 8.
17. Amy Hilliard-Jones, "Consumers of Color are Changing the American Marketplace," *Marketing News* 30(24) (November 18, 1996): 8.
18. Carol Post, "Marketing Data Marts Help Companies Stay Ahead of the Curve and in Front of the Competition," *Direct Marketing* 59(12) (April 1997): 42–4.
19. Greg R. Notess, "Searching the Hidden Internet," *Database* 20(3) (June/July 1997): 37–40.
20. Barbara Quint, "Assume the Position, Take the Consequences," *Information Today* 13(6) (June 1996): 11–13.
21. Christopher C. Brown, "Creating Automated Bibliographies Using Internet-Accessible On-line Library Catalogs," *Database* 17(1) (February 1994): 67–71.
22. Mary Ellen Bates, "American, Business Information: Here, There, and Everywhere," *Database* 20(2) (April/May 1997): 45–50.
23. Greg R. Notess, "The Internet as an On-line Service: Bibliographic Databases on the Net," *Database* 19(4) (August/September 1996): 92–5.
24. For a recent application of PIMS database, see J. Zif and D.J. McCarthy, "The Research-and-Development Cycle: The Influence of Product and Process Research-and-Development on Short Term ROI," *IEEE Transactions on Engineering Management* 44(2) (May 1997): 114–23; Venkatram Ramaswamy, Hubert Gatignon, and David J. Reibstein, "Competitive Marketing Behavior," *Journal of Marketing* 58 (April 1994): 45–56.
25. For a recent application of computerized databases, see Vicki Lane and Robert Jacobson, "Stock Market Reactions to Brand Extension Announcements: The Effects of Brand Attitude and Familiarity," *Journal of Marketing* 59 (January 1995): 63–77.
26. "The Monitor™ Service," brochure prepared by Yankelovich and Partners.
27. For a recent application of DDB Needham Life Style Study, see L. J. Shrum, John A. McCarty, and Tina M. Lowrey, "Buyer Characteristics of the Green Consumer and Their Implications for Advertising Strategy," *Journal of Advertising* 24(2) (Summer 1995): 71–82.
28. Leon G. Schiffman and Leslie Lazar Kanuk, *Consumer Behavior,* 6th. ed. (Upper Saddle River, NJ: Prentice Hall, 1997): 68–71.
29. Christina Merrill, "Roper Expands Testing," *Adweek* (Eastern Ed) 37(45) (November 4, 1996): 6; *Starch Readership Report: Scope, Method, and Use* (Mamaroneck, NY: Starch INRA Hooper, undated).
30. "Roper Custom Question Service: A Unique Omnibus Research Facility," brochure prepared by the Roper Organization, Inc., One Park Avenue, New York, NY 10016.
31. Panel descriptions supplied by Rita E. Turgeon, *We Make the Market Perfectly Clear* (New York: NPD Research, Inc. undated).
32. Information provided by A. C. Nielsen.
33. Associated Press, "Nielsen Test Rating Service for TV Commercials," *Marketing News* 31 (May 12, 1997): 22.
34. Donna Petrozzello, "Arbitron Offers Custom Fit," *Broadcasting & Cable* 127(8) (February 24, 1997): 46.
35. "Why Consumer Mail Panel Is the Superior Option," (Chicago: Market Facts, Inc. undated); John H. Parfitt and B.J.K. Collins, "Use of Consumer Panels for Brand-Share Predictions," *Journal of Market Research Society* 38(4) (October 1996): 341–67; Venkatram Ramaswamy and Wayne S. DeSarbo, "SCULPTURE: A New Methodology for Deriving and Analyzing Hierarchical Product-Market Structures from Panel Data," *Journal of Marketing Research* 27 (November 1990): 418–27.
36. R. Tim Coupe and Nnadi M. Onodu, "Evaluating the Impact of CASE: An Empirical Comparison of Retrospective and Cross-Sectional Survey Approaches," *European Journal of Information Systems* 6(1) (March 1997): 15–24; Seymour Sudman, "On the Accuracy of Recording of Consumer Panels II," *Learning Manual* (New York: Neal-Schumen Publishers, 1981).
37. Tim Bowles and Claude Charbit, "Can Scanner Data Achieve Their Potential in Europe? New Questions, New Solutions," *Marketing & Research Today* 25(2) (May 1997): 121–4. A recent study investigating the accuracy of UPC scanner pricing systems found that both underring and overring rates were significantly higher than retailers' expectations: Ronald C. Goodstein, "UPC Scanner Pricing Systems: Are They Accurate?" *Journal of Marketing* 58 (April 1994): 20–30.
38. S. Baron and A. Lock, "The Challenges of Scanner Data," *Journal of the Operational Research Society* 46(1) (January 1995): 95; Rick L. Andrew and T. C. Srinivasan, "Studying Consideration Effects in Empirical Choice Models Using Scanner Panel Data," *Journal of Marketing Research* 32 (February 1995): 30–41.
39. It is possible to combine store-level scanner data with scanner panel data to do an integrated analysis. See for example, Gary J. Russell, and Wagner A. Kamakura, "Understanding Brand Competition Using Micro and Macro Scanner Data," *Journal of Marketing Research* 31 (May 1994): 289–303.
40. Examples of recent applications of scanner data include Markus Christen, Sachin Gupta, John C. Porter, Richard Staelin, and Dick R. Wittink, "Using Market-Level Data to Understand Promotion Effects in a Nonlinear Model,"

7. Sharon Munger, "Premium Medium," *Marketing Research: A Magazine of Management & Applications* 8(1) (Spring 1996): 10–12.
8. Gail Gaboda, "For Business Travelers, There's No Place Like Home," *Marketing News* 31(19) (September 15, 1997): 19, 21; Courtyard Hotels' Web site (www.courtyard.com).
9. Thomas T. Semon, "Reality Is Unfair to Small Fry," *Marketing News* 30(24) (November 18, 1996): 18.
10. "Cause Related Marketing Sends a Multiplicity of Messages," *Entertainment Marketing Letter* 10(2) (February 1997): 6; *Quirk's Marketing Research Review* (February 1988): 57.
11. "Auto-Mania at the Mall," *American Demographics* (Marketing Tools Supplement) (June 1997): 6+; A. J. Bush and J. F. Hair Jr., "An Assessment of the Mall-Intercept as a Data Collection Method," *Journal of Marketing Research* (May 1985): 158–67.
12. Cyndee Miller, ". . . And Baby Gets Brand," *Marketing News* 30(6) (March 11, 1996): 18; "Research Basic to Baby-Wear Business," *Marketing News* (February 13, 1987): 26.
13. Laurence N. Gold, "Do-it-Yourself Interviewing," *Marketing Research: A Magazine of Management & Applications* 8(2) (Summer 1996): 40–41; John P. Liefeld, "Response Effects in Computer-Administered Questioning," *Journal of Marketing Research* 25 (November 1988): 405–409.
14. "Anytime, Anywhere, Anyhow: Retail Banking by 2005 Will be Different from Today with More Emphasis on Consumer Convenience Expected," *Bank Marketing International* 70 (April 1996): 14; Nicolaos E. Synodinos and Jerry M. Brennan, "Computer Interactive Interviewing in Survey Research," *Psychology and Marketing* 5 (Summer 1988): 117–38.
15. "Primary Results: Audits & Surveys (New York, NY) Proposes to Initiate Primary Audience Research Founded on Equal Sample Sizes from Any Given Magazine's Database of Subscribers and Newsstand Buyers," *Inside Media* 8(10) (May 15, 1996): 30; Jeffrey S. Conant, Denise T. Smart, and Bruce J. Walker, "Mail Survey Facilitation Techniques: An Assessment and Proposal Regarding Reporting Practices," *Journal of Market Research Society* (UK) 32 (October 1990): 569–80.
16. Mail surveys are common in institutional and industrial marketing research. See, for example, H. L. Brossard, "Information Sources Used by an Organization during a Complex Decision Process: An Exploratory Study," *Industrial Marketing Management* 27(1) (January 1998): 41–50.
17. Rob Yoegei, "List Marketers Head to Cyberspace," *Target Marketing* 20(8) (August 1997): 54–5.
18. "SOFRES Group SA," *Marketing News* 31(17) (August 18, 1997): H7; Robert Arnett, "Mail Panel Research in the 1990s," *Applied Marketing Research* 30(2) (Second Quarter 1990): 8–10.
19. "YM Magazine Subscribes to Co-Op," *Promo IX* (7) (June 1996): 19; *Seventeen* magazine. Retail Survey.
20. Jim Stevens and John Chisholm, "An Integrated Approach: Technology Firm Conducts Worldwide Satisfaction Research Survey Via E-Mail, Internet," *Quirk's Marketing Research Review* 11(8) (October 1997): 12–13, 64–65.
21. "Demonstrating Control: More Retailers Are Calling the Shots in Choosing Sampling and Demonstration Firms," *Supermarket News* (Brand Marketing Supplement) (March 4, 1996): 1; Terry L. Childers and Steven J. Skinner, "Theoretical and Empirical Issues in the Identification of Survey Respondents," *Journal of the Market Research Society* 27 (January 1985): 39–53.
22. Wayne Smith, Paul Mitchell, Karin Attebo, and Stephen Leeder, "Selection Bias from Sampling Frames: Telephone Directory and Electoral Rolls Compared to Door-to-Door Population Census: Results from the Blue Mountain Eye Study," *Australian & New Zealand Journal of Public Health* 21(2) (April 1997): 127–33.
23. "One Less Hurdle for Caller ID in California," *New York Times* (National Edition) CXLV (50434) (May 21, 1996): C17; Survey Sampling, Inc., "Sacramento is Top Unlisted Market," *The Frame* (February 1995): 1.
24. Scott Keeter, "Estimating Telephone Noncoverage Bias with a Telephone Survey," *Public Opinion Quarterly* 59(2) (Summer 1995): 196–217.
25. C. Muntaner and P. E. Parsons, "Income, Social Stratification, Class, and Private Health Insurance—A Study of the Baltimore Metropolitan Area," *International Journal of Health Services* 26(4) (1996): 655–71; Johnny Blair and Ronald Czaja, "Locating a Special Population Using Random Digit Dialing," *Public Opinion Quarterly* 46 (Winter 1982): 585–90; E. L. Landon Jr. and S. K. Banks, "Relative Efficiency and Bias of Plus-One Telephone Sampling," *Journal of Marketing Research* 14 (August 1977): 294–99.
26. David O. Schwartz, "Mailing List Owners and the Millennium," *Marketing News* 31(11) (May 26, 1997): 4; Paul M. Biner and Deborah L. Barton, "Justifying the Enclosure of Monetary Incentives in Mail Survey Cover Letters," *Psychology and Marketing* (Fall 1990): 153–62; "Lists Make Targeting Easy," *Advertising Age* (July 9, 1984): 20.
27. Best Mailing Lists, Inc., *Catalog 1998*. Reprinted with permission of Best Mailing Lists, Inc.
28. Jenny Printz and Dwight Maltby, "Beyond Personalization: When Handwriting Makes a Difference," *Fund Raising Management* 28(3) (May 1997): 16–19; Jeffrey S. Conant, Denise T. Smart, and Bruce J. Walker, "Mail Survey Facilitation Techniques: An Assessment and Proposal Regarding Reporting Practices," *Journal of Market Research Society* (UK) 32 (October 1990): 569–80.
29. Jack Edmonston, "Why Response Rates are Declining," *Advertising Age's Business Marketing* 82(8) (September 1997): 12; Raymond Hubbard and Eldon L. Little, "Promised Contributions to Charity and Mail Survey Responses: Replications with Extension," *Public Opinion Quarterly* 52 (Summer 1988): 223–30; Paul L. Erdos and Robert Ferber, ed., "Data Collection Methods: Mail Surveys," *Handbook of Marketing Research* (New York: McGraw-Hill, 1974): 102.
30. Robert Grey, "Speeding Up the Process," *Campaign-London* (Information Interpretation) (October 18, 1996): 7; Pamela G. Guengel, Tracy R. Berchman, and Charles F. Cannell, *General Interviewing Techniques: A Self-Instructional Workbook for Telephone and Personal Interviewer Training* (Ann Arbor, MI: Survey Research Center, University of Michigan, 1983).
31. Betsy V. Boze and Charles R. Patton, "The Future of Consumer Branding as Seen from the Picture Today," *Journal of Consumer Marketing* 12(4) (1995): 20–41.

32. Karen Fletcher, "Jump on the Omnibus," *Marketing* (June 15, 1995): 25–8.
33. William L. Nicholls, II, "Highest Response," *Marketing Research: A Magazine of Management & Applications* 8(1) (Spring 1996): 5–7; Julie Yu and Harris Cooper, "A Quantitative Review of Research Design Effects on Response Rates to Questionnaires," *Journal of Marketing Research* 20 (February 1983): 36–44. See also Jeannine M. James, and Richard Bolstein, "The Effect of Monetary Incentives and Follow-Up Mailings on the Response Rate and Response Quality in Mail Surveys," *Public Opinion Quarterly* 54 (Fall 1990): 346–61.
34. Deniz Ones, Angelika D. Reiss, Chockalingam Viswesvaran, "Role of Social Desirability in Personality Testing for Personnel Selection: The Red Herring," *Journal of Applied Psychology* 81(6) (December 1996): 660–79.
35. Gerald Vinten, "The Threat in the Question," *Credit Control* 18(1) (1997): 25–31; Priya Raghubir and Geeta Menon, "Asking Sensitive Questions: The Effects of Type of Referent and Frequency Wording in Counterbiasing Method," *Psychology & Marketing* 13(7) (October 1996): 633–52.
36. Chad Rubel, "Researcher Praises On-Line Methodology," *Marketing News* 30(12) (June 3, 1996): H18; Charles F. Cannell, Peter U. Miller, Lois Oksenberg, and Samuel Leinhardt, eds., "Research on Interviewing Techniques," *Sociological Methodology* (San Francisco: Jossey-Bass, 1981); Peter U. Miller and Charles F. Cannell, "A Study of Experimental Techniques for Telephone Interviewing," *Public Opinion Quarterly* 46 (Summer 1982): 250–69.
37. "How the Survey Was Designed," *Management Accounting* 79(8) (February 1998): 48; and Arlene Fink, *A Survey Handbook* (Thousand Oaks, CA: Sage Publications, 1995).
38. Hybrid methods, which combine the features of these basic methods, are also being employed. For example, disk-by-mail (DBM) involves mailing the questionnaire on a disk to the respondents. This method is growing in popularity as it offers the benefits of both computer-assisted and mail surveys. "Disk-by-Mail Data Collection: A Researcher's Notes," *Sawtooth News* 10 (Winter 1994/1995): 3–4. See also David Chaudron, "The Right Approach to Employee Surveys," *HR Focus* 74(3) (March 1997): 9–10.
39. Ruth N. Bolton, "Covering the Market," *Marketing Research: A Magazine of Management & Applications* 6(3) (Summer 1994): 30–5; Stanley L. Payne, "Combination of Survey Methods," *Journal of Marketing Research* (May 1964): 62.
40. Judann Pollack, "Oscar Mayer Plans Taco Bell–Branded Lunchables Products," *Advertising Age* 68(29) (July 21, 1997): 3, 37; Charlie Etmekjian and John Grede, "Marketing Research in a Team-Oriented Business: The Oscar Mayer Approach," *Marketing Research: A Magazine of Management and Applications* 2 (December 1990): 6–12.
41. Stephen B. Wilcox, "Trust, But Verify," *Appliance Manufacturer* 46(1) (January 1998): 8, 87; Langbourne Rust, "How to Reach Children in Stores: Marketing Tactics Grounded in Observational Research," *Journal of Advertising Research* 33 (November/December 1993): 67–72.
42. "Keeping Track of the Customer," *Retail Business-Market Surveys* (475) (September 1997): 1–11; Cliff Scott, David M. Klein, and Jennings Bryant, "Consumer Response to Humor in Advertising: A Series of Field Studies Using Behavioral Observation," *Journal of Consumer Research* 16 (March 1990): 498–501; Fred N. Kerlinger, *Foundations of Behavioral Research*, 3rd ed. (New York: Holt, Rinehart & Winston, 1986): 538.
43. A. V. Seaton, "Unobtrusive Observational Measures as a Qualitative Extension of Visitor Surveys at Festivals and Events: Mass Observation Revisited," *Journal of Travel Research* 35(4) (Spring 1997): 25–30; E. J. Webb, D. T. Campbell, K. D. Schwarts, and L. Sechrest, *Unobtrusive Measures: Nonreactive Research in the Social Sciences* (Chicago: Rand McNally, 1966): 113–14.
44. Keith Naughton, Emily Thornton, Kathleen Kerwin, and Heidi Dawley, "Can Honda Build a World Car?" *BusinessWeek* (September 8, 1997): 100–8.
45. Laurence N. Gold, "Technology in Television Research: The Meter," *Marketing Research: A Magazine of Management & Applications* 6(1) (Winter 1994): 57–8.
46. J. Edward Russo and France Leclerc, "An Eye-Fixation Analysis of Choice Processes for Consumer Nondurables," *Journal of Consumer Research* 21 (September 1994): 274–90.
47. For recent applications of GSR, see Priscilla A. LaBarbera and Joel D. Tucciarone, "GSR Reconsidered: A Behavior-Based Approach to Evaluating and Improving the Sales Potency of Advertising," *Journal of Advertising Research* 35(5) (September/October 1995): 33–53; Piet Vanden Abeele and Douglas L. MacLachlan, "Process Tracing of Emotional Responses to TV Ads: Revisiting the Warmth Monitor," *Journal of Consumer Research* 20 (March 1994): 586–600.
48. S. Gregory, S. Webster, and G. Huang, "Voice Pitch and Amplitude Convergence as a Metric of Quality in Dyadic Interviews," *Language & Communication* 13(3) (July 1993): 195–217; Glen A. Buckman, "Uses of Voice-Pitch Analysis," *Journal of Advertising Research* 20 (April 1980): 69–73.
49. John N. Bassili and B. Stacey Scott, "Response Latency as a Signal to Question Problems in Survey Research," *Public Opinion Quarterly* 60(3) (Fall 1996): 390–99; David A. Aaker, Richard P. Bagozzi, James M. Carman, and James M. MacLachlan, "On Using Response Latency to Measure Preference," *Journal of Marketing Research* 17 (May 1980): 237–44.
50. Howard Rachlin, "Can We Leave Cognition to Cognitive Psychologists? Comments on an Article by George Loewenstein," *Organizational Behavior & Human Decision Processes* 65(3) (March 1996): 300–4; and David W. Stewart, "Physiological Measurement of Advertising Effects," *Psychology and Marketing* (Spring 1984): 43–8.
51. "Equal Spoonful Granulated Sweetener with NutraSweet," *Lookout-Foods* (February 11, 1997): 021F-97; "Plenty of Prime Pickings in New-Package Potpourri," *Packaging* 39(2) (February 1994): 23–4; *Quirk's Marketing Research Review* (October–November 1987): 6–8.
52. Sean Stokes, "Compaq Leapfrogs Over Rivals," *Computing Canada* 20(10) (May 11, 1994): 26.
53. Peter A. Manickas and Linda J. Shea, "Hotel Complaint Behavior and Resolution: A Content Analysis," *Journal of Travel Research* 36(2) (Fall 1997): 68–73; Rebecca Morris, "Computerized Content Analysis in Management Research: A Demonstration of Advantages and Limitations," *Journal of Management* 20(4) (Winter 1994): 903–31; Richard H. Kolbe and Melissa S. Burnett, "Content-Analysis Research:

An Examination of Applications with Directives for Improving Research Reliability and Objectivity," *Journal of Consumer Research* 18 (September 1991): 243–50.

54. Subir Sengupta, "The Influence of Culture on Portrayals of Women in Television Commercials: A Comparison between the United States and Japan," *International Journal of Advertising* 14(4) (1995): 314–33; Charles S. Madden, Marjorie J. Caballero, and Shinya Matsukubo, "Analysis of Information Content in U.S. and Japanese Magazine Advertising," *Journal of Advertising* 15, 3(1986): 38–45.
55. Ellen Messmer, "ISP Software Track Customers' Every Move," *Network World* 14(39) (September 29, 1997): 17.
56. Gerald Berstell and Denise Nitterhouse, "Looking 'Outside the Box'," *Marketing Research: A Magazine of Management & Applications* 9(2) (Summer 1997): 4–13.
57. Michael Hartnett, "In-Store Sign Systems Target Shopper Buying Decisions," *Stores* 79(7) (July 1997): 83–8; *Marketing News* (March 27, 1987): 38.
58. C. L. Hung, "Canadian Business Pursuits in the PRC, Hong Kong, and Taiwan and Chinese Perception of Canadians as Business Partners," *Multinational Business Review* 6(1) (Spring 1998): 73–82; C. Min Han, Byoung-Woo Lee, and Kong-Kyun Ro, "The Choice of a Survey Mode in Country Image Studies," *Journal of Business Research* 29(2) (February 1994): 151–62.
59. Sarah Jones, "Re-Evaluating Reebok," *Adweek* (New England Ed.) 34(43) (October 27, 1997): 2.
60. Wade Leftwich, "How Researchers Can Win Friends and Influence Politicians," *American Demographics* (August, 1993): 9.
61. Marla Royne Stafford and Thomas F. Stafford, "Participant Observation and the Pursuit of Truth: Methodological and Ethical Considerations," *Journal of the Market Research Society* 35 (January 1993): 63–76.
62. C. N. Smith and J. A. Quelch, *Ethics in Marketing* (Homewood, IL: Richard D. Irwin, 1993).
63. Brad Edmondson, "The Wired Bunch," *American Demographics* (June 1997): 10–15; Decisive Technology Corporation Web site, www.decisive.com

Chapter 7

1. "LeSportsac Announces Latest International Expansion," *Showcase* 20(6) (December 1995): 67; "Surveys Help Settle Trade Dress Infringement Case," *Quirk's Marketing Research Review* (October–November 1987): 16, 17, 33.
2. Robert Dwek, "Prediction of Success," *Marketing* (POP & Field Marketing Supplement) (April 17, 1997): XII–XIII; "POP Radio Test Airs the Ads In-store," *Marketing News* (October 24, 1986): 16.
3. R. Barker Bausell, *Conducting Meaningful Experiments* (Thousand Oaks, CA: Sage Publications, Inc., 1994).
4. Robert F. Boruch, *Randomized Experiments for Planning and Evaluation* (Thousand Oaks, CA: Sage Publications, Inc., 1994).
5. Michele Witthaus, "POP Stars," *Marketing Week* 20(16) (July 17, 1997): 37–41.
6. Gordon A. Wyner, "Experimental Design," *Marketing Research: A Magazine of Management & Applications* 9(3) (Fall 1997): 39–41; Steven R. Brown and Lawrence E. Melamed, *Experimental Design and Analysis* (Newbury Park, CA: Sage Publications, 1990).
7. A recent study employing experimental designs is Mark T. Spence and Merrie Brucks, "The Moderating Effect of Problem Characteristics on Experts' and Novices' Judgments," *Journal of Marketing Research* 34 (May 1997): 233–47.
8. Alice Ann Love, "Companies Want to Cut Coupons, But Consumers Demand Bargains," *Marketing News* 31(10) (May 12, 1997): 15; Robert W. Shoemaker and Vikas Tibrewala, "Relating Coupon Redemption Rates to Past Purchasing of the Brand," *Journal of Advertising Research* 25 (October–November 1985): 40–7.
9. In addition to internal and external validity, there also exist construct and statistical conclusion validity. Construct validity addresses the question of what construct, or characteristic, is in fact being measured and is discussed in chapter 9 on measurement and scaling. Statistical conclusion validity addresses the extent and statistical significance of the covariation that exists in the data and is discussed in the chapters on data analysis.
10. Prashant Bordia, "Face-to-Face Computer-Mediated Communication: A Synthesis of the Experimental Literature," *Journal of Business Communication* 34(1) (January 1997): 99–120; David M. Bowen, "Work Group Research: Past Strategies and Future Opportunities," *IEEE Transactions on Engineering Management* 42(1) (February 1995): 30–8; John G. Lynch Jr., "On the External Validity of Experiments in Consumer Research," *Journal of Consumer Research* 9 (December 1982): 225–44.
11. Chris Argyris, "Actionable Knowledge: Design Causality in the Service of Consequential Theory," *Journal of Applied Behavioral Science* 32(4) (December 1966): 390–406; John G. Lynch Jr. "The Role of External Validity in Theoretical Research," B. J. Calder, L. W. Phillips, and Alice Tybout, "Beyond External Validity," and J. E. McGrath and D. Brinberg, "External Validity and the Research Process," *Journal of Consumer Research* (June 1983): 109–11, 112–14, and 115–24.
12. Alan R. Hirsch, "Effects of Ambient Odors on Slot-Machine Usage in a Las Vegas Casino," *Psychology & Marketing* 12(7) (October 1995): 585–94.
13. C. Durier, H. Monod, and A. Bruetschy, "Design and Analysis of Factorial Sensory Experiments with Carry-Over Effects," *Food Quality and Preference* 8(2) (March 1997): 141–49; Lloyd S. Nelson, "Notes on the Use of Randomization in Experimentation," *Journal of Quality Technology* 28(1) (January 1996): 123–26.
14. Marcus Selart, "Structure Compatability and Restructuring in Judgment and Choice," *Organizational Behavior & Human Decision Processes* 65(2) (February 1996): 106–16; R. Barker Bausell, *Conducting Meaningful Experiments* (Thousand Oaks, CA: Sage Publications, Inc., 1994).
15. Betsy Spethmann, "Choosing a Test Market," *Brandweek* 36(19) (May 8, 1995): 42–3; Andrew M. Tarshis, "Natural Sell-in Avoids Pitfalls of Controlled Tests," *Marketing News* (October 24, 1986): 14.
16. Other experimental designs are also available. See Bert Gunter, "Fundamental Issues in Experimental Design," *Quality Progress* 29(6) (June 1996): 105–13; R. S. Winer, "Analysis of Advertising Experiments," *Journal of Advertising Research* (June 1980): 25–31.

17. For an application of the Solomon four-group design, see Richard W. Mizerski, Neil K. Allison, and Stephen Calvert, "A Controlled Field Study of Corrective Advertising Using Multiple Exposures and a Commercial Medium," *Journal of Marketing Research* 17 (August 1980): 341–48.
18. C. Moorman, "A Quasi-Experiment to Assess the Consumer and Informational Determinants of Nutrition Information-Processing Activities—The Case of the Nutrition Labeling and Education Act," *Journal of Public Policy and Marketing* 15(1) (Spring 1996): 28–44.
19. Leonard M. Lodish, Magid M. Abraham, Jeanne Livelsberger, Beth Lubetkin, et al., "A Summary of Fifty-Five In-Market Experimental Estimates of the Long-Term Effects of TV Advertising," *Marketing Science* (Summer 1995): G133–G140; Lakshman Krishnamurthi, Jack Narayan, and S. P. Raj, "Intervention Analysis of a Field Experiment to Assess the Buildup Effect of Advertising," *Journal of Marketing Research* 23 (November 1986): 337–45.
20. See, for example, M. G. Weinberger, H. Spotts, L. Campbell, and A. L. Parsons, "The Use and Effect of Humor in Different Advertising Media," *Journal of Advertising Research* 35(3) (May–June 1995): 44–56.
21. For a recent application of factorial designs see Wendy J. Bryce, Rachel Day, and Thomas J. Olney, "Commitment Approach to Motivating Community Recycling: New Zealand Curbside Trial," *Journal of Consumer Affairs* 31(1) (Summer 1997): 27–52.
22. Gwen E. Jones and Michael J. Kavanagh, "An Experimental Examination of the Effects of Individual and Situational Factors on Unethical Behavioral Intentions in the Workplace," *Journal of Business Ethics* 15(5) (May 1996): 511–23.
23. John R. Dickson and Carolyn P. Wilby, "Concept Testing with and without Product Trial," *Journal of Product Innovation Management* 14(2) (March 1997): 117–25; James B. Miller, Norman T. Bruvold, and Jerome B. Kernan, "Does Competitive-Set Information Affect the Results of Concept Tests?" *Journal of Advertising Research* (April–May 1987): 16–23.
24. Paula F. Bone, "Word-of-Mouth Effects on Short-Term and Long-Term Product Judgments," *Journal of Business Research* 32(3) (March 1995): 213–23; J. H. Barnes Jr. and D. T. Seymour, "Experimenter Bias: Task, Tools, and Time," *Journal of the Academy of Marketing Science* (Winter 1980): 1–11.
25. J. Perrien, "Repositioning Demand Artifacts in Consumer Research," *Advances in Consumer Research* 24 (1997): 267–71; T. A. Shimp, E. M. Hyatt, and D. J. Snyder, "A Critical Appraisal of Demand Artifacts in Consumer Research," *Journal of Consumer Research* 18(3) (December 1991): 272–83.
26. Yasuhiro Monden, Mahmuda Akter, and Naoto Kubo, "Target Costing Performance Based on Alternative Participation and Evaluation Method: A Laboratory Experiment," *Managerial & Decision Economics* 18(2) (March 1997): 113–29.
27. Richard M. Alston and Clifford Nowell, "Implementing the Voluntary Contribution Game: A Field Experiment," *Journal of Economic Behavior & Organization* 31(3) (December 1996): 357–68.
28. Aris Spanos, "On Theory Testing in Econometrics: Modeling with Nonexperimental Data," *Journal of Econometrics* 67(1) (May 1995): 189–226; Hurbert M. Blalock Jr., *Causal Inferences in Nonexperimental Research* (Chapel Hill, NC: University of North Carolina Press, 1964).
29. In some situations, surveys and experiments can complement each other and may both be used. For example, the results obtained in laboratory experiments may be further examined in a field survey. See Wesley J. Johnston and Keysuk Kim, "Performance, Attribution, and Expectancy Linkages in Personal Selling," *Journal of Marketing* 58 (October 1994): 68–81.
30. Peter Romeo, "Testing, Testing," *Restaurant Business* 97(2) (January 15, 1998): 12. Reprinted with permission from *Marketing News* published by the American Marketing Association, Chicago, IL, p. 15, March 1, 1985.
31. Stephanie Thompson, "Tetley Tests Higher-Value Pitches," *Brandweek* 38(47) (December 15, 1997): 8; Ed Rubinstein, "7-Eleven Tests Internet Kiosks in Seattle Market," *Nation's Restaurant News* 31(42) (October 20, 1997): 24.
32. Tara Parker-Pope, "Frito-Lay to Begin Selling Wow! Chips Made with Olestra Later This Month," *Wall Street Journal* (February 10, 1998): B2.
33. Sean Mehegan, "Vaseline Ups Ante Via Anti-Bacterial," *Brandweek* 38(21) (May 26, 1997): 1, 6.
34. "Why New Products are Bypassing the Market Test," *Management Today* (October 1995): 12.
35. Jack Neff, "Ivory Extension Targets Families," *Advertising Age* 68(9) (March 3, 1997): 39.
36. Dermot J. Hayes, Jason F. Shogren, John A. Fox, and James B. Kliebenstein, "Test Marketing New Food Products Using a Multitrial Nonhypothetical Experimental Auction," *Psychology & Marketing* 13(4) (July 1996): 365–79.
37. "Simulated Test Marketing," *Sloan Management Review* 36(2) (Winter 1995): 112.
38. David Woodruff and Karen Nickel, "When You Think Deluxe Think East Germany," *Business Week* (May 26, 1997): 124E2.
39. Bernard H. Schmitt, "Contextual Priming of Visual Information in Advertisements," *Psychology & Marketing* 11(1) (January/February 1994): 1–14.
40. Betsy Peterson, "Ethics, Revisited," *Marketing Research: A Magazine of Management & Applications* 8(4) (Winter 1996): 47–8.
41. Isabelle Sender, "Internet Coupons Driving Store Traffic," *Chain Store Age* 73(9) (September, 1997): 127–8.

Chapter 8

1. "India End at 112," *Indian Express* (December 24, 1997): 15.
2. Warren Shoulberg, "Mall People," *Home Textiles Today* 18(49) (August 18, 1997): 16; "The Malling of America," *Quirk's Marketing Research Review* (May 1990): 15.
3. Ken Gofton, "If It Moves Measure It," *Marketing* (Marketing Technique Supplement) (September 4, 1997): 17; Jum C. Nunnally, *Psychometric Theory*, 2nd ed. (New York: McGraw-Hill, 1978): 3.
4. V. Srinivasan and Chan Su Park, "Surprising Robustness of the Self-Explicated Approach to Customer Preference Structure Measurement," *Journal of Marketing Research* 34 (May 1997): 286–91; Stanley S. Stevens, "Mathematics, Measurement and Psychophysics," in Stanley S. Steven (ed.), *Handbook of Experimental Psychology* (New York: John Wiley, 1951).

5. Wade D. Cook, Moshe Kress, and Lawrence M. Seiford, "On the Use of Ordinal Data in Data Envelopment Analysis," *Journal of the Operational Research Society* 44(2) (February 1993): 133–40; William D. Perreault Jr. and Forrest W. Young, "Alternating Least Squares Optimal Scaling: Analysis of Nonmetric Data in Marketing Research," *Journal of Marketing Research* 17 (February 1980): 1–13.
6. Anne Fisher, "The World's Most Admired Companies," *Fortune* 136(8) (October 27, 1997): 220. Used with permission of *Fortune* magazine. All rights reserved.
7. Michael Lynn and Judy Harris, "The Desire for Unique Consumer Products: A New Individual Difference Scale," *Psychology & Marketing* 14(6) (September 1997): 601–16.
8. For a discussion of these scales, refer to Christian Genest and Shuang-Shuang Zhang, "A Graphical Analysis of Ratio-Scaled Paired Comparison Data," *Management Science* 42(3) (March 1996): 335–49; C. H. Coombs, "Theory and Methods of Social Measurement," in L. Festinger and D. Katz (eds.), *Research Methods in the Behavioral Sciences* (New York: Holt, Rinehart & Winston, 1953).
9. However, there is some controversy regarding this issue. See Moonsig Kang and Antonie Stam, "PAHAP: A Pairwise Aggregated Hierarchical Analysis of Ratio-Scale Preferences," *Decision Sciences* 25(4) (July/August 1994): 607–24.
10. Deborah L. Kellogg and Richard B. Chase, "Constructing an Empirically Derived Measure for Customer Contact," *Management Science* 41(11) (November 1995): 1734–49; Kim P. Corfman, "Comparability and Comparison Levels Used in Choices among Consumer Products," *Journal of Marketing Research* 28 (August 1991): 368–74.
11. Leah Rickard, "Remembering New Coke," *Advertising Age* 66(16) (April 17, 1995): 6; "Coke's Flip-Flop Underscores Risks of Consumer Taste Tests," *Wall Street Journal* (July 18, 1985): 25.
12. However, it is not necessary to evaluate all possible pairs of objects. Procedures such as cyclic designs can significantly reduce the number of pairs evaluated. A treatment of such procedures may be found in Naresh K. Malhotra, Arun K. Jain, and Christian Pinson, "The Robustness of MDS Configurations in the Case of Incomplete Data," *Journal of Marketing Research* 25 (February 1988): 95–102.
13. For an advanced application involving paired comparison data see Christian Genest and Shuang-Shuang Zhang, "A Graphical Analysis of Ratio-Scaled Paired Comparison Data," *Management Science* 42(3) (March 1996): 335–49.
14. Rensis Likert, Sydney Roslow, and Gardner Murphy, "A Simple and Reliable Method of Scoring the Thurstone Attitude Scales," *Personnel Psychology* 46(3) (Autumn 1993): 689–90; L. L. Thurstone, *The Measurement of Values* (Chicago: University of Chicago Press, 1959). For an application of the case V procedure, see Naresh K. Malhotra, "Marketing Linen Services to Hospitals: A Conceptual Framework and an Empirical Investigation Using Thurstone's Case V Analysis," *Journal of Health Care Marketing* 6 (March 1986): 43–50.
15. Thomas T. Semon, "Design of Taste Tests Depends on Product, Research Purpose," *Marketing News* 28(19) (September 12, 1994): 5, 14; Tim Davis, "Taste Tests: Are the Blind Leading the Blind?" *Beverage World* (April 1987): 43–48, 85.
16. Michael W. Herman and Waldemar W. Koczkodaj, "A Monte Carlo Study of Pairwise Comparison," *Information Processing Letters* 57(1) (January 15, 1996): 25–29.
17. Noel M. Noel and Nessim Hanna, "Benchmarking Consumer Perceptions of Product Quality with Price: An Exploration," *Psychology & Marketing* 13(6) (September 1996): 591–604; E. Jan-Benedict, M. Steenkamp, and Dick R. Wittink, "The Metric Quality of Full-Profile Judgments and the Number of Attribute Levels Effect in Conjoint Analysis," *International Journal of Research in Marketing* 11(3) (June 1994): 275–86.
18. For recent applications of verbal protocols see David A. Harrison, Mary E. McLaughlin, and Terry M. Coalter, "Context, Cognition, and Common Method Variance: Psychometric Properties and Verbal Protocol Evidence," *Organizational Behavior & Human Decision Processes* 68(3) (December 1996): 246–61; S. F. Gardial, D. S. Clemons, R. B. Woodruff, D. W. Schumann, and M. J. Burns, "Comparing Consumers' Recall of Prepurchase and Postpurchase Product Evaluation Experiences," *Journal of Consumer Research* 20 (March 1994): 548–60.
19. David Glen Mick, "Levels of Subjective Comprehension in Advertising Processing and Their Relations to Ad Perceptions, Attitudes, and Memory," *Journal of Consumer Research* 18 (March 1992): 411–24; Peter L. Wright, "Cognitive Processes Mediating Acceptance of Advertising," *Journal of Marketing Research* 10 (February 1973): 53–62; Peter L. Wright, "Cognitive Responses to Mass Media Advocacy and Cognitive Choice Processes," in R. Petty, T. Ostrum, and T. Brock (eds.), *Cognitive Responses to Persuasion* (New York: McGraw-Hill, 1978).
20. Joseph Marinelli and Anastasia Schleck, "Collecting, Processing Data for Marketing Research Worldwide," *Marketing News* (August 18, 1997): 12, 14; Naresh K. Malhotra, "A Methodology for Measuring Consumer Preferences in Developing Countries," *International Marketing Review* 5 (Autumn 1988): 52–66.
21. Rachel Miller, "On the Right Track," *Marketing* (October 9, 1997): 29–31; *Business Week* (December 14, 1992).
22. I. P. Akaah, "Differences in Research Ethics Judgments between Male and Female Marketing Professionals," *Journal of Business Ethics* 8 (1989): 375–81. See also Anusorn Singhapakdi, Scott J. Vitell, Kumar C. Rallapalli, and Kenneth L. Kraft, "The Perceived Role of Ethics and Social Responsibility: A Scale Development," *Journal of Business Ethics* 15(11) (November 1996): 1131–40.
23. www.dominos.com.

Chapter 9

1. Chuck Ross, "TVB, Nielsen Examining TV Sweeps Alternatives," *Advertising Age* 68(19) (May 12, 1997): 10, 8; Douglas M. Stayman and David A. Aaker, "Continuous Measurement of Self-Report of Emotional Response," *Psychology & Marketing* 10(3) (May/June 1993): 199–214.
2. Heidi Tolliver, "A Tale of Four Cities: How Paris, London, Florence and New York Measure—and React—to What Riders Want," *Mass Transit* XXII (2) (March/April 1996): 22–30, 107.
3. Patrick Dalton, "What Would You Do?" *Bank Marketing* 28(2) (February 1996): 12, 49; "Americans Voice Opinions

on the Services Industry," *Marketing News* (November 20, 1987): 18.

4. Ian P. Murphy, "RAMS Helps Best Western Tout Worldwide Positioning," *Marketing News* 31(1) (January 6, 1996): 25.
5. ORTEK Data Systems, Inc.
6. G. Albaum, "The Likert Scale Revisited—An Alternate Version," *Journal of the Market Research Society* 39(2) (April 1997): 331–48; C. J. Brody and J. Dietz, "On the Dimensionality of 2-Question Format Likert Attitude Scales," *Social Science Research* 26(2) (June 1997): 197–204; Rensis Likert, "A Technique for the Measurement of Attitudes," *Archives of Psychology* 140(1932).
7. However, when the scale is multidimensional, each dimension should be summed separately. See Jennifer L. Aaker, "Dimensions of Brand Personality," *Journal of Marketing Research* 34 (August 1997): 347–56.
8. Joel Herche and Brian Engelland, "Reversed-Polarity Items and Scale Unidimensionality," *Journal of the Academy of Marketing Science* 24(4) (Fall 1996): 366–74.
9. John P. Walsh and Shu-Fen Tseng, "The Effects of Job Characteristics on Active Effort at Work," *Work & Occupations* 25(1) (February 1998): 74–96; George H. Lucas Jr., A. Parasuraman, Robert A. Davis, and Ben M. Enis, "An Empirical Study of Salesforce Turnover," *Journal of Marketing* 51 (July 1987): 34–59.
10. T. A. Chandler and C. J. Spies, "Semantic Differential Comparisons of Attributions and Dimensions Among Respondents From 7 Nations," *Psychological Reports* 79(3 pt 1) (December 1996): 747–758.
11. R. Millar and C. Brotherton, "Measuring the Effects of Career Interviews on Young People—A Preliminary Study," *Psychological Reports* 79(3 pt 2) (December 1996): 1207–215.
12. Naresh K. Malhotra, "A Scale to Measure Self-Concepts, Person Concepts and Product Concepts," *Journal of Marketing Research* 18 (November 1981): 456–64. See also Jennifer L. Aaker, "Dimensions of Brand Personality," *Journal of Marketing Research* 34 (August 1997): 347–56.
13. However, there is little difference in the results based on whether the data are ordinal or interval. See M. D. Garciapena, et al., "Development and Validation of an Inventory for Measuring Job Satisfaction among Family Physicians," *Psychological Reports* 79(1) (August 1996): 291–301; John Gaiton, "Measurement Scales and Statistics: Resurgence of an Old Misconception," *Psychological Bulletin* 87 (1980): 564–67.
14. Timothy H. Reisenwitz and G. Joseph Wimbish Jr., "Over-the-Counter Pharmaceuticals: Exploratory Research of Consumer Preferences Toward Solid Oral Dosage Forms," *Health Marketing Quarterly* 13(4) (1996): 47–61; S. Malhotra, S. Van Auken, and S. C. Lonial, "Adjective Profiles in Television Copy Testing," *Journal of Advertising Research* (August 1981): 21–25.
15. Jan Stapel, "About 35 Years of Market Research in the Netherlands," *Markonderzock Kwartaalschrift* 2 (1969): 3–7.
16. Robert F. Devellis, *Scale Development: Theories and Applications* (Thousand Oaks, CA: Sage Publications, 1991); Michael J. Etzel, Terrell G. Williams, John C. Rogers, and Douglas J. Lincoln, "The Comparability of Three Stapel Scale Forms in a Marketing Setting," in Ronald F. Bush and Shelby D. Hunt (eds.), *Marketing Theory: Philosophy of Science Perspectives* (Chicago: American Marketing Association, 1982): 303–06.
17. A. M. Coleman, C. E. Norris, and C. C. Peterson, "Comparing Rating Scales of Different Lengths—Equivalence of Scores from 5-Point and 7-Point Scales," *Psychological Reports* 80(2) (April 1997): 355–62; Madhubalan Viswanathan, Mark Bergen, and Terry Childers, "Does a Single Response Category in a Scale Completely Capture a Response?" *Psychology & Marketing* 13(5) (August 1996): 457–79; Eli P. Cox III, "The Optimal Number of Response Alternatives for a Scale: A Review," *Journal of Marketing Research* 17 (November 1980): 407–22.
18. D. F. Alwin, "Feeling Thermometers versus 7-Point Scales—Which Are Better," *Sociological Methods & Research* 25(3) (February 1997): 318–40; M. M. Givon and Z. Shapira, "Response to Rating Scales: A Theoretical Model and Its Application to the Number of Categories Problem," *Journal of Marketing Research* (November 1984): 410–19; D. E. Stem Jr. and S. Noazin, "The Effects of Number of Objects and Scale Positions on Graphic Position Scale Reliability," in R. F. Lusch, et al., *1985 AMA Educators' Proceedings* (Chicago: American Marketing Association, 1985): 370–72.
19. D. Watson, "Correcting for Acquiescent Response Bias in the Absence of a Balanced Scale—An Application to Class-Consciousness," *Sociological Methods & Research* 21(1) (August 1992): 52–88; H. Schuman and S. Presser, *Questions and Answers in Attitude Surveys* (New York: Academic Press, 1981): 179–201.
20. G. J. Spagna, "Questionnaires: Which Approach Do You Use?" *Journal of Advertising Research* (February–March 1984): 67–70.
21. Kathy A. Hanisch, "The Job Descriptive Index Revisited: Questions about the Question Mark," *Journal of Applied Psychology* 77(3) (June 1992): 377–82; and K. C. Schneider, "Uninformed Response Rate in Survey Research," *Journal of Business Research* (April 1985): 153–62.
22. K. M. Gannon and T. M. Ostrom, "How Meaning is Given to Rating Scales—The Effects of Response Language on Category Activation," *Journal of Experimental Social Psychology* 32(4) (July 1996): 337–60; H. H. Friedman and J. R. Leefer, "Label versus Position in Rating Scales," *Journal of the Academy of Marketing Science* (Spring 1981): 88–92.
23. D. F. Alwin, "Feeling Thermometers versus 7-Point Scales—Which Are Better," *Sociological Methods & Research* 25(3) (February 1997): 318–40.
24. For a recent construction of a multiitem scales, see Jennifer L. Aaker, "Dimensions of Brand Personality," *Journal of Marketing Research* 34 (August 1997): 347–56.
25. For example, see Anusorn Singhapakdi, Scott J. Vitell, Kumar C. Rallapalli, and Kenneth L. Kraft, "The Perceived Role of Ethics and Social Responsibility: A Scale Development," *Journal of Business Ethics* 15(11) (November 1996): 1131–40.
26. Stephania H. Davis, "Smart Products for Smart Marketing," *Telephony* 34(9) (March 2, 1998): 66; Erin Anderson, Wujin Chu, and Barton Weitz, "Industrial Purchasing: An Empirical Exploration of the Buyclass Framework," *Journal of Marketing* 51 (July 1987): 71–86.
27. K. Kim and Gary L. Frazier, "Measurement of Distributor Commitment in Industrial Channels of Distribution," *Journal*

of Business Research 40(2) (October 1997): 139–54; Eric A. Greenleaf, "Improving Rating Scale Measures by Detecting and Correcting Bias Components in Some Response Styles," *Journal of Marketing Research* 29 (May 1992): 176–88.

28. E. J. Wilson, "Research Design Effects on the Reliability of Rating Scales in Marketing—An Update on Churchill and Peter," *Advances in Consumer Research* 22 (1995): 360–65; William D. Perreault Jr. and Laurence E. Leigh, "Reliability of Nominal Data Based on Qualitative Judgments," *Journal of Marketing Research* 25 (May 1989): 135–48; J. Paul Peter, "Reliability: A Review of Psychometric Basics and Recent Marketing Practices," *Journal of Marketing Research* 16 (February 1979): 6–17.
29. Simon S. K. Lam and Ka S. Woo, "Measuring Service Quality: A Test-Retest Reliability Investigation of SERVQUAL," *Journal of the Market Research Society* 39(2) (April 1997): 381–96.
30. David Armstrong, Ann Gosling, John Weinman, and Theresa Marteau, "The Place of Inter-Rater Reliability in Qualitative Research: An Empirical Study," *Sociology: The Journal of the British Sociological Association* 31(3) (August 1997): 597–606; M. N. Segal, "Alternate Form Conjoint Reliability," *Journal of Advertising Research* 4 (1984): 31–8.
31. Robert A. Peterson, "A Meta-Analysis of Chronbach's Coefficient Alpha," *Journal of Consumer Research* 21 (September 1994): 381–91; L. J Cronbach, "Coefficient Alpha and the Internal Structure of Tests," *Psychometrika* 16 (1951): 297–334.
32. David M. Zeitlin and Richard A. Westwood, "Measuring Emotional Response," *Journal of Advertising Research* (October–November 1986): 34–44.
33. D. G. McTavish, "Scale Validity—A Computer Content-Analysis Approach," *Social Science Computer Review* 15(4) (Winter 1997): 379–93; Peter, J. Paul, "Construct Validity: A Review of Basic Issues and Marketing Practices," *Journal of Marketing Research* 18 (May 1981): 133–45.
34. For further details on validity, see M. Joseph Sirgy, Dhruv Grewal, Tamara F. Mangleburg, Jae-ok Park, et al., "Assessing the Predictive Validity of Two Methods of Measuring Self-Image Congruence," *Journal of the Academy of Marketing Science* 25(3) (Summer 1997): 229–41; Rosann L. Spiro and Barton A. Weitz, "Adaptive Selling: Conceptualization, Measurement, and Nomological Validity," *Journal of Marketing Research* 27 (February 1990): 61–9.
35. For a discussion of generalizability theory and its applications in marketing research, see Shuzo Abe, Richard P. Bagozzi, and Pradip Sadarangani, "An Investigation of Construct Validity and Generalizability of the Self-Concept: Self-Consciousness in Japan and the United States," *Journal of International Consumer Marketing* 8(3, 4) (1996): 97–123; Joseph O. Rentz, "Generalizability Theory: A Comprehensive Method for Assessing and Improving the Dependability of Marketing Measures," *Journal of Marketing Research* 24 (February 1987): 19–28.
36. Timothy R. Hinkin, "A Review of Scale Development Practices in the Study of Organizations," *Journal of Management* 21(5) (1995): 967–88.
37. Michael R. Mullen, George R. Milne, and Nicholas M. Didow, "Determining Cross-Cultural Metric Equivalence in Survey Research: A New Statistical Test," *Advances in International Marketing* 8 (1996): 145–57; E. Gencturk, T. L. Childers, and R. W. Ruekert, "International Marketing Involvement—The Construct, Dimensionality, and Measurement," *Journal of International Marketing* 3(4) (1995): 11–37.
38. Alan L. Unikel, "Imitation Might Be Flattering, but Beware of Trademark Infringement," *Marketing News* 21(19) (September 11, 1997): 20021; Betsy Mckay, "Xerox Fights Trademark Battle," *Advertising Age International* (April 27,1992): 1–39.
39. Scott J. Vitell and Foo Nin Ho, "Ethical Decision Making in Marketing: A Synthesis and Evaluation of Scales Measuring the Various Components of Decision Making in Ethical Situations," *Journal of Business Ethics* 16(7) (May 1997): 699–717; R. E. Reidenbach and Donald P. Robin, "Some Initial Steps toward Improving the Measurement of Ethical Evaluations of Marketing Activities," *Journal of Business Ethics* 7 (1988): 871–9; and R. Eric Reidenbach and Donald P. Robin, "A Response to 'On Measuring Ethical Judgments'," *Journal of Business Ethics* 14 (February 1995): 159–62.

Chapter 10

1. Shari Sanders, "Kids & Teens Show Who's Boss in Purchasing Power," *Discount Store News* 34(7) (April 3, 1995): 22, 30.
2. "Channel 5 Scores with Child Viewers," *Marketing Week* 20(45) (February 19, 1998): 14; Joseph Rydholm, "Omnibus Study Talks to Kids," *Quirk's Marketing Research Review* 5, 6 (June/July 1991): 42, 41.
3. S. L. Payne, *The Art of Asking Questions* (Princeton, NJ: Princeton University Press, 1951).
4. These guidelines are drawn from several books on questionnaire design. See for example, Howard Schuman and Stanley Presser, *Questions & Answers in Attitude Survey* (Thousand Oaks, CA: Sage Publications, 1996); Arlene Fink, *How to Ask Survey Questions* (Thousand Oaks, CA: Sage Publications, 1995); Floyd J. Fowler Jr., *Improving Survey Questions* (Thousand Oaks, CA: Sage Publications, 1995).
5. Howard Schuman and Stanley Presser, *Questions & Answers in Attitude Survey* (Thousand Oaks, CA: Sage Publications, 1996); Jagdip Singh, Roy D. Howell, and Gary K. Rhoads, "Adaptive Designs for Likert-Type Data: An Approach for Implementing Marketing Surveys," *Journal of Marketing Research* 27 (August 1990): 304–21.
6. Linda B. Bourque and Eve P. Fielder, *How to Conduct Self-Administered and Mail Surveys* (Thousand Oaks, CA: Sage Publications, 1995); James H. Frey and Sabine M. Oishi, *How to Conduct Interviews by Telephone and in Person* (Thousand Oaks, CA: Sage Publications, 1995).
7. Thomas T. Semon, "Asking 'How Important' Is Not Enough," *Marketing News* 31(16) (August 4, 1997): 19.
8. "Brand Imaging Drives Niketown," *Chain Store Age* 72(4) (April 1996): 46–54.
9. Arthur Sterngold, Rex H. Warland, and Robert O. Hermann, "Do Surveys Overstate Public Concerns?" *Public Opinion Quarterly* 58(20) (Summer 1994): 255–63; D. I. Hawkins and K. A. Coney, "Uninformed Response Error in Survey Research," *Journal of Marketing Research* (August 1981): 373.

10. Jan Stapel, "Observations: A Brief Observation about Likability and Interestingness of Advertising," *Journal of Advertising Research* 34(2) (March/April 1994): 79–80; George F. Bishop, Robert W. Oldendick, and Alfred J. Tuchfarber, "Effects of Filter Questions in Public Opinion Surveys," *Public Opinion Quarterly* 46 (Spring 1982): 66–85.
11. Kenneth C. Schneider and James C. Johnson, "Link between Response-Inducing Strategies and Uninformed Response," *Marketing Intelligence & Planning* 12(1) (1994): 29–36.
12. Solomon Dutka and Lester R. Frankel "Measuring Response Error," *Journal of Advertising Research* 37(1) (January/February 1997): 33–9; Terry Haller, *Danger: Marketing Researcher at Work* (Westport, CT: Quorum Books, 1983): 149.
13. Geeta Menon, Priya Raghubir, and Norbert Schwarz, "Behavioral Frequency Judgments: An Accessibility-Diagnosticity Framework," *Journal of Consumer Research* 22(2) (September 1995): 212–28; William A. Cook, "Telescoping and Memory's Other Tricks," *Journal of Advertising Research* (February–March 1987): 5–8.
14. R. P. Hill, "Researching Sensitive Topics in Marketing—The Special Case of Vulnerable Populations," *Journal of Public Policy & Marketing* 14(1) (Spring 1995): 143–8.
15. Roger Tourangeau and Tom W. Smith, "Asking Sensitive Questions: The Impact of Data Collection Mode, Question Format, and Question Context," *Public Opinion Quarterly* 60(20) (Summer 1996): 275–304; Kent H. Marquis, et al., *Response Errors in Sensitive Topic Survey: Estimates, Effects, and Correction Options* (Santa Monica, CA: Rand Corporation, 1981).
16. Priya Raghubir and Geeta Menon, "Asking Sensitive Questions: The Effects of Type of Referent and Frequency Wording in Counterbiasing Methods," *Psychology & Marketing* 13(7) (October 1996): 633–52.
17. For a recent application, see Brian K. Burton and Janet P. Near, "Estimating the Incidence of Wrongdoing and Whistle-Blowing: Results of a Study Using Randomized Response Technique," *Journal of Business Ethics* 14 (January 1995): 17–30.
18. P. Mukhopadhyay, "A Note on UMVU-Estimation under Randomized-Response Model," *Communications in Statistics—Theory and Methods* 26(10) (1997): 2415–20; D. E. Stem Jr. and R. K. Steinhorst, "Telephone Interview and Mail Questionnaire Applications of the Randomized Response Model," *Journal of the American Statistical Association* (September 1984): 555–64.
19. Lynn M. Newman, "That's a Good Question," *American Demographics* (Marketing Tools) (June 1995): 10–13.
20. Serge Luyens, "Coding Verbatims by Computers," *Marketing Research: A Magazine of Management & Applications* 7(2) (Spring 1995): 20–5.
21. Based on a marketing research project conducted by the author.
22. Kevin W. Mossholder, Randall P. Settoon, Stanley G. Harris, and Achilles A. Armenakis, "Measuring Emotion in Open-Ended Survey Responses: An Application of Textual Data Analysis," *Journal of Management* 21(2) (1995): 335–55.
23. Floyd J. Fowler Jr., *Improving Survey Questions* (Thousand Oaks, CA: Sage Publications, 1995); Jon A. Krosnick and Duane F. Alwin, "An Evaluation of a Cognitive Theory of Response-Order Effects in Survey Measurement," *Public Opinion Quarterly* (Summer 1987): 201–19.
24. Niels J. Blunch, "Position Bias in Multiple-Choice Questions," *Journal of Marketing Research* 21 (May 1984): 216–20, has argued that position bias in multiple-choice questions cannot be eliminated by rotating the order of the alternatives. This viewpoint is contrary to the common practice.
25. Howard Schuman and Stanley Presser, *Questions & Answers in Attitude Survey* (Thousand Oaks, CA: Sage Publications, 1996).
26. Joseph A. Herriges and Jason F. Shogren, "Starting Point Bias in Dichotomous Choice Valuation with Follow-up Questioning," *Journal of Environmental Economics & Management* 30(1) (January 1996): 112–31; R. W. Mizerski, J. B. Freiden, and R. C. Green Jr., "The Effect of the 'Don't Know' Option on TV Ad Claim Recognition Tests," in *Advances in Consumer Research* 10 (Association for Consumer Research, 1983); 283–7.
27. Michael McBurnett, "Wording of Questions Affects Responses to Gun Control Issue," *Marketing News* 31(1) (January 6, 1997): 12; M. Wanke, N. Schwarz, and E. Noelle-Neumann, "Asking Comparative Questions: The Impact of the Direction of Comparison," *Public Opinion Quarterly* 59(3) (Fall 1995): 347–72.
28. J. F. Etter and T. V. Perneger, "Analysis of Nonresponse Bias in a Mailed Health Survey," *Journal of Clinical Epidemiology* 50(10) (October 1997): 1123–28; G. S. Omura, "Correlates of Item Nonresponse," *Journal of the Market Research Society* (October 1983): 321–30; S. Presser, "Is Inaccuracy on Factual Survey Items Item-Specific or Respondent-Specific?" *Public Opinion Quarterly* (Spring 1984): 344–55.
29. Nancy Johnson Stout, "Questionnaire Design Workshop Helps Market Researchers Build Better Surveys," *Health Care Strategic Management* 12(7) (July 1994): 10–11.
30. Lida C. Saltz, "How to Get Your News Release Published," *Journal of Accountancy* 182(5) (November 1996): 89–91.
31. Brad Edmondson, "How to Spot a Bogus Poll," *American Demographics* 8(10) (October 1996): 10–15; John O'Brien, "How Do Market Researchers Ask Questions?" *Journal of the Market Research Society* 26 (April 1984): 93–107.
32. Thomas T. Semon, "Ask Simple Question to Improve Analysis of Value Perception," *Marketing News* 29(5) (February 27, 1995): 32.
33. Paul R. Abramson and Charles W. Ostrom, "Question Wording and Partisanship," *Public Opinion Quarterly* 58(1) (Spring 1994): 21–48.
34. "Don't Lead: You May Skew Poll Results," *Marketing News* 30(12) (June 3, 1996): H37.
35. Raymond J. Adamek, "Public Opinion and Roe v. Wade: Measurement Difficulties," *Public Opinion Quarterly* 58(3) (Fall 1994): 409–18; E. Noelle-Neumann and B. Worcester, "International Opinion Research," *European Research* (July 1984): 124–31.
36. Jacob Jacoby and George J. Szybillo, "Consumer Research in FTC versus Kraft (1991): A Case of Heads We Win, Tails You Lose?" *Journal of Public Policy & Marketing* 14(1) (Spring 1995): 1–14; E. D. Jaffe and I. D. Nebenzahl, "Alternative Questionnaire Formats for Country Image Studies," *Journal of Marketing Research* (November 1984): 463–71.

37. Howard Schuman and Stanley Presser, *Questions & Answers in Attitude Survey* (Thousand Oaks, CA: Sage Publications, 1996); Jon A. Krosnick and Duane F. Alwin, "An Evaluation of a Cognitive Theory of Response-Order Effects in Survey Measurement," *Public Opinion Quarterly* (Summer 1987): 201–19.
38. Rating a brand on specific attributes early in a survey may affect responses to a later overall brand evaluation. For example, see Barbara A. Bickart, "Carryover and Backfire Effects in Marketing Research," *Journal of Marketing Research* 30 (February 1993): 52–62. See also Ian McAllister and Martin P. Wattenberg, "Measuring Levels of Party Identification: Does Question Order Matter?" *Public Opinion Quarterly* 59(2) (Summer 1995): 259–68.
39. Fern K. Willits and Bin Ke, "Part–Whole Question Order Effects: Views of Rurality," *Public Opinion Quarterly* 59(3) (Fall 1995): 392–403; Donald J. Messmer and Daniel J. Seymour, "The Effects of Branching on Item Nonresponse," *Public Opinion Quarterly* 46 (Summer 1982): 270–77.
40. George R. Milne, "Consumer Participation in Mailing Lists: A Field Experiment," *Journal of Public Policy & Marketing* 16(2) (Fall 1997): 298–309.
41. Linda Friedman and Hershey H. Friedman, "A Comparison of Vertical and Horizontal Rating Scales," *Mid-Atlantic Journal of Business* 30(1) (March 1994): 107–11.
42. "A World Press Model Debuts," *Graphic Arts Monthly* 66(6) (June 1994): 66.
43. E. Martin and A. E. Polivka, "Diagnostics for Redesigning Survey Questionnaires—Measuring Work in the Current Population Survey," *Public Opinion Quarterly* 59(4) (Winter 1995): 547–67.
44. M. G. Mohrle, "Empirical Testing of a Computer-Based Dialog Questionnaire—11 Design Rules for Successful Usage," *Wirtschaftsinformatik* 39(5) (October 1997): 461.
45. Adamantios Diamantopoulos, Nina Reynolds, and Bodo B. Schlegelmilch, "Pretesting in Questionnaire Design: The Impact of Respondent Characteristics on Error Detection," *Journal of the Market Research Society* 36 (October 1994): 295–314.
46. Nina Reynolds, Adamantios Diamantopoulos, and Bodo B. Schlegelmilch, "Pretesting in Questionnaire Design: A Review of the Literature and Suggestions for Further Research," *Journal of the Market Research Society* 35 (April 1993): 171–82.
47. Jack Neff, "S. C. Johnson Sees Extension Opportunities with DowBrands," *Advertising Age* 68(44) (November 3, 1997): 17; Julie Skur Hill, "Japan Hatches New Brands for Johnson," *Advertising Age* (September 2, 1991): 36.
48. M. H. Morris, A. S. Marks, J. A. Allen, and N. S. Peery, "Modeling Ethical Attitudes and Behaviors under Conditions of Environmental Turbulence—Case of South Africa," *Journal of Business Ethics* 15(10) (October 1996): 1119–30; G. R. Laczniak and P. E. Murphy, *Ethical Marketing Decisions the Higher Road* (Needhan Heights, MA: Allyn and Bacon, 1993).
49. R. W. Armstrong, "The Relationship between Culture and Perception of Ethical Problems in International Marketing," *Journal of Business Ethics* 15(11) (November 1996): 1199–1208; R. W. Armstrong, "An Empirical Investigation of International Marketing Ethics: Problems Encountered by Australian Firms," *Journal of Business Ethics* 11(1992): 161–71.
50. Marshall Rice, "What Makes Users Revisit a Web Site?" *Marketing News* 31 (March 17, 1997): 12.

Chapter 11

1. Marc Gunther, "This Gang Controls Your Kids' Brains," *Fortune* 136(8) (October 27, 1997): 172–82.
2. Carol Krol, "Survey: Friends Lead Pack in Kids' Spending Decisions," *Advertising Age* 68(10) (March 10, 1997): 16; The Warner-Lambert Company, The American Chicle Youth Poll.
3. V. Verma and T. Le, "An Analysis of Sampling Errors for the Demographic and Health Surveys," *International Statistical Review* 64(3) (December 1966): 265–94; H. Assael and J. Keon, "Nonsampling versus Sampling Errors in Sampling Research," *Journal of Marketing* (Spring 1982): 114–23.
4. Barbara A. Bailar, "Does Sampling Work?" *Business Economics* 32(1) (January 1997): 47–53; "Frequently Asked Questions about Census 2000," *Indiana Business Review* 72(8) (Summer 1997): 10.
5. Arlene Fink, *How to Sample in Surveys* (Thousand Oaks, CA: Sage Publications, 1995); Martin R. Frankel, "Sampling Theory," in Peter H. Rossi, James D. Wright, and Andy B. Anderson (eds.), *Handbook of Survey Research* (Orlando, FL: Academic Press, 1983): 21–67; R. M. Jaeger, *Sampling in Education and the Social Sciences* (New York: Longman, 1984): 28–9.
6. Gary T. Henry, *Practical Sampling* (Thousand Oaks, CA: Sage Publications, 1995); Seymour Sudman, "Applied Sampling," in Peter H. Rossi, James D. Wright, and Andy B. Anderson (eds.), *Handbook of Survey Research* (Orlando, FL: Academic Press, 1983): 145–94.
7. Robert Cage, "New Methodology for Selecting CPI Outlet Samples," *Monthly Labor Review* 119(12) (December 1996): 49–83.
8. Wayne Smith, Paul Mitchell, Karin Attebo, and Stephen Leeder, "Selection Bias from Sampling Frames: Telephone Directory and Electoral Roll Compared with Door-to-Door Population Census: Results from the Blue Mountain Eye Study," *Australian & New Zealand Journal of Public Health* 21(2) (April 1997): 127–33.
9. For the effect of sample frame error on research results, see Kelly E. Fish, James H. Barnes, and Benjamin F. Banahan III, "Convenience or Calamity: Pharmaceutical Study Explores the Effects of Sample Frame Error on Research Results," *Journal of Health Care Marketing* 14 (Spring 1994): 45–9.
10. "The Many Faces of Florida," *Association Management* (A Guide to Florida Supplement) (April 1997): 3; "Florida Travel Habits Subject of Phone Survey," *Quirk's Marketing Research Review* (May 1987): 10, 11, 31, 56, 60.
11. For a recent application of convenience sampling see Nin Foo Ho, Beng Soo Ong, and Seonsu, "A Multicultural Comparison of Shopping Patterns among Asian Consumers," *Journal of Marketing Theory & Practice* 5(1) (Winter 1997): 42–51.
12. Richard Zelade, "Money Isn't Quite Everything," *International Business* 10(4) (May/June 1997): 9; "Students Seek

Good Careers, Successful Marriages," *Quirk's Marketing Research Review* (June–July 1988): 26.

13. Brian OToole, "Have You Had Your Quota of Nearest Birthdays," *Australian & New Zealand Journal of Public Health* 21(2) (April 1997): 117–19; Catherine Marsh and E. Scarbrough, "Testing Nine Hypotheses about Quota Sampling," *Journal of Market Research Society* (UK), 32 (October 1990): 485–506; Leslie Kish, *Survey Sampling* (New York: John Wiley, 1965): 552.
14. John Curtice and Nick Sparrow, "How Accurate Are Traditional Quota Opinion Polls," *Journal of the Market Research Society* 39(3) (July 1997): 433–48.
15. "Public Opinion: Polls Apart," *Economist* 336(7927) (August 12, 1995): 48; Seymour Sudman, "Improving the Quality of Shopping Center Sampling," *Journal of Marketing Research* 17 (November 1980): 423–31.
16. For a recent application of snowball sampling, see Gary L. Frankwick, James C. Ward, Michael D. Hutt, and Peter H. Reingen, "Evolving Patterns of Organizational Beliefs in the Formation of Strategy," *Journal of Marketing* 58 (April 1994): 96–110.
17. If certain procedures for listing members of the rare population are followed strictly, the snowball sample can be treated as a probability sample. See Gary T. Henry, *Practical Sampling* (Thousand Oaks, CA: Sage Publications, 1995); Graham Kalton and Dallas W. Anderson. "Sampling Rare Populations," *Journal of the Royal Statistical Association* (1986): 65–82.
18. Gale D. Muller and Jane Miller, "Interviewers Make the Difference," *Marketing Research: A Magazine of Management & Applications* 8(1) (Spring 1996): 8–9; Raymond F. Barker, "A Demographic Profile of Marketing Research Interviewers," *Journal of the Market Research Society* (July 1987): 279–92.
19. When the sampling interval, *i*, is not a whole number, the easiest solution is to use as the interval the nearest whole number below or above *i*. If rounding has too great an effect on the sample size, add or delete the extra cases.
20. For recent applications of systematic random sampling, see Hailin Qu and Isabella Li, "The Characteristics and Satisfaction of Mainland Chinese Visitors to Hong Kong," *Journal of Travel Research* 35(4) (Spring 1997): 37–41; Goutam Chakraborty, Richard Ettenson, and Gary Gaeth, "How Consumers Choose Health Insurance," *Journal of Health Care Marketing* 14 (Spring 1994): 21–33.
21. Mark Adams, "Court Marshall," *Mediaweek* 6(12) (March 18, 1996): 22; "Readership Survey Serves *Tennis* Magazine's Marketing Needs," *Quirk's Marketing Research Review* (May 1988): 75–6.
22. For a recent application of stratified random sampling, see Samaradasa Weerahandi and Soumyo Moitra, "Using Survey Data to Predict Adoption and Switching for Services," *Journal of Marketing Research* 32 (February 1995): 85–96.
23. "Purchasing Smarts Pay Off in Travel Buying," *Purchasing* 121(9) (December 12, 1996): 30–1; "Vacations High Priority Among Americans, Survey Shows," *Quirk's Marketing Research Review* (May 1988): 16–19.
24. "Niche Marketing to the Wealthy," *Health Care Strategic Management* 15(9) (September 1997): 12; Thomas J. Stanley and Murphy A. Sewall, "The Response of Affluent Consumers to Mail Surveys," *Journal of Advertising Research* (June–July 1986): 55–8.
25. Geographic clustering of rare populations, however, can be an advantage. See James C. Raymondo, "Confessions of a Nielsen Household," *American Demographics* 19(3) (March 1997): 24–7; Seymour Sudman, "Efficient Screening Methods for the Sampling of Geographically Clustered Special Populations," *Journal of Marketing Research* 22 (February 1985): 20–9.
26. June S. Park, Michael Peters, and Kwei Tang, "Optimal Inspection Policy in Sequential Screening," *Management Science* 37(8) (August 1991): 1058–61; E. J. Anderson, K. Gorton, and R. Tudor, "The Application of Sequential Analysis in Market Research," *Journal of Marketing Research* 17 (February 1980): 97–105.
27. For more discussion of double sampling, see David H. Baillie, "Double Sampling Plans for Inspection by Variables When the Process Standard Deviation Is Unknown," *International Journal of Quality & Reliability Management* 9(5) (1992): 59–70; Martin R. Frankel and Lester R. Frankel, "Probability Sampling," in Robert Ferber (ed.), *Handbook of Marketing Research* (New York: McGraw-Hill, 1974): 2-230–2-246.
28. Steven Murphy, "Moving Targets," *Business Latin America* 31(13) (April 1, 1996): 4–5. For the use of different nonprobability and probability sampling techniques in cross-cultural research, see Samiee Saeed and Insik Jeong, "Cross-Cultural Research in Advertising: An Assessment of Methodologies," *Journal of the Academy of Marketing Science* 22 (Summer 1994): 205–15.
29. Margaret E. Grosh and Paul Glewwe, "Household Survey Data from Developing Countries: Progress and Prospects," *American Economic Review* 86(2) (May 1996): 15–19.
30. Taylor Humphrey, "Horses for Courses: How Survey Firms in Different Countries Measure Public Opinion with Different Methods," *Journal of the Market Research Society* 37(3) (July 1995): 211–19; B. J. Verhage, U. Yavas, R. T. Green, and E. Borak, "The Perceived Risk Brand Loyalty Relationship: An International Perspective," *Journal of Global Marketing* 3(3) (1990): 7–22.
31. Satish P. Deshpande, "Managers' Perception of Proper Ethical Conduct: The Effect of Sex, Age, and Level of Education," *Journal of Business Ethics* 16(1) (January 1997): 79–85; I. P. Akaah, "Differences in Research Ethics Judgments between Male and Female Marketing Professionals," *Journal of Business Ethics* 8 (1989): 375–81.
32. Marshall Rice, "What Makes Users Revisit a Web Site?" *Marketing News* 31 (March 17, 1997): 12.

Chapter 12

1. Jan Larson, "The Bicycle Market," *American Demographics* 17(3) (March 1995) 42–8; and *Bicycling* magazine, *Bicycling Magazine's 1997 Semiannual Study of U.S. Retail Bicycle Stores*. See also Ann M. Kerwin, "MRI Makes Sampling Changes," *The Magazine for Magazine Management* 26(3) (March 1, 1997): 15.
2. Bruce Nussbaum, "A Camera in a Wet Suit," *BusinessWeek* (June 2,1997): 109.
3. A discussion of the sampling distribution may be found in any basic statistics textbook. For example, see Mark L.

1997): 28; Laurel Wentz, "Poll: Europe Favors U.S. Products," *Advertising Age* (September 23, 1991).

22. James E. Nelson and Pamela L. Kiecker, "Marketing Research Interviewers and Their Perceived Necessity of Moral Compromise," *Journal of Business Ethics* 15(10) (October 1996): 1107–17.
23. Glen J. Nowak and Joseph Phelps, "Direct Marketing and the Use of Individual-Level Consumer Information: Determining How and When Privacy Matters," *Journal of Direct Marketing* 11(4) (Autumn 1997): 94–108.

Chapter 14

1. Kevin T. Higgins, "Never Ending Journey," *Marketing Management* 6(1) (Spring 1997): 4–7; Joann Harristhal, "Interviewer Tips," *Applied Marketing Research* 28 (Fall 1988): 42–45.
2. Kofi Q. Dadzie, "Demarketing Strategy in Shortage Marketing Environment," *Journal of the Academy of Marketing Science* (Spring 1989): 157–65. See also Fred Davidson, *Principles of Statistical Data Handling* (Thousand Oaks, CA: Sage Publications, 1996).
3. Colin McDonald, "Linguistic Coding—A New Solution to an Old Problem," *Journal of the Market Research Society* 38(4) (October 1996): 505–24; Philip S. Sidel, "Coding," in Robert Ferber (ed.), *Handbook of Marketing Research* (New York: McGraw-Hill, 1974): 2-178–2-199.
4. Arlene Fink, *How to Analyze Survey Data* (Thousand Oaks, CA: Sage Publications, 1995); Pamela L. Alreck and Robert B. Settle, *The Survey Research Handbook*, second edition (Homewood, IL: Irwin Professional Publishing, 1994).
5. Serge Luyens, "Coding Verbatims by Computer," *Marketing Research: A Magazine of Management & Applications* 7(2) (Spring 1995): 20–5.
6. Norman Frendberg, "Scanning Questionnaires Efficiently," *Marketing Research: A Magazine of Management & Applications* 5(2) (Spring 1993): 38–42.
7. Eric L. Einspruch, *An Introductory Guide to SPSS for Windows* (Thousand Oaks, CA: Sage Publications, 1998); Paul E. Spector, *SAS Programming for Researchers and Social Scientists* (Thousand Oaks, CA: Sage Publications, 1993); Mohamed Afzal Norat, "Software Reviews," *Economic Journal: The Journal of the Royal Economic Society* 107(442) (May 1997): 857–82.
8. Vicki A. Freedman and Douglas A. Wolf, "A Case Study on the Use of Multiple Imputation," *Demography* 32(3) (August 1995): 459–70; Naresh K. Malhotra, "Analyzing Marketing Research Data with Incomplete Information on the Dependent Variable," *Journal of Marketing Research* 24 (February 1987): 74–84.
9. A meaningful and practical value should be imputed. The value imputed should be a legitimate response code. For example, a mean of 3.86 may not be practical, if only single-digit response codes have been developed. In such cases, the mean should be rounded to the nearest integer.
10. Ali Kara, Christine Nielsen, Sundeep Sahay, and Nagaraj Sivasubramaniam, "Latent Information in the Pattern of Missing Observations in Global Mail Surveys," *Journal of Global Marketing* 7(4) (1994): 103–26; Naresh K. Malhotra, "Analyzing Marketing Research Data with Incomplete Information on the Dependent Variable," *Journal of Marketing Research* 24 (February 1987): 74–84.
11. Some weighting procedures require adjustments in subsequent data-analysis techniques. See Llan Yaniv, "Weighting and Trimming: Heuristics for Aggregating Judgments under Uncertainty," *Organizational Behavior & Human Decision Processes* 69(3) (March 1997): 237–49; Humphrey Taylor, "The Very Different Methods Used to Conduct Telephone Surveys of the Public," *Journal of the Market Research Society* 39(3) (July 1997): 421–32.
12. Rajiv M. Rao, "Nielsen's Internet Survey: Does It Carry Any Weight?" *Fortune* 133(5) (March 18, 1996): 24.
13. Arch G. Woodside, Robert L. Nielsen, Fred Walters, and Gale D. Muller, "Preference Segmentation of Health Care Services: The Old-Fashioneds, Value Conscious, Affluents, and Professional Want-It-Alls," *Journal of Health Care Marketing* (June 1988): 14–24. See also Rama Jayanti, "Affective Responses toward Service Providers: Implications for Service Encounters," *Health Marketing Quarterly* 14(1) (1996): 49–65.
14. See B. Swift, "Preparing Numerical Data," in Roger Sapsford and Victor Jupp (eds.), *Data Collection and Analysis* (Thousand Oaks, CA: Sage Publications, 1996); Ronald E. Frank, "Use of Transformations," *Journal of Marketing Research* (August 1966): 247–53, for specific transformations frequently used in marketing research.
15. Bivariate techniques have been included here with multivariate techniques. Whereas bivariate techniques are concerned with pairwise relationships, multivariate techniques examine more complex simultaneous relationships among phenomena. See Jacques Tacq, *Multivariate Analysis Techniques in Social Science Research Analysis* (Thousand Oaks, CA: Sage Publications, 1996).
16. Fred Davidson, *Principles of Statistical Data Handling* (Thousand Oaks, CA: Sage Publications, 1996). For a similar data analysis strategy, see Naresh K. Malhotra, "Modeling Store Choice Based on Censored Preference Data," *Journal of Retailing* (Summer 1986): 128–44.
17. J. Douglass Carroll and Paul E. Green, "Psychometric Methods in Marketing Research: Part II: Multidimensional Scaling," *Journal of Marketing Research* 34(2) (May 1997): 193–204.
18. David Kilburn, "Haagen-Dazs Is Flavor of Month," *Marketing Week* 20(23) (September 4, 1997): 30; Mark Maremont, "They're All Screaming for Haagen Dazs," *Business Week* (October 14, 1991).
19. Pertti Alasuutari, *Researching Culture* (Thousand Oaks, CA: Sage Publications, 1995); C. T. Tan, J. McCullough, and J. Teoh, "An Individual Analysis Approach to Cross-Cultural Research," in Melanie Wallendorf and Paul Anderson (eds.), *Advances in Consumer Research* 14 (Provo, UT: Association for Consumer Research, 1987): 394–7.
20. See for example, Lisa D. Spiller and Alexander J. Campbell, "The Use of International Direct Marketing by Small Businesses in Canada, Mexico, and the United States: A Comparative Analysis," *Journal of Direct Marketing* 8 (Winter 1994): 7–16; Mee-Kau Nyaw and Ignace Ng, "A Comparative Analysis of Ethical Beliefs: A Four Country Study," *Journal of Business Ethics* 13 (July 1994): 543–56.
21. Dianna L. Newman and Robert D. Brown, *Applied Ethics for Program Evaluation Analysis* (Thousand Oaks, CA:

Sage Publications, 1996); G. M. Zinkhan, M. Bisesi, and M. J. Saxton, "MBAs' Changing Attitudes toward Marketing Dilemmas: 1981–1987," *Journal of Business Ethics* 8 (1989): 963–74.

Chapter 15

1. Chow-Hou Wee, Mei-Lan Choong, and Siok-Kuan Tambyah, "Sex Role Portrayal in Television Advertising," *International Marketing Review* 12(1) (1995): 49–64; Mary C. Gilly, "Sex Roles in Advertising: A Comparison of Television Advertisements in Australia, Mexico, and the United States," *Journal of Marketing* 52 (April 1988): 75–85.
2. Melissa Dowling, "To Go Direct—or Not," *Catalog Age* 14(9) (September 1, 1997): 5; Troy A. Festervand, Don R. Snyder, and John D. Tsalikis, "Influence of Catalog vs. Store Shopping and Prior Satisfaction on Perceived Risk," *Journal of the Academy of Marketing Science* (Winter 1986): 28–36.
3. Saviour L. S. Nwachukwu, Scott J. Vitell Jr., Faye W. Gilbert, and James H. Barnes, "Ethics and Social Responsibility in Marketing: An Examination of the Ethical Evaluation of Advertising Strategies," *Journal of Business Research* 39(2) (June 1997): 107–18; Shelby D. Hunt and Lawrence B. Chonko, "Ethical Problems of Advertising Agency Executives," *Journal of Advertising* 16 (Fall 1987): 16–24.
4. For an application of frequencies and descriptive statistics, see Mary Jo Bitner, Bernard H. Booms, and Lois A. Mohr, "Critical Service Encounters: The Employee's Viewpoint," *Journal of Marketing* 58 (October 1994): 95–106.
5. See any introductory statistics book for a more detailed description of these statistics, for example, Mark L. Berenson and David M. Levine, *Basic Business Statistics: Concepts and Applications*, 6th ed., (Englewood Cliffs, NJ: Prentice Hall, 1996).
6. For our purposes, no distinction will be made between formal hypothesis testing and statistical inference by means of confidence intervals.
7. Thomas T. Semon, "Let's Hear It for Disaggregate Analysis," *Marketing News* 30(7) (March 25, 1996): 10. Excellent discussions of ways to analyze cross-tabulations can be found in O. Hellevik, *Introduction to Causal Analysis: Exploring Survey Data by Crosstabulation* (Beverly Hills, CA: Sage Publications, 1984).
8. Lawrence F. Feick, "Analyzing Marketing Research Data with Association Models," *Journal of Marketing Research* 21 (November 1984): 376–86. For a recent application, see Wagner A. Kamakura and Michel Wedel, "Statistical Data Fusion for Cross-Tabulation," *Journal of Marketing Research* 34(4) (November 1997): 485–98.
9. Wayne Lenell and Robert Boissoneau, "Using Causal-Comparative and Correlational Designs in Conducting Market Research," *Journal of Professional Services Marketing* 13(2) (1996): 59–69.
10. R. Mark Sirkin, *Statistics for the Social Sciences* (Thousand Oaks, CA: Sage Publications, 1994).
11. Marjorie A. Pett, *Nonparametric Statistics for Health Care Research* (Thousand Oaks, CA: Sage Publications, 1997). For a more extensive treatment see H. O. Lancaster, *The Chi-Squared Distribution* (New York: John Wiley, 1969).
12. Mark L. Berenson and David M. Levine, *Basic Business Statistics: Concepts and Applications*, 6th ed. (Upper Saddle River, NJ: Prentice Hall, 1996).
13. Some statisticians, however, disagree. They feel that a correction should not be applied. See, for example John E. Overall, "Power of Chi-Square Tests for 2 × 2 Contingency Tables with Small Expected Frequencies," *Psychological Bulletin* (January 1980): 132–5.
14. Significance tests and confidence intervals are also available for either asymmetric-lambda or symmetric-lambda. See L. A. Goodman and W. H. Kruskal, "Measures of Association for Cross Classification: Appropriate Sampling Theory," *Journal of the American Statistical Association* 88 (June 1963): 310–64.
15. Rohit Verma and John C. Goodale, "Statistical Power in Operations Management Research," *Journal of Operations Management* 13(2) (August 1995): 139–52; Michael Cowles and Caroline Davis, "On the Origins of the .05 Level of Statistical Significance," *American Psychologist* (May 1982): 553–8.
16. Technically, a null hypothesis cannot be accepted. It can be either rejected or not rejected. This distinction, however, is inconsequential in applied research.
17. The condition when the variances cannot be assumed to be equal is known as the Behrens-Fisher problem. There is some controversy over the best procedure in this case.
18. Anne L. Balazs, "Positioning the Retail Shopping Center for Aging Customers," *Stores* 77(4) (April 1995): RR10–RR11; James R. Lumpkin and James B. Hunt, "Mobility as an Influence on Retail Patronage Behavior of the Elderly: Testing Conventional Wisdom," *Journal of the Academy of Marketing Science* (Winter 1989): 1–12.
19. Eleftheria Parpis, "Playing for the Ring," *Adweek* (Eastern Edition) 39(3) (January 19, 1998): 29–31; Larry Dunst, "Is It Possible to Get Creative in 15 Seconds?" *Advertising Age* 64(50) (November 29, 1993): 18; Jerry A. Rosenblatt and Janet Mainprize, "The History and Future of 15-Second Commercials: An Empirical Investigation of the Perception of Ad Agency Media Directors," in William Lazer, Eric Shaw, and Chow-Hou Wee (eds.), *World Marketing Congress, International Conference Series*, Vol. IV (Boca Raton, FL: Academy of Marketing Science, 1989), pp. 169–77.
20. Gopal K. Kanji, *100 Statistical Tests* (Thousand Oaks, CA: Sage Publications, 1993); Donald L. Harnett, *Statistical Methods*, 3rd ed. (Reading, MA: Addison-Wesley, 1982).
21. Marjorie A. Pett, *Nonparametric Statistics for Health Care Research* (Thousand Oaks, CA: Sage Publications, 1997).
22. There is some controversy over whether nonparametric statistical techniques should be used to make inferences about population parameters. See also Y. K. Cheung and J. H. Klotz, "The Mann-Whitney-Wilcoxon Distribution Using Linked Lists," *Statistica Sinica* 7(3) (July 1997): 805–13.
23. The t test in this case is equivalent to a chi-square test for independence in a 2 × 2 contingency table. The relationship is $\chi^2_{.95\,(1)} = t^2_{.05\,(n_1 + n_2 - 2)}$. For large samples, the t distribution approaches the normal distribution and so the t test and the z test are equivalent.
24. James R. Krum, Pradeep A. Rau, and Stephen K. Keiser, "The Marketing Research Process: Role Perceptions of Researchers and Users," *Journal of Advertising Research*

(December–January 1988): 9–21. See also Cyndee Miller, "Gallup Brothers Analyze the Research Industry," *Marketing News* 31(1) (January 6, 1997): 2.

25. For a recent application of Wilcoxon matched-pairs signed ranks test, see Manohar U. Kalwani and Narakesari Narayandas, "Long-Term Manufacturer-Supplier Relationships: Do They Pay Off for Supplier Firms?" *Journal of Marketing* 59 (January 1995): 1–16.
26. Marjorie A. Pett, *Nonparametric Statistics for Health Care Research* (Thousand Oaks, CA: Sage Publications, 1997); J. G. Field, "The World's Simplest Test of Significance," *Journal of the Market Research Society* (July 1971): 170–2.
27. Eric L. Einspruch, *An Introductory Guide to SPSS for Windows* (Thousand Oaks, CA: Sage Publications, 1998); Paul E. Spector, *SAS Programming for Researchers and Social Scientists* (Thousand Oaks, CA: Sage Publications, 1993); Mohamed Afzal Norat, "Software Reviews," *Economic Journal: The Journal of the Royal Economic Society* 107(442) (May 1997): 857–82; John Wass, "How Statistical Software Can be Assessed," *Scientific Computing and Automation* (October 1966).
28. Leslie de Chernatony, Chris Halliburton, and Ratna Bernath, "International Branding: Demand or Supply Driven," *International Marketing Review* 12(2) (1995): 9–21.
29. Lawrence B. Chonko, *Ethical Decision Making in Marketing* (Thousand Oaks, CA: Sage Publications, 1995); G. R. Laczniak and P. E. Murphy, "Fostering Ethical Marketing Decisions," *Journal of Business Ethics* 10 (1991): 259–71.

Chapter 16

1. Thomas Kiely, "The Internet: Fear and Shopping in Cyberspace," *Harvard Business Review* 75(4) (July/August 1997): 13–14; Pradeep Korgaonkar and George P. Moschis, "The Effects of Perceived Risk and Social Class on Consumer Preferences for Distribution Outlets," in Paul Bloom, Russ Winer, Harold H. Kassarjian, Debra L. Scammon, Bart Weitz, Robert Spekman, Vijay Mahajan, and Michael Levy (eds.), *Enhancing Knowledge Development in Marketing*, Series No. 55 (Chicago, IL: American Marketing Association, 1989): 39–43.
2. Michael Wilke, "Health Reports in Vogue Again for Drug Advertisers," *Advertising Age* 68(33) (August 18, 1997): 31; Easwar S. Iyer, "The Influence of Verbal Content and Relative Newness on the Effectiveness of Comparative Advertising," *Journal of Advertising* 17 (1988): 15–21.
3. For recent applications of ANOVA, see Sajeev Varki and Rowland T. Rust, "Satisfaction Is Relative," *Marketing Research: A Magazine of Management & Applications* 9(2) (Summer 1997): 14–19; Rohit Deshpande and Douglas M. Stayman, "A Tale of Two Cities: Distinctiveness Theory and Advertising Effectiveness," *Journal of Marketing Research* 31 (February 1994): 57–64.
4. Daniel B. Wright, *Understanding Statistics* (Thousand Oaks, CA: Sage Publications, 1993); M. J. Norusis, *The SPSS Guide to Data Analysis for SPSS/PC+* (Chicago: SPSS Inc., 1991).
5. Wade C. Driscoll, "Robustness of the ANOVA and Tukey-Kramer Statistical Tests," *Computers & Industrial Engineering* 31(1, 2) (October 1996): 265–8; Richard K. Burdick, "Statement of Hypotheses in the Analysis of Variance," *Journal of Marketing Research* (August 1983): 320–4.
6. The F test is a generalized form of the t test. If a random variable is t distributed with n degrees of freedom, then t^2 is F distributed with 1 and n degrees of freedom. Where there are two factor levels or treatments, ANOVA is equivalent to the two-sided t test.
7. Although computations for the fixed-effects and random-effects models are similar, interpretations of results differ. A comparison of these approaches is found in Amir Erez, Matthew C. Bloom, and Martin T. Wells, "Using Random Rather Than Fixed Effects Models in Meta-Analysis: Implications for Situational Specificity and Validity Generalization," *Personnel Psychology* 49(2) (Summer 1996): 275–306; John W. Neter, *Applied Linear Statistical Models*, 4th ed. (Burr Ridge, IL: Irwin, 1996).
8. Dawn Wilensky, "Cents and Sensibility," *Discount Store News* 35(5) (March 4, 1996): 18–19; Denise T. Smart, James E. Zemanek Jr., and Jeffrey S. Conant, "Videolog Retailing: How Effective Is This New Form of Direct Mail Marketing?" in Paul Bloom, Russ Winer, Harold H. Kassarjian, Debra L. Scammon, Bart Weitz, Robert Spekman, Vijay Mahajan, and Michael Levy (eds.), *Enhancing Knowledge Development in Marketing*, Series No. 55 (Chicago, IL: American Marketing Association, 1989): 85.
9. We consider only the full factorial designs, which incorporate all possible combinations of factor levels. For example, see Geeta Menon, "Are the Parts Better Than the Whole? The Effects of Decompositional Questions on Judgments of Frequent Behaviors," *Journal of Marketing Research* 34 (August 1997): 335–46.
10. James Jaccard, *Interaction Effects in Factorial Analysis of Variance* (Thousand Oaks, CA: Sage Publications, 1997); Jerome L. Mayers, *Fundamentals of Experimental Design*, 3rd ed. (Boston, MA: Allyn & Bacon, 1979). See also Mark T. Spence and Merrie Brucks, "The Moderating Effects of Problem Characteristics on Experts' and Novices' Judgments," *Journal of Marketing Research* 34 (February 1997): 233–47.
11. Jacques Tacq, *Multivariate Analysis Techniques in Social Science Research* (Thousand Oaks, CA: Sage Publications, 1997); Wayne W. Daniel and James C. Terrell, *Business Statistics*, 7th ed. (Boston, MA: Houghton Mifflin, 1995).
12. See James Jaccard, *Interaction Effects in Factorial Analysis of Variance* (Thousand Oaks, CA: Sage Publications, 1997).
13. Robert A. Peterson and Alain J. P. Jolibert, "A Meta-Analysis of Country-of-Origin Effects," *Journal of International Business Studies* 26(4) (Fourth Quarter 1995): 883–900; Paul Chao, "The Impact of Country Affiliation on the Credibility of Product Attribute Claims," *Journal of Advertising Research* (April–May 1989): 35–41.
14. Although this is the most common way in which analysis of covariance is performed, other situations are also possible. For example, covariate and factor effects may be of equal interest, or the set of covariates may be of major concern. For a recent application, see Kevin Lane Keller and David A. Aaker, "The Effects of Sequential Introduction of Brand Extensions," *Journal of Marketing Research* 29 (February 1992): 35–50.
15. For a more detailed discussion, see John W. Neter, *Applied Linear Statistical Models*, 4th ed. (Burr Ridge, IL: Irwin,

1996); A. R. Wildt and O. T. Ahtola, *Analysis of Covariance* (Beverly Hills, CA: Sage Publications, 1978).

16. See U. N. Umesh, Robert A. Peterson, Michelle McCann-Nelson, and Rajiv Vaidyanathan, "Type IV Error in Marketing Research: The Investigation of ANOVA Interactions," *Journal of the Academy of Marketing Science* 24(1) (Winter 1966): 17–26; William T. Ross Jr. and Elizabeth H. Creyer, "Interpreting Interactions: Raw Means or Residual Means," *Journal of Consumer Research* 20(2) (September 1993): 330–8; J. H. Leigh and T. C. Kinnear, "On Interaction Classification," *Educational and Psychological Measurement* 40 (Winter 1980): 841–3.
17. James Jaccard, *Interaction Effects in Factorial Analysis of Variance* (Thousand Oaks, CA: Sage Publications, 1997); Brian Wansink, "Advertising's Impact on Category Substitution," *Journal of Marketing Research* 31 (November 1994): 505–15; Laura A. Peracchio and Joan Meyers-Levy, "How Ambiguous Cropped Objects in Ad Photos Can Affect Product Evaluations," *Journal of Consumer Research* 21 (June 1994): 190–204.
18. Rohit Verma and John C. Goodale, "Statistical Power in Operations Management," *Journal of Operations Management* 13(2) (August 1995): 139–52; Gordon A. Wyner, "The Significance of Marketing Research," *Marketing Research: A Magazine of Management & Applications* 5(1) (Winter 1993): 43–5; Alan Sawyer and J. Paul Peter, "The Significance of Statistical Significance Tests in Marketing Research," *Journal of Marketing Research* 20 (May 1983): 125; R. F. Beltramini, "A Meta-Analysis of Effect Sizes in Consumer Behavior Experiments," *Journal of Consumer Research* 12 (June 1985): 97–103.
19. This formula does not hold if repeated measurements are made on the dependent variable. See Edward F. Fern and Kent B. Monroe, "Effect-Size Estimates: Issues and Problems in Interpretation," *Journal of Consumer Research* 23(2) (September 1996): 89–105; David H. Dodd and Roger F. Schultz, Jr., "Computational Procedures for Estimating Magnitude of Effect for Some Analysis of Variance Designs," *Psychological Bulletin* (June 1973): 391–5.
20. The ω^2 formula is attributed to Hays. See W. L. Hays, *Statistics for Psychologists* (New York, NY: Holt, Rinehart & Winston, 1963). For a recent application, see S. Ratneshwar and Shelly Chaiken, "Comprehension's Role in Persuasion: The Case of Its Moderating Effect on the Persuasive Impact of Source Cues," *Journal of Consumer Research* 18 (June 1991): 52–62. For an alternative approach, see also Adam Finn and Ujwal Kayande, "Reliability Assessment and Optimization of Marketing Measurement," *Journal of Marketing Research* 34 (February 1997): 262–75.
21. Edward F. Fern and Kent B. Monroe, "Effect-Size Estimates: Issues and Problems in Interpretation," *Journal of Consumer Research* 23(2) (September 1996): 89–105; Jacob Cohen, *Statistical Power Analysis for the Behavioral Sciences* (New York, NY: Academic Press, 1969).
22. John W. Neter, *Applied Linear Statistical Models*, 4th ed. (Burr Ridge, IL: Irwin, 1996); B. J. Winer, Donald R. Brown, and Kenneth M. Michels, *Statistical Principles in Experimental Design*, 3rd ed. (New York, NY: McGraw-Hill, 1991).
23. It is possible to combine between-subjects and within-subjects factors in a single design. See, for example, Michael K. Mount, Marcia R. Sytsma, Joy F. Hazucha, and Katherine E. Holt, "Rater-Ratee Effects in Developmental Performance Ratings of Managers," *Personnel Psychology* 50(1) (Spring 1997): 51–69; Susan M. Broniarczyk and Joseph W. Alba, "The Importance of the Brand in Brand Extension," *Journal of Marketing Research* 31 (May 1994): 214–28; Aradhna Krishna, "The Effect of Deal Knowledge on Consumer Purchase Behavior," *Journal of Marketing Research* 31 (February 1994): 76–91.
24. See Thomas P. Novak, "MANOVAMAP: Geographical Representation of MANOVA in Marketing Research," *Journal of Marketing Research* 32(3) (August 1995): 357–74; J. H. Bray and S. E. Maxwell, *Multivariate Analysis of Variance* (Beverly Hills, CA: Sage Publications, 1985). For an application of MANOVA see Sajeev Varki, "Satisfaction is Relative," *Marketing Research: A Magazine of Management & Applications* 9(2) (Summer 1997): 14–19.
25. Neil R. Abramson, Robert J. Keating, and Henry W. Lane, "Cross-National Cognitive Process Differences: A Comparison of Canadian, American and Japanese Managers," *Management International Review* 36(2) (Second Quarter 1996): 123–47; Ishmael P. Akaah, "A Cross-National Analysis of the Perceived Commonality of Unethical Practices in Marketing Research," in William Lazer, Eric Shaw, and Chow-Hou Wee (eds.), *World Marketing Congress*, International Conference Series Vol. IV (Boca Raton, FL: Academy of Marketing Science, 1989): 2–9.
26. Eric L. Einspruch, *An Introductory Guide to SPSS for Windows* (Thousand Oaks, CA: Sage Publications, 1998); Paul E. Spector, *SAS Programming for Researchers and Social Scientists* (Thousand Oaks, CA: Sage Publications, 1993); Mohamed Afzal Norat, "Software Reviews," *Economic Journal: The Journal of the Royal Economic Society* 107(442) (May 1997): 857–82; John Wass, "How Statistical Software Can be Assessed," *Scientific Computing and Automation* (October 1966).
27. Patricia L. Smith and Ellwood F. Oakley, "Gender-Related Differences in Ethical and Social Values of Business Students: Implications for Management," *Journal of Business Ethics* 16(1) (January 1997): 37–45; Ishmael P. Akaah, "Differences in Research Ethics Judgments between Male and Female Marketing Professionals," *Journal of Business Ethics* 8 (1989): 375–81.

Chapter 17

1. Jennifer Zajac, "Avon's Finally Glowing Thanks to Global Sales—and New Lip-Shtic," *Money* 26(9) (September 1997): 60; Cyndee Miller, "Computer Modeling Rings the Right Bell for Avon," *Marketing News* (May 9, 1988): 14.
2. Lauren Freedman, "Brand Names Will Bring New Velocity to On-Line Sales," *Discount Store News* 36(16) (August 18, 1997): 12; Pradeep K. Korgaonkar and Allen E. Smith, "Shopping Orientation, Demographic and Media Preference Correlates of Electronic Shopping," in Kenneth D. Bahn (ed.), *Developments in Marketing Science* vol. 11 (Blacksburg, VA: Academy of Marketing Science, 1988): 52–5.
3. N. R. Draper and H. Smith, *Applied Regression Analysis*, 3rd ed. (New York, NY: John Wiley, 1998); Michael E. Doherty and James A. Sullivan, "rho: = *p*," *Organizational*

Behavior & Human Decision Processes 43(1) (February 1989): 136–44; W. S. Martin, "Effects of Scaling on the Correlation Coefficient: Additional Considerations," *Journal of Marketing Research* 15 (May 1978): 304–8; K. A. Bollen and K. H. Barb, "Pearson's *R* and Coarsely Categorized Measures," *American Sociological Review* 46 (1981): 232–9.

4. Jacques Tacq, *Multivariate Analysis Techniques in Social Science Research* (Thousand Oaks, CA: Sage Publications, 1997); John Neter, William Wasserman, and Michael J. Kutner, *Applied Linear Statistical Methods*, 3rd ed. (Burr Ridge, IL: Richard D. Irwin, 1990): 501–3.
5. Although the topic is not discussed here, partial correlations can also be helpful in locating intervening variables and making certain types of causal inferences.
6. "Bates Saatchi & Saatchi, Budapest: Accounting for Change," *Accountancy* 116(224) (August 1995): 31; Ken Kasriel, "Hungary's Million-Dollar Slap," *Advertising Age* (June 8, 1992).
7. Another advantage to τ is that it can be generalized to a partial correlation coefficient. Marjorie A. Pett, *Nonparametric Statistics for Health Care Research* (Thousand Oaks, CA: Sage Publications, 1997); Sidney Siegel and N. J. Castellan, *Nonparametric Statistics*, 2nd ed. (New York: McGraw-Hill, 1988).
8. In a strict sense, the regression model requires that errors of measurement be associated only with the criterion variable and that the predictor variables be measured without error. For serially correlated errors, see Eugene Canjels and Mark W. Watson, "Estimating Deterministic Trends in the Presence of Serially Correlated Errors," *Review of Economics and Statistics* 79(2) (May 1997): 184–200.
9. See any text on regression, such as N. R. Draper and H. Smith, *Applied Regression Analysis*, 3rd ed. (New York, NY: John Wiley, 1998); John Neter, William Wasserman, and Michael H. Kutner, *Applied Linear Regression Models*, 3rd ed. (Burr Ridge, IL: Richard D. Irwin, 1990).
10. Technically, the numerator is $b - \beta$. However, because it has been hypothesized that $\beta = .0$, it can be omitted from the formula.
11. The larger the SEE, the poorer the fit of the regression.
12. The assumption of fixed levels of predictors applies to the "classical" regression model. It is possible, if certain conditions are met, for the predictors to be random variables. However, their distribution is not allowed to depend on the parameters of the regression equation. See N. R. Draper and H. Smith, *Applied Regression Analysis*, 3rd ed. (New York, NY: John Wiley, 1998).
13. For an approach to handling the violations of these assumptions, see Gary S. Dispensa, "Use Logistic Regression with Customer Satisfaction Data," *Marketing News* 31(1) (January 6, 1997): 13; S. K. Reddy, Susan L. Holak, and Subodh Bhat, "To Extend or Not to Extend: Success Determinants of Line Extensions," *Journal of Marketing Research* 31 (May 1994): 243–62.
14. Jon Rees, "Tight Ship Keeps Coke on Top of the World," *Marketing Week* 20(6) (May 8, 1997): 28–9; Nancy Giges, "Europeans Buy Outside Goods, but Like Local Ads," *Advertising Age* 63(17) (April 27, 1992) I1–I26.
15. For other recent applications of multiple regression, see Abbie Griffin, "The Effect of Project and Process Characteristics on Product Development Cycle Time," *Journal of Marketing Research* 34 (February 1997): 24–35; Hubert Gatignon and Jean-Marc Xuereb, "Strategic Orientation of the Firm and New Product Performance," *Journal of Marketing Research* 34 (February 1997): 77–90; Nirmalya Kumar, Lisa K. Scheer, and Jan-Benedict E. M. Steenkamp, "The Effects of Supplier Fairness on Vulnerable Resellers," *Journal of Marketing Research* 32 (February 1995): 54–65.
16. Yet another reason for adjusting R^2 is that, as a result of the optimizing properties of the least squares approach, it is a maximum. Thus, to some extent, R^2 always overestimates the magnitude of a relationship. For a recent application of adjusted R^2, see N. Craig Smith and Elizabeth Cooper-Martin, "Ethics and Target Marketing: The Role of Product Harm and Consumer Vulnerability," *Journal of Marketing* 61(3) (January 1997): 1–20; Morris A. Cohen, Jehoshua Eliashberg, and Teck H. Ho, "An Anatomy of a Decision Support System for Developing and Launching Line Extensions," *Journal of Marketing Research* 34 (February 1997): 117–29.
17. If R^2_{pop} is zero, then the sample R^2 reflects only sampling error, and the F ratio will tend to be equal to unity.
18. Another approach is the hierarchical method, in which the variables are added to the regression equation in an order specified by the researcher.
19. A. C. Atkinson, S. J. Koopman, and N. Shephard, "Detecting Shocks: Outliers and Breaks in Time Series," *Journal of Econometrics* 80(2) (October 1997): 387–422; George C. S. Wang and Charles K. Akabay, "Autocorrelation: Problems and Solutions in Regression Modeling," *Journal of Business Forecasting Methods & Systems* 13(4) (Winter 1994/1995): 18–26; David Belsley, *Conditioning Diagnostics: Collinearity and Weak Data in Regression* (New York: John Wiley, 1980); David Belsley, Edwin Kuh, and Roy. E. Walsh, *Regression Diagnostics* (New York, NY: John Wiley, 1980).
20. The Durbin-Watson test is discussed in virtually all regression textbooks. See for example, Hiroyuki Hisamatsu and Koichi and Maekawa, "The Distribution of the Durbin-Watson Statistic in Integrated and Near-Integrated Models," *Journal of Econometrics* 61(2) (April 1994): 367–82; N. R. Draper and H. Smith, *Applied Regression Analysis*, 3rd ed. (New York, NY: John Wiley, 1998).
21. Helen Berman, "Selling the Advertising/Trade Show Partnership," *Folio: The Magazine for Magazine Management* (Special Sourcebook Issue for 1997 Supplement) 25(18) (1997): 214–15; Lawrence Soley and R. Krishnan, "Does Advertising Subsidize Consumer Magazine Prices?" *Journal of Advertising* 16 (Spring 1987): 4–9.
22. John Fox, *Applied Regression Analysis, Linear Models and Related Methods* (Thousand Oaks, CA: Sage Publications, 1997); Shelby H. McIntyre, David B. Montgomery, V. Srinivasan, and Barton A. Weitz, "Evaluating the Statistical Significance of Models Developed by Stepwise Regression," *Journal of Marketing Research* 20 (February 1983): 1–11.
23. For recent applications of stepwise regression, see Christopher D. Ittner and David F. Larcker, "Product Development Cycle Time and Organizational Performance," *Journal of Marketing Research* 34 (February 1997): 13–23; Michael Laroche and Robert Sadokierski, "Role of Confidence in a Multi-Brand Model of Intentions for a High-Involvement Service," *Journal of Business Research* 29 (January 1994): 1–12.

24. Diane Crispell, "Hispanics at the Mall," *American Demographics* 19(10) (October 1997): 35–6; Glen R. Jarboe and Carl D. McDaniel, "A Profile of Browsers in Regional Shopping Malls," *Journal of the Academy of Marketing Science* (Spring 1987): 46–53.
25. Edward Greenberg and Robert P. Parks, "A Predictive Approach to Model Selection and Multicollinearity," *Journal of Applied Econometrics* 12(1) (January/February 1997): 67–75; Chezy Ofir and Andre Khuri, "Multicollinearity in Marketing Models: Diagnostics and Remedial Measures," *International Journal of Research in Marketing* 3 (1986): 181–205.
26. Possible procedures are given in George C. S. Wang, "How to Handle Multicollinearity in Regression Modeling," *Journal of Business Forecasting Methods & Systems* 15(1) (Spring 1996): 23–7; Charlotte H. Mason and William D. Perreault Jr., "Collinearity, Power, and Interpretation of Multiple Regression Analysis," *Journal of Marketing Research* 28 (August 1991): 268–80; R. R. Hocking, "Developments in Linear Regression Methodology: 1959–1982," *Technometrics* 25 (August 1983): 219–30; Ronald D. Snee, "Discussion," *Technometrics* 25 (August 1983): 230–7.
27. R. James Holzworth, "Policy Capturing with Ridge Regression," *Organizational Behavior and Human Decision Processes* 68(2) (November 1996): 171–9; Albert R. Wildt, "Equity Estimation and Assessing Market Response," *Journal of Marketing Research* 31 (February 1994): 437–51; Subhash Sharma and William L. James, "Latent Root Regression: An Alternative Procedure for Estimating Parameters in the Presence of Multicollinearity," *Journal of Marketing Research* (May 1981): 154–61.
28. Only relative importance can be determined, because the importance of an independent variable depends on all the independent variables in the regression model.
29. Robert Rugimbana, "Predicting Automated Teller Machine Usage: The Relative Importance of Perceptual and Demographic Factors," *International Journal of Bank Marketing* 13(4) (1995): 26–32; Paul E. Green, J. Douglas Carroll, and Wayne S. DeSarbo, "A New Measure of Predictor Variable Importance in Multiple Regression," *Journal of Marketing Research* (August 1978): 356–60; Barbara Bund Jackson, "Comment on 'A New Measure of Predictor Variable Importance in Multiple Regression,'" *Journal of Marketing Research* (February 1980): 116–18.
30. In the rare situation in which all the predictors are uncorrelated, simple correlations = partial correlations = part correlations = betas. Hence the squares of these measures will yield the same rank order of the relative importance of the variables.
31. For more on cross-validation, see Mark S. Litwin, *How to Measure Survey Reliability and Validity* (Thousand Oaks, CA: Sage Publications 1997); X. Michael Song and Mark E. Perry, "The Determinants of Japanese New Product Success," *Journal of Marketing Research* 34 (February 1997): 64–76; Bruce Cooil, Russell S. Winer, and David L. Rados, "Cross-Validation for Prediction," *Journal of Marketing Research* (August 1987): 271–9.
32. For a recent application of dummy variable regression see U. Yavas, "Demand Forecasting in a Service Setting," *Journal of International Marketing and Marketing Research* 21(1) (February 1996): 3–11; for further discussion on dummy variable coding, see Jacob Cohen and Patricia Cohen, *Applied Multiple Regression Correlation Analysis for the Behavioral Sciences*, 2nd ed. (Hillsdale, NJ: Lawrence Erlbaum Associates, 1983): 181–222.
33. John Fox, *Applied Regression Analysis, Linear Models, and Related Methods* (Thousand Oaks, CA: Sage Publications 1997); for an application of regression analysis to conduct analysis of covariance, see Peter A. Dancin and Daniel C. Smith, "The Effect of Brand Portfolio Characteristics on Consumer Evaluations of Brand Extensions," *Journal of Marketing Research* 31 (May 1994): 229–42.
34. Geoffrey I. Crouch, "Demand Elasticities in International Marketing: A Meta-Analytical Application to Tourism," *Journal of Business Research* 36(2) (June 1996): 117–36; Andrew Geddes, "Asian Airlines Try Loyalty Offers," *Advertising Age* 63(51) (December 14, 1992): 10.
35. Lynne M. Andersson and Thomas S. Bateman, "Cynicism in the Workplace: Some Causes and Effects," *Journal of Organizational Behavior* 18(5) (September 1997): 449–69; I. P. Akaah and E. A. Riordan, "The Incidence of Unethical Practices in Marketing Research: An Empirical Investigation," *Journal of the Academy of Marketing Science* 18 (1990): 143–52.
36. Eric L. Einspruch, *An Introductory Guide to SPSS for Windows* (Thousand Oaks, CA: Sage Publications, 1998); Paul E. Spector, *SAS Programming for Researchers and Social Scientists* (Thousand Oaks, CA: Sage Publications, 1993); Mohamed Afzal Norat, "Software Reviews," *Economic Journal: The Journal of the Royal Economic Society* 107(442) (May 1997): 857–82; Seiter Charles, "The Statistical Difference," *Macworld* 10(10) (October 1993): 116–21.

Chapter 18

1. Donald R. Lichtenstein, Scot Burton, and Richard G. Netemeyer, "An Examination of Deal Proneness across Sales Promotion Types: A Consumer Segmentation Perspective," *Journal of Retailing* 73(2) (Summer 1997): 283–97; Marvin A. Jolson, Joshua L. Wiener, and Richard B. Rosecky, "Correlates of Rebate Proneness," *Journal of Advertising Research* (February–March 1987): 33–43.
2. A detailed discussion of discriminant analysis may be found in Jacques Tacq, *Multivariate Analysis Techniques in Social Science Research* (Thousand Oaks, CA: Sage Publications, 1996); P. A. Lachenbruch, *Discriminant Analysis* (New York, NY: Hafner Press, 1975). For a recent application, see Ken Deal, "Determining Success Criteria for Financial Products: A Comparative Analysis of CART, Logit and Factor/Discriminant Analysis," *Service Industries Journal* 17(3) (July 1997): 489–506.
3. See Richard A. Johnson and Dean W. Wichern, *Applied Multivariate Statistical Analysis*, 4th ed. (Upper Saddle River, NJ: Prentice Hall, 1998); W. R. Klecka, *Discriminant Analysis* (Beverly Hills, CA: Sage Publications, 1980). See also Steven A. Sinclair and Edward C. Stalling, "How to Identify Differences between Market Segments with Attribute Analysis," *Industrial Marketing Management* 19 (February 1990): 31–40.
4. For a recent application, see Zafar Khan, Sudhir K. Chawla, and S. Thomas A. Cianciolo, "Multiple Discriminant Analysis: Tool for Effective Marketing of Computer Information

Systems to Small Business Clients," *Journal of Professional Services Marketing* 12(2) (1995): 153–62; J. K. Sager and Ajay Menon, "The Role of Behavioral Intentions in Turnover of Salespeople," *Journal of Business Research* 29 (March 1994): 179–88; Valerie Kijewski, Eunsang Yoon, and Gary Young, "How Exhibitors Select Trade Shows," *Industrial Marketing Management* 22 (November 1993): 287–98.

5. Vincent-Watne Mitchell, "How to Identify Psychographic Segments: Part 2," *Marketing Intelligence & Planning* 12(7) (1994): 11–16; M. R. Crask and W. D. Perreault Jr., "Validation of Discriminant Analysis in Marketing Research," *Journal of Marketing Research* 14 (February 1977): 60–8.
6. Strictly speaking, before testing for the equality of group means, the equality of group covariance matrices should be tested. Box's M test can be used for this purpose. If the equality of group covariance matrices is rejected, the results of discriminant analysis should be interpreted with caution. In this case, the power of the test for the equality of group means decreases.
7. See Lillian Fok, John P. Angelidis, Nabil A. Ibrahim, and Wing M. Fok, "The Utilization and Interpretation of Multivariate Statistical Techniques in Strategic Management," *International Journal of Management* 12(4) (December 1995): 468–81; D. G. Morrison, "On the Interpretation of Discriminant Analysis," *Journal of Marketing Research* 6 (May 1969): 156–63. For use of other techniques in conjunction with discriminant analysis to aid interpretation, see Rajiv P. Dant, James R. Lumpkin, and Robert P. Bush, "Private Physicians or Walk-In Clinics: Do the Patients Differ?" *Journal of Health Care Marketing* (June 1990): 23–35.
8. Jon M. Hawes, C. P. Rao, and Thomas L. Baker, "Retail Salesperson Attributes and the Role of Dependability in the Selection of Durable Goods," *Journal of Personal Selling & Sales Management* 13(4) (Fall 1993): 61–71; Edward F. Fern, Ramon A. Avila, and Dhruv Grewal, "Salesforce Turnover: Those Who Left and Those Who Stayed," *Industrial Marketing Management* (1989): 1–9.
9. For the validation of discriminant analysis, see Robert P. Bush, David J. Ortinau, and Alan J. Bush, "Personal Value Structures and AIDS Prevention," *Journal of Health Care Marketing* 14 (Spring 1994): 12–20.
10. Joseph F. Hair Jr., Ralph E. Anderson, Ronald L. Tatham, and William C. Black, *Multivariate Data Analysis with Readings*, 5th ed. (Upper Saddle River, NJ: Prentice Hall, 1999).
11. Vincent-Wayne Mitchell, "How to Identify Psychographic Segments: Part 2," *Marketing Intelligence and Planning* 12(7) (1994): 11–16.
12. Don R. Rahtz, M. Joseph Sirgy, and Rustan Kosenko, "Using Demographics and Psychographic Dimensions to Discriminate between Mature Heavy and Light Television Users: An Exploratory Analysis," in Kenneth D. Bahn (ed.), *Developments in Marketing Science*, Vol. 11 (Blacksburg, VA: Academy of Marketing Science, 1988): 2–7.
13. Richard A. Johnson and Dean W. Wichern, *Applied Multivariate Statistical Analysis*, 4th ed. (Upper Saddle River, NJ: Prentice Hall, 1998). For an application, see Rajiv P. Dant and Patrick L. Schul, "Conflict Resolution Processes in Contractual Channels of Distribution," *Journal of Marketing* 56 (January 1992): 38–54.
14. Constantine Loucopoulos and Robert Pavur, "Computational Characteristics of a New Mathematical Programming Model for the Three-Group Discriminant Problem," *Computers & Operations Research* 24(2) (February 1997): 179–91. For a recent application of multiple discriminant analysis, see Stephen J. O'Connor, Richard M. Shewchuk, and Lynn W. Carney, "The Great Gap," *Journal of Health Care Marketing* 14 (Summer 1994): 32–9.
15. Kathryn H. Dansky and Diane Brannon, "Discriminant Analysis: A Technique for Adding Value to Patient satisfaction Surveys," *Hospital & Health Services Administration* 41(4) (Winter 1996): 503–13; Jeen-Su Lim and Ron Zallocco, "Determinant Attributes in Formulation of Attitudes toward Four Health Care Systems," *Journal of Health Care Marketing* (June 1988): 25–30.
16. Richard A. Johnson and Dean A. Wichern, *Applied Multivariate Statistical Analysis*, 4th ed. (Upper Saddle River, NJ: Prentice Hall, 1998); Joseph F. Hair Jr., Ralph E. Anderson, Ronald L. Tatham, and William C. Black, *Multivariate Data Analysis with Readings*, 5th ed. (Upper Saddle River, NJ: Prentice Hall, 1999): 178–255.
17. Jeryl Whitelock, Carole Roberts, and Jonathan Blakeley, "The Reality of the Eurobrand: An Empirical Analysis," *Journal of International Marketing* 3(3) (1995): 77–95; Charlotte Klopp and John Sterlicchi, "Customer Satisfaction Just Catching on in Europe," *Marketing News* 24(11) (May 28, 1990): 5.
18. David J. Fritzsche, "Personal Values: Potential Keys to Ethical Decision Making," *Journal of Business Ethics* 14(11) (November 1995): 909–22; Paul R. Murphy, Jonathan E. Smith, and James M. Daley, "Executive Attitudes, Organizational Size, and Ethical Issues: Perspectives on a Service Industry," *Journal of Business Ethics* 11 (1992): 11–19.
19. Eric L. Einspruch, *An Introductory Guide to SPSS for Windows* (Thousand Oaks, CA: Sage Publications, 1998); Paul E. Spector, *SAS Programming for Researchers and Social Scientists* (Thousand Oaks, CA: Sage Publications, 1993); Mohamed Afzal Norat, "Software Reviews," *Economic Journal: The Journal of the Royal Economic Society* 107(442) (May 1997): 857–82; Charles Seiter, "The Statistical Difference," *Macworld* 10(10) (October 1993): 116–21.

Chapter 19

1. Gerhard Mels, Christo Boshoff, and Deon Nel, "The Dimensions of Service Quality: The Original European Perspective Revisited," *Service Industries Journal* (January 1997): 173–89; James M. Sinukula and Leanna Lawtor, "Positioning in the Financial Services Industry: A Look at the Decomposition of Image," in Jon M. Hawes and George B. Glisan (eds.), *Developments in Marketing Science* Vol. 10 (Akron, OH: Academy of Marketing Science, 1987): 439–42.
2. For a detailed discussion of factor analysis, see Jacques Tacq, *Multivariate Analysis Techniques in Social Science Research* (Thousand Oaks, CA: Sage Publications, 1996); George H Dunteman, *Principal Components Analysis* (Newbury Park, CA: Sage Publications, 1989). For a recent application, see Jennifer L. Aaker, "Dimensions of Brand Personality," *Journal of Marketing Research* 34 (August 1997): 347–56.

3. See, for example, Shirely Bo Edvardsson, Gerry Larsson, and Sven Setterlind, "Internal Service Quality and the Psychosocial Work Environment: An Empirical Analysis of Conceptual Interrelatedness," *Service Industries Journal* 17(2) (April 1997): 252–63; Shirley Taylor, "Waiting for Service: The Relationship between Delays and Evaluations of Service," *Journal of Marketing* 58 (April 1994): 56–69.
4. See Sanjay Gaur, "Adelman and Morris Factor Analysis of Developing Countries," *Journal of Policy Modeling* 19(4) (August 1997): 407–15; John L. Lastovicka and Kanchana Thamodaran, "Common Factor Score Estimates in Multiple Regression Problems," *Journal of Marketing Research* 28 (February 1991): 105–12; W. R. Dillon and M. Goldstein, *Multivariate Analysis: Methods and Applications* (New York, NY: John Wiley, 1984): 23–99.
5. For a recent application of factor analysis, see Christopher D. Ittner and David F. Larcker, "Product Development Cycle Time and Organizational Performance," *Journal of Marketing Research* 34 (February 1997): 13–23.
6. Alexander Basilevsky, *Statistical Factor Analysis & Related Methods: Theory & Applications* (New York: John Wiley, 1994); Joseph F. Hair Jr., Ralph E. Anderson, Ronald L. Tatham, and William C. Black, *Multivariate Data Analysis with Readings*, 5th ed. (Upper Saddle River, NJ: Prentice Hall, Inc., 1999).
7. Factor analysis is influenced by the relative size of the correlations rather than by the absolute size.
8. See James A. Roberts and Donald R. Beacon, "Exploring the Subtle Relationships between Environmental Concern and Ecologically Conscious Behavior," *Journal of Business Research* 40(1) (September 1997): 79–89; Sangit Chatterjee, Linda Jamieson, and Frederick Wiseman, "Identifying Most Influential Observations in Factor Analysis," *Marketing Science* (Spring 1991): 145–60; Frank Acito and Ronald D. Anderson, "A Monté Carlo Comparison of Factor Analytic Methods," *Journal of Marketing Research* 17 (May 1980): 228–36.
9. Other methods of orthogonal rotation are also available. The quartimax method minimizes the number of factors needed to explain a variable. The equamax method is a combination of varimax and quartimax.
10. James E. Zemanek Jr., "Manufacturer Influence versus Manufacturer Salesperson Influence over the Industrial Distributor," *Industrial Marketing Management* 26(1) (January 1997): 59–66; Ronald C. Curhan and Robert J. Kopp, "Obtaining Retailer Support for Trade Deals: Key Success Factors," *Journal of Advertising Research* (December 1987–January 1988): 51–60.
11. William M. Bulkeley, "Rebates' Secret Appeal to Manufacturers: Few Consumers Actually Redeem Them," *Wall Street Journal* (February 10, 1998): B1–B2; Donald R. Lichtenstein, Nancy M. Ridgway, and Richard G. Netemeyer, "Price Perceptions and Consumer Shopping Behavior: A Field Study," *Journal of Marketing Research* 30(2) (May 1993): 234–45; Peter Tat, William A. Cunningham III, and Emin Babakus, "Consumer Perceptions of Rebates," *Journal of Advertising Research* (August–September 1988): 45–50.
12. "Return of the Beetle," *The Economist* 346(8050) (January 10, 1998): 54.
13. William J. Bigoness and Gerald L. Blakely, "A Cross-National Study of Managerial Values," *Journal of International Business Studies* 27(4) (Fourth Quarter 1996): 739–52; Ishmael P. Akaah and Edward A. Riordan, "The Incidence of Unethical Practices in Marketing Research: An Empirical Investigation," *Journal of the Academy of Marketing Science* 18 (1990): 143–52.
14. Eric L. Einspruch, *An Introductory Guide to SPSS for Windows* (Thousand Oaks, CA: Sage Publications, 1998); Paul E. Spector, *SAS Programming for Researchers and Social Scientists* (Thousand Oaks, CA: Sage Publications, 1993); Mohamed Afzal Norat, "Software Reviews," *Economic Journal: The Journal of the Royal Economic Society* 107(442) (May 1997): 857–82; Seiter Charles, "The Statistical Difference," *Macworld* 10(10) (October 1993): 116–21.

Chapter 20

1. Liz Stuart, "Haagen-Dazs Aims to Scoop a Larger Share," *Marketing Week* 19(46/2) (February 21, 1997): 26; Dwight J. Shelton, "Birds of a Geodemographic Feather Flock Together," *Marketing News* (August 28, 1987): 13.
2. For an application of cluster analysis, see Sudhir H. Kale, "Grouping Euroconsumers: A Culture-Based Clustering Approach," *Journal of International Marketing* 3(3) (1995): 35–48.
3. Overlapping clustering methods that permit an object to be grouped into more than one cluster are also available. See Anil Chaturvedi, J. Douglass Carroll, Paul E. Green, and John A. Rotondo, "A Feature-Based Approach to Market Segmentation via Overlapping K-Centroids Clustering," *Journal of Marketing Research* 34 (August 1997): 370–7.
4. Excellent discussions on the various aspects of cluster analysis may be found in B. Everitt, *Cluster Analysis*, 3rd ed. (New York, NY: Halsted Press, 1993); H. Charles Romsburg, *Cluster Analysis for Researchers* (Melbourne: Krieger Publishing Company, 1990).
5. Vicki Douglas, "Questionnaires Too Long? Try Variable Clustering," *Marketing News* 29(5) (February 27, 1995): 38; Girish Punj and David Stewart, "Cluster Analysis in Marketing Research: Review and Suggestions for Application," *Journal of Marketing Research* 20 (May 1983): 134–48.
6. For use of cluster analysis for segmentation, see Mark Peterson and Naresh K. Malhotra, "Comparative Marketing Measures of Societal Quality of Life: Substantive Dimensions in 186 Countries," *Journal of Macromarketing* 17(1) (Spring 1997): 25–38; Tung-Zong Chang and Su-Jane Chen, "Benefit Segmentation: A Useful Tool for Financial Investment Services," *Journal of Professional Services Marketing* 12(2) (1995): 69–80; "Using Cluster Analysis for Segmentation," *Sawtooth News* 10 (Winter 1994/1995): 6–7.
7. Chul-Min Mo, Mark E. Havitz, and Dennis R. Howard, "Segmenting Travel Markets with the International Tourism Role (ITR) Scale," *Journal of Travel Research* 33(1) (Summer 1994): 24–31; George P. Moschis and Daniel C. Bello, "Decision-Making Patterns among International Vacationers: A Cross-Cultural Perspective," *Psychology & Marketing* (Spring 1987): 75–89.
8. B. Everitt, *Cluster Analysis*, 3rd ed. (New York, NY: Halsted Press, 1993).
9. For a detailed discussion on the different measures of similarity and formulas for computing them, see Victor Chepoi

and Feodor Dragan, "Computing a Median Point of a Simple Rectilinear Polygon," *Information Processing Letters* 49(6) (March 22, 1994): 281–5; H. Charles Romsburg, *Cluster Analysis for Researchers* (Melbourne: Krieger Publishing Company, 1990).

10. Tomio Hirata, "A Unified Linear-Time Algorithm for Computing Distance Maps," *Information Processing Letters* 58(3) (May 13, 1996): 129–33; Joseph F. Hair Jr., Ralph E. Anderson, Ronald L. Tatham, and William C. Black, *Multivariate Data Analysis with Readings*, 5th ed. (Upper Saddle River, NJ: Prentice Hall, Inc., 1999).
11. For further discussion of the issues involved in standardization, see H. Charles Romsburg, *Cluster Analysis for Researchers* (Melbourne: Krieger Publishing Company, 1990).
12. Richard A. Johnson and Dean A. Wichern, *Applied Multivariate Statistical Analysis*, 4th ed. (Upper Saddle River, NJ: Prentice Hall, 1998); G. Milligan, "An Examination of the Effect of Six Types of Error Perturbation on Fifteen Clustering Algorithms," *Psychometrika* 45 (September 1980): 325–42.
13. B. Everitt, *Cluster Analysis*, 3rd ed. (New York, NY: Halsted Press, 1993); Punj Girish and David Stewart, "Cluster Analysis in Marketing Research: Review and Suggestions for Application," *Journal of Marketing Research* 20 (May 1983): 134–8.
14. For a formal discussion of reliability, validity, and significance testing in cluster analysis, see S. Dibbs and P. Stern, "Questioning the Reliability of Market Segmentation Techniques," *Omega* 23(6) (December 1995): 625–636; G. Ray Funkhouser, "A Note on the Reliability of Certain Clustering Algorithms," *Journal of Marketing Research* 30 (February 1983): 99–102; T. D. Klastorin, "Assessing Cluster Analysis Results," *Journal of Marketing Research* 20 (February 1983): 92–8; S. J. Arnold, "A Test for Clusters," *Journal of Marketing Research* 16 (November 1979): 545–51.
15. John Saunders, Veronica Wong, and Peter Doyle, "The Congruence of Successful International Competitors: A Study of the Marketing Strategies and Organizations of Japanese and U.S. Competitors in the UK," *Journal of Global Marketing* 7(3) (1994): 41–59; Peter Doyle, John Saunders, and Veronica Wong, "International Marketing Strategies and Organizations: A Study of U. S., Japanese, and British Competitors," in Paul Bloom, Russ Winer, Harold H. Kassarjian, Debra L. Scammon, Bart Weitz, Robert E. Spekman, Vijay Mahajan, and Michael Levy (eds.), *Enhancing Knowledge Development in Marketing* Series No. 55 (Chicago, IL: American Marketing Association, 1989): 100–4.
16. Edward J. Holohean Jr., Steven M. Banks, and Blair A. Maddy, "System Impact and Methodological Issues in the Development of an Empirical Typology of Psychiatric Hospital Residents," *Journal of Mental Health Administration* 22(2) (Spring 1995): 177–88; Arch G. Woodside, Robert L. Nielsen, Fred Walters, and Gale D. Muller, "Preference Segmentation of Health Care Services: The Old-Fashioneds, Value Conscious, Affluents, and Professional Want-It-Alls," *Journal of Health Care Marketing* (June 1988): 14–24.
17. Vicki Douglas, "Questionnaire Too Long? Try Variable Clustering," *Marketing News* 29(5) (February 27, 1995): 38.
18. Thorolf Helgesen, "The Power of Advertising—Myths and Realities," *Marketing & Research Today* 24(2) (May 1996): 63–71; David A. Aaker, Douglas M. Stayman, and Richard Vezina, "Identifying Feelings Elicited by Advertising," *Psychology & Marketing* (Spring 1988): 1–16.
19. Fred Zandpour and Katrin R. Harich, "Think and Feel Country Clusters: A New Approach to International Advertising Standardization," *International Journal of Advertising* 15(4) (1996): 325–44; Nancy Giges, "World's Product Parity Perception High," *Advertising Age* (June 20, 1988).
20. Ishmael P. Akaah, "Organizational Culture and Ethical Research Behavior," *Journal of the Academy of Marketing Science* 21(1) (Winter 1993): 59–63; R. E. Reidenbach and D. P. Robin, "Some Initial Steps toward Improving the Measurement of Ethical Evaluations of Marketing Activities" *Journal of Business Ethics* 7 (1988): 871–9.
21. Eric L. Einspruch, *An Introductory Guide to SPSS for Windows* (Thousand Oaks, CA: Sage Publications, 1998); Paul E. Spector, *SAS Programming for Researchers and Social Scientists* (Thousand Oaks, CA: Sage Publications, 1993); Mohamed Afzal Norat, "Software Reviews," *Economic Journal: The Journal of the Royal Economic Society* 107(442) (May 1997): 857–82; Seiter Charles, "The Statistical Difference," *Macworld* 10(10) (October 1993): 116–21.

Chapter 21

1. Paul E. Green, Frank J. Carmone, Jr., and Scott M. Smith, *Multidimensional Scaling: Concepts and Applications* (Boston, MA: Allyn & Bacon, 1989): 16–17. See also Nikhil Deogun, "Coke Claims Dominance in the Mideast and North Africa, but Pepsi Disagrees," *Wall Street Journal* (March 3, 1998): A4.
2. Ali Kara, Erdener Kaynak, and Orsay Kucukemiroglu, "Credit Card Development Strategies for the Youth Market: The Use of Conjoint Analysis," *International Journal of Bank Marketing* 12(6) (1994): 30–6; Mary Tonnenberger, "In Search of the Perfect Plastic," *Quirk's Marketing Research Review* 5 (May 1992): 6–7, 37.
3. For a review of MDS studies in marketing research, see J. Douglass Carroll and Paul E. Green, "Psychometric Methods in Marketing Research: Part II, Multidimensional Scaling," *Journal of Marketing Research* 34 (February 1997): 193–204; Lee G. Cooper, "A Review of Multidimensional Scaling in Marketing Research," *Applied Psychological Measurement* 7 (Fall 1983): 427–50.
4. An excellent discussion of the various aspects of MDS may be found in Mark L. Davison, *Multidimensional Scaling* (Melbourne, Krieger Publishing Company, 1992).
5. The data are commonly treated as symmetric. For an asymmetric approach see Wayne S. Desarbo and Ajay K. Manrai, "A New Multidimensional Scaling Methodology for the Analysis of Asymmetric Proximity Data in Marketing Research," *Marketing Science* 11(1) (Winter 1992): 1–20. For other approaches to MDS data, see Tammo H. A. Bijmolt and Michel Wedel, "The Effects of Alternative Methods of Collecting Similarity Data for Multidimensional Scaling," *International Journal of Research in Marketing* 12(4) (November 1995): 363–71.
6. See Ingwer Borg and Patrick J. Groenen, *Modern Multidimensional Scaling Theory and Applications* (New York, NY: Springer-Verlag, 1996); Naresh K. Malhotra, Arun K. Jain, and Christian Pinson, "The Robustness of MDS Con-

figurations in the Case of Incomplete Data," *Journal of Marketing Research* 25 (February 1988): 95–102; Jan-Benedict E.M. Steenkamp and Hans C. M. Van Trijp, "Task Experience and Validity in Perceptual Mapping: A Comparison of Two Consumer-Adaptive Techniques," *International Journal of Research in Marketing* 13(3) (July 1996): 265–76.

7. See T. Cox, *Multidimensional Scaling* (New York: Routledge, Chapman & Hall, 1994).
8. Kruskal's stress is probably the most commonly used measure for lack of fit. See Ingwer Borg and Patrick J. Groenen, *Modern Multidimensional Scaling Theory and Applications* (New York, NY: Springer-Verlag, 1996). For the original article, see J. B. Kruskal, "Multidimensional Scaling by Optimizing Goodness of Fit to a Nonmetric Hypothesis," *Psychometrika* 29 (March 1964): 1–27.
9. J. Douglass Carroll and Paul E. Green, "Psychometric Methods in Marketing Research: Part II, Multidimensional Scaling," *Journal of Marketing Research* 34 (February 1997): 193–204; Naresh K. Malhotra, "Validity and Structural Reliability of Multidimensional Scaling," *Journal of Marketing Research* 24 (May 1987): 164–73.
10. For a recent examination of the reliability and validity of MDS solutions, see Jan-Benedict E. M. Steenkamp, Hans C. M. Van Trijp, and Jos M. F. Ten Berge, "Perceptual Mapping Based on Idiosyncratic Sets of Attributes," *Journal of Marketing Research* 31 (February 1994): 15–27.
11. Joseph F. Hair Jr., Ralph E. Anderson, Ronald L. Tatham, and William C. Black, *Multivariate Data Analysis with Readings*, 5th ed. (Upper Saddle River, NJ: Prentice Hall, Inc., 1999): 484–555.
12. See, for example, Wayne S. DeSarbo, M. R. Young, and Arvind Rangaswamy, "A Parametric Multidimensional Unfolding Procedure for Incomplete Nonmetric Preference/Choice Set Data Marketing Research," *Journal of Marketing Research* 34(4) (November 1997): 499–516; David B. Mackay, Robert F. Easley, and Joseph L. Zinnes, "A Single Ideal Point Model for Market Structure Analysis," *Journal of Marketing Research* 32(4) (November 1995): 433–43.
13. Ian P. Murphy, "Downscale Luxury Cars Drive to the Heart of Baby Boomers," *Marketing News* 30(21) (October 1997): 1, 19.
14. For a recent application of correspondence analysis, see J. J. Math, M. Candel, and Eric Maris, "Perceptual Analysis of Two-Way Two-Mode Frequency Data: Probability Matrix Decomposition and Two Alternatives," *International Journal of Research in Marketing* 14(4) (October 1997): 321–39; Paul E. Green and Abba M Krieger, "A Simple Approach to Target Market Advertising Strategy," *Journal of the Market Research Society* 35 (April 1993): 161–70.
15. Ali Kara, Erdener Kaynak, and Orsay Kucukemiroglu, "Positioning of Fast Food Outlets in Two Regions of North America: A Comparative Study Using Correspondence Analysis," *Journal of Professional Services Marketing* 14(2) (1996): 99–119; Terrence V. O'Brien, "Correspondence Analysis," *Marketing Research: A Magazine of Management & Applications* 5(4) (Fall 1993): 54–6.
16. See Jorg Blasius and Michael L. Greenacre, *Visualization of Categorical Data* (Academic Press, 1998); Michael J. Greenacre, *Correspondence Analysis in Practice* (New York, NY: Academic Press, 1993); Michael J. Greenacre, "The Carroll-Green-Schaffer Scaling in Correspondence Analysis: A Theoretical and Empirical Appraisal," *Journal of Marketing Research* 26 (August 1989): 358–65; Michael J. Greenacre, *Theory and Applications of Correspondence Analyses* (New York, NY: Academic Press, 1984); Donna L. Hoffman and George R. Franke, "Correspondence Analysis: Graphical Representation of Categorical Data in Marketing Research," *Journal of Marketing Research* 23 (August 1986): 213–27.
17. For the use of factor analysis in constructing spatial maps, see Larry Hasson, "Monitoring Social Change," *Journal of the Market Research Society* 37 (January 1995): 69–80.
18. John R. Hauser and Frank S. Koppelman, "Alternative Perceptual Mapping Techniques: Relative Accuracy and Usefulness," *Journal of Marketing Research* 16 (November 1979): 495–506. Hauser and Koppelman conclude that factor analysis is superior to discriminant analysis. See also Ingwer Borg and Patrick J. Groenen, *Modern Multidimensional Scaling Theory and Applications* (New York, NY: Springer-Verlag, 1996).
19. For recent applications and issues in conjoint analysis, see V. Srinivasan and Chan Su Park, "Surprising Robustness of the Self-Explicated Approach to Customer Preference Structure Measurement," *Journal of Marketing Research* 34 (May 1997): 286–91; Paul E. Green and Abba M. Krieger, "Segmenting Markets with Conjoint Analysis," *Journal of Marketing* 55 (October 1991): 20–31.
20. F. J. Danaher, "Using Conjoint Analysis to Determine the Relative Importance of Service Attributes Measured in Customer Satisfaction Surveys," *Journal of Retailing* 73(2) (Summer 1997): 235–60.
21. For an overview of conjoint analysis in marketing, see J. Douglass Carroll and Paul E. Green, "Psychometric Methods in Marketing Research: Part I, Conjoint Analysis," *Journal of Marketing Research* 32 (November 1995): 385–91; Paul E. Green and V. Srinivasan, "Conjoint Analysis in Marketing: New Developments with Implications for Research and Practice," *Journal of Marketing* 54 (October 1990): 3–19; Paul E. Green and V. Srinivasan, "Conjoint Analysis in Consumer Research: Issues and Outlook," *Journal of Consumer Research* 5 (September 1978): 102–23.
22. Judith Thomas Miller, James R. Ogden, and Craig A. Latshaw, "Using Trade-Off Analysis to Determine Value-Price Sensitivity of Custom Calling Features," *American Business Review* 16(1) (January 1998): 8–13.
23. Dick R. Wittink, Marco Vriens, and Wim Burhenne, "Commercial Uses of Conjoint Analysis in Europe: Results and Critical Reflections," *International Journal of Research in Marketing* 11(1) (January 1994): 41–52; Dick R. Wittink and Philippe Cattin, "Commercial Use of Conjoint Analysis: An Update," *Journal of Marketing* 53 (July 1989): 91–7. For using conjoint analysis to measure price sensitivity, see "Multi-Stage Conjoint Methods to Measure Price Sensitivity," *Sawtooth News* 10 (Winter 1994/1995): 5–6.
24. These three attributes are a subset of five attributes used by Michael Etgar and Naresh K. Malhotra, in "Determinants of Price Dependency: Personal and Perceptual Factors," *Journal of Consumer Research* 8 (September 1981): 217–22. See also Jan-Benedict E. M. Steenkamp and Dick R. Wittink, "The Metric Quality of Full-Profile Judgments

and the Number of Attribute Levels Effect in Conjoint Analysis," *International Journal of Research in Marketing* 11(3) (June 1994): 275–86.

25. Gerard H. Loosschilder, Edward Rosbergen, Marco Vriens, and Dick R. Wittink, "Pictorial Stimuli in Conjoint Analysis-to Support Product Styling Decisions," *Journal of the Market Research Society* 37 (January 1995): 17–34.
26. See J. Douglass Carroll and Paul E. Green, "Psychometric Methods in Marketing Research: Part I, Conjoint Analysis," *Journal of Marketing Research* 32 (November 1995): 385–91; Warren F. Kuhfeld, Randall D. Tobias, and Mark Garratt, "Efficient Experimental Designs with Marketing Applications," *Journal of Marketing Research* 31 (November 1994): 545–57; Sidney Addleman, "Orthogonal Main-Effect Plans for Asymmetrical Factorial Experiments," *Technometrics* 4 (February 1962): 21–36; Paul E. Green, "On the Design of Choice Experiments Involving Multifactor Alternatives," *Journal of Consumer Research* 1 (September 1974): 61–8.
27. More complex conjoint designs are also possible. See Harmen Oppewal, Jordan J. Louviere, and Harry J. P. Timmermans, "Modeling Hierarchical Conjoint Processes with Integrated Choice Experiments," *Journal of Marketing Research* 31 (February 1994): 15–27.
28. J. Douglass Carroll and Paul E. Green, "Psychometric Methods in Marketing Research: Part I, Conjoint Analysis," *Journal of Marketing Research* 32 (November 1995): 385–91; Arun K. Jain, Franklin Acito, Naresh K. Malhotra, and Vijay Mahajan, "A Comparison of the Internal Validity of Alternative Parameter Estimation Methods in Decompositional Multiattribute Preference Models," *Journal of Marketing Research* (August 1979): 313–22.
29. H. Oppewal, H. J. Timmermans, and J. J. Louviere, "Modeling the Effect of Shopping Center Size and Store Variety in Consumer Choice Behavior," *Environment and Planning* 29(6) (June 1997): 1073–90.
30. Markus Christen, Sachin Gupta, John C. Porter, Richard Staelin, and Dick R. Wittink, "Using Market-Level Data to Understand Promotion Effects in a Nonlinear Model," *Journal of Marketing Research* 34(3) (August 1997): 322–34; William L. Moore, "Levels of Aggregation in Conjoint Analysis: An Empirical Comparison," *Journal of Marketing Research* 17 (November 1980): 516–23. See also Roger Brice, "Conjoint Analysis: A Review of Conjoint Paradigms and Discussion of the Outstanding Design Issues," *Marketing & Research Today* 25(4) (November 1997): 260–6.
31. J. Douglass Carroll and Paul E. Green, "Psychometric Methods in Marketing Research: Part I, Conjoint Analysis," *Journal of Marketing Research* 32 (November 1995): 385–91; Frank J. Carmone and Paul E. Green, "Model Misspecification in Multiattribute Parameter Estimation," *Journal of Marketing Research* 18 (February 1981): 87–93.
32. For a recent application of conjoint analysis using OLS regression, see Amy Ostrom and Dawn Iacobucci, "Consumer Trade-Offs and the Evaluation of Services," *Journal of Marketing* 59 (January 1995): 17–28; Peter J. Danaher, "Using Conjoint Analysis to Determine the Relative Importance of Service Attributes Measured in Customer Satisfaction Surveys," *Journal of Retailing* 73(2) (Summer 1997): 235–60.
33. J. Douglass Carroll and Paul E. Green, "Psychometric Methods in Marketing Research: Part I, Conjoint Analysis," *Journal of Marketing Research* 32 (November 1995): 385–91; Naresh K. Malhotra, "Structural Reliability and Stability of Nonmetric Conjoint Analysis," *Journal of Marketing Research* 19 (May 1982): 199–207; Thomas W. Leigh, David B. MacKay, and John O. Summers, "Reliability and Validity of Conjoint Analysis and Self-Explicated Weights: A Comparison," *Journal of Marketing Research* 21 (November 1984): 456–62; Madhav N. Segal, "Reliability of Conjoint Analysis: Contrasting Data Collection Procedures," *Journal of Marketing Research* 19 (February 1982): 139–43.
34. Del I. Hawkins, Roger J. Best, and Kenneth A. Coney, *Consumer Behavior Implications for Marketing Strategy*, 7th ed. (Boston, MA: McGraw Hill, 1998).
35. Clark Hu and Stephen J. Hiemstra, "Hybrid Conjoint Analysis as a Research Technique to Measure Meeting Planners Preferences in Hotel Selection," *Journal of Travel Research* 35(2) (Fall 1996): 62–9; Paul E. Green and Abba M. Krieger, "Individualized Hybrid Models for Conjoint Analysis," *Management Science* 42(6) (June 1996): 850–67; Paul E. Green, "Hybrid Models for Conjoint Analysis: An Expository Review," *Journal of Marketing Research* 21 (May 1984): 155–69.
36. S. Pfeifer, B. Gain, and K. Walsh, "Managing Specialties: How to Grow When Prices Stall," *Chemical Week* 159(47) (December 10, 1997): 30–4; Diane Schneidman, "Research Method Designed to Determine Price for New Products, Line Extensions," *Marketing News* (October 23, 1987): 11.
37. "Luxury Car Makers Assemble World View," *Corporate Location* (January/February 1997): 4.
38. Linda Grant, "Outmarketing P & G," *Fortune* 137(1) (January 12, 1998): 150–2; David Butler, "Thai Superconcentrates Foam," *Advertising Age* 64(3) (January 18, 1993): I11.
39. S. J. Vitell and F. N. Ho, "Ethical Decision-Making in Marketing: A Synthesis and Evaluation of Scales Measuring the Various Components of Decision-Making in Ethical Situations," *Journal of Business Ethics* 16(7) (May 1997): 699–717.

Chapter 22

1. Joseph Rydholm, "Surveying the Friendly Skies," *Marketing Research* (May 1996); Karen Schwarz, "Airline Food Is No Joke," *Marketing News* 31(21) (October 13, 1997): 1, 10.
2. Thomas L. Greenbaum, *The Handbook for Focus Group Research* (Thousand Oaks, CA: Sage Publications, 1997); Thomas L. Greenbaum, "Using 'Ghosts' to Write Reports Hurts Viability of Focus Group," *Marketing News* 27(19) (September 13, 1993): 25.
3. Edward R. Tufte, *Visual Explanations: Images and Quantities, Evidence and Narrative* (Cheshire, CT: Graphic Press, 1997); Arlene Fink, *How to Report on Surveys* (Thousand Oaks, CA: Sage Publications, 1995).
4. Theodore Keys Jr., "Report Writing," *Internal Auditor* 53(4) (August 1996): 65–6.
5. S. H. Britt, "The Writing of Readable Research Reports," *Journal of Marketing Research* (May 1971): 265. See also Simon Mort, *Professional Report Writing* (Brookfield, IL: Ashgate Publishing Company, 1995); David I. Shair, "Report Writing," *HR Focus* 71(2) (February 1994): 20.

6. Ann Boland, "Got Report-O-Phobia?: Follow These Simple Steps to Get Those Ideas onto Paper," *Chemical Engineering* 103(3) (March 1996): 131–2.
7. L. Deane Wilson, "Are Appraisal Reports Logical Fallacies," *Appraisal Journal* 64(2) (April 1996): 129–33; John Leach, "Seven Steps to Better Writing," *Planning* 59(6) (June 1993): 26–7; A. S. C. Ehrenberg, "The Problem of Numeracy," *American Statistician* 35 (May 1981): 67–71.
8. Anders Wallgren, Britt Wallgren, Rolf Persson, Ulf Jorner, and Jan-Age Haaland, *Graphing Statistics and Data* (Thousand Oaks, CA: Sage Publications, 1996); Edward R. Tufte, *Visual Display of Quantitative Information* (Cheshire, CT: Graphic Press, 1992).
9. Neal B. Kauder, "Pictures Worth a Thousand Words," *American Demographics* (Tools Supplement) (November/December 1996): 64–8.
10. Sue Hinkin, "Charting Your Course to Effective Information Graphics," *Presentations* 9(11) (November 1995): 28–32.
11. Mark T. Chen, "An Innovative Project Report," *Cost Engineering* 38(4) (April 1996): 41–5; Gene Zelazny, *Say It with Charts: The Executive's Guide to Visual Communication*, 3rd ed. (Burr Ridge, IL: Irwin Professional Publishing, 1996).
12. "Get Visual with Modeling Tools," *Insurance & Technology* 20(6) (June 1995): 30; Patricia Ramsey and Louis Kaufman, "Presenting Research Data: How to Make Weak Numbers Look Good," *Industrial Marketing* 67 (March 1982): 66, 68, 70, 74.
13. Sharon Johnson and Michael Regan, " A New Use for an Old Tool," *Quality Progress* 29(11) (November 1996): 144; Gary L. Parr, "Pretty-Darned-Quick Flowchart Creation," *Quality* (August 1996): 62–3.
14. S. Paul Verluyten, "Business Communication and Intercultural Communication in Europe: The State of the Art," *Business Communication Quarterly* 60(2) (June 1997): 135–43; Geraldine E. Hynes and Vinita Bhatia, "Graduate Business Students' Preferences for the Managerial Communication Course Curriculum," *Business Communication Quarterly* 59(2) (June 1996): 45–55.
15. Daniel M. Hrisak, "Key Presentation Principles," *Chartered Accountants Journal of New Zealand* (April 1997): 76(3) (April 1997): 24; Paul Piscitelli, "How to Wow an Audience," *Sales & Management* 149(6) (June 1997): 63–9; Dorothy Sarnoff, *Never Be Nervous Again* (New York, NY: Fawcett Book Group, 1997).
16. Information provided by Roger L. Bacik, senior vice president, Elrick & Lavidge, Atlanta.
17. Lawrence F. Locke, Stephen Silverman, and Wannen W. Spirduso, *Reading and Understanding Research* (Thousand Oaks, CA: Sage Publications, 1998).
18. Ross Garnaut, "Australian Cars in a Global Economy," *Australian Economic Review* 30(4) (December 1997): 359–73; Geoffrey Lee Martin, "Aussies Chicken Fries Ford," *Advertising Age* (January 18, 1993).
19. John Milton-Smith, "Business Ethics in Australia and New Zealand," *Journal of Business Ethics* 16(14) (October 1997): 1485–97; Lawrence B. Chonko, *Ethical Decision Making in Marketing* (Thousand Oaks, CA: Sage Publications, 1995).
20. Edward J. O'Boyle and Lyndon E. Dawson Jr., "The American Marketing Association Code of Ethics: Instructions for Marketers," *Journal of Business Ethics* 11(12) (December 1992): 921–32; "AMA Adopts New Code of Ethics," *Marketing News* (September 11, 1987): 1, 10.
21. Cheryl Fenelle, "Tobacco Liability: Can Your Company Get Smoked," *Risk Management* 44(5) (May 1997): 56; Kirk Davidson, "Sure It's Legal, but Is It Legitimate?" *Marketing*, 30(13) (June 17, 1996): 13; S. Rapp, "Cigarettes: A Question of Ethics," *Marketing News* (November 5, 1992): 17.

Chapter 23

1. See Naresh K. Malhotra, James Agarwal, and Mark Peterson, "Cross-Cultural Marketing Research: Methodological Issues and Guidelines," *International Marketing Review* 13(5) (1996): 7–43; Naresh K. Malhotra, "Administration of Questionnaires for Collecting Quantitative Data in International Marketing Research," *Journal of Global Marketing* 4(2) (1991): 63–92; Naresh K. Malhotra, "Designing an International Marketing Research Course: Framework and Content," *Journal of Teaching in International Business* 3 (1992): 1–27.
2. Ian P. Murphy, "RAMS Helps Best Western Tout Worldwide Positioning," *Marketing News* 31(1) (January 6, 1997): 25; "Hotel Chains Capitalize on International Travel Market," *Hotels and Restaurants International* (June 1989): 81S–86S; "Target Marketing Points to Worldwide Success," *Hotels and Restaurants International* (June 1989): 87S.
3. Stephanie Thompson, "Blue Diamond Puts Crunch in a Munch," *Brandweek* 38(22) (June 2, 1997): 4; "Every Market Needs a Different Message," *IABC Communication World* (April 1990): 16–18.
4. "Top 25 Global Marketing/Ad/Opinion Research Firms Profiled," *Marketing News* 30(20) (September 23, 1996): H2–H19.
5. Lisa S. Howard, "Your Competition Is in Every Corner of the Globe," *National Underwriter* (Life/Health/Financial Services) 100(27) (July 1, 1996): 4; Associated Press, "Regional Markets are International Order of the Day," *Marketing News* (March 1, 1993): IR–10; Thomas T. Semon, "Red Tape is Chief Problem in Multinational Research," *Marketing News* (March 1, 1993): 7.
6. Emma Donnellan, "Changing Perspectives on Research Methodology in Marketing," *Irish Marketing Review—Dublin* 8 (1995): 81–90.
7. George W. Trivoli, Robert Glenn Graham, and Paul A. Herbig, "Determinants for Trading and Investing in Latin America by U.S. Businesses," *American Business Review* (January 1998): 53–63; Jack Honomichl, "Research Cultures are Different in Mexico, Canada," *Marketing News* 27(10) (May 10,1993): 12–13.
8. Masaru Ariga, M. Yasue, and Gu Xiang Wen, "China's Generation III: Viable Target Segment Implications for Marketing Communication," *Marketing & Research Today* 25(1) (February 1997) 17–24; Cyndee Miller, "China Emerges as Latest Battleground for Marketing Researchers," *Marketing News* (February 14, 1994): 1.
9. For a recent example of international marketing research, see Mark Peterson and Naresh K. Malhotra, "Comparative Marketing Measures of Societal Quality of Life: Substantive Dimensions in 186 Countries," *Journal of Macromarketing* 17(1) (Spring 1997): 25–38.
10. Tanya Clark, "China's Challenges," *Industry Week* 246(19) (October 20, 1997): 126–34.

11. Thomas L. Greenbaum, "Understanding Focus Group Research Abroad," *Marketing News* 30(12) (June 3, 1996): H14, H36; "Will Sheiks Take to Burgers and Fries?" *D&B Reports* (January–February 1986): 10–13.
12. See Niraj Dawar and Philip Parker, "Marketing Universals: Consumers' Use of Brand Name, Price, Physical Appearance, and Retailer Reputation as Signals of Product Quality," *Journal of Marketing* 58 (April 1994): 81–95.
13. The section on survey methods is drawn from Naresh K. Malhotra, "Administration of Questionnaires for Collecting Quantitative Data in International Marketing Research," *Journal of Global Marketing* 4(2) (1991): 63–92. See also Nadia G. Mitevska and Michelle Meyer, "The Role of Marketing Research in Bulgaria: Activities, Scope, and Importance," *Journal of Euromarketing* 6(2) (1997): 57–73.
14. Thomas T. Semon, "Select Local Talent When Conducting Research Abroad," *Marketing News* 31(19) (September 15, 1997): 28.
15. Humphrey Taylor, "The Very Different Methods Used to Conduct Telephone Surveys of the Public," *Journal of the Market Research Society* 39(3) (July 1997): 421–32.
16. Louella Miles, "The Fast Track to Knowledge," *Marketing* (Choosing and Using Market Research Supplement) (May 23, 1996): VIII–XI.
17. Clive Fletcher, "Just How Effective Is a Telephone Interview?" *People Management* 3(13) (June 26, 1997): 49; Minoo Farhangmehr and Paula Veiga, "The Changing Consumer in Portugal," *International Journal of Research in Marketing* 12(5) (December 1995): 485–502.
18. Kathleen Cox, "Hello. Hello. Hello. In India, There Is Still a Busy Signal," *Worldbusiness* 2(3) (May/June 1996): 5.
19. Peter H. Wertheim and Dayse Abrantes, "Brazil: New Take on Telecom," *Data Communications* 26(5) (April 1997): 42; P. Pinheiro de Andrade, "Market Research in Brazil," *European Research* (August 1987): 188–97.
20. Trish Shukers, "Integrated Interviewing," *Marketing Research: A Magazine of Management & Applications* 8(1) (Spring 1996): 20–1.
21. Karen Fletcher, "Jump on the Omnibus," *Marketing* (June 15, 1995): 25–8.
22. Naresh K. Malhotra, James Agarwal, and Mark Peterson, "Cross-Cultural Marketing Research: Methodological Issues and Guidelines," *International Marketing Review* 13(5) (1996): 7–43.
23. Jonathan Holburt, "Global Tastes, Local Trimmings," *Far Eastern Economic Review* 160(1) (December 26, 1996–January 2, 1997): 24; Julie Skur Hill, "Coke Tops in Americas," *Advertising Age* (November 12, 1990).
24. Ellen Gregory, "Cost/Quality Issues Plague Mall Intercepts," *Marketing Research: A Magazine of Management & Applications* 8(2) (Summer 1996): 46–7.
25. Peter Jones and John Polak, "Computer-Based Personal Interviewing: State-of-the-Art and Future Prospects," *Journal of Market Research Society* 35(3) (July 1993): 221–3.
26. Francis Buttle and Gavin Thomas, "Questionnaire Color and Mail Survey Response Rate," *Journal of Market Research Society* 39(4) (October 1994): 625-6.
27. Paul Lewis, "Do Your Homework!" *Successful Meetings* 46(3) (March 1997): 120–1; T. Vahvelainen, "Marketing Research in the Nordic Countries," *European Research* (April 1985): 76–9; T. Vahvelainen, "Marketing Research in Finland," *European Research* (August 1987): 62–6.
28. Ian Darby, "The Meaning of Life," *Marketing* (August 14, 1997): 21–2; Lewis C. Winters, "International Psychographics," *Marketing Research: A Magazine of Management & Applications* 4(3) (September 1992): 48–9; "We Are the World," *American Demographics* (May 1990): 42–3.
29. Jorge Zamora, "Management of Respondents' Motivation to Lower the Desertion Rates in Panels in Emerging Countries: The Case of Talca, Chile," *Marketing & Research Today* 25(3) (August 1997): 191–8; "TSMS and AGB Set up Ad Effectiveness Panel," *Marketing Week* 18(27) (September 22, 1995): 15.
30. See also C. Min-Han, Byoung-Woo Lee, and Kong-Kyun Ro, "The Choice of a Survey Mode in Country Image Studies," *Journal of Business Research* 29 (February 1994): 151–62.
31. Naresh K. Malhotra, James Agarwal, and Mark Peterson, "Cross-Cultural Marketing Research: Methodological Issues and Guidelines," *International Marketing Review* 13(5) (1996): 7–43.
32. Michael L. Maynard and Charles R. Taylor, "A Comparative Analysis of Japanese and U.S. Attitudes toward Direct Marketing," *Journal of Direct Marketing* 10(1) (Winter 1996): 34–44; J. Craig Andrews, Srinivas Durvasula, and Richard G. Netemeyer, "Testing the Cross-National Applicability of U.S. and Russian Advertising Belief and Attitude Measures," *Journal of Advertising* 23 (March 1994): 17–26.
33. Naresh K. Malhotra, James Agarwal, and Mark Peterson, "Cross-Cultural Marketing Research: Methodological Issues and Guidelines," *International Marketing Review* 13(5) (1996): 7–43. For a recent application of back translation, see Robert Wharton, Inga S. Baird, and Marjorie A. Lyles, "Conceptual Frameworks among Chinese Managers: Joint Venture Management and Philosophy," *Journal of Global Marketing*, 5(1–2) (1991): 163–81.
34. John Shannon, "National Values Can be Exported," *Marketing Week* 19(45) (February 7, 1997): 20; S. C. Grunert and G. Scherhorn, "Consumer Values in West Germany: Underlying Dimensions and Cross-Cultural Comparison with North America," *Journal of Business Research* 20 (1990): 97–107. See also H. C. Triandis, *Culture and Social Behavior* (New York, NY: McGraw-Hill, Inc. 1994).
35. Rebecca Sykes, "Privacy Debates Get More Complicated Overseas," *InfoWorld* 19(44) (November 3, 1997): 111; Simon Chadwick, "Data Privacy Legislation All the Rage in Europe," *Marketing News* 27(17) (August 16, 1993); A7.
36. Hewlett-Packard Web site: www.hp.com. Hewlett-Packard's chemical analysis survey (English): www.hp.com/chem_survey/english/index.html.

Chapter 24

1. This chapter draws heavily from Naresh K. Malhotra and Gina Miller, "An Integrated Model for Ethical Decisions in Marketing Research," *Journal of Business Ethics* 17 (1998): 263–80.
2. William B. Carlin and Kelly C. Strong, "A Critique of Western Philosophical Ethics: Multidisciplinary Alternatives for Framing Ethical Dilemmas," *Journal of Business Ethics* 14(5) (May 1995): 387–96; A. E. Singer, S. Lysonski, M. Singer,

and David Hayes "Ethical Myopia: The Case of 'Framing' by Framing," *Journal of Business Ethics* 10 (1991): 29–36.

3. Beng Soo Ong, Foo-Nin Ho, and Kenneth E. Clow, "Ethical Perceptions of Reference Price Advertising," *American Business Review* 15(1) (January 1997): 7–14; Gwendolyn K. Ortmeyer, "Ethics in Marketing, Retail Promotion Pricing: When is a Sale Really a Sale?" *Harvard Business School* Case N9-591-111 (1991).
4. Betsy Peterson, "Ethics, Revisited," *Marketing Research: A Magazine of Management & Applications* 8(4) (Winter 1996): 47–8; Gene R. Laczniak and Patrick E. Murphy, "Fostering Ethical Marketing Decisions," *Journal of Business Ethics* 11 (1991): 259–71.
5. A. Singhapakdi, S. J. Vitell, and K. L. Kraft, "Moral Intensity and Ethical Decision-Making of Marketing Professionals," *Journal of Business Research* 36(3) (July 1996): 245–55; Morris B. Holbrook, "Ethics in Consumer Research—An Overview and Prospects," *Advances in Consumer Research* 21 (1994): 566–71; L. T. Hosmer, *The Ethics of Management*, 2nd ed. (Homewood, IL: Irwin, 1991): 13–15.
6. Alan Mitchell, "The Power of Ethical Branding," *Marketing Week* 20(8) (May 22, 1997): 26–7; Lynn Sharp Paine, "Managing for Organizational Integrity," *Harvard Business Review* 94 (March/April 1994): 106–17.
7. N. C. Smith and E. Coopermartin, "Ethics and Target Marketing—The Role of Product Harm and Consumer Vulnerability," *Journal of Marketing* 61(3) (July 1997): 1–20; Gene R. Laczniak and Patrick E. Murphy, *Marketing Ethics: Guidelines for Managers* (Lexington, MA: Lexington Books, 1985): 57.
8. Naresh K. Malhotra and Gina L. Miller, "Ethical Issues in Marketing Managed Health Care," *Journal of Health Care Marketing* 16(1) (1996): 60–5; Stephen B. Knouse and Robert A. Giacalone, "The Six Components of Successful Ethics Training," *Business & Society Review* (98) (1997): 10–13.
9. P. J. Dean, "Examining the Profession and the Practice of Business Ethics," *Journal of Business Ethics* 16(15) (November 1997): 1637–49; Patrick E. Murphy and Gene R. Laczniak, "Traditional Ethical Issues Facing Marketing Researchers," *Marketing Research: A Magazine of Management and Applications* 4 (March 1992): 8–19; Kenneth C. Schneider, "Ethics and Marketing Research," in James E. Nelson (ed.), *The Practice of Marketing Research* (Boston, MA: Kent Publishing Company, 1982): 608.
10. J. E. Nelson and P. L. Kiecker, "Marketing Research Interviewers and Their Perceived Necessity of Moral Compromise," *Journal of Business Ethics* 15(10) (October 1996): 1107–17; Gene R. Laczniak and Patrick E. Murphy, *Ethical Marketing Decisions: The Higher Road* (Needham Heights, MA: Allyn & Bacon, 1993): 61; N. C. Smith and J. A. Quelch, *Ethics in Marketing* (Homewood, IL: Irwin, 1993): 161–73.
11. Betsy Peterson, "Ethics Revisited," *Marketing Research: A Magazine of Management & Applications* 8(4) (Winter 1996): 47–8; "AMA Adopts New Code of Ethics," *Marketing News* (September 11, 1987): 1, 10. This code is given in Appendix 3A of Gene R. Laczniak and Patrick E. Murphy, *Ethical Marketing Decisions: The Higher Road* (Needham Heights, MA: Allyn & Bacon, 1993): 76–7.
12. Patrick E. Murphy and Gene R. Laczniak, "Emerging Ethical Issues Facing Marketing Researchers," *Marketing Research: A Magazine of Management and Applications* 4 (June, 1992): 6–11; Stephen B. Castleberry and Warren French, "The Ethical Framework of Advertising/Marketing Research Practitioners: A Moral Development Perspective," Working Paper (August 1991).
13. C. J. Thompson, "Contextualist Proposal for the Conceptualization and Study of Marketing Ethics," *Journal of Public Policy & Marketing* 14(2) (Fall 1995): 177–91; Gene R. Laczniak and Patrick E. Murphy, *Ethical Marketing Decisions: The Higher Road* (Needham Heights, MA: Allyn & Bacon, 1993): 61.
14. J. R. Shannon and R. L. Berl, "Are We Teaching Ethics in Marketing—A Survey of Students' Attitudes and Perceptions," *Journal of Business Ethics* 16(10) (July 1997): 1059–75; Gene R. Laczniak and Patrick E. Murphy, *Ethical Marketing Decisions: The Higher Road* (Needham Heights, MA: Allyn & Bacon, 1993): 66–8; N. C. Smith and J. A. Quelch, *Ethics in Marketing* (Homewood, IL: Irwin, 1993): 180–1.
15. T. Teal "The Human Side of Management," *Harvard Business Review* 74(6) (November/December 1996): 35; Laura Nash, "Ethics without the Sermon," *Harvard Business Review* (November/December 1981): 88.
16. J. Kevin Quinn, J. David Reed, M. Neil Browne, and Wesley J. Hiers, "Honesty, Individualism, and Pragmatic Business Ethics: Implications for Corporate Hierarchy," *Journal of Business Ethics* 16(12/13) (September 1997): 1419–30; J. Bowditch and A. Buono, *A Primer on Organizational Behavior*, 2nd ed. (New York, NY: John Wiley and Sons, 1990).
17. Belinda Archer, "Why Moral Crusades May Be Good for Business," *Campaign-London* (September 19, 1997): 13; Patrick E. Murphy and Gene R. Laczniak, "Emerging Ethical Issues Facing Marketing Researchers," *Marketing Research: A Magazine of Management and Applications* 4 (June, 1992): 6–11. Adapted from Wade Worth, *Industrial Espionage and Mis-Use of Trade Secrets* (Ardmore, PA: Advance House, 1965).
18. Naresh K. Malhotra and Gina Miller, "An Integrated Model for Ethical Decisions in Marketing Research," *Journal of Business Ethics* 17 (1998): 263–80; Elaine Sternberg, "The Moral is Not to Moralize," *Management Today* (December 1996): 88.
19. John Fraedrich, Debbie M. Thorne, and O. C. Ferrell, "Assessing the Application of Cognitive Moral Development Theory to Business Ethics" *Journal of Business Ethics*, 13 (October 1994): 829–38.
20. Foo Nin Ho, Scott J. Vitell, James H. Barnes, and Rene Desborde, "Ethical Correlates of Role Conflict and Ambiguity in Marketing: The Mediating Role of Cognitive Moral Development," *Journal of the Academy of Marketing Science* 25(2) (Spring 1997): 117–26; O. C. Ferrell and J. Fraedrich, *Business Ethics: Ethical Decision Making and Cases* (Boston, MA: Houghton Mifflin Company, 1991).
21. F. Neil Brady and Craig P. Dunn, "Business Meta-Ethics: An Analysis of Two Theories," *Business Ethics Quarterly* 5(3) (July 1995): 385–98; W. H. Shaw and V. Barry, *Moral Issues in Business* (Belmont, CA: Wadsworth, 1992).
22. James E. MacDonald and Caryn L. Beck-Dudley, "Are Deontology and Teleology Mutually Exclusive?" *Journal of Business Ethics* 13 (August 1994): 615–24.

23. Ishmael P. Akaah, "Influence of Deontological and Teleological Factors on Research Ethics Evaluations," *Journal of Business Research* 39(2) (June 1997): 71–80; Shelby D. Hunt and Arturo Z. Vasquez-Parraga, "Organizational Consequences, Marketing Ethics, and Salesforce Supervision," *Journal of Marketing Research* 30 (February 1993): 78–90.
24. David A. Griffith and Michael A. Mayo, "Integrating Ethics into International Marketing Strategy: An Extension of Robin and Reidenbach's Framework," *International Executive* 39(6) (November/December 1997): 745–63; R. Eric Reidenbach and Donald P. Robin, "A Response to 'On Measuring Ethical Judgments'," *Journal of Business Ethics* 14 (February 1995): 159–62.
25. Iwao Taka and Thomas W. Dunfee, "Japanese Moralogy as Business Ethics," *Journal of Business Ethics* 16(5) (April 1997): 507–19; Robert W. Armstrong, and Jill Sweeney, "Industry Type, Culture, Mode of Entry and Perceptions of International Marketing Ethics Problems: A Cross-Cultural Comparison," *Journal of Business Ethics* 13 (October 1994): 787–94.
26. M. Cecilia Arruda, "Business Ethics in Latin America," *Journal of Business Ethics* 16(14) (October 1997): 1597–1603; R. Maxwell, "Ethics and Identity in Global Market Research," *Cultural Studies* 10(2) (May 1996): 218–36.
27. Stuart C. Gilman and Carol W. Lewis, "Public Service Ethics: A Global Dialog," *Public Administration Review* 56(6) (November/December 1996): 517–24; Scott J. Vitell, S. L. Nwachukwu, and J. H. Barnes, "The Effects of Culture on Ethical Decision Making: An Application of Hofstede's Typology," *Journal of Business Ethics* 12 (1993): 753–60.
28. John B. Ford, Michael S. LaTour, Scott J. Vitell, and Warren A. French, "Moral Judgments and Market Negotiations: A Comparison of Chinese and American Managers," *Journal of International Marketing* 5(2) (1997): 57–76; Michael A. Mayo, "Ethical Problems Encountered by U.S. Small Businesses in International Marketing," *Journal of Small Business Management* (April 1991): 51–9.

Indexes

SUBJECT INDEX

D

COMPANY INDEX

NAME INDEX

G

H

I

J

K

Credits

CHAPTER 1 **3** NKM Photo/Burke, Inc.; **6** Courtesy of Chrysler Corporation; **8** Brian Johnson; **15** Federal Express Corperation; **20** Samsonite Corporation; **23 (top left)** Courtesy of the Gallup Organization; **23 (top right)** Courtesy of the SABRE Group; **23 (bottom left)** Courtesy of Smith Hanely Associates, Inc.; **23 (bottom right)** Courtesy of BAI Behavioral Analysis, Inc.; **26** Sears, Roebuck & Co.

CHAPTER 2 **33** NKM Photo/Burke, Inc.; **34** Ron Kimball Photography; **41** K. Knudson/Photo Disc, Inc.; **44** Jon Anderson/Black Star; **49** NKM Photo/Burke, Inc.; **54** Teri Stratford/Simon & Schuster/PH College; **56** Pan American World Airways.

PROFESSIONAL PERSPECTIVES **65** NKM Photo/Burke, Inc.; **68** New York American Marketing Association; **71** NKM Photo/Burke, Inc.

CHAPTER 3 **81** NKM Photo/Burke, Inc.; **82** Fotopic/Omni-Photo Communications, Inc.; **86** Microsoft Corporation; **91** Courtesy of Market Facts, Inc.; **92** Gorge Rose/Liaison Agency, Inc.; **96** Chip Henderson/Chip Henderson Photography; **99** John Lei/Stock Boston.

CHAPTER 4 **109** NKM Photo/Burke, Inc.; **110** Boston Chicken, Inc.; **129** Eric Mencher; **134** Churchill & Klehr Photography; **136** This map was provided by National Decision Systems, ©1998 San Diego, CA. All rights reserved.

CHAPTER 5 **145** NKM Photo/Burke, Inc.; **149** Elrick & Lavidge Marketing Research; **153** NKM Photo/Burke, Inc.; **158** Chase Manhattan Bank; **162** Teri Stratford/Simon & Schuster/PH College; **164** Greg Davis/The Stock Market.

CHAPTER 6 **176** NKM Photo/Burke, Inc.; **180** NKM Photo/Burke, Inc.; **182, 184** Elrick & Lavidge Marketing Research; **185** Paul Lange; **196** Churchill & Klehr Photography.

CHAPTER 7 **212** NKM Photo/Burke, Inc.; **213** Eckerd Corporation; **218** Irene Springer/Simon & Schuster/PH College; **236** Frito-Lay, Inc.; **241** Lee Snider/The Image Works.

CHAPTER 8 **246** NKM Photo/Burke, Inc.; **247** Bergen Mall; **250** David Madison/Tony Stone Images; **257** Elrick & Lavidge Marketing Research; **259** Colgate-Palmolive Company.

CHAPTER 9 **266** NKM Photo/Burke, Inc.; **267** Courtesy of New York City Transit; **268** Lucky Stores, Inc.; **270** ORTEK Data Systems, Inc.; **272** Rhoda Sidney; **285** Jeff Greenberg/PhotoEdit.

CHAPTER 10 **292** NKM Photo/Burke, Inc.; **294** Michael Weisbrot/Stock Boston; **299** Steve Hall/Hedrick Blessing/Nike Town; **306** Bob Daemmrich/The Image Works; **307** C.J. Allen/Stock Boston.

CHAPTER 11 **326** NKM Photo/Burke, Inc.; **333** Vision Impact Photography; **337** Margot Granilsas/Photo Researchers, Inc.; **341** American Express Travel Related Services Company, Inc.; **343** Gary Russ/The Image Bank.

CHAPTER 12 **354** NKM Photo/Burke, Inc.; **355** Jean-Claude LeJeune/Stock Boston; **360** New York Convention & Visitors Bureau; **367** Jacksonville Symphony Orchestra and Chorus; **374** Chromo Sohm/Sohm/Unicorn Stock Photos.

PROFESSIONAL PERSPECTIVES **383** NKM Photo/Burke, Inc.; **386** NKM Photo/Burke, Inc.; **388** NKM Photo/Burke, Inc.

CHAPTER 13 **403** NKM Photo/Burke, Inc.; **404** Courtesy of the Council for Marketing and Opinion Research; **407** Simon & Schuster/PH College; **411** NKM Photo/Burke, Inc.

CHAPTER 14 **418** NKM Photo/Burke, Inc.; **428 (left)** NKM Photo/Burke, Inc.; **428 (right)** Simon & Schuster/PH College; **430** Laima E. Druskis/Simon & Schuster/PH College; **432** Barbara Rios/Photo Researchers, Inc.; **437** James Leynse/SABA Press Photo, Inc.

CHAPTER 15 **444** NKM Photo/Burke, Inc.; **445** Pepsi Co., Inc; **446** Teri Stratford; **449** Churchill & Klehr Photography; **482** Colgate-Palmolive Company.

CHAPTER 16 **488** NKM Photo/Burke, Inc.; **490** Teri Stratford/Simon & Schuster/PH College; **500** Teri Stratford/Simon & Schuster/PH College.

CHAPTER 17 **519** NKM Photo/Burke, Inc; **520** Avon Products, Inc.; **545** Teri Stratford/Simon & Schuster/PH College; **547** Laima E. Druskis/Simon & Schuster/PH College; **551** Singapore Airlines.

CHAPTER 18 **559** NKM Photo/Burke, Inc; **560** Reprinted with permission of Business Week; **566** R. Ford Smith/The Stock Market; **577** Peter Menzel/Stock Boston.

CHAPTER 19 **585** NKM Photo/Burke, Inc; **597** Bic Corporation; **601** Courtesy of SC Johnson & Son, Inc.

CHAPTER 20 **610** NKM Photo/Burke, Inc; **611** Robert Freck/Tony Stone Images; **613** Tony Stone Images; **626** Cathy Cheny/Stock Boston.

CHAPTER 21 **633** NKM Photo/Burke, Inc; **634** Teri Stratford/Simon & Schuster/PH College; **646** General Motors; **651** Reebok; **658** Courtesy of International Business Machines Corporation. Unauthorized use not permitted.

PROFESSIONAL PERSPECTIVES **667** Courtesy of Burke, Inc.; **670** NKM Photo/Burke, Inc.

CHAPTER 22 **693** NKM Photo/Burke, Inc; **702** General Motors; **705** NKM Photo/Burke, Inc; **706** NKM Photo/Burke, Inc.

CHAPTER 23 **714** NKM Photo/Burke, Inc; **715** Best Western International; **717** Christopher Brown/Stock Boston; **721** Stuart Cohen/Comstock; **724** Monkmeyer Press; **729** Reproduced with permission of Hewlett-Packard Company.

CHAPTER 24 **732** NKM Photo/Burke, Inc; **733** Phil Lauro/ProfilesWest/Index Stock Imagery, Inc.; **737** Richard Falco/Photo Researchers, Inc.; **739** Courtesy of Chrysler Corporation; **748** F. Hibon/Sygma.

PROFESSIONAL PERSPECTIVES **753** NKM Photo/Burke, Inc; **757** NKM Photo/Burke, Inc. **758** Courtesy of Burke, Inc.